Guide to the U.S. Supreme Court

Guide to the U.S. Supreme Court

FOURTH EDITION • VOLUME II

DAVID G. SAVAGE

CQ PRESS   A Division of Congressional Quarterly Inc.

Washington, D.C.

David G. Savage is the Supreme Court reporter for the *Los Angeles Times*. He joined the paper in 1981 and moved to its Washington bureau in 1986. He is the author of *Turning Right: The Making of the Rehnquist Supreme Court,* published in 1992.

CQ Press
1255 22nd Street, N.W., Suite 400
Washington, D.C. 20037
202-729-2900; toll-free, 1-866-4CQ-PRESS (1-866-427-7737)
Copyright © 2004 CQ Press, a division of Congressional Quarterly Inc.

∞ The paper used in this publication exceeds the requirements of the American National Standard for Information Sciences—Permanence of Paper for Printed Library Materials, ANSI Z39.48-1992.

Printed and bound in the United States of America

08   07   06   05   04   5   4   3   2   1

Acknowledgments: HoweData Supreme Court Reports provided the text of *Marbury v. Madison, McCulloch v. Maryland,* and *Brown v. Board of Education of Topeka* appearing in Appendix A. Lee Epstein and Thomas G. Walker contributed their research on natural courts, which is part of Appendix B. This research was published previously in their *Constitutional Law for a Changing America: Institutional Powers and Constraints,* 2d ed. (Washington, D.C.: CQ Press, 1995), 617. Lee Epstein, Jeffrey A. Segal, Harold J. Spaeth, and Thomas G. Walker provided the map of the federal court system in Appendix B. The map was published previously in their *Supreme Court Compendium: Data, Decisions, and Developments,* 2d ed. (Washington, D.C.: Congressional Quarterly, 1996), 651.

Illustration credits and acknowledgements begin on page 1259, Volume 2, which is to be considered an extension of the copyright page.

LIBRARY OF CONGRESS CATALOGING-IN-PUBLICATION DATA
Savage, David G.
  Guide to the U.S. Supreme Court / David G. Savage.—4th ed.
    p.   cm.
  Rev. ed. of: Guide to the U.S. Supreme Court / Joan Biskupic and Elder Witt. 3rd ed. c1997.
  Includes bibliographical references and index.
  ISBN 1-56802-743-5 (set; casebound : alk. paper) — ISBN 1-56802-744-3 (vol 1; casebound : alk. paper)—ISBN 1-56802-745-1 (vol 2; casebound : alk. paper)
    1. United States. Supreme Court.   I. Title: Guide to the US Supreme Court.   II. Title: Guide to the United States Supreme Court.   III. Biskupic, Joan. Guide to the U.S. Supreme Court.   IV. Title.

KF8742.W567 2004
347.73'26—dc22   2004001572

Summary Table of Contents

Table of Contents

PART IV

Pressures on the Court

Congressional Pressure

ONGRESS AND THE JUDICIARY are separate but interdependent branches of the federal government. The Supreme Court defines the limits of congressional authority under the terms of the Constitution, while Congress confirms the Court's members, sets its jurisdiction, and pays its bills. Just as the Court has used its judicial review powers to influence the shape of federal legislation, so Congress has tried from time to time to use its powers over the Court to influence the outcome of particular rulings.

Congressional Influence

Congress can influence the Supreme Court in three general ways—through selection, confirmation, and impeachment of individual justices; through institutional and jurisdictional changes; and through direct reversal of the effects of specific Court decisions.

The Justices

Congress has limited influence over the president's choice of a Supreme Court nominee. There is no established procedure for Congress to advise the president on the choice of a nominee, although a majority in both houses at least twice has successfully petitioned the chief executive to nominate a particular person to a Court vacancy.

The Constitution does, however, require Senate confirmation of all Supreme Court nominees, and the Senate takes this responsibility seriously. Of the 148 nominations to the Court, 28 have failed to win confirmation. All but 6 of these rejections, most of them for partisan political reasons, occurred in the eighteenth and nineteenth centuries.

For a variety of reasons, Congress's power to impeach Supreme Court justices has been of little significance. Only one justice has been impeached—Samuel Chase in 1804—and he was acquitted by the Senate. Another justice, Abe Fortas, resigned in 1969 under threat of impeachment, but Justice William O. Douglas, accused a year later of committing similar improprieties, not only did not resign but also was cleared of all the charges. Through its appropriations process, Congress controls all of the money for the operation and maintenance of the federal judicial system, including the Supreme Court. It also sets the levels of the justices' salaries. Congress has never tried to pressure the Court by deliberately withholding operational funds. In 1964, however, after the Court handed down a series of controversial rulings, a majority in Congress voted to deny the justices as large a pay increase as other high-ranking federal employees received.

The Institution

Congress has been least successful in influencing the Court by making changes in the institution itself and in its procedures and functions. Only once has it stopped the Court from taking action by revoking its power to review a case while the case was pending. Proposals to limit the Court's jurisdiction so that it may not review federal legislation on specific subjects are offered whenever the Court issues a particularly controversial decision or series of rulings, but none of these proposals has been approved.

Congress has tried to influence the philosophical composition of the Court by changing its size. This ploy apparently worked once. In 1869, after the Court found a particular statute unconstitutional by a 4-3 vote, Congress increased the size of the Court by two members; the case was reconsidered, and the earlier decision was reversed by a 5-4 vote. Proposals to require unanimity or a two-thirds vote of the justices to declare federal statutes or state laws unconstitutional also have been made in Congress throughout the Court's history, but none has ever passed.

The Decisions

Congress has been far more adept at reversing specific Court decisions than at eliminating whole areas from Supreme Court review. Reversal may come about through legislation, if the Court's decision is based on statutory construction and interpretation, or through constitutional amendment, if the decision is an interpretation of a constitutional provision. The first constitutional amendment overturning a Supreme Court decision was the Eleventh, ratified in 1795; the first legislative reversal came in 1852.

Periods of Confrontation

There have been several major periods of confrontation between Congress and the Court. The first of these occurred in the early 1800s, when the national leadership passed from the Federalists to the Democratic-Republicans. The last confrontational period occurred in the mid-1950s and 1960s, when conservative members of Congress constantly challenged the liberal decisions on social issues handed down by the Warren Court.

In the 1800 elections, the Federalists lost to the Democratic-Republicans, and Thomas Jefferson was elected to replace President John Adams. In the final days of the Adams administration in 1801, to ensure that they would have some influence in the national government, the Federalists passed legislation creating sixteen new circuit court judgeships and several justice of the peace positions. The Federalists also stipulated that when the next vacancy occurred on the Court, it would go unfilled and the number of justices would be reduced by one. President Adams quickly appointed Federalists to the new judgeships, but his midnight appointments came so late that some of the appointees never received their commissions. Their suit to force the Jefferson administration to honor the Adams appointments resulted in the famous *Marbury v. Madison* decision. *(See details of this case, pp. 80–83.)*

In 1802, after the Democratic-Republicans were ensconced in office, they repealed the new judgeships and raised the number of justices back to six. They also postponed the next Supreme Court term so that the Court would be unable to hear quickly an anticipated suit challenging the validity of the repeal. When the Court did meet again in 1803, it sustained the repeal. Still not satisfied, the Democratic-Republicans decided to attack the Federalists on the Supreme Court through impeachment, selecting as their first target Justice Samuel Chase, a man who had used his position on the bench to advance Federalist doctrine.

The House impeached Chase on a party-line vote, but the Democratic-Republicans did not hold together in the Senate, and he was acquitted. The House then passed a bill to authorize the president to remove a justice at the request of a majority of the House and Senate, but that effort also died in the Senate. After those two defeats, Democratic-Republicans ended their broadside attack on the Federalist judiciary, choosing instead to fill vacancies with individuals of their own persuasion as opportunities arose.

Federal Power versus States' Rights

In the 1820s and early 1830s controversial decisions expanded the powers of the national government at the expense of state sovereignty. This situation led Congress to try unsuccessfully to remove the Court's jurisdiction to hear cases challenging the validity of state laws. Repeal of this power would have prevented the Court from reviewing the validity of any state law and would have resulted in conflict and confusion among the states. The proposals were, however, soundly defeated in the House in 1831.

Reconstruction

Congress had its greatest successes in curbing the Court during the post–Civil War Reconstruction era. In addition to reducing the number of justices, as vacancies occurred, from ten to seven to prevent President Andrew Johnson from making any appointments to the Court, Congress repealed the Court's jurisdiction to review certain denials of writs of habeas corpus. The repeal, which the Court ultimately sustained (but which

Congress eventually reversed), prevented it from rendering an opinion in a pending case on the constitutionality of the congressional program of Reconstruction.

Once Johnson left office, Congress quickly raised the number of justices to nine. The additional seats proved critical to the Court's reversal of its decision that Congress could not make paper money a substitute currency for gold in the payment of debts.

Progressives

In the early 1920s Progressives in Congress tried to pressure the economically and socially conservative Court into rendering more liberal decisions, but these attempts were singularly unsuccessful. Indeed, few of their proposals won any consideration at all. Among the proposals were legislation to require two-thirds of the justices to concur in decisions declaring federal statutes unconstitutional and a measure to permit Congress to overrule a Court decision invalidating a federal law by repassing the statute with a two-thirds majority.

New Deal Crisis

Although an economically conservative Court clashed with Congress when it declared most of the early New Deal legislation invalid in the 1930s, the Court's real confrontation was with President Franklin D. Roosevelt, who sought to moderate the Court's conservatism by "packing" it with additional members. The plan was extremely unpopular; a majority in Congress opposed it, enacting instead legislation making retirement for elderly justices more financially attractive. Even though Roosevelt's plan to increase the size of the Court was defeated, at the cost of a serious rift in the Democratic Party, his goal of more economic power for the federal government was achieved.

In decisions reached before the Court-packing plan was unveiled but not announced, the Court indicated that it was adopting a broader view of federal economic regulatory powers. The Court reinforced its new stance by sustaining reenactment of much of the New Deal legislation it had previously found unconstitutional. Then, within months of enactment of the liberalized retirement bill, one of the conservative stalwarts on the Court announced his resignation. From that point on, Roosevelt was able to gradually make appointments that strengthened the liberal faction on the Court.

The Warren Court

During the fifteen years Earl Warren was chief justice (1954–1969), the Court consistently sustained individual and minority interests against what many citizens considered to be the best interests of the community. Warren began his career on the Court by writing the opinion declaring segregation in public schools unconstitutional. Under his guidance, the Court—often by narrow margins—sustained procedural rights for alleged wrongdoers and criminals, upheld the civil rights of blacks and other racial minorities, granted First Amendment protections to alleged subversives, narrowly defined what material was obscene and could therefore be banned, prohibited officially prescribed prayer and religious observances in public schools, and ordered state legislatures to reapportion on the basis of "one person, one vote."

Each of these decisions outraged some segment of the population. Complaints that the Court was too permissive and that its decisions would lead to the moral downfall of the country abounded, and billboards all across the country demanded Warren's impeachment.

Responding to their constituents and their own more conservative political and social philosophies, several groups in Congress tried to curb the Warren Court, but very few of these attempts were successful, and even fewer had any real effect on the Court. Efforts to cut back the Court's jurisdiction to review certain kinds of federal and state legislation failed, as did several attempts to reverse specific decisions by legislation or through constitutional amendment. Congress did succeed in reversing one decision relating to subversive activities and in modifying three decisions relating to criminal procedures in federal courts. The Court itself—under Warren and his successors, Warren E. Burger, then William H. Rehnquist—modified more of the disputed decisions than did Congress.

The Contemporary Court

Although the Burger Court (1969–1986) was significantly more conservative than the Warren Court, a few of its decisions, including acceptance of forced busing as a method to achieve racial desegregation in public schools and its bar on state prohibition of abortions, elicited loud but ineffective calls from Congress for statutory reversal and jurisdictional curbs on the Court. In the 1980s, however, two conservative decisions

by the Court on questions of civil rights were reversed by congressional statute. In the area of voting rights, the Court made challenges to discriminatory laws more difficult, while Congress amended the 1965 Voting Rights Act to contradict the Court. A later Court ruling that limited the impact of a sex discrimination ban, and affected similar language in other civil rights laws, was reversed by Congress, although the effort took several years to move through the legislative process. After Rehnquist became chief justice in 1986 and the Court in 1989 cut back on the reach of federal laws against job discrimination, another protracted legislative battle ensued, concluding in 1991 with passage of a broad-based reversal of several Court decisions.

In the second half of the 1990s, the Rehnquist Court struck down or limited a series of congressional measures that had been championed by liberal Democrats, including the Violence against Women Act, the Brady Handgun Control Act, and the Americans with Disabilities Act. Senators Joseph Biden, D-Del., and Hillary Rodham Clinton, D-N.Y., spoke out against what they called "conservative judicial activism" by the Court. But Congress as a whole took no action seeking to reverse the decisions.

Although Congress rarely has been successful—outside of reversing decisions through legislation—in directly pressuring the Court, it is impossible to measure how much, if any, indirect pressure is placed on the Court by consideration of Court-limiting proposals. Perhaps the overall impact of such congressional efforts has been not to weaken the Court's authority but to strengthen it. Each time Congress attempts to curb the Supreme Court and fails, the public perception is heightened that the Court as an institution is unassailable and that its decisions, except in extreme circumstances, are final.

Congress as an institution has little influence on the selection of nominees to the Supreme Court. Although the Constitution in Article II, section 2, stipulates that the president shall appoint Supreme Court justices by and with the advice and consent of the Senate, the advisory role usually occurs after the fact as the Senate considers confirmation.

SELECTION AND REJECTION

An individual senator or representative, particularly one who is personally close to the president, may wield some unofficial influence in the selection process. And because the Senate adheres to the custom of senatorial courtesy—a custom that reflects its reluctance to confirm a nominee who is repugnant to a senator of the nominee's home state—presidents do well to assure themselves in advance that their nominees will not be objectionable to the pertinent senators.

In at least two instances, a majority of the Senate and House successfully petitioned the president to nominate a specific individual. In 1862, 129 of 140 House members and all but four senators signed a petition urging President Abraham Lincoln to nominate Samuel F. Miller of Iowa to the vacancy created by the death of Justice Peter V. Daniel. The Senate confirmed Miller's nomination half an hour after receiving it.[1] After Justice Robert C. Grier announced his resignation in December 1869, members of Congress submitted a petition to President Ulysses S. Grant asking him to name former secretary of war Edwin M. Stanton to the seat. Already pending in the Senate was the nomination of Grant's attorney general, Ebenezer R. Hoar, to a second vacancy on the Court—Hoar's nomination had run into some difficulty. Although Stanton was not Grant's first choice, the president acceded to the congressional request, thinking that the Stanton nomination might enhance Hoar's confirmation chances. Grant's strategy never bore fruit, however. Confirmed immediately upon nomination, Stanton died four days later of heart trouble. The Senate rejected Hoar in February 1870.[2]

Qualifications

Although the Constitution specifies qualifications that the president and members of Congress must meet, it sets no corresponding requirements for Supreme Court justices. Proposals to establish qualifications for the Court have been made throughout the nation's history, but few have received more than passing attention in Congress.

The most frequent recommendations are that justices be natural-born citizens, of a minimum age, and have a certain number of years of judicial experience. This last suggestion may grow into an informal requirement. Pressure from the legal community and the increasing complexity of the law have made experience on the bench an important consideration in the

selection of nominees. Although the Senate does not play a significant role in the selection of justices, it plays a crucial one in the confirmation of Supreme Court nominees. Article II, section 2, of the Constitution provides that no nominee shall be seated unless confirmed by the Senate. Of the 148 individuals nominated to a seat on the Supreme Court, 28, nearly one-fifth, have failed to win confirmation. By contrast, the Senate has denied confirmation to only ten cabinet nominees.

Competence

Only two Supreme Court nominees have gone unconfirmed primarily on the grounds that they were not professionally qualified.[3] In 1873 President Grant nominated his attorney general, George H. Williams, to be chief justice. Williams had served as chief justice of the Oregon Territory, but his record was undistinguished. When the Senate showed signs of balking at the nomination, Williams asked that his name be withdrawn.

Nearly one hundred years later President Richard Nixon's 1970 appointment of G. Harrold Carswell was rejected largely because of Carswell's mediocre juridical record. A second Nixon nominee, Clement F. Haynsworth Jr., although well qualified judicially, was rejected in part because he appeared insensitive to ethical improprieties and participated in cases where his financial interest might have involved him in conflicts of interest. Similar allegations of impropriety led to the resignation in 1969 of Justice Abe Fortas, nominated to the Court four years earlier by President Lyndon B. Johnson. (See "Fortas Resignation," p. 769.)

Partisan Politics

By far, most Senate rejections of Supreme Court nominees have been grounded in political considerations. A primary factor in the rejection of fourteen nominees was the "lame-duck" status of the nominating president or the fact that the party in control of the Senate was confident that its presidential candidate would win the next election.

Both of these problems afflicted the Court nominations of President John Tyler, who has the dubious distinction of having more nominees rejected than any other president. Tyler had an opportunity to fill two vacancies, but only one of his six nominations was confirmed by the Senate. One nominee was rejected because his politics offended the party ruling the Senate. Two appointments were killed because the Senate—anticipating correctly that Tyler, a Whig, would not be his party's candidate for election—wanted to hold the vacancies open. And two others, including one whom Tyler renominated, were rejected after the election of 1844, before the victor—Democrat James K. Polk—assumed office.

Ironically, Tyler made his only confirmed nomination during this period. As historian Charles Warren observed, Tyler's choice

SUPREME COURT NOMINATIONS NOT CONFIRMED BY THE SENATE

In the more than two centuries from 1789 to 1996, the Senate has rejected Supreme Court nominees twenty-eight times. One nominee, Edward King, twice failed to win Senate confirmation. A dozen have been rejected outright, and the remainder have been withdrawn or allowed to lapse when Senate rejection seemed imminent. Three were renominated later and confirmed. Following is the complete list of nominees failing to receive confirmation:

Nominee	President	Date of Nomination	Senate Action	Date of Senate Action
William Paterson	Washington	February 27, 1793	Withdrawn[1]	
John Rutledge[2]	Washington	July 1, 1795	Rejected (10-14)	December 15, 1795
Alexander Wolcott	Madison	February 4, 1811	Rejected (9-24)	February 13, 1811
John J. Crittenden	J. Q. Adams	December 17, 1828	Postponed	February 12, 1829
Roger Brooke Taney	Jackson	January 15, 1835	Postponed (24-21)[3]	March 3, 1835
John C. Spencer	Tyler	January 9, 1844	Rejected (21-26)	January 31, 1844
Reuben H. Walworth	Tyler	March 13, 1844	Withdrawn	
Edward King	Tyler	June 5, 1844	Postponed	June 15, 1844
Edward King	Tyler	December 4, 1844	Withdrawn	
John M. Read	Tyler	February 7, 1845	Not acted upon	
George W. Woodward	Polk	December 23, 1845	Rejected (20-29)	January 22, 1846
Edward A. Bradford	Fillmore	August 16, 1852	Not acted upon	
George E. Badger	Fillmore	January 10, 1853	Postponed	February 11, 1853
William C. Micou	Fillmore	February 24, 1853	Not acted upon	
Jeremiah S. Black	Buchanan	February 5, 1861	Rejected (25-26)	February 21, 1861
Henry Stanbery	A. Johnson	April 16, 1866	Not acted upon	
Ebenezer R. Hoar	Grant	December 15, 1869	Rejected (24-33)	February 3, 1870
George H. Williams[2]	Grant	December 1, 1873	Withdrawn	
Caleb Cushing[2]	Grant	January 9, 1874	Withdrawn	
Stanley Matthews	Hayes	January 26, 1881	Not acted upon[1]	
William B. Hornblower	Cleveland	September 19, 1893	Rejected (24-30)	January 15, 1894
Wheeler H. Peckham	Cleveland	January 22, 1894	Rejected (32-41)	February 16, 1894
John J. Parker	Hoover	March 21, 1930	Rejected (39-41)	May 7, 1930
Abe Fortas[2]	L. Johnson	June 26, 1968	Withdrawn	
Homer Thornberry	L. Johnson	June 26, 1968	Not acted upon	
Clement F. Haynsworth Jr.	Nixon	August 18, 1969	Rejected (45-55)	November 21, 1969
G. Harrold Carswell	Nixon	January 19, 1970	Rejected (45-51)	April 8, 1970
Robert H. Bork	Reagan	July 1, 1987	Rejected (42-58)	October 23, 1987

1. Later nominated and confirmed.
2. Nominated for chief justice.
3. Later nominated for chief justice and confirmed.

SOURCE: Congressional Research Service, Library of Congress.

of Samuel Nelson "was so preeminently a wise one that the Senate at once confirmed it."[4] But the Senate's refusal to confirm any of Tyler's nominations to the second seat helped to create the longest vacancy in Supreme Court history. (*See box, Empty Chairs: Vacancies on the Court, p. 906.*) Other lame-duck presidents whose nominees were rejected include John Quincy Adams, Millard Fillmore, James Buchanan, and Lyndon B. Johnson. (*See "The 'Save-the-Seat' Syndrome," pp. 806–807.*)

President Ronald Reagan was in the next to the last year of his eight-year stay at the White House when his nomination of Robert H. Bork was defeated by the Senate after one of the most vociferous confirmation battles in history. Bork's rejection stemmed largely from his often-articulated and well-known conservative views and the fact that he had been named to replace a "swing vote" on the Court, Justice Lewis F. Powell Jr. (Reagan's later selection of Douglas H. Ginsburg came to naught as well. Before his nomination was official, Ginsburg asked that his name be withdrawn because of the questions being raised about his possible conflicts of interest and his past drug use.[5] Reagan's third choice, Anthony M. Kennedy, was confirmed unanimously by the Senate in 1988.)

Several other nominations also were rejected because a majority of the Senate objected to specific political views or actions of the nominee. George Washington's nomination of John Rutledge for chief justice was refused because Rutledge had publicly attacked the Jay Treaty. Although it became apparent during the confirmation process that Rutledge suffered from occasional fits of insanity, "[t]he excited political situation was such that irrespective of Rutledge's mental condition his rejection by the Senate was certain," wrote Warren.[6]

Senate Whigs rejected future chief justice Roger B. Taney twice—first as Treasury secretary, forcing him to resign his recess appointment, and then as an associate justice because he had carried out President Andrew Jackson's orders to remove government deposits from the Bank of the United States.

James Madison's appointment of Alexander Wolcott failed in part because of his strict enforcement of the embargo and non-intercourse laws during his tenure as customs collector. James K. Polk's nomination of George W. Woodward did not succeed in part because Woodward held what were described as "native American sentiments" offensive to Irish Americans and other ethnic groups.

The distinguished lawyer Jeremiah S. Black had two strikes against him. He was a lame-duck appointment; President Buchanan nominated him a month before Abraham Lincoln was inaugurated. He also was a northerner whose views on slavery were unacceptable to abolitionists. The Senate objected to Ebenezer Hoar for several reasons, two of which were that he had opposed the impeachment of President Andrew Johnson and had supported civil service reform. Rutherford B. Hayes's nomination of Stanley Matthews was initially rejected for political reasons and ethical considerations, but upon renomination he was confirmed.

In 1930 the American Federation of Labor (AFL) and the National Association for the Advancement of Colored People (NAACP) mounted a successful lobbying campaign against confirmation of Herbert C. Hoover's appointee, John J. Parker. A well-qualified federal judge from North Carolina, Parker was accused of insensitivity to labor and racial problems. Civil rights activists might well have rued their success. Parker continued as a judge on the Fourth Circuit Court of Appeals where he handed down some of the earliest and most influential decisions in favor of rights for African Americans. The man elevated to the Supreme Court in his stead, Owen J. Roberts, was not so supportive on civil rights issues.

One nominee was denied the position of chief justice because the Senate could not decide what his political views were. In addition to being seventy-four years old at the time of his nomination in 1874, Caleb Cushing had been a Whig, a Tyler Whig, a Democrat, a Johnson Constitutional Conservative, and a Republican. Those shifting allegiances gained him so many political enemies that Senate opposition forced President Grant to withdraw the nomination.

Perhaps the most pointed political rejection of a nominee was the treatment of Henry Stanbery, President Andrew Johnson's attorney general. Stanbery was well liked, but the president was not. To deny Johnson any opportunity to make appointments to the Court, Radical Republicans in Congress engineered the passage of legislation that reduced the number of justices from ten to seven as vacancies occurred. The seat to which Stanbery had been appointed in 1865 was thus abolished and his nomination was never considered. *(See "Size of the Court," pp. 773–774.)*

Senatorial Courtesy

A feud between a president and a senator prompted the only two rejections made solely on the grounds of senatorial courtesy. When Justice Samuel Blatchford died in 1893, President Grover Cleveland sought to replace him with another New Yorker. Sen. David B. Hill, D-N.Y., made several suggestions, but because he and Cleveland opposed each other on patronage matters, Cleveland ignored his recommendations and nominated New York attorney William B. Hornblower. Hill prevailed upon his colleagues, and the Senate rejected the nomination.

Undaunted, Cleveland next proposed another New Yorker, Wheeler Peckham. Again Hill objected and again the Senate followed his wishes. To Hill's surprise, Cleveland abandoned his intention to nominate a New Yorker and instead named Edward D. White of Louisiana, then serving as the Senate's Democratic majority leader. He was confirmed the same day he was nominated. In most instances, the Senate confirms sitting or former senators with little or no inquiry or opposition. One exception to that tradition was the rejection of North Carolina senator George E. Badger to fill the seat left vacant when Justice John McKinley died. President Fillmore, a Whig, named Badger, also a Whig, to the Court just three months before the inauguration of Democrat Franklin Pierce. Although it was highly irregular to reject one of its own members, the Democrat-controlled Senate wanted Pierce to fill the vacancy. As a result, Badger's nomination was postponed on February 11, 1853, by a one-vote margin, 26–25. Pierce took office the following month and nominated a fellow Democrat, John A. Campbell, who was confirmed.

CONTROVERSIAL CONFIRMATIONS

Perhaps because there has been some effort to submerge political considerations in favor of judicial experience when selecting and confirming Supreme Court nominees, fewer rejections have occurred in modern times. The Senate has refused to confirm only five nominees as associate justices and one as chief justice in the twentieth century, compared with a total of twenty-two appointees rejected in the nineteenth century.

Six other twentieth-century nominations, however, have faced stiff opposition—those of Louis D. Brandeis as associate justice in 1916, Harlan Fiske Stone as associate justice in 1925, Charles Evans Hughes as chief justice in 1930, Hugo L. Black as associate justice in 1937, William H. Rehnquist as chief justice in 1986, and Clarence Thomas as associate justice in 1991. To this list might be added Thurgood Marshall, the first black named to the Court. The Senate Judiciary Committee in 1961 and 1962 held up Marshall's confirmation as a judge of the Second Circuit Court of Appeals for a year before approving the nomination. In 1965 the same committee approved Marshall's appointment as solicitor general in less than a month. But when

The nomination of Louis D. Brandeis to the Supreme Court in January 1916 set off a four-month confirmation battle, in which conservative forces in industry and finance vigorously fought to keep Brandeis off the bench. President Woodrow Wilson and a host of progressive reform groups prevailed, and the Senate confirmed him by a wide margin.

Hughes's nomination as chief justice in 1930 was attacked primarily because the country was entering the Great Depression, and his views were considered too conservative for the times. Black encountered difficulties because he had once been a member of the Ku Klux Klan. Black repudiated his Klan involvement in a dramatic radio broadcast, and criticism waned.

Like the controversy over the nomination of Hughes as chief justice, the controversy that surrounded President Reagan's nomination of Justice Rehnquist as chief justice was in part a function of the point in time—and in the Court's history—at which it came. Reagan, who believed federal judges had become too activist and were interfering with civil rights and social policy that should be controlled by legislators, had made no secret of his desire to use his nominations to shape a more conservative Court. When he chose Rehnquist to succeed retiring chief justice Warren E. Burger, he moved the Court's most conservative member to its center chair. Rehnquist had been easily confirmed fifteen years earlier, but this time three months and five days of Senate debate passed before he won confirmation, 65–33. During that time, civil rights groups mounted an all-out effort to defeat his nomination as chief justice.[7]

The thirty-three votes cast against Rehnquist were the most ever cast against a Supreme Court nominee who won confirmation—until five years later when Clarence Thomas was nominated. Thomas, selected by President George Bush, was narrowly confirmed, 52-48, on October 15, 1991, after months of controversy over Thomas's conservative record and unprecedented

President Johnson named him to the Supreme Court in 1967, southern members of the Senate committee subjected Marshall to intense questioning about his opinions and judicial philosophy. Marshall was nonetheless confirmed as an associate justice by a comfortable 69-11 vote.

Action on the Brandeis nomination a half-century earlier was delayed for months by the Senate Judiciary Committee as it pondered the nominee's "radical views." Although opposition to the nomination centered on Brandeis's liberal economic, political, and social posture, there is evidence that much of it was motivated by anti-Semitic prejudice.

At the time of his nomination, Stone was attorney general and was in the midst of prosecuting Burton K. Wheeler, a recently elected and influential Democratic senator from Montana, for oil land fraud. Wheeler was eventually acquitted of the charges, but with the aid of his home state colleague, Sen. Thomas J. Walsh, he fought Stone's nomination so vigorously on the Senate floor that it was recommitted for further investigation by the Judiciary Committee. Stone then personally appeared before the committee, something no previous Supreme Court nominee had done. Subjected to hostile questioning, Stone's performance was impressive, and the committee again recommended that he be confirmed. The full Senate concurred by a vote of 71-6.

Clarence Thomas prepares to give testimony at a Senate Judiciary Committee hearing on his Supreme Court nomination, September 10, 1991. Thomas was narrowly confirmed, 52–48, after months of controversy.

last-minute hearings into a former Thomas employee's allegations of sexual harassment.

The harassment charges by Anita F. Hill, a law professor at the University of Oklahoma, had received only a cursory behind-the-scenes examination before the Senate Judiciary Committee deadlocked, 7-7, on the Thomas nomination on September 27. But the weekend before the full Senate's scheduled October 8 vote on the nomination, word of the allegations leaked out to reporters. Hill had submitted an affidavit to the Judiciary Committee outlining Thomas's unwelcome sexual advances to her when she worked with him in the early 1980s at the Department of Education and the Equal Employment Opportunity Commission.

The disclosure of the allegations—and the failure of the committee to investigate them thoroughly—touched off a storm of criticism and demands for more hearings. The Judiciary Committee reopened its proceedings and took testimony from both Hill and Thomas, who denied the charges. The committee's awkward handling of the sexual harassment allegations, played out before a nationwide television audience, and the lack of resolution of the charges prompted an outpouring of public anger and scorn, particularly from women against senators. For several years after Thomas made it onto the Court his name continued to be associated with the sexual harassment issue, although nothing was ever proven.[8]

REMOVAL FROM OFFICE

The Constitution stipulates that Supreme Court justices, like all other federal judges, are appointed for life "during good behavior." A judge may die in office or retire, but the only method specified by the Constitution for forcible removal of a federal judge is through impeachment in the House and conviction by two-thirds of the Senate.

From time to time the other two branches of the federal government have thought to change the philosophical direction of the Supreme Court by proposing that justices serve a limited number of years. Thomas Jefferson, for example, wanted to limit the tenure of justices to six years, with reappointment subject to approval of both the House and Senate. Such a scheme would have allowed the Democratic-Republican president and Congress to replace the Federalists on the Court with justices more in keeping with their political philosophy.

In 1957 Sen. James O. Eastland, D-Miss., and Rep. Thomas G. Abernethy, D-Miss., offered a constitutional amendment to limit terms of justices to four years and to require Senate approval of incumbent justices within six months of the ratification of the proposed amendment. This proposal showed the Mississippians' displeasure with some of the Warren Court's liberal rulings, including its decisions striking down state-imposed racial segregation.

None of the proposals to limit tenure has come close to passage. But proposals suggesting ways other than impeachment to remove judges who are physically or mentally incompetent or who conduct themselves unethically or improperly have received serious consideration. The Senate approved such a proposal in 1978, but the House took no action.

Impeachment

Article II, section 4, of the Constitution states that "all Civil Officers of the United States shall be removed from office on Impeachment for, and conviction of, Treason, Bribery, or other high Crimes and Misdemeanors." The crimes of treason and bribery as grounds for impeachment have roused little debate, because treason is defined elsewhere in the Constitution and bribery is well defined in the criminal code. But throughout the nation's history there has been much debate about what the Constitution's authors meant by the phrase "high crimes and misdemeanors." Did they intend it to be read narrowly to mean that a judge could be removed from office only if he or she committed some indictable offense? Or did the Framers intend that the phrase be construed broadly so that impeachment might be used as a political weapon?

The broad construction was the one held by the members of Congress who brought the only successful impeachment action against a Supreme Court justice. In 1804 Democratic-Republican members of the House of Representatives impeached Federalist justice Samuel Chase for misconduct. Their intent, if the Senate convicted Chase, was to then impeach other Federalist members of the Supreme Court, including the Democratic-Republicans' *bête noire*, Chief Justice John Marshall. But the Senate failed to convict Chase, Democratic-Republicans abandoned their plan, and Marshall's Federalist philosophy dominated the Court until his death in 1835.

Only two other justices have faced serious impeachment threats. Abe Fortas resigned from the Court in 1969 after the House threatened to begin an impeachment inquiry into his association with an industrialist convicted of securities irregularities. On two separate occasions the House investigated impeachment charges against William O. Douglas, first in 1953 because of his temporary stay of execution of two convicted spies, and again in 1970. The second attempt was spurred by conservative Republicans in part to retaliate for the Senate's rejection of two Nixon appointees, in part to reprimand the Court for issuing several decisions that conservatives disliked, and in part to punish Douglas for what they considered his inappropriate judicial and extrajudicial behavior. In neither instance did proceedings progress beyond the inquiry stage.

Chase Impeachment

The impeachment and trial of Justice Chase for partisan, harsh, and unfair judicial treatment while riding circuit had its roots in the Democratic-Republicans' desire to rid the federal judiciary of Federalist influence. When Jefferson was elected president and Democratic-Republicans gained control of Congress in 1800, the judiciary became the last Federalist stronghold in the national government.

The efforts of Rep. John Randolph *(right)* of Roanoke, Virginia, to prosecute Samuel Chase *(left)* in his 1805 impeachment trial before the Senate were no match for the defense, and Chase was acquitted. The House of Representatives had earlier voted to impeach Chase, a Federalist, for showing bias against Democratic-Republican defendants in circuit court trials.

Outgoing Federalist president John Adams sought to ensure continuation of his party's judicial influence by having Congress enact laws creating sixteen new circuit court judgeships and several justice of the peace positions. He then filled these new posts with last-minute appointments, who quickly became known as "midnight judges."

In 1802 the Democratic-Republican Congress repealed the 1801 Judiciary Act creating the circuit court judgeships, and the Supreme Court upheld the repeal in 1803.[9] In the same year, Chief Justice Marshall, an ardent Federalist, announced the Court's unanimous decision in *Marbury v. Madison*, the case in which one of Adams's midnight appointees sued the Court to order the Jefferson administration to give him his commission. Marshall ruled that the Court did not have the constitutional authority to issue such an order, but in so doing he sharply rebuked President Jefferson and asserted for the Court the power to declare acts of Congress unconstitutional.[10] *(See "Marbury v. Madison," pp. 80–83.)* This decision convinced Democratic-Republicans that they should move against the Court. They had already used impeachment as a tool of intimidation, threatening to institute impeachment inquiries if the Court refused to approve repeal of the 1801 act or ruled against Jefferson in the *Marbury* case.

Other events were conspiring to make the idea of impeachment attractive. In January 1803 the Pennsylvania legislature had impeached and convicted a state judge of high crimes and misdemeanors, even though it was evident his only "crime" was being an active Federalist. In early February of the same year, Jefferson sent to the House of Representatives documents complaining of the behavior of U.S. District Judge John Pickering of New Hampshire. As one commentator described it, Pickering "was making a daily spectacle of himself on the bench because of intoxication aggravated by copious and blasphemous profanity."[11] The House responded immediately, passing on March 2, 1803, a resolution that impeached Pickering. He was later convicted and removed from office.

Then, in May 1803, Justice Chase provided the Democratic-Republicans with the excuse they needed to move against a member of the Supreme Court.

The Charges. An active patriot during the Revolutionary War, Chase was a signer of the Declaration of Independence and chief justice of Maryland before his appointment to the Supreme Court by President Washington in 1796. Chase's legal ability and integrity were unquestioned. But his personality made him unpopular with contemporaries; they found him arrogant, arbitrary, and guilty of using his position as a judge to advance his Federalist beliefs. As an associate justice, Chase openly approved passage of the despised Alien and Sedition Acts and actively campaigned for Adams's reelection in 1800. These activities drew the enmity of many, but the greatest opprobrium fell on Chase for some of his judicial decisions.

Chase was severely condemned for his arbitrary and intemperate treatment of the sedition trial of Democratic-Republican printer James T. Callender, who was indicted for writing during the 1800 presidential campaign, "Take your choice, then, between Adams, war and beggary, and Jefferson, peace and competency."

Chase was apparently so rude to Callender's attorneys that they left the courtroom. Chase also was sharply criticized for his conduct of the trial of John Fries, the Pennsylvania farmer who had organized the Whiskey Rebellion against payment of the 1798 "war taxes" to the federal government. Although Fries and his men were armed, there was little violence during the uprising. Chase nonetheless insisted that the grand jury indict Fries for treason; he then found Fries guilty and sentenced him to death. To avoid public outrage, Adams later pardoned Fries.

On yet another occasion, Chase refused to discharge a Delaware grand jury that had ignored his hints that it should indict a Wilmington publisher Chase thought guilty of publishing seditious statements. Finally, in May 1803 Chase delivered what was described as a political harangue to a Baltimore grand jury in which he denounced the Democratic-Republican administration and its policies. Enraged at this extrajudicial behavior, Jefferson wrote on May 13, 1803, to Rep. Joseph R. Nicholson of Maryland:

> You must have heard of the extraordinary charge of Chace [sic] to the Grand Jury at Baltimore? Ought this seditious and official attack on the principles of our Constitution, and on the proceedings of a state, to go unpunished? and to whom so pointedly as yourself will the public look for the necessary measures? I ask these questions for your consideration, for myself it is better that I should not interfere.[12]

House Democratic-Republicans took Jefferson's broad hint. In January 1804, just as the Senate was beginning Judge Pickering's impeachment trial, Rep. John Randolph of Virginia introduced an impeachment resolution against Chase in the House. Randolph brought eight specific charges against Chase. Six of them dealt with his conduct of the Callender and Fries trials, the seventh with his conduct before the Delaware grand jury, and the eighth with his diatribe to the Baltimore grand jury.

Just an hour after the Senate voted on March 12 to remove Pickering from office, the full House voted to impeach Chase. The vote was 73-32, along strictly partisan lines.

Senate Trial. The Senate chamber was filled with spectators, including Chief Justice Marshall and the associate justices, as Chase's trial began on January 2, 1805. Vice President Aaron Burr, who had recently killed Alexander Hamilton in a duel, presided over the trial. John Randolph led the team of House managers who prosecuted Chase; Randolph's associates included Nicholson, George W. Campbell of Tennessee, Caesar Rodney of Delaware, and Peter Early of Georgia. Defending Chase was a battery of able lawyers, including a celebrated orator, Maryland attorney general Luther Martin, former representative Robert Goodloe Harper, Philip Barton Key, Joseph Hopkinson, and former U.S. attorney general Charles Lee.

Chase appeared before the Senate on the opening day of the trial to read a statement in which he maintained he had not engaged in impeachable conduct.

> To these articles ... I say that I have committed no crime or misdemeanor ... for which I am subject to impeachment according to the Constitution of the United States. I deny, with a few exceptions, the acts with which I am charged; I shall contend, that all acts admitted

to have been done by me were legal, and I deny, in every instance, the improper intentions with which the acts charged are alleged to have been done, and in which their supposed criminality altogether consists.[13]

Chase asked for a delay in the trial so that he could prepare his defense and was granted a month. When the proceedings resumed in February, fifty-two witnesses, including Marshall, testified before the Senate. Marshall's principal biographer, Albert J. Beveridge, wrote that the chief justice's performance was marked by trepidation and that his responses were not favorable to Chase's cause. Marshall's demeanor may have been caused by his worry that should Chase be convicted, Marshall was sure to be the next target. In a letter to Chase dated January 23, 1804, Marshall even suggested that impeachment might be avoided by giving Congress the authority to reverse Court decisions that declared federal laws unconstitutional.[14] *(See quote from letter, p. 820.)* Once testimony was complete, the major debate centered on whether a justice must have committed an indictable crime to be impeached and convicted. Although Chase may have behaved in a highly questionable manner, he had not violated any federal law.

The House managers argued that offensive conduct was sufficient for impeachment. Representative Campbell contended:

> Impeachment, ... according to the meaning of the Constitution, may fairly be considered a kind of inquest into the conduct of an officer [of the United States], merely as it regards his office; the manner in which he performs the duties thereof; and the effects that his conduct therein may have on society. It is more in the nature of a civil investigation than of a criminal prosecution.[15]

In Chase's behalf, attorney Hopkinson argued that

> no judge can be impeached and removed from office for any act or offense for which he could not be indicted.... I maintain as a most important and indispensable principle, that no man should be criminally accused, no man can be criminally condemned, but for the violation of some known law by which he was bound to govern himself. Nothing is so necessary to justice and to safety as that the criminal code should be certain and known. Let the judge, as well as the citizen, precisely know the path he has to walk in, and what he may or may not do.[16]

On March 1, 1805, the Senate was ready to vote. Of the thirty-four members present, twenty-five were Democratic-Republicans, and nine were Federalists. Because twenty-three votes were needed for conviction, the Democratic-Republicans could carry the day if they voted together. But at least six Democratic-Republicans sided with the Federalists on each vote, and Chase was acquitted of all eight charges. On one charge the vote was unanimous in Chase's favor. The closest vote came on the complaint that triggered the impeachment—Chase's political harangue to the grand jury. Eighteen senators found Chase guilty; sixteen, not guilty.

Several factors accounted for Chase's acquittal. Manager Randolph's popularity in the House did not extend to the Senate. He may have reduced his influence further by boastfulness and by his extremely broad interpretation of the power of impeachment. There is also evidence that more moderate Democratic-

Republicans were miffed at his opposition in the House to some of their legislative proposals. By all accounts, the case presented by the House managers was inept compared with that of Chase's defenders. Besides, Jefferson, having goaded the House into initiating impeachment, had taken no further part in the proceedings.

Randolph's response to the acquittal was immediate. He strode to the House floor and offered a constitutional amendment to provide for the removal of Supreme Court justices by the president at the request of a majority of both houses of Congress. The House approved the amendment by a 68-33 vote, but the proposal never emerged from the Senate.

The outcome of the trial meant that the Democratic-Republicans were forced to give up their plans for further impeachments and that Federalist judges on both the Supreme Court and inferior federal courts were secure for the first time since Jefferson's election. The exercise probably proved that impeachment and conviction could not succeed if the motivations were primarily partisan ones. But the episode did not resolve the fundamental constitutional question of whether only indictable offenses are impeachable. Some 165 years later, when members of Congress sought to impeach Justice Douglas primarily for political reasons, the leader of the movement raised the identical question when he argued that "an impeachable offense is whatever a majority of the House of Representatives considers it to be at a given moment in history." [17]

Fortas Resignation

In 1969 Abe Fortas became the first Supreme Court justice to resign under threat of impeachment. Only eight months earlier the Senate had refused to act on President Johnson's proposal to elevate Fortas from associate justice to chief justice to replace retiring Earl Warren.

Fortas resigned on May 14, 1969, just ten days after an article about him was published in *Life* magazine. *Life* reported that in January 1966 Fortas had accepted a $20,000 check from a family foundation established by multimillionaire industrialist Louis E. Wolfson. Fortas had agreed to act as an adviser to the foundation, which worked to improve community relations and racial and religious cooperation. In September 1966 Wolfson was indicted (and later convicted) for selling unregistered securities. According to the article, Fortas had returned the $20,000 to Wolfson in December 1966 and severed his connection with the foundation.

The same day the *Life* article was published, Fortas issued a statement declaring that he did not feel the fee implied any inducement for him to try to influence Wolfson's case. But his statement did not reassure many members of Congress; they thought that Fortas had violated Canon 25 of "The Canons of Judicial Ethics," prepared in 1922 for the American Bar Association by a committee headed by Chief Justice William Howard Taft. Canon 25 said that a "judge should avoid giving any ground for any reasonable suspicion that he is utilizing the power or prestige of his office to persuade or coerce others to patronize or contribute, either to the success of private business, or to charitable enterprises."

On May 11, Rep. H. R. Gross, R-Iowa (1949–1975), announced that he had prepared articles of impeachment against Fortas to present to the House within a "reasonable" time if the justice did not resign. The articles, Gross said, accused Fortas of malfeasance, misconduct, and impropriety. Calls for resignation began to come not only from the conservative Republicans and southern Democrats who had blocked his confirmation as chief justice, but also from liberal Democrats who had supported him in the earlier fight.

On May 13 Rep. Clark MacGregor, R-Minn., apparently with the blessing of the Nixon administration, proposed a preliminary inquiry into the affair by the House Judiciary Committee. The next day Fortas tendered his resignation to President Nixon, who promptly accepted it.

In a letter of explanation to Chief Justice Warren, Fortas maintained that he had done nothing wrong. But he said he feared that continued controversy over his association with the foundation would "adversely affect the work and position of the Court" and that his resignation "will enable the Court to proceed with its vital work free from extraneous stress." [18]

Douglas Impeachment Attempts

Twice during Justice William O. Douglas's unprecedentedly long tenure on the Supreme Court bench (thirty-six years), the House initiated unsuccessful impeachment proceedings against him. Appointed to the Court in 1939, Douglas quickly became one of the most controversial justices in history. His staunchly

William O. Douglas

liberal views, his outspoken opinions, and his several marriages, two to women considerably younger than he, made him the target of continuing criticism.

The first attempt to impeach Douglas stemmed from his temporary stay, on June 17, 1953, of the executions of convicted spies Julius and Ethel Rosenberg. One day later, Rep. W. M. "Don" Wheeler, D-Ga., introduced a resolution of impeachment, and the House Judiciary Committee immediately appointed a special subcommittee of inquiry. On June 19 the full Supreme Court overruled Douglas, setting aside the stay, and the Rosenbergs were executed. At the single subcommittee hearing, Wheeler was the only witness to testify, and on July 7 the full committee tabled the impeachment resolution.

The second attempt to impeach Douglas came on the heels of the resignation under threat of impeachment of Abe Fortas in 1969 and the Senate rejections in 1969 and 1970 of two Nixon nominees, Clement F. Haynsworth Jr. and G. Harrold Carswell, to fill the vacancy. On April 15, 1970, House minority leader Gerald R. Ford, R-Mich., made five major charges against Douglas in a floor speech. Douglas, Ford said, had engaged in "gross impropriety" when he did not disqualify himself from sitting on obscenity cases involving publisher Ralph Ginzburg. (In March 1969 one of Ginzburg's publications, *Evergreen Review*, had paid Douglas $350 for an article.) Ford also objected that an article by Douglas and photographs of nudes had appeared in an issue of the same publication.

The minority leader also charged that a book written by Douglas, *Points of Rebellion*, could be construed to advocate the violent overthrow of the existing political order and therefore violated the standard of good behavior.

The most serious charge against Douglas was that—in violation of federal law—he practiced law through his association with Albert Parvin and the Albert Parvin Foundation. Parvin was a multimillionaire industrialist who had an interest in a Las Vegas hotel and gambling casino; his foundation was established to promote international cooperation through education. There were allegations that the foundation received a substantial portion of its funding from gambling interests.

Ford charged that Douglas had assisted in the incorporation of the foundation and gave the institution legal advice in dealing with an Internal Revenue Service (IRS) investigation. Douglas maintained that he acted only as an adviser to the foundation, for which he received $12,000 a year plus travel expenses. The justice voluntarily ended his association with the foundation in May 1969.

Finally, Ford criticized Douglas's role as a consultant to the Center for the Study of Democratic Institutions at the same time the center was a recipient of Parvin Foundation funds. Ford urged creation of a special House committee to investigate these charges, but Rep. Andrew Jacobs Jr., D-Ind., a Douglas supporter, successfully offered an impeachment resolution to be referred to the House Judiciary Committee, where Douglas was likely to receive sympathetic treatment.

RETIREMENT

Congressional inaction on salary and benefits for the Supreme Court can exert pressure on the members of the Court. For example, for the first eighty years of the Court's existence Congress made no pension provisions for justices who wished to retire. As a result, several stayed on the Court until death even though they were physically and mentally incapable of performing their duties.

That situation was somewhat remedied by congressional passage on April 10, 1869, of an act that provided that any federal justice who reached seventy years of age and had ten years of service could resign and receive a pension equal to his salary at the time of resignation.

In 1936, when President Franklin D. Roosevelt announced a plan to rid the Court of aged conservatives who were blocking implementation of most of his economic recovery program, all members of the federal judiciary except Supreme Court justices were allowed to retire from regular service rather than resign. Judges who retired were still entitled to the salary of the office, including the increases in salary given to active judges.

Supreme Court justices, however, had to resign, and their pensions were subject to the same fluctuations as other retired government officials. When Justice Oliver Wendell Holmes Jr. was prevailed upon to resign in 1932, his pension was $10,000 a year—half his annual pay as a justice—because the Hoover administration, thinking to economize, set that amount as the maximum pension for former government employees.

Chief Justice Charles Evans Hughes thought later that two of the more conservative members of the Court would have joined Holmes and retired if Congress had not been so penurious. As it was, Justices Willis Van Devanter and George Sutherland remained on the Court, forming the nucleus of the conservative majority that struck down one New Deal law after another.

In response to Roosevelt's "Court-packing" proposal, which it opposed, Congress quickly approved the Supreme Court Retirement Act of 1937, which permitted justices aged seventy with ten years of service—or at age sixty-five with fifteen years of service—to retire at full salary rather than resign.

The statute quickly proved effective. Roosevelt signed it into law March 1, 1937, and on May 18 Justice Van Devanter announced his retirement.

SOURCES: William F. Swindler, *Court and Constitution in the Twentieth Century, The New Legality, 1932–1968* (Indianapolis: Bobbs-Merrill, 1970); Charles Fairman, *History of the Supreme Court of the United States*, vol. 6, *Reconstruction and Reunion, 1864–88*, part 1 (New York: Macmillan, 1971); Leonard Baker, *Back to Back: The Duel between FDR and the Supreme Court* (New York: Macmillan, 1967).

On April 21, 1970, the Judiciary Committee established a special five-member subcommittee to investigate Ford's charges. After months of hearings and deliberations, on December 3 the subcommittee voted 3-1, with one abstention, that it had found no grounds for impeachment of Douglas.

In its formal report the subcommittee said that Douglas had not violated either judicial ethics or federal law when he failed to disqualify himself from the Ginzburg obscenity cases or when he received payment from one of the Ginzburg publications for the article he had written. Nor was Douglas guilty of practicing law on behalf of the Parvin Foundation. Another attorney had assumed responsibility for incorporating the foundation, and it had retained outside tax counsel during the IRS investigation.

Douglas had done nothing unethical or illegal when he accepted payment from the foundation in return for his consulting services. The subcommittee said it considered other charges made against Douglas on the basis of his relationship to Parvin and the foundation but found them "difficult to analyze because of the extreme tenuousness of the circumstantial evidence." And the committee cleared Douglas of the charges related to his association with the Center for the Study of Democratic Institutions.

The subcommittee also found that Douglas had no control over publication by *Evergreen Review* of his writings; the arrangements had been made by Douglas's publisher without his knowledge. The charges that *Points of Rebellion* encouraged violence were based on a misinterpretation of the book, the subcommittee concluded.[19]

Douglas remained on the Court another five years, retiring in November 1975 after a stroke made it impossible for him to maintain his rigorous work schedule.

Other Means of Discipline

Is impeachment the only permissible method for removing a Supreme Court justice or other federal judge from office?

Because impeachment is so seldom used—only thirteen federal judges have been impeached, and, of those, seven were convicted (but two impeached judges left office before the Senate could take up their cases)—it is widely viewed as an inadequate deterrent to misconduct on the bench. "[A]n impracticable thing—a mere scarecrow," Thomas Jefferson called it after the impeachment attempt against Justice Chase failed.

Furthermore, a judge may be impeached and convicted only for commission of treason, bribery, or high crimes and misdemeanors. But there has never been a conclusive answer to the question of what constitutes a high crime or misdemeanor. Can a judge be impeached for noncriminal but nevertheless improper judicial conduct? How can a judge who is physically or mentally unable to continue in office be removed?

These questions have prompted Congress to explore alternative methods for removal of judges. After Chase's acquittal in 1805, for example, Representative Randolph, the chief House prosecutor, rushed to the House floor and proposed a constitutional amendment that would permit the president to remove a justice at the request of a majority of both houses of Congress. The proposal was not approved.

Congress approved a modern alternative to impeachment in 1980 (Public Law 96-458). It gave the federal judiciary procedures for disciplining judges without going as far as impeaching them. The new law empowered the chief judge and the governing council of each judicial circuit to hear and investigate complaints against federal judges. The council could then certify that the judge was disabled; it could ask the judge to retire; it could suspend the judge temporarily. It could also refer cases to the Judicial Conference, which served as the review body for the council's disciplinary decisions and had the authority to send cases to the House of Representatives for possible impeachment.[20]

SALARIES

Article III, section 1, of the Constitution bars Congress from reducing the salaries of Supreme Court justices, but the legislature has absolute control over increases in wages and over appropriations for the operation of the Court itself. Only once—in 1964—has Congress deliberately exercised its power of the purse to show its displeasure with Court rulings.

In 1789 Congress set the initial salary of the associate justices at $3,500 per year. As of 2003 associate justices were paid $190,000 a year. Traditionally, the chief justice has been paid more than the associate justices. John Jay earned $4,000 as the first chief justice; as of January 1, 2003, William H. Rehnquist earned a salary of $198,600 as chief justice. *(See box, Justices' Salaries, p. 900.)*

Like most working people, the justices have not always been satisfied with the level of their compensation. At least one justice resigned from the Court partially because he was unable to support his family in the manner he desired on his Court salary. *(See box, Compensation Complaint, p. 772.)*

During congressional debate in 1866 over reducing the size of the Court, Chief Justice Salmon P. Chase urged a three-seat reduction so that the salaries of the remaining justices might be raised. In a June 15, 1866, letter to Associate Justice Samuel F. Miller, Chase wrote:

> It is very important—if it is important that adequate salaries should be paid to the Judges of the Supreme Court—that the number of Judges should be reduced proportionally as vacancies may occur, to seven. I think that the salaries of the highest Judicial Officers of the Nation ought not to be less than those of the highest Military Officers: and at least an approximation might be made if the number were not so large, and especially if by the reduction of the number the means of increase would ultimately be supplied.[21]

In 1866 the chief justice was paid $6,500 a year; associate justices, $6,000. Chase apparently wished an increase to $12,000 for himself and to $10,000 for his associates. Congress did reduce the size of the Court to seven as justices either died or retired, but it did not increase their salaries. The next pay raise occurred in 1871, when the salary of associate justices was increased to $8,000 and that of the chief justice to $8,500. *(See "Size of the Court," pp. 773–774.)*

In 1964 Congress considered legislation authorizing the first increases in pay since 1955 for top-level federal employees. The House approved a $7,500 increase for members of Congress and all federal judges, including Supreme Court justices. But when the bill reached the Senate, it, by a vote of 46-40, adopted an amendment to reduce the increase for the justices to $2,500. A

COMPENSATION COMPLAINT

Supreme Court justices are very well paid compared with most American workers in the private or public sector. Compared with other prominent lawyers, however, they do not fare so well. The official salaries of the justices are only a fraction of those earned by the partners in well-established law firms.

At least one justice resigned from the Supreme Court because he found the salary too low. Justice Benjamin R. Curtis resigned on September 30, 1857, at the age of forty-eight. As an associate justice he earned $4,500 a year. An abolitionist, Curtis also was greatly disturbed by the Court's decision in the Dred Scott case in March 1857. Curtis wrote to his friend George Ticknor, a Boston historian and educator:

Before [September] I shall have to come to a decision upon a matter of great moment to myself,—whether to continue to hold my present office. The expenses of living have so largely increased, that I do not find it practicable to live on my salary, even now; and, as my younger children will soon call for much increased expenses of education, I shall soon find it difficult to meet expenses by my entire income. Indeed I do not think I can do so without changing, in important particulars, my mode of life. Added to this, I cannot have a house in Washington, and I must either live apart from my family for four to six months every year while I go there, or subject them to a kind of migrant life in boarding-houses, neither congenial or useful. I had hoped it would prove otherwise, and looked forward to being able to have a house there for six months in a year. But what with the increase of luxury and the greatly enhanced prices there, I have now no hope of being able to do this. I can add something to my means by making books, but at the expense of all my vacations, when perhaps I ought not to labor hard. The constant labor of the summer has told on my health during the last two years. Such is the actual state of the case as respects my duty to my family. Then as regards the court and the public, I say to you in confidence, that I can not feel that confidence in the court, and that willingness to cooperate with them which are essential to the satisfactory discharge of my duties as a member of that body; and I do not expect its condition to be improved. On the other hand, I suppose there is a pretty large number of conservative people in the Northern, and some of the Southern States, who would esteem my retirement a public loss, and who would think that I had disappointed reasonable expectations in ceasing to hold the office; and particularly in my own circuit I believe my retirement would be felt to be a loss.... But I do not myself think it of great public importance that I should remain where I believe I can exercise little beneficial influence and I think all might abstain from blaming me when they remember that I have devoted six of the best years of my life to the public service.... I have no right to blame the public for not being willing to pay a larger salary; but they have not right to blame me for declining it on account of its inadequacy.

SOURCES: Benjamin R. Curtis, *The Life and Writings of Benjamin Robbins Curtis* (Boston: Little, Brown, 1879), 155; quoted by John R. Schmidhauser and Larry L. Berg, *The Supreme Court and Congress: Conflict and Interaction, 1945–1968* (New York: Free Press, 1972), 64–65.

---

compromise was struck in House-Senate conference, and the increase for the justices was set at $4,500—$3,000 less than the increase for other federal executives.

The amendment's chief sponsor, Sen. Gordon Allott, R-Colo., insisted that the reduced increase would establish a "semblance of equity" between justices and members of Congress. With the $7,500 increase, members of Congress would receive $30,000; with the $4,500 increase, associate justices would earn $39,500. But there was little doubt in anyone's mind that the amendment was approved out of congressional pique over several decisions handed down by the Warren Court on issues such as obscenity, school prayer, desegregation, and loyalty-security programs. The *American Bar Association Journal* published an editorial that said:

The reason for this discriminating provision seems inescapably an effort on the part of Congress to punish members of our highest Court for performing their constitutional duty of deciding cases as they see them. If indeed this was the purpose, it was unworthy of the principle of the division of powers of our government. But even worse it is an affront to the principle of the independence of the judiciary.[22]

Congress was not to be intimidated by such criticisms. In 1965 the House, after heated debate, rejected a measure that would have increased Supreme Court salaries by $3,000 retroactive to January 1, 1965. This bill would have provided the justices with the same increase awarded to members of Congress and other federal judges. The Supreme Court justices did not receive another raise until 1969.

Pressures on the Institution

Congress sometimes tries to influence the Supreme Court by enacting legislation that affects the Court as an institution rather than its individual members. To influence the outcome of certain decisions, Congress has changed the size of the Court, repealed its jurisdiction over certain kinds of cases, and even abolished a Court term.

But Congress has considered many more efforts to pressure the Court than it has approved. Proposals to require two-thirds of the Court to concur to declare an act of Congress or state statute unconstitutional have never been approved and seldom were even seriously considered. The major proposal for a change in the size of the Court—President Franklin D. Roosevelt's plan to add six new members—failed because a majority in Congress opposed it. And only once has Congress successfully removed a threat to its legislative policies by repealing the Court's jurisdiction; several other attempts have been defeated, most of them by large margins.

SIZE OF THE COURT

Congress has increased or reduced the number of justices on the Supreme Court seven times in the Court's 215-year history. Generally, laws decreasing the number of justices have been motivated by a desire to punish the president; increases have been aimed at influencing the philosophical balance of the Court itself.[1]

The Judiciary Act of 1789 set the number of Supreme Court seats at six. In the last days of John Adams's presidency, however, Congress reduced the number to five. Justice William Cushing was ill and not expected to live much longer, and the outgoing Federalists wanted to deny incoming Democratic-Republican president Thomas Jefferson an opportunity to name Cushing's replacement. The reduction in size never occurred. In 1802 the Democratic-Republican–controlled Congress repealed the 1801 law and restored the number of justices to six. (Cushing lived until 1810, and it was James Madison who named his successor.)

In 1807 Congress increased the number of justices by one, to seven, primarily because of the population growth in Kentucky, Tennessee, and Ohio. Justice Thomas Todd of Kentucky was the first justice to fill this new seat.

In 1837 Congress increased the Court by two, to nine, again because of the increasing population and expansion of the country into the West and Southwest. Presidents James Madison, James Monroe, and John Quincy Adams each had urged Congress to enlarge the Court so that the additional judges might ease some of the backlog of cases in the circuit courts, but Congress refused because it did not want the sitting president to name the justices. (See box, Circuit-Riding, p. 875.)

The Judiciary Act of 1837 was passed on the last day of President Andrew Jackson's term. Jackson signed the bill and immediately named John Catron and William Smith to the seats. Both men were confirmed, but Smith then declined the appointment. The next increase, to ten justices, came in the midst of the Civil War. On the surface the increase was justified again by the westward expansion. The law created a tenth circuit comprising California and Oregon and later Nevada. But the additional seat meant that President Abraham Lincoln could appoint a justice who would help to ensure that the Court majority would decide issues in favor of the Union. Lincoln already had made three appointments in 1862, but his control of the Court was still not firm. The same day that the 1863 Judiciary Act went into effect, the Court upheld Lincoln's extraordinary exercise of his war powers by a slim 5-4 vote. To the new seat Lincoln appointed Californian Stephen J. Field, who supported the president on war issues. (See "Prize Cases," pp. 206–208.)

Congress was not so accommodating of Lincoln's successor, Andrew Johnson. When Justice Catron died in 1865, Johnson nominated Attorney General Henry Stanbery, who was exceptionally well qualified for the position. However, the majority in Congress was so opposed to Johnson's Reconstruction policies, and so fearful that his appointments to the Court might rule against Congress's Reconstruction programs, that it responded by reducing the number of seats on the Court from ten to seven. The vacancy to which Stanbery was nominated therefore no longer existed, and no action was taken on his appointment. The Court was reduced to eight members when Justice James M. Wayne died in July 1867.

No further vacancies occurred during Johnson's tenure. Little more than a month after President Ulysses S. Grant was inaugurated in March 1869, Congress passed another judiciary act raising the number of justices to nine. Because the Court had fallen to only eight in number, Grant had only one new seat to fill. But the resignation of Justice Robert C. Grier gave Grant two vacancies to fill during his first year in office. The president's first appointee was rejected; his second died just four days after confirmation. (See details, pp. 801–802.)

Grant then nominated William Strong and Joseph P. Bradley just hours after the Court declared in *Hepburn v. Griswold* (1870) that the substitution of paper money for gold as legal tender for the payment of contracts entered into before 1862 was unconstitutional. Shortly after Strong and Bradley were confirmed in February and March, respectively, the Court voted to reconsider its decision in the legal tender case. Fifteen months after declaring "greenbacks" unconstitutional, the Court reversed itself by a 5-4 vote and held that paper money was legal for the payment of all contracts. Because both of Grant's appointees voted in favor of reversal and because of the timing of their appointments, Grant was charged with "packing the Court," but these allegations have since been considered unwarranted. *(See "The 'Court-Packers,'" pp. 801–804; see Legal Tender Cases, pp. 135–139.)*

Congress has not changed the number of seats on the Supreme Court since 1869, although members of Congress frustrated by Court decisions have continued to propose such changes. The most serious of these proposals in the twentieth century came not from Congress but from the president. Franklin Roosevelt proposed in 1937 that the number of justices be raised to fifteen. Ostensibly to improve the efficiency of the Court, the increase was in reality designed to allow Roosevelt to appoint new justices who could be depended upon to support the constitutionality of his New Deal programs, several of which the Court had struck down.

The plan was unpopular with both the public and Congress and was not enacted, but much of the threat to the Court's independence was defused by the Court itself. Shortly after the proposal was made public, the Court upheld in quick succession a Washington State minimum wage law and the federal National Labor Relations Act. These rulings indicated that the Court was now willing to sanction broad federal regulation of private enterprise. *(See "The 'Court-Packers,'" pp. 801–804.)*

EXTRAORDINARY MAJORITY

Members of Congress occasionally have sought to restrain exercise of the Court's review powers by requiring that it find acts of Congress or state laws unconstitutional only if an extraordinary majority of the justices concurs in the decision. Most of these proposals have required that two-thirds of the justices concur; some of the more extreme proposals have urged that such decisions be unanimous.

The first proposal requiring an extraordinary majority to be considered seriously by Congress was offered in the 1820s after the Court ruled against the states in two controversial land claim suits.[2] Although the Court's vote was not announced, it was widely thought that because of absences and dissents the cases had been decided by a vote of less than a full majority of the Court.

At the behest of Kentucky, one of the states affected by the decisions, Sen. Richard M. Johnson, D-Ky., asked the Senate Judiciary Committee to consider increasing the number of justices to ten and requiring seven of them to agree in decisions rendering state laws invalid. The committee recommended against increasing the size of the Court, but it did report a bill to require five of the seven members to concur before the Court could nullify state laws. However, the full Senate voted to recommit this bill.

Similar bills offered in both the House and Senate during the next few years also failed, but their consideration may have had the intended effect on the Court. In 1834 Chief Justice John Marshall announced that the Court would delay a decision in the case of *New York v. Miln*, saying, "The practice of this Court is not (except in cases of absolute necessity) to

---

MORE IS LESS

In March 1838, at the end of the first term after the addition of two seats to the Supreme Court, Justice Joseph Story implied in a letter that the increased number had led to decreased efficiency:

You may ask how the Judges got along together? We made very slow progress, and did less in the same time than I ever knew. The addition to our number has most sensibly affected our facility as well as rapidity of doing business. Many men of many minds require a great deal of discussion to compel them to come to definite results; and we found ourselves often involved in long and very tedious debates. I verily believe, if there were twelve Judges, we should do no business at all, or at least very little.

SOURCE: Charles Warren, *The Supreme Court in United States History*, rev. ed., 2 vols. (Boston: Little, Brown, 1926), 2:42.

---

deliver any judgment in cases where constitutional questions are involved unless four [of the seven] judges concur in opinion, thus making the decision that of a majority of the whole Court." The case was not decided until 1837; then five of the seven justices concurred in the judgment.[3] *(See details of New York v. Miln, p. 346.)*

Other proposals would give Congress the final authority to determine the validity of its own legislation. One such proposal, offered by Sen. Robert M. La Follette, R-Wis., would have allowed Congress to reverse Supreme Court decisions holding federal legislation invalid by repassing it with a two-thirds majority vote. Like similar proposals, it died in committee.

TERMS

Congress has absolute power to set the terms of the Supreme Court. It once used this power to delay a particular decision by abolishing a term altogether.

In 1802 the Democratic-Republican–dominated Congress repealed the 1801 Judiciary Act. The statute, enacted by the Federalist lame-duck Congress, created several new federal judgeships. Outgoing president John Adams promptly filled the judgeships with Federalists, who in 1802 challenged the repeal. Concerned that the Supreme Court—which was composed completely of Federalists—would find the 1802 repeal unconstitutional, possibly on grounds that the Constitution forbids Congress to reduce judges' salaries, the Democratic-Republicans postponed the Court's next term.

During debate on the legislation, Delaware Federalist representative James A. Bayard opposed the delay, asking the House:

Could a more dangerous precedent than this be established? May it not lead to the virtual abolition of a Court, the existence of which is guaranteed by the Constitution? If the functions of the Court can be extended by law for fourteen months, what time will arrest us before we arrive at ten or twenty years?[4]

When the Court convened fourteen months later, in February 1803, it upheld the repeal in *Stuart v. Laird* (1803). Since then Congress has not resorted to this method to restrain the Court.

REMOVAL OF JURISDICTION

Removal of the Supreme Court's authority to review certain categories of cases has been considered throughout U.S. history as one of the more serious threats to the independence of the Court. The Constitution authorizes Congress "to make exceptions" to the Court's appellate jurisdiction. Although this language probably was not intended as a political weapon, Congress has viewed it as such during three major confrontations with the Court.

An attempt to remove some of the Court's jurisdiction came in the 1820s and 1830s when Congress sought unsuccessfully to repeal Section 25 of the Judiciary Act of 1789. This section gave the Court power to review high state-court decisions upholding state laws challenged as in conflict with the federal Constitution, federal law, or treaties.

Only once has Congress repealed the Supreme Court's jurisdiction as a way of stopping the Court from issuing a decision. In 1868 Congress repealed the Court's power to review federal court denials of writs of habeas corpus. The repeal was specifically intended to prevent the Court from hearing a habeas corpus appeal that called into question the constitutionality of the Reconstruction Acts of 1867.

Since then Congress has considered legislation to repeal the Court's authority to review specific subjects, such as internal security programs, certain criminal procedures, local education problems such as desegregation and school prayer, and state laws forbidding abortions. Although the Court's decisions in all of these areas were controversial and generated an outpouring of opposition from the public and members of Congress, none of the jurisdictional repeal attempts was successful.

There has been much scholarly debate on whether the Constitution's authors intended to give Congress absolute control over the Court's authority to take appeals from lower-court decisions. Justice Felix Frankfurter was one constitutional expert who believed that Congress could "withdraw appellate jurisdiction once conferred" even if the withdrawal affected a pending case.[5] Justice William O. Douglas, on the other hand, thought it unlikely that the Court would uphold the constitutionality of repeal legislation.[6] Justice Owen J. Roberts in 1949 and the American Bar Association in 1950 sought to resolve the dilemma by recommending adoption of a constitutional amendment to make the Court and not Congress the determiner of the Court's appellate jurisdiction.

In his book analyzing Congress's failure to curb the Court during the mid- and late-1950s, constitutional historian C. Herman Pritchett makes the argument that the constitutional grant of authority to control the Court's appellate jurisdiction is now largely an anachronism, having been repealed in effect

by the passage of time and by the recognition that exercise of such power would be in the truest sense subversive of the American tradition of an independent judiciary. Congress can no longer claim

with good conscience the authority granted by Article III, Section 2, and every time proposals to exercise such authority are rejected … the Court's control over its appellate jurisdiction is correspondingly strengthened.[7]

The first congressional attempts to repeal the Supreme Court's jurisdiction were prompted by the Court's early decisions overturning state laws. Section 25 of the Judiciary Act of 1789 authorized the Supreme Court to review, and therefore declare invalid, decisions of the states' highest courts that upheld state laws challenged as conflicting with the federal Constitution, federal statutes, or treaties. With each successive ruling striking down a state law, opposition to Section 25 grew among proponents of states' rights. After the Supreme Court emphatically upheld its review power under Section 25 in the case of *Cohens v. Virginia* (1821), several states appealed to their congressional delegations to remove this review power from the Court.[8]

The first proposal along these lines was introduced in the Senate in 1821. Senator Johnson of Kentucky proposed a constitutional amendment to give the Senate appellate jurisdiction in cases raising a federal question where a state was a party. This suggestion, however, received little support, primarily because small states held the balance of power in the Senate and were considered likely to prefer a strong national government.

The next year, legislation to repeal the Court's Section 25 review power was introduced, but it received little attention then or in the next few years. However, the Court's rulings against state sovereignty in *Craig v. Missouri* (1830) and *Cherokee Nation v. Georgia* (1831), coupled with Georgia's outright defiance of the Court, generated a major clash over the proper balance of power between the states and the federal government.[9]

As part of that confrontation the House ordered its Judiciary Committee to report a measure repealing Section 25. The committee made its report on January 24, 1831, declaring that it was

no more necessary to the harmonious action of the Federal and State governments, that the Federal court should have power to control the decisions of State courts by appeal, than that the Federal legislature should have power to control the legislation of the States, or the Federal Executive a State Executive.[10]

Repeal of Section 25 was viewed as a grave threat by members of the Court. Chief Justice John Marshall wrote that the "crisis of our Constitution is now upon us," while Justice Joseph Story lamented that "if the Twenty-Fifth Section is repealed, the Constitution is practically gone."[11]

In a letter written after the crisis had passed, former president James Madison commented on its seriousness:

The jurisdiction claimed for the Federal Judiciary is truly the only defensive armor of the Federal Government, or rather for the Constitution and laws of the United States. Strip it of that armor, and the door is wide open for nullification, anarchy and convulsion.[12]

The measure was never fully debated in the House. Using parliamentary tactics, Court supporters were able to repulse the repeal movement by a wide margin. Moves to repeal the section were made in later years, but none came any closer to passage.

Although Marshall's Court feared the consequences of a successful repeal drive, a later Court resisted efforts to expand its Section 25 appellate jurisdiction. In the Act of February 5, 1867, Congress changed the wording of the section so that it could be interpreted to allow the Supreme Court to review all errors of law in high state-court decisions and not just those concerned with federal questions. It appeared that Congress might well have intended such an expansion to counter any obstruction to the federal judicial system from the recently rebellious states. Nonetheless, in *Murdock v. Memphis* (1875) the Court held that the 1867 law had not changed Section 25 in any way. Congress did not explicitly amend the section until 1914.[13] *(See "Appellate Jurisdiction," pp. 286–288.)*

THE *McCARDLE* CASE

Only once in the nation's history has Congress prevented the Supreme Court from deciding a pending case by repealing its appellate jurisdiction over the subject matter of the case. This extraordinary action was taken by a Congress dominated by Radical Republicans who wanted to prohibit the Supreme Court from reviewing the constitutionality of the Reconstruction Acts of 1867. The acts substituted military rule for civilian government in the ten southern states that initially refused to rejoin the Union. The acts also established procedures for those states to follow to gain readmittance and representation in the federal government.

The Supreme Court twice avoided ruling on the constitutionality of the Reconstruction Acts. In April 1867, just before the acts were scheduled to take effect, the state of Mississippi asked the Court for permission to seek an injunction to stop the president from implementing them. The Court unanimously rejected the request in *Mississippi v. Johnson* (1867), holding that the president's duties under the acts were political, and therefore the Court was without jurisdiction to order the injunction.[14]

In 1868 the Court dismissed a similar request by Georgia and Mississippi officials asking that the secretary of war and the commanders of the five military districts be stopped from enforcing the Reconstruction Acts. The Court again held that the suit raised political questions over which it had no jurisdiction.[15]

Reconstruction Attacked

It was not until November 1867, several months after military rule was established in the southern states, that the events that would touch off the confrontation between the Court and Congress began. Mississippian William H. McCardle, the editor of the *Vicksburg Times*, was not loath to express editorially his distaste for Reconstruction and his views that blacks should be excluded from participation in government and that the Fourteenth Amendment should be left unratified.

His editorials continually attacked the imposition of military government in the South and the actions of the commanding

generals. In one editorial he called the five district commanders "infamous, cowardly, and abandoned villains who should have their heads shaved, their ears cropped, their foreheads branded, and their precious persons lodged in a penitentiary."

In other columns the editor tried to rouse white Mississippians to oppose black political participation and promised to publish the names of the "sneaks" and "scoundrels" who ignored this advice.[16]

McCardle reserved his bitterest criticisms for Maj. Gen. Edward O. C. Ord, the commanding general of the Fourth Military District, which included Mississippi and Arkansas. Ord finally had McCardle arrested and held for trial by a military tribunal, charging him with disturbing the peace, inciting insurrection, slowing the pace of Reconstruction, and printing libelous statements.

The Tables Turned

A protection against illegal imprisonment, a writ of habeas corpus orders a person holding a prisoner to explain why the prisoner is being held. Seeking to protect blacks and federal officials in the South from harassment by white southerners, Congress in February 1867 enacted a statute expanding the Supreme Court's jurisdiction to review denials of writs of habeas corpus.

Prior to enactment of the 1867 law, the Supreme Court had no appellate jurisdiction over writs of habeas corpus. The 1867 statute permitted appeals from federal circuit courts to the Supreme Court in "all cases where any person may be restrained of his or her liberty in violation of the Constitution or of any treaty or law of the United States" and sought release through a writ of habeas corpus.

The statute was not intended to protect southern whites, but McCardle sought a writ of habeas corpus in a federal circuit court, charging that the Reconstruction Acts that allowed his arrest and trial by military tribunal were unconstitutional. When the circuit court denied the writ, he appealed directly to the Supreme Court.

Rumors abounded that the Supreme Court would use McCardle's case to declare the Reconstruction Acts unconstitutional. In 1866 the Court had held unanimously that it was illegal for a military commission to try a civilian when civilian courts were available, and five of the justices had gone so far as to say they did not think Congress had the power under any circumstances to authorize military trials of civilians where civilian courts were open. Many observers interpreted this decision in *Ex parte Milligan* (1866) to indicate that the Court would not respond favorably to the military rule imposed in the South.[17]

But the Radical Republicans could not afford to have the Reconstruction Acts declared unconstitutional until after they had solidified their political power in the South and had forced the southern states to ratify the Fourteenth Amendment as the price for readmittance to the Union. Thus when McCardle's attorney, Jeremiah S. Black, appealed to the Supreme Court in December 1867 to act quickly on the case, Republicans in the House moved just as quickly to stave off an adverse ruling. In January 1868 the House Judiciary Committee reported, and the House passed, a bill to require two-thirds of the justices to concur in opinions finding federal laws unconstitutional.

According to historian Charles Warren, this measure had little public support, and the Senate postponed action on it indefinitely.[18] Moreover, it was widely believed that the measure would have failed to accomplish its purpose; of the eight justices then on the Court, at least five were thought to believe the Reconstruction Acts invalid.

Meanwhile, the Supreme Court agreed to Black's request and set arguments for the first week in March. The government's attorney, Sen. Lyman Trumbull, R-Ill., sought to end the matter by moving for a dismissal of the case on the grounds that the Supreme Court did not have jurisdiction. But the Court denied the motion on February 17, 1868.

Arguments on the merits in *Ex parte McCardle* began on March 2, the same day the House approved the first of the articles of impeachment against President Andrew Johnson.[19] McCardle's attorneys included Black, who had been nominated as an associate justice of the Supreme Court by President James Buchanan in the last months of his term but was rejected by the Senate in 1861 largely because Senate Republicans wanted to hold the vacancy open for President Abraham Lincoln to fill. Another attorney for McCardle was David Dudley Field, brother of Justice Stephen J. Field, who was sitting on the case.

Because he considered the Reconstruction Acts unconstitutional, Attorney General Henry Stanbery refused to argue the government's position; his place was taken by Trumbull and the eminent attorney Matthew Hale Carpenter. By all accounts, the arguments by both sides were impressive.

Jurisdiction Repealed

Arguments concluded on March 9. On March 12 the Radical Republicans in Congress made their move. Pending in the House was an insignificant Senate-passed bill to expand the Supreme Court's appellate jurisdiction to cases concerning customs and revenue officers. James F. Wilson, R-Iowa, chairman of the House Judiciary Committee, offered an amendment to repeal the 1867 grant of appellate jurisdiction over habeas corpus writs and to prohibit the Court from acting on any appeals then pending. Democrats and moderate Republicans who might have opposed Wilson's measure apparently did not understand what was happening, and the amendment was passed without debate or objection. The bill as amended was then returned to the Senate, which approved it later in the same day by a 32-6 vote.

President Johnson waited as long as possible before vetoing the bill to see if the Supreme Court would defy Congress and decide the *McCardle* case before its jurisdiction was removed. Although the Court met in conference on March 21, it announced no decision on the case, taking note instead of the repeal bill and saying it would postpone a decision on the case until action on the legislation was concluded. Justices Field and Robert C. Grier objected to the postponement. Field later wrote that the "judges had all formed their conclusions, and no excuse was urged that more time was wanted for examination."[20] Johnson vetoed the

bill on March 25, declaring that the repeal "establishes a precedent which, if followed, may eventually sweep away every check on arbitrary and unconstitutional legislation."[21]

March 30 was the Court's next opinion day. When it became obvious that the justices would say nothing about the *McCardle* case, attorney Black asked that the effect of the repeal legislation on the case be argued formally before the Court. The Court agreed, but it also agreed to a postponement until the December 1868 term to give government attorneys time to prepare their arguments.

Justice Grier objected to this delay and read the following statement in open Court:

> This case was fully argued in the beginning of this month. It is a case which involves the liberty and rights, not only of the appellant, but of millions of our fellow citizens. The country and the parties had a right to expect that [the case] would receive the immediate and solemn attention of the Court. By the postponement of this case, we shall be subject ourselves, whether justly or unjustly, to the imputation that we have evaded the performance of a duty imposed on us by the Constitution, and waited for the Legislative interposition to supersede our action, and relieve us from responsibility. I am not willing to be a partaker of the eulogy or opprobrium that may follow. I can only say … I am ashamed that such opprobrium should be cast upon the Court, and that it cannot be refuted.[22]

Grier was not the only one to decry the Court's apparent submission to Congress. Gideon Welles, Lincoln's secretary of the navy and close ally and a noted diarist, wrote that the "judges of the Supreme Court have caved in, fallen through, failed in the *McCardle* case."[23] Former justice Benjamin R. Curtis, who defended President Johnson at his impeachment trial, said, "Congress with the acquiescence of the country, has subdued the Supreme Court, as well as the President."[24] And Black in an April 1868 letter wrote that "the Court stood still to be ravished and did not even hallo while the thing was getting done."[25]

Final Submission, Aftermath

Final arguments in the *McCardle* case were anticlimactic. On April 12 the Court issued a unanimous decision upholding the repeal measure and dismissing the case for lack of jurisdiction. Chief Justice Salmon P. Chase wrote that the Constitution gave Congress authority to make exceptions to the Court's appellate jurisdiction and that Congress had expressly exercised that authority when it repealed the Court's right to review denials of writs of habeas corpus:

> We are not at liberty to inquire into the motive of the legislature. We can only examine into its power under the Constitution, and the power to make exceptions to the appellate jurisdiction of this Court is given by express words. What, then, is the effect of the repealing act upon the case before us? We cannot doubt as to this. Without jurisdiction the Court cannot proceed at all in any cause. Jurisdiction is power to declare the law, and when it ceases to exist, the only function remaining to the Court is that of announcing the fact and dismissing the cause.[26]

Less than a month later Chase confirmed the belief that the Court would have declared at least part of the Reconstruction Acts unconstitutional. "I may say to you," he wrote to a district judge, "that had the merits of the *McCardle* Case been decided the Court would doubtless have held that his imprisonment for trial before a military commission was illegal."[27]

As it turned out, McCardle was never brought to trial. By the time the Supreme Court dismissed his case in 1869, Major General Ord was no longer the commanding officer in McCardle's military district. His replacement dropped the charges.

Historian Charles Fairman points out one major irony of the *McCardle* case. Had the Supreme Court defied Congress and issued a decision declaring the Reconstruction Acts invalid, it is possible that the Fourteenth Amendment to the Constitution would not have been ratified. One of the provisions of the Reconstruction Acts required the ten recalcitrant southern states to approve the amendment to gain reentry into the Union. Ratification of the amendment could occur only if some of the southern states approved it. As Fairman wrote, "one must believe that if Congress had failed to bring the weight of its authority to bear upon the ten States as then organized, there would have been no Fourteenth Amendment."[28]

Ex Parte Yerger

A McCardle-type confrontation between Congress and the Court about jurisdiction over habeas corpus granted the Court by the Judiciary Act of 1789 was narrowly avoided late in 1869. *Ex parte Yerger* concerned the imprisonment, conviction for murder, and sentencing of another Mississippi newspaper editor by a military tribunal.[29] Edward M. Yerger applied to the Supreme Court for an original writ of habeas corpus, charging, like McCardle, that it was unconstitutional for military tribunals to try civilians for civilian crimes.

When the Court agreed to hear the case, a bill was introduced in the Senate to remove the Court's jurisdiction in cases involving the constitutionality of the Reconstruction Acts and over writs of habeas corpus until Reconstruction was completed. A second proposal would have prohibited Supreme Court review of any federal act.

Before the Senate could act, a compromise was struck between Yerger's lawyers and the attorney general. His case was removed to civilian court and his petition for the writ of habeas corpus withdrawn. No further congressional action was taken on the proposed jurisdictional limitations.

COURT JURISDICTION: MODERN REPEAL EFFORTS

The 1954 appointment of former California governor Earl Warren as chief justice of the United States initiated a period unique in the nation's history when the Court led other government institutions in protecting individual rights from majority discrimination. The first major ruling of the Warren Court struck down segregation in public schools, overturning sixty years of officially sanctioned racial discrimination.

These Warren Court decisions inspired a series of anti-Court efforts by members of Congress. Perhaps the most serious of these occurred in 1957 and 1958 when southerners opposed to desegregation allied with other conservative members of Congress who thought the Court's decisions protecting individuals alleged to have participated in communist activities threatened to undermine the nation's security. In addition to trying to reverse the individual decisions, the groups launched two major attacks on the Court's power to review certain classes of cases. But despite the conservative alliance and widespread opposition to the Court's decisions, Congress ultimately refused to adopt either proposal.

Jenner-Butler Bill

The broader of the two assaults on the jurisdiction of the Court during this uneasy period was initiated in the Senate by William E. Jenner, R-Ind.[30] His bill (S. 2646), introduced in July 1957, would have barred the Supreme Court from accepting appeals in five categories:

- Cases involving the powers of congressional investigating committees and contempt of Congress proceedings. This provision was aimed at *Watkins v. United States* (1957), in which the Court ruled that a witness before the House

William E. Jenner

Un-American Activities Committee had not been guilty of contempt of Congress for refusing to answer certain questions, because the scope of the committee's inquiry had not been clearly defined by Congress and the committee had failed to show the pertinence of its question to its investigation.[31] *(See "Watkins v. United States," p. 174.)*

- Cases involving federal laws and regulations governing hiring and firing of government employees on loyalty grounds. This provision was directed at the Court's ruling in *Cole v. Young* (1956), which held that loyalty-security procedures under the Summary Suspension Act of 1950 applied only to "sensitive" jobs and not to all federal employment.[32] *(See "Federal Loyalty Programs," pp. 583–584.)*

- Cases involving school regulations dealing with subversive activities by teachers. This provision was directed at the Court's jurisdiction to review cases like *Slochower v. Board of Higher Education of New York City* (1956), in which the Court ruled that New York City could not dismiss a city college professor from his job merely for refusing to cooperate with a congressional committee investigating subversive activities. Rather, it had to grant him all the procedural rights due under state and city laws regulating employment of teachers suspected of engaging in forbidden activities.[33] *(See details of Slochower v. Board of Higher Education of New York City, p. 589.)*

- Cases involving state laws and regulations punishing subversive activities directed against the federal government. This provision was aimed at the Court's ruling in *Pennsylvania v. Nelson* (1956), in which it held that provisions of the Pennsylvania Sedition Act punishing subversive activities directed against the federal government were invalid because Congress had preempted this field of legislation when it passed the 1940 Smith Act.[34] *(See box, The Court and State Sedition Laws, p. 580.)*

- Cases involving state regulations for admission to the bar, aimed at cases such as *Konigsberg v. State Bar of California* (1957), in which the Court ruled that an applicant could not be denied admission to a state bar solely because he refused to answer questions about past or present membership in the Communist Party.[35] *(See box, Politics and Loyalty at the Bar, p. 587.)*

The "extreme liberal wing of the court" has "become a majority," said Senator Jenner on August 7, 1957, the opening day of hearings, "and we witness a court constantly changing the law, and even changing the meaning of the Constitution, in an apparent determination to make the law of the land what the court thinks it should be."[36]

But solving the problem by removing the Court's jurisdiction proved too strong a medicine for many witnesses, who perceived this threat to the independence of the judiciary as a graver danger to national security than that posed by communists. At the suggestion of Sen. John Marshall Butler, R-Md., Jenner's bill was substantially amended by the Senate Judiciary

PRESSURE ON CONGRESS TO CURB THE COURT

In the middle of the 1957–1959 congressional effort to reverse Supreme Court decisions on internal security measures and to limit the Court's jurisdiction over such cases, Congress received outside pressure from two influential sources.

The first of these was the states' Conference of Chief Justices, which charged that recent Supreme Court decisions in some areas were significantly eroding the power of the states in the federal system. In a document entitled "Report of the Committee on Federal-State Relationships as Affected by Judicial Decisions," adopted on August 23, 1958, the chief justices contended that "the overall tendency of the Supreme Court over the last 25 years or more has been to press the extension of federal power and to press it rapidly" and that the Court "too often has tended to adopt the role of policy-maker without proper judicial restraint." In conclusion, the conference stated its "grave concern as to whether individual views of the members of the court as from time to time constituted, or of a majority thereof, as to what is wise or desirable do not unconsciously override a more dispassionate consideration of what is or is not constitutionally warranted."

A second report, this one a set of resolutions urging Congress to "correct legislative defects in the field of internal security revealed by particular [Court] decisions," was adopted by the House of Delegates of the American Bar Association (ABA) on February 24, 1959. The ABA specifically opposed legislation to remove any Court jurisdiction, but it urged adoption of legislation to reverse the Court's rulings in *Cole v. Young* (1956), *Pennsylvania v. Nelson* (1956), *Yates v. United States* (1957), and *Watkins v. United States* (1957).

Because these reports coincided with the views of members of Congress opposed to the Court, they were cited frequently throughout the debate on the Jenner-Butler bill as expert testimony to buttress arguments to curb the Court.

Committee. As reported in May 1958, only one section of the original Jenner proposal—the provision barring the Supreme Court from reviewing state bar admission rules—was retained. Instead of repealing the Court's jurisdiction to review the other categories of cases, the committee recommended language to overturn the particular offending decisions.

To nullify the *Nelson* decision, the reported bill provided that no past or future federal antisubversive laws should be construed by the courts as prohibiting enforcement of otherwise valid state laws punishing seditious activities directed at the state or federal government. To nullify the *Watkins* decision, the bill provided that each chamber of Congress would be the final judge of whether questions put to witnesses by investigating committees were pertinent to the authorized purpose of the committee's inquiry. The measure also provided that a person accused of contempt of Congress could not argue that the questions were not pertinent unless he had raised that objection at the time the questions were asked.

DOMESTIC SECURITY RULINGS: ONLY ONE REVERSED

Distressed by many of the Supreme Court's rulings in domestic security cases, Congress tried between 1957 and 1959 not only to remove the Court's jurisdiction to review such cases but also to reverse the rulings. Only one of these attempts—modifying the decision in *Jencks v. United States* (1957)—was successful. The rest failed, most of them in the Senate, where the two efforts to repeal jurisdiction also foundered.[1]

THE VICTORY

In June 1957 the Supreme Court reversed the conviction of labor leader Clinton E. Jencks, charged with perjury for swearing he was not a communist.[2] The five-justice majority held that reports filed by FBI-paid informants alleging Jencks's participation in Communist Party activities should have been made available to Jencks's defense attorneys when requested. The majority ruled that the prosecution either must turn over to the defense directly any portion of statements previously made by government witnesses that related to their trial testimony or drop the case.

Justice Tom C. Clark, a former U.S. attorney general, dissented, along with Justices Harold H. Burton and John Marshall Harlan. (Justice Charles E. Whittaker did not participate.) Clark said that unless Congress nullified the decision through new legislation, "those intelligence agencies of our government engaged in law enforcement may as well close up shop." He added that the decision would result in a "Roman holiday" for criminals to "rummage" through secret files.

Clark's dissent was seized upon by those in Congress opposed to the Court's decision. They also drew strength from the fact that the majority had not specified any right of the prosecution to withhold from the defense any irrelevant portions of testimony requested by the defense. As a result, lower courts were left to their own interpretations of the ruling, and the government was ordered in a number of subsequent trials to produce entire files in a case, regardless of relevancy. Several important prosecutions were dismissed because the government refused to produce the requested files.

At the behest of the White House, the Justice Department, and the Federal Bureau of Investigation, the House and Senate Judiciary Committees moved quickly to report bills to narrow the impact of the *Jencks* decision. The Senate passed its version by voice vote on August 26, 1957; the House passed its measure a day later with only seventeen dissenting votes. Both chambers agreed overwhelmingly on August 30 to a compromise version, and President Dwight D. Eisenhower signed the bill into law on September 2.[3]

Public Law 85-269 did not reverse *Jencks* but restricted it. After testimony by a government witness, a defendant in a criminal case

Cartoon of June 28, 1957, expressing frustration with the Court's decision in *Jencks v. United States*. Congress later restricted the ruling's impact on criminal prosecutions.

could request relevant pretrial statements made by that witness if they were written and signed by the witness or if they were a transcription of oral statements made at the time. The statute authorized the trial judge to screen requested statements for relevance.

THE DEFEATS

Reversal of another Court decision came within a whisker of passage. In *Cole v. Young* (1956) the Court held that federal employee security procedures applied only to sensitive jobs and that government employees in nonsensitive jobs could not be summarily dismissed for suspected disloyalty.[4]

In August 1957 the Senate approved a bill (S. 1411) to permit government supervisors to transfer suspected security risks from sensitive to nonsensitive jobs instead of suspending them. In July

The Butler amendment left the *Slochower* and *Cole* decisions standing. But it moved to overturn a Court ruling that the original Jenner bill had not touched. In *Yates v. United States* (1957), the Court ruled that the 1940 Smith Act did not prohibit "advocacy of forcible overthrow of the government

as an abstract doctrine" but only as an incitement to action. The Court also held that the act's prohibition against organizing a group seeking to overthrow the government by force applied only to the original act of bringing the group into being and not to continued organizational activity such as

1958 the House approved an amended version of S. 1411 that extended federal employee security procedures to all government employees so that anyone suspected of subversive activities could be summarily dismissed.

The final compromise version was identical to the House amendment but limited to one year. The House passed it by voice vote, but the compromise was never taken up in the Senate and died at adjournment. In 1959 House and Senate committees held hearings on the issue; however, no further action was taken.[5]

YATES BILL

In 1958 and 1959 the House approved measures to reverse the portion of the Court ruling in *Yates v. United States* (1957) that defined the word organize to mean only the act of initially bringing together a group of people.[6] The legislation would have redefined the word to make it a crime not only to bring into being a group seeking to overthrow the government by force but also to conduct continuing organizational activities. A similar provision was included in the Jenner-Butler bill killed in the Senate in 1958. The Senate took no action on the 1958 House-passed bill; in 1959 a Senate subcommittee approved the House bill, but the full Senate Judiciary Committee did not act on it.

PASSPORT CONTROL

After the Supreme Court held in *Kent v. Dulles* (1958) that Congress had not authorized the State Department to deny passports to American citizens affiliated with the Communist Party, the department proposed legislation to Congress to overturn the decision.[7] The House passed an amended version of the proposal by voice vote, but a threatened filibuster in the Senate blocked consideration there. The House passed similar legislation again in 1959. Although three Senate subcommittees held hearings on the issue, no bill was reported to the Senate floor.[8]

1. See C. Herman Pritchett, *Congress versus the Supreme Court, 1957–60*, reprint ed. (New York: Da Capo Press, 1973); and Walter F. Murphy, *Congress and the Court: A Case Study in the American Political Process* (Chicago: University of Chicago Press, 1962).

2. *Jencks v. United States*, 353 U.S. 657 (1957).

3. *Congressional Quarterly Almanac 1957* (Washington, D.C.: Congressional Quarterly, 1958).

4. *Cole v. Young*, 351 U.S. 536 (1956).

5. See *Congressional Quarterly Almanac, 1957, 1958, 1959,* (Washington, D.C.: Congressional Quarterly, 1958, 1959, 1960).

6. *Yates v. United States*, 354 U.S. 298 (1957); see also *Congressional Quarterly Almanac*, 1958 and 1959.

7. *Kent v. Dulles*, 357 U.S. 116 (1958).

8. *Congressional Quarterly Almanac 1960* (Washington, D.C.: Congressional Quarterly, 1961).

recruitment of members.[37] *(See "Yates v. United States (1957)," pp. 577–578.)*

As reported, the compromise Jenner-Butler bill made all teaching and advocacy of forcible overthrow of the government a crime under the Smith Act. It also redefined the term organize to include both initial and continuing organizational activities.

The bill did not come to the Senate floor until August 20, 1958, one of the last days of the session. Senate majority leader Lyndon B. Johnson, D-Texas, apparently had hoped he could avoid bringing it up for consideration altogether, but under pressure from southern colleagues and knowing that he had the votes to defeat it, he allowed it to be offered as an amendment to a minor House-passed bill (H.R. 6789) dealing with appeals from rulings of federal administrative agencies. After long supporting speeches by Jenner and Butler and rebuttals by Judiciary Committee opponents Thomas C. Hennings Jr., D-Mo., and Alexander Wiley, R-Wis., Hennings offered a motion to table the Jenner-Butler bill. The motion was adopted, 49-41, and the bill was killed. Measures similar to individual parts of it were subsequently considered in the House and Senate, but none was enacted. *(See box, Domestic Security Rulings, left.)*

Implied Preemption

The second attempt during this period to repeal Supreme Court jurisdiction was more limited in scope but came closer to passage. Under the preemption doctrine—based on Article IV, section 2, of the Constitution, which makes federal laws the "supreme law of the land"—courts have invalidated state laws for several reasons: because Congress stated an intention to preempt a given field of legislation, because a conflict emerged between the federal and state law, or because the court inferred an intention by Congress to preempt the field.

It was to prohibit this "preemption by implication" that H.R. 3, the most important of several antipreemption proposals, was offered. Its primary provision stated: "No act of Congress shall be construed as indicating an intent on the part of Congress to occupy the field in which such act operates, to the exclusion of all state laws on the same subject matter, unless such act contains an express provision to that effect or unless there is a direct and positive conflict between such act and a state law so that the two cannot be reconciled or consistently stand together."

H.R. 3 was introduced in the House in 1955 by Rules Committee chairman Howard W. Smith, D-Va., after the Pennsylvania Supreme Court held in 1954 that the 1940 Smith Act preempted provisions of state antisedition laws that punished persons found guilty of subversive activities directed against the federal government.

The ruling, when affirmed by the U.S. Supreme Court in *Pennsylvania v. Nelson* (1956), affected the antisubversive laws of forty-three states. Smith, who wrote the 1940 act affected by the ruling, said the Court decision was "the first intimation I have ever had that Congress ever had the faintest notion of nullifying the concurrent jurisdiction of the respective sovereign states to pursue also their own prosecution for subversive activities."[38]

After his bill failed to pass, Smith reintroduced H.R. 3 in 1957. Spurred by opposition to the Supreme Court's ruling in *Nelson,* the House Judiciary Committee reported both a modified version of H.R. 3 and a bill that would overturn only the *Nelson* decision. The full House adopted H.R. 3 on July 17, 1958, by a 241-155 vote after merging it with the narrower bill.

Similar bills were reported to the full Senate. When one was called up for consideration on August 20, 1958, immediately after the Senate voted to table the Jenner-Butler bill, Sen. John L. McClellan, D-Ark., offered an amendment to substitute the House-passed version of H.R, 3 for the Senate bill. Over protests from the measure's supporters, Majority Leader Johnson won adjournment until the next day. Although it looked as though the McClellan amendment had enough votes for adoption, Johnson and other opponents of H.R. 3 lobbied hard throughout August 21. The lobbying paid off when a motion to recommit the bill to the Judiciary Committee was agreed to by a one-vote margin, 41-40.

Recommittal ended further consideration of H.R. 3 in the Eighty-fifth Congress. In 1959 the House again approved H.R. 3, although with diminished enthusiasm. Smith continued to introduce the measure for several more years, but it was never again considered by the full House or Senate.

The change in the congressional attitude on the preemption issue between 1958 and 1959 has been attributed to several factors, including an influx of "pro-Court" northern Democrats into the Senate after the 1958 elections, a series of rulings giving the states wider latitude over business matters, and Court affirmation that the states could prosecute subversive activities directed against them rather than the federal government.

Reversals of Rulings

Of all its methods of influencing the Supreme Court, Congress has had most success in reversing individual rulings through adoption of a constitutional amendment or passage of legislation.

Four of the twenty-seven amendments to the Constitution were adopted specifically to overrule the Supreme Court's interpretation of that document. The amendments reversed the Court's rulings on the ability of citizens of one state to bring suit against another state, on the application of the Bill of Rights to the states, on income taxes, and on the right of eighteen-year olds to vote.

It is difficult and time-consuming to amend the Constitution. Each chamber of Congress must approve the proposed amendment by a two-thirds vote, and it must then be ratified by three-fourths of all the states. Moreover, there is long-standing and deeply held sentiment that amendments to the Constitution should not be adopted every time there is a significant disagreement with a Supreme Court ruling. As a result, most proposals to amend the Constitution never emerge from Congress.

The more common way of reversing the Supreme Court is for Congress to repass an offending statute after modifying it to meet the Court's objections. In such cases the Court in its opinion will suggest rewording the legislation to achieve its original purpose. This kind of reversal through simple legislation is easily accomplished if the Court has interpreted a statute contrary to the construction intended by Congress. The House and Senate may then pass new legislation explicitly setting forth their intention.

Reversal is not so easily accomplished when the Court and Congress are at philosophical odds. For example, twice Congress passed legislation to end child labor, and twice the Supreme Court ruled that such legislation was not within Congress's powers to enact. That its interpretation was based on philosophical differences rather than purely constitutional considerations was evident when the Court reversed these two decisions several years later. In the mid-1930s it appeared that a similar confrontation would develop over New Deal legislation, but the Court retreated and upheld congressional authority to regulate economic matters, which eased the crisis.

In several instances Congress has passed reversal legislation that has had only a symbolic effect because Congress has not had comprehensive jurisdiction over the subject in question. In 1968, for example, Congress passed additions to an anticrime bill overturning several Court rulings on the admissibility into evidence of criminal confessions. However, the legislation affected only federal courts, which hear a very small fraction of all criminal cases; procedures for confessions in state courts were left untouched.

Whether such limited reversals have an indirect effect by warning the Court that it may be reaching politically unacceptable limits probably depends on a multitude of factors, including the nature of the issue involved, the strength of the congressional opposition, the position of the president, and public consensus.

CONSTITUTIONAL AMENDMENTS

Congress and the states have allied on four occasions to overturn Supreme Court decisions through constitutional amendments. Several other proposed amendments to nullify unpopular high court rulings have been offered, but have not been approved either by the requisite two-thirds majority of both the House and Senate or by three-fourths of the states.

States' Rights

The Eleventh Amendment, ratified in 1795, was the first amendment adopted to negate a Supreme Court decision; it is the only constitutional amendment that actually removed part of the jurisdiction of the federal courts. The other three overturned specific rulings of the Court.

Article III, section 2, of the Constitution gave the Supreme Court jurisdiction over cases arising between a state and citizens of another state or of a foreign country. During the writing of the Constitution, opponents of a strong central government opposed this grant, claiming that it would jeopardize the sovereignty of the individual states. But these fears were successfully allayed when proponents of the grant argued that it would only permit suits where the state was the plaintiff. As historian Charles Warren explained:

> The right of the Federal Judiciary to summon a State as defendant and to adjudicate its rights and liabilities had been the subject of deep apprehension and of active debate at the time of the adoption of the Constitution; but the existence of any such right had been disclaimed by many of the most eminent advocates of the new Federal Government, and it was largely owing to their successful dissipation of the fear of the existence of such Federal power that the Constitution was finally adopted.[1]

The Federalists' assurances, however, proved empty promises. The first case brought to the Supreme Court in the February 1791 term was a suit by Dutch bankers against the state of Maryland.[2] The case that would lead directly to adoption of the Eleventh Amendment was brought to the Court in the August 1792 term.

A South Carolinian named Chisholm, acting as executor for a British creditor, sued the state of Georgia for property confiscated from an Englishman. Chisholm had as his attorney Edmund Randolph, who, despite his position as the first U.S. attorney general, continued his private law practice.

The Court postponed arguments in *Chisholm v. Georgia* until February 1793. When the time came, Georgia officials refused to appear before the Court, claiming that the federal judiciary had no jurisdiction over the case. Randolph made his case in behalf of Chisholm, and when he was finished the justices asked if anyone would like to respond. No one did. The Court announced its decision on February 18, 1793, upholding the right of citizens of one state to sue in federal court another state for breach of contract.[3] *(See "Resistance: Chisholm v. Georgia," pp. 332–333.)*

The decision, according to Warren, "fell upon the country with a profound shock."[4] Anti-Federalists argued that the decision compromised the sovereignty of the states and made them nothing more than corporations. But the real fear was that the decision would lead to a proliferation of citizen suits against the states that would further jeopardize their already precarious financial plights. Warren wrote:

> In the crucial condition of the finance of most of the States at that time, only disaster was to be expected if suits could be successfully maintained by holders of State issues of paper and other credits, or by Loyalist refugees to recover property confiscated or sequestered by the States; and that this was not theoretical danger was shown by the immediate institution of such suits against the States in South Carolina, Georgia, Virginia and Massachusetts.[5]

The day after the *Chisholm* decision was announced, a resolution proposing a constitutional amendment to bar citizen suits against states was offered in the House. A similar resolution proposed in the Senate was tabled on February 25. That resolution was reintroduced in the Senate on January 2, 1794, and passed twelve days later by a 23-2 vote. The House approved it on March 4, 1794, by an 81-9 vote.

Three-fourths of the states approved the amendment in less than a year, but almost four years passed before its ratification was officially recognized. President John Adams sent a message to Congress on January 8, 1798, stating that three-fourths of the states having acted, the amendment "may now be deemed to be a part of the Constitution."

The Supreme Court acquiesced in the amendment in February 1798 when it dismissed the case of *Hollingsworth v. Virginia.* Shareholders of a company were suing for losses resulting from Virginia's nullification of the company's title to land in the state. The Court said that ratification of the Eleventh Amendment had removed its jurisdiction "in any case, past or future, in which a State was sued by citizens of another State, or by citizens or subjects of any foreign States."[6] In the 1990s the Rehnquist Court expanded the reach of this amendment and said it gave the states a "sovereign immunity" from some federal laws, even when the states were sued by their own citizens.

Citizenship and Civil Rights

After the surrender of the Confederacy in 1865, one of Congress's first actions was adoption of the Thirteenth Amendment abolishing slavery. The states ratified the amendment late in 1865, but expectations that it would compel the rebel states to protect the civil rights of former black slaves went unfulfilled. The South adopted black codes and continued its oppressive treatment of the former slaves.

Congress responded by enacting federal laws to give blacks some measure of protection, but because the constitutionality of one of the most important of these laws—the Civil Rights Act of 1866—was in doubt, the legislature looked to enactment of a constitutional amendment to force the South to give blacks their civil rights.

A specially created Joint Committee on Reconstruction drafted the Fourteenth Amendment in early 1866. Although the political attention of the day was focused on the amendment's second section, which unsuccessfully sought to ensure black voting rights, the first section of the amendment ultimately provided more protection to both blacks and whites.

As proposed by Rep. John A. Bingham, R-Ohio, this section gave Congress power to make laws "to secure to the citizens of each state all privileges and immunities of citizens in the several states, and to all persons in the several states equal protection in the rights of life, liberty and property."[7] Representative Bingham's intention was to undo the effect of the Supreme Court's ruling in the 1833 case of *Barron v. Baltimore,* which held that the first eight amendments to the Constitution protected individual rights only against infringement by the federal government and not by the states.[8]

As amended by the joint committee, passed by Congress, and ratified by the states, the first section did not give Congress a positive grant of power to guard against infringement by the states but simply prohibited the states from making any law that abridged the privileges and immunities of citizens of the United States; deprived any persons of life, liberty, or property without due process of the law; or denied anyone equal protection of the laws.

Although the record indicates that Bingham expected this amended version to have the same effect as his initial proposal, several rulings by the Supreme Court in the 1870s and 1880s so narrowly construed the language of the first section that it afforded little of its intended protection to any citizens. It was not until 1925 that the Court began to use the Fourteenth Amendment to secure the guarantees of the Bill of Rights against state action, and it was not until the middle of the twentieth century that the Court began to extend equal protection of the laws to blacks. *(See "Rights and the States," pp. 432–433; see also the introduction to Chapter 12, pp. 667–672.)*

The first section of the Fourteenth Amendment overturned another Supreme Court ruling—the Dred Scott decision of 1857—which held that blacks were not and could never become U.S. citizens.[9] Adding a single sentence to the language already approved by the House, the Senate declared that all persons born or naturalized in the United States and subject to its jurisdiction are citizens of the United States. Although the Dred Scott case was not mentioned during debate, it was clear that the Senate addition was intended to nullify that unfortunate Court ruling. *(See "Dred Scott," p. 150.)*

The debate shows that there was some opposition to the provision because it applied to Chinese and other ethnic groups that were discriminated against by the white majority. Nonetheless, it was approved by both the House and Senate and, upon ratification of the Fourteenth Amendment in 1868, became the only definition of citizenship to appear in the Constitution.

Income Taxes

When the Supreme Court struck down a federal income tax law in 1895 because the tax was not apportioned according to constitutional dictates, Chief Justice Melville W. Fuller invited Congress to overturn the Court's ruling. "If it be true that the Constitution should have been so framed that a tax of this kind could be laid, the instrument defines the way for its amendment," Fuller wrote in *Pollock v. Farmers' Loan and Trust Co.* (1895).[10]

Article I, section 9, clause 4, of the Constitution forbids Congress to levy any direct tax that is not apportioned by population. For the first one hundred years of the nation's life, the Court held that only per capita taxes and taxes on land were direct taxes. But in the 1895 income tax cases the Court held that taxes on income from real estate were also direct and must be levied proportionately among the states. *(See "The Income Tax Cases," pp. 125–128.)* The decisions were highly unpopular with both laborers and farmers who felt they were burdened with payment of disproportionately high amounts of indirect taxes, such as tariffs. With each election they returned to Congress more and more Democrats and progressive Republicans who favored enactment of an income tax. But nothing concrete happened until 1909. Then a two-year-long depression, which had depleted government revenues, and a Republican campaign promise to do something about the high tariffs made consideration of an income tax imperative.

When the Republicans' tariff bill was introduced, Democrats seized on it, offering an amendment almost identical to the income tax law that had been declared unconstitutional in 1895. Conservative Republicans opposed to the tax countered with a proposal for a constitutional amendment to permit an income tax without apportionment. For support they turned to President William Howard Taft, who favored an amendment over legislation. In a message to Congress he observed that simple reenactment of the income tax law would undoubtedly encounter "protracted litigation" before it could take effect. President Taft also suggested that congressional defiance of the Court's rulings would "not strengthen public confidence in the stability of judicial construction of the Constitution."[11]

Conservative Republicans banked on the hope that even if the amendment were approved by Congress, not enough state legislatures would ratify it. Democrats and progressive Republicans largely agreed with this analysis, but felt philosophically compelled to vote for the amendment anyway.

The amendment was submitted to the states in 1909. Contrary to all expectations, the requisite number of state legislatures ratified the amendment in less than four years, and it became part of the Constitution on February 25, 1913. *(See box, The "Income Tax" Amendment, p. 127.)*

The Right to Vote

Adoption of the fourth amendment to overturn a Supreme Court decision occurred with the apparent cooperation of the Court itself. As one of the amendments to the Voting Rights Act of 1965, Congress enacted in 1970 a provision lowering the voting age for federal, state, and local elections to eighteen years. President Richard Nixon objected to the provision even as he signed it into law in June 1970. He said he favored lowering the voting age but believed "along with most of the Nation's leading constitutional scholars—that Congress has no power to enact it by simple statute, but rather it requires a constitutional amendment."[12]

The Nixon administration quickly brought suit to test the validity of the legislative measure, and the Supreme Court cooperated by deciding the case just six months after the measure was signed into law. By a 5-4 vote, the Court ruled in December 1970 that Congress had the authority to lower the voting age for federal elections but not for state and local elections.[13]

This decision created immense administrative difficulties for the forty-seven states that did not allow eighteen-year-olds to vote. State election officials and legislators said the task of producing dual registration books, ballots, and voting machines could not be completed in time for the 1972 elections. Amendments to state constitutions changing voting age requirements would have been difficult, if not impossible, for some states to approve before 1972.

To assist the states, an amendment to the Constitution to lower the voting age to eighteen years in all elections was introduced in both houses of Congress in early 1971. The Senate approved the amendment unanimously on March 10, 1971. The House adopted it by a 401-19 vote on March 23. The states also acted in record time, ratifying the amendment by July 1, 1971, just three months and seven days after it was submitted to them.

Child Labor Amendment

Although Congress adopted an amendment to overturn a pair of Supreme Court decisions on child labor, the amendment failed to win ratification by a sufficient number of states before the Supreme Court itself overruled its earlier decisions.

In 1916 Congress sought to discourage employment of children by enacting a law forbidding the shipment in interstate commerce of goods made by child laborers. The validity of the statute was challenged, and the Supreme Court declared it unconstitutional in *Hammer v. Dagenhart* (1918).[14] In passing the statute, the Court said, Congress was attempting to regulate not interstate commerce but labor, which was a matter reserved to the states for regulation under the Tenth Amendment. *(See "Child Labor," pp. 108–109.)*

Congress reacted to this ruling in February 1919 by passing a second child labor law that placed a tax of 10 percent on the net profits of any company employing children. But, in *Bailey v. Drexel Furniture Co.* (1922), the Court declared this statute unconstitutional as well, ruling that the tax was intended not to raise revenue but to penalize employers.[15] *(See "Child Labor," pp. 129–131.)*

Still unwilling to concede the fight to the Court, Congress in June 1924 submitted to the states a constitutional amendment that would give Congress authority to outlaw child labor. By 1938, however, only twenty-eight of the forty-eight states had ratified the amendment. In that year Congress again utilized its constitutional power to regulate interstate commerce and enacted a child labor law as part of the federal minimum wage statute. In 1941 the Supreme Court upheld the 1938 law in *United States v. Darby Lumber Co.*, specifically reversing its 1918 ruling in *Dagenhart*. The effort to pass an amendment then faded.[16] *(See details of Darby case, p. 115.)*

Other Proposed Amendments

Other proposed constitutional amendments to invalidate Supreme Court decisions have failed to win congressional approval. The Court's controversial decisions on reapportionment, school prayer, school busing, abortion, and flag burning have prompted these efforts to amend the Constitution.

Reapportionment

A revolution in the apportionment of state legislatures was precipitated by the Supreme Court in 1962 when it held in *Baker v. Carr* that the judiciary could entertain suits challenging malapportionment. The decision overturned a line of legal precedent holding that the makeup of state legislatures was not a justiciable matter—rather, it was a political one—and that citizens had no standing to sue to effect a change.[17]

That decision did not generate much congressional opposition, but in 1964 the Court in *Reynolds v. Sims* applied its "one person, one vote" rule to state legislatures, holding that both chambers must be apportioned on a basis of substantial equality of population.[18] The decision struck not only at malapportioned state legislatures but also at those apportioned—sometimes under terms of the state constitution—on the basis of one state senator for each city, town, and county, regardless of population. *(See details of Reynolds v. Sims, pp. 558–559.)* The decision was opposed by many rural organizations and state legislators whose strength in the state legislatures was bound to be undermined by the ruling. They lost no time in making their views known to Congress, which responded quickly but ineffectively to the Court ruling. Within two months of the decision, the House passed a bill denying federal courts jurisdiction over state reapportionment, but it died at the end of the session when the Senate failed to act. In the Senate a six-week filibuster by liberals stymied an attempt by Senate minority leader Everett McKinley Dirksen, R-Ill., to require the Court to delay reapportionment orders until January 1966. Dirksen said such a delay would give Congress time to consider a constitutional amendment overturning the Court decision.

In 1965 and again in 1966 Dirksen tried to secure Senate passage of a constitutional amendment that would allow states to apportion one chamber of their legislatures on the basis of factors other than population. In both years, although a majority of the Senate approved the proposal, Dirksen's effort fell seven

---

TERM LIMITS AMENDMENT

The term limits movement exploded onto the national political scene in the early 1990s with repercussions in Congress and at the Supreme Court. Twenty-three states enacted laws limiting the time a senator or representative could represent the state in Congress. Proponents of these term limits contended that they offered an antidote for the gridlock and special interest politics ailing Washington. Opponents of term limits countered that term limits would deprive Congress of some of its most able and seasoned lawmakers.

The Supreme Court on May 22, 1995, put an end to state efforts to impose term limits. The Court in *U.S. Term Limits Inc. v. Thornton* said states have no constitutional role in determining the qualifications for serving in Congress.[1] *(See details of this case, p. 389.)* That left a constitutional amendment as the only route for advocates of term limits.

Although the Republican-dominated Congress had touted term limits as part of its 1995 agenda, a proposed constitutional amendment stalled. The House of Representatives on March 29, 1995, rejected, 227-204, a proposed amendment to limit senators and House members to twelve years in office (two six-year terms for senators, and six two-year terms for representatives). The vote fell short of the two-thirds majority required for adoption. Most Republicans supported the amendment, but the opposition of senior Republicans combined with Democrats' distaste for the proposal contributed to its defeat.[2] Afterward, the fervor for term limits quickly faded, as even the Republicans, who controlled Congress, lost enthusiasm for the idea of legislating themselves out of office.

1. *U.S. Term Limits v. Thornton*, 115 S. Ct. 1842 (1995).
2. *Congressional Quarterly Almanac 1995* (Washington, D.C.: Congressional Quarterly, 1996), 1-35–1-36, 6-37.

---

votes short of the two-thirds needed for approval of a constitutional amendment.

Discouraged by failure to win Senate approval, advocates of the constitutional amendment turned to the state legislatures themselves. By 1969 thirty-three states—one short of the two-thirds necessary—had submitted petitions to Congress calling for a constitutional convention to propose a reapportionment amendment. No further action has occurred.

School Prayer and School Busing

At about the same time it was causing havoc with the state legislatures, the Supreme Court created additional public controversy by ruling in 1962 and again in 1963 that the First Amendment's prohibition against establishment of religion barred officially prescribed or supported religious observances in public schools.[19] *(See "School Prayer" and "Bible Readings," pp. 520–523.)* Although most major religious organizations were opposed to any constitutional amendments overriding these decisions, mail advocating them flooded into congressional offices. The House Judiciary Committee reluctantly held hearings on proposed amendments in 1964, but took no further action. In the Senate, Minority Leader Dirksen offered a proposed amendment in 1966, but the Senate failed by nine votes to approve it by the necessary two-thirds majority.

Little more happened on the proposals until 1971, when an intense two-year grassroots campaign succeeded in dislodging a school prayer amendment from the House Judiciary Committee. But this effort, too, was ultimately unsuccessful when the House failed to approve the amendment. *(See box, School Prayer and Congressional Backlash, p. 525.)*

In the 1980s the support of the Reagan administration for a constitutional amendment permitting organized prayer in school revived efforts in Congress to win passage of such a proposal. In 1984 an amendment came to the Senate floor with administration backing. It failed, however, to win the necessary two-thirds approval; at 56-44, the vote was eleven short of the sixty-seven needed.

The next year, after the Court in *Wallace v. Jaffree* (1985) struck down Alabama's moment-of-silence law, the Senate Judiciary Committee approved an amendment to permit silent prayer in public schools, but the measure did not come to the floor.[20]

In 1979 congressional supporters of an amendment to ban school busing for desegregation purposes managed to bypass the House Judiciary Committee, but the amendment ultimately failed when the House on July 24 rejected it 209-216.

School prayer amendments were introduced intermittently in Congress through the 1980s and 1990s, and they became a priority for Republican lawmakers after they won majorities in both the House and Senate in the 1994 elections. No proposal to permit organized school prayer passed the floor of either chamber, however.

Abortion

Despite intense controversy over abortion, almost a decade passed after the Supreme Court's landmark decision in *Roe v. Wade* (1973) before a congressional committee approved a constitutional amendment nullifying the decision. The proposed language approved by the Senate Judiciary Committee in 1982 declared that the Constitution did not protect the right to have an abortion.

The full Senate did not vote on the amendment that year. When a similar amendment came to the Senate floor in 1983, it was rejected, 49-50, falling eighteen votes short of the two-thirds required to approve a constitutional amendment.

Flag Burning

In 1989 the Court touched off a public and political outcry with a 5-4 ruling that effectively invalidated existing state and federal laws against desecration of the U.S. flag. The decision in *Texas v. Johnson* (1989), which held that flag burning was a form of political expression protected by the First Amendment, brought swift demands from President George Bush for a constitutional amendment to reverse it.[21]

The Court's ruling in *Texas v. Johnson,* which held that flag burning was a form of political expression protected by the First Amendment, touched off a public and political outcry. Congress in 1989 and 1990 considered a constitutional amendment that would have permitted it to outlaw flag desecration; the amendment was defeated in both the House and the Senate.

Yet despite an initial outpouring of protest and patriotic rhetoric, anger over the Court's ruling soon began to fade. Many people who had demanded reversal of the decision reconsidered their support for a constitutional amendment reversing it after Congress began debating the wisdom of amending the Bill of Rights. The Senate eventually voted in October 1989 on a proposed constitutional amendment to permit Congress to outlaw flag desecration, but the 51-48 vote was fifteen short of the required two-thirds of those present and voting.

A proposed amendment also failed in 1990. The furor over flag burning continued that year after the Court in *United States v. Eichman* invalidated a 1989 federal statute designed to protect the flag. The Court by 5-4 cited *Texas v. Johnson* in that opinion. The invalidated statute had been a second-best attempt by Congress to ban flag burning after the constitutional amendment plan failed in 1989. The 1990 case repeated the split from the 1989 case of *Texas v. Johnson.* William J. Brennan Jr., writing again for the majority, said, "Although Congress cast the Flag Protection Act in somewhat broader terms than the Texas statute at issue in *Johnson*, the Act still suffers from the same fundamental flaw: it suppresses expression out of concern for its likely communicative impact."[22]

When the proposal for an amendment came to the House in June 1990, the House vote was 254-177, or thirty-four votes short of the two-thirds necessary for passage of an amendment. Within a week the Senate also defeated a resolution for such an amendment. The measure failed 58-42, nine votes short of the required two-thirds of senators present and voting.[23]

In 2003, after the Court struck down a Texas law that singled out gays and lesbians for criminal prosecutions in *Lawrence v. Texas,* social conservatives feared the next step would be to give homosexuals a right to marry.[24] They rallied behind a constitutional amendment (H.J. Res. 56) that would define marriage as the union of a man and a woman.

LEGISLATIVE REVERSALS

A speedier and frequently more successful method than the constitutional amendment for reversing Supreme Court decisions is congressional reversal or modification by legislative enactment. The Court generally acquiesces in such legislative overrides. Its opinions often actually suggest that Congress reenact the measure in question after tailoring it to remove the Court's objections to its validity.

The justices do not, however, always bow to congressional efforts to void Court decisions by legislation. After the Court declared the 1916 child labor law unconstitutional—it barred the shipment in interstate commerce of goods made by children—Congress passed a second measure that placed a prohibitively high tax on profits from such goods. The Court proceeded to declare this law invalid as well. Congress then approved a constitutional amendment forbidding child labor, but fewer than the necessary two-thirds of the states ratified it before the Supreme Court itself reversed its earlier holdings. *(See "Child Labor," pp. 108–109, and "Wages and Hours," pp. 114–115.)*

Early Examples

According to historian Charles Warren, Congress first reversed the Supreme Court by legislation in 1852. In *Pennsylvania v. Wheeling and Belmont Bridge Co.* (1852) the Court ruled that because a bridge built across the Ohio River obstructed interstate commerce and violated a congressionally sanctioned compact between Kentucky and Virginia, it must be either raised so that ships could pass under it or taken down.

Congress immediately passed a law reversing this decision by declaring that the bridge did not obstruct interstate commerce and requiring instead that ships be refitted so that they could pass under the bridge. In 1856 the Court sustained this legislative reversal.[25]

Congressional reversal by legislation occurred again after the Court held in 1890 that in the absence of congressional authorization, liquor in its original container imported into a state through interstate commerce was not subject to state prohibition laws. Accepting the Court's implicit invitation, Congress later in the year permitted the states to prohibit such shipments of liquor, and the Court upheld that statute in 1891.[26]

Another early example of legislative reversal of Supreme Court decisions concerns the Interstate Commerce Commission (ICC). Congress was able to modify the Court's rulings on the powers of the commission. In 1887 Congress had created the ICC, the first federal regulatory agency, to provide uniform regulation of interstate railroad rates and to end unethical rebate and price-fixing practices. In 1894 the Supreme Court sustained the authority of Congress to create the agency. But in a series of cases decided over the next three years, the Court, which was dominated by men opposed to any governmental regulation impinging on the free development of business and industry, stripped the agency of all of its essential regulatory powers. The most damaging ruling held that the ICC had no rate-making powers and implied that Congress could not constitutionally delegate such powers to it.[27] The decisions led to a resumption of all the unsavory practices that prompted creation of the agency in the first place.

In the face of growing demands for reform from the public—and even from some of the railroad companies—Congress decided to confront the Court. In 1906 it enacted the Hepburn Act, which specifically authorized the ICC to adjust rates it judged to be unreasonable and unfair.

The Court upheld that grant of power in 1910. Changing Court personnel and shifting attitudes of sitting justices may explain the Court's new stance toward the ICC. Encouraged, Congress then gave the ICC authority to set original rates. Several railroads challenged this statute as an unconstitutional delegation of power, but the Court in 1914 said that contention was "without merit," thus completely reversing its earlier decisions.[28] *(See "Creation of the ICC," pp. 98–99.)*

Civil Rights

In one area more than eighty years passed between a Supreme Court decision and its reversal by legislation. In 1883 the Court held unconstitutional the Civil Rights Act of 1875, which made it a misdemeanor for any individual to discriminate against another individual on account of race in the use of public accommodations, transportation, or public entertainment. The Court specifically ruled that Congress had exceeded its power under the Thirteenth and Fourteenth Amendments when it enacted the statute.[29]

Congress did not reverse the 1883 ruling until passage of the 1964 Civil Rights Act. In that statute Congress used its authority to regulate interstate commerce to bar racial discrimination in public accommodations that serve interstate travelers or that sell goods or provide entertainment, a substantial portion of which moves through interstate commerce. Six months after this statute was signed into law, the Court unanimously sustained its constitutionality.[30] *(See details of Heart of Atlanta Motel v. United States, p. 700.)*

Unions and Antitrust

One particularly prolonged and hostile confrontation between the Court and Congress centered on whether labor unions were exempt from federal antitrust law. The 1894 statute making combinations in restraint of trade illegal was silent on the question of labor unions, and in 1908 the Court ruled that certain union practices, including the boycott, were illegal restraints of trade punishable under the antitrust law.[31]

That decision impelled Congress to add provisions to the Clayton Act of 1914 that specifically exempted labor unions pursuing lawful objectives from the reach of the antitrust law. The Clayton Act also stipulated that federal courts could not issue injunctions in any labor disputes unless necessary to prevent irreparable property damage.

Seven years later the Supreme Court subverted the intent of the Clayton Act. In a 1921 decision it interpreted the anti-injunction language of the act so narrowly that injunctions against striking workers became almost commonplace. The Court also held that, the Clayton Act notwithstanding, certain union practices illegally interfered with commerce and still fell afoul of the antitrust law.[32]

Congress made the next move, enacting the Norris-LaGuardia Act in 1932 to reverse the Court's 1921 decision and restore the vitality of the Clayton Act's provisions. A challenge to the 1932 statute did not reach the Court until 1938, a year after the majority conceded that Congress as part of its authority to regulate interstate commerce had broad powers to regulate labor relations. Then, in a pair of cases, the Court upheld the constitutionality of the Norris-LaGuardia Act, ruling that Congress had clearly passed it to "obviate the results of the judicial construction" of the Clayton Act.[33]

New Deal Legislation

The New Deal period saw Congress overturn the Court on more important measures than in any other period in the country's history. At President Franklin D. Roosevelt's instigation, Congress in the 1930s enacted several statutes aimed at ending the Great Depression and restoring the nation's economic well-being. Of eight major statutes, the Supreme Court upheld only two—an act establishing the Tennessee Valley Authority and legislation abolishing gold clauses in public and private contracts.

At first frustrated by the economically conservative Court majority's unwillingness to sustain most of the New Deal programs and then encouraged by the Court's apparent economic liberalization in 1937, Congress revised five of the six laws the Court had declared invalid. The Court subsequently sustained all of the modified versions that were challenged. In lieu of the National Industrial Recovery Act, Congress enacted the National Labor Relations Act, which the Court also sustained.

The six original statutes, the cases striking them down, the revised laws, and the cases sustaining their validity were:

- National Industrial Recovery Act of 1933, struck down in *Panama Refining Co. v. Ryan* (1935) and *Schechter Poultry Co. v. United States* (1935), replaced by the National Labor Relations Act of 1935, upheld in *National Labor Relations Board v. Jones & Laughlin Steel Corp.* (1937).[34]
- Railroad Retirement Pension Act of 1934, struck down in *Railroad Retirement Board v. Alton* (1935), replaced by railroad retirement acts adopted in 1935, 1937, and 1938, which were never challenged before the Supreme Court.[35]
- Frazier-Lemke Farm Mortgage Act of 1934, struck down in *Louisville Joint Stock Land Bank v. Radford* (1935), modified by Frazier-Lemke Act of 1935, upheld in *Wright v. Vinton Branch* (1937).[36]
- Agricultural Adjustment Act of 1933, struck down in *United States v. Butler* (1936), modified in Agricultural Adjustment Act of 1937, upheld in *Mulford v. Smith* (1939).[37]

- Bituminous Coal Conservation Act of 1935, struck down by *Carter v. Carter Coal Co.* (1936), modified in Bituminous Coal Act of 1937, upheld in *Sunshine Anthracite Coal Co. v. Adkins* (1940).[38]
- Municipal Bankruptcy Act of 1934, struck down in *Ashton v. Cameron County District* (1936), modified in Municipal Bankruptcy Act of 1937, upheld in *United States v. Bekins* (1938).[39]

Insurance and Oil

Congress has used its power to reverse the Court to rid itself of regulatory functions it has not wanted. In 1944, for example, the Supreme Court issued a ruling that gave Congress control over insurance, a matter that traditionally had been regulated by the states, even though transactions were often conducted through interstate commerce.[40] Congress wanted no part of this new responsibility and in 1945 passed a law returning the authority to regulate insurance to the states. The Court upheld this delegation of control in 1946.[41]

Congress in one instance successfully overruled both the Court and a president. In *United States v. California* (1947) the Court ruled that the federal government, not the states, owned the three-mile strip of oil-rich submerged land adjacent to the ocean shores. Legislation to reverse this ruling was introduced in 1948, 1949, and 1950 but was not approved. After the Court reaffirmed its 1947 ruling in two 1950 cases affecting Louisiana and Texas, Congress in 1951 passed a law giving ownership of the tidelands to the states.[42] President Harry S Truman, whose administration had brought the 1947 suit claiming federal ownership, vetoed it.

No attempt was made to override the veto, but the question of who was to control the submerged lands became a major campaign issue in the 1952 presidential elections, with Republicans promising to restore the lands and their oil deposits to the states. The Republicans won the election, and Congress in 1953 enacted the Submerged Lands Act ceding to the states the mineral rights to lands lying offshore between the low tide mark and the states' historic boundaries. The Supreme Court upheld this cession in 1954.[43]

Criminals and Confessions

Congress tried for decades to reverse some of the Supreme Court's decisions that seemed to enlarge the rights of criminal suspects and hamper law enforcement. Then, in 1968, rising crime rates, urban riots, and the assassinations of civil rights leader Martin Luther King Jr. and Democratic presidential candidate Robert F. Kennedy supplied the necessary impetus, and Congress, over the objection of President Lyndon B. Johnson, enacted legislation modifying the impact of these decisions. Most criminals, however, are prosecuted in state courts, and Congress has no jurisdiction to set their rules. Thus, because this legislation affected only federal courts, its effect was largely symbolic.

The Mallory Decision

In 1943 the Court in *McNabb v. United States* ruled that a confession obtained by police during an "unnecessary delay" in a suspect's arraignment could not be used as evidence in federal court, even if the confession had been given voluntarily.[44]

In 1957 the Supreme Court sparked controversy when it reaffirmed the *McNabb* decision and overturned the rape conviction of Andrew Mallory.[45] Because police had not complied with the *McNabb* doctrine requiring prompt arraignment, the Court determined that Mallory had been detained illegally, and his confession was therefore inadmissible as evidence. *(See details of Mallory v. United States, p. 635.)*

Reaction to the *Mallory* decision was immediate and widespread. The House in July 1958 passed "corrective" legislation by an overwhelming vote, 294-79. The House measure barred federal courts from disqualifying confessions otherwise admissible as evidence in criminal cases solely because of delay in arraigning the suspect. The Senate passed the bill, but it died before final passage.

The Miranda and Wade Decisions

In *Miranda v. Arizona* (1966) the Court expanded and formalized a new procedure for procuring confessions. Under the so-called "Miranda rights" rule, confessions were inadmissible as evidence in state or federal criminal trials if the persons accused had not been informed of their right to remain silent, if they had not been warned that any statement they made might be used against them, and if they had not been informed of their right to have an attorney present during the police interrogation.[46] *(See "Confessions and Counsel," pp. 638–641.)*

The next year in *United States v. Wade* (1967) the Court held that identification of a defendant based solely on a police lineup staged when the defendant's attorney was not present was inadmissible.[47]

These two decisions angered the public, which pressured the president and Congress to reverse the Court. Congress in 1968

- modified the *Miranda* decision by making confessions admissible in evidence if voluntarily given;
- modified the *Mallory* decision to provide that a confession made by a person in custody of law officers was not to be inadmissible as evidence solely because of delay in arraigning the defendant;
- modified the *Wade* decision to provide that the testimony of an eyewitness that he or she saw the accused commit the crime for which the accused was being tried was to be admissible in evidence in any federal criminal trial.

The bill, known as the Omnibus Crime Control Act of 1968, came to the House floor just hours after an assassin shot Robert Kennedy in a Los Angeles hotel kitchen. Although opponents of some Senate amendments moved to send the bill to a House-Senate conference where they hoped the provisions could be deleted, the House adopted the Senate bill unchanged. President Johnson signed the bill into law on June 19, 1968.

The congressional effort to reverse the *Miranda* decision proved, however, to be a failure. From the 1970s through the 1990s U.S. attorneys did not rely on the 1968 law to defend the use of confessions that were "voluntarily given." Most prosecutors believed—and judges held—that confessions could not be admitted as evidence unless the defendant had been warned of his or her rights, as required by *Miranda v Arizona*.

More than three decades after its enactment, the 1968 law was finally put to a test in the Court, thanks to Paul Cassell, a University of Utah law professor and a veteran of the Reagan administration's Justice Department. He had written critically of the refusal of federal prosecutors to invoke the 1968 law, and he intervened as a friend of the court in the case of a Virginia bank robber to argue that voluntary statements to FBI agents should be admitted as evidence. Cassell won a 2-1 decision from the U.S. court of appeals in Richmond, Va., but lost 7-2 in the Supreme Court.

In *Dickerson v. United States* (2000), Chief Justice William H. Rehnquist, long a critic of the *Miranda decision*, nonetheless described the 1966 decision as having set a "constitutional rule" that Congress "may not legislatively supercede."[48] Although the scope of the *Miranda* decision remained in some dispute, the *Dickerson* ruling made clear that the Court, not Congress, would resolve the disputes.

Sex Discrimination, Environmental Issues

During the 1970s two congressional reversals of Supreme Court decisions concerned pregnant women and small fish. In 1978 Congress required employers to include benefits for pregnancy, childbirth, and related medical conditions in their health insurance and temporary disability plans. This measure overturned a 1976 Court ruling.[49] In another 1978 statute Congress modified the Endangered Species Act of 1973 to reverse the Court's 1978 ruling that a Tennessee Valley Authority dam could not be put into operation because it would destroy the only habitat of a tiny fish called the snail darter.[50] The modification authorized a special cabinet-level board to decide whether to allow operation of federally funded public works projects even if they threatened the existence of an endangered species.

Congress was less receptive to proposals to reverse the controversial Court decisions upholding abortion and forced school busings to overcome racial segregation. Unable to overturn the Court's 1973 decision forbidding states to deny abortions, Congress since 1975 has prohibited federal funds from being used to pay for abortions except under certain circumstances. The legislation, however, primarily affects poor women receiving Medicaid payments; privately funded abortions are not touched by the measures.

Since 1975 Congress also has approved language to prohibit the Department of Education from requiring busing of any student beyond the school closest to his home that offers the course of study sought by the student. The legislation had no effect on federal courts that order most busing to alleviate racial segregation in schools.

Voting Rights and Civil Rights

Concern about ensuring the right to vote and the right to fair treatment has brought about notable congressional reversals of Supreme Court rulings.

In 1980 the Court ruled in *City of Mobile, Ala. v. Bolden* that those who wished to prove that an election law, practice, or procedure violated the Voting Rights Act of 1965 had to prove that it was intentionally discriminatory.[51] Effect alone—the fact that no blacks had won election in a particular jurisdiction, for example—was insufficient to prove a violation of the law.

When Congress amended the Voting Rights Act in 1982, it specifically included language declaring that a law or practice that resulted in discrimination could be held to violate the act, whether it was intended to discriminate or not.[52] The Reagan administration had opposed this change, preferring the "intent" test. The Court, however, acknowledged and implemented the will of Congress. When it applied the amended law for the first time, in 1986, it agreed that the effect of certain multimember electoral districts—those that elect certain officials by means of at-large elections—was to dilute black votes in violation of the Voting Rights Act.[53]

In 1984 the Court was persuaded by the Reagan administration to give a narrow interpretation to language barring sex discrimination by schools that received federal aid. The language at issue, contained in Title IX of the 1972 education act amendments, forbade discrimination "under any education program or activity receiving federal financial assistance."

Since its enactment, the ban had been consistently interpreted to cover all programs and departments at any recipient school. But over the objections of fifty members of Congress, the Court in *Grove City College v. Bell* (1984) accepted the administration's view that the ban applied only to the specific part of the school receiving federal aid.[54]

Civil rights advocates were alarmed by the ruling, noting that the same language so narrowly construed in Title IX was also included in three other major civil rights laws—Title VI of the 1964 Civil Rights Act, barring discrimination by race, color, or national origin in all federally assisted programs; Section 504 of the Rehabilitation Act of 1973, barring discrimination against the disabled; and the 1975 Age Discrimination Act. They immediately began to urge Congress to overturn the *Grove City* decision.

The effort took four years; in early 1988 Congress cleared legislation that specified that if one part of an institution or entity received federal aid, the discrimination ban applied to the entire institution. President Reagan vetoed the bill, saying that it would vastly expand federal power over the decisions of private organizations and state and local governments. The veto was overridden 73-24 in the Senate and 292-133 in the House.[55]

When Congress passed the Civil Rights Act of 1991, it countered the effects of nine Supreme Court decisions restricting the reach and remedies of federal antidiscrimination law. Most of the Court decisions had been announced in 1989. They interpreted the law to put a greater burden on workers charging bias. The compromise bill strengthened antidiscrimination laws and provided new guarantees of money damages and reimbursement of court costs for aggrieved workers who prevailed in lawsuits. President George Bush had vetoed a 1990 version of the legislation after a battle with Democratic sponsors over whether the earlier version would induce employers to hire certain "quotas" of racial minorities and women to avoid lawsuits.[56]

Religious Exercise

With wide bipartisan support, Congress in 1993 reversed a controversial 1990 Court decision that made it easier for states or the federal government to pass general laws that incidentally restricted individual religious rights. The Court held in *Employment Division v. Smith* that states could impose laws that incidentally limited religious freedom as long as they served a valid state purpose and were not aimed at inhibiting religion.[57] Before that ruling, government regulations affecting religion had to meet a stricter legal standard of serving a "compelling" government interest and posing the least possible burden on religious freedom.

The *Smith* decision involved two American Indians who were fired from jobs at a drug rehabilitation clinic for using the illegal hallucinogenic drug peyote during a religious ceremony. The state of Oregon refused to grant the men unemployment compensation benefits because they were fired for illegal behavior. The men sued, claiming the state's interest was not compelling enough to warrant infringement on their religious rights. But the Court ruled against them and effectively eliminated the compelling interest test for such free exercise cases.

Congress restored that "compelling interest" standard in 1993 when the Senate passed a bill 97-3 and the House approved the measure by voice vote. The government need not meet that standard to justify every law or action affecting a person's religious rights, stated the Religious Freedom Restoration Act, but only those that placed a "substantial burden" on their free exercise of religion.[58]

But the Court was determined to have the last word, and it struck down the Religious Freedom Restoration Act as unconstitutional in 1997. The 6-3 majority characterized Congress's action as an affront to the Court's authority to define the substance of the Constitution—in this instance, the meaning of "free exercise" of religion in the First Amendment. Although Congress may "enforce" constitutional rights through "appropriate legislation," it "does not enforce a constitutional right by changing what the right is," said Justice Anthony M. Kennedy.[59]

The decisions in the *City of Boerne* case defining religious rights and the *Dickerson* ruling upholding *Miranda* rights made clear the Court would insist on determining the meaning of constitutional rights. Acts of Congress were another matter. When the Court narrowly interpreted voting rights in the *City of Mobile* case or the Title IX law in the *Grove City College* case, lawmakers in Congress moved quickly to correct what they saw as an error in interpretation by the Court. The justices, chastened, then applied the amended law.

CONGRESS AND THE COURT'S WORKLOAD

For most of the Supreme Court's history, its members have complained that the workload is too heavy and that Congress should act to ease the burden. Only in 1988, the Court's 199th year, did the Court gain nearly complete control over which cases it chooses to hear. The first major complaint centered on the justices' circuit-riding duties. Congress removed them, but by then the number of appeals the Court was required by law to hear had swollen to almost unmanageable proportions. Congress gave the Court more discretion to choose the cases it reviews on the merits, but for decades several categories of cases required mandatory review. Although Congress in 1988 allowed the Court greater discretion over its docket, Congress continues intermittently to enact laws that require expedited judicial review by the high court.

CIRCUIT COURT DUTIES

In addition to establishing the size and jurisdiction of the Supreme Court, the Judiciary Act of 1789 required the justices to "ride circuit." Under the terms of the act, two justices sat with one district court judge at circuit courts in each of three circuits. In 1792 the six justices were required to attend a total of twenty-seven circuit courts a year and two sessions of the Supreme Court.

As the country expanded westward, circuit-riding duties grew more burdensome. One justice reported that he traveled ten thousand miles in 1838 to fulfill these responsibilities.[1] But Congress refused to do much more than tinker with the federal court system until 1891, when it established a separate system of circuit courts of appeals. Even then the appeals courts were composed of one justice and two circuit judges, although the law allowed a district judge to sit instead of the justice. This exception soon became the rule, and in 1911 Congress finally relieved Supreme Court justices of all circuit court duties.

MANDATORY JURISDICTION

The Supreme Court's caseload began to increase dramatically after the Civil War. Factors involved in this increase included a rise in the number of diversity cases (cases involving citizens of different states), suits stemming from Reconstruction legislation, and congressional enlargement of the Court's jurisdiction.

In 1914 Congress began to ease this caseload by increasing the kinds of cases the Supreme Court could review at its own discretion by writ of certiorari. At about the same time, it began to cut back on the categories of cases that the Court was required to review. This shift from largely mandatory to primarily discretionary judicial review culminated in the Judiciary Act of 1925. The act increased the Court's jurisdiction and expanded the number of cases appealed to the Court, but it reduced considerably the percentage of cases the Court was required to review on the merits. In its 1923 term, 39 percent of the cases that were filed required review by the Court. In the 1930 term, that proportion had fallen to 15 percent.[2]

The solution was only temporary. By 1976 less than 10 percent of the petitions for review at the Supreme Court fell within its mandatory jurisdiction. However, these cases comprised slightly less than half of all cases argued and decided with full opinions that year.[3] In the 1970s Congress began to seriously consider recommendations that it abolish the remaining categories the Court was obliged to review. After almost a decade, Congress in 1988 gave the Court greater discretion to decide what cases to hear. It eliminated the Court's mandatory jurisdiction over direct appeals from decisions invalidating acts of Congress; appeals from courts of appeals finding state statutes unconstitutional; and final judgments of the highest state courts questioning the validity of a federal treaty or law.[4]

LEGISLATED BURDENS

Congress created much of the modern explosion in the federal court workload. Its legislation places new burdens on federal courts, and its complex regulatory schemes are challenged by businesses and individuals nearly as soon as they are adopted. The Speedy Trial Act of 1974, for example, required that by 1980 all federal criminal defendants be tried within 180 days of their arrest.

To alleviate some of the crush of this work, Chief Justice Warren E. Burger urged Congress to include with the legislation a "court impact statement." If every committee reporting a measure that would affect the federal courts wrote such a statement, Burger said, Congress would be aware of those consequences and might more readily provide the system more resources with which to deal with the judicial impact of new laws.

Federal judges also contend that the workload could be relieved if Congress would make the difficult policy decisions in the course of enacting legislation, rather than passing them on to administrators to make under judicial supervision. "The prevailing passion of Congress for judicial review is the central fact of life at the moment for federal judges at all levels of the system," wrote Judge Carl McGowan in 1976.[5] Chief Justice William H. Rehnquist said in 1989 that the Court's ability to maintain a uniform body of federal law would be strained "beyond the breaking point" if Congress created any new federal causes of action.[6] Some justices have been similarly critical of complex legislation. For example, legislation in the areas of disability rights, telecommunications, and campaign finance reform immediately produced litigation in the federal courts.

1. Felix Frankfurter and James M. Landis, *The Business of the Supreme Court: A Study in the Federal Judicial System* (New York: Macmillan, 1928), 49.

2. Gerhard Casper and Richard A. Posner, *The Workload of the Supreme Court* (Chicago: American Bar Foundation, 1976), 20.

3. U.S. Senate, *The Supreme Court Jurisdiction Act of 1979*, S. Rept. 96-35 to Accompany S. 450, 96th Cong., 1st sess., 1979, 6.

4. *Congressional Quarterly Weekly Report*, June 11, 1988, 1596.

5. Quoted in Congressional Quarterly, "Judicial Workload: The Courtroom Explosion," *The Supreme Court: Justice and the Law*, 2d ed. (Washington, D.C.: Congressional Quarterly, 1977), 130.

6. *Congressional Quarterly Weekly Report*, June 3, 1989, 1324.

The Court showed no deference, however, when lawmakers tried to revise a constitutional interpretation handed down by the justices. "Our national experience teaches that the Constitution is preserved best when each part of the government respects both the Constitution and the proper actions and determination of the other branches," wrote Justice Kennedy in the *City of Boerne* decision. "When the Court has interpreted the Constitution, it has acted within the province of the Judicial Branch, which embraces the duty to say what the law is."[60]

NOTES

PRESSURES ON THE JUSTICES (PP. 762–772)

1. Henry J. Abraham, *Justices and Presidents: A Political History of Appointments to the Supreme Court*, 3d ed. (New York: Oxford University Press, 1992), 118–119.

2. Ibid., 118; see also Charles Warren, *The Supreme Court in United States History*, rev. ed., 2 vols. (Boston: Little, Brown, 1926), 2:501.

3. Sources for the information contained in this section on rejections came primarily from Abraham, *Justices and Presidents;* Warren, *Supreme Court in United States History;* and *Congress and the Nation*, 4 vols. (Washington, D.C.: Congressional Quarterly, 1965, 1969, 1973, 1977).

4. Warren, *Supreme Court in United States History*, 2:119.

5. *CQ Almanac 1987* (Washington, D.C.: Congressional Quarterly, 1988), 271–276.

6. Warren, *Supreme Court in United States History*, 1:137.

7. *CQ Almanac 1986* (Washington, D.C.: Congressional Quarterly, 1987), 67–72.

8. *CQ Almanac 1991* (Washington, D.C.: Congressional Quarterly, 1992), 274–285.

9. *Stuart v. Laird*, 1 Cr. (5 U.S.) 299 (1803).

10. *Marbury v. Madison*, 1 Cr. (5 U.S.) 137 (1803).

11. Irving Brant, *Impeachment: Trials and Errors* (New York: Knopf, 1972), 48.

12. Leonard Baker, *John Marshall: A Life in Law* (New York: Macmillan, 1974), 418.

13. Brant, *Impeachment*, 64.

14. Beveridge's account of Chase's impeachment is found in Albert J. Beveridge, *The Life of John Marshall*, 4 vols. (Cambridge, Mass.: Houghton Mifflin, Riverside Press, 1919), 3:157–222.

15. Brant, *Impeachment*, 65.

16. Ibid., 67–68.

17. House minority leader Gerald R. Ford's statement, quoted in Brant, *Impeachment*, 79–80.

18. For a summary of events leading to resignation, see *CQ Almanac 1969* (Washington, D.C.: Congressional Quarterly, 1970), 136–139.

19. For a summary of impeachment proceedings, see *CQ Almanac 1970* (Washington, D.C.: Congressional Quarterly, 1971), 1025–1027.

20. *Congress and the Nation*, vol. 5 (Washington, D.C.: Congressional Quarterly, 1981), 744–745.

21. Charles Fairman, *History of the Supreme Court of the United States*, vol. 6, *Reconstruction and Reunion, 1864–88*, part 1 (New York: Macmillan, 1971), 163–164.

22. *American Bar Association Journal* (1964): 1151, quoted by John R. Schmidhauser and Larry L. Berg, *The Supreme Court and Congress: Conflict and Interaction, 1945–68* (New York: Free Press, 1972), 9.

PRESSURES ON THE INSTITUTION (PP. 773–782)

1. Sources for the information on changes in the size of the Court include Henry J. Abraham, *Justices and Presidents: A Political History of Appointments to the Supreme Court*, 3d ed. (New York: Oxford University Press, 1992); and Charles Warren, *The Supreme Court in United States History*, rev. ed., 2 vols. (Boston: Little, Brown, 1926).

2. *Martin v. Hunter's Lessee*, 1 Wheat. (14 U.S.) 304 (1816); *Green v. Biddle*, 8 Wheat. (21 U.S.) 1 (1823).

3. Quoted by Walter F. Murphy in *Congress and the Court: A Case Study in the American Political Process* (Chicago: University of Chicago Press, 1962), 23.

4. Warren, *Supreme Court in United States History*, 1:223.

5. *National Mutual Insurance Co. v. Tidewater Transfer Co.*, 337 U.S. 582 at 655 (1949).

6. *Glidden Co. v. Zdanok*, 370 U.S. 530 (1962).

7. C. Herman Pritchett, *Congress versus the Supreme Court, 1957–60*, reprint ed. (New York: Da Capo Press, 1973), 122–123.

8. *Cohens v. Virginia*, 6 Wheat. (19 U.S.) 264 (1821); major sources for the information on attempts to repeal Section 25 are Warren, *Supreme Court in United States History*, and Murphy, *Congress and the Court*.

9. *Craig v. Missouri*, 4 Pet. (29 U.S.) 410 (1830); *Cherokee Nation v. Georgia*, 5 Pet. (30 U.S.) 1 (1831).

10. Murphy, *Congress and the Court*, 24.

11. Warren, *Supreme Court in United States History*, 1:727–740.

12. Ibid., 1:740.

13. *Murdock v. Memphis*, 20 Wall. (87 U.S.) 590 (1875).

14. *Mississippi v. Johnson*, 4 Wall. (71 U.S.) 475 (1867).

15. *Georgia v. Stanton*, 6 Wall. (73 U.S.) 50 (1868).

16. Charles Fairman, *History of the Supreme Court of the United States:* vol. 6, *Reconstruction and Reunion, 1864–88, part 1* (New York: Macmillan, 1971), 416, 420–421.

17. *Ex parte Milligan*, 4 Wall. (71) 2 (1866).

18. Warren, *Supreme Court in United States History*, 2:466–467.

19. *Ex parte McCardle*, 7 Wall.(74 U.S.) 506 (1869).

20. Julius J. Marke, *Vignettes of Legal History* (South Hackensack, N.J.: Fred B. Rothman, 1965), 157.

21. President Andrew Johnson's veto message to Congress, March 25, 1868, quoted by Ralph R. Martig, "Congress and the Appellate Jurisdiction of the Supreme Court," *Michigan Law Review* 34 (1936): 664.

22. Warren, *Supreme Court in United States History*, 2:482.

23. Ibid., 2:483.

24. Ibid.

25. Fairman, *Reconstruction and Reunion*, 478.

26. *Ex parte McCardle*, 7 Wall. (74 U.S.) 506 at 514–515 (1869).

27. Fairman, *Reconstruction and Reunion*, 494.

28. Ibid., 510.

29. *Ex parte Yerger*, 8 Wall. (U.S. 75) 85 (1869).

30. Major sources for the material included in this section are Murphy, *Congress and the Court;* Pritchett, *Congress versus the Supreme Court;* John R. Schmidhauser and Larry L. Berg, *The Supreme Court and Congress: Conflict and Interaction, 1945–1968* (New York: Free Press, 1972); *CQ Almanac*, 1956, 1957, 1958, 1959 (Washington, D.C.: Congressional Quarterly, 1957, 1958, 1959, 1960).

31. *Watkins v. United States*, 354 U.S. 178 (1957).

32. *Cole v. Young*, 351 U.S. 536 (1956).

33. *Slochower v. Board of Higher Education of New York City*, 350 U.S. 551 (1956).

34. *Pennsylvania v. Nelson*, 350 U.S. 497 (1956).

35. *Konigsberg v. State Bar of California*, 366 U.S. 252 (1957).

36. *CQ Almanac 1958*, 294.

37. *Yates v. United States*, 354 U.S. 298 (1957).

38. *CQ Almanac 1956*, 586.

REVERSALS OF RULINGS (PP. 783–793)

1. Charles Warren, *The Supreme Court in United States History*, rev. ed., 2 vols. (Boston: Little, Brown, 1926), 1:91.

2. *Vanstophorst v. Maryland*. No report of this case was made in the February 1791 term; see Warren, *Supreme Court in United States History*, 1:91.

3. *Chisholm v. Georgia*, 2 Dall. (2 U.S.) 419 (1793).

4. Warren, *Supreme Court in United States History*, 1:96.

5. Ibid., 99.

6. *Hollingsworth v. Virginia*, 3 Dall. (3 U.S.) 378 at 381 (1798).

7. Carl Brent Swisher, *American Constitutional Development*, 2d ed. (Boston: Houghton Mifflin, 1974), 331.

8. *Barron v. Baltimore*, 7 Pet. (33 U.S.) 243 (1833).

9. *Scott v. Sandford*, 19 How. (60 U.S.) 393 (1857).

10. *Pollock v. Farmers' Loan and Trust Co.*, 158 U.S. 601 at 635 (1895).

11. Alfred H. Kelly and Winfred A. Harbison, *The American Constitution: Its Origins and Development*, 5th ed. (New York: Norton, 1976), 586.

12. Richard M. Nixon, *Public Papers of the Presidents of the United States, 1970* (Washington, D.C.: U.S. Government Printing Office, 1971), 521.

13. *Oregon v. Mitchell*, 400 U.S. 112 (1970).

14. *Hammer v. Dagenhart*, 247 U.S. 251 (1918).

15. *Bailey v. Drexel Furniture Co.*, 259 U.S. 20 (1922).

16. *United States v. Darby Lumber Co.*, 312 U.S. 100 (1941).

17. *Baker v. Carr*, 369 U.S. 186 (1962).

18. *Reynolds v. Sims*, 377 U.S. 533 (1964).

19. *Engel v. Vitale*, 370 U.S. 421 (1962); *School District of Abington Township v. Schempp*, 374 U.S. 203 (1963).

20. *Wallace v. Jaffree*, 472 U.S. 38 (1985).

21. *Texas v. Johnson*, 491 U.S. 397 (1989).

22. *United States v. Eichman*, 496 U.S. 310 (1990); see also *CQ Almanac 1989* (Washington, D.C.; Congressional Quarterly, 1990), 307–314.

23. *CQ Almanac 1990* (Washington, D.C.: Congressional Quarterly, 1991), 524–528.

24. *Lawrence v. Texas*, __ U.S. __ (2003).

25. *Pennsylvania v. Wheeling and Belmont Bridge Co.*, 13 How. (54 U.S.) 518 (1852); 18 How. (59 U.S.) 421 (1856).

26. *Leisy v. Hardin*, 135 U.S. 100 (1890); *In re Rahrer*, 140 U.S. 545 (1891).

27. *Interstate Commerce Commission v. Brimson*, 154 U.S. 447 (1894); *Interstate Commerce Commission v. Cincinnati, New Orleans & Texas Pacific Railway Co.*, 167 U.S. 479 (1897); *Interstate Commerce Commission v. Alabama-Midland Railway Co.*, 168 U.S. 144 (1897).

28. *Interstate Commerce Commission v. Chicago, Rock Island and Pacific Railway Co.*, 218 U.S. 88 (1910); *United States v. Atchison, Topeka and Santa Fe Railroad Co.*, 234 U.S. 476 at 486 (1914).

29. *Civil Rights Cases*, 109 U.S. 3 (1883).

30. *Heart of Atlanta Motel v. United States*, 379 U.S. 241 (1964).

31. *Loewe v. Lawlor (The Danbury Hatters Case)*, 208 U.S. 274 (1908).

32. *Duplex Printing Press Co. v. Deering*, 254 U.S. 443 (1921).

33. *Lauf v. E. G. Shinner & Co.*, 303 U.S. 315 (1938); *New Negro Alliance v. Sanitary Grocery Co.*, 303 U.S. 552 (1938).

34. *Panama Refining Co. v. Ryan*, 293 U.S. 388 (1935); *Schechter Poultry Co. v. United States*, 295 U.S. 495 (1935); *National Labor Relations Board v. Jones & Laughlin Steel Corp.*, 301 U.S. 1 (1937).

35. *Railroad Retirement Board v. Alton*, 295 U.S. 330 (1935).

36. *Louisville Joint Stock Land Bank v. Radford*, 295 U.S. 555 (1935); *Wright v. Vinton Branch*, 300 U.S. 440 (1937).

37. *United States v. Butler*, 297 U.S. 1 (1936); *Mulford v. Smith*, 307 U.S. 38 (1939).

38. *Carter v. Carter Coal Co.*, 298 U.S. 238 (1936); *Sunshine Anthracite Coal Co. v. Adkins*, 310 U.S. 381 (1940).

39. *Ashton v. Cameron County District*, 298 U.S. 513 (1936); *United States v. Bekins*, 304 U.S. 27 (1938).

40. *United States v. South-Eastern Underwriters Assn.*, 322 U.S. 533 (1944).

41. *Prudential Insurance Co. v. Benjamin*, 328 U.S. 408 (1946).

42. *United States v. California*, 332 U.S. 19 (1947); *United States v. Louisiana*, 339 U.S. 699 (1950); *United States v. Texas*, 339 U.S. 707 (1950).

43. *Alabama v. Texas*, 347 U.S. 272 (1954); see also *United States v. Louisiana*, 363 U.S. 1 (1960).

44. *McNabb v. United States*, 318 U.S. 332 (1943).

45. *Mallory v. United States*, 354 U.S. 449 (1957); on Congress's reaction to the *Mallory* decision, see *CQ Almanac 1958*, and *CQ Almanac 1959* (Washington, D.C.: Congressional Quarterly, 1959, 1960).

46. *Miranda v. Arizona*, 384 U.S. 436 (1966).

47. *United States v. Wade*, 388 U.S. 218 (1967); on Congress's reaction to the *Miranda* and *Wade* decisions, see *CQ Almanac 1968* (Washington, D.C.: Congressional Quarterly, 1969), 226, 233.

48. *Dickerson v. United States*, 530 U.S. 428 (2000)

49. *General Electric Co. v. Gilbert*, 429 U.S. 125 (1976).

50. *Tennessee Valley Authority v. Hill*, 437 U.S. 153 (1978).

51. *City of Mobile, Ala. v. Bolden*, 446 U.S. 55 (1980).

52. *CQ Almanac 1982* (Washington, D.C.: Congressional Quarterly, 1983), 373–377.

53. *Thornburg v. Gingles*, 478 U.S. 30 (1986).

54. *Grove City College v. Bell*, 465 U.S. 555 (1984).

55. *Congressional Quarterly Weekly Report*, March 26, 1988, 774–776.

56. *CQ Almanac 1991* (Washington, D.C.: Congressional Quarterly, 1992), 251–261.

57. *Employment Division v. Smith*, 494 U.S. 872 (1990).

58. *CQ Almanac 1993* (Washington, D.C.: Congressional Quarterly, 1994), 315.

59. *City of Boerne v. Flores*, 521 U.S. 507 at 519 (1997).

60. Id. at 535–536.

CHAPTER 14

Presidential Pressure

THE MAJOR WAY a president exerts influence over the Supreme Court's work is through the power to select its members. And presidents throughout history have been well aware that the justices they select will shape public policy.

All presidents attempt to place on the Court justices—usually from their political party—whose views coincide with their own. But this effort has met with varying degrees of success. Presidents Thomas Jefferson, Andrew Jackson, Abraham Lincoln, Franklin D. Roosevelt, Richard Nixon, and Ronald Reagan have been the most successful in influencing the Court's conduct through judicial appointments.

During presidential election campaigns, presidents also have attempted to influence the Court by criticizing the judiciary or earlier decisions by the Court. In at least seven campaigns (1800, 1860, 1896, 1924, 1936, 1968, and 1980), presidential candidates challenged the Court's effect on public policy.

Political scientist Robert G. Scigliano has described the intersecting relationship between the Court and the president:

> In their contemporary relationship, the Presidency has gained considerable influence over the Supreme Court.
>
> Yet the President cannot be said to dominate the Court....
>
> Tension continues to exist between the two institutions....A President cannot be sure that he is getting what he thinks he is getting in his appointments, a person may change his views after joining the Court, and the judicial obligation calls upon a justice to heed the Constitution and the laws, and not Presidential positions.[1]

A vacancy on the Supreme Court has occurred, on the average, about every two years. A president can expect to have at least one appointment per term.[2] At times, however, the Court has seemed to defy the actuarial tables, and its membership has remained stable for a much longer period, denying the incumbent president the opportunity to make an appointment to the Court. Jimmy Carter was the first full-term president denied the opportunity to name anyone to the Court; no vacancy occurred during his four years in the White House (1977–1981). Barring unforeseen circumstances, President George W. Bush also will have no opportunity to appoint a justice to the Court before the 2004 presidential election.

President Nixon, by contrast, had an opportunity to appoint a new chief justice during his first year in office. Nixon then made three more appointments to the Court during his first term. During his eight years as president, Reagan had several opportunities: he named three associate justices and a new chief justice to the Court.

Qualifications

Presidents consider a variety of criteria in selecting justices. Among the most consistent are merit, friendship, geographic and religious balance, and ideology.

Almost all presidents have agreed that a Court nominee should have some legal training, but until the last half of the twentieth century judicial experience had not been considered particularly important. Many distinguished appointees—including eight chief justices—had no prior judicial experience.[3]

Of the modern presidents, Franklin Roosevelt appointed six men who had no judicial experience: Chief Justice Harlan Fiske Stone and Associate Justices Stanley F. Reed, Felix Frankfurter, William O. Douglas, James F. Byrnes, and Robert H. Jackson. President Dwight D. Eisenhower, after appointing Earl Warren chief justice of the United States, insisted that all future nominees have judicial experience. (Warren had none.)

Harry S Truman appointed two men without judicial experience: Harold H. Burton and Tom C. Clark. Neither of President John F. Kennedy's two appointees, Arthur J. Goldberg and Byron R. White, had judicial experience. Nor did a Lyndon B. Johnson appointee, Abe Fortas, or a Nixon nominee, William H. Rehnquist.

Merit

Almost every one of the 108 individuals who have served on the Court had some record of public service prior to their appointment. Many had held offices in the executive branch or had served as state or federal judges, senators, members of the House, governors, or law professors.[4]

High ethical standards, as well as experience in public life, are criteria presidents seek in a nominee. Louis D. Brandeis's nomination successfully weathered a challenge from charges that he had engaged in improper practices as an attorney. But the nominations of Clement F. Haynsworth Jr. and Abe Fortas as chief justice failed to win approval by the Senate because of questions raised about possible conflicts of interest.

Friendship

Personal friendship has been the reason for several nominations to the Court. William Howard Taft's nomination of Horace H. Lurton, Woodrow Wilson's selection of Brandeis, Truman's choice of Harold Burton, and Kennedy's preference for Byron White all had some basis in personal friendship.

President Johnson selected a reluctant Abe Fortas for the bench in 1965 on the basis of personal friendship. And in 1968

Johnson unsuccessfully proposed an old Texas political associate, Homer Thornberry, to fill Fortas's seat.

Geographic Representation

Justices have come from thirty-one of the fifty states, and states have not been represented in any substantially equal appointment pattern. New York has been the home of sixteen justices. Among the other states that have been home to five or more justices are Pennsylvania, Massachusetts, Ohio, Virginia, Kentucky, and Tennessee.[5]

Early in the Court's history, geographic balance was a major consideration in the selection of nominees. Because the justices functioned as circuit judges, conventional thinking was that each geographic area should have a spokesman on the Court. Until the Civil War, this kind of thinking resulted in a "New England" seat, a "Virginia" seat, a "New York" seat, and a "Pennsylvania" seat. With the nation's post–Civil War expansion and the end of the justices' circuit-riding duties, this tradition faded.

Religious Balance

The notion of sectarian religious representation developed out of the fact that Americans are a pluralistic society and a politically group-conscious people. Thus the idea of a "Roman Catholic" seat and a "Jewish" seat on the Court developed as a way of acknowledging the role of these religious minority groups in the nation. By the late twentieth century, however, this idea seemed to have faded, although in 2003 two Catholics and two Jews were serving on the Court.

Chief Justice Roger B. Taney was the first to hold the Catholic seat. Since Grover Cleveland appointed Edward D. White to that seat in 1894, it has been held by Joseph McKenna, Pierce Butler, Frank Murphy, and William J. Brennan Jr. Truman's appointment of Tom Clark in 1949 after Murphy's death interrupted the tradition, but Eisenhower's appointment of Brennan in 1956 restored the notion of a "Catholic seat." The selection was regarded in part as an appeal to Catholic voters. But when President Reagan nominated Antonin Scalia and Anthony M. Kennedy in 1986 and 1987, respectively, their Catholicism was hardly an issue.

The Jewish seat, established in 1916 with the appointment of Louis D. Brandeis, was filled by Justices Felix Frankfurter (1938), Arthur Goldberg (1963), and Abe Fortas (1965). (Benjamin N. Cardozo, also Jewish, served along with Brandeis.) In 1969 President Nixon again broke the tradition by nominating three Protestants in succession to the seat Fortas vacated. President Clinton appointed two Jewish justices, Ruth Bader Ginsburg and Stephen G. Breyer. The latter filled the seat once occupied by Fortas. Nixon appointee Harry A. Blackmun had held the Fortas seat in the intervening years.

Subtler Influences

The special representational concerns of the Republican and Democratic Parties may govern, to some extent, the choice of nominees to the Court. Black and Jewish support of the Democratic Party enhances the likelihood that Democratic presidents will continue to consider those groups in making their selections.

In 1967 President Lyndon Johnson nominated Thurgood Marshall as the first black justice of the Supreme Court. Marshall had been counsel for the National Association for the Advancement of Colored People (NAACP) and one of the attorneys responsible for arguing successfully the 1954 Court decision in *Brown v. Board of Education*, the school desegregation case. Marshall served as solicitor general of the United States prior to appointment to the Court. Johnson said as he nominated Marshall, "It is the right thing to do, the right time to do it, the right man and the right place."[6]

As the political power and professional participation of women grew in the mid-twentieth century, it became clear that it was time for a woman to sit on the Supreme Court. During

Thurgood Marshall is sworn in as solicitor general August 24, 1965. Two years later President Lyndon B. Johnson (shown here on Marshall's right) nominated Marshall as the first black justice of the Supreme Court.

the 1980 campaign, Reagan pledged he would name a woman to the Court, and within his first year in office he made good on that pledge. In July 1981 he named Arizona judge Sandra Day O'Connor as the first woman justice; she was easily confirmed in September.[7]

Scholar Henry J. Abraham soon after observed: "There is no doubt that there now exists a 'black seat' on the bench that is, in effect, far more secure than a 'Catholic seat' or a 'Jewish seat.' That is unquestionably also true of a 'woman's seat,' to all intents and purposes established with President Reagan's dramatic appointment of Judge Sandra Day O'Connor."[8]

Indeed, when Marshall retired in 1991, President Bush appointed Clarence Thomas, an African American appeals court judge and former chairman of the Equal Employment Opportunity Commission. More possibilities opened for women, however, when President Clinton replaced the retiring Byron White in 1993 with Ruth Bader Ginsburg, an appeals court judge and former women's rights advocate. The second woman justice joined O'Connor, by then a veteran of twelve years on the Court.

Ideology has been a significant factor in several presidents' appointments to the high bench. During the consideration of Horace Lurton, a Democrat, for appointment to the Court, Republican president Theodore Roosevelt wrote to Sen. Henry Cabot Lodge, R-Mass., explaining that Lurton was "right" on all the important issues:

> The nominal politics of the man has nothing to do with his actions on the bench. His real politics are all important.... On every question that would come before the bench, he has so far shown himself to be in much closer touch with the policies in which you and I believe.[9]

Lodge agreed, but wondered why a Republican who held the same opinions could not be found. He suggested William H. Moody, the attorney general of Massachusetts, and Roosevelt appointed Moody in 1906. In 1909 Lurton was finally nominated to the Court, by William Howard Taft, a Republican who, like Roosevelt, thought Lurton was right for the job despite his Democratic Party affiliation.

More recently, the Reagan administration systematically screened the judicial philosophy of candidates for all federal courts. Reagan looked for judges and justices who would eschew the liberal "activism" of earlier decades, defined most notably by rulings establishing a constitutional right to abortion, prohibiting prayer in public schools, and expanding the rights of defendants in criminal cases. Ironically, Justice Anthony Kennedy, President Reagan's last appointee, penned one of the Court's most recent "activist" opinions. The 2003 *Lawrence v. Texas* decision struck down state anti-sodomy laws directed against the sexual privacy rights of homosexuals.[10]

Party Loyalty

Presidents generally nominate members of their party to the Court. As noted, however, occasionally they nominate members of the opposition party.

Republican presidents have appointed nine Democratic justices to the Court, and Democratic presidents have named three Republicans. John Tyler, a Whig, appointed Democrat Samuel Nelson. Republican presidents Abraham Lincoln, Benjamin Harrison, William Howard Taft, Warren G. Harding, Herbert Hoover, Dwight Eisenhower, and Richard Nixon appointed nominal Democrats to the Court.

Taft appointed Democrats Horace Lurton, Edward D. White (promoted to chief justice), and Joseph R. Lamar. The other GOP presidents who successfully nominated Democrats were Lincoln (Stephen J. Field), Benjamin Harrison (Howell E. Jackson), Harding (Pierce Butler), Hoover (Benjamin Cardozo), Eisenhower (William Brennan), and Nixon (Lewis F. Powell Jr.).

Among Democratic presidents, Woodrow Wilson appointed Louis Brandeis, Franklin Roosevelt appointed Harlan F. Stone chief justice, and Harry Truman appointed Republican senator Harold Burton to the Court.

Outside Influences

The appointment of a justice to the Supreme Court involves a complex pattern of personal and political transactions between the president and the individuals and groups seeking to influence that nomination.

Among the more important influence groups are the members of the president's administration, the legal community, and even the Court's sitting justices.

The Attorney General

Presidents normally seek the advice of their chief legal officer, the attorney general. In 1840 the attorney general assumed responsibility for judicial appointments, taking over the function from the secretary of state. Since that time the attorney general has become the president's liaison with the principal interest groups and individuals involved in the screening and selection of qualified candidates for appointment to the Court.

The White House counsel's office has been an equally active player in judicial selection since the 1980s. In the George Bush and Clinton administrations, White House lawyers took the lead in the selection of Court nominees and in the promotion of the candidates with the Senate and public.[11] The same pattern has emerged in the judicial selection process of George W. Bush's administration. Alberto R. Gonzales, the White House counsel, has played a role in vetting Bush's nominees for the federal judiciary, and has even been mentioned as a possible Bush appointee to the Court should a vacancy occur.

The Senate's Role

The Senate's power to confirm or reject presidential nominees to the Court has resulted in the rejection of 28 out of 148 nominations in the two centuries of the Court's history. In the nineteenth century one out of three nominees was rejected by the Senate. In the twentieth century only six nominees have been rejected. The Senate has rejected the presidents' choices because of the appointee's position on public issues, political characteristics, perceived lack of judicial qualifications, or opposition to the prevailing views on the Court.

In the tradition of senatorial courtesy, the Senate will not confirm a nominee opposed by the senators from the nominee's home state, at least if they are members of the president's political party. Application of senatorial courtesy accounted for several rejections of Supreme Court nominees in the nineteenth century, but that tradition has rarely been mentioned in connection with Supreme Court nominations in modern times. Instead, it is a more established practice with lower federal court nominations, especially to federal district courts.

In 1894 the Senate rejected President Cleveland's nominees, William B. Hornblower and Wheeler H. Peckham, both of New York. Sen. David B. Hill, D-N.Y., invoked senatorial courtesy to block the nominations in each instance because Cleveland had failed to consult with him about their selection. Cleveland then refused to name a third New Yorker and chose instead Edward White, D-La., the Democratic majority leader in the Senate.

Senatorial courtesy was a prominent factor in the rejection of Reuben H. Walworth of New York, the choice of President John Tyler. And it was a factor in the negative vote the Senate gave to James K. Polk's nomination of Pennsylvanian George W. Woodward in 1846.[12]

The Justices' Role

Until recent years sitting justices rarely hesitated to voice their suggestions of especially qualified nominees for vacant seats. Some have offered negative advice. Joseph P. Bradley prepared a report about those who would be qualified to succeed him, and concluded that no candidate from his home state of New Jersey possessed the necessary qualifications for the post.

In the nineteenth century, justices often lobbied effectively with presidents to urge appointment of certain candidates. Justices John Catron and Benjamin R. Curtis, for example, urged President Franklin Pierce to nominate John A. Campbell to the Court. Their communications to Pierce included letters of support for Campbell from all the remaining sitting justices.[13] Other justices who successfully urged presidents to appoint certain individuals to the Court include Robert C. Grier for William Strong in 1870, Noah H. Swayne for Joseph Bradley in 1870, Morrison R. Waite for William B. Woods in 1880, Samuel F. Miller for David J. Brewer in 1889, and Henry B. Brown for Howell Jackson in 1893.[14]

In 1981 Chief Justice Warren E. Burger suggested to President Reagan the judge who became the first woman justice, Sandra Day O'Connor. O'Connor also happened to be a classmate of Rehnquist at Stanford University Law School.[15]

Taft: Champion Influencer

William Howard Taft was the only president to become chief justice of the United States, thus enjoying a unique double opportunity to influence its personnel and work. Taft, the twenty-seventh president of the United States (1909–1913), served as chief justice from 1921 to 1930. During Warren G. Harding's presidency (1921–1923), Taft either selected or approved three of the four men Harding appointed to the Court—George Sutherland, Pierce Butler, and Edward T. Sanford.

Taft had lobbied for his own appointment as chief justice. In 1920 the ex-president let it be known to newly elected president Harding that he wanted the job. Taft had named Edward White chief justice and, Taft told Harding, "many times in the past [White] had said he was holding the office for me and that he would give it back to a Republican administration."[16] On June 30, 1921, Harding appointed Taft chief justice.

Taft's most prodigious lobbying effort on presidential appointments resulted in Pierce Butler's appointment to the Court. Taft orchestrated a letter-writing campaign recommending Butler and played down the talents of other potential nominees. Taft dismissed the candidacy of Judge Benjamin Cardozo of the New York Court of Appeals because, Taft wrote, Cardozo was "a Jew and a Democrat [and] a progressive judge." Judge Learned Hand, Taft warned, "would almost certainly herd with Brandeis and be a dissenter."[17]

The chief justice sought and obtained endorsements for Butler from the Minnesota congressional delegation, members of the church hierarchy (Butler was a Roman Catholic), and from local bar associations across the nation. Harding succumbed to the pressure and sent Butler's nomination to the Senate where, despite considerable opposition from Senate progressives, he won approval.

When Mahlon Pitney resigned from the Court in 1922, Taft heartily approved of Harding's choice, Edward Sanford. Taft and Sanford had been acquaintances since Theodore Roosevelt's administration. Some observers felt that Sanford was so close to Taft that the chief justice had two votes on the bench. Their friendship and judicial affinity had a final coincidence: they died on the same day in 1930.[18]

Chief Justice Taft's influence over Harding's appointments to the Court gave that body a decidedly conservative majority during the 1920s—ending only with Franklin Roosevelt's appointments to the Court after 1937.

Hughes and Stone

Other chief justices have influentially advised presidents on Supreme Court appointments.

Charles Evans Hughes counseled three presidents on appointments. Herbert C. Hoover sought Hughes's advice in naming a replacement for Oliver Wendell Holmes Jr. in 1931. The president particularly wanted to know Hughes's opinion of fellow New Yorker Benjamin Cardozo.[19] In 1941 Hughes wanted President Franklin Roosevelt to name Harlan Fiske Stone as his successor as chief justice. President Harry Truman also consulted Hughes, in 1946, on his choice of a chief justice after Stone's death.[20]

Hoover also sought and obtained Stone's advice on filling Holmes's seat. Stone was so convinced of Cardozo's qualifications that he sent several memoranda to Hoover recommending

Cardozo in preference to alternate candidates. Stone tried to overcome Hoover's reservations about appointing another Jewish justice, even offering his own resignation from the Court to make room for Cardozo.[21]

Hoover appointed Cardozo on February 15, 1932; he was confirmed nine days later. Of the Cardozo nomination one author wrote:

> The appointment and confirmation of Benjamin Cardozo . . . violated nearly all the "rules of the game." Judge Cardozo was a New Yorker, and there were already two judges from that state on the bench—Stone and Hughes. He was a nominal Democrat, and his "real" politics, highly tinged with liberalism, differed sharply from those of President Hoover. Moreover, he was a Jew and there was already one Jewish judge in the person of Louis Brandeis. Cardozo's selection is inexplicable except in terms of his pre-eminent position among American jurists and the overwhelming pressures on his behalf from leaders of the bench and bar throughout the land.[22]

The Role of the ABA

Through its standing committee on the federal judiciary, the American Bar Association (ABA) has played a role in passing on the legal and intellectual qualifications of those selected for consideration as Supreme Court justices.

Established in 1945–1946, the committee began, with the nomination of William Brennan in 1956, to rate prospective justices as professionally qualified or unqualified. These ratings were used until Harry Blackmun's appointment in 1970.

Blackmun was confirmed to a seat for which the Senate had rejected Clement Haynsworth in 1969 and G. Harrold Carswell in 1970. The ABA committee had rated Haynsworth as "highly qualified" and Carswell as "qualified." Public criticism resulted in a change in the ABA rating system to three categories— "highly qualified," "not opposed," and "not qualified." Twenty years later, the ABA again revised its rating system to use the labels "well qualified," "qualified," and "not qualified."

After the embarrassment of the Haynsworth and Carswell rejections, Attorney General John N. Mitchell wrote the chairman of the committee in July 1970 to say that the Nixon administration would submit names of potential Supreme Court nominees to the ABA for preliminary screening prior to sending the president's choice to the Senate. But the agreement dissolved almost immediately when the names of prospective Nixon nominees to fill the next vacant seats reached the press while the ABA committee was studying their qualifications. The administration, suspecting a news leak in the committee, withdrew support of the practice.

Despite this rebuff, the ABA conducted its own investigation of the qualifications of nominees Lewis Powell and William Rehnquist. The ABA approved both men—Powell unanimously as "one of the best lawyers available." Rehnquist received nine votes for a highly qualified rating, but three committee members said merely that they were "not opposed" to his appointment.

During the Reagan years, the ABA committee received harsh criticism from liberals and conservatives alike. Reagan halted the practice of submitting a name to the committee before the nomination was made, sending it only after the nomination was official. The committee's approval of some controversial lower-court nominations drew liberal criticism, while its split, 10-5, on Robert H. Bork's Supreme Court nomination infuriated Bork's supporters who felt that the division on the committee, once made public, made it respectable to oppose the nomination and thus contributed to its defeat.[23]

During the George Bush administration, the bar association continued to fend off charges from the Justice Department and some members of the Senate Judiciary Committee that its evaluation process was biased.

During the Clinton administration, the White House continued to seek the ABA's review of potential nominees. But in 2001, shortly after President George W. Bush took office, his White House counsel, Alberto Gonzales, said the administration would no longer give the ABA advance notice of its nominees for the courts. Gonzales said that while his office would be glad to receive advice from the ABA, the bar association did not deserve a special role in the nomination process.

Politics and Appointments

Politics has always been a primary motivation in a president's selection of a Supreme Court nominee. It has also been a primary moving force in the process of senatorial confirmation. The oft-repeated disclaimer—that this process is, or should be, above politics—is simply not a true account.

In the early days of the republic the Court was an open political battlefield between the competing interests of Federalists and Democratic-Republicans as each party sought to impose its ideology on the government of the new nation. George Washington, W. D. Coles wrote, "initiated the system of appointing political adherents only, to places on the Supreme Bench. That system has seldom been departed from." [1]

In modern times the political element has become less openly partisan and manipulative, with a few notable exceptions, as the Court has evolved into a more equal and autonomous branch of the federal system. The evolution of the Court into such a relatively independent institution can be attributed in part to its growing stature under the weight of experience and tradition, and to the justices' sense of destiny and momentous undertaking as they assume their duties. In any event, service on the Court, however politically determined, began to engender a spirit of higher motive and unpredictable judgment that came more and more to confound the political expectations of those who made it possible. Meanwhile, the rigid party-line ideology of the Senate became more amorphous, with liberal and conservative factions of each party uniting on common ideological ground in considering Court appointees.

In the beginning, however, the president's power to appoint Supreme Court justices was considered an out-and-out political opportunity—and soon proved to be a political hornet's nest.

PRESIDENTIAL REASONING

On January 20, 1801, about two months before he left the White House and with little consultation and no fanfare, President John Adams appointed John Marshall chief justice of the United States, because he wanted a loyal Federalist on the bench who would preserve the party's principles in the wake of Democratic-Republican Thomas Jefferson's election as president in 1800. Marshall was not Adams's first choice, however. He had appointed John Jay chief justice, but Jay declined the post because he dreaded circuit-riding duties and felt the fledgling Court lacked "energy, weight, and dignity."

The Senate exhibited little enthusiasm for Marshall—less because its members opposed Marshall than because they preferred to see Associate Justice William Paterson elevated to the post of chief justice. Yet Adams remained firm. The Federalist-dominated Senate realized that if they rejected Marshall, Adams might send them a "spite" nominee, or worse, and the post would be left vacant for Jefferson to fill. [2]

The Senate approved Marshall's nomination on January 27, 1801. No other single appointment affected the early Court or the young nation more profoundly. From the Court, Marshall championed the principles of federalism for thirty-four years. His dominance over the Court is indicated by the fact that he wrote 519 of the 1,215 decisions handed down between 1801 and 1835. Marshall wrote thirty-six of the sixty-two decisions on major constitutional questions announced during his tenure. [3]

Unlike many of his successors, Adams was proud of his nominee. In 1826 he observed: "My gift of John Marshall to the people of the United States was the proudest act of my life. There is no act of my life on which I reflect with more pleasure." [4]

McLean and Taney

President Andrew Jackson's appointment of John McLean to the Supreme Court illustrates how easily Court nominees may break political promises to presidents.

McLean, a constant and persistent aspirant to high office, had been postmaster general under Presidents James Monroe and John Quincy Adams. In the tumultuous presidential election of 1828, McLean somehow maintained cordial ties with the forces of both Adams (a National-Republican) and Jackson (a Democratic-Republican). Jackson kept McLean on as postmaster general even though he did not really trust him. He knew McLean was a popular figure in the West, and he did not wish to risk a political fight with McLean early in his administration.

In return for McLean's promise to abandon his presidential aspirations, Jackson nominated him to the vacant seat on the Supreme Court in 1829. McLean, however, failed to live up to his end of the bargain. While on the bench he was a serious contender for a presidential nomination three times, taking on the colors of a political chameleon. In 1832 Anti-Mason Party leaders tried to persuade him to become their nominee; they eventually settled on William Wirt of Maryland. In 1848 he was in the running for both the Whig and Free Soil Party nominations, but he was twice defeated. He suffered a similar fate in 1856, when he failed to win the Republican Party nomination. Unsuccessful in all four efforts, he served on the Court until his death in 1861. [5]

In contrast to the McLean selection was Jackson's appointment of Roger B. Taney as chief justice. With the resignation of Justice Gabriel Duval in January 1835, Jackson appointed Taney, his loyal supporter and Treasury secretary, to the vacant seat. Taney had demonstrated his loyalty by complying with Jackson's controversial order to remove government deposits from the Bank of the United States during the president's war against the bank.

The Senate countered the Taney nomination by postponing consideration on the last day of the 1835 session—effectively killing it. The same day, moreover, the Senate passed a bill abolishing the vacant seat. The House of Representatives refused to go along with that move.

Then, on July 6, 1835, Chief Justice John Marshall died. Now Jackson had two seats to fill. Daniel Webster and Associate Justice Joseph Story were mentioned as candidates for the chief justice's chair. Jackson also received suggestions that he promote John McLean.

In December Jackson nominated Philip P. Barbour of Virginia to fill the Duval seat and Taney to succeed Marshall as chief justice. After three months of debate the Senate confirmed both appointments in March 1836.

Taney presided as chief justice for twenty-eight years, earning a reputation as a great champion of states' rights. His best-known opinion, however, was an aberration in an otherwise notable judicial career. This 1857 ruling in the case of the slave Dred Scott said blacks could not be citizens of the United States. The decision hastened the onset of the Civil War and contributed to the Court's loss of public esteem during and after the conflict. *(See "The Election of 1860," p. 807.)*

Salmon P. Chase

Chief Justice Taney died on October 12, 1864. In the midst of civil war, President Abraham Lincoln sought as a replacement for Taney a chief justice who would support him on matters of war policy and who could help close the widening breach in the Republican Party over Lincoln's conduct of the war.

Salmon Portland Chase was, from the outset, a serious candidate. Chase had been governor, senator from Ohio, and Lincoln's secretary of the Treasury. He was a talented public servant and seemed to hold the "right" opinions on the issues Lincoln considered important. But Chase was a political schemer, and he wanted desperately to be president. He had sought the Republican nomination in 1856 and in 1860, and even after becoming chief justice he vied for the 1868 presidential nomination of both parties.

Lincoln considered other political candidates for the post, including Associate Justices James M. Wayne and Noah H. Swayne, Secretary of State William H. Seward, Secretary of War Edwin M. Stanton, and Montgomery Blair, Lincoln's former postmaster general. Blair was Lincoln's personal choice for the post. He was a distinguished public servant with roots in the original Free Soil movement that became the Republican Party and a bitter foe of Chase.

But Lincoln appointed Chase—whom he did not trust—and not Blair—whom he trusted implicitly—because he believed that Chase commanded greater respect among Republicans and Unionists of all varieties and would help to unify the party and the nation. The Senate immediately confirmed the nomination in 1864.

Lincoln was assassinated four months later. Chief Justice Chase found himself presiding over challenges both to the slain president's wartime policies and postwar plans for conciliation with the South, and to Congress's punitive Reconstruction legislation. By most accounts, Chase—notwithstanding his continuing political ambitions—acted with even-handed judicial restraint aimed at forestalling the Court's involvement in politics. His reluctance to preside at the trial for treason of Jefferson Davis, the president of the Confederacy, contributed to the eventual dismissal of charges against Davis; and his fair handling of the impeachment trial of Andrew Johnson is considered an important factor in Johnson's acquittal.

As chief justice, Chase joined the Court majority in *Ex parte Milligan* (1866), which limited the authority of military tribunals over civilians. In the *Slaughterhouse Cases* he dissented from the opinion allowing the maintenance of civil rights under state jurisdiction. *(See details of Ex parte Milligan, p. 209; on the Slaughterhouse Cases, see pp. 369–370.)*

Chase's main apostasy from Lincoln's doctrines came in the 1870 "legal tender" cases. Chase delivered the opinion that the act issuing Civil War currency without providing for redemption was unconstitutional—even though Chase had been Treasury secretary when the greenbacks were issued. He dissented when the decision was reversed in 1871.

THE "COURT-PACKERS"

The term *Court-packing* is usually associated not with Ulysses Grant's appointments but with Franklin Roosevelt's blatant but unsuccessful bid in 1937 to reshape the Court into an instrument of his will. Nevertheless, the most successful, if unintentional, Court-packing ever accomplished by a president came in 1870.

Grant and Legal Tender

President Ulysses Grant's two appointees to the Court in 1870 played a role in the rapid reversal of a major decision involving the government's power to make paper money legal tender.

In April 1869 Congress increased the size of the Court to nine, giving Grant the opportunity to fill an extra seat. Then in December 1869 Justice Robert Grier resigned, giving Grant another vacancy to fill. Grant chose Edwin Stanton and Attorney General Ebenezer Hoar to fill the vacancies. Stanton was quickly confirmed but died suddenly, only four days after his confirmation. The Senate then rejected Hoar's nomination.

In February 1870 Grant nominated Joseph Bradley and William Strong to the vacancies. Bradley was a Republican railroad lawyer, and Strong was a former Pennsylvania Supreme Court justice. Grant made the nominations even as the Court was announcing its decision in the case of *Hepburn v. Griswold*.[6] By 4–3, the Court declared unconstitutional the Legal Tender Act of 1862, which had made greenbacks—paper money—legal tender for payment of debts. Those supporting the gold standard for currency opposed the Court's ruling, arguing that it permitted debtors to pay off their debts in cheap currency.

Chief Justice Chase wrote the majority opinion, holding the law invalid insofar as it allowed the use of paper money to pay off debts contracted before its passage. Three Republican justices—Miller, Swayne, and Davis, all Lincoln appointees—

APPOINTMENTS AND DISAPPOINTMENTS PRESIDENTS AND JUDGES

Despite their best efforts to name individuals to the Court who share their views, presidents frequently have been disappointed. Their appointees failed to follow presidential political philosophy in their Court opinions. Donning the Court robe does seem to make a difference in the appointees' views. Justice Felix Frankfurter, when asked if appointment to the Court changed a person's views, allegedly retorted: "If he is any good, it does."[1]

Chief Justice Earl Warren, reflecting on sixteen years' service on the Court, said he did not see "how a man could be on the Court and not change his views substantially over a period of years for change you must if you are to do your duty on the Supreme Court."[2]

Historian Charles Warren wrote that "nothing is more striking in the history of the Court than the manner in which the hopes of those who expected a judge to follow the political views of the President appointing him are disappointed."[3]

JEFFERSON AND MARSHALL

Presidents Thomas Jefferson and James Madison repeatedly registered their disappointment at the failure of those they appointed to the Court to resist the powerful and dominating influence of Chief Justice John Marshall. Madison failed to heed Jefferson's advice against appointing Joseph Story to the Court. Jefferson warned Madison that Story would side with Marshall on important legal questions—and Jefferson proved correct. Story not only joined Marshall in his interpretation of the Constitution but occasionally showed himself even more nationalistic than the chief justice.

ROOSEVELT AND HOLMES

Theodore Roosevelt named Oliver Wendell Holmes Jr. to the Court. Holmes then voted against the administration's antitrust efforts, most notably in the 1904 case of *Northern Securities v. United States*. Holmes's unexpected dissent left the government with a narrow 5-4 majority upholding the dissolution of the Northern Securities Company railroad conglomerate.

Following the decision, Roosevelt, referring to Holmes's defection, said that he "could carve out of a banana a Judge with more backbone than that!" Holmes reportedly smiled when told of the remark. Later, at a White House dinner, Holmes remarked to a labor leader and fellow guest: "What you want is favor, not justice. But when I am on my job, I don't give a damn what you or Mr. Roosevelt want."[4]

Woodrow Wilson had reason to regret the appointment of James C. McReynolds to the bench when that justice proved to hold the opposite of Wilson's viewpoint on almost every question the administration argued before the Court.

COOLIDGE AND TRUMAN

Calvin Coolidge's sole appointee, Harlan F. Stone, sided within a year of his appointment with the liberal Holmes-Brandeis wing of the Court.

President Harry S Truman noted that "packing the Supreme Court simply can't be done I've tried and it won't work. Whenever you put a man on the Supreme Court he ceases to be your friend."[5]

And Truman should have known. In the important *Steel Seizure Case* (1952) the four Truman appointees divided 2-2 in the case that ruled the president's seizure of the steel mills unconstitutional. *(See details, p. 265, in Chapter 5, Vol. I.)*

EISENHOWER AND NIXON

President Dwight D. Eisenhower later suggested it was a mistake to appoint Earl Warren as chief justice. Warren's leadership commenced a judicial "revolution" that greatly disturbed the Republican president. But Warren's appointment made good political sense in 1953. Warren had delivered California delegates to Eisenhower at the Republican National Convention in 1952. Warren's removal from the California political scene, where he had

dissented, arguing that a federal power with respect to money included the right to make paper money legal tender.

The Senate confirmed Bradley and Strong, and they took their seats in the spring of 1870, during which the Court agreed to hear a second legal tender case argued. A year later the Court, in *Knox v. Lee*, reversed *Hepburn v. Griswold*.[7] The vote was 5-4. Justices Bradley and Strong joined the three dissenters in *Hepburn* to form a majority in *Knox*.

Scholars later debated whether Grant intentionally packed the Court to get the legal tender ruling reversed. Charles Warren, historian of the Supreme Court, absolved Grant of the charge, saying that the president did not know in advance of the Court's ruling when he appointed Bradley and Strong and that, under any circumstances, Grant would have appointed men to the Court who agreed with his views on the money question.

But evidence not available when Warren wrote his history indicates that Grant did have prior knowledge of the outcome of the *Hepburn* case. Grant's secretary of the Treasury, George S. Boutwell, received word from Chief Justice Chase two weeks before the decision was announced what the outcome would be. That information most likely was passed to Grant. Moreover, several years after the event, Grant said he had desired in his appointments of Strong and Bradley a Court decision that would sustain the constitutionality of legal tender. He got his wish.[8]

Roosevelt's Would-Be Court

The selection and confirmation of individual nominees to the Court have not been the only factors in the struggle between the president and Congress for a politically acceptable Court. Both from time to time have attempted to juggle the size of the Court's membership in order to achieve a judicial consensus proven an immensely popular three-term governor, placated conservative California Republican leaders, including Vice President Richard Nixon and Senate Majority Leader William F. Knowland, both of whom disliked Warren's progressive Republican views.

But Eisenhower reportedly regretted the liberalism of Warren and that of another of his appointees, Justice William J. Brennan Jr. Henry J. Abraham writes: "To Eisenhower, the new Warren represented all but a betrayal of older beliefs and understandings and his recognition of the chief justice's judicial independence, which he regarded as judicial legislating, was bitter and frustrating."[6]

President Richard Nixon had cause to regret some of the selections he made for the Court. Although the justices' views, on the whole, comported with the president's on "law and order" issues, some of the four appointees' opinions rejected Nixon's positions on abortion, aid to parochial schools, desegregation, and electronic surveillance. And in 1974 the Court, in an 8-0 opinion, handed down the decision in the tapes case that led to Nixon's resignation from office.[7] *(See "Nixon, Watergate, and the Court," pp. 266–270, in Chapter 5, Vol. I.)* Both Justice Harry A. Blackmun and Justice Lewis F. Powell Jr. carved out more moderate legacies than would have been expected by Pres. Nixon when he appointed them.

REAGAN AND BUSH

Ronald Reagan, whose administration engaged in a concerted effort to make the federal bench more conservative, enjoyed results as mixed as his Republican predecessors'. During his two terms (1981–1985, 1985–1989), Reagan appointed three reputed conservatives as associate justices (Sandra Day O'Connor, Antonin Scalia, and Anthony M. Kennedy) and elevated William H. Rehnquist to chief justice.

All told, these four appointments did move the Court into a more conservative era. The Court more narrowly interpreted the Constitution and federal statutes, reinvigorated federalism and state sovereignty, restricted appeals by prisoners sentenced to death, cut back use of affirmative action, and allowed greater

government involvement with religion. But on the most symbolic constitutional issue of the era—abortion—two Reagan appointees, Justices O'Connor and Kennedy, cast decisive votes in 1992 to affirm *Roe v. Wade*, a position directly contrary to the desires of the president who had chosen them.[8] President George H. W. Bush's first appointee, David H. Souter, would disappoint conservative partisans even more than had O'Connor and Kennedy. Not only did he vote with those two justices to uphold abortion rights, but by the mid-1990s, he was firmly ensconced in the Court's liberal wing on most controversial issues.

A DIFFERENT VIEW

In his book *God Save This Honorable Court*, Laurence H. Tribe argues against what he calls the "myth of the surprised president," contending that "for the most part, and especially in areas of particular and known concern to a President, Justices have been loyal to the ideals and perspectives of the men who have nominated them."[9]

Tribe's qualification—"in areas of known concern to a President"—points out the most significant reason for presidential disappointment. Issues change over time. As legal scholar Alexander Bickel once said, "You shoot an arrow into a far-distant future when you appoint a Justice and not the man himself can tell you what he will think about some of the problems he will face."[10]

1. Henry J. Abraham, *Justices and Presidents: A Political History of Appointments to the Supreme Court*, 3d ed. (New York: Oxford University Press, 1992), 70.

2. Anthony Lewis, "A Talk with Warren on Crime, the Court, the Country," *New York Times Magazine*, October 19, 1969, 128–129.

3. Charles Warren, *The Supreme Court in United States History*, rev. ed., 2 vols. (Boston: Little, Brown, 1922, 1926), I: 22.

4. Abraham, *Justices and Presidents*, 69.

5. Ibid., 70.

6. Ibid., 258, 266.

7. *United States v. Nixon*, 418 U.S. 683 (1974).

8. *Planned Parenthood of Southeastern Pennsylvania v. Casey*, 505 U.S. 833 (1992).

9. Laurence Tribe, *God Save This Honorable Court* (New York: Random House, 1985), 50.

10. *Time*, May 23, 1969, 24.

more to their liking. Franklin Roosevelt's attempt to increase the Court's membership was the most transparent example yet of a president's political pressure on the Court—and it landed Roosevelt in his biggest political controversy up to that time.

In 1935 and 1936 the Court, in a series of 5-4 and 6-3 decisions, struck down every important measure of Roosevelt's New Deal program. The so-called "Four Horsemen"—Justices William Van Devanter, James C. McReynolds, George Sutherland, and Pierce Butler—were totally antagonistic to New Deal philosophy that called for government spending and work projects to help farmers, labor, and business survive the depression. They were often joined by Chief Justice Charles Evans Hughes and Justice Owen J. Roberts to form an anti-New Deal majority. *(See "New Deal and Old Court," pp. 261–262.)*

Roosevelt won a stunning reelection victory in 1936 and on the strength of that popular mandate redoubled his efforts to

prevent the "nine old men" on the Supreme Court from obstructing his legislative programs. But his "Court reform" bill—permitting a president to add a justice to the Supreme Court for every justice over seventy who refused to retire, for a total of fifteen justices—was really a plan to pack the Court, and it offended some of FDR's ardent supporters in the Congress and on the bench.

A confrontation was, however, averted. By the time the bill was unfavorably reported by the Senate Judiciary Committee, Roosevelt had begun to get more cooperation from a Court suddenly more amenable to his legislation, and he had gained the opportunity to appoint new justices to recently vacated seats. The bill never reached the Senate floor, and the scheme was allowed to die.

The Court had signaled a more hospitable attitude toward the New Deal in three decisions in the spring of 1937 upholding

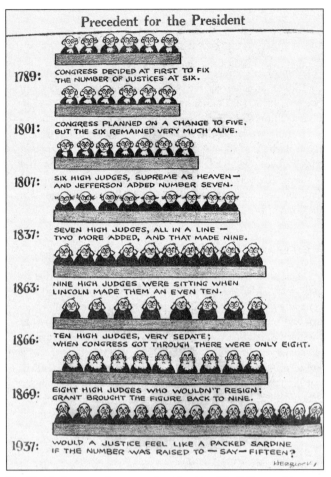

This Herblock cartoon lampoons President Franklin D. Roosevelt's proposal to enlarge the Supreme Court's membership.

major administration acts. And Van Devanter's retirement announcement came while the Judiciary Committee was considering the Court-packing bill. Van Devanter's retirement gave Roosevelt a chance to name his first appointee to the Court, and he nominated a full-fledged New Dealer, Alabama senator Hugo L. Black—the first of nine appointments he would make before the end of 1943. As a result of Roosevelt's new appointments, the thrust and focus of the Court's decisions changed drastically in the next few years.

The retirement of Chief Justice Charles Evans Hughes in 1941 gave President Roosevelt an opportunity to name the person of his choice to that position. Eventually, he picked a Republican in the hope of increasing bipartisan political support for his administration in the face of World War II.

When the eighty-year-old chief justice announced on June 2, 1941, that he would be retiring as of July 1, 1941, Roosevelt felt no urgency to move quickly to fill the post. The president had two candidates in mind: Associate Justice Harlan Fiske Stone and Attorney General Robert Jackson. Roosevelt preferred Jackson, his attorney general and a New Deal loyalist. The retiring Hughes, on the other hand, felt Stone's record on the Court merited his elevation to chief justice.

Roosevelt also discussed the nomination with Justice Felix Frankfurter. When asked which of the two men he preferred, Frankfurter told the president:

> On personal grounds I'd prefer Bob [Jackson]. While I've known Stone longer and our relations are excellent and happy, I feel closer friendship with Bob. But from the national interest I am bound to say that there is no reason for preferring Bob to Stone—quite the contrary. Stone is senior and qualified professionally to be C. J. But for me the decisive consideration, considering the fact that Stone is qualified, is that Bob is of your personal and political family, as it were, while Stone is a Republican.... When war does come, the country should feel you are the Nation's ... President, and not a partisan President. Few things would contribute as much to confidence in you as a national and not as a partisan president than for you to name a Republican, who has the profession's confidence, as chief justice.[9]

Roosevelt discussed the nomination with Jackson, who assured the president he agreed with Frankfurter's analysis. And Jackson personally delivered the news to Stone of his appointment as chief justice. Stone was confirmed in the Senate by a voice vote. The president later appointed Jackson to Stone's vacant justice seat.

ROUTES TO THE COURT

After Stone's death in 1946, President Harry Truman appointed Fred M. Vinson chief justice of the United States. Truman selected him because Vinson was an able administrator with broad experience in public service and he was a friend. Vinson had served with Truman in the Senate. When Truman became president, Vinson served as his Treasury secretary and ex officio adviser.

At the time of Stone's death the Court was seriously divided by personality clashes among the justices, especially the feud between Justices Robert Jackson and Hugo Black described by one of Black's biographers as "the bitterest internecine controversy in the court's history."[10] Among other things, the long-simmering antagonism involved Jackson's charges that Black was guilty of conflict of interest by participating in two decisions in 1944 and 1945.[11] Meanwhile Black criticized Jackson's leave of absence from the Court in 1945–1946 to serve as U.S. prosecutor at the Nazi war crimes trial at Nuremberg, Germany—a trial Black called a "high-grade lynching party."[12]

Truman sought the advice of former chief justice Charles Evans Hughes and former associate justice Owen Roberts about the chief justice appointment. Both men urged Truman to appoint someone who could restore peace among the members of the Court, which apparently ruled out Jackson, believed by many, evidently including Jackson himself, to be next in line for the chief justiceship.[13] Truman nominated Fred Vinson on June 7, 1946, and he was confirmed, uncontested, two weeks later amid a further volley of mutual public criticism between Jackson and Black.

In seven years as chief justice Vinson muted the clashes between members of the Court, but he did not restore harmony.

There were proportionally more 5-4 opinions during the Vinson period than in any other era in the Court's history until the unprecedented division on the Rehnquist Court.[14] Vinson died in 1953, disappointed with the results of his term as chief justice.[15]

Creating a Vacancy

In 1965 President Lyndon Johnson persuaded Arthur Goldberg to leave the Court to create a vacancy to which Johnson could appoint his friend and trusted adviser Abe Fortas. Appealing to Goldberg's sense of duty and public service, Johnson urged him to resign from the Court so that he could serve as U.S. ambassador to the United Nations. Goldberg allowed himself to be persuaded, genuinely hoping that the UN forum would be the arena in which to negotiate an end to the war in Vietnam.

Goldberg, from a poor immigrant family background, had been general counsel for the nation's largest labor unions before becoming secretary of labor in the Kennedy administration. Both Chief Justice Earl Warren and Justice Felix Frankfurter approved of Goldberg's appointment in 1962 as Frankfurter's successor. But Goldberg was to serve only three years. President Johnson, fresh from an election victory, wanted to put his choice on the Court.

After coaxing Goldberg off the Court, Johnson had to persuade a reluctant Abe Fortas to take the seat. Johnson invited Fortas to the White House on July 18, 1965, on the pretext of seeking his advice on another matter. The president then simply informed Fortas that he was going over to the East Wing of the White House to nominate Fortas for the Supreme Court.

The prearranged session included Goldberg and his family. The resigning justice did not hide his disappointment at leaving the Court, saying, "I shall not, Mr. President, conceal the pain with which I leave the Court after three years of service. It has been the richest and most satisfying period of my career."[16]

Delaying a Vacancy

When Chief Justice Earl Warren announced in 1968 his intention to retire, he gave President Johnson an opportunity to appoint his successor in the nation's highest judicial post. But Johnson had become a lame-duck president, declaring in March 1968 that he would not be a candidate for reelection. Nevertheless, Johnson took advantage of the Warren retirement announcement and nominated Justice Fortas as chief justice.

The Senate rejected Fortas. Republicans, hopeful of winning the White House in 1968, wanted to "save" the vacancy for the Republican president-to-be to fill. Fortas's continuing role as an

At the request of Lyndon B. Johnson, Arthur J. Goldberg (above) resigned from the Supreme Court in 1965 to become the ambassador to the United Nations. Johnson persuaded his friend and adviser Abe Fortas to fill the vacancy. In the picture on the right, Fortas is subjected to a friendly dose of the well-known Johnson "treatment."

unofficial adviser to the president on policy matters while on the Court and his acceptance of fees for a series of university seminars created enough doubts among enough senators to forestall confirmation in 1968. Fortas's nomination cleared the Senate Judiciary Committee but ran into a filibuster on the floor. A motion to end the filibuster failed, and Fortas then asked President Johnson to withdraw his name from nomination.

Richard Nixon, the Republican candidate, won election as president soon thereafter, and in May 1969 he named his choice, Warren E. Burger, chief justice. By the time Burger was sworn in, Fortas had left the Court. In May 1969 *Life* magazine reported that Fortas in 1966 had accepted, and then returned, a large fee from the Louis E. Wolfson family foundation. Millionaire Wolfson later was sent to prison for illegal stock manipulations.[17] Rather than face a full-scale inquiry and possibly impeachment proceedings, Fortas resigned on May 15, 1969.

THE "SAVE-THE-SEAT" SYNDROME

The refusal of the Senate to confirm Fortas's nomination as chief justice was a modern example of the "save-the-seat" stratagem. During the nineteenth century the Senate denied confirmation to many late-term nominees to the Court simply because the Senate, for partisan reasons, wished to save the seat for the incoming president to fill and thereby place his stamp on the Court at the outset of his term. In early 1829, for example, the Senate refused to confirm lame-duck president John Quincy Adams's nomination of John J. Crittenden to the Court, thus saving the vacancy for President Andrew Jackson to fill.

The unluckiest president for Court appointments was John Tyler. Five of his nominations failed to win Senate approval. Tyler, a Whig, was without a solid political base of his own after President William Henry Harrison died in office in 1841.

Tyler's first four nominees met Senate rejection after the president's policies collided with those advocated by Henry Clay's rival Whig Party supporters in the Senate. Tyler's fifth nominee—announced in February 1845 after Democrat James K. Polk won the 1844 presidential election—was a well-known Philadelphia lawyer, John M. Read, who had political ties with both the Whigs and Democrats. The Senate postponed consideration of the nomination made by the lame-duck Tyler and adjourned. President Polk therefore began his term in office with an opportunity to fill Henry Baldwin's still-vacant seat. After rejecting Polk's first nominee, George W. Woodward, the Senate confirmed Robert Grier in August 1846.

After Franklin Pierce won the 1852 election, President Millard Fillmore, by then a lame duck, named Sen. George E. Badger of North Carolina to the post of justice. The Senate postponed the nomination—an unusual breach of a senatorial practice that usually grants immediate confirmation to a senator appointed to the Court. Fillmore, however, refused to accept defeat and named a prominent Louisiana lawyer, William C. Micou. But the Senate again refused to act, allowing Pierce to fill that vacancy at the outset of his administration.

In 1861, at the end of his presidential term, President James Buchanan, a Democrat, tried to fill the seat vacated by Peter V. Daniel. Buchanan found a worthy candidate in Pennsylvanian Jeremiah S. Black—a strong believer in the Union but not an abolitionist. Moreover, Black had been chief justice of the Pennsylvania Supreme Court and attorney general of the United States. But it was too late. In less than a month Lincoln would assume the presidency. Republicans in the Senate were not anxious to deny the first Republican president the opportunity to make the Court appointment. Black was denied confirmation, 25–26.

Rutherford B. Hayes, an avowed one-term president, nominated in late January 1881 his friend and former college classmate Stanley Matthews of Ohio to the seat made vacant by Noah Swayne's retirement. Matthews had a successful career as a public servant, but he was a political maverick. The major drawback to his candidacy, however, was that Matthews served as a prominent counsel to financier Jay Gould. The Senate Judiciary Committee refused to report the nomination for floor action, and it appeared Matthews's nomination was dead until Hayes's successor, James A. Garfield, renominated Matthews for the post in March 1881. He was confirmed by the narrowest of margins, 24–23.

William Howard Taft laid the groundwork for his own subsequent appointment as chief justice in 1921 when, as president in 1910, he chose the veteran justice Edward White for the post rather than the younger candidate, Justice Charles Evans Hughes. Earlier, in 1910, Taft had appointed Hughes associate justice, filling the vacancy created by David J. Brewer's death. Taft had considered Hughes a threat to his own presidential nomination in 1908. And Hughes was recognized as presidential "timber" within Republican ranks. At the time of Hughes's appointment Taft dangled before him the prospect of becoming chief justice when that vacancy occurred. Taft wrote Hughes that he had no reservations about promoting an associate justice to chief justice. Then, in an equivocal addendum, Taft wrote:

> Don't misunderstand me as to the Chief Justiceship. I mean if that office were now open, I should offer it to you and it is probable that if it were to become vacant during my term, I should promote you to it; but, of course, conditions change, so that it would not be right for me to say by way of promise what I would do in the future. Nor, on the other hand, would I have you think that your declination now would prevent my offering you the higher position, should conditions remain as they are.[18]

Hughes got the message and accepted, but conditions did change. In July 1910 Chief Justice Melville W. Fuller died, and in December 1910 Taft appointed Louisianan Edward White, age sixty-five, a Catholic, and a Democrat, to replace him. The public—not to mention Hughes—had expected Taft to name Hughes to the post. In 1916 Hughes resigned from the Court to run for the presidency.[19]

White had already served on the Court seventeen years when Taft named him chief justice. He was an able administrator whose views coincided with those of Taft. And because White was not a young man, the president counted on White's retirement, resignation, or death—preferably during a Republican administration—to create a vacancy in the Court's top spot, which Taft hoped to fill.

Taft did not conceal his ambitions. When he signed White's commission as chief justice he remarked aloud: "There is nothing I would have loved more than being Chief Justice of the United States. I cannot help seeing the irony in the fact that I, who desired that office so much, should now be signing the commission of another man."[20]

White died on May 21, 1921. After considerable lobbying by Taft in his own behalf, President Warren G. Harding appointed him chief justice. He served until 1930, when President Hoover appointed the man Taft had decided not to make chief justice—Charles Evans Hughes.

THE COURT AS A CAMPAIGN ISSUE

The Supreme Court—its personnel as well as its positions—has been a recurring issue in presidential campaigns since 1800. The candidates of both major parties, and those of some third parties, have found the Court's rulings on a variety of issues, from slavery to taxes to criminal procedure—all handy targets for election year rhetoric. Presidents Jefferson, Lincoln, Franklin Roosevelt, Richard Nixon, and Ronald Reagan most successfully implemented their campaign criticism of the Court. Each of those presidents influenced the Court's decisions through his appointments and policies.

Thomas Jefferson

During the election of 1800, Jeffersonian Democratic-Republicans charged that the federal judiciary was a solid Federalist phalanx intent upon destroying republican liberties. Jeffersonians also criticized both Chief Justice John Jay and his successor in that post, Oliver Ellsworth, for accepting diplomatic assignments from Presidents Washington and Adams, respectively. Moreover, Jay had then negotiated the treaty that bore his name, a treaty reviled by all Jeffersonians as too pro-British. James T. Callender, the notorious Jeffersonian pamphleteer, wrote in his 1800 election campaign pamphlet, *The Prospect Before Us:* "Think of the gross and audacious prostitution of the federal bench by the successive selection of foreign ambassadors from that body."[21]

When Jefferson became president, he launched an attack on the judicial branch, encouraging Congress first to repeal the Judiciary Act of 1801 and then to impeach an associate justice, Samuel Chase, for his "crimes" of making political diatribes from the bench. The Jeffersonians succeeded in repealing the 1801 act but failed in their efforts to impeach Chase. *(See "Chase Impeachment," pp. 766–769.)*

On the whole, Jefferson got what he wanted. The judges toned down their statements from the bench and the appointment of Jeffersonian Democratic-Republicans to all levels of the judiciary ended charges that the federal bench was a Federalist sanctuary. Nevertheless, all of Jefferson's Court appointees sub-

sequently succumbed to the influence of Jefferson's Federalist archenemy, Chief Justice John Marshall.

The Election of 1860

The Court's decision in *Scott v. Sandford* (1857) permanently disrupted the fragile structure of political compromise and adjustment between North and South on the issue of the expansion of slavery into the territories beyond the Mississippi River.[22] The decision gave Abraham Lincoln an issue that carried him to the White House. The whole existence of the Republican Party rested on the twin pillars of free land and free men in the territories west of the Mississippi.

Republicans chose Lincoln as their standard-bearer in 1860—in large part because of his simple and eloquent refutation of the slavery expansion argument made by Sen. Stephen A. Douglas in the 1858 Illinois Senate race. Lincoln refused to compromise on the expansion question:

> Now, I confess myself as belonging to the class in the country who contemplates slavery as a moral, social, and political evil, having due regard for its actual existence among us and the difficulties of getting rid of it in any satisfactory way, and to all constitutional obligations which have been thrown about it; but nevertheless, [I] desire a policy that looks to the prevention of it as a wrong, and looks hopefully to the time when as a wrong it may come to an end.[23]

The Dred Scott decision left antislavery advocates in a dilemma. If Congress could not act to halt the spread of slavery, then who could? The decision—and the Court—were primary campaign issues in 1860. Republicans argued that the Court's statements on the power of Congress were simply *dicta*—comments extraneous to resolution of the case itself and thus not binding as constitutional law. They also argued that the Dred Scott ruling could be overturned by a future Court if Republicans gained control of both Congress and the White House, thus winning the opportunity to appoint loyal Republicans to the Court. Several Republicans demanded that the Court be packed with Republicans should Lincoln win the election.

The Republican platform of 1860 sharply criticized the Dred Scott decision:

> [T]he new dogma that the Constitution, of its own force, carries slavery into any or all of the territories of the United States, is a dangerous political heresy, at variance with the explicit provisions of that instrument itself, with contemporaneous exposition, and with legislative and judicial precedent; is revolutionary in its tendency, and subversive of the peace and harmony of the country.... [T]he normal condition of all territory of the United States is that of freedom.[24]

Lincoln won the election, but war, rather than his nominations to the Court, ultimately overruled the Dred Scott decision.

The Income Tax Issue

In 1895 the Court held the federal income tax unconstitutional in *Pollock v. Farmers' Loan and Trust Co.* The decision angered progressives in Congress and other reformers who felt that it protected private vested rights and frustrated Congress's

The Court's decision in *Dred Scott v. Sandford* set the tenor of the 1860 presidential contest. The four presidential candidates of the battered national parties dance with members of their respective constituencies in this campaign cartoon. Clockwise from upper left are southern Democrat John C. Breckinridge, Republican Abraham Lincoln, Constitutional party candidate John Bell, and Democrat Stephen A. Douglas.

attempts to make the wealthy pay their fair share of taxes. Farmers and laborers considered the decision another victory of the rich and powerful. *(See "The Income Tax Cases," pp. 125–128.)*

The income tax ruling became an issue in the 1896 presidential campaign. The Democratic Party favored the income tax and decried such judicial "usurpation" of legislative power. Its candidate, William Jennings Bryan, championed the tax at the Democratic National Convention in Chicago in July 1896:

> They criticize us for our criticism of the Supreme Court of the United States. . . . They say that we passed an unconstitutional law; we deny it. The income tax law was not unconstitutional when it was passed; it was not unconstitutional when it went before the Supreme Court for the first time; it did not become unconstitutional until one of the judges changed his mind, and we cannot be expected to know when a judge will change his mind. The income tax is just. It simply intends to put the burdens of government justly upon the backs of the people. I am in favor of an income tax. When I find a man who is not willing to share of the burdens of government which protects him, I find a man who is unworthy to enjoy the blessings of a government like ours.[25]

Bryan lost, and not until ratification of the Sixteenth Amendment in 1913 did Congress overturn the effect of the Court's 1895 decision.

La Follette on the Attack

In the 1924 presidential election Progressives made the Supreme Court's opposition to reform legislation a campaign issue. Sen. Robert M. La Follette, R-Wis., was the Progressive Party's candidate. He argued that the day had come

when the Federal judiciary must be made—to some extent at least—subject to the will of the people, or we must abandon the pretense that the people rule in this country. . . . We cannot live under a system of government where we are forced to amend the Constitution every time we want to pass a progressive law. The remedy must adequately cope with the disease, or there is no use applying it.[26]

La Follette's remedy was a single constitutional amendment that sharply curtailed the power of judicial review, denying any lower federal court authority to declare an act of Congress unconstitutional and providing that when the Supreme Court declared an act of Congress unconstitutional, Congress could override that decision by reenacting the law. The 1924 Progressive Party platform stated: "We favor submitting to the people, for their considerate judgment, a constitutional amendment providing that Congress may by enacting a statute make it effective over a judicial veto."[27]

But 1924 was not a year for reformers. Prosperity and "normalcy" were on the rise, and the nation voted to keep President Calvin Coolidge at the helm. The Court, Coolidge said in response to La Follette's criticism, was the chief defender of the American way of life—the chief obstacle preventing "breakdown [of] the guarantees of our fundamental law."[28]

"Fighting Bob" La Follette died in 1925. His constitutional amendment was never adopted.

The Election of 1968

In the presidential campaign of 1968, Richard Nixon made clear that if elected he intended to use his power of appointment to remake the Warren Court in the image of his own conservative value system. Nixon sharply criticized the Warren Court during a "law and order" campaign alleging that the Court's decisions on criminal procedure were "seriously hamstringing the peace forces in our society and strengthening the criminal forces."[29]

Once elected, Nixon nominated Warren Earl Burger chief justice of the United States on May 21, 1969. Burger had a reputation as a hard-line "law and order" judge on the court of appeals for the District of Columbia.[30] He was quickly confirmed. Nixon's effort to name a second conservative ran into trouble, however. The difficulty came when he tried to fill the seat left vacant by the resignation of Abe Fortas on May 14, 1969.

During the campaign Nixon had said he would nominate a southerner to the Court who had a conservative judicial philosophy. In November 1969 the Senate rejected Nixon's first southern nominee, Judge Clement F. Haynsworth of the Fourth Circuit Court of Appeals, because of his participation in deciding cases in which, it was charged, he had a financial interest. Nixon then submitted the name of G. Harrold Carswell, another conservative southerner who was a judge of the Fifth Circuit Court of Appeals. Aware of Carswell's record as a staunch segregationist and his lack of intellectual qualities, the Senate rejected his nomination. Nixon later filled the Fortas seat with Minnesotan Harry A. Blackmun, a conservative member of the Eighth Circuit Court of Appeals.

In 1971 the retirements of Hugo Black and John Marshall Harlan gave Nixon two more seats to fill on the Court. He named Lewis Powell to Black's seat. Powell was a distinguished Virginia lawyer who had criticized some of the Warren Court's civil liberties decisions. To Harlan's seat Nixon nominated William Rehnquist of Arizona, who was seen as both very conservation and brilliant, having graduated first in his Stanford law school class. Both men were confirmed in 1971.

By the end of 1971—his third year as president—Nixon had appointed four members of the Court. He had fulfilled his campaign pledges. The Court's rulings on criminal law reflected the conservative views of Burger and the new associate justices.

The Reagan Revolution

To win the White House in 1980, and again in 1984, Ronald Reagan said what the nation's most conservative voters wanted to hear: that he would work for the reversal of the Supreme Court's 1973 decision permitting abortion (*Roe v. Wade*) and its earlier rulings forbidding officially prescribed prayers in public schools (*Engel v. Vitale*, 1962; *Abington School District v. Schempp*, 1963).

These decisions were just a few that Reagan hoped to persuade the Court to disavow. In addition, he wanted the Court to abandon the use of affirmative action, relax the Warren Court's rulings denying police and prosecutors the use of illegally obtained evidence, and lower the barrier separating church and state, particularly when the issue was state aid to parochial schools.

ARGUING THE PRESIDENT'S CASE

When the White House wants the Supreme Court to take a certain position on an issue, it is the solicitor general, or one of the solicitor general's staff, who argues the administration's case to the Supreme Court. When the government is a party to a case, the solicitor general argues the government's side. When it is not a party, but nevertheless wishes to make its views known on the issue, the solicitor general files an amicus curiae—friend of the court—brief.

The government has been very successful in arguing cases before the Court. One study of the Court's opinions shows that the government won more than 60 percent of its cases in the eighteenth and nineteenth centuries. From 1953 through 1983 it won almost 70 percent of its cases.[1] Subsequent studies have found that success rate continuing through the late 1980s but dropping off slightly in the 1990s.[2]

The government's record in cases where it filed as amicus curiae is even better. The position endorsed by the government prevailed in as many as 87 percent of the cases in some terms after World War II. For the terms between 1958 and 1967 the government's rate of success in such cases averaged 71 percent.[3]

In recent terms, the solicitor general's office has participated in most of the cases heard before the Court and has been on winning side most of the time. In the 2001–2002 term, Solicitor General Theodore B. Olson took sides in seventy-five of the eighty-eight cases decided by the Court, and, of those, was on the winning side in sixty-three and on the losing side in twelve for an 84 percent success rate. Olson did nearly as well in his second term, in 2002–2003. He filed briefs in seventy-one of the eighty-four cases that were decided, and was on the winning side of fifty-six and on the losing side in fourteen, with one nondecision, for a 79 percent winning record.

SOURCES: Office of Solicitor General, Department of Justice.
1. Lincoln Caplan, *The Tenth Justice: The Solicitor General and the Rule of Law* (New York: Knopf, 1987), 295.
2. Statistics compiled by Office of Solicitor General, 1996.
3. Robert G. Scigliano, *The Supreme Court and the Presidency* (New York: Free Press, 1971), 180.

Like all presidents, Reagan had two ways to effect these changes in the Court—the power to appoint new members when vacancies occurred and the power to argue his point of view through the solicitor general. He used both to the maximum extent possible; in the end the former proved more effective than the latter.

Jimmy Carter had spent four years in the White House without any vacancy occurring on the Court; Reagan had to wait only five months. Justice Potter Stewart retired in June 1981, and Reagan made good on another campaign pledge, naming the first woman justice of the U.S. Supreme Court, Judge Sandra Day O'Connor of the Arizona Court of Appeals. O'Connor quickly allied herself with Rehnquist, her Stanford law school classmate, and the Court's other conservative members. She became an articulate voice for the conservative wing of the Court.

During Reagan's first term his solicitor general, Rex E. Lee, argued the administration's case for change in cases concerning criminal law, deregulation, affirmative action, and abortion, but with only limited success.

In the October 1983 term the administration seemed to make some headway, winning favorable rulings on affirmative action, the exclusionary rule, and deregulation. But its success in those rulings was significantly diluted in the next two terms when the Court—in some cases with O'Connor's help—rejected the administration's position on school prayer, aid to parochial schools, and affirmative action.[31]

Then in the summer of 1986 Chief Justice Burger retired, giving Reagan the chance to name a new chief. Reagan selected Rehnquist, the Court's most conservative member, and, to the seat Rehnquist vacated, he named Antonin Scalia, a highly respected conservative judge who was the first justice of Italian descent.

But even three Reagan justices were not enough to swing the Court firmly in a conservative direction. It took one more nomination, and Justice Powell provided the opportunity when he retired in 1987. Reagan's first choice, Robert H. Bork, was soundly defeated in the Senate. Opposition to Bork's nomination was led by civil rights groups who criticized his views, and it was intensified by awareness of the pivotal role the new justice would play in some of the Court's most controversial decisions.

In February 1988 Anthony Kennedy, Reagan's third choice to fill Powell's seat, was sworn in as the nation's 104th justice. The next term, Reagan's campaign for change finally bore fruit. In the October 1988 term the Supreme Court issued decisions limiting the use of affirmative action, and for the first time since *Roe v. Wade* it upheld a state law imposing significant restrictions on a woman's right to have an abortion.[32]

Opposition to abortion remained a priority for the administration of George Bush (1989–1993). In 1992, when the Supreme Court again considered a constitutional right of privacy for abortion, the Court noted that five times in the past decade the president, first Reagan then Bush, had asked the Court to overturn *Roe v. Wade*. Emphasizing the need for stability in key areas of constitutional liberties, the Court affirmed the right to an abortion, declaring that "liberty finds no refuge in the jurisprudence of doubt."[33]

President Bill Clinton, who as a candidate said abortion should be "safe, legal and rare," appointed two new justices who supported the right to abortion: Ruth Bader Ginsburg in 1993 and Stephen G. Breyer in 1994.

During the 2000 general election campaign, the candidates for president went further and named names in describing their intended nominees to the Court. Texas governor George W. Bush, the Republican nominee, told an interviewer he would choose new justices in the mold of Justices Antonin Scalia and Clarence Thomas, the Court's most conservative members. Vice President Al Gore, the Democratic nominee, responded by saying his models would be Justices William Brennan and Thurgood Marshall, who were the most liberal members of the Court when they retired.

When the battle for Florida's electoral votes reached the Court in the case of *Bush v. Gore* (2000), Scalia and Thomas cast decisive votes to grant Bush's emergency appeal and to halt the hand recount of the remaining ballots that had gone uncounted by the tabulating machines. Their decision ensured Bush's narrow electoral college victory (Gore had won the popular vote). However, as President Bush launched his reelection campaign in 2004, he still had not had a chance to fill a vacancy on the Court.

NOTES

INTRODUCTION (PP. 795–799)

1. Robert G. Scigliano, *The Supreme Court and the Presidency* (New York: Free Press, 1971), 207–208.

2. Ibid., 86.

3. Henry J. Abraham, *Justices and Presidents: A Political History of Appointees to the Supreme Court*, 3d ed. (New York: Oxford University Press, 1993), 56–59.

4. Ibid., Table 3, 62.

5. Ibid., Table 4, 62.

6. Ibid., 64.

7. Elder Witt, *A Different Justice: Reagan and the Supreme Court* (Washington, D.C.: Congressional Quarterly, 1986), chap. 3.

8. Abraham, *Justices and Presidents*, 64–65.

9. Henry Cabot Lodge, *Selections from the Correspondence of Theodore Roosevelt and Henry Cabot Lodge, 1884–1918*, 2 vols. (New York: Scribner's, 1925), 2:228, 230–231.

10. Lawrence v. Texas, 539 (U.S.) __ (2003).

11. Daniel S. McHargue, "Appointments to the Supreme Court of the United States: The Factors that Have Affected Appointments, 1789–1932," Ph.D. diss., University of California at Los Angeles, 1949, 549; Sheldon Goldman, "Bush's Judicial Legacy: The Final Imprint," *Judicature* 76 (April–May 1993): 282–298, and "Judicial Selection under Clinton: A Midterm Examination," *Judicature* 78 (May–June 1995): 276–292.

12. Abraham, *Justices and Presidents*, 40–41.

13. Ibid., 29.

14. Ibid., 10.

15. Ibid., 8.

16. Alpheus T. Mason, *William Howard Taft: Chief Justice* (New York: Simon and Schuster, 1965), 76ff.

17. Ibid., 170–171.

18. Leon Friedman and Fred L. Israel, eds., *The Justices of the United States Supreme Court, 1789–1969*, 4 vols. (New York: Chelsea House, R. R. Bowker, 1969), 3:2209.

19. Abraham, *Justices and Presidents*, 31.

20. Ibid.

21. Alpheus T. Mason, *Harlan Fiske Stone: Pillar of the Law* (New York: Viking, 1956), 336.

22. Peter Odegaard, *American Politics*, 2d ed. (New York: Harper and Bros., 1947), 172.

23. For details on the ABA role, see Herman Schwartz, *Packing the Courts: The Conservative Campaign to Rewrite the Constitution* (New York: Scribner's, 1988).

POLITICS AND APPOINTMENTS (PP. 800–810)

1. Quoted by Peter Odegaard in *American Politics*, 2d ed. (New York: Harper and Bros., 1947), 169.

2. Charles Warren, *The Supreme Court in United States History*, rev. ed., 2 vols. (Boston: Little, Brown, 1926), 1:176–177.

3. Robert J. Steamer, *The Supreme Court in Crisis: A History of Conflict* (Amherst: University of Massachusetts Press, 1971), 35.

4. Warren, *Supreme Court in United States History*, 1:178.

5. Henry J. Abraham, *Justices and Presidents: A Political History of Appointees to the Supreme Court*, 3d ed. (New York: Oxford University Press, 1992), 97.

6. *Hepburn v. Griswold*, 8 Wall. (75 U.S.) 603 (1870).

7. *Knox v. Lee*, 12 Wall. (79 U.S.) 457 (1871).

8. Warren, *Supreme Court in United States History*, 2:515–527; Sidney Ratner, "Was the Supreme Court Packed by President Grant?" *Political Science Quarterly* 50 (September 1935): 343–358.

9. Alpheus T. Mason, *Harlan Fiske Stone: Pillar of the Law* (New York: Viking, 1956), 566–567.

10. Gerald T. Dunne, *Hugo Black and the Judicial Revolution* (New York: Simon and Schuster, 1977), 225.

11. *Tennessee Coal, Iron and Railroad Co. v. Muscola Local 123*, 321 U.S. 590 (1944); *Jewell Ridge Coal Corp. v. Local 6167 U.M.W.*, 325 U.S. 161 (1945).

12. Dunne, *Hugo Black*, 241.

13. Ibid., 240–248.

14. Lee Epstein, Jeffrey A. Segal, Harold J. Spaeth, and Thomas G. Walker, *The Supreme Court Compendium: Data, Decisions, and Developments*, 3d ed. (Washington, D.C.: CQ Press, 2003), 224–225.

15. Abraham, *Justices and Presidents*, 245.

16. Ibid., 287.

17. Robert Shogan, *A Question of Judgment: The Fortas Case and the Struggle for the Supreme Court* (Indianapolis: Bobbs-Merrill, 1972), 233–236.

18. Merlo J. Pusey, *Charles Evans Hughes*, 2 vols. (New York: Macmillan, 1951), 1:271.

19. Henry F. Pringle, *The Life and Times of William Howard Taft* (New York: Farrar and Rinehart, 1939), 535.

20. Alpheus T. Mason, *William Howard Taft: Chief Justice* (New York: Simon and Schuster, 1965), 39.

21. Warren, *Supreme Court in United States History*, 1:167.

22. *Scott v. Sandford*, 19 How. (60 U.S.) 393 (1857).

23. Arthur M. Schlesinger Jr. and Fred L. Israel, eds., *History of American Presidential Elections, 1789–1968*, 4 vols. (New York: Chelsea House, 1971), 2:1110–1111.

24. Ibid., 1126.

25. Ibid., 1847.

26. William F. Swindler, *Court and Constitution in the Twentieth Century*, vol. 1, *The Old Legality 1889–1932* (Indianapolis: Bobbs-Merrill, 1969), 283–284.

27. Schlesinger and Israel, *American Presidential Elections*, 3:2520.

28. Alfred H. Kelly and Winfred A. Harbison, *The American Constitution: Its Origins and Development*, 7th ed. (New York: Norton, 1991).

29. Ibid., 981.

30. Stephen J. Wasby, *The Supreme Court in the Federal Judicial System* (New York: Holt, Rinehart, and Winston, 1978), 95.

31. Elder Witt, *A Different Justice: Reagan and the Supreme Court* (Washington, D.C.: Congressional Quarterly, 1986), chaps. 6 and 7.

32. *City of Richmond v. J. A. Croson Co.*, 488 U.S. 469 (1989); *Martin v. Wilks*, 490 U.S. 755 (1989); *Wards Cove Packing Co. v. Atonio*, 490 U.S. 642 (1989); *Webster v. Reproductive Health Services*, 492 U.S. 490 (1989).

33. *Planned Parenthood of Southeastern Pennsylvania v. Casey*, 505 U.S. 833 (1992).

CHAPTER 15

The Court, the Press, and the Public

THE REACTION of the people to judicially-declared law has been an especially important factor in the development of the country, wrote Charles Warren, the noted Supreme Court historian, "for while the judges' decision makes law, it is often the people's view of the decision that makes history. Hence, the effect produced on contemporary public opinion has frequently been of more consequence than the actual decision itself." [1]

More than any other part of the American government, the courts rely on the consent of the governed. The Supreme Court, the highest and most powerful court in the land, has no enforcement power. The extent to which its decisions are implemented or ignored depends almost entirely on public opinion, on whether those affected by the decisions choose to abide by them.

Few institutions have as much effect on public opinion as the press. Warren acknowledged that phenomenon as well: "[R]egard must be paid to the fact that, while the law comes to lawyers through the official reports of judicial decisions, it reaches the people of the country filtered through the medium of the news columns and editorials of partisan newspapers and often exaggerated, distorted and colored by political comment." [2]

This assessment in the 1920s, while not entirely flattering to the reporters and media outlets that today attempt to cover the Supreme Court seriously and accurately, acknowledged that the mass media have played a role in the process by which word of major decisions reaches the people, in the understanding of what the Court has done, and to some extent from time to time in the justices' understanding of how those decisions affect the world outside.

There have been long stretches in the nation's history when the Supreme Court made little news, when its members deferred with regularity to the actions of the executive and legislative branches. It interpreted the Constitution as narrowly and infrequently as possible and kept busy debating legal niceties that were largely of interest to small groups of lawyers and merchants.

As a result, when the Court roused itself to assertive action, as it did during the years under Chief Justice Earl Warren (1953–1969), much of the public was astonished and not infrequently angered to discover that this relatively obscure group of nine people held immense power over their lives.

Correspondingly, covering the Supreme Court for a media outlet has been considered an up-and-down sort of assignment. When the Court has bold members and when broad social ferment presents them with important disputes to resolve, the Court can be one of the most demanding and rewarding beats for a Washington reporter.

At any time, exciting or routine, it is entirely different from almost any other kind of journalistic beat. A reporter who covers the White House or Congress normally has access to senior and junior staff members and to trained public information aides, if not to the principals themselves, when background is needed. The leak of theoretically private information by someone whose purpose may be thereby served is a way of life.

At the Supreme Court, there are few staff sources, access to the justices is limited, and, only since the 1980s has the public information officer distributed much information beyond the official statements of the Court. Unauthorized leaks about Court activities are regarded as roughly equivalent to breaches of national security. A law professor can sometimes help to assess the impact of a ruling in his or her area of specialty. Otherwise, covering the Court involves papers—briefs and opinions—rather than people.

Media coverage has its most demonstrable effect on the modern Court during confirmation controversies. Reports on the alleged liabilities of candidates, sometimes originating from special-interest groups and sometimes uncovered by the media itself, have clearly influenced voting in the Senate and therefore directly affected the makeup of the Court.

The extent of influence of the media on the actual deliberations of the Court is much more difficult to chart. The justices are almost inescapably aware of widespread public interest in a particular highly publicized case; large numbers of friend-of-the-court briefs signal this situation just as clearly as do numerous news reports.

Legally trained and normally well experienced as judges, members of the Court are highly unlikely to be influenced by prior media accounts of a case or of its oral argument, as opposed to their own reading of the record. Moreover, media reaction to argument of a case, whether in news accounts or editorials, has very little time to make itself felt, if at all. Ordinarily, the justices vote on a case, at least tentatively, within two to three days after they hear it.

The long-range impact of media reaction to a controversial decision poses yet another question, one not so easily answered. Even though judicial purists would deny it, there seems little doubt that public opinion, shaped to some degree by the media, has some effect on the way courts decide cases. This process is much more gradual and imperceptible than, for example, the way media coverage and viewpoint may affect an election after an intensive campaign.

The doctrine of *stare decisis*, "let the decision stand," expresses the institutional conservatism of the judicial process. Although this doctrine severely limits policy reversals that reflect public opinion, such reversals do occur. In 1943 the Supreme Court reversed its 1940 ruling that compulsory flag salute laws for public schools violated constitutional freedom-of-religion guarantees. More than 150 newspapers had editorialized against the first ruling.

More often than not public opinion, and the public's need for stability in the law, work against reversals. In 1992 when the Court upheld a constitutional right to abortion, the controlling plurality opinion said *Roe v. Wade* (1973) should be affirmed, in part, because the public had come to count on it. Justices O'Connor, Kennedy, and Souter wrote:

> [F]or two decades of economic and social developments, people have organized intimate relationships and made choices that define their views of themselves and their places in society, in reliance on the availability of abortion in the event that contraception should fail. The ability of women to participate equally in the economic and social life of the nation has been facilitated by their ability to control their reproductive lives.... The Constitution serves human values, and while the effect of reliance on *Roe* cannot be exactly measured, neither can the certain cost of overruling *Roe* for people who have ordered their thinking and living around that case be dismissed.[3]

An equally surprising example came in 2000 when Chief Justice William H. Rehnquist spoke for the Court in reaffirming the requirement that police give the "Miranda warnings" to crime suspects before questioning them. For most of his career on the bench, Rehnquist had criticized the *Miranda* decision as poor constitutional law and bad police policy. But decades of police dramas on television had made the *Miranda* warnings familiar to millions of Americans. They also became standard practice for the police, the chief justice said, who concluded that it was too late to reverse such a well-accepted precedent.[4]

The Court and the Media

For more than two hundred years, all but a very small percentage of Americans learned about the Supreme Court exclusively through the mass media—first, newspapers and, later, radio and television. The history of the institution has been written largely by the reporters who have covered its activities and commented on them—before that role passed to the editorial writers. In recent years, however, the formerly closed circle of justices and Court reporters has been opened to millions of others, thanks to the Internet. The Court's opinions are available almost instantly online to be read and analyzed by all who have an interest. Commentary on the Court, formerly the province of columnists and opinion writers, has been enlivened by an array of self-appointed experts who post daily blogs on legal matters, including the rulings of the high court.

EARLY YEARS, 1790–1850

In the early days of the republic, information about cases before the Supreme Court and its decisions reached the public in somewhat irregular fashion, as did most information about government. In a classic example, the first sentence of the official record of the Court in 1790 was wrong. It called the body "the Supreme Judicial Court of the United States," following the nomenclature of Massachusetts, but not that of the Constitution.

Coverage

Not until 1804 was the first volume issued of what were to become the official reports of Court decisions, an absolute necessity for anyone attempting to practice law. William Cranch, chief justice of the Circuit Court of the District of Columbia, took it upon himself to assemble and publish the decisions of the 1801–1804 terms, and succeeding ones.

Until that time, it had been very difficult for judges and lawyers, much less the general public, to obtain copies of the Court's rulings. A rare exception was *Marbury v. Madison* in 1803; a summary of Chief Justice John Marshall's opinion was widely printed in the newspapers, arousing considerable comment.

In a preface to his first volume of reports, Cranch emphasized the need for uniformity in the law, with an accurate record of Supreme Court decisions enabling judges everywhere to conform. "Every case decided is a check upon the Judge," Cranch wrote. "He cannot decide a similar case differently without strong reasons, which, for his own justification, he will wish to make public. The avenues of corruption are thus obstructed and the sources of litigation closed." [1]

Until 1874 this service for the new nation's judges and lawyers was continued by a series of private decision compilers, whose names are preserved in the formal citations used to identify a decision or a quotation from it, such as 4 Cranch 94. Then the compilation became the *United States Reports,* prepared by the Government Printing Office, and the volume and page citations became impersonal—1 U.S. 12 and so on. *(See box, How to Read a Court Citation, p. 1205, in Reference Materials.)*

For years, newspaper coverage of arguments before the Court and its subsequent decisions was sporadic, concentrating on a few controversial cases and all but ignoring many of the rest. In 1819, for the first time, the *National Intelligencer* began printing a daily list of all cases argued and decisions handed down.

Inaccurate reporting and misinterpretation of Supreme Court decisions by the press were serious problems almost from the start. In 1803 several papers printed an erroneous account of the Court's reasoning in *Marbury v. Madison,* which said the Court had made a distinction between its authority within the District of Columbia and in the states elsewhere. This mistake originally appeared in the *Alexandria Advertiser* and was picked up, as was the custom then, by the *Georgia Republican* and the *Boston Gazette.* The error did little damage, however, because all three papers correctly reported the outcome of the decision.

A more serious example of inaccurate reporting occurred in 1819 when the justices ruled on a challenge to the constitutionality of a New York State bankruptcy law. Because no federal law governed that subject at the time, the issues in the case were critically important to businessmen as well as other citizens. The Court invalidated the state law, insofar as it enabled a debtor to free himself from a debt that had been contracted before the statute went into effect. But the first newspaper accounts of an admittedly murky opinion said the Court had held that states had no authority to pass bankruptcy laws generally.

"This opinion has given much alarm to many persons," the *Niles Register* of Baltimore declared.[2] According to a New York paper, the inaccurate version "caused a very considerable sensation in the city, and we do not wonder at it." [3] A Baltimore paper cautioned that "nothing but the publication of the entire opinion can possibly allay the fermentation that is excited." [4]

Twelve days after the decision, an accurate article was printed in a New York paper, and the furor began to subside. But the full text of the opinion in the case, *Sturges v. Crowinshield,* was not published for some time, and a simultaneous period of economic uncertainty in the nation compounded problems created by the initial mistake. *(See "Bankruptcy Laws," pp. 341–344.)*

Errors aside, the chief characteristic of press coverage of the Court during its formative years was political partisanship. Most of the papers were closely allied with a party—the Federalists or the Democratic-Republicans during the early days, later the Whigs or the Jacksonian Democrats—and their accounts were highly colored by this alignment. Indeed, objectivity was not the style of the day, either in reporting arguments before the Court by noted lawyers or in presenting the facts behind a controversial decision. This unabashed bias was particularly notable in accounts of stormy confirmation battles in the Senate and the highly political attempt to impeach Justice Samuel Chase in 1804.

But the newspapers of this period, incomplete and partisan as they were, were the principal means of informing the public and influencing opinion. They printed little of what is called news today, and their circulation was very limited, largely by the absence of transportation.

As the republic grew, so did the influence of the press. Historical scholar Julius Goebel Jr. noted: "Relying as they did for filler upon clippings from whatever out-of-town newspapers that might come to hand, it was possible for a subscriber to a Boston or New York journal to learn belatedly of an event or opinion published weeks earlier in South Carolina or Virginia."[5]

Confirmation Battles

In these early years the press occasionally played a role in determining the Supreme Court's membership by serving as an open forum for criticism of controversial nominees, some of whom were later rejected by the Senate. During this period, most American newspapers were, as noted, highly partisan, containing much outspoken opinion as fact and making little attempt to distinguish between editorials and news accounts.

In 1795, when the first chief justice, John Jay, resigned to become governor of New York, John Rutledge of South Carolina sought and obtained President George Washington's nomination

John Rutledge

for the vacant seat. Rutledge had served as an associate justice from 1789 until his resignation in 1791. He was sworn in by virtue of a recess appointment as chief justice on August 12, 1795.

Just before the August term was to begin, newspaper accounts reached the North of a speech Rutledge had given in Charleston, denouncing the treaty Jay had negotiated with Britain a month earlier, which had already been ratified by the Senate. Some of the stories were clearly inaccurate; a Boston paper described Rutledge as having spoken "mounted upon the head of a hogshead, haranguing a mob," when the speech was actually delivered in a Charleston church. But Federalist treaty supporters were outraged and accused Rutledge of insanity and bringing "ruin and disgrace" to the country.[6] The *Columbian Centinel* of Boston, a leading Federalist paper, attacked the nominee's character and charged he could not pay his debts. Other papers, in the South and elsewhere, defended him.

Rutledge sat as a recess appointee on the Court, which proceeded to decide only two cases during a short session. But he never returned. The president sent his nomination to the Senate, which rejected it, 10-14, on December 15, 1795. The *Columbian Centinel* rejoiced that the senators had considered Rutledge's treaty speech an "impudent and virulent attack" on them "by a very unfit person for a Chief Justice."[7]

In 1811 President James Madison nominated for a vacancy on the Court a Connecticut Democratic-Republican whose political credentials were considerably stronger than his legal qualifications. He was Alexander Wolcott, a onetime customs collector.

Once again the Federalist press charged into the breach. The *Columbian Centinel* observed that "even those most acquainted with modern degeneracy were astounded at this abominable nomination."[8] The *Connecticut Courant* said it had hoped for a nominee "less disgusting to the moral sense of the community and whose private virtues or legal knowledge might have afforded some security from his personal depravity."[9] Other papers commented adversely on his personal habits and morals.

Even Democratic-Republican leaders were hard-put to defend Wolcott, and the Senate denied him confirmation, 9-24. Historian Charles Warren, noting that Wolcott later endorsed the expulsion of any judge who declared a law unconstitutional, concluded that "it was fortunate for the course of American legal history that he did not secure this position on the Supreme Bench."[10]

In 1835 another controversy erupted when President Andrew Jackson nominated Roger B. Taney to the Court. The Senate earlier had refused to confirm Taney as secretary of the Treasury because he had removed government deposits from the United States Bank, at Jackson's behest. Taney's acknowledged legal skills—he had also served as attorney general—were virtually ignored during the ensuing political debate.

A Boston Whig paper argued that the Senate could not confirm him for the Court without reversing in the process "the sentence they passed on Mr. Taney's outrageous violation of the law and the Constitution when he was in the cabinet."[11] A New York paper said that judgeships "are not in the gift solely of the

Executive and that subservancy to his will or truckling to his behests is not enough to secure them." [12] After two months of maneuvering, the Senate shelved the Taney nomination by a 21-24 vote on the last day of its session in March 1835.

Nine months later, however, Jackson nominated Taney to succeed John Marshall as chief justice. A somewhat realigned Senate confirmed him, 29-15, and he served with considerable distinction until his death twenty-eight years later. *(See details, pp. 800–801.)*

The role of the press in these early confirmation battles was very different from its role today. Newspapers then were the principal means of serious public and political communication. They circulated, though somewhat slowly, up and down the coast of the narrow new nation, rather than only locally. A week-old article from one city that struck a responsive chord with an editor elsewhere would be reprinted in full, sometimes in several different papers. Frequently, papers also printed ostensibly private letters that proved influential in shaping political reaction.

Cases

Marbury v. Madison (1803) was a squabble over presidential patronage that escalated into a contest for authority between Congress and the Supreme Court. It involved an attempt to force President Thomas Jefferson to award minor judgeships to men chosen by President John Adams in the closing hours of his administration. The case attracted considerable attention from the pro-Adams Federalist press, including the *New York Evening Post*, the *Connecticut Courant*, and the *Columbian Centinel*.

Although the decision is remembered today for establishing the Court's power to declare an act of Congress unconstitutional, contemporary press coverage focused instead on the political conflict between Chief Justice Marshall and the Federalist would-be justices of the peace, on one hand, and President Jefferson and his fellow Democratic-Republicans on the other.

Marshall held that the Adams appointees were entitled to their commissions as judges but that Congress had gone beyond constitutional limits in authorizing the Supreme Court to order cabinet officers to issue those commissions. *(See "Marbury v. Madison," pp. 80–83; see also "Jefferson Versus Marshall," pp. 256–258.)*

Federalist newspapers, not surprisingly, regarded the ruling as a rebuke of Jefferson. But some of the most prominent Democratic-Republican papers, which could have been expected to defend the president and denounce the Court's validation of the commissions, were strangely silent. As a group, they did not feel compelled to criticize Marshall's holding that the Court had the right to review the constitutionality of acts of Congress. One Democratic-Republican paper, the *Virginia Argus*, ran a series of articles questioning Marshall's power to rule against Jefferson on the issue of the judges' commissions in one breath while denying Supreme Court jurisdiction over the case in the next.

The *Washington Federalist* printed a series of letters from "an unlearned layman," who contended that the justices lacked the power to review acts of Congress. The paper then printed a reply that argued, "[I]f a law conflict with the Constitution, the judges are bound to declare which is paramount. The judges here arrogate no power. It is not they who speak—it is the Constitution, or rather, the people." [13] That was virtually the only contemporary commentary published on the issue of judicial review, which history has come to regard as the chief legacy of *Marbury*.

In some instances the highly partisan press of this period devoted more attention to the Supreme Court than newspapers do today. The *Charleston Courier*, a leading Federalist paper, published in a little more than a month in 1803 two news reports and four lengthy editorials on *Marbury v. Madison*, plus a summary of the decision taken from the *National Intelligencer* and later the full text of the opinion.

Dartmouth College v. Woodward (1819) attracted very little attention when it was argued and decided, apparently because neither the bar nor the press anticipated how important the issue in the case would become in the economic development of the country. The question before the Supreme Court was whether the New Hampshire legislature, having granted Dartmouth College a corporate charter, could later rewrite that charter without impairing a contract, conduct forbidden by the federal Constitution. (For generations of loyal Dartmouth alumni, this case was immortalized by the response of Daniel Webster, one of the winning attorneys, to an inquiring justice: "It is, sir, as I have said, a small college, and yet there are those who love it.")

When the case was argued in 1818, the Court was stalemated. The *National Intelligencer* said that a decision would be postponed until the next term; there was no majority because "some of the judges have not come to an opinion on the case. Those of the judges who have formed opinions do not agree." [14] Only the Boston and New Hampshire papers covered the arguments, and their accounts illustrate the highly subjective reporting of the era.

The *Columbian Centinel* of Boston informed its readers that "our friend Webster never made a happier effort. To a most elaborate and lucid argument he united a dignified and pathetic peroration which charmed and melted his hearers." [15] The *Boston Daily Advertiser* said that Webster "enchained the Court and the audience with an argument which, for weight of authority, force or reasoning and power of eloquence, has seldom been equalled." [16]

Nearly a year later when the 1819 term opened, the justices decided the case, holding 5-1 that the charter of a private corporation was a contract, thus invalidating the legislature's attempt to change the Dartmouth charter. The result was significant not only in confirming the supremacy of the Constitution over state legislation but also in giving business corporations security against improper interference by lawmakers. *(See "Private Corporate Charters," pp. 340–341.)*

Corporations were still in their infancy at the time, and the press paid scant attention. There was no mention of the decision in the *Niles Register*, a Baltimore weekly that normally summarized all legal events of consequence. The New York papers barely

In 1819 John Marshall wrote the decision in *Dartmouth College v. Woodward,* which forbade the New Hampshire legislature to alter the charter of the college (pictured here in 1793) because the charter was a "contract." The case, which attracted little attention when it was argued and decided, played an important role in the nation's economic development.

touched on the case, merely calling the opinion "a most able and elaborate production" and "a learned and able paper."[17]

The decision overruled the state courts, which had upheld the New Hampshire legislature, and the *New Hampshire Gazette* was bold enough to suggest incompetence by the losing attorneys. "Had the case been fairly laid before the Court, no man, without impeaching their integrity or their common sense, can doubt but their decision would have confirmed that of the Superior Court in this state."[18]

McCulloch v. Maryland (1819), by contrast, aroused widespread interest around the country from the beginning, and the Court's opinion was reprinted in full by many papers, whether they agreed with the outcome or not. At issue, as several papers emphasized, was the power of states to tax the Bank of the United States. The case was obviously important to the determination of state and federal rights, and the justices heard arguments for nine days. But it took them only three days to rule unanimously that Congress had exclusive jurisdiction over the bank, which it had chartered as a federal agency, and that the state tax was invalid. *(See details of McCulloch v. Maryland, pp. 83–86.)*

The press reacted along political and geographical lines, with the Federalist papers of the North and East generally favorable. Typical was the *Boston Daily Advertiser,* whose Washington correspondent called the ruling "one of the most able judgments, I will venture to say, ever delivered in this Court, and when it is read will satisfy all minds."[19]

That prediction proved false: most Democratic-Republican papers in the South and West denounced the decision as an unwarranted invasion of states' rights. The *Natchez Press* observed that "our privileges as a people have of late been so frittered away that we may as well inter at once the form of a Constitution, of which the spirit has been murdered."[20] The *Niles Register* in Maryland also attacked the ruling. "[A] deadly blow has been struck at the sovereignty of the states and from a quarter so far removed from the people as to be hardly accessible to public opinion," it charged, an early example of the accusations of unresponsiveness that the Court still confronts today.[21]

The *General Advertiser* in Philadelphia went beyond the issues in the case to attack editorially Chief Justice Marshall's opinion for displaying "a most lamentable sophistry, a most lame and impotent logic, and . . . the most flimsy and false attempt at reasoning that can be found in the annals of any nation."[22]

Gibbons v. Ogden (1824) represented a direct confrontation between states' rights advocates and a strong federal government. It was a legal challenge to a long-standing steamboat monopoly granted two prominent Republican politicians by the New York legislature. The challenge was brought by a would-be competitor who refused to obtain a license from them for his New York–New Jersey ferry line. Other states had granted similar monopolies, and some had retaliated with bans on ships licensed by adjacent states. As a result, arguments before the Court attracted detailed newspaper coverage. "You can form no idea what interest this decision excites at Washington," the *New York Statesman* reported.[23] The Court's opinion was ready in three weeks. Chief Justice Marshall announced the Court's finding that the New York law was an unconstitutional

JOURNALISTIC EXTREMISM: EARLY YEARS

In the early nineteenth century, American newspapers felt very little restraint about printing the most vituperative attacks on the Supreme Court and its decisions. A favorite vehicle for such unbridled criticism was a series of letters signed with a pseudonym. A particularly virulent but typical example of this species appeared in 1819 in the *General Advertiser* of Philadelphia, signed "Brutus" and commenting on *McCulloch v. Maryland*. In that controversial opinion written by Chief Justice John Marshall, Congress won and the states lost: Congress had exclusive jurisdiction over the Bank of the United States, and the states could not tax its operations. "The opinion of that tribunal now before the world," wrote Brutus,

is a perfect model of that prejudiced judgment and *ex parte* consideration of a subject that springs from a predetermined resolution to accomplish a desired object, which shows but one side of the question, views but one relation of the principles in controversy and studiously avoids all allusion to the most essential and the principal leading features in the discussion: the foundation of social obligation, the purpose of government, the rights of the people and the liberty of the states.

These principles and rights are rigorously excluded from all consideration in this argument; and the power, the authority and the supremacy of the Federal government is made the irrefutable, the original source and the sole origin, and the despotic arbiter of a question which challenges and denies the extent of that supremacy of power, that unresisting vigor of authority.

Never was a bad cause worse supported by constellated talents, learning and wisdom of a Bench of supreme Judges. It seems as if nature had revolted from the debasing task assigned them; and that their reason and their judgment had forsaken them, upon an instinctive horror and disgust from the destructive purposes they were pledged to fulfill, in defiance of all human rights, human joys and divine commandments.

interference with Congress's right to regulate commerce. *(See "Gibbons v. Ogden," pp. 94–96.)*

For once, newspaper reaction was largely nonpartisan, with journals all over the country praising the Marshall opinion whatever their political affiliation. New Yorkers particularly resented the state-imposed monopoly, and the *New York Evening Post* called the ruling "one of the most able and solemn opinions that has ever been delivered in any Court."[24] For the *New York Commercial Advertiser*, it was "one of the most powerful efforts of the human mind that has ever been displayed from the bench of any Court."[25]

Reaction elsewhere in the country was similar. The *National Gazette* called the decision a "masterpiece of judicial reasoning,"[26] and the *Georgia Journal* published the entire opinion because it found the case "one of such vast interest and importance to our country."[27] Some concern for state authority was voiced; the *Richmond Enquirer* foresaw the possibility that "the state governments would moulder into ruins."[28]

The Cherokee Cases (1830–1832) involved the refusal of a state to honor an order of the Court, a precursor of the doctrine of nullification that precipitated the Civil War. A 1791 federal treaty had granted the Cherokees land in Georgia, but the state legislature attempted to take it away in 1829. When the Indians filed an original suit in the Supreme Court, state officials refused to participate. Later, the Georgia governor ignored another Supreme Court writ after state authorities arrested a Cherokee for murder within Indian property.

The *Boston Courier*, a Whig paper, charged that "the integrity and permanence of the union are at stake."[29] Representing the Jackson administration, the *United States Telegraph* contended that the confrontation demonstrated "the absurdity of the doctrine which contends that the court is clothed with supreme and absolute control over the states."[30] But the *New York Daily Advertiser* saw a concerted effort "to curtail the constitutional jurisdiction and destroy the influence and independence of the Supreme Court."[31]

The Court ruled in 1831 that it had no jurisdiction to decide the Cherokee case, but a second challenge to the Georgia laws arose later in the year when Georgia arrested two missionaries living in Indian country without a license. In March 1832 the Court struck down the state licensing law as unconstitutional, holding that the federal government had exclusive jurisdiction over the Cherokees and their reservation. *(See "Repeal and Resistance," pp. 336–337.)*

President Jackson is supposed to have responded, "Well, John Marshall has made his decision, now let him enforce it," but there is considerable doubt about the authenticity of that quote. Georgia officials continued to ignore the Supreme Court, and Whig papers supported the Court, while those backing Jackson counseled moderation. *(See box, Did Jackson Really Say That? p. 259.)*

The Georgia legislature later passed a nullification ordinance, rejecting Supreme Court jurisdiction. Congress, at President Jackson's behest, countered with the Force Bill to give federal authorities adequate power to deal with the situation. At that point, Georgia, realizing that Jackson was adamant, pardoned the two missionaries, and the constitutional crisis was averted.

Impeachment Efforts

Only once, in 1805, was a Supreme Court justice formally charged by the House of Representatives with impeachable offenses and tried by the Senate. Justice Samuel Chase survived this largely political attack, in part with the assistance of the press of the period, including some Democratic-Republican papers presumably dedicated to his removal. The abortive impeachment effort against Chase was important because it freed the justices from the threat of congressional retaliation for one or more decisions that had angered a president and the lawmakers of his party.

Chase had won the enmity of the Democratic-Republicans both for actively opposing Jefferson in the 1800 presidential campaign and for his conduct of the sedition trials of two prominent party members. Charging that the judge's disposition was arbitrary and his temper ferocious, the *Aurora* observed that "few men, perhaps, hold a humbler estimation among his fellow citizens."[32]

With the full approval of President Jefferson, the Democratic-Republicans focused on a lengthy oration that Justice Chase had delivered in charging a Baltimore grand jury in 1803. They used it as evidence that Chase should be removed from the bench. The *National Intelligencer* printed an account of Chase's charge, in which the judge attacked congressional legislation and called the administration "weak, relaxed and not adequate to a discharge of their functions" and primarily interested in "a continuance in unfairly acquired power."[33]

Although its accuracy was later disputed, this article was widely reprinted around the country, and the Chase charge was attacked or defended according to the partisan position of the reprinting paper. The *Charleston Courier*, for example, accused the president and his allies of "conspiring for the overthrow of that third branch of the Constitution—the judiciary."[34]

In January 1804 the House named a committee to investigate impeachment of Justice Chase, and the debate continued to rage in the press. "Never, never was the bench so much disgraced as by Judge Chase," declared the *Aurora*,[35] while the *Connecticut Courant* accused Congress of attempting "to level with the dust the national judiciary, or at least to render it completely subordinate."[36]

The House voted articles of impeachment in March 1804, citing misconduct during the sedition trial and the Baltimore grand jury charge. The Senate heard the case, then found Chase not guilty. *(See details of Chase trial, pp. 766–769.)*

According to Charles Warren, the refusal of the Senate to impeach Chase had a "profound effect . . . on the course of American legal history."[37] It sidetracked contemporary Republican plans to move against other justices and discredited the theory that impeachment could be used to remove justices with whom Congress disagreed, without any proof of crime or misdemeanor.

MIDDLE YEARS, 1851–1900

The Supreme Court was a participant, all too passively in the eyes of some, in the tumultuous events of the last half of the nineteenth century. The issue of slavery tore the country apart, and the Civil War ultimately left a legacy of institutionalized discrimination smoldering beneath the surface of reconstituted national self-satisfaction.

Coverage

Throughout the crisis, the press held a mirror up to the deep emotional divisions in the nation that ultimately produced armed camps, literally as well as figuratively. The abolitionist and Radical Republican papers subjected the Court to an unprecedented level of substantive, professional, and political criticism during the course of the Dred Scott case in 1856–1857. Opposition papers replied in kind.

If *Scott v. Sandford* showed a Democratic majority on the Court lining up politically behind the South and slavery, the *Legal Tender Cases* two dozen years later demonstrated that judicial venality was bipartisan, with a freshly minted Republican majority promptly reversing a fifteen-month-old Supreme Court ruling and sending shock waves through the press and public. But time slowly brought the country back together, and the bitterness engendered by the slavery issue subsided. The rights of blacks again were relegated to the margins. By 1883, when the Court declared federal antidiscrimination laws unconstitutional in the *Civil Rights Cases*, only one justice dissented, and a good deal of the press reaction was favorable. By 1896, when the Court upheld state Jim Crow laws in *Plessy v. Ferguson*, newspapers—apart from the black press of the day—were paying little attention.

During these fifty years, the press continued to play an instrumental role in Senate confirmation of new justices. Two lame-duck presidents, Millard Fillmore and James Buchanan, tried but failed to place their choices on the bench. The Senate's refusal to confirm these nominees was attributed, at least in part, to newspaper criticism.

Copies of Court opinions remained in short supply. When in 1842 the *Newark Daily Advertiser* could not get the text of a fugitive slave ruling, it suggested that the official reporter publish it in pamphlet form "as a mere matter of pecuniary speculation."[38] Lack of the same opinion did not deter the *Baltimore Sun* from saying that the decision was "all that Maryland can desire, and will be particularly agreeable to the slaveholders of the South."[39]

Newspapers were not the only ones inconvenienced by the Court's primitive information policy. When the federal fugitive slave law was upheld against state interference in *Ableman v. Booth* (1859), Chief Justice Taney ordered the clerk not to give out copies of the opinion until it had been printed in the official reports. Six weeks after the decision had been handed down, Attorney General J. S. Black had to get special permission from the chief justice to obtain a copy for his official use. Reporters continued to include in their Supreme Court stories comments that today would be regarded as highly editorial. Discussing the arguments in a martial law case, the *New York Tribune* called one attorney's presentation "long beyond the patience of most listeners."[40]

The justices themselves sometimes responded to newspaper criticism in unorthodox fashion. After the Court had decided to reaffirm the constitutionality of the federal fugitive slave act, but before the opinion was printed, Justice John McLean wrote an anonymous letter to a newspaper, protesting criticism of the decision and defending the Court against accusations that it universally favored owners over slaves.

During this era of strong feelings on the slavery issue, the attention of the public became a widely sought commodity, and partisans on both sides sought space in any kind of publication. In one of the fugitive slave cases, arguments by the antislavery lawyers, Salmon P. Chase and William H. Seward, were privately printed and widely circulated for propaganda purposes.

But the official Supreme Court reporter of the period, Benjamin Howard, refused to include the arguments in full in his *U.S. Reports,* arousing some suspicion that his personal sympathies on the fugitive slave question were involved. Historian Carl Swisher noted that in the past Howard had "often incurred widespread criticism for dumping into the reports materials of all kinds to expand the size of his volumes (but) here reversed his usual custom."[41]

Cases

Scott v. Sandford (1857) launched the Court—and the country—into one of the stormier periods in its history. The decision in the slavery case aroused bitter criticism in the press, and the Court as an institution sank to its lowest level of public esteem and confidence before or since. Throughout the controversy, newspapers as the dominant means of communication played a major role in highlighting the issues before the Court and later in reflecting the outrage that the decision inspired in many areas, foreshadowing the division of the Civil War.

Scott was a slave from Missouri who went to court in 1846 claiming that he had become a free man when his former master took him into free territory, irrespective of his return to Missouri later. After losing in state court in 1852, then in U.S. Circuit Court two years later, he carried an appeal to the Supreme Court. At issue were whether a slave could be a citizen with power to sue in the federal courts and whether Congress had the authority to prohibit slavery in the territories, as it originally had in the Missouri Compromise.

The leading abolitionist paper of the North, the *New York Tribune*, printed a running account of the Court's secret deliberations after the case had been argued. At one early juncture, the paper reported, apparently with considerable accuracy, the position of each justice. In retrospect, it seems clear that Justice John McLean was providing regular leaks to one of the *Tribune*'s Washington reporters, a highly unusual practice even for a politically inclined justice in those days.

After three months without a decision, the justices called for reargument and were praised by the *New York Courier* for deliberative wisdom. The case was largely ignored during the 1856 presidential campaign, but when it came before the Court again in December, the *Courier* said "it may well be regarded as the most important that has been brought before that tribunal."[42]

The political issue of slavery had become inflammatory. In the reargument, "the prejudices of the judges were appealed to," reported a correspondent of the *New York Independent*. " . . . I came to the realization of the fact that our supreme court is composed of men, mere men after all, with the like passions and prejudices of the masses."[43]

The justices did not take up the case in conference for another two months, but the newspapers were filled with rumors and conjecture. With southern Democrats making up a majority of the Court, the abolitionist *New York Tribune* declared: "If the

Court is to take a political bias, and to give a political decision, then let us by all means have it distinctly, and now. The public mind is in a condition to receive it with the contempt it deserves."[44]

Early in March 1857 Chief Justice Taney handed down the majority opinion in the 7-2 decision, holding that Negroes were not citizens and thus unable to sue in the courts. Not content to rest there, the Court declared that Congress had no power to exclude slavery from the territories. From contemporary accounts, it appears that the Court had no idea what a firestorm of opposition the ruling would set off.

One day later the *New York Independent* said, "If there be not aroused a spirit of resistance and indignation which shall wipe out this decision and all its results, as the lightning wipes out the object it falls upon, then indeed are the days of our republic numbered, and the patriot shall see might only beyond the storms of revolution and blood."[45] The *New York Evening Post* charged that a majority of the justices "consented to become parties to a combination with the Administration to transfer the political control of the government to the hands of the slave oligarchy."[46]

But Democratic papers in both the North and South defended the Court against its fervent attackers and counseled moderation. The *New York Herald* warned that disobedience of the Court's ruling would constitute "rebellion, treason and revolution."[47] The *Pennsylvanian* attacked the "black Republican press, brimful of elements of sedition, treason and insurrection."[48] The administration's voice in Washington, the *Daily Union*, predicted, somewhat rashly as events proved, that the decision "would exert the most powerful and salutary influence throughout the United States."[49] And the *St. Louis Evening News* observed that the decision "has roused the lately torpid Northern pulpit into a factious frenzy on the stale Negro question and incited the preachers to a fresh crusade against the judges."[50]

In this critical case, the justices became their own publicists. The McLean dissent was read in church the day after he delivered it, obviously with his cooperation, and printed in the *Cincinnati Gazette*, enabling the justice to circulate copies around the country. Justice John Catron, who had voted with the majority but split with Chief Justice Taney on some pivotal question, assumed—incorrectly as it developed—that the *Daily Union* would not carry his opinion, and so he had it separately printed in the *Nashville Daily Union and American*.

Some conservative historians have since argued that press coverage of the Dred Scott decision was more responsible for inflaming public opinion and ultimately precipitating the Civil War than was the decision itself. Charles Warren, writing in 1922, quoted with approval a *Harper's Weekly* prediction that "however repugnant the Dred Scott decision may be to the feelings of a portion of the Northern states, it can have no practical effects injurious to our tranquility or to our institutions."[51]

"Had the country been influenced by editorials like these," Warren commented, "rather than by the hysterical, virulent and false outpourings of the *Tribune* and the *Independent*, the

Court's action would have had less effect on history, but it was otherwise destined."[52]

Six months later the *North American Review* concluded, "The country will feel the consequences of the decision more deeply and more permanently in the loss of confidence in the sound judicial integrity and strictly legal character of their tribunals than in anything beside."[53] But Warren insisted sixty-five years later that "the loss of confidence in the court was due not merely to the court's decision but to the false and malignant criticisms and portrayals of the court which were spread widely through the North by influential newspapers."[54]

The Legal Tender Cases of 1870–1871

These decisions brought the Court again to a low level of public esteem. Once again press coverage played a significant part in creating the widespread view that the Court was not only undependable but also subject to the most obvious political manipulation.

The issue here, while not as inflammatory as slavery, was an outgrowth of the Civil War: Did Congress have the power to make paper treasury notes as good as gold for the payment of debts? The financial stakes were high. If the wartime acts were sustained, debtors could settle with depreciated paper money; if not, they would need much more costly gold. (*See "The Currency Powers," pp. 134–139.*)

State courts generally had upheld the Legal Tender Acts, according to the *Nation*, "being in closer dependence on popular opinion . . . on such an exceedingly delicate subject as the value and power of the currency."[55] The *Chicago Republican* suggested

---

COURT REPORTERS

Intense public interest in the Dred Scott decision of 1857 focused attention on the informal monopoly enjoyed by the reporter of the Supreme Court, in this instance Benjamin Howard. His public salary was only $1,300 a year, but a banner case enabled him to sell more copies of the volume in which it appeared and even print it separately in pamphlet form.

The Democratic-controlled Senate, strongly supporting the majority opinion and anxious to publicize it broadly, decided to print twenty thousand copies. Howard protested that his income would suffer as a result, so the Senate voted to pay him $1,500 and agreed not to distribute its reprint until after his bound volume and pamphlet version had appeared.

The Court had ruled in 1834 that its opinions could not be copyrighted, but the Senate concluded that Howard had a fair claim to compensation.

SOURCE: Charles Grove Haines and Foster H. Sherwood, *The Role of the Supreme Court in American Government and Politics: 1835–64* (Berkeley: University of California Press, 1957), 432.

---

that the Court "should not now work universal ruin" but instead withhold any decision that would invalidate paper money.[56]

Hepburn v. Griswold was argued in 1867 and reargued a year later, but a majority did not result because of vacancies on the Court. By November 1869 a majority had agreed privately that the law was unconstitutional but delayed announcement while opinions were being reconciled.

Meanwhile, press speculation was conspicuously inaccurate. In January 1870 the *New York Times* said that "no consideration has yet been had in the case by the Court" and predicted another reargument.[57] On February 1 the *New York Tribune* said "there is ground for believing that the decision will not go into the question of the constitutionality of the law."[58]

A week later a 4-3 majority of the Court decided *Hepburn*, holding that the Legal Tender Acts exceeded Congress's war powers, impaired the obligation of contracts, and were therefore unconstitutional. Early reaction was mild, apparently because it was assumed that only contracts signed before the laws were passed were affected. When lawyers concluded that the ruling invalidated paper money for all contracts, before and after, panic set in among those who foresaw disastrous financial consequences for the entire nation.

On the same day the Court decided *Hepburn v. Griswold* (1870), President Ulysses S. Grant sent two new Supreme Court nominations to the Senate. Within two months they were confirmed, and the government had moved for rehearing of two other pending legal tender cases that dealt with contracts made after the acts, thus reopening an issue that had been widely regarded as settled. The revamped Court granted the motion by a 5-4 vote.

The press reacted strongly, with the *Nation* observing, "We find very little difference of opinion in the press as to the gross impropriety (to use a very mild term) of the reopening of the Legal Tender decision. It is, in every way one looks at it, a blunder."[59] The *Springfield Republican* expressed a hope that "the country is to be spared this great wrong and scandal of a reversal."[60] The *American Law Review* warned that the Court could not reverse the ruling in *Hepburn* "without degrading itself in the eyes of all intelligent men, and this fact we should think the new members of the Court would recognize quite as distinctly as the old."[61]

But the Court ordered yet another reargument of the constitutional question, and on May 1, 1871, by a 5-4 vote it narrowly reversed *Hepburn*, decided fifteen months earlier. In this second Legal Tender case—*Knox v. Lee* and *Parker v. Davis*—the two new Grant justices joined with the former minority in *Hepburn*.

The reversal "will greatly aggravate the growing contempt for what has long been the most respected and the most influential department of our government, its judiciary," predicted the *Springfield Republican*.[62] The *Nation* said the move would "weaken popular respect for all decisions of the court, including this last one."[63] Despite its outspoken Republican position, the *New York Tribune* said "it will not be easy to restore public respect and reverence for the tribunal which this decision has sacrificed." [64]

A collection of papers, influenced more by economic stability than judicial impartiality, defended both the outcome of the case and the character of the new justices. But Charles Warren concluded that the reversal was "a very grave mistake—and a mistake which for many years impaired the people's confidence, not in the honesty but in the impartiality and good sense of the court." [65]

The Civil Rights Cases

By 1883, when the Court decided the *Civil Rights Cases*, the climate of public opinion had begun to shift away from the fevered antagonism of the Civil War. The Court, with a single dissent by Justice John Marshall Harlan, struck down as unconstitutional an 1875 statute that had prohibited discrimination of any kind in places of public accommodation.

The majority held that the Fourteenth Amendment had not given Congress authority to invade areas of state authority, concluding that "it would be running the slavery argument into the ground to make it apply to every act of discrimination which a person may see fit to make as to the guest he will entertain." *(See "Civil Rights Cases," pp. 695–696.)*

Press reaction was generally favorable. "The fact is," observed the *New York Times*, "that as long as we have state governments, within their field of action we cannot by national authority prevent the consequences of misgovernment." [66] The once-radical *New York Independent* acknowledged that "several leading colored men have expressed great indignation and disappointment," but concluded that "the court is clearly right." [67] The *Chicago Tribune*, the *Washington Post*, and the *Louisville Courier-Journal* all expressed support for the ruling.

However, the case did provoke considerable public debate, including editorials, rallies, and proposals for countervailing legislation. Frederick C. Douglass, the black editor, protested that the Court had exposed the black to any kind of treatment his oppressors could devise: "They can put him in a smoking car or baggage car. . . take him or leave him at a railroad station, exclude him from inns, drive him from all places of amusement or instruction, without the least fear that the national government will interfere for the protection of his liberty." [68]

This era of public indignation and strong conviction, in which the Court became a major target, drew to an ignominious close in 1896 with the decision of *Plessy v. Ferguson*, which upheld the constitutionality of separate-but-equal facilities for blacks. State legislatures enacting Jim Crow laws, the Court held, were entitled to take into consideration "the established usages, customs and traditions of the people and . . . the promotion of their comfort and the preservation of the public peace and good order."

REPORTING OPINIONS

The divisive character of the Dred Scott decision was dramatically illustrated by the Court itself in a dispute over making public the language of the majority opinion and dissents. The day after Chief Justice Roger B. Taney had read the majority opinion in Court, Justice Benjamin Curtis, one of the two dissenters, filed his opinion with the clerk based on what he had heard said from the bench. He gave a copy to a Boston newspaper, and it was widely reprinted.

Nearly a month later Curtis heard that Taney was revising the majority opinion. He asked the clerk for a copy and was told that the chief justice had forbidden its release until all opinions were printed in the official reports. For the next two months the two justices engaged in an angry exchange of letters over the issue.

Taney was obviously reacting bitterly to comparisons being made in the abolitionist press between his oral opinion and Curtis's written dissent. The chief justice wrote his colleague that "the opinion of the court on former occasions has been assailed in political journals and by political partisans before the opinion itself could be published, yet this is the first instance in the history of the Supreme Court in which the assault was commenced by the publication of the opinion of a dissenting judge."

Curtis already had given some thought to leaving the Court, where his $6,000 salary compared unfavorably with the rewards of private practice. His dispute with the chief justice settled the matter, and he resigned on September 1, 1857. President James Buchanan refused to issue the customary statement of praise for the justice's service that the attorney general had prepared.

"And so the Dred Scott case further deepened its impact of ill will," historian Carl B. Swisher wrote, "and on the Supreme Court an able jurist withdrew to be replaced for more than two decades by a mediocre Buchanan appointment (Nathan Clifford)."

Chief Justice Taney still tried to have the last word. He drafted for the official report of the case a headnote three pages long that summarized his opinion, including those parts that did not enjoy the support of a majority of his colleagues.

SOURCES: Charles Grove Haines and Foster H. Sherwood, *The Role of the Supreme Court in American Government and Politics: 1835–64* (Berkeley: University of California Press, 1956), 425–429; Carl B. Swisher, *History of the Supreme Court of the United States," vol. 5,* The Taney Period, 1836–64 (New York: Macmillan, 1971), 657.

Outside the black press, newspapers paid scant if any attention to the ruling, and there were almost no editorials. It remained for the *Richmond Times*, four years later, to sum up the case: "God Almighty drew the color line, and it cannot be obliterated. The negro must stay on his side of the line, and the white man must stay on his side, and the sooner both races recognize this fact, and accept it, the better it will be for both."[69] *(See details of Plessy v. Ferguson, pp. 696–697.)*

Confirmation Battles

During the latter half of the nineteenth century, presidents did not hesitate to make appointments to the Supreme Court during their last days in office, and the press was instrumental on several occasions in calling public attention to the political factors involved.

Franklin Pierce, a Democrat, was elected president in 1852, but before he was to take office in March 1853, outgoing president Millard Fillmore nominated a Whig, Sen. George Badger of North Carolina, to a vacancy on the Court. An earlier Fillmore nomination for the seat had died when the Senate adjourned without acting on it. Democrats controlled the Senate, but Fillmore had hoped a fellow senator, even of the minority party, might be confirmed. An Alabama paper saw this as "a corrupt effort to seduce the independence of the Senate by the kindly sentiments that exist in that body for one of its members."[70]

The Democratic papers of the South attacked Badger as less acceptable on the slavery issue than a Northern abolitionist. Even the Whig press was less than enthusiastic. The *New York Tribune* called for his confirmation but conceded that "as a statesman, he is of no account, and as a politician detestable."[71]

A month after the nomination, the Senate voted 26-24 to postpone consideration for another three weeks, a clear indication that Badger would not be confirmed. The *New York Times* protested that it was "one of those purely party operations . . . [and] there was no possible objection . . . except that he is a Whig."[72] After Pierce took office, he immediately nominated a Democrat, John Archibald Campbell of Alabama, who won Senate confirmation in four days.

Eight years later the political tables were turned. President James Buchanan, a Democrat with only one month left in his term, named Jeremiah Black, his secretary of state and former attorney general, to a vacancy on the Court. Republicans insisted that the selection should be made by their incoming president, Abraham Lincoln.

The situation was complicated by vacancies in the Senate caused by resignations of members from seceding states and by the bitter opposition to Black of Stephen A. Douglas and his Democratic followers. Echoing the position of the antislavery press, the *New York Tribune* observed, "In all the extensive range of his most unhappy selections for office, Mr. Buchanan has never hit upon a single nomination more eminently unfit to be made."[73] The Senate rejected Black by a 25-26 vote, and President Lincoln, after delays caused by the outbreak of war, filled

the vacancy. *(See details, p. 764; see also box, Empty Chairs: Vacancies on the Court, p. 906.)*

Just after the war, Congress reduced the number of Supreme Court seats to seven to deprive President Andrew Johnson of a nomination, but when he was succeeded by President Grant in 1869, Congress restored the number to nine. Grant named his attorney general, Ebenezer Rockwood Hoar of Massachusetts, to the vacancy. Initial reaction was favorable.

The *Nation* called the appointment "an admirable one."[74] The *New York Times* said of Hoar, "His distinguished abilities are conceded and his elevation to the supreme Bench is received with profound satisfaction by all."[75] *Harper's Weekly* called the choice "one of the best that could have been made."[76]

But as attorney general, Hoar had offended a number of senators by persuading President Grant to reject their political selections for judgeships and by his personal attitude toward the lawmakers. Charles Warren said his "brusque manners had given great offense."[77] The *New York Herald* said he treated the senators with "supercilious contempt."[78]

The president attempted to rescue the Hoar nomination by appeasing the Senate with the selection, five days later, of Edwin M. Stanton of Pennsylvania for a second Court vacancy created by a sudden resignation. The former secretary of war was confirmed immediately, but died of a heart attack four days later, and Hoar's prospects for Senate approval failed to improve. Six weeks later the Senate refused to confirm him by a 24-33 vote.

President Grant did not fare any better with another attorney general when he nominated George H. Williams of Oregon as chief justice in 1873 to succeed Salmon Chase. The move startled both the organized bar and the public, which had been little impressed by the nominee as a senator or cabinet officer. The *American Law Review* called the selection "a disappointment to all who had hoped that the seat of Marshall might be filled by a fitting successor" and said that Grant "has not improved the opportunity to make such a choice from the eminent lawyers of the country as the people had a right to expect."[79] The *Nation* called it "rather odd that the chief of a court which has to pass on the most complicated controversies of a great commercial country should be chosen from the bar of a frontier state like Oregon."[80] The *New York Independent* observed that "the general feeling of the public is that the President might and should have done better."[81]

So widespread was public protest that the Senate Judiciary Committee voted to reconsider its approval of confirmation. Five weeks after he had put forth the nomination, Grant withdrew it, at Williams's request. Twenty-five years later Williams wrote that he had been nominated "without my knowledge or consent" and that "the reasons for the Republican opposition to me in the Senate were not such as were given to the public by the newspapers."[82]

Undaunted, President Grant turned to Caleb Cushing of Massachusetts as his new candidate for chief justice. The nominee also had served as attorney general and had experience on the supreme court of his home state. He was, however, seventy-four years old

LEAKS AT THE COURT

The intense atmosphere of security that envelops the decisions and procedures of the Court is bound to present a challenge to some enterprising reporters. In all other agencies of government, news leaks—the private release of information in advance of official schedule—are regarded as regrettable but unavoidable. At the Supreme Court, they are regarded as a violation of sacred trust.

Meticulous precautions against premature disclosure of Court decisions are based on the well-grounded fear that unscrupulous investors could profit at the expense of the innocent if they had advance knowledge of the outcome of one of the many cases with great economic impact. Especially in modern times, some of the Court's most celebrated leaks, however, have involved closely watched controversies over social issues such as abortion.

One early leak dates to 1852, ten days before the Court announced its decision in the *Wheeling Bridge Case.* The *New York Tribune* reported that the majority would require removal or elevation of a bridge across the Ohio River because it interfered with interstate commerce. The story, which identified Justice John McLean as author of the opinion, proved accurate. Two years later, after Congress had preserved the bridge by legislation, it was destroyed by a windstorm. Ignoring an injunction, the bridge company began reconstruction, and the case came back before the Court.

In February 1856 the *Tribune* said a majority would hold the protective statute constitutional, effectively reversing its earlier ruling. In April the Court did just that. *(See "Commerce and Navigation," pp. 96–98.)* Observing that the *Tribune* "seems to have had a trustworthy pipeline to the Supreme Court," historian Carl B. Swisher wrote that the paper "was well served by its news source—from the nature of the comment apparently one of the dissenting justices." One of the dissenters was Justice McLean.

Later in the same year the *Tribune* was able to provide its readers with a running account of the Court's secret discussions of the Dred Scott case. Once again the leak apparently came from a dissenting justice who sympathized with the paper's antislavery position. The only justice who dissented in both cases was McLean.[1]

In the contemporary era *Time* magazine predicted in 1973 the gist of the Court's historic abortion decision and the 7-2 vote more than a week before it was handed down. (The magazine appears on Sunday, and the chief justice, wanting to confound *Time,* reportedly held back the opinion, which was to have been released the following day, for a week.) The news business took this scoop in stride, but the Court did not. Among various new security measures, Chief Justice Warren E. Burger ordered all the Court clerks—top-ranking young law school graduates who serve each justice for a year as part of a very exclusive apprenticeship—not to speak to or be seen with reporters in the future.

Nevertheless, four years later the secrecy of the Court conference was violated again. National Public Radio made headlines by reporting that the justices had voted 3-5 against reviewing the convictions of three defendants in the Watergate cover-up case, and that Chief Justice Burger had personally delayed for a week the scheduled announcement of the decision in hope of recruiting the necessary fourth vote to obtain review. Three of the four men named to the Court by President Nixon, the account went, supported reexamining the Watergate convictions, but the fourth disqualified himself.

The story, obtained by NPR reporter Nina Totenberg, was confirmed by the *New York Times,* with a cautionary note that it was not unusual for any justice to seek and obtain a week's postponement of any tentative decision of the conference. The source of the Totenberg leak was not identified, but the episode served notice to a startled Court that anything smacking of political maneuver inside the sacrosanct conference might find its way into the news.

In the spring of 1979, an ABC-TV reporter correctly reported in advance the outcome of a Supreme Court opinion on the rights of courts to question reporters about their thoughts while writing stories. Soon after this incident, a Government Printing Office typesetter assigned to the Court's printing unit was reassigned, without disciplinary action or loss of civil service status, at the request of Chief Justice Burger. The typesetter denied any disclosure of information.

1. *New York Tribune,* February 19, 1856, quoted by Carl B. Swisher in *History of the Supreme Court of the United States," vol. 5,* The Taney Period, 1836–64 (New York: Macmillan, 1971), 416.

and, according to Warren, "a man of exceedingly unstable character," having switched political parties four or five times.[83]

Press reaction, especially among Republican papers, was strongly negative. The *New York Tribune* called the nomination "incongruous" and "objectionable."[84] *Harper's Weekly* attacked Cushing as "a pro-slavery Democrat whose views have been notoriously in opposition to those by virtue of which the war was carried on."[85] The *Nation* said that "the President has at last entered the small circle of eminent lawyers, and then with great care has chosen the worst man in it."[86]

The president and the Senate were spared a decision on Cushing's merits, however, when a thirteen-year-old letter of recommendation from the nominee to Jefferson Davis, then president of the Confederate States, came to light. Although the letter contained no evidence of disloyalty, several senators said it compelled them to vote against Cushing, and Grant withdrew the nomination four days after he had made it.

TWENTIETH CENTURY, 1901–1950

During the first half of the twentieth century, the Supreme Court moved through a phase of relative somnolence that reflected national prosperity and wartime unity into one of its most critical eras as an institution. The Great Depression brought radical changes in the role of the federal government and sharp constitutional challenges to those changes.

Generally, during the first three decades of the new century, the Court did not play a major part in governing the country and, as a result, received relatively little attention from the newspapers. But the advent of the depression brought sweeping change. President Franklin D. Roosevelt persuaded Congress that powerful government intervention was required in the nation's economic and social affairs, and the challenges posed to the resulting legislation focused a strong spotlight on the justices and their work. Press coverage broadened and deepened as the nation realized that the fate of the New Deal hung on the response of the Court.

The resulting story was good fodder for the news media of the day. First, the relatively conservative Court, which had been all but invisible during the terms of Calvin Coolidge and Herbert C. Hoover, made news by consistently finding New Deal measures unconstitutional. Then the president launched an unprecedented attack against the justices, proposing that the Court be enlarged with the obvious expectation that his appointees would shift its philosophical balance.

Coverage

The ensuing controversy turned Supreme Court reporters into combat correspondents. The justices attempted to defend their institution. Editorial pages around the country, generally Republican, erupted with charges that Roosevelt was trying to trample on the Constitution. Then, for whatever reason, the Court shifted and began upholding New Deal legislation. It was a journalistic field day.

Roughly around the turn of the century, newspaper reporting of the Court, as of other government activities, had begun to come of age, shifting its emphasis from the highly opinionated articles that were common during the 1800s to more or less straight accounts of the facts. The trend was faster and more pronounced in some areas of the country than others, but the old personalized journalism was largely a thing of the past by the time the New Deal revived the Court's prominence.

After this period, press commentary on Supreme Court rulings moved from the news columns of the nation's papers to their editorial pages. To the extent that the Court responds to public opinion in reaching its decisions or in modifying past decisions to conform to changed conditions—a controversial matter from the nation's earliest days to the present—such movement must

be measured today against newspapers' editorial comment rather than news stories.

Also during the New Deal period, a new and timelier source of news reporting—radio broadcasting—began to play a major role in coverage of the Court. Generally, then as now, radio news accounts tended to lose in detail what they gained in immediacy, leaving newspapers and specialized legal journals as the principal source of information about all but the simplest cases decided by the Court.

Cases

President Roosevelt's New Deal presented the Supreme Court with the most serious challenges in its history, in both judicial and political terms. Congress, at the president's behest,

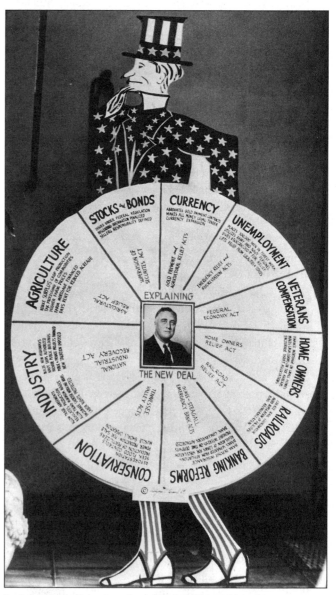

In the 1930s the Court issued a dozen decisions within a three-year period striking down parts of President Franklin D. Roosevelt's New Deal program, explained in this 1933 chart. Roosevelt responded by proposing that the membership of the Court be enlarged to as many as fifteen justices, provoking a largely critical reaction from the media.

had enacted an imposing body of innovative legislation; many of the new laws aroused sufficient public opposition to wind up in the Courts, where they posed a series of issues of great complexity and controversy.

When, from the viewpoint of the White House, the Court proved too inflexible to adjust to new concepts of executive and legislative authority aimed at meeting the economic crisis of the depression, the president launched a frontal attack on the institution itself. Nominally, that attack failed: Roosevelt's attempt to reshape the philosophy of the Court by expanding its membership aroused nearly fanatical opposition and never won congressional endorsement. But the mere proposal apparently had such impact on the Court that the president achieved his underlying goal of more favorable consideration for his programs. Or so it appears today.

Press coverage of this fascinating era, while very different from that of earlier years, played a role in the unfolding events, if only by informing the public of the daily skirmishes between the White House and the justices and their defenders. The opinions of the press, now emanating from the editorial pages of the nation's newspapers rather than from their news columns, were not always a steady guide to the controversy.

The NRA Decision of 1935

In May 1935, when the Court declared the National Recovery Administration (NRA) unconstitutional, the *Washington Star* exulted: "The Supreme Court, almost in the twinkling of an eye, yesterday re-established the Constitution of the United States." The justices "turned back those who have sought to set Federal power above law" and reversed "a tendency toward government domination . . . that bordered on dictatorship." [87] *(See details of Panama Refining Co. v. Ryan and Schechter Poultry Corp. v. United States, p. 87 and pp. 110–111.)*

Comparable enthusiasm was voiced elsewhere. The *New York Herald-Tribune* said with satisfaction of President Roosevelt, "The damage to his prestige is great. He is shown . . . to have been leading the country down a blind alley." [88] The *Los Angeles Times*: "The days of a virtually uncontrolled one-man dictatorship in the United States are at an end." [89] The *Denver Post*: "The Constitution still stands and cannot be stretched by any group of well-meaning but visionary theorists to set up any kind of a political despotism." [90]

Even papers more favorable to the Roosevelt administration expressed little sorrow at the passing of the NRA. "Perhaps the decision will mean the end of slovenly legislative procedure," the *Boston Herald* observed. [91] Refusing to become excited, the *New York Times* said, "The judges simply pronounced to be dead a statute which the great mass of the people had already decided to be dead," and their ruling "seems so far to have met with general approval." [92]

The AAA Decision of 1936

Eight months later, when the Court pulled down another pillar of the New Deal, the Agricultural Adjustment Administration (AAA), the president's press critics took it in stride. The *Washington Star* predicted that the ruling "presages the ultimate invalidation of many more New Deal laws," observing that the decision "should not come as a surprise to the nation. . . . [I]ndeed, the surprising thing would have been for the Court to uphold the A.A.A." [93] *(See details of United States v. Butler, pp. 133–134.)*

The *New York Herald-Tribune* praised the opinion, saying "the unceremonious fashion in which it sweeps aside the various subterfuges of the law would be a warning to those optimistic New Dealers who had thought to hoodwink the court and evade the Congress by trick or glibly stated purpose." [94]

Other newspapers reacted by reflecting more localized interests. The *Kansas City Star* said the ruling had "precipitated an immediate crisis" among farmers who had participated in the program. [95] The *Chattanooga Times* called for a constitutional amendment to continue the AAA and the Tennessee Valley Authority, which now appeared threatened. [96] The *Lincoln (Neb.) State Journal* inveighed against farmers who "took those checks, swapped away the right to manage their own properties, voted as A.A.A. agents told them to and pretended to be grateful." [97]

"Packing" the Court

The turning point in this conflict came on February 5, 1937, when President Roosevelt proposed enlarging the membership of the Court to as many as fifteen justices. He argued that the federal courts as a whole needed manpower, but his transparent purpose was to dilute the Supreme Court majority hostile to his legislation into a minority by new appointments. *(See "Counterattack" and "A Court Reversal," pp. 263–265.)*

Press reaction was swift and largely critical, ranging from outrage on the right to mannerly questioning by papers that had generally supported the New Deal. The *Washington Star* accused the president of "indirection, savoring strongly of subterfuge" and questioned whether the nine-man Court "will have enough to do to keep it busy through March." [98] The *New York Herald-Tribune* said the Court plan would "end the American state as it has existed throughout the long years of its life" and reduce the Constitution to "a paper shell." [99] The *Hartford Courant* suggested that the president might better have said openly, "Let me appoint six judges to the Supreme Court, and they will see to it that the Constitution does not stand in the way of what I want to do." [100]

Calling the plan "a program of almost devilish ingenuity," the *Los Angeles Times* declared, "It is a hard thing to say of the President of the United States, but the fact remains this program cannot be offered in good faith." [101] The *San Francisco Chronicle* said it was "an open declaration of war on the Supreme Court, which is none the less direct because its first attack is on the flank." [102]

Roosevelt sympathizers were hard put to defend the plan. "The historic truth is," the *Des Moines Register* observed, "that no matter how great and good a man may be, executive aggrandisement is not safe for democracy." [103] The *New York Times* said Roosevelt had laid himself open to charges that he was trying

---

LYNDON AND FRANKLIN

While the controversy over President Franklin D. Roosevelt's plan to increase the size of the Supreme Court was at its height, a special election was held in the Tenth Congressional District of Texas. Of the eight candidates competing, only one endorsed the president's "packing" proposal, and he won. His victory was "a vote of confidence" in the Court plan, the new representative, Lyndon B. Johnson, told the *New York Times*.

SOURCE: *New York Times*, April 11, 1937, quoted by Leonard Baker in *Back to Back* (New York: Macmillan, 1967), 188.

"to do by indirection what he cannot do directly," and it raised the question of whether this amounted to "political sharp practice, a thing Americans are not yet ready to condone under the name of judicial reform." [104]

The *Kansas City Star* and the *St. Paul Pioneer Press* argued that such a change in the Court should be accomplished, if at all, by constitutional amendment rather than statute. Otherwise, the Minnesota paper said, "the Constitution is to be reduced to a mere generality and the Court to become a changeling." [105] The *Star* maintained the people should decide such a drastic shift in power and called the packing legislation "a short cut . . . in the specious guise of expediting justice." [106]

Support for the New Deal

Then, with almost dazzling swiftness, the entire situation changed: the Court began handing down decisions upholding instead of dismantling the New Deal. Little more than two months after the plan to pack the Court with six new justices was unveiled, the justices upheld a state minimum wage law for women, almost the same as a state law it had overturned ten months earlier. In April 1937 the Court again sided with the president when it upheld the federal Wagner Act, guaranteeing collective bargaining rights to workers.

"The majority of the Court has made legal history," proclaimed the *New York Times*. "What more can the Roosevelt Administration reasonably ask?" the *Times* inquired, suggesting that the Wagner Act ruling provided "an excellent opportunity to . . . withdraw with good grace from the packing proposal." [107] There was general agreement elsewhere about this decision in *National Labor Relations Board v. Jones and Laughlin Steel Corp* (1937). The *Los Angeles Times* said the Court had "disproved the President's contention that it is biased and prejudiced against New Deal legislation." [108] The *San Francisco Chronicle* observed that if the ruling doomed "Mr. Roosevelt's rash anti-constitutional revolutionary coup d'état, believers in representative democratic government breathe easier." [109] The *Chattanooga Times* said, "After these decisions . . . there seems to be left little ground on which the President can stand." [110]

Six weeks later, when the Court upheld the new Social Security system in *Helvering v. Davis* (1937), the *New York Times* news account said the ruling "showed that the majority of the Court now tends to favor the liberal aims of the Administration," and the paper editorially called the decision "another historic step in the process of adapting the great character of American democracy to the changing needs of the times." [111]

Somewhat more skeptically, the *Wall Street Journal* pointed out that "the Court passes only upon its wisdom or the rightness of a complex law as it stands." The *Journal* argued that the decision "again enhances the Federal domain; it impairs state sovereignty to the extent that no state can now assert its right to hold its industries free of social burdens like these." [112]

The *Washington Star* questioned the need for any further debate on the "discredited" Court reorganization plan, "a dangerous redesign of the American form of government." [113] The *Washington Post* agreed, saying the Court "has driven another nail in the coffin of the President's plan to enlarge the Court's membership . . . removing the last flimsy argument." [114]

Whether public reaction to the packing plan, reflected by the press, had been overwhelmingly hostile or whether President Roosevelt felt he had achieved his aim by threat, the proposal to expand the Court was never pressed seriously again.

The Court and the Stars and Stripes

During the World War II years, a pair of Supreme Court decisions suggested that the justices were indeed attentive to adverse, widespread press reaction. In June 1940 the Court held 8-1 that public schools can compel pupils to salute the American flag, even if the salute violates their religious beliefs.

Initial press response to *Minersville School District v. Gobitis* (1840) was supportive. The *New York Times* was not disturbed that the Court upheld the compulsory salute law; it observed that "reverence for which the flag stands is more important than any gesture." [115] The *Washington Star* cautioned its readers that the decision "does not mean that the safeguards against impairment of freedom of worship have been relaxed in the slightest degree." [116]

But, as time passed, more and more reflective editorial writers concluded that the decision had been a mistake, and more than 150 papers ended up criticizing the decision. For example, the *St. Louis Post Dispatch* concluded: "We think [the Court's] decision is a violation of American principle. We think it is a surrender to popular hysteria. If patriotism depends on such things as this—upon violation of a fundamental right of religious freedom—then it becomes not a noble emotion of love for country but something to be rammed down our throats by the law." [117]

Three years later, in *West Virginia State Board of Education v. Barnette* (1943), the justices reversed their former decision and invalidated flag salute laws as a violation of religious freedom. The *New York Times* remained cautious, acknowledging that the earlier ruling had aroused "an emotion of dislike" and concluding that "the voluntary principle is the essence of civil rights as

The Court ruled in *Minersville School District v. Gobitis* (1940) that the government can require public school students to salute the U.S. flag, even if the salute violates their religious beliefs. The press was initially supportive of the decision, but the tide of editorial opinion later turned against the ruling. The Court reversed itself three years later in *West Virginia Board of Education v. Barnette.*

of common sense." [118] *(See details of Gobitis and Barnette, pp. 513–515.)*

The *Washington Star* agreed with the majority that "the tribute to the flag becomes a meaningless gesture when forced" but was otherwise not enthusiastic. "There will be grave doubts," the paper concluded, as to the wisdom of the ruling "that compliance with a reasonable regulation, applied almost universally to promote good citizenship, depends on nothing more than the whim of the individual. By that logic the dissidents become the rulemakers, and no regulation is safe." [119]

THE MODERN ERA, 1951–2004 AND BEYOND

The Supreme Court probably has made news more consistently in the years since 1950 than at any other time in the nation's past. Under Chief Justice Earl Warren (1953–1969), the Court became a mighty engine of government in a way it rarely had been before. Under Chief Justices Warren Burger and William Rehnquist, that machine slowed somewhat but did not stop.

Coverage

Because of the sweeping and controversial nature of many of the modern Court's decisions, contemporary press coverage has been among the most intensive the institution ever has received. As in the past, the news media conveyed the pronouncements of the Court to the public, analyzed the impact on the nation, and relayed citizens' reaction back to the nine justices if they chose to read, watch, and listen.

The second half of the twentieth century added a new dimension to coverage of the Court: television. Although TV cameras are barred from Supreme Court sessions, television stations have hired reporters with legal training and have worked to encapsulate and illustrate major decisions for their broad audience. In the late 1950s, newspapers, increasingly aware of television competition, tended to compress the kind of exhaustive coverage given landmark cases of the past, but more papers assigned more reporters with better legal knowledge to cover the Court's overall activities in a thorough fashion.

It is no more possible at present than it ever has been to prove or disprove Finley Peter Dunne's dictum that "the Supreme Court follows the election returns." The most that can be said is that a highly sophisticated communications system makes more information, opinion, and reaction available to the Court than ever before, for whatever judicial notice its members might take.

The sixteen years of the activist Warren Court produced news that tested the press's reportorial ability: the abolition of public school segregation, the requirement that members of Congress and both houses of all state legislatures be elected from districts accurately balanced in population, and a long series of rulings protecting the constitutional rights of criminal defendants against abuse by law enforcement officials.

The Burger Court—and the Rehnquist Court after it—continued to make news, moving incrementally away from the Warren Court's positions on criminal law and in other areas, winning applause in some legal circles and criticism in others. Their decisions on abortion, obscenity, capital punishment, and affirmative action presented as large a challenge to reporters and editorial writers as had many rulings by the preceding Court.

These years also brought controversy over Court nominations. In the mid-1980s the press covered closely, and some would say intensified, the battle over President Ronald Reagan's effort to fill the "swing" seat on the Court vacated by Justice Lewis F. Powell Jr. The press also played a role in the confirmation hearings for

THE COURT AND PUBLIC OPINION

The Supreme Court, whose members are not chosen by popular election, was intended as a check on the political branches of the federal government, whose members are chosen by election. To that end the men who wrote the Constitution insulated the Court from the more passionate and evanescent extremes of public sentiment. The Constitution—with its checks and balances and guarantee of a fair trial—was designed to prevent the new republic from becoming a tyranny of the majority. The independence of a Supreme Court, its members appointed for life, also reflected suspicion of truly "popular" government.

It is usually difficult to determine whether, or to what extent, a particular decision has been influenced by public opinion. The justices rarely admit that they are swayed by popular, rather than judicial, considerations. To base an interpretation of the Constitution on public opinion would seem to vitiate the purpose of assigning the function of interpretation to an unelected body and to undermine the Supreme Court's credibility even with the public whose opinion it sought to follow.

Still, the same historical events and trends that shape public opinion also influence judges, and the judges' opinions may resemble those of the public not because they are following popular views but because they have shared the same historical experience.

The fact that public opinion is usually divided, often ambivalent, and generally subject to change gives the justices considerable latitude in responding to it. It is only natural that a justice tends to be more responsive to the sentiments of the sector of society that shaped his or her pre-Court experiences. But elevation to the Supreme Court may broaden an individual's awareness of, and sympathy for, elements of the public not previously considered. So might moments when those two worlds come together—such as cases involving racial discrimination or affirmative action programs in law school settings.

The traditional image of the Supreme Court also exerts pressure on the justices' behavior. However responsive a justice may be to prevailing opinions, the public generally expects his or her behavior to be judicious. That appearance of dignity and reason is central to the Court's function of reassuring the people of the permanence and stability of their political system.

In the public eye the Court is aloof from the haggling of politicians, above the compromising among selfish interests that is so much a part of democratic politics. This image of the Supreme Court, however, is double-edged. Because the justices' opinions can be influenced by the interests of major sections of the public, popular expectations that the Court will be motivated solely by reason and high ideals often are disappointed. Quickest to see a betrayal of principle in the Court's reasoning are those whose ox has just been gored by one of its decisions.

President George Bush's 1991 nominee, Clarence Thomas. The Senate Judiciary Committee had tried to keep secret an allegation of sexual harassment against Thomas. But when the information was leaked to the press and disclosed shortly before a scheduled confirmation vote, a public uproar forced the Senate to hold an unprecedented second round of nationally televised hearings on the nomination.

Cases

The Supreme Court has never been far from the spotlight of press attention since 1954, the year that the Warren Court issued its first major ruling, *Brown v. Board of Education of Topeka*. With the exception of the New Deal Court-packing controversy, the Court was probably never the focus of such intense public attention and criticism as it was during the years after Earl Warren become chief justice in 1953. In the post–Warren era the criticism was less intense; supporters and critics exchanged roles, but the Court itself continued as a major center of controversy.

Desegregating the Public Schools

The high mark of the Court's prominence as a powerful agency of government almost certainly came in May 1954 when the justices ruled unanimously that racial segregation in the public schools was unconstitutional. Recognizing that revolutionary forces had been set in motion, the great majority of the nation's newspapers reacted with caution rather than with exultation or outrage. Most significantly, few of the bitterest critics raised the prospect of resistance. *(See details of Brown v. Board of Education, pp. 680–685.)*

The *New York Times* was so restrained that today its view might seem rather equivocal. "The Court is not talking of that sort of equality which produces interracial marriage," the paper assured the nation. "It is not talking of a social system at all." Acknowledging serious problems ahead, the *Times* concluded that "little by little . . . we move toward a more perfect democracy." [120]

The *Washington Post* said the decision "affords all Americans an occasion for pride and gratification" and will ultimately prove "profoundly healthy and healing." [121] The more conservative *Washington Star* observed that "concern over a dubious assumption of power by the Court . . . does not alter the fact that this decision finds much support in wisdom and fairness." [122]

Reaction from the South was, understandably, less favorable. The *New Orleans Times-Picayune* predicted that in "the immediate future, the decision will do no service either to education or racial accommodation" and concluded that "the disappointment and frustration of the majority of southerners at the revolutionary overturn of practice and usage cannot immediately result in the improvement of race relations." [123] The *Louisville Courier-Journal* said that "the end of the world has not come for the South or for the nation. The Supreme Court's ruling is not itself a revolution. It is rather acceptance of a process that has been going on a long time—people everywhere could well match the Court's moderation and caution."[124] The *Atlanta Constitution* observed that the ruling "does not mean that Negro and white children will go to school together this fall."[125] The *Chicago Tribune* salvaged something from the ruling in a grudging editorial. "The principle established by this decision is not that anybody has to give up any of his prejudices," the paper said. "The principle is the much simpler one that the state governments, North and South, must regard all men as created equal so far as opportunities at the disposal of the state are concerned."[126]

The *Houston Chronicle* warned that "racial friction may be increased rather than diminished and . . . endless litigation may arise to plague the southern states" as they comply.[127] The *Jackson (Miss.) Clarion-Ledger* said, "May 17, 1954, may be recorded by future historians as a black day of tragedy for the South and for both races, but we can conduct ourselves in such fashion as to cause historians to record that we faced that tragedy and crisis with wisdom, courage, faith and determination."[128]

A year later, when the Court ordered compliance with its desegregation edict with "all deliberate speed," southern newspapers were considerably less exercised than they had been at the original decision. The Court, said the *Raleigh News and Observer*, "has gone about as far as any Southerner could have expected" in refusing to set an arbitrary timetable.[129] The *Atlanta Constitution* called the ruling "much more mild and less specific in tone than had been anticipated."[130]

The *New York Times* said the implementing decision was "perhaps not wholly satisfactory for anybody," but concluded that "the error of a static and ineffective edict has been avoided."[131] The *Wilmington (Del.) Morning News* called it "a pretty sensible decision" that displayed "no lack of firmness" but "understanding of local feelings and respect for local control."[132]

"One Man, One Vote"

The Warren Court had more than one revolution in store for the American people. In 1964 the Court ruled that both houses of state legislatures must be apportioned according to population rather than geography or custom. The result was a massive redistribution of power away from rural areas to the cities and suburbs, and press response was sharply divided.

The *New York Times* declared that "as a matter of equity, the Court is clearly right" in correcting the "historic injustice" that limited the influence of cities in state legislatures.[133] Echoing this reaction, the *Washington Post* said the ruling "goes a long way toward establishing democracy in America" and "will be magnificently liberating" because "rural domination in the state legislatures has created a paralyzing tyranny."[134] *(See details of Reynolds v. Sims, p. 561.)*

But the *Wall Street Journal* was unhappy. "It was clearly wrong for the states for so many years to deny effective voice to their urban minorities," the *Journal* conceded. "But it is hardly less wrong for the nation now to go to the other extreme of muzzling rural minorities."[135]

The *Washington Star* observed that there was "no longer cause for surprise that the Court makes its decisions . . . on the basis of its personalized idea of what is right—what is good for us. . . . We may wonder whether our system of government benefits when justices do what voters will not do." The paper concluded, however, that "the practical and moral effects of the rulings probably will be for the good."[136]

Criminal Justice

The vigor with which the press praised or belabored the Warren Court was nowhere more visible than in the highly controversial area of law enforcement. The Court's dedication to ensuring the rights of the accused to fair treatment in criminal prosecutions, at the possible expense of convictions, sharply divided commentary in the news media. A classic example was the 1966 *Miranda* case, in which the Court mandated a code of protection for suspects who were to be interrogated by the police.

The decision, said the *Washington Star*, "will be received with rejoicing by every thug in the land" and "will grievously handicap the police and make it much easier for a criminal to beat the rap." Chief Justice Warren's opinion was "a murky torrent of words" that "will largely destroy the traditional police function at least as far as interrogation is concerned."[137] Across town, the *Washington Post* observed with satisfaction that "the Supreme Court is determined to take all this jazz about civil liberty seriously" and "insists upon reading the Constitution as though it had been intended as a charter of freedom." *(See details of Miranda v. Arizona, pp. 639–641.)*

But even the Court's supporters could not agree entirely. The *Post* called the Warren opinion "admirable" for specifying permissible police procedures "with clarity and accuracy."[138] But the *New York Times*, while supporting the decision as a whole, found the listing of procedures "regrettable" as an "over-hasty trespass into the legislative area." The *Times* also criticized the majority for "downgrading the reliability and worth of all confessions." While predicting that the *Miranda* ruling "will erase some of the discrimination against the poor" in criminal cases, the *Times* said that "experience may well validate the fear expressed by the dissenting justices that law enforcement will be handicapped."[139]

The Burger Court: Abortion, Then Watergate

The most enduringly controversial decision of the Warren Burger era was *Roe v. Wade*, the 1973 ruling that made abortion legal nationwide. Newspapers published stories in the decision's immediate aftermath that pitted religious leaders who called the ruling "shocking" and "horrifying" against birth control advocates who hailed it as a "triumph." News organizations themselves were equally divided on the merits of the decision detailing a new right to abortion.

The *New York Times* wrote an editorial calling the decision a major contribution to the preservation of individual liberties. But the newspaper also predicted that the decision would lead to resolution of the issue that had long divided America. As the *Times*'s own pages would demonstrate, strife over abortion and *Roe v. Wade* would not subside during the next two decades.[140]

Another famous case that came before Chief Justice Burger and his colleagues during their early years was the dispute over President Richard Nixon's tape recordings. In 1974 a unanimous Court required the president to surrender tapes of sixty-four White House conversations for use as evidence in the Watergate burglary cover-up trial. This decision led directly to the conviction of several high administration officials and to the resignation of the president to avoid a House vote on articles of impeachment against him. *(See details of United States v. Nixon, Nixon v. United States, p. 254 and p. 269.)*

Press coverage of the case was intensive. When the Supreme Court agreed to hear it on an accelerated basis on May 31, the story was played as the most important of the day. The exchange of briefs and oral arguments on July 8 produced front-page stories.

When the decision came down on July 24, the nation's newspapers voiced a thundering chorus of grateful affirmation. The *Wall Street Journal*, for example, saw the ruling as "a common sense resolution of the immediate problems involved" rather than the rescue of the republic. "Surely it is healthier," the *Journal* observed, "to have the President's arguments based not in defiance of the courts but in compliance with them." The paper expressed editorial gratitude for President Nixon's announcement that he would surrender the tapes, on behalf of "those of us who have been struggling to keep an open mind." [141]

Similarly, the *Washington Star* called the decision "historic, definitive and above all correct" and was able to take some solace from the Court's recognition, for the first time, of the existence of executive privilege in the White House. That recognition will make for "a more careful and cleaner presidency"; otherwise the courts "would have required the President and his advisors to conduct the nation's business in a fishbowl, a situation that would be intolerable and unworkable." [142]

The *New York Times* praised the Court for reaffirming "the supremacy of law over Presidential pretensions" and establishing that "the presidency cannot be used as a sanctuary for miscreants." The *Times* said, "If this nation was to remain the Republic established by the authors of the Constitution, the court could only have ruled as it did." [143]

The *Washington Post* paid one of its relatively rare tributes to Chief Justice Burger, for "a particularly sound and skillful opinion . . . nicely reconciling the conflicting interests of confidentiality for the President and the right of due process for criminal defendants." The paper concluded ruefully that "it is a measure of how far we have come when a President of the United States can hope to earn favor by not defying a decision by the Supreme Court." [144]

The Rehnquist Court: Abortion Again

After nineteen years of highly emotional public controversy over the right to abortion, the Supreme Court in 1992 tried to stake out a firm middle ground on the issue. It upheld most of a Pennsylvania law regulating a woman's access to abortion while affirming what it described as the "essential holding" of *Roe v. Wade*.

The 1992 Court said states could not impose an "undue burden" on a women's right to end a pregnancy. Because the decision in *Planned Parenthood of Southeastern Pennsylvania v. Casey* gave states more leeway to restrict abortion, many abortion rights advocates insisted that it sounded the death knell for abortion rights. [145] But the language of the opinion did not support such a conclusion, as Harvard University law professor Kathleen M. Sullivan pointed out in an opinion piece in the *New York Times:* "Roe opponents have won some skirmishes, but so far they are still losing the war. For the anti-abortion movement, yesterday's Supreme Court decision in the Pennsylvania abortion case was a rout." [146]

The media cut through the rhetoric. Syndicated columnist Joan Beck wrote in the *Chicago Tribune*, "Both sides are unhappy with the decision." Referring to claims that *Roe v. Wade* was dead, the columnist continued, "That's not what happened. But it illustrates the overblown rhetoric and self-righteous anger endemic to both sides of this weary controversy." [147]

Unlike the reception given *Roe v. Wade* two decades earlier, media on both sides of the ideological spectrum accepted the outcome. A *Wall Street Journal* editorial reflected:

> The sun rose this morning just as it rises every other day of the year, and we feel confident that come evening it will also set. We feel equally confident in stating that despite the Supreme Court's ruling . . . regulation of abortion in this society will not go back to the prohibitions of the 1950s. What the ruling does mean is that Americans will now be allowed a greater say in the most contentious issue in the country today, a say they lost in *Roe v. Wade*, the 1973 Supreme Court decision that unearthed a right to abortion in a document that didn't even mention that word. [148]

A more liberal voice, the *Washington Post*, weighed in:

> The most important thing about the Supreme Court's ruling in the Pennsylvania abortion case . . . is what it doesn't do. In spite of the fervent arguments of antiabortion forces and the Bush administration, and notwithstanding the appointment of a series of justices thought to be safe votes on this question, the court refused to overturn *Roe v. Wade* outright. Moreover, it is possible that those who oppose that 1973 ruling have peaked in terms of their impact on the judicial aspect of this debate, for the longer *Roe* remains a valid precedent, the harder it will be to dislodge. [149]

Editorial reaction to the *Bush v. Gore* ruling of 2000 was as divided as that of the country after the disputed presidential election. The 5-4 ruling to end the recount in Florida "comes at a considerable cost to the public trust and the tradition of fair elections," said the *New York Times*. [150] "The ruling of the court's five-justice majority—the same five who suspended the recount last week—read as if it came straight from the pages of 'Catch 22,'" said *USA Today*. [151] Others hailed the ruling as bringing the right result to a fractured nation. "We are extremely pleased that seven members of the Supreme Court recognized the illegitimacy of the recounting carnival in Florida," said the *Atlanta Constitution*. [152]

The Court's split decision in 2003 upholding some affirmative action in colleges and universities was hailed on many editorial pages. "A compelling interest indeed! If universities are the training grounds for America's future leaders, as Justice Sandra Day O'Connor suggested in the court's 5-4 ruling, schools must strive to create a diverse educational environment for students," said the *Baltimore Sun*.[153] But the *Wall Street Journal* predicted the ruling would lead to "another generation of polarizing race-based public policy." [154]

The Court's decision a week later upholding gay rights and striking down a Texas antisodomy law was also praised by the editorial pages of most large newspapers, including in Houston, where the case, *Lawrence v. Texas* had originated. "Good for the U.S. Supreme Court" for declaring "Texas' 120-year old, archaic and discriminatory anti-sodomy law an unconstitutional invasion of privacy," said the *Houston Chronicle*.[155]

Confirmation Battles

The Senate confirmation battles over two of President Richard Nixon's nominees for the Supreme Court—first, Clement F. Haynsworth Jr., chief judge of the U.S. Court of Appeals for the Fourth Circuit, and then G. Harrold Carswell, a junior judge on the U.S. Court of Appeals of the Fifth Circuit—provided dramatic examples of the influence of the news media.

During the confirmation disputes, newspapers, and to a lesser extent radio and television, served two functions. They circulated growing criticism of the two Nixon nominees to the public, which, in turn, brought pressure on members of the Senate from their constituents to vote against the president's choices. But some of that critical information was actually the product of investigative reporting into the backgrounds of the two judges, producing far more significant information than the Federal Bureau of Investigation had furnished to the White House.

Unforeseen Opposition

No one really anticipated either of the controversies. The Senate had not denied confirmation to a Supreme Court nominee since 1930. Nixon's first choice, Chief Justice Burger, had aroused little opposition in the Democratic-controlled Senate, despite his relatively conservative judicial views. When Haynsworth was named in 1969 to fill Abe Fortas's seat, he appeared headed for the same sort of gentle treatment.

Newspaper reaction at first was guarded but not hostile. The *Washington Star* called the choice of the South Carolinian "both a logical and an excellent one" if the president's purpose was "to bring the Court back to a more balanced, a more central position." The newspaper acknowledged that the nominee was "something of an unknown quantity" and observed prophetically that possible conflict of interest questions were "not without troublesome aspects." [156]

The *New York Times* said the candidate was "disappointing . . . an obscure judge with little reputation for . . . depth, social sensitivity and philosophic insight." The *Times* also said his record was "marked by an extremely cautious reluctance to interpret the Constitution in the light of changing conditions." [157] The *Washington Post* agreed that Haynsworth was "not particularly

---

THE PRESS AND JUSTICE FORTAS

Only one justice has resigned from the Supreme Court under public pressure. He was Abe Fortas, who, in less than five years on the high bench, almost rose to the pinnacle of chief justice. Eleven months later, however, he was forced to step down under circumstances that bordered on disgrace. His rise and fall were extensively chronicled, and in some ways influenced, by the press. Although Fortas had been a controversial figure throughout his judicial service, it was journalistic enterprise that effectively ended his career. William Lambert, an investigative reporter for *Life* magazine, uncovered the fact that Fortas had agreed to accept $20,000 a year for his lifetime, and then for his wife's, from a foundation in return for "continuing services."

What made the charges of unethical behavior even more damning was that the foundation's head was Louis E. Wolfson, who was serving a prison term for selling unregistered securities. The American Bar Association later declared that Fortas's retention of a high-paying client while on the bench had been "clearly contrary" to the canons of ethics.

For Fortas it was a mighty fall. When he was named to the Court by President Lyndon B. Johnson in 1965, the *New York Times* said the move "gives every promise of providing an exceptional appointment," since the nominee had "many qualities other than

political shrewdness and presidential gratitude." The *Washington Post* praised Fortas for "his intellectual capacity, his legal experience and his deep concern over civil liberties and civil rights," and the strongly Republican *Washington Star* called him "a most able, respected and scholarly lawyer."

Three years later, an attempt by President Johnson to make Fortas chief justice foundered in a Senate filibuster amid charges that he had accepted high lecture fees while on the bench and had continued to serve as a major White House adviser, raising obvious conflict of interest problems.

When he resigned in 1969, the *New York Times* approved, saying the justice had "helped preserve the reputation for the integrity of the nation's highest court, which his own actions had so severely shaken." The *Washington Star* agreed that the move "should free the court of the shadow cast upon it by the Fortas indiscretions, and this is the most important thing." Calling the resignation "imperative," the *Washington Post* said that "the outcome is tragic in the true dramatic sense of the term for it entails the destruction of a man of great stature and great promise."

SOURCES: *New York Times*, July 29, 1965; *Washington Post*, July 30, 1965; *Washington Star*, July 29, 1965; *New York Times*, May 16, 1969; *Washington Star*, May 16, 1969; *Washington Post*, May 16, 1969.

distinguished . . . a symbol rather than a man" and found his record that of "a competent jurist . . . nothing more, nothing less."[158]

Then, gradually, conflict charges against the nominee began to mount, based on his considerable stock holdings. He had ruled for a corporation in a labor case while he owned stock in a company that did business with the corporation. He bought stock in a corporation after he had voted in its favor on a case but before the decision was announced. Organized labor came out against his confirmation, as did some civil rights groups.

Backers of the nomination held rallying news conferences and spoke out on the Senate floor. The Senate Judiciary Committee approved the nomination, but the vote was 10-7. Finally, in late November 1969 after some Republican defections, the Senate rejected Judge Haynsworth, 45-55.

The *Washington Star*, which had supported Haynsworth throughout the three-month debate, insisted that there had been "insufficient evidence to brand Judge Haynsworth as anti-Negro, anti-labor or unethical in his financial dealings."[159] The *New York Times*, however, called the Senate vote "a political setback of stunning proportions" for Nixon. The *Times* had called on the president to withdraw the nomination, but had not urged senators to vote against Haynsworth because the president's right to select his own Court nominees "outweighs the inadequacies and improprieties alleged against Judge Haynsworth." The paper concluded it was "better for the court and the country" that the nomination had been defeated rather than approved by a narrow margin.[160]

Judicial Competence

Two months later President Nixon sent the Senate the nomination of another southern conservative, G. Harrold Carswell of Florida, to fill the continuing vacancy. Both the candidate and the controversy his confirmation debate aroused proved to be even more astonishing than the Haynsworth affair.

Press reaction to Judge Carswell fell short of enthusiasm by varying degrees. The *Washington Star* saw the nominee's philosophy as "several degrees to the right of our own . . . but no red-necked reactionary." The paper predicted that "this time the nomination [of a southerner] will stick" because "Carswell, from all accounts, has been investigated with uncommon diligence."[161] The *Star* news stories displayed comparable foresight. "Fast Okay Likely for Carswell," the front-page headline read.

The *Washington Post* called it "unfortunate" that the president "did not see fit to reward one of the truly distinguished judges [of the South]," maintaining that Carswell's performance on the bench "does not lift him even to the top layer" of the Republicans named to judgeships in the South during the 1950s by President Dwight D. Eisenhower.[162] Even more pointedly, the *New York Times* expressed "shock" that the president had proposed a nominee "totally lacking in professional distinction . . . wholly unknown for cogent opinions or learned writing." But the editorial more or less conceded his confirmation, saying he "may in time grow in wisdom."[163]

But Carswell's nomination was in trouble almost immediately. Two days after his designation, a television reporter uncovered a militant white-supremacist speech he had made in 1948 and printed on the front page of a weekly newspaper he owned. Then came the story of how he had participated in converting a public golf course in Tallahassee into an all-white private club rather than desegregate it. Feminist groups joined the labor and civil rights coalition that had formed to resist Haynsworth's nomination and rallied to fight Carswell.

Witnesses told of Judge Carswell's hostility from the bench to black civil rights attorneys. The dean of the Yale Law School said Carswell had "the most slender credentials of any man put forward in this century for the Supreme Court." The Judiciary Committee supported him, 13-4, but a floor vote was delayed as reports accumulated of the nominee's participation in discriminatory activities.

The *Washington Star* remained steadfast, saying that the judge "certainly should be approved. His apparent lack of judicial brilliance is not the point." The *Star* claimed, "His detractors have not made a convincing case against him."[164] But the *New York Times* called his participation in the golf course transaction "shameful" and urged "a rejection of this unworthy nominee" who had displayed "callous disregard of both the law and civil rights."[165]

Late in March both the *Washington Post* and the *New York Times* reported Senate support for Carswell ebbing but probably not seriously enough to prevent his confirmation. Opponents launched delaying tactics to allow wider circulation of adverse information about the nominee. Some Republican backers shifted to an undecided posture. The White House mustered a statement of support by southern judges. President Nixon charged the Senate with trying to usurp his constitutional powers.

"Chances are, it's all over but the confirmation," predicted the *Washington Star* on the eve of the final vote, while acknowledging that "our enthusiasm for Judge Carswell is, quite frankly, restrained."[166] The *Washington Post*, which had favored Judge Haynsworth's confirmation, said Carswell should be rejected because "he lacks the essential qualities."[167] The *New York Times*, two days before the vote, called confirmation "simply incomprehensible."[168] On the morning of the vote, the paper called the nomination "an insult to the Congress, a denigration of the Court and an affront to the faith of the American people in the quality of their government.[169]

After the Senate rejected the Carswell nomination, 45–51 on April 8, 1970, the newspapers reacted more or less predictably. The *Star* reaffirmed its belief that Judge Carswell had been properly qualified and said that the Senate had been "wrong" if its vote was based on "his social or judicial philosophy." The paper said, "Mr. Nixon should stick to his guns" in picking still another conservative Supreme Court candidate.[170] The *Washington Post* urged the president to choose someone with "impeccable credentials" like Chief Justice Burger, "a man of quality in his intellectual capacity as well as his personal life."[171] The *New York Times* called the Senate decision "a triumph of constitutional responsibility over political partisanship" and observed that "the dismal experience of past weeks must emphasize to the president the urgency of turning quickly to the nomination of a first-rate jurist."[172]

Nixon's third choice for Fortas's seat, Harry A. Blackmun, fit this description. He was confirmed unanimously on May 12, 1970.

Challenging Conservatism

The nomination of Robert H. Bork by President Reagan in 1987—eighteen years after the Haynsworth and Carswell battles—set off one of the most intense and vociferous confirmation battles in history. The media, both broadcast and print, covered the battle intensely and in doing so played their own role in the eventual defeat of Bork's nomination after a three-and-a-half month debate. But the role of the press was different from that it had played eighteen years earlier. While newspaper editorials once again endorsed or opposed confirmation, press coverage of this nomination afforded the public a fuller picture of the nominee.

Ronald Reagan's 1987 nomination of Robert H. Bork, a federal appeals court judge of pronounced conservative views, to succeed Lewis F. Powell Jr., touched off an epic battle. The groups defending and opposing the nomination used the media to a degree not before seen in confirmation battles.

In large part, the scholarly, gray-bearded Bork—who lacked a telegenic face or personality—was his own worst enemy when it came to the media. The television networks covered the confirmation hearings, and the more viewers saw of this precise, intellectual man, the less they liked. Newspaper and radio coverage was also intense, and the more Bork said, the more citizens found to complain about.

The groups defending and opposing Bork also used the media—through paid advertisements for and against confirmation—to a degree not seen before in confirmation battles. These messages had an impact similar to that of the coverage of the events themselves, galvanizing public opinion and keeping the issue alive.

No one questioned Bork's qualifications for the job: he had taught in law schools, practiced law, served as solicitor general, and served on the U.S. Court of Appeals for the District of Columbia Circuit since 1981. He had been a leading contender for a Supreme Court nomination for several years; his name always surfaced in any discussion of probable Reagan nominees. What intensified public attention was that the vacancy had been created by the retirement of Justice Lewis F. Powell Jr., a man of generally conservative views who had voted with the Court's more liberal justices to affirm prior rulings on school prayer, abortion, and affirmative action. In other words, his vote had often been the key swing vote. Because Powell had been the steadying influence on a sharply divided Court, his successor would be positioned to tip the balance.

Liberal groups, led by Ralph G. Neas of the Leadership Conference on Civil Rights, declared their opposition to Bork as soon as the nomination was announced on July 1, 1987. The battle was immediately joined. Sen. Edward M. Kennedy, D-Mass., announced he would lead the opposition. Both the opposition and the defense, led by several conservative organizations, including the American Conservative Union, mounted media advertising campaigns using newspaper, television, and radio to convince Congress and the public of their point of view.

By the time the Senate Judiciary Committee moved to vote in early October, the coverage and media campaigns had had their effect. The *Atlanta Constitution* published a Roper poll that showed that southerners, who were expected to favor Bork's confirmation, opposed him 51 percent to 31 percent. The committee voted 5-9 against confirmation.

Stung by the impending defeat of the nomination by the full Senate, Republican senator Gordon J. Humphrey criticized the media coverage. Holding up the front page of the *Washington Post*, he complained that stories about supporters were buried inside the paper. Sen. Joseph Biden, chairman of the Judiciary Committee, responded that the American people, who saw Bork for themselves during the televised hearings, did not like what they saw. He repeated this point in the debate that preceded the formal vote, 42-58, on October 23, 1987, rejecting the nomination. He pointed out that after Bork's televised testimony, public opinion turned against him. "All the money spent on advertising against Judge Bork could not have purchased one half of a day of the live coverage the networks gave to Bork," he said. "They covered everything Judge Bork did live and in color. . . . I am told that tens of millions of people watched Judge Bork . . . unfiltered by the news media, and drew a conclusion."

Reporters played an even larger role in the contentious hearings on Clarence Thomas, President George Bush's 1991 nominee. He was the Court's second black nominee—intended to succeed the first, the retiring Thurgood Marshall—but Thomas was nonetheless opposed by the same liberal groups that helped to defeat Bork. Thomas was a chairman of the Equal Employment Opportunity Commission (EEOC) under Ronald Reagan and then a federal appeals judge, appointed by Bush. Over his career, Thomas had amassed a large body of extracurricular conservative writings: he was personally opposed to affirmative action and favored narrow interpretations of constitutional individual rights and congressional power. He also had suggested that Roe v. Wade was wrongly decided.

Thomas completed the usual round of Senate Judiciary Committee hearings in early October 1991, and despite a 7-7 vote by the committee on whether to recommend the candidate to the full Senate, he appeared headed for confirmation. But the weekend before the full Senate's scheduled Tuesday, October 8, vote on the nomination, word of sexual harassment allegations against Thomas leaked to Newsday, a Long Island, New York, newspaper, and to a National Public Radio reporter. The NPR reporter, Nina Totenberg, arranged an interview with Anita F. Hill, a University of Oklahoma law professor, in which Hill confirmed that she had submitted an affidavit to the Judiciary Committee outlining Thomas's unwelcome sexual advances to her when she worked with him in the early 1980s at the Department of Education and at the EEOC.

The disclosure of the allegations—and the committee's failure to investigate them thoroughly—touched off a storm of criticism and demands for a delay in the Senate vote. Some in the press and public barraged senators with accusations that lawmakers were insensitive to women and out of touch with America. The Senate Judiciary Committee reluctantly held a second round of hearings to air Hill's complaint and Thomas's defense.

When the hearings opened on October 11, the accuser and accused delivered some of the most extraordinary public testimony ever offered to a congressional committee. Here were two individuals—both black, who shared backgrounds of poverty and prejudice and had built successful and highly respected careers—blaming each other for devastating wrongs. Both spoke convincingly and with great emotion, and both told their stories to a huge national television audience that found it hard to turn away. Thomas declared his innocence and "categorically" denied that he had ever harassed Hill or, indeed, even tried to date her. He lashed out at the committee, telling Sen. Biden,

> Mr. Chairman, I am a victim of this process. My name has been harmed. My character has been harmed. My family has been harmed. My friends have been harmed. There is nothing this committee, this body or this country can do to give me my good name back. Nothing.

> I will not provide the rope for my own lynching or for further humiliation. I am not going to engage in discussions, nor will I submit to roving questions, of what goes on in the most intimate parts of my private life or the sanctity of my bedroom. These are the most intimate parts of my privacy, and they will remain just that: private.[173]

Then Hill spent seven hours telling her story, how Thomas had humiliated her with lewd comments and unwanted advances. She said she believed he wanted to have sexual intercourse with her. She provided embarrassing details of what she said were Thomas's comments to her on the job: talk of women's breasts, the size of his penis, accounts of movies of group sex and bestiality. Hill spoke of the anguish she had suffered since being contacted by the committee about her experiences with Thomas. "It is only after a great deal of agonizing consideration that I am able to talk of these unpleasant matters to anyone except my closest friends."

Each side brought character witnesses and corroborating witnesses. The rhetoric from senators and the nominee himself escalated. Thomas called the episode a "high-tech lynching." In the end the Senate voted 52-48 to confirm Thomas. Most senators said Hill's charges and Thomas's defense were inconclusive. Senators fell back on their previous positions based on Thomas's judicial philosophy or his determined character and rise from poverty.

A special counsel was hired by the Senate to investigate the leaks to NPR's Totenberg and Newsday reporter Timothy Phelps. But, after a four-month investigation that included interviews with more than two hundred witnesses, the counsel was unable to identify how Hill's allegations, supposedly revealed only to the committee, got to the press.[174]

COVERING THE HIGH COURT

The relationship between the Supreme Court and the news media has been an uneasy one over the years. This is not surprising since the Court, almost by definition, is an insular, tradition-bound, secretive institution, while the press is, by necessity, adaptive, exploratory, and devoted as a matter of principle to the elimination of secrecy.

Historically, the Court has made the minimum possible accommodation to the need for public information. For many years the justices regarded other judges and lawyers as their proper constituency and felt they could and should be reached through legal publications. The lay public was largely ignored. At one time during the nineteenth century, Chief Justice Roger Taney ordered that no Court opinions be made public until they had been printed in the official bound reports. Only some thirty years ago, reporters with deadline problems—which meant all of them—had to sit in the courtroom and take notes while opinions were being read in full, because texts were not handed out until the justices had concluded, often well into the afternoon.

Conflict between the two institutions, the judiciary and the press, peaked during the Warren Court when cross-complaints of botched reporting and impossible working conditions were freely exchanged. Chief Justice Burger concerned himself with public access to the Court's rulings more than any of his predecessors, and, during the latter part of his tenure, significant improvements were made in the amount of assistance provided to reporters by the Court through the Public Information Office. In addition, Burger made himself available from time to time to discuss with reporters the problems they faced in covering the Court—a considerable advance, although few additional changes emerged as a result of these discussions. Chief Justice Rehnquist has continued this practice, periodically inviting the standing press corps to lunch in one of the Court's ceremonial conference rooms.

Several of the reporters who cover Court have legal training, and many of them have written about the Court and the law for more than a decade. The current roster lists nearly fifty reporters who devote all or part of their time to Court. Some of them are also assigned to cover the Department of Justice, which is another good reason for such a reporter to have a background in the law. The major news organizations that assign full-time reporters to cover the Court include the wire services—Associated Press, Bloomberg, Dow Jones, Reuters, and United Press International—and the *Chicago Tribune*, Knight-Ridder, *Los Angeles Times*, National Public Radio, NBC, *New York Times*, *USA Today*, *Wall Street Journal*, *Washington Post*, and *Washington Times*.

Keeping their Distance

Direct contact between the justices and the reporters who cover their pronouncements is very limited. Print journalists may sit in the courtroom and observe the justices as they present summaries of their opinions and question attorneys during oral argument. Broadcast journalists have the same right, but no additional ones; they may not record any of the proceedings for radio or television.

Press seating in the courtroom is adequate for thirty-seven reporters. When major cases attract larger attendance, many reporters are seated where they can hear but not see the bench, and identifying a speaking justice is often difficult. (The police officers present generally help out by whispering to reporters which justice is speaking.)

The Court provides an office for its public information officer, a separate room for staff and documents, and a room for reporters, which is frequently crowded on decision days. Those who cover the Court regularly have semiprivate alcoves for their own desks and telephones. Others must scramble for a limited number of public telephones and table space. A computer terminal is available in the pressroom so reporters can access the Court's docket electronically.

Only one set of briefs on each of the cases before the Court is available to assist the press corps. (The major wire services have one set apiece, which are jealously but not always successfully guarded against pilferage.) A reporter can run into long delays in getting access to briefs on a newsworthy case. There is a single photocopier in the pressroom and often long lines to make copies of briefs.

A separate room is provided in which radio correspondents can record their news broadcasts, but there is no provision for television at all. Cameras were rarely allowed in the building during the 1970s and 1980s. The few instances included a news conference by Justice William O. Douglas in 1975 when he returned to duty after suffering a stroke; a conference by Potter Stewart in 1981 when he retired; and a Cable News Network (CNN) interview with Justice Harry A. Blackmun in 1982. Cameras are now permitted under limited circumstances. Crews still cannot film courtroom proceedings, but they are allowed to film elsewhere in the building. Cameras may be used in the courtroom when no official proceedings are under way, but no one other than a justice may be filmed in the courtroom. Furthermore, no one may be filmed in the justices' conference room.

Some lawyers, including former attorney general Griffin B. Bell, have proposed that television be permitted to record oral arguments and decision ceremonies in the courtroom. Chief Justice Burger opposed the idea of televising oral arguments. Chief Justice Rehnquist and a majority on the bench continue to resist entreaties from television. In March 1996 when Justice David H. Souter testified before a House Committee on an unrelated judicial topic, the subject of cameras in the courtroom arose. The Associate Press reported that Souter said cameras would come into the courtroom "over my dead body."

The Court's public information officer hands out copies of the Court's orders and opinions, supervises the small library of briefs and past decisions, and answers a wide range of inquiries from the public at large. Copies of opinions are distributed in the information office as soon as the author begins reading a précis from the bench. Sometimes a justice will ad-lib a colorful phrase or even a small joke in the summary, but a reporter must be in the courtroom to catch it; there are no transcripts of Court proceedings available until days later. Reporters who want a same-day transcript of arguments in an important case must make their own private arrangements.

Although the public information officer does not interpret the legal rationale or the impact of a Supreme Court decision, he or she does provide reporters with information about how the Court operates and what its technical actions mean. The office has developed a "reporter's guide" to covering the Court, which serves as a primer for newcomers, giving them a basic set of definitions for Court terminology and outlining the Court's procedures. The office also provides a separate guide for journalists on emergency applications, or requests, to the Court, especially those arising in death penalty cases.

A Tough Beat

During some periods in the history of Supreme Court, such as the latter days of the Warren Court, inaccurate or simply wrong reporting has been more prevalent than at other times. Usually such periods provoke some self-criticism by the press and generate efforts to improve working conditions that can contribute to inaccuracy.

Volume

To help the press deal with the thousands of cases on its docket, the Court provides limited advance warning on which cases it will announce on a given Monday that it has accepted or denied for review. A week or so before these "orders" are handed down, a list of case numbers is given reporters on a not-for-publication basis. (Actually, any interested party could find out such information by contacting the clerk's office; the clerk also operates an automated response system that provides case information by telephone.) The case numbers are those of cases the Court proposes to take up at its conference that Friday. Not every case on the list will be accepted or rejected the following Monday, but the Court is committed to not departing from the list and springing surprises.

No comparable warning is provided, however, when the Court decides a case it has accepted and heard argued. The public information officer tells reporters a few days in advance how many decisions will be handed down on a given day without any hint of which ones they will be. (The night before the Court's decision in the 1978 *Bakke* "reverse discrimination" case, a semi-official source, who may or may not have been acting for the Court, tipped off a few reporters about the timing but not the result of the decision. Such tips, however, are very rare.)

Unlike other branches of government, the Court announces its decisions at a regular time: at ten a.m., and usually on Monday, Tuesday or Wednesday. Reporters appreciate the fact that decisions are not handed at five p.m. on a Friday evening or on the weekends. But there are exceptions to every rule. One of the most momentous decisions in the Court's history, the *Bush v. Gore* ruling that decided the disputed presidential election of 2000, was handed down at ten p.m. on Tuesday, December 12.

Timing

Most of the mistakes in Supreme Court reporting are made by reporters for wire services or afternoon newspapers who must file stories as rapidly as possible after decisions are handed down. Radio correspondents normally have a little more time in which to compose much shorter dispatches.

When the ruling in *Bush v. Gore* was handed down, television reporters rushed in front of the cameras to announce the news. Several of them quickly looked at the end of opinion, which said the case had been "remanded" to the Supreme Court of Florida. From this, they mistakenly assumed the Court was sending the dispute back to Florida for a further hearing or more recounts. But a reading of the whole opinion revealed that the 5-4 majority had closed the door to further recounts or more litigation.

Still, the *Bush v. Gore* case was exceptional in every way—including its lack of headnotes. Normally the Court's opinions begin with a set of headnotes that summarize the ruling in one or two pages. Also included is how the various justices voted. This summary gives reporters with short deadlines a news capsule from which to work. Formerly, these headnotes

appeared only when the Court opinions were published in bound volumes, months—even years—later.

For some time reporters have urged Court officials to institute a "lock-up." Under this plan, Court officials would distribute opinions or an order list to reporters in advance of a strict release time two hours later. In this way the hectic, error-prone rush into print or onto the air could be avoided. Highly sensitive to untimely security leaks, the Court has not been willing to test this system, even when reporters agreed to be literally locked up.

While not so critical, time can be a serious problem for morning newspaper reporters as well. On heavy decision days, particularly at the end of a term, a reporter for a morning paper that expects full Supreme Court coverage often can expect to work without a break from 10 a.m. to an early evening deadline to handle the day's material.

Complexity

In the uncherished past all Supreme Court decisions for a given week were handed down on Monday, along with orders accepting or rejecting cases, and the result was often chaos. Sometimes there was simply too much material to be read, analyzed, and reported adequately. Mistakes resulted, and significant cases went unreported.

In 1965 the Court began spacing out its decisions, handing down a few on Tuesday and Wednesday mornings when it was in session for oral arguments. This practice improved the accuracy and balance of Court coverage substantially, but congestion remains a problem at term's end, when a tired Court is unwilling to sit a few days longer merely to time its decisions in the interest of better public understanding.

The growth of the Internet has improved the quality of reporting on the Court's work. Prior to the 1990s the Court's decisions were not widely seen on the day they were issued, and news reporters often had to rely on their own best judgment about the significance of a decision in a complex case. With the arrival of the Internet, however, the Court's opinions can be read and analyzed by legal experts around the nation, and their reactions inform the daily news coverage of the ruling.

Secret Chambers

One dilemma in Supreme Court coverage that appears to be nearly insoluble involves secrecy and security. In virtually every agency of the executive and legislative branches, reporters have access to the men and women who make the news and an opportunity to question them about public business and to learn something, in the process, about their character and personality.

At the Supreme Court, this is not true. Justices obviously cannot discuss a case pending before the Court. If they talk about a recent decision, their comments have a tendency to revise the decision's content or to prejudge the next similar case, or both. If they talk for the record about any issue that may come before the Court, they put their impartiality in question. As a result, members of the Court seldom talk with reporters at all, rarely grant on-the-record interviews, and almost never hold news conferences.

Sometimes, however, their public comments in news stories can cause them a problem. In January 2003 Justice Antonin Scalia spoke in Fredericksburg, Virginia, at a Religious Freedom Day celebration and criticized a recent appeals court ruling in California that had declared unconstitutional the use of "under God" in the Pledge of Allegiance. "I have no problem with that philosophy being adopted democratically. . . . Then we could eliminate 'under God' from the Pledge of Allegiance," he said in a Associated Press report. But courts should not require its elimination, which would be "contrary to our whole tradition," he added. That fall, when the pledge case was appealed to the Supreme Court, Scalia felt obliged to withdraw from the case, because he would no longer be seen as an "impartial" jurist.

Reporters sometimes encounter justices at Washington social events, but the conversations are closely circumscribed, tending to be limited to sports, hobbies, and the weather. After the resignation of Justice Abe Fortas following revelation of his extrajudicial financial entanglements, members of the Court became even more reclusive, limiting public appearances of any kind. In the 1990s, however, some of the justices were more visible outside the Court—in particular, Sandra Day O'Connor, Antonin Scalia, Ruth Bader Ginsburg, and Stephen G. Breyer.

What amounts to a communications barrier between the justices and the media has been particularly vexing to reporters when a member of the Court disqualifies himself or herself from participating in a decision. The motive is almost always praiseworthy, and the reason is usually routine—a past association with a lawyer or organization involved or stock holdings that might suggest a conflict of interest. But, by tradition, the Court refuses to explain why one of its nine members has abstained. Scalia's recusal in the Pledge of Allegiance case was an exception because the plaintiff, Michael Newdow, filed a motion asking him to step aside because of his public comments about an issue pending before the Court. An abstention can result in a deadlocked Court (4-4), which has the effect of denying the appealing party the Supreme Court review that the justices had agreed to provide, a situation that would seem to merit some modest public explanation.

NOTES

INTRODUCTION (PP. 813–814)

1. Charles Warren, *The Supreme Court in United States History*, rev. ed., 2 vols. (Boston: Little, Brown, 1922, 1926), 1:3.

2. Ibid.

3. *Planned Parenthood of Southeastern Pennsylvania v. Casey*, 505 U.S. 833 (1992).

4. *Dickerson v. United States*, 539 U.S. 428 (2000).

THE COURT AND THE MEDIA (PP. 815–839)

1. Charles Warren, *The Supreme Court in United States History*, rev. ed., 2 vols. (Boston: Little, Brown, 1926), 1:288.

2. *Niles Register*, February 27, 1819, quoted in ibid., 1:494.

3. *New York Evening Post*, February 20, 1819, quoted in Warren, 1:494.

4. *Baltimore Federal Republican*, cited in *Independent Chronicle*, March 6, 1819, quoted in Warren, 1:494.

5. Julius Goebel Jr., *History of the Supreme Court of the United States:* vol. 1, *Antecedents and Beginnings to 1801* (New York: Macmillan, 1971), 255.

6. Letter of Oliver Wolcott, July 28, 1795, quoted in Warren, 1:131.

7. *Columbian Centinel*, December 26, 1795, quoted in Warren, 1:137.

8. *Columbian Centinel*, February 23, 1811, quoted in Warren, 1:411.

9. *Connecticut Courant*, February 20, 1811, quoted in Warren, 1:411.

10. Ibid., 1:413.

11. *Columbian Centinel*, January 22, 1835, quoted in Warren, 1:799.

12. *New York Courier*, January 19, 1835, quoted in Warren, 1:799.

13. *Washington Federalist*, April 29, 1803, quoted in Warren, 1:253.

14. *National Intelligencer*, March 13, 1818, quoted in Warren, 1:480.

15. *Columbian Centinel*, March 24, 1818, quoted in Warren, 1:482.

16. *Boston Daily Advertiser*, March 23, 1818, quoted in Warren, 1:482.

17. *New York Evening Post*, February 5, 1819; *New York Commercial Advertiser*, February 6, 1819, quoted in Warren, 1:488.

18. Ibid., 1:489.

19. *Boston Daily Advertiser*, March 13, 1819, quoted in Warren, 1:512.

20. *Natchez Press* quoted in *Niles Register*, May 22, 1819, quoted in Warren, 1:519.

21. *Niles Register*, March 13, 1819, quoted in Warren, 1:522.

22. *General Advertiser*, March 17, 1819, quoted in Warren, 1:523.

23. *New York Statesman*, February 9, 1824, quoted in Warren, 1:604.

24. *New York Evening Post*, March 5, 1824, quoted in Warren, 1:612.

25. *New York Commercial Advertiser*, March 12, 1824, quoted in Warren, 1:612.

26. *National Gazette*, March 29, 1824, quoted in Warren, 1:613.

27. *Georgia Journal*, April 6, 1824, quoted in Warren, 1:614.

28. *Richmond Enquirer*, March 16, 1824, quoted in Warren, 1:618.

29. *Boston Courier*, January 21, 1831, quoted in Warren, 1:734.

30. *United States Telegraph*, January 7, 1831, quoted in Warren, 1:734.

31. *New York Daily Advertiser*, January 13, 1831, quoted in Warren, 1:736.

32. *Aurora*, January 15, 1801, quoted in Warren, 1:273.

33. *National Intelligencer*, May 20, 1803, quoted in Warren, 1:276.

34. *Charleston Courier*, June 9, 1803, quoted in Warren, 1:277.

35. *Aurora*, March 22, 1804, quoted in Warren, 1:280.

36. *Connecticut Courant*, February 27, 1804, quoted in Warren, 1:280.

37. Ibid., 1:292–293.

38. *Newark Daily Advertiser*, March 5, 1842, quoted by Carl B. Swisher in *History of the Supreme Court of the United States*, vol. 5, *The Taney Period, 1836–64* (New York: Macmillan, 1971), 543.

39. *Baltimore Sun*, March 3, 1842, quoted in ibid., 543.

40. *New York Tribune*, January 5, 1849, quoted in Swisher, 526.

41. Ibid., 552.

42. *New York Courier*, December 18, 1856, quoted in Warren, 1:286.

43. *New York Independent*, January 1, 1857, quoted in Warren, 1:287.

44. *New York Tribune*, January 9, 1857, quoted by Swisher, 615.

45. *New York Independent*, March 12, 1857, quoted in Warren, 1:306.

46. *New York Evening Post*, March 7, 1858, quoted in Warren, 1:307.

47. *New York Herald*, March 12, 1857, quoted in Warren, 1:309.

48. *Pennsylvanian*, quoted in Warren, 1:311.

49. *Daily Union*, March 7, 1857, quoted in Warren, 1:312.

50. *St. Louis Evening News*, April 15, 1857, quoted by Charles Grove Haines and Foster H. Sherwood in *The Role of the Supreme Court in American Government and Politics: 1835–64* (Berkeley: University of California Press, 1957), 431.

51. *Harper's Weekly*, March 28, 1857, quoted in Warren, 1:315.

52. Warren, 1:315.

53. *North American Review*, vol. 85, 1857, quoted in Warren, 1:316.

54. Warren, 1:317.

55. *Nation*, February 10, 1869, quoted in Warren, 1:500.

56. *Chicago Republican*, December 21, 1868, quoted in Warren, 1:500.

57. *New York Times*, January 4, 1870, quoted in Warren, 1:509.

58. *New York Tribune*, February 1, 1870, quoted in Warren, 1:510.

59. *Nation*, April 17, 1870, quoted in Warren, 1:521.

60. *Springfield Republican*, April 8, 1870, quoted in Warren, 1:522.

61. *American Law Review*, vol. 5 (1870), quoted in Warren, 1:523.

62. *Springfield Republican*, May 5, 1871, quoted in Warren, 1:525.

63. *Nation*, May 27, 1871, quoted in Warren, 1:525.

64. *New York Tribune*, May 2, 1871, quoted in Warren, 1:526.

65. Warren, 1:522.

66. *New York Times*, January 24, 1883, quoted in Warren, 1:522.

67. *New York Independent*, October 25, 1883, quoted in Warren, 1:614.

68. John A. Garraty, ed., *Quarrels That Have Shaped the Constitution* (New York: Harper and Row, 1964), 138.

69. *Richmond Times*, January 1, 1900, quoted in ibid., 158.

70. *Mobile Register*, quoted in *Washington Union*, February 3, 1853, quoted in Warren, 1:243.

71. *New York Tribune*, January 8, 1853, quoted in Warren, 1:244.

72. *New York Times*, February 16, 1853, quoted in Warren, 1:245.

73. *New York Tribune*, January 29, 1861, quoted in Warren, 1:364.

74. *Nation*, December 2, 1869, quoted in Warren, 1:502.

75. *New York Times*, December 16, 1869, quoted in Warren, 1:502.

76. *Harper's Weekly*, January 1, 1870, quoted in Warren, 1:502.

77. Warren, 1:503.

78. *New York Herald*, December 21, 1869, quoted in Warren, 1:503.

79. *American Law Review*, January 1874, quoted in Warren, 1:553–555.

80. *Nation*, December 4, 1873, quoted in Warren, 1:555.

81. *New York Independent*, December 12, 1873, quoted in Warren, 1:556.

82. *Yale Law Journal*, vol. 8 (1899), quoted in Warren, 1:556.

83. Warren, 1:557.

84. *New York Tribune*, January 10, 12, 1874, quoted in Warren, 1:557.

85. *Harper's Weekly*, February 7, 1874, quoted in Warren, 1:557.

86. *Nation*, January 15, 1874, quoted in Warren, 1:557.

87. *Washington Star*, May 28, 1935.

88. *New York Herald-Tribune*, May 28, 1935.

89. *Los Angeles Times*, May 28, 1935.

90. *Denver Post*, May 28, 1935.

91. *Boston Herald*, May 28, 1935.

92. *New York Times*, May 28, 1935.

93. *Washington Star*, January 7, 1936.

94. *New York Herald-Tribune*, January 7, 1936.

95. *Kansas City Star*, January 7, 1936.

96. *Chattanooga Times*, January 7, 1936.

97. *Lincoln (Neb.) State Journal*, January 7, 1936.

98. *Washington Star*, February 5, 1937.

99. *New York Herald-Tribune*, February 6, 1937.

100. *Hartford Courant*, February 6, 1937.

101. *Los Angeles Times*, February 6, 1937.

102. *San Francisco Chronicle*, February 6, 1937.

103. *Des Moines Register*, February 6, 1937.

104. *New York Times*, February 6, 1937.

105. *St. Paul Pioneer Press*, February 6, 1937.

106. *Kansas City Star*, February 6, 1937.

107. *New York Times*, April 13, 1937.

108. *Los Angeles Times*, April 13, 1937.

109. *San Francisco Chronicle*, April 13, 1937.

110. *Chattanooga Times*, April 13, 1937.

111. *New York Times*, May 25, 1937.

112. *Wall Street Journal*, May 25, 1937.

113. *Washington Star*, May 25, 1937.

114. *Washington Post*, May 25, 1937.

115. *New York Times*, June 5, 1940.

116. *Washington Star*, June 4, 1940.

117. *St. Louis Post Dispatch*, as quoted in Garraty, *Quarrels That Have Shaped the Constitution*, 234.

118. *New York Times*, June 19, 1943.

119. *Washington Star*, June 16, 1943.

120. *New York Times*, May 18, 1954.

121. *Washington Post*, May 18, 1954.

122. *Washington Star*, May 18, 1954.

123. *New Orleans Times-Picayune*, May 18, 1954.

124. *Louisville Courier-Journal*, May 18, 1954.

125. *Atlanta Constitution*, May 18, 1954.

126. *Chicago Tribune*, May 18, 1954.

127. *Houston Chronicle*, May 18, 1954.

128. *Jackson (Miss.) Clarion-Ledger*, May 18, 1954.

129. *Raleigh News and Observer*, June 1, 1955.

130. *Atlanta Constitution*, June 1, 1955.

131. *New York Times*, June 1, 1955.

132. *Wilmington (Del.) Morning News*, June 1, 1955.

133. *New York Times*, June 16, 1964.

134. *Washington Post*, June 17, 1964.

135. *Wall Street Journal*, June 16, 1964.

136. *Washington Star*, June 16, 1964.

137. *Washington Star*, June 15, 1966.

138. *Washington Post*, June 15, 1966.

139. *New York Times*, June 14, 1966.

140. *New York Times*, January 24, 1973.

141. *Wall Street Journal*, July 25, 1974.

142. *Washington Star*, July 25, 1974.

143. *New York Times*, July 25, 1974.

144. *Washington Post*, July 25, 1974.

145. *CQ Almanac 1992* (Washington, D.C.: Congressional Quarterly, 1993), 398–399.

146. *New York Times*, June 20, 1992.

147. *Chicago Tribune*, July 2, 1992.

148. *Wall Street Journal*, June 30, 1992.

149. *Washington Post*, June 30, 1992.

150. *New York Times*, December 13, 2000.

151. *USA Today*, December 13, 2000.

152. *Atlanta Constitution*, December 13, 2000.

153. *Baltimore Sun*, June 24, 2003.

154. *Wall Street Journal*, June 24, 2003.

155. *Houston Chronicle*, June 17, 2003.

156. *Washington Star*, August 19, 1969.

157. *New York Times*, August 18, 1969.

158. *Washington Post*, August 19, 1969.

159. *Washington Star*, November 22, 1969.

160. *New York Times*, November 22, 1969.

161. *Washington Star*, January 20, 1970.

162. *Washington Post*, January 21, 1970.

163. *New York Times*, January 21, 1970.

164. *Washington Star*, February 18, 1970.

165. *New York Times*, February 27, 1970.

166. *Washington Star*, April 7, 1970.

167. *Washington Post*, April 6, 1970.

168. *New York Times*, April 6, 1970.

169. *New York Times*, April 8, 1970.

170. *Washington Star*, April 9, 1970.

171. *Washington Post*, April 9, 1970.

172. *New York Times*, April 9, 1970.

173. *CQ Almanac 1991* (Washington, D.C.: Congressional Quarterly, 1992), 27–285.

174. *CQ Almanac 1992*, 72–73.

PART V

The Court at Work

CHAPTER 16

Operations and Traditions of the Court

CONSTITUTIONALLY and politically, the Supreme Court is at the helm of a branch of the federal government co-equal with Congress and the executive. In some ways the judiciary appears to be the most powerful of the three: the Court can declare the actions of the president illegal and acts of Congress unconstitutional.

Organizationally, however, the Supreme Court is dwarfed by the sprawling bureaucracies of the other branches. The Court is, after all, only nine people, housed in a single building at One First Street Northeast in the nation's capital. Its budget is but a fraction of the size of those required to fund Congress and the executive branch.

Nevertheless, the Court is hardly aloof from the problems of management, procedure, maintenance, and personnel faced by any other institution. Like Congress—or the local department store, for that matter—it must be administered, budgeted, staffed, and locked up after work each day. Moreover, it is the apex of a substantial federal judicial system that includes ninety-four district courts, thirteen courts of appeal, and two special courts, along with their judges and attendant staff.

The administrative aspects of the Court's operations are considerable, even if they do not rival those that have spawned the huge bureaucracies that serve the executive branch and Congress. Chief justices from John Jay to William H. Rehnquist have wrestled with the problems of ensuring the smooth functioning of the Court's managerial machinery to allow the judges to concentrate on dispassionate consideration of matters of law.

The ideal tableau of the Court—and certainly the image that it has sought to perpetuate over the years—is of nine wise, just, and serene jurists sitting to render, with irreproachable integrity, decisions crucial to the conduct of national life.

That this image has been maintained so well for more than two centuries is, to a remarkable degree, a testament to its accuracy. The high standards requisite for both effective judicial performance and public trust have indeed been consistently maintained by a succession of mostly able jurists who also were individuals of exemplary personal demeanor. There have been few scandals involving the justices, and any embarrassments the Court has suffered have been resolved openly and expeditiously. With some notable exceptions, the political affinities of the justices have been more implicit than overt.

But to some extent the Court's sacrosanct image is also more apparent than real. The Court has no public relations mechanism as such; the long-standing internal traditions of the institution effectively serve that function. The secrecy of its deliberations, in particular, protects the justices from disclosure of any of the fractiousness or ineptitude that certainly must occur from time to time. The elaborate courtesy and obeisance to seniority on the Court also serve its image as an august deliberative body aloof from contentious bickering and disharmony. Its imposing headquarters, the "marble palace," has erased the memory of the many years during which the justices were shunted from one "mean and dingy" makeshift office to another.

The image notwithstanding, the Court as a bureaucracy and administrative body continues to face many workaday challenges. These challenges involve matters much more pressing than the mere operation and upkeep of the Court itself. Most important, the Court must select which cases to review. Between 1975 and 2002 the number of new cases filed in federal district courts rose from 160,602 to 344,546, and thus it is from this mountain of work that the Supreme Court is expected to cull the legal issues most worthy of its judgment. The Court's own docket also has been steadily climbing for the past quarter-century. By 2002 over 8,000 petitions for review were presented to the Court each year.[1]

So the august tribunal of justices is also, by necessity, a beleaguered bureaucracy that must decide how to allocate its resources. Chief Justice Warren E. Burger was a forceful, if unsuccessful, advocate of finding a solution to the problem of the Court's mushrooming workload. In remarks to the sixtieth annual meeting of the American Law Institute in May 1983, Burger recalled that

> in the 1920s, one of the Justices wrote . . . that he dreaded the thought of returning to the Court and having to cope with the weeks' burden of argued cases and in addition as many as 12 or 14 petitions for certiorari. . . . I wonder what that worthy gentleman would have thought of a conference list which every week contains more than 100 items! When we look at these Supreme Court figures . . . the increase in the docket . . . one must be forgiven for being puzzled by the irrational, unreasoning resistance we encounter to making any change in the system. We remember the tale of the farm boy who had acquired a new pony and vowed . . . he would increase his own strength by lifting that pony every morning. He did so for a long time, but obviously there came a day when the boy could no longer carry out his promise. Lifting a horse of 1,000 or 2,000 pounds . . . presents an unmanageable problem. Just when the bar and Congress will discover what the little boy discovered remains to be seen.

Chief Justice Rehnquist voiced similar concerns in 1996 about the steady stream of laws federalizing crimes long thought to be matters of concern only to the states. In a speech to an audience

843

at American University's centennial celebration of its law school, Rehnquist recalled:

> Forty-some years ago when I began the practice of law in Arizona, there were not many federal criminal statutes on the books. There were some very esoteric crimes, but the staple of the criminal business of federal courts outside of the metropolitan areas was confined to prosecutions for transporting a stolen car in interstate commerce, using the mails for interstate communications to commit fraud, and a very few other similar crimes. But that landscape has entirely changed in the last forty years. Congress, understandably concerned with the increasing trafficking of drugs and the violence resulting from the use of guns, has legislated again and again to make what once were only state crimes federal offenses. The same sort of dissatisfaction with state treatment of the cases in this area of the law has obtained as obtained earlier with welfare legislation and civil rights laws.

The result, lamented the chief justice, is an ever-increasing wave of litigation before the Supreme Court and federal courts of appeals. The Constitution makes the Supreme Court the final arbiter in "cases" and "controversies" arising under the Constitution or the laws of the United States. As the interpreter of the law, the Court is often viewed as the least mutable and most tradition-bound of the three branches of the federal government. Yet the Supreme Court, now into its third century, has undergone innumerable changes. A few of these changes have been mandated by law. Almost all of them, however, were made because members of the Court felt such changes would provide a more efficient or a more equitable way of dealing with the Court's responsibilities. Some of the changes are embodied in Court rules; others are informal adaptations to needs and circumstances.

THE SCHEDULE OF THE TERM

The Court's annual schedule reflects both continuity and change. During its formal annual sessions, certain times are set aside for oral argument, for conferences, for writing opinions, and for announcing decisions. Because of the ever-increasing number of petitions arriving at the Court each year, the justices are confronted with a tremendous—some say excessive—amount of work during the regular term, which now lasts nine months.

Their work does not end when the session is finished, however. During the summer recess, the justices receive new cases to consider. About a fourth of the applications for review filed during the term are read by the justices and their law clerks during the summer interim.

Annual Terms

By law, the Supreme Court begins its regular annual term on the first Monday in October.[2] The regular session, known as the October term, lasts nine months. The summer recess, which is not determined by statute or Court rules, generally begins in late June or early July of the next year, just after the Court has

taken action on the last case argued before it during the term. The Court's growing caseload has resulted in longer terms. For example, in 1955 the Court began its summer recess on June 6, while in the mid-1990s it did not recess until the last week of June each term.

Until 1979 the Court actually adjourned its session when the summer recess began. The adjournment occurred when the chief justice announced in open court, "All cases submitted and all business before the Court at this term in readiness for disposition having been disposed of, it is ordered by this Court that all cases on the docket be, and they are hereby, continued to the next term." Since 1979, however, the Court has been in continuous session throughout the year, marked by periodic recesses; the October 1994 term, for example, did not adjourn until the first Monday in October 1995 when the new term began. This system makes it unnecessary to convene a special term to deal with matters arising in the summer.[3]

Over the years the annual sessions of the Court have been changed several times. During the first decade of its existence, 1790–1801, the Court met twice a year, in February and August. The justices had few cases during these years, and the early sessions were devoted largely to organization and discussions of lawyers' qualifications. The first case did not reach the Court until 1791; the first formal opinion was not handed down until 1792, in the Court's third year.

Despite the dearth of casework during the early semiannual sessions, the chief justice and five associate justices had enough to do. The Judiciary Act of 1789, in addition to mandating the February and August sessions, required the justices to travel through the country to preside over the circuit courts—a time-consuming task that continued, except for a brief period, until circuit riding was finally abolished in 1891 and circuit courts of appeal were established.

The Judiciary Act of 1801 called for Court terms beginning in June and December. The Judiciary Act of 1802 restored the February term of the Court but not the August term, which resulted in a fourteen-month adjournment—from December 1801 until February 1803.

At the beginning of the 1827 term, Congress changed the opening day of the new term to the second Monday in January. This change was made to give the justices more time to ride their circuits.

The opening day of the term was changed to the second Monday in December by an act of June 17, 1844. By this statute, wrote Supreme Court historian Charles Warren, the justices "were relieved of holding more than one Term of the Circuit Court within any District of such Circuit, in any one year. The result of this provision was to enable the Court to sit later each spring in Washington; and in alternate years thereafter it made a practice of sitting through March, adjourning through April and sitting again in May."[4]

An act of January 24, 1873, moved the beginning of the term from the first Monday in December to the second Monday in

October. Since 1917 terms have begun on the first Monday in October.

Special Sessions

The statute and rule covering the annual session of the Court also permit the justices to hold special terms after the regular session is over. Special sessions are called to deal with urgent matters that cannot be postponed until the next session.

There have been few special sessions in the Court's history; it has been far more common for the Court to consider important cases that arise toward the end of the term simply by delaying the end of the regular term until action is completed. Only four cases have been decided in special session:[5]

• *Ex parte Quirin.* The Court convened a special term on July 29, 1942; heard arguments on July 29 and July 30; and on July 31 upheld a military court's conviction of a group of Nazi saboteurs smuggled ashore from a German submarine. A formal opinion in the case was released on October 29, 1942.

• *Rosenberg v. United States.* Three days after the end of the October 1952 term, on June 18, 1953, the Supreme Court convened a special term to consider a stay of execution ordered by Justice William O. Douglas for Ethel and Julius Rosenberg, convicted of divulging information about the atomic bomb to the Soviet Union. Arguments were heard on June 18, and the Court vacated the stay on June 19. The Rosenbergs were executed that day. The Court's opinion in the case was released on July 16, 1953.[6]

• *Cooper v. Aaron.* In a special session convened on August 28, 1958, the Court unanimously upheld a lower-court order enforcing a desegregation plan for Central High School in Little Rock, Arkansas. The order was opposed by state officials. The Court heard arguments on August 28 and September 11 and issued its decision on September 12. City schools were to open in Little Rock on September 15, but Gov. Orval Faubus closed them after the Court's decision. A formal opinion in the case was released on September 29, 1958.[7]

• *O'Brien v. Brown.* The Court convened a special session on July 6, 1972, to consider the seating of delegates from California and Illinois at the Democratic National Convention, which was to open on July 10. On July 7 the Court decided, 6–3, to return the California and Illinois cases to the convention and to let the convention rather than the Court decide the matter.[8]

• *McConnell v. Federal Election Commission.* When Congress passed the Bipartisan Campaign Reform Act in 2002, it urged the Court to review speedily its many changes in the laws that govern federal elections. The measure, known popularly as the McCain-Feingold Act for its sponsors Sen. John McCain, R-Ariz., and Russell Feingold, D-Wis., prohibited political parties from raising and spending money from corporations and unions. On September 8, 2003, the Court heard four hours of oral argument on the issue.

• On December 10 the Court, by 5–4, upheld the heart of the McCain-Feingold law. Justices John Paul Stevens and Sandra Day O'Connor, writing for the Court, said Congress had the power to stop the flow of unregulated "soft money" to the political parties and for campaign-style ads. They rejected a First Amendment challenge to the law, saying the money limits will have only a "marginal impact" on free expression, since all persons remained free to give $2,000 to the federal candidate of their choice. The case was named *McConnell v. Federal Election Commission* after its lead plaintiff, Sen. Mitch McConnell, R-Ky., who had battled McCain and Feingold for years in the Senate.[9]

Among the decisions made by the modern Court after postponing adjournment of the regular term, the most famous is *United States v. Nixon.* In that case the Court on July 24, 1974, unanimously denied President Richard Nixon's claim of absolute executive privilege to withhold documents requested by the Watergate special prosecutor.

Other important decisions delivered after delaying adjournment include *Wilson v. Girard,* handed down on July 11, 1957; *New York Times v. United States, United States v. Washington Post,* June 30, 1971; and *Dames and Moore v. Regan,* July 2, 1981. The first case involved an earlier stage of the Little Rock school desegregation case; the second rebuffed the effort by the Nixon administration to bar publication of the Pentagon Papers; and the third resolved a major challenge to the agreements with which President Jimmy Carter had won release of American hostages by Iran.[10]

Opening Day

Opening day ceremonies of the new term have changed considerably since the Court first met on February 1, 1790. Chief Justice Jay was forced to postpone the first formal session for a day because some of the justices were unable to reach New York City—at that time the nation's capital and home of the Court. It began proceedings the next day in a crowded courtroom but with an empty docket.

From 1917 to 1975, when the annual session began on the first Monday in October, the opening day and week were spent in conference. The justices discussed cases that had not been disposed of during the previous term and some of the petitions that had reached the Court during the summer recess. The decisions made during this initial conference on which cases to accept for oral argument were announced on the second Monday of October.

At the beginning of the October 1975 term, this practice was changed. That year the justices reassembled for this initial conference during the last week in September. When the justices convened formally on Monday, October 6, 1975, oral arguments began.

Schedule of Arguments and Conferences

At least four justices must request that a case be argued before it can be approved for a hearing. Until 1955 the Court often heard oral arguments five days a week. Friday arguments were excluded when the Court's conference was moved to that day. Arguments are now heard on Monday, Tuesday, and Wednesday for seven two-week sessions, beginning in the first week in October and ending in the last week of April. The two-week sessions are separated by two-week or longer recesses during which the justices consider the cases and deal with other Court business.

Since the early 1800s, when justices heard arguments from eleven in the morning until four or five in the afternoon, the schedule for hearing arguments has been changed several times to achieve a more manageable daily calendar. The present schedule for oral arguments, 10 a.m. to noon and 1 p.m. to 3 p.m., began during the 1969 term. Because most cases receive one hour apiece for argument, the Court could hear twelve cases a week. By the mid-1990s, however, the Court was hearing only about half that number, not because of time constraints but because the justices were granting fewer petitions for review.

Under a rule of the Court adopted on March 12, 1849, the time provided for oral argument had been limited to two hours—one hour for each side. Cases that the Court felt could be covered in a shorter period were placed on a "summary calendar," under which arguments were limited to a half-hour for each side. That practice was revived during the 1940s, and a one-hour argument became the current limit in 1970. Exceptions to the hour-per-case time limit must be sought and granted before arguments begin.

In the Court's early years, conferences were often held in the evenings or on weekends, sometimes in the common boardinghouse the justices shared. The number of cases for which review was sought and the cases awaiting a final decision determined when and how often conferences were held. Later, Saturday was set aside as the regular conference day. Under a 1955 Court order that ended Friday oral arguments, Friday became conference day.

Until 1975 the Court held its first conferences during opening week, after its formal call to order on the first Monday in October. To streamline the procedure, the justices began meeting in the last week in September, before the official convening of the annual session. At its initial conference, the Court attempts to resolve leftover matters—appeals, petitions for certiorari, and so forth—from the previous session. The September conference allows the Court to announce its orders on these matters by opening day rather than a week after the formal convening.

In 1993 the justices began the practice of releasing the initial orders list of the term—announcing which cases they had accepted for oral argument—shortly after they completed their first conference in late September. This practice broke with the notion of opening the Court's term on the first Monday in October. Under the new schedule, the first major action of the new Court term is the announcement in late September of new cases to be heard. However, the first public session of the Court, and its opening round of arguments, still occurs on the first Monday in October.

During its term, the Court holds conferences each Friday during the weeks when arguments are heard, and on the Friday just before the two-week oral argument periods. To reduce the workload of its Friday sessions, the Court also holds Wednesday conferences during the weeks when oral arguments are scheduled.

At the conferences the justices consider cases heard in oral argument during the preceding week and resolve other business before the Court. Prior to each of the Friday conferences, the chief justice circulates a "discuss list"—a list of cases deemed important enough for discussion and a vote. Other justices are free to add cases to the chief's "discuss list." Appeals (of which there are now only a small number) are placed on the discuss list almost automatically, but as many as three-quarters of the petitions for certiorari are summarily denied a place on the list and simply disappear. No case is denied review during conference, however, without an initial examination by the justices and their law clerks. Any one of the justices can have a case placed on the Court's conference agenda for review. Most of the cases scheduled for the discuss list are also denied review in the end, but only after discussion by the justices during the conference.

Although the last oral arguments have been heard by late April or early May of each year, the Friday and Monday conferences of the justices continue until the end of the term to consider cases remaining on the Court's agenda.

All conferences are held in strict secrecy, with no legal assistants or staff present. The attendance of six justices constitutes a quorum. Conferences begin with handshakes all around. In discussing a case, the chief justice speaks first, followed by each justice in order of seniority.

Decision Days and Orders Days

In the Court's earliest years, decisions were announced whenever they were ready, with no formal schedule for making them known. The tradition of announcing decisions on Monday—"Decision Monday"—began in 1857, apparently without any formal announcement or rule to that effect. This practice continued until the Court said on April 5, 1965, that "commencing the week of April 26, 1965, it will no longer adhere to the practice of reporting its decisions only at Monday sessions and that in the future they will be reported as they become ready for decision at any session of the Court." [11]

At present, opinions are released mostly on Tuesdays and Wednesdays during the weeks that the Court is hearing oral arguments; during other weeks they are released on Mondays along with the orders.

Like the announcement of opinions, the day for release of the Court's "orders list"—the summary of the Court's action granting or denying review—has changed over the years. During the nineteenth century, the Court's summary orders were often announced on Friday, which was called "Motion Day." The practice of posting orders on Monday evolved gradually.

During the first three months of the 1971 term, orders were announced on Tuesday, but on January 10, 1972, Monday was reinstated as the day for posting orders. When urgent or important matters arise, the Court's summary orders may be announced on a day other than Monday. And when the last oral arguments of the term have been presented, the Court may release decisions and written opinions, as well as the orders list, on Mondays.

At present, the orders list is released at the beginning of the Monday session. It is not announced orally, but can be obtained from the clerk and the public information officer.

Unlike its orders, decisions of the Court are announced orally in open court. The justice who wrote the opinion announces the Court's decision, and justices writing concurring or dissenting opinions may state their views as well. When more than one decision is to be rendered, the justices who wrote the opinion make their announcements in reverse order of seniority. Typically, the justice who is the author of the Court's opinion will summarize the decision and read a portion of the opinion. On occasion, a dissenting justice will follow with a part of his or her reasons for disagreeing with the majority.

REVIEWING CASES

In determining whether to accept a case for review, the Court has considerable discretion, subject only to the restraints imposed by the Constitution and Congress. Article III, section 2, of the Constitution states: "In all Cases affecting Ambassadors, other public Ministers and Consuls, and those in which a State shall be Party, the Supreme Court shall have original jurisdiction. In all the other Cases . . . the Supreme Court shall have appellate Jurisdiction, both as to Law and Fact, with such Exceptions, and under such Regulations as the Congress shall make."

Original jurisdiction refers to the right of the Supreme Court to hear a case before any other court does. Appellate jurisdiction is the right to review the decision of a lower court. The vast majority of cases reaching the Supreme Court are appeals from rulings of the lower courts; generally only a handful of original jurisdiction cases are filed each term.

After Congress enacted the Judiciary Act of 1925, the Supreme Court had broad discretion to decide for itself what cases it would hear. Since Congress in 1988 virtually eliminated the Court's mandatory jurisdiction through which it was obliged to hear most appeals, that discretion has been nearly unlimited.[12]

Methods of Appeal

Cases come to the Supreme Court in several ways—through petitions for writs of certiorari, appeals, and requests for certification. In petitioning for a writ of certiorari, a litigant who has lost a case in a lower court sets out the reasons why the Supreme Court should review his or her case. If it is granted, the Court requests a certified record of the case from the lower court. Supreme Court rules state:

> Whenever the Court grants a petition for a writ of certiorari, the Clerk will prepare, sign, and enter an order to that effect and will

notify forthwith counsel of record and the court whose judgment is to be reviewed. The case then will be scheduled for briefing and oral argument. If the record has not previously been filed in this Court, the Clerk will request the clerk of the court having possession of the record to certify and transmit it. A formal writ will not issue unless specially directed.[13]

The main difference between the certiorari and appeal routes is that the Court has complete discretion to grant a request for a writ of certiorari, but is under an obligation to accept and decide a case that comes to it on appeal. *(See "Federal Jurisdiction," pp. 279–290.)*

Most cases reach the Supreme Court by means of the writ of certiorari. In the relatively few cases to reach the Court by means of appeal, the appellant must file a jurisdictional statement explaining why his or her case qualifies for review and why the Court should grant it a hearing. With increasing frequency in recent years, the justices have been disposing of these cases by deciding them summarily, without oral argument or formal opinion.

Those whose petitions for certiorari have been granted by the Court must pay a $300 fee for placement of the case on the Court's docket. The U.S. government does not have to pay this fee, nor do persons too poor to afford it. The latter may file an *in forma pauperis* (in the character or manner of a pauper) petition. The law governing *in forma pauperis* proceedings states:

> [A]ny court of the United States may authorize the commencement, prosecution or defense of any suit, action or proceeding, civil or criminal, or appeal therein, without prepayment of fees and costs or security therefor, by a person who makes affidavit that he is unable to pay such costs or give security therefor. Such affidavit shall state the nature of the action, defense or appeal and affiant's belief that he is entitled to redress. . . . An appeal may not be taken in forma pauperis if the trial court certifies in writing that it is not taken in good faith.[14]

Another, but seldom used, method of appeal is certification, the request by a court of appeals for a final answer to questions of law in a particular case. The Supreme Court, after examining the certificate, may order the case argued before it.

Process of Review

Each year the Court is asked to review about eight thousand cases. All petitions are examined by the clerk of the Court and his staff; those found to be in reasonably proper form are placed on the docket and given a number. Before 1970 there were two dockets: an appellate docket for petitions for certiorari and appeals in cases where the docketing fee was paid, and a miscellaneous docket for *in forma pauperis* petitions and appeals and other requests not qualifying for the appellate docket. When a case on the miscellaneous docket was accepted for review, it was transferred to the appellate docket and renumbered.

Since 1970 all cases except those falling within the Court's original jurisdiction are placed on a single docket, known simply as "the docket." Only in the numbering of the cases is a distinction made between prepaid and *in forma pauperis* cases on the docket. Beginning with the 1971 term, prepaid cases were labeled with the year and the number. The first case filed in 1995, for example, would have been designated 95-1. *In forma pauperis* cases contain the year and begin with the number 5001. The second *in forma pauperis* case filed in 1995 would be number 95-5002.[15]

Cases on the original docket were unaffected by the 1970 revision. The original docket remains separate and distinct, but cases on it that are carried over to the next term are no longer renumbered; they retain the docket numbers assigned to them when they were filed.

Each justice, aided by his or her law clerks, is responsible for reviewing all cases on the dockets. Since the late 1970s, some justices have used a "cert pool" system in this review. Their clerks work together to examine cases, writing a pool memo on several petitions. The memo is then given to the justices who determine if more research is needed. (Some of the other justices have preferred to use a system in which they or their clerks review each petition themselves.)

Justice Douglas called the review of cases on the dockets "in many respects the most important and interesting of all our functions." Others apparently have found it time-consuming and tedious, and they support the cert pool as a mechanism to reduce the burden on the justices and their staffs. After the retirement of Justice William J. Brennan in 1990, Justice John Paul Stevens was the only one of the nine sitting justices who did not use the cert pool.

The delegation of power to the clerks has raised a few eyebrows, as Chief Justice Rehnquist acknowledged in his 1987 book *The Supreme Court: How It Was, How It Is*:

> Recently I was asked whether or not the use of law clerks in a cert pool didn't represent the abandonment of the justices' responsibilities to a sort of internal bureaucracy. I certainly do not think so. The individual justices are of course quite free to disregard whatever recommendation the writer of the pool memo may have made, as well as the recommendation of his own law clerks, but this is not a complete answer to the criticism. It is one thing to do the work yourself, and it is another thing to simply approve the recommendation of another person who has done the work. But the decision as to whether to grant certiorari is a much more "channeled" decision than the decision as to how a case should be decided on the merits; there are really only two or three factors comprised in the certiorari decision—conflict with other courts, general importance, and perception that the decision is wrong in the light of Supreme Court precedent. Each of these factors is one that a well-trained law clerk is capable of evaluating, and the justices, of course, having been in the certiorari-granting business term after term, are quite familiar with many of the issues that come up.[16]

Petitions on the docket vary from elegantly printed and bound documents, of which multiple copies are submitted to the Court, to single sheets of prison stationery scribbled in pencil and filled with grammatical and spelling errors. All are considered by the justices, however, in the process of deciding which merit review.

To Grant or Deny Review: The Discuss List and the Orders List

The decisions to grant or deny review of cases are made in conferences, which are held in the conference room adjacent to the chief justice's chambers. Justices are summoned to the conference room by a buzzer, usually between 9:30 and 10 a.m. They shake hands with each other, take their appointed seats, and the chief justice begins the discussion.

A few days before the conference convenes, the chief justice compiles a "discuss list"—a list of cases deemed important enough for discussion and a vote. As many as three-quarters of the petitions for certiorari are denied a place on the list and thus rejected without further consideration. Any justice can have a case placed on the discuss list simply by requesting that it be placed there.

Conferences are held in strict secrecy: only the justices attend, and no legal assistants or staff are present. The junior associate justice acts as doorkeeper and messenger, sending for reference material and receiving messages and data at the door. The secrecy has worked well; unlike other parts of the federal government, there have been very few leaks about what transpires during the conferences. (*See box, Leaks at the Court, p. 825.*)

At the start of the conference, the chief justice makes a brief statement outlining the facts of each case. Then each justice, beginning with the senior associate justice, comments on the case, usually indicating in the course of the comments how he or she intends to vote. A traditional but unwritten rule specifies that four affirmative votes are needed to schedule a case for oral argument.

Petitions for certiorari, appeal, and *in forma pauperis* that are approved for review or denied review during conference are placed on a certified orders list to be released the following Monday in open court.

ARGUMENTS

Once the Court announces it will hear a case, the clerk of the Court arranges the schedule for oral argument. Generally, cases are argued roughly in the order in which they were granted review, but that is subject to change, in the light of availability of appendices and other documents, extensions of time to file briefs, and other relevant factors. Cases generally are heard not sooner than three months after the Court has agreed to review them. Under special circumstances, the date scheduled for oral argument can be advanced or postponed.

Well before oral argument takes place, the justices receive the briefs and records from counsel in the case. The measure of attention the brief receives—from a thorough and exhaustive study to a cursory glance—depends both on the nature of the case and the work habits of the justice.

As one of the two public functions of the Court, oral arguments are viewed by some as very important. Others dispute their significance, contending that by the time a case is heard most of the justices have already made up their minds.

THE "RULE OF FOUR"

In 1925 Congress gave the Supreme Court broad discretion over the decision to review or deny review in most of the cases brought to its attention. The Court has adopted certain rules to guide the exercise of this discretion. One is the "Rule of Four"—a case is accepted for review only if four justices feel that it merits the Court's full consideration. Since 1925 that rule has governed decisions to grant or deny review through use of the writ of certiorari.

More formal and official is the portion of the Rules of the Supreme Court of the United States that states:

Review on a writ of certiorari is not a matter of right, but of judicial discretion. A petition for writ of certiorari will be granted only for compelling reasons. The following, although neither controlling nor fully measuring the Court's discretion, indicate the character of the reasons the Court considers:

• a United States court of appeals has entered a decision in conflict with the decision of another United States court of appeals on the same important matter; has decided an important federal question in a way that conflicts with a decision by a state court of last resort; or has so far departed from the accepted and usual course of judicial proceedings, or sanctioned such a departure by a lower court, as to call for an exercise of this Court's supervisory power;

• a state court of last resort has decided an important federal question in a way that conflicts with the decision of another state court of last resort or of a United States court of appeals;

• a state court or United States court of appeals has decided an important question of federal law that has not been, but should be, settled by this Court, or has decided an important federal question in a way that conflicts with relevant decisions of this Court.

A petition for a writ of certiorari is rarely granted when the asserted error consists of erroneous factual findings or the misapplication of a properly stated rule of law.

SOURCE: Rule 10 of the Rules of the Supreme Court of the United States, adopted July 26, 1995; effective October 2, 1995.

Some justices have indicated that oral arguments serve a useful purpose. Chief Justice Charles Evans Hughes wrote that "the desirability . . . of a full exposition by oral argument in the highest court is not to be gainsaid" because it provides "a great saving of time of the court in the examination of extended records and briefs, to obtain the grasp of the case that is made possible by oral discussion and to be able more quickly to separate the wheat from the chaff."[17]

In 1967 Justice William J. Brennan Jr. said, "Oral argument is the absolute indispensable ingredient of appellate advocacy. Often my whole notion of what a case is about crystallizes at oral argument. This happens even though I read the briefs before oral argument."[18]

Chief Justice Rehnquist has on occasion questioned the value of oral arguments, but he nevertheless has said, "I think that in a significant minority of the cases in which I have heard oral argument, I have left the bench feeling different about the case than I did when I came on the bench. The change is seldom a full one-hundred-and-eighty-degree swing, and I find that it is most likely to occur in cases involving areas of law with which I am least familiar."[19]

Time Limits

Like many other aspects of the Court's operations, the time allotted for oral arguments, as well as the atmosphere in which arguments were heard, have undergone considerable change over the years. In the early years of the Court, arguments in a single case often would continue for days.

For the spectators who crowded the courtroom, oral arguments provided high entertainment. In the nineteenth century, women in Washington flocked to hear the popular and dashing Henry Clay argue before the Court. Arguments at least once were adjourned so that counsel could sober up. John P. Frank reported that one time a case was reargued so that a late-arriving woman could hear the part she had missed.[20]

The increasing number of cases heard by the Court made the continuation of such practices impossible. Under a rule the Court adopted on March 12, 1849, counsel was allowed no more than two hours to present his argument. The two-hour allowance for oral argument continued until the early twentieth century. In between his terms on the Court, Charles Evans Hughes wrote in 1928:

In the early period when cases were few, the Court could permit extended argument. At a more recent time, and until a few years ago, two hours was the regular allowance to each side and in very important cases, that time was extended. This allowance has been reduced to an hour, unless special permission is granted, and even in cases of great importance the Court has refused to hear arguments for more than an hour and a half on each side. This restriction is due to the crowded calendar of the Court.[21]

In 1970 the time allowed each side for oral argument was reduced from one hour to thirty minutes to save the Court's time. Since the time allotted must accommodate any questions the justices may wish to ask, the actual time for presentation may be considerably shorter than thirty minutes.

Under the current rules of the Court, as revised in 1995, only one counsel is heard for each side, except by special permission when there are several parties on the same side and additional time has been granted. When cases were allowed one hour per party, the Court allowed two counsel to be heard for each side. Generally, the Court does not favor divided arguments.

An exception is made for an amicus curiae—a person who volunteers or is invited to take part in matters before a court but is not a party in the case. Counsel for an amicus curiae may participate in oral argument if the party supported by the amicus allows him or her to use part of its argument time or the Court grants a motion allowing argument by counsel for the "friend of the court." The motion must show, the rules state, that the amicus's argument "would provide assistance to the Court not otherwise available."[22]

Because the Court is reluctant to extend the time that each side is given for oral argument and because amicus curiae participation in oral argument would often necessitate such an extension, the Court is generally unreceptive to such motions. And counsel in a case is usually equally unreceptive to a request to give an amicus counsel any of the precious minutes allotted to argue the case.

Court rules provide advice to counsel appearing before the justices: "Oral argument should emphasize and clarify the written arguments in the briefs on the merits. Counsel should assume that all Justices have read the briefs before oral argument. Oral argument read from a prepared text is not favored."[23] On rare occasions, justices have been known to interrupt an attorney reading from a prepared text and call his attention to the rule. Most attorneys appearing before the Court use an outline or notes to make sure they cover the important points.

Recording the Argument

The Supreme Court has tape-recorded oral arguments since 1955. In 1968 the Court, in addition to its own recording, began contracting with private firms to tape and transcribe all oral arguments. The contract stipulates that the transcript "shall include everything spoken in argument, by Court, counsel, or others, and nothing shall be omitted from the transcript unless the Chief Justice or Presiding Justice so directs." But "the names of Justices asking questions shall not be recorded or transcribed; questions shall be indicated by the letter 'Q.'"[24]

The marshal of the Court keeps the Court's tape during the term when oral arguments are presented. During that time use of these tapes is usually limited to the justices and their law clerks. However, a transcribed copy of the argument is usually available from the Court or on its web site two weeks after the case is heard. At the end of the term, the tapes are sent to the National Archives. In 1993 the Court announced that the audio tapes would be available to the public on a generally unrestricted basis. They can be purchased from the National Archives.

The Court's handling of *Bush v. Gore*, the presidential election cases in December 2000, did not set a true legal precedent because, as the justices explained, the issues of a recount in a presidential race were extraordinary and unlikely to recur. However, the extraordinary interest in the case helped to set a new precedent for public transmission of the Court's argument. The justices voted to release an audio tape of the oral arguments in the Florida election cases immediately after the session.

A CROWDED DOCKET, FEWER DECISIONS, AND A CONTINUING DEBATE

The Supreme Court sits atop the nation's court system. For parties who lose in the lower court, it is the final stop. They may appeal all the way up the Supreme Court, as many disgruntled losers vow to do. But the justices are not obliged or expected to review and decide every case that comes through the courts. Instead, their duty is to decide legal questions and to resolve disputes over the meaning of the U.S. Constitution and federal laws. Unlike other judges on lower courts, the justices of the Supreme Court are free to choose which cases they will decide. Those key facts explain a persistent trend in the docket. While the number of cases reaching the Court steadily increases, the number of written decisions has remained steady, or shrunk.

After Warren E. Burger replaced Earl Warren as chief justice in 1969, the number of cases heard by the Court rose steadily. Burger presided over a fractured Court whose justices bitterly disagreed on many constitutional issues. By the early 1980s they were hearing and deciding more than 150 cases per term, nearly double the workload during the Warren era. A frustrated Burger said it was perhaps time to create a new, midlevel appeals court to resolve disputes before they reached the Supreme Court.

When William H. Rehnquist replaced Burger in 1986, he soon found a solution to the overwork problem: take fewer cases. In the Court's conferences, Rehnquist stressed the need to resolve significant issues of law, not to reconsider every case that was decided wrongly in the lower courts. Several thousand persons each year file a petition for a writ of certiorari—a formal plea asking the Court to review the case. Law clerks review each one and write a memo describing the legal issue being appealed.

"The great majority of petitions for certiorari are never even discussed at conference and are simply denied without being taken up by the justices as a group," Rehnquist wrote. "There are really two or three factors involved in the certiorari decision—conflict with other courts, general importance and perception that the decision is wrong in the light of Supreme Court precedent." Unless the appeal petition raises an important, unresolved issue, the Court is not interested in considering it, he said.[1] The number of decisions with written opinions fell steadily, from 145 in 1987, the first year of the Rehnquist Court, to 112 in 1990, 82 in 1995, and 77 in 2000. By then the Court had settled on a pattern of deciding between 75 and 80 cases per term with a written opinion.

All the while, the number of cases appealed to the Court continued its inexorable rise. Most of them were from prison inmates who, with lots of time and nothing to lose, petitioned the Court to review their cases. Typically, inmates are permitted to file their appeals as paupers and therefore need not pay the $300 fee for filing a case. In 1950, 1,321 cases reached the Court docket; in 1960, 2,296; in 1970, 4,212; in 1980, 4,781; in 1990, 6,316; and in 2000, 8,965. Of the latter, 6,651—about three-fourths of the total—were appeals from indigents who could not pay the filing fee.

1. *The Supreme Court* (New York: Vintage Book, Random House, 2001), 235.

In 2003 the Court gave the public immediate access to the audio tape of the oral arguments in the pair of affirmative action cases from the University of Michigan that were heard in April and in the campaign finance cases that were heard in September.

The OYEZ Project, with funding from the National Science Foundation and National Endowment for the Humanities as well as private grants, has digitized over two thousand hours of Supreme Court oral arguments. Selections in the collection are available at www.oyez.org. All cases recorded since 1995 are available, as well as a selective list of cases before 1995.

Use of Briefs

The Supreme Court rules state that "Counsel should assume that all Justices have read the briefs before oral argument."[25] In 1960 Justice Brennan wrote that

> most of the members of the present Court follow the practice of reading the briefs before argument. Some of us, and I am one, often have a bench memorandum prepared before argument. This memorandum digests the facts and the arguments of both sides, highlighting the matters about which I may want to question counsel at the argument. Often I have an independent research made in advance of argument and incorporate the results in the bench memorandum.[26]

Nevertheless, an attorney cannot be sure that all the justices will devote such attention to his brief. If the brief has been thoroughly digested by the justices, the attorney can use his or her arguments to highlight certain elements. But if it has been merely scanned—and perhaps largely forgotten—in the interval between the reading and the oral argument, the attorney will want to go into considerable detail about the nature of the case and the facts involved. Many lawyers therefore prepare their argument on the assumption that the justices know relatively little about their particular case but are well-acquainted with the general principles of relevant law.

Except for *in forma pauperis* cases, the petitioner or appellant must file forty copies of the brief within forty-five days of the Court's announced decision to hear the case. For *in forma pauperis* proceedings, the party must file one typed copy with the clerk and send one typed copy to each of the other parties in the case. The opposing brief from the respondent or appellee is to be filed within thirty days of receipt of the brief of the petitioner or appellant. Either party may appeal to the clerk for an extension of time in filing the brief.

The form and organization of the brief are covered by Rules 33 and 34 of the Court. The rules limit the number of pages in briefs, specifying that the major brief in a case, the brief on the merits, should not exceed fifty pages. Separately, Rule 24 gives general guidance on briefs, stating that they "shall be concise, logically arranged with proper headings, and free of irrelevant, immaterial, or scandalous matter. The Court may disregard or strike a brief that does not comply with this paragraph."[27]

In a 1974 case, for example, the Court declared that one party's brief did not comply with Court rules with respect to conciseness, statement of questions without unnecessary detail, and printing of appendices. Accordingly, the Court directed counsel to file a brief complying with the rules within twenty days.[28]

Rule 24 sets forth the elements that a brief should contain. These are: the questions presented for review; a list of all parties to the proceeding; a table of contents and table of authorities; citations to the opinions and judgments delivered in the courts below; "a concise statement of the basis for jurisdiction

Throughout much of the Court's history the justices have felt burdened by a heavy caseload, as depicted in this 1885 *Puck* cartoon.

in this Court"; constitutional provisions, treaties, statutes, ordinances, and regulations involved; "a concise statement of the case, setting out the facts material to the consideration of the questions presented"; a summary of argument; the argument, "exhibiting clearly the points of fact and of law being presented and citing the authorities and statutes relied on"; and a conclusion "specifying with particularity the relief the party seeks."

The rules also set out a color code for the covers of different kinds of briefs. Petitions are white; motions opposing them are orange. Petitioner's briefs on the merits are light blue, while those of respondents are to be light red. Reply briefs are yellow; amicus curiae, green; and documents filed by the United States, gray. All other documents should have a tan cover.

Questioning

During oral argument the justices may interrupt with questions or remarks as often as they wish. In fact, in the Rehnquist Court justices' questions consume much of a counsel's allotted half-hour of argument. Unless counsel has been granted special permission extending the thirty-minute limit, he or she can continue talking after the time has expired only to complete a sentence.

The frequency of questioning, as well as the manner in which questions are asked, depends on the style of the justices and their interest in a particular case. Chief Justice Burger asked very few questions, as did Justice Brennan. Justice Clarence Thomas has gone entire terms without asking more than one or two questions. At the other extreme, Justices Antonin Scalia, Ruth Bader Ginsburg, and Stephen G. Breyer have from their first days on the bench peppered attorneys with questions.

Questions from the justices may upset and unnerve counsel by interrupting a well-rehearsed argument and introducing an unexpected element. Nevertheless, questioning has several advantages. It serves to alert counsel about what aspects of the case need further elaboration or more information. For the Court, questions can bring out weak points in an argument—and sometimes strengthen it.

In 1928 Chief Justice Hughes wrote:

> The judges of the Supreme Court are quite free in addressing questions to counsel during argument. The Bar is divided as to the wisdom of this practice in courts of last resort. Some think that as a rule the court will get at the case more quickly if counsel are permitted to present it in their own way. Well-prepared and experienced counsel, however, do not object to inquiries from the bench, if the time allowed for argument is not unduly curtailed, as they would much prefer to have the opportunity of knowing the difficulties in the minds of the court and of attempting to meet them rather than to have them concealed and presented in conference when counsel are not present. They prefer an open attack to a masked battery. From the standpoint of the bench, the desirability of questions is quite obvious as the judges are not there to listen to speeches but to decide the case. They have an irrepressible desire for immediate knowledge as to the points to be determined.[29]

It is politic for attorneys to answer the justices' questions immediately and directly. Several justices have expressed their annoyance when informed by counsel that their inquiry will be answered later in the oral argument. Justice Robert H. Jackson advised in 1951, "never . . . postpone answer to a question, for that always gives an impression of evasion. It is better immediately to answer the question, even though you do so in short form and suggest that you expect to amplify and support your answer later."[30]

Anecdotes probably tell as much about the proceedings of the Court during oral argument as does any careful study of the rules and procedures. Perhaps the most famous story concerns Chief Justice Hughes, who was a stickler for observance of the time limit for oral argument. He is reported to have informed a leader of the New York Bar that his argument was over when the lawyer was in the middle of the word "if."[31] In the 1990s Chief Justice Rehnquist was equally concerned with punctuality, halting lawyers in midsentence when their time was up. When counsel would ask if he or she could complete the thought, the answer often was a firm "no."

Rehnquist's 1987 book, which characterizes the broad range of talent that appears before the Court daily, also relates his own experience at the lectern: "My adrenaline was up, and I sat like a greyhound in the slip waiting for my chance to begin. After the one argument I made before the Supreme Court of the United States when I was an assistant attorney general in the Justice Department, I was drenched with sweat."[32]

In the late nineteenth century when arguments went on for a full day, the justices occasionally left to have lunch behind a curtain in back of the bench when argument was particularly lengthy and inconsequential. Argument proceeded without the justices and amidst a clatter of china.[33] Justice Felix Frankfurter was renowned for treating counsel, as well as his fellow justices, much as he had his students when he was a professor. This annoyed many lawyers presenting arguments and was resented by other justices who complained about Frankfurter's professorial questioning and his pedantic, if erudite, lectures.[34] Justice Douglas was known to write opinions or articles during the presentation of oral argument.[35]

CONFERENCES

Cases on which oral argument has been heard are discussed in conference. During the Wednesday afternoon conference, the cases that were argued the previous Monday are discussed and decided. At the Friday conference, the cases argued on the preceding Tuesday and Wednesday are discussed and decided. These conferences also consider new motions, appeals, and petitions.

Conferences are conducted in complete secrecy. No secretaries, clerks, stenographers, or messengers are allowed into the room. This practice began many years ago when the justices became convinced that there was a leak, a premature report of a

On Mondays and Wednesdays when the Court is in session, the justices meet in this conference room to discuss cases on which oral argument has been heard and to consider new motions, appeals, and petitions.

decision. Suspicion focused on two page boys who waited upon the justices in the conference room. Despite the fact that the pages were later cleared when a member of the bar confessed that he had merely made an educated guess about the Court's decision in a particular case, conferences have since been attended only by the justices themselves. In 1979 the substance of an opinion—and even the identity of its author—were correctly reported in the press several days before its announcement. A typesetter assigned to the Court was then reassigned. *(See Inside the Conference Room, p. 861.)*

In the Court's early years conferences were held in the Washington boardinghouses in which the justices resided. The justices now meet in an elegant, oak-paneled, book-lined conference chamber adjacent to the chief justice's suite. Nine chairs are placed around the large rectangular table, each bearing the nameplate of the justice who sits there. The chief justice sits at the east end of the table, and the senior associate justice at the west end. The other justices take their places in order of seniority. The junior justice is charged with sending for and receiving documents or other information the Court needs. Justice Tom C. Clark, the junior justice from 1949 until 1954, once remarked: "For five years, I was the highest paid doorkeeper in the world."[36] Confirmed in 1994, Justice Stephen G. Breyer set a new record in the fall of 2000 as the longest-serving junior justice in modern Court history.

On entering the conference room the justices shake hands, a symbol of harmony that began in the 1880s. The chief justice begins the conference by calling the first case to be decided and discussing it. When the chief justice is finished, the senior associate justice speaks, followed by the other justices in order of seniority.

In theory, the justices can speak for as long as they wish. Even so, Chief Justice Hughes—impatient with long and occasionally irrelevant discourses during conference—convinced the other justices to limit the time they spent discussing a case. The record of the number of cases decided during Hughes's tenure as chief justice indicates that discussion and debate of the cases were considerably curtailed. As the number of cases considered during conference has grown, later Courts have tended to follow Hughes's example.

Similarly, no one is supposed to interrupt the justice whose turn it is to speak during conference. But according to an often-repeated story, Justice Oliver Wendell Holmes Jr. did just that to Justice John Marshall Harlan early in the twentieth century. As Harlan was presenting his argument in a particular case, Holmes broke in with "That won't wash! That won't wash!" Chief Justice Melville W. Fuller allegedly relieved the tension with the remark "Well, I'm scrubbing away, anyhow."[37]

Other than these procedural arrangements, little is known about what actually transpires in conference. Although discussions generally are said to be polite and orderly, they occasionally can be acrimonious. Likewise, consideration of the issues in a particular case may be full and probing, or perfunctory, leaving the real debate on the question to go on in the written drafts of opinions circulating up and down the Court's corridors between chambers.

Generally, it is clear—and often explicit—in the discussion of the case how a justice plans to vote on it. It takes a majority vote to decide a case—five votes if all nine justices are participating.

OPINIONS

After the justices have voted on a case, the writing of the opinion or opinions begins. An opinion is a reasoned argument explaining the legal issues in the case and the precedents on which the opinion is based.

Soon after a case is decided in conference, the task of writing the majority opinion is assigned. The chief justice assigns the task in cases in which he voted in the majority. In cases in which the chief justice was in the minority, the senior associate justice voting with the majority assigns the job of writing the majority opinion.

Any justice can decide to write a separate opinion. A justice who agrees with the Court's decision but disagrees with some of the reasoning in the majority opinion may write a concurring opinion giving the reasoning. A justice who disagrees with the majority may write a dissenting opinion or simply go on record as a dissenter without an opinion. More than one justice can sign a concurring or a dissenting opinion.

The amount of time consumed between the vote on a case and the announcement of the decision varies from case to case. In simple cases where few points of law are at issue, the opinion sometimes can be written and cleared by the other justices in two or three weeks. In more complex cases, especially those with several dissenting or concurring opinions, it can take six months or more. Some cases may have to be reargued or the initial decision reversed after the drafts of opinions have been circulated.

Writing opinions is often a long and tedious process but a highly important one. The way in which a majority opinion is written can have a tremendous impact on the lives of Americans. The impact of a particular opinion depends to some extent on who writes it, how it is written, and the extent of support for or dissent from the opinion by the other justices.

In 1993, when the papers of the late Justice Thurgood Marshall were unexpectedly made public at the Library of Congress, reporters gained access to numerous private memos and drafts of decisions. The *Washington Post* described the decision-making process revealed in the papers as

> a continuing conversation among nine distinct individuals on dozens of issues simultaneously. The exchanges are serious, sometimes scholarly, occasionally brash and personalized, but generally well-reasoned and most often cast in understated, genteel language.... The months-long internal debate on a case often focuses on how much law to

change or make. Sometimes, cases come right down to the wire.... In other cases, a majority of justices start down one path, only to reverse direction.... This is the kind of internal debate that the justices have argued should remain confidential, taking the position that only their final opinions have legal authority. They have expressed concern that premature disclosure of their private debates and doubts may undermine the court's credibility and inhibit their exchange of ideas.[38]

The assigning justice may consider the points made by majority justices during the conference discussion, the workload of the other justices, the need to avoid the more extreme opinions within the majority, and expertise in the particular area of law involved in a case. For example, the Court's landmark ruling on abortion was explained through a majority opinion written by Justice Harry A. Blackmun, who developed his expertise in medical law while in private practice, including work with the famous Mayo Clinic in Minnesota, his home state. Chief Justice Hughes sometimes assigned conservative opinions to liberal justices and liberal opinions to conservative justices to avoid giving any impression that the Court was divided along ideological lines.

The assignment of opinions can create morale problems among members of the Court. Justices have become annoyed and angered when not assigned to write opinions in cases of particular interest to them or directed to write them in routine, uninteresting cases. In 1898 Justice Harlan wrote to Chief Justice Fuller and complained: "Two Saturdays in succession you have not assigned to me any case but have assigned cases and important ones to Justice [Horace] Gray. I was in the majority in each case assigned to him."[39]

Rumors circulated about ill will between Chief Justice Burger and Justice Douglas. In a 1972 abortion case, Douglas was said to believe that Burger had abused his power by voting with the majority in order to assign the writing of the majority opinion, although, Douglas alleged, Burger's sympathies lay with the minority. Douglas threatened to file a scathing dissent on Burger's alleged misuse of the assignment powers but was dissuaded from doing so by his colleagues, who argued that the Court's reputation would suffer if the dissent were publicized.[40]

The style of writing a Court opinion—a majority opinion or a concurring or dissenting opinion—depends primarily on the individual justice. In some cases, the justice may prefer to write a restricted and limited opinion; in others, he or she may prefer a broader approach to the subject. The decision is likely to be influenced by the need to satisfy the other justices who voted with the writer.

The time spent to prepare an opinion varies from justice to justice. Justice Holmes was reportedly able to write an opinion over a weekend. Justices Hugo L. Black and Louis D. Brandeis were noted for reading widely on all aspects of a case before writing their opinions. Justice Frankfurter was a perfectionist who often prepared as many as thirty or more drafts for each opinion. On the contemporary Court, Justice Sandra Day O'Connor is known for her speed at producing opinions.

Justices use their law clerks to obtain and sift through the material needed to write an opinion. There has been speculation that some clerks actually ghostwrite a justice's opinion—or at least that justices sometimes tell a clerk what they want in an opinion and allow the clerk to write the first draft.

At the other extreme, Justice Douglas was said to give his clerks little or nothing to do in writing or organizing his written opinions. The traditional secrecy that surrounds each justice's office and work habits makes verification of such reports about the clerks' role in opinion writing very difficult.

Circulation of Drafts

The circulation of the drafts—whether computer-to-computer or on paper—provokes considerable discussion in many cases. Often the suggestions and criticisms require the author to carefully juggle opposing views. To retain a majority, the author of the draft opinion may have to make major emendations to oblige justices who are unhappy with the initial draft. Some opinions must be rewritten repeatedly before the majority is satisfied.

One illustration of the difficulty of writing a majority opinion is provided by Chief Justice Burger's problems in the case of the Nixon White House tapes. In mid-1974 the Court voted unanimously that the president must turn over the tapes sought as evidence in the Watergate "cover-up" case, rejecting the argument that he could invoke executive privilege to withhold them. After the decision had been reached, Burger assigned himself the opinion. To save time, he circulated the draft opinion piece by piece. The other justices were dissatisfied with what they were seeing. Many began writing their own version of the opinion. Burger, while annoyed, was forced to compromise. The final result, handed down on July 24, 1974, in *United States v. Nixon*,[41] was therefore a rather unusual joint product written by several justices. Nevertheless, it was issued in Burger's name.[42]

One reason for the secrecy surrounding the circulation of drafts is that one or more of the justices who voted with the majority may find the majority draft opinion so unpersuasive—or a dissenting draft so convincing—that votes may be switched. If enough justices alter their votes, the majority may shift, so that what was a dissent becomes instead the majority opinion. When a new majority emerges from this process, the task of writing and the process of circulating a new majority draft begin again.

The papers of the late Thurgood Marshall reveal that in 1989, when Chief Justice Rehnquist was circulating drafts of his proposed majority opinion in an abortion case, *Webster v. Reproductive Health Services*, he was proceeding as if he held a majority (at least four other justices).[43] His draft opinion would have come close to overturning the landmark abortion rights decision *Roe v. Wade* (1973) and would have enhanced state legislatures' ability to pass laws restricting abortion. But shortly before the opinion was to be released, Justice O'Connor, who was the critical fifth vote, declined to agree with Rehnquist's attack on *Roe*. In the end, the majority, including O'Connor, agreed to uphold the restrictive Missouri abortion law at issue, leaving Rehnquist with no majority for a major constitutional attack on abortion rights.

Similarly in 1989 Justice Brennan thought he had five votes in a racial harassment case that tested the breadth of a federal civil rights law. After the justices began exchanging draft opinions, however, Justice Anthony Kennedy decided he could not join Brennan's liberal view of the law and switched sides. Kennedy ended up writing the majority opinion concluding that racial harassment was not covered under the particular law at issue. The *Washington Post* reported the exchange of memos found in Marshall's files:

> The defeat did not sit well with Brennan. In an uncharacteristic display, he drafted a biting dissent attacking the Court: "The Court's fine phrases about our commitment to the eradication of racial discrimination . . . seem to count for little in practice."
>
> Kennedy responded in kind, adding a footnote aimed at Brennan. Brennan, he said, "thinks it judicious to bolster his position by questioning the Court's understanding of the necessity to eradicate racial discrimination. The commitment to equality, fairness, and compassion is not a treasured monopoly of our colleagues in dissent."[44]

Those comments in draft opinions circulated among justices made their way into Marshall's private papers but not into the final public version of the opinions.

When a justice is satisfied that the opinion he or she has written is conclusive or "unanswerable," it goes into print. In the past this process occurred at a print shop in the Court's basement, where the draft was printed under rigid security, with each copy numbered to prevent the removal of extra copies from the premises. In the 1980s, however, new technology arrived at the Court, and the October 1982 term was the last in which the Court's opinions were set on hot-lead typesetters. Computerization of the Court's output began in 1973, when the Clerk's Office began using a word processor for form letters. When an employee from the Clerk's Office moved into Justice Lewis F. Powell's chambers in the mid-1970s, she convinced him to put in a similar word processor there. That was so successful that a pilot project was begun in 1978 to customize word processors to meet the Court's needs. In 1980 the first set of fifty-five terminals was installed for the drafting of opinions; soon some of the justices—Byron R. White and Stevens among them—were writing on computers. For the first year the system was used only for drafting opinions. But within several years hot lead was dead and the draft opinions were circulated, revised, and printed on the computerized typesetting system.

As the new century began, the Court had its own secure computer network so opinions and drafts could be shared among the justices. However, paper and pens had not disappeared. Many of the justices continued to review and edit paper copies of opinions.

The Tradition of Unanimous Opinions

Over the past few decades there has been considerable concern about the lack of unanimity in Court decisions and the frequent use of dissenting and concurring opinions. The chief argument in favor of greater unanimity is that it increases the authority of—

and thus the respect for—the Court's decisions. Decades ago Judge Learned Hand wrote that "disunity cancels the impact of monolithic solidarity on which the authority of a bench of judges so largely depends."[45]

Such disunity actually has a long tradition, at odds with the relative harmony the Court likes to project. It was not until the fourth chief justice, John Marshall of Virginia, took his seat on the Court in 1801 that the aspiration toward unanimity became the norm. Before Marshall, each justice would announce his own independent opinion and the reason for it. These separate (or *seriatim*) opinions were the custom during the first decade of the Court's existence.

During Marshall's thirty-five years on the Court, the practice of *seriatim* opinions was largely abandoned. In his first four years as chief justice, Marshall delivered twenty-four opinions and the senior associate justice only two of the twenty-six handed down. The Court's ostensible unanimity was disturbed only once during these four years, by a one-sentence concurring opinion by Justice Samuel Chase in 1804.[46]

Although Marshall's insistence on unanimity did much to dispel the early Court's image as a bickering and dissension-filled forum and to increase its respect and esteem by the public, it did not meet with universal approval. One of Marshall's strongest critics was President Thomas Jefferson, a Democratic-Republican who often—and vociferously—expressed displeasure over the Court's decisions under Marshall, a Federalist.

In a letter to Thomas Richie, dated December 25, 1820, Jefferson wrote that he had long favored a return to "the sound practice of the primitive court" of delivering *seriatim* opinions. Of Marshall's changes, he wrote, "An opinion is huddled up in conclave, perhaps by a majority of one, delivered as if unanimous, and with the silent acquiescence of lazy or timid associates, by a crafty chief judge, who sophisticates the law to his own mind, by the turn of his own reasoning."[47]

The Tradition of Dissent

During the first decade of its existence, the Court followed the custom of the King's Bench of Great Britain in issuing *seriatim* opinions. Unlike the King's Bench, however, the Supreme Court delivered *seriatim* opinions in reverse order of seniority. The first case in which a full opinion was published was *State of Georgia v. Brailsford* (1792). The first opinion in the published record of that case was given by a justice who disagreed with the majority in the case.

The first real dissent, and most of the few other dissents to surface during Marshall's tenure, came from William Johnson of South Carolina, a Jefferson appointee. Soon after coming to the Court, Johnson delivered what amounted to a dissenting opinion in *Huidekoper's Lessee v. Douglass* (1805).

In a letter to Jefferson, dated December 10, 1822, Johnson complained about the adverse reaction to his concurring or dissenting opinions. "Some Case soon occurred in which I differed from my Brethren, and I felt it a thing of Course to deliver my Opinion. But, during the rest of the Session, I heard nothing but lectures on the Indecency of Judges cutting at each other."[48]

Under Marshall's successor, Chief Justice Roger B. Taney, dissent became more frequent. Unlike Marshall, Taney did not insist on delivering the sole opinion for the Court and the use of *seriatim* opinions was even resumed. Nevertheless, Marshall's tradition of unity continued for many years after his death. Until the early twentieth century, the Court generally gave single opinions with only an occasional concurrence or dissent. Concurring or dissenting opinions were issued in only about a tenth of the cases decided in the middle and late nineteenth century.

Although the increasing use of concurring and dissenting opinions after Marshall's death has been criticized, it was, according to some observers, almost inevitable. Charles P. Curtis Jr., for example, has written that "if you require unanimity, you make compromise inevitable, in the Court as everywhere else. Compromise is as alien to the feelings of the judicial process as what Solomon offered to do with the baby was to the feelings of the mother."[49] Even Marshall, the high apostle of unanimity, filed nine dissents and one special concurrence during his thirty-five years as chief justice.

Dissenting opinions usually are defended by a recitation of cases in which a carefully reasoned dissent became, in time, the basis of a new majority opinion. But such turnabouts are infrequent. Justice Holmes, the "Great Dissenter," issued 173 formal dissents, but fewer than 10 percent of them had any impact on subsequent reversals of Court decisions.

A dissenting justice may hope that his or her dissent will convince a majority of the other justices that the dissenting opinion is the correct one or that a later Court will vindicate the views expressed in it. Unlike the author of the majority opinion, a dissenting justice is able to avoid the process of revising and compromising his or her opinion. Dissenters generally have only themselves to please, a fact that makes many well-reasoned and well-written dissents more memorable or more enjoyable to read than the majority opinion.

The most frequently quoted defense of dissent on the Court was given by Chief Justice Hughes, who wrote, "A dissent in a court of last resort is an appeal to the brooding spirit of the law, to the intelligence of a future day, when a later decision may possibly correct the error into which the dissenting judge believes the court to have been betrayed."[50] Hughes was by no means an unqualified advocate of dissent; in fact, it is believed that on some occasions he yielded his dissent to join the majority without further argument. The words preceding his statement about "an appeal to the brooding spirit of the law" are probably more indicative of Hughes's feelings about dissent:

> There are some who think it desirable that dissents should not be disclosed as they detract from the forces of the judgment. Undoubtedly, they do. When unanimity can be obtained without sacrifice or coercion, it strongly commends the decision to public confidence. But unanimity which is merely formal, which is recorded at the expense of strong conflicting views, is not desirable in a court of last resort, whatever may be the effect upon public opinion at

the time. This is so because what must ultimately sustain the court in public confidence is the character and independence of the judges. They are not there simply to decide cases, but to decide them as they think they should be decided, and while it may be regrettable that they cannot always agree, it is better that their independence should be maintained and recognized than that unanimity should be secured through its sacrifice.[51]

A list of the "great dissenters" compiled by Karl M. Zobell includes those few who exercised dissent "in a manner which was—either because of a particular notable dissenting opinion, or because of the sheer weight of dissents filed—of historical or jurisprudential significance." According to Zobell, the great dissenters were

• Justice William Johnson (1804–1834), who "did not choose to conceal his ideas when they differed from those of the majority." He wrote almost half of the seventy dissenting opinions filed while he served on the Court. Johnson differed with the majority most frequently in three areas: judicial versus legislative power, the sanctity of property, and the role of the states.

• Justice Benjamin R. Curtis (1851–1857), who "seldom dissented" during his six years on the Court. But his last opinion—a dissent in the case of *Scott v. Sandford* (1857)—"was subsequently vindicated by the will of the people, and constitutional amendment; it is thus recalled as a landmark opinion in the history of American judicature."

• Justice John Marshall Harlan (1877–1911), a prodigious dissenter who delivered 380 dissents. He is most famous for his lone dissent against the "separate but equal" doctrine upheld in *Plessy v. Ferguson* (1896). "It was Harlan's lot to read the law differently from the majority of his brethren in numerous cases, only to have his views adopted by the legislature or by the Court years after his death," Zobell said.

• Justice Oliver Wendell Holmes Jr. (1902–1932), who "actually dissented less frequently during his tenure than did the average of his brethren—once in every 33 cases." But "Holmes' dissents had a way of later becoming correct expositions of the law, as defined by the court or as effected by the Legislature, not only more frequently, but sooner than did those of Harlan." The effect of Holmes on the use of dissent cannot be overestimated. During the so-called Holmes era, "Dissent became an instrument by which Justices asserted a personal, or individual, responsibility which they viewed as of a higher order than the institutional responsibility owed by each to the court, or by the court to the public."[52]

Other justices who almost certainly should be added to any list of great dissenters are Louis Brandeis (1916–1939), Benjamin N. Cardozo (1932–1938), Chief Justice Harlan Fiske Stone (1925–1946), Felix Frankfurter (1939–1962), William Brennan (1956–1990), Thurgood Marshall (1967–1991), and Antonin Scalia (1986–). All served during a time of increasing Court division and dissension.

Although Scalia does not dissent with great frequency, his dissents are memorable because of his strong, caustic attacks on the logic and the legal conclusions of his colleagues. "Today's opinion is the product of a Court, which is the product of a law-profession culture, that has largely signed on to the so-called homosexual agenda," Scalia said in a dissent he read from the bench in *Lawrence v. Texas* (2003). Scalia took issue with some of his colleagues as well in his dissent in *McConnell v. Federal Election Commission* (2003):

This is a sad day for the freedom of speech. Who could have imagined that the same court which, within the past four years, has sternly disapproved of restrictions upon such inconsequential forms of expression as virtual child pornography, tobacco advertising, dissemination of illegally intercepted communications, and sexually explicit cable programming would smile with favor upon a law that cuts to the heart of what the First Amendment is meant to protect: the right to criticize the government.

Concurring Opinions

For those convinced that dissents damage the prestige of the Court and the impact of its decisions, concurring opinions are also distasteful. Concurrence is, in many ways, a variation on the *seriatim* opinions of the 1790s. A concurring opinion indicates that the justice who wrote it agrees in general with the majority opinion but has reservations about the way it was written, the reasoning behind it, or specific points in it.

During John Marshall's tenure as chief justice, dissents were often masked as concurring opinions. Justice William Johnson was a master at this, too, but he also wrote concurring opinions supporting decisions of the Federalist majority but not the reasoning behind the decisions. In *Martin v. Hunter's Lessee*, for example, Johnson wrote in a concurring opinion: "I flatter myself that the full extent of the constitutional revisory power may be secured to the United States, and the benefits of it to the individual, without ever resorting to compulsory or restrictive process upon the state tribunals; a right which, I repeat again, Congress has not asserted; nor has this court asserted, nor does there appear any necessity for asserting."[53]

Modern-day justices are more likely than their predecessors to write concurrences, explaining how their legal reasoning differs from the majority's approach. Such concurring opinions are often used to emphasize the limits of the majority's opinion or to address distinct concerns not embraced by other justices. As of 2003 Justice Stevens had written 298 concurring opinions, the highest number of any justice in history. Stevens, who was appointed in 1975 and was still on the Court in 2003, also had the opportunity to add more separate opinions to his record.[54]

United States v. United Mine Workers, decided in 1947, provides one example of the problems and vexations accounting for and arising from the use of concurring opinions.[55] Chief Justice Fred M. Vinson and Justices Stanley F. Reed and Harold H. Burton voted against the United Mine Workers for two reasons. Justices

Wiley B. Rutledge and Frank Murphy both dissented on the same grounds. Justices Frankfurter and Jackson agreed with Vinson, Reed, and Burton on one of the grounds but rejected the other. Justices Black and Douglas concurred with Vinson for the reason that Frankfurter and Jackson had rejected, but rejected the argument that Frankfurter had approved. The result was that five justices supported the decision for one reason, five justices supported it for another reason, and four justices were opposed for both reasons.

Issuing the Opinion

When the drafts of an opinion—including dissents and concurring views—have been written, circulated, discussed, and revised, if necessary, the final versions are printed.

Before computerization, final opinions were typed by the justices' secretaries and given to the printer in the Supreme Court building where they were kept under security. Now the whole process takes place internally in the Court's computer system, but security is still tight. Before the opinion is produced, the reporter of decisions adds a "headnote" or syllabus summarizing the decision and a "lineup" at the end showing how each justice voted.

As the decision is announced in Court, the "bench opinion" is distributed to journalists and others in the Public Information Office. Another copy that includes any necessary corrections is sent to the U.S. Government Printing Office, which prints the more than four thousand "slip opinions" distributed to federal and state courts and agencies. Copies of the slip opinions are available to the public free through the Public Information Office. The Government Printing Office also prints the opinion for inclusion in *United States Reports*, the official record of Supreme Court opinions.

The public announcement of opinions in Court is probably the Court's most dramatic function. It also may be the most expendable. Depending on who delivers the opinion and how, announcements can take a considerable amount of the Court's time. Opinions are simultaneously given to the public information officer for distribution.

Those in the courtroom to hear the announcement of a ruling are participating in a very old tradition. The actual delivery may be tedious or exciting, depending on the nature of the case and the eloquence of the opinion and the style of its oral delivery. Differences between the opinion as actually spoken and its written counterpart, while of little legal or practical importance, can add a certain interest. Once, Justice James C. McReynolds allegedly became so agitated in delivering a dissent that he added, "The Constitution is gone."[56]

In this century, the Court has reduced the amount of time spent in delivering opinions. Before Hughes became chief justice in 1930, the Court generally read long opinions word for word. Early in the Court's history some opinions took days to announce. As the workload increased, this practice came to be regarded as a waste of the Court's time. Hughes encouraged the delivery of summaries of the opinion. The justice who has written the majority opinion now generally delivers only a summary, and dissenting justices often do the same with their opinions.

Reporting of Decisions

The importance—and difficulty—of adequately reporting Supreme Court decisions cannot be underestimated. Few people read the full Supreme Court opinions, and accounts in the news media often are superficial.

Justice Frankfurter was acutely aware of this problem. "The evolution of our constitutional law is the work of the initiate," he wrote in 1932. "But its ultimate sway depends upon its acceptance by the thought of the nation. The meaning of the Supreme Court decisions ought not therefore to be shrouded in esoteric mystery. It ought to be possible to make clear to lay understanding the exact scope of constitutional doctrines that underlie decisions."[57]

In a 1967 magazine article Gilbert Cranberg of the Des Moines, Iowa, *Register and Tribune* quoted a columnist who described the Supreme Court as

> the worst reported and the worst judged institution in the American system of government. . . .
>
> The wholesale shunning of what the Court says leaves most of the country dependent on second-hand reports. It would be difficult to devise handicaps more devastating to an understanding of the Court than those that hobble news reporting of its rulings. . . . Where Congressmen, subordinate administrators and Presidents are frequently eager to explain and defend their policies, Justices of the Supreme Court emerge from isolation only to read their opinions. . . . No Justice is available to discuss or clarify the opinion he has written.[58]

Cranberg estimated that in 1967 the total circulation of Supreme Court opinions was probably no more than 20,000, and he pointed out that most of the texts were placed "in forbidding legal libraries and inaccessible private law offices." He asserted that "even many of the nation's attorneys do not actually read the court opinions."[59]

Although the total circulation of formal Court opinions is now considerably higher than it was in 1967, the psychological impediments to reading them are still there. Cranberg noted that "poring over Supreme Court texts seemed about as inviting as an evening of wading through a technical manual. Indeed, the deadly, all-but-indigestible legalese I expected to find was there in abundance, but to my delighted surprise there was also a gold mine of information and often exciting, absorbing reading."[60]

Even as computerization has changed the way the opinions are drafted, polished, and produced, it has also made them much more accessible to interested persons across the nation. Several months used to elapse between the decision's release and its availability in the preliminary prints of the *United States Reports*.

Today, the opinions are available shortly after their release on the Court's Web site, www.supremecourtus.gov, and on other sites such as www.findlaw.com. A limited number of printed copies of the Court's most recent decisions also are available from its Public Information Office. The weekly editions of *United States Law Week*, published by the Bureau of National Affairs, and *Supreme Court Bulletin*, published by the Commerce Clearing House, also carry the Court's opinions.

News Media

Relatively few people make the effort or take the time to read the opinions of the Court, so most Americans must rely on the news media to learn what the Court has decided. Since the late eighteenth century, however, many—perhaps most—of the opinions handed down by the Court have not even been reported. *(See Chapter 15, p. 813.)*

Efforts were made in the mid-twentieth century to improve media coverage of the Supreme Court. Justice Frankfurter played a considerable role in that improvement. As one of his biographers wrote,

> Frankfurter's concern for public understanding of the Supreme Court took him into a long running fight with the *New York Times*. The press, Frankfurter believed, had a semipublic function and a semipublic responsibility. The *Times*, as the one documentary paper in the nation, should, he thought, furnish its readers the kind of competence in its reporting of the Supreme Court that it furnished in other fields. It should, Frankfurter was fond of saying, cover the Supreme Court at least as well as the World Series.

Beginning in 1933, Frankfurter barraged Arthur Hays Sulzberger, publisher of the *Times*, with letters in which he was outspokenly critical of its failings—and equally outspokenly congratulatory of its triumphs. Finally, in the mid-1950s, a young reporter and Pulitzer Prize winner named Anthony Lewis was sent to Harvard Law School for a year, then assigned to cover the Supreme Court. The *Times* expanded and deepened its Court coverage; a significant by-product of this development was the effect on other prominent newspapers which, encouraged by the *Times*, sought to improve their reporting of Court news and bring it up to World Series levels.[61]

Supreme Court justices have long felt that their opinions must speak for themselves and that efforts by the justices or by the Court's Public Information Office to explain or interpret the Court's opinions are unnecessary. Nevertheless, the Court has taken some steps to make it easier for the news media to digest the written opinions in the limited time available. These changes include:

• Announcement of opinions on days other than Monday so that the press would have a smaller list of cases to report on each day.

• The use of headnotes since 1970, which makes it easier for reporters to plow through hundreds of pages of written opinions.

• The availability of the *Preview of United States Supreme Court Cases*, a background analysis of the cases pending before the Court.

SOURCES OF SUPREME COURT DECISIONS

PAPER SOURCES OF DECISIONS

The primary paper source for Supreme Court decisions is *United States Reports*, the official record of Supreme Court decisions and opinions published by the U.S. Government Printing Office.

This source can be supplemented by *United States Law Week*, published by the Bureau of National Affairs; *Supreme Court Reporter*, published by West Publishing Company; and *United States Supreme Court Reports, Lawyers' Edition*, published by Lawyers Cooperative Publishing Company.

ONLINE SOURCES OF DECISIONS

Using the Internet, it is possible to read the full text of recent Supreme Court opinions as well as decisions from the past. Here are four web sites that offer decisions and other Court information at no cost.

U.S. Supreme Court
www.supremecourtus.gov
This site includes easy access to the Court's recent decisions as well as links to other sites that have opinions prior to 1990. This site also offers information on the Court's rules and procedures, its current cases, transcripts of oral arguments, and a description and history of the Court's building.

Findlaw
www.findlaw.com/casecode/supreme.html
This site offers the Court's opinions dating back to 1893. They may be retrieved by name, by year, or by the volume and page citations in the *United States Reports*. The site also includes information on the Court's calendar and current cases, including the key briefs on the opposing sides.

Cornell Law
http://supct.law.cornell.edu/supct
This popular site is easy to use. It offers the text of Supreme Court opinions from 1990 to the present, and they may be accessed by the topic, as well by the name of a party, the date, or the official citation. The site features fifty historic Supreme Court decisions since World War II, including *Brown v. Board of Education, New York Times v. Sullivan, Gideon v. Wainwright,* and *Roe v. Wade*. Links also access to other Court opinions dating back to the 1890s.

OYEZ
www.oyez.org/oyez/frontpage
In addition to offering access to the Court's decisions, this web site, Sponsored by Northwestern University offers multimedia presentations, including audio versions of past arguments before the Court, and previews of upcoming cases that are written for nonlawyers.

The *Preview* is published regularly, from September through April, by the Public Education Division of the American Bar Association. Prepared by law school professors and active practitioners of the law, it outlines the background, issues, and importance of all cases awaiting a final Court decision.

The Court's public information officer releases opinions to the news media shortly after they are announced. Many of the country's major newspapers and national news media have reporters on hand so that news in the Court opinions can be relayed quickly to their headquarters. (See "Covering the High Court," pp. 836–839.)

Other Channels

In addition to the formal and press reporting of Court opinions, other, often impromptu methods are used to publicize its rulings. Various lobbying groups are not shy about speaking out on Court opinions that meet with their approval or provoke their disapproval. Decisions on issues such as school desegregation, prayer in the schools, capital punishment, and abortion always produce an avalanche of publicity from groups both supportive of and hostile to the opinions.

When Supreme Court justices were still riding circuit, they usually maintained strong contacts with people, particularly lawyers and local judges, in the communities they served. Through these contacts, they were able to inform community leaders about recent Court rulings and the legal principles on which those opinions were based. And even until this day the legal fraternity provides a forum for discussing and clarifying Court opinions through meetings of bar associations and publication of scholarly articles.

TRADITIONS OF THE COURT

Tradition plays a major role in the operations of the Supreme Court. The Court's insistence on the historic continuity of its procedures, and its strict adherence to conventions of secrecy and formal decorum, have yielded little to the changing moods and social patterns of the contemporary world outside its chambers.

At best, this overlapping network of traditions gives the Supreme Court an aura of substance, dignity, and caution that befits the nation's highest institution of law—and the public's confidence in the integrity, sobriety of purpose, and independence from outside pressure of its justices. But to some critics, much of the Court's tenacious adherence to its formal traditions of procedure and behavior reflect an anachronistic set of values that constrict the effective functioning of the modern Court.

Despite continuing efforts to streamline its procedures and find more efficient ways to cope with change, the Court remains the most traditional of the three major branches of government. Some traditional aspects of the Court seem merely quaint. The elevators in the Court building are operated by hand, and until the early 1990s the justices employed a part-time seamstress to

mend their robes. White quill pens are placed at each chair at the attorneys' tables in the courtroom on argument days, available for removal as mementos. Although most lawyers no longer don frock coats and striped trousers to appear before the Court, male attorneys from the solicitor general's office still dress in cutaways.

Other traditions are much more substantive and more controversial. Proposed changes in convention such as the mandatory retirement of justices or televising Court sessions continue to generate debate. No tape recorders are allowed in the chamber, and visitors generally are not allowed to take notes of the oral arguments.

Even the more informal or irreverent of the justices have found the traditions of the Court of sufficient importance to observe and preserve them. Justice Frankfurter, for example, was a man who

> brought a sense of informality and impish humor to the august tribunal. He would wave from the bench at friends among the spectators. He once escorted the child of a visiting Australian law school dean into the empty courtroom and let her sit on each of the justices' chairs. When Mrs. Charles Fahy once came to court to hear her husband, the solicitor general, argue a case, Frankfurter teased her with this note scribbled from the bench: "Anyhow—I'm for your hat!" He teased his own law clerks incessantly. He whistled in the marble halls, anything from "The Stars and Stripes Forever" to the sextet from "Lucia."

But "underneath the gaiety and banter there was a seriousness of purpose equal to anything Frankfurter had undertaken in his life. He approached the court with a kind of religious awe; he was indefatigable in guarding its traditions, and he felt, said Chief Justice Earl Warren, 'the burden of carrying on the traditions of the court more than any man.'"[62]

Secrecy

Among the Court's most important traditions is secrecy, which applies not only to formal deliberations but also to disclosure of personal disagreements and animosities among the justices. The unwritten code of secrecy has made the Court the most leak-proof of Washington institutions. Nevertheless, there have been and continue to be occasional glimpses into its inner workings and conflicts.

The practice of allowing no one except the justices in the conference room began years ago with the mistaken impression that a page, secretary, clerk, or stenographer had leaked a decision. Subsequent leaks, including instances in 1973, 1977, and 1979, have moved the justices to take measures to prevent further premature disclosures or unwarranted gossip. (See box, Leaks at the Court, p. 825.)

In addition to the rather infrequent revelations by an inquisitive press, justices and their law clerks have occasionally revealed something about the Court's inner workings and conflicts in their writings and speeches. Probably the three best-known examples were the use of the papers of Chief Justice Stone, Justice Brandeis, and Justice Thurgood Marshall.

INSIDE THE CONFERENCE ROOM

An unusual and well-publicized leak from the Supreme Court occurred in 1979 when ABC-TV news reporter Tim O'Brien broadcast the results of two cases that had not yet been formally announced. On April 16 O'Brien revealed that Justice Byron R. White would deliver the majority opinion in an important libel case that would allow public figures offended by a report to inquire into the journalist's "state of mind."

Two days later the Court, with Justice White speaking for the majority, ruled that public figures could indeed look into the "state of mind" of a journalist and the editorial process when suing for allegedly libelous reporting. O'Brien also reported that during the conference discussion of the case, the justices became involved in an angry and vociferous shouting match about the decision.

On April 17 O'Brien reported that Chief Justice Warren E. Burger had written the opinion in a still unannounced case in which the Court ruled against the effort of prison inmates to expand their "due process" rights in parole hearings. After the two ABC-TV broadcasts, Burger was said by Court sources to have ordered an immediate investigation.

The Court made no public comment about the O'Brien reports, and O'Brien refused to reveal how or from whom he obtained the information. Within a week, however, it was reported that Chief Justice Burger had fired a typesetter in the Court's print shop. The typesetter, John Tucci, worked for the U.S. Government Printing Office in the Court's basement printing shop. Tucci, who would have had access to the opinion before it was released in Court, denied that he had leaked the information to O'Brien, but he was transferred to another job outside the Court.

Seven years later O'Brien once again broadcast the results of a decision *before* it was released by the Court. On Sunday, June 15, 1986, O'Brien reported on ABC News that the Court had voted 7-2 to strike down part of the Gramm-Rudman-Hollings deficit reduction law, and that the Court would issue its decision the next day.

The Court was expected to announce three decisions on June 16, but only two were announced, and the Gramm-Rudman-Hollings decision was not one of them. Three weeks later the decision in *Bowsher v. Synar* was announced, and the vote was 7-2. The law was struck down.

When Stone died in 1946, his widow turned over all his files and papers to Alpheus T. Mason. In his biography of Stone, Mason revealed much of the Court's day-to-day operations, including feuds between liberal and conservative justices.[63] Alexander Bickel used Brandeis's papers to show the justice's contribution to Court solidarity, quoting Chief Justice William Howard Taft as saying of Brandeis, "He thinks much of the court and is anxious to have it consistent and strong, and he pulls his weight in the boat."[64]

Marshall's papers were made public by the Library of Congress within months of his death in 1993. The files covered Marshall's twenty-four years on the Court and showed the draft-by-draft evolution of opinions and the critical negotiations that occurred as individual justices—most of them still on the Court when the papers were made public—tried to win a majority in a particular case. A *Washington Post* series based on the previously secret information on the Court's deliberations prompted protest from Marshall's family and some of the sitting justices. They asserted that Marshall likely did not want his papers made available to the general public. But the Library of Congress maintained that the opening of the once-confidential files was part of an arrangement with him and refused to change the status of the papers.[65]

The justices believe they have good reason to maintain the veil of secrecy that surrounds their conference deliberations and their personal relations with other members of the Court. Widespread disclosure of what goes on in conference could reduce public esteem for the Court and its rulings. When leaks occur, the Court refuses to confirm or deny their accuracy, and the justices are loath to reveal instances of infighting and conflict among themselves lest they demean the dignity of the Court and encourage further quarreling among the justices.

Courtesy

Both in and out of Court the justices seek to present an image of formality and courtesy. Before they go into the courtroom and at the beginning of their private conferences, the justices shake hands with each other. This practice began in the late nineteenth century when Chief Justice Fuller decided that it was a good idea to remind the justices that differences of opinion did not preclude overall harmony of purpose.[66] In court and in their written opinions, the justices traditionally addressed each other as "my brother" or "my dissenting brothers." On the contemporary Court, with two women justices, members refer to each other simply as "Justice." But the image of fraternal harmony is occasionally undermined by personal, ideological, and legal differences among justices with strong views and even stronger egos.

In his book on Justice Samuel F. Miller (1862–1890), Charles Fairman quoted Miller as having told a friend that Chief Justice Morrison R. Waite (1874–1888) was "mediocre" and that "I can't make a great Chief Justice out of a small man." Miller was equally critical of fellow justices Nathan Clifford, Noah Haynes Swayne, and David Davis. "I can't make Clifford and Swayne, who are too old, resign, or keep the Chief Justice from giving them cases to write opinions in which their garrulity is often mixed with mischief. I can't hinder Davis from governing every act of his life by his hope of the Presidency."[67]

More than a decade before his appointment as chief justice, President Taft indicated his distaste for some of the justices. "The condition of the Supreme Court is pitiable, and yet those old fools hold on with a tenacity that is most discouraging," Taft said in 1910. "Really, the Chief Justice Fuller is almost senile; Harlan does no work; Brewer is so deaf that he cannot hear and has got beyond the point of the commonest accuracy in writing his opinions; Brewer and Harlan sleep almost through all the arguments. I don't know what can be done. It is most discouraging to the active men on the bench."[68]

Once he became chief justice in 1921, Taft was far less publicly critical of the other justices. Still, Taft's efforts to control the disputes and acrimony among them "at times exhausted his supply of good nature, and he sometimes betrayed his own irritations by very sharp remarks in letters." One of these letters, written in 1929, when Justice Stone was being considered as Taft's successor, alleged that "Stone is not a leader and would have a good deal of difficulty in massing the Court." John Frank recounts how, when Stone was first appointed in 1925, "he was welcomed into the little extra-court meetings of the Taft bloc of conservative justices, and then, after a time, was dropped from those conventions when it appeared that he might be dangerously 'progressive.'"[69]

Perhaps the most publicized public airing of judicial antagonisms was the attack by Justice Robert Jackson against Justice Hugo Black in 1946. Jackson had wanted and expected to become chief justice when Harlan Stone died. Instead, President Harry S. Truman nominated Fred M. Vinson; Jackson blamed Black for blocking his appointment as chief justice.

When Vinson was nominated, Jackson was serving as chief of a tribunal trying German war criminals in Nuremberg. Jackson responded to news of the appointment with a vitriolic letter to the Senate and House Judiciary Committees. In that letter, Jackson denounced Black for participating in a case in which, Jackson charged, Black should have disqualified himself. The case involved the United Mine Workers, who were being represented by a former law partner of Black's, Crampton Harris. Unmentioned in the letter was the fact that Black and Harris had ceased being partners nineteen years earlier and had seen each other hardly at all since that time. Black did not reply to the charge, nor did he mention that he had disqualified himself in all cases involving the Federal Communications Commission because his brother-in-law was a member of the commission.

An earlier example of lack of judicial courtesy involved Chief Justice Taney and Justice Curtis in the *Scott v. Sandford* decision of 1857.[70] Nine separate opinions were filed in the case, with Taney speaking for the majority of the Court. Taney represented the southern point of view, and Curtis the northern, or abolitionist, side on the question of slavery in the territories. The chief justice made Curtis's dissent in the case far more difficult by allowing Curtis to see the other opinions before completing his dissent. Shortly after the opinions were released, Curtis resigned from the Court.

Justice McReynolds is often cited as a man whose lack of courtesy made life on the Court difficult for his fellow justices. McReynolds was appointed by President Woodrow Wilson in 1914 and served until 1941, but he was described by John Frank as "the total antithesis of everything Wilson stood for and ... the most fanatic and hard-bitten conservative extremist ever to grace the Court."[71] McReynolds showed considerable antagonism to the more liberal members of the Court and particularly to the Jewish justices, Brandeis and Cardozo.

Frank noted that "far more striking than the Court's disputes over the years is the absence of personal friction among the judges, and the extent to which normal tendencies of irritability are controlled rather than exposed. When one considers how easily a bench of nine could march off in nine different directions, one's principal impression may well be not how often but how seldom this occurs. An instance of a McReynolds snarling in bare-toothed anti-Semitic hostility at his Jewish brothers on the Court is overbalanced by the real personal sympathy" among the justices. "This degree of respectful personal interrelations is by no means restricted to Justices who were ... essentially like-minded."[72]

The desire of most justices to maintain these "respectful personal interrelations" has made outbursts like Justice Jackson's rare. Disagreements among justices are far more likely to be exhibited in subtler ways. A common method of criticizing another justice is to cite his or her words or previous opinions to prove the inconsistency of views on a particular issue or opinion. Jackson, for example, was fond of quoting the statements that Black had made when he was a senator from Alabama. Many of these criticisms are so subtle that they go unnoticed by everyone except those privy to the relationships between the justices.

On the modern Court, Justice Scalia is known for his brash style and confrontations with colleagues. Justice Powell's biographer wrote of Powell's reaction to Scalia when Scalia joined the bench in 1986:

> Politically, Powell and Scalia were not so far apart, but personally they were like oil and water. Scalia's cheerful lack of deference rubbed his senior colleague the wrong way. His volubility struck Powell as bad manners. In Scalia's first oral argument he asked so many questions that Powell finally leaned over to Marshall and whispered, "Do you think he knows that the rest of us are here?"[73]

Despite the occasional sharp comments in their opinions, the justices regularly say they enjoy a friendly and collegial relationship with all the members of the Court. Justices Clarence Thomas and Stephen G. Breyer rarely agree in major cases, but the two sit together on the bench and can often be seen talking and joking together. Both have made nearly identical statements in speeches attesting to the fact they have never heard a harsh personal comment or a raised voice in the private conferences of the justices.

Seniority

The system of seniority affects Supreme Court procedures such as conference discussion and voting, announcement of opinions, and seating in the courtroom. It is also a determining factor in assignment of office space. Only the chief justice is exempt from such traditional obeisance to seniority.

During conferences, discussion of cases begins with the chief justice and proceeds down the line of seniority to the junior associate justice. The junior justice has the task of sending for and receiving documents or other information the Court may need.

When opinions are announced in the courtroom, the justices who wrote the opinions announce them in reverse order of seniority. The chief justice is seated in the center of the winged mahogany table. The senior associate justice sits at his immediate right and the second senior associate justice at his immediate left. In alternating order of seniority, the other justices take their places, with the junior associate justice at the far left of the bench and the second newest appointee at the far right.

Like the seating on the bench, the offices of the justices are assigned according to seniority. Because there were only six suites inside the so-called "golden gates"—the large bronze doors that seal the justices off from the public—the three junior justices usually occupy the offices on the corridor just outside. One exception to this rule was Justice Douglas who until 1962 chose to keep the office he had been assigned as the most junior justice when he came to the Court in 1939. Over the next twenty-three years, twelve justices with less seniority than Douglas moved to suites inside the door. In 1962, when Justice Frankfurter retired, Douglas at last decided to move inside the golden gates.

The suites were reconfigured early in the 1970s and now stretch entirely around the first floor of the Court. The offices occupied in 1996 by Justices O'Connor and Kennedy were originally offices for other purposes, converted into justices' chambers in a renovation during the 1970s. All the old chambers had working fireplaces, so fireplaces were added to these redesigned offices—but they do not work. When Justice Ginsburg joined the Court in 1993 she broke tradition and moved into an office on the second floor. She chose roomier, sunnier chambers so that all of her clerks could be nearby. She also said she was seeking a better atmosphere than she would have had in the smaller first-floor suite that was available.

Continuity

Continuity is not merely an image that the Court seeks to perpetuate; it is inherent in the nature of the institution. The main factor in the continuity of the Court is that its justices are appointed for life, and for most members that has been literally true. The majority of justices have either died while still on the bench or retired near the end of their lives.

Only 108 justices have been confirmed for Court service in little more than two centuries. (One—Edwin M. Stanton—died after confirmation before taking his seat on the bench.) None has been removed from the bench involuntarily, although several have resigned under pressure, and few have given up the prestige and accoutrements of the Court for another career. Just as change is central to Congress and the presidency through periodic elections, continuity is built into the Court through longevity of service. The average length of service of all justices of the Court, including sitting members, has been about fifteen years. More than half of them served for at least that long.

William Douglas served longer than any other justice in the Court's history. When he retired on November 12, 1975, he had been on the high bench for more than thirty-five years. Sen.

Augustus H. Garland, D-Ark., reportedly told President Grover Cleveland, who wished to appoint him to the Court, that he thought himself unqualified because a justice should serve for at least twenty years and he doubted that he would live that long. In January 1972 forty-seven-year-old William Rehnquist took his seat on the Supreme Court, and he told friends that he did not intend to remain on the Court as a doddering old man. But after his wife died in 1991, Rehnquist said he found retirement less appealing. And in January 2004 he began his thirty-third year on the Court, putting himself in range of Douglas's record for longevity on the bench.

Turnover

The justices' long service on the Court is the most integral aspect of its continuity. With a new member added only every two years or so on average, successive Courts assume their own collective identity as the same justices work together over the space of decades. Each new member, however different in ideology and temperament from his or her associates, can make only an incremental difference. A new member is influential as an instrument of change by a factor of only one-ninth—less so, in fact, given the deferential role imposed on the newcomer by the tradition of seniority.

Even though it is customary to refer to influential Courts by the names of their chief justices—the "Marshall Court" or the "Warren Court"—such designations are somewhat misleading. Although the leadership and judicial ideology of each chief justice is without doubt a strong element in the direction "his" Court takes and the innovations it generates, the makeup of each Court is to a large degree fortuitous.

The chief justice, after all, usually inherits his associates when he takes office and does not himself choose replacements as vacancies occur—although his counsel may be covertly sought by a president. For the most part, a chief justice works with the associates he has been given, often nominated by a president and confirmed by a Congress of a different political persuasion.

The Warren Court, for example, is considered the most liberal and activist of modern times. Yet its chief, Earl Warren, was a Republican appointee who took command of a bench manned entirely by eight veteran justices appointed by the liberal Democratic Roosevelt-Truman administrations. In subsequent years—although the Court absorbed four nominees of Warren's sponsor, Dwight Eisenhower—the Warren Court's membership also came to include four appointees of Democrats John F. Kennedy and Lyndon B. Johnson.

The direction of the Warren Court's successor—the clearly more conservative Burger Court—can easily be attributed to the judicial attitudes of its chief justice, Warren Burger, and the three justices named by President Richard Nixon. But it also encompassed three Eisenhower-Kennedy-Johnson holdovers and a moderate, Justice Stevens, appointed by Nixon's successor, Gerald R. Ford.

In other words, whether tending to be monolithic in its judgments or closely divided along liberal/conservative lines—or simply unpredictable—the membership of the Court is determined in large part by slowly evolving circumstances: by the political party in power as vacancies occur, by the length of time a Court has sat together, and finally by the durability of each justice, surviving changes in the Court and in the times.

Precedent

Another substantive factor in the Court's essential continuity is its reliance on precedent in arriving at decisions. Except in rare cases where there is no judicial opinion to be cited, any decision is based primarily on earlier relevant opinions of the Supreme Court or lower courts as interpreted in light of the case under consideration. *(See "The Role of Precedent," pp. 320–322.)*

The most dramatic and far-reaching of the Court's decisions have been those in which a Court has arrived at a clear-cut reversal of an earlier Court's landmark opinion, especially where basic constitutional questions are involved. The 1954 decision in *Brown v. Board of Education* represented a watershed reversal of more than a century of earlier Court decisions in civil rights cases—decisions that the Warren Court, in effect, declared to have been unconstitutional.

But whatever the Court's decision—and it is far more common to uphold or modify an earlier Court's judgment than to reverse it outright—it is so rooted in precedent that it marks a further stage in a judicial continuum rather than an original judgment that stands on its own.

For some justices, precedent has been the only consideration. Justice Owen J. Roberts, for example, issued this scathing dissent in January 1944 when the Court overturned an admiralty case it had decided sixteen years earlier. "The evil resulting from overruling earlier considered decisions must be evident," Roberts contended. "The law becomes not a chart to govern conduct but a game of chance. . . . [T]he administration of justice will fall into disrepute. Respect for tribunals must fall when the bar and the public come to understand that nothing that has been said in prior adjudication has force in a current controversy."[74]

Justice Frankfurter joined in Roberts's dissent. Yet four years earlier, Frankfurter had this to say about reversing previous Court decisions:

> We recognize that stare decisis [adherence to precedent] embodies an important social policy. It represents an element of continuity in law, and is rooted in the psychologic need to satisfy reasonable expectations. But stare decisis is a principle of policy and not a mechanical formula of adherence to the latest decision, however recent and questionable, when such adherence involves collision with a prior doctrine more embracing in its scope, intrinsically sounder, and verified by experience. . . . This Court, unlike the House of Lords, has from the beginning rejected a doctrine of disability at self-correction.[75]

NOTES

1. Harold W. Stanley and Richard G. Niemi, *Vital Statistics on American Politics 2003–2004* (Washington, D.C.: CQ Press, 2003), Table 7-9, 289.

2. Supreme Court Rule 3.

3. Robert L. Stern, Eugene Gressman, Stephen M. Shapiro, and Kenneth S. Geller, *Supreme Court Practice*, 7th ed. (Washington, D.C.: Bureau of National Affairs, 1993), 3–4.

4. Charles Warren, *The Supreme Court in United States History*, rev. ed., 2 vols. (Boston: Little, Brown, 1926), 2:148.

5. *Ex parte Quirin*, 317 U.S. 1 (1942).

6. *Rosenberg v. United States*, 346 U.S. 273 (1953).

7. *Cooper v. Aaron*, 358 U.S. 1 (1958).

8. *O'Brien v. Brown*, 409 U.S. 1 (1972).

9. *McConnell v. Federal Election Commission*, __ U.S. __ (2003).

10. *United States v. Nixon*, 418 U.S. 683 (1974); *Wilson v. Girard*, 354 U.S. 524 (1957); *New York Times Co. v. United States, United States v. Washington Post*, 403 U.S. 713 (1971); *Dames and Moore v. Regan*, 453 U.S. 654 (1981).

11. *Supreme Court Journal*, April 5, 1965, quoted by Stern et al. in *Supreme Court Practice*, 8.

12. John P. Frank, *Marble Palace: The Supreme Court in American Life* (New York: Knopf, 1958), 15. See also PL 100-352, passed in 1988, eliminating much of the Court's mandatory jurisdiction.

13. Supreme Court Rule 16.2.

14. 928 U.S.C. 1915.

15. Rules of the Supreme Court of the United States, adopted July 29, 1995.

16. William H. Rehnquist, *The Supreme Court: How It Was, How It Is* (New York: Quill, William Morrow, 1987), 265–266.

17. Charles Evans Hughes, *The Supreme Court of the United States* (New York: Columbia University Press, 1928), 62–63.

18. Quoted in Harvard Law School Occasional Pamphlet Number Nine (1967), 22.

19. Rehnquist, *Supreme Court*, 276.

20. Frank, *Marble Palace*, 91–92.

21. Hughes, *Supreme Court*, 61.

22. Supreme Court Rule 28.7.

23. Supreme Court Rule 28.1.

24. Stern et al, *Supreme Court Practice*, 584.

25. Supreme Court Rule 28.1.

26. William J. Brennan Jr., "State Court Decisions and the Supreme Court," *Pennsylvania Bar Association Quarterly* 31 (1960): 403–404.

27. Supreme Court Rule 24.6.

28. *Huffman v. Pursue, Ltd.*, 419 U.S. 892 (1974).

29. Hughes, *Supreme Court*, 62.

30. Robert H. Jackson, "Advocacy before the Supreme Court: Suggestions for Effective Case Presentations," *American Bar Association Journal* 101 (1951): 862.

31. Frank, *Marble Palace*, 92.

32. Rehnquist, *Supreme Court*, 283.

33. Frank, *Marble Palace*, 93.

34. Ibid., 105.

35. Ibid.

36. Quoted by Richard L. Williams, "Justices Run 'Nine Little Law Firms' at Supreme Court," *Smithsonian*, February 1977.

37. Willard L. King, *Melville Weston Fuller* (New York: Macmillan, 1950), 290.

38. *Washington Post*, May 23, 1993, 1.

39. King, *Melville Weston Fuller*, 245. See also Bernard Schwartz, *Super Chief* (New York: New York University Press, 1983), 418.

40. Glen Elsasser and Jay Fuller, "The Hidden Face of the Supreme Court," *Chicago Tribune Magazine*, April 23, 1978, 50.

41. *United States v. Nixon*, 418 U.S. 683 (1974).

42. Elsasser and Fuller, "Hidden Face," 50–57.

43. *Washington Post*, May 23, 1993, 1.

44. *Washington Post*, May 24, 1993, 1.

45. Learned Hand, *The Bill of Rights* (Cambridge: Harvard University Press, 1958), 72.

46. *Head and Amory v. Providence Ins. Co.*, 2 Cr. (6 U.S.) 127 (1804).

47. Quoted in Warren, *Supreme Court in United States History*, 1:654.

48. Ibid., 1:655.

49. Charles P. Curtis Jr., *Lions under the Throne* (Fairfield, N.J.: Kelley Press, 1947), 76.

50. Hughes, *Supreme Court*, 68.

51. Ibid., 67–68.

52. Karl M. Zobell, "Division of Opinion in the Supreme Court: A History of Judicial Disintegration," *Cornell Law Quarterly* 44 (1959): 186–214.

53. *Martin v. Hunter's Lessee*, 1 Wheat. (14 U.S.) 304, 381 (1816).

54. Lee Epstein, Thomas G. Walker, Jeffrey A. Segal, and Harold J. Spaeth, *The Supreme Court Compendium: Data, Decisions, and Developments*, 3d ed. (Washington, D.C.: CQ Press, 2002).

55. *United States v. United Mine Workers*, 330 U.S. 258 (1947).

56. Frank, *Marble Palace*, 121.

57. *New York Times*, November 13, 1932.

58. Gilbert Cranberg, "What Did the Supreme Court Say?" *Saturday Review*, April 8, 1967.

59. Ibid.

60. Ibid.

61. Liva Baker, *Felix Frankfurter* (New York: Coward-McCann, 1969), 218.

62. Ibid., 216–217.

63. Alpheus T. Mason, *Harlan Fiske Stone* (New York: Viking Press, 1956).

64. Alexander Bickel, *The Unpublished Opinions of Justice Brandeis* (Cambridge: Harvard University Press, 1957), 203.

65. *Washington Post*, May 25, 1993, 1.

66. Mary Ann Harrell, *Equal Justice under Law: The Supreme Court in American Life* (Washington, D.C.: The Foundation of the American Bar Association, with the cooperation of the National Geographic Society, 1975), 127.

67. Charles Fairman, *Mr. Justice Miller* (Cambridge: Harvard University Press, 1939), 373–374.

68. Henry F. Pringle, *Life and Times of William Howard Taft*, 2 vols. (New York: Farrar and Rinehart, 1939), 1:529–530.

69. Frank, *Marble Palace*, 76, 81, 264–265.

70. *Scott v. Sandford*, 19 How. (60 U.S.) 393 (1857).

71. Frank, *Marble Palace*, 45.

72. Ibid., 259.

73. John C. Jeffries Jr., *Justice Lewis F. Powell, Jr.: A Biography* (New York: Scribner's, 1994), 534.

74. *Mahnich v. Southern Steamship Co.*, 321 U.S. 96 at 112–113 (1944).

75. *Helvering v. Hallock*, 309 U.S. 106 at 119, 121 (1940).

CHAPTER 17

The People of the Court

MORE THAN TWO CENTURIES after the creation of the federal government, the Supreme Court is only nine people—the chief justice and eight associate justices. Even when the Court's supporting personnel are included, the numbers add up to hundreds, not thousands, of people.

The Court is not a vast bureaucracy, but an organization with well-defined jobs and responsibilities. That point remains valid even though the number of Court offices has grown. The clerk of the Court holds a position as old as the Court itself; the marshal's post is only half as old. The Public Information Office has been a part of the Court for more than fifty years; the curator and the legal officer hold positions about two decades old.

THE CHIEF JUSTICE

The office of chief justice of the United States has developed in large part through the leadership, initiative, and inclinations of the men (and so far, only men) who have held the job. The Constitution mentions the title only once: "When the President of the United States is tried, the Chief Justice shall preside." [1] The Judiciary Act of 1789 specifies only "[t]hat the supreme court of the United States shall consist of a chief justice and five associate justices." *(See Judiciary Act of 1789, pp. 1039, in Appendix A.)*

Indeed, in the very early years of the Court there was little indication that the title of chief justice would become so important and prestigious. As John P. Frank noted.

> The great and yet intangible difference between the Chief and his Associates is the prestige that, rightly or wrongly, tradition attaches to the Chief Justiceship. Popular mythology makes the Chief Justiceship much of what it is, in part because there have been some very great Chief Justices whose personal glory has rubbed off on the office, and partly because of popular esteem for the very idea of "Chief." [2]

Yet because of tradition, popular perception of the office, or other intangible factors, the chief justice is widely perceived as more than *primus inter pares*, or "first among equals." Although he casts only one vote in accepting and deciding cases, Frank pointed out,

> his formal title is a trifle different: he is Chief Justice of the United States, and his fellows are Justices of the Supreme Court. He administers the oath of office to the President. He presides when the Court is in public session, and at its secret conferences. He also presides over the judicial conference of the judges of the lower courts,

and he has the not inconsiderable duty of assigning the writing of most of the opinions of his brothers. He is the chief administrative officer of the Court. [3]

First Among Equals

The first three chief justices were not held in especially high esteem. The first, John Jay, came to the Court in 1789 and resigned six years later, on June 29, 1795, after concluding the peace treaty with England and being elected governor of New York. [4]

His successor, John Rutledge, had first been appointed to the Court in 1790, but resigned as a justice the next year to accept the post of chief justice of South Carolina. After Jay's election, Rutledge wrote to President George Washington that he would accept the chief justiceship "if you think me as fit as any other person and have not made choice of one to succeed him [Jay]." [5]

Washington immediately accepted the suggestion, and Rutledge was sworn in as chief justice on August 12, 1795. But before the Senate came back into session to confirm him, reports of Rutledge's earlier criticism of the Jay Treaty provoked a storm of controversy. When the Senate returned in December, there were, in addition to that controversy, persistent rumors that the new chief justice was mentally unbalanced. Later that month the Senate rejected the nomination 10–14.

Washington next offered the chief justiceship to Henry Clay, but Clay declined the offer, as did Justice William Cushing. Washington then nominated Oliver Ellsworth, who served from 1796 until he resigned in 1800. President John Adams named Jay to succeed Ellsworth, but Jay refused to return to his old post, largely because of the onerous circuit duties imposed upon the justices. Adams then chose John Marshall.

John Marshall

John Marshall's great achievement was to increase public respect for the Supreme Court. When he became chief justice in 1801 the Court was held in low esteem, and its rulings, embodied in often unclear and confusing *seriatim* opinions, did little to enhance the prestige of the third branch of the government.

By his insistence on unanimity and the avoidance of dissenting and concurring opinions, Marshall—and, to a far lesser extent, his successor, Roger B. Taney (1836–1864)—gave the Court the prestige it needed to deal effectively with many of the conflicts and controversies facing the country. President Thomas Jefferson, who sought to break Federalist control of the Court, encouraged dissent but was successful only in his appointment of Jeffersonian loyalist William Johnson. After the deaths of Justices

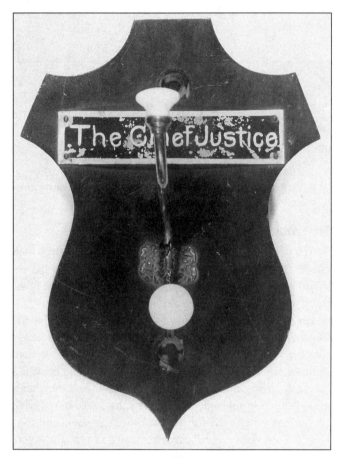

One of the five coathooks used by the justices when the Court occupied the basement of the U.S. Capitol Building (1810–1860).

William Cushing and Samuel Chase, Jefferson wrote to his successor, James Madison, in 1811 that "it will be difficult to find a character of firmness enough to preserve his independence on the same bench with Marshall."

According to Frank, a chief justice

> must get his real eminence not from the office but from the qualities he brings to it. He must possess the mysterious quality of leadership. In this respect the outstanding Chief was Marshall, who for 35 years presided over a Court largely populated by Justices of an opposing political party. Moreover, his Court, because of the very newness of the Constitution it was expounding, dealt with some of the greatest questions of history. Nonetheless, Marshall dominated his Court as has no other Chief Justice. He wrote most of its important opinions, and his dissents are remarkable for their rarity.... More important, Marshall brought a first-class mind and a thoroughly engaging personality into second-class company. The Court when he came to it was lazy and quite willing to let him do the work.[6]

William Howard Taft

The only chief justice who had served as president (1909–1913), William Howard Taft came to the Court in 1921 and immediately embarked on efforts to modernize the U.S. judicial system. His greatest contributions to the Court came in his role as administrator rather than as judge or legal scholar.

A year after his appointment, Taft succeeded in persuading Congress to establish the Judicial Conference of Circuit Court Judges—now the Judicial Conference of the United States—the governing body for the administration of the federal judicial system. (See "Judicial Conference," pp. 890–891.)

More important to the Court was Taft's work in convincing Congress to enact the Judiciary Act of 1925. That law gave the Court—then suffering a severe backlog of cases—almost unlimited discretion in deciding which cases to accept for review. As a result, the caseload, at least for a time, became more manageable, and the Court was able to devote more time and energy to constitutional issues and important questions of federal law.

James F. Simon noted Taft's contribution as chief justice:

> Some experts rate Chief Justice William Howard Taft as one of the Court greats, not because of his opinions, but because of his devoted efforts to reform an antiquated court system.... In his first year as Chief Justice Taft crisscrossed the country in a whistle stop campaign for reform of the courts. He spoke to bar associations, argued his case in legal periodicals and testified at length before the House and Senate judiciary committees. His efforts were handsomely rewarded the next year when Congress passed a judicial reform act that streamlined the federal judicial system by coordinating the activities of the far-flung federal districts and bringing them under surer executive control of the Chief Justice. That accomplished, Taft turned his attention to the problem of court congestion in the Supreme Court docket. "We made our preparations with care," he later said, "and it proved to be easier than we supposed." (Taft's reward was the Judges Bill of 1925....) Before he was through, Chief Justice Taft's arm-twisting (he thought nothing of calling the chairman of the judiciary committee or even talking to the president about his reforms) had succeeded in winning the Court its first permanent home—the present Supreme Court building.[7]

Before winning the presidency and, later, joining the Supreme Court as chief justice, William Howard Taft *(right)* served as governor general of the Philippines and as secretary of war in the administration of President Theodore Roosevelt.

Charles Evans Hughes

Another great chief justice, Charles Evans Hughes, called attention to the "personality and character" of the office before he assumed it in 1930:

> The Chief Justice as the head of the Court has an outstanding position, but in a small body of able men with equal authority in the making of decisions, it is evident that his actual influence will depend upon the strength of his character and the demonstration of his ability in the intimate relations of the judges. It is safe to say that no member of the Supreme Court is under any illusion as to the mental equipment of his brethren. Constant and close association discloses the strength and exposes the weaknesses of each. Courage of conviction, sound learning, familiarity with precedents, exact knowledge due to painstaking study of the cases under consideration cannot fail to command that profound respect which is always yielded to intellectual power conscientiously applied. That influence can be exerted by any member of the Court, whatever his rank in order of precedence.[8]

Hughes served as an associate justice from 1910 to 1916 under the often indecisive, occasionally rambling Chief Justice Edward D. White. During those years, Hughes became acutely aware of the need for leadership by a chief justice in conference discussions and in the assignment of opinions. He also came to appreciate the value of harmony among the nine justices.

Years after Hughes's death, former justice Owen J. Roberts described Hughes as "the greatest of a great line of Chief Justices." During conferences, Roberts said,

> his presentation of the facts of a case was full and impartial. His summary of the legal questions arising out of the facts was equally complete, dealing with opposing contentions so as to make them stand out clearly. . . . After the Chief Justice had finished his statement of the case and others took up the discussion, I have never known him to interrupt or to get into an argument with the Justice who was speaking. He would wait until the discussion had closed and then briefly and succinctly call attention to the matters developed in the discussion as to which he agreed or disagreed, giving his reasons.[9]

During oral argument and in assigning opinions, Hughes was said to show similar control and consideration. Counsel who were nervous or long-winded were often saved by a simple question from Hughes that sought to clarify or rephrase arguments they had presented poorly. "I know of no instance," Justice Roberts said, "where a lawyer had reason to feel rebuked or hurt by anything the Chief Justice said or did."[10]

Hughes described the assigning of opinions as "my most delicate task. . . . I endeavored to do this with due regard to the feelings of the senior Justices and to give each Justice the same proportion of important cases while at the same time equalizing so far as possible the burden of work. Of course, in making assignments I often had in mind the special fitness of a Justice for writing in the particular case."[11] In assigning opinions, Hughes also tried to avoid extreme points of view and let the centrist view prevail. As Merlo Pusey pointed out in his study of Hughes, "When a Justice with a reputation as a liberal voted with the majority on the conservative side of a question, he usually got the opinion to write. The same was true in the case of a conservative voting on the liberal side. Hughes' constant effort was to enhance public confidence in the entire Court as an independent and impartial tribunal."[12]

Hughes also could be considerate in more personal ways. When he had voted with the majority at the Saturday conference, he usually had the opinion-writing assignment delivered to the appropriate justice that same night. Knowing that Justice Benjamin Cardozo, who had suffered a heart attack before coming to the Court in 1932, would begin work on an assignment immediately after getting it, Hughes delayed the delivery of Cardozo's assignments until Sunday. And—so that Cardozo would not be aware of this practice—he also delayed delivering the assignments to Justice Willis Van Devanter, who lived in the same apartment house as Cardozo. Similar tact was used when the other justices gave Hughes "the highly unpleasant duty" of asking for the resignation of the ninety-year-old justice Oliver Wendell Holmes Jr.

Earl Warren

Chief Justice Earl Warren was nominated by President Dwight D. Eisenhower in October 1953 and confirmed unanimously by the Senate on March 1, 1954. Three days after Warren's confirmation, columnist James Reston of the *New York Times* wrote that the new chief justice appeared to display "an ability to concentrate on the concrete; a capacity to do his homework; a sensitive, friendly manner, wholly devoid of pretense, and a self-command and natural dignity so useful in presiding over the court."[13]

Warren's affability and low-key persuasiveness—as much as the liberal affinities of the associate justices he inherited from Democratic presidents—were responsible for leading the Supreme Court into a revolutionary era of ideological decision making. *Brown v. Board of Education*[14] and other opinions of the Warren era were catalysts of social reform. They also unleashed a storm of protest from those who feared expanding the rights of blacks, the poor, criminals, and the underprivileged.

Despite his amiable relationships with his fellow justices, Warren did show at times a gritty leadership. On two occasions

---

EARL WARREN AND THE *BROWN* DECISION

Chief Justice Earl Warren's personal qualities and his amiable relationship with the other justices played a major role in the Court's unanimous ruling in *Brown v. Board of Education*. That landmark decision, written by Warren and handed down May 17, 1954, declared racial segregation in public schools inherently discriminatory and therefore in contravention of the equal protection clause of the Fourteenth Amendment.

The *Brown* decision was a catalyst for the civil rights revolution of the late 1950s and 1960s. The opinion doubtless would have been far less important and far-reaching had it not been unanimous. Had there been dissenting or concurring opinions, the impact of the decision would have been reduced, and opponents of desegregation would have been given the opening to challenge the decision. Warren's achievement in securing unanimity was remarkable in itself. Equally remarkable was the fact that he had been chief justice only a few months when the decision was handed down.

In his book on the *Brown* decision, Richard Kluger wrote that

some time between late February and late March, the Court voted at one of its Saturday conferences on the school-segregation cases. The date is in doubt because the justices had agreed that the case was of such magnitude that no word ought to leak out before the decision was announced. The vote was apparently eight to strike down segregation and one, Reed, to uphold it. But it was far from certain whether Jackson was going to file a separate concurrence or whether Frankfurter might or whether the two of them might agree on one. Warren, of course, wished to avoid concurring opinions; the fewer voices with which the Court spoke, the better. And he did not give up his hope that Stanley Reed, in the end, would abandon his dissenting position. The Chief assigned himself the all-important task of writing the majority opinion.

On March 30 Justice Jackson suffered a serious heart attack. It was suspected that Jackson, along with Frankfurter, might issue a concurring opinion in the case.

Warren, who had been working on the majority opinion, did not circulate his draft until May 7. Justices Burton, Black, Douglas, Minton, and Clark responded quickly and enthusiastically, making only a few minor suggestions for change.

"It was with the three remaining members of the Court [Frankfurter, Jackson, Reed] that Warren could have anticipated problems: any of them might still choose to write his own opinion," Kluger wrote. But Frankfurter "had from the beginning been working for a unified Court. Nothing could have been worse, for the

Court or the nation itself, than a flurry of conflicting opinions that would confuse and anger the American people. So long as the Chief was willing to fashion his opinion in a frank, carefully modulated way, Frankfurter had intended to go along." Warren's draft apparently met with Frankfurter's approval.

"Warren personally delivered his draft opinions to Jackson's hospital room and left them for the ailing Justice to study." After having his clerk, Barrett Prettyman, read the draft, Jackson "was willing to settle for one whose principal virtue seemed to be its temperate tone." Prettyman was quoted by Kluger as saying that the "genius of the Warren opinion was that it was so simple and unobtrusive. [Warren] had come from political life and had a keen sense of what you could say in this opinion without getting everybody's back up. His opinion took the sting off the decision, it wasn't accusatory, and it didn't pretend that the Fourteenth Amendment was more helpful than the history suggested—he didn't equivocate on that point."

Justice Reed then remained the only holdout. According to Kluger, Reed's position on the *Brown* case "stemmed from a deeply held conviction that the nation had been taking big strides in race relations and that the Court's decision to outlaw separate schools threatened to impede that march, if not halt it altogether." Warren met many times with Reed and, according to Reed's clerk, George Mickum, had this to say in one of their last meetings: "Stan, you're all by yourself in this now. You've got to decide whether it's really the best thing for the country."

Warren, according to Mickum, "was not particularly eloquent and certainly not bombastic. Throughout, the chief justice was quite low-key and very sensitive to the problems that the decision would present to the South. He empathized with Justice Reed's concern. But he was quite firm on the Court's need for unanimity on a matter of this sensitivity." Mickum added that "I really think he [Reed] was really troubled by the possible consequences of his position. Because he was a Southerner, even a lone dissent by him would give a lot of people a lot of grist for making trouble. For the good of the country, he put aside his own basis for dissent." At a conference on May 15 the justices at last accepted—unanimously—Warren's opinion in the *Brown* case.

SOURCES: Richard Kluger, *Simple Justice: Brown v. Board of Education and Black America's Struggle for Equality* (New York: Alfred A. Knopf, 1976); Bernard Schwartz, *Super Chief: Earl Warren and His Supreme Court, A Judicial Biography* (New York: New York University Press, 1983), chap. 3.

in early 1961 Warren publicly rebuked senior justice Felix Frankfurter for expanding his written opinion as he announced it in open court and for lecturing the other justices when he delivered a dissenting opinion. Such rebukes were superficial signals of the deep differences between Warren and Frankfurter about the proper posture for the Court. Warren espoused an activist role; Frankfurter a restrained one. Upon his retirement, Warren cited the Court's 1962 decision in *Baker v. Carr* as the most significant of his tenure; Frankfurter wrote one of his most oft-quoted dissents in that case, which was announced just two weeks before a stroke ended his judicial career.

Marshall, Hughes, and Warren are generally considered the three greatest chief justices in American history. In his study of the office, Robert J. Steamer pointed out that despite dissimilar backgrounds and temperaments, these three men shared certain traits, chief among them a willingness "to stretch judging—in different degrees—to accommodate their own convictions." "They were serious men who did not take themselves seriously," Steamer continued, but "perhaps most important, all were straightforward, moral men, personally, professionally, and publicly uncorruptible. . . . None of them was a scheming, petty politician; none was an aggressive office seeker." [15]

"Warren," Steamer wrote, "was neither scholar nor lawyer preeminent, but no matter; he created an ambiance that was to give the Court a unique and exciting character. . . . Under Earl Warren's leadership the Supreme Court became the refuge for those who had been ignored by the president, the Congress, and by governors and state legislatures, with mixed consequences both for the future of constitutional law and for the future of the nation." [16]

Warren E. Burger

A Minnesota native who had been an outspoken "law and order" judge during the turbulent days of the late 1960s, Warren Burger was chosen chief justice by President Richard Nixon in 1969 and was given a mission: halt or reverse the liberal activism of the Warren Court. However, Burger, unlike Warren, did not have a group of like-minded justices who were prepared to follow him. He inherited a solid core of liberal justices, including William O. Douglas, William J. Brennan, and Thurgood Marshall, who were determined to maintain the Court's progressive agenda.

Burger won praise for improving and modernizing the federal court system, as well as the day-to-day operations at the Supreme Court, but he was considered by many a failure as chief justice. He had a pompous and starchy demeanor that alienated some of his colleagues, and his presentations in their closed-door conferences were criticized as rambling and unpersuasive. Rather than lead a conservative revival, the Burger Court was best known for liberal advances such as the recognition of women's rights, the 1973 *Roe v. Wade* ruling that confirmed a woman's right to an abortion, and the 1978 decision in *Board of Regents of the University of California v. Bakke* that upheld affirmative action in colleges and universities.

William H. Rehnquist

An Arizonan, William H. Rehnquist came to Washington in 1969 to join the Nixon administration, and he soon developed a reputation as the most intellectually gifted lawyer—and one of the more conservative ones—in the Justice Department. Nixon appointed Rehnquist to the Court in 1971, and he lived up to his billing as a both as a powerful thinker and an unflinching conservative. President Reagan elevated him to the position of chief justice in 1986. Unlike his predecessor, Warren Burger, Rehnquist established himself as the unquestioned leader of the Court. He combined a firm grasp of constitutional law, a clear conservative philosophy, and a genial manner. His colleagues always knew where the chief justice stood, and a majority usually agreed with him. But the Rehnquist Court was not as conservative as its chief justice would have preferred. Even though he was able to engineer a revival of states' rights and new limits on Congress's power, Rehnquist failed to win a majority to overturn the abortion right or the ban on prayer and other religious activities in the public schools.

Head of the Judicial System

In addition to his duties on the Supreme Court, the chief justice serves as chairman of the Judicial Conference of the United States and the board of the Federal Judicial Center and supervises the Administrative Office of the United States Courts. Chief Justice Burger estimated that he spent about a third of his time on administrative tasks that did not directly involve the other justices.

The Judicial Conference of the United States, the body that governs administration of the federal judicial system, was set up in 1922 by Chief Justice Taft. A former lower-court judge as well as a former president, Taft felt the federal judiciary needed a forum for coordination. The conference consists of the chief justice, its chairman, and twenty-six members—the thirteen chief judges of the U.S. courts of appeal, a district court judge elected by his or her peers in each of the twelve geographic circuits, and the chief judge of the Court of International Trade.

The Federal Judicial Center was created by Congress in 1967 as the research, training, and planning arm of the federal judiciary. Headquartered in Washington, D.C., the center has a seven-member board that meets four times a year. It was in his capacity as chairman of the Federal Judicial Center that Chief Justice Burger established the Study Group on the Caseload of the Supreme Court in 1972. *(See "Federal Judicial Center," p. 891.)*

The Administrative Office of the United States Courts serves as the "housekeeper" and statistician for the federal court system. It was established by Congress in 1939 to take over the administrative duties that had been performed by the attorney general's office.

Extrajudicial Roles

The Constitution gives justices of the Supreme Court no other duty than to serve as justices and the chief justice no other duty than to preside over Senate impeachment proceedings. Congress, however, has given chief justices numerous additional tasks in addition to heading the Supreme Court and the federal judicial system. For example, Congress has made the chief justice a member of the board of regents of the Smithsonian Institution and a member of the board of trustees of the National Gallery of Art and of the Joseph H. Hirshhorn Museum and Sculpture Garden. Even with all these duties, over the years some chief justices have found time to assume voluntarily various nonjudicial roles that have engendered some controversy.

Political Involvement

It could be that chief justices have taken on nonjudicial tasks because so many of them were prominent in politics before their nomination and they retained an activist political temperament upon assuming command of the high court. John Marshall, Roger Taney, Salmon P. Chase, Charles Evans Hughes, Harlan Fiske Stone, and Fred M. Vinson had been cabinet members. Taft had been president. Edward White had been a U.S. senator. Earl Warren had been governor of California. In fact, only two chief justices have come essentially from the bar: Morrison R. Waite (1874–1888) and Melville W. Fuller (1888–1910).

Advising the President

During his first term, President Washington, without judicial advisers of his own, sent the Court twenty-nine questions on international law and treaties. At the time Washington was trying to keep the new country out of the war between Britain and France. The Court refused to give advice, maintaining that the Constitution gave them no authority to share executive power or to issue advisory opinions to a president. But as Chief Justice Burger pointed out, "Although the members of the first Supreme Court wisely resisted President Washington's request for advisory opinions and declined to perform other functions which they deemed to be executive in nature, there is little doubt that Chief Justice Jay gave advice to Washington over the dinner table and even in writing."[17]

Diplomatic Missions

Jay did more for President Washington than offer occasional advice. During his first six months as chief justice, he also served as secretary of state. At the president's request, Jay undertook a successful diplomatic mission to Great Britain in 1794 to try to patch up quarrels over British troops in the American Northwest and private debts to British creditors. The Jay Treaty, which the chief justice negotiated during the visit, may have prevented another war between Britain and the United States, but it involved Jay and the Court in partisan controversy. (So did Jay's subsequent decision to run for governor of New York while still chief justice.)

Although on April 19, 1794, the Senate confirmed, 18–8, Jay's nomination as envoy to Britain, there were strenuous objections to his acceptance of the post while serving as chief justice. During three days of Senate debate on the nomination, one resolution offered maintained that "to permit Judges of the Supreme Court to hold at the same time any other office of employment emanating from and holden at the pleasure of the Executive is contrary to the spirit of the Constitution and as tending to expose them to the influence of the Executive, is mischievous and impolitic."

Similar, but more subdued, criticism befell Jay's successor Oliver Ellsworth for accepting President John Adams's appointment as envoy to France in early 1799.

Chief Justice Stone referred to the impact on the Court of the Jay and Ellsworth missions in a letter to President Franklin D. Roosevelt on July 20, 1942. "We must not forget that it is the judgment of history that two of my predecessors, Jay and Ellsworth, failed in the obligation of their office and impaired their legitimate influence by participation in executive action in the negotiation of treaties," Stone wrote. "True, they repaired their mistake in part by resigning their commissions before resuming their judicial duties, but it is not by mere chance that every chief justice since has confined his activities strictly to the performance of his judicial duties."[18]

Investigatory Commissions

Stone's letter to Roosevelt was written in response to the president's suggestion that the chief justice conduct an investigation into the uses of rubber during World War II. Stone declined the offer, saying, "I cannot rightly yield to my desire to render for you a service which as a private citizen I should not only feel bound to do but one which I should undertake with zeal and enthusiasm."

Stone's main reason for rejecting the assignment was that "a judge and especially the Chief Justice cannot engage in political debate or make public defense of his acts. When his action is judicial he may always rely upon the support of the defined record upon which his action is based and of the opinion in which he and his associates unite as stating the grounds for decision. But when he participates in the action of the executive or legislative departments of government he is without those supports. He exposes himself to attack and indeed invites it, which because of his peculiar situation, inevitably impairs his value as a judge and the appropriate influence of his office."[19]

Chief Justice Warren proved more willing to accept a nonjudicial public duty after the assassination of President John F. Kennedy in 1963. But, for heading the Warren Commission, which investigated and reported on the assassination, he was subjected to considerable criticism. Justice Frankfurter, who had retired in 1962, made little secret of his opposition to the chief justice's participation on the commission. Frankfurter predicted that as a result of Warren's participation in what was primarily a political investigation, the Court would suffer a considerable loss of public respect.[20]

Perquisites

The chief justice has special perquisites. In addition to an annual salary of $198,600 (in 2003) and the attention and respect that surrounds the office, the chief justice may have up to four law clerks, three secretaries, and a messenger. The chief justice is also provided with a car and driver, paid for by the government.

In 1972 Congress authorized the chief justice to "appoint an Administrative Assistant who shall serve at the pleasure of the Chief Justice and shall perform such duties as may be assigned to him by the Chief Justice." The statute authorizing the appointment of an administrative assistant says nothing about the functions and duties of such a position; it is left to the chief justice to determine how and in what areas he or she will work. Both Burger and Rehnquist had their administrative assistants operate in areas outside the chief justice's judicial functions. The administrative assistants provided research and analysis for the justices' speeches, monitored literature and developments in judicial administration, and helped with internal matters such as preparation of the court budget.

THE JUSTICES

Since 1790 only 108 men and women have served as Supreme Court justices (as of early 2004). On average, a new justice joins the Court every twenty-two months. Every president who has served a full term or more, except Jimmy Carter and George W. Bush (as of early 2004), has made at least one appointment. That so few justices have served stems from their appointment for life; most of them are loath to give up a position of such prestige and influence.

Another factor in the low turnover has been the Court's consistent size (nine justices) since 1869. In the Judiciary Act of 1789 Congress set the number of justices, including the chief justice, at six. The Circuit Court Act of 1801, enacted one month before President John Adams's term expired, reduced the number to five to prevent the newly elected president, Thomas Jefferson, from filling any vacancies. In 1802 Congress repealed the 1801 law, bringing the number of Supreme Court justices back to six.

The Judiciary Act of 1807 increased the number to seven, primarily because of the growing judicial workload. In 1837 Congress added two more new seats, bringing the number to nine, the size it has remained ever since, except during the Civil War period. The Judiciary Act of 1863 increased the number of justices to ten, but in 1866 Congress cut the Court's size down to seven to prevent President Andrew Johnson from filling vacancies with appointees who would reflect his views about the unconstitutionality of Reconstruction legislation.

The last adjustment in Court size came with the Judiciary Act of 1869, which increased it to nine seats. The act mandated "[t]hat the Supreme Court of the United States shall hereafter consist of the Chief Justice of the United States and eight associate justices, any six of whom shall constitute a quorum; and for the purposes of this act there shall be appointed an additional associate justice of said court."

The last major effort to change the number of members of the Court was President Franklin Roosevelt's aborted "Court-packing" attempt in 1937 to add justices who ostensibly would

The Royal Exchange, New York City, first home of the U.S. Supreme Court

be more sympathetic to his New Deal legislative proposals than were the sitting justices. In opposition to the plan, several justices argued

> that a Court of nine is as large a court as is manageable. The Court could do its work, except for writing of the opinions, a good deal better if it were five rather than nine. Every man who is added to the Court adds another voice in counsel, and the most difficult work of the Court . . . is that that is done around the counsel table; and if you make the Court a convention instead of a small body of experts, you will simply confuse counsel. It will confuse counsel within the Court, and will cloud the work of the Court and deteriorate and degenerate it.[21]

Since the failure of Roosevelt's plan, there have been no further efforts to increase the number of justices, nor are there likely to be any—for the moment, at least. During the nineteenth century, the main reason for increasing the number of justices was the burden of circuit duty: as new circuits were added, more justices were needed to attend sessions of the courts in these circuits. The circuit-riding duties of the justices ended in 1891. *(See box, Circuit Riding, right.)*

In the past, a Supreme Court justice usually was appointed from the circuit in which he was to serve, but today geographic considerations are not a factor. Factors a president generally considers in nominating someone to the Court are the likelihood of the person winning Senate confirmation and the individual's ability, reputation, ideological position, and political affiliation and beliefs.

Throughout the Court's history the Senate has formally rejected twenty-eight nominees to the Court (the last was President Ronald Reagan's nominee Robert H. Bork in 1987). In addition to the nominees the Senate has formally rejected, fifteen others have been denied confirmation without a vote.

A Judicial "Family"

Depending on shifting traditions and circumstances, members of the Court have sometimes behaved more like a close-knit, chummy family, at other times more like a group of dignitaries on their most scrupulously formal behavior.

In the early years of the Court, particularly after John Marshall became chief justice in 1801, the justices usually lived in the same boardinghouse during the term and shared their meals together. During the Marshall years, when the Court was in session, the justices were together during oral arguments, usually from eleven in the morning until four in the afternoon each day, and during conference after seven in the evening. After the conferences the justices often dined and socialized with each other.

About the justices of the early nineteenth century, Charles Warren has written, "The Judges of the Court appear to have been assiduous diners-out." John Quincy Adams, then secretary of state, wrote in his diary on March 8, 1821: "We had the Judiciary company to dine with us, this day. Chief Justice Marshall, the Judges Johnson, Story and Todd, the Attorney-General Wirt, and late District Attorney Walter Jones; also Messrs. Harper, Hopkinson, D. B. Ogden, J. Sergeant, Webster, Wheaton and

Winder, all counsellors of the Court. . . . We had a very pleasant and convivial party."[22] At this time, the justices "lived for the most part in the same lodgings," Warren continued, and "their intercourse was necessarily of the closest kind, off as well as on the bench."

Charles Sumner, later the Radical Republican senator from Massachusetts and outspoken abolitionist, wrote in a letter of March 3, 1834:

> All the judges board together, having rooms in the same house and taking their meals from the same table, except Judge McLean whose wife is with him, and who consequently has a separate table, though in the same house. I dined with them yesterday. . . . No conversation is forbidden, and nothing which goes to cause cheerfulness, if not hilarity. The world and all its things are talked of as much as on any other day.[23]

In a letter of March 8, 1812, Justice Joseph Story described the life of the justices in their common boardinghouse. "It is certainly true, that Judges here live with perfect harmony, and as agreeably as absence from friends and families could make our residence. Our intercourse is perfectly familiar and unrestrained, and our social hours, when undisturbed with the labors of the law, are passed in gay and frank conversation, which at once enlivens and instructs."[24]

Many of the justices continued to share a common boardinghouse until after the Civil War. In the late nineteenth century, however, as the terms of the Court grew longer, the justices abandoned the boardinghouses, moved their families to Washington, and set up their own households.

Some of the familial aspects of the earlier days remain. It is rare for one justice to allow his or her animosity toward another to come to public attention. Justices rarely criticize the views of their colleagues, except in their written opinions. And there have been repeated instances when the other justices have taken on extra work or exhibited extra kindness toward a justice who was physically or mentally unwell. Still, the secrecy and isolation of the Court tend to make the camaraderie of the boardinghouse days all but impossible today.

Individualism

History, tradition, and the nature of the Court's work limit the opportunities of its members to demonstrate their individual views and traits.

In the early years of the Court several factors encouraged the growth of individualism. One was the practice of delivering *seriatim* opinions, resulting in the issuance of no single opinion of the Court. Chief Justice Marshall ended *seriatim* opinions, but after his tenure the increasing use of dissenting and concurring opinions had a similar effect. Of judicial independence and individualism Wesley McCune wrote:

> Were it not for one institution, the dissenting opinion, anyone who accepted appointment to the Court would almost immediately lose his individual identity, except for what he could retain in Washington society or during summer vacations. If justices

CIRCUIT-RIDING: BURDENS AND HAZARDS

Circuit-riding was a tremendous burden for most justices, and they frequently complained about the intolerable conditions that circuit duties imposed on them. For example, in a letter to the president dated August 19, 1792, the justices wrote:

We really, sir, find the burdens laid upon us so excessive that we cannot forbear representing them in strong and explicit terms. . . . That the task of holding twenty-seven Circuit Courts a year, in the different States, from New Hampshire to Georgia, besides two sessions of the Supreme Court at Philadelphia, in the two most severe seasons of the year, is a task which, considering the extent of the United States and the small number of Judges, is too burdensome. That to require of the Judges to pass the greater part of their days on the road, and at inns, and at a distance from their families, is a requisition which, in their opinion, should not be made unless in cases of necessity.

The president transmitted the letter to Congress, but Congress, then and for almost one hundred years thereafter, refused to abolish the circuit-riding duties. Therefore, the justices, many of them old and in ill health, faced days of difficult travel, inadequate lodging, bad food, and epidemics and disease.

Many unsuccessful bills were introduced in Congress to free Supreme Court justices from this onerous task. In a speech on the Senate floor on January 12, 1819, Sen. Abner Lacock, D-Pa., summed up the major reasons for congressional defeat of the bills. If the justices were relieved of circuit duties, Lacock argued, they would become "completely cloistered within the City of Washington, and their decisions, instead of emanating from enlarged and liberalized minds, would assume a severe and local character." They might also become "another appendage of the Executive authority" and be subjected to the "dazzling splendors of the palace and the drawing room" and the "flattery and soothing attention of a designing Executive."

Congress finally ended the justices' circuit-riding duties when it approved the Circuit Court Act of 1891, which established intermediate—or circuit—courts between the district courts and the Supreme Court. *(See "Circuit Court of Appeals Act of 1891," p. 1079, in Appendix A.)* That long-desired action came in the wake of the attempted murder of Justice Stephen Field by a litigant unhappy with one of Field's decisions as a circuit judge.

In 1888 Field, sitting as a circuit judge in California, his home state, held invalid a marriage contract between Sarah Althea Hill and William Sharon. Sharon, a wealthy mine owner and senator from Nevada (R), had died by the time of the ruling. Hill, who had later married David Terry, one of Justice Field's former colleagues on the California Supreme Court, was incensed at Field's ruling. As a result of their conduct in the courtroom when the ruling was announced, she and Terry were imprisoned for contempt of court.

Justice Stephen Field

The next year Field returned to California to hold circuit court. Concerned about Field's safety, the attorney general authorized protection for him in the form of David Neagle, an armed federal marshal. As Field and Neagle were traveling by train to Los Angeles where Field was to hold court, the Terrys boarded the train. While Field was eating breakfast at a station restaurant, Terry accosted him and struck him. Neagle, thinking that Terry was reaching for a knife with the intent of attacking Field, shot and killed Terry. Neagle was then arrested and charged with murder by state officials. He contested his detention, arguing to the federal courts that the state could not hold him for actions taken in the performance of his duties under federal law.

The case came to the Supreme Court in 1890. Justice Field did not participate in the matter, but the Court agreed with Neagle's argument and ordered his release. *(In re Neagle, 135 U.S. 1 [1890]).*

Although today's justices do not preside over circuit courts, they still have jurisdiction over one or more of the federal circuits and may issue injunctions, grant bail, or stay an execution in these circuits. Requests for an injunction, bail, or a stay of execution go first to the presiding justice in that circuit. If denied, the application may then be made to one of the other justices.

wrote only majority opinions, blended to fit the views of five or more justices, the name of the opinion would mean little and the Court would become as impersonal as a big bank. But through dissents justices have asserted their personal views. Thus, each justice can build a reputation even after arriving on the Court, in addition, of course, to shaping future law by protesting that of the present.[25]

The justices' early circuit-riding responsibilities also encouraged individualism. While on the circuit, the justices operated not as a group but as individual judges with as much discretionary power as they wished to exert.

Another factor favoring independence was the lack of office space before the new Court building was completed in 1935. Until then, most of the justices worked in their own homes, seeing the other justices only when oral arguments were heard or conferences held.

Even after the Court had its own building, some justices continued to work at home. Hugo L. Black was the first justice to move into his Court office and work there—in 1937, two years after the building was occupied. Justice Stone was already in the habit of working at home when he became chief justice in 1941, and he continued to do so. Not until Fred Vinson became chief justice in 1946 did all nine justices work regularly in their court chambers.

Never again, however, has the Court approached the "old boy" closeness of the boardinghouse days. After taking his seat on the Court in 1972, Justice Lewis F. Powell Jr. confessed:

> I had thought of the Court as a collegial body in which the most characteristic activities would be consultation and cooperative deliberation, aided by a strong supportive staff. I was in for more than a little surprise.... The Court is perhaps one of the last citadels of jealously preserved individualism.... Indeed a justice may go through an entire term without being once in the chambers of all the other members of the Court.

Powell described the justices and their staffs as "nine small independent law firms."[26]

Retirement

Neither the Constitution nor the law states when or under what circumstances a justice should retire from service on the Supreme Court. Justices are appointed for life and "shall hold their Offices during good Behaviour," according to Article III, section 1, of the Constitution.

Seventeen justices have resigned from the Court to move on to other careers. Thirty-one justices have resigned to take up retirement. One, Charles Evans Hughes, resigned, served a second time, and then retired. Reasons for resigning have included matters of conscience, the desire to do other work, retirement, and the threat of scandal or impeachment.

Forty-eight justices died while on the Court. Three who had announced their retirements died before their resignations took effect.

Until 1869 many older justices stayed on the job to keep drawing a salary, because a retired justice received no compensation. The Judiciary Statute of 1869 provided that any judge who had served on any federal court for at least ten years and was seventy or older could retire from the bench and continue to receive his regular salary until he died. The law now provides that a justice, if he or she wishes, may retire at age seventy after having served ten years or at age sixty-five after fifteen years of service, with compensation commensurate with his salary.

Even though suffering from old age or poor health, some justices have resisted leaving their seats until subjected to considerable pressure from their colleagues on the Court.

After the election of President Andrew Jackson in 1832, Chief Justice Marshall and Justice Gabriel Duvall (1811–1835), both in

Justices Oliver Wendell Holmes Jr. and Louis D. Brandeis. Holmes retired from the Court at age ninety after twenty-nine years of service.

failing health, were reluctant to resign because they feared that the "radical" new president would choose equally "radical" new justices to take their places. Marshall remained on the Court until his death in 1835, and Duvall submitted his resignation the same year after learning that Jackson intended to nominate as his successor Roger Taney, of whom Duvall approved. (In the end, however, Taney was not confirmed by the Senate to Duvall's seat; after Marshall's death, Jackson named Taney chief justice, and Philip Barbour of Virginia took Duvall's chair.)

By 1869 it was apparent that Justice Robert C. Grier (1846–1870) was both physically and mentally unable to carry out his duties. Early the next year all the other justices formed a committee to tell Grier that "it was their unanimous opinion that he ought to resign." Soon after meeting with the committee Grier retired.

In his book on the Supreme Court Hughes recounts the difficulties that certain justices had in convincing Justices Grier and Stephen J. Field (1863–1897) to retire:

> Some justices have stayed too long on the bench. An unfortunate illustration was that of Justice Grier who had failed perceptibly at the time of the first argument of the legal tender case. As the decision

There have been repeated—if so far unsuccessful—suggestions that a constitutional amendment be enacted to require justices of the Supreme Court to retire at age seventy or seventy-five. Justice Owen J. Roberts expressed his support for such a proposal more than thirty years ago:

I believe it is a wise provision. First of all, it will forestall the basis of the last attack on the Court, the extreme age of the justices, and the fact that superannuated old gentlemen hung on there long after their usefulness had ceased. More than that, it tends to provide for each administration an opportunity to add new personnel to the Court, which, I think, is a good thing.[1]

Charles Fairman wrote that "there are two distinct reasons for urging some scheme for compulsory retirement" of Supreme Court justices:

There is, first, the actual impairment of mental and physical powers. . . . A second reason for insuring renewal of the Court involves considerations of a different order. Rigidity of thought and obsolescence of social outlook, though more objective, may be no less real than the waning of bodily powers. When a majority of the Court cling to views of public policy no longer entertained by the community or shared by the political branches of government, a conflict arises which must be resolved.[2]

1. Speech to the Association of the Bar of the City of New York, December 11, 1948.
2. Charles Fairman, "The Retirement of Federal Judges," *Harvard Law Review* (January 1938): 397.

was delayed, he did not participate in it. A committee of the Court waited upon Justice Grier to advise him of the desirability of his retirement and the unfortunate consequences of his being in a position to cast a deciding vote in an important case when he was not able properly to address himself to it.

Justice Field tarried too long on the bench. . . . It occurred to the other members of the Court that Justice Field had served on a committee which waited upon Justice Grier to suggest his retirement, and it was thought that recalling that to his memory might aid him to decide to retire. Justice Harlan was deputed to make the suggestion. He went over to Justice Field, who was sitting alone on a settee in the robing room apparently oblivious of his surroundings, and after arousing him gradually approached the question, asking if he did not recall how anxious the Court had become with respect to Justice Grier's condition and the feeling of the other Justices that in his own interest and in that of the Court he should give up his work. Justice Harlan asked if Justice Field did not remember what had been said to Justice Grier on that occasion. The old man listened, gradually became alert and finally, with his eyes blazing with the old fire of youth, he burst out:

"Yes! And a dirtier day's work I never did in my life!"

That was the end of that effort of the brethren of the Court to induce Justice Field's retirement; he did resign not long after.[27]

In recounting the Grier and Field retirements, Hughes also described the "agreeable spectacle of Justice Holmes at eighty-five doing his share of work, or even more, with the same energy and brilliance that he showed twenty years ago."[28] But in 1932 and after he had become chief justice, Hughes was obliged to suggest to Holmes, then ninety years old, that he retire. Holmes, doubtless recalling the Grier and Field cases, retired immediately.

At least three justices have resigned because of the dictates of conscience. Justice John A. Campbell (1853–1861) resigned soon after the outbreak of the Civil War to return to his native Alabama, even though he had opposed secession and had freed all of his own slaves. Justice Benjamin R. Curtis (1851–1857) resigned after disagreeing with Chief Justice Taney over the Dred Scott decision; Curtis, a strong advocate of freedom for slaves once they were on free territory, felt he could no longer serve on a Court that had issued such a decision, and so he retired, for that and other reasons. *(See box, Compensation Complaint, p. 772.)* Justice Tom C. Clark (1949–1967) retired to avoid any possible charges of conflict of interest after his son, Ramsey Clark, was appointed attorney general.

Some justices have left the Court to run for elective office or to take other work. John Jay resigned in 1795 to become governor of New York. Five years later he declined reappointment as chief justice because he felt that the Court lacked "the energy, weight and dignity which are essential to its affording due support to the national government."[29] Justice Charles Evans Hughes resigned in 1916 to run unsuccessfully for the presidency. Fourteen years later he returned as chief justice. Arthur J. Goldberg resigned in 1965 when President Johnson asked him to become U.S. ambassador to the United Nations.

Abe Fortas, the only justice ever to resign amidst charges of judicial misconduct, submitted his resignation on May 14, 1969, a few weeks after *Life* magazine published reports that Fortas, during his first year on the Court, had received the first of what were to be annual fees of $20,000 from the Wolfson Foundation. Louis Wolfson was later convicted of violating federal securities laws. In submitting his resignation Fortas denied any wrongdoing, saying that the fee in question had been returned and the relationship terminated. He was resigning nevertheless, he said, to quiet the controversy and enable the Court to "proceed with its work without the harassment of debate concerning one of its members."[30]

Impeachment Attempts

Only a few justices have faced impeachment. The first was Samuel Chase (1796–1811). Of the eight articles of impeachment the House voted against him in late 1804, six concerned his alleged arbitrary and improper actions at the treason and sedition trials of John Fries and James G. Callender in 1800. In its articles of impeachment the House charged that his partisan behavior in and out of court amounted to "high Crimes and Misdemeanors" under the Constitution.

The Senate trial began on February 4, 1805. Although twenty-five of the thirty-four members of the Senate were Republicans, Chase, a Federalist, was acquitted on all counts on March 1. Soon after the acquittal, Chase's and Marshall's adversary, President

Jefferson, acknowledged that the impeachment of justices was "a farce which will not be tried again."

Jefferson proved prophetic, except for several inchoate efforts to impeach Justice William O. Douglas (1939–1975) and Chief Justice Earl Warren.

The first impeachment attempt against Douglas came after he stayed the execution of convicted spies Julius and Ethel Rosenberg in 1953. That resolution was tabled by the House Judiciary Committee after a one-day hearing. The second effort came on April 15, 1970, a week after the Senate's rejection of President Nixon's nomination of G. Harrold Carswell to the Supreme Court. In a speech on the House floor that day, Minority Leader Gerald R. Ford, R-Mich., charged that Douglas (1) had not disqualified himself from a 1970 Supreme Court case involving Ralph Ginzburg, publisher of *Eros* magazine, although Douglas had received $350 for a 1969 article in another magazine published by Ginzburg; (2) had allegedly sanctioned revolution in his book *Points of Rebellion*;[31] (3) was the author of an article entitled "Redress in Revolution" in the April 1970 issue of *Evergreen Review*, which contained nude photographs; (4) practiced law in violation of federal statutes by assisting in the establishment of the Albert Parvin Foundation in 1960 and in giving the foundation legal advice; and (5) served as a consultant to the "leftish" Center for the Study of Democratic Institutions at a time when the center was the recipient of Parvin Foundation funds. On December 3 a special House subcommittee created to investigate the charges against Douglas concluded that there were no grounds for impeachment.

The efforts to impeach Chief Justice Warren never got as far as those against Douglas. Most of the opposition to Warren came from right-wing groups angered over the Warren Court's expansion of individual, civil, and criminal rights. The demand for Warren's impeachment was confined, for the most part, to the fulminations of the John Birch Society and to a grassroots bumper sticker campaign throughout the South.

Extrajudicial Activities

Supreme Court justices cannot be compelled to take any extrajudicial assignments, but they are free to engage in such activities if they wish. The use of this freedom has sparked considerable controversy both inside the Court and among its critics. It was Justice Douglas's extrajudicial activities that prompted the 1970 impeachment effort against him.

A Yen for Politics

The extrajudicial activities that cause the most concern are those in which a political motive is suspected. Before 1900 the political activities of the justices involved a generally less-than-subtle quest for elective office or outright endorsement of or opposition to political candidates. As Justice Owen Roberts pointed out in a 1948 speech, "every justice who has ever sat on that Court who was bitten by political ambition and has actively promoted his own candidacy for office has hurt his own career as a judge and has hurt the Court."[32]

The early justices did not hesitate to campaign openly for their party's candidates. Justices Samuel Chase and Bushrod Washington (1799–1829) campaigned actively for presidential candidates John Adams and Charles Pinckney, respectively, in 1800. Chase's campaigning was denounced by the anti-Federalist press, which complained, somewhat disingenuously, that he was neglecting his Court duties.

Other political-minded nineteenth-century justices included Smith Thompson (1823–1843), John McLean (1830–1861), Salmon Chase (the chief justice, 1864–1873, who presided over the Senate impeachment trial of President Andrew Johnson), David Davis (1862–1877), and Stephen Field (1863–1897).

Like Chief Justice Jay before him, Justice Thompson, a Democrat, ran for governor of New York in 1828 but, unlike Jay, conducted an all-out campaign—which he lost. Justice McLean, who before coming to the Court in 1830 had served in the cabinets of Presidents James Monroe and John Quincy Adams, sought and failed to receive his party's presidential nomination in 1836, 1848, 1852, and 1856. Referring to McLean specifically and to the tendency of justices during that period to become involved in politics, Alexander Bickel wrote that "the recurrence of justices with manifest political aspirations would in time destroy an institution whose strength derives from consent based on confidence." The conduct of justices acting upon their "manifest political aspirations," Bickel continued, "is awkward, unseemly and may give occasion for dire suspicions."[33]

Before his appointment as chief justice in 1864, Salmon Chase had been a U.S. senator, a governor, a cabinet member, and a presidential candidate. His political activities did not cease on the Court. From the bench in 1868 he unsuccessfully sought the presidential nomination of both parties. Justice Davis accepted nomination as a minor-party candidate for president in 1872 before resigning from the Court in 1877 to serve in the Senate. Justice Field periodically indicated his availability for the Democratic presidential nomination.

Far fewer justices have sought elective office in the twentieth century. Justice Robert H. Jackson (1941–1954) was approached to run for governor of New York, largely as a possible springboard for a run for the presidency. Franklin D. Roosevelt in 1944 and Harry S. Truman in 1948 both considered Justice Douglas as a running mate. After President Dwight D. Eisenhower suffered a heart attack, Chief Justice Warren was widely considered a possible Republican presidential nominee in 1956. Eisenhower recovered, ran again, and won.

1876 Electoral Commission

One ostensibly public-spirited activity on the part of five justices ended up involving the Court in one of its most serious political controversies. Justices Nathan Clifford (1858–1881), Samuel F. Miller (1862–1890), Stephen Field (1863–1897), William Strong (1870–1880), and Joseph P. Bradley (1870–1892) were appointed to serve on the electoral commission that resolved the disputed presidential election between Democratic candidate Samuel J. Tilden and Republican candidate Ruther-ford B. Hayes in 1876.

Congress set up the commission in January 1877 and speci-fied that it be composed of fifteen members: three Republicans and two Democrats from the Senate, two Republicans and three Democrats from the House, and two Democrats and two Re-publicans from the Supreme Court. The Court itself was to choose a fifth justice. The Court finally selected Bradley, a Re-publican. Dexter Perkins and Glyndon G. Van Deusen wrote: "Justice Bradley, at first in favor of giving Florida's electoral vote to Tilden, changed his mind between midnight and the morn-ing of the day the decision was announced; there is considerable evidence that he yielded to Republican pressure." [34] The com-mission's vote, announced February 10, 1877, favored Hayes, and Congress acquiesced on March 2, 1877.

Charles Warren pointed out that the justices' service on this commission did not enhance the Court's prestige. "The partisan excitement caused by this election and by the inauguration of Hayes led some newspapers to assert that public confidence in the judges had been weakened, and that the country would be the less willing to accept the doctrines laid down by the Court." [35]

"Public Service"

Some twentieth-century justices ignored the lesson of the Hayes-Tilden Electoral Commission that participation in sup-posedly nonpartisan commissions or investigative bodies could involve the Court in political controversy. Among these in-stances were the participation of Justice Joseph R. Lamar (1911–1916) in international arbitration cases; Justice Owen Roberts's role in the German-American Mixed Claims Commis-sion and the Pearl Harbor Review Commission; and, the most controversial, Justice Robert Jackson's prosecution of Nazi war criminals at the Nuremberg trials and Chief Justice Earl War-ren's role as head of a seven-member commission to investigate the assassination of President John Kennedy.

Jackson at Nuremberg. Several justices were troubled by Jack-son's one-year absence from the Court because of his war trial duties. Chief Justice Stone had opposed Jackson's acceptance of the assignment, and some of the other justices were angry about the extra work that Jackson's absence imposed on them. The sit-uation became even worse after Stone's death in early 1946. As John Frank wrote: "Taking a justice away from his primary duty can be done only at the expense of that duty. Stone's acute bit-terness over the burdens placed upon the court by the absence of Jackson (who, Stone sputtered, was off running a lynching bee at Nuremberg) is understandable. Such extra-judicial work may also involve justices in controversies that lower the prestige so valuable to the court." [36]

But the fact that the Court did suffer some loss of prestige because of Jackson's role at Nuremberg had less to do with the workload burdens placed on the other justices than with Jack-son's assault on Justice Hugo Black, issued from Nuremberg. According to Frank, "The most recent direct outbreak of one justice against another was Jackson's attack on Black at the time

of the appointment of Chief Justice Vinson in 1946. Jackson, who was abroad at Nuremberg trying German war criminals at the time and who had deeply desired the place for himself, apparently felt that Black was in some way responsible for the appointment of Vinson. He issued a vitriolic public statement denouncing Black for having participated in a certain case in which Jackson felt that Black should have disqualified himself." Amidst the publicity that the statement received, Justice Black "maintained a complete silence." [37]

Somewhat surprisingly, Justice Frankfurter did not share his colleagues' resentment of Jackson's role in the Nuremberg trials. Years before his appointment to the Supreme Court in 1939 and after his retirement in 1962, Justice Frankfurter opposed the par-ticipation of justices in any public activities that were not strictly relevant to their judicial responsibilities. In 1929, for ex-ample, Professor Frankfurter wrote: "In suggesting that judges engage in public activities off the bench, we are in danger of for-getting that it is the business of judges to be judges. . . . It is nec-essary for judges to be less worldly than others in order to be more judicial." [38] After his retirement from the Court, Frank-furter also criticized Chief Justice Warren's decision to head the investigation of President Kennedy's assassination.

Although Frankfurter resigned immediately from the Ameri-can Civil Liberties Union, the National Association for the Ad-vancement of Colored People, and even the Harvard Club when named to the Court, he nevertheless served on several presiden-tial and national commissions while a sitting justice.

Warren Commission. To ascertain all the facts and circum-stances related to the assassination of President Kennedy, Presi-dent Lyndon B. Johnson created a seven-man investigating commission on November 29, 1963. Chief Justice Warren agreed to head the commission, which also included Sens. Richard B. Russell, D-Ga., and John Sherman Cooper, R-Ky.; Reps. Hale Boggs, D-La., and Gerald Ford, R-Mich.; Allen W. Dulles, for-mer director of the CIA; and John J. McCloy, former disarma-ment adviser to President Kennedy.

The Warren Commission released its findings on September 27, 1964, concluding that Lee Harvey Oswald, "acting alone and without advice or assistance," had shot President Kennedy. Be-fore the report was released, critics of Warren's performance on the Court denounced the chief justice for neglecting his judicial duties and for participating in such a "political" undertaking. After the findings were released, those convinced that there had been a conspiracy to assassinate Kennedy joined in the criticism.

White House Advisers

Justice Frankfurter's continuing interest in political and other nonjudicial matters was particularly evident in his role as adviser to President Franklin Roosevelt on a variety of mat-ters, foreign and domestic. During the spring and summer of 1939, for example, Frankfurter sent almost three hundred notes to Roosevelt warning of the threat posed by Hitler and advising the president of the actions that should be taken to counter the German threat. These and later actions led observers to label Frankfurter the "outside insider in the Roosevelt administration."[39]

Supreme Court justices have been giving advice to presidents and other elected officials since the time of John Jay. This informal relationship generally has resulted in criticism of the justices and the Court. When President Roosevelt indicated at a press conference in September 1939 that he had discussed the situation in Europe with Justices Stone and Frankfurter, there was a storm of protest over the involvement of justices in the foreign policy deliberations and decisions of the executive branch. Stone thereafter refused all invitations to confer with the president. Frankfurter, however, continued advising Roosevelt and his successors.

In the 1960s Justice Fortas continued to advise President Johnson after his appointment to the Court. This role as adviser to Johnson was a major factor in Fortas's failure to win Senate confirmation as chief justice in 1968. It likely played some part in his resignation from the Court on May 14, 1969. James Simon described the circumstances leading to Fortas's resignation. In the summer of 1968,

> President Johnson named Associate Justice Abe Fortas to succeed Chief Justice Warren. At first, anti-Fortas forces, led by Republican Senator Robert P. Griffin of Michigan, opposed the nomination primarily because it had been made by a "lame duck" president. At the Senate's confirmation hearings, Fortas ran into deeper trouble. The chief justice-designate, it was learned, had counseled the president on national policy and had even done some behind-the-scenes lobbying on the president's behalf while sitting on the Supreme Court. Later, when Fortas admitted that he had received $15,000 for conducting a series of seminars at American University, his ethics as well as his politics were brought into question. As a result, his nomination as Chief Justice languished and was finally withdrawn by President Johnson.[40]

Fortas retained his seat as an associate justice. But in May 1969 *Life* Magazine revealed that since becoming a justice Fortas had accepted—and then returned several months later—$20,000 from a charitable foundation controlled by the family of indicted stock manipulator Louis E. Wolfson. Shortly thereafter Fortas resigned. In a letter to Chief Justice Warren on May 14, 1969, Fortas stated:

> There has been no wrongdoing on my part. . . .
> There has been no default in the performance of my judicial duties in accordance with the high standards of the office I hold. So far as I am concerned, the welfare and maximum effectiveness of the Court to perform its critical role in our system of government are factors that are paramount to all others. It is this consideration that prompts my resignation which, I hope, by terminating the public controversy, will permit the Court to proceed with its work without the harassment of debate concerning one of its members.[41]

Perquisites

The scandal surrounding Justice Fortas's acceptance of a fee from the Wolfson foundation prompted Chief Justice Warren, shortly before his resignation, to urge adoption of a judicial code of ethics requiring judges to file an annual report on investments, assets, income, gifts, and liabilities and prohibiting them from accepting compensation other than their judicial salaries.

In 1973 the Judicial Conference, under Chief Justice Burger, adopted resolutions asking judges to report gifts of more than $100 and any income from outside work. Supreme Court justices today file annual financial disclosure reports of assets and income earned from activities off the bench.

In 2003 each associate justice was paid an annual salary of $190,100—the chief justice makes $198,600—so there is little need for a justice to seek outside sources of income. This was not always the case, however. Some of the early justices were so strapped for money and so badly reimbursed for their services on the Court that they were obliged to find ways to supplement their earnings. *(See box, Justices' Salaries, p. 900.)*

Justices have various perquisites. They include four law clerks, two secretaries, and a messenger. All the justices can make use of the Court's barber, for which they pay, as well as the Court's dining room, exercise room, and library. The Court maintains a small fleet of cars for the official use of the justices, but most of the justices drive themselves to and from work.

SUPPORTING PERSONNEL

Compared with the executive and legislative branches of the federal government, the Supreme Court employs few people and spends relatively little money. About 325 people work for the Court, and its annual budget in 2003 was in the comparatively modest $46 million range.

The Court's statutory employees—clerk, marshal, reporter of decisions, and librarian—are appointed by the Court. The justices select their own clerks and other personal staff. All other support personnel are appointed by the chief justice. In addition, several other groups work with the Court but are not employees of it. These include the Federal Judicial Center, the Administrative Office of the United States Courts, the Judicial Conference of the United States, and the Supreme Court Historical Association.

The solicitor general and that official's staff, while closely involved with the work of the Court, are part of the executive branch, specifically the Department of Justice. The solicitor general and staff select which cases the government brings to the Court and advise the Court, when asked, on the government's view of various other cases. The Supreme Court bar, the attorneys who argue before the Court, are also independent yet important parts of the Court's support system.

Clerk of the Court

The clerk of the Court is the Court's judicial business manager. The clerk ensures that the Court is able to carry out its constitutional duty, its judicial business, in an orderly fashion. The office was established by the first formal rule of the Court, adopted in February 1790. Through the years the clerk's duties have increased enormously. The clerk now has a staff of thirty people.

CLERKS OF THE COURT

Name	Term	State of Origin
John Tucker	1790–1791	Massachusetts
Samuel Bayard	1791–1800	Pennsylvania
Elias B. Caldwell	1800–1825	New Jersey
William Griffith	1826–1827	New Jersey
William T. Carroll	1827–1863	Maryland
D. W. Middleton	1863–1880	D.C.
J. H. McKenney	1880–1913	Maryland
James D. Maher	1913–1921	New York
William R. Stansbury	1921–1927	D.C.
C. Elmore Cropley	1927–1952	D.C.
Harold B. Willey	1952–1956	Oregon
John T. Fey	1956–1958	Virginia
James R. Browning	1958–1961	Montana
John F. Davis	1961–1970	Maine
E. Robert Seaver	1970–1972	Missouri
Michael Rodak Jr.	1972–1981	West Virginia
Alexander Stevas	1981–1985	Virginia
Joseph F. Spaniol Jr.	1985–1991	Ohio
William K. Suter	1991–	Virginia

The responsibilities of the clerk of the Court include:

• administering the Court's dockets and argument calendars;
• receiving and recording all motions, petitions, jurisdictional statements, briefs, and other documents filed on the various dockets;
• distributing those various papers to the justices;
• collecting filing fees and assessing costs;
• preparing and maintaining the Court's order list and journal, in which are entered all the Court's formal judgments and mandates;
• preparing the Court's formal judgments and mandates;
• notifying counsel and lower courts of all formal actions taken by the Court, including written opinions;
• supervising the printing of briefs and appendices after review has been granted in *in forma pauperis* cases;
• requesting and securing the certified record below upon the grant of review or other direction of the Court;
• supervising the admission of attorneys to the Supreme Court bar, as well as their occasional disbarments; and
• giving procedural advice by telephone, mail, and in person to those counsel and litigants who need assistance with or assurance about the Court's rules and procedures.

To help the clerk and the clerk's staff carry out these many functions, a computerized information system was installed in 1976.[42]

To date, there have been only nineteen clerks of the Court. Four of them served for a quarter of a century or more: Elias B. Caldwell (1800–1825), William T. Carroll (1827–1863); J. H. McKenney (1880–1913), and C. Elmore Cropley (1927–1952). The first clerk, John Tucker, was selected on the third day of the Court's first session, February 3, 1790, to oversee the courtroom and library, manage subordinate employees, collect the salaries of the justices, and find them lodgings when necessary. The clerk in early 2004 was William K. Suter, who has held that position since 1991.

The 1790 rule that established the position of clerk prohibited him from practicing law before the Court while he was a clerk. In the early years the clerk performed many of the duties later taken over by the reporter and the marshal. So varied were the responsibilities of the early clerks that they were described as a combination business manager–errand boy for the justices and the lawyers who appeared before the Court.

The importance of the clerk was summed up nearly a century ago by a man who had had considerable experience with the Clerk's Office, Augustus H. Garland, former governor of Arkansas, former Democratic senator from that state, and former U.S. attorney general. Garland wrote:

> It is well to note that it is quite important for lawyers practicing in that Court to see much of the Clerk's office and to know its workings. If any motion is to be had or proceedings asked in Court not specifically provided for by law or rule, it is wise to seek advice there beforehand.... Many useless and sometimes unpleasant collisions between the Court and counsel are avoided by this precaution. Even the oldest and most experienced attorneys are not ashamed to consult the Clerk's office and they do not hesitate to do so.[43]

Although the Office of the Clerk of the Court was established in 1790, no provision was made for a salary until nine years later. In 1799 Congress provided that "the compensation to the Clerk of the Supreme Court of the United States shall be as follows, to wit: for his attendance in Court, ten dollars per day, and for his other services, double the fees of the clerk of the Supreme Court of the state in which the Supreme Court of the United States shall be holden."[44]

For almost one hundred years the Office of the Clerk was self-supporting. It paid salaries and other expenses of its operations out of filing fees. The generous fees and other allowances gave some of the early clerks a handsome annual stipend. In 1881, for example, the clerk's net income was almost $30,000 a year—only slightly less than the president's and considerably more than the justices'.[45] Strict accountability for the Court's funds was not imposed until 1883. The filing fees now go to the U.S. Treasury, and Congress appropriates the money for the salaries and expenses of the Clerk's Office.

Marshal of the Court

The Judiciary Act of 1867 gave the Court authority to appoint a marshal, to remove a marshal, and to fix that official's compensation. Today the marshal oversees the operations of

MARSHALS OF THE COURT

Name	Term
Richard C. Parsons	1867–1872
John C. Nicolay	1872–1887
John Montgomery Wright	1888–1915
Frank Key Green	1915–1938
Thomas E. Waggaman	1938–1952
T. Perry Lippitt	1952–1972
Frank M. Hepler	1972–1976
Alfred Wong	1976–1994
Dale E. Bosley	1994–2000
Pamela Talkin	2001–

the Court building as its general manager, its paymaster, and its chief security officer. Before the office was created, these duties were performed either by the clerk or the marshal of the district in which the Court was located. Between 1801 and 1867, for example, the twelve men who served as marshal of the District of Columbia also served, informally, as marshal of the Court.

The present-day marshal attends all the Court's sessions, manages more than two hundred employees, supervises the federal property used by the Court, pays the justices and other employees, oversees telecommunications, orders supplies, and pays the Court's bills. The marshal, whose original duties were to keep order in the courtroom, also oversees the Supreme Court Police Force, which consists of a chief of police and about eighty officers. They police the building, grounds, and adjacent streets; they may make arrests and carry firearms. The marshal and the marshal's aides also receive visiting dignitaries and escort the justices to formal functions outside the Court.

During public sessions of the Court, the marshal (or his deputy) and the clerk—both dressed in morning coats or cutaways—station themselves at opposite ends of the bench. At exactly 10 a.m., on a signal from the chief justice, the marshal pounds the gavel and announces: "The Honorable, the Chief Justice and the Associate Justices of the Supreme Court of the United States." As the justices take their seats, he calls for silence by crying "Oyez" ("Hear ye") three times and announces: "All persons having business before the Honorable, the Supreme Court of the United States, are admonished to draw near and give their attention, for the Court is now sitting. God save the United States and this honorable Court." During oral argument, the marshal or his assistant flashes the white and red lights to warn counsel that the time for presenting arguments is about to expire.

Until recently, the marshal also was directed to "serve and execute all process and orders issued by the Court or a member thereof." The marshal would delegate the actual serving of papers—usually disbarment orders—to U.S. marshals. The only time this function drew attention came during the tenure of

Marshal Frank Key Green (1915–1938). Green served a subpoena on business tycoon J. Pierpont Morgan Jr. when government officials were trying to regain possession of Martha Washington's will, which Morgan's father allegedly had stolen. Upon receiving the subpoena, Morgan returned the will. The process-and-orders function has passed to the Clerk's Office.

Like the other statutory officers of the Court—the clerk, the reporter, and the librarian—the marshal's salary in 2003 was about $118,000. Pamela Talkin was serving as marshal in early 2004; she has served in that position since 2001.

Reporter of Decisions

The reporter of decisions is responsible for editing the opinions of the Court and supervising their printing and publication in the official *United States Reports*. The reporter and the reporter's staff of nine check all citations after the opinions of the justices have been delivered, correct typographical and other errors in the opinions, and add the headnotes, the voting lineup of the justices, and the names of counsel that appear in the published version of the opinions.

The Court's orders and decisions are first circulated as "Preliminary Prints." Users of these preliminary prints are "requested to notify the reporter of decisions . . . of any typographical or other formal errors, in order that corrections may be made before the bound volume goes to press." The orders and decisions are printed under the auspices of the U.S. Government Printing Office and sold by the Superintendent of Documents.

The post of reporter of decisions had informal beginnings. The first reporter, Alexander J. Dallas (1790–1800), was self-appointed. Before the Supreme Court moved to Philadelphia, Dallas had published a volume on Pennsylvania court decisions.

REPORTERS OF DECISIONS

Name	Term
Alexander J. Dallas	1790–1800
William Cranch	1801–1815
Henry Wheaton	1816–1827
Richard Peters Jr.	1828–1843
Benjamin C. Howard	1843–1861
Jeremiah S. Black	1861–1862
John W. Wallace	1863–1875
William T. Otto	1875–1883
J. C. Bancroft Davis	1883–1902
Charles Henry Butler	1902–1916
Ernest Knaebel	1916–1944
Walter Wyatt	1946–1963
Henry Putzel Jr.	1964–1979
Henry C. Lind	1979–1987
Frank D. Wagner	1987–

When the Court began meeting in Philadelphia in 1791, Dallas's book contained the cases of both the Pennsylvania court and the Supreme Court. Most accounts of the early Supreme Court indicate that Dallas, a lawyer, undertook the first reports as a labor of love and a public service. Dallas, who was also a journalist, editor, patron of the arts, and secretary of the Treasury (1814–1816), published four volumes of decisions covering the Supreme Court's first decade.

Dallas was succeeded unofficially by William Cranch in 1801. Like Dallas—who served as Treasury secretary while reporting on the Court's decisions—Cranch continued to sit as a judge and later chief justice of the circuit court in Washington, D.C.

During Cranch's service as reporter of decisions, the justices began supplementing their oral opinions with written texts in important cases. This was of immeasurable assistance to Cranch and subsequent reporters. Cranch, whose reports were highly praised for their accuracy and clarity, believed that public scrutiny of opinions was needed to keep the justices from making arbitrary decisions.

Cranch's successor, Henry Wheaton, was the first reporter formally appointed by the Court. In 1816 Congress provided for publication of Court decisions, and a year later set the reporter's salary at $1,000 a year. The Judiciary Act of 1817 mandated that, for this salary, the reporter had to publish each opinion within six months of a decision and provide eighty copies to the secretary of state for distribution. The reports continued to be sold to the public, at $5 a volume, and the reporter was still able to share in the profits, such as they were.

After he retired in 1827 to become minister to Denmark, Wheaton and his successor, Richard Peters Jr., became involved themselves in a Supreme Court case.[46] Peters was determined to increase the meager sales of the reports and his own profits as well. He therefore decided to revise and streamline the earlier reports and publish them in "Peters' Condensed Reports" at a price of $36. Because the purchase of Peters's reports would make it unnecessary for the interested public to purchase Wheaton's reports, the former reporter of decisions sued Peters, charging a violation of copyright. The Court ruled, however, that Court opinions were in the public domain.

As Garland noted, "The office of the Reporter is not a . . . bed of roses. The work is constant, arduous and exacting. A failure to give full scope in the syllabus . . . to the utterances of a judge brings wrath upon him."[47] Reporters Benjamin C. Howard (1843–1861) and John W. Wallace (1863–1875) felt the wrath of several justices. In 1855 Justice Peter V. Daniel (1842–1860) wrote to reporter Howard complaining that his name had not been inserted at the beginning of his dissenting opinion and that he was henceforth uncertain that he would allow his dissents to be published in the reports. Justices Noah H. Swayne (1862–1881) and Nathan Clifford complained that reporter Wallace failed to publish their opinions or butchered them.

Wallace was the last reporter to have his name on the cover of the Court's published reports. The first ninety volumes of the reports were titled Dall. 1–4; Cranch 1–15; Wheat. 1–12; Pet. 1–16;

How. 1–24; Black 1–2, and Wall. 1–23. After 1874 the name of the reporter of decisions appeared only on the title page of the reports.

The reporter in early 2004 was Frank D. Wagner; he assumed that position in 1987.

Librarian

The Supreme Court library, which contains more than 450,000 volumes in print, microform, and electronic formats, is located on the third floor of the Court building. (A private library for the justices, with 65,000 volumes, is on the second floor. There are also small core libraries in each chamber plus an offsite annex library containing 50,000 books.) Use of the main Supreme Court library is limited to Court personnel, members of the Court bar, members of Congress and their legal staffs, and government attorneys. Usually, however, the library will grant access to its books to members of the public or press who specify a particular research interest.

Since 1887, when the post of librarian was created, there have been eleven Court librarians. The library has a staff of twenty-five, of whom twelve are professional librarians and some also are lawyers. As of early 2004 Judith A. Gaskell was librarian of the Court. She assumed that position in 2003.

In the early years of the Court the justices had no library of their own, and it was not until 1812 that Congress allowed the justices to use the Library of Congress. In 1832, after repeated refusals to give the Court its own library, Congress gave the justices the 2,011 law books in the Library of Congress, but insisted that members of Congress retain the right to use them as well. Because the Court had no librarian at the time, the clerk of the Court was put in charge of the books. By 1863 the number of law books had increased to almost 16,000. In 1884 the marshal of the Court was given responsibility for the Court's collection of books. The post of librarian, created in 1887, remained in the marshal's department until Congress made it a separate office in 1948.

LIBRARIANS OF THE COURT

Name	Term
Henry Deforest Clarke	1887–1900
Frank Key Green	1900–1915
Oscar Deforest Clarke	1915–1947
Helen C. Newman	1947–1965
Henry Charles Hallam Jr.	1965–1972
Edward G. Hudon	1972–1976
Betty H. Clowers (acting)	1976–1978
Roger F. Jacobs	1978–1985
Stephen G. Margeton	1985–1988
Shelley L. Dowling	1989–2003
Judith A. Gaskell	2003–

The library has the most complete set available of the printed briefs, records, and appendices of Court cases. It also contains all federal, state, and regional reports, federal and state statutory codes, legal periodicals, legal treatises, and digests and legislative and administrative source materials. And it has special collections in international law, military law, British law, patent and trademark law, and Supreme Court history.

When the clerk was in charge of the library in the nineteenth century, lawyers and others allowed to use the library could borrow no more than three books at a time. The books had to be returned within a "reasonable" time. For books that were not returned within a reasonable time, the clerk imposed a fine of $1 a day on the borrower. If a book was lost, the borrower had to pay twice the value of the lost book. This rule later was changed to protect the Court's collection. Books and other materials now cannot be removed from the building, although members of the Supreme Court bar may request that materials be sent to them when they are arguing a case.

Public Information Officer

The Court's Public Information Office is responsible for answering questions from the public, facilitating competent coverage of the Court by the news media, and distributing information about the Court and the justices. The public information officer is the Court's public spokesperson on matters other than the interpretation of its opinions and orders. The justices believe that their opinions and orders must speak for themselves.

The Public Information Office releases the opinions and orders of the Court to the press as soon as they are announced in open court, and then serves as the public's source for these documents. The schedule of Court sessions and conferences, the activities of the justices, and changes in Court procedures are usually placed on a bulletin board in the press room adjoining the Public Information Office. Special announcements about the Court or the justices are released by the office.

In 1982 the press room was modernized and expanded. It houses carrels for eighteen major news organizations covering the Court on a regular basis and facilities for other journalists. In addition, the major television and radio networks have separate broadcast booths on the ground floor where reporters tape record their news stories and then transmit them directly to their offices.

The Public Information Office also maintains petitions, motions, briefs, responses, and jurisdictional statements on all current cases for the use of Court staff and the media. It supervises the assignment of Court press credentials and admission to the press section of the courtroom, and serves as liaison between the media and all other offices of the Court, including the chambers of the justices.

The Public Information Office serves as the source of news and information within the Court, circulating news items and publishing an employee newsletter, *Oyez! Oyez!*, and an occasional features publication, *The Docket Sheet*.

The current (as of early 2004) public information officer, Kathleen L. Arberg, is the fifth person to hold that post since it was established in 1935. Her predecessors were Ned Potter, Banning E. Whittington, Barrett McGurn, and Toni House. The office has a staff of four.

Legal Office and Law Clerks

As the number of cases has increased over the years, the justices have relied more and more on their law clerks. In recent years thirty-four law clerks were serving nine justices, about twice the number employed in the mid-1960s. Most of the justices have four clerks each. Chief Justice William Rehnquist and Justice John Paul Stevens have chosen to have only three.

The justices have complete discretion in hiring the law clerks they want. The clerks are generally selected from candidates who were at the top of their classes in the country's most prestigious law schools. Many have already clerked for a lower-court judge. The nature and amount of a clerk's work depends on the work habits of his or her particular justice. Years ago Justice Louis Brandeis once asked his clerk to check every page of every volume of *United States Reports* for information that Brandeis wanted. Justice Black insisted that some of his clerks play tennis with him. Chief Justice Stone liked his clerks to accompany him on his walks. On the contemporary Court, Justice Sandra Day O'Connor has been known to take her clerks whitewater rafting.

As John Frank, who clerked for Justice Black in the early 1950s, pointed out, "The tasks of the clerks are very much the product of the whims of their justices. In general, it is the job of the clerk to be eyes and legs for his judge, finding and bringing in useful materials."[48] The two major functions of the clerks are to read, analyze, and often prepare memoranda for the justices on the thousands of cases that reach the Court each year and to help otherwise in whatever way a justice expects in preparing the opinion that he or she will deliver.

It has been charged that law clerks have on occasion written the opinion issued in the name of the justices, but there has been no proof that any clerk has actually been the author of an opinion. How much of the preliminary writing a clerk may do is a well-guarded secret.

Three of the current justices served as law clerks: John Paul Stevens clerked for Wiley B. Rutledge in 1947 and 1948; Rehnquist clerked for Robert Jackson in 1952 and 1953; and Stephen G. Breyer clerked for Arthur Goldberg in 1964 and 1965.

All three tend to minimize the influence the clerks have on the justices and their opinions. Stevens has written that "an interesting loyalty develops between clerks and their Justices. It is much like a lawyer-client relationship, close and confidential. Like a lawyer, a clerk can't tell his client, the Justice, what to do. He can only suggest what can happen if he does or doesn't do something."[49]

Byron R. White (1962–1993), who was a law clerk for Chief Justice Vinson in 1946 and 1947, said, "We couldn't get our work done without the clerks. But I don't think they influence the results here all that much. I like 'em around to hear their various views. When I served as a clerk, I don't think anything I ever did or said influenced my Justice. I felt I was doing Chief Justice Vinson a service by making sure that relevant considerations were placed before him, such as opinions from other courts, law journals, ideas of my own—things he wouldn't have time to dig up on his own." [50]

In 1957 Rehnquist described his activities as clerk to Justice Jackson:

> On a couple of occasions each term, Justice Jackson would ask each clerk to draft an opinion for him along lines which he suggested. If the clerk were reasonably faithful to his instructions and reasonably diligent in his work, the Justice would be quite charitable with his black pencil and paste pot. The result reached in these opinions was no less the product of Justice Jackson than those he drafted himself; in literary style, these opinions generally suffered by comparison with those which he had drafted. . . . The specter of the law clerk as a legal Rasputin, exerting an important influence on the cases actually decided by the Court, may be discarded at once. No published biographical materials dealing with any of the Justices suggest any such influence. I certainly learned of none during the time I spent as Clerk. [51]

Thirty years later, when Rehnquist wrote a book about how the Court works, he noted that he always asks a law clerk to prepare a first draft of a Court opinion and said,

> The practice of assigning the task of preparing first drafts of Court opinions to law clerks who are usually just one or two years out of law school may undoubtedly and with some reason cause raised eyebrows in the legal profession and outside of it. Here is the Supreme Court of the United States, picking and choosing with great care one hundred and fifty of the most significant cases out of the four or five thousand presented to it each year, and the opinion in the case is drafted by a law clerk! I think the practice is entirely proper: The justice must retain for himself control not merely of the outcome of the case, but the explanation for the outcome, and I do not believe this practice sacrifices either. [52]

Whatever the impact of the clerks on the justices and their opinions has been, they almost always remain in the shadows, inaccessible to the public and the press. The clerks talk among themselves about the views and personalities of their justices, but rarely has a clerk discussed clashes among the justices or leaked news about an opinion until it is announced. Such unwritten rules, as well as the clerks' loyalty to the justices they serve, account for the anonymity that surrounds the clerks during their time as staff members of the Court.

That tradition of anonymity was punctured in 1998 when Edward Lazarus, a former clerk to Justice Harry Blackmun, published a highly critical account of the Court, based in part on the experience of his year there. In *Closed Chambers: The First Eyewitness Account of the Epic Struggles Inside the Supreme Court,* Lazarus described a Court that was torn by the "destructive pathologies" of deceit and partisanship. He spoke of the "warping factors of polarization and a failure of integrity" among the justices. "The story of the Court in the late 1980s and early 1990s is of this spirit of faction and recrimination," Lazarus

concluded. [53] Although the Court had no official response to the book, the chief justice stressed to newly arriving clerks that they owed a duty of loyalty and confidentiality to the Court.

Because of the steady volume of new appeals and the need for legal research, the justices long ago recognized that they required the aid of a well-trained legal assistant. The first law clerk was hired by Justice Horace Gray in 1882. As early as 1850 the justices had sought congressional approval for the hiring of an "investigating clerk" to help each justice and to copy opinions. When that request was not granted, some of the justices used employees of the Court Clerk's Office to help them.

Justice Gray's law clerk, who had been the top graduate of Harvard Law School, served primarily as a servant and a barber, paid by the justice himself. It was not until 1886 that Congress provided $1,600 a year for a "stenographic clerk" for each justice. In the years that followed, clerks often served considerably longer than the one year they generally serve now. Chief Justices Hughes and Taft and Justice Frank Murphy employed law clerks who served for five years or more.

In 1973 the Court's Legal Office was established. It serves in part to act as "house counsel" on questions directly concerning the Court and its building and in part to provide permanent and specialized help to the justices in addition to the more transient assistance they receive from their law clerks.

The office consists of two attorneys (the Court counsel and staff counsel) and a legal assistant. The lawyers prepare memoranda for the justices' conference on a variety of matters, including petitions for extraordinary writs, issues related to original cases, and Supreme Court bar admissions and disbarment questions. They also advise the clerk of the Court and the justices' offices on requests that the Court expedite its consideration of a case. In addition, they provide legal services for Court officers on problems ranging from personnel grievances and contracts to proposed changes in the Court's rules. They work with outside counsel on legislation and litigation of concern to the Court.

Curator's Office

In 1973 the Court created another new office, that of curator. Its responsibilities include caring for the Court's historical papers and possessions, developing exhibits about the Court, offering educational programs for the public about the Court's history and its collections, and recording events at the Court for future researchers.

The Supreme Court's collections include antique furnishings; archives of documents, photographs, and cartoons; other memorabilia; and art. In 1994 the curator's staff installed a permanent exhibit portraying the architecture and construction of the Supreme Court building.

Nearly 800,000 people visit the Supreme Court building each year. The Curator's Office provides courtroom lectures and tours Monday through Friday. A twenty-three-minute film on the Court is shown continuously during visiting hours in the theater on the ground floor. Up-to-date information on visiting hours and special exhibits is available on the Court's Web site at www.supremecourtus.gov.

The first curator was Catherine Hetos Skefos, who served from 1973 to 1976; the second curator, Gail Galloway, served from 1976 to 2002. The curator in early 2004 was Catherine Fitts.

The Chief Justice's Administrative Assistant

Since 1972 the chief justice of the United States has had an administrative assistant to help with the increasingly complex administrative duties that devolve upon the office in addition to its strictly judicial functions.

Under Chief Justice Rehnquist, the administrative assistant acts as a senior court manager, assisting the chief in the internal management of the Court with responsibilities for personnel, budget, information systems, public information, general organization policy, and other administrative matters. The assistant also helps the chief justice in his responsibilities involving the Judicial Conference of the United States, the Federal Judicial Center, the Administrative Office of the United States Courts, and the Smithsonian Institution. The assistant serves as a liaison with the executive branch, Congress, and the other state and private organizations involving the administration of justice.

The administrative assistant also oversees the judicial fellows program and the judicial internship program at the Court. The first administrative assistant was Mark Cannon; the second, Noel J. Augustyn; the third, Larry Averill; the fourth, Robb M. Jones; and the fifth, Harvey Rishikof. The current administrative assistant is Sally Rider.

SUPREME COURT LAWYERS

The advocates—the lawyers who argue before the Supreme Court—do not work for the Court, but without them the Court would have no work. These lawyers counsel the clients, file the petitions, write the briefs, and argue the cases before the Court. They represent the federal government, the states, the individuals, and the businesses whose disputes come to the Court. Their skill—or lack of it—in presenting a client's claim and the issues it raises can make the Court's work easier or more difficult.

The Supreme Court bar is not an organized group, but its undisputed leader is the U.S. solicitor general. Because the U.S. government is involved in so many of the cases that come to the Court, the solicitor general and staff appear there more than any other "law firm" in the country. Indeed, the solicitor general is sometimes called the "tenth justice" and has a permanent office in the Court building.

Supreme Court Bar

When the Supreme Court first convened in February 1790, one of its first actions was to establish qualifications for lawyers who wished to practice before it. The current version of that rule says: "To qualify for admission to the Bar of this Court, an applicant must have been admitted to practice in the highest court of a State, Commonwealth, Territory or Possession, or the

---

JOHN S. ROCK: FIRST AFRICAN AMERICAN ADMITTED TO THE U.S. SUPREME COURT BAR

"Wherever the colored man is elevated it will be by his own exertions."

—John S. Rock

In his forty-one years of life, John S. Rock managed to become a teacher, dentist, doctor, and a lawyer, all during a time when millions of African American men were still enslaved in the South. Rock was born in New Jersey, and his parents, who early on recognized his intelligence and insatiable desire to learn, ensured that he completed his secondary education. After his first career as a teacher, Rock began studying medicine but later turned to dentistry, most likely when he was denied entrance to medical colleges because of his race.

While practicing dentistry in Philadelphia, Rock took up the cause of racial justice as a political lecturer and abolitionist speaker. He expressed pride in himself and was among the first African American activists to publicly acknowledge pride in his race. He was ultimately able to complete his medical education and graduated from the American Medical College in 1852. The following year, he and his wife moved to Boston, the epicenter of the abolitionist movement. Persistent ill health forced him to abandon his medical and dental practice and led him instead to study law. He was admitted to the Massachusetts Bar in 1861.

During the Civil War, Rock practiced law and continued to serve as a community leader and orator and worked with other activists to create an African American militia. In 1865 on the day that Congress approved the Thirteenth Amendment ending slavery, Massachusetts senator Charles Sumner introduced a motion to make Rock the first African American attorney admitted to the U.S. Supreme Court Bar. Gaining admittance to practice before the highest court in the country was unfortunately to be one of Rock's final achievements. He died less than a year later.

SOURCE: National Park Service, Boston African-American National Historic Site, Biographies, www.nps.gov/boaf/johnsrock.htm.

District of Columbia for a period of at least three years immediately before the date of application; must not have been the subject of any adverse disciplinary action pronounced or in effect during that three-year period; and must appear to the Court to be of good moral and professional character." [54]

The two requirements for admission to the Supreme Court bar—acceptable personal and professional character, and qualification to practice before a state's or territory's highest court—have remained the same since 1790. It is not known how many attorneys were admitted to the Supreme Court bar between 1790 and 1852. From 1853 to 1924, 25,097 were admitted. Since 1925 another 215,000 lawyers have been admitted, for a total of about 240,000 members since records began being kept. About 5,000 are now admitted each year.

The Supreme Court bar has been called "a heterogeneous collection of individual lawyers located in all parts of the

BELVA LOCKWOOD: FIRST WOMAN ADMITTED TO THE U.S. SUPREME COURT BAR

"The glory of each generation is to make its own precedents."
—Belva Lockwood

A lawyer, reformer, and women's rights advocate, Belva Lockwood was not only the first woman to practice law before the United States Supreme Court, she was also one of the first female presidential candidates. When her husband's death left her with an infant daughter to support, the nineteen-year-old teacher resumed her education and graduated from Genesee College (now Syracuse University) in New York. After relocating to Washington, D.C., remarrying, and returning to teaching, Lockwood decided to study law. She fought for admission and was finally accepted at the National University Law School (now George Washington University Law School). She graduated in 1873 but was denied her diploma until a direct appeal to President Ulysses S. Grant, who was the titular head of the school, led to its release.

Graduating from law school and being admitted to the District of Columbia Bar, however, were not lofty enough accomplishments for Lockwood. When one of her cases reached the Supreme Court, she was refused admission to practice before the Court, leading her to spend the next five years lobbying Congress to allow women to practice law before the highest court in the land. In 1879 Lockwood had the honor of becoming the first woman admitted to the U.S. Supreme Court Bar.

Although Belva Lockwood is best known for her work in opening the legal profession to women, she was also an advocate of equal rights for women, minorities, and the poor. Indeed, she argued before the Court in support of an African American man whose law degree was withheld from him because of his color. In 1884 and 1888 Lockwood was the candidate of the Equal Rights Party for the presidency of the United States.

SOURCES: Barbara Babcock, *Belva Lockwood: For Peace, Justice, and President*, Women's Legal Biography Project, Stanford University, 1997, www.stanford.edu/group/WLHP/papers/lockwood.htm; National Women's Hall of Fame, www.greatwomen.org/women.php?action=viewone&id=99.

In 1879 Belva Lockwood became the first woman lawyer to be admitted to the Supreme Court bar. In 1906 she became the first woman to argue before the Court.

nation. There is no permanent organization or formal leadership."[55] Although some lawyers seek admission to the Supreme Court bar merely for personal prestige, membership does have a real function. Except in limited circumstances, any attorney seeking to file any legal document with the Court and to argue a case before the Court must be a member of the Court's bar. A nonmember may work on a case, but at least one member of the bar must sponsor any case filed with the Court.

A lawyer who believes he or she meets the two requirements for admission to the bar must submit two documents to the clerk of the Court:

(1) a certificate from the presiding judge, clerk, or other authorized official of that court evidencing the applicant's admission to practice there and the applicant's current good standing, and (2) a

completely executed copy of the form approved by this Court and furnished by the Clerk containing (a) the applicant's personal statement, and (b) the statement of two sponsors endorsing the correctness of the applicant's statement, stating that the applicant possesses all the qualifications required for admission, and affirming that the applicant is of good moral and professional character. Both sponsors must be members of the Bar of this Court who personally know, but are not related to, the applicant.[56]

Applications are screened by the Clerk's Office, and lawyers whose applications are in order are notified by the clerk. There is a $100 admission fee.

Since 1970 there have been two ways to gain formal admission to the bar. Previously, attorneys had only the route of an oral motion in open court. The attorney selects a day when the Court is in public session and notifies the clerk. The applicant then finds a standing member of the Supreme Court bar who is willing and able to appear in Court with the applicant. When the Court convenes, the chief justice announces that admissions will be entertained at that time. The clerk then calls the sponsor to the rostrum, the sponsor requests that the applicant be admitted to the bar, and the chief justice announces that the motion is granted.

After all the motions have been made and granted, the new members are welcomed by the chief justice, and the clerk of the Court administers the oath to the group. Each newly admitted member of the bar is asked to "solemnly swear that as an attorney and counselor of this Court, you will conduct yourself uprightly and according to law, and that you will support the Constitution of the United States. So help you God." The applicants reply in unison, "I do."

In 1970, largely as a result of the increasing amount of time being spent on the oral motions in open session, the Court began allowing applicants to submit written motions without making a formal appearance. These so-called mail-order admissions now constitute 80 percent or more of all admissions to the Supreme Court bar. Applicants choosing the written-motion form also must sign the oath of admission and have it notarized and send their checks to the clerk of the Court. If an applicant's papers are in order and the Court approves the admission, the clerk notifies the applicant and informs him or her that the certificate of admission will be mailed.

Attorneys can be disbarred from the Supreme Court Bar after disbarment in some jurisdiction or "conduct unbecoming a member of the Bar or for failure to comply with" the rules of the Court.[57] An attorney may also resign from the bar. No reason need be given.

To some observers, including John Frank, modern members of the Supreme Court bar lack the dramatic flair and oratorical genius of nineteenth-century advocates like Daniel Webster, Henry Clay, John C. Calhoun, and Augustus Garland. "In the 19th century, there was a Supreme Court bar, a group of lawyers in or about Washington . . . to whom other lawyers sent their cases in the same fashion that a New York lawyer today might send a piece of San Francisco business to a San Francisco lawyer," Frank wrote. But, he continued:

> The ease of modern transportation coupled with the desire of individual lawyers to have the experience of appearing in the Supreme Court have almost totally destroyed the system of a Supreme Court bar, so that today a very small number of appearances makes a man an unusually experienced Supreme Court practitioner. The number of lawyers under the age of sixty engaged solely in private practice who have appeared before the court a substantial number of times could be quickly counted. Today the lawyer from Little Rock takes in his own case, whereas in 1880 he would have retained A. H. Garland, who as attorney general and private counsel argued 130 cases. Jeremiah Sullivan Black presented 16 cases between 1861 and 1865 and won 13, including eight reversals of lower courts. Today a very experienced private practitioner may have argued five cases in a lifetime.[58]

But in 1993 political scientist Kevin T. McGuire accurately documented a discrete, reemerging Supreme Court bar:

> Who are these lawyers? They are former members of the solicitor general's staff who now utilize their enormous Supreme Court expertise in private practice. They are former clerks to the justices who have seen the Court from the inside. They are well-educated, talented litigators who work in some of the nation's largest, most prestigious law firms and who represent a sophisticated clientele in the Court. They are counsel to any number of organized interests that have established offices throughout the neighboring streets of the capital community and that use appellate litigation to further their policy goals. These lawyers position cases in lower courts for possible appeals. They file briefs at the agenda stage and argue cases on the merits. They strategize with amici curiae and consult with less experienced counsel. They are, in sum, central actors in the politics of the Supreme Court.[59]

Three attorneys in the twentieth century stood out as the most experienced Supreme Court advocates. John W. Davis, who was the solicitor general from 1913 to 1918, made 140 arguments before the Court both as the solicitor general and as a private attorney. Erwin N. Griswold, who was the solicitor general from 1967 to 1973, made 118 arguments as the solicitor general and as a private lawyer. Lawrence G. Wallace, an assistant solicitor general whose tenure began in 1968 and was continuing in the mid-1990s, had already made 133 arguments by early 1996.

Solicitor General

The solicitor general is appointed by the president to represent the U.S. government before the Supreme Court. It is the solicitor general who usually decides which cases the government should ask the Court to review and what the government's legal position on them will be. He (so far, all have been men) and his staff of some two dozen attorneys prepare the government's briefs and argue the government's case before the Court. Often the solicitor general himself argues the case. In most years, he does so six or seven times per term. The rest of the time the solicitor general is represented by one of the lawyers on his staff. On rare occasions an important case may be argued by the attorney general, the solicitor general's superior.

One observer who spent many years in the Office of the Solicitor General wrote that the solicitor general

> may not unfairly be described as the highest government official who acts primarily as a lawyer. He has few administrative responsibilities; he can devote his time to studying the legal problems which come before him. Moreover, he must stand on his own feet when he is presenting the most important government cases to the Supreme Court. . . . The solicitor general regards himself—and the Supreme Court regards him—not only as an officer of the executive branch but also as an officer of the Court.[60]

The principal duties of the solicitor general's office, which is part of the Department of Justice, are to review hundreds of briefs from government agencies, to decide which cases the government should appeal, and to argue the government's position to the Court. The briefs that are reviewed usually are amended

SOLICITORS GENERAL, 1870–2003

Name	Term	State of Origin	President
Benjamin H. Bristow	October 11, 1870–November 15, 1872	Kentucky	Grant
Samuel F. Phillips	November 15, 1872–May 3, 1885	North Carolina	Grant
John Goode	May 1, 1885–August 5, 1886	Virginia	Cleveland
George A. Jenks	July 30, 1886–May 29, 1889	Pennsylvania	Cleveland
Orlow W. Chapman	May 29, 1889–January 19, 1890	New York	B. Harrison
William Howard Taft	February 4, 1890–March 20, 1892	Ohio	B. Harrison
Charles H. Aldrich	March 21, 1892–May 28, 1893	Illinois	B. Harrison
Lawrence Maxwell Jr.	April 6, 1893–January 30, 1895	Ohio	Cleveland
Holmes Conrad	February 6, 1895–July 8, 1897	Virginia	Cleveland
John K. Richards	July 1, 1897–March 6, 1903	Ohio	McKinley
Henry M. Hoyt	February 25, 1903–March 31, 1909	Pennsylvania	T. Roosevelt
Lloyd Wheaton Bowers	April 1, 1909–September 9, 1910	Illinois	Taft
Frederick W. Lehman	December 12, 1910–July 15, 1912	Missouri	Taft
William Marshall Bullitt	July 16, 1912–March 11, 1913	Kentucky	Taft
John William Davis	August 30, 1913–November 26, 1918	West Virginia	Wilson
Alexander C. King	November 27, 1918–May 23, 1920	Georgia	Wilson
William L. Frierson	June 11, 1920–June 30, 1921	Tennessee	Wilson
James M. Beck	June 30, 1921–June 7, 1925	New Jersey	Harding
William D. Mitchell	June 4, 1925–April 5, 1929	Minnesota	Coolidge
Charles Evans Hughes Jr.	May 27, 1929–March 16, 1930	New York	Hoover
Thomas D. Thacher	March 22, 1930–May 4, 1933	New York	Hoover
James Crawford Biggs	May 4, 1933–March 24, 1935	North Carolina	F. Roosevelt
Stanley Reed	March 23, 1935–January 30, 1938	Kentucky	F. Roosevelt
Robert H. Jackson	March 5, 1938–January 17, 1940	New York	F. Roosevelt
Francis Biddle	January 22, 1940–September 4, 1941	Pennsylvania	F. Roosevelt
Charles Fahy	November 15, 1941–September 27, 1945	New Mexico	F. Roosevelt
J. Howard McGrath	October 4, 1945–October 7, 1946	Rhode Island	Truman
Philip B. Perlman	July 30, 1947–August 15, 1952	Maryland	Truman
Walter J. Cummings Jr.	December 2, 1952–March 1, 1953	Illinois	Truman
Simon E. Sobeloff	February. 10, 1954–July 19, 1956	Maryland	Eisenhower
J. Lee Rankin	August 4, 1956–January 23, 1961	Nebraska	Eisenhower
Archibald Cox	January 24, 1961–July 31, 1965	Massachusetts	Kennedy
Thurgood Marshall	August 11, 1965–August 30, 1967	New York	L. Johnson
Erwin N. Griswold	October 12, 1967–June 25, 1973	Massachusetts	L. Johnson
Robert H. Bork	June 19, 1973–January 20, 1977	Connecticut	Nixon
Wade Hampton McCree Jr.	March 28, 1977–August 5, 1981	Michigan	Carter
Rex E. Lee	August 6, 1981–May 31, 1985	Utah	Reagan
Charles Fried	October 25, 1985–January 20, 1989	Massachusetts	Reagan
Kenneth Starr	May 27, 1989–January 20, 1993	Virginia	Bush
Drew S. Days III	June 7, 1993–June 30, 1996	Florida	Clinton
Seth P. Waxman	Nov. 13, 1997–Jan. 20, 2001	Connecticut	Clinton
Theodore B. Olson	June 11, 2001–	California	Bush

and on occasion are totally rewritten. Most are revised and modified to some extent in collaboration with the author of the draft.

The Office of the Solicitor General has a heavy workload. During the October 2002 term, for example, the solicitor general participated in 71 of 84 cases fully considered by the Court and was on the winning side in 56 of them. Over many decades, the solicitor general's office has won about 70 percent of the cases it argued.

The solicitor general is under considerable pressure to limit the number of cases that he asks the Court to take. As Robert L. Stern noted, this pressure is "partly self-serving and partly not." On the more objective level, as Lincoln Caplan noted, the solicitor general

Theodore B. Olson

As far as the general public is concerned, solicitors general are fairly anonymous figures, although several—William Howard Taft, Stanley Reed, Robert Jackson, and Thurgood Marshall—later became justices of the Supreme Court. One exception was Robert H. Bork (1973–1977). Bork's notoriety, however, had nothing to do with his Court-related duties but with his role in the infamous "Saturday night massacre" following President Nixon's decision to fire special Watergate prosecutor Archibald Cox—himself a former solicitor general (1961–1965)—on October 20, 1973. Attorney General Elliot Richardson and Deputy Attorney General William Ruckelshaus resigned rather than obey Nixon's order to fire Cox, at which point Bork, as the highest-ranked official left in the Justice Department, took command and fired Cox.

President Reagan's aggressive push to convince the Court to change its views on major social issues—such as abortion, affirmative action, and school prayer—thrust the solicitor general back into the national limelight. Charles Fried, Reagan's second solicitor general, particularly drew much attention, and considerable criticism, as he carried the president's arguments on these questions to the Court.[63] Theodore B. Olson is the forty-second solicitor general of the United States. Appointed by President George W. Bush, he took office in June 2001.

SUPPORTING ORGANIZATIONS

Four other organizations have an impact directly or indirectly on how the Court operates, on its workload, and on the amount of public interest in the Court. These organizations are the Judicial Conference of the United States, the Administrative Office of the United States Courts, the Federal Judicial Center, and the Supreme Court Historical Society. The first three organizations were created by Congress and, with the chief justice, are involved in the administration of the federal courts. They are located in the Thurgood Marshall Federal Judiciary Center just a few blocks north of the Supreme Court building.

Judicial Conference

The Judicial Conference of the United States is the policy-making body for the administration of the federal judicial system, the system's "board of trustees" or "board of directors." The conference is composed of the chief judges of the thirteen courts of appeals, a district court judge from each of the twelve geographic (or regional) circuits, and the chief judge of the Court of International Trade. The chief justice serves as the presiding officer. By law, the conference is charged with carrying on "a continuous study of . . . the general rules of practice and procedure" and recommending "such changes in and addition to those rules as the Conference may deem desirable to promote simplicity in procedure, fairness in administration, the just determination of litigation and the elimination of unjustifiable expense and delay."[64]

In 2003 the conference had committees on the Administrative Office, automation and technology, bankruptcy, budget,

is aware of the necessity from the standpoint of the effective administration of the judicial system of restricting the number of cases taken to the Supreme Court to the number that the Court can hear. This alone permits the Court to give adequate consideration to the important matters which the highest tribunal in the land should decide. . . . A heavy additional burden would be imposed on the Court if the government, with its great volume of litigation, disregarded that policy and acted like the normal litigant who wants to take one more shot at reversing a decision which is obviously wrong because he lost.

The selfish reason for the Solicitor General's self-restraint in petitioning for certiorari is to give the Court confidence in government petitions. It is hoped and believed—although no one who has not been on the Court can be sure—that the Court will realize that the Solicitor General will not assert that an issue is of general importance unless it is—and that confidence in the Solicitor General's attempt to adhere to the Court's own standards will cause the Court to grant more government petitions.[61]

The post of solicitor general was created by Congress in 1870 when the Department of Justice was established. Before 1870 the functions of the solicitor general were carried out by the attorney general. Congress explained that its purpose in establishing the new office was to provide "a staff of law officers sufficiently numerous and of sufficient ability to transact this law business of the Government in all parts of the United States." The law also said that the solicitor general should be "a man of sufficient learning, ability and experience that he can be sent . . . into any court wherever the government has any interest in litigation, and there present the case of the United States as it should be presented."[62]

codes of conduct, court administration, criminal law, defender services, federal-state jurisdiction, financial disclosure, intercircuit assignments, international judicial relations, the judicial branch, judicial resources, long-range planning, magistrates, circuit council conduct and disability orders, rules of practice and procedure, and space and facilities.

The conference was created by Congress, at the urging of Chief Justice Taft, in 1922. It was then called the Judicial Conference of Senior Circuit Judges. It originally consisted of the chief justice of the United States, the chief judges of the nine circuit courts of appeal, and the attorney general, who was at that time responsible for the administrative affairs of the courts.

Until 1940 the reports of the conference were included in the annual reports of the attorney general. When the Administrative Office of the United States Courts was created in 1939, administrative responsibility over the courts was transferred from the attorney general to the new office. The administrative office has operated under the supervision and direction of the judicial conference ever since.

The number of members on the conference has more than doubled since 1922. In the 1950s a district court judge representing each regional circuit joined the judicial conference. In late 1986 the chief judge of the U.S. Court of International Trade was added. The conference has no separate budget of its own, and whatever staff assistance is needed is provided by the Administrative Office of the United States Courts.

Administrative Office

As its name indicates, the Administrative Office of the United States Courts performs many of the support functions needed for the federal court system. The duties and functions of the office have expanded considerably since it was created in 1939.

The office prepares and submits to Congress the budget and legislative agenda for the courts. It provides administrative assistance to the clerical staffs of the courts, the probation officers, bankruptcy judges, magistrate judges, and other court staff. It also audits and disburses funds for the operation of the courts.

The Administrative Office also provides support to the committees of the Judicial Conference of the United States. It compiles and publishes statistics on the work and workloads of the federal courts, conducts various studies of the courts as directed by the conference, and maintains liaison with various groups, including Congress and the executive branch. The director and deputy director are appointed by the chief justice in consultation with the Judicial Conference.

Since its creation, the Administrative Office of the United States Courts has operated under the direction of the Judicial Conference. The director submits a report on the activities of the office and the situation of the federal courts, and any recommendations for improvement to the annual meeting of the Judicial Conference, to Congress, and to the attorney general. Nearly seven hundred people work in the Administrative Office. In fiscal year 2003 the office had a budget of $66.9 million.

Federal Judicial Center

The Federal Judicial Center was created by Congress in 1967 "to further the development and adoption of improved judicial administration in the courts of the United States." The center serves as the research, training, and development arm of the federal judiciary. Its seven-member board, headed by the chief justice, includes two judges from the U.S. circuit courts, three from the U.S. district courts, and the director of the Administrative Office of the United States Courts. The board meets four times a year, and the center's policy decisions are made at these meetings.

The center provides a two-week orientation to new federal judges and offers continuing education programs on topics ranging from docket management to criminal sentencing. It provides training to improve the management practices of the 25,000 supporting personnel of the courts, helps clerks' offices process cases, and teaches probation officers techniques for supervising defendants and preparing bail and sentencing recommendations.

The results of the center's research projects are often passed on to the Judicial Conference of the United States to assist it in making recommendations for improvements in the federal court system. The center's staff is made up of about 140 lawyers, educators, and social scientists. The center's annual budget in fiscal year 2003 was $22.9 million.

Historical Society

The Supreme Court Historical Society was founded in November 1974 as a nonprofit group to increase public interest in and knowledge about the Supreme Court and the federal court system. The society collects and preserves data and memorabilia related to the Court's history. It also supports historical research, publishing the results of that research in scholarly works and publications for the general public.

The society is funded through membership contributions from its five thousand members as well as from gifts, grants, and sales of Court-related books and memorabilia in a gift shop it operates on the Court's ground floor. Regular membership dues are $50 a year; life memberships begin at $5,000. Students pay $25 a year. The society has an active volunteer structure with committees on acquisitions, programs, development, publications, and membership, among others. It publishes a quarterly newsletter, an annual journal, and various books and pamphlets.

The society has cosponsored with the Court *The Documentary History of the Supreme Court of the United States, 1789–1800*, a comprehensive documentary collection of material relating to the first decade of the Court's history. The society's Web site is www.supremecourthistory.org.

NOTES

1. Article I, section 3, clause 6.
2. John P. Frank, *Marble Palace: The Supreme Court in American Life* (New York: Knopf, 1958), 71.

3. Ibid.

4. Charles Warren, *The Supreme Court in United States History*, rev. ed., 2 vols. (Boston: Little, Brown, 1926), 1:124.

5. Quoted in ibid., 1:127.

6. Frank, *Marble Palace*, 78–79.

7. James F. Simon, *In His Own Image: The Supreme Court in Richard Nixon's America* (New York: David McKay, 1973), 92–93.

8. Charles Evans Hughes, *The Supreme Court of the United States* (New York: Columbia University Press, 1928), 57.

9. Address to the Association of the Bar of the City of New York, December 12, 1948.

10. Ibid.

11. Merlo Pusey, *Charles Evans Hughes*, 2 vols. (New York: Columbia University Press, 1963), 2:678.

12. Ibid., 2:679.

13. *New York Times*, March 4, 1954.

14. *Brown v. Board of Education*, 347 U.S. 483 (1954).

15. Robert J. Steamer, *Chief Justice: Leadership and the Supreme Court* (Columbia: University of South Carolina Press, 1986), 36–38.

16. Ibid., 50.

17. Address to the National Archives, September 21, 1978.

18. Letter to Franklin D. Roosevelt, July 20, 1942.

19. Ibid.

20. Bruce Allen Murphy, *The Brandeis/Frankfurter Connection: The Secret Political Activities of Two Supreme Court Justices* (New York: Oxford University Press, 1982), 340.

21. Charles Evans Hughes, letter to Congress, March 21, 1937.

22. Warren, *Supreme Court in United States History*, 1:87, 471.

23. Ibid., 1:792.

24. Ibid., 1:473.

25. Wesley McCune, *The Nine Young Men* (New York: Harper and Brothers, 1947), 238.

26. Quoted by Richard L. Williams, "Justices Run 'Nine Little Law Firms' at Supreme Court," *Smithsonian*, February 1977, 89.

27. Hughes, *Supreme Court*, 75–76.

28. Ibid., 76.

29. Warren, *Supreme Court in United States History*, 1:173.

30. Letter to Chief Justice Earl Warren, May 14, 1969.

31. William O. Douglas, *Points of Rebellion* (New York: Random House, 1970).

32. Address to the Association of the Bar of the City of New York, December 11, 1948.

33. Alexander Bickel, *Politics and the Warren Court* (New York: Harper and Row, 1965), 137.

34. Dexter Perkins and Glyndon G. Van Deusen, *The United States of America*, 2 vols. (New York: Macmillan, 1962), 2:64. But see also Charles Fairman, *Five Justices and the Electoral Commission of 1877*, supplement to

vol. 7 of the Oliver Wendell Holmes Devise *History of the Supreme Court of the United States* (New York: Macmillan, 1988).

35. Warren, *Supreme Court in United States History*, 2:583.

36. Frank, *Marble Palace*, 269.

37. Ibid., 258–259.

38. *Boston Herald*, November 15, 1929. But also see Murphy, *Brandeis/Frankfurter Connection*.

39. Liva Baker, *Felix Frankfurter* (New York: Coward-McCann, 1969), 237. See also Joseph P. Lash, *From the Diaries of Felix Frankfurter* (New York: Norton, 1975).

40. Simon, *In His Own Image*, 102.

41. Letter to Chief Justice Earl Warren, May 14, 1969.

42. Robert L. Stern, Eugene Gressman, Stephen M. Shapiro, and Kenneth S. Geller, *Supreme Court Practice*, 7th ed. (Washington, D.C.: Bureau of National Affairs, 1993), 14.

43. Augustus H. Garland, *Experience in the Supreme Court of the United States, with Some Reflections and Suggestions as to That Tribunal* (Washington, D.C.: John Byrne, 1898), 12.

44. 1 Stat. 624, 625.

45. Charles Fairman, "The Retirement of Federal Judges," *Harvard Law Review* (January 1938): 417.

46. *Wheaton v. Peters*, 8 Pet. (33 U.S.) 591 (1834).

47. Garland, *Experience in the Supreme Court*, quoted in Supreme Court Information Office, *The Docket Sheet* 13 (summer 1976): 4.

48. Frank, *Marble Palace*, 116.

49. Quoted by Williams in "Justices Run 'Nine Little Law Firms,' " 88.

50. Ibid., 90–91.

51. William H. Rehnquist, "Who Writes Decisions of the Supreme Court?" *U.S. News and World Report*, December 13, 1957, 74.

52. William H. Rehnquist, *The Supreme Court: How It Was, How It Is* (New York: Quill and William Morrow, 1987), 299–300.

53. Edward Lazarus, *The First Eyewitness Account of the Epic Struggles Inside the Supreme Court* (New York: Times Books, 1998), 13, 510

54. Supreme Court Rule 5.1.

55. Stern et al., *Supreme Court Practice*, 733.

56. Supreme Court Rule 5.2.

57. Supreme Court Rule 8.2.

58. Frank, *Marble Palace*, 93–94.

59. Kevin T. McGuire, *The Supreme Court Bar: Legal Elites in the Washington Community* (Charlottesville: University Press of Virginia, 1993), 21–22.

60. Robert L. Stern, "The Solicitor General and Administrative Agency Litigation," *American Bar Association Journal* (February 1960): 154–155.

61. Caplan, *Tenth Justice*, 156.

62. 28 U.S.C. 505.

63. Caplan, *Tenth Justice*.

64. 28 U.S.C. 331, as amended in 1961.

CHAPTER 18

Courtrooms and Costs

FOR THE FIRST 145 YEARS of its existence, the Supreme Court of the United States was a tenant in buildings intended for other purposes. The Court did not move into its own building until 1935. Today, nearly seventy years later, the Court is still housed in a single building. In contrast to Congress, its neighbor on Capitol Hill, the Court has no additional buildings or wings.

The costs of the Court likewise are comparatively small. In fiscal year 2003 the Supreme Court's budget was about $46 million, and the budget of the full federal judiciary's was projected to be $5.3 billion, out of a total U.S. budget of $2.1 trillion.

HOUSING THE COURT

Between its first meeting in New York City and its first session in its present building at One First Street, Northeast, in Washington, D.C., the Supreme Court convened in about a dozen different places. During the Court's first 145 years, the justices moved, on average, once every 12 years.

Early Days

Some of the early courtrooms were shared with other courts. After the Court moved to Washington in 1801, it held formal sessions in various rooms of the Capitol and, according to some sources, in two taverns as well.[1] Some of the premises provided for the Court in the Capitol were described by commentators of that time as "mean and dingy" and "little better than a dungeon."[2] Their present headquarters, by contrast, has been called a "marble palace."[3]

New York City

The Supreme Court first met on February 1, 1790, in New York City, then the nation's temporary capital. The Court held session at the Royal Exchange Building at the intersection of Broad and Water Streets in what is now Manhattan's financial district. The courtroom occupied the second floor of the gambrel-roofed, cupola-topped building; an open-air market occupied the first floor. The courtroom was sixty feet long with a vaulted ceiling.

The justices stayed in New York for two terms. The first lasted from February 1 to February 10, 1790, and the second for only two days, August 2 and 3, 1790. There were no cases on the Court's docket during these two terms, and the justices spent their time at duties such as appointing a Court crier and admitting lawyers to the bar.

Philadelphia

Congress voted on July 16, 1790, to move the capital from New York to Philadelphia. The Supreme Court joined the rest of the federal government there for its next session, which began on February 7, 1791, at Independence Hall, then known as the "State House." With no cases to attend to, the Court adjourned the next day.

When the Court moved to Philadelphia, it was understood that the justices would sit in City Hall, but that building was not completed until the summer of 1791, in time for the Court's August 1791 term. The justices met in the east wing of the new City Hall, which also housed the state and municipal courts.

Those courts usually met at times different from the Supreme Court. In March 1796, however, the "Mayor's Court" was scheduled to hold a session in the same first-floor courtroom that the Supreme Court was using. As a result, the Supreme Court vacated the courtroom and held session in the chambers of the Common Council on the second floor of the building.

The Court remained in City Hall until the end of the August 1800 term. City Hall also housed the U.S. Congress, which occupied the west wing, and the Pennsylvania legislature, which met in the central part of the building. The records indicate that while in City Hall the justices often kept late hours to hear oral arguments and that there they began wearing robes for the first time.

Washington, D.C.

The act of July 16, 1790, that transferred the seat of the federal government from New York to Philadelphia, also provided for a subsequent and permanent move to Washington, D.C. The law specified that the final move would take place on the "first Monday in December, in the year one thousand eight hundred." By that time, enough of the Capitol and the White House had been completed for the government to move. Congress and the president were subjected to considerable criticism because the buildings they were to occupy were dubbed too palatial and extravagant for a young democracy.

The Supreme Court, however, had no accommodations whatsoever. In 1796 a House committee had pointed out that a "building for the Judiciary" was needed, and in 1798 Alexander White, a commissioner for the federal city, had suggested appropriating funds for it. But two weeks before the Court moved to Washington, it was still seeking a place to conduct its business.

Courtrooms in the Capitol

Faced with the imminent convening of the homeless Supreme Court in Washington, Congress on January 23, 1801, passed a resolution providing that "leave be given to the Commissioners of the City of Washington to use one of the rooms on the first floor of the Capitol for holding the present session of the Supreme Court of the United States."

Because only the north wing of the Capitol was ready for occupancy at that time, Congress assigned the Court a small room—twenty-four feet by thirty feet, thirty-one feet high, and rounded at the south end—in the east basement, or first floor, entrance hall. There, the Court held its first session in Washington on February 2, 1801. It was the first of a series of often makeshift, hand-me-down quarters assigned by Congress to the Court before the completion of its present building in 1935.

By 1807 the north wing of the Capitol was in need of renovation. In a letter to Chief Justice John Marshall on September 17, Benjamin Henry Latrobe, the architect of the Capitol and surveyor of public buildings, suggested that the Court move "for the next session into the Library formerly occupied by the House of Representatives."

There the Court remained for the February and summer 1808 terms. But as Latrobe indicated in a letter to President James Monroe on September 6, 1809, "the Library became so inconvenient and cold that the Supreme Court preferred to sit at Long's Tavern" during the February 1809 term. Long's Tavern, where the first inaugural ball was held, was located on First Street, Southeast, where the Library of Congress now stands.

On February 5, 1810, the Court returned to the Capitol and met in a courtroom especially designed for it. Located in the basement beneath the new Senate chamber, the courtroom was also used by the U.S. Circuit Court and probably by the Orphan's Court of the District of Columbia. The noted Philadelphia lawyer Charles J. Ingersoll provided this description of the new courtroom:

> Under the Senate Chamber, is the Hall of Justice, the ceiling of which is not unfancifully formed by the arches that support the former. The Judges in their robes of solemn black are raised on seats of grave mahogany; and below them is the bar; and behind that an arcade, still higher, so contrived as to afford auditors double rows of terrace seats thrown in segments round the transverse arch under which the Judges sit.... When I went into the Court of Justice yesterday, one side of the fine forensic colonnade was occupied by a party of ladies, who, after loitering some time in the gallery of the Representatives, had sauntered into the hall, and, were, with their attendants, sacrificing some impatient moments to the inscrutable mysteries of pleading. On the opposite side was a group of Indians, who are here on a visit to the President in their native costume, their straight black hair hanging in plaits down their tawny shoulders, with mockassins [sic] on their feet, rings in their ears and noses, and large plates of silver on their arms and breasts.[4]

The Court remained in the new courtroom until the Capitol was burned by the British on August 24, 1814, during the War of

The Supreme Court occupied this chamber in the U.S. Capitol from 1860 until it moved to its permanent home in 1935.

1812. The British are said to have used Supreme Court documents to start the fire. When the Capitol was burned, Congress moved to the temporary "Brick Capitol" at the site of the present Supreme Court building, and then, during the two years that the Capitol was being restored, to a house rented from Daniel Carroll. That house, which the Court used from February 6, 1815, until July 1, 1816, later became Bell Tavern.

The Court returned to the Capitol for its February 1817 term and occupied an undestroyed section in the north wing until 1819. This is the room that was described as "mean and dingy" and "little better than a dungeon."[5] The Court remained in that room until the February 1819 term, when it moved back into its regular courtroom beneath the Senate chamber, now repaired.

That courtroom, which the justices were to occupy until 1860, was the object of both praise and criticism. It was on the Court's first day in the restored courtroom—February 2, 1819—that the decision in *Dartmouth College v. Woodward* was announced, a decision that made the Court headline news throughout the country.[6] On the same day that *Dartmouth College* was decided, the *National Intelligencer* reported:

> We are highly pleased to find that the Court-room in the Capitol is in a state fit for the reception of the Supreme Court. . . . It is . . . considerably more agreeable than that which was produced on entering the same apartment, previous to the re-modification of it made necessary by the conflagration of the interior of the Capitol.[7]

Many observers saw the courtroom in a less favorable light. The *New York Statesman*, for example, described it as

> not in a style which comports with the dignity of that body, or which wears a comparison with the other halls of the Capitol. In the first place, it is like going down cellar to reach it. The room is on the basement story in an obscure part of the north wing. In arriving at it, you pass a labyrinth, and almost need the clue of Ariadne to guide you to the sanctuary of the blind goddess. A stranger might traverse the dark avenues of the Capitol for a week, without finding the remote corner in which Justice is administered to the American Republic.[8]

Other critics noted that the chamber was so small that the justices had to put on their robes in full view of the spectators.

Whatever its shortcomings, the courtroom at least lent a new aura of stability and permanence to the previously peripatetic Court. The Court remained in its basement courtroom for forty-one years, surviving fires in 1851 and 1852. After the Court moved to new chambers in 1860, the courtroom became part of the law library of Congress.

In 1860, with the Civil War imminent, the Court moved from the basement to the old Senate chamber on the first floor of the Capitol. The new courtroom was located on the east side of the main corridor between the rotunda and the current Senate chamber. The large room, with a dozen anterooms for office space and storage, was by far the most commodious and imposing quarters the Court had occupied. The galleries had been removed when the Senate moved to its new chambers, giving the courtroom an aura of spaciousness.

The justices sat on a raised platform behind a balustrade. In back of the balustrade was an arched doorway topped by a gilded American eagle and flanked by ten marble columns. The justices faced a large semicircular colonnaded chamber. The area just in front of the bench was used for the presentation of arguments, and it was ringed by wooden benches for the spectators. There were red drapes and carpets, and busts of former chief justices lined the walls.

Despite the dignity and spaciousness of the courtroom, the adjoining office space was cramped and inadequate. There was no dining hall, for example, and the justices were forced to use the robing room for their meals. The conference room, where the justices met to discuss cases and render their decisions, also served as the Court's library. Because of the reluctance of some of the justices to have the conference room windows open, the room was frequently close and stuffy. The Clerk's Office was similarly close and cluttered.

None of the justices had individual office space in the Capitol; each had to provide for his own and his staff's working quarters at a time when spacious housing in Washington was difficult to find. Nevertheless, the justices held sessions in these quarters for seventy-five years, with two exceptions. An explosion of illuminating gas on November 6, 1898, forced the Court to hold the November 7 and November 14 sessions in the Senate District of Columbia Committee room. During reconstruction of the courtroom from October to December 9, 1901, sessions were held in the Senate Judiciary Committee room.

President William Howard Taft began promoting the idea of a separate building for the Supreme Court around 1912. He continued to advocate the construction of a Supreme Court building when he became chief justice in 1921. At Taft's persistent urging, Congress finally relented in 1929 and authorized funds for the construction of a permanent dwelling for the Court. During the construction of the new building, the Court continued to sit in the old Senate chamber. Its last major decision announced there, at the end of the 1934 term, was that of striking down President Franklin D. Roosevelt's National Industrial Recovery Act.

New Court Building

The Supreme Court held its first session in the new building at One First Street, Northeast, across the plaza from the Capitol, on October 7, 1935. One hundred and forty-five years after it first met in New York City, 134 years after it moved to Washington, and 6 years after Congress had appropriated $9,740,000 for a permanent residence, the nation's highest tribunal finally had a home of its own.

In laying the cornerstone for the new building on October 13, 1932, Chief Justice Charles Evans Hughes paid tribute to his predecessor, William Taft, who had died two years before. "This building," Hughes said, "is the result of his intelligent persistence." The site chosen for the Court was occupied by the Brick Capitol, which had been used by Congress after the British burned the Capitol in 1814.

A model of the Supreme Court building is inspected by Justices Louis D. Brandeis, Willis Van Devanter, Chief Justice William Howard Taft, Justices Oliver Wendell Holmes Jr., Pierce Butler, George Sutherland, and Harlan Fiske Stone. Taft died in 1930 before his plan for a separate building for the Court was fulfilled.

Architect Cass Gilbert was commissioned to design the building, and in May 1929 he submitted a plan for "a building of dignity and importance suitable for its use as a permanent home of the Supreme Court of the United States." Gilbert died in 1934, and the project was continued under Chief Justice Hughes and architects Cass Gilbert Jr. and John R. Rockart, under the supervision of Architect of the Capitol David Lynn.

VISITING THE COURT

The Supreme Court is open for visitors year-round, Monday through Friday from 9 A.M. to 4:30 P.M. Annually, about 800,000 people visit the Court. Arguments are held from 10 A.M. to noon on Monday, Tuesday, and Wednesday, and on rare occasions from 1 to 3 P.M. The afternoon argument depends on whether the justices agreed to hear more cases than can be heard in the mornings alone. In the 1980s the Court nearly always held afternoon arguments, but by the late 1990s they had become a rarity.

During the weeks when the Court is not in session, lectures are presented regularly by the staff of the Curator's Office from 9:30 A.M. to 3:30 P.M. On the ground floor there are exhibits, portraits of all former justices, a gift shop, and a cafeteria. In addition, visitors can see a film about the Court in a ground floor room. In 1994 the Curator's office began organizing extensive, permanent exhibits that are open to the public—the first was on the building's form and function. The exhibit included a model and pictures of the private conference room where justices vote on cases and historical items such as a snuff box, inkwells, and the chair used by Chief Justice John Marshall (1801–1835).

The architects chose the Corinthian style of Greek architecture, which would blend most harmoniously with the congressional buildings on Capitol Hill. The dimensions of the building were 385 feet east and west, from front to back, and 304 feet north and south. As for its height, the building rises four stories above ground level.

Marble was selected as the primary building material, with the result that more than $3 million—almost a third of the building's cost—was spent on domestic and foreign marble. A thousand freight cars were needed to bring in the Vermont marble used for the exterior of the building. Georgia marble flecked with crystal was quarried for the four inner courts, and a creamy Alabama marble was used for most of the walls and floors of corridors and entrance halls.

For the Court's Great Hall—its showcase—and the courtroom at the end of the Great Hall, architect Gilbert insisted on Ivory Vein Marble from Spain for the walls and Light Sienna Old Convent marble from the Montarrenti quarry in Italy for the huge columns. The Italian marble was shipped to finishers in Knoxville, Tennessee, and they made the blocks into thirty-foot columns and shipped them to Washington. Darker Italian and African marble was used for the floor.

Most of the floors elsewhere in the building are oak, and the doors and walls of most offices are American-quartered white oak. Bronze and mahogany were also used. The roof was made from cream-colored Roman tile set on bronze strips over lead-coated copper on a slab of watertight concrete. As Wesley McCune noted, the "Court might succumb to a political storm, but it will never be driven out by any kind of inclement weather." [9] The building includes two self-supporting marble spiral staircases

Supreme Court building, completed in 1935.

from the garage to the top floor. The only other spiral staircases like those in the Court are in the Vatican and the Paris Opera.

Since its completion in 1935 the Supreme Court building has been a subject of both outspoken criticism (a "marble mausoleum") and praise (a "marble palace"). Its admirers speak in terms of structural simplicity, austerity, beauty, and dignity. For them, it is a fitting monument epitomizing the words on the front entrance of the building, "Equal Justice under Law."

But at the time its detractors were numerous, despite general public approval of the new building. In the 1930s the authors of the Federal Writers' Project *Guide to Washington* wrote that "the building has a cold, abstract, almost anonymous beauty but is lacking in that power which comes from a more direct expression of purpose." Chief Justice Harlan Fiske Stone called it "almost bombastically pretentious" and "wholly inappropriate for a quiet group of old boys such as the Supreme Court." Another justice said that the Court would be "nine black beetles in the Temple of Karnak." Another asked: "What are we supposed to do, ride in on nine elephants?" [10]

The building was designed so that the justices need not enter public areas except when hearing oral arguments and announcing their opinions. A private elevator connects the underground garage with the corridor, closed to the public, where the justices' offices are located.

The basement of the Supreme Court building contains—in addition to the garage—the offices of the facilities manager and a staff of thirty-two electricians, plumbers, painters, air-conditioning and heating specialists, and groundskeepers. The basement also houses a carpentry shop, laundry, and police roll-call room.

The ground floor contains the Public Information Office, the Clerk's Office, the publications unit, police "headquarters," and other administrative offices, in addition to the exhibit halls,

cafeteria, and gift shop. This floor also is the location of a bronze larger-than-life statue of Justice John Marshall (1801–1835). The sculptor was William Wetmore Story, the son of Justice Joseph Story (1812–1845).

The first floor contains the courtroom, the conference room, and all of the justices' chambers except Ruth Bader Ginsburg's. She chose a roomier office on the second floor. The second floor contains the justices' dining room and library, the office of the reporter of decisions, the legal office, and law clerks' offices. On the third floor is the library, paneled in hand-carved oak, and on the fourth floor there is a gymnasium and storage area. The public is allowed to see only the ground floor and part of the first floor.

When Congress in 1929 authorized $9,740,000 for the construction of the Supreme Court building, it was expected then that extra funds would have to be appropriated for furnishings. In the end, though the final and complete cost of the building, in addition to that of all the furnishings, was below the authorization, and $94,000 was returned to the U.S. Treasury.

On the steps to the main entrance of the building are a pair of huge marble candelabra with carved panels representing justice, holding sword and scales, and the "three fates," who are weaving the thread of life. On either side of the steps are two marble figures by sculptor James Earle Fraser. On the left side is a female—the contemplation of justice—and on the right is a male—the guardian or authority of law.

Above the entrance of the building is a pediment filled with sculptures representing, at the center, "Liberty Enthroned," guarded by "Order" and "Authority." On either side are groups depicting "Council and Research" in the guise of modern figures: the three on the left are a reclining Chief Justice William Howard Taft (1921–1930), who is portrayed as a student at Yale University and represents "Research Present"; New York Republican senator

The bronze doors of the Supreme Court building depict significant events in the development of law and justice.

"safeguard of the rights of the people" and "genii of wisdom and statescraft." At the far right is the "defense of human rights."

On the wall to the right of incoming visitors are figures of historical lawmakers of the pre-Christian era—Menes, Hammurabi, Moses, Solomon, Lycurgus, Solon, Draco, Confucius, and Octavian. Moses is seen carrying a tablet on which some numbering is visible. This represents the Ten Commandments. The procession of ancient lawgivers is flanked by figures symbolizing "fame" and "history." To the left of visitors are lawmakers of the Christian era—Napoleon, Marshall, Blackstone, Grotius, Saint Louis, King John, Charlemagne, Mohammed, and Justinian. They are flanked by figures representing "liberty," "peace," and "philosophy." The Office of the Curator at the Court has put together a four-page information sheet on these marble "friezes." It is also posted on the Court's web site at www.supremecourtus.gov.

Little has changed in the physical appearance of the Court building since 1935. The courtroom was renovated in 1992, the first time since the building was opened. The new gold-fringed deep-red draperies and red, gold, and black carpet replaced worn-out furnishings, yet remained consistent with the original interior's style. Toni House, the public information officer, said the cost of the renovation was $264,000, of which about $69,000 came from funds appropriated by Congress and the other $195,000 derived from Supreme Court bar membership fees. Justices Sandra Day O'Connor and Anthony M. Kennedy oversaw the refurbishing.

In 2003 the Court began a five-year, $122 million modernization project that will, among many other things, update the wiring and electrical systems throughout the building. The first phase called for constructing a two-story underground annex on the Maryland Avenue side of the building to house the Court police.

COST OF THE COURT

Compared with its two coequal branches of the government, the executive branch and Congress, the Supreme Court seems to operate on a shoestring. In fiscal year 2003, for example, the Court received about $46 million to pay the salaries of the nine justices and Court employees, and to cover operating costs, including care of the building and grounds. For the same fiscal year, Congress had an appropriation of about $3.5 billion.

The Supreme Court budget for each fiscal year is drawn up in the Office of the Marshal of the Court. It is submitted by October 15—nearly a year in advance—to the Office of Management and Budget (OMB). (The fiscal year begins the following October 1.)

The OMB is prohibited by statute from making any changes in the proposed budget for the federal judiciary before submitting it—along with proposed executive and legislative budgets—to Congress in January.

The Court's requests in the President's Budget Document have been divided into two categories—salaries and expenses of the Supreme Court and care of buildings and grounds—since

Elihu Root (1909–1915), who sponsored legislation creating a fine arts commission; and building architect Cass Gilbert. The three figures grouped to the right of the truly allegorical forms are Justice Charles Evans Hughes (1910–1916, 1930–1941), the pediment's sculptor Robert Aitken; and Chief Justice John Marshall (1801–1835), representing "Research Past."

Panels on the main door were sculptured by John Donnelly Jr. and depict scenes in the development of the law. Along both sides of the Great Hall are busts of former chief justices, heraldic devices, and medallion profiles of lawgivers.

From the Great Hall, oak doors open into the courtroom, or court chamber. Measuring eighty-two feet by ninety-one feet with a forty-four-foot ceiling, the room has twenty-four columns of Italian marble. Directly above the bench are two seated male figures who symbolize "majesty of the law" and "power of government," according to a letter from sculptor Adolph A. Weinman to architect Gilbert that described the scene. Between the two figures is a pylon carved with the Roman numerals I to X, symbolizing the first ten amendments to the Constitution known as the Bill of Rights. At the far left is a group representing fiscal year 1977. Before that, there were five categories: salaries, printing, miscellaneous expenses, car for the chief justice, and books for the Supreme Court.

Federal Judiciary Budget

For the ninety-four federal district courts and thirteen courts of appeals, the budget process, before submission to Congress, involves several steps that are not applicable to the Supreme Court. The budget of each lower court is sent to the Administrative Office of the United States Courts by the court's

---

SUPREME COURT BUDGET APPROPRIATIONS, SELECTED FISCAL YEARS, 1950–2004

Fiscal Year	Salaries and Expenses[a]	Building and Grounds[b]	Total
1950	944,100	152,000	1,096,100
1960[c]	1,536,000	347,000	1,883,000
1970	3,138,000	410,000	3,548,000
1980	10,363,000	2,182,000	12,545,000
1990	17,497,000	4,369,000	21,866,000
2000	36,000,000	6,000,000	42,000,000

Budgetary Categories	2002 (actual)	2003 (estimated)	2004 (estimated)
Court operations			
Personnel compensation	24,000,000	27,000,000	30,000,000
Civilian personnel benefits	6,000,000	7,000,000	7,000,000
Printing and reproduction	1,000,000	1,000,000	2,000,000
Other services	5,000,000	5,000,000	7,000,000
Supplies and materials	1,000,000	1,000,000	4,000,000
Equipment	3,000,000	5,000,000	7,000,000
Total operations	40,000,000	46,000,000	57,000,000
Care of buildings and grounds	78,000,000[d]	54,000,000[d]	5,000,000
Total budget authorization	118,000,000	100,000,000	62,000,000

[a]Includes salaries for Court employees, printing and binding of decisions, purchase of books and periodicals (1940–2000), committees on the preparation of rules for criminal and civil procedure (1950), automobile and driver for the chief justice (1960–2000), and miscellaneous expenses.

[b]Includes improvements, maintenance, repairs, equipment, supplies, materials, special clothing for workers, snow removal, and miscellaneous expenses.

[c]Beginning with fiscal year 1960, budgetary figures are stated in thousands of dollars rather than actual expenditures.

[d]The substantial increase in funds for buildings and grounds is due to the first major renovation of the building since its construction, as well as the government's response to increased security concerns following the September 11, 2001, attacks on the United States.

SOURCE: Lee Epstein, et al., *The Supreme Court Compendium: Data, Decisions, and Developments*, 3d ed. (Washington, D.C.: CQ Press, 2003); Office of Management and Budget, *Budget of the United States Government* (Washington, D.C.: Government Printing Office, 1932–1962), and Office of Management and Budget, *Appendix to the Budget* (Washington, D.C.: Government Printing Office, 1963–2004).

---

chief judge. It is consolidated into a national budget by the Administrative Office and then approved by the Judicial Conference of the United States, which has no jurisdiction over the Supreme Court's budget. The conference is composed of the chief judges of the thirteen courts of appeals, a district court judge from each of the twelve geographic (or regional) circuits, and the chief judge of the Court of International Trade. The chief justice serves as the presiding officer.

In the budget process, the chief judge of the twelve geographic circuit courts has been assisted since 1972 by a "circuit executive" whose duties include preparing the budgets. Like those of the district, bankruptcy, and special courts, the proposed budget for the circuits must be submitted to the Administrative Office by May 1.

Budget requests are evaluated by specialists on the basis of program and project needs, in May and June. The conclusions are reviewed by the director of the Administrative Office and then sent to committees of judges for review before they are delivered to the Judicial Conference for approval. Committees of the Judicial Conference review the requests, make recommendations, and send them to the budget committee for evaluation and further recommendations. The Judicial Conference, usually in September, meets to consider the committees' recommendations and prepare a final version of the requests. The Administrative Office submits the final versions to OMB by October 15. The appropriation for the federal judiciary was $5.3 billion in 2003.

Before the president sends the budget to Congress, the Administrative Office of the United States Courts submits justifications for the funds requested to the subcommittees of the congressional appropriations committees that will first consider the requests—the Senate and House subcommittees on Commerce, Justice, State, the Judiciary, and Related Agencies. Subcommittee hearings on the proposed budget generally begin in the spring of each year.

The subcommittees hold public hearings at which a justice of the Supreme Court, the chairman of the Judicial Conference Budget Committee, the chief judges of the special courts, and the director of the Administrative Office of the United States Courts are called to justify the budget requests. When the hearings are over, the subcommittees vote on appropriations bills and send them to a vote by the full Senate and House Appropriations Committees, followed by a final vote on the floors of the House and Senate. The judiciary's budget requests are often reduced by Congress, but not in ways that significantly differ from reductions applied to executive agencies.

The funds Congress appropriates for the Supreme Court now go directly to the Court and are spent by the marshal for salaries of the justices and other employees and for Court needs. Before 1935 Congress channeled money for the Court through the Justice Department. The allocation of funds for the other federal courts is handled by the Office of Finance and Budget of the Administrative Office of the United States Courts. The division submits recommendations on the allocation to the director of the Administrative Office and the executive committee of the Judicial Conference, who make the final decision on how the money is disbursed.

SALARIES OF THE JUSTICES

The salary of the chief justice of the United States was $198,600 in 2003 and that of the associate justices was $190,100.

Service on the Supreme Court was not always so remunerative. On September 23, 1789, Congress set the salary of an associate justice at $3,500 a year and for the chief justice at $4,000 a year.

JUSTICES' SALARIES

Years	Chief Justice	Associate Justices
1789–1819	$4,000	$3,500
1819–1855	5,000	4,500
1855–1871	6,500	6,000
1871–1873	8,500	8,000
1873–1903	10,500	10,000
1903–1911	13,000	12,500
1911–1926	15,000	14,500
1926–1946	20,500	20,000
1946–1955	25,500	25,000
1955–1964	35,500	35,000
1964–1969	40,000	39,500
1969–1975	62,500	60,000
1975	65,625	63,000
1976*	68,800	66,000
1977	75,000	72,000
1978*	79,100	76,000
1979*	84,700	81,300
1980*	92,400	88,700
1981*	96,800	93,000
1982–1983*	100,700	96,700
1984	104,700	100,600
1985–1986	108,400	104,100
1987	115,000	110,000
1990	124,000	118,600
1991	160,600	153,600
1992	166,200	159,000
1993–1998	171,500	164,100
1999	175,400	167,900
2000	181,400	173,600
2001	186,300	178,300
2002	192,600	184,400
2003	198,600	190,100

*A cost-of-living adjustment equal to 5 percent of regular salary.

That salary was not increased until 1819. When Congress was urged to raise the salaries in 1816, Justice Joseph Story (1812–1845) prepared a memorandum complaining that "the necessaries and comforts of life, the manner of living and the habits of ordinary expenses, in the same rank of society, have, between 1789 and 1815, increased in price from one hundred to two hundred percent. The business of the Judges of the Supreme Court, both at the Law Term in February and on the Circuits, has during the same period increased in more than a quadruple ratio and is increasing annually."[11] Congress was unreceptive at that time to Story's and other pleas for a pay raise for the justices.

The failure of Congress in early 1989 to approve a recommended raise for federal judges and other high-level federal officeholders, including members of Congress, moved Chief Justice William H. Rehnquist to do some serious lobbying as head of the judicial system. Breaking precedent, he appeared before a congressional committee, met privately with congressional leaders, and held a press conference to urge Congress to increase the salaries of federal judges. When he appeared before the House Post Office and Civil Service Committee in May 1989, he was the first sitting chief justice to appear to testify before Congress. In 1990 the judges were given a raise.[12]

Retirement System

From the establishment of the Supreme Court and for almost a century, many justices were caught in a dilemma: low salaries and no retirement plan. Many solved the problem by leaving the bench to accept more lucrative employment elsewhere. Justice Story, for one, did not. In 1816, when Congress refused to increase his and the other associate justices' salaries from $3,500, Story declined an offer to take over Charles Pinckney's law practice in Baltimore. Had he accepted, he would have been assured of an income of at least $10,000 a year.

Until 1869 justices who were unable to carry out their duties because of age or disability often hesitated to submit their resignations because there were no retirement benefits. It was in large measure the incapacity of Justices Robert C. Grier (1846–1870) and Samuel Nelson (1845–1872) that prompted Congress to provide in the Judiciary Act of April 10, 1869, that "any judge of any court of the United States, who, having held his commission as such at least ten years, shall, after having attained the age of seventy years, resign his office, shall thereafter, during the residue of his natural life, receive the same salary which was by law payable to him at the time of his resignation."

The Judiciary Act of 1869 made no provisions for retirement benefits for a justice who became incapacitated before reaching age seventy or before ten years of service on the Court. That omission was subsequently remedied, and the U.S. Code now contains provisions for resignation or retirement for age and retirement for disability.

Before 1937, justices who left the Court for any reason had to resign rather than retire, which meant that their pensions were subject to fluctuating civil service guidelines. That policy was changed with the Supreme Court Retirement Act of 1937. *(See "Retirement," pp. 867–868.)* The law now provides the following

> Any justice or judge of the United States appointed to hold office during good behavior may retire from the office after attaining the age and meeting the service requirements, whether continuous or otherwise, of [the law] and shall, during the remainder of his lifetime, receive an annuity equal to the salary he was receiving at the time he retired.[13]

The age and years-of-service requirements delineated in the law are sixty-five years of age and fifteen years of service. The years of service required decrease by one as a justice's age increases by one. At age seventy, a justice needs only ten years of service to retire.[14]

> Any justice or judge of the United States appointed to hold office during good behavior who becomes permanently disabled from performing his duties may retire from regular active service, and the President shall, by the advice and consent of the Senate, appoint a successor. Any justice or judge of the United States desiring to retire under this section shall certify to the President his disability in writing.[15]

A justice of the Supreme Court who is unable to perform his duties cannot be forced to resign. Congress, however, has provided that other federal judges deemed to be "unable to discharge efficiently all the duties of his office by reason of permanent mental or physical disability" can be replaced by the president with Senate approval.[16]

NOTES

1. "The Supreme Court—Its Homes Past and Present," *American Bar Association Journal* 27 (1941): 283–289.

2. Charles Warren, *The Supreme Court in United States History*, rev. ed., 2 vols. (Boston: Little, Brown, 1926), 1:164.

3. John P. Frank, *Marble Palace: The Supreme Court in American Life* (New York: Knopf, 1958).

4. Quoted by Warren in *Supreme Court in United States History*, 1:457–458.

5. Ibid., 1:459.

6. *Dartmouth College v. Woodward*, 4 Wheat. (17 U.S.) 519 (1819).

7. *National Intelligencer*, February 2, 1819, quoted by Warren in *Supreme Court in United States History*, 1:460.

8. *New York Statesman*, February 7, 1824, quoted in ibid.

9. Wesley McCune, *The Nine Young Men* (New York: Harper and Brothers, 1947), 2.

10. Quoted by Mary Ann Harrell in *Equal Justice Under Law: The Supreme Court in American Life* (Washington, D.C.: Foundation of the American Bar Association, with the cooperation of National Geographic Society, 1975), 116.

11. William Waldo Story, ed., *Life and Letters of Joseph Story*, 2 vols. (Boston: Little, Brown, 1851), 1:302.

12. *Congressional Quarterly, Weekly Report*, June 3, 1989, 1325.

13. 28 U.S.C. 371 (a).

14. 28 U.S.C. 371 (c).

15. 28 U.S.C. 372 (a).

16. 28 U.S.C. 372 (b).

PART VI

Members of the Court

CHAPTER 19

Members of the Court

SINCE ITS ESTABLISHMENT in 1789, the Supreme Court has had only 108 members, making it one of the most exclusive and enduring of judicial bodies. All but two members have been men, and all but two have been white. Only sixteen have not been Protestant.

The Court has, however, exhibited diversity in other ways—politically, geographically, and in the age, personality, and previous service of its individual members. Indeed, in periodic breakthroughs an appointee with a controversial viewpoint or a different background has attained a seat on the Court. The first Roman Catholic was appointed in 1835, the first Jew in 1916, the first black in 1967, and the first woman in 1981.

There are no constitutional or statutory qualifications at all for serving on the Supreme Court. The Constitution's Article III simply states that "the judicial power of the United States shall be vested in one supreme Court" as well as any lower federal courts Congress may establish. Article II directs that the president "by and with the Advice and Consent of the Senate, shall appoint . . . Judges of the Supreme Court." There is no age limit, no requirement that judges be native-born citizens—in fact, the Constitution does not even specify that appointees must have a legal background.

Nevertheless, informal criteria for membership developed quickly. Every nominee to the Court has been a lawyer—although it was not until the twentieth century that most justices were law school graduates. And over the years many other factors have entered into the process of presidential selection. Some of them became long-lasting traditions with virtually the force of a formal requirement. Others were as fleeting as the personal friendship between an incumbent president and his nominee.

THE PRESIDENT SHALL APPOINT . . .

George Washington, as the first president, had the responsibility of choosing the original six justices of the Supreme Court. The type of men he chose and the reasons he chose them foreshadowed the process of selection carried out by his successors.

In naming the first justices, Washington paid close attention to their politics, which at that time primarily meant loyalty to the new Constitution. Of the six original appointees, three had attended the Philadelphia convention that formulated the Constitution, and the other three had supported its adoption. John Jay, the first chief justice, was coauthor with Alexander Hamilton and

James Madison of *The Federalist Papers*, a series of influential essays published in New York supporting ratification of the Constitution. During his two terms of office, Washington had occasion to make five additional Supreme Court appointments. All were staunch supporters of the Constitution and the new federal government.

Another of Washington's major considerations was geography. The new states were a disparate group that barely had held together during the fight for independence and the confederation government of the 1780s. To bind them more closely together, Washington consciously tried to represent each geographical area of the country in the nation's new supreme tribunal.

His first six appointees were three northerners—Chief Justice John Jay from New York and Associate Justices William Cushing of Massachusetts and James Wilson of Pennsylvania—and three southerners—John Blair of Virginia, James Iredell of North Carolina, and John Rutledge of South Carolina. The five later appointees were Oliver Ellsworth of Connecticut, Thomas Johnson and Samuel Chase of Maryland, William Paterson of New Jersey, and Rutledge, appointed a second time. By the time Washington left office, nine of the original thirteen states had achieved representation on the Supreme Court.

With a total of eleven, Washington still holds the record for the number of Supreme Court appointments made by any president. The second highest total—nine—belongs to President Franklin D. Roosevelt, the only president to serve more than two terms. Roosevelt also came closest since Washington to naming the entire membership of the Court—only two justices who served prior to the Roosevelt years were still on the Court at the time of his death. Roosevelt elevated one of them, Harlan Fiske Stone, from associate justice to chief justice.

With six each, Presidents Andrew Jackson (1829–1837) and William Howard Taft (1909–1913) appointed the next highest number of justices. Taft holds the record for a one-term president. Next in order are Abraham Lincoln (1861–1865) and Dwight D. Eisenhower (1953–1961) with five each.

Four presidents, William Henry Harrison, Zachary Taylor, Andrew Johnson, and Jimmy Carter, made no appointments to the Supreme Court. Harrison (1841) and Taylor (1849–1850) both died in office before any vacancies occurred. Johnson (1865–1869), who served just six weeks short of a full term, had no chance to make a Court appointment because of his rancorous political battle with Congress over Reconstruction. So bitter did the struggle become that Congress in effect took away

Johnson's power of appointment by passing legislation in 1866 to reduce the Court from ten to seven members as vacancies should occur.

The legislation was occasioned by the death of Justice John Catron in 1865 and Johnson's nomination in 1866 of Henry Stanbery to replace him. The Senate took no action on Stanbery's nomination and instead passed the bill reducing the size of the Court. When Justice James Wayne died in 1867, the membership of the Court automatically dropped to eight.

In 1869, when the Republicans recaptured the White House, Congress passed legislation increasing the Court to nine seats and allowing President Ulysses S. Grant to make a nomination.

Jimmy Carter is the only full-term president who has been denied the opportunity to nominate a member of the Court. No deaths or resignations occurred on the Court during his term.

Party Lines

As political parties became an established fact of American political life, the major parties sought to promote the appointment to the Court of members who would espouse their view of what the federal government should and should not do. As Washington had appointed supporters of the new Constitution, so most presidents have selected nominees with whom they felt comfortable—philosophically and politically.

EMPTY CHAIRS: VACANCIES ON THE COURT

Twice in the Court's history a seat has been vacant for more than two years. The longest vacancy lasted for two years, three months, and twenty-three days. During that period the Senate rejected four nominations by two presidents, and a future president, James Buchanan, declined three invitations to the seat.

When Justice Henry Baldwin died on April 21, 1844, John Tyler was president. Elected vice president on the Whig ticket in 1840, Tyler had broken with the party after he became president following William Henry Harrison's death in 1841. From then on, he was a president without a party or personal popularity. At the time of Baldwin's death, one Tyler nomination to the Court had already been rejected, and a second was pending. Tyler first offered the Baldwin vacancy to Buchanan, who, like Baldwin, was a Pennsylvanian. When he declined, the president nominated Philadelphia attorney Edward King.

Followers of Henry Clay, however, who controlled the Senate, thought Clay would win the presidency in that year's election, and they voted in June 1844 to postpone consideration of both King's nomination and Tyler's pending appointment of Reuben H. Walworth to the second vacancy. Tyler resubmitted King's name in December. Again the Senate refused to act, and Tyler was forced to withdraw the appointment.

By this time, Tyler was a lame-duck president and Clay had lost the election to Democrat James K. Polk. Nonetheless, in February 1845 Tyler named John M. Read, a Philadelphia attorney who had support among the Democrats and the Clay Whigs in the Senate. But the Senate failed to act on the nomination before adjournment, and the vacancy was left for Polk to fill.

Polk had only slightly better luck. After six months in office he offered the position to Buchanan, who again refused it. Another few months passed before Polk formally nominated George W. Woodward to the Baldwin vacancy in December 1845. Woodward turned out to be a hapless choice. He was opposed by one of the senators from his home state, Pennsylvania, and his extreme "American nativist" views made him unpopular with many other senators. His nomination was rejected on a 20-29 vote in January 1846.

Polk asked Buchanan once again to take the seat. Buchanan accepted, but later changed his mind and declined a third time. The president then turned to Robert C. Grier, a district court judge from Pennsylvania who proved acceptable to almost everyone. The Senate confirmed him on August 4, 1846, the day after his nomination.

The second-longest vacancy lasted almost as long as the first—two years, one month, and sixteen days. It occurred when Justice Peter V. Daniel of Virginia died on May 31, 1860. At this point four of the remaining justices were from the North, and four were from the South. Naturally, the South wanted Buchanan, now the president, to replace Daniel with another southerner; the North urged a nomination from one of its states.

Buchanan took a long time making up his mind. In February 1861, nearly eight months after the vacancy occurred, he nominated Secretary of State Jeremiah S. Black, a former chief justice of the Pennsylvania Supreme Court and U.S. attorney general. Black might have proved acceptable to southern senators, but many of them had already resigned from the Senate to join the Confederacy. Although he supported the Union, Black was not an abolitionist, and his nomination drew criticism from the northern antislavery press. Black also was opposed by Democrat Stephen A. Douglas, who had just lost the presidential election to Abraham Lincoln. Finally, Republicans in the Senate were not anxious to help fill a vacancy that they could leave open for the incoming Republican president. Had Buchanan acted earlier, it is likely that Black would have been confirmed. As it was, the Senate rejected his nomination by a one-vote margin, 25-26.

Buchanan made no further attempt to fill the Daniel vacancy. Lincoln, who soon had two more seats on the Court to fill, did not name anyone to the Daniel seat until July 1862—more than a year after his inauguration. His choice was Samuel F. Miller, a well-respected Iowa attorney. Miller's nomination had been urged by a majority of both the House and Senate and by other politicians and members of the legal profession. On July 16, 1862, the Senate confirmed his nomination within half an hour of receiving it.

SOURCES: Henry J. Abraham, *Justices and Presidents: A Political History of Appointments to the Supreme Court*, 3d ed. (New York: Oxford University Press, 1992); and Charles Warren, *The Supreme Court in United States History*, rev. ed., 2 vols. (Boston: Little, Brown, 1926).

It is the exception when a president goes to the opposite political party to find a nominee. The first clear-cut instance of a president of one party appointing a member of the other to the Supreme Court was Republican Abraham Lincoln's selection of Democrat Stephen J. Field of California in 1863. President John Tyler, who was elected vice president as a Whig in 1840, appointed Democrat Samuel Nelson to the Court in 1845. But by that time Tyler was no longer identified with either major political party.

After Lincoln's example, Republican presidents occasionally appointed Democrats to the Court. President Benjamin Harrison selected Howell Jackson of Tennessee in 1893; Warren G. Harding appointed Pierce Butler in 1922; Herbert Hoover appointed Benjamin Cardozo in 1932; Dwight D. Eisenhower appointed William J. Brennan Jr. in 1956; and Richard Nixon appointed Lewis F. Powell Jr. in 1971. Republican William Howard Taft was the only president to appoint more than one member of the opposite party to the Court. Three of his six nominees to the Court were Democrats—Edward D. White, whom he elevated from associate justice to chief justice, and Horace Lurton and Joseph R. Lamar, southern Democrats appointed in 1909 and 1910, respectively.

The only two Democrats ever to appoint Republicans to the Supreme Court were Franklin D. Roosevelt and Harry S. Truman. Roosevelt elevated Justice Stone, a Republican, to chief justice in 1941. Truman appointed Sen. Harold H. Burton, R-Ohio, an old friend and colleague from Truman's Senate days, in 1945.

Seeking a Seat

Before a president finally decides on a nominee, a process of balancing and sifting usually goes on, sometimes involving many participants and sometimes only a few. Occasionally, however, a president's choice has all but been made by overwhelming pressure for a particular nominee.

One of the more dramatic instances of this process occurred in 1853 when President Franklin Pierce nominated John A. Campbell of Alabama for a seat on the Court. Campbell was a forty-one-year-old lawyer who had such a brilliant reputation that the justices decided they wanted him as a colleague. The entire membership of the Court wrote to Pierce requesting Campbell's nomination. To emphasize their point, two justices delivered the letters in person. Pierce complied, and Campbell was confirmed within four days.

In 1862 President Lincoln was looking for a new justice from the Midwest. The Iowa congressional delegation began pressing for the appointment of Samuel Miller, a doctor and lawyer who had helped form the Iowa Republican Party and who had a strong reputation for moral and intellectual integrity. The movement grew rapidly until 129 of 140 House members and all but four senators had signed a petition for Miller's nomination. With such massive and unprecedented congressional support, Miller received Lincoln's approval despite his lack of any judicial experience. He became the first justice from west of the Mississippi River.

In 1932 a strong national movement began for the appointment of Benjamin Cardozo, chief judge of the New York Court of Appeals, to the Supreme Court. Cardozo was a Democrat, while the president who was to make the appointment, Herbert C. Hoover, was a Republican. Furthermore, Cardozo was Jewish and there was already one Jew on the Court, Louis D. Brandeis. Under these circumstances, it was considered unlikely Hoover would make the nomination.

But Cardozo's record was so impressive that it created a groundswell of support. Deans and faculty members of the nation's leading law schools, chief judges of other state courts, labor and business leaders, and powerful senators all urged Hoover to choose Cardozo. Despite his desire to appoint a western Republican, Hoover finally yielded and nominated Cardozo, who was confirmed without opposition.

States of Origin

The tradition begun by George Washington of weighing geographic factors in appointing justices continued for more than a century. It was reinforced by the justices' duty under the Judiciary Act of 1789 to ride and preside over circuit court sessions. Presidents not only strove for geographic balance in their appointments but also considered it important that each justice be a native of the circuit over which he presided.

The burdensome attendance requirement was curtailed by legislation during the nineteenth century until it became optional in 1891 and was abolished altogether in 1911. In the twentieth century, geography became a less important consideration in Supreme Court nominations, although as recently as 1970 President Nixon made an issue of it when the Senate refused to confirm two southerners—Clement Haynsworth Jr. and G. Harrold Carswell—to the Court. Nixon claimed the Senate would not confirm a conservative southerner and turned to Harry A. Blackmun of Minnesota instead.

In its heyday the geographic factor was sometimes almost sacrosanct. The longest-lasting example, which endured from 1789 to 1932, was the so-called New England seat, usually occupied by an appointee from Massachusetts. There was also a seat for a New Yorker from 1806 to 1894 and a Maryland-Virginia seat from 1789 to 1860.

Geography had strong political ramifications as well, especially for the South. With the growth of sectional differences, particularly over the slavery issue before the Civil War, the South felt itself to be on the defensive. One of the ways it sought to protect its interests was to gain a majority on the Supreme Court. And, indeed, five of the nine justices in 1860 were from slaveholding states.

With the coming of the Civil War, the sectional balance of power shifted. Four of the five southern justices died between 1860 and 1867, and another—Justice John A. Campbell of Alabama—resigned to join the Confederate cause.

Not one of these justices was replaced by a southerner, and by 1870 every Supreme Court seat was held by a northerner or westerner. But with the gradual decline of bitterness over the

---

THE IMPORTANCE OF BEING EASTERN . . . OR SOUTHERN

Geography was a prime consideration in the appointment of Supreme Court justices throughout the nineteenth century. Presidents found it expedient to have each of the expanding nation's rival sections represented on the Court.

THE "NEW ENGLAND" SEAT

The most notable example of geographic continuity was the seat traditionally held by a New Englander. William Cushing of Massachusetts was appointed an associate justice by President George Washington in 1789. For the next 143 years, that seat was held by a New Englander.

When Cushing died, President James Madison selected Joseph Story of Massachusetts. Story served thirty-four years. When he died in 1845, President James K. Polk appointed Levi Woodbury of New Hampshire, a prominent Jacksonian who had served as governor, senator, secretary of the navy, and secretary of the Treasury.

Woodbury's tenure lasted less than six years, and it fell to President Millard Fillmore to find a successor. He chose Benjamin Curtis, another Massachusetts native. Curtis resigned in 1857, and President James Buchanan chose Nathan Clifford of Maine, a former attorney general, to fill the seat.

Clifford served until his death in July 1881, shortly after President James A. Garfield was shot. When Garfield died in September, Chester A. Arthur chose Horace Gray, the chief justice of the Massachusetts Supreme Court. Gray served until 1902, when he was succeeded by another Massachusetts Supreme Court chief justice, Oliver Wendell Holmes Jr., appointed by President Theodore Roosevelt.

By the time of Holmes's appointment, however, the significance of geography had declined, and it was mostly accidental that Holmes came from Massachusetts. Nevertheless, his selection extended for another thirty years the tradition of the "New England" seat. After Holmes resigned in 1932, President Herbert C. Hoover chose as his successor Benjamin Cardozo, chief judge of New York State's highest court, and ended the Supreme Court's longest-lasting geographic tradition.

THE "NEW YORK" SEAT

The appointment of Justice Henry Brockholst Livingston by President Thomas Jefferson in 1806 began a tradition of a New York seat that continued for almost ninety years.

Livingston served until his death in 1823. President James Monroe then chose Smith Thompson of New York, his secretary of the navy. Thompson served for twenty years. His death in 1843 came at an inopportune moment politically: President John Tyler was disliked by both Democrats and Whigs and had little political leverage. His attempts to choose a successor to Thompson met with repeated failure. Finally, just before leaving office in 1845, Tyler found a New Yorker acceptable to the Senate, Justice Samuel Nelson, who served until 1872. After Nelson's retirement, two more New Yorkers held the seat, Ward Hunt from 1873 to 1882 and Samuel Blatchford from 1882 to 1893. But then a bitter quarrel between New Yorkers ended the tradition.

The New York antagonists were President Grover Cleveland and Sen. David B. Hill, old political enemies. Cleveland twice nominated a New Yorker for the post, and twice Hill used senatorial courtesy to object to the nominees. In both cases, the Senate followed its tradition of honoring a senator's objection to a nominee of his own party from his home state and rejected Cleveland's choices. On his third try to fill the vacancy, Cleveland abandoned New York and chose Sen. Edward D. White of Louisiana, who was confirmed immediately by his colleagues.

THE "VIRGINIA-MARYLAND" SEAT

Virginia and Maryland shared representation on the Court from 1789 until the Civil War. John Blair of Virginia, appointed by Washington, was succeeded by Samuel Chase of Maryland. After Chase's death in 1811, another Marylander, Gabriel Duvall, was given the seat. He resigned in 1835, and the seat went back to Virginia, with Philip Barbour holding it from 1836 to 1841, and Peter V. Daniel from 1841 to 1860. The Maryland-Virginia tradition was ended when President Abraham Lincoln appointed Samuel Miller of Iowa as Daniel's successor.

---

war, southerners again began to reappear on the Court. President Rutherford B. Hayes, who sought to reconcile relations between the North and South, made the first move by appointing William B. Woods of Georgia in 1880. Woods was not a native southerner; he had moved South after the Civil War. But despite this "carpetbagger" background, he was never identified with the corruption and profligacy associated with the Reconstruction era. As a federal judge for the Fifth Circuit, in the Deep South, he gained the respect of his neighbors for his fairness and honesty.

The first native southerner appointed to the Court after the Civil War was Woods's successor, Lucius Q. C. Lamar of Mississippi, appointed by President Grover Cleveland in 1888. Lamar had personally drafted the ordinance of secession for

Mississippi in 1861 and had served the Confederacy both as a military officer and as a diplomatic envoy to Europe. So his accession to the Court was an even more significant symbol of reconciliation than Woods's appointment eight years earlier.

Thirty-one states have contributed justices to the Supreme Court. New York has by far the highest total with fourteen, two of whom, Charles Evans Hughes and Harlan Stone, served as both associate justice and chief justice, followed by Ohio with ten and Massachusetts and Virginia with eight. Several major states have had only one justice, including Texas, Indiana, and Missouri—as have less-populated states such as Utah, Maine, and Wyoming.

Nineteen states, mostly western states with small populations, have never had a native on the Court. Only six of the nineteen are east of the Mississippi River. The largest state never to have had a justice is Florida.

The lack of representation on the Court from some of the less densely populated states resulted in a controversy during the 1950s when North Dakota's outspoken maverick senator, Republican William Langer, began opposing all non-North Dakotan Supreme Court nominees as a protest against big-state nominees. Langer was chairman of the Senate Judiciary Committee during the Eighty-third Congress (1953–1955). In 1954 he joined in delaying tactics against the nomination of Earl Warren as chief justice, managing to hold off confirmation for two months. He continued his struggle until his death in 1959.

JUSTICES' CHARACTERISTICS

All of President Washington's appointees were lawyers, and no president has deviated from this precedent. Legal education has changed radically over the years, however. Until the mid-nineteenth century, it was traditional for aspiring lawyers to study privately in a law office until they had learned the law sufficiently to pass the bar. There were no law schools as such in the early years, although some universities had courses in law. John Marshall, for example, attended a course of law lectures at William and Mary College in the 1770s. Two of the earliest justices, John Rutledge and John Blair, received their legal education in England, at the Inns of Court. A modern justice, Frank Murphy (1940–1949), also studied there. Three justices, Henry Baldwin, Levi Woodbury, and Ward Hunt, attended law lectures by Federalist judge Tapping Reeve in Lichtfield, Connecticut.

Of the sixty-one justices (including Rutledge and Blair) who attended law school, by far the largest number (sixteen) attended Harvard. Yale taught nine justices law, and Columbia six. The first justice to receive a law degree from an American university was Benjamin Curtis, who got his from Harvard in 1832.

It was not until 1957 that the Supreme Court was composed, for the first time, entirely of law school graduates. Before that, many had attended law school but had not received degrees. The last justice never to have attended law school was James F. Byrnes, who served from 1941 to 1942. The son of poor Irish immigrants, Byrnes never even graduated from high school. He left school at the age of fourteen, worked as a law clerk, and eventually became a Court stenographer. Reading law in his spare time, Byrnes passed the bar at the age of twenty-four.

The last justice not to have a law degree was Stanley F. Reed, who served from 1938 to 1957. He attended both the University of Virginia and Columbia law schools, but received no law degree.

Life Before the Court

Most justices were politicians or judges before coming to the Supreme Court. In fact, only one justice, George Shiras Jr., had never engaged in political or judicial activities before his appointment. A total of sixty-seven justices had some judicial experience—federal or state—before coming to the Supreme Court. Surprisingly, there have been more (forty-four) who

had experience on the state level than on the federal level (thirty-one).

All except two of President Washington's appointees had state judicial experience. Washington believed such experience was important for justices of the new federal court. But not until 1826 was a federal judge appointed to the Court. Robert Trimble had served nine years as a U.S. district judge before being elevated to the Supreme Court.

Even after Trimble's appointment, judges with federal judicial experience continued to be a rarity on the Supreme Court. By 1880 only two other federal judges, Philip P. Barbour in 1836 and Peter V. Daniel in 1841, had made it to the high court. After 1880, when federal circuit judge William Woods was appointed, the pace picked up, and federal judicial experience became an increasingly important criterion for appointment to the Supreme Court. By 1995, seven of the nine justices had served as federal judges before coming to the Court. An eighth had served as a state judge before her appointment.

Many justices had political careers, serving in Congress, as governors, or as members of a cabinet. One president, William Howard Taft, was later appointed to the Court, as chief justice, in 1921. As of 1995, a fourth of all justices, twenty-seven, had served in Congress before their elevation to the Court. An additional six justices sat in the Continental Congress in the 1770s or 1780s.

The first justice with congressional background was William Paterson, who had served in the Senate from 1789 to 1790. Chief Justice John Marshall was the first justice with cabinet experience, having held the post of secretary of state from 1800 to 1801. Only a few justices have come directly from Congress to the Court. Only one incumbent House member, James M. Wayne in 1835, has been named to the Court, and five incumbent senators: John McKinley in 1837, Levi Woodbury in 1846, Edward D. White in 1894, Hugo L. Black in 1937, and Harold H. Burton in 1945.

The Senate traditionally has confirmed its own members without much debate. But in January 1853, when lame-duck president Millard Fillmore nominated Whig senator George Badger of North Carolina to the Court, the Democratic Senate postponed the nomination until the close of the congressional session in March. Then the new Democratic president, Franklin Pierce, was able to nominate his own man. The postponement of Badger's nomination was a polite way of defeating a colleague's nomination, avoiding an outright rejection.

Senator White's nomination came about after a bitter quarrel between President Grover Cleveland and Sen. David B. Hill of New York resulted in the Senate's rejection of two Cleveland nominees from New York. Cleveland then turned to the Senate for one of its own members, and that body quickly approved him. (*See "Senatorial Courtesy," p. 764.*)

Hugo Black's 1937 nomination was surrounded by controversy. Sen. Joseph T. Robinson of Arkansas, the Senate majority leader who had led the fight for President Franklin D. Roosevelt's so-called Court-packing plan, was expected to get the nomination, but he died suddenly. Roosevelt picked Black, one of the few southern senators other than Robinson who had championed the president in the Court battle. Black's support of the controversial bill—plus what some felt was his general lack of qualifications for the Supreme Court—led to a brief but acrimonious fight over his nomination. After he was confirmed, publicity grew over his onetime membership in the Ku Klux Klan, and charges were made that he was still a member. In a nationwide radio address, Black denied having any racial or religious intolerance and defused the criticism.

The last Supreme Court appointee with any previous congressional service was Sherman Minton in 1949. He had served as a U.S. senator from Indiana from 1935 to 1941, then was appointed to a circuit court of appeals judgeship. Since the retirement of Justice Black in 1971, no Supreme Court member has had any congressional experience.

Since John Adams's secretary of state, John Marshall, was appointed to the Supreme Court, twenty-two other cabinet members have become justices, thirteen of them appointed while still serving in the cabinet. Heading the list of cabinet positions that led to Supreme Court seats is that of attorney general. Nine attorneys general, including seven incumbents, have been appointed to the Court. Next come secretaries of the Treasury (four), secretaries of state (three), and secretaries of the navy (three). One postmaster general, one secretary of the interior, one secretary of war, and one secretary of labor have been appointed to the Court.

The appointment of incumbent attorneys general was largely a twentieth-century phenomenon, at least for the first half; six of the seven appointments occurred after 1900. The other occurred in 1897, when President William McKinley appointed his attorney general, Joseph McKenna. The twentieth-century incumbents named to the Court were William H. Moody, appointed by Theodore Roosevelt in 1906; James C. McReynolds (Wilson, 1914); Harlan Fiske Stone (Coolidge, 1925); Frank Murphy (Franklin Roosevelt, 1940); Robert H. Jackson (Roosevelt, 1941); and Tom C. Clark (Truman, 1949).

CATHOLIC AND JEWISH JUSTICES

All but sixteen Supreme Court justices have been of Protestant background. The first break with Protestant tradition came in 1835 when President Andrew Jackson nominated Roger B. Taney, a Roman Catholic, as chief justice. Taney's religion caused no controversy at the time; however, his close alliance with Jackson, whom he served as attorney general and Treasury secretary, was an issue.

After Taney's death in 1864, it was thirty years before another Catholic was appointed. In that year President Grover Cleveland chose Edward D. White of Louisiana as associate justice. Sixteen years later President William Howard Taft made White chief justice. As with Taney, White's religion attracted no particular notice. Both Taney and White were from traditional Catholic areas of the country, and both had long been engaged in politics. In 1897 President William McKinley chose Joseph McKenna, his attorney general and a Catholic, as associate justice. In that appointment geography was the overriding factor—McKenna came from California, the same state as his predecessor, Stephen J. Field.

Pierce Butler was the next Catholic appointee, named by Warren G. Harding in 1922. On Butler's death in late 1939, Franklin D. Roosevelt picked as his successor Frank Murphy, an Irish Catholic who had been mayor of Detroit, governor of Michigan, and was then serving as Roosevelt's attorney general. In 1949, when Murphy died, Harry S. Truman named a Protestant, Tom C. Clark. For the first time since 1894 there was no Catholic on the Court.

Of all Catholic appointments, that of William J. Brennan Jr. by President Dwight D. Eisenhower in 1956 attracted the most notice, although it was relatively noncontroversial. But it was an election year, and the Republicans were making a strong appeal to normally Democratic Catholic voters in the big cities. Some saw Brennan's appointment as part of that GOP strategy, although Eisenhower insisted it was an appointment made purely on merit.

President Ronald Reagan named two Catholics to the Court—Anthony M. Kennedy and Antonin Scalia. Their religious beliefs seemed significant only insofar as the Catholic church, like Reagan, steadfastly opposed abortion. The link between Catholicism and that particular position, however, is not indissoluble. Justice Brennan had steadily supported abortion rights.

Much more controversial than any of the Catholic nominees was Louis D. Brandeis, the first Jewish justice, named by Woodrow Wilson in 1916. Brandeis was already a figure of great controversy because of his views on social and economic matters. Conservatives bitterly fought his nomination, raising an element of anti-Semitism. When Brandeis took his seat on the Court, Justice James McReynolds refused to speak to him for three years and once refused to sit next to him for a Court picture-taking session.

Herbert C. Hoover's nomination of Benjamin Cardozo in 1932 established a so-called Jewish seat on the Supreme Court. Justice Felix Frankfurter replaced Cardozo in 1939. He in turn was replaced by Justice Arthur J. Goldberg in 1962. And when Goldberg resigned his Court position to become U.S. ambassador to the United Nations, President Lyndon B. Johnson chose Abe Fortas to replace him. But with Justice Fortas's resignation in 1969, President Richard Nixon broke the tradition of a "Jewish" seat by choosing Harry A. Blackmun of Minnesota, a Protestant.

A quarter of a century then passed before the Court had another Jewish member and then, in quick succession, President Bill Clinton named two Jewish justices: Ruth Bader Ginsburg in 1993 and Stephen G. Breyer in 1994. Religion was not an issue for either of the nominees, both of whom were long-serving judges on lower federal courts.

Clarence Thomas was an Episcopalian when named to the Court in 1991, but in 1996 he announced that he had returned to Catholicism, the faith of his youth. That personal decision made history: for the first time, a majority of the justices were not Protestant. Thomas, Scalia, and Kennedy were Catholic; Breyer and Ginsburg, Jewish.

During the nineteenth century two men who had served as attorney general eventually were elevated to the Supreme Court, but in both cases appointment came after their cabinet service. They were Roger B. Taney, appointed chief Justice by President Andrew Jackson in 1835, after serving as Jackson's attorney general from 1831 to 1833, and Nathan Clifford, appointed to the Court by President James Buchanan in 1857 after service as James K. Polk's attorney general from 1846 to 1848. The last justice with cabinet experience was Clark, who served on the Court from 1949 to 1967.

Six men have been appointed to the Supreme Court after serving as governor of their state. The first was William Paterson, who served as governor of New Jersey from 1790 to 1793. The most recent—and the most famous—was California governor Earl Warren, appointed chief justice by President Eisenhower in 1953. Warren had a long political career behind him, having served as attorney general of California before winning three terms as governor. In 1948 he was the Republican nominee for vice president and ran a brief campaign for the presidential nomination in 1952.

Charles Evans Hughes of New York was appointed to the Court by President Taft in 1910. Hughes was a reform governor who had conducted investigations into fraudulent insurance practices in New York before being elected governor in 1906. He left the Court in 1916 to run for president on the Republican ticket, losing narrowly to Woodrow Wilson. Later he served as secretary of state under Harding and Coolidge and returned to the Court in 1930 as chief justice, appointed by President Hoover.

The three other former governors appointed to the Supreme Court were Levi Woodbury of New Hampshire in 1846 (governor, 1823–1824), Salmon P. Chase of Ohio in 1864 (governor, 1856–1860), and Frank Murphy of Michigan in 1940 (governor, 1937–1939). One chief justice, John Jay, left the Court to become governor of New York.

James Byrnes followed Jay's path, leaving the Court in 1942, after only sixteen months in the post, for other positions in federal and state government, the last of which was that of governor of South Carolina, an office he held from 1951 to 1955.

Generation Gaps

The age at which justices join the Court varies widely. Oldest at the time of his initial appointment was Horace H. Lurton, who was sixty-five when he went on the Court in 1910. Two chief justices were older than that when they achieved their office, but they had previously served on the Court: in 1941 Harlan Fiske Stone was sixty-eight, and in 1930 Charles Evans Hughes was sixty-seven.

Representing the younger generation, Justices William Johnson and Joseph Story were only thirty-two when they were appointed in 1804 and 1811, respectively. Story was younger than Johnson by about a month.

Only two other justices were under forty when appointed: Bushrod Washington, nephew of the president, who was thirty-six

when appointed in 1798, and James Iredell, who was thirty-eight when appointed in 1790. Iredell also was the youngest justice to die on the Court—forty-eight when he died in 1799. The youngest twentieth-century justice was William O. Douglas, who was forty when appointed in 1939.

The oldest justice to serve was Oliver Wendell Holmes Jr., who retired at ninety in 1932, the Court's only nonagenarian. The second oldest member, Chief Justice Roger Taney, was eighty-seven when he died in 1864. Of the current justices, John Paul Stevens turns eighty-four in April 2004 and Chief Justice William H. Rehnquist turns eighty in October 2004. All the other justices who had served past the age of eighty retired from the bench and did not die in office. They were Harry Blackmun, eighty-five when he retired; William Brennan, eighty-four; Thurgood Marshall, eighty-three; Louis Brandeis and Gabriel Duvall, both eighty-two; Joseph McKenna and Stephen Field, both eighty-one; and Samuel Nelson, eighty.

The youngest member to leave the Court was Benjamin Curtis, who resigned in 1857 at forty-seven. Others who left the Court before the age of fifty were Justices Iredell, dead at forty-eight, Alfred Moore, who retired at forty-eight, and John Jay and John Campbell, who retired at forty-nine. Jay also holds the record for number of years survived after leaving the Court—thirty-four. In modern times, James Byrnes lived twenty-nine years after resigning from the Court in 1942.

Length of Service

Length of service on the Court also has varied greatly, from fifteen months to thirty-six years. Byrnes served the shortest time; he was confirmed by the Senate on June 12, 1941, and resigned on October 3, 1942, to become director of the World War II Office of Economic Stabilization. Justice Thomas Johnson, who served from 1791 to 1793, was on the Court only sixteen months. Although he retired because of ill health, he lived another twenty-six years, dying at the age of eighty-seven.

In January 1974 Justice Douglas broke the record for service on the Court, held since December 1897 by Stephen Field, who had served thirty-four years and nine months when he resigned. Douglas served until November 1975, when he resigned after thirty-six years and seven months on the Court. Chief Justice Marshall established the first longevity record by serving for thirty-four years and five months between 1801 and 1835. That record held until Field broke it in 1897. Chief Justice Rehnquist may yet set the record for longevity on the court. As of January 2004 he had served for thirty-two years.

Other justices who served thirty years or longer include Brennan (thirty-three years, nine months), Black (thirty-four years, one month), the first John Marshall Harlan and Joseph Story (thirty-three years each), James Wayne (thirty-two years), Byron R. White (thirty-one years, two months), John McLean (thirty-one years), and Bushrod Washington and William Johnson (thirty years each). John Paul Stevens will have served for thirty years if he is still on the Court in December 2005.

SIX FOREIGN-BORN JUSTICES

The Constitution does not require that Supreme Court justices be native-born Americans, and so presidents are free to name foreign-born persons to the Court. In all, six Supreme Court justices have been born outside the United States, one the son of an American missionary abroad. Of the remaining five, four were born in the British Isles. Only one—Felix Frankfurter—was born in a non-English-speaking country, Austria.

President George Washington appointed three of the foreign-born justices. The others were selected by Presidents Benjamin Harrison, Warren G. Harding, and Franklin D. Roosevelt.

The six justices born outside the United States are:

• James Wilson, born on September 14, 1742, in Caskardy, Scotland. Wilson grew up in Scotland and was educated at St. Andrews University in preparation for a career in the ministry. But in 1765 he sailed for America, where he studied law and became a land speculator. A signer of the Declaration of Independence, Wilson also was a member of the 1787 Constitutional Convention and its Committee of Detail, which was responsible for writing the first draft of the Constitution. In 1789 President Washington appointed Wilson one of the original members of the Supreme Court.

• James Iredell, born on October 5, 1751, in Lewes, England. Iredell was born into an old English family allegedly descended from Oliver Cromwell's son-in-law. Through family connections, Iredell received an appointment as colonial comptroller of customs at Edenton, North Carolina, at age seventeen. After six years he was promoted to collector of the port of Edenton. But Iredell identified with the colonial cause and resigned his job as collector in 1776. While serving in his colonial offices, Iredell had studied law and began practice in 1770. By 1788 he had become a strong supporter of the new federal Constitution and worked for its ratification by North Carolina. President Washington appointed him a Supreme Court justice in 1790.

• William Paterson, born on December 24, 1745, in County Antrim, Ireland. Paterson emigrated to America with his parents when he was only two years old. He received his education at the College of New Jersey (now Princeton University) and then read law, opening his own law practice in 1769. Paterson was active in New Jersey affairs during the Revolutionary and Confederation periods, and he served as a delegate to the Constitutional Convention in 1787. He was a member of the First Senate from 1789 to 1790 and, as a member of the Judiciary Committee, helped to write the Judiciary Act of 1789. Later, he codified the laws of the state of New Jersey and, in association with Alexander Hamilton, laid out plans for the industrial city of Paterson. He was appointed to the Supreme Court by President Washington in 1793.

• David Brewer, born on June 20, 1837, in Smyrna, Asia Minor, where his father was serving as a Congregational missionary. Brewer's mother was the sister of Justice Stephen J. Field (1863–1897) and Cyrus W. Field, promoter of the first Atlantic cable. The family returned to the United States soon after Brewer's birth. Brewer sought his fortune in Kansas and spent most of his career in the Kansas court system and lower federal courts. He was elevated to the Supreme Court by President Benjamin Harrison in 1890.

• George Sutherland, born on March 25, 1862, in Buckinghamshire, England. Sutherland's father converted to Mormonism about the time of George's birth and moved his family to the Utah Territory. Although the senior Sutherland soon deserted the Mormons, the family remained in Utah, where George was educated at Brigham Young Academy (now Brigham Young University). When Utah entered the Union as a state in 1896, Sutherland was elected to the state legislature. In 1900 he won a seat in the U.S. House and served two terms in the U.S. Senate (1905–1917) before being defeated for reelection. While in the Senate, he formed a close friendship with a fellow senator, Warren G. Harding of Ohio. When Harding became president, he appointed Sutherland to the Supreme Court.

• Felix Frankfurter, born on November 15, 1882, in Vienna, Austria. Frankfurter came to the United States with his parents in 1894 and grew up on the lower East Side of New York City. He had a brilliant academic record at City College and Harvard Law School, after which he practiced law for a time in New York City. In 1914 he joined the Harvard Law faculty and remained there, with time out for government service during World War I, until his appointment to the Supreme Court by President Franklin D. Roosevelt in 1939.

Four or five years is usually the longest the Court goes without a change in justices, which makes the current Court's length of continuous service, over nine years as of January 2004, unusual. The long terms of Black and Douglas spanned an era of such changing membership on the Court that they each served with more than a quarter of the Court's entire membership throughout its history. But there was one lengthy period—twelve years—when the Court's membership remained intact. That was from 1811, when Joseph Story was confirmed, to 1823, when Justice Henry Brockholst Livingston died.

Long service sometimes leads to questions of disability as justices age and are no longer capable of carrying a full load of casework. By early 1870 Justice Robert C. Grier was nearly seventy-six. His mental and physical powers were obviously impaired, and often he seemed confused and feeble. Grier complied when a committee of his fellow justices finally approached him to urge his resignation. He died eight months later.

Justice Field was among those urging Grier's retirement. Ironically, a quarter of a century later, Field found himself in the same position as Grier. His powers had visibly declined, and he was frequently absent from the Court. The other justices finally began hinting strongly that Field should resign. But Field insisted on staying on long enough to break Chief Justice Marshall's record for length of service.

In 1880 the Court was manned by an especially infirm set of justices; three of the nine—Ward Hunt, Nathan Clifford, and Noah Swayne—were incapacitated. Hunt had suffered a paralytic stroke in 1879 and took no further part in Court proceedings, but he refused to resign because he was not eligible for a full pension under the law then in effect. Finally, after three years, Congress passed a special law exempting Hunt from the terms of the pension law and granting him retirement at full pay if he would resign from the Court within thirty days of enactment of the exemption. Hunt resigned the same day.

Justice Clifford also had suffered a stroke that prevented him from participating in Court activities. But Clifford also refused to resign, hoping to live long enough for a Democratic president to name a successor. At the time, Clifford was the only Democrat left on the Court who had been named by a Democratic president. But he died while Republicans were still in power.

Justice Swayne's mental acuity was noticeably declining. He was finally persuaded to resign by President Hayes, with the promise that Swayne's friend and fellow Ohioan Stanley Matthews would be chosen as his successor.

The most recent case of a Court disability was that of Justice Douglas, who suffered a stroke in January 1975. At first, Douglas attempted to continue his duties, but in November 1975 he resigned, citing pain and physical disability.

CONTROVERSIAL JUSTICES

Only once has a justice been driven from the Court by outside pressure. That occurred in 1969, when Justice Abe Fortas resigned. The resignation followed by less than eight months a successful Senate filibuster against President Lyndon B. Johnson's nomination of Fortas to be chief justice. Fortas's departure from the Court climaxed a furor brought on by the disclosure early in May 1969 that he had received and held for eleven months a $20,000 fee from the family foundation of a man later imprisoned for illegal stock manipulation.

A year after Fortas's resignation, an attempt was made to bring impeachment charges against Justice William Douglas. General dissatisfaction with Douglas's liberal views and controversial lifestyle—combined with frustration over the Senate's rejection of two of President Nixon's conservative southern nominees—seemed to spark the action. House Republican leader Gerald R. Ford of Michigan, who led the attempt to impeach Douglas, charged among other things that the justice had practiced law in violation of federal law, had failed to disqualify himself in cases in which he had an interest, and had violated standards of good behavior by allegedly advocating revolution. A special House Judiciary subcommittee created to investigate the charges found no grounds for impeachment.

RELATIVE JUSTICES

Service on the Court has sometimes been a family tradition. The two justices named John Marshall Harlan were grandfather and grandson. The elder Harlan, a Kentucky politician, was put on the Court by President Rutherford B. Hayes in 1877 and served until 1911—one of the longest periods of service in Court history. His grandson and namesake was born and grew up in Chicago and made his career as a highly successful Wall Street lawyer. His service extended from his appointment by President Dwight D. Eisenhower in 1955 until his resignation in September 1971.

Stephen J. Field was appointed to the Supreme Court by President Abraham Lincoln in 1863. Twenty-seven years later, in 1890, he was joined by his nephew on the Court when President Benjamin Harrison named David Brewer as an associate justice. Brewer was Field's sister's son. The two served together on the Court for seven years, until Field retired in 1897.

Justice Stanley Matthews was four years older than his colleague Justice Horace Gray, both of whom were appointed in 1881. They served together for eight years until Matthews's death in March 1889. Three months later, Gray, a sixty-one-year-old bachelor, married Matthews's daughter Jane.

The two Lamars who served on the Court—Lucius Quintus Cincinnatus Lamar of Mississippi and Joseph Rucker Lamar of Georgia—were cousins, descendants of a Huguenot family that settled in the colonies in the 1600s. Lucius was also a cousin of John A. Campbell, who served on the Court from 1853 to 1861. Lucius served from 1888 to 1893 and was the first native-born southerner to be appointed after the Civil War. Joseph, appointed by President William Howard Taft, served from 1911 to 1916.

The only Supreme Court justice ever to be impeached was Samuel Chase. A staunch Federalist who had rankled Jeffersonians with his partisan political statements and his vigorous prosecution of the Alien and Sedition Acts, Chase was impeached by the House in 1804. But his critics failed to achieve the necessary two-thirds majority in the Senate for conviction. (*See "Removal from Office," pp. 766–771.*)

Other, less heralded cases of questionable behavior have occurred from time to time. In 1857, when the nation was awaiting the Court's decision in *Scott v. Sandford*, Justices Robert Grier and John Catron wrote privately to the incoming president, James Buchanan, detailing the Court's discussions and foretelling the final decision. Buchanan was glad of the news and was able to say in his inaugural address that the decision was expected to come soon and that he and all Americans should acquiesce in it. But divulging the Court's decision before it is publicly announced is generally considered to be unethical.

Another controversy arose fourteen years later in the so-called *Legal Tender Cases*. The Court, with two vacancies, had found the Civil War legal tender acts unconstitutional. But then President Grant named two justices to fill the vacancies, and the Court voted to rehear the case. With the two new justices—

William Strong and Joseph P. Bradley—voting with the majority, the Court now found the legal tender acts constitutional. It was charged that Grant had appointed the two knowing in advance that they would vote to reverse the Court's previous decision. Historians have no evidence of any explicit arrangements.

Although political activity by Supreme Court justices usually has been frowned on, it has not been unknown, especially during the nineteenth century when several justices manifested a hunger for their party's presidential nomination. Justice John McLean entertained presidential ambitions throughout his long Supreme Court career (1829–1861) and flirted with several political parties at various stages. In 1856 he received 190 votes on an informal first ballot at the first Republican national convention. He also sought the Republican presidential nomination in 1860.

Chief Justice Salmon Chase had aspired to the presidency before going on the bench, losing the Republican nomination to Lincoln in 1860. In 1864, while serving as Lincoln's secretary of Treasury, he allowed himself to become the focus of an anti-Lincoln group within the Republican Party. During his service on the Court, in both 1868 and 1872, he made no secret of his still-burning presidential ambitions and allowed friends to maneuver politically for him.

In 1877 the Supreme Court was thrust into the election process when a dispute arose about the outcome of the 1876 presidential election. To resolve the problem, Congress created a special electoral commission that included five Supreme Court justices. Each House of Congress also chose five members, the Democratic House selecting five Democrats and the Republican Senate five Republicans.

The five justices were supposed to be divided evenly politically—two Democrats, Clifford and Field; two Republicans, Miller and Strong; and independent David Davis. Davis, however, withdrew from consideration because he had been elected a U.S. senator from Illinois. Justice Bradley, a Republican, was substituted for Davis, making the overall lineup on the commission eight to seven in favor of the Republicans.

The three Republican justices loyally supported the claims of Republican presidential aspirant Rutherford Hayes on all questions, and the two Democratic justices backed Democratic nominee Samuel J. Tilden. The result was the election of Hayes. Justice Clifford, the chairman of the commission, was so contemptuous of the outcome that he called Hayes an illegitimate president and refused to enter the White House during his term.

CHAPTER 20

Brief Biographies

THE FOLLOWING PAGES include vital statistics and brief accounts of the lives and public careers of each of the 108 individuals who to date have served as justices of the Supreme Court of the United States. They are listed in order of their appointment; the dates beneath each name indicate the period of service on the Court, beginning with the year he or she took the judicial oath.

Biographies of the individual justices were consulted, including those contained in *The Justices of the United States Supreme Court 1789–1969: Their Lives and Major Opinions*, ed. Leon Friedman and Fred L. Israel (New York: R. R. Bowker, 1969); *The Supreme Court Justices: Illustrated Biographies, 1789–1995*, 2d ed., ed. Clare Cushman (Washington, D.C.: Congressional Quarterly, 1995); and Lee Epstein et al., *The Supreme Court Compendium: Data, Decisions, and Developments*, 2d ed. (Washington, D.C.: Congressional Quarterly, 1996). The standard reference works used were the *Dictionary of American Biography* (New York: Charles Scribner's Sons, 1928–1936); *Encyclopedia of American Biography*, ed. John A. Garraty (New York: Harper and Row, 1974); *Encyclopedia Americana* (New York: Americana, 1968); *Encyclopaedia Britannica* (Chicago: Encyclopaedia Britannica, 1973); *Who Was Who in America* (Chicago: Marquis-Who's Who, 1968). Several Supreme Court histories were also referenced, chiefly Charles Warren, *The Supreme Court in United States History*, 2 vols. (Boston: Little, Brown, 1926).

JOHN JAY

(1789–1795)

BIRTH: December 12, 1745, New York City.

EDUCATION: privately tutored; attended boarding school; graduated from King's College (later Columbia University), 1764; clerked in law office of Benjamin Kissam; admitted to the bar in 1768.

OFFICIAL POSITIONS: secretary, Royal Boundary Commission, 1773; member, New York Committee of 51, 1774; delegate, Continental Congress, 1774, 1775, 1777, president, 1778–1779; delegate, New York provincial congress, 1776–1777; chief justice, New York State, 1777–1778; minister to Spain, 1779; secretary of foreign affairs, 1784–1789; envoy to Great Britain, 1794–1795; governor, New York, 1795–1801.

SUPREME COURT SERVICE: nominated chief justice by President George Washington September 24, 1789; confirmed by the Senate September 26, 1789, by a voice vote; took judicial oath October 9, 1789; resigned June 29, 1795; replaced by Oliver Ellsworth, nominated by President Washington.

FAMILY: married Sarah Van Brugh Livingston, April 28, 1774; died 1802; five daughters, two sons.

DEATH: May 17, 1829, Bedford, New York.

John Jay, the first chief justice of the United States, was descended from two of New York's most prominent families. His mother, Mary Van Cortlandt Jay, was Dutch, and his father, Peter Jay, was a wealthy merchant descended from French Huguenots.

The youngest of eight children, Jay grew up on the family farm at Rye, New York. He was taught Latin by his mother and attended a boarding school in New Rochelle for three years. Following more private tutoring, he entered King's College and graduated at the age of nineteen. He was admitted to the bar four years later.

In 1774 Jay married Sarah Van Brugh Livingston, daughter of William Livingston, later governor of New Jersey during the Revolution. The couple had seven children, one of whom became a lawyer and active abolitionist. John Jay, Jay's grandson, served as minister to Austria in the early 1870s.

In retirement, Jay pursued an interest in agriculture and devoted time to the Episcopal Church. He was one of the founders of the American Bible Society and was elected its president in 1821. He opposed the War of 1812.

John Jay

During his many years of public service, Jay developed a reputation for fairness and honesty. Prior to the presidential election of 1800, Alexander Hamilton urged Governor Jay to call a special session of the New York legislature and change the state's election laws to ensure that New York would deliver Federalist votes. Although a strong Federalist, Jay refused, writing to Hamilton that he would be "proposing a measure for party purposes which I think it would not become me to adopt."

Jay represented his state at both the first and second Continental Congresses. Although he was not present for the signing of the Declaration of Independence, he worked for its ratification in New York. At this time he also helped to draft the new state constitution.

In December 1778 Jay was elected president of the Continental Congress. The following September, he was sent to Spain in an attempt to win diplomatic recognition and large amounts of economic aid. Although the mission was at best only a modest success, it provided Jay with important diplomatic experience. In 1783 Jay helped negotiate the Treaty of Paris, which formally ended the Revolutionary War.

Although he was not a member of the Constitutional Convention in 1787, Jay recognized the need for a stronger union while serving as secretary of foreign affairs. He contributed five essays to the *Federalist Papers* urging support of the new Constitution. In the presidential election of 1789 Jay received nine electoral votes.

While organizing his first administration, George Washington first offered Jay the position of secretary of state. When Jay declined, the president named him chief justice of the new Supreme Court. In this position, Jay helped pave the way for a strong, independent national judiciary.

In 1794 Jay, while still chief justice, was sent to England in an effort to ease growing hostilities between that country and the United States. The result was the controversial Jay Treaty, which outraged many at home who felt it surrendered too many American rights.

When he returned from the treaty negotiations Jay discovered he had been elected governor of New York, a position he had run for and lost in 1792. He promptly resigned as chief justice and served as governor for two three-year terms.

During his tenure Jay supported the gradual freeing of slaves and instituted a revision of the state criminal code. He became interested in prisoner welfare and recommended the construction of a model penitentiary. He also reduced the number of crimes carrying the death penalty.

Following the resignation of Oliver Ellsworth, President Adams, in December 1800, nominated Jay for a second term as chief justice. Although he was immediately confirmed by the Senate, Jay refused the office for health reasons and, as he wrote Adams, because the Court lacked "the energy, weight, and dignity which are essential to its affording due support to the national government."

Jay lived in retirement on his eight hundred-acre estate in Westchester County, New York, for twenty-eight years until his death at eighty-three in 1829.

THE OATHS OF OFFICE

As he or she is sworn into office, every justice of the U.S. Supreme Court has taken two oaths: the Constitutional Oath and the Judicial Oath. Article VI of the Constitution requires of all federal employees to pledge to support the Constitution. The oath reads,

"I, ———, do solemnly swear that I will support and defend the Constitution of the United States against all enemies, foreign and domestic; that I will bear true faith and allegiance to the same; that I take this obligation freely, without any mental reservation or purpose of evasion; and that I will well and faithfully discharge the duties of the office on which I am about to enter. So help me God."

The Judicial Oath is required by Section 8 of the Judiciary Act of 1789. The original oath included the phrase "according to the best of my abilities and understanding, agreeably to the constitution." The oath was amended in 1990 to say "under the Constitution." The oath reads,

"I, ———, do solemnly swear (or affirm) that I will administer justice without respect to persons, and do equal right to the poor and to the rich, and that I will faithfully and impartially discharge and perform all the duties incumbent upon me as ——— under the Constitution and laws of the United States. So help me God."

JOHN RUTLEDGE
(1790–1791, 1795)

BIRTH: September 1739, Charleston, South Carolina.

EDUCATION: privately tutored; studied law at the Middle Temple in England; called to the English bar February 9, 1760.

OFFICIAL POSITIONS: member, South Carolina Commons House of Assembly, 1761–1776; South Carolina attorney general pro item, 1764–1765; delegate, Stamp Act Congress, 1765; member, Continental Congress, 1774–1776, 1782–1783; president, South Carolina General Assembly, 1776–1778; governor, South Carolina, 1779–1782; judge of the Court of Chancery of South Carolina, 1784–1791; chief, South Carolina delegation to the Constitutional Convention, 1787; member, South Carolina convention to ratify U.S. Constitution, 1788; chief justice, South Carolina Supreme Court, 1791–1795; member, South Carolina Assembly, 1798–1799.

SUPREME COURT SERVICE: nominated associate justice by President George Washington September 24, 1789; confirmed by the Senate September 26, 1789, by a voice vote; took judicial oath February 15, 1790; resigned March 5, 1791; replaced by Thomas Johnson, nominated by President Washington. Later sworn in by virtue of recess appointment as chief justice August 12, 1795; appointment not confirmed, and service terminated December 15, 1795.

FAMILY: married Elizabeth Grimke, May 1, 1763; died 1792; ten children.

DEATH: July 18, 1800, Charleston, South Carolina.

John Rutledge

Sarah Hext Rutledge was only fifteen years old when she gave birth to her first son, John. When her husband, Dr. John Rutledge, died in 1750, she was left a wealthy twenty-six-year-old widow with seven children.

As a youth, John Rutledge studied law in the office of his uncle, Andrew Rutledge, Speaker of the South Carolina Commons House of Assembly. Later he read for two years under Charleston lawyer James Parsons and then sailed for England, where he studied at the Inns of Court in London.

The wealthy Rutledge family, together with the Pinckneys, exerted great influence over South Carolina politics toward the end of the eighteenth century. John Rutledge's brother Edward, a law partner of Thomas Pinckney, was a signer of the Declaration of Independence and a delegate to the Constitutional Convention in Philadelphia; he was elected governor of South Carolina in 1798. Hugh Rutledge, another brother, also was a member of the South Carolina bar.

In 1763 Rutledge married Elizabeth Grimke, a member of an old Charleston family and aunt of Angelina and Sarah Moore Grimke, two of South Carolina's most famous abolitionists and reformers. One of Rutledge's children, John Jr., became a member of the U.S. House of Representatives.

Almost immediately upon his return to South Carolina from England in 1761, Rutledge became a leading member of the local bar. He had been home only three months when he was elected to the provincial legislature. In 1764 he was appointed attorney general by the king's governor in an attempt to win his support in a power struggle between the Crown and the assembly. Rutledge held the position for ten months but did not take sides against the assembly.

At the age of twenty-five Rutledge was the youngest delegate to the Stamp Act Congress in New York in 1765. There he served as chairman of the committee that drafted a petition to the king demanding repeal of the Stamp Act. The demand was met the following year.

In 1774 Rutledge headed the South Carolina delegation to the Continental Congress, which included his brother Edward and Edward's father-in-law, Henry Middleton. At the Congress in Philadelphia, Rutledge allied with other conservatives in supporting colonial rights but opposing separation from the mother country. When the Congress proposed an economic boycott against Britain, he convinced them to allow one product to continue to be traded—South Carolina's principal export, rice.

Rutledge continued to serve in the Continental Congress in 1775 but returned to South Carolina in December of that year to help form a new state government. A new constitution was written, calling for the formation of a new state assembly. Rutledge was elected president of the assembly in March 1776. In 1778 he resigned rather than accept a new, more liberal and democratic state constitution. In the face of a British invasion the following year, however, he was made governor by the assembly and given broad emergency powers.

South Carolina fell to the British in the summer of 1780. After the British army moved to Virginia in 1781, Rutledge returned to South Carolina to help restore civil authority. In 1784 he was appointed chief judge of the new state court of chancery.

At the Constitutional Convention in 1787 Rutledge served on the select committee that produced the first draft of the Constitution. He is responsible for writing the Supremacy Clause, which states that the Constitution and laws of the United States "shall be the supreme Law of the Land."

Most of his attention, however, was directed toward protecting wealthy, antidemocratic interests. He successfully opposed, for example, an immediate ban on the slave trade. In 1789 South Carolina's electors cast their vice-presidential votes for Rutledge, in recognition of his service to the state.

Rutledge accepted President Washington's offer to become an associate justice of the Supreme Court in 1789. Although he participated in circuit court duties, he never sat as a justice due to personal illness and the inactivity of the Court. In February 1791 Rutledge resigned to accept what he considered to be a more prestigious position—chief justice of the Supreme Court of South Carolina.

The importance of the U.S. Supreme Court was gradually increasing, however, and in 1795 Rutledge wrote Washington of his desire to succeed John Jay as chief justice. He presided unofficially over the August term of the Court, but his nomination as chief justice was rejected by the Senate in December 1795 because of his public opposition to the Jay Treaty with England.

Rutledge attempted to drown himself after hearing news of his Senate rejection and suffered lapses of sanity until the end of his life. He died July 18, 1800, at the age of sixty.

MARGINS OF VICTORY

For most of the Supreme Court's history, the Senate's confirmation of a nominee to the bench has been a simple formality. Deference to the president, who selects the new justice, usually has prevailed over any reservations senators may have. Indeed, seventy-three justices have been approved by voice vote with no recorded opposition. Five of these, however, subsequently declined the seat.

Six justices—including three of President Ronald Reagan's nominees—were confirmed by unanimous roll-call votes. In two other cases, the nominee was officially confirmed by voice vote, but each time one senator wanted his opposition recorded. Sen. Joseph McCarthy, R-Wis., opposed confirmation of Justice William J. Brennan Jr. (1957), and Sen. Strom Thurmond, R-S.C., opposed the nomination of Arthur J. Goldberg (1962.)

There have been numerous close votes on confirmation to the Court. Stanley Matthews won confirmation by the barest of margins—one vote, 24-23—in 1881. Nathan Clifford was confirmed in 1858 by a 26-23 vote, and Lucius Q. Lamar squeaked by with a 32-28 vote in 1888. In the twentieth century, Clarence Thomas won confirmation by the closest margin, 52-48. Some nominees were confirmed over substantial opposition, here considered more than ten votes:

Chief Justice Roger B. Taney, 29-15 (1836)
PHILIP P. BARBOUR, 30-11 (1836)
William Smith, 23-18 (1837) (declined the seat)
John Catron, 28-15 (1837)
Edwin M. Stanton, 46-11 (1869)
Roscoe Conkling, 39-12 (1882) (declined the seat)

Chief Justice Melville W. Fuller, 41-20 (1888)
David J. Brewer, 53-11 (1889)
Mahlon Pitney, 50-26 (1912)
Louis D. Brandeis, 47-22 (1916)
Chief Justice Charles E. Hughes, 52-26 (1930)
Hugo L. Black, 63-16 (1937)
Sherman Minton, 48-16 (1949)
John M. Harlan, 71-11 (1955)
Potter Stewart, 70-17 (1959)
Thurgood Marshall, 69-11 (1967)
William H. Rehnquist, 68-26 (1971) and as chief justice, 65-33 (1986)
Clarence Thomas, 52-48 (1991)

Some nominees were rejected by the barest of margins. Jeremiah S. Black was defeated by a single vote, 25-26, in 1861. Those who came close to confirmation only to lose it were as follows:

John Rutledge, as chief justice, 10-14 (1795)
JOHN C. SPENCER, 21-26 (1844)
George W. Woodward, 20-29 (1845)
Ebenezer R. Hoar, 24-33 (1870)
Jeremiah S. Black, 25-26 (1861)
William B. Hornblower, 24-30 (1894)
Wheeler H. Peckham, 32-41 (1894)
Clement Haynsworth Jr., 45-55 (1969)

WILLIAM CUSHING

(1790–1810)

BIRTH: March 1, 1732, Scituate, Massachusetts.

EDUCATION: graduated Harvard, 1751, honorary LL.D., 1785; honorary A.M., Yale, 1753; studied law under Jeremiah Gridley; admitted to the bar in 1755.

OFFICIAL POSITIONS: judge, probate court for Lincoln County, Massachusetts (now Maine), 1760–1761; judge, Superior Court of Massachusetts Bay province, 1772–1777; chief justice, Superior Court of the Commonwealth of Massachusetts, 1777–1780, Supreme Judicial Court, 1780–1789; member, Massachusetts Constitutional Convention, 1779; vice president, Massachusetts Convention, which ratified U.S. Constitution, 1788; delegate to electoral college, 1788.

SUPREME COURT SERVICE: nominated associate justice by President George Washington September 24, 1789; confirmed by the Senate September 26, 1789, by a voice vote; took judicial oath February 2, 1790; served until September 13, 1810; replaced by Joseph Story, nominated by President James Madison.

FAMILY: married Hannah Phillips, 1774.

DEATH: September 13, 1810, Scituate, Massachusetts.

William Cushing, the son of Mary Cotton Cushing and John Cushing, was a member of one of the oldest and most prominent

William Cushing

families of colonial Massachusetts. He was descended on his mother's side from John Cotton, the seventeenth-century Puritan minister. Both his father and grandfather served in the government of the Massachusetts Bay province.

Cushing graduated from Harvard in 1751. After teaching for a year in Roxbury, Massachusetts, he began studying law under Jeremiah Gridley in Boston. In 1755 he set up a private practice in his hometown of Scituate.

In 1760 Cushing moved to what is now Dresden, Maine, to become justice of the peace and judge of probates. He was not an accomplished lawyer and seemed unable to make decisions. Before long, he had lost most of his corporate business to other lawyers. In 1774 Cushing married Hannah Phillips of Middletown, Connecticut.

Cushing is known as the last American judge to wear a full wig, a habit he did not abandon until 1790.

When Cushing's father, John Cushing, decided to retire from the provincial superior court in 1772, he insisted that his son succeed him as judge. Although William Cushing was not the colonial government's first choice, he nonetheless was appointed to the position that year.

In 1774 Cushing reluctantly allied himself with the colonials by refusing to accept his salary through the British government. Although his decision did not come until the state legislature began preparing impeachment proceedings against him, he now began to be perceived as a supporter of the revolutionary cause. This belief was strengthened when he was denied a seat on the governor's council because of his stand.

In 1775 the new revolutionary government of Massachusetts reorganized the judicial system but retained Cushing as senior associate justice of the superior court. In 1777 he was elevated to chief justice.

Although Cushing played only a small role in the state constitutional convention of 1779, he actively supported ratification of the Constitution. He also served as vice president of the state convention that ratified the document in 1788.

Cushing was one of Washington's original appointees to the Supreme Court in 1789. In 1794 he was persuaded to run against Samuel Adams for governor of Massachusetts—while retaining his Court seat—but lost by a two-to-one margin. In 1795 he declined an offer from Washington to succeed John Jay as chief justice. As senior associate justice, however, he presided over the court when Chief Justice Ellsworth was absent.

Cushing remained on the bench until his death in 1810, the longest term of the original members of the Court.

JAMES WILSON

(1789–1798)

BIRTH: September 14, 1742, Caskardy, Scotland.

EDUCATION: attended University of St. Andrews (Scotland); read law in office of John Dickinson; admitted to the bar in 1767; honorary M.A., College of Philadelphia, 1776; honorary LL.D., 1790.

James Wilson

OFFICIAL POSITIONS: delegate, first Provincial Convention at Philadelphia, 1774; delegate, Continental Congress, 1775–1777, 1783, 1785–1787; delegate, U.S. Constitutional Convention, 1787; delegate, Pennsylvania convention to ratify U.S. Constitution, 1787.

SUPREME COURT SERVICE: nominated associate justice by President George Washington September 24, 1789; confirmed by the Senate September 26, 1789, by a voice vote; took judicial oath October 5, 1789; served until August 21, 1798; replaced by Bushrod Washington, nominated by President John Adams.

FAMILY: married Rachel Bird, November 5, 1771; died 1786; six children; married Hannah Gray, September 19, 1793; one son died in infancy.

DEATH: August 21, 1798, Edenton, North Carolina.

James Wilson was born in the Scottish Lowlands, the son of a Caskardy farmer, also named James. His mother was Alison Lansdale Wilson. Although the family had little money, his devout Calvinist parents were determined that James be educated for the ministry.

After study in local grammar schools, Wilson at fourteen won a scholarship to St. Andrews University and matriculated in the fall of 1757. During his fifth year, he entered the university's divinity school but was forced to leave for financial reasons when his father died.

To help support his family, he took a job as a private tutor but left the position to study accounting and bookkeeping in Edinburgh. In 1765 he decided against becoming a clerk and sailed for America.

After studying law in the new country, Wilson became one of its foremost legal scholars. Described as a man of extreme energy, he was driven by a desire for wealth and fame, constantly involved in various speculation schemes, primarily in land. He was part-owner of the Somerset Mills on the Delaware River and president of the Illinois and Wabash Company, which had vast western land holdings.

From 1777 to 1787 Wilson devoted most of his energy to developing new business interests. As his financial commitments built, he continued to seek new investments. The credit cycle eventually caught up with Wilson, however. As an associate justice, he traveled the southern circuit in constant fear of being thrown in jail for bad debts.

Wilson arrived in Philadelphia in the fall of 1765 and immediately obtained a tutorship at the College of Philadelphia. Teaching tired him, however, and he saw a better opportunity in law. He soon began reading law in the office of John Dickinson, a prominent attorney who had studied at the Inns of Court.

In 1768 Wilson opened private practice in Reading, Pennsylvania. Two years later, he moved west to Carlisle, where his practice expanded rapidly. By 1774 he was practicing in seven counties, specializing in land law.

In 1775 Wilson was elected a delegate to the Continental Congress, where he served on several committees. He aligned himself with other members of the Pennsylvania delegation in opposing separation from England. In the end, however, he followed the state assembly's instructions and signed the Declaration of Independence.

Wilson's opposition to the Pennsylvania constitution of 1776 attracted criticism from state populists and earned him a reputation as a conservative aristocrat. That reputation grew when he developed an active practice in Philadelphia defending wealthy Tories and other rich businessmen. In 1779 he was forced to barricade his home against an armed attack by a riotous mob angered over high inflation and food shortages. He eventually had to go into hiding.

At the Constitutional Convention in 1787, Wilson was a member of the committee of detail, responsible for writing the first draft of the Constitution. Although his populist foes refused to believe it, Wilson was a fervent advocate of popular sovereignty and democracy who supported popular election of the president and members of both the Senate and House. One of the first to envision the principle of judicial review, Wilson fought for a strong national judiciary and a powerful presidency. He saw no conflict between the ideal of popular rule and a strong national government because, in his view, the national government existed only by virtue of the popular will. Wilson is credited with incorporating this idea of popular sovereignty into the Constitution.

As the new national government was being formed, Wilson hoped for federal office and offered his name to Washington as chief justice of the United States. Washington appointed John Jay instead and named Wilson an associate justice.

Of the original Washington appointees to the Supreme Court, Wilson was its most accomplished legal scholar. A pamphlet he had published in 1774 presaged the concept of "dominion status" that serves today as the official guiding principle of the British Commonwealth.

His defense of the Bank of North America in 1785 anticipated constitutional opinions delivered by Chief Justice Marshall at least twenty-five years later. Associate Justice Hugo Black in *Wesberry v. Sanders* (1964) cited Wilson as a supporting source for the "one-man-one-vote" principle.

Around 1796 Wilson's investment schemes began to collapse around him. While riding circuit, he was chased by angry creditors who caught up with him at least once and had him jailed. He then sought refuge in Edenton, North Carolina—the hometown of fellow justice James Iredell—but was soon discovered and imprisoned again. Eventually released, he remained in Edenton in ill health. He died at fifty-five in a dingy inn next to the Edenton Court House.

JOHN BLAIR JR.

(1790–1796)

BIRTH: 1732, Williamsburg, Virginia.

EDUCATION: graduated with honors from College of William and Mary, 1754; studied law at Middle Temple, London, 1755–1756.

OFFICIAL POSITIONS: member, Virginia House of Burgesses, 1766–1770; clerk, Virginia Governor's Council, 1770–1775; delegate, Virginia Constitutional Convention, 1776; member, Virginia Governor's Council, 1776; judge, Virginia General Court, 1777–1778; chief justice, 1779; judge, first Virginia Court of Appeals,

John Blair Jr.

1780–1789; delegate, U.S. Constitutional Convention, 1787; judge, Virginia Supreme Court of Appeals, 1789.

SUPREME COURT SERVICE: nominated associate justice by President George Washington September 24, 1789; confirmed by the Senate September 26, 1789, by a voice vote; took judicial oath February 2, 1790; resigned January 27, 1796; replaced by Samuel Chase, nominated by President Washington.

FAMILY: married Jean Blair, December 26, 1756; died 1792.

DEATH: August 31, 1800, Williamsburg, Virginia.

John Blair Jr. was the son of one of Virginia's most prominent colonial officials, a member of the House of Burgesses, and a member of the Governor's Council. He was also acting governor of the state in 1758 and 1768.

The family owned rich land holdings, and young John—one of ten children of John Blair Sr. and Mary Monro Blair—was given an excellent education. In 1754 he graduated from the College of William and Mary, which had been founded by his great-uncle James Blair. After studying law at the Middle Temple in London, he returned home to Williamsburg and began practicing law.

A slightly built man, six feet tall with thinning red hair, Blair toward the end of his life suffered from chronic headaches, possibly brought on by the rigors of riding circuit.

Blair entered the Virginia House of Burgesses in 1766 at the age of thirty-four. A conservative, he opposed the defiant resolutions of Patrick Henry condemning the Stamp Act, but joined with leading merchants in agreeing to boycott specific British imports.

In 1770 Blair resigned his seat to become clerk of the Governor's Council, the first of several state offices and judgeships. In 1782, while serving as a judge on the state's first court of appeals, he sided with the majority decision in *Commonwealth v. Caton* that the court could declare legislative acts unconstitutional.

Although not a leading participant in the Constitutional Convention of 1787, Blair firmly supported ratification and was one of three Virginia delegates who signed the new document. When the Virginia judicial system was reorganized in 1789, Blair sat on the new supreme court of appeals for three months until his appointment as one of the original justices of the U.S. Supreme Court. Because of his wife's illness and the relative inactivity of the Court, he did not attend all its sessions. He resigned in January 1796, four years after his wife's death.

In 1799 Blair wrote to his sister of being "struck with a strange disorder . . . depriving me of nearly all the powers of mind." He died August 31, 1800, at his home in Williamsburg.

JAMES IREDELL

(1790–1799)

BIRTH: October 5, 1751, Lewes, England.

EDUCATION: educated in England; read law under Samuel Johnston of North Carolina; licensed to practice, 1770–1771.

OFFICIAL POSITIONS: comptroller of customs, Edenton, North Carolina, 1768–1774; collector of customs, Port of North

RECESS APPOINTMENTS

Fifteen men have been nominated to the Supreme Court while the Senate was not in session and have received "recess" appointments. These appointments permit the individual to be sworn in and to take part in the Court's work before the nomination is confirmed. Once the Senate returns, the president must then formally nominate the individual, who is then subject to confirmation. If confirmed, he or she is sworn in a second time.

Only five of the fifteen people who received such appointments took their seats on the bench before confirmation. Four were eventually confirmed: Benjamin R. Curtis, appointed and confirmed in December 1851; Earl Warren, appointed as chief justice in September 1953 and confirmed in March 1954; William J. Brennan Jr., appointed in October 1956 and confirmed in March 1957; and Potter Stewart, appointed in October 1958 and confirmed in May 1959. The fifth, John Rutledge, was rejected by the Senate. Rutledge, who had served as an associate justice from 1790 to 1791, was given a recess appointment as chief justice in the summer of 1795. He presided over the Court's August 1795 term, at which two cases were heard and decided. On December 15 the Senate refused, 10-14, to confirm him. Ten people received recess appointments but waited to be seated until after confirmation:

> Thomas Johnson, confirmed in 1791
> BUSHROD WASHINGTON, 1798
> Alfred Moore, 1799
> Brockholst Livingston, 1806
> Smith Thompson, 1823
> John McKinley, 1837
> Levi Woodbury, 1846
> David Davis, 1862
> John Marshall Harlan, 1877
> Oliver Wendell Holmes Jr., 1902

Carolina, 1774–1776; judge, Superior Court of North Carolina, 1778; attorney general, North Carolina, 1779–1781; member, North Carolina Council of State, 1787; delegate, North Carolina convention for ratification of federal Constitution, 1788.

SUPREME COURT SERVICE: nominated associate justice by President George Washington February 8, 1790; confirmed by the Senate February 10, 1790, by a voice vote; took judicial oath May 12, 1790; served until October 20, 1799; replaced by Alfred Moore, nominated by President John Adams.

FAMILY: married Hannah Johnston, July 18, 1773; two daughters, one son.

DEATH: October 20, 1799, Edenton, North Carolina.

James Iredell, the son of Francis Iredell and Margaret McCulloch Iredell, was born into an English family reputedly descended from Oliver Cromwell's son-in-law, Henry Ireton. The family was forced to change its name, so the story goes, following the return of Charles II to the throne.

James Iredell

When James's merchant father became ill in the early 1760s, James was able through his mother's family connections to acquire a position in America in 1768 as comptroller of the customs in Edenton, North Carolina. During his six years in that job he read law in the office of Samuel Johnston and began practice in December 1770. In 1773 he married his mentor's sister, Hannah Johnston.

Because of a slight lisp, Iredell was not effective as a public speaker but was a prolific writer of letters and essays. Many of these writings survive today and reveal a clear, candid style.

Although a new immigrant and an employee of the British, Iredell nevertheless soon found himself in support of the American revolutionary cause. In 1776 he resigned from his job as collector for the Crown at the port of Edenton.

Iredell then served on a commission to redraft North Carolina law in conformance with the state's new independent status. When a new state judicial court system was created the following year, he was chosen one of three Superior Court judges, a position he reluctantly accepted. The rigors of traveling circuit were burdensome for him, however, and he resigned after a few months to return to private law practice.

From 1779 to 1781 Iredell served as state attorney general. In 1787 the legislature appointed him to collect and revise all state laws; the new code appeared in 1791.

After the war Iredell had aligned himself with conservative leaders who favored a strong government and adherence to the peace treaty terms of 1783. In 1786 he said that the state

constitution had the power to limit the state legislature—a novel idea at the time.

Iredell's most influential work, written under the pen name Marcus, was his defense of the new federal Constitution. The tract, which appeared at the same time as the first issues of the Jefferson-Hamilton-Jay proconstitutional *Federalist Papers*, refuted George Mason's eleven objections to the document.

At the state ratification convention in 1788, Iredell served as floor leader of the Federalists, a position that brought him to the attention of George Washington. When Robert Harrison declined to serve on the Supreme Court in 1790, the president decided to appoint Iredell because, as Washington noted in his diary, "In addition to the reputation he sustains for abilities, legal knowledge and respectability of character, he is of a State of some importance in the Union that has given no character to a federal office."

Iredell served on the Court for nine years, riding the southern circuit, covering the eighteen hundred miles five times between 1790 and 1794. In dissent from *Chisholm v. Georgia,* he argued that a state could not be sued in federal court by a citizen from another state—a position later added to the Constitution by the Eleventh Amendment. In 1798 he set a precedent for *Marbury v. Madison* in arguing for the right of courts to declare laws unconstitutional (*Calder v. Bull*).

Iredell died in 1799 at the age of forty-eight at his home in Edenton.

THOMAS JOHNSON

(1792–1793)

BIRTH: November 4, 1732, Calvert County, Maryland.

EDUCATION: educated at home; studied law under Stephen Bordley; admitted to the bar, 1760.

OFFICIAL POSITIONS: delegate, Maryland Provincial Assembly, 1762; delegate, Annapolis Convention of 1774; member, Continental Congress, 1774–1777; delegate, first constitutional convention of Maryland, 1776; first governor of Maryland, 1777–1779; member, Maryland House of Delegates, 1780, 1786, 1787; member, Maryland convention for ratification of the federal Constitution, 1788; chief judge, general court of Maryland, 1790–1791; member, board of commissioners of the Federal City, 1791–1794.

SUPREME COURT SERVICE: nominated associate justice by President George Washington November 1, 1791, to replace John Rutledge, who resigned; confirmed by the Senate November 7, 1791, by a voice vote; took judicial oath August 6, 1792; resigned February 1, 1793; replaced by William Paterson, nominated by President Washington.

FAMILY: married Ann Jennings, February 16, 1766; died 1794; three boys, five girls, one of whom died in infancy.

DEATH: October 26, 1819, Frederick, Maryland.

Born to Thomas and Dorcas Sedgwick Johnson, Thomas Johnson was one of twelve children. He received no formal education as a youth but trained in the office of Thomas Jennings, clerk of the Maryland provincial court in Annapolis. Following

Thomas Johnson

During the Revolution Johnson served three consecutive terms as governor of Maryland and played a major role in keeping Washington's army manned and equipped.

Declining to serve a fourth term as governor, Johnson entered the Maryland House of Delegates in 1780, where he helped prepare legislation determining the jurisdiction of the state admiralty court. As a member of the state ratification convention in 1788, he worked for approval of the new federal Constitution. Two years later he became chief judge of the Maryland general court.

Johnson was nominated associate justice of the Supreme Court in August 1791. Hesitant because of the rigors of riding circuit, he was assured by Chief Justice Jay that every attempt would be made to bring him relief. When assigned to the southern circuit, however, including all territory south of the Potomac, he was unable to persuade Jay to rotate assignments. Citing ill health, he resigned from the bench after serving little more than a year. He wrote only one opinion during his tenure.

Johnson, however, continued in public life as a member of the commission appointed by Washington to plan the new national capital on the Potomac. That commission selected the design submitted by Pierre L'Enfant and voted to name the new city "Washington." Johnson was present when the cornerstone of the new Capitol building was laid in September 1793.

In 1795 Johnson refused an offer from President Washington to serve as secretary of state. He retired to Frederick, Maryland, where he died at the age of eighty-six.

that apprenticeship, Johnson worked and studied in the office of Stephen Bordley, an Annapolis attorney. He was admitted to the bar in 1760.

During the Revolution Johnson served as first brigadier-general of the Maryland militia. In 1777 he was responsible for leading almost two thousand men from Frederick, Maryland, to General Washington's headquarters in New Jersey.

After the war Johnson revived a plan he had dreamed of as early as 1770—to improve navigation along the Potomac River and open a passageway to the west coast. To this end, he helped organize the state-chartered Potomac Company in 1785, with his good friend George Washington as its president. The company eventually proved unprofitable.

In 1766 Johnson married Ann Jennings, the daughter of his old employer in the provincial court. They were married for twenty-eight years, until her death in 1794.

Johnson began his career as a Maryland statesman in 1762 when he was chosen a delegate to the Maryland Provincial Assembly from Anne Arundel County. As a member of the first Continental Congress in Philadelphia, he served on the committee that drafted a petition of grievances to King George III. In 1775 Johnson placed the name of George Washington in nomination before the Congress for the position of commander in chief of the Continental Army.

Johnson was absent from Philadelphia the day the Declaration of Independence was signed. However, he thoroughly supported the document and voted for Maryland's independence on July 6, 1776. He also helped to write the new state constitution that year.

WILLIAM PATERSON

(1793–1806)

BIRTH: December 24, 1745, County Antrim, Ireland.

EDUCATION: graduated from College of New Jersey (Princeton), 1763; M.A., 1766; studied law under Richard Stockton; admitted to the bar, 1769.

OFFICIAL POSITIONS: member, New Jersey Provincial Congress, 1775–1776; delegate, New Jersey State Constitutional Convention, 1776; New Jersey attorney general, 1776–1783; delegate, U.S. Constitutional Convention, 1787; U.S. senator, 1789–1790; governor, New Jersey, 1790–1793.

SUPREME COURT SERVICE: nominated associate justice by President George Washington March 4, 1793, to replace Thomas Johnson, who resigned; confirmed by the Senate March 4, 1793, by a voice vote; took judicial oath March 11, 1793; served until September 9, 1806; replaced by Henry B. Livingston, nominated by President Thomas Jefferson.

FAMILY: married Cornelia Bell, February 9, 1779; died 1783; three children; married Euphemia White, 1785.

DEATH: September 9, 1806, Albany, New York.

Born in Ireland, William Paterson emigrated to America with his parents when he was two years old. The family lived in several places before settling in Princeton, New Jersey, where William's father, Richard, began manufacturing tin plate and

THOSE WHO DID NOT SERVE

Eight men were nominated and confirmed as Supreme Court justices, but did not serve. President Washington selected Robert H. Harrison to serve on the newly created Supreme Court in 1789, but Harrison refused. In 1796 Washington asked William Cushing to become the chief justice, and the Senate confirmed him. Cushing held the post for a week before he resigned it, citing poor health. Nevertheless, he served as an associate justice until 1810. John Jay, the first chief justice, refused President John Adams's offer to serve on the Court a second time. Adams sent Jay's name to the Senate when Oliver Ellsworth resigned, but Jay declined the seat.

When Cushing's seat became available, President James Madison offered it to Levi Lincoln, Alexander Wolcott, and John Quincy Adams. Lincoln and Adams were confirmed by the Senate on January 3, 1811, and February 22, 1811, respectively, but neither accepted the post. The Senate rejected Wolcott, 24-9. In 1837 President Andrew Jackson named William Smith of Alabama to one of two new seats, but Smith turned it down. Edwin M. Stanton, President Abraham Lincoln's fiery secretary of war, was named to the Court in 1869 by President Ulysses S. Grant. Stanton was in failing health at the time of the appointment and died just four days after his confirmation. He never took his seat on the bench. President Chester A. Arthur named Roscoe Conkling of New York to fill Ward Hunt's seat on the Court. Conkling, an influential Republican, had served in the House of Representatives and the Senate. Conkling was more interested in the presidency, however, and therefore declined a place on the Court.

William Paterson

selling general merchandise. He also made successful real estate investments, which helped to pay for William's education. Little is known about his mother, whose name was Mary.

At the college of New Jersey (Princeton), Paterson was a fellow student of Oliver Ellsworth, who would later become chief justice. With Ellsworth and others, Paterson founded the Well-Meaning Society (later the Cliosophic Club) as a forum for lively discussions on the political issues of the day.

In 1766 Paterson received a Master of Arts degree from Princeton and the same year began reading law in the office of Richard Stockton. In 1769 he opened his own practice in New Bromley, about thirty miles from Princeton. There was little demand for his services, however, and in 1772 he returned to the college town. With his first wife, Cornelia Bell, Paterson lived on a farm on the Raritan River west of New Brunswick. She died in 1783 after the birth of their third child. Two years later Paterson married her close friend, Euphemia White.

Paterson was elected as a delegate from Somerset County to the First Provincial Congress of New Jersey in 1775, where he served as assistant secretary and later secretary. In 1776 he helped write the state constitution and was chosen attorney general. During this period Paterson also was a member of the

state legislative council, an officer with the county minutemen, and a member of the council of safety.

In May 1787 Paterson was chosen a delegate to the Constitutional Convention in Philadelphia, where he was responsible for introducing the New Jersey Plan, proposing a unicameral legislature giving each state an equal vote. Despite failure of that plan, Paterson signed the Constitution and worked for its adoption in New Jersey.

As a member of the judiciary committee of the new U.S. Senate, Paterson was responsible, along with his old classmate Oliver Ellsworth, for writing the Judiciary Act of 1789. He left the Senate in 1790 when he was chosen governor and chancellor of the state of New Jersey.

In this capacity, Paterson codified the laws of the state and updated the procedural rules for the common-law and chancery courts. With the assistance of Alexander Hamilton, he laid plans for an industrial town on the Passaic River, to be named Paterson.

Appointed to the Supreme Court in 1793, Paterson—while riding circuit—tried several cases arising out of the Whiskey Rebellion in western Pennsylvania. He took the Federalist position in a number of sedition trials.

When Oliver Ellsworth resigned as chief justice in 1800, President Adams refused to elevate Paterson to the position because of his close alliance with Alexander Hamilton. In 1804 Paterson missed a session of the Court because of failing health and in 1806 decided to travel to Ballston Spa, New York, for treatment. He died at his daughter's home in Albany, on September 9.

SAMUEL CHASE

(1796–1811)

BIRTH: April 17, 1741, Somerset County, Maryland.

EDUCATION: tutored by father; studied law in Annapolis law office; admitted to bar in 1761.

official positions: member, Maryland General Assembly, 1764–1784; delegate, Continental Congress, 1774–1778, 1784–1785; member, Maryland Committee of Correspondence, 1774; member, Maryland Convention and Council of Safety, 1775; judge, Baltimore Criminal Court, 1788–1796; chief judge, General Court of Maryland, 1791–1796.

SUPREME COURT SERVICE: nominated associate justice by President George Washington January 26, 1796, to replace John Blair, who resigned; confirmed by the Senate January 27, 1796, by a voice vote; took judicial oath February 4, 1796; served until June 19, 1811; replaced by Gabriel Duvall, nominated by President James Madison.

FAMILY: married Anne Baldwin May 21, 1762; seven children, three of whom died in infancy; married Hannah Kitty Giles, March 3, 1784; two daughters.

DEATH: June 19, 1811, Baltimore, Maryland.

Samuel Chase's mother, Martha Walker, died when he was still a child. His father, Thomas Chase, an Episcopal clergyman, tutored him at home and gave him a foundation in the classics. At eighteen Chase began studying law in the office of Hammond and Hall in Annapolis. Two years later, in 1761, he was admitted to the bar and began practicing in the mayor's court of Annapolis. Chase lived in the state capital until 1786, when he moved to Baltimore.

During his lifetime Chase invested in several business schemes that later caused him embarrassment. In 1778, when his efforts to corner the flour market through speculation were discovered, he was dismissed as a member of the Maryland delegation to the Continental Congress for two years.

Chase also was involved in two war-supply partnerships and owned many iron and coal properties. These businesses were largely failures, and in 1789 he was forced to declare personal bankruptcy.

About six feet in height, Chase had a large head and brownish-red complexion that earned him the nickname "bacon face" among his law colleagues. He was a signer of the Declaration of Independence and a fervent patriot whose career was marked by turbulence and controversy.

When Chase entered the Maryland General Assembly in 1764 he immediately opposed the policies of the British-appointed governor of the colony. As a member of the "Sons of Liberty," he participated in riotous demonstrations, incurring the wrath of the Annapolis mayor and aldermen who called him a "busy, restless incendiary, a ringleader of mobs, a foul-mouthed and inflaming son of discord."

In 1778 Chase served on no fewer than thirty committees of the Continental Congress. As a delegate from Maryland, he urged that the colonies unite in an economic boycott of England. He served with Benjamin Franklin and Charles Carroll on a commission sent to Montreal to persuade Canada to join with the colonies against Great Britain. The mission failed.

Instrumental in achieving support in Maryland for the Declaration of Independence, Chase did not favor adoption of the new Constitution, arguing it would institute an elitist government and not a government of the people. He wrote a series of articles against ratification under the pen name Caution.

As a judge, his abusive and overbearing manner won him few friends. Displeased over the fact that Chase held two judgeships simultaneously, the Maryland Assembly at one point tried to strip from him all public offices, but the vote fell short.

By the time Chase reached the Supreme Court he had become a radical Federalist. As an associate justice, he took an active part in Federalist politics and campaigned hard for the Alien and Sedition Acts. Biased and dogmatic, he sought the indictment of Republican editors who sided against the Federalists.

Chase's greatest political impropriety came on May 2, 1803, when he gave an impassioned speech to a grand jury against democratic "mobocracy." He was impeached by the House on March 12, 1804. Although most senators agreed that Chase had acted poorly on the bench, there were not enough votes to convict him of "high crimes," and he kept his seat on the Court.

Following the trial, Chase sank into oblivion. He was often ill from gout and unable to attend the Court's sessions. He died in 1811.

OLIVER ELLSWORTH
(1796–1800)

BIRTH: April 29, 1745, Windsor, Connecticut.

EDUCATION: A.B., Princeton, 1766; honorary LL.D., Yale (1790), Princeton (1790), Dartmouth (1797).

OFFICIAL POSITIONS: member, Connecticut General Assembly, 1773–1776; state's attorney, Hartford County, 1777–1785; delegate to Continental Congress, 1777–1784; member, Connecticut Council of Safety, 1779; member, Governor's Council, 1780–1785, 1801–1807; judge, Connecticut Superior Court, 1785–1789; delegate, Constitutional Convention, 1787; U.S. senator, 1789–1796; commissioner to France, 1799–1800.

SUPREME COURT SERVICE: nominated chief justice by President George Washington March 3, 1796, to replace John Jay, who had resigned; confirmed by the Senate March 4, 1796, by a 21-1 vote; took judicial oath March 8, 1796; resigned September 30, 1800; replaced by John Marshall, nominated by President John Adams.

FAMILY: married Abigail Wolcott, 1771; four sons, three daughters survived infancy.

DEATH: November 26, 1807, Windsor, Connecticut.

Oliver Ellsworth's great-grandfather emigrated in the middle of the seventeenth century from Yorkshire, England, to Windsor, Connecticut, where the future chief justice was born to Capt. David Ellsworth and Jemima Leavitt Ellsworth in 1745.

After studying under a Bethlehem, Connecticut, minister, Ellsworth entered Yale at seventeen. He left Yale at the end of his sophomore year and enrolled in Princeton, where he engaged in lively discussions about colonial politics and sharpened his debating skills.

After graduating from Princeton, Ellsworth began studying for the ministry at the urging of his father. Theology did not hold his interest long, however, and he soon turned to law. After four years of training he was admitted to the bar in 1777.

Ellsworth had little money in the early years of his practice. After marrying sixteen-year-old Abigail Wolcott, he settled on a farm that had belonged to his father and worked the land himself. When the Hartford court was in session, he walked to the town and back, a total of twenty miles.

Ellsworth's financial situation changed dramatically, however, as his practice grew. By 1780 he had become a leading member of the Connecticut bar and was well on his way toward acquiring a large fortune.

According to contemporary accounts, Ellsworth was a good conversationalist and elegant dresser who enjoyed frequent pinches of snuff. A tall, robust man, he was in the habit of talking to himself and was prone to obstinacy. Aaron Burr is said to have remarked: "If Ellsworth had happened to spell the name of the Deity with two d's, it would have taken the Senate three weeks to expunge the superfluous letter."

Deeply religious, Ellsworth was an active member of the Congregationalist Church and returned to the study of theology after his retirement from the Court. He also advocated improved farming techniques for Connecticut and wrote a regular advice column on the subject.

Although his name is not among the signers of the Constitution, Ellsworth deserves to be included in any list of the nation's Founding Fathers. Principal author of the Judiciary Act of 1789 and coauthor of the Connecticut Compromise, Ellsworth originated the name for the new American government when he suggested the appellation "United States" in a resolution being considered by the Constitutional Convention.

Ellsworth's political career began in 1773 when he was elected to the Connecticut General Assembly. In 1775 he was appointed one of five members of the Committee of the Pay Table, which controlled the state's Revolutionary War expenditures. He also was a Connecticut delegate to the Continental Congress during the Revolution and served on many of its committees, including one that heard appeals from admiralty courts.

In 1787 Ellsworth was elected a member of the Connecticut delegation to the Constitutional Convention and helped devise the famous Connecticut Compromise that ended the dispute between large and small states over representation in the federal legislature.

Ellsworth had to leave the convention before it ended to attend to judicial business in Connecticut and was not present for the signing of the newly drafted Constitution. He worked hard for its ratification in Connecticut, however.

In 1789 Ellsworth became one of Connecticut's first two U.S. senators. His administrative skills were immediately put to use as he helped draft the first set of Senate rules and organize the army, a U.S. Post Office, and a census. Ellsworth engineered the conference report on the Bill of Rights and helped draft the measure that admitted North Carolina to the Union. It was Ellsworth's idea to force Rhode Island to join the federation by imposing an economic boycott.

A staunch supporter of Hamilton's monetary policies, Ellsworth had by this time become a strong Federalist. His most important work in the Senate came when he was chosen to head a committee to draft a bill organizing the federal judiciary. The bill, which provided for the Supreme Court, the district courts, and the circuit courts, became the Judiciary Act of 1789.

When John Jay resigned as chief justice in 1795, President Washington appointed John Rutledge as his successor. The Senate refused to confirm Rutledge, however, and Washington chose to elevate Associate Justice William Cushing. When Cushing declined, the nomination fell to Ellsworth.

Ellsworth had been on the Court only three years when President Adams sent him to France with two other envoys in an effort to soften hostilities between France and the United States. The mission, plagued by transportation difficulties and only partially successful, took its toll on Ellsworth's health.

Before returning home, Ellsworth notified Adams of his resignation as chief justice. He lived on his estate in Windsor until his death in 1807.

Bushrod Washington

BUSHROD WASHINGTON

(1799–1829)

BIRTH: June 5, 1762, Westmoreland County, Virginia.

EDUCATION: privately tutored; graduated College of William and Mary, 1778; read law under James Wilson; member, Virginia bar; honorary LL.D. degrees from Harvard, Princeton, and University of Pennsylvania.

OFFICIAL POSITIONS: member, Virginia House of Delegates, 1787; member, Virginia convention to ratify U.S. Constitution, 1788.

SUPREME COURT SERVICE: nominated associate justice by President John Adams December 19, 1798, to replace James Wilson, who had died; confirmed by the Senate December 20, 1798, by a voice vote; took judicial oath February 4, 1799; served until November 26, 1829; replaced by Henry Baldwin, nominated by President Andrew Jackson.

FAMILY: married Julia Ann Blackburn, 1785.

DEATH: November 26, 1829, in Philadelphia, Pennsylvania.

Bushrod Washington received his first name from his mother, Hannah Bushrod, a member of one of Virginia's oldest colonial families. His father, John Augustine Washington, was a brother of George Washington and served as a member of the Virginia legislature and magistrate of Westmoreland County, Virginia.

As a boy Bushrod was privately tutored. He graduated from the College of William and Mary at sixteen and was a founding member of Phi Beta Kappa, then a secret social club. He was a student in George Wythe's law course at the same time as John Marshall.

Toward the end of the Revolution, Washington enlisted as a private in the Continental Army. He was present when Cornwallis surrendered at Yorktown in October 1781. After the war, Washington studied law for two years under Philadelphia lawyer James Wilson, whom he would later succeed on the Supreme Court.

Washington was a confirmed user of snuff and an untidy dresser, blind in one eye. According to most accounts, he also was a diligent and methodical student of the law. In the words of his colleague, Justice Joseph Story, "His mind was solid, rather than brilliant; sagacious and searching, rather than quick or eager; slow, but not torpid."

In 1785 Washington married Julia Ann Blackburn, the daughter of an aide-de-camp to General Washington during the Revolution. She is said to have been at his side constantly, even when he made his rounds as a circuit judge. She was with him when he died in Philadelphia and died herself during the trip home to attend the funeral.

When George Washington died in 1799 with no children of his own, he left his Mount Vernon estate, including all his public and private papers, to his nephew Bushrod. The former president had provided that his slaves be freed when his wife Martha died. Bushrod Washington brought his own slaves to Mount Vernon, where his lack of farming experience pushed the estate into debt. In 1821 he sold more than half the Mount Vernon slaves, separating families in the process.

For this action he was bitterly attacked in several journals of the day. He dismissed the criticism by arguing the slaves were his property to do with as he saw fit. In 1816 Washington had been elected the first president of the American Colonization Society, established to transport free blacks to Africa, a movement that was criticized by abolitionists.

Washington began private law practice in Westmoreland County, Virginia, and later in Alexandria, Virginia, where he specialized in chancery cases. In 1787, with encouragement from his uncle, he ran for the Virginia House of Delegates and was elected. The following year he was sent as a delegate to the state ratification convention and successfully argued, along with Marshall and Madison, for state approval of the new federal Constitution.

Around 1790 Washington moved to Richmond, where he developed a successful law practice and trained many law students, including Henry Clay. During this period he also served as reporter for the court of appeals and spent much of his time writing two volumes of reports of cases argued before the court.

During his tenure on the Supreme Court, Washington was often allied with Chief Justice Marshall and Justice Story. Indeed, Justice William Johnson, another member of the Marshall Court, once complained that Marshall and Washington "are commonly estimated as a single judge." Washington disagreed with Marshall only three times during the twenty-nine years they were on the Court together.

He died November 26, 1829, while on circuit court business in Philadelphia. Julia Washington died while bringing her husband's body to Mount Vernon for burial.

Alfred Moore

ALFRED MOORE

(1800–1804)

BIRTH: May 21, 1755, New Hanover County, North Carolina.

EDUCATION: educated in Boston; studied law under his father; received law license, 1775.

OFFICIAL POSITIONS: member, North Carolina legislature, 1782, 1792; North Carolina attorney general, 1782–1791; trustee, University of North Carolina, 1789–1807; judge, North Carolina Superior Court, 1799.

SUPREME COURT SERVICE: nominated associate justice by President John Adams December 6, 1799, to replace James Iredell, who had died; confirmed by the Senate December 10, 1799, by a voice vote; took judicial oath April 21, 1800; resigned January 26, 1804; replaced by William Johnson, nominated by President Thomas Jefferson.

FAMILY: married Susanna Eagles.

DEATH: October 15, 1810, Bladen County, North Carolina.

Alfred Moore was the son of Maurice Moore, a North Carolina colonial judge, and Anne Grange Moore. He was descended from Roger Moore, a leader of the 1641 Irish Rebellion, and James Moore, governor of South Carolina in the early eighteenth century.

Following his mother's death and his father's remarriage, Moore was sent to school in Boston. His studies there completed,

Moore returned home and read law under his father. At the age of twenty he was licensed to practice law.

During the Revolution Moore served as a captain in a Continental regiment commanded by his uncle, Col. James Moore. He saw action in several successful battles, but, after his father died in 1777, left the army and returned to the family plantation. He continued his activities against the British by joining the local militia and participating in raids on troops stationed in Wilmington. The British plundered his property in retaliation.

Following brief service in the North Carolina legislature, Moore became state attorney general in 1782, succeeding James Iredell, his predecessor on the Supreme Court, and during that time became a leader of the state bar. In one major case, Moore argued in support of the North Carolina Confiscation Act, which allowed the state to confiscate all land that had been abandoned by Loyalists during the Revolution.

A strong Federalist, Moore lost election as a delegate to the state constitutional ratifying convention, but was instrumental in getting the state finally to approve in 1789.

Moore resigned as attorney general in 1791 when the state legislature created a new office of solicitor general, giving it the same powers and salary as the attorney general. Moore claimed the new office was unconstitutional.

In 1792 Moore was elected to the state legislature again, but three years later lost a race for the U.S. Senate by one vote in the legislature. In 1798 he was appointed by President John Adams as one of three commissioners to negotiate a treaty with the Cherokee Indians, but he withdrew from the discussions before the treaty was signed. In 1799 he served as a judge on the North Carolina Superior Court.

When Justice James Iredell died in 1799, Adams looked to North Carolina for a replacement. William R. Davie was apparently the first choice, but he had just been made a diplomatic agent to France, so the nomination went to Moore.

Moore exerted little influence during his five years on the Court and wrote only one opinion. He resigned in 1804, citing ill health, and returned home to work on the development of the University of North Carolina. He died in North Carolina on October 15, 1810, at the home of his son-in-law.

JOHN MARSHALL
(1801–1835)

BIRTH: September 24, 1755, Germantown, Virginia.

EDUCATION: tutored at home; self-taught in law; attended one course of law lectures at College of William and Mary, 1780.

OFFICIAL POSITIONS: member, Virginia House of Delegates, 1782–1785, 1787–1790, 1795–1796; member, Executive Council of State, 1782–1784; recorder, Richmond City Hustings Court, 1785–1788; delegate, state convention for ratification of federal Constitution, 1788; minister to France, 1797–1798; U.S. representative, 1799–1800; U.S. secretary of state, 1800–1801; member, Virginia Constitutional Convention, 1829.

SUPREME COURT SERVICE: nominated chief justice by President John Adams January 20, 1801, to replace Oliver Ellsworth, who had resigned; confirmed by the Senate January 27, 1801, by a voice vote; took judicial oath February 4, 1801;

John Marshall

served until July 6, 1835; replaced by Roger B. Taney, nominated by President Andrew Jackson.

FAMILY: Married Mary Willis Ambler, January 3, 1783; died December 25, 1831; ten children.

DEATH: July 6, 1835, Philadelphia, Pennsylvania.

The first of fifteen children, John Marshall was born in a log cabin on the Virginia frontier near Germantown. His father, Thomas Marshall, was descended from Welsh immigrants, was an assistant surveyor to George Washington and member of the Virginia House of Burgesses. His mother, Mary Randolph Keith Marshall, was the daughter of an educated Scottish clergyman.

As a youth, Marshall was tutored by two clergymen, but his primary teacher was his father, who introduced him to the study of English literature and Blackstone's *Commentaries.*

During the Revolutionary War, young Marshall participated in the siege of Norfolk as a member of the Culpeper Minute Men and was present at Brandywine, Monmouth, Stony Point, and Valley Forge as a member of the third Virginia Regiment. In 1779 he returned home to await another assignment but was never recalled. He left the Continental Army with the rank of captain in 1781.

Marshall's only formal instruction in the law came in 1780 when he attended George Wythe's course of law lectures at the College of William and Mary. He was admitted to Phi Beta Kappa, after returning to Fauquier County, to the Virginia bar. He gradually developed a lucrative practice, specializing in defending Virginians against their pre–Revolutionary War British creditors.

In January 1783 Marshall married Mary Willis Ambler, daughter of the Virginia state treasurer, and established a home in Richmond. The couple had ten children, only six of whom survived to maturity. Marshall spent many years attending to the needs of Polly, as his wife was called. She suffered from nervous disorders and chronic illness.

From 1796 until about 1806, Marshall's life was dominated by the pressures of meeting debts incurred by a land investment he had made in the northern neck of Virginia. It has been speculated that his need for money motivated him to write *The Life of George Washington,* which appeared in five volumes from 1804 to 1807. The book was written too quickly, and when Jefferson ordered federal postmasters not to take orders for it, the opportunity for large sales was lost.

The leisurely pace of the Supreme Court in its early days was well suited to Marshall, who had grown to enjoy relaxation and the outdoors as a boy. The chief justice enjoyed socializing in the clubs and saloons of Richmond and kept a fine supply of personal wines. He is said to have excelled at the game of quoits (similar to horseshoes), and was also known to take a turn at whist, backgammon, and tenpins.

Marshall was master of his Masonic lodge in Richmond and served as Masonic Grand Master of Virginia for several years. He was a member of the American Colonization Society, which worked toward the transfer of freed slaves to Africa, and belonged to the Washington Historical Monument Society and several literary societies.

Marshall was elected to the Virginia House of Delegates from Fauquier County in 1782 and 1784. He reentered the House in 1787 and was instrumental in Virginia's ratification of the new U.S. Constitution. At the state ratifying convention his primary attention was directed to the need for judicial review. By 1789 Marshall was considered to be a leading Federalist in the state.

Marshall refused many appointments in the Federalist administrations of Washington and Adams, including U.S. attorney general in 1795, associate justice of the Supreme Court in 1798, and secretary of war in 1800. In 1796 he refused an appointment by President Adams as minister to France, but the following year agreed to serve as one of three special envoys sent to smooth relations with that country. This mission, known as the XYZ Affair, failed when French diplomats demanded a bribe as a condition for negotiation. Congress, however, was greatly impressed by the stubborn resistance of the American emissaries, and Marshall received a generous grant as a reward for his participation.

In 1799 Marshall was persuaded by Washington to run for the U.S. House of Representatives as a Federalist from Richmond. His career in the House was brief, however, for in 1800 he became secretary of state under Adams. When Adams retired to his home in Massachusetts for a few months that year, Marshall served as the effective head of government.

Oliver Ellsworth resigned as chief justice in 1800, and Adams offered the position to John Jay, who had been the Court's first chief justice. Jay declined, and the Federalists urged Adams to elevate Associate Justice William Paterson. Adams instead nominated Marshall.

As the primary founder of the American system of constitutional law, including the doctrine of judicial review, Marshall participated in more than one thousand Supreme Court decisions, writing more than five hundred of them himself. In 1807 he presided over the treason trial of Aaron Burr in the Richmond Circuit Court, locking horns with Jefferson, who sought an absolute conviction. Burr was acquitted.

In 1831, at age seventy-six, Marshall underwent successful surgery in Philadelphia for the removal of kidney stones. Three years later, he developed an enlarged liver, and his health declined rapidly. When Marshall died on July 6, 1835, three months short of his eightieth birthday, the Liberty Bell cracked as it tolled in mourning.

WILLIAM JOHNSON

(1804–1834)

BIRTH: December 27, 1771, Charleston, South Carolina.

EDUCATION: graduated Princeton, 1790; studied law under Charles Cotesworth Pinckney; admitted to bar in 1793.

OFFICIAL POSITIONS: member, South Carolina House of Representatives, 1794–1798; Speaker, 1798; judge, Court of Common Pleas, 1799–1804.

SUPREME COURT SERVICE: nominated associate justice by President Thomas Jefferson March 22, 1804, to replace Alfred

William Johnson

Moore, who had resigned; confirmed by the Senate March 24, 1804, by a voice vote; took judicial oath May 7, 1804; served until August 4, 1834; replaced by James M. Wayne, nominated by President Andrew Jackson.

FAMILY: married Sarah Bennett, March 20, 1794; eight children, six of whom died in childhood; two adopted children.

DEATH: August 4, 1834, Brooklyn, New York.

William Johnson's father, also named William, was a blacksmith, legislator, and Revolutionary patriot who moved from New York to South Carolina in the early 1760s. His mother was Sarah Nightingale Johnson. When the British captured Charleston during the war, the Johnson family was exiled from their home, and William's father sent to detention in Florida. After several months, the family was reunited in Philadelphia and returned to South Carolina together.

Young William graduated first in his class from Princeton in 1790. Returning to Charleston, he began reading law under Charles Cotesworth Pinckney, a prominent adviser to President Washington who had studied at the Inns of Court. Johnson joined the bar in 1793.

The following year, Johnson married Sarah Bennett, sister of Thomas Bennett, who later would become governor of South Carolina. The couple had eight children, but only two survived to maturity. They eventually adopted two refugee children from Santo Domingo.

A member of the American Philosophical Society, Johnson retained an interest in education and literature all his life. He was one of the primary founders of the University of South Carolina and in 1822 published a two-volume biography of

Revolutionary War general Nathanael Greene. Johnson also published *Eulogy of Thomas Jefferson* in 1826.

Johnson's political career began in 1794 when he entered the South Carolina House of Representatives as a member of Jefferson's new Republican Party. Following service as Speaker in 1798, Johnson was chosen one of three judges to sit on the state's highest court, the Court of Common Pleas. Here, he gained experience riding circuit and dealing with the burgeoning judicial questions concerning federal-state relations. In 1804 Johnson became Jefferson's first Republican nominee to the Supreme Court.

At least until 1830, Johnson was the most independent of the justices on the Marshall Court, and he has been called "the first great Court dissenter." Fighting against the wishes of powerful—some would say dictatorial—Chief Justice John Marshall, Johnson succeeded in establishing the Court's tradition of dissenting opinions.

Johnson once wrote Jefferson that the Court was no "bed of roses," and in the first part of his career on the bench tried to obtain another appointment. He remained on the Court, however, until his death following surgery in 1834.

HENRY BROCKHOLST LIVINGSTON

(1807–1823)

BIRTH: November 25, 1757, New York City.

EDUCATION: graduated from College of New Jersey (Princeton), 1774; honorary LL.D., Harvard (1810), Princeton; studied law under Peter Yates; admitted to bar in 1783.

OFFICIAL POSITIONS: member, New York Assembly, Twelfth, Twenty-fourth, and Twenty-fifth sessions; judge, New York State Supreme Court, 1802–1807.

SUPREME COURT SERVICE: nominated associate justice by President Thomas Jefferson December 13, 1806, to replace William Paterson, who had died; confirmed by the Senate December 17, 1806, by a voice vote; took judicial oath January 20, 1807; served until March 18, 1823; replaced by Smith Thompson, nominated by President James Monroe.

FAMILY: married Catherine Keteltas, five children; married Ann Ludlow, three children; married Catharine Kortright, three children.

DEATH: March 18, 1823, Washington, D.C.

As a member of the powerful Livingston family of New York, Brockholst Livingston was born into the colonial aristocracy. His father, William Livingston, was governor of New Jersey and a leader in the New York opposition to British colonial policies. His mother was Susanna French Livingston.

Young Livingston was graduated from Princeton in 1774, where he was a classmate of James Madison, and joined the Continental Army at the outbreak of the Revolution. As a commissioned major, he served under Generals Schuyler and St. Clair and participated in the siege of Ticonderoga. He was also an aide to Benedict Arnold during the Saratoga campaign and was present at Gen. John Burgoyne's surrender in 1777. Livingston left the army with the rank of lieutenant colonel.

After the war, Livingston traveled to Spain to serve as private secretary to his brother-in-law, John Jay, then serving as the American minister there. During this time, Livingston began to dislike Jay.

Although Livingston was considered an affable and genial man, there appears to have been a violent side to his personality. He killed one man in a duel in 1798 and is believed to have fought several others. An assassination attempt was made on his life in 1785.

Livingston married three times and had a total of eleven children. A devotee of history, he was cofounder of the New York Historical Society and one of its vice presidents. He served as trustee and treasurer of Columbia University from 1784 until the end of his life and was instrumental in organizing the New York public school system. Livingston was an original member of the Society of the Cincinnati.

Livingston—who began using the middle name Brockholst, probably to avoid confusion with two cousins also named Henry—was elected to the New York Assembly in 1786. He also began practicing law at this time, working closely with Alexander Hamilton.

During these years, Livingston began a conversion, along with other members of his family, from Federalism to anti-Federalism. By 1792 he was bitterly attacking Jay's campaign for the New York governorship and succeeded in denying him a crucial bloc of votes. When Jay returned from negotiating a treaty with England in 1794, Livingston was at the forefront of voices critical of it.

As the New York anti-Federalist alliance of the Burr, Clinton, and Livingston factions reached its height around 1800, several Livingstons received high appointments. In 1802 Brockholst Livingston joined two of his relatives by marriage on the New York Supreme Court. He served for five years, specializing in commercial law.

In 1804 Livingston was considered seriously for an opening on the U.S. Supreme Court, but the position went instead to William Johnson. In 1806, however, Livingston was nominated by Jefferson to fill the vacancy created by the death of William Paterson.

Livingston died in 1823, after serving sixteen years on the high court.

THOMAS TODD

(1807–1826)

BIRTH: January 23, 1765, King and Queen County, Virginia.

EDUCATION: graduated from Liberty Hall (now Washington and Lee University), Lexington, Virginia, 1783; read law under Harry Innes; admitted to bar in 1788.

OFFICIAL POSITIONS: clerk, federal district for Kentucky, 1792–1801; clerk, Kentucky House of Representatives, 1792–1801; clerk, Kentucky Court of Appeals (Supreme Court), 1799–1801; judge, Kentucky Court of Appeals, 1801–1806; chief justice, 1806–1807.

SUPREME COURT SERVICE: nominated associate justice by President Thomas Jefferson February 28, 1807, to fill a newly created seat; confirmed by the Senate March 3, 1807, by a voice vote; took judicial oath May 4, 1807; served until February 7, 1826;

Thomas Todd

replaced by Robert Trimble, nominated by President John Quincy Adams.

FAMILY: married Elizabeth Harris, 1788; died 1811; five children; married Lucy Payne, 1812; three children.

DEATH: February 7, 1826, Frankfort, Kentucky.

Thomas Todd was only eighteen months old when his father, Richard Todd, died. His mother, Elizabeth Richards Todd, died when Thomas was eleven, and from then on he was raised by a guardian. The family owned large tracts of land handed down since the seventeenth century, but, because Thomas was not the oldest son, he was excluded from inheriting any of these holdings.

Todd's mother, Elizabeth, managed to leave her son money she had accumulated through her successful boardinghouse, and Thomas used it to acquire a solid education in the classics. Most of the inheritance, however, was eventually lost because of mismanagement by his guardian.

At age sixteen Todd served in the Revolutionary War for six months, returning home to attend Liberty Hall (now Washington and Lee University) in Lexington, Virginia. After graduation, he accepted an invitation from Harry Innes, a distant relative and respected member of the Virginia legislature, to tutor Innes's daughters in exchange for room, board, and law instruction.

In 1784, when Innes was asked to move to Danville, Kentucky, (then part of Virginia) to set up a district court in the area, Todd made the move with the family. It was at this time that the Kentucky area of Virginia held the first of five conventions seeking admission to the Union as a separate state. Through his friendship with Innes, Todd was able to act as clerk for each convention.

With his first wife, Elizabeth, Todd had five children, one of whom, Charles Stewart, became minister to Russia in 1841. Elizabeth died in 1811, and Todd married Dolley Madison's sister, Lucy Payne, in the East Room of the White House the following year. Todd lived in Danville until 1801 and then moved about forty miles north to Frankfort, Kentucky. During his lifetime, Todd accumulated more than 7,200 acres in Kentucky. He also owned stock in the Kentucky River Company, which promoted water navigation, and Kentucky Turnpike, one of the first public highways west of the Allegheny Mountains.

Todd joined the Virginia bar in 1788 and soon developed a specialty in land law. When Kentucky became a state in 1792, he served as secretary to the new Kentucky legislature. In 1799, when the state supreme court was created, Todd was chosen to be its chief clerk.

In 1801 Kentucky governor James Garrard appointed Todd to fill a newly created fourth seat on the state court. At the age of forty-one, Todd was named its chief justice. Most of the cases handled by the court during his tenure involved land title disputes, and the chief justice developed a reputation for being fair and honest in settling complicated land controversies.

In 1807 the federal Judiciary Act of 1789 was amended to create a new federal court circuit made up of Tennessee, Kentucky, and Ohio. On the recommendation of the members of Congress from those states, President Jefferson chose Todd to preside over this new circuit as the sixth associate justice on the Supreme Court.

During his years on the bench, Todd missed five entire Court sessions because of personal and health reasons. He delivered only fourteen opinions during his tenure, including one dissent.

He died in February 1826, leaving a considerable fortune.

GABRIEL DUVALL

(1811–1835)

BIRTH: December 6, 1752, Prince George's County, Maryland.

EDUCATION: classical preparatory schooling; studied law.

OFFICIAL POSITIONS: clerk, Maryland Convention, 1775–1777; clerk, Maryland House of Delegates, 1777–1787; member, Maryland State Council, 1782–1785; member, Maryland House of Delegates, 1787–1794; U.S. representative, 1794–1796; chief justice, General Court of Maryland, 1796–1802; presidential elector, 1796, 1800; first comptroller of the Treasury, 1802–1811.

SUPREME COURT SERVICE: nominated associate justice by President James Madison November 15, 1811, to replace Samuel Chase, who had died; confirmed by the Senate November 18, 1811, by a voice vote; took judicial oath November 23, 1811; resigned January 14, 1835; replaced by Philip Barbour, nominated by President Andrew Jackson.

FAMILY: married Mary Brice, July 24, 1787; died March 24, 1790; one son; married Jane Gibbon, May 5, 1795; died April 1834.

DEATH: March 6, 1844, Prince George's County, Maryland.

Descended from a family of French Huguenots, Gabriel Duvall was the sixth of ten children born to Benjamin and Susanna Tyler

Gabriel Duvall

Duvall on the family plantation "Marietta." The farmland, located on the South River near Buena Vista, Maryland, had been assigned to Gabriel's great-grandfather by Lord Baltimore.

Duvall was active in the Revolutionary War, serving as mustermaster and commissary of stores for the Maryland troops, and later as a private in the Maryland militia. Toward the end of the war, he helped protect confiscated British property.

In 1787, at the age of thirty-five, Duvall married Mary Brice, daughter of Captain Robert Brice of Annapolis. She died three years later, after the birth of their son. In 1795 Duvall married Jane Gibbon, who died in 1834 shortly before Duvall resigned from the Supreme Court.

Duvall's first public appointment came in 1775 when he was made clerk of the Maryland Convention. When the Maryland state government was created in 1777, he was named clerk for the House of Delegates.

In 1787 Duvall was elected to the Maryland House of Delegates, where he served until 1794. He was also chosen to attend the Constitutional Convention in Philadelphia, but decided along with the four others elected from Maryland not to attend.

Duvall entered the Third Congress of the United States in 1794 as a Republican-Democrat. Two years later he resigned to become chief justice of the General Court of Maryland. As chief justice, Duvall also served as recorder of the mayor's court in Annapolis, and it was in this capacity that he heard Roger Taney deliver his first speech as a member of the bar.

Duvall was chosen by President Thomas Jefferson to be the first comptroller of the Treasury in 1802. Nine years later he was nominated by President James Madison to serve on the Supreme Court.

During his twenty-three years on the bench, Duvall generally voted with Chief Justice Marshall. His most notable dissent came in *Dartmouth College v. Woodward* (1819), although he wrote no formal opinion.

By the end of his tenure on the Court, Duvall was eighty-two years old. His deafness and frequent absences had become an embarrassment, and his resignation in 1835 came as a great relief. Duvall spent his last years working on his family history and devoting attention to his son and nieces and nephews. He died in 1844 at the age of ninety-one.

JOSEPH STORY

(1812–1845)

BIRTH: September 18, 1779, Marblehead, Massachusetts.

EDUCATION: attended Marblehead Academy; graduated from Harvard, 1798; LL.D., 1821; read law under Samuel Sewall and Samuel Putnam; admitted to bar, 1801.

OFFICIAL POSITIONS: member, Massachusetts legislature, 1805–1808; Speaker of the House, 1811; U.S. representative, 1808–1809; delegate, Massachusetts Constitutional Convention, 1820.

SUPREME COURT SERVICE: nominated associate justice by President James Madison November 15, 1811, to replace William

Joseph Story

Cushing, who had died; confirmed by the Senate November 18, 1811, by a voice vote; took judicial oath February 3, 1812; served until September 10, 1845; replaced by Levi Woodbury, nominated by President James K. Polk.

FAMILY: married Mary Lynde Oliver, December 9, 1804; died June 1805; married Sarah Waldo Wetmore, August 27, 1808; seven children.

DEATH: September 10, 1845, Cambridge, Massachusetts.

Joseph Story was descended on both sides from old New England families. His father, Elisha Story, was a participant in the Boston Tea Party in 1773. His mother was Mehitable Pedrick Story.

Following a disagreement with a fellow classmate, Joseph was forced to leave Marblehead Academy before completing his college preparatory studies. By constantly studying on his own through the fall of 1794, however, he was able to enroll in Harvard in time for the 1795 term. Such drive and diligence were to characterize much of Story's life.

After graduating (second in his class) from Harvard in 1798, Story began reading law, sometimes for fourteen hours a day, in the Marblehead office of Samuel Sewall, later chief justice of the Massachusetts Supreme Court. When Sewall was appointed to a judgeship, Story completed his studies under Samuel Putnam in Salem, Massachusetts.

Admitted to the bar in 1801, Story began practice in Salem. The county bar was dominated by the Federalist establishment, however, and Story, a Republican-Democrat, was exposed to a good deal of prejudice. In the beginning he considered moving to Baltimore, but as his practice grew in prestige and influence, he chose to remain in Salem.

Story was an ardent poetry lover throughout his life. He was known by his hometown friends as "the poet of Marblehead." In 1805 he published "The Power of Solitude," a long, effusive poem written in heroic couplets. When his father and his wife of only seven months both died that year, Story, in a fit of sorrow, burned all copies of the poem he could find. He experienced further tragedy losing five of his seven children by his second marriage.

An avid conversationalist, Story enjoyed music, drawing, and painting. Besides being a writer, Story was an able public speaker and eulogist. He delivered the annual Fourth of July oration in Salem in 1804 and in 1826 delivered the Phi Beta Kappa oration at Harvard.

Story served for three years in the Massachusetts legislature and then entered the U.S. Congress in 1808. During his one term of service in the House, he was blamed by Jefferson for the repeal of Jefferson's foreign trade embargo, and he lost more points with his party by calling for a plan to strengthen the U.S. Navy. In January 1811 Story returned to the Massachusetts legislature and was elected Speaker of the House. By November of that year he had become one of the two youngest men ever to sit on the Supreme Court. (The other was William Johnson.)

Only thirty-two years old and with no court experience, Story had not been Madison's first choice for the job, but Levi Lincoln and John Quincy Adams had both declined, and Alexander Wolcott had been rejected by the Senate. Although he had a few financial reservations about taking the job, Story accepted the position as a great honor.

A supporter of higher learning for women, Story retained an active interest in education for most of his life. In 1819 he was elected to the Harvard Board of Overseers and became a fellow of the Harvard Corporation six years later. In 1829 Story moved from Salem to Cambridge, Massachusetts, to become professor of law at his alma mater. He played a major role in the foundation of Harvard Law School. He is also credited, along with Chancellor James Kent of New York, with founding the equity system of jurisprudence as practiced in the United States today.

While at Harvard, Story wrote his famous nine *Commentaries* on the law. Each of these works went through many editions, and one—*Commentaries on the Constitution* (1833)—was published in French, Spanish, and German, enhancing Story's international reputation.

In addition to the *Commentaries*, Story wrote legal essays for the *North American Review* and the *American Law Review*, and contributed unsigned articles to the *Encyclopedia Americana*. His Court opinions, though often accused of being tedious, are seminal works in the history of American national law.

On the Court, Story rarely broke from the strong nationalism of Chief Justice Marshall. In fact, it was Story's opinion in *Martin v. Hunter's Lessee* (1816) that established the appellate supremacy of the Supreme Court over state courts in civil cases involving federal statutes and treaties.

When Marshall died in 1835, Story undoubtedly coveted the chief justiceship, and his colleagues generally agreed he should be appointed. Story, however, was anathema to Andrew Jackson (he once called Story the "most dangerous man in America"), and Roger Taney received the nomination instead.

Story's nine years on the Taney Court were spent largely in dissent and by the beginning of the 1845 term he was prepared to resign. He refused to leave until he had attended to all his unfinished business, however. He died September 10, 1845, after a sudden illness.

SMITH THOMPSON

(1823–1843)

BIRTH: January 17, 1768, Dutchess County, New York.

EDUCATION: graduated Princeton, 1788; read law under James Kent; admitted to the bar, 1792; honorary law doctorates from Yale, 1824; Princeton, 1824; and Harvard, 1835.

OFFICIAL POSITIONS: member, New York state legislature, 1800; member, New York Constitutional Convention, 1801; associate justice, New York Supreme Court, 1802–1814; appointed to New York State Board of Regents, 1813; chief justice, New York Supreme Court, 1814–1818; secretary of the Navy, 1819–1823.

SUPREME COURT SERVICE: nominated associate justice by President James Monroe December 8, 1823, to replace Brockholst Livingston, who had died; confirmed by the Senate December 19, 1823, by a voice vote; took judicial oath February 10, 1823; served until December 18, 1843; replaced by Samuel Nelson, nominated by President John Tyler.

FAMILY: married Sarah Livingston, 1794; died September 22, 1833; two sons, two daughters; married Eliza Livingston; two daughters, one son.

DEATH: December 18, 1843, Poughkeepsie, New York.

Smith Thompson's public career was inevitably shaped by his personal ties and social connections. His father, Ezra Thompson, was a successful New York farmer and a well-known Anti-Federalist in state politics. His mother was Rachel Smith Thompson. More important, however, was Thompson's link through marriage to the Livingston family, albeit to a less-prominent branch. The Livingstons were a powerful force in New York politics at the end of the eighteenth century.

Thompson was born in 1768 in Dutchess County, New York, between the Hudson River and the Connecticut border. After graduating from Princeton in 1788, he taught school and read law under James Kent, a well-respected jurist then working in Poughkeepsie. In 1793 Thompson joined the law practice of Kent and Gilbert Livingston, an old friend of his father.

Thompson married Livingston's daughter, Sarah, in 1794. When Sarah died in 1833, he married her first cousin, Eliza Livingston. By this time, however, the family's influence was on the decline.

Thompson's public career got off to a quick start in 1800 when he entered the state legislature as a member of the Livingston wing of the Anti-Federalist Republican party. The next year he attended the state constitutional convention and received an appointment as district attorney for the middle district of New York. Before he had a chance to assume those duties, however, he was appointed to the state supreme court and immediately assumed that position.

During his tenure on the state bench, Thompson served with two of his cousins by marriage. He replaced one of these men, Brockholst Livingston, on the U.S. Supreme Court. Thompson was also joined on the state court by James Kent, his old friend and mentor. When Kent stepped down as its chief justice in 1814 to become chancellor of New York, Thompson succeeded him.

Thompson became secretary of the Navy under President Monroe in 1819, probably through the influence of Martin Van Buren, a rising young New York politician and ally of Thompson. As Navy secretary, Thompson had few administrative duties and spent a good deal of his time dabbling in New York politics, working, at times, with Van Buren. He also made no secret of his presidential ambitions during this period.

When Brockholst Livingston died in 1823, Thompson was immediately thought of as a contender for the vacancy on the Supreme Court, along with Chancellor Kent. Thompson delayed expressing formal interest in the seat, however, hoping with Van Buren's help to mount a campaign drive for the 1824 presidential election. Van Buren outwitted him in the end, however, and Thompson accepted the Court appointment from Monroe. Thompson continued to foster political ambitions while on the Supreme Court and in 1828 decided to run for governor of New York. He lost to his old friend, Martin Van Buren, in a bitter and dramatic campaign.

While on the Court, Thompson became part of a group that began to pull away from the strong nationalism of Chief Justice John Marshall. He voted with the majority against Marshall in

Ogden v. Saunders (1827) supporting state bankruptcy laws. His most notable opinion came in *Kendall v. United States* (1838), in which he argued against President Jackson that the executive branch was not exempt from judicial control. The passage was later omitted from the printed opinion at the request of the U.S. attorney general.

ROBERT TRIMBLE

(1826–1828)

BIRTH: November 17, 1776, Berkeley County, Virginia.

EDUCATION: Bourbon Academy; Kentucky Academy; read law under George Nicholas and James Brown; admitted to the bar in 1803.

OFFICIAL POSITIONS: Kentucky state representative, 1802; judge, Kentucky Court of Appeals, 1807–1809; U.S. district attorney for Kentucky, 1813–1817; U.S. district judge, 1817–1826.

SUPREME COURT SERVICE: nominated associate justice by President John Quincy Adams April 11, 1826, to replace Thomas Todd, who had died; confirmed May 9, 1826, by a 27-5 vote; took judicial oath June 16, 1826; served until August 25, 1828; replaced by John McLean, nominated by President Andrew Jackson.

FAMILY: married Nancy Timberlake, August 18, 1803; at least ten children.

DEATH: August 25, 1828, Paris, Kentucky.

Robert Trimble was the son of William Trimble, an early Kentucky pioneer who hunted game and scouted for Indians, and Mary McMillan Trimble. It appears young Trimble studied at the Bourbon Academy in Kentucky and after teaching for a short time attended the Kentucky Academy (later Transylvania University) in Woodford County. Following his study at the Kentucky Academy, Trimble read law under George Nicholas, the first attorney general of Kentucky, and James Brown, who later became minister to France.

Trimble began private practice in Paris, Kentucky, in about 1800. In 1802 he entered the Kentucky House of Representatives and in 1807 was appointed justice of the Kentucky Court of Appeals. He resigned the judgeship in 1808, claiming the yearly salary of $1,000 was too low to support his growing family.

Trimble also refused the chief justiceship of Kentucky in 1810 for financial reasons and declined to run for the U.S. Senate in 1812. Although he twice refused to accept the law professorship at Transylvania University, he served as a trustee of the school for many years.

Trimble's decision to concentrate on his private law practice instead of public service proved profitable. By 1817 he had earned a sizable amount of money and owned a number of slaves. That year he decided to accept the nomination by President Madison to be the federal district judge for Kentucky. He served for eight years.

Trimble—John Quincy Adams's only appointment to the U.S. Supreme Court—was chosen for his belief in strong national power, a position that had not won him many friends in Kentucky. During his two years on the Supreme Court bench, he was a strong supporter of Chief Justice Marshall, but disagreed with him in *Ogden v. Saunders,* voting to sustain the power of the states to apply insolvency laws.

JOHN McLEAN

(1830–1861)

BIRTH: March 11, 1785, Morris County, New Jersey.

EDUCATION: attended local school; privately tutored; read law with John S. Gano and Arthur St. Clair Jr.

OFFICIAL POSITIONS: examiner, U.S. Land Office, 1811–1812; U.S. representative, 1813–1816, chairman, Committee on Accounts; judge, Ohio Supreme Court, 1816–1822; commissioner, General Land Office, 1822–1823; U.S. postmaster general, 1823–1829.

SUPREME COURT SERVICE: nominated associate justice by President Andrew Jackson March 7, 1829, to replace Robert Trimble, who had died; confirmed by the Senate March 7, 1829, by a voice vote; took judicial oath January 11, 1830; served until April 3, 1861; replaced by Noah H. Swayne, nominated by President Abraham Lincoln.

FAMILY: married Rebecca Edwards, 1807; died 1840; four daughters, three sons; married Sarah Bella Ludlow Garrard, 1843; one son, died at birth.

DEATH: April 3, 1861, Cincinnati, Ohio.

John McLean's father, Fergus McLain, was a Scotch-Irish weaver who immigrated to New Jersey in 1775. After his marriage to Sophia Blackford of Middlesex County, New Jersey, and the birth of several children, Fergus moved his family first to

John McLean

western Virginia, then Kentucky; finally in 1797 they settled on a farm near Lebanon, Ohio, about forty miles north of Cincinnati. Young John attended the county school and later earned enough money as a farmhand to hire two Presbyterian ministers to tutor him.

In 1804 he began two years of work as an apprentice to the clerk of the Hamilton County Court of Common Pleas in Cincinnati. At the same time, he was able to study with John S. Gano and Arthur St. Clair, two respected Cincinnati lawyers.

Following his admission to the bar in 1807, McLean married Rebecca Edwards of Newport, Kentucky, and returned to Lebanon, where he opened a printing office. In a short time, he began publishing the Lebanon *Western Star* newspaper, a weekly journal supportive of Jeffersonian politics. In 1810, however, McLean relinquished the print shop to his brother, Nathaniel, and devoted all of his time to law practice.

McLean experienced a profound religious conversion in 1811 and remained a devout Methodist for the rest of his life. He participated actively in church affairs and was chosen honorary president of the American Sunday School Union in 1849.

McLean was elected to Congress in 1812. During his two terms in service, he supported the war measures of the Madison administration and opposed creation of a second Bank of the United States. In 1816 McLean resigned from the House and was elected to one of four judgeships on the Ohio Supreme Court, serving from 1816 to 1822.

McLean worked hard for the nomination and election of James Monroe to the presidency in 1816, and in 1822 Monroe returned the favor by appointing McLean commissioner of the General Land Office. A year later he was made postmaster general. McLean was well liked by the postal employees and proved to be a skilled administrator. The postal service greatly expanded under his leadership, and by 1828 the department was the largest agency in the executive branch.

By this time, McLean had become an astute politician. He managed to keep his job as postmaster general under John Quincy Adams while establishing ties with many of Andrew Jackson's men at the same time. When Jackson became president in 1829, Robert Trimble's seat on the Supreme Court was still vacant because of Senate political maneuverings, and McLean was nominated to fill it. His most famous opinion during his thirty-two years on the bench was his dissent in *Scott v. Sandford*, which was eventually reflected in the Fourteenth Amendment to the Constitution.

McLean entertained presidential ambitions throughout his Supreme Court career and flirted with several political parties at various stages. In 1856 he received 190 votes on an informal presidential ballot taken at the first Republican national convention in Philadelphia. Thaddeus Stevens pushed his candidacy four years later, but the effort was blocked by Ohio Republicans.

McLean died of pneumonia in 1861.

HENRY BALDWIN

(1830–1844)

BIRTH: January 14, 1780, New Haven, Connecticut.

EDUCATION: Hopkins Grammar School, 1793; Yale College, 1797, LL.D., 1830; attended the law lectures of Judge Tapping Reeve; clerked for Alexander James Dallas.

Henry Baldwin

OFFICIAL POSITIONS: U.S. representative; chairman, Committee on Domestic Manufactures.

SUPREME COURT SERVICE: nominated associate justice by President Andrew Jackson January 4, 1830, to replace Bushrod Washington, who had died; confirmed by the Senate January 6, 1830, by a 41-2 vote; took judicial oath January 18, 1830; served until April 21, 1844; replaced by Robert C. Grier, nominated by President James K. Polk.

FAMILY: married Marianna Norton, 1802; died 1803; one son; married Sally Ellicott, 1805.

DEATH: April 21, 1844, Philadelphia, Pennsylvania.

Baldwin was the product of a New England family dating back to the seventeenth century. His parents were Michael and Theodora Wolcott Baldwin. His half-brother, Abraham, was a representative to both the Continental Congress and the Constitutional Convention and a U.S. senator from Georgia.

As a boy, Henry lived on the family farm near New Haven, but moved to the city when he entered Yale College. Upon graduation in 1797, he attended law lectures at Judge Tapping Reeve's school in Litchfield, Connecticut. He clerked in the law office of Alexander James Dallas, a prominent Philadelphia attorney, and was soon admitted to the bar. Baldwin decided to settle in Pittsburgh, a young city that afforded opportunities for a beginning lawyer.

Baldwin settled easily and quickly into the Pittsburgh community, joining the county bar and making many friends. With Tarleton Bates and Walter Forward, he formed a successful law firm known as the "Great Triumvirate of Early Pittsburgh." During this period, Baldwin developed a reputation for his well-written law briefs, which he prepared in his large personal law library, considered to be one of the finest in the "West."

In only a short time, Baldwin and his law partners became known for their political leadership as well as their legal skill. Together, they published a newspaper called *The Tree of Liberty,* which supported a faction of the Republican Party in western Pennsylvania. Through his work in the party and in Pittsburgh civic affairs, Baldwin became a popular and prominent leader in the community by his mid-twenties. Before long, he was affectionately known as the "Idol of Pennsylvania" and the "Pride of Pittsburgh."

Despite his political and legal activities, Baldwin found time to involve himself in business affairs. He was part-owner of at least three mills in Pennsylvania, in addition to a profitable woolen mill in Steubenville, Ohio.

Baldwin, the manufacturer, entered Congress in 1817 as a supporter of higher tariffs and as a spokesman for Pittsburgh's economic growth interests. He resigned from the House in 1822 for health reasons, but after two years of rest returned to his role as unofficial political leader of Allegheny County. In 1823 he urged Andrew Jackson to run for the presidency and throughout John Quincy Adams's administration was a close adviser to Jackson on western Pennsylvania politics.

When Justice Bushrod Washington died in 1829, President Jackson decided to nominate Baldwin to fill the seat, against the wishes of Vice President John C. Calhoun, who supported another candidate.

Baldwin's career on the bench has been characterized as erratic. In the beginning, he supported the liberal interpretations of Chief Justice Marshall, but later refused to embrace either strict or broad construction of the Constitution.

Baldwin is reported to have suffered temporary mental derangements toward the end of his life. Biographical sources do not elaborate on his illness except to say he did not get along well with other justices on the bench, and his closest friends were suspicious of his nonconforming and peculiar habits. As early as 1832, Roger Taney had advised President Jackson not to take legal action against the Bank of the United States because the case would be tried in Philadelphia and Baldwin would be unreliable as presiding judge. Baldwin, then fifty-two, had already begun to suffer lapses of reason.

Baldwin was said to be occasionally violent and ungovernable on the bench toward the end of his life. In 1844, when he died of paralysis, he was deeply in debt, and his friends had to take up a collection to pay his funeral expenses.

JAMES MOORE WAYNE

(1835–1867)

BIRTH: 1790, Savannah, Georgia.

EDUCATION: College of New Jersey (Princeton University), 1808, honorary LL.B., 1849; read law under three lawyers, including Judge Charles Chauncey of New Haven; admitted to the bar January 1811.

James Moore Wayne

OFFICIAL POSITIONS: member, Georgia House of Representatives, 1815–1816; mayor, Savannah, 1817–1819; judge, Savannah Court of Common Pleas, 1820–1822; Georgia Superior Court, 1822–1828; U.S. representative, 1829–1835; chairman, Committee on Foreign Relations.

SUPREME COURT SERVICE: nominated associate justice by President Andrew Jackson January 7, 1835, to replace William Johnson, who had died; confirmed by the Senate January 9, 1835 by a voice vote; took judicial oath January 14, 1835; served until July 5, 1867; replaced by Joseph Bradley, nominated by President Ulysses S. Grant.

FAMILY: married Mary Johnson Campbell, 1813; three children.

DEATH: July 5, 1867, Washington, D.C.

James Wayne was the son of Richard Wayne, a British army officer, and Elizabeth Clifford Wayne. He was the twelfth of their thirteen children. As a boy, James lived on the family rice plantation outside of Savannah and was educated by an Irish tutor. He progressed so quickly in his studies that he was ready to enter the College of New Jersey (now Princeton) at the age of fourteen. Shortly after his graduation in 1808, James's father died and his brother-in-law, Richard Stites, became his guardian.

Wayne had begun to study law under a prominent Savannah lawyer, John Y. Noel, and, after his father's death, he studied at Yale under Judge Charles Chauncey for almost two years. Upon returning to Savannah, he read in the office of his brother-in-law and in 1810 went into partnership with Samuel M. Bond.

During the War of 1812, Wayne served as an officer in a volunteer Georgia militia unit called the Chatham Light Dragoons. In 1813 he married Mary Johnson Campbell of Richmond, Virginia. The couple had three children.

In 1815 Wayne was elected to the Georgia legislature, serving two years. At age twenty-seven he became mayor of Savannah, but resigned after two years to resume his law practice. At the end of 1819, he was elected to sit on the Savannah Court of Common Pleas and in 1822 was appointed to a superior court judgeship. The court provided him with much hard work and the opportunity for public recognition.

Wayne entered Congress in 1829 and served for three terms. During this period he became a strong ally of the Jackson administration. By 1835 he was considered a leading Unionist Democrat and was nominated to the Supreme Court by President Jackson.

Unlike his colleague, Justice Campbell of Alabama, Wayne refused to leave the bench when secession came and remained a strong Union supporter throughout the Civil War. It was an agonizing period for the justice, who was disowned by his home state and accused of being an enemy alien by a Confederate court.

At war's end, Wayne opposed the punitive Reconstruction measures taken against the South and refused to hold circuit court in states under military Reconstruction rule. He did not live to see the end of Reconstruction, dying of typhoid in 1867.

ROGER BROOKE TANEY

(1836–1864)

BIRTH: March 17, 1777, Calvert County, Maryland.

EDUCATION: graduated from Dickinson College in Pennsylvania, 1795, honorary LL.D.; read law in office of Judge Jeremiah Chase in Annapolis.

OFFICIAL POSITIONS: member, Maryland House of Delegates, 1799–1800; Maryland state senator, 1816–1821; Maryland attorney general, 1827–1831; chairman, Jackson Central Committee for Maryland, 1827–1828; U.S. attorney general, 1831–1833; acting secretary of war, 1831; U.S. secretary of the Treasury, 1833–1834 (appointment rejected by Senate).

SUPREME COURT SERVICE: nominated chief justice by President Andrew Jackson December 28, 1835, to replace John Marshall, who had died; confirmed by Senate on March 15, 1836, by a 29-15 vote; took judicial oath March 28, 1836; served until October 12, 1864; replaced by Salmon P. Chase, nominated by President Abraham Lincoln.

FAMILY: married Anne Phoebe Carlton Key, January 7, 1806; died 1855; six daughters; one son, died in infancy.

DEATH: October 12, 1864, Washington, D.C.

Roger Taney was descended on both sides from prominent Maryland families. Monica Brooke Taney's family first arrived in the state in 1650, complete with foxhounds and other trappings of aristocracy. Michael Taney's forebear immigrated to America around 1660 as an indentured servant but eventually acquired a large amount of property and became a member of the landed Maryland tidewater gentry.

Taney was born in Calvert County, Maryland, on his father's tobacco plantation. He was educated in local rural schools and privately tutored by a Princeton student. In 1795, at the age of eighteen, he graduated first in his class from Dickinson College in Pennsylvania.

As his father's second son, Taney was not in line to inherit the family property and so decided on a career in law and politics. For three years, he was an apprentice lawyer in the office of Judge Jeremiah Chase of the Maryland General Court in Annapolis. He was admitted to the bar in 1799.

In 1806 Taney married Anne Key, daughter of a prominent farmer and the sister of Francis Scott Key. Because Taney was a devout Roman Catholic and his wife an Episcopalian, they agreed to raise their sons as Catholics and their daughters as Episcopalians. The couple had six daughters and a son who died in infancy. In 1855, the year *Scott v. Sandford* came before the Supreme Court, Taney's wife and youngest daughter died of yellow fever.

Taney began his political career as a member of the Federalist Party, serving one term in the Maryland legislature from 1799 to 1800. After being defeated for reelection, he moved from Calvert County to Frederick, where he began to develop a profitable law practice.

In 1803 Taney was beaten again in an attempt to return to the House of Delegates. Despite this setback, he began to achieve prominence in the Frederick community as a lawyer and politician. He lived there for twenty years.

In supporting the War of 1812, Taney split with the majority of his state's Federalists. In 1816, as a result of shifting political loyalties, he was elected to the Maryland Senate and became a dominant figure in party politics.

Taney's Senate term expired in 1821. In 1823 he settled in Baltimore, where he continued his successful law practice and political activities. By this time, the Federalist Party had virtually disintegrated, and Taney threw his support to the Jackson Democrats, leading Jackson's 1828 presidential campaign in Maryland. Taney served as the state's attorney general from 1827 until 1831 when he was named U.S. attorney general for the Jackson administration and left Baltimore for Washington.

Taney played a leading role in the controversy over the second Bank of the United States, helping to write Jackson's message in 1832 vetoing the bank's recharter. The next year, when Treasury Secretary William Duane refused to withdraw federal deposits from the bank, Duane was dismissed and replaced by Taney, who promptly carried out the action.

Taney held the Treasury job for nine months, presiding over a new system of state bank depositories called "pet banks." Jackson, who had delayed as long as he could, was eventually forced to submit Taney's nomination as Treasury secretary to the Senate. In June 1834 the Senate rejected Taney, and he was forced to resign.

In 1835 Jackson appointed Taney to replace aging Supreme Court justice Gabriel Duvall, but the nomination was indefinitely postponed by a close Senate vote. Ten months later, Jackson proposed Taney's name again, this time to fill the seat left vacant by the death of Chief Justice Marshall. To the horror of the Whigs, who considered him much too radical, Taney was confirmed as chief justice on March 15, 1836.

Taney's reputation rests almost entirely on his opinion in *Scott v. Sandford,* in which he held that slaves had no legal rights and could not become citizens. This decision hastened the Civil War and damaged the standing of the Court. Taney is also, however, responsible for a much earlier and more socially responsible decision in *Charles River Bridge v. Warren Bridge* (1837), in which the Court asserted that contracts made by a state legislature should benefit the public good.

PHILIP PENDLETON BARBOUR

(1836–1841)

BIRTH: May 25, 1783, Orange County, Virginia.

EDUCATION: read law on his own; attended one session at College of William and Mary, 1801.

OFFICIAL POSITIONS: member, Virginia House of Delegates from Orange County, 1812–1814; U.S. representative, 1814–1825, 1827–1830; Speaker of the House, 1821–1823; state judge, General Court for the Eastern District of Virginia, 1825–1827; president, Virginia Constitutional Convention, 1829–1830; U.S. district judge, Court of Eastern Virginia, 1830–1836.

SUPREME COURT SERVICE: nominated associate justice by President Andrew Jackson February 28, 1835, to replace Gabriel Duvall, who had resigned; confirmed by the Senate, March 15, 1836, by a 30-11 vote; took judicial oath May 12, 1836; served until

Philip Barbour

February 25, 1841; replaced by Peter V. Daniel, nominated by President Martin Van Buren.

FAMILY: married Frances Todd Johnson, 1804; seven children.

DEATH: February 25, 1841, Washington, D.C.

Philip Barbour was a country gentleman from one of Virginia's oldest families. Descended from a Scottish merchant who settled in the state in the seventeenth century, Philip's father, Thomas Barbour, was a member of the Virginia House of Burgesses and an Orange County planter. His mother was Mary Pendleton Thomas Barbour, the daughter of a well-to-do farmer. James Barbour, Philip's older brother, was a Virginia governor, a U.S. senator, and secretary of war under President John Quincy Adams.

Because of his family's financial difficulties, Philip received his early education in the local schools, rather than the private schools attended by his social peers. He excelled in languages and classical literature. At the age of seventeen, he read law for a short time and then moved to Kentucky to begin practice. He soon returned to his home state, however, and borrowed money to enroll in the College of William and Mary. He attended only one session and left to resume his law practice. After two years, he had earned enough money to marry Frances Johnson, the daughter of an Orange County landowner. James Barbour had married Frances's sister twelve years earlier.

Philip Barbour was elected to the Virginia House of Delegates in 1812. Two years later he won a seat in the U.S. Congress and, in a philosophical split with his brother, allied with a group of older Republicans who espoused strict construction and limited federal power.

Barbour served as Speaker of the House from 1821 until he was defeated by Henry Clay in 1823. In 1824 he chose not to run for reelection to his House seat.

After declining an offer from Thomas Jefferson to teach law at the University of Virginia, Barbour became a state judge on the General Court for the Eastern District of Virginia, serving for almost two years. In 1827 he returned to Congress and ran again for Speaker, losing this time to fellow Virginian Andrew Stevenson.

By this time Barbour was politically aligned with the Democratic forces of Andrew Jackson. After being passed over for a Jackson cabinet position in 1829, he was chosen president of the Virginia Constitutional Convention to replace the ailing James Monroe. In votes taken by the convention, he sided with the landed interests of the conservative eastern slaveholders against the claims of the westerners who later were to form a separate state, West Virginia.

In 1830 Barbour accepted an appointment as judge of the Federal District Court for Eastern Virginia. During the national election of 1832, he was touted as a vice-presidential candidate over Jackson's choice, Martin Van Buren. Party regulars, fearing the election might be thrown into the Senate, persuaded Barbour to withdraw his candidacy and support Van Buren as the nominee.

Barbour became an associate justice at the age of fifty-three. In his short term on the bench—only five years—he generally followed the Taney Court's drift toward a narrowing of corporate immunity and greater consideration of social and economic concerns.

Barbour became ill in early February 1841. By the end of the month, however, his health seemed to have improved, and on February 24 he attended a conference with other justices until ten o'clock at night. The next morning he was found dead of a heart attack.

JOHN CATRON

(1837–1865)

BIRTH: ca. 1786, Pennsylvania or Virginia.

EDUCATION: self-educated.

OFFICIAL POSITIONS: judge, Tennessee Supreme Court of Errors and Appeals, 1824–1831; first chief justice of Tennessee, 1831–1834.

SUPREME COURT SERVICE: nominated associate justice by President Andrew Jackson March 3, 1837, to fill a newly created seat; confirmed by the Senate March 8, 1837, by a 28-15 vote; took judicial oath May 1, 1837; served until May 30, 1865; seat abolished by Congress.

FAMILY: married Matilda Childress.

DEATH: May 30, 1865, Nashville, Tennessee.

Little is known about John Catron's early years. Born around 1786, of German ancestry, he is believed to have lived first in Virginia and then Kentucky. His father's name was Peter Catron. The family was poor, and young Catron probably had little if any formal education. In 1812 Catron moved to the Cumberland Mountain region of Tennessee and served under Andrew Jackson

John Catron

in the War of 1812. He joined the bar in 1815 and practiced in the Cumberland Mountain area until 1818, when he settled in Nashville and became an active member of the Davidson County bar. By this time he had developed a specialty in land law.

Catron was a successful businessman as well as a lawyer. With his brother George and a third partner, he owned and operated the profitable Buffalo Iron Works from 1827 until 1833 when he sold his interest in the business. He later reinvested in the company but kept himself out of its management.

In 1824 the Tennessee legislature created a new seat on the Supreme Court of Errors and Appeals—the state's highest court—and Catron was elected to fill the post. In 1831 he became the court's first chief justice but resigned in 1834 when the court was abolished by judicial reorganization.

After leaving the bench, Catron turned his attention to private practice and politics. In 1836 he directed Martin Van Buren's presidential campaign in Tennessee. As a result of his party loyalty and diligence, Catron was picked by Jackson, the outgoing president, in 1837 to fill one of two newly created seats on the Supreme Court. (The other was filled by John McKinley.) The appointment came on Jackson's final day in office.

On the Court, Catron supported states' rights and in 1857 sided with the "prosouthern" majority in *Scott v. Sandford*. He refused to support the Confederacy, however, and was forced to leave Nashville after Tennessee seceded from the Union. He returned home as soon as it was possible to resume his judicial duties, but by this time he was in failing health and died shortly thereafter.

JOHN McKINLEY

(1838–1852)

BIRTH: May 1, 1780, Culpeper County, Virginia.

EDUCATION: read law on his own; admitted to the bar in 1800.

OFFICIAL POSITIONS: Alabama state representative, sessions of 1820, 1831, and 1836; U.S. senator, 1826–1831 and 1837; U.S. representative, 1833–1835.

SUPREME COURT SERVICE: nominated associate justice by President Martin Van Buren September 18, 1837, for a newly created Supreme Court seat; confirmed by the Senate September 25, 1837, by a voice vote; took judicial oath January 9, 1838; served until July 19, 1852; replaced by John A. Campbell, nominated by President Franklin Pierce.

FAMILY: married Juliana Bryan; married Elizabeth Armistead.

DEATH: July 19, 1852, Louisville, Kentucky.

Born in Virginia, McKinley at an early age moved to Lincoln County on the Kentucky frontier where his mother's family was prominent. His father, Andrew McKinley, was a physician. His mother's name was Mary Logan McKinley. Little is known about McKinley's early education; he read law on his own and was admitted to the bar in 1800.

After practicing in Frankfort, the state capital, and in Louisville, the state's main commercial center, McKinley set out for Alabama, a newly thriving territory about to be admitted to the Union. He settled in Huntsville and soon became a part of

John McKinley

the so-called Georgia machine, a group of locally prominent lawyers, planters, and businessmen, mostly from Georgia, who dominated northern Alabama socially and politically.

Once settled in Huntsville, McKinley entered politics. He was elected to the Alabama legislature for the session of 1820. Then, in 1822, he missed election by the state legislature to the U.S. Senate by only one vote. Four years later, the seat opened up again with the death of the incumbent, and this time McKinley took it, by a margin of three votes.

During his term in the Senate, he stood for strict construction of the Constitution and a liberal reform of federal land policies, defending small landholders against speculators. McKinley was defeated for reelection to the Senate by Alabama governor Gabriel Moore in 1831.

During the 1820s McKinley had switched from support of Henry Clay to Andrew Jackson. Thereafter, he remained an ardent Jacksonian. In 1832 he was elected to the U.S. House and supported Jackson's campaign against the Bank of the United States. McKinley further proved his loyalty to Jackson by supporting Martin Van Buren, Jackson's choice for the vice presidency in 1832 and for the presidency in 1836.

Elected once again to the U.S. Senate in 1837, McKinley was picked for the Supreme Court by President Van Buren before the new Congress met, so he never got to serve his second Senate term. Congress had enacted a bill increasing the Court from seven members to nine in the waning days of Jackson's term. After William Smith of Alabama had turned down Jackson's nomination to one of the new seats, it fell to the newly inaugurated President Van Buren to pick another man. His choice was McKinley.

In his fifteen years on the bench, McKinley wrote only nineteen majority opinions, four dissents, and two concurrences. He suffered poor health during his last seven years on the Court, no doubt aggravated by the rigors of attending to the vast southern circuit. To the last, he stood by his states' rights and proslavery views.

PETER VIVIAN DANIEL

(1841–1860)

BIRTH: April 24, 1784, Stafford County, Virginia.

EDUCATION: privately tutored; attended Princeton University, 1802–1803.

OFFICIAL POSITIONS: member, Virginia House of Delegates, 1809–1812; Virginia Privy Council, 1812–1835; lieutenant governor of Virginia, 1818–1835; U.S. district judge, Eastern District of Virginia, 1836–1841.

SUPREME COURT SERVICE: nominated associate justice by President Van Buren February 26, 1841, to replace Justice Philip Barbour, who had died; confirmed by the Senate March 2, 1841, by a 22-5 vote; took judicial oath January 10, 1842; served until May 31, 1860; replaced by Samuel F. Miller, nominated by President Abraham Lincoln.

FAMILY: married Lucy Randolph, 1809; died 1847; married Elizabeth Harris, 1853; two children.

DEATH: May 31, 1860, Richmond, Virginia.

Peter Daniel, the son of Travers and Frances Moncure Daniel, was a member of an old Virginia family which went back to the early days of the colony. It was a landed family, with a sizable estate, "Crow's Nest," where Daniel was born and brought up. His early education was by private tutors. He spent one year at Princeton, but returned to Virginia and moved to Richmond to study law in the office of Edmund Randolph.

Randolph had been both attorney general and secretary of state in George Washington's administration, and Daniel's association with him gained him access to the inner circle of Virginia political power. Daniel's marriage to Randolph's daughter Lucy further cemented the connection.

In 1809 Daniel was elected to the Virginia House of Delegates, where he served until elected to the Virginia Privy Council, an executive advisory and review body, in 1812. In 1818 he was chosen lieutenant governor of Virginia while continuing to serve on the Privy Council. He remained in both posts for the next seventeen years.

A loyal Jacksonian Democrat, Daniel supported President Andrew Jackson in his attack on the Bank of the United States. At one point, Jackson offered him the post of attorney general, but Daniel turned it down because of its inadequate salary. Because of his support of Jackson, Daniel was denied reelection in 1835 to his positions as privy councilor and lieutenant governor. The next year, Jackson appointed him federal district judge for the Eastern District of Virginia.

Daniel's elevation to the Supreme Court came suddenly. Justice Philip Barbour died February 24, 1841, only a week before President Martin Van Buren was to turn over his office to the new Whig administration of William Henry Harrison. To ensure that the Court seat remained in Democratic hands, Van Buren nominated Daniel only two days after Barbour's death, and the Democratic-controlled Senate confirmed the appointment on March 2, two days before adjournment.

Daniel remained on the Court for nineteen years, a vestige of the Jeffersonian school's advocacy of states' rights and a weak central government. He died on the eve of the Civil War and was not replaced on the Court for two years. The delay occurred because the Republicans took power and restructured the circuit court system to reduce the number of southern circuits and increase those in the Midwest and West.

Peter Vivian Daniel

SAMUEL NELSON

(1845–1872)

BIRTH: November 11, 1792, Hebron, New York.

EDUCATION: graduated, Middlebury College, 1813.

OFFICIAL POSITIONS: postmaster, Cortland, New York, 1820–1823; presidential elector, 1820; judge, Sixth Circuit of New York, 1823–1831; associate justice, New York Supreme Court, 1831–1837; chief justice, New York Supreme Court, 1837–1845; member, *Alabama* Claims Commission, 1871.

SUPREME COURT SERVICE: nominated associate justice by President John Tyler February 4, 1845, to replace Justice Smith Thompson, who had died; confirmed by the Senate February 14, 1845, by a voice vote; took judicial oath February 27, 1845; retired

Samuel Nelson

November 28, 1872; replaced by Ward Hunt, nominated by President Ulysses S. Grant.

FAMILY: married Pamela Woods, 1819; died 1822; one son; married Catherine Ann Russell, ca. 1825; two daughters, one son.

DEATH: December 13, 1873, Cooperstown, New York.

Samuel Nelson's grandparents were Scotch-Irish immigrants to America in the 1760s. His parents were John Rogers Nelson and Jean McCarter Nelson. Samuel spent his boyhood on farms in upstate New York. He attended local district schools, where his interest in his studies at first led him to plan a career in the ministry.

After graduation from Middlebury College in 1813, Nelson decided to study law instead. He clerked in a law office in Salem, New York, was admitted to the bar in 1817, and settled in Cortland, a small but thriving county seat in central New York. After establishing a successful law practice there, Nelson became involved in politics, identifying with the Democratic-Republicans and later with the Jackson-Van Buren wing of the Democratic Party.

In 1820 Nelson served as a presidential elector, voting for President James Monroe, and was appointed postmaster of Cortland, a position he held for three years. Also during that period, in 1821, Nelson was a delegate to the state constitutional convention, where he advocated the abolition of property qualifications for voting.

Beginning in 1823, Nelson embarked on a career in the judiciary which was to last for nearly fifty years. His first judicial position was as a judge of the Sixth Circuit of New York

(1823–1831). In 1831 he was elevated to the state supreme court and in 1837 became chief justice. From there he went to the U.S. Supreme Court in 1845.

Nelson's nomination for the Supreme Court in the waning days of the Tyler administration came as a complete surprise. Two previous Tyler nominees had been turned down by the Senate, and several other prominent persons had declined offers of appointment. Nelson's reputation as a careful and uncontroversial jurist, combined with his Democratic background, were received favorably, and the Democratic-controlled Senate confirmed him with little contention.

Most of Nelson's twenty-seven years on the Court were unspectacular. He achieved some brief notoriety in the secession crisis of 1860–1861 when he joined with Justice John A. Campbell to try to conciliate the North and South and avoid the Civil War. Nelson was also considered for the Democratic presidential nomination in 1860, but nothing came of it.

In 1871 President Grant appointed Nelson a member of the commission to settle the *Alabama* claims dispute against Great Britain. His hard work on the commission broke Nelson's health, and he retired from the Court the next year.

LEVI WOODBURY

(1845–1851)

BIRTH: December 22, 1789, Francestown, New Hampshire.

EDUCATION: Dartmouth College, graduated with honors, 1809; Tapping Reeve Law School, ca. 1810.

Levi Woodbury

OFFICIAL POSITIONS: clerk, New Hampshire Senate, 1816; associate justice, New Hampshire Superior Court, 1817–1823; governor, New Hampshire, 1823–1824; Speaker, New Hampshire House, 1825; U.S. senator, 1825–1831, 1841–1845; secretary of the Navy, 1831–1834; secretary of the Treasury, 1834–1841.

SUPREME COURT SERVICE: nominated associate justice by President James K. Polk December 23, 1845, to replace Justice Joseph Story, who had died; confirmed by the Senate January 3, 1846, by voice vote; took judicial oath September 23, 1845; served until September 4, 1851; replaced by Benjamin R. Curtis, nominated by President Millard Fillmore.

FAMILY: married Elizabeth Williams Clapp, June 1819; four daughters, one son.

DEATH: September 4, 1851, Portsmouth, New Hampshire.

The second of ten children, Woodbury was born into an old New England family that traced its American roots back to 1630. Originally settled in Massachusetts, some of the family's descendants moved to New Hampshire in the late 1700s, where Woodbury was born in 1789. His parents were Peter and Mary Woodbury. His mother's maiden name was also Woodbury.

Woodbury graduated from Dartmouth College with honors in 1809 and then began the study of law. While he studied privately with practicing lawyers—as was then the custom—he also briefly attended a law school in Litchfield, Connecticut, making him one of the first Supreme Court justices to attend a law school.

After being admitted to the bar in 1812, Woodbury practiced in his native Francestown and in nearby Portsmouth, the main commercial center of the state, from 1812 to 1816. His interests soon turned to politics, and he held some kind of political office almost constantly from 1816 until his appointment to the Supreme Court in 1845.

Woodbury started his climb up the political ladder in 1816 when he was appointed clerk of the state Senate. After serving a year, he was put on the New Hampshire Superior Court, where he remained until 1823, when he became a successful insurgent candidate for the governorship, beating the entrenched Democratic-Republican machine of Isaac Hill.

Woodbury was defeated for reelection in 1824, but came back the next year to win a seat in the state House and was elected Speaker. Shortly thereafter, the legislature elected him to the U.S. Senate, where he served from 1825 to 1831.

Woodbury was appointed secretary of the Navy in President Andrew Jackson's cabinet reorganization of 1831. He made little mark in that office, but in 1834 he was suddenly elevated to the crucial post of secretary of the Treasury in the midst of Jackson's war on the Bank of the United States. Jackson had gone through three Treasury secretaries in just over a year. Woodbury loyally cooperated with Jackson's policies, although with some reservations, and remained as head of the Treasury through the administration of Martin Van Buren (1837–1841).

Upon leaving the cabinet, Woodbury was chosen to serve once again in the U.S. Senate, where he was sitting when Polk used a recess appointment to place him on the Supreme Court

just days after Justice Story's death. Woodbury' official nomination and confirmation came several months later.

He served for less than six years on the Court, dying in 1851. He was a contender for the Democratic presidential nomination in 1848, but lost to Lewis Cass.

ROBERT COOPER GRIER

(1846–1870)

BIRTH: March 5, 1794, Cumberland County, Pennsylvania.

EDUCATION: Dickinson College, graduated 1812.

OFFICIAL POSITIONS: president judge, District Court of Allegheny County, Pennsylvania, 1833–1846.

SUPREME COURT SERVICE: nominated associate justice by President James K. Polk August 3, 1846, to replace Justice Henry Baldwin, who had died; confirmed by the Senate August 4, 1846, by a voice vote; took judicial oath August 10, 1846; retired January 31, 1870; replaced by William Strong, nominated by President Ulysses S. Grant.

FAMILY: married Isabella Rose, 1829.

DEATH: September 25, 1870, Philadelphia, Pennsylvania.

The eldest of eleven children, Grier was born into a family of Presbyterian ministers. Both his father, Isaac Grier, and his maternal grandfather followed that vocation. His mother was Elizabeth Cooper Grier.

Grier was taught by his father until the age of seventeen, when he entered Dickinson College as a junior and finished in one year. He taught at Dickinson before becoming a teacher in

Robert Cooper Grier

the Northumberland Academy, his father's school, where he succeeded the elder Grier as principal in 1815.

Grier's interests turned to the law, which he studied privately, passing the bar in 1817. He set up practice first in Bloomsburg, but soon moved to the county seat of Danville, where he became a prominent local attorney.

A solid Jacksonian Democrat, Grier came to the attention of the Democratic politicians in Harrisburg. As a result, he got a patronage appointment as president judge of the District Court of Allegheny County in 1833, a job he held for the next thirteen years, establishing a reputation as a thorough and knowledgeable judge.

In 1844 Supreme Court justice Henry Baldwin of Pennsylvania died, and a long effort began to fill his seat. It took more than two years for the spot to be filled finally by Grier. President Tyler had made two nominations; the first was withdrawn and the second got no action from the Democratic Senate. Tyler left office in March 1845, and the task of filling the vacancy fell to President Polk.

Polk also had difficulty finding a justice, first offering the position to future president James Buchanan. When Buchanan turned it down, Polk nominated George Woodward, but the Senate refused to confirm him. Finally, Polk selected Grier, who was confirmed.

Grier served on the Court for nearly a quarter of a century. He wrote the majority opinion in the *Prize Cases* (1863), upholding the legality of President Lincoln's blockade of southern ports. This action had taken place three months before Congress authorized the war. Grier stated that a formal declaration of war was unnecessary because a civil war is never "solemnly declared."

Toward the end of his service, his mental and physical powers waned to the point that he was barely functioning. Finally, a committee of his colleagues called on him to urge his retirement. He took their advice and retired in January 1870. He died seven months later.

BENJAMIN ROBBINS CURTIS

(1851–1857)

BIRTH: November 4, 1809, Watertown, Massachusetts.

EDUCATION: Harvard University, graduated 1829 with highest honors; Harvard Law School, graduated 1832.

OFFICIAL POSITIONS: Massachusetts state representative, 1849–1851.

SUPREME COURT SERVICE: nominated associate justice by President Millard Fillmore December 11, 1851, to replace Justice Levi Woodbury, who had died; confirmed by the Senate December 20, 1851, by a voice vote; took judicial oath October 10, 1851; resigned September 30, 1857; replaced by Nathan Clifford, nominated by President James Buchanan.

FAMILY: married Eliza Maria Woodward, 1833; died 1844; five children; married Anna Wroe Curtis, 1846; died 1860; three children; married Maria Malleville Allen, 1861; four children.

DEATH: September 15, 1874, Newport, Rhode Island.

Benjamin Robbins Curtis

Curtis was the son of a Massachusetts ship captain whose ancestors settled New England in the 1630s. His father, Benjamin Curtis III, died while on a voyage abroad when Curtis was a child. He was raised by his mother, Lois Robbins Curtis, with help from his half-uncle, George Ticknor, a Harvard professor and author.

When Curtis was ready to enter Harvard University in 1825, his mother moved to Cambridge and ran a boarding school for students there to support herself and her family. Curtis graduated from Harvard in 1829 and immediately entered Harvard Law School, from which he graduated in 1832 after taking a year off in 1831 to set up a law practice in Northfield, Massachusetts, a small town in the Connecticut River Valley.

In 1834 Curtis moved to Boston to join the law practice of his distant cousin, Charles Pelham Curtis. After the death of his first wife, Curtis married his law partner's daughter in 1846.

Curtis was elected to the Massachusetts House in 1849 and chaired a commission that designed a sweeping reform of judicial proceedings in the state. A conservative Whig, he was a strong supporter of Sen. Daniel Webster. He rallied behind Webster during the crisis of 1850 when the senator was working for compromise of the territorial and slave issues and was being denounced for his efforts by Massachusetts abolitionists.

In 1851, when President Fillmore was looking for a replacement for the late Justice Levi Woodbury, Webster, then serving as Fillmore's secretary of state, recommended Curtis. Curtis, however, found life in the capital uncomfortable and the salary, despite a raise of one-third in 1855, inadequate to support his large family. Adding to his difficulties was his perceived obligation to uphold the constitutionality of the Fugitive Slave Act of 1850, while he was on circuit duty in New England. The press attacked Curtis, labeling him "the slave-catcher judge," even though he was a strong abolitionist and abhorred slavery. Curtis's relations with his colleagues on the Court, especially with Chief Justice Taney, became so acrimonious during Court arguments over *Scott v. Sandford* and other pre–Civil War controversies that he decided to resign. Curtis and Justice John McLean were the only dissenters in *Scott*. Curtis pointed out that blacks were citizens and had voting rights in 1787. He left the Court on September 30, 1857.

Curtis devoted the remainder of his life to a lucrative law practice in Boston. He appeared before the Supreme Court on numerous occasions to argue for his clients. Politically, he remained a conservative, objecting to some of the emergency measures taken by President Abraham Lincoln, including the Emancipation Proclamation and the suspension of habeas corpus. He also opposed the radical Reconstruction policies of congressional Republicans during Andrew Johnson's administration. In 1868 he served as the leading counsel for President Johnson during the impeachment proceedings. Johnson offered Curtis the position of attorney general, but he declined.

John Archibald Campbell

JOHN ARCHIBALD CAMPBELL

(1853–1861)

BIRTH: June 24, 1811, Washington, Georgia.

EDUCATION: Franklin College (now the University of Georgia), graduated with first honors, 1825; attended U.S. Military Academy at West Point, 1825–1828.

OFFICIAL POSITIONS: Alabama state representative, sessions of 1837 and 1843; assistant secretary of war, Confederate States of America, 1862–1865.

SUPREME COURT SERVICE: nominated associate justice by President Franklin Pierce March 21, 1853, to replace Justice John McKinley, who had died; confirmed by the Senate March 25, 1853, by a voice vote; took judicial oath April 11, 1853; resigned April 30, 1861; replaced by David Davis, nominated by President Abraham Lincoln.

FAMILY: married Anna Esther Goldthwaite in the early 1830s; four daughters, one son.

DEATH: March 12, 1889, Baltimore, Maryland.

Born into a family of Scotch and Scotch-Irish descent, Campbell was the son of Duncan and Mary Williamson Campbell. A child prodigy, he entered college at the age of eleven, graduating at fourteen. He then attended West Point for three years before withdrawing to return home to support the family after the death of his father. A year later, at the age of eighteen, he was admitted to the bar by special act of the Georgia legislature.

In 1830 Campbell moved to Alabama to begin his legal career, settling first in Montgomery, where he met and married Anna

Esther Goldthwaite, a New Hampshire native who had moved to the South with her brothers. The couple moved to Mobile in 1837, and Campbell was elected to the first of two terms in the state legislature.

Campbell quickly became one of the leading lawyers in Alabama, and before long his reputation spread nationally. Twice he declined appointment to the Alabama Supreme Court. He was a delegate to the Nashville convention of 1850, convened to protect southern rights in the face of what they saw as northern encroachment, especially on the slavery question. Campbell was a moderating influence at the convention, writing many of the resolutions that finally were adopted.

Campbell was selected for the Supreme Court after a Democratic Senate had refused to act on three choices nominated by Whig president Millard Fillmore. When Fillmore was replaced by Democrat Franklin Pierce in March 1853, Democrats were able to appoint one of their own to the Court. Campbell's selection was made in an unprecedented fashion. The Supreme Court justices wanted the new president to nominate Campbell and sent a delegation to Pierce to make their wish known. Pierce complied.

Campbell's service on the bench was cut short by the Civil War. He opposed secession and believed that slavery would slowly disappear if the South were left alone. He freed all his slaves upon his Supreme Court appointment and thereafter hired only free blacks as servants. During the secession crisis, he attempted to serve as a mediator between the seceding states and the new Lincoln administration.

When the die was cast and hostilities broke out, he resigned his Court position and returned to the South, settling in New Orleans. In 1862 he was invited to join the Confederate government and accepted the position of assistant secretary of war in charge of administering the conscription law. He remained in that position until the fall of the Confederacy in 1865.

After a few months of detention by the Union, Campbell was freed and returned to New Orleans, where he built up a prosperous and prestigious law practice. He argued before the Supreme Court on numerous occasions in the quarter-century before his death.

NATHAN CLIFFORD
(1858–1881)

BIRTH: August 18, 1803, Rumney, New Hampshire.

EDUCATION: Haverhill Academy; studied law in office of Josiah Quincy in Rumney; admitted to New Hampshire bar, 1827.

OFFICIAL POSITIONS: Maine state representative, 1830–1834; attorney general of Maine, 1834–1838; U.S. representative, 1839–1843; U.S. attorney general, 1846–1848; minister to Mexico, 1848–1849.

SUPREME COURT SERVICE: nominated associate justice by President James Buchanan December 9, 1857, to replace Benjamin R. Curtis, who had resigned; confirmed by the Senate January 12, 1858, by a 26-23 vote; took judicial oath January 21, 1858; served until July 25, 1881; replaced by Horace Gray, nominated by President Chester A. Arthur.

Nathan Clifford

FAMILY: married Hannah Ayer, ca. 1828; six children.

DEATH: July 25, 1881, Cornish, Maine.

Nathan Clifford was the son of Lydia Simpson Clifford and Nathaniel Clifford, a New Hampshire farmer whose American roots went back three generations. His grandfather was an officer in the Revolutionary War.

Clifford attended the local academies for his early education, then studied law in the office of Josiah Quincy, a prominent attorney in Rumney, New Hampshire. Clifford was admitted to the bar in 1827 and moved to Newfield, Maine, to begin practice. There he met and married a local woman, Hannah Ayer.

He was a staunch Jacksonian Democrat, maintaining his early political beliefs throughout his long life and political career.

Clifford entered public life soon after beginning his law practice in Maine. In 1830, at the age of twenty-seven, he was elected to the lower house of the Maine legislature. He was reelected for three additional one-year terms and served the last two years as Speaker. He was then elected attorney general of the state by the legislature, serving four years. After that, he won two terms in the U.S. House, but was defeated for reelection to a third term.

Clifford's defeat in 1843 marked the end of the first phase of his political career. He then returned to law practice in Maine for three years. He had earned a reputation as a hard worker and received attention for the thoroughness of his preparation.

In 1846 President Polk chose Clifford as attorney general. Polk needed New England representation in his cabinet, and Clifford supported his ideas. During his service in the Polk cabinet, Clifford played a major role in mediating the many disputes between Polk and his secretary of state, James Buchanan. Polk was vigorously pursuing his war with Mexico, while Buchanan advocated a more cautious policy. Buchanan liked and trusted Clifford.

In 1848 Polk entrusted Clifford with a diplomatic mission. He was sent to Mexico with the purpose of getting Mexico to ratify the peace treaty ending the war. Clifford did so and stayed on to become U.S. minister to the Mexican government from 1848 to 1849. With a new Whig administration in Washington in 1849, Clifford returned to Maine to resume law practice, this time in the more populous and prosperous city of Portland.

When a Supreme Court vacancy occurred in late 1857, President Buchanan chose Clifford to fill it. There was strong criticism against the nomination; Clifford was looked upon in the North as a "doughface"—a northern man with southern principles. Clifford had supported Buchanan policies that many northerners thought favored the South. He, however, was confirmed in a close vote.

In 1877 Clifford—still on the Court—served as chairman of the electoral commission set up to decide the disputed presidential election of 1876. He voted with the Democrats for Tilden, but the Republican, Rutherford B. Hayes, won by one vote. Clifford always considered Hayes an illegitimate president and refused to enter the White House during his presidency.

In 1880 Clifford suffered a stroke, which prevented him from taking any further active role in Court proceedings. He refused to resign, however, hoping to live until a Democratic president could name his successor. He died, however, while the Republicans were still in power.

NOAH HAYNES SWAYNE

(1862–1881)

BIRTH: December 7, 1804, Frederick County, Virginia.

EDUCATION: studied law privately; admitted to the bar in Warrenton, Virginia, in 1823.

OFFICIAL POSITIONS: Coshocton County (Ohio) prosecuting attorney, 1826–1829; Ohio state representative, 1830 and 1836; U.S. attorney for Ohio, 1830–1841; Columbus city councilman, 1834.

SUPREME COURT SERVICE: nominated associate justice by President Abraham Lincoln January 21, 1862, to replace John McLean, who had died; confirmed by the Senate January 24, 1862, by a 38-1 vote; took judicial oath January 27, 1862; retired January 24, 1881; replaced by Stanley Matthews, nominated by President Rutherford B. Hayes and renominated by President James A. Garfield.

FAMILY: married Sarah Ann Wager, 1832; four sons, one daughter.

DEATH: June 8, 1884, New York City.

Although born in the slave-holding state of Virginia, Noah Swayne was the son of antislavery Quaker parents, Joshua and Rebecca Smith Swayne, who came from Pennsylvania. Noah studied medicine as a youth, but after the death of his teacher he switched to law.

Following his admission to the bar, Swayne migrated to the free state of Ohio because of his opposition to slavery. During

Noah Haynes Swayne

his long legal career in that state, he was involved in cases defending runaway slaves. When he married Sarah Ann Wager, a Virginian who owned slaves, she agreed to free them.

Shortly after settling in Ohio, Swayne became involved in politics as a Jacksonian Democrat. He was elected prosecuting attorney of Coshocton County in 1826 and to the Ohio legislature in 1829. In 1830 President Andrew Jackson appointed him U.S. attorney for Ohio, and he served throughout the rest of Jackson's administration as well as that of Martin Van Buren. During his service as U.S. attorney, he also developed a successful private law practice and served on the Columbus City Council and once again in the state legislature.

Swayne's political activity ebbed in the 1840s, but reemerged in the 1850s when the slavery issue began tearing the nation apart. Swayne's antislavery convictions drove him from the Democratic Party, and he supported the presidential candidate of the new Republican Party, John Charles Fremont, in 1856. Swayne also served in the 1850s as a member of a state committee overseeing Ohio's finances, which had fallen into disorder.

Although Swayne had no judicial experience and was not well known outside Ohio, Lincoln nevertheless made him his first appointment to the Supreme Court. The vacancy was caused by the death of Justice John McLean, a close friend of Swayne's, and McLean had let it be known that he wanted Swayne to succeed him on the Court. In addition, Swayne was close to the governor of Ohio, William Dennison, who traveled to Washington to lobby for him. The Ohio congressional delegation also recommended him.

Swayne fulfilled Republican hopes that he would uphold the extraordinary Civil War measures of the national government, and he continued to take a generally nationalist stance in his decisions throughout his years on the Court. He also lobbied for passage of the Fifteenth Amendment, guaranteeing voting rights for blacks. His own state of Ohio was crucial to the ratification of the amendment, and Swayne used all his influence in his adopted state on behalf of approval.

Twice Swayne maneuvered for the chief justiceship—in 1864, when Roger B. Taney died, and again in 1873, when Salmon P. Chase died. Swayne, however, was disappointed both times. With his mental acuity noticeably declining by 1881, Swayne was persuaded by President Hayes to retire with the promise that his friend and fellow-Ohioan Stanley Matthews would be chosen as his successor.

SAMUEL FREEMAN MILLER

(1862–1890)

BIRTH: April 5, 1816, Richmond, Kentucky.

EDUCATION: Transylvania University, M.D., 1838; studied law privately; admitted to the bar in 1847.

OFFICIAL POSITIONS: justice of the peace and member of the Knox County, Kentucky, court, an administrative body, in the 1840s.

SUPREME COURT SERVICE: nominated associate justice by President Abraham Lincoln July 16, 1862, to replace Justice Peter V.

Samuel Freeman Miller

Daniel, who had died; confirmed July 16, 1862, by a voice vote; took judicial oath July 21, 1862; served until October 13, 1890; replaced by Henry B. Brown, nominated by President Benjamin Harrison.

FAMILY: married Lucy Ballinger, November 8, 1842; died 1854; three children; married Elizabeth Winter Reeves, widow of his law partner, 1857; two children.

DEATH: October 13, 1890, Washington, D.C.

Samuel Miller was the eldest son of Frederick Miller, a Pennsylvania-German, and Patsy Freeman Miller, a North Carolinian, both of whom migrated to Kentucky at the turn of the nineteenth century. Young Miller began his career as a medical doctor. After graduating from the medical department of Transylvania University in 1838, he set up practice in Barboursville in Kentucky's small, mountainous Knox County.

Miller soon developed an interest in legal and political matters. He joined a debating society and studied law on the side, passing his bar exam in 1847. He favored gradual emancipation of slaves, and when the Kentucky constitutional convention of 1849 strengthened the position of slavery in the state, Miller freed his own slaves and moved west to Iowa, a free state.

In Iowa Miller abandoned medicine and set up a prosperous law practice in Keokuk. With political tensions rising in the 1850s, he joined the public arena and helped organize the Republican Party in Iowa, serving as chairman of the Keokuk County GOP organization.

By 1860 Miller was one of the leading Republican figures in the state and a strong backer of Abraham Lincoln for the party's presidential nomination. In 1861 Miller made a try for the

Republican gubernatorial nomination but was defeated by incumbent governor Samuel J. Kirkwood.

Miller's appointment to the Supreme Court came despite his lack of judicial experience. With the creation of a new circuit west of the Mississippi, western members of Congress and politicians, including a unanimous Iowa delegation, pressed for Miller's appointment. Lincoln's agreement made Miller the first Supreme Court justice from west of the Mississippi. His best-known opinion came in the landmark *Slaughterhouse Cases* (1873), in which the Court decided that the right to do business did not derive from U.S. citizenship and therefore was not protected by the Fourteenth Amendment.

Miller was one of the five justices to serve on the electoral commission in 1877 to resolve the disputed presidential election of 1876 between Democrat Samuel J. Tilden and Republican Rutherford B. Hayes. Miller voted with his party to give the presidency to Hayes.

Twice Miller was considered for chief justice—in 1873 and 1888—but was passed over both times. His name was also mentioned for the presidency in 1880 and 1884, but no significant movement developed. Miller died October 13, 1890, just before the start of a new term.

DAVID DAVIS

(1862–1877)

BIRTH: March 9, 1815, Cecil County, Maryland.

EDUCATION: graduated Kenyon College, 1832; Yale Law School, 1835.

David Davis

OFFICIAL POSITIONS: Illinois state representative, 1845–1847; member, Illinois constitutional convention, 1847; Illinois state circuit judge, 1848–1862; U.S. senator, 1877–1883.

SUPREME COURT SERVICE: nominated associate justice by President Abraham Lincoln December 1, 1862, to replace John A. Campbell, who had resigned; confirmed by the Senate December 8, 1862, by a voice vote; took judicial oath December 10, 1862; resigned March 4, 1877; replaced by John Marshall Harlan, nominated by President Rutherford B. Hayes.

FAMILY: married Sarah Walker, October 30, 1838; died 1879; one son (two children died in infancy); married Adeline Burr, March 14, 1883; two daughters.

DEATH: June 26, 1886, Bloomington, Illinois.

David Davis was born in Maryland of Welsh ancestry and named for his father, a doctor, who had died before Davis was born. When his mother, Ann Mercer Davis, remarried, David went to live with an uncle in Annapolis. After studying law, he sought his fortune in the West.

Settling first in Pekin, Illinois, he moved within a year to Bloomington, which became his lifelong home. He was active in Whig politics, running a losing race for the state Senate in 1840 but winning a state House seat in 1844. During this period he became acquainted with Abraham Lincoln; this relationship deepened over the years and had a major effect on Davis's life.

After one term in the state legislature, Davis was chosen a member of the Illinois constitutional convention of 1847. At the convention, he fought for a popularly elected judiciary, replacing the system of election by the legislature. Davis's position prevailed, and in 1848 he was elected a judge of the Illinois Eighth Circuit, a position to which he was twice reelected and which he held until his appointment to the Supreme Court.

Among the prominent lawyers who practiced before Judge Davis in Illinois were Abraham Lincoln and Stephen Douglas. Davis became close to Lincoln in the 1850s and joined the new Republican Party with him when their Whig Party fell apart. Davis became Lincoln's campaign manager in 1860 and was perhaps the most important person in securing Lincoln the Republican presidential nomination that year.

Lincoln appointed Davis to the Supreme Court vacancy created by the resignation of Justice John A. Campbell, an Alabaman who withdrew to join the Confederate effort. Davis's opinion in *Ex parte Milligan* (1866) established that constitutional rights do not disappear during wartime and that military courts have no jurisdiction where civilian courts are operating.

Davis's interest in politics never faded. After Lincoln's death, he became disenchanted with the Republican Party. In 1872 he was nominated for president by the Labor Reform Party, a splinter group. Davis hoped to use this nomination to further his candidacy for the Liberal Republicans, a group opposing Grant. When the Liberals chose Horace Greeley instead, Davis declined the Labor Reform nomination.

Tired of his career on the Supreme Court, Davis accepted his election in 1877 by the Illinois legislature to the U.S. Senate and re-signed from the Court. Davis had been expected to be a member of the electoral commission set up to decide the disputed presidential election of 1876. Davis's political independence would have made him the swing vote on an otherwise evenly divided commission. His replacement was a Republican, Justice Joseph P. Bradley, who voted with the Republicans and gave the election to Republican Rutherford B. Hayes. At the time, it was thought that Davis might have voted with the Democrats on at least some of the disputed electoral votes, but he indicated later that he did not disagree with the commission's decisions.

Davis served one term in the Senate (1877–1883), voting independently, and then retired. From 1881 to 1883, he was president pro tem of the Senate, which under the succession law then in effect made him next in line for the presidency if anything had happened to President Chester A. Arthur.

STEPHEN JOHNSON FIELD

(1863–1897)

BIRTH: November 4, 1816, Haddam, Connecticut.

EDUCATION: graduated Williams College, 1837, class valedictorian; studied law in private firms; admitted to the bar in 1841.

OFFICIAL POSITIONS: Alcalde of Marysville, 1850; California state representative, 1850–1851; justice, California Supreme Court, 1857–1863.

SUPREME COURT SERVICE: nominated associate justice by President Abraham Lincoln March 6, 1863, for a newly created seat; confirmed by the Senate March 10, 1863, by a voice vote; took judicial oath May 20, 1863; retired December 1, 1897;

Stephen Johnson Field

replaced by Joseph McKenna, nominated by President William McKinley.

FAMILY: married Sue Virginia Swearingen, June 2, 1859.

DEATH: April 9, 1899, in Washington, D.C.

The son of Submit Dickinson Field and David Dudley Field, a New England Congregational clergyman, Stephen Johnson Field was born into a family that produced several prominent people. His brothers included David Dudley Field, a noted New York lawyer and politician; Cyrus West Field, a promoter of the first Atlantic cable; and Henry Martyn Field, a leading clergyman and author. Field's nephew, David J. Brewer, was a Supreme Court justice (1889–1910) and served with Field for the last eight years of his uncle's term.

Field studied law with his brother Dudley and with John Van Buren, son of President Martin Van Buren. He was admitted to the New York bar in 1841 and for the next seven years practiced in partnership with his brother.

In 1849, after a trip to Europe, he decided to strike out on his own and moved to California. Settling in Marysville, in the heart of the gold fields, Field lived the rough-and-tumble life of a frontier entrepreneur.

Field served in 1850 as Marysville's alcalde, the chief local administrative office under the old Spanish system. He quarreled with a local judge and was twice disbarred and once sent to jail for contempt of court.

Field was elected to the California Assembly, the lower house of the legislature, in 1850 and during his year of service was the chief drafter of the civil and criminal codes for the new state. After being defeated in a bid for the state Senate in 1851, he resumed his legal career for a time and then was elected to the California Supreme Court as a Democrat in 1857.

In 1863 Congress authorized an additional seat on the U.S. Supreme Court, partly to gain a new justice who would support the Civil War measures of the federal government, and partly because there was a need for a new circuit for the West Coast. Many cases concerning land and mineral issues were coming to the Court from California, and westerners wanted someone familiar with those issues.

Lincoln crossed party lines to appoint Field to the new seat. The California and Oregon congressional delegations unanimously recommended him, even though he was a Democrat. Field had staunchly supported the Union cause and was an acknowledged expert in land and mining issues.

It is rare for a Supreme Court justice to be involved in a case before the Court, but it happened to Field. David Neagle, a federal marshal assigned to protect Field shot and killed a would-be assassin—an old enemy of Field's—during a circuit court trip to California. The state charged Neagle with murder, but the Court ruled that California could not try him for actions carried out under federal law. Field did not participate in the case.

During his term on the Court, Field served, in 1877, on the electoral commission that decided the contested presidential election in favor of Republican Rutherford B. Hayes. Field voted on the losing Democratic side on all questions.

Field's name was mentioned for the Democratic presidential nomination in 1880 and 1884, but his candidacy did not advance very far. He aspired to be chief justice in 1888, when Morrison Waite died, but President Cleveland picked Melville W. Fuller instead.

In the 1890s Field's mental powers were visibly declining, and he was taking less and less part in Court proceedings. Finally, the other justices strongly hinted that he retire. Ironically, Field had been part of an effort to get an aging justice, Robert C. Grier, to retire in 1877. Field finally quit the Court in late 1897, but only after he had surpassed Chief Justice John Marshall's record of thirty-four years and five months of service.

SALMON PORTLAND CHASE

(1864–1873)

BIRTH: January 13, 1808, Cornish, New Hampshire.

EDUCATION: Dartmouth College, 1826.

OFFICIAL POSITIONS: U.S. senator, 1849–1855, 1861; governor of Ohio, 1856–1860; secretary of the Treasury, 1861–1864.

SUPREME COURT SERVICE: nominated chief justice by President Abraham Lincoln December 6, 1864, to replace Chief Justice Roger B. Taney, who had died; confirmed by the Senate December 6, 1864, by a voice vote; took judicial oath December 15, 1864; served until May 7, 1873; replaced by Morrison R. Waite, appointed by President Ulysses S. Grant.

Salmon Portland Chase

FAMILY: married Katherine Jane Garniss, March 4, 1834; died December 1, 1835; married Eliza Ann Smith, September 26, 1839; died September 29, 1845; one daughter; married Sara Belle Dunlop Ludlow, November 6, 1846; died January 13, 1852; one daughter.

DEATH: May 7, 1873, New York City.

Chase, the son of Ithamar and Janette Ralston Chase, was born in New Hampshire of a prominent family that traced its American roots back to 1640. An uncle, Dudley Chase, served as a U.S. senator for Vermont (1813–1817 and 1825–1831), and another uncle, Philander Chase, was the Protestant Episcopal Bishop of Ohio (1818–1831). Chase's father was a tavern-keeper who held various local political offices. Chase grew up and made his career in Ohio.

Upon his father's death in 1817, Chase went to live with his Uncle Philander in Ohio and was brought up under his stern discipline. Throughout his life, Chase retained a strong and righteous religious streak, inculcated in his early years by his uncle.

After graduation from Dartmouth, Chase went to Washington, D.C., opened a private school, and studied law under Attorney General William Wirt. He was admitted to the bar in 1829, then moved west to Cincinnati to begin his legal career.

Chase became involved early in the antislavery movement and took a prominent role in defending runaway slaves, arguing one case up to the Supreme Court. For his activities, he became known as the "attorney general for runaway Negroes."

Chase's opposition to slavery soon moved him into politics, and he became a leader of the antislavery Liberty Party in the 1840s. In 1848 he joined the Free Soilers and helped write part of the party's platform. The following year, when the Free Soilers held the balance of power in the Ohio legislature, they helped the Democrats organize the legislature in return for the Democrats' support in electing Chase to the U.S. Senate.

In the Senate Chase joined antislavery stalwarts such as William Seward and Benjamin Wade. When the old party system broke up, he helped to form the new Republican Party.

In 1855 Chase was elected governor of Ohio by a coalition headed by Republicans, and was reelected in 1857. He was mentioned for the Republican presidential nomination in both 1856 and 1860, but did not receive many votes. In 1861 he was elected once again to the U.S. Senate, but resigned after only two days to become secretary of the Treasury, a position he held during most of Lincoln's administration. Chase was responsible for financing the Civil War, first with large borrowings and then with the issue of paper money. He also devised a new federal banking system that became the cornerstone of American finance for the next half-century. He received high marks from political enemies as well as friends for his management of the Treasury during a time of national crisis.

Chase was not, however, happy with Lincoln's leadership and allowed himself to become the focus of an anti-Lincoln group within the Republican Party, which wanted to deny the president renomination in 1864. Twice that year, efforts were made to substitute Chase for Lincoln, but they were unsuccessful. Chase also had a number of running disagreements with Lincoln over other matters and submitted his resignation several times. Lincoln finally accepted it in the summer of 1864.

When Chief Justice Taney died in October, Chase was Lincoln's first choice for the post. Despite their differences, Lincoln had high regard for Chase's abilities, and the Republicans wanted someone on the Court they believed would sustain the extraordinary measures taken by the federal government during the war and others contemplated for the postwar period.

Chase was probably the most politically involved chief justice in American history, both because of his own ambitions and because of the tumultuous state of the country. In the spring of 1865 he made a tour of the South to study conditions there and report to President Andrew Johnson. Later, in 1868, Chase presided at the impeachment trial of Johnson and fought with the radical Republicans for his rights as presiding officer of the trial.

In both 1868 and 1872, Chase made no secret of his still-burning presidential ambitions and allowed friends to maneuver politically for him. As in the past, however, he was disappointed in his hopes for the nation's highest elected office.

WILLIAM STRONG

(1870–1880)

BIRTH: May 6, 1808, Somers, Connecticut.

EDUCATION: Yale College, A.B., 1828; M.A., 1831.

OFFICIAL POSITIONS: U.S. representative, 1847–1851; Pennsylvania Supreme Court justice, 1857–1868.

SUPREME COURT SERVICE: nominated associate justice by President Ulysses S. Grant February 7, 1870, to replace Robert C. Grier, who had retired; confirmed by the Senate February 18,

1870, by a voice vote; took judicial oath March 14, 1870; retired December 14, 1880; replaced by William B. Woods, nominated by President Rutherford B. Hayes.

FAMILY: married Priscilla Lee Mallery, November 28, 1836; died 1844; two daughters, one son; married Rachel Davis Bull, a widow, November 22, 1849; two daughters, two sons.

DEATH: August 19, 1895, Lake Minnewaska, New York.

Strong was born into an old New England family that traced its ancestry in America back to 1630. He was the eldest of eleven children of Harriet Deming Strong and William Lighthouse Strong, a Presbyterian clergyman. After graduating from Yale in 1831, Strong taught school in New Jersey to pay his student debts. He studied with a local attorney before returning to Yale for a master's degree in law. He was admitted to the Connecticut and Pennsylvania bars in 1832. He began his practice in Reading, a thriving industrial town in the heart of the rich Pennsylvania-Dutch country. Since many of his clients did not speak English, Strong mastered the local German dialect and soon developed a thriving practice.

After establishing himself as a member of Reading's elite through his successful law career, Strong was elected to two terms in the U.S. House as an antislavery Democrat (1847–1851). In 1857 he was elected to a fifteen-year term on the Pennsylvania Supreme Court. With the coming of the Civil War, Strong joined the Republican Party.

In 1864, when Chief Justice Roger B. Taney died, Lincoln considered Strong as a potential replacement, but chose Salmon P. Chase instead. Strong resigned from the Pennsylvania court in 1868 to devote himself to making money, but in 1869 his name came up again for a Court vacancy, this time as an associate justice. Justice Grier had announced his retirement because of age and infirmity, and President Grant's advisers recommended Strong for the spot. There was, however, great sentiment in the country and the Congress for Edwin M. Stanton, the former secretary of war. Members of Congress circulated a petition for Stanton which was signed by a large majority of both houses; as a result Grant sent up Stanton's name instead of Strong's. Stanton was confirmed December 20, 1869, but died suddenly four days later, never having had a chance to participate in Court proceedings.

With Stanton's death, the way was clear for Strong's appointment. His selection was clouded by charges that Grant was trying to "pack" the Court to reverse a decision unfavorable to the Civil War legal tender acts.

During his Court service, Strong was known for his keen intellect and the forceful and articulate manner in which he presented his arguments. He was appointed a member of the electoral commission that in 1877 decided the disputed presidential election of 1876 in favor of Republican Rutherford B. Hayes. Strong supported Hayes on all the votes of the commission.

Strong retired from the Court at age seventy-two, while he was still in good health. He devoted himself to religious work, something he had begun while on the bench. From 1883 to 1895, he was president of the American Sunday School Union; he also served as vice president of the American Bible Society from 1871 to 1895, and was president of the American Tract Society from 1873 to 1895.

JOSEPH P. BRADLEY

(1870–1892)

BIRTH: March 14, 1813, Berne, New York.

EDUCATION: Rutgers University, graduated 1836.

OFFICIAL POSITIONS: none.

SUPREME COURT SERVICE: nominated associate justice by President Ulysses S. Grant February 7, 1870, succeeding James Wayne, who died in 1867 and whose seat remained vacant by act of Congress until 1870; confirmed by the Senate March 21, 1870, by a 46-9 vote; took judicial oath March 23, 1870; served until January 22, 1892; replaced by George Shiras Jr., nominated by President Benjamin Harrison.

FAMILY: married Mary Hornblower in 1844; seven children.

DEATH: January 22, 1892, Washington, D.C.

Bradley's life and career exemplify the traditional American "Horatio Alger" success story. The eldest of the twelve children of Philo and Mercy Gardiner Bradley, Joseph Bradley was raised on a small farm in penurious circumstances. He showed an early aptitude for learning and after going to a country school, began teaching at the age of sixteen. A local minister took an interest in him and sponsored his entrance to Rutgers University, where he was graduated in 1836.

Joseph P. Bradley

Bradley then studied law in the office of Archer Gifford, collector of the port of Newark, New Jersey, and passed the bar in 1839. His assiduous legal work soon paid off in a successful law practice. Specializing in patent, commercial, and corporate law, he became counsel for various railroads, the most important being the powerful Camden and Amboy Railroad. In 1844 he married Mary Hornblower, daughter of the chief justice of the New Jersey Supreme Court.

Bradley had a lifelong interest in mathematics and geology. He devised a perpetual calendar designed to determine the day of the week any date fell on throughout history. He also researched and wrote a treatise on the origins of the steam engine. Always an avid reader, Bradley had a library numbering sixteen thousand volumes. The middle initial "P" did not stand for a name; Bradley adopted its use some time during his early life, perhaps after his father's name, Philo.

Bradley was a Whig before the Civil War, and went to Washington, D.C., in the winter of 1860–1861 to lobby for a compromise settlement of issues between the North and South. Once the war broke out, however, he supported the Union cause and the Lincoln administration unreservedly. He ran a losing race for the U.S. House as a Unionist in 1862. After the war, he identified with the radical wing of the Republican Party and ran unsuccessfully as a Grant presidential elector in 1868.

Grant nominated Bradley for a seat on the Court in February 1870, the same day he chose William Strong for another Court vacancy. The choices raised a storm later because they made possible the reversal of a crucial Court decision, *Hepburn v. Griswold,* involving the validity of the Civil War legal tender acts.

The other major controversy of Bradley's Court career came in 1877 when he served on the electoral commission established to determine the outcome of the disputed presidential election of 1876. With the commission divided seven-to-seven along partisan lines, Supreme Court justice David Davis, an independent, was to have been the fifteenth and deciding member. Davis, however, withdrew from the commission because the Illinois legislature had chosen him to be a U.S. senator, and Bradley was substituted as the next least partisan justice. He voted with the Republicans on all the issues, awarding all twenty disputed electoral votes to Republican Rutherford B. Hayes, making him president by one vote. Although he was excoriated in the Democratic press, Bradley always contended that he voted on the basis of the legal and constitutional questions and not on a partisan basis.

The rest of Bradley's career on the Court was quieter. He was known for careful research and thoughtful analysis. He worked until almost the day he died, January 22, 1892.

WARD HUNT

(1873–1882)

BIRTH: June 14, 1810, Utica, New York.

EDUCATION: graduated with honors from Union College, 1828; attended Tapping Reeve law school.

Ward Hunt

OFFICIAL POSITIONS: member, New York Assembly, 1839; mayor of Utica, 1844; member, New York Court of Appeals, 1866–1869; New York State commissioner of appeals, 1869–1873.

SUPREME COURT SERVICE: nominated associate justice by President Ulysses S. Grant December 3, 1872, to replace Samuel Nelson, who had retired; confirmed by the Senate December 11, 1872, by a voice vote; took judicial oath January 9, 1873; retired January 27, 1882; replaced by Samuel Blatchford, nominated by President Chester A. Arthur.

FAMILY: married Mary Ann Savage, 1837; died 1845; three children; married Marie Taylor, 1853.

DEATH: March 24, 1886, Washington, D.C.

Hunt was born and made his career in the upstate New York city of Utica. His father, Montgomery Hunt, was a banker there and descended from early New England settlers. His mother was Elizabeth Stringham Hunt. After graduation from Union College, Hunt studied law, first at Tapping Reeve's academy in Litchfield, Connecticut, and then with a local Utica judge, Hiram Denio. After admission to the bar in 1831, he formed a partnership with Denio and built a lucrative practice.

While practicing law, Hunt became actively engaged in politics. He was elected to the New York Assembly as a Jacksonian Democrat in 1838, and served a one-year term. He served a year as mayor of Utica in 1844.

Hunt's ties with the Democratic Party began to loosen in the 1840s, when he opposed the annexation of Texas and the expansion of slavery. In 1848 he broke with the party to back Martin Van Buren's presidential bid on the antislavery Free Soil ticket.

In 1853 Hunt lost a bid for the state supreme court (the state court of original jurisdiction in New York) as a Democrat, partly because many Democrats refused to back him because of his disloyalty in 1848. With the slavery issue becoming more contentious, Hunt broke permanently with the Democrats and helped found the Republican Party in New York in 1855. During the process, he formed an alliance with fellow Utica native Roscoe Conkling, later the boss of New York Republican politics to whom Hunt was to owe his Supreme Court appointment.

In 1865 Hunt was elected to the New York Court of Appeals, the state's highest court, becoming its chief judge in 1868. Following a court reorganization in 1869, he became commissioner of appeals, a position he held until his Supreme Court appointment.

Several other more famous names were presented to President Grant for the vacancy created by Justice Nelson's retirement, but Conkling, Grant's close ally, prevailed on the president to choose Hunt. Hunt's service is considered one of the more inconspicuous in the Court's history, and he was responsible for few major opinions. In January 1879 he suffered a paralytic stroke that incapacitated him from further service, but he did not retire for another three years. The law then in effect granted a full pension only to justices who had reached the age of seventy and had served on the Court for ten years.

Finally, with the Court in danger of becoming bogged down because of Hunt's illness and the increasing age of several other justices, Congress passed a special law exempting Hunt from the terms of the pension law, granting him retirement at full pay if he would retire from the Court within thirty days of enactment of the exemption. He retired the day the law went into effect and died four years later.

Morrison Remick Waite

MORRISON REMICK WAITE

(1874–1888)

BIRTH: November 27, 1816, Lyme, Connecticut.

EDUCATION: graduated from Yale College, 1837.

OFFICIAL POSITIONS: Ohio state representative, 1850–1852; representative to the Geneva Arbitration, 1871; president of the Ohio Constitutional Convention, 1873–1874.

SUPREME COURT SERVICE: nominated chief justice by President Ulysses S. Grant January 19, 1874, to replace Salmon P. Chase, who had died; confirmed by the Senate January 21, 1874, by a 63-0 vote; took judicial oath March 4, 1874; served until March 23, 1888; replaced by Melville W. Fuller, nominated by President Grover Cleveland.

FAMILY: married his second cousin, Amelia C. Warner, September 21, 1840; five children.

DEATH: March 23, 1888, Washington, D.C.

Born into an old New England family, Waite counted among his forebears a chief justice of the Connecticut Supreme Court, a prominent Connecticut justice of the peace, and a Revolutionary War hero. He was the eldest son of Henry Matson Waite and Maria Selden Waite. He attended one of New England's most

prestigious institutions of higher learning, Yale College, graduating in the class of 1837, which included Samuel J. Tilden, later governor of New York and Democratic presidential nominee in 1876; William Evarts, later secretary of state under President Hayes (1877–1881); and Edwards Pierrepont, later attorney general under President Grant (1875–1876).

Seeing greater opportunities in the frontier, Waite moved to northwest Ohio in 1838 and studied law with Samuel D. Young, a prominent attorney in Maumee City. Waite was admitted to the bar in 1839 and practiced in Maumee City until 1850, when he and his family moved to the booming city of Toledo on Lake Erie. There he made a name for himself as a specialist in railroad law and developed a large business clientele.

Although Waite came to the Supreme Court as one of the least experienced and least known chief justices—he had never held a judicial position nor practiced before the Supreme Court before his appointment—he nevertheless had been involved in public affairs on and off for almost thirty years. He ran for Congress from the northwest Ohio district encompassing Toledo, as a Whig in 1846 and as an independent Republican in 1862, but lost both times. He was elected to the Ohio General Assembly in 1849, serving one term. Throughout the Civil War, Waite was strongly pro-Union and, with his speeches and writing, attempted to rally the population to the Union cause.

Waite was offered a seat on the Ohio Supreme Court in 1863 but declined in favor of an informal advisory role to the governor. The major break that brought Waite to the attention of the national administration headed by President Grant occurred in 1871 when he was appointed a member of the U.S. delegation to the Geneva Arbitration, which was to settle the *Alabama* claims case. The United States was demanding compensation from Great Britain for allowing Confederate vessels to be fitted out in British ports and operate from them during the Civil War. Waite's hard work during the arbitration proceedings and the final award to the United States of $15.5 million brought him a measure of national attention and praise.

When he returned to the United States, Waite was elected to the Ohio Constitutional Convention in 1873 and unanimously chosen its president. While he was presiding over the convention, he received word that President Grant had nominated him as chief justice. The selection came as a complete surprise to both the nation and to Waite. Waite was Grant's fourth choice for the post—the first refused to accept the job and the next two withdrew under threat of rejection by the Senate.

At first, Waite was treated with some condescension by his fellow Court members because of his inexperience, but he soon asserted his authority. He issued 872 opinions in fourteen years, a remarkably high number. Among the better known are *Minor v. Happersett* (1875), upholding a state's right to deny women the right to vote; *Reynolds v. United States* (1878), in which the Court said that the practice of polygamy was not protected by the First Amendment; and *Munn v. Illinois* (1877), in which the Court said that private property could be regulated for the public good. By the end of his service he received praise for his industriousness if not his imaginativeness.

Waite also made efforts to protect his post from being involved in national politics, as it had during the tenure of his predecessor, Salmon P. Chase. Waite refused to allow his name to be considered for the 1876 Republican presidential nomination. He also declined to make himself available for service on the electoral commission formed in 1877 to determine the outcome of the disputed 1876 presidential contest.

Even while fulfilling his duties on the Court, Waite assumed an additional load of civic responsibilities. He served as trustee of the Peabody Education Fund from 1874 to 1888 and was a member of the Yale Corporation from 1882 to 1888.

JOHN MARSHALL HARLAN I

(1877–1911)

BIRTH: June 1, 1833, Boyle County, Kentucky.

EDUCATION: Centre College, A.B., 1850; studied law at Transylvania University, 1851–1853.

OFFICIAL POSITIONS: adjutant general of Kentucky, 1851; judge, Franklin County, 1858; state attorney general, 1863–1867; member, Louisiana Reconstruction Commission, 1877; member, Bering Sea Tribunal of Arbitration, 1893.

SUPREME COURT SERVICE: nominated associate justice by President Rutherford B. Hayes October 17, 1877, to replace David Davis, who had resigned; confirmed by the Senate November 29, 1877, by a voice vote; took judicial oath December 10, 1877;

John Marshall Harlan I

served until October 14, 1911; replaced by Mahlon Pitney, nominated by President William Howard Taft.

FAMILY: married Malvina F. Shanklin, December 23, 1856; six children.

DEATH: October 14, 1911, Washington, D.C.

Harlan was born into a prominent Kentucky political family. Both his ancestors and his descendants played important roles in public life. His mother was Eliza Davenport Harlan. His father, James Harlan, an admirer of Henry Clay's patriotism and John Marshall's leadership on the Court, was a U.S. representative from Kentucky (1835–1839) and also served as attorney general and secretary of state of Kentucky. Justice Harlan's son, John Maynard Harlan (1864–1934), became a prominent Chicago lawyer and was the unsuccessful Republican nominee for mayor of Chicago in 1897 and 1905. His grandson and namesake John Marshall Harlan (1899–1971) was himself a Supreme Court justice (1955–1971).

Young Harlan studied law at Transylvania University, known as the "Harvard of the West," and then completed his legal education in his father's law office. He was admitted to the bar in 1853.

Harlan's only judicial experience before his appointment to the Supreme Court was his first office, Franklin County judge, from 1858 to 1859. After that one-year experience on the bench, Harlan turned to politics. He ran for the U.S. House in 1859 as the candidate of a coalition of anti-Democratic groups, including the Whigs and Know-Nothings, but lost by sixty-seven votes.

As a slaveholder and a member of the southern aristocracy, Harlan had difficulty following many of the nation's Whigs into the new Republican Party. In the presidential election of 1860, he backed the Constitutional Union Party, which stood for a compromise settlement of the increasingly bitter sectional conflict. When the Civil War came, however, Harlan chose to stay loyal to the Union and served as an officer in the northern forces.

When his father died in 1863, Harlan resigned his commission and ran successfully for attorney general of Kentucky on the pro-Union ticket. Although opposed to many policies of the Lincoln administration—he supported Democrat George B. McClellan against Lincoln in 1864—and believing the postwar constitutional amendments ending slavery and attempting to guarantee the rights of blacks were a mistake, Harlan eventually gravitated into the Republican Party and was its nominee for governor of Kentucky in 1875. He was also prominently mentioned as a Republican vice-presidential candidate in 1872.

The major impact Harlan had on the national political scene came in 1876, when he headed the Kentucky delegation to the Republican National Convention. At a critical moment during the deadlocked proceedings, Harlan swung the state's votes to Ohio governor Rutherford B. Hayes, helping to start a bandwagon moving in Hayes's direction. Hayes was nominated and elected and acknowledged his debt to Harlan by considering him for appointment as attorney general.

Although other political considerations intervened so that no cabinet post was open for Harlan, Hayes kept him in mind. The new president appointed him to head a commission to settle the rival claims of two factions for control of Louisiana in the spring of 1877. Then, when Supreme Court Justice Davis resigned to enter the U.S. Senate, Hayes nominated Harlan to fill the vacancy.

Harlan's tenure—almost thirty-four years—was one of the longest in the Court's history, being exceeded by only four other justices. During his service on the Court, he was called on by President Benjamin Harrison in 1892 to serve as the U.S. representative in the arbitration of the Bering Sea controversy with Great Britain.

He had a lively temperament, often delivering his opinions extemporaneously, in the style of an old-fashioned Kentucky stump speech. His vigorous attacks on several famous majority decisions earned him the title of "great dissenter." Most notable was his eloquent dissent in *Plessy v. Ferguson* (1896), the case that upheld Louisiana's "separate but equal" law with respect to public accommodations.

WILLIAM BURNHAM WOODS

(1881–1887)

BIRTH: August 3, 1824, Newark, Ohio.

EDUCATION: attended Western Reserve College for three years; graduated from Yale University, 1845.

William Burnham Woods

OFFICIAL POSITIONS: mayor of Newark, Ohio, 1856; Ohio state representative, 1858–1862, Speaker in 1858–1860 and minority leader in 1860–1862; chancellor, middle chancery district of Alabama, 1868–1869; U.S. circuit judge for the Fifth Circuit, 1869–1880.

SUPREME COURT SERVICE: nominated associate justice by President Rutherford B. Hayes December 15, 1880, to replace William Strong, who had retired; confirmed by the Senate December 21, 1880, by a 39-8 vote; took judicial oath January 5, 1881; served until May 14, 1887; replaced by Lucius Q. C. Lamar, nominated by President Grover Cleveland.

FAMILY: married Anne E. Warner, June 21, 1855; one son, one daughter.

DEATH: May 14, 1887, Washington, D.C.

Woods was born in Newark in the central part of Ohio. His father, Ezekiel Woods, was a farmer and merchant from Kentucky. His mother, Sarah Burnham Woods, came from New England. Following his education at Western Reserve University and Yale, Woods studied law with S.D. King, a prominent lawyer in his hometown of Newark. Woods passed the bar in 1847 and joined in partnership with his mentor, King, until the Civil War changed the course of his life.

Following a rise to local prominence through the practice of law in Newark, the county seat of Licking County, Ohio, Woods was chosen mayor of his native city in 1856. The following year, he was elected to the state legislature, and was chosen Speaker. An ardent Democrat, he opposed the rise of the newly established Republican Party. When the Democrats lost control of the state House in the 1859 elections, Woods became the minority leader.

At first, he opposed the war policy of President Lincoln, but as the conflict continued Woods became convinced of the necessity of victory over the South. He joined the Union army in 1862, seeing action in the battles of Shiloh and Vicksburg and marching with Sherman through Georgia. He rose to the rank of brigadier general in 1865 and was brevetted a major general just before being mustered out of service in February 1866. His brother, Charles Robert Woods (1827–1885), was a well-known officer in the Union army.

After the war, Woods settled in Alabama, engaging in cotton planting, investing in an iron works, and resuming the practice of law. His decision to reside in the South invited the charge of "carpetbagger," but his name was never linked to the corruption and profligacy associated with that term.

By this time, Woods had become a Republican and was elected chancellor of the middle chancery division of Alabama on his new party's ticket in 1868. When President Grant and the national Republican Party came to power the next year, Woods received an appointment as a circuit court judge for the Fifth Circuit (Florida, Georgia, Alabama, Mississippi, Louisiana, and Texas). Despite his northern origins and Union military background, he gained the respect of his southern neighbors and colleagues. To master his job he had to learn Louisiana law, which was based on the Napoleonic code. In 1877 Woods moved to Atlanta.

In 1880, when President Hayes was looking for a southerner to appoint to the Court, he decided on Woods. Hayes made a constant effort throughout his administration to bring southerners back into the federal government. Woods became the first Supreme Court justice appointed from a southern Confederate state since 1853.

Woods wrote 159 opinions during his six and a half years on the Court. He is best known for two. In *United States v. Harris* (1883) the Court struck down the federal statute known as the "Ku Klux Law," which was designed to protect blacks against terrorism in the South. In *Presser v. State of Illinois* (1886) the Court supported the right of state authorities alone to maintain militias and to determine the conditions for individuals to carry arms.

Woods was partially incapacitated by illness during the last months. The tradition of a new southern seat on the Court was continued when President Cleveland picked as Woods's successor Lucius Q. C. Lamar of Mississippi.

STANLEY MATTHEWS

(1881–1889)

BIRTH: July 21, 1824, Cincinnati, Ohio.

EDUCATION: Kenyon College, graduated with honors, 1840.

OFFICIAL POSITIONS: assistant prosecuting attorney, Hamilton County, 1845; clerk, Ohio House of Representatives, 1848–1849; judge, Hamilton County Court of Common Pleas, 1851–1853; member, Ohio Senate, 1855–1858; U.S. attorney for

Stanley Matthews

southern Ohio, 1858–1861; judge, Superior Court of Cincinnati, 1863–1865; counsel, Hayes-Tilden electoral commission, 1877; U.S. senator, 1877–1879.

SUPREME COURT SERVICE: nominated associate justice by President Rutherford B. Hayes January 26, 1881, to replace Noah Swayne, who had retired; no action by Senate; renominated by President James A. Garfield, March 14, 1881; confirmed by Senate May 12, 1881, by a 24-23 vote; took judicial oath May 17, 1881; served until March 22, 1889; replaced by David J. Brewer, nominated by President Benjamin Harrison.

FAMILY: married Mary Ann Black, February 1843; died 1885; eight children; married Mary Theaker, 1887.

DEATH: March 22, 1889, Washington, D.C.

Thomas Johnson and Isabella Brown Matthews's first child, born in Cincinnati in 1824, was named Thomas Stanley. He preferred to be called Stanley and dropped his first name when he became an adult. His maternal grandfather, Col. William Brown, was an Ohio pioneer who settled in Hamilton County in 1788. His father, a Virginian, served as Morrison professor of mathematics and natural history at Transylvania University in Lexington, Kentucky, for a number of years before becoming president of Cincinnati's Woodward High School, which his son attended.

Matthews entered Kenyon College as a junior and graduated in 1840. After reading law for two years in Cincinnati, he left Ohio because he was too young to take the bar exam there. He moved to Maury County, Tennessee, where he passed the bar at the age of eighteen and began his legal practice and the editorship of the *Tennessee Democrat,* a weekly paper supporting James K. Polk for president.

In 1844 Matthews married Mary Ann Black, the daughter of a prosperous Tennessee farmer. They had eight children. After her death in 1885 he married Mary Theaker of Washington, D.C.

Matthews left Tennessee when he was twenty and returned to Cincinnati. Within a year he was appointed assistant prosecuting attorney for Hamilton County and made editor of the *Cincinnati Morning Herald.* His strong stance against slavery won him election as clerk of the Ohio House of Representatives in 1848. Three years later he was elected one of three judges of the Hamilton County Court of Common Pleas. Matthews served in the Ohio Senate from 1855 to 1858 and as U.S. attorney for southern Ohio from 1858 to 1861, a post to which he was appointed by President Buchanan. Although personally opposed to slavery, as U.S. attorney Matthews upheld the Fugitive Slave Act and prosecuted W. B. Connelly, a reporter who had helped two slaves escape.

An officer in Ohio's Twenty-third and Fifty-first Regiment of volunteers, Matthews resigned his command in 1863 to accept election to the Cincinnati Superior Court. Two years later he returned to his private practice of railroad and corporate law. During Reconstruction Matthews was active in Republican politics as a presidential elector in 1864 and 1868, temporary chairman of the Liberal Republican Convention in 1872, and GOP congressional candidate in 1876. He was defeated in part because of the unpopularity of his prosecution of Connelly before the war.

Matthews campaigned for presidential candidate Rutherford B. Hayes and was one of the principal spokesmen on his behalf at the 1877 electoral commission. When Sen. John Sherman of Ohio was appointed secretary of Treasury in Hayes's cabinet, Matthews was elected by the legislature to fill Sherman's Senate seat. In January 1878 he introduced the "Matthews resolution" for the remonetization of silver.

Matthews's nomination to the Supreme Court by President Hayes upon the resignation of Justice Swayne of Ohio was not confirmed by the Senate. The appointment was criticized as merely a reward for Matthews's aid in Hayes's disputed victory over Samuel J. Tilden. The president was accused of cronyism—he and Matthews were fellow students at Kenyon College, lawyers in Cincinnati, and officers in the Twenty-third Ohio Infantry.

Matthews was renominated by President Garfield, Hayes's successor, but received continued opposition. Some feared Matthews's defense of large corporations and railroads during his legal practice would hinder his ability to dispense justice impartially on the Court. A vote on the nominee was finally taken on May 12, 1881; he was confirmed 24-23. One of his best-known opinions was that for a unanimous Court in *Yick Wo v. Hopkins* (1886). The Court struck down a city ordinance that, Matthews said, was fair on its face, but administered to discriminate against a particular group.

Matthews died in Washington, D.C., during his eighth year on the Court.

HORACE GRAY

(1882–1902)

BIRTH: March 24, 1828, Boston, Massachusetts.

EDUCATION: Harvard College, A.B., 1845; Harvard Law School, 1849.

OFFICIAL POSITIONS: reporter, Massachusetts Supreme Court, 1854–1864; associate justice, 1864–1873; chief justice, 1873–1881.

SUPREME COURT SERVICE: nominated associate justice by President Chester A. Arthur December 19, 1881, to replace Nathan Clifford, who had died; confirmed by Senate December 20, 1881, by a 51-5 vote; took judicial oath January 9, 1882; served until September 15, 1902; replaced by Oliver Wendell Holmes Jr., nominated by President Theodore Roosevelt.

FAMILY: married Jane Matthews, June 4, 1889.

DEATH: September 15, 1902, Nahant, Massachusetts.

Harriet Upham Gray gave birth to her first child March 24, 1828, and named him Horace after his father, a businessman in the iron industry. His grandfather, Lt.-Gov. William Gray, was the son of a poor New England shoemaker. He made his fortune as one of the first American merchants and shipowners to trade with Russia, India, and China. Horace Gray's uncle, Francis Calley Gray, was a Massachusetts legal historian and his younger half-brother, John Chipman Gray, a renowned professor at Harvard Law School.

Gray graduated from Harvard in 1845 and traveled abroad. Reversals in the family business forced him to return to Boston to choose a career. Although Gray's chief interest had always been natural history, he chose the law and studied industriously at Harvard Law School. Reading law with Judge John Lowell and clerking in the firm of Sohier and Welch completed Gray's preparation for the bar, which he passed in 1851. He practiced in Boston for thirteen years.

As a young Boston lawyer, Gray was a member of the Free Soil Party, which advocated free homesteads and opposed the expansion of slavery into the territories. Late in his life Gray married Jane Matthews, the daughter of Supreme Court Justice Stanley Matthews.

Gray's career in the Massachusetts judiciary began in 1854 as a reporter for the state supreme court. After six years as a reporter he ran for state attorney general but failed to obtain the nomination of the Republican Party, which he joined soon after its founding. Gov. John A. Andrews promoted Gray to the position of associate justice on August 23, 1864. Gray was thirty-six years old, the youngest appointee in the history of the Massachusetts Supreme Court. The death or resignation of senior justices elevated Gray to the chief justiceship in 1873.

During his seventeen years of service on the state court, Gray dissented only once and during his lifetime none of his decisions was overruled. Gray was respected for his careful historical research and knowledge of legal precedent. As chief justice he employed as his law clerk a bright young Harvard student named Louis D. Brandeis.

President James A. Garfield considered nominating Horace Gray to the Supreme Court after the death of Justice Nathan Clifford on July 25, 1881. Prior to making the appointment, however, Garfield died. His successor, Chester Alan Arthur, appointed Gray associate justice on December 19, 1881. The Senate, anxious to fill Clifford's seat, which had been vacant for five months, confirmed Arthur's nominee the following day by a 51-5 vote.

On the Court Gray became known as a strong nationalist, partly because of his opinion in *Juilliard v. Greenman* (1884). In this case the Court affirmed the right of the federal government to issue currency, even in the form of paper money. Gray is also known for his opinion in *United States v. Wong Kim Ark* (1898), in which the Court ruled that all Chinese born in the United States were citizens.

On July 9, 1902, after twenty years of service, the seventy-four-year-old justice informed President Theodore Roosevelt of his intention to retire. He died in September, before his retirement became effective, in Nahant, Massachusetts.

SAMUEL BLATCHFORD

(1882–1893)

BIRTH: March 9, 1820, New York City.

EDUCATION: Columbia College, A.B., 1837.

OFFICIAL POSITIONS: judge, Southern District of New York, 1867–1872; judge, Second Circuit of New York, 1872–1882.

SUPREME COURT SERVICE: nominated associate justice by President Chester Arthur March 13, 1882, to replace Ward Hunt, who had retired; confirmed by Senate March 27, 1882, by a voice

Samuel Blatchford

vote; took judicial oath April 3, 1882; served until July 7, 1893; replaced by Edward D. White, nominated by President Grover Cleveland.

FAMILY: married Caroline Appleton, December 17, 1844.

DEATH: July 7, 1893, Newport, Rhode Island.

Samuel Blatchford was the son of the former Julia Ann Mumford, daughter of a well-known publicist, and Richard M. Blatchford, counsel for the Bank of England and the Bank of the United States and a Whig in the New York legislature. His paternal grandfather, a British clergyman and the father of seventeen children, immigrated to Lansingburg, New York, in 1795.

At the age of thirteen, Blatchford entered Columbia College and four years later graduated at the top of his class. From 1837 to 1841 he prepared for the bar as the private secretary of his father's friend, New York governor William H. Seward. Blatchford passed the bar in 1842, practiced law with his father for three years, and joined Seward's law firm in Auburn, New York. In 1844 he married Caroline Appleton of Lowell, Massachusetts.

After nine years as a partner with Seward and Morgan, Blatchford and Seward's nephew established the New York City firm Blatchford, Seward, and Griswold. He declined a seat on the New York Supreme Court in 1855 to devote himself to his admiralty and international law practice.

During his legal career Blatchford reported extensively on federal court decisions. *Blatchford's Circuit Court Reports* (1852) included cases from New York's Second Circuit since 1845 and *Blatchford's and Howland's Reports* (1855) contributed to the extant knowledge of admiralty cases in the Southern District.

His extensive research into the state's judicial history as well as his expertise in admiralty law qualified Blatchford for the post of district judge for Southern New York to which he was appointed in 1867 and for his subsequent appointment to the Second Circuit Court in 1872.

After fifteen years in the federal judiciary, Blatchford was nominated to the Supreme Court by President Chester A. Arthur to fill the vacancy created by the retirement of Justice Ward Hunt of New York. Two other nominees had refused the post. Roscoe Conkling, a New York lawyer and politician, was the president's first choice. The Senate confirmed him, but Conkling declined. Arthur's second choice, Sen. George F. Edmunds of Vermont, also declined. Blatchford accepted, and the Senate readily confirmed him.

During Blatchford's tenure, a steady stream of admiralty and patent cases inundated the Court. His expertise in these areas proved invaluable, and Blatchford earned a reputation as a workhorse.

Blatchford served as trustee of Columbia University from 1867 until his death in 1893 in Newport, Rhode Island.

LUCIUS QUINTUS CINCINNATUS LAMAR

(1888–1893)

BIRTH: September 17, 1825, Eatonton, Georgia.

EDUCATION: Emory College, A.B., 1845.

OFFICIAL POSITIONS: member, Georgia House of Representatives, 1853; U.S. representative, 1857–1860, 1873–1877; U.S. senator, 1877–1885; secretary of interior, 1885–1888.

SUPREME COURT SERVICE: nominated associate justice by President Grover Cleveland December 6, 1887, to replace William Woods, who had died; confirmed by U.S. Senate January 16, 1888, by a 32-28 vote; took judicial oath January 18, 1888; served until January 23, 1893; replaced by Howell Edmunds Jackson, nominated by President Benjamin Harrison.

FAMILY: married Virginia Longstreet, July 15, 1847; died 1884; one son, three daughters; married Henrietta Dean Holt, January 5, 1887.

DEATH: January 23, 1893, Macon, Georgia.

Of French Huguenot ancestry, Lamar was born into the landed aristocracy of the pre-Civil War South in 1825. The fourth of Lucius Quintus Cincinnatus and Sarah Bird Lamar's eight children, he attended the Georgia Conference Manual Labor School, an institution that combined farm work with academics. Lamar graduated from Emory College in 1845 and two years later married its president's daughter, Virginia Longstreet.

Lamar read law in Macon, Georgia, passed the bar in 1847, and shortly thereafter followed his father-in-law to Oxford, Mississippi. The Reverend Augustus B. Longstreet became president of the University of Mississippi, and Lamar taught mathematics and practiced law. The two men were devoted to one another. Longstreet had lost his only son, and Lamar's father had committed suicide when Lamar was nine years old.

In 1852 Lamar returned to Georgia and established a successful legal practice in Covington. The following year he was elected to the state legislature. The dissolution of his law partnership and his failure to obtain the Democratic nomination to Congress prompted Lamar's return to Mississippi in 1855. He settled on a plantation and began practicing law and participating in state politics. A Jefferson Davis supporter and states' rights extremist, Lamar was elected to Congress in 1857 but resigned before his term expired. He personally drafted the state's ordinance of secession at the Mississippi Secession Convention of 1861.

Lamar served the Confederacy as colonel of the Eighteenth Mississippi Regiment until an attack of apoplexy, an ailment since childhood, forced him to retire from active duty in May 1862. As special envoy to Russia he attended diplomatic briefings in Europe in 1863, but never went to Russia. He spent the remainder of the war as a judge advocate for the Army of Northern Virginia.

When General Lee surrendered, Lamar was forty years old. Two of his brothers had died in battle; his friend Jefferson Davis was in prison; and he was in debt. Disqualified from public office, he returned to Mississippi to practice law and teach metaphysics at the university.

Although a partisan sectionalist before the war, Lamar publicly advocated reconciliation and cooperation during the difficult days of Reconstruction. Pardoned for his role in the Confederacy, he was reelected to Congress in 1872. His eulogy of Massachusetts Unionist Charles Sumner, heralded by the Boston *Advertiser* as the most significant and hopeful word from the South since the war, won Lamar national acclaim as the Great Pacificator. A representative of the new South, Lamar reached the Senate in 1877. His reputation as a politician guided by more than sectional interests was strengthened by his refusal to follow the directive of the Mississippi legislature to support a bill authorizing the free coinage of silver.

Anxious to demonstrate the South's desire to serve the entire nation, Lamar resigned from his second Senate term to accept a cabinet appointment. As Grover Cleveland's secretary of the interior, he directed the reclamation of thousands of acres of public lands and the establishment of a new Indian policy. While in office Lamar married Henrietta Dean Holt.

The death in 1887 of Justice William Woods, a Georgia Republican, created the first vacancy on the Supreme Court in six years. Although Lamar's appointment by President Cleveland was strongly opposed by many Republicans, Senators Stanford of California and Stewart of Nevada argued persuasively that Lamar's rejection would be interpreted as a ban against all Confederate veterans. The sixty-three-year-old nominee was narrowly confirmed by the Senate, 32-28.

Lamar served on the Court for five years, voting consistently to uphold the rights of business. In *Kidd v. Pearson* (1888), one of his best-known opinions, Lamar defined commerce to exclude manufacturing, which made it more difficult for Congress to regulate.

He died from apoplexy in his native Georgia on January 23, 1893.

MELVILLE WESTON FULLER

(1888–1910)

BIRTH: February 11, 1833, Augusta, Maine.

EDUCATION: Bowdoin College, A.B., 1853; studied at Harvard Law School and read law, 1853–1855.

OFFICIAL POSITIONS: member, Illinois House of Representatives, 1863–1864; member, Venezuela-British Guiana Border Commission, 1899; member, Permanent Court of Arbitration at the Hague, 1900–1910.

SUPREME COURT SERVICE: nominated chief justice by President Grover Cleveland April 30, 1888, to replace Morrison R. Waite, who had died; confirmed by Senate July 20, 1888, by a 41-20 vote; took judicial oath October 8, 1888; served until July 4, 1910; replaced as chief justice by Edward D. White, nominated by President William Howard Taft.

FAMILY: married Calista Ophelia Reynolds, June 28, 1858; died 1864; two daughters; married Mary Ellen Coolbaugh, May 30, 1866; eight children, seven of whom survived childhood.

DEATH: July 4, 1910, Sorrento, Maine.

Melville Weston Fuller was the second son of Frederick Augustus Fuller and Catherine Martin Weston. When he was two months old, his mother divorced his father on the grounds of adultery and took her sons to live with their grandfather, a judge on the Maine Supreme Court. Although she remarried when Fuller was eleven, he and his brother continued to live with Judge Weston in Augusta.

Melville Weston Fuller

Fuller attended Bowdoin College, where he was active in politics and a prolific writer of verse. He graduated Phi Beta Kappa in 1853 and, like his father and both his grandfathers, chose the legal profession. Fuller read law in Bangor and after six months at Harvard Law School passed the bar. He began to practice in Augusta at the age of twenty-two and the same year took an editorial position on *The Augusta Age,* a local Democratic paper owned by his father's brother. At the age of twenty-four he was elected president of the Common Council and appointed city solicitor.

Like many young men in the 1850s, Fuller was lured west by the promise of a better life on the frontier. He settled in the booming railroad town of Chicago and started practicing real estate and commercial law.

Fuller married twice. His first wife, Calista Ophelia Reynolds, died of tuberculosis six years after they were married. In 1866 he married Mary Ellen Coolbaugh, the daughter of the president of Chicago's Union National Bank. They had eight children, losing one during childhood. Fuller also had two daughters by his previous marriage.

In Chicago Fuller pursued a political as well as a legal career. He managed Stephen Douglas's senatorial campaign against Abraham Lincoln in 1858, attended the Illinois Constitutional Convention three years later, and served in the Illinois House of Representatives from 1863 to 1864.

Meanwhile, Fuller's legal practice and real estate investments on the North Shore prospered; his earnings by the 1880s reached an estimated $30,000 a year. Fuller acted as Chicago's counsel in litigation over the city's rights to Lake Michigan shore property. He also defended—in a nationally publicized case—the

Reverend Charles E. Cheney, rector of Christ Church in Chicago, who was accused of canonical disobedience by an ecclesiastical tribunal because of his "low church" practices. A high Episcopalian himself, Fuller opened the way for the founding of the Reformed Protestant Episcopal Church in America.

Grover Cleveland met Melville Fuller during a western presidential tour and was impressed by his "sound money," low-tariff economic philosophy. Although Fuller had previously declined the positions of civil service chairman and solicitor general in Cleveland's administration, he accepted the appointment of chief justice on April 30, 1888. The Republican Senate soon voiced their objections to the Democratic nominee. Midwesterners were wary of his ties with big corporations. Northerners accused him of anti-Union sentiment and circulated the pamphlet "The War Record of Melville Fuller," which was discredited only after Robert T. Lincoln, son of the former president, attested to his loyalty. The Philadelphia *Press* claimed that Cleveland's nominee was the most obscure man ever appointed chief justice.

Although Fuller had never held federal office, his professional credentials were sound and his appointment geographically expedient. Moreover, the Seventh Circuit, comprising Illinois, Indiana, and Wisconsin, had been unrepresented on the bench since Justice David Davis's resignation in 1877. Fuller was confirmed by the Senate, 41-20, nearly three months after his appointment.

During his Court tenure, Fuller served on the Venezuela-British Guiana Border Commission and the Permanent Court of Arbitration in the Hague. An efficient and courteous leader of the Court for twenty-two years, he was well respected by his colleagues on the bench, particularly by Justice Oliver Wendell Holmes Jr.

Fuller's best-known opinions are *Pollock v. Farmers' Loan and Trust Co.* and *United States v. E.C. Knight,* both decided in 1895. In *Pollock* the Court invalidated a general income tax. This decision was overturned by passage and ratification of the Sixteenth Amendment. In *E.C. Knight* the Court ruled that the Sherman Antitrust Act did not apply to manufacturing, even though the company in question refined more than 90 percent of the sugar sold in the United States.

When Cleveland returned to the presidency he offered Fuller the position of secretary of state, but Fuller declined, believing his acceptance would lower the dignity of the Court in the mind of the public. He died of heart failure at the age of seventy-seven at his summer home in Sorrento, Maine.

DAVID JOSIAH BREWER
(1890–1910)

BIRTH: June 20, 1837, Smyrna, Asia Minor.

EDUCATION: Wesleyan University, 1852–1853; Yale University, A.B., 1856; Albany Law School, LL.B., 1858.

OFFICIAL POSITIONS: commissioner, U.S. Circuit Court, Leavenworth, Kansas, 1861–1862; judge of probate and criminal

David Josiah Brewer

courts, Leavenworth County, 1863–1864; judge, First District of Kansas, 1865–1869; Leavenworth city attorney, 1869–1870; justice, Kansas Supreme Court, 1870–1884; judge, Eighth Federal Circuit, 1884–1889; president, Venezuela-British Guiana Border Commission, 1895.

SUPREME COURT SERVICE: nominated associate justice by President Benjamin Harrison December 4, 1889, to replace Stanley Matthews, who had died; confirmed by Senate, December 18, 1889, by a 53-11 vote; took judicial oath January 6, 1890; served until March 28, 1910; replaced by Charles Evans Hughes, nominated by President William Howard Taft.

FAMILY: married Louise R. Landon, October 3, 1861; died 1898; married Emma Miner Mott, June 5, 1901.

DEATH: March 28, 1910, Washington, D.C.

Brewer was born in the part of Asia Minor that is now Izmir, Turkey, where his father was a Congregational missionary. With his infant son and wife Emilia Field Brewer, the daughter of a New England clergyman, Reverend Josiah Brewer returned to America to become chaplain of St. Francis Prison, in Wethersfield, Connecticut. Young Brewer had three notable uncles: David Dudley Field, a jurist; Cyrus W. Field, a financier and promoter of the transatlantic telegraph cable; and Stephen J. Field, a Supreme Court justice from California (1863–1897).

Brewer attended Wesleyan University for two years before enrolling in his father's alma mater, Yale University, from which he graduated with honors in 1856. After reading law for a year in David Field's office, Brewer attended Albany Law School. He passed the New York bar in 1858 and, deciding to go west as his Uncle Stephen had done, the Kansas bar the following year.

When he was twenty-four Brewer married Louise R. Landon of Burlington, Vermont. She died after thirty-seven years of marriage, and Brewer, at the age of sixty-four, married Emma Miner Mott of Washington, D.C.

Brewer's first official position was administrative. He was appointed commissioner of the U.S. Circuit Court for the District of Kansas in Leavenworth in 1861. After two years he was nominated judge of probate and criminal courts. From 1865 to 1869 Brewer served as state district attorney and the following year as city attorney for Leavenworth until his election at the age of thirty-three to the Kansas Supreme Court. When Kansas passed a prohibition amendment in 1881, Judge Brewer sought to defend the rights of manufacturers against the confiscation of their property without compensation. Brewer's fourteen years of service on the state court ended in 1884 when he was appointed to the Eighth Federal Circuit by President Chester A. Arthur.

When Justice Stanley Matthews died, Republican senators Preston B. Plumb and John J. Ingalls of Kansas urged President Benjamin Harrison to appoint Brewer to the Supreme Court. During his consideration of the nomination, the president received a letter from Brewer recommending the appointment of Henry B. Brown, a Michigan district court judge who had been in his class at Yale. Impressed by these generous comments about Brown, Harrison nominated Brewer instead. Although his appointment was opposed by some prohibitionists, Brewer was confirmed by the Senate by a 53–11 vote.

During his twenty years on the Supreme Court, Brewer spoke out freely on the issues of the day. He advocated independence for the Philippines, suffrage for women, and residency rights for Chinese aliens in America. He may be best known for his opinion in *Muller v. Oregon* (1908), in which the Court decided that a state could limit women's working hours for health reasons.

Brewer was one of the original officers in the American Society of International Law and in 1895 presided over the congressional commission to oversee the disputed Venezuela-British Guiana boundary. A lecturer on American citizenship at Yale and corporate law at Columbian, now George Washington, University, Brewer also edited collections of the world's best orations and essays and wrote numerous books and articles. He was a lifelong member of the Congregational Church and active in missionary work.

Brewer died suddenly on March 28, 1910, in Washington, D.C.

HENRY BILLINGS BROWN

(1891–1906)

BIRTH: March 2, 1836, South Lee, Massachusetts.

EDUCATION: Yale University, A.B., 1856; studied briefly at Yale Law School and Harvard Law School.

OFFICIAL POSITIONS: U.S. deputy marshal for Detroit, 1861; assistant U.S. attorney, 1863–1868; circuit judge, Wayne County, Michigan, 1868; federal judge, Eastern District of Michigan, 1875–1890.

Henry Billings Brown

SUPREME COURT SERVICE: nominated associate justice by President Benjamin Harrison December 23, 1890, to replace Samuel Miller, who had died; confirmed by the Senate December 29, 1890, by a voice vote; took judicial oath January 5, 1891; retired May 28, 1906; replaced by William H. Moody, nominated by President Theodore Roosevelt.

FAMILY: married Caroline Pitts, July 1864; died 1901; married Josephine E. Tyler, June 25, 1904.

DEATH: September 4, 1913, Bronxville, New York.

The son of a prosperous merchant, Brown was born in a small town and raised in a middle-class Protestant home. His parents, Billings and Mary Tyler Brown prepared their son for the legal career they had chosen for him with a private secondary school and Yale University education. A moderately good student, he graduated from Yale in 1856 and went abroad for a year.

Brown began his legal education as a law clerk in Ellington, Connecticut. After a few months he returned to Yale to attend lectures at the law school. Brown also studied briefly at Harvard Law School.

In 1859 the twenty-three-year-old law student moved to Detroit. Within a year he finished his legal apprenticeship and passed the bar. Wealthy enough to hire a substitute, Brown escaped military service in the Civil War and immediately began his private practice.

He married Caroline Pitts, a member of a prosperous Detroit family, in 1864. She died in 1901. Three years later, at the age of sixty-seven, Brown married Josephine E. Tyler from Crosswicks, New Jersey, the widow of a lieutenant in the U.S. Navy.

In the early days of the Lincoln administration, Brown was appointed deputy U.S. marshal for Detroit, his first official position. After two years he was promoted to assistant U.S. attorney for the Eastern District of Michigan. Detroit was a busy Great Lakes port, and Brown became an expert in admiralty law.

Republican governor Henry H. Crapo appointed Brown interim circuit judge for Wayne County in 1868. Defeated in his bid for election to a full term, Brown returned to private practice and formed a partnership with John S. Newberry and Ashley Pond that specialized in shipping cases. After an unsuccessful congressional campaign in 1872, he resumed his practice until President Grant appointed him district judge of Eastern Michigan.

During his fourteen years as district judge, Brown won a national reputation as an authority on admiralty law. Howell E. Jackson, a judge on the Sixth Federal Circuit Court, urged President Benjamin Harrison to appoint Brown to the Supreme Court after the death of Justice Samuel Miller. Harrison had served with Jackson in the Senate and followed the advice of his former colleague. Nominated associate justice December 23, 1890, Brown was confirmed by the Senate within the week. Three years later Justice Brown returned Jackson's favor by recommending his appointment to the Court.

Brown's best-known opinion for the Court is *Plessy v. Ferguson* (1896), which established the legality of "separate but equal" facilities. This decision was overturned in 1954 by *Brown v. Board of Education.*

Despite an attack of neuritis in 1890 that blinded him in one eye, Brown served on the Court for fifteen years. At the age of seventy, severely handicapped by his impaired vision, he retired. He lived in semiretirement in Bronxville, New York, until his death on September 14, 1913, at the age of seventy-seven.

GEORGE SHIRAS JR.

(1892–1903)

BIRTH: January 26, 1832, Pittsburgh, Pennsylvania.

EDUCATION: Ohio University, 1849–1851; Yale University, B.A., 1853, honorary LL.D., 1883; studied law at Yale and privately; admitted to the bar in 1855.

OFFICIAL POSITIONS: none.

SUPREME COURT SERVICE: nominated associate justice by President Benjamin Harrison July 19, 1892, to replace Joseph P. Bradley, who had died; confirmed by the Senate July 26, 1892, by a voice vote; took judicial oath October 10, 1892; retired February 23, 1903; replaced by William R. Day, nominated by President Theodore Roosevelt.

FAMILY: married Lillie E. Kennedy, December 31, 1857; two sons.

DEATH: August 2, 1924, Pittsburgh, Pennsylvania.

George Shiras Jr. was born into a family that had been in America since the 1760s. His father, of Scotch ancestry, married a

George Shiras Jr.

Presbyterian minister's daughter, Eliza Herron, and was successful enough in the family brewery business to retire in his early thirties to a farm near the Ohio River. Here young Shiras, with his two brothers, spent his early years helping in his father's orchards.

In 1849 he left to attend Ohio University at Athens, Ohio, but after two years transferred to Yale where he graduated in 1853. He then read law at Yale (without graduating) and in the Pittsburgh law office of Judge Hopewell Hepburn before being admitted to the Allegheny County bar in November 1855. Before settling down in Pittsburgh in 1858 to become Judge Hepburn's law partner, he spent several years practicing law in Dubuque, Iowa, with his brother, Oliver Perry Shiras, who later became a federal district judge in northern Iowa.

On December 31, 1857, he married a Pittsburgh manufacturer's daughter, Lillie E. Kennedy, with whom he had two sons. Both offspring followed him into the law profession, and one, George Shiras III, served as U.S. representative from Pennsylvania in the Fifty-eighth Congress from 1903 to 1905.

Judge Hepburn died in 1862, and Shiras carried on a successful practice until his appointment to the Supreme Court in 1892. The years Shiras practiced law in Pittsburgh were those when the iron and steel, coal, and railroad magnates were amassing their fortunes. In more than thirty years as a lawyer in his native city, Shiras maintained a reputation of absolute integrity, of moderation in politics and manner, of restraint and good judgment, and of dignity and wit. Despite his financial success, Shiras remained modest, unostentatious, and respected by his peers. In 1883 he received an honorary LL.D. degree from Yale, the first alumnus to do so.

To the end he preferred quiet living among family and friends and his pursuits as a naturalist rather than seeking the limelight. His moderation seemed to be reflected in both his professional and personal lives.

Shiras's professional life was centered mainly in the private sector; he held no public offices until his Supreme Court appointment. In 1881 he refused the Pennsylvania state legislature's offer of the U.S. Senate nomination. A moderate Republican, he remained aloof from party politics and the state political machine. In 1888 he served as a presidential elector.

In July 1892, at the age of sixty, he was nominated by President Benjamin Harrison to be an associate justice of the Supreme Court to replace Joseph P. Bradley of New Jersey, who had died in January. Although Shiras had the support of the Pennsylvania bar, of the iron and steel interests (including Andrew Carnegie's personal support), and of U.S. representative John Dalzell, the U.S. senators who headed the state Republican machine vigorously opposed his appointment. President Harrison had sent Shiras's name to the Senate without first consulting Senators James Donald Cameron and Matthew S. Quay as senatorial courtesy dictated. However, when the press and prominent persons, including former Yale classmates, came to his defense and the opposition was shown to be purely political, the matter was resolved and he was confirmed unanimously.

Respected for his analytical powers and as a legal technician, Shiras exhibited a quiet competence and bore his share of the workload during his ten years on the Court. Although he wrote 259 majority opinions, he may be best remembered for switching his vote when *Pollock v. Farmers' Loan and Trust Co.* (1895) was reargued, a change that resulted in the decision that struck down a general income tax. The decision was overturned by ratification of the Sixteenth Amendment in 1913.

He retired, as he had earlier resolved to do, at the age of seventy-one, and lived out the years of his retirement in quiet comfort, shuttling between homes in Florida and the Lake Superior region of northern Michigan until his death in 1924 at age ninety-two.

HOWELL EDMUNDS JACKSON

(1893–1895)

BIRTH: April 8, 1832, Paris, Tennessee.

EDUCATION: West Tennessee College, A.B., 1850; University of Virginia, 1851–1852; Cumberland University, 1856.

OFFICIAL POSITIONS: custodian of sequestered property for Confederate states, 1861–1865; judge, Court of Arbitration for Western Tennessee, 1875–1879; state legislature, 1880; U.S. senator, 1881–1886; judge, Sixth Federal Circuit Court, 1886–1891, U.S. Circuit Court of Appeals, 1891–1893.

SUPREME COURT SERVICE: nominated associate justice by President Benjamin Harrison February 2, 1893, to replace Lucius Q. C. Lamar, who had died; confirmed by the Senate February 18, 1893, by a voice vote; took judicial oath March 4, 1893; served

Howell Edmunds Jackson

until August 8, 1895; replaced by Rufus W. Peckham, nominated by President Grover Cleveland.

FAMILY: married Sophia Malloy in 1859; died 1873; six children, two died in infancy; married Mary E. Harding in April 1874; three children.

DEATH: August 8, 1895, Nashville, Tennessee.

In 1830 Alexander Jackson left his medical practice in Virginia and moved to Paris, Tennessee, with his wife Mary Hurt Jackson, the daughter of a Baptist minister. Two years later their eldest son, Howell Edmunds, was born. Howell grew up in Jackson, Tennessee, and studied classics at West Tennessee College, graduating at the age of eighteen. He continued his education at the University of Virginia from 1851 to 1852. After completing a year in the law school of Cumberland University in Lebanon, Tennessee, Jackson passed the bar and began practicing law in his hometown.

In 1859 Jackson moved to Memphis and formed the partnership Currin and Jackson, specializing in corporate, railroad, and banking cases, and he married a local woman, Sophia Malloy. After her death in 1873, Jackson wed Mary E. Harding, the daughter of General W. G. Harding, the owner of a three-thousand-acre thoroughbred stock farm near Nashville. The western part of the property, West Meade, became Jackson's home, where he lived with his second wife, their three children, and the four surviving children of his previous marriage.

Although opposed to secession, Jackson served the Confederacy as the receiver of confiscated property and after the Civil War was twice appointed to the Court of Arbitration of Western Tennessee. His younger brother, William Hicks Jackson—the husband of General Harding's daughter Selene, who inherited the Belle Meade plantation—was a famous brigadier general in the Confederate Army, known by his men as the "red fox."

In 1880 Jackson, a respected lawyer and antirepudiation Tennessean during Reconstruction, was elected to the state House of Representatives. Because of factions and fighting within the Democratic Party over the state debt, he was elected the following year to the U.S. Senate. A Whig before the war, Jackson had been able to win the needed support of Republicans and "state-credit" Democrats. In the Senate he served on the Post Office, Pensions, Claims, and Judiciary Committees and loyally defended President Grover Cleveland's tariff measures.

In 1886, at the president's request, Jackson reluctantly resigned before his Senate term expired to fill a vacancy on the Sixth Judicial Federal Circuit. When the U.S. Circuit Court of Appeals was established in 1891, Jackson became its first presiding judge.

In the Senate chamber, Jackson had been seated next to Benjamin Harrison, a Republican senator from Indiana. As president, Harrison remembered his former colleague and friend and nominated him to the Supreme Court on February 2, 1893, to fill the vacancy created by the death of Justice Lucius Q. C. Lamar. Grover Cleveland had been elected to a second term in November, and the lame-duck president realized Senate confirmation of a Republican nominee was unlikely. With the strong backing of Justice Henry B. Brown, who had known him on the Sixth Federal Circuit, Jackson was confirmed by the Senate February 18, 1893.

One year after his appointment, Jackson contracted a severe case of tuberculosis. Hoping to recuperate in the West, he took a leave from the Court in October 1894. In May 1895, however, a full Court was needed to hear a reargument of the case testing the constitutionality of income taxes because the eight active justices had been evenly divided on the question. Unwell but unwilling to resign, Jackson returned to Washington. Three months after his dissent from the Court's decision ruling income taxes unconstitutional, Jackson succumbed to tuberculosis at his home in Nashville.

EDWARD DOUGLASS WHITE

(1894–1910, 1910–1921)

BIRTH: November 3, 1845, Lafourche Parish, Louisiana.

EDUCATION: Mount St. Mary's College, Emmitsburg, Maryland, 1856; Georgetown College (University), Washington, D.C., 1857–1861; studied law at University of Louisiana (Tulane) and with Edward Bermudez; admitted to the bar in 1868.

OFFICIAL POSITIONS: Louisiana state senator, 1874; associate justice, Louisiana Supreme Court, 1878–1880; U.S. senator, 1891–1894.

SUPREME COURT SERVICE: nominated associate justice by President Grover Cleveland February 19, 1894, to replace Samuel Blatchford, who had died; confirmed by the Senate February 19,

Edward Douglass White

1894, by a voice vote; took judicial oath March 12, 1894. Nominated chief justice of the United States by President William Howard Taft, December 12, 1910, to replace Melville Fuller, who had died; confirmed by the Senate December 12, 1910, by a voice vote; took judicial oath December 19, 1910; served until May 19, 1921; replaced as chief justice by former president Taft, appointed by President Warren G. Harding.

FAMILY: married Virginia Montgomery Kent, November 1894.
DEATH: May 19, 1921, in Washington, D.C.

White was born and raised in the deep South. His Irish-Catholic ancestors originally settled in Pennsylvania, but his peripatetic father, Edward White, moved his wife, Catherine Ringgold White, and their family farther into frontier country until they finally reached Louisiana. There they prospered on a large farm. White's father, a Whig, spent four years as a judge on the New Orleans city court and served five terms in the U.S. House of Representatives (1829–1834; 1839–1843) and one term as governor of Louisiana (1834–1838).

White received his early education at local Jesuit schools. In 1856 he enrolled for one year at Mount St. Mary's College in Emmitsburg, Maryland, and then entered Georgetown College (now University) in Washington, D.C. His academic career was interrupted by the Civil War. White left Georgetown in 1861, returned home, and joined the Confederate Army. He was captured in 1863 at Port Hudson, Louisiana, on the lower Mississippi River and spent the remainder of the war as a prisoner.

After the war, he began his legal career by reading law under the direction of Edward Bermudez, a successful New Orleans lawyer. Admitted to the Louisiana bar in 1868, White established a lucrative practice in New Orleans and became involved in Democratic politics. He was elected to the state Senate in 1874, and his support of Francis T. Nicholls in the 1877 gubernatorial election gained him, at age thirty-three, an appointment to the Louisiana Supreme Court the next year. Nicholls's successor, however, engineered White's removal from the court in 1880 through the passage of a law setting a minimum age requirement for justices that the youthful White failed to meet. Retribution came in 1888 when Nicholls was again elected governor and the state legislature gave one of Louisiana's U.S. Senate seats to Edward D. White.

White's short Senate career was marked by efforts to restrict the power of the federal government, except in matters protecting sugar farmers in the South from foreign competition. White himself farmed a large sugar-beet plantation. His unexpected appointment to the Supreme Court came in 1894. The beleaguered President Grover Cleveland had sought to replace Justice Samuel Blatchford, who had died July 7, 1893, with appointees from New York, Blatchford's home state. On two separate occasions, however, Cleveland's choices were rejected by the Senate in deference to the wishes of New York's senators, who were among his severest detractors. In frustration, Cleveland nominated White, who was approved immediately.

White's appointment to the chief justiceship was equally surprising. Chief Justice Melville Fuller died July 4, 1910, and President Taft, on December 12, 1910, elevated White to the post. He was the first associate justice successfully promoted to chief justice.

Historians tend to explain Taft's selection of White as chief justice in different ways. One side holds that Taft chose White, a southern Catholic, as a symbol of the president's desire to reduce lingering anti-South and anti-Catholic sentiments and to gain southern and Catholic support in the next election. The other, less sympathetic, view argues that Taft reckoned that he would have a better chance to become the chief justice himself (a lifelong ambition) after he left the White House if he appointed the aging White instead of the other contender for the post, the relatively young Charles Evans Hughes.

White's greatest legal contribution was his introduction of the "rule of reason" into the Court's interpretation of the Sherman Antitrust Act. The act outlawed all monopolies in restraint of trade, but White, from his earliest days on the Court, objected to a literal reading of the law; and he gradually persuaded his colleagues that only "unreasonable" restraints were prohibited.

In *Standard Oil v. United States* (1911) White wrote the opinion for a unanimous Court that broke up the oil company's monopoly on the grounds that it restricted free trade.

White wrote the opinion in *Guinn v. United States* (1915). In this case the Court struck down Oklahoma's "grandfather clause," a provision that exempted from a qualifying literacy test those whose ancestors had voted in the 1866 election. The law was intended to prevent blacks, who could not vote before ratification of the Fifteenth Amendment in 1870, from voting.

White was seventy-five years old and had been on the Court for twenty-six years, ten of them as chief justice, when he was taken ill May 13, 1921. He died May 19. His replacement was indeed William Howard Taft.

RUFUS WHEELER PECKHAM
(1896–1909)

BIRTH: November 8, 1838, Albany, New York.

EDUCATION: Albany Boys' Academy; studied privately in Philadelphia.

OFFICIAL POSITIONS: district attorney, Albany County, 1869–1872; corporation counsel, City of Albany, 1881–1883; judge, New York Supreme Court, 1883–1886; judge, New York Court of Appeals, 1886–1895.

SUPREME COURT SERVICE: nominated associate justice by President Grover Cleveland December 3, 1895, to replace Howell E. Jackson, who had died; confirmed by Senate December 8, 1895, by a voice vote; took judicial oath January 6, 1896; served until October 24, 1909; replaced by Horace Harmon Lurton, nominated by President William Howard Taft.

FAMILY: married Harriette M. Arnold, November 14, 1866; two sons.

DEATH: October 24, 1909, Altamont, New York.

Rufus Wheeler Peckham was the son of Rufus Wheeler Peckham Sr. and Isabella Lacey Peckham, both members of old New York families. His father and his older brother, Wheeler Hazard

Rufus Wheeler Peckham

Peckham, were both prominent lawyers and active in state Democratic politics. As district attorney for Albany County, the senior Rufus Peckham was elected to the U.S. House of Representatives. He also served on the state supreme court and the New York Court of Appeals. During a vacation in 1873, Judge Peckham was lost at sea.

Young Rufus Peckham was educated at the Albany Boys' Academy and studied privately in Philadelphia. After a year in Europe with his brother, Rufus returned to Albany to read law in his father's firm, Peckham and Tremain. He joined the firm at the age of twenty-seven and in 1866 married Harriette M. Arnold, the daughter of a wealthy New York merchant.

Wheeler Peckham, a one-time president of the New York Bar Association, served as special counsel in the prosecution of the Tweed Ring in the city's political corruption trials.

Like his father before him, Peckham began his public career as district attorney for Albany County. In this post he gained recognition for his skillful prosecution and conviction of criminals involved in railroad express-car robberies. First as county attorney and then as corporation counsel for the city of Albany, 1881–1883, Peckham participated actively in upstate New York politics and became well acquainted with Gov. Grover Cleveland. Peckham's political connections, his legal reputation, and his respected name helped win him election to the state supreme court in 1883 and to the New York Court of Appeals three years later.

After Justice Howell E. Jackson's death, President Grover Cleveland nominated his friend associate justice of the Supreme Court. Peckham was confirmed without objection, although his brother's nomination two years earlier to fill Justice Blatchford's seat had been rejected due to political infighting. (Sen. David B. Hill, D-N.Y., Wheeler's chief opponent, also succeeded in blocking the confirmation of William B. Hornblower, President Cleveland's earlier choice for the Blatchford seat.)

During his thirteen years on the bench, Peckham vigorously upheld the individual's right to contract and favored state regulation only when interstate commerce was directly and substantially affected. He wrote the Court's opinion in *Lochner v. New York* (1905), which struck down a state law limiting the hours bakers could work. Three years later, however, he voted to uphold an Oregon law regulating women's work hours.

Peckham died in Altamont, New York, on October 24, 1909, at the age of seventy.

JOSEPH McKENNA

(1898–1925)

BIRTH: August 10, 1843, Philadelphia, Pennsylvania.

EDUCATION: Benicia Collegiate Institute, graduated in 1864; admitted to the bar in 1865.

OFFICIAL POSITIONS: district attorney, Solano County, California, 1866–1870; member, California Assembly, 1875–1876; U.S. representative, 1885–1892; judge, U.S. Ninth Judicial Circuit, 1892–1897; U.S. attorney general, 1897.

Joseph McKenna

SUPREME COURT SERVICE: nominated associate justice by President William McKinley December 16, 1897, to replace Stephen J. Field, who had retired; confirmed by Senate January 21, 1898, by a voice vote; took judicial oath January 26, 1898; retired January 5, 1925; replaced by Harlan F. Stone, nominated by President Calvin Coolidge.

FAMILY: married Amanda Frances Bornemann, June 10, 1869; three daughters, one son.

DEATH: November 21, 1926, Washington, D.C.

Joseph McKenna, the first child of Irish immigrants John and Mary Ann Johnson McKenna, was born in the Irish quarter of Philadelphia. The growing popularity in Philadelphia of the staunchly anti-immigrant, anti-Catholic American Party contributed to the failure of John McKenna's bakery business. Hoping for success on the frontier, he took his family west, traveling third class on a Panamanian steamship to Benicia, California. In this small coastal town he succeeded in obtaining a better life for his family. He died when Joseph was fifteen years old.

Young McKenna attended public schools, graduated from the law department of the Benicia Collegiate Institute in 1864, and the following year was admitted to the California bar. The Republicans were becoming increasingly powerful in California and in 1861 elected railroad pioneer Leland Stanford the state's first Republican governor. McKenna switched his membership to the Republican Party, became acquainted with Stanford, and participated actively in political affairs. He was elected district attorney for Solano County in 1866. Three years later he married Amanda Frances Bornemann of San Francisco, his wife for fifty-five years.

For the ten years following his election to the state legislature in 1875, McKenna's political future was uphill. He was an unsuccessful candidate for the speakership of the California Assembly, from which he resigned after one term. Although twice nominated by his party for the U.S. Congress, he suffered two defeats prior to his election in 1885.

During four terms in the House, McKenna won passage of legislation extending railroad land grants, improving port facilities, and restricting the freedoms of Chinese workers. Considering his own immigrant parentage, McKenna's support for the latter is surprising, despite its popularity with his constituents.

As a member of the House Ways and Means Committee, McKenna became friends with its chairman, William McKinley. Another political ally in Congress was Sen. Leland Stanford. On Stanford's recommendation, President Benjamin Harrison appointed McKenna to California's Ninth Judicial Circuit. A circuit court judge for five years, McKenna was then promoted to attorney general. Within a year of assuming the post, he was nominated to the Supreme Court. When Justice Field resigned, President McKinley chose McKenna, another Californian and a trusted friend, to fill the vacancy. Over the objections of many to McKenna's ties with Stanford and western railroad interests, the Senate confirmed the appointment.

Realizing his own need for further legal training, McKenna studied for a few months at Columbia University Law School before taking office. Nevertheless, his early years on the bench proved difficult because of his lack of knowledge of the law and his inability to construct an opinion that expressed the convictions of his colleagues.

Scholars have pointed to McKenna's lack of judicial consistency, but in one area—the broad sweep of the Commerce Clause—he was consistent. In 1903 McKenna joined the majority in *Champion v. Ames,* a 5-4 decision upholding a federal law prohibiting the distribution of lottery tickets through the mail. In *Hipolite Egg Company v. United States* (1911) McKenna spoke for a unanimous Court in upholding the constitutionality of the Pure Food and Drug Act. In *Hoke v. United States* (1913) McKenna wrote the unanimous opinion upholding the Mann Act, which prohibited the interstate transportation of women for immoral purposes. All three of these cases were based on the federal government's ability to regulate interstate commerce.

McKenna served on the Court for twenty-six years. He was eighty-one years old and in failing health when Chief Justice Taft and the other members of the Court finally persuaded him to step down. The following year he died in his sleep at his home in Washington, D.C.

OLIVER WENDELL HOLMES JR.

(1902–1932)

BIRTH: March 8, 1841, Boston, Massachusetts.

EDUCATION: Harvard College, A.B., 1861; LL.B., 1866.

OFFICIAL POSITIONS: associate justice, Massachusetts Supreme Court, 1882–1899; chief justice, 1899–1902.

Oliver Wendell Holmes Jr.

SUPREME COURT SERVICE: nominated associate justice by President Theodore Roosevelt December 2, 1902, to replace Horace Gray, who had died; confirmed by Senate December 4, 1902, by a voice vote; took judicial oath December 8, 1902; retired January 12, 1932, replaced by Benjamin N. Cardozo, nominated by President Herbert Hoover.

FAMILY: married Fanny Bowdich Dixwell, June 17, 1872.

DEATH: March 6, 1935; Washington, D.C.

Oliver Wendell Holmes Jr.'s father was a professor of anatomy at Harvard Medical School as well as a poet, essayist, and novelist in the New England literary circle that included Longfellow, Emerson, Lowell, and Whittier. Dr. Holmes's wife, Amelia Lee Jackson Holmes, was the third daughter of Justice Charles Jackson of the Massachusetts Supreme Court. Young Holmes attended a private school in Cambridge run by Epes Sargent Dixwell and received his undergraduate education at Harvard, graduating as class poet in 1861 as had his father thirty-two years before him.

Commissioned after graduation a second lieutenant in the Massachusetts Twentieth Volunteers, known as the Harvard Regiment, Holmes was wounded in three Civil War battles in three years. He was mustered out of the Army July 17, 1864, with the rank of captain in recognition of his bravery and gallant service. After the war, Holmes returned to Harvard to study law despite his father's conviction that "a lawyer can't be a great man."

He was admitted to the Massachusetts bar in 1867 and practiced in Boston for fifteen years, beginning with the firm of Chandler, Shattuck, and Thayer and later forming with Shattuck his own partnership. In 1872 Holmes married Fanny Bowdich Dixwell, the daughter of his former schoolmaster and a friend since childhood. They were married fifty-seven years.

During his legal career Holmes taught constitutional law at his alma mater, edited the *American Law Review,* and lectured on common law at the Lowell Institute. His twelve lectures were compiled in a volume entitled *The Common Law* and published shortly before his fortieth birthday after more than ten years of work. The London *Spectator* heralded Holmes's treatise as the most original work of legal speculation in decades. *The Common Law* was translated into German, Italian, and French.

In 1882 the governor of Massachusetts appointed Holmes—then a full professor at the Harvard Law School in a chair established by Boston lawyer Louis D. Brandeis—an associate justice of the Massachusetts Supreme Court. Holmes served on the state court for twenty years, the last three as chief justice, and wrote more than one thousand opinions, many of them involving labor disputes. Holmes's progressive labor views, criticized by railroad and corporate interests, were favorably considered by President Theodore Roosevelt during his search in 1902 for someone to fill the "Massachusetts seat" on the Supreme Court, vacated by the death of Horace Gray. Convinced of his compatibility with the administration's national policies, Roosevelt nominated Holmes, who was sixty-one years old. The Senate confirmed him without objection two days later.

Holmes's twenty-nine years of service on the Supreme Court spanned the tenures of Chief Justices Fuller, White, Taft, and Hughes and the administrations of Presidents Roosevelt, Taft, Wilson, Harding, Coolidge, and Hoover. For twenty-five years he never missed a session and walked daily the two and a half miles from his home to the Court. Like Justice Brandeis, Holmes voluntarily paid an income tax despite the majority's ruling that exempted federal judges. Unlike the idealistic and often moralistic Brandeis, with whom he is frequently compared, Holmes was pragmatic, approaching each case on its own set of facts without a preconceived notion of the proper result.

Although a lifelong Republican, on the Court Holmes did not fulfill Roosevelt's expectations as a loyal party man. Shortly after his appointment, he dissented from the Court's decision in 1904 to break up the railroad trust of the Northern Securities Company; his opinion surprised the nation and angered the president.

In his years on the Court, Holmes wrote 873 opinions and, although he is known as one of the great dissenters, he wrote proportionately fewer dissents than many other justices. His reputation rests on the clear writing and forcefulness of his dissents. In 1905 Holmes dissented in *Lochner v. New York.* Holmes argued for the right of a state to regulate working hours, in this case for bakers, some of whom were required to work one hundred hours per week.

Holmes is also known for the "clear and present danger" test for seditious speech in *Schenck v. United States* (1919). This unanimous decision upheld the conviction of a Socialist Party member who printed and distributed antidraft pamphlets at a time when the country was preparing for war. However, in *Abrams v. United States,* decided seven months later, Holmes dissented. In this case, the offensive material was a leaflet protesting American intervention in Russia. Holmes declared that the First Amendment protected speech unless it posed such a threat that an immediate response was necessary.

At the suggestion of Chief Justice Hughes and his colleagues on the bench, Holmes retired on January 12, 1932, at the age of ninety. A widower since 1929, he continued to spend his winters in Washington, D.C., and his summers in Beverly Farms, Massachusetts. He died at his Washington home two days before his ninety-fourth birthday.

WILLIAM RUFUS DAY

(1903–1922)

BIRTH: April 17, 1849, Ravenna, Ohio.

EDUCATION: University of Michigan, A.B., 1870; University of Michigan Law School, 1871–1872.

OFFICIAL POSITIONS: judge, Court of Common Pleas, Canton, Ohio, 1886; first assistant U.S. secretary of state, 1897–1898; U.S. secretary of state, 1898; member, United States delegation, Paris Peace Conference, 1898–1899; judge, U.S. Court of Appeals for the Sixth Circuit, 1899–1903; umpire, Mixed Claims Commission, 1922–1923.

SUPREME COURT SERVICE: nominated associate justice by President Theodore Roosevelt February 19, 1903, to replace

William Rufus Day

George Shiras Jr., who had resigned; confirmed by the Senate February 23, 1903, by a voice vote; took judicial oath March 2, 1903; resigned November 13, 1922; replaced by Pierce Butler, nominated by President Warren G. Harding.

FAMILY: married Mary Elizabeth Schaefer, 1875; four sons.
DEATH: July 9, 1923, Mackinac Island, Michigan.

William Day, the son of Luther Day and Emily Spalding Day, was raised in a family with a strong judicial background. His maternal great-grandfather, Zephania Swift, was the chief justice of Connecticut; his grandfather, Rufus Spalding, was a member of the Ohio Supreme Court; his father, Luther Day, served as chief justice of Ohio. It seemed predetermined, then, that William Day, after receiving his A.B. from the University of Michigan in 1870, should enter the law school at his alma mater, which he did after studying law for one year in his hometown of Ravenna, Ohio. He attended law school for a year at the University of Michigan. He returned home to Ohio in 1872 and set up a law practice in Canton, about twenty-five miles from Ravenna.

Day established a solid reputation and a lucrative law practice in Canton, where he also became a good friend of another young attorney, William McKinley. Day and McKinley traveled in the same Republican circles, and McKinley soon came to rely on Day for help and counsel.

While McKinley's political fortunes took him to the U.S. House of Representatives (1877–1884; 1885–1891) and the governor's mansion (1892–1896), Day remained in Canton, married a local woman, and raised a family of four boys.

Day's popularity was so great in the Canton area that he was elected in 1886 judge of the Court of Common Pleas after receiving both the Democratic and Republican nominations. Three years later he was appointed to the U.S. District Court by President Benjamin Harrison. However, his frail health prevented him from serving in that position.

When his friend McKinley was elected president, Day was named first assistant secretary of state. His job was to assist the aged and failing secretary of state, John Sherman, in performing the country's diplomatic chores. After the war between the United States and Spain over Cuba officially began April 11, 1898, Sherman was eased out of the State Department and replaced by Day, who had been closely involved in the events leading up to the outbreak of hostilities. Day served as secretary of state only from April 26, 1898, to August 26; during his brief tenure, however, he oversaw the delicate negotiations between the United States and Spain and was able to obtain assurances of neutrality and goodwill from the countries of Western Europe.

In August McKinley named Day to the U.S. commission to negotiate the terms of the peace with Spain. Day is credited with the plan to pay Spain $20 million for the Philippines instead of outright annexation.

His work on the peace commission finished, Day was named by McKinley in 1899 to the U.S. Court of Appeals for the Sixth Circuit, located in Cincinnati. Day enjoyed his four years on the bench—it was close to home, and his colleagues

included William Howard Taft, the future president and Supreme Court chief justice, and Horace H. Lurton, a future associate justice.

Day was deeply shocked by the 1901 assassination of President McKinley. As a tribute to his longtime friend and patron, he began to mark McKinley's birthday with an annual memorial service. At one of these services, on January 29, 1903, Day first learned that McKinley's successor, Theodore Roosevelt, intended to name him to the Supreme Court. After Day introduced the president to the audience, Roosevelt surprised the crowd by referring to Day as "Mr. Justice Day." His appointment was announced officially February 19, 1903.

Day wrote the majority opinion in *Hammer v. Dagenhart* (1918), in which the Court overturned a federal law prohibiting the interstate shipment of goods made by child labor. However, he had ruled in a 1916 case that the federal government could regulate interstate commerce when moral and health hazards were involved.

Day retired from the Court November 13, 1922. He accepted an appointment from President Warren G. Harding to serve as an umpire on the Mixed Claims Commission, a board established to settle claims remaining from World War I. Day worked on the commission only until May 1923. He died July 9, 1923, at his summer home on Mackinac Island, Michigan.

WILLIAM HENRY MOODY

(1906–1910)

BIRTH: December 23, 1853, Newbury, Massachusetts.
EDUCATION: Harvard College, A.B., cum laude, 1876; Harvard Law School, 1876–1877; read law with Richard Henry Dana.

William Henry Moody

OFFICIAL POSITIONS: city solicitor, Haverhill, 1888–1890; district attorney, Eastern District of Massachusetts, 1890–1895; U.S. representative, 1895–1902; secretary of the Navy, 1902–1904; U.S. attorney general, 1904–1906.

SUPREME COURT SERVICE: nominated associate justice by President Theodore Roosevelt December 3, 1906, to replace Henry B. Brown, who had retired; confirmed by the Senate December 12, 1906, by a voice vote; took judicial oath December 17, 1906; retired November 20, 1910; replaced by Joseph R. Lamar, nominated by President William Howard Taft.

FAMILY: unmarried.

DEATH: July 2, 1917, Haverhill, Massachusetts.

William Moody was born to Henry L. Moody and Melissa A. Emerson Moody in a house that had been his family's home for more than two hundred years. He was raised in nearby Danvers, attended Phillips Academy in Andover, and, after a poor start at Harvard, graduated with honors in 1876. In the fall of that year he entered the Harvard School of Law but left in January 1877. To prepare for his entry to the bar he began an eighteen-month course of study in the law offices of Boston lawyer and author Richard Henry Dana. Although three years of study were normally required before an applicant was allowed to take the oral examination, an exception was made in Moody's case, and he passed easily.

Moody left Boston after his admittance to the bar in 1878 and established a private practice in Haverhill, Massachusetts. His clientele soon included most of the industries and manufacturers in the region. As his prestige grew, Moody became involved in Republican politics and in 1888 began his public career as city solicitor for Haverhill.

Two years later he was named district attorney for the Eastern District of Massachusetts. His most famous case (and that spread his name across the country) was the prosecution of Lizzie Borden, the alleged ax murderer of Fall River. Fall River was beyond Moody's venue, but he was called in to assist with the 1892 case, in which the defendant was acquitted by a sympathetic jury. Despite his loss, his adept handling of the state's case brought him to the attention of Massachusetts Republican Party leaders, notably Sen. Henry Cabot Lodge (1893–1924).

In 1895 Moody won a special election to fill the U.S. House seat in Massachusetts's Sixth Congressional District vacated by the death of Rep. William Cogswell (1887–1895). The same year, Moody met New York police commissioner Theodore Roosevelt, and the two men became close friends over the next few years.

In the House, Moody was respected for his mastery of details and facts. When Roosevelt became president after the assassination of William McKinley, Moody was one of the new president's first choices for his cabinet. As secretary of the Navy, Moody won increased congressional appropriations to enlarge and improve the U.S. fleet, which met with the hearty approval of President Roosevelt. He said of Moody, "We have never had as good a Secretary of the Navy."

Moody's next assignment in the Roosevelt administration was to replace Attorney General Philander Knox in 1904 and to continue the administration's prosecution of trusts. A dedicated progressive Republican, Moody personally argued for the government in the successful suit against the beef trust, *Swift and Company v. United States* (1905).

Moody's appointment to the Supreme Court was not without controversy; he was thought to be too radical. Opponents pointed to his eager prosecution of trusts and his enthusiasm for progressive reforms. Criticism notwithstanding, Moody was confirmed by the Senate December 12, 1906, to replace Justice Henry B. Brown.

Moody's Supreme Court career was shortened by the onslaught of a crippling form of arthritis that forced his retirement in 1910. In his brief career he wrote sixty-seven opinions, including five dissents. An important dissent came in *First Employers' Liability Case* (1908). Moody argued to uphold federal legislation designed to make common carriers engaged in interstate commerce liable for deaths and injuries suffered by their employees on the job. Moody is also known for his opinion in *Twining v. New Jersey* (1908). In this case the Court refused to extend the Fifth Amendment protection against self-incrimination to state defendants.

Moody left the Court November 20, 1910. He returned home to Haverhill, where he died July 2, 1917.

HORACE HARMON LURTON

(1910–1914)

BIRTH: February 26, 1844, Newport, Kentucky.

EDUCATION: Douglas University (University of Chicago), 1860; Cumberland Law School, L.B., 1867.

OFFICIAL POSITIONS: chancellor in equity, 1875–1878; judge, Tennessee Supreme Court, 1886–1893; judge, U.S. Court of Appeals for the Sixth Circuit, 1893–1909.

SUPREME COURT SERVICE: nominated associate justice by President William Howard Taft December 13, 1909, to replace Rufus W. Peckham, who had died; confirmed by Senate December 20, 1909, by a voice vote; took judicial oath January 3, 1910; served until July 12, 1914; replaced by James C. McReynolds, nominated by President Woodrow Wilson.

FAMILY: married Mary Francis Owen, September 1867; three sons, two daughters.

DEATH: July 12, 1914, Atlantic City, New Jersey.

Horace Harmon Lurton was born the same year Democrat James K. Polk defeated Whig Henry Clay for the presidency over the issue of annexation of the Republic of Texas. His parents, Sarah Ann Harmon Lurton and Dr. Lycurgus Leonidas Lurton, a physician who later became an Episcopal minister, moved the family to Clarksville, Tennessee, a town of fifteen thousand on the Cumberland River. When Lurton was sixteen the family moved again, this time to Chicago where he attended Douglas University until the outbreak of the Civil War.

Lurton served in the Confederate Army in both the Kentucky and Tennessee infantries before his capture during General

Horace Harmon Lurton

Grant's siege of Fort Donelson. He escaped from Camp Chase in Columbus, Ohio, and joined General John Hunt Morgan's daredevil marauders, famous throughout the South for their surprise attacks on Union railroads, bridges, and telegraph stations. Lurton was captured again in July 1863. During his incarceration in one of the northernmost camps on Lake Erie he contracted tuberculosis. Fearing for her son's life, Sarah Ann Lurton went to Washington and succeeded in persuading President Lincoln to let her son return with her to Clarksville before the end of the war.

After his recuperation at home, Lurton attended law school at Cumberland University in Lebanon, Tennessee. He graduated in 1867, married Mary Francis Owen, the daughter of a local physician, and returned to Clarksville to practice law. Through his partner, James A. Bailey, who was elected to the U.S. Senate in 1877, Lurton became involved in Democratic politics. He was appointed by the governor to the Sixth Chancery Division of Tennessee, becoming at thirty-one the youngest chancellor in the state's history.

In 1878 Lurton returned to the practice of law in an eight-year partnership with ex-chancellor Charles G. Smith. During this period Lurton became a prosperous and well-respected Clarksville citizen as president of the Farmers' and Merchants' National Bank, vestryman of Trinity Episcopal Church, and trustee of the University of the South.

Lurton was elected to the Tennessee Supreme Court in 1886 and served for seven years. Immediately following his promotion to chief justice, he was appointed to the U.S. Court of Appeals for the Sixth Circuit by President Grover Cleveland. William Howard Taft was the presiding judge. Lurton succeeded him in office when Taft left to become governor general of the Philippines. In addition to his judicial responsibilities, Lurton taught constitutional law at Vanderbilt University from 1898 to 1905 and served as dean the following four years.

Close personal friendship as well as respect for his judicial ability prompted President Taft to make Lurton, then sixty-five, his first Supreme Court appointment. "There was nothing I had so much at heart in my whole administration," Taft said of his choice.

Lurton took a symbolic train ride northward to assume his new responsibilities. Explaining the personal significance of the trip he stated, "I felt that in appointing me, President Taft, aside from manifestations of his friendship, had a kindly heart for the South; that he wished to draw the South to him with cords of affection. So, being a southerner myself, I determined to go to Washington through the South—every foot of the way."

Lurton served only five years on the Court. He died of a heart attack July 12, 1914, in Atlantic City, New Jersey.

CHARLES EVANS HUGHES
(1910–1916, 1930–1941)

BIRTH: April 11, 1862, Glens Falls, New York.

EDUCATION: Madison College (now Colgate University), 1876–1878; Brown University, A.B., 1881, A.M., 1884; Columbia Law School, LL.B., 1884.

Charles Evans Hughes

OFFICIAL POSITIONS: special counsel, New York state investigating commissions, 1905–1906; governor of New York, 1907–1910; U.S. secretary of state, 1921–1925; U.S. delegate, Washington Armament Conference, 1921; U.S. member, Permanent Court of Arbitration, 1926–1930; judge, Permanent Court of International Justice, 1928–1930.

SUPREME COURT SERVICE: nominated associate justice by President William Howard Taft April 25, 1910, to replace David J. Brewer, who had died; confirmed by Senate May 2, 1910, by a voice vote; took judicial oath October 10, 1910; resigned June 10, 1916, to become Republican presidential candidate; replaced by John H. Clarke, nominated by President Woodrow Wilson; nominated chief justice February 3, 1930, by President Herbert Hoover, to replace Chief Justice Taft, who had retired; confirmed by Senate February 13, 1930, by a 52-26 vote; took judicial oath February 24, 1930; retired July 1, 1941; replaced by Harlan F. Stone, nominated by President Franklin D. Roosevelt.

FAMILY: married Antoinette Carter, December 5, 1888; one son, three daughters.

DEATH: August 27, 1948, Osterville, Massachusetts.

Born during the Civil War, Charles Evans Hughes was the only child of David Charles Hughes, an abolitionist minister, and his wife Mary Catherine Connelly Hughes. When the Reverend Hughes became secretary of the American Bible Union in 1873, the family left the Adirondacks and moved to New York City. Charles was taught at home by his parents until age fourteen when he enrolled in Madison College (now Colgate University). Before his junior year he transferred to Brown University, chosen because of its Baptist tradition, which appealed to his parents, and its city location, which appealed to him. After graduation Hughes taught Greek, Latin, and algebra at the Delaware Academy in Delhi, New York, and clerked for the Wall Street firm Chamberlin, Carter, and Hornblower to earn money for law school. He graduated from Columbia in 1884 and passed the bar at age twenty-two with a score of ninety-nine and one-half.

Hughes then returned to Chamberlin, Carter, and Hornblower and married Antoinette Carter, the daughter of one of the partners. Two years later the firm became Carter, Hughes, and Cravath. Hughes's legal practice in New York City continued for twenty years, with an interim of three years teaching law at Cornell University.

In 1905 Hughes began investigating illegal rate-making practices and fraudulent insurance activities in New York as special counsel for the Stevens Gas Commission and the Armstrong Insurance Committee, established by the state legislature. His successful exposure of racketeering won him national recognition. Endorsed by President Theodore Roosevelt, Hughes defeated William Randolph Hearst in a 1906 race for governor and was reelected two years later.

When President William Howard Taft appointed Hughes to the Supreme Court to fill the vacancy left by Justice David Brewer's death in 1910, his nomination met with approval by the Court and the press. According to the liberal paper *The World*, "Mr. Taft could not have made a better or more popular selection." Justifying his acceptance of the seat on the Supreme Court to New York Republicans who envisioned for him a great political future, Hughes explained, "I had no right to refuse. A refusal on the ground that some time or other I might be a candidate for the Presidency . . . would have been absurd."

After six years on the Court, Hughes became a presidential candidate, endorsed by both the Republican Party and the Progressive Party. "Wilson with Peace and Honor or Hughes with Roosevelt and War?" was a popular slogan of the Democrats, critical of Hughes's advocacy of military preparedness against Germany. The former Supreme Court justice lost the 1916 election by only twenty-three electoral votes. He returned to the practice of law as senior partner in the New York firm Hughes, Rounds, Schurman, and Dwight.

When Warren G. Harding became president, he appointed Hughes secretary of state, a post he also held during the Coolidge administration. At the Washington Armament Conference in 1921 Hughes was instrumental in the agreement reached by the major powers to limit the naval race, end the Anglo-Japanese Alliance, and recognize China's open door diplomacy.

Unlike the general acclaim that greeted Hughes's Supreme Court appointment in 1910, his nomination as chief justice by President Herbert Hoover twenty years later met considerable opposition in the Senate. "No man in public life so exemplifies the influence of powerful combinations in the political and financial worlds as does Mr. Hughes," Sen. George W. Norris of Nebraska objected. Critics felt Hughes's representation of America's largest corporations after he left the State Department jeopardized his ability to defend the rights of the ordinary citizen on the Court. Supporters, on the other hand, pointed to his efforts on behalf of world peace during his legal career as a member of the Permanent Court of Arbitration in the Hague and the Permanent Court of International Justice. The Senate confirmed him February 13, 1930, by a 52-26 vote. His son, Charles Evans Hughes Jr., resigned the same day from his position as solicitor general.

Among Hughes's most important opinions as associate justice was the *Shreveport Rate Case* (1914). This opinion extended the federal government's regulation of rail rates to intrastate railroads, if the two were so intertwined that it would be impossible to regulate one without regulating the other. As chief justice, Hughes wrote the Court's opinion in several of the cases (that overturned New Deal legislation), including *Schechter Poultry Corp. v. United States* and *Panama Refining Co. v. Ryan,* both decided in 1935. In *Home Building and Loan Assn. v. Blaisdell* (1934), however, Hughes upheld a state's emergency law designed to keep people from losing their homes during the Great Depression.

Hughes is also the author of the landmark freedom of the press case, *Near v. Minnesota* (1931). In *Near* the Court ruled, 5-4, that a law barring future publication of a newspaper that prints malicious or defamatory material is a prior restraint in violation of the First Amendment.

After eleven years of service as chief justice, Hughes informed President Franklin Roosevelt of his wish to retire due to "considerations of health and age." Justice Felix Frankfurter likened Hughes's ability to marshal the Court to "Toscanini lead[ing] an orchestra," and Justice William O. Douglas praised his "generosity, kindliness and forbearance."

In 1942, a year after his retirement, Hughes was awarded the American Bar Association medal for conspicuous service to jurisprudence. He died at his summer cottage on Cape Cod at the age of eighty-six.

WILLIS VAN DEVANTER

(1911–1937)

BIRTH: April 17, 1859, Marion, Indiana.

EDUCATION: Indiana Asbury University, A.B., 1878; University of Cincinnati Law School, LL.B., 1881.

OFFICIAL POSITIONS: city attorney, Cheyenne, 1887–1888; member, Wyoming territorial legislature, 1888; chief justice, Wyoming Territory Supreme Court, 1889–1890; assistant attorney general, Department of the Interior, 1897–1903; judge, U.S. Court of Appeals for the Eighth Circuit, 1903–1910.

SUPREME COURT SERVICE: nominated associate justice by President William Howard Taft December 12, 1910, to replace Edward D. White, who became chief justice; confirmed by U.S. Senate December 15, 1910, by a voice vote; took judicial oath January 3, 1911; retired June 2, 1937; replaced by Hugo L. Black, nominated by President Franklin D. Roosevelt.

Willis Van Devanter

FAMILY: married Dellice Burhans, October 10, 1883; two sons.

DEATH: February 8, 1941, in Washington, D.C.

Willis Van Devanter, the eldest of eight children of Isaac and Violetta Spencer Van Devanter, was born in Marion, Indiana. He attended Indiana Asbury (now DePauw) University and the University of Cincinnati Law School. After receiving his degree in 1881, Van Devanter joined his father's law firm in Marion. He married Dellice Burhans of Michigan, and in 1884 they moved to Cheyenne in the Wyoming Territory. There he established a practice and became involved in Republican politics by cultivating a close friendship with Gov. Francis E. Warren, who also became a U.S. senator. Warren served as head of the Republican Party in Wyoming and remained an influential friend.

Van Devanter served as city attorney in Cheyenne in 1887 and the following year was elected to the territorial legislature. He codified the territorial laws and statutes, which became the basis for the future state's constitution. In 1889, when Van Devanter was just thirty years old, President Benjamin Harrison named him chief justice of the Wyoming Territory Supreme Court. He served for only one year before resigning to resume private practice.

Van Devanter enjoyed a thriving practice and remained active in Republican politics, serving as chairman of the Wyoming state committee (1892–1894) and as a member of the Republican National Committee (1896–1900). His service to the party was rewarded in 1897 when President William McKinley named him as assistant attorney general assigned to the Interior Department. There he relied on his years of experience in Wyoming to specialize in legal questions regarding public lands and Indian matters. He also found time to lecture at Columbian (now George Washington) University.

In 1903 President Theodore Roosevelt appointed Van Devanter to the U.S. Court of Appeals for the Eighth Circuit. His years on the bench were marked by a concern for jurisdictional questions, land claims, rights of railroads, and other complex technical areas.

President William Howard Taft December 12, 1910, named Van Devanter to the vacancy created by the promotion of Edward D. White to chief justice. Van Devanter's nomination was strongly opposed by several liberals, particularly William Jennings Bryan, who said that Van Devanter was "the judge that held that two railroads running parallel to each other for two thousand miles were not competing lines, one of the roads being that of Union Pacific," one of Van Devanter's former clients.

As one of the so-called Four Horsemen, the most consistently conservative members of the Court, Van Devanter voted to strike down several of President Roosevelt's measures aimed at stimulating the economy. He is also known for his opinion in *McGrain v. Daugherty* (1927), in which the Court affirmed Congress's subpoena power.

He retired from the Court June 2, 1937, and died February 8, 1941, in Washington, D.C.

JOSEPH RUCKER LAMAR

(1911–1916)

BIRTH: October 14, 1857, Elbert County, Georgia.

EDUCATION: University of Georgia, 1874–1875; Bethany College, A.B., 1877; Washington and Lee University, 1877.

OFFICIAL POSITIONS: member, Georgia legislature, 1886–1889; commissioner to codify Georgia laws, 1893; associate justice, Georgia Supreme Court, 1903–1905; member, mediation conference, Niagara Falls, Canada, 1914.

SUPREME COURT SERVICE: nominated associate justice by President William Howard Taft December 12, 1910, to replace William Henry Moody, who had retired; confirmed by the Senate December 15, 1910, by a voice vote; took judicial oath January 3, 1911; served until January 2, 1916; replaced by Louis D. Brandeis, nominated by President Woodrow Wilson.

FAMILY: married Clarinda Huntington Pendleton, January 30, 1879; two sons, one daughter.

DEATH: January 2, 1916, Washington, D.C.

Joseph Rucker Lamar was named after his maternal grandfather on whose antebellum plantation, Cedar Grove in Ruckersville, Georgia, he was born and raised. Both the Ruckers and the Lamars were socially prominent Georgia families. Mary, the youngest daughter of Joseph Rucker, merchant, planter, banker, and founder of Ruckersville, married James Sanford Lamar of French Huguenot ancestry. Other notable family members were Mirabeau Buonaparte Lamar, president of the

Republic of Texas from 1838 to 1841, and Lucius Quintus Cincinnatus Lamar, associate justice of the Supreme Court from 1888 to 1893.

After his mother's death when he was eight, Joseph Lamar left Cedar Grove and moved to Augusta, where his father became a minister in the Disciples of Christ Church, a new Protestant denomination founded by Alexander Campbell, the president of Bethany College during James Lamar's attendance. Greatly influenced by Campbell, Joseph's father left his legal career to join the ministry. Woodrow Wilson's father was the minister of the leading Presbyterian church in Augusta, and the two boys became close friends.

Lamar attended Martin Institute and Richmond Academy in Georgia and the Penn Lucy Academy in Baltimore before enrolling in the University of Georgia. Consenting to his father's wishes, he transferred to Bethany College, from which he graduated in 1877. After reading law at Washington and Lee University and clerking for the well-known Augusta lawyer, Henry Clay Foster, Lamar passed the Georgia bar. He married Clarinda Huntington Pendleton, the daughter of the president of Bethany College, and they lived with her family for one year while he taught Latin at the college.

Lamar's legal practice began in 1880 when Foster asked him to become a partner. During their joint practice for more than ten years, Lamar served for two terms in the Georgia legislature. As elected representative for Richmond County, he continued studying the state's history of jurisprudence, his special field of interest, and wrote a number of essays. Lamar's research on Georgia's legal history was recognized in 1893 by the governor, who asked him to help rewrite Georgia's law codes.

During his legal practice, Lamar also served on the examining board for applicants to the Georgia bar. This experience helped prepare him for a seat on the Georgia Supreme Court, which he occupied from 1903 to 1905. Overworked and homesick for Augusta, Lamar resigned before his term expired and returned to private law practice, this time in a partnership specializing in railroad law with E. H. Callaway, a former superior court judge.

President William Howard Taft nominated Lamar associate justice of the Supreme Court December 12, 1910, much to the Georgian's surprise. He had become acquainted with the president during two brief vacations in Augusta. Lamar did not expect to be confirmed: not only was he little known outside of the South but also he was a Democrat. Only in the appointments of Justices Stephen J. Field, Howell E. Jackson, and Horace Lurton had party lines been crossed. The Senate, however, confirmed him five days after his nomination.

His best-known opinion came in *Gompers v. Bucks Stove and Range Company* (1911). In keeping with the times, the Court upheld the legality of an injunction against boycotts, one of the labor movement's most powerful weapons.

During his last term Justice Lamar overworked himself in the performance of his judicial responsibilities. He suffered a stroke in September 1916 and died three months later at fifty-eight after only five years on the bench.

"The whole country has reason to mourn," President Wilson telegraphed Clarinda Lamar. "It has lost an able and noble servant. I have lost in him one of my most loved friends."

MAHLON PITNEY

(1912–1922)

BIRTH: February 5, 1858, Morristown, New Jersey.

EDUCATION: College of New Jersey (Princeton), A.B., 1879; A.M., 1882.

OFFICIAL POSITIONS: U.S. representative, 1895–1899; New Jersey State senator, 1899–1901; president, New Jersey Senate, 1901; associate justice, New Jersey Supreme Court, 1901–1908; chancellor of New Jersey, 1908–1912.

SUPREME COURT SERVICE: nominated associate justice by President William Howard Taft February 19, 1912, to replace John Marshall Harlan, who had died; confirmed by the Senate March 13, 1912, by a 50-26 vote; took judicial oath March 18, 1912; retired December 31, 1922; replaced by Edward T. Sanford, nominated by President Warren G. Harding.

FAMILY: married Florence T. Shelton, November 14, 1891; two sons, one daughter.

DEATH: December 9, 1924, Washington, D.C.

The second son of Henry Cooper Pitney and Sarah Louisa Halsted Pitney was born on his family's farm in Morristown,

Mahlon Pitney

New Jersey. At least four of his forebears fought in the Revolutionary War, including his great-grandfather, for whom he was named. Pitney attended the College of New Jersey, now Princeton University, and graduated in 1879. Woodrow Wilson was a classmate. He received his legal education from his father, "a walking encyclopedia of law," and after passing the New Jersey bar in 1882 practiced for seven years in the industrial iron town of Dover. When his father was appointed vice-chancellor of New Jersey in 1889, Pitney moved back to Morristown to take over his legal practice. At the age of thirty-three he married Florence T. Shelton.

The popular choice among New Jersey Republicans, Pitney was elected to a Fourth District congressional seat in 1894. As a member of Congress, he endorsed conservative monetary policies and easily won a second term with the additional support of Democrats who favored gold-backed currency. Pitney resigned January 5, 1899, after his election to the New Jersey Senate.

Party leader William J. Sewall advised Pitney to remain in the legislature for a few years before running for governor, the political office to which he most aspired. When Republicans gained control of the New Jersey senate, Pitney was elected its president. Appointment to the New Jersey Supreme Court by Governor Foster M. Voorhees in 1901 altered his gubernatorial ambitions. For the next twenty years Pitney pursued a judicial career, the culmination of which was the position of chancellor of New Jersey. His father had been vice-chancellor nineteen years before.

Pitney was greatly surprised when, on February 19, 1912, President William Howard Taft named him to the U.S. Supreme Court. They had met just seven days before at a dinner party in Newark and discussed another associate justice of the New Jersey Supreme Court, Francis J. Swayze, who was being considered for the bench. After the Pitney nomination, Taft acknowledged, "I did consider with a good deal of care another lawyer from New Jersey."

Confirmation by the Senate followed in less than a month, although liberal senators and union leaders objected to him because of his antilabor record as a New Jersey judge. After the 50-26 vote in favor of confirmation, Pitney received a congratulatory telegram from New Jersey governor and former Princeton classmate Woodrow Wilson, who assured him "a better choice could not have been made."

His opposition to expanding the rights of workers continued during his tenure on the Court. He wrote the Court's opinion in *Coppage v. Kansas* (1915), which overturned a statute outlawing "yellow dog" contracts. Pitney wrote that a worker has no right to join a union and stay in the employ of a business that does not hire union members.

Mental and physical stress forced Pitney to resign at age sixty-four, after ten years of service. He suffered a stroke in August 1922 and retired in December. Pitney's death two years later in Washington, D.C., has been attributed to the strain of overwork while on the Court.

JAMES CLARK McREYNOLDS

(1914–1941)

BIRTH: February 3, 1862, Elkton, Kentucky.

EDUCATION: Vanderbilt University, B.S., 1882; University of Virginia, LL.B., 1884.

OFFICIAL POSITIONS: assistant U.S. attorney, 1903–1907; U.S. attorney general, 1913–1914.

SUPREME COURT SERVICE: nominated associate justice by President Woodrow Wilson August 19, 1914, to replace Horace H. Lurton, who died; confirmed by the Senate August 29, 1914, by a 44-6 vote; took judicial oath October 12, 1914; retired January 31, 1941; replaced by James F. Byrnes, nominated by President Franklin D. Roosevelt.

FAMILY: unmarried.

DEATH: August 24, 1946, in Washington, D.C.

James McReynolds was born to John McReynolds, a noted surgeon, and Ellen Reeves McReynolds in a Kentucky community that exhibited considerable sympathy for the Confederacy during the Civil War. He was raised on a plantation by highly moral parents who were members of the fundamentalist Campbellite religious sect.

After receiving his B.S. from Vanderbilt University, where he was class valedictorian, McReynolds studied law at the University of Virginia. He received his LL.B. in 1884 and returned to Nashville to practice law. His legal business in Nashville went uninterrupted until 1903, except for two years as secretary to Sen. Howell E. Jackson, a Tennessee Democrat who later served on the Supreme Court. Representing primarily corporate clients, McReynolds gained a reputation as a meticulous lawyer, if a weak advocate. In 1900 he took a part-time position teaching commercial law at Vanderbilt University.

McReynolds ran for Congress in 1896 as a "Gold Democrat" with some Republican support, but his arrogant and standoffish manners while campaigning alienated a majority of the voters. His candidacy, however, provided him with a measure of prominence in the Democratic Party.

In 1903 he was appointed an assistant U.S. attorney in Theodore Roosevelt's administration. During his four years at the Justice Department, McReynolds handled several antitrust prosecutions, including the court battles with the anthracite coal trust and the tobacco trust. So involved was he in trustbusting that he once referred to the American Tobacco Company as a group of "commercial wolves and highwaymen."

He resigned from the U.S. attorney's office in 1907 and took up law practice in New York City. He continued, however, to assist the Justice Department with antitrust cases over the next several years. A Wilson supporter in the election of 1912, he was named U.S. attorney general in the new administration. Although he served in the post for little more than a year, McReynolds managed to anger several members of Congress and executive branch officials with his temper and haughtiness. To show his continued support for McReynolds and, at the same time, remove him from a political position, Wilson named him to the Supreme Court August 19, 1914. He replaced Justice Horace H. Lurton, also from Tennessee, who had died in July.

McReynolds was part of the voting bloc known as the Four Horsemen. They earned the nickname because of their unfailing opposition to President Franklin D. Roosevelt and the economic recovery legislation he had pushed through Congress. When the judicial tide began to turn against McReynolds, he retired from the Court January 31, 1941. He died August 24, 1946, in Washington, D.C.

LOUIS DEMBITZ BRANDEIS

(1916–1939)

BIRTH: November 13, 1856, Louisville, Kentucky.

EDUCATION: Harvard Law School, LL.B., 1877.

OFFICIAL POSITIONS: "people's attorney," Public Franchise League and Massachusetts State Board of Trade, 1897–1911; counsel, New England Policyholders' Protective Committee, 1905; special counsel, wage and hour cases in California, Illinois, Ohio, and Oregon, 1907–1914; counsel, Ballinger-Pinchot investigation, 1910; chairman, arbitration board, New York garment workers' labor disputes, 1910–1916.

SUPREME COURT SERVICE: nominated associate justice by President Woodrow Wilson January 28, 1916, to replace Joseph R. Lamar, who had died; confirmed by the Senate June 1, 1916, by a 47-22 vote; took judicial oath June 15, 1916; retired February 13, 1939; replaced by William O. Douglas, nominated by President Franklin D. Roosevelt.

Louis Dembitz Brandeis

FAMILY: married Alice Goldmark, March 23, 1891; two daughters.

DEATH: October 5, 1941, Washington, D.C.

Louis Dembitz Brandeis was the son of Adolph and Fredericka Dembitz Brandeis, Jews who emigrated from Bohemia after the unsuccessful democratic revolts of 1848. His father was a prosperous grain merchant who provided his family with comfort, education, and culture. Having completed two years of preparatory studies at the Annen-Realschule in Dresden, but without a college degree, Brandeis enrolled at Harvard Law School when he was eighteen years of age. He graduated in 1877 with the highest average in the law school's history. After eight months practicing law in St. Louis, Brandeis returned to Cambridge—for him "the world's center"—and with Bostonian Samuel D. Warren Jr., who ranked second in their law school class, opened a one-room office downtown.

Warren and Brandeis and the successor firm Brandeis, Dunbar, and Nutter handled a variety of cases and were highly successful. By the time he was thirty-five, Brandeis was earning more than $50,000 a year. He and his wife, Alice Goldmark of New York, preferred to live simply, however, and set a ceiling on their personal expenditures of $10,000 a year. As a young lawyer Brandeis devoted many hours to his alma mater. He helped raise funds for a teaching post for Oliver Wendell Holmes Jr. and was one of the founders of the *Harvard Law Review.*

The turn of the century marked the rapid growth in America of corporate monopolies—the "curse of bigness," as Brandeis described it. He chose to protect the rights not of special interest groups but of the general public, and usually without a fee for his services. Brandeis initiated sliding scale gas rates in Boston that lowered consumer costs while raising corporate dividends and instituted savings bank insurance policies, another reform later implemented in the rest of the country. He defended municipal control of Boston's subway system and opposed the monopolistic practices of the New Haven Railroad. He arbitrated labor disputes in New York's garment industry and established the constitutionality of state maximum hour and minimum wage statutes. For thirty-seven years Brandeis devoted his time, energy, and talents to a host of public causes. He called himself an "attorney for the situation," but the press adopted the popular title "people's attorney."

President Wilson respected Brandeis and often sought his opinion. He nominated him associate justice of the Supreme Court January 28, 1916, to fill the vacancy left by Justice Joseph Lamar's death. Vicious opposition to his appointment ensued. One particularly vituperative critic described Brandeis as a "business-baiter, stirrer up of strife, litigious lover of hate and unrest, destroyer of confidence, killer of values, commercial coyote, spoiler of pay envelopes."

Factory owners paying higher wages, New Haven Railroad stockholders, moguls in the Boston transit system, insurance and gas industries—in short, all the losers in court—united to voice their objections to the appointment. Among those seeking satisfaction for past injuries was William Howard Taft. His administration had been embarrassed by an investigation led in part by Brandeis of the conservation practices of Secretary of the Interior Richard A. Ballinger.

The former president, ambitious for a justiceship himself, described the nomination as "one of the deepest wounds that I have had as an American and a lover of the Constitution" and spoke of the "indelible stain" on the Wilson administration that confirmation would bring.

Another critic, Clarence W. Barron, editor and publisher of the *Wall Street Journal,* also felt the choice was unwise: "There is only one redeeming feature in the nomination and that is that it will assist to bury Mr. Wilson in the next Presidential election." The president viewed the political climate differently. He believed Brandeis was a smart choice who would attract the needed Progressive vote. Wilson could not count on a divided Republican Party to ensure his reelection.

During four months of acrimonious debate over his appointment, Brandeis quietly pursued his legal practice. He went to the office every day and did not resort to personal attacks against his opponents. "Your attitude while the wolves yelp is sublime," his young nephew wrote.

The hearings in the Senate Judiciary Committee turned up no valid grounds for rejection. According to Sen. Thomas J. Walsh, Brandeis's only "real crime" was that "he had not stood in awe of the majesty of wealth." One of his supporters from the Harvard Law School, Arthur Hill, attributed the opposition to the fact that "Mr. Brandeis is an outsider, successful and a Jew."

Brandeis was confirmed by the Senate on June 1, 1916, by a vote of 47-22, becoming the first Jewish justice.

His prolabor positions led to many dissents in cases favoring employers' rights over those of workers. A staunch believer in the rights of the individual, Brandeis also dissented when the Court upheld the government's right to wiretap. He said the Founding Fathers had included in the Constitution the "right to be let alone."

At eighty-two, Brandeis resigned from the Court but not from public service. After twenty-two years on the bench, he devoted the last two years of his life to the Zionist movement and a boycott of German products. As the *New York Times* noted upon his retirement in 1939, "the storm against him . . . seems almost incredible now."

JOHN HESSIN CLARKE

(1916–1922)

BIRTH: September 18, 1857, Lisbon, Ohio.

EDUCATION: Western Reserve University, A.B., 1877, A.M., 1880.

OFFICIAL POSITIONS: federal judge, U.S. District Court for Northern District of Ohio, 1914–1916.

SUPREME COURT SERVICE: nominated associate justice by President Woodrow Wilson July 14, 1916, to replace Charles Evans Hughes, who had resigned; confirmed by the Senate July 24, 1916, by a voice vote; took judicial oath October 9, 1916; resigned September 18, 1922; replaced by George Sutherland, nominated by President Warren G. Harding.

FAMILY: unmarried.

DEATH: March 22, 1945, San Diego, California.

John Hessin Clarke

John Hessin Clarke was the son of John and Melissa Hessin Clarke, Irish Protestants. His father had left Ireland in 1830 and settled in Lisbon, Ohio, the county seat, where he practiced law and participated in liberal Democratic politics. His son graduated Phi Beta Kappa from Western Reserve College in Hudson, Ohio, and returned to Lisbon to study law under his father's tutelage. He passed the bar with honors in 1878 and joined his father's practice.

In 1880 Clarke moved to Youngstown where his career in corporate law began. Under his ownership and direction, the town newspaper the *Vindicator* became a strong voice for progressive reform. A member of the Youngstown literary society, Clarke lectured on Shakespeare and James Russell Lowell. He was an honorary life trustee of the Youngstown Public Library and bequeathed the library $100,000 in his will.

Clarke left Youngstown and his legal practice of seventeen years to join the Cleveland firm of Williamson and Cushing in 1897. Although he represented corporate clients such as the Nickel Plate Railroad and the makers of Pullman railway cars, he remained true to his liberal politics and advocated antitrust and antirebate legislation. He even favored municipal ownership of street railways. A progressive reformer, Clarke supported suffrage for women, direct election of senators, and public disclosure of campaign expenditures.

In 1894 he ran for the U.S. Senate but was defeated by incumbent Calvin S. Brice. As chairman of the Ohio State Democratic Sound Money Convention, Clarke disagreed with William Jennings Bryan's free silver populism and split from the Democrats at the 1896 national convention over that issue. He ran for the Senate a second time in 1914 but withdrew when another Irishman, Timothy Hogan, announced his candidacy.

After more than thirty-five years in the legal profession and progressive politics, Clarke received his first federal post. In 1914 President Wilson appointed him federal judge for the Northern District of Ohio.

When Charles Evans Hughes resigned from the Court to run against Wilson, the president considered nominating Attorney General Tom Gregory or Republican senator Warren G. Harding to fill the vacancy. He decided instead on John Clarke because he wanted a decidedly progressive justice with an antitrust record on Chief Justice White's staid court.

After his nomination, Clarke was described by the *New York World* as "singularly like Brandeis in having been a successful corporation lawyer whose practice served only to quicken his sympathies and activities for the causes of political and social justice." Indeed, President Wilson had hoped that Clarke would join Brandeis "to restrain the court from the extreme reactionary course which it seem[ed] inclined to follow." He was therefore greatly disappointed when Clarke resigned from the Court to promote American participation in the League of Nations, even though the league was Wilson's own dream. Clarke informed the president he would "die happier" working for world peace rather than devoting his time "to determining whether a drunken Indian had been deprived of his land before he died or whether the digging of a ditch was constitutional or not."

From 1922 to 1930 Clarke presided over the League of Nations' Non-Partisan Association of the United States and—against the advice of his physician, who was concerned about his heart—spoke on its behalf across the country.

At the age of eighty, Clarke emerged unexpectedly from his retirement in San Diego to endorse over nationwide radio President Franklin D. Roosevelt's Court-packing plan. He died March 22, 1945, shortly before the convening of the San Francisco conference that created the United Nations.

WILLIAM HOWARD TAFT

(1921–1930)

BIRTH: September 15, 1857, Cincinnati, Ohio.

EDUCATION: Yale University, A.B., class salutatorian, 1878; Cincinnati Law School, LL.B., 1880.

OFFICIAL POSITIONS: assistant prosecuting attorney, Hamilton County, Ohio, 1881–1883; assistant county solicitor, Hamilton County, 1885–1887; judge, Ohio Superior Court, 1887–1890; U.S. solicitor general, 1890–1891; judge, U.S. District Court for the Sixth Circuit, 1892–1900; chairman, Philippine Commission, 1900–1901; governor general of the Philippines, 1901–1904; secretary of war, 1904–1908; president of the United States, 1909–1913; joint chairman, National War Labor Board, 1918–1919.

SUPREME COURT SERVICE: nominated chief justice by President Warren G. Harding June 30, 1921, to replace Chief Justice

William Howard Taft

Edward D. White, who had died; confirmed by the Senate June 30, 1921, by a voice vote; took judicial oath July 11, 1921; retired February 3, 1930; replaced by Chief Justice Charles Evans Hughes, nominated by President Herbert Hoover.

FAMILY: married Helen Herron, June 19, 1886; two sons, one daughter.

DEATH: March 8, 1930, in Washington, D.C.

Public service was a tradition in the Taft family; William Howard Taft extended it to its limit during his lifetime. His grandfather, Peter Rawson Taft, was a judge on the probate and county courts in Windham County, Vermont. His father, Alphonso Taft, served two terms on the Ohio Superior Court before he was named secretary of war in the last months of the administration of Ulysses S. Grant. He also served briefly in the Grant administration as attorney general, and later was ambassador to Austria-Hungary and Russia under President Chester A. Arthur. Taft's mother, Louisa Maria Torrey Taft, was Alphonso's second wife. William's brother, Charles Phelps Taft, a Republican from Ohio, served a term in the U.S. House of Representatives, 1895–1897.

Born in Cincinnati, Taft received an A.B. in 1878 from Yale University, where he was the salutatorian of his graduating class. He entered Cincinnati Law School and took a job as a law reporter for the *Cincinnati Commercial* He continued to report for the newspaper through 1880, the year in which he received his LL.B. and was admitted to the bar.

In 1886 he married Helen Herron. They had one daughter and two sons, one of whom, Robert A. Taft, served in the U.S. Senate, from 1939 until his death in 1953, and was one of its most powerful leaders. Taft's grandson, Robert Taft Jr., served several terms in the House of Representatives and the Senate from 1971 to 1976.

In 1881 Taft plunged into Republican politics and gave his support to a candidate for county prosecutor. After his candidate won, Taft was selected to be an assistant county prosecutor. He went back to private practice in 1883.

Taft was named to a two-year term as assistant county solicitor for Hamilton County in 1885 and, in 1887, when he was barely thirty years old, was appointed to the Ohio Superior Court.

He sat on the superior court bench until President Benjamin Harrison in 1890 named him solicitor general. In 1892, after Congress created additional judgeships for the federal circuit courts, Taft sought and received appointment to the Sixth Circuit.

Taft remained on the circuit court for eight years. He left reluctantly in 1900 when President William McKinley asked him to head a commission established to ensure the smooth transition from military to civilian government in the Philippines in the aftermath of the Spanish-American War. In 1901 he was made governor general of the Philippines, a position he held until President Theodore Roosevelt named him secretary of war to replace Elihu Root in 1904.

Once in the cabinet, Taft became one of Roosevelt's closest advisers; the president increasingly relied on Taft to handle important matters for the administration. As secretary of war Taft was in command of the Panama Canal project and made a goodwill tour of the site. He also was dispatched in 1906 to Cuba to investigate reports of revolutionary activity.

As Taft's prestige grew, so did his influence in the Republican Party. With Roosevelt's backing he won the party's nomination for president and the subsequent election in 1908. He was sworn in as the twenty-ninth president of the United States March 4, 1909.

The presidency was a post that Taft did not particularly covet—he would have preferred a seat on the Supreme Court as chief justice, but he ran at the urging of his wife and Republican Party regulars. His single term in office was not controversial. It saw the institution of the postal savings system and the Tariff Board, the intervention of American troops in the Dominican Republic, the ratification of the Sixteenth Amendment to the Constitution, and a continuation of the trustbusting begun under Theodore Roosevelt.

Taft also named six men to the Supreme Court, including a chief justice, Edward D. White. The others were Horace H. Lurton, Charles Evans Hughes (who resigned from the Court to run for president in 1916, lost, and was named chief justice in 1930 by President Herbert Hoover to replace Taft), Willis Van Devanter, Joseph R. Lamar, and Mahlon Pitney. When Taft was named chief justice in 1921, only two of his appointees, Van Devanter and Pitney, were still on the bench.

Soon after he was elected president, Taft began to fall out of favor with former president Roosevelt. The two men came to represent opposing sides of a division within the Republican Party. When Taft was renominated in 1912, Roosevelt ran for president under the banner of the Bull Moose Party and effectively splintered the Republican vote. After the election, which was won by Democrat Woodrow Wilson, Taft described Roosevelt as "the most dangerous man that we have had in the country since its origin."

After leaving the White House, Taft taught constitutional law at Yale University, served a year as president of the American Bar Association, wrote magazine articles and was a frequent participant on the lecture circuit. He was elected president of the League to Enforce Peace in 1915. In 1916 he and four other former presidents of the American Bar Association joined with current president Elihu Root in writing to the U.S. Senate to register their disapproval of President Wilson's nomination of Louis D. Brandeis to the Supreme Court. During this period Taft also continued discreetly to publicize his desire to be named to the Court, especially as chief justice.

Taft served as the joint chairman of the National War Labor Board, 1918–1919. An enthusiastic advocate of the League of Nations, he embarked on a fifteen-state tour in an attempt to rally support for it. His greatest ambition was achieved when President Harding named him chief justice June 30, 1921, to replace Chief Justice White.

Taft can be credited with modernizing procedures at the Court and cutting down on its workload. He created the Judicial Conference of the United States, which fosters cooperation among the federal judiciary's many courts. He secured passage of the Judiciary Act of 1925, giving the Supreme Court greater power to decide which cases to hear. He also lobbied Congress to provide funds for the Supreme Court building, but he did not live to see it completed. The only person in U.S. history to hold both the presidency and the chief justiceship, Taft died March 8, 1930.

GEORGE SUTHERLAND

(1922–1938)

BIRTH: March 25, 1862, Buckinghamshire, England.

EDUCATION: Brigham Young (University) Academy, 1879–1881; University of Michigan Law School, 1882.

OFFICIAL POSITIONS: Utah state senator, 1896–1900; U.S. representative, 1901–1903; U.S. senator, 1905–1917; chairman, advisory committee to the Washington Conference for the Limitation of Naval Armaments, 1921; U.S. counsel, Norway-United States arbitration, The Hague, 1921–1922.

SUPREME COURT SERVICE: nominated associate justice by President Warren G. Harding September 5, 1922, to replace Justice John H. Clarke, who had resigned; took judicial oath October 2, 1922; confirmed by the Senate September 5, 1922, by a voice vote; retired January 17, 1938; replaced by Stanley F. Reed, nominated by President Franklin D. Roosevelt.

FAMILY: married Rosamund Lee, June 18, 1883; two daughters, one son.

DEATH: July 18, 1942, Stockbridge, Massachusetts.

Sutherland was brought to the United States in 1863 by his parents, Alexander George Sutherland and Frances Slater Sutherland.

George Sutherland

His father, a recent convert to the Church of Jesus Christ of Latter-day Saints, settled his family in Springville in the Utah Territory. The senior Sutherland soon deserted the Mormons and moved the family to Montana. They returned to Utah in 1869, settling in Provo. George Sutherland learned the value of thrift and hard work in his childhood—he left school at age twelve to help support the family. By the time he was sixteen, however, he had saved enough money to enroll at Brigham Young Academy in Provo, where he stayed for three years. He then worked a year for the company building the Rio Grande Western Railroad and in 1882 entered the University of Michigan Law School. He studied law for only one year before passing the bars in Michigan and Utah. He started a law practice in Provo and married Rosamund Lee of Beaver, Utah.

After ten years in Provo, Sutherland in 1893 moved to Salt Lake City. The next year he helped found the Utah Bar Association. When the territory achieved statehood in 1896, Sutherland, running as a Republican, was elected to the first state senate. In 1900 he was elected to the U.S. House of Representatives. He declined to run for a second term in the House, but was elected in 1904 to the U.S. Senate.

During his first term in the Senate, Sutherland endorsed several reform measures, including the Pure Food and Drug Act (1906), the Postal Savings Act (1910), and a compensation bill for workers injured in interstate commerce (1911–1912). He also played a major role in the revision and codification of federal criminal statutes. Among the bills he opposed were statehood for Arizona and New Mexico (1912)—because their constitutions provided for recalls, initiatives, and referenda—the Federal Reserve Act (1913), the Sixteenth Amendment (1913), the Clayton Antitrust Act (1914), and the Federal Trade Commission Act (1914). He also opposed the nomination of Louis D. Brandeis to the Supreme Court.

In 1916 Sutherland failed in his attempt to be renominated by the Utah Republican Party. He stayed in Washington, D.C., practiced law, and remained in touch with his former Senate colleague, Warren Harding. Sutherland developed into one of Harding's closest advisers and worked on his successful presidential campaign in 1920. Soon thereafter Sutherland represented the Harding administration as chairman of the advisory committee to the Washington Conference for the Limitation of Naval Armaments in 1921 and as counsel in arbitration between Norway and the United States over matters of shipping.

President Harding named Sutherland to the Supreme Court when Justice John H. Clarke unexpectedly resigned to work for the cause of world peace. Sutherland joined Justices James McReynolds, Willis Van Devanter, and Pierce Butler (on the Court in 1923) to form a bloc known as the Four Horsemen. The bloc voted consistently to void regulatory and social legislation, which they saw as infringing the rights of individuals to make contracts. For example, in 1923 Sutherland wrote the opinion in *Adkins v. Children's Hospital*, in which the Court ruled unconstitutional the District of Columbia's minimum wage law for women.

Sutherland retired from the Court January 17, 1938, and died in Stockbridge, Massachusetts, July 18, 1942.

PIERCE BUTLER

(1923–1939)

BIRTH: March 17, 1866, Pine Bend, Minnesota.

EDUCATION: Carleton College, A.B., B.S., 1887.

OFFICIAL POSITIONS: assistant county attorney, Ramsey County, Minnesota, 1891–1893; county attorney, 1893–1897.

SUPREME COURT SERVICE: nominated associate justice by President Warren G. Harding November 23, 1922, to replace William R. Day, who had retired; confirmed by Senate December 21, 1922, by a 61-8 vote; took judicial oath January 2, 1923; served until November 16, 1939; replaced by Frank Murphy, nominated by President Franklin D. Roosevelt.

FAMILY: married Annie M. Cronin, August 25, 1891; eight children.

DEATH: November 16, 1939, Washington, D.C.

Pierce Butler, born on St. Patrick's Day, was the sixth of Patrick and Mary Gaffney Butler's eight children. His parents, Roman Catholics, settled on a farm in Minnesota after emigrating from Ireland during the potato famine of the 1840s. With money earned at a nearby dairy, Pierce attended Carleton College in Northfield, graduating in 1887 with a bachelor of arts and a bachelor of science degree. He read law with a St. Paul firm, Pinch and Twohy, and was admitted to the bar in 1888 at age twenty-two.

Pierce Butler

Butler began his legal career practicing law with Stan Donnelly, the son of Ignatius Donnelly, a member of Congress from Minnesota and future vice-presidential candidate of the People's Party.

In 1891 Butler was elected assistant attorney of Ramsey County, which included St. Paul. While county attorney he formed the firm How, Butler, and Mitchell and later became senior partner of Butler, Mitchell, and Doherty. Attorney General George Wickersham chose Butler to represent the federal government in a number of antitrust cases around 1910. His skillful prosecution won him the attorney general's praise as the "foremost lawyer in his part of the country" and brought him to President Harding's attention.

When Justice William Day's resignation in 1922 left a vacancy on the Court, Butler was Chief Justice Taft's top choice for the seat. During arbitration in Canada the year before, Taft had been favorably impressed with Butler and recommended him to Harding. There were other reasons for Taft's strong preference, however. He wanted to obtain a conservative majority on the Court. Butler's conservative judicial past made Taft confident that if appointed he would align himself with Justices Van Devanter, McReynolds, and Sutherland. The president also was reminded by Taft of the political advantages of a Butler appointment: Taft, a Protestant, had replaced Chief Justice White, a Catholic, and another Catholic was needed on the bench.

Although Taft succeeded in convincing President Harding of Butler's merits, Senate liberals were not so easily persuaded. Their primary objection concerned Butler's defense of several railroads—the Northern Pacific, the Great Northern, and the Chicago, Burlington, and Quincy—during his legal practice. Also criticized were Butler's actions as regent of the University of Minnesota from 1907 to 1924. Faculty members whose economic or political views differed from his own had been dismissed or refused tenure. The liberal academics claimed he was a reactionary with no tolerance for dissent. Despite the opposition to Butler's appointment, only eight senators voted against his confirmation December 21, 1922.

As predicted, Pierce allied himself with the three most conservative members of the Court, completing the voting bloc known as the Four Horsemen. He maintained that government should not interfere in economic matters, even during the worst days of the Great Depression. He opposed social welfare legislation in all its forms, writing the Court's opinion in a 1936 case striking down a New York law that provided a minimum wage for women.

Butler died in Washington, D.C., during his seventeenth year of service on the Court.

EDWARD TERRY SANFORD

(1923–1930)

BIRTH: July 23, 1865, Knoxville, Tennessee.

EDUCATION: University of Tennessee, B.A. and Ph.B., 1883; Harvard, B.A., 1884, M.A., 1889; Harvard Law School, LL.B., 1889.

Edward Terry Sanford

OFFICIAL POSITIONS: special assistant to the U.S. attorney general, 1906–1907; assistant U.S. attorney general, 1907–1908; federal judge, U.S. District Court for the Middle and Eastern Districts of Tennessee, 1908–1923.

SUPREME COURT SERVICE: nominated associate justice by President Warren G. Harding January 24, 1923, to replace Mahlon Pitney, who had retired; confirmed by the Senate January 29, 1923, by a voice vote; took judicial oath February 19, 1923; served until March 8, 1930; replaced by Owen J. Roberts, nominated by President Herbert Hoover.

FAMILY: married Lutie Mallory Woodruff, January 6, 1891; two daughters.

DEATH: March 8, 1930, Washington, D.C.

Born three months after the South had surrendered to the Union armies, Sanford grew up in one of the few Republican enclaves in the post–Civil War South. His father, Edward J. Sanford, had come to Tennessee in 1852 from Connecticut where his family had lived since 1634. In Tennessee he rose from poverty to make a fortune in the lumber and construction business and became a prominent member of the Republican Party. Sanford's mother, Emma Chavannes, was the daughter of French-Swiss parents, who had emigrated from Switzerland in 1848.

Following his education at the University of Tennessee and Harvard, where he was editor of the *Law Review,* Sanford studied in France and Germany for a year. He returned to Knoxville, settled into the practice of law, and married Lutie Mallory Woodruff.

Throughout his life, Sanford retained an interest in higher education. He served as trustee of the University of Tennessee from 1897 to 1923 and as trustee of the George Peabody College for Teachers from 1909 until his death in 1930. He also served as president of both the University of Tennessee and Harvard alumni associations.

Sanford's first official position came in 1905 at the age of forty-one when he accepted the post of special assistant to U.S. Attorney General William H. Moody (later appointed to the Supreme Court). Sanford's task—as one of President Theodore Roosevelt's "trustbusters"—was to prosecute the fertilizer trust under the Sherman Antitrust Act of 1890. In 1907 he became assistant attorney general. A year later Roosevelt nominated him as federal district judge for the Middle and Eastern Districts of Tennessee, a post Sanford held until his nomination to the Supreme Court in 1923.

After World War I, Sanford worked to mobilize support for the Treaty of Versailles and U.S. membership in the League of Nations. Although the treaty was defeated in the Senate, Sanford's efforts brought him to the attention of Chief Justice Taft—with whom he had become acquainted during his Justice Department service—and of Attorney General Harry M. Daugherty. They suggested his name to President Harding when Justice Mahlon Pitney retired on December 31, 1922, giving Harding a fourth vacancy on the Court to fill during his term.

During his seven-year tenure, Sanford delivered the opinion of the Court in 130 cases. Among them was *Gitlow v. New York* (1925), in which the Court upheld the conviction of Benjamin Gitlow under a state criminal anarchy law. Even though the decision went against Gitlow, Sanford wrote that "freedom of speech and of the press . . . are among the . . . "liberties" protected by the due process clause of the Fourteenth Amendment." The ruling was the first to extend the guarantees of the Bill of Rights to state action.

Sanford died suddenly March 8, 1930, only a few hours before the death of William Howard Taft.

HARLAN FISKE STONE

(1925–1941, 1941–1946)

BIRTH: October 11, 1872, Chesterfield, New Hampshire.

EDUCATION: Amherst College, A.B., 1894, M.A., 1897, LL.D., 1913; Columbia University, LL.B., 1898.

OFFICIAL POSITIONS: U.S. attorney general, 1924–1925.

SUPREME COURT SERVICE: nominated associate justice by President Calvin Coolidge January 5, 1925, to replace Joseph McKenna, who had retired; confirmed by the Senate February 5, 1925, by a 71-6 vote; took judicial oath March 2, 1925; nominated chief justice by President Franklin D. Roosevelt June 12, 1941, to replace Chief Justice Hughes, who had retired; confirmed by the Senate June 27, 1941, by a voice vote; took judicial oath July 3, 1941; served until April 22, 1946; replaced by Fred M. Vinson, nominated by President Harry S. Truman.

FAMILY: married Agnes Harvey, September 7, 1899; two sons.

DEATH: April 22, 1946, Washington, D.C.

Harlan Fiske Stone

Harlan Fiske Stone was the son of Frederick Lawson Stone, a New England farmer, and Ann Sophia Butler Stone. Phi Beta Kappa and president of his class at Amherst College, Stone graduated with an A.B. in 1894, one year before Calvin Coolidge, and with an M.A. three years later.

A Columbia University Law School graduate, Stone was admitted to the New York bar, married Agnes Harvey, whom he had known since childhood, and began his legal practice with the firm Sullivan and Cromwell in 1899. For the next twenty-five years he divided his time between his Wall Street practice and a career as professor of law and dean at Columbia.

In 1924 President Coolidge appointed his fellow Republican and Amherst alumnus to succeed the controversial Harry M. Daugherty as attorney general. Stone began a reorganization of the Justice Department and recommended J. Edgar Hoover to head the FBI. The Supreme Court resignation of Justice Joseph McKenna in 1925 gave Coolidge the opportunity to promote his old friend to the bench after only a year in his cabinet.

Despite reservations over Stone's moderate conservatism and ties to Wall Street wealth (five years before he had been J. P. Morgan's counsel), the Senate confirmed him February 5, 1925. A spokesman for judicial restraint on the Taft and Hughes Courts, Stone was nominated chief justice by President Franklin D. Roosevelt sixteen years later.

When the Agricultural Adjustment Act was declared unconstitutional by a 6-3 majority in 1936, Stone had sided with the president, declaring that the Court was not "the only agency of government that must be assumed to have the capacity to govern." Stone recognized the danger of the Court's becoming a "legislative

Constitution-making body," and Roosevelt needed a chief justice who would not thwart his programs. Moreover, a Republican appointment, the president felt, would show him to be a nonpartisan leader. Favored by the press and bar, Stone's selection as chief justice was well received. Archibald MacLeish described the nomination as "the perfect word spoken at the perfect moment."

For Stone the appointment was not the culmination of a lifelong ambition: "I cannot say I had any thought of being a member of the Supreme Court or any other court," said Stone recalling his ambitions as a twenty-one-year-old college student, "for I believed then, as I do now, that the best insurance of a happy life and reasonable success in it is devotion to one's immediate job and happiness in doing it."

Stone achieved far more than "reasonable success." Progressing from the most junior to senior associate justice and finally to chief justice, he occupied consecutively, as none of his predecessors had done, every seat on the bench.

Stone may be the only member of the Court who is known for a famous footnote. In Footnote Four of *United States v. Carolene Products Corp.* (1938), Stone introduced the idea that statutes aimed at restricting fundamental rights would be regarded as suspect. Two years later, in *Minersville School District v. Gobitis,* Stone was the lone dissenter when the Court decided that the children of Seventh-day Adventists were required to salute the flag in school even though their religion forbade it. Three years later, the justices took his arguments to heart when they overruled the decision.

His twenty-one years of service on the Court ended suddenly. On April 22, 1946, while reading a dissent in a naturalization case, he was stricken and died later in the day.

OWEN JOSEPHUS ROBERTS

(1930–1945)

BIRTH: May 2, 1875, Germantown, Pennsylvania.

EDUCATION: University of Pennsylvania, A.B. with honors, 1895; LL.B. cum laude, 1898.

OFFICIAL POSITION: assistant district attorney, 1903–1906; special deputy attorney general, Eastern District of Pennsylvania, 1918; special U.S. attorney, 1924–1930; umpire, Mixed Claims Commission, 1932; chairman, Pearl Harbor Inquiry Board, 1941–1942.

SUPREME COURT SERVICE: nominated associate justice by President Herbert Hoover May 9, 1930, to replace Edward Terry Sanford, who had died; confirmed by the Senate May 20, 1930, by a voice vote; took judicial oath June 2, 1930; resigned July 31, 1945; replaced by Harold H. Burton, nominated by President Harry S. Truman.

FAMILY: married Elizabeth Caldwell Rogers, 1904; one daughter.

DEATH: May 17, 1955, West Vincent Township, Pennsylvania.

Roberts's ancestors left Wales in 1808 and settled in southeastern Pennsylvania. His parents were Josephus and Emma

Owen Josephus Roberts

Laferty Roberts. Owen Roberts was a quiet youngster who displayed a love for books and an aptitude for debating. He attended the University of Pennsylvania and graduated Phi Beta Kappa in 1895. He went on to the University of Pennsylvania Law School, where for two years he was the associate editor of the *American Law Register* (now the *University of Pennsylvania Law Review*). He graduated cum laude in 1898. In addition to starting private practice the same year, Roberts also taught at his former law school, rising from lecturer to full professor. He continued to teach part-time at the university until 1919.

In 1903 Roberts was named assistant district attorney in Philadelphia. He returned to private practice in 1906 and built a prosperous business representing a large clientele, including several corporations.

Appointed a special deputy attorney general in 1918, Roberts prosecuted several cases in the Philadelphia area under the terms of the Espionage Act. In 1924 President Calvin Coolidge named him and former senator Atlee Pomerene, D-Ohio (1911–1923), as special U.S. attorneys to investigate the Teapot Dome Scandal of the Harding administration. Roberts uncovered a network of bribes to administration officials, several of whom were convicted but received relatively short prison sentences.

In May 1930 the Senate refused to confirm President Hoover's nomination of North Carolina judge John J. Parker to the Supreme Court because of Parker's rulings upholding "yellow dog" labor contracts and his derogatory comments on blacks. Roberts was Hoover's next choice, and the Senate confirmed him May 20.

Roberts joined a Court that was divided between a conservative group nicknamed the Four Horsemen and a more liberal group. As a swing vote, he could decide the outcome of a case. He is generally regarded as more conservative than liberal. For example, he wrote the 1936 opinion in *Butler v. United States,* which struck down one of the pillars of the New Deal, the Agricultural Adjustment Act. He also, however, voted to uphold a Minnesota law that provided mortgage relief to homeowners suffering financial difficulties due to the depression. In *Nebbia v. New York* (1934) he came out in favor of price regulation.

It is a popular myth that Roberts made the "switch in time that saved the Nine." Just months after President Franklin D. Roosevelt proposed adding more members to the Court, the story goes, Roberts changed his vote in a case involving a Washington State law providing a minimum wage for women. In truth, Roberts had voted before the "court-packing" plan became known.

In addition to his Court duties, Roberts oversaw an investigation of the attack on Pearl Harbor and headed the Commission for the Protection and Salvage of Artistic and Historic Monuments in Europe. The commission traced and catalogued art objects stolen or destroyed by the Germans during World War II.

After resigning from the Court, Roberts returned to his alma mater and served as dean of the University of Pennsylvania Law School from 1948 to 1951. He was involved in the world federalist movement and served in 1953 as the chairman of the Fund for the Advancement of Education. He died May 17, 1955, in Pennsylvania.

BENJAMIN NATHAN CARDOZO

(1932–1938)

BIRTH: May 24, 1870, New York City.

EDUCATION: Columbia University, A.B., 1889; A.M., 1891; Columbia Law School, 1891, no degree.

OFFICIAL POSITIONS: justice, New York Supreme Court, 1913; judge, New York State Court of Appeals, 1913–1932; chief judge, 1926–1932.

SUPREME COURT SERVICE: nominated associate justice by President Herbert Hoover February 15, 1932, to replace Oliver Wendell Holmes Jr., who had retired; confirmed by the Senate February 24, 1932, by a voice vote; took judicial oath March 14, 1932; served until July 9, 1938; replaced by Felix Frankfurter, nominated by President Franklin D. Roosevelt.

FAMILY: unmarried.

DEATH: July 9, 1938, Port Chester, New York.

Benjamin Nathan Cardozo and his twin sister Emily were the youngest children of Albert and Rebecca Nathan Cardozo, descendants of Sephardic Jews who had settled in New York in the mid-eighteenth century. A cousin, Emma Lazarus, wrote the verse at the base of the Statue of Liberty. Cardozo's childhood was spent in the aftermath of the Boss Tweed scandal, which

Benjamin Nathan Cardozo

implicated his father, a Tammany Hall judge, in the political corruption of the city government. Charged with graft, Albert Cardozo resigned rather than face impeachment.

At age fifteen Benjamin Cardozo was admitted to Columbia University. He graduated with honors in 1889 and completed his master's degree while also studying law. In 1891 he was admitted to the New York bar without a law degree—a not uncommon practice at that time—and began work in the law firm where his brother Albert was a partner. Cardozo remained a bachelor and drew his friends from among his legal colleagues. He was very fond of his older unmarried sister Ellen and lived with her until her death in 1929.

After years as a private lawyer, Cardozo ran against Tammany Hall in 1913 and was elected by a narrow margin to the New York Supreme Court, the state's trial bench. Shortly thereafter, Gov. Martin A. Glynn appointed him to a temporary position on the New York Court of Appeals, on which he was to serve until 1932. Elected to a full term as associate judge in 1917, he became chief judge in 1926 and won for the court its reputation as the leading state court in the country.

Cardozo's early judicial writings were used by lawyers as a handbook, and his lectures at Yale Law School on a number of topics were extended and published as *The Nature of the Judicial Process* in 1921, *The Growth of the Law* in 1924 and *The Paradoxes of Legal Science* four years later.

When ninety-year-old Justice Oliver Wendell Holmes Jr. announced his retirement, Sen. Robert F. Wagner, D-N.Y., presented Cardozo's name to President Hoover. University faculty, journalists, political leaders, and members of the bar all voiced their endorsement of the New York judge. Within ten days of Holmes's resignation, a tally of names received at the White House showed Cardozo a clear favorite. The *New York Times* described the unanimity of support for him as "quite without precedent."

Hoover was unconvinced, however. Two justices from New York, Hughes and Stone, and one Jew, Brandeis, were quite enough, he thought. Only after Stone offered his resignation (which was not accepted) on Cardozo's behalf did Hoover make his decision, appointing him February 15, 1932. Harvard professor Zechariah Chafee Jr. praised the momination: the president's choice "ignored geography and made history."

In his six years as a liberal on a primarily conservative Court, Cardozo is well remembered for his dissents, but he also wrote more than one hundred opinions for the Court. In *Steward Machine Co. v. Davis* and *Helvering v. Davis,* both 1937, he affirmed the constitutionality of the Social Security Act. He wrote the opinion in *Palko v. Connecticut* (1937), in which the Court chose not to apply the Bill of Rights' prohibition against double jeopardy to the states.

Cardozo died in 1938 after a long illness. In *Nine Old Men,* columnists Drew Pearson and Robert S. Allen described the silver-haired justice as "the hermit philosopher." The Court, in its memorial testimony described "the strangely compelling power of that reticent, sensitive and almost mystical personality."

Hugo Lafayette Black

HUGO LAFAYETTE BLACK

(1937–1971)

BIRTH: February 27, 1886, Harlan, Alabama.

EDUCATION: Birmingham Medical School, 1903–1904; University of Alabama Law School, LL.B., 1906.

OFFICIAL POSITIONS: police court judge, Birmingham, 1910–1911; county solicitor, Jefferson County, Alabama, 1914–1917; U.S. senator, 1927–1937.

SUPREME COURT SERVICE: nominated associate justice by President Franklin D. Roosevelt August 12, 1937, to replace Willis Van Devanter, who had retired; confirmed by the Senate August 17, 1937, by a 63-16 vote; took judicial oath August 19, 1937; retired September 17, 1971; replaced by Lewis F. Powell Jr., nominated by President Richard Nixon.

FAMILY: married Josephine Foster, February 1921; died 1951; two sons, one daughter; married Elizabeth Seay DeMerritte, September 11, 1957.

DEATH: September 25, 1971, Washington, D.C.

Hugo Black was the eighth child of William Lafayette Black, a Baptist storekeeper and farmer, and Martha Ardella Toland Black. He spent the first years of his life in the hill country near Harlan, Alabama. When he was still a youngster, his family moved to Ashland, a larger community where his father's business prospered.

Black attended the local schools in Ashland and after trying one year at Birmingham Medical School, decided to study law. At eighteen he entered the University of Alabama Law School at Tuscaloosa.

Graduating in 1906, Black returned to Ashland and set up his first law practice. The following year a fire destroyed his office and library, and Black moved to Birmingham. There he quickly established a relationship with labor by defending the United Mine Workers strikers in 1908. He also developed an expertise for arguing personal injury cases.

Black was named a part-time police court judge in Birmingham in 1911 and was elected county solicitor (public prosecutor) for Jefferson County in 1914. As solicitor, he gained a measure of local fame for his investigation of reports of the brutal means the police employed while questioning suspects at the notorious Bessemer jail.

When he left the solicitor's post to enter the army in World War I, Black had succeeded in emptying a docket that had once held as many as three thousand pending cases.

His brief military career kept him within the borders of the United States. He returned to practice in Birmingham in 1918, married the following year, and continued to expand his practice, still specializing in labor law and personal injury cases. In 1923 he joined the Ku Klux Klan, but resigned from the organization two years later just before announcing his intention to run for the Democratic nomination for the Senate. Campaigning as the poor man's candidate, Black won not only the party's endorsement but also the election. He entered the Senate in 1927 and immediately began to study history and the classics at the Library of Congress to compensate for his lack of formal education.

During his two terms in the Senate, Black used committee hearings to investigate several areas, including abuses of marine and airline subsidies and the activities of lobbying groups. In 1933 he introduced a bill to create a thirty-hour work week. This legislation, after several alterations, was finally passed in 1938 as the Fair Labor Standards Act. One of the Senate's strongest supporters of President Franklin D. Roosevelt, Black spoke out in favor of the 1937 Court-packing scheme and other New Deal programs. His support for the administration and his strong liberal instincts led the president to pick Black as his choice to fill the Supreme Court seat vacated by the retirement of Willis Van Devanter.

Black's previous affiliation with the Ku Klux Klan was widely reported in the national news media after his Senate confirmation. The furor quickly quieted, however, when the new justice admitted in a dramatic radio broadcast that he had indeed been a member of the Klan but added that he had resigned many years before and would comment no further.

Black is remembered for his reverence for the U.S. Constitution—he always carried a copy of it in his pocket. He believed the courts should protect the weak, minorities, and those who held unpopular views. He was passionate about the First Amendment, interpreting the language literally to mean that Congress shall pass *no law* abridging the freedoms the amendment guarantees.

He retired from the Court September 17, 1971, after suffering an impairing stroke. He died eight days later.

Stanley Forman Reed

STANLEY FORMAN REED

(1938–1957)

BIRTH: December 31, 1884, Minerva, Kentucky.

EDUCATION: Kentucky Wesleyan University, A.B., 1902; Yale University, A.B., 1906; legal studies, University of Virginia and Columbia University (no degree); graduate studies, University of Paris, 1909–1910.

OFFICIAL POSITIONS: representative, Kentucky General Assembly, 1912–1916; general counsel, Federal Farm Board, 1929–1932; general counsel, Reconstruction Finance Corporation, 1932–1935; special assistant to attorney general, 1935; solicitor general, 1935–1938.

SUPREME COURT SERVICE: nominated associate justice by President Franklin D. Roosevelt January 15, 1938, to replace George Sutherland, who had retired; confirmed by Senate January 25, 1938, by a voice vote; took judicial oath January 31, 1938; retired February 25, 1957; replaced by Charles E. Whittaker, appointed by President Dwight D. Eisenhower.

FAMILY: married Winifred Elgin, May 11, 1908; two sons.

DEATH: April 2, 1980, New York City.

Stanley Forman Reed was born in tobacco-rich Mason County, Kentucky, to John A. Reed, a physician, and Frances Forman Reed. Reed received undergraduate degrees from Kentucky Wesleyan and Yale universities and studied law at the University of Virginia and Columbia University. He married Winifred Elgin from Maysville, Kentucky, May 11, 1908, and they left the following year for Paris where he took graduate courses in civil and international law at the Sorbonne.

Returning in 1910 to Maysville, Reed read law with a local attorney before passing the Kentucky bar. He set up a private practice, then closed it to serve in an army intelligence unit during World War I. Once his tour of duty was over, Reed joined a law firm and served in the Kentucky General Assembly for four years. Among the firm's clients were the Chesapeake and Ohio Railroad and the Burley Tobacco Growers Cooperative Association, which he helped organize.

In 1929 Reed's experience with the tobacco cooperative in market control through group sales became needed in Washington. Following the recommendation of Burley's president, James C. Stone, President Herbert Hoover appointed Reed general counsel for the Federal Farm Board, newly established to resell surpluses of American farm commodities abroad. After two years with the board, Reed was promoted to general counsel for the Reconstruction Finance Corporation, Hoover's loan-granting agency in the Great Depression to help banks, businesses, and agricultural enterprises.

When Franklin Roosevelt became president, one of his most controversial economic policies was to raise prices by reducing the gold content of the dollar. He appointed Reed special assistant to the attorney general with the unique task of defending the government's legal right to change the requirement of certain private companies for payment in gold. Reed argued the *Gold Clause Cases* before the Supreme Court in 1935; his success with this assignment made Roosevelt confident that as solicitor general Reed would be able to argue persuasively before the

Supreme Court the constitutionality of his New Deal legislation. Despite defeats such as the Court's decision to invalidate the Agricultural Adjustment Act (AAA) in 1936, Solicitor General Reed succeeded in upholding the constitutionality of the National Labor Relations Act and other important measures of the Roosevelt era.

When Justice Sutherland retired in 1938, Roosevelt had the opportunity to choose his second justice. Reed's ten years of government experience under both Republican and Democratic administrations and seventeen years in private practice made him well qualified for the bench.

On the Court, Reed's opinions reflected his belief in social welfare and government regulation of the economy. He had the satisfaction of seeing the AAA upheld just three years after it was declared unconstitutional. He wrote the opinion in the landmark *Smith v. Allwright* (1944), in which the Court invalidated the white-only primary, a common practice in the southern states to keep blacks from running for elective office.

From 1939 to 1941 Justice Reed chaired President Roosevelt's Commission on Civil Service Improvement. After his resignation from the Court in 1957, he served as chairman of President Eisenhower's U.S. Civil Rights Commission. Reed left the commission because he felt his continued involvement with the federal judiciary disqualified him. Reed argued thirty-five cases before the Court of Claims and twenty-five cases before the Court of Appeals in the District of Columbia during his retirement. He maintained an office in the Supreme Court until his move to New York, where he died on April 2, 1980, twenty-three years after leaving the Supreme Court.

Felix Frankfurter

FELIX FRANKFURTER

(1939–1962)

BIRTH: November 15, 1882, Vienna, Austria.

EDUCATION: College of the City of New York, A.B., 1902; Harvard Law School, LL.B., 1906.

OFFICIAL POSITIONS: assistant U.S. attorney, Southern District of New York, 1906–1909; law officer, Bureau of Insular Affairs, War Department, 1910–1914; assistant to the secretary of war, 1917; secretary and counsel, President's Mediation Commission, 1917; assistant to the secretary of labor, 1917–1918; chairman, War Labor Policies Board, 1918.

SUPREME COURT SERVICE: nominated associate justice by President Franklin D. Roosevelt January 5, 1939, to replace Benjamin Cardozo, who had died; confirmed by the Senate January 17, 1939, by a voice vote; took judicial oath January 30, 1939; retired August 28, 1962; replaced by Arthur Goldberg, nominated by President John F. Kennedy.

FAMILY: married Marion A. Denman, December 20, 1919.

DEATH: February 22, 1965, Washington, D.C.

An Austrian Jew, Felix Frankfurter came to the United States with his parents, Leopold and Emma Winter Frankfurter, in 1894 and was raised amidst the squalor of New York's Lower East Side. He attended City College and, after an impressive three years at the Harvard University School of Law, took a job with a New York law firm. He was soon recruited away by Henry L. Stimson, the U.S. attorney for the Southern District of New York.

Stimson had been appointed by President Theodore Roosevelt. At the end of the Roosevelt administration in 1909, Stimson went into private practice for a short time and brought Frankfurter with him. After an unsuccessful bid for the governorship of New York, Stimson was named secretary of war under President William Howard Taft.

Frankfurter accompanied his mentor to Washington, D.C., and was appointed legal officer in the War Department's Bureau of Insular Affairs.

In 1913 Harvard University offered Frankfurter a teaching post in the law school, and he happily returned to his alma mater. Passionate about teaching, Frankfurter trained two generations of students devoted to the law and public service. He also became involved in the Zionist movement, argued a number of minimum and maximum wage cases for the National Consumers League, and helped found the *New Republic*.

Frankfurter returned to Washington in 1917 as an assistant to Secretary of War Newton D. Baker. That same year, President Woodrow Wilson named a mediation commission to handle the rash of strikes obstructing the defense industry; Frankfurter was named its secretary and counsel. While serving on the commission, Frankfurter investigated the handling of the case of Tom Mooney, the alleged Preparedness Day Parade bomber, and the Bisbee, Arizona, deportation case wherein approximately one thousand miners were taken roughly from their labor camps in Arizona and dropped in a deserted town in New Mexico. In both instances Frankfurter found that the rights of the individuals involved had been violated.

These cases, as well as his highly publicized arguments in defense of Sacco and Vanzetti, his work with the National Association for the Advancement of Colored People, and the fact that he was a founding member of the American Civil Liberties Union earned him a reputation as a die-hard liberal that would follow him throughout his career.

He also served as chairman of the War Labor Policies Board. This position first introduced him to Franklin Roosevelt who, as assistant secretary of the navy, sat on the board.

At war's end, Frankfurter attended the Paris Peace Conference as a representative of the American Zionist movement and then returned to Cambridge. In 1919 he married Marion A. Denman. The ceremony took place in Judge Learned Hand's chambers and was performed by Judge Benjamin Cardozo of the New York Court of Appeals, later Frankfurter's predecessor on the U.S. Supreme Court.

At Harvard, Frankfurter enjoyed a growing reputation as an expert on the Constitution and the Supreme Court. He was offered a seat on the Massachusetts Supreme Court in 1932, which he declined. His friendship with Roosevelt grew closer, and in 1933 the newly elected president asked him to be solicitor general, another post Frankfurter declined.

He remained, however, a close adviser to the president and recommended to him a number of Harvard graduates eager to work in the Roosevelt administration, including Thomas G. Corcoran, one of the most influential New Dealers.

Named to the Supreme Court in 1939 to replace Justice Cardozo, Frankfurter was Roosevelt's third appointment. Despite his support for liberal causes, Frankfurter's voting on the Court was considered conservative. He joined with the majority in *Korematsu v. United States* (1944), upholding the exclusion of Japanese Americans from the West Coast. He argued that the country was engaged in a world war against horrific foes, and he believed the claims of the nation were stronger than those of individuals. He dissented in *Board of Education v. Barnette* (1943), the case that overturned an earlier ruling that had said children could be expelled from school for declining to salute the flag for religious reasons. As an immigrant to the United States, Frankfurter felt it was important to show patriotism.

Frankfurter continued to advise the president on a number of issues until Roosevelt's death in 1945. Frankfurter remained on the Court until he suffered a debilitating stroke in 1962. He died in Washington, D.C., in 1965.

Frankfurter was the author of *The Case of Sacco and Vanzetti*, 1927; *The Business of the Supreme Court*, with James M. Landis, 1928; *The Labor Injunction*, with Nathan Greene, 1930; *The Public and Its Government*, 1930; *The Commerce Clause under Marshall, Taney and Waite*, 1937; *Mr. Justice Holmes and the Supreme Court*, 1939; and the editor of several volumes on various areas of law.

WILLIAM ORVILLE DOUGLAS

(1939–1975)

BIRTH: October 16, 1898, Maine, Minnesota.

EDUCATION: Whitman College, B.A., 1920; Columbia Law School, LL.B., 1925.

OFFICIAL POSITIONS: member, Securities and Exchange Commission, 1936–1939; chairman, 1937–1939.

SUPREME COURT SERVICE: nominated associate justice by President Franklin D. Roosevelt March 20, 1939, to replace Louis D. Brandeis, who had retired; confirmed by the Senate April 4, 1939, by a 62-4 vote; took judicial oath April 17, 1939; retired November 12, 1975; replaced by John Paul Stevens, nominated by President Gerald R. Ford.

FAMILY: married Mildred Riddle, August 16, 1923; divorced 1953; one son, one daughter; married Mercedes Hester Davison, December 14, 1954; divorced 1963; married Joan Martin, August 1963; divorced 1966; married Cathleen Ann Heffernan, July 1966.

DEATH: January 19, 1980, Washington D.C.

Born into an impoverished farm family in Minnesota shortly before the turn of the twentieth century, William Douglas was the son of Rev. William Douglas and Julia Bickford Douglas. He spent his early years in Yakima, Washington. A polio attack as a child sparked Douglas's lifelong passion for the outdoors, as he hiked the mountains near his home to build strength in his weakened legs.

After graduating Phi Beta Kappa from Whitman College in Walla Walla, Washington, in 1920, Douglas decided to pursue a law career. Despite his lack of funds, he decided to study law at Columbia University Law School. Douglas quickly became one of the school's top students and graduated second in his class in 1925.

Following law school, a two-year stint with a prestigious Wall Street law firm convinced Douglas that representing corporate clients was not to his liking. After a year back in Yakima, Douglas joined the law faculty of Columbia University. In 1929 he moved to New Haven, Connecticut, to teach law at Yale.

By the time the Great Depression struck in 1929, Douglas had already developed a reputation as one of the country's foremost financial law experts. So when President Franklin D. Roosevelt needed members for the newly formed Securities and Exchange Commission (SEC), created in 1934, he called on Douglas, who joined the commission in 1936 and became chairman the following year.

Douglas's 1939 Supreme Court nomination sailed through the Senate. Such easy relations with Congress, however, were not to mark his years in Washington. Three times he faced the threat of impeachment, although only in 1970 did the effort gain any real support.

Douglas's lifestyle and liberal political views—plus conservative resentment at the Senate's rejection of two of President Richard Nixon's Supreme Court nominees—were the main spur behind the 1970 impeachment attempt. The justice's relations with the Parvin Foundation, recipient of considerable income from gambling interests, were held up for scrutiny. Antiestablishment sentiments expressed in one of his many books further fueled the attack. His marital history also raised congressional eyebrows, but a special House Judiciary Subcommittee created to investigate the charges found no grounds for impeachment.

Although he voted with the Court in the Japanese exclusion cases, after World War II Douglas became known for his defense of civil liberties. He wrote the opinion in *Terminiello v. Chicago* (1949), in which the Court reversed a speaker's conviction for causing a near riot. He dissented in *Dennis v. United States* (1951), which upheld the convictions of American Communist Party members for conspiracy to overthrow the government. Douglas may be best remembered, however, for his opinion for the Court in *Griswold v. Connecticut* (1965). Finding an implicit right to privacy in the Constitution, Douglas overturned a state law prohibiting the sale of birth control devices to married people.

Douglas suffered a paralytic stroke in January 1975. He attempted to continue his work on the Court, but in November 1975 he retired, citing the pain and physical disability resulting from the stroke.

At the time of his retirement, he had served thirty-six years and seven months, longer than any other justice in history. He died four years and a few months later, in January 1980.

FRANCIS WILLIAM MURPHY

(1940–1949)

BIRTH: April 13, 1890, Sand (now Harbor) Beach, Michigan.

EDUCATION: University of Michigan, A.B., 1912, LL.B., 1914; graduate study, Lincoln's Inn, London, and Trinity College, Dublin.

Francis William Murphy

OFFICIAL POSITIONS: chief assistant U.S. attorney, Eastern District of Michigan, 1919–1920; judge, Recorder's Court, Detroit, 1924–1930; mayor of Detroit, 1930–1933; governor general of the Philippines, 1933–1935; U.S. high commissioner to the Philippines, 1935–1936; governor of Michigan, 1937–1939; U.S. attorney general, 1939–1940.

SUPREME COURT SERVICE: nominated associate justice by President Franklin D. Roosevelt January 4, 1940, to replace Pierce Butler, who had died; confirmed by the Senate January 16, 1940, by a voice vote; took judicial oath February 5, 1940; served until July 19, 1949; replaced by Tom C. Clark, nominated by President Harry S. Truman.

FAMILY: unmarried.

DEATH: July 19, 1949, Detroit, Michigan.

Francis William Murphy, called Frank, was the third child of Irish Catholic parents, John T. Murphy, a country lawyer, and his wife Mary Brennan Murphy. As a young boy, Frank promised his mother he would never smoke or drink and he kept that promise until adulthood. He received his undergraduate and law degrees from the University of Michigan and after his admission to the bar in 1914 worked for the Detroit firm Monaghan and Monaghan for three years, teaching law at night school. During World War I Murphy served with the American Expeditionary Force in France and with the Army of Occupation in Germany. He did not return home immediately after the war but took graduate courses at Lincoln's Inn in London and Trinity College in Dublin.

Murphy began his career in Michigan as chief assistant U.S. attorney for the Eastern District. After practicing law in Detroit for three years, he became judge for the Recorder's Court, the principal criminal court in Detroit. In the midst of the Great Depression, Murphy, a prolabor Democrat and advocate of federal relief, was elected mayor of Detroit and served from 1930 to 1933.

Franklin Roosevelt was governor of New York during this period. Murphy supported Roosevelt's bid for the presidency in 1932 and, when Roosevelt was elected, wholeheartedly endorsed the Works Progress Administration (WPA).

In recognition of this support, Roosevelt named Murphy governor general of the Philippine Islands and in 1935, when commonwealth status was won, appointed him U.S. high commissioner. In the Far East as in the Midwest, Murphy enacted New Deal policies such as maximum hour and minimum wage laws. Once the independent government was working smoothly, he returned to Michigan, but his high regard for the people of the Philippines continued. The American and Philippine flags hung side by side in his Supreme Court office.

From 1937 to 1939 Murphy served as governor of Michigan. Immediately upon taking office, he was faced with a sit-down strike of 135,000 automotive workers. Murphy's refusal to call out the state troopers earned him many critics and cost him reelection in 1938.

Murphy aspired to be secretary of war in Roosevelt's cabinet. A bit of political juggling landed him the position of attorney general instead. Roosevelt had many people to please. To Solicitor General (later Supreme Court justice) Robert H. Jackson he wrote, "I want you for my attorney general, Bob, but I want to name Murphy immediately to something and since I can't name him to what he himself wants, it is desirable to use the attorney generalship temporarily for that purpose." During his one year in that office, Murphy indicted a number of Democratic political bosses, most notably Tom Pendergast of Kansas City, brought suit against numerous trust companies, and established the first civil liberties unit in the Justice Department.

When Justice Butler died in 1939, President Roosevelt filled the vacancy in kind by appointing another Democrat and Catholic—Frank Murphy. Murphy did not want the job. To his parish priest he wrote, "I am not too happy about going on the court. A better choice could have been made." So anxious was he for involvement in the war effort that during Court recesses Murphy served as an infantry officer in Fort Benning, Georgia, much to the dismay of Chief Justice Stone.

On the Court, described by Murphy as the "Great Pulpit," he preached civil liberties, and his moralizing rhetoric gave birth to the phrase "justice tempered with Murphy." Murphy's Catholicism did not influence his decision making even where Jehovah's Witnesses, a strongly anti-Catholic sect, was concerned. He upheld their right to proselytize door to door and, in the Court's second flag-salute decision, voted with the majority to invalidate the salute as a compulsory requirement in schools.

Murphy continued to defend civil rights during World War II, arguing that for the Court to do otherwise would rob the war of its meaning. He concurred in *Hirabayashi v. United States* (1943), the case that upheld a wartime curfew for Japanese Americans living on the West Coast. The next year, however, he wrote a moving dissent in *Korematsu v. United States,* in which the Court agreed that the removal of Japanese Americans from the West Coast to relocation centers inland was within the war powers granted to the president and Congress. Murphy claimed the action went beyond constitutional power and fell into the "ugly abyss of racism."

Murphy died July 19, 1949, in Detroit, Michigan, at the age of fifty-nine. With the sudden deaths that year of Murphy and Wiley B. Rutledge, the Court lost two of its most consistently liberal spokesmen.

JAMES FRANCIS BYRNES

(1941–1942)

BIRTH: May 2, 1879, Charleston, South Carolina.

EDUCATION: St. Patrick's Parochial School (never graduated); studied law privately; admitted to the bar in 1903.

OFFICIAL POSITIONS: court reporter, Second Circuit of South Carolina, 1900–1908; solicitor, Second Circuit of South Carolina, 1908–1910; U.S. representative, 1911–1925; U.S. senator, 1931–1941; director, Office of Economic Stabilization, 1942–1943; director, Office of War Mobilization, 1943–1945; secretary of state, 1945–1947; governor of South Carolina, 1951–1955.

SUPREME COURT SERVICE: nominated associate justice by President Franklin D. Roosevelt June 12, 1941, to replace James McReynolds, who had retired; confirmed by the Senate June 12, 1941, by a voice vote; took judicial oath July 8, 1942; resigned

James Francis Byrnes

October 3, 1942; replaced by Wiley B. Rutledge, appointed by President Roosevelt.

FAMILY: Married Maude Perkins Busch, May 2, 1906.

DEATH: April 9, 1972, Columbia, South Carolina.

The son of Irish immigrants, James Francis Byrnes was born in the Charleston of the post-Reconstruction South. He was named after his father, who had died shortly before his birth. Elisabeth E. McSweeney Byrnes supported the family as a dressmaker.

At age fourteen, Francis left school to work as a law clerk in a Charleston firm for $2 a week. With his mother's help he learned shorthand and won an exam for a court stenographer's job in Aiken, South Carolina, where he served as official court reporter for the Second Circuit for eight years, reading law in his spare time. Byrnes passed the bar in 1903, the same year he bought the Aiken newspaper, *Journal and Review,* and became its editor.

As solicitor, or district attorney, for South Carolina's Second Circuit, Byrnes unexpectedly won a seat in the U.S. House of Representatives in 1910. "I campaigned on nothing but gall, and gall won by fifty-seven votes," he later reminisced. During his second term, he became well acquainted with Franklin Roosevelt, Woodrow Wilson's assistant secretary of the Navy, who often appeared before Byrnes's House Appropriations Committee.

A speechwriter and political strategist for Roosevelt's campaign in 1932, he continued his loyal support of the administration during two terms in the Senate, despite his objections to certain New Deal labor and welfare policies. The president twice considered his friend as a running mate but decided in favor of Henry Wallace in 1940 and Sen. Harry S. Truman four years later. Byrnes's failure to obtain the vice-presidential nomination was attributable in part to his unpopularity with northern liberals and, despite his conversion to the Episcopal faith, anti-Catholic sentiment.

Roosevelt rewarded Byrnes for his loyalty by nominating him to the Supreme Court in June 1941. However, so valuable was Byrnes to the president as a troubleshooter behind the scenes in the Senate that after Justice James McReynolds announced his retirement in January, Roosevelt kept Byrnes in the Senate for six months before naming him as McReynolds's successor.

Byrnes served only sixteen months on the Court, during which he wrote sixteen opinions. Best known is *Edwards v. California* (1941), in which the Court invalidated a California law that had made it illegal to transport indigents into California from other states. He based his opinion on the Commerce Clause, which, he said, guarantees free movement across state borders.

He was restless on the Court. "My country's at war and I want to be in it," he wrote. "I don't think I can stand the abstractions of jurisprudence at a time like this." Late in 1942 he resigned to take a more active part in the administration's war effort. Both as director of the Office of Economic Stabilization from 1942 to 1943 and as director of the Office of War Mobilization and Reconversion the following two years, Byrnes exercised great power in the administration. As the president stated when he called Byrnes from the Court to the White House, "I want you to act as a judge and I will let it be known that your decision is my decision and that there is no appeal. For all practical purposes, you will be assistant President." In 1945 Byrnes accompanied Roosevelt to the meeting in Yalta with Stalin and Churchill, and, as secretary of state in the Truman administration, he attended the Potsdam Conference.

Critical of the concentration of power in the Fair Deal government and criticized for his firm hand with the Soviets as secretary of state, Byrnes resigned from Truman's cabinet in 1947. For four years he practiced law in South Carolina and in Washington, D.C., with the firm Hogan and Hartson.

A proponent of states' rights and separate-but-equal schooling for blacks, Byrnes was elected governor of South Carolina in 1950, the last public office of his distinguished career. Few justices held so many positions of responsibility after leaving the bench.

Byrnes' autobiography, *All in a Lifetime* (1958), was written during his retirement. His first book, *Speaking Frankly,* published in 1947, described his firsthand experience with postwar diplomacy.

Byrnes died of a heart attack April 9, 1972, in Columbia, South Carolina.

ROBERT HOUGHWOUT JACKSON

(1941–1954)

BIRTH: February 13, 1892, Spring Creek, Pennsylvania.

EDUCATION: Local schools in Frewsburg, New York; Albany Law School, 1912.

OFFICIAL POSITIONS: general counsel, Bureau of Internal Revenue, 1934–1936; assistant U.S. attorney general, 1936–1938; U.S. solicitor general, 1938–1939; U.S. attorney general, 1940–1941; chief U.S. prosecutor, Nuremberg war crimes trial, 1945–1946.

SUPREME COURT SERVICE: nominated associate justice by President Franklin D. Roosevelt June 12, 1941, to replace Harlan F. Stone, who was promoted to chief justice; confirmed by the Senate July 7, 1941, by a voice vote; took judicial oath July 11, 1941; served until October 9, 1954; replaced by John Marshall Harlan, nominated by President Dwight D. Eisenhower.

FAMILY: married Irene Alice Gerhardt, April 24, 1916; one daughter, one son.

DEATH: October 9, 1954, Washington, D.C.

A descendant of eighteenth-century settlers of Warren County, Pennsylvania, Robert Jackson was the son of William Eldred Jackson and Angelina Houghwout Jackson. He grew up across the border near Jamestown, New York, where at eighteen he apprenticed in a local law firm. After a year at Albany Law School, he was admitted to the New York bar in 1913. He then began his career in earnest, laying the foundation for a lucrative general practice.

Robert Houghwout Jackson

Jackson entered politics at twenty-one when he was elected a Democratic state committeeman. His term as committeeman, marked by controversy over dispensing patronage posts, convinced Jackson that he preferred law to politics, and he refused to run for reelection. He said later that politics had "filled my office with people who came there asking political favors and waging political fights."

His early contact with Roosevelt and his growing reputation as a talented advocate brought Jackson to Washington in 1934 as the counsel to the Bureau of Internal Revenue, where he won a highly publicized $750,000 judgment in an income tax suit brought against Andrew W. Mellon, the fabulously wealthy former secretary of the Treasury. Jackson rose quickly in the Roosevelt administration: he was named assistant attorney general in 1936, solicitor general in 1938, and attorney general in 1940.

During that time, Jackson also became one of Roosevelt's closest advisers and supporters. He campaigned for the president's reelection in 1936 and was a chief assistant at the 1940 Democratic convention. He supported the president's Court-packing scheme. He devised the legal means for Roosevelt in 1940 to give destroyers to Great Britain in exchange for American bases on British territories in the Caribbean, the West Indies, and the North Atlantic.

Named in June 1941 to the Supreme Court seat vacated after Justice Stone was appointed chief justice, Jackson's opinions reflected his strong support for the rights of individuals. He wrote the majority opinion in *Board of Education v. Barnette* (1943), overturning an earlier decision that had compelled school children to salute the flag. "The very purpose of the Bill of Rights

was to withdraw certain subjects from the vicissitudes of political controversy, to place them beyond the reach of majorities and officials and establish them as legal principles to be applied by courts," he wrote. In 1944 he dissented from the Court's decision in *Korematsu v. United States.* Expressing his disapproval of the government's removal of Japanese Americans from the West Coast, Jackson said it was a fundamental principle of the American system that guilt was personal and not inheritable.

Jackson also served as the chief U.S. prosecutor at the Nuremberg war crimes trial in 1945 and 1946. He originated the concept upon which the successful prosecution of the Nazi leaders was based: that it is a crime against international society to plan and wage an aggressive war. While Jackson was in Germany, growing dissension among the Supreme Court justices reached a climax; it was reported that, on the death of Chief Justice Stone, two justices had threatened to resign if Jackson was elevated to chief justice. Jackson exacerbated the controversy by releasing a letter he had written to President Truman castigating Justice Hugo L. Black for his participation in a case argued by Black's former law partner.

Jackson remained on the Court until his death. He was the author of *The Struggle for Judicial Supremacy,* 1941; *Full Faith and Credit: The Lawyer's Clause of the Constitution,* 1945; *The Case against the Nazi War Criminals,* 1946; *The Nuremberg Case,* 1947; and *The Supreme Court in the American System of Government,* 1955.

WILEY BLOUNT RUTLEDGE
(1943–1949)

BIRTH: July 20, 1894, Cloverport, Kentucky.

EDUCATION: University of Wisconsin, A.B., 1914; University of Colorado, LL.B., 1922.

OFFICIAL POSITIONS: judge, U.S. Court of Appeals for the District of Columbia, 1939–1943.

SUPREME COURT SERVICE: nominated associate justice by President Franklin D. Roosevelt January 11, 1943, to replace James F. Byrnes, who had resigned; confirmed by the Senate February 8, 1943, by a voice vote; took judicial oath February 15, 1943; served until September 10, 1949; replaced by Sherman Minton, nominated by President Harry S. Truman.

FAMILY: married Annabel Person, August 28, 1917; two daughters, one son.

DEATH: September 10, 1949, York, Maine.

Wiley Blount Rutledge was the first son of Mary Lou Wiggington Rutledge, who named him for his father, a circuit-riding Baptist preacher. His mother's tuberculosis condition and his father's search for a pastorate caused the Rutledge family to move to Texas to Louisiana to North Carolina, finally settling in Asheville, where Pastor Rutledge found a position. When Wiley was nine years old, his mother died, whereupon his father took his three children and headed west again, settling in Maryville, Tennessee. Although raised in the conservative Christian tradition, Wiley later adopted the Unitarian faith.

Wiley Blount Rutledge

An ancient languages major and debating team captain, Rutledge transferred his junior year from Maryville College to the University of Wisconsin, from which he graduated in 1914. Unable to afford legal studies there, he attended the Indiana University Law School part-time, while supporting himself as a high school teacher in Bloomington.

Law school and teaching responsibilities proved too strenuous for Rutledge's health. He contracted a serious case of tuberculosis and went to recover in the mountains near Asheville, where his mother had died twelve years earlier. Two years later he married Annabel Person, a classmate at Maryville. They lived in New Mexico and Colorado, where he taught high school and continued to recuperate. Despite financial and physical setbacks, Rutledge was determined to become a lawyer. He resumed his legal studies full-time at the University of Colorado and graduated in 1922, seven years after receiving his undergraduate degree. For the next two years Rutledge practiced law with the Boulder law firm Goss, Kimbrough, and Hutchinson before returning to academia. He served as a professor of law and dean for more than fifteen years.

Rutledge first came to Franklin Roosevelt's attention because of his outspoken support for the president's Court-packing plan as dean of the University of Iowa College of Law from 1935 to 1939. So unpopular was the proposed judicial reorganization in the Midwest that several Iowa state legislators threatened to withhold university salary increases to protest Dean Rutledge's unorthodox liberal stand. In a letter to his friend Irving Brant of the *St. Louis Star-Times* in 1936, Rutledge expressed confidence that Roosevelt would be able to gain control of the Court if

reelected: "I feel sure he will have the opportunity to make a sufficient number of liberal appointments to undo the major harm."

Recommended by Justice Frankfurter and Irving Brant, Rutledge was appointed to the Court seven years later. Although he had four years of federal judicial experience as a Roosevelt appointee to the Court of Appeals for the District of Columbia, some doubted his legal qualifications for the job. During Senate confirmation hearings Sen. William Langer of North Dakota challenged "the wisdom of the choice of this inexperienced member of the bar. Second-best generals and admirals will not bring us victory and peace. Second-best justices or legal mediocrities will not insure justice in our land."

Judicial experience, however, was not the president's deciding criterion. As he explained to his eighth and last Supreme Court appointee, "Wiley, we had a number of candidates for the court who were highly qualified, but they didn't have geography—you have that."

Rutledge served only six years on the Court, during which he wrote 171 opinions, among them *Thomas v. Collins* (1945), invalidating a Texas law requiring a labor union to seek prior permission from a government official before soliciting members. Despite his sympathy for Jehovah's Witnesses and the discrimination they faced, Rutledge wrote the majority opinion in *Prince v. Massachusetts* (1944). He sustained the conviction of a woman who permitted her nine-year-old niece to sell religious literature on the street. Rutledge is also known for his dissents, especially in *Everson v. Board of Education* (1947) and *In re Yamashita* (1946).

He died suddenly on September 10, 1949.

HAROLD HITZ BURTON

(1945–1958)

BIRTH: June 22, 1888, Jamaica Plain, Massachusetts.

EDUCATION: Bowdoin College, A.B., 1909; Harvard University LL.B., 1912.

OFFICIAL POSITIONS: member, Ohio House of Representatives, 1929; director of law, Cleveland, 1929–1932; acting mayor of Cleveland, November 9, 1931–February 20, 1932; mayor of Cleveland, 1935–1940; U.S. senator, 1941–1945.

SUPREME COURT SERVICE: nominated associate justice by President Harry S. Truman September 19, 1945, to replace Owen J. Roberts, who had resigned; confirmed by the Senate September 19, 1945, by a voice vote; took judicial oath October 1, 1945; retired October 13, 1958; replaced by Potter Stewart, appointed by President Dwight D. Eisenhower.

FAMILY: married Selma Florence Smith, June 15, 1912; two daughters, two sons.

DEATH: October 28, 1964, Washington, D.C.

Burton grew up in Jamaica Plain, a suburb of Boston, in a Republican Unitarian family. His father, Alfred E. Burton, was the dean of faculty at Massachusetts Institute of Technology. His

Harold Hitz Burton

Justice Roberts's retirement from the Court July 31, 1945, gave President Truman his first opportunity to appoint a Supreme Court justice. The membership of the "New Deal" Court was heavily Democratic, with the single exception of Chief Justice Harlan Fiske Stone, who had been appointed an associate justice by Republican president Calvin Coolidge. He had been named chief justice, however, by President Roosevelt. Truman was under considerable pressure to name a Republican to the vacant seat. By naming Burton, the president not only improved his relationship with Republican congressional leaders but also gained a justice who, although he was a member of the opposition, was also a former colleague.

One of Burton's best-known opinions is his dissent in *Louisiana ex rel. Francis v. Resweber* (1947). In a 5-4 decision, the Court said it was neither double jeopardy nor cruel and unusual punishment to carry out an electrocution after a first attempt to do so failed. Burton pointed out that repeated attempts to electrocute a prisoner would certainly be considered cruel if the failures were intentional, so why should there be a distinction for an unintentional failure?

After thirteen years on the bench, Burton, suffering from debilitating Parkinson's disease, retired October 13, 1958. He died six years later in Washington, D.C.

mother, Gertrude Hitz Burton, was the granddaughter of a Swiss diplomat. Burton received a B.A. from Bowdoin College in Brunswick, Maine, in 1909, and an LL.B. from Harvard University in 1912. He married Selma Florence Smith of West Newton, Massachusetts, and together they headed to Ohio, where Burton believed it would be easier to establish a law practice than in the East.

During the next five years, Burton engaged in private practice in Ohio (1912–1914), worked for a Utah public utility (1914–1916), and was an attorney for an Idaho public utility (1917). When World War I began, he was assigned to the 361st Infantry, U.S. Army, where he rose to the rank of captain. After the war Burton returned to Cleveland and private practice.

Burton served a one-year term as a Republican representative to the Ohio state legislature in 1929 and that same year was named Cleveland's director of law, a position he held until 1932. After a brief term as acting mayor of Cleveland in 1931–1932, he won the 1935 mayoral election running as a reformer who would rid the city of gangsters. Twice reelected by the largest majorities in the city's history, he was then elected to the U.S. Senate in 1941. There he gained a reputation as an internationalist, particularly for his sponsorship of the "B_2H_2" resolution of 1943 that urged U.S. participation in a postwar international peace organization. (The resolution was named after its four sponsors, Senators Burton, Joseph Ball, R-Minn., Carl Hatch, D-N.M., and Joseph Lister Hill, D-Ala.) Burton was also a member of the "Truman Committee," which investigated fraudulent war claims against the government.

FREDERICK MOORE VINSON

(1946–1953)

BIRTH: January 22, 1890, Louisa, Kentucky.

EDUCATION: Kentucky Normal College, 1908; Centre College, A.B., 1909; LL.B., 1911.

OFFICIAL POSITIONS: commonwealth attorney, Thirty-second Judicial District of Kentucky, 1921–1924; U.S. representative, 1924–1929, 1931–1938; judge, U.S. Court of Appeals for the District of Columbia, 1938–1943; director, Office of Economic Stabilization, 1943–1945; administrator, Federal Loan Agency, 1945; director, Office of War Mobilization and Reconversion, 1945; secretary of the Treasury, 1945–1946.

SUPREME COURT SERVICE: nominated chief justice by President Harry S. Truman June 6, 1946, to replace Chief Justice Harlan F. Stone, who had died; confirmed by the Senate June 20, 1946, by a voice vote; took judicial oath June 24, 1946; served until September 8, 1953; replaced by Earl Warren, nominated by President Dwight D. Eisenhower.

FAMILY: married Roberta Dixson, January 24, 1923; two sons.

DEATH: September 8, 1953, Washington, D.C.

Frederick Moore Vinson was born in a small Kentucky town to James Vinson, the county jailer, and his wife, Virginia Ferguson Vinson. He worked his way through school, graduating with an A.B. from Centre College, Kentucky, in 1909 and from law school two years later. Passing the bar at age twenty-one, he began seventeen years of legal practice in the state.

Vinson's first official position came as commonwealth attorney for the Thirty-second Judicial District of Kentucky. When a

Frederick Moore Vinson

vacancy occurred for the seat representing Kentucky's Ninth Congressional District, Vinson, a resident for thirty-three years and well known for his grocery, milling, and banking enterprises as well as for his legal practice, was elected. He served in the House from 1924 to 1929 and from 1931 to 1938 and spent the intervening years practicing law in Ashland, Kentucky. An influential member of the House Ways and Means Committee, Vinson worked for passage of President Franklin D. Roosevelt's tax and coal programs.

He resigned his seat in 1938 to become judge for the U.S. Court of Appeals in the District of Columbia, a position to which he was appointed by Roosevelt in recognition of his New Deal support. After twelve years of legislative experience and five years in the federal judiciary, Vinson began his career in the executive branch as director of the Office of Economic Stabilization in the Roosevelt Administration. His knowledge of tax matters and his ties with Congress made him highly qualified for this position.

Vinson gained further administrative experience as federal loan administrator and director of the Office of War Mobilization and Reconversion, a post previously held by former member of Congress and Supreme Court justice James F. Byrnes.

When Harry Truman became president in 1945, he recognized his need for experienced advisers. Vinson's two years in the previous administration as a political organizer and congressional liaison made him valuable to Truman, who appointed him secretary of the Treasury. In this position Vinson administered the last of the war bond drives and recommended the Revenue Act of 1945 to raise taxes.

After the death of Harlan F. Stone, Truman appointed Vinson chief justice on June 6, 1946. Truman recognized in his friend and adviser someone who realized the need for strong government by the executive. As a member of Congress, Vinson had endorsed President Roosevelt's Court-packing plan. Truman had hoped that Vinson would bring calm leadership to a badly fractured Court, where disagreements among the justices had become public knowledge.

On the Court Vinson usually supported presidential authority. He dissented from the Court's opinion in *Youngstown Sheet and Tube Co. v. Sawyer* (1952), which struck down Truman's seizure of the nation's steel mills. The president was attempting to keep the mills operating while a labor dispute was settled.

Vinson wrote some of the Court's most important opinions concerning race relations and civil rights. In *Shelley v. Kraemer* (1948) the Court ruled that restrictive covenants in housing were unenforceable. In *McLaurin v. Oklahoma State Regents* (1950) the Court said that, once admitted to a state university, blacks may use all the facilities. In *Sweatt v. Painter* (1950) the justices ruled that a state may not deny a black admission to law school, even if there is a "black" law school available. This case set the stage for *Brown v. Board of Education,* which in 1954 overturned the separate but equal principle that had kept schools segregated.

Vinson died of a heart attack September 8, 1953, ending seven years of service on the Court.

TOM C. CLARK

(1949–1967)

BIRTH: September 23, 1899, Dallas, Texas.

EDUCATION: Virginia Military Institute, 1917–1918; University of Texas, A.B., 1921; LL.B., 1922.

OFFICIAL POSITIONS: assistant district attorney, Dallas County, 1927–1932; special assistant, Justice Department, 1937–1943; assistant U.S. attorney general, 1943–1945; U.S. attorney general, 1945–1949; director, Federal Judicial Center, 1968–1970; judge, U.S. Court of Appeals, various circuits, by special arrangement, 1967–1977.

SUPREME COURT SERVICE: nominated associate justice by President Harry S. Truman August 2, 1949, to replace Frank Murphy, who had died; confirmed by the Senate August 18, 1949, by a 73-8 vote; took judicial oath August 24, 1949; retired June 12, 1967; replaced by Thurgood Marshall, nominated by President Lyndon B. Johnson.

FAMILY: Married Mary Jane Ramsey, November 8, 1924; one daughter, two sons.

DEATH: June 13, 1977, New York City.

Thomas Campbell Clark was the son of Virginia Falls Clark and William Clark, a prominent Dallas lawyer active in Democratic politics in Texas. Tom C. Clark, as he preferred to be known, maintained a close relationship with the Democratic Party throughout his life. During World War I Clark served in the national guard after the regular army rejected him. He

Tom C. Clark

entered the University of Texas, where he received his A.B. in 1921 and his LL.B. a year later. While a student he met Mary Jane Ramsey, the daughter of a Texas Supreme Court justice. They were married in 1924.

Clark practiced law with his father, whose connections to the Democratic Party helped him forge good relationships with the party's leaders, particularly Tom Connally (House 1917–1929, Senate 1929–1953). Clark was appointed an assistant district attorney for Dallas County in 1927. He returned to private practice in 1932.

With Connally's backing, Clark was named a special assistant in the Justice Department in 1937. He worked in antitrust matters, was the civilian coordinator of the program to evacuate Japanese-Americans from the West Coast, a task he later described as "the biggest mistake of my life." He also prosecuted fraudulent war claims, which brought him into contact with Sen. Harry Truman, D-Mo., head of the Senate War Investigating Committee. Clark was promoted to assistant attorney general in 1943 and the following year cultivated his friendship with Truman by supporting his vice-presidential bid at the Democratic convention. When Truman assumed the presidency after the death of Franklin Roosevelt in 1945, he chose Clark as his attorney general. During his four years at the Justice Department, Clark led the administration's effort to prosecute the American leaders of the Communist Party and other alleged subversives. The department also drafted the first attorney general's list of dangerous political organizations. Truman relied on these activities by the Justice Department to counter charges of being "soft" on communism in the 1948 presidential campaign.

Truman nominated Clark to the Supreme Court August 2, 1949, to replace Justice Frank Murphy, the only Roman Catholic then on the bench. The president was criticized for his choice of Clark, a Presbyterian, but Truman argued that religious considerations should not apply to the selection of Supreme Court justices.

On the Court, Clark showed his independence by voting against Truman's attempt to seize the nation's steel mills during the Korean War. Although he continued to side with the government in loyalty and national security cases, he also wrote some major opinions defending civil rights and civil liberties. In *Mapp v. Ohio* (1961) Clark ruled that evidence obtained through an illegal search could not be used at trial. In *Abington School District v. Schempp* (1963) the Court banned Bible reading and the recitation of prayers in public schools. He also wrote the Court's opinion in *Heart of Atlanta Motel v. United States* (1964), which outlawed segregation in hotels, motels, and restaurants that deal in interstate commerce.

To avoid any appearance of a conflict of interest, Clark resigned from the Court in 1967 when President Johnson named his son, William Ramsey Clark, attorney general.

Clark was a founder of the Federal Judicial Center, a unit within the judicial branch that studies ways to improve the administration of the courts, and he served as its first director, 1968–1970. Until his death in June 1977, he accepted assignments to sit on various circuits of the U.S. Court of Appeals to help ease the federal caseload.

SHERMAN MINTON

(1949–1956)

BIRTH: October 20, 1890, Georgetown, Indiana.

EDUCATION: Indiana University, LL.B., 1915; Yale University, LL.M., 1917.

OFFICIAL POSITIONS: public counselor, Public Service Commission, 1933–1934; U.S. senator, 1935–1941; assistant to president, 1941; judge, Seventh Circuit Court of Appeals, 1941–1949.

SUPREME COURT SERVICE: nominated associate justice by President Harry S. Truman September 15, 1949, to replace Wiley B. Rutledge, who had died; confirmed by the Senate October 4, 1949, by a 48-16 vote; took judicial oath October 12, 1949; retired October 15, 1956; replaced by William J. Brennan Jr., nominated by President Dwight D. Eisenhower.

FAMILY: married Gertrude Gurtz, August 11, 1917; two sons, one daughter.

DEATH: April 9, 1965 in New Albany, Indiana.

Sherman Minton, the son of John Evan and Emma Lyvers Minton, was born eight miles from New Albany, Indiana, which would be his home for much of his life. Tall and broad-shouldered, Shay, as he was called by his friends, attended Indiana University, where he excelled in football and basketball as well as his studies. In 1925 he graduated at the top of his class at the law college. His classmates included future GOP presidential candidate Wendell L. Willkie and Paul V. McNutt, who later became gover-

Sherman Minton

nor of Indiana. After graduation, Minton left the state with a $500 scholarship to attend Yale Law School for a year of graduate studies, where one of his teachers was William Howard Taft.

McNutt appointed his former classmate and fellow liberal Democrat to his first official position, as a public counselor, in 1933. The next year Minton successfully ran for the Senate on the New Deal ticket. "Sure I'm a New Dealer," he explained. "I'd be ashamed to be an old dealer." Minton became the assistant Democratic whip and forged friendships with the other freshman senators, particularly Harry Truman.

Beginning his third term as president, Franklin D. Roosevelt remembered Minton's Senate endorsement of his plan to pack the Court with justices of his choosing and his support for other New Deal policies. In 1941 the president asked Minton to join his staff as an adviser in charge of coordinating military agencies; in that capacity he backed Truman's efforts in the Senate to establish a new committee to investigate defense activities. Later that year Roosevelt appointed him to the U.S. Court of Appeals for the Seventh Circuit.

After Wiley Rutledge's death it took Truman only five days to name Minton, his friend of nearly fifteen years, to the Court. Although a liberal legislator, Minton proved to be a conservative justice. Most of his decisions favored the restrictive powers of the government over the civil liberties of the individual. For example, he wrote the majority opinion in *United States v. Rabinowitz* (1950). He found that it was not a violation of the Fourth Amendment's prohibition against unreasonable search and seizure for the police to conduct a warrantless search, during a lawful arrest, of the area within the suspect's control.

Pernicious anemia forced Minton to resign October 15, 1956, after seven years of service. His retirement announcement suggests that perhaps his career on the Court had not been as influential as he might have hoped. "There will be more interest in who will succeed me than in my passing," he wrote. "I'm an echo." He spent the last nine years of his life in retirement in New Albany, Indiana, where he died in 1965.

EARL WARREN

(1953–1969)

BIRTH: March 19, 1891, Los Angeles, California.

EDUCATION: University of California, B.L., 1912; J.D., 1914.

OFFICIAL POSITIONS: deputy city attorney, Oakland, California, 1919–1920; deputy district attorney, Alameda County, 1920–1925; district attorney, Alameda County, 1925–1939; California attorney general, 1939–1943; governor, 1943–1953.

SUPREME COURT SERVICE: nominated chief justice by President Dwight D. Eisenhower September 30, 1953, to replace Chief Justice Fred M. Vinson, who had died; confirmed March 1, 1954, by a voice vote; took judicial oath October 5, 1953; retired June 23, 1969; replaced by Warren E. Burger, nominated by President Richard Nixon.

FAMILY: married Nina P. Meyers, October 14, 1925; three sons, three daughters.

DEATH: July 9, 1974, Washington, D.C.

Earl Warren was the son of Scandinavian immigrant parents, Methias and Chrystal Hernlund Warren. Soon after his birth, the family moved to Bakersfield, where his father worked as a

Earl Warren

railroad car repairman. In 1938, after Warren had become active in politics, his father was bludgeoned to death in a crime that was never solved.

Warren worked his way through college and law school at the University of California. After graduation, he worked in law offices in San Francisco and Oakland, the only time in his career that he engaged in private practice.

From 1919 until his resignation from the Supreme Court in 1969, Warren served without interruption in public office. His first post was deputy city attorney for Oakland. Then he was named a deputy district attorney for Alameda County, which embraces the cities of Oakland, Alameda, and Berkeley.

In 1925 Warren was appointed district attorney when the incumbent resigned. He won election to the post in his own right in 1926, 1930, and 1934. During his fourteen years as district attorney, Warren developed a reputation as a crime fighter, sending a city manager and several councilmen to jail on graft charges and smashing a crooked deal on garbage collection.

A Republican, Warren decided in 1938 to run for state attorney general. He cross-filed and won three primaries—his own party's, as well as the Democratic and Progressive Party contests.

In 1942 he ran for governor of California. Although at first rated an underdog, Warren wound up defeating the incumbent Democratic governor, Culbert Olson, by a margin of 342,000, winning 57.1 percent of the vote. He was reelected twice, winning the Democratic as well as the Republican nomination in 1946 and defeating Democrat James Roosevelt, son of President Franklin D. Roosevelt, by an almost two-to-one margin in 1950.

At first viewed as a conservative governor—he denounced "communistic radicals" and supported the wartime federal order to move all persons of Japanese ancestry away from the West Coast—Warren developed a progressive image after the war. In 1945 he proposed a state program of prepaid medical insurance and later championed liberal pension and welfare benefits.

Warren made two bids for national political office. In 1948 he ran for vice president on the Republican ticket with Gov. Thomas E. Dewey of New York. In 1952 he sought the Republican presidential nomination. With little chance to win, however, he threw his support at a crucial moment behind Gen. Dwight D. Eisenhower, helping him win the battle with Sen. Robert A. Taft of Ohio for the nomination.

That support resulted in Eisenhower's political indebtedness to Warren, which the president repaid in 1953. After the death of Chief Justice Fred M. Vinson, Eisenhower nominated Warren to replace him. Reflecting on his choice years later in light of the Warren Court's liberal record, Eisenhower reportedly said that the appointment of Warren was the biggest mistake he made as president.

The Warren Court is credited with a large number of landmark decisions, many written by the chief justice. Best known is the Court's unanimous decision in *Brown v. Board of Education* (1954), which said that separate schools for blacks and whites were inherently unequal and violated the equal protection guarantee of the Fourteenth Amendment. Warren also wrote the majority opinion in *Miranda v. Arizona* (1966). Here the Court said that those held in police custody must be told of their constitutional rights before they can be questioned. Warren said, however, that the crowning achievement of his tenure was *Baker v. Carr,* a 1962 opinion written by Justice William Brennan. The decision in *Baker v. Carr* opened the federal courts to litigants who had been unable to convince their states to reapportion state legislative and congressional districts.

In addition to his work on the Court, Warren headed the commission that investigated the assassination of President John F. Kennedy.

In 1968 Warren submitted his resignation, conditional on confirmation of a successor. The Senate, however, became bogged down in the fight to confirm President Johnson's nomination of Associate Justice Abe Fortas to succeed him, so Warren agreed to serve another year. In 1969, when Richard Nixon assumed office, he chose Warren E. Burger as the new chief justice, and Warren stepped down.

JOHN MARSHALL HARLAN II
(1955–1971)

BIRTH: May 20, 1899, Chicago, Illinois.

EDUCATION: Princeton University, B.A., 1920; Rhodes scholar, Oxford University, Balliol College, B.A. in jurisprudence, 1923; New York Law School, LL.B., 1924.

OFFICIAL POSITIONS: assistant U.S. attorney, Southern District of New York, 1925–1927; special assistant attorney general, New York, 1928–1930; chief counsel, New York State Crime

John Marshall Harlan II

Commission, 1951–1953; judge, U.S. Court of Appeals for the Second Circuit, 1954–1955.

SUPREME COURT SERVICE: nominated associate justice by President Dwight D. Eisenhower November 8, 1954, to replace Robert Jackson, who had died; confirmed by the Senate March 16, 1955, by a 71-11 vote; took judicial oath March 28, 1955; retired September 23, 1971; replaced by William H. Rehnquist, nominated by President Richard Nixon.

FAMILY: married Ethel Andrews, November 10, 1928; one daughter.

DEATH: December 29, 1971, Washington D.C.

The namesake and grandson of Justice John Marshall Harlan (Supreme Court, 1877–1911) was born in Chicago, where his father, John Maynard Harlan, was a prominent attorney. John Maynard Harlan was also engaged in politics, running two losing races for mayor of Chicago near the turn of the century. The future justice's mother was Elizabeth Palmer Flagg Harlan.

The younger Harlan, who went by John M. Harlan, to distinguish himself from his famous forebear, attended Princeton University, graduating in 1920. Awarded a Rhodes scholarship, he spent the next three years studying jurisprudence at Balliol College, Oxford. Returning to the United States, he earned his law degree in 1924 from New York Law School.

For the next twenty-five years Harlan was a member of a prominent Wall Street law firm, but he took periodic leaves to serve in various public positions. In 1925 he became an assistant U.S. attorney for the Southern District of New York. He returned to private practice but soon left again, this time to serve as one of the special prosecutors in a state investigation of municipal graft.

During World War II, Harlan served as head of the Operational Analysis Section of the Eighth Air Force, even though he was well past the usual age of service. After the war he returned to private practice, but was again called to public service. From 1951 to 1953 he was chief counsel to the New York State Crime Commission, which Gov. Thomas E. Dewey had appointed to investigate the relationship between organized crime and state government. During the same period, Harlan also became active in various professional organizations, serving as chairman of the committee on professional ethics of the Association of the Bar of the City of New York and later as chairman of its committee on the judiciary and as vice president of the association.

A lifelong Republican, Harlan was nominated in January 1954 by President Eisenhower to the U.S. Court of Appeals for the Second Circuit. Harlan had hardly begun his work there, however, when the president named him in November 1954 to the U.S. Supreme Court. The Senate, then in special session to consider the censure of Sen. Joseph R. McCarthy, postponed consideration of his nomination until the new Congress met in 1955. Harlan remained on the appeals court until confirmed by the Senate in March 1955.

Harlan did not share the activist views of the Warren Court. He allied himself with Felix Frankfurter—they agreed in more than 80 percent of the cases they heard together—but he was much more of a moderate than a doctrinaire conservative. In the First Amendment area, his views were more liberal. In *NAACP v. Alabama ex rel. Patterson* (1958) he upheld the right of the organization to keep its membership lists private. In *Cohen v. California* (1971) he wrote the majority opinion, which extended to a rude message on the back of a jacket the constitutional protection afforded to speech.

Suffering from cancer of the spine, Harlan resigned from the Court in September 1971 and died December 29.

WILLIAM JOSEPH BRENNAN JR.

(1956–1990)

BIRTH: April 25, 1906, Newark, New Jersey.

DEATH: July 24, 1997, Arlington, Virginia

EDUCATION: University of Pennsylvania, B.S., 1928; Harvard Law School, LL.B., 1931.

OFFICIAL POSITIONS: judge, New Jersey Superior Court, 1949–1950; judge, appellate division, New Jersey Superior Court, 1950–1952; associate judge, New Jersey Supreme Court, 1952–1956.

SUPREME COURT SERVICE: recess appointment as associate justice by President Dwight D. Eisenhower October 16, 1956, to replace Sherman Minton, who had resigned; nominated as associate justice by President Eisenhower January 14, 1957; confirmed by the Senate March 19, 1957 by a voice vote; took judicial oath October 16, 1956; retired July 20, 1990; replaced by David H. Souter, nominated by President George Bush.

FAMILY: married Marjorie Leonard, May 5, 1928, died 1982; two sons, one daughter; married Mary Fowler, March 9, 1983.

William Joseph Brennan Jr.

William J. Brennan Jr. was the second of eight children of Irish parents who immigrated to the United States in 1890. His mother was Agnes McDermott Brennan. William displayed impressive academic abilities early in life. He was an outstanding student in high school, an honors student at the University of Pennsylvania's Wharton School of Finance, and in the top 10 percent of his Harvard Law School class in 1931.

After law school Brennan returned to Newark, where he joined a prominent law firm. Following passage of the Wagner Labor Act in 1935, Brennan began to specialize in labor law. With the outbreak of World War II, Brennan entered the Army, serving as a manpower troubleshooter on the staff of the undersecretary of war, Robert B. Patterson. At the conclusion of the war, Brennan returned to his old law firm. As his practice swelled, however, Brennan, a dedicated family man, began to resent the demands it placed on his time.

A desire to temper the pace of his work was one of the reasons Brennan accepted an appointment to the newly created New Jersey Superior Court in 1949. Because Brennan had been a leader in the movement to establish the court as part of a large program of judicial reform, it was not a surprise when Republican governor Alfred E. Driscoll selected him, even though he was a registered Democrat, to serve on it.

During his tenure on the superior court, Brennan's use of pretrial procedures to speed up the disposition of cases brought him to the attention of New Jersey Supreme Court justice Arthur T. Vanderbilt. It was reportedly at Vanderbilt's suggestion that Brennan was moved first in 1950 to the appellate division of the superior court and then in 1952 to the state supreme court. Late in 1956, when President Eisenhower was looking for a justice to replace Sherman Minton, Vanderbilt and others strongly recommended Brennan for the post, and Eisenhower gave him a recess appointment in October. There was some criticism that Eisenhower was currying favor with voters by nominating a Roman Catholic Democrat to the bench so close to the election, but Brennan's established integrity and nonpolitical background minimized the impact of the charges.

In his time on the Court, thirty-four years and nine months, it was hard to find an area of American life that Brennan did not affect. Among his most important opinions is *Baker v. Carr* (1962). Ruling that federal courts could consider cases of disproportionate voting districts, he said that states that fail to reapportion may be in violation of the Equal Protection Clause. In the area of free speech, Brennan ruled in *New York Times v. Sullivan* (1964) that to sue for libel public figures had to prove actual malice on the part of the media. Brennan also influenced thinking on the right to privacy. In *Eisenstadt v. Baird* (1972) Brennan wrote the opinion in which the Court expanded on its ruling in *Griswold v. Connecticut* (1965). *Eisenstadt* said that a ban on distribution of contraceptives to unmarried persons was unconstitutional.

Even after his many years on the Court, it was with reluctance that Brennan retired July 20, 1990. He had suffered a small stroke and was advised that the combination of his medical condition and his age, eighty-four at the time, would make it difficult to keep up his rigorous Court schedule. In the years immediately after his retirement, Brennan continued to go to his office every day. He kept busy with federal appeals court work, law school lectures, and speeches.

CHARLES EVANS WHITTAKER

(1957–1962)

BIRTH: February 22, 1901, Troy, Kansas.

EDUCATION: University of Kansas City Law School, LL.B., 1924.

OFFICIAL POSITIONS: judge, U.S. District Court for Western District of Missouri, 1954–1956; judge, Eighth Circuit Court of Appeals, 1956–1957.

SUPREME COURT SERVICE: nominated associate justice by President Dwight D. Eisenhower March 2, 1957, to replace Stanley Reed, who had retired; confirmed by the Senate March 19, 1957, by a voice vote; took judicial oath March 25, 1957; retired March 31, 1962; replaced by Byron R. White, nominated by President John F. Kennedy.

FAMILY: married Winifred R. Pugh, July 7, 1928; three sons.

DEATH: November 26, 1973, Kansas City, Missouri.

Charles Evans Whittaker's beginnings were humble. The son of Charles and Ida Miller Whittaker, he was born in eastern Kansas and raised on his father's farm. After his nomination to

Charles Evans Whittaker

the Supreme Court, Whittaker described to the Senate Judiciary Committee his early life: "I went to school in a little white school house on the corner of my father's farm through nine grades and then I went to high school in Troy, Kansas, and rode a pony to school through six miles of mud night and morning for about a year and a half."

Whittaker quit school after his mother died on his sixteenth birthday. Four years later he applied to the University of Kansas City Law School and was accepted only after agreeing to private tutoring in the high school subjects he had missed. His education was financed from the sale of pelts of animals he trapped on the Kansas plains and from part-time work as an office boy in the law firm Watson, Gage, and Ess. In 1923 he passed the Missouri bar examination, a year before he graduated from law school.

Whittaker joined the law firm where he had been the office boy. He became a full partner in 1932. He represented many corporate clients including Union Pacific and Montgomery Ward. Another client was the *Kansas City Star,* a newspaper controlled by Roy Roberts. Whittaker and Roberts became friends. Roberts was also a friend and political supporter of Gen. Dwight D. Eisenhower. As president, Eisenhower appointed Whittaker to the U.S. District Court for the Western District of Missouri from 1954 to 1956 and on the U.S. Court of Appeals for the Eighth Circuit in 1956 and 1957.

Eisenhower considered previous judicial experience one of the most important criteria for a Supreme Court justice. Whittaker's outstanding qualifications as well as his ties to the Republican Party made him a likely choice to fill the vacancy left by Stanley Reed's retirement. On March 19, 1957, Charles Whittaker became the first Supreme Court justice born in Kansas and appointed from Missouri.

As the junior justice, who traditionally votes last, Whittaker often had the unenviable task of breaking ties on a sharply divided Court. He tended to side with the liberals in cases dealing with individual liberties, such as *Green v. United States* (1957), which concerned double jeopardy, and *Moore v. Michigan* (1957), which dealt with the right to counsel. He, however, was on the side of the conservatives in two 1958 cases that upheld the convictions of defendants who claimed their confessions were coerced.

Exhausted from overwork, Whittaker suffered a nervous breakdown in 1962. He followed his doctor's advice and resigned from the Court at the age of sixty-one after only five years of service. Whittaker did not return to his former legal practice, nor was he active in public life. In 1965 he served on the legal staff of General Motors and the following year was asked by the Senate Committee on Standards and Conduct to help devise a code of senatorial ethics. The spread of civil disobedience in the 1960s particularly disturbed him, and he addressed the American Bar Association on various occasions concerning the need for "redress in the courts rather than in the streets."

He died November 26, 1973, in Kansas City.

POTTER STEWART

(1958–1981)

BIRTH: January 23, 1915, Jackson, Michigan.

EDUCATION: Yale College, B.A., cum laude, 1937; Yale Law School, LL.B., cum laude, 1941; fellow, Cambridge University, Cambridge, England, 1937–1938.

OFFICIAL POSITIONS: member, Cincinnati, Ohio, city council, 1950–1953; vice mayor of Cincinnati, 1952–1953; judge, Sixth Circuit Court of Appeals, 1954–1958.

SUPREME COURT SERVICE: received recess appointment as associate justice by President Dwight D. Eisenhower October 14, 1958, to replace Harold H. Burton, who had retired; nominated associate justice by President Eisenhower January 17, 1959; confirmed by the Senate May 5, 1959, by a 70-17 vote; took judicial oath October 14, 1958; retired July 3, 1981; replaced by Sandra Day O'Connor, nominated by President Ronald Reagan.

FAMILY: married Mary Ann Bertles, April 24, 1943; two sons, one daughter.

DEATH: December 7, 1985, Hanover, New Hampshire.

Stewart was the son of an established middle-class Cincinnati family with a strong tradition of public service and a respect for the benefits of a good education. His father, James Garfield Stewart, was mayor of Cincinnati from 1938 to 1947 and was the Republican nominee for governor of Ohio in 1944. He served on the Ohio Supreme Court from 1947 until his death in 1959. His mother, Harriet Potter Stewart, served as president of the League of Women Voters in Cincinnati.

Stewart attended two of the most prestigious eastern schools—Hotchkiss (preparatory) and Yale, where he received numerous academic honors and graduated Phi Beta Kappa in 1937. After completing his undergraduate work, he spent a year doing postgraduate work at Cambridge University in England. He returned to the United States in 1938 and began law school at Yale. He graduated in 1941 and moved to New York, where he joined a Wall Street law firm. He had hardly begun work there, however, when World War II broke out, and he joined the Navy. Stewart served as a deck officer aboard oil tankers in the Atlantic and Mediterranean. He married Mary Ann Bertles April 24, 1943, while his ship was in port. The couple eventually had three children.

After the war, Stewart returned to his New York law practice but soon moved to his hometown of Cincinnati, where he joined one of its leading law firms. In Cincinnati he took up the family's tradition of public service. He was twice elected to the city council and served one term as vice mayor. He was also involved in the 1948 and 1952 Republican presidential campaigns. In both years he supported the efforts of his friend, Sen. Robert A. Taft, to secure the Republican presidential nomination. When Eisenhower won the party's endorsement instead in 1952, Stewart actively supported him in the fall campaign.

Stewart's appointment in 1954 to the U.S. Court of Appeals for the Sixth Circuit ended his direct participation in politics. He was President Eisenhower's fifth and last appointment to the Supreme Court. He received a recess appointment in 1958, and Eisenhower sent his nomination to the new Congress early in 1959.

On the Court Stewart was described as a "swing justice," moving between the liberal and conservative factions. He, however, disliked the characterization of swing justice, saying that judges should be free of political, religious, and moral ideology when they make their decisions. He dissented from the Court's decision in *Griswold v. Connecticut* (1965), saying the statute in question, which prevented married couples from obtaining contraceptives, was "an uncommonly silly law," but not unconstitutional. He wrote more than six hundred opinions, many concerning the Fourth Amendment protection against unreasonable search and seizure—for example, the landmark *Katz v. United States* (1967), in which the Court extended such protection to the interception by police of telephone conversations.

Stewart retired July 3, 1981, after twenty-three years of service. He said he wanted to leave the Court while he was still relatively young and healthy enough to enjoy time with his family. He died four years later following a stroke in Hanover, New Hampshire December 7, 1985.

BYRON RAYMOND WHITE

(1962–1993)

BIRTH: June 8, 1917, Fort Collins, Colorado.

DEATH: April 15, 2000, Denver, Colorado

EDUCATION: University of Colorado, B.A., 1938; Rhodes Scholar, Oxford University, 1939; Yale Law School, LL.B., magna cum laude, 1946.

Byron Raymond White

OFFICIAL POSITIONS: law clerk to Chief Justice Fred M. Vinson, 1946–1947; deputy U.S. attorney general, 1961–1962.

SUPREME COURT SERVICE: nominated associate justice by President John F. Kennedy March 30, 1962, to replace Charles E. Whittaker, who had retired; confirmed by the Senate April 11, 1962, by a voice vote; took judicial oath April 16, 1962; retired June 28, 1993; replaced by Ruth Bader Ginsburg, nominated by President Bill Clinton.

DEATH: April 15, 2002, Denver, Colorado

FAMILY: married Marion Stearns, 1946; one son, one daughter.

White was born in Fort Collins, but grew up in Wellington, Colorado, a small town in the sugar beet area of the state. His father, Alpha Albert White, was in the lumber business and served as a Republican mayor of Wellington. His mother was Maude Burger White.

Ranking first in his high school class, White in 1934 won a scholarship to the University of Colorado, where he earned a reputation as an outstanding scholar-athlete. He was first in his class, a member of Phi Beta Kappa, and the winner of three varsity letters in football, four in basketball, and three in baseball. By the end of his college career in 1938 he had been dubbed "Whizzer" White for his prowess as a football player, a performance that earned him both a national reputation and a one-year contract with the old Pittsburgh Pirates professional football team.

After a year in football, White sailed for England to attend Oxford University, where he had received a coveted Rhodes Scholarship. When World War II broke out in September 1939, White returned to the United States and enrolled in Yale Law

School, alternating law study with playing professional football for the Detroit Lions.

When the United States entered the war, White joined the Navy, serving in the South Pacific. He returned to Yale after the war, earning his law degree magna cum laude.

White then served as law clerk to the new chief justice, Fred M. Vinson. In 1947 he returned to his native Colorado, where for the next fourteen years he practiced law with a prominent Denver law firm.

Several times during his adult life, White had crossed paths with John F. Kennedy. The two first met when White was studying at Oxford and Kennedy's father, Joseph, was ambassador to the Court of St. James's. They met again during White's wartime service in the South Pacific. When White was clerking for Vinson, he renewed his acquaintance with Kennedy, then a freshman U.S. representative.

In 1960, when Kennedy decided to run for president, White joined the campaign and headed the preconvention Kennedy effort in Colorado. After Kennedy's nomination, White became chairman of the National Citizens for Kennedy organization, designed to attract independents and Republicans. President Kennedy named White to the post of deputy attorney general, a position White held until Kennedy named him to the Supreme Court in 1962.

Joining a Court with a solid liberal bloc, White quickly gained a reputation for strong dissents. Indeed, he dissented from some of the most influential decisions of the late twentieth century, among them *Escobedo v. Illinois* (1964) and *Miranda v. Arizona* (1966), in the criminal justice field, and *Roe v. Wade* (1973), which guarantees a woman's right to have an abortion. He wrote the majority opinion in *Bowers v. Hardwick* (1986), in which the Court upheld a state law prohibiting sodomy.

White retired from the Court June 28, 1993, after thirty-one years and two months of service. He was seventy-six years old at the time but in good health, still enjoying various athletic activities. "It has been an interesting and exciting experience to serve on the Court," he said, adding that he was retiring because it was time that "someone else be permitted to have a like experience."

Nine years after retiring, White died at age eighty-four. The last survivor of the Warren Court (1953–1969) passed away April 15, 2002, in Denver, Colorado.

ARTHUR JOSEPH GOLDBERG

(1962–1965)

BIRTH: August 8, 1908, Chicago, Illinois.

EDUCATION: Northwestern University, B.S.L., 1929; J.D., summa cum laude, 1930.

OFFICIAL POSITIONS: secretary of labor, 1961–1962; U.S. ambassador to the United Nations, 1965–1968.

SUPREME COURT SERVICE: nominated associate justice by President John F. Kennedy August 29, 1962, to replace Felix Frankfurter, who had retired; confirmed by the Senate September 25,

Arthur Joseph Goldberg

1962, by a voice vote; took judicial oath October 1, 1962; resigned July 25, 1965; replaced by Abe Fortas, nominated by President Lyndon B. Johnson.

FAMILY: married Dorothy Kurgans, July 18, 1931; one daughter, one son.

DEATH: January 19, 1990, Washington, D.C.

The youngest of eleven children born to his Russian Jewish parents, Joseph and Rebecca Perlstein Goldberg, Arthur Goldberg was admitted to the Illinois bar at age twenty. He first gained national attention as counsel to the Chicago Newspaper Guild during its 1938 strike. After serving as a special assistant in the Office of Strategic Services during World War II, Goldberg returned to the practice of labor law, representing both the Congress of Industrial Organizations (CIO) and the United Steelworkers of America. He played a major role in the 1955 merger of the CIO with the American Federation of Labor and worked as a special counsel to the new AFL-CIO until 1961.

Appointed secretary of labor in the first year of the Kennedy administration, Goldberg's tenure saw the passage of the Area Redevelopment Act of 1961, congressional approval of an increase in the minimum wage, and the reorganization of the Office of Manpower Administration (now the Employment and Training Administration).

President Kennedy's second Supreme Court appointment, Goldberg was named August 29, 1962, to replace Felix Frankfurter, who had held the "Jewish seat" since 1939. It had been occupied formerly by Justice Benjamin N. Cardozo, 1932–1938.

Although his service on the Court was brief, Goldberg wrote a number of significant majority opinions. Among the best known is *Escobedo v. Illinois* (1964), in which the Court overturned the conviction of a man for murder because he had not been informed of his right to remain silent and not incriminate himself.

President Johnson asked Goldberg to leave the Court and become U.S. ambassador to the United Nations July 20, 1965. Goldberg replaced Adlai Stevenson, who had died July 14 in London. He resigned the post in 1968. After an unsuccessful race for governor of New York against Republican incumbent Nelson Rockefeller in 1970, Goldberg returned to Washington, D.C., where he remained in private practice. A frequent guest instructor at universities and colleges, he was the author of *AFL-CIO Labor United*, 1956; *Defenses of Freedom*, 1966; and *Equal Justice: The Warren Era of the Supreme Court*, 1972.

Goldberg died January 19, 1990 in Washington, D.C.

ABE FORTAS

(1965–1969)

BIRTH: June 19, 1910, Memphis, Tennessee.

EDUCATION: Southwestern College, A.B., 1930; Yale Law School, LL.B., 1933.

OFFICIAL POSITIONS: assistant director, corporate reorganization study, Securities and Exchange Commission, 1934–1937; assistant director, Public Utilities Division, Securities and Exchange Commission, 1938–1939; general counsel, Public Works Administration, 1939–1940, and counsel to the Bituminous Coal Division, 1939–1941; director, Division of Power, Department of the Interior, 1941–1942; undersecretary of the interior, 1942–1946.

Abe Fortas

SUPREME COURT SERVICE: nominated associate justice by President Lyndon B. Johnson July 28, 1965, to replace Arthur J. Goldberg, who had resigned; confirmed by the Senate August 11, 1965, by a voice vote; took judicial oath October 4, 1965; resigned May 14, 1969; replaced by Harry A. Blackmun, nominated by President Richard Nixon.

FAMILY: married Carolyn Eugenia Agger, July 9, 1935.

DEATH: April 5, 1982, in Washington, D.C.

Fortas was the youngest of five children born to Ray Berson Fortas and William Fortas, an English immigrant cabinetmaker. After working his way through Southwestern College in Memphis, from which he graduated first in his class in 1930, Fortas entered Yale Law School, where he met William O. Douglas, a young professor. Fortas served as editor of the school's law journal and graduated in 1933.

As a child Fortas had developed an interest in music and learned the violin, a skill he used to earn money while in school. Throughout his adult life he played in various string quartets. In 1935 he married Carolyn Eugenia Agger, who became a renowned tax lawyer.

Upon graduation, Fortas joined the faculty at Yale as an associate professor of law. The excitement and activity generated by President Franklin D. Roosevelt's New Deal in Washington soon enticed the young lawyer away from academic pursuits and into public office.

During the 1930s Fortas held a series of jobs in the Roosevelt administration, mostly involving detailed legal work in newly created agencies such as the Securities and Exchange Commission (with Douglas) and the Public Works Administration. In 1942 he was appointed undersecretary of the interior, serving under the controversial and irascible Harold L. Ickes.

Following World War II, Fortas helped found the law firm of Arnold, Fortas, and Porter, which quickly became one of Washington's most prestigious legal institutions. The firm specialized in corporate law, but its members, including Fortas, found time to litigate some important civil and individual rights cases as well. He defended Owen Lattimore against charges of disloyalty and argued Clarence Earl Gideon's case before the Supreme Court.

In 1948 Fortas successfully defended a member of Congress from Texas—Lyndon B. Johnson—in a challenge to Johnson's election victory in the Texas Democratic senatorial primary. That defense was the basis for an enduring friendship between the two men, and Fortas became one of Johnson's most trusted advisers.

Preferring his role as confidential adviser, Fortas in 1964 declined Johnson's offer to name him attorney general. In 1965 Johnson persuaded Justice Arthur J. Goldberg to resign from the Supreme Court to become the U.S. ambassador to the United Nations, which created a vacancy on the Court for Fortas. Johnson ignored Fortas's opposition and appointed him to the Court.

He is best known for two cases involving the rights of juveniles. In 1967 he held in *In re Gault* that the privilege against self-incrimination and the right to counsel extended to those accused in juvenile court. In *Tinker v. Des Moines Independent Community School District* (1969) Fortas said that the wearing of black armbands to school to protest the Vietnam War was "closely akin" to "pure speech" protected by the First Amendment.

When Chief Justice Earl Warren voiced his intention to resign in 1968, Johnson decided to elevate Fortas to the chief justiceship, but amid charges of "cronyism," events began to unfold that ultimately led to Fortas's undoing.

In the face of strong opposition from Republicans and conservative Democrats, Johnson was finally forced to withdraw the nomination, but not before it was revealed that Fortas had received $15,000 to teach a course at a local university.

Then, in May 1969, *Life* magazine revealed that since becoming a justice Fortas had accepted—and then returned several months later—$20,000 from a charitable foundation controlled by the family of an indicted stock manipulator. The allegations touched off talk of impeachment proceedings against Fortas. In mid-May, denying any "wrongdoing on my part," Fortas resigned from the Court. He then returned to private law practice in Washington in partnership with another attorney, a practice he maintained until his death in 1982.

Thurgood Marshall

THURGOOD MARSHALL

(1967–1991)

BIRTH: July 2, 1908, Baltimore, Maryland.

EDUCATION: Lincoln University, A.B., cum laude, 1930; Howard University Law School, LL.B., 1933.

OFFICIAL POSITIONS: judge, Second Circuit Court of Appeals, 1961–1965; U.S. solicitor general, 1965–1967.

SUPREME COURT SERVICE: nominated associate justice by President Lyndon B. Johnson June 13, 1967, to replace Tom C. Clark, who had retired; confirmed by the Senate August 30, 1967, by a 69-11 vote; took judicial oath October 2, 1967; retired October 1, 1991; replaced by Clarence Thomas, nominated by President George Bush.

FAMILY: married Vivian Burey, September 4, 1929, died February 1955; married Cecilia Suyat, December 17, 1955; two sons.

DEATH: January 24, 1993, Bethesda, Maryland.

Marshall was the son of Norma Williams Marshall, a primary school teacher, and William Canfield Marshall, a club steward. In 1926 he left Baltimore to attend the all-black Lincoln University in Chester, Pennsylvania, where he developed a reputation as an outstanding debater. After graduating cum laude in 1930, Marshall decided to study law and entered Howard University in Washington, D.C.

While he was in college, Marshall developed a lifelong interest in civil rights. After graduating first in his law school class in 1933, he began a long and historic involvement with the National Association for the Advancement of Colored People (NAACP). In 1940 he became the head of the newly formed

NAACP Legal Defense and Education Fund, a position he held for more than twenty years.

Over those two decades, Marshall coordinated the fund's attack on segregation in voting, housing, public accommodations, and education. The culmination of his career as a civil rights attorney came in 1954 as chief counsel in a series of cases grouped under the title *Brown v. Board of Education*. In that historic case, which Marshall argued before the Supreme Court, civil rights advocates convinced the Court to declare segregation in public schools unconstitutional.

In 1961 Marshall was appointed by President Kennedy to the Second Circuit Court of Appeals, but because of heated opposition from southern Democratic senators, he was not confirmed for a year.

Four years after he was named to the appeals court, Marshall was chosen by President Lyndon B. Johnson to be the nation's first black solicitor general. During his years as the government's chief advocate before the Supreme Court, Marshall scored impressive victories in the areas of civil and constitutional rights. He won Supreme Court approval of the 1965 Voting Rights Act, voluntarily informed the Court that the government had used electronic eavesdropping devices in two cases, and joined in a suit that successfully overturned a California constitutional amendment that prohibited open housing legislation.

On June 13, 1967, President Johnson chose Marshall to become the first black justice of the Supreme Court. He is known for his majority opinion in *Stanley v. Georgia* (1969), which held that the Constitution protects a person's right to read anything he chooses in the privacy of his home. In *Benton v. Maryland*

(1969) he wrote the opinion that applies the Double Jeopardy Clause of the Constitution to state actions. Always opposed to the death penalty, Marshall joined his colleague William Brennan in dissenting in every case that upheld it.

After nearly a quarter century of service on the Court, Marshall retired October 1, 1991. When he announced he would be stepping down, he said his advancing age and worsening health prevented him from continuing on the bench. Marshall, who had championed civil rights and individual liberties, had become the bitter voice of dissent on a Court that was becoming more conservative. He died less than two years later, in January 1993.

WARREN EARL BURGER

(1969–1986)

BIRTH: September 17, 1907, St. Paul, Minnesota.

EDUCATION: attended the University of Minnesota, 1925–1927; St. Paul College of Law (now William Mitchell College of Law), LL.B., magna cum laude, 1931.

OFFICIAL POSITIONS: assistant U.S. attorney general, Civil Division, Justice Department, 1953–1956; judge, U.S. Court of Appeals for the District of Columbia, 1956–1969.

SUPREME COURT SERVICE: nominated chief justice by President Richard Nixon May 21, 1969, to replace Chief Justice Earl Warren, who had retired; confirmed by the Senate June 9, 1969, by a 74-3 vote; took judicial oath June 23, 1969; retired September 26, 1986; replaced as chief justice by William H. Rehnquist, named by President Ronald Reagan.

Warren Earl Burger

FAMILY: married Elvera Stromberg, November 8, 1933; one son, one daughter.

DEATH: June 25, 1995, Washington, D.C.

Burger was the fourth of seven children born to Charles J. Burger and Katharine Schnittger Burger. His Swiss-German-Austrian grandparents had come to the Middle West before the Civil War. Financially unable to attend college full-time, Burger spent the years following his 1925 graduation from high school attending college and law school evening classes—two years at the University of Minnesota and four at St. Paul College of Law, now William Mitchell College of Law. To support himself, Burger worked full-time as an accountant for a life insurance company.

After graduating with honors from law school in 1931, Burger joined a respected law firm in Minnesota, where he practiced until 1953. He also taught part-time at his alma mater from 1931 to 1948.

As a schoolboy Burger developed an interest in art and was an accomplished sculptor; as chief justice, he served as chairman of the board of the National Gallery of Art. He was an antiques buff and a connoisseur of fine wines. He also served as chancellor of the Smithsonian Institution.

Soon after beginning his law career in Minnesota, Burger became involved in Republican state politics. In 1938 he helped in the successful campaign of Harold E. Stassen for governor of Minnesota.

During Stassen's unsuccessful bid for the Republican presidential nomination ten years later, Burger first met a man who was to figure prominently in his future—Herbert Brownell, then campaign manager for GOP presidential nominee Thomas E. Dewey. Brownell, who became attorney general during the Eisenhower administration, brought Burger to Washington in 1953 to serve as assistant attorney general in charge of the Justice Department's Civil Division.

Burger's stint as assistant attorney general from 1953 to 1956 was not without controversy. His decision to defend the government's action in the dismissal of John F. Peters, a part-time federal employee, on grounds of disloyalty—after Solicitor General Simon E. Sobeloff had refused to do so on grounds of conscience—won Burger the enmity of many liberals.

Burger's overall record as assistant attorney general, however, apparently met with President Eisenhower's approval, and in 1956 the president appointed Burger to the U.S. Court of Appeals for the District of Columbia Circuit. As an appeals court judge, Burger developed a reputation as a conservative, especially in criminal justice cases.

Off the bench, Burger began to speak out in support of major administrative reform of the judicial system—a cause he continued to advocate as chief justice. Due in large part to Burger's efforts, the American Bar Association and other legal groups established the Institute of Court Management to train court executive officers, bring new management techniques to the courts, and relieve judges of paperwork. During Burger's years as chief justice, Congress also approved a number of measures to modernize the operations of the federal judiciary.

President Nixon's appointment of Burger as chief justice on May 21, 1969, caught most observers by surprise because, despite the nominee's years of service in the Justice Department and the court of appeals, he was little known outside the legal community. Nixon apparently was impressed by Burger's consistent argument as an appeals judge that the Constitution should be read narrowly, a belief Nixon shared.

In an odd twist of fate, Burger announced the unanimous decision of the Court that led to Nixon's resignation. In *United States v. Nixon* (1974) the Court ruled that the president must surrender tapes of conversations recorded in the Oval Office. The tapes had been subpoenaed in a criminal conspiracy trial, the culmination of the Watergate scandal. Burger's opinion argued that a president's privileges and immunities were not absolute but depended on the circumstances. In this case the need for evidence to conduct a fair trial outweighed presidential privilege.

Burger served for seventeen years as chief justice, resigning in 1986 to devote full-time to the chairmanship of the commission planning the Constitution's bicentennial celebration in 1987. He continued to write and speak about judicial administration and reform of the legal system until his death in Washington on June 25, 1995. Just a few months earlier, he had published a book entitled *It is So Ordered: A Constitution Unfolds*.

Harry Andrew Blackmun

HARRY ANDREW BLACKMUN

(1970–1994)

BIRTH: November 12, 1908, Nashville, Illinois.

EDUCATION: Harvard College, B.A., summa cum laude, 1929; Harvard Law School, LL.B., 1932.

OFFICIAL POSITIONS: clerk, Eighth Circuit Court of Appeals, 1932–1933; judge, Eighth Circuit Court of Appeals, 1959–1970.

SUPREME COURT SERVICE: nominated associate justice by President Richard Nixon April 14, 1970, to replace Abe Fortas, who had resigned; confirmed by the Senate May 12, 1970, by a 94-0 vote; took judicial oath June 9, 1970; retired August 3, 1994; replaced by Stephen G. Breyer, nominated by President Bill Clinton.

FAMILY: married Dorothy E. Clark, June 21, 1941; three daughters.

DEATH: March 4, 1999, Arlington, Virginia

Harry Blackmun was born in Nashville, Illinois, to Corwin Blackmun and Theo Reuter Blackmun. He spent most of his early years in the Minneapolis-St. Paul area. In grade school Blackmun began a lifelong friendship with Warren Burger, with whom he was later to serve on the Supreme Court.

Showing an early aptitude for mathematics, Blackmun went east after high school to attend Harvard College on a scholarship. At Harvard Blackmun majored in mathematics and thought briefly of becoming a physician, but chose the law instead. He graduated Phi Beta Kappa from Harvard in 1929 and entered Harvard Law School, from which he graduated in 1932. During his school years, Blackmun supported himself with a variety of odd jobs, including tutoring in math and driving the launch for the college crew team.

Blackmun returned to St. Paul, where he served for a year and a half as clerk to Judge John B. Sanborn, whom Blackmun was to succeed on the U.S. circuit court in 1959. He left the clerkship in 1933 to enter private practice with a Minneapolis law firm, where he remained for sixteen years. During that time he also taught at the St. Paul College of Law, Burger's alma mater, and at the University of Minnesota Law School.

In 1950 he accepted a post as counsel for the world-famous Mayo Clinic in Rochester, Minnesota. There, Blackmun quickly developed a reputation among his colleagues as a serious man totally engrossed in his profession.

This reputation followed him to the bench of the Eighth Circuit Court of Appeals, to which Blackmun was appointed by President Eisenhower in 1959. As an appeals court judge, Blackmun became known for his scholarly and thorough opinions.

Blackmun's nomination to the Supreme Court was President Nixon's third try to fill the seat vacated by Justice Abe Fortas's resignation. When the Senate refused to confirm Nixon's first two nominees—Clement F. Haynsworth Jr. of South Carolina and G. Harrold Carswell of Florida—Nixon said that he had concluded that the Senate "as it is presently constituted" would not confirm a southern nominee who was also a judicial conservative.

Nixon then turned to Chief Justice Burger's friend, Harry Blackmun, who was confirmed without opposition. During his first years on the Court, Blackmun was frequently linked with Burger as the "Minnesota Twins," who thought and voted alike, but, beginning with his authorship of the Court's 1973 ruling in *Roe v. Wade*, legalizing abortion, Blackmun moved in a steadily more liberal direction. Reinforcing his commitment to the concept of privacy, Blackmun dissented from *Bowers v. Hardwick* (1986), in which the majority upheld Georgia's law prohibiting sodomy. Blackmun declared that the case concerned not whether sodomy was constitutionally protected, but whether an individual has the right to be let alone.

Blackmun's liberal transformation continued into his last term on the Court when he surprised observers by announcing that he could no longer support capital punishment because it could not be fairly administered. By the time he retired in 1994, he was its most liberal member, a statement as revealing of the conservative transformation of the Court in the 1980s and early 1990s as of Blackmun's own shift to the liberal side.

LEWIS FRANKLIN POWELL JR.

(1972–1987)

BIRTH: September 19, 1907, Suffolk, Virginia.

EDUCATION: Washington and Lee University, B.S., 1929; Washington and Lee University Law School, LL.B., 1931; Harvard Law School, LL.M., 1932.

OFFICIAL POSITIONS: president of the Richmond School Board, 1952–1961; member, 1961–1969, and president, 1968–1969, Virginia State Board of Education; president of the American Bar Association, 1964–1965; president, American College of Trial Lawyers, 1968–1969.

SUPREME COURT SERVICE: nominated associate justice by President Richard Nixon October 22, 1971, to replace Hugo L. Black, who had retired; confirmed by the Senate December 6, 1971, by an 89-1 vote; took judicial oath January 6, 1972; retired June 26, 1987; replaced by Anthony Kennedy, nominated by President Ronald Reagan.

FAMILY: married Josephine M. Rucker, May 2, 1936; three daughters, one son.

DEATH: August 25, 1998, Richmond, Virginia

Powell was born to Lewis F. Powell Sr. and Mary Gwathmey Powell in Suffolk, in Tidewater Virginia, but spent most of his life in Richmond. He attended Washington and Lee University in Lexington, Virginia, where he earned a B.S. and election to Phi Beta Kappa. He stayed at Washington and Lee for law school, graduating in two years instead of the usual three. He then obtained a master's degree from Harvard Law School in 1932.

Turning down an offer from a top New York law firm, Powell returned to Virginia and joined one of the state's oldest and most prestigious law firms, located in Richmond. After a two-year association, Powell joined another firm and eventually became a

Lewis Franklin Powell Jr.

senior partner. Except for three years as an Air Force intelligence officer during World War II, Powell worked at this firm until his nomination to the Supreme Court.

Powell's practice included both corporate law and litigation experience. As attorney for a number of national corporations, he was no stranger to blue-chip boardrooms. He represented his profession on the national level as president of the American Bar Association and the American College of Trial Lawyers.

Powell's reputation as a moderate stemmed from his work as president of the Richmond School Board (1952–1961) and as a member and president of the Virginia State Board of Education. In the face of intense pressure for "massive" resistance to desegregation, Powell consistently advocated keeping the schools open.

A one-year stint from 1964 to 1965 as president of the American Bar Association provided Powell with a national platform from which to express his views on a variety of subjects and enhanced his reputation as a moderate. On the liberal side, Powell spoke out against inadequate legal services for the poor and worked to create the legal services program of the Office of Economic Opportunity. A more conservative tone characterized his view of social ills caused by parental permissiveness and his stern denunciations of civil disobedience and other forms of civil demonstrations. As a member in 1966 of President Lyndon B. Johnson's Crime Commission, Powell participated in a minority statement criticizing Supreme Court rulings upholding the right of criminal suspects to remain silent.

During Powell's sixteen years on the Court, it became more closely balanced between liberals and conservatives, and he became the single most important member, able to cast the deciding vote on a long list of issues, including abortion and affirmative action.

Powell retired on the last day of the October 1986 term. He said he had served longer than the decade he had originally intended and that a recent illness had made him aware of how the prolonged absence of one justice handicapped the Court. Powell's health improved after he stepped down, and he often volunteered to sit on federal appeals court cases. In the decade that followed, Powell frequently remarked that he wished he had not retired so soon.

WILLIAM HUBBS REHNQUIST

(1972–1986, 1986–)

BIRTH: October 1, 1924, Milwaukee, Wisconsin.

EDUCATION: Stanford University, B.A., 1948, M.A., 1948; Harvard University, M.A., 1950; Stanford University Law School, LL.B., 1952.

OFFICIAL POSITIONS: law clerk to Supreme Court Justice Robert H. Jackson, 1952–1953; assistant U.S. attorney general, Office of Legal Counsel, 1969–1971.

SUPREME COURT SERVICE: nominated associate justice by President Richard Nixon October 21, 1971, to replace John Marshall Harlan, who had retired; confirmed by the Senate December 10, 1971, by a 68-26 vote; took judicial oath January 7, 1972; nominated chief justice by President Ronald Reagan June 20, 1986; confirmed by the Senate, 65-33, September 17, 1986; took judicial oath September 26, 1986; replaced as associate justice by Antonin Scalia, nominated by President Reagan.

FAMILY: married Natalie Cornell, August 29, 1953; died October 17, 1991; one son, two daughters.

William Rehnquist was born and grew up in Milwaukee. His mother was Margery Peck Rehnquist and his father was William B. Rehnquist, a paper salesman. After World War II service in the Air Force, he attended Stanford University on the G.I. Bill and received both a B.A. and an M.A. in political science in 1948. He earned another M.A. in government at Harvard University (conferred in 1950) before returning to Stanford to attend law school. He graduated first in his class in 1952. One of his classmates was Sandra Day, who later joined him on the Supreme Court.

After finishing law school, Rehnquist clerked for Justice Robert H. Jackson. In 1952 he wrote a memorandum for Jackson that was much discussed during his Senate confirmation hearings. The memorandum favored separate but equal schools for blacks and whites. Asked about those views by the Senate Judiciary Committee in 1971, Rehnquist repudiated them, declaring that they were Justice Jackson's, not his own.

In 1953, following his clerkship, Rehnquist married Natalie Cornell, whom he had met at Stanford, and began his law practice in Phoenix, Arizona, He also became immersed in Republican state politics. From his earliest days in Arizona, Rehnquist was associated with the party's most conservative wing. A 1957 speech denouncing the liberalism of the Warren Court typified his views at the time.

During the 1964 presidential campaign, Rehnquist campaigned ardently for Barry Goldwater, the GOP candidate. He also met and worked with Richard G. Kleindienst, who, as President Nixon's deputy attorney general, would later appoint Rehnquist to head the Justice Department's Office of Legal Counsel.

Rehnquist quickly became one of the Nixon administration's chief spokesmen on Capitol Hill, commenting on issues ranging from wiretapping to rights of the accused. It was Rehnquist's job to review the legality of all presidential executive orders and other constitutional law questions in the executive branch. He frequently testified before congressional committees in support of the administration's policies—most of which matched his own conservative philosophy. So tightly reasoned and articulate was his testimony—backing controversial matters such as government surveillance of American citizens and tighter curbs on obscene materials—that members of Congress from both parties acknowledged his ability.

In 1971 President Nixon nominated him to the Supreme Court. As an associate justice, Rehnquist voted consistently in favor of law enforcement over the rights of suspects and for states' rights over the power of the federal government, votes that usually put him in the minority. After serving on the Court for fifteen years, he was promoted to chief justice by President

Ronald Reagan, the third sitting associate justice in history to be elevated to chief justice.

Controversy surrounded his 1986 nomination. His views on civil rights were questioned, and he was accused of harassing black voters in Phoenix during the 1950s and early 1960s. He was approved by a vote of 65-33, which in 1986 was more opposition than any other successful Supreme Court nominee in the twentieth century had survived.

Since becoming chief justice in 1986, Rehnquist has been the Court's unquestioned leader and its most dominant figure. He has made the Court into a reliable supporter of law enforcement and of the death penalty. He also has edged the Court toward greater support for public aid to religious schools and restrictions on the use of affirmative action and the "racial gerrymandering" of electoral districts.

Rehnquist led a revival of states' rights and breathed new life into the principle that the Court has a duty to limit the power of Congress and the federal government. "We start with first principles. The Constitution creates a Federal government [whose] powers are few and defined," he said in *United States v. Lopez,* a 1995 ruling striking down a federal gun control law. In later rulings, the chief justice set out his view that the states are "sovereign entities" whose core powers cannot be infringed by the federal government. All of these decisions in the area of federalism came by 5-4 votes, however, suggesting that their future depends on the ideological leanings of future justices.

In 1997 Rehnquist spoke for the Court in two decisions that rejected the notion of a constitutional "right to die." This sensitive matter should be decided by the states, he said in *Washington v. Glucksberg* and *Vacco v. Quill.* He also spoke for the Court in 2002 in upholding a state voucher program for students in religious schools, but he dissented when the Court struck down the death penalty for mentally retarded defendants. The chief justice dissented as well in 2003 when the Court upheld the use of affirmative action in state colleges and when the 6-3 majority struck down antisodomy laws in a Texas case.

In 1999 Rehnquist presided over the Senate during the impeachment trial of President Bill Clinton and announced his acquittal on all the charges. An amateur historian, he wrote three popular books while serving as chief justice: *The Supreme Court: How It Was, How It Is* (1988), *Grand Inquests: The Historic Impeachments of Justice Samuel Chase and President Andrew Johnson* (1992), and *All the Laws but One: Civil Liberties in Wartime* (1998).

JOHN PAUL STEVENS

(1975–)

BIRTH: April 20, 1920, Chicago, Illinois.

EDUCATION: University of Chicago, B.A., 1941; Northwestern University School of Law, J.D., magna cum laude, 1947.

OFFICIAL POSITIONS: law clerk to Justice Wiley B. Rutledge, 1947–1948; associate counsel, Subcommittee on the Study of Monopoly Power, House Judiciary Committee, 1951; member,

John Paul Stevens

U.S. Attorney General's National Committee to Study the Antitrust Laws, 1953–1955; judge, Seventh Circuit Court of Appeals, 1970–1975.

SUPREME COURT SERVICE: nominated associate justice by President Gerald R. Ford November 28, 1975, to replace William O. Douglas, who had retired; confirmed by the Senate December 17, 1975, by a 98-0 vote; took judicial oath December 19, 1975.

FAMILY: married Elizabeth Jane Sheeren, 1942, divorced 1979; one son, three daughters; married Maryan Mulholland Simon, 1980.

John Paul Stevens is the youngest of the four sons of Ernest James Stevens and Elizabeth Street Stevens. His family was prominent in Chicago. Stevens graduated Phi Beta Kappa from the University of Chicago in 1941. After a wartime stint in the Navy during which he earned the Bronze Star, he returned to Chicago to enter Northwestern University Law School, graduating in 1947. Stevens then served as a law clerk to Justice Wiley B. Rutledge. He left Washington to join a prominent Chicago law firm that specialized in antitrust law.

Stevens developed a reputation as a preeminent antitrust lawyer, and after three years formed his own law firm, Rothschild, Stevens, Barry, and Myers. He remained there, also teaching part-time at Northwestern University and the University of Chicago law schools until his appointment by President Nixon in 1970 to the Seventh Circuit Court of Appeals.

Stevens for a time flew his own small airplane. He was also a nationally competitive bridge player and a golf and tennis enthusiast.

Stevens developed a reputation as a political moderate during his undergraduate days at the University of Chicago, then an overwhelmingly liberal campus. A registered Republican, he was never active in partisan politics. Nevertheless, Stevens served as Republican counsel in 1951 to a House Judiciary subcommittee's study of monopoly power. He also served from 1953 to 1955, during the Eisenhower administration, as a member of the attorney general's National Committee to Study the Antitrust Laws.

When President Ford nominated Stevens to the Supreme Court seat vacated by veteran liberal William O. Douglas, observers struggled to pin an ideological label on the new nominee. On the whole, however, they decided that he was neither a doctrinaire liberal nor a conservative, but a centrist whose well-crafted scholarly opinions made him a "judge's judge." He was unanimously confirmed.

On the Court, Stevens has proved the observations correct—he has been pragmatic and independent rather than ideological. For example, in writing the Court's opinion in *Federal Communications Commission v. Pacifica Foundation* (1978), Stevens chose to focus on the practical aspects of the case rather than freedom of speech in the abstract. He concluded that the FCC could regulate language that was broadcast at times when young children were likely to be listening.

With the conservative appointments of the Reagan and Bush years, Stevens, despite his lack of definitive ideology, is now considered one of the liberal justices. He wrote the Court's 1995 decision throwing out state term limits for members of Congress, saying that permitting such tenure restrictions would lead to a patchwork of state qualifications and undermine the uniformity and national character of the U.S. government.

Stevens strongly dissented from rulings that curbed the powers of Congress and revived what he referred to as the discredited doctrine of states' rights. He mocked his conservative colleagues for having invented the principle of state "sovereign immunity," which the framers of 1787 had forgotten to mention in the text of the Constitution. In 2002 Stevens spoke for the Court in *Atkins v. Virginia*, declaring an end to the execution of mentally retarded defendants. He has also been a longtime advocate of the separation of church and state and a more recent convert to the cause of affirmative action and gay rights. Well into his early eighties, Stevens continued to be a lively presence during the Court's oral arguments and a writer of energetic and fresh opinions.

SANDRA DAY O'CONNOR

(1981–)

BIRTH: March 26, 1930, El Paso, Texas.

EDUCATION: Stanford University, B.A., 1950, Stanford University Law School, LL.B., 1952.

OFFICIAL POSITIONS: deputy county attorney, San Mateo, California, 1952–1953; assistant attorney general, Arizona, 1965–1969; Arizona state senator, 1969–1975, majority leader,

Sandra Day O'Connor

state Senate, 1973–1974; judge, Maricopa County Superior Court, 1975–1979; judge, Arizona Court of Appeals, 1979–1981.

SUPREME COURT SERVICE: nominated associate justice by President Ronald Reagan August 19, 1981, to replace Potter Stewart, who had retired; confirmed by the Senate by a 99–0 vote, September 21, 1981; took judicial oath September 26, 1981.

FAMILY: married John O'Connor, 1952; three sons.

Sandra Day, the daughter of Harry A. Day and Ada Mae Wilkey Day, was born a pioneer. She is the grandchild of a man who left Kansas in 1880 to take up farming in the desert Southwest. She was born in El Paso because her mother had gone there to stay with her parents, rather than give birth at the Lazy B Ranch, which was far from any hospital. Day grew up dividing her time between El Paso, where she lived with her grandmother and attended school, and summers on the 162,000-acre ranch that her grandfather had founded in southeastern Arizona.

After graduating from high school at sixteen, Day attended Stanford University, earning a degree in economics, magna cum laude, in 1950. She stayed at Stanford for her law degree, which she received in 1952. At law school, she met two men who would figure largely in her adult life—John J. O'Connor III, whom she married in December 1952, and William H. Rehnquist, whom she joined as a colleague on the U.S. Supreme Court in 1981.

Her law school record was outstanding. She was an editor of the *Stanford Law Review* and a member of Order of the Coif, a legal honorary society. She, however, was a woman in a field where women were oddities, and so it was difficult for her to find a job as an attorney. She applied, among other places, to the

firm in which William French Smith was a partner, and was offered a job as a secretary. Smith, as U.S. attorney general, later
played a part in her nomination to the U.S. Supreme Court.

O'Connor found a job as deputy county attorney for San
Mateo County, California. When her husband finished school,
he joined the Army, and the O'Connors moved to Germany
where she worked as a civilian attorney for the U.S. Army.

The O'Connors returned to civilian life in 1957 and settled in
Phoenix, Arizona. For eight years, O'Connor combined child
rearing with volunteer work and some private practice of law
and a number of miscellaneous legal tasks part-time. She also
became active in Republican politics.

In 1965 O'Connor became an assistant attorney general of
Arizona, the first woman to hold the position. After four years,
she was appointed to the state Senate, and the following year she
won election to that body. During her six years as a state senator,
she served for two years as majority leader—the first woman in
the nation to hold such a post of legislative leadership.

Having served in the executive and legislative branches of
state government, O'Connor rounded out her experience by
moving to the bench in 1974, elected to the superior court of
Maricopa County. Five years later, Gov. Bruce Babbitt—acting,
some said, to remove a potential rival—appointed her to the Arizona Court of Appeals. A year earlier Arizona Republican leaders
had pushed O'Connor to make a gubernatorial bid, but she had
declined. It was from that state appeals court seat that President
Reagan chose her as his first nominee to the Supreme Court.
Once again, Sandra Day O'Connor was "the first woman"—this
time, the first of her sex to sit on the U.S. Supreme Court.

On the Court, O'Connor was at first solidly in the conservative wing, voting in most cases with fellow Arizonian William H.
Rehnquist. Over time she has moved to the center. After the retirement of Justice Lewis F. Powell Jr. in 1987, O'Connor became
the Court's pivotal justice, the one whose vote decides the crucial cases. She has defined the Court's position in areas such as
religion, abortion, affirmative action, and the death penalty. In
1992 O'Connor joined David Souter and Anthony Kennedy in a
plurality opinion that affirmed *Roe v. Wade* (1973), which guarantees a woman's right to have an abortion. While states may
regulate abortion, they may not place an "undue burden" before
women who seek an abortion prior to the time a fetus may live
on its own, O'Connor decided.

As an advocate of federalism, O'Connor played a key role in
the long line of decisions that limited federal power and upheld
states' rights. In 2000 she cast the deciding fifth vote in *United
States v. Morrison* to strike down the federal Violence Against
Women Act, believing that it crossed the line by authorizing
federal courts to decide state and local offenses. In *Kimel v.
Florida* (2000) and *Board of Trustees of the University of Alabama
v. Garrett* (2001), O'Connor also spoke for the Court in shielding
states from being sued by state employees who alleged that they
were victims of discrimination because of their age or disability.

O'Connor has usually supported the death penalty, but in
2002 she cast a key vote to outlaw its use against mentally

retarded defendants. Her crucial role was apparent in 2003,
when the Court narrowly upheld affirmative action in colleges
and university admissions. "In a society, like our own, in which
race unfortunately still matters," universities may give extra consideration to qualified minority applicants, she said for the 5-4
majority in *Grutter v. Bollinger*.

While serving on the Court, O'Connor wrote two popular
books: *Lazy B: Growing Up on a Cattle Ranch in the American
Southwest* (2002), the story of her childhood along the Arizona–New Mexico border, and *The Majesty of the Law: Reflections of a Supreme Court Justice* (2003), her thoughts on the
work of the Court.

ANTONIN SCALIA

(1986–)

BIRTH: March 11, 1936, Trenton, New Jersey.

EDUCATION: Georgetown University, A.B., summa cum
laude, 1957; Harvard Law School, LL.B., magna cum laude, 1960.

OFFICIAL POSITIONS: general counsel, White House Office of Telecommunications Policy, 1971–1972; chairman, Administrative Conference of the United States, 1972–1974; assistant attorney general, Office of Legal Counsel, 1974–1977; judge,
U.S. Court of Appeals for the District of Columbia Circuit,
1982–1986.

SUPREME COURT SERVICE: nominated associate justice by
President Ronald Reagan June 24, 1986, to replace William H.

Antonin Scalia

Rehnquist, who had been promoted to chief justice; confirmed by a 98-0 vote of the Senate, September 17, 1986; took judicial oath September 26, 1986.

FAMILY: married Maureen McCarthy, 1960; nine children.

Antonin Scalia was the first person of Italian ancestry to be appointed to the Supreme Court and the first Roman Catholic since William J. Brennan Jr. was named in 1956. Born in Trenton, New Jersey, Scalia was the only child of Eugene Scalia, a professor of Romance languages who had emigrated from Italy, and Catherine Panaro Scalia, a schoolteacher whose parents also had emigrated from Italy. Scalia grew up in Queens where he attended Jesuit schools.

Scalia graduated from Georgetown University and Harvard Law School. The year he graduated from law school, he married Maureen McCarthy. Scalia spent seven years in private practice in Cleveland, Ohio, with the law firm of Jones, Day, Reavis, and Pogue, but left practice to teach law at the University of Virginia law school late in the 1960s. Early in his career, he developed a strong individual style marked by a keen legal intellect and a certain whimsicality. He made playful use of the language, would sometimes sing at public appearances, and liked to entertain friends with his piano playing.

Scalia was drawn to government service during the Nixon administration, which he joined in 1971 as general counsel of the White House Office of Telecommunications Policy. From that post, he became chairman of the Administrative Conference of the United States, and in 1974 he joined the Justice Department as assistant attorney general in charge of the Office of Legal Counsel, the same post William H. Rehnquist held from 1969 to 1971.

Scalia remained in that position through the Nixon and Ford administrations. He returned to teaching and held posts at Georgetown University Law School, the University of Chicago Law School, and Stanford University Law School. He was then named by President Reagan to the U.S. Court of Appeals for the District of Columbia Circuit in 1982.

Scalia developed a reputation as an outspoken conservative with very definite views of the law. He believed the power of the courts was limited. He also took a strong interest in the interpretation of statutes, arguing that the only legitimate guide for judges is the actual text of a statute and its related provisions. In 1986 Reagan promoted him to the U.S. Supreme Court. True to his reputation, Scalia has established himself as the most consistently conservative and outspoken member of the Court. He has insisted that the Constitution be interpreted strictly in line with its words and the intent of its framers in 1787. He strongly rebuked his colleagues when they announced a right to abortion, a ban on executions for mentally retarded murderers, and a prohibition on criminal laws that target homosexuals.

Though Scalia has been a conservative on a conservative-leaning Court, he has written few important opinions. Rather, he is best known for his dissents. In *Cruzan v. Missouri*, a 1990 case from Missouri on the "right to die," Scalia said the right answers to these difficult questions "are neither set forth in the Constitution nor known to the nine justices of this Court any better than they are known to nine people picked at random from the Kansas City telephone directory." In his most caustic dissents, he has accused his colleagues of taking their cues from "elite" opinion. "Today's opinion is the product of a Court, which is the product of a law-profession culture, that has largely signed on to the so-called homosexual agenda," he said dissenting from the ruling in *Lawrence v. Texas* (2003) that struck down antisodomy laws.

ANTHONY McLEOD KENNEDY
(1988–)

BIRTH: July 23, 1936, Sacramento, California.

EDUCATION: Stanford University, A.B., 1958; London School of Economics, 1957–1958; Harvard Law School, J.D., 1961.

OFFICIAL POSITIONS: judge, U.S. Court of Appeals for the Ninth Circuit, 1976–1988.

SUPREME COURT SERVICE: nominated associate justice by President Ronald Reagan November 30, 1987, to replace Lewis F. Powell Jr., who had retired; confirmed by a 97-0 vote of the Senate, February 3, 1988; took judicial oath February 18, 1988.

FAMILY: married Mary Davis, 1963; three children.

Until called to serve as a justice of the U.S. Supreme Court, Anthony Kennedy's life centered around his hometown, Sacramento. His father, Anthony J. Kennedy, was a lawyer and lobbyist, well known in that state capital. Kennedy, like his father, was

Anthony McLeod Kennedy

both Catholic and Republican. Earl Warren, who would become a chief justice of the United States, was a family friend. Kennedy's mother was born Gladys McLeod.

Kennedy graduated from McClatchy High School in Sacramento and went on to Stanford, his mother's alma mater. He graduated in 1958 and was elected to Phi Beta Kappa. He spent his final undergraduate year at the London School of Economics before entering Harvard Law School, gaining his degree in 1961.

During his first year as a lawyer, he worked for a firm in San Francisco, but his father's sudden death brought him back to Sacramento. He took over his father's practice, including the lobbying activities, which he found less to his taste than the legal work. He also taught part time at the McGeorge School of Law at the University of the Pacific.

Kennedy's legal abilities brought him to the attention of the administration of Ronald Reagan, then governor of California. That connection won Kennedy a nomination by President Gerald R. Ford to a seat on the Ninth Circuit Court of Appeals in 1975. Easily confirmed, he took his seat in 1976 and remained on the court for a dozen years.

He earned a reputation as a conservative, diligent, and even-handed jurist. In one of his most controversial opinions as an appeals court judge, he invalidated a federal statute that allowed either house of Congress to cancel administration action on a deportation order. The Supreme Court in 1983 endorsed Kennedy's view when it rejected the one-house legislative veto in the important case of *Immigration and Naturalization Service v. Chadha.*

Kennedy became Ronald Reagan's choice for the Court in 1987 after the Senate had rejected the nomination of Robert H. Bork and Douglas Ginsburg's name was withdrawn.

From the start, Kennedy proved to be a pivotal member of the Court. He has joined Chief Justice William H. Rehnquist to form a conservative majority limiting federal power, upholding the principle of state "sovereign immunity," allowing limited public aid to religious schools, and prohibiting "racial gerrymanders" in electoral districts. Kennedy was credited with being the author of the Court's unsigned opinion in *Bush v. Florida* (2000), which ended the Florida recount and delivered the White House to George W. Bush.

Kennedy has, however, proven to be independent and unpredictable in other areas. A strong advocate of free speech, he joined the opinion of William J. Brennan Jr. to strike down a Texas law forbidding flag burning. The majority held that flag burning is symbolic speech protected by the First Amendment. One of Kennedy's most surprising votes came when he joined with Justices David H. Souter and Sandra Day O'Connor to write the Court's opinion in *Planned Parenthood of Southeastern Pennsylvania v. Casey* (1992) upholding the basic right to abortion while permitting certain state regulations.

In *U.S. Term Limits v. Thornton* (1995) Kennedy cast the decisive fifth vote to strike down state term limits on federal officeholders, asserting that they violate the principle that

states cannot intrude on federal standards set in the Constitution. Though a defender of religious rights, Kennedy spoke for the Court in outlawing school-sponsored prayers and invocations at graduation ceremonies in *Lee v. Weisman* (1992). In perhaps his most powerfully written opinion—in *Lawrence v. Texas* (2003)—Kennedy spoke for the Court in striking down state antisodomy laws. In the opinion he declared that law may not "demean" the private lives of gays and lesbians.

DAVID HACKETT SOUTER

(1990–)

BIRTH: September 17, 1939, Melrose, Massachusetts.

EDUCATION: Harvard College, B.A., 1961; Oxford University (Rhodes Scholar), 1961–1963; Harvard University Law School, LL.B., 1966.

OFFICIAL POSITIONS: assistant attorney general, New Hampshire, 1968–1971; deputy attorney general, New Hampshire, 1971–1976; attorney general, New Hampshire, 1976–1978; associate justice, New Hampshire Superior Court, 1978–1983; associate justice, New Hampshire Supreme Court, 1983–1990; judge, U.S. Court of Appeals for the First Circuit, 1990.

SUPREME COURT SERVICE: nominated associate justice by President George Bush July 23, 1990, to replace William J. Brennan Jr., who had retired; confirmed by the Senate, October 2, 1990, by a 90-9 vote; took judicial oath October 9, 1990.

FAMILY: Unmarried.

David Hackett Souter

David Souter was born in Melrose, Massachusetts, the only child of Joseph A. Souter, a banker, and Helen Hackett Souter. He spent most summers at his maternal grandparents' farmhouse in Weare, New Hampshire. The family moved there when he was eleven years old. Except for his college years, Souter lived in Weare until 1990. He attended Harvard College where he majored in philosophy and wrote his senior honors thesis on the jurisprudence of Justice Oliver Wendell Holmes Jr. He was elected to Phi Beta Kappa and graduated magna cum laude in 1961. Souter attended Oxford University on a Rhodes scholarship from 1961 to 1963. He then attended Harvard Law School. He graduated in 1966 and worked for two years in a Concord law firm, Orr and Reno. Souter's practice included corporate law, real estate, and taxation.

In 1968 Souter became an assistant attorney general for the state's criminal division. He rose to deputy attorney general in 1971 and in 1976 was appointed attorney general. Under Gov. Meldrim Thomson Jr., Souter defended a number of controversial orders, including the lowering of state flags to half-staff on Good Friday to commemorate the death of Jesus. He prosecuted Jehovah's Witnesses who obscured the state motto "Live Free or Die" on their license plates. He also was responsible for the prosecution of protesters who took over the Seabrook nuclear power plant in 1977.

Souter served as attorney general until 1978, when he was named to the state's trial court. Five years later, Gov. John H. Sununu selected Souter for the state supreme court. Sununu later become President Bush's chief of staff and, when Bush had the opportunity to name a successor to retiring justice William J. Brennan Jr., Sununu suggested Souter's name. Just three months earlier, Bush had named Souter to the U.S. Court of Appeals for the First Circuit, but in July 1990 he nominated him to the U.S. Supreme Court. During Souter's confirmation hearings, he stressed that his years on state courts had taught him two lessons that he thought would help him as a justice. The first was that "at the end of our task some human being is going to be affected, some human life is going to be changed in some way by what we do." The second (and related) lesson: "We had better use every power of our minds and our hearts and our beings to get those rulings right."

On the Court Souter has shown a respect for precedent. He was one of the three authors (with Sandra Day O'Connor and Anthony M. Kennedy) of the Court's 1992 opinion in *Planned Parenthood of Southeastern Pennsylvania v. Casey* that upheld *Roe v. Wade* (1973).

Initially part of the conservative bloc, Souter has moved to the left of center on the modern conservative Court. By the mid-1990s he voted more often with Clinton appointees Ruth Bader Ginsburg and Stephen G. Breyer than with any of the justices appointed by Presidents Ronald Reagan and George Bush. He dissented from the series of rulings that diminished the power of Congress and endorsed states' rights. Souter argued that the Constitution gave Congress broad power to shape national law. Moreover, it nowhere says that the states have a "sovereign immunity" that shields them from federal laws, he contended. When Souter dissented in the 1996 case of *Seminole Tribe of Florida v. Florida*, he took the extraordinary step of reading his opinion from the bench. He declared that the majority opinion, which said that Congress had exceeded its authority in trying to force state officials to negotiate gaming contracts with Indian tribes, "flies in the face of the Constitution's text."

Souter has been devoted to the principle of church-state separation, and he wrote long dissents when the Court's conservative majority upheld the flow of taxpayers' money to religious schools. He also played a key role in defending the principle that the government can limit the effect of big money in politics, speaking for the Court in 2000 and 2001 in rulings upholding state and federal campaign contribution limits. If money can flow freely to politicians, it will feed "the cynical assumption that large donors call the tune," Souter wrote in *Nixon v. Shrink Missouri PAC* (2000). His opinions formed the basis for the Court's 5-4 ruling in 2003 that upheld the McCain-Feingold Act, which banned unregulated soft money from flowing to the political parties.

CLARENCE THOMAS

(1991–)

BIRTH: June 23, 1948, Pin Point, Georgia.

EDUCATION: Immaculate Conception Seminary, 1967–1968; Holy Cross College, B.A., 1971; Yale University Law School, J.D., 1974.

OFFICIAL POSITIONS: assistant attorney general, Missouri, 1974–1977; assistant secretary of education for civil rights, 1981–1982; chairman, Equal Employment Opportunity Commission, 1982–1990; judge, U.S. Court of Appeals for the District of Columbia, 1990–1991.

SUPREME COURT SERVICE: nominated associate justice by President George Bush July 1, 1991, to replace Thurgood Marshall, who had retired; confirmed by the Senate, October 15, 1991, by a 52-48 vote; took judicial oath October 23, 1991.

FAMILY: married Kathy Grace Ambush, 1971; one son; divorced 1984; married Virginia Lamp, 1987.

Clarence Thomas, the son of Leola Williams and M. C. Thomas, was born in an enclave of five hundred inhabitants south of Savannah, Georgia. He overcame great odds to reach a seat on the U.S. Supreme Court. His father abandoned the family when Thomas was two years old, and his mother struggled to provide for her three children, working as a maid. After their house burned down, Thomas and his only brother were sent to live with their grandfather, Myers Anderson, in Savannah. Thomas has often spoken of his grandfather's lessons of hard work and determination. Thomas attended an all-black school run by white nuns, whom he credited with instilling in him a strong sense of the possibilities of life. Intending to become a priest, he enrolled in Immaculate Conception Seminary in northwestern Missouri in 1967. The prejudice of other students convinced him to leave the seminary, and in 1968 he transferred

Clarence Thomas

to Holy Cross College in Worcester, Massachusetts. Thomas graduated in 1971 with honors in English. In 1974 he graduated from Yale Law School.

Thomas joined the staff of John C. Danforth, Missouri's attorney general. Danforth, a Republican, became Thomas's political mentor. Following a three-year stint as an assistant attorney general, Thomas worked as a staff attorney for Monsanto Company from 1977 to 1979. He returned to public service to work from 1979 to 1981 as a legislative assistant to Danforth, who had been elected to the U.S. Senate. Thomas then accepted a position in the Reagan administration as assistant secretary for civil rights in the Department of Education. In 1982 Reagan named him chairman of the Equal Employment Opportunity Commission.

President Bush appointed Thomas to the Court of Appeals for the District of Columbia Circuit in 1990. Eighteen months later Bush selected Thomas, whose judicial record was notably conservative, for the Supreme Court. Thomas was critical of abortion rights and opposed affirmative action. Those positions and controversy over other substantive issues, however, were eclipsed during the confirmation hearings by the allegations of Anita Hill, a former employee of Thomas's, that he had sexually harassed her. The charges were never proved, but Thomas said the ordeal, shown on national television, dramatically changed him. The Senate's 52-48 vote on Thomas was the closest Supreme Court confirmation vote in more than a century. Thomas succeeded Thurgood Marshall, whose six-decade legal career had shaped the country's civil rights struggle. Marshall was the first black justice, and Thomas became the second.

From the start, Thomas became a member of the conservative bloc, opposing abortion rights and favoring law enforcement, states' rights, and a more accommodating approach to religion. He has voted most often with Justice Antonin Scalia and Chief Justice William H. Rehnquist. He joined them in rulings that curbed federal antidiscrimination laws, and he dissented with them when the Court prohibited school-sponsored prayers at graduation ceremonies and football games.

Thomas has been a strong voice against race-based remedies for past discrimination, including affirmative action and "majority-minority" voting districts. He wrote in *Holder v. Hall* (1994) that the Court's earlier cases upholding racially designated voting districts disserved the country: "In doing so we have collaborated in what may aptly be termed the racial balkanization of the Nation." In 2003 he dissented when the Court upheld the limited use of affirmative action at the nation's colleges and universities. "The Constitution abhors classifications based on race," he wrote in *Grutter v. Bollinger*. "Every time the government places citizens on racial registers and makes race relevant to the provision of burdens and benefits, it demeans us all."

Thomas wrote the dissent to *U.S. Term Limits v. Thornton* (1995), in which the Court declared that states may not limit the number of terms their representatives serve in Congress. He said the Constitution is "simply silent" on term limits, so under the Tenth Amendment, the states retained the authority to prescribe "eligibility requirements" for Congress.

RUTH BADER GINSBURG

(1993–)

BIRTH: March 15, 1933, Brooklyn, New York.

EDUCATION: Cornell University, B.A., 1954; attended Harvard University Law School, 1956–1958; graduated Columbia Law School, J.D., 1959.

OFFICIAL POSITIONS: judge, U.S. Court of Appeals for the District of Columbia, 1980–1993.

SUPREME COURT SERVICE: nominated associate justice by President Bill Clinton June 22, 1993, to replace Byron R. White, who had retired; confirmed by the Senate, August 3, 1993, by a 96-3 vote; took judicial oath August 10, 1993.

FAMILY: married Martin D. Ginsburg, 1954; one daughter, one son.

Born into a Jewish family of modest means in Brooklyn, Ruth Bader Ginsburg is the daughter of Nathan Bader and Celia Amster Bader. Ruth was greatly influenced by her mother, who imparted a love of learning and a determination to be independent. Celia Bader died of cancer on the eve of her daughter's high school graduation in 1948. Ruth Bader attended Cornell University, where she graduated first among the women in her class and was elected to Phi Beta Kappa. She also met her future husband, Martin Ginsburg.

Clinton's choice for the Supreme Court. Clinton said he was moved by her nontraditional life and predicted she would bring consensus to the Court. Ginsburg was the first Supreme Court justice appointed by a Democratic president in twenty-six years, since Lyndon Johnson appointed Thurgood Marshall in 1967.

The Court she joined was composed of eight justices, all of whom had been appointed by Republican presidents. She became the second woman to serve on the Court and its first Jewish member since the resignation of Justice Abe Fortas in 1969. Ginsburg has proved herself to be a liberal-leaning justice on a conservative-leaning Court. She has supported the separation of church and state, civil rights, and the right to abortion, and she dissented from the series of states' rights rulings that began in the mid-1990s. In her most important opinion, *United States v. Virginia* (1996), she spoke for the Court in striking down state policies that exclude individuals from state universities based on their sex. Ginsburg asserted that such gender discrimination is unconstitutional and violates the Equal Protection Clause.

STEPHEN GERALD BREYER

(1994–)

BIRTH: August 15, 1938, San Francisco, California.

EDUCATION: Stanford University, A.B., 1959; Oxford University, B.A., 1961; Harvard Law School, LL.B., 1964.

OFFICIAL POSITIONS: Law clerk to Justice Arthur J. Goldberg, 1964–1965; assistant to assistant attorney general, Antitrust

Ruth Bader Ginsburg

At Harvard Law School Ruth Ginsburg made law review, cared for an infant daughter, and helped her husband complete his studies after he was diagnosed with cancer. Martin Ginsburg recovered, graduated, and got a job in New York, and she transferred to Columbia for her final year of law school. Ginsburg was tied for first place in her class when she graduated. She won a two-year clerkship with a federal district court judge. She then accepted a research position at Columbia that took her to Sweden, where she studied civil procedure. Ginsburg taught at Rutgers University Law School in New Jersey from 1963 to 1972. She also worked for the American Civil Liberties Union (ACLU), where her caseload included several early sex discrimination complaints. In 1972 Ginsburg became the first woman to be named to a tenured position on the Columbia Law School faculty. Then, as director of the national ACLU's newly established Women's Rights Project, she also handled the cases that over time led the Supreme Court to require heightened scrutiny of legal classifications based on sex. Ginsburg won five of the six cases she argued before the Court.

As an advocate, Ginsburg gained nationwide attention in the 1970s for developing the legal strategy that established constitutional principles against sex discrimination. In 1980 President Jimmy Carter named her to the U.S. Court of Appeals for the District of Columbia. She developed a moderate judicial record, following the letter of the law and believing that judging has its limits. "Measured motions seem to me right, in the main, for constitutional as well as common law adjudication," she wrote in an article that criticized the broad sweep of the Court's 1973 *Roe v. Wade* decision. In 1993 Ginsburg became President Bill

Stephen Gerald Breyer

Division, U.S. Justice Department, 1965–1967; assistant special prosecutor, Watergate Special Prosecution Force, 1973; special counsel, Senate Judiciary Committee, 1974–1975; chief counsel, Senate Judiciary Committee, 1979–1980; judge, U.S. Court of Appeals for the First Circuit, 1980–1994.

SUPREME COURT SERVICE: nominated associate justice by President Bill Clinton May 13, 1994, to replace Harry A. Blackmun, who had retired; confirmed by the Senate, July 29, 1994, by a 87-9 vote; took judicial oath August 3, 1994.

FAMILY: married Joanna Hare, 1967; two daughters, one son.

Stephen Breyer was born in 1938 in San Francisco, the first of two sons of Irving G. Breyer and Anne Roberts Breyer. Breyer's father was a lawyer for the San Francisco public school system, and his mother was active in local Democratic politics and community activities. They encouraged their son to do well academically but also, in his mother's words, to learn how "to work with other people." Breyer excelled at Lowell High School, especially in math and science, and was voted "most likely to succeed" when he graduated in 1955. He then graduated Phi Beta Kappa from Stanford University in 1959 and went to Oxford as a Marshall Scholar, completing course work in 1961. Breyer graduated from Harvard Law School in 1964. While working in Washington, he met his wife, Joanna Hare, the daughter of a former high-ranking official in Britain's Conservative Party and heir to a wealthy media company. They were married in 1967. Breyer is a prolific author, avid bird watcher, bicyclist, and gourmet cook.

Breyer acquired early Supreme Court experience as a law clerk to Justice Arthur J. Goldberg during the 1964–1965 term. That term produced a decision establishing the right of married couples to use contraceptives, and Breyer helped draft Goldberg's influential concurring opinion finding a right of personal privacy in the Constitution. Breyer then served two years in the Justice Department's Antitrust Division. In 1967 he obtained a teaching position at Harvard Law School, beginning an association that would continue through his various tours in public service until he was named to the Supreme Court.

Breyer took leave from Harvard to serve as an assistant prosecutor in the Watergate investigation in 1973, to be a special counsel to the Judiciary Committee's Administrative Practices Subcommittee from 1974 to 1975, and to serve as the full Judiciary Committee's chief counsel, 1979 to 1980. He helped write major legislation to deregulate the airline industry in the mid-1970s and then to standardize federal criminal sentences in 1980.

Breyer worked for the Democratic committee chairman, Sen. Edward M. Kennedy of Massachusetts, but established good relationships with Republican committee members, too. Those ties proved beneficial when President Jimmy Carter nominated Breyer to be a judge on the U.S. Court of Appeals for the First Circuit in November 1980. Although Ronald Reagan had been elected president and would soon have the opportunity to name his own judges, Republican senators allowed a vote to confirm Breyer's nomination.

On the appeals court, Breyer continued to be interested in regulatory reform. His academic writings focused on government's failure to work out health and environmental problems. He asserted that federal regulation sometimes imposed millions of dollars in extra costs for only marginal health improvements. Breyer served as a member of the U.S. Sentencing Commission from 1985 to 1989.

In 1993 President Clinton considered Breyer for a Supreme Court vacancy, but at the last minute chose Ruth Bader Ginsburg. When Breyer was nominated the following year, his selection was embraced by both Democrats and Republicans, and he was easily confirmed, 87-9.

In Breyer's first decade on the Court, he proved himself a strong advocate for congressional authority, particularly when balanced against the powers of the states. He wrote the main dissenting opinion when a five-justice majority struck down a federal ban on guns near public schools. Breyer contended that the gun law "falls well within the scope of the commerce power as this Court has understood that power over the last half-century." The majority said the ban had nothing to do with commerce or any sort of economic enterprise.

Breyer has supported the separation of church and state and the right to abortion. In 2000 he wrote the Court's opinion for the 5-4 majority in *Stenberg v. Carhart* that struck down a Nebraska law banning so-called "partial birth abortions." Breyer held that the ban would force doctors in some instances to subject patients to riskier surgery.

Reference Materials

APPENDIX A Chronological Documents and Texts

Declaration of Independence

On June 11, 1776, the responsibility to "prepare a declaration" of independence was assigned by the Continental Congress, meeting in Philadelphia, to five members: John Adams, Benjamin Franklin, Thomas Jefferson, Robert Livingston, and Roger Sherman. Impressed by his talents as a writer, the committee asked Jefferson to compose a draft. After modifying Jefferson's draft the committee turned it over to Congress on June 28. On July 2 Congress voted to declare independence; on the evening of July 4, it approved the Declaration of Independence.

The declaration is best remembered for its ringing preamble, which affirms the "self-evident" truths that "all men are created equal, that they are endowed by their Creator with certain unalienable Rights, that among these are Life, Liberty, and the pursuit of Happiness." Besides asserting this natural law, the declaration also elevated the importance of public will: "Governments are instituted among Men, deriving their just powers from the consent of the governed." Many later Supreme Court decisions attempted to find a balance these two fundamental pillars of American democracy: unalienable rights and popular will.

In Congress, July 4, 1776,

THE UNANIMOUS DECLARATION OF
THE THIRTEEN UNITED STATES OF AMERICA,

When in the Course of human events, it becomes necessary for one people to dissolve the political bands which have connected them with another, and to assume among the Powers of the earth, the separate and equal station to which the Laws of Nature and of Nature's God entitle them, a decent respect to the opinions of mankind requires that they should declare the causes which impel them to the separation.

We hold these truths to be self-evident, that all men are created equal, that they are endowed by their Creator with certain unalienable Rights, that among these are Life, Liberty and the pursuit of Happiness. That to secure these rights, Governments are instituted among Men, deriving their just powers from the consent of the governed. That whenever any form of Government becomes destructive of these ends, it is the Right of the People to alter or to abolish it, and to institute new Government, laying its foundation on such principles and organizing its powers in such form, as to them shall seem most likely to effect their Safety and Happiness. Prudence, indeed, will dictate that Government long established should not be changed for light and transient causes; and accordingly all experience hath shown, that mankind are more disposed to suffer, while evils are sufferable, than to right themselves by abolishing the forms to which they are accustomed. But when a long train of abuses and usurpations, pursuing invariably the same Object evinces a design to reduce them under absolute Despotism, it is their right, it is their duty, to throw off such Government, and to provide new Guards for their future security. — Such has been the patient sufferance of these Colonies; and such is now the necessity which constrains them to alter their former Systems of Government. The history of the present King of Great Britain is a history of repeated injuries and usurpations, all having in direct object the establishment of an absolute Tyranny over these States. To prove this, let Facts be submitted to a candid world.

He has refused his Assent to Laws, the most wholesome and necessary for the public good.

He has forbidden his Governors to pass Laws of immediate and pressing importance, unless suspended in their operation till his Assent should be obtained; and when so suspended, he has utterly neglected to attend to them.

He has refused to pass other Laws for the accommodation of large districts of people, unless those people would relinquish the right of Representation in the Legislature, a right inestimable to them and formidable to tyrants only.

He has called together legislative bodies at places unusual, uncomfortable, and distant from the depository of their Public Records, for the sole purpose of fatiguing them into compliance with his measures.

He has dissolved Representative Houses repeatedly, for opposing with manly firmness his invasions on the rights of the people.

He has refused for a long time, after such dissolutions, to cause others to be elected; whereby the Legislative Powers, incapable of Annihilation, have returned to the People at large for their exercise; the State remaining in the mean time exposed to all the dangers of invasion from without, and convulsions within.

He has endeavored to prevent the population of these States; for that purpose obstructing the Laws of Naturalization of Foreigners; refusing to pass others to encourage their migration hither, and raising the conditions of new Appropriations of Lands.

He has obstructed the Administration of Justice, by refusing his Assent to Laws for establishing Judiciary Powers.

He has made Judges dependent on his Will alone, for the tenure of their offices, and the amount and payment of their salaries.

He has erected a multitude of New Offices, and sent hither swarms of Officers to harass our People, and eat out their substance.

He has kept among us, in times of peace, Standing Armies without the Consent of our legislature.

He has affected to render the Military independent of and superior to the Civil Power.

He has combined with others to subject us to a jurisdiction foreign to our constitution, and unacknowledged by our laws; giving his Assent to their acts of pretended legislation:

For quartering large bodies of armed troops among us:

For protecting them, by a mock Trial, from Punishment for any Murders which they should commit on the Inhabitants of these States:

For cutting off our Trade with all parts of the world:

For imposing taxes on us without our Consent:

For depriving us in many cases, of the benefits of Trial by Jury:

For transporting us beyond Seas to be tried for pretended offences:

For abolishing the free System of English Laws in a neighbouring Province, establishing therein an Arbitrary government, and enlarging its Boundaries so as to render it at once an example and fit instrument for introducing the same absolute rule into these Colonies:

For taking away our Charters, abolishing our most valuable Laws, and altering fundamentally the Forms of our Governments:

For suspending our own Legislature, and declaring themselves invested with Power to legislate for us in all cases whatsoever.

He has abdicated Government here, by declaring us out of his Protection and waging War against us.

He has plundered our seas, ravaged our Coasts, burnt our towns, and destroyed the lives of our people.

He is at this time transporting large armies of foreign mercenaries to compleat the works of death, desolation and tyranny, already begun with circumstances of Cruelty & perfidy scarcely parallel in the most barbarous ages, and totally unworthy the Head of a civilized nation.

He has constrained our fellow Citizens taken Captive on the high Seas to bear Arms against their Country, to become the executioners of their friends and Brethren, or to fall themselves by their Hands.

He has excited domestic insurrections amongst us, and has endeavoured to bring on the inhabitants of our frontiers, the merciless Indian Savages, whose known rule of warfare, is an undistinguished destruction of all ages, sexes and conditions.

In every stage of these Oppressions We have Petitioned for Redress in the most humble terms: Our repeated Petitions have been answered only by repeated injury. A Prince, whose character is thus marked by every act which may define a Tyrant, is unfit to be the ruler of a free People.

Nor have We been wanting in attention to our British brethren. We have warned them from time to time of attempts by their legislature to extend an unwarrantable jurisdiction over us. We have reminded them of the circumstances of our emigration and settlement here. We have appealed to their native justice and magnanimity, and we have conjured them by the ties of our common kindred to disavow these usurpations, which would inevitably interrupt our connections and correspondence. They too have been deaf to the voice of justice and of consanguinity. We must, therefore, acquiesce in the necessity, which denounces our Separation, and hold them, as we hold the rest of mankind, Enemies in War, in Peace Friends.

We, therefore, the Representatives of the United States of America, in General Congress, Assembled, appealing to the Supreme Judge of the world for the rectitude of our intentions, do, in the Name, and by Authority of the good People of these Colonies, solemnly publish and declare, That these United Colonies are, and of Right ought to be Free and Independent States; that they are Absolved from all Allegiance to the British Crown, and that all political connection between them and the State of Great Britain, is and ought to be totally dissolved; and that as Free and Independent States, they have full Power to levy War, conclude Peace, contract Alliances, establish Commerce, and to

do all other Acts and Things which Independent States may of right do. And for the support of this Declaration, with a firm reliance on the Protection of Divine Providence, we mutually pledge to each other our Lives, our Fortunes and our sacred Honor.

John Hancock.

New Hampshire:
Josiah Bartlett,
William Whipple,
Matthew Thornton.

Massachusetts-Bay:
Samuel Adams,
John Adams,
Robert Treat Paine,
Elbridge Gerry.

Rhode Island:
Stephen Hopkins,
William Ellery.

Connecticut:
Roger Sherman,
Samuel Huntington,
William Williams,
Oliver Wolcott.

New York:
William Floyd,
Philip Livingston,
Francis Lewis,
Lewis Morris.

Pennsylvania:
Robert Morris,
Benjamin Harris,

Benjamin Franklin,
John Morton,
George Clymer,
James Smith,
George Taylor,
James Wilson,
George Ross.

Delaware:
Caesar Rodney,
George Read,
Thomas McKean.

Georgia:
Button Gwinnett,
Lyman Hall,
George Walton.

Maryland:
Samuel Chase,
William Paca,
Thomas Stone,
Charles Carroll of
   Carrollton.

Virginia:
George Wythe,
Richard Henry Lee,
Thomas Jefferson,
Benjamin Harrison,

Thomas Nelson Jr.,
Francis Lightfoot
   Lee,
Carter Braxton.

North Carolina:
William Hooper,
Joseph Hewes,
John Penn.

South Carolina:
Edward Rutledge,
Thomas Heyward
   Jr.,
Thomas Lynch Jr.,
Arthur Middleton.

New Jersey:
Richard Stockton,
John Witherspoon,
Francis Hopkinson,
John Hart,
Abraham Clark.

Articles of Confederation

On June 11, 1776, the same day that it created a five-member committee to prepare the Declaration of Independence, the Continental Congress appointed a thirteen-member committee (one from each state) to draft a "plan of confederation." The two decisions were closely connected: a new and independent nation needed a government of some sort. The committee recommended the Articles of Confederation to Congress on July 12; Congress adopted the plan on November 15, 1777; and unanimous ratification by the states finally came on March 1, 1781.

The Articles of Confederation, which did not provide for a system of national courts, created a weak central government with no executive at all and made Congress the sole organ of the new national government. The Articles provided a barely adequate framework for fighting and winning the Revolutionary War: the presence of a common enemy fostered a certain amount of unity among the states. But when the British were defeated in 1783, the national government found it increasingly difficult to unite the country to confront the new challenges of peace. The lack of a federal court system also remained a major source of embarrassment for the young nation.

To all to whom these Presents shall come, we the undersigned Delegates of the States affixed to our Names send greeting. Whereas the Delegates of the United States of America in Congress assembled did on the fifteenth day of November in the Year of our Lord One Thousand Seven Hundred and Seventy seven, and in the Second Year of the Independence of America agree to certain articles of Confederation and perpetual Union between the States of Newhampshire, Massachusetts-bay, Rhodeisland and Providence Plantations, Connecticut, New York, New Jersey, Pennsylvania, Delaware, Maryland, Virginia, North-Carolina, South-Carolina and Georgia in the Words following, viz. "Articles of Confederation and perpetual Union between the states of Newhampshire, Massachusetts-bay, Rhodeisland and Providence Plantations, Connecticut, New-York, New-Jersey, Pennsylvania, Delaware, Maryland, Virginia, North-Carolina, South-Carolina and Georgia.

Article I. The Stile of this confederacy shall be "The United States of America."

Article II. Each state retains its sovereignty, freedom and independence, and every Power, Jurisdiction and Right, which is not by this confederation expressly delegated to the United States, in Congress assembled.

Article III. The said states hereby severally enter into a firm league of friendship with each other, for their common defence, the security of their Liberties, and their mutual and general welfare, binding themselves to assist each other, against all force offered to, or attacks made upon them, or any of them, on account of religion, sovereignty, trade, or any other pretence whatever.

Article IV. The better to secure the perpetuate mutual friendship and intercourse among the people of the different states in this union, the free inhabitants of each of these states, paupers, vagabonds and fugitives from Justice excepted, shall be entitled to all privileges and immunities of free citizens in the several states; and the people of each state shall have free ingress and regress to and from any other state, and shall enjoy therein all the privileges of trade and commerce, subject to the same duties, impositions and restrictions as the inhabitants thereof respectively, provided that such restriction shall not extend so far as to prevent the removal of property imported into any state, to any other state of which the Owner is an inhabitant; provided also that no imposition, duties or restriction shall be laid by any state, on the property of the united states, or either of them.

If any Person guilty of, or charged with treason, felony, or other high misdemeanor in any state, shall flee from Justice, and be found in any of the united states, he shall upon demand of the Governor or executive power, of the state from which he fled be delivered up and removed to the state having jurisdiction of his offence.

Full faith and credit shall be given in each of these states to the records, acts and judicial proceedings of the courts and magistrates of every other state.

Article V. For the more convenient management of the general interests of the united states, delegates shall be annually appointed in such manner as the legislature of each state shall direct, to meet in Congress on the first Monday in November, in every year, with a power reserved to each state, to recall its delegates, or any of them, at any time within the year, and to send others in their stead, for the remainder of the Year.

No state shall be represented in Congress by less than two, nor by more than seven Members; and no person shall be capable of being a delegate for more than three years in any term of six years; nor shall any person, being a delegate, be capable of holding any office under the united states, for which he, or another for his benefit receives any salary, fees or emolument of any kind.

Each state shall maintain its own delegates in a meeting of the states, and while they act as members of the committee of the states.

In determining questions in the united states, in Congress assembled, each state shall have one vote.

Freedom of speech and debate in Congress shall not be impeached or questioned in any Court, or place out of Congress, and the members of congress shall be protected in their persons from arrests and imprisonments, during the time of their going to and from, and attendance on congress, except for treason, felony, or breach of the peace.

Article VI. No state without the Consent of the united states in congress assembled, shall send any embassy to, or receive any embassy from, or enter into any conference, agreement, or alliance or treaty with any King, prince or state; nor shall any person holding any office of profit or trust under the united states, or any of them, accept of any present, emolument, office or title of any kind whatever from any king, prince or foreign state; nor shall the united states in congress assembled, or any of them, grant any title of nobility.

No two or more states shall enter into any treaty, confederation or alliance whatever between them, without the consent of the united states in congress assembled, specifying accurately the purposes for which the same is to be entered into, and how long it shall continue.

No state shall lay any imposts or duties, which may interfere with any stipulations in treaties, entered into by the united states in congress assembled, with any king, prince or state, in pursuance of any treaties already proposed by congress, to the courts of France and Spain.

No vessels of war shall be kept up in time of peace by any state, except such number only, as shall be deemed necessary by the united states in congress assembled, for the defence of such state, or its trade; nor shall any body of forces be kept up by any state, in time of peace, except such number only, as in the judgment of the united states, in congress assembled, shall be deemed requisite to garrison the forts necessary for the defence of such state; but every state shall always keep up a well regulated and disciplined militia, sufficiently armed and accoutred, and shall provide and constantly have ready for use, in public stores, a due number of field pieces and tents, and a proper quantity of arms, ammunition and camp equipage.

No state shall engage in any war without the consent of the united states in Congress assembled, unless such state be actually invaded by enemies, or shall have received certain advice of a resolution being formed by some nation of Indians to invade such state, and the danger is so imminent as not to admit of a delay, till the united states in congress assembled can be consulted: nor shall any state grant commissions to any ships or vessels of war, nor letters of marque or reprisal, except it be after a declaration of war by the united states in congress assembled, and then only against the kingdom or state and the subjects thereof, against which war has been so declared, and under such regulations as shall be established by the united states in congress assembled, unless such state be infested by pirates, in which case vessels of war may be fitted out for that occasion, and kept so long as the danger shall continue, or until the united states in congress assembled shall determine otherwise.

Article VII. When land-forces are raised by any state for the common defence, all officers of or under the rank of colonel, shall be appointed by the legislature of each state respectively by whom such forces shall be raised, or in such manner as such state shall direct, and all vacancies shall be filled up by the state which first made the appointment.

Article VIII. All charges of war, and all other expences that shall be incurred for the common defence or general welfare, and allowed by the united states in congress assembled, shall be defrayed out of a common treasury, which shall be supplied by the several states, in proportion to the value of all land within each state, granted to or surveyed for any Person, as such land and the buildings and improvements thereon shall be estimated according to such mode as the united states in congress assembled, shall from time to time direct and appoint. The taxes for paying that proportion shall be laid and levied by the authority and direction of the legislatures of the several states within the time agreed upon by the united states in congress assembled.

Article IX. The united states in congress assembled, shall have the sole and exclusive right and power of determining on peace and war, except in the cases mentioned in the sixth article—of sending and receiving ambassadors—entering into treaties and alliances, provided that no treaty of commerce shall be made whereby the legislative power of the respective states shall be restrained from imposing such imposts and duties on foreigners, as their own people are subjected to, or from prohibiting the exportation or importation of any species of goods or commodities whatsoever—of establishing rules for deciding in all cases, what capture on land or water shall be legal, and in what manner prizes taken by land or naval forces in the service of the united states shall be divided or appropriated—of granting letters of marque and reprisal in times of peace—appointing courts for the trial of piracies and felonies committed on the high seas and establishing courts for receiving and determining finally appeals in all cases of captures, provided that no member of congress shall be appointed a judge of any of the said courts.

The united states in congress assembled shall also be the last resort on appeal in all disputes and differences now subsisting or that hereafter may arise between two or more states concerning boundary, jurisdiction or any other cause whatever; which authority shall always be exercised in the manner following. Whenever the legislative or executive authority or lawful agent of any state in controversy with another shall present a petition to congress, stating the matter in question and praying for a hearing, notice thereof shall be given by order of congress to the legislative or executive authority of the other state in controversy, and a day assigned for the appearance of the parties by their lawful agents, who shall then be directed to appoint by joint consent, commissioners or judges to constitute a court for hearing and determining the matter in question: but if they cannot agree, congress shall name three persons out of each of the united states, and from the list of such persons each party shall alternately strike out one, the petitioners beginning, until the number shall be reduced to thirteen; and from that number not less than seven, nor more than nine names as congress shall direct, shall in the presence of congress be drawn out by lot, and the persons whose names shall be so drawn or any five of them, shall be commissioners or judges, to hear and finally determine the controversy, so always as a major part of the judges who shall hear the cause shall agree in the determination: and if either party shall neglect to attend at the day appointed, without shewing reasons, which congress shall judge sufficient, or being present shall refuse to strike, the congress shall proceed to nominate three persons out of each state, and the secretary of congress shall strike in behalf of such party absent or refusing; and the judgment and sentence of the court to be appointed, in the manner before prescribed, shall be final and conclusive; and if any of the parties shall refuse to submit to the authority of such court, or to appear to defend their claim or cause, the court shall nevertheless proceed to pronounce sentence, or judgment, which shall in like manner be final and decisive, the judgment or sentence and other proceedings being in either case transmitted to congress, and lodged among the acts of congress for the security of the parties concerned: provided that every commissioner, before he sits in judgment, shall take an oath to be administered by one of the judges of the supreme or superior court of the state, where the cause shall be tried, "well and truly to hear and determine the matter in question, according to the best of his judgment, without favour, affection or hope of reward:" provided also that no state shall be deprived of territory for the benefit of the united states.

All controversies concerning the private right of soil claimed under different grants of two or more states, whose jurisdictions as they may respect such lands, and the states which passed such grants are adjusted, the said grants or either of them being at the same time claimed to have originated antecedent to such settlement of jurisdiction, shall on the petition of either party to the congress of the united states, be finally determined as near as may be in the same manner as is before prescribed for deciding disputes respecting territorial jurisdiction between different states.

The united states in congress assembled shall also have the sole and exclusive right and power of regulating the alloy and value of coin struck by their own authority, or by that of the respective states—fixing the standard of weights and measures throughout the united states—regulating the trade and managing all affairs with the Indians, not members of any of the states, provided that the legislative right of any state within its own limits be not infringed or violated—establishing and regulating post-offices from one state to another, throughout all the united states, and exacting such postage on the papers passing thro' the same as may be requisite to defray the expences of the said office—appointing all officers of the land forces, in the service of the united states, excepting regimental officers—appointing all the officers of the naval forces, and commissioning all officers whatever in the service of the united states—making rules for the government and regulation of the said land and naval forces, and directing their operations.

The united states in congress assembled shall have authority to appoint a committee, to sit in the recess of congress, to be denominated "A Committee of the States," and to consist of one delegate from each state; and to appoint such other committees and civil officers as may be necessary for managing the general affairs of the united states under their direction—to appoint one of their number to preside, provided that no person be allowed to serve in the office of president more than one year in any term of three years; to ascertain the necessary sums of Money to be raised for the service of the united states, and to appropriate and apply the same for defraying the public expences—to borrow money, or emit bills on the credit of the united states, transmitting every half year to the respective states an account of the sums of money so borrowed or emitted,—to build and equip a navy—to agree upon the number of land forces, and to make requisitions from each state for its quota, in proportion to the number of white inhabitants in such state; which requisition shall be binding, and thereupon the legislature of each state shall appoint the regimental officers, raise the men and cloath, arm and equip them in a soldier like manner, at the expence of the united states, and the officers and men so cloathed, armed and equipped shall march to the place appointed, and within the time agreed on by the united states in congress assembled: But if the united states in congress assembled shall, on consideration of circumstances judge proper that any state should not raise men, or should raise a smaller number than its quota, and that any other state should raise a greater number of men than the quota thereof, such extra number shall be raised, officered, cloathed, armed and equipped in the same manner as the quota of such state, unless the legislature of such state shall judge that such extra number cannot be safely spared out of the same, in which case they shall raise, officer, cloath, arm and equip as many of such extra number as they judge can be safely spared. And the officers and men so cloathed, armed and equipped, shall march to the place appointed, and within the time agreed on by the united states in congress assembled.

The united states in congress assembled shall never engage in a war, nor grant letters of marque and reprisal in time of peace, nor enter into any treaties or alliances, nor coin money, nor regulate the value thereof, nor ascertain the sums and expences necessary for the defence and welfare of the united states, or any of them, nor emit bills, nor borrow money on the credit of the united states, nor appropriate money, nor agree upon the number of vessels of war, to be built or purchased, or the number of land or sea forces to be raised, nor appoint a commander in chief of the army or navy, unless nine states assent to the same: nor shall a question on any other point, except for adjourning from day to day be determined, unless by the votes of a majority of the united states in congress assembled.

The congress of the united states shall have power to adjourn to any time within the year, and to any place within the united states, so that no period of adjournment be for a longer duration than the space of six Months, and shall publish the Journal of their proceedings monthly, except such parts thereof relating to treaties, alliances or military operations as in their judgment require secresy; and the yeas and nays of the delegates of each state on any question shall be entered on the Journal, when it is desired by any delegate; and the delegates of a state, or any of them, at his or their request shall be furnished with a transcript of the said Journal, except such parts as are above excepted, to lay before the legislatures of the several states.

Article X. The committee of the states, or any nine of them, shall be authorised to execute, in the recess of congress, such of the powers of congress as the united states in congress assembled, by the consent of nine states, shall from time to time think expedient to vest them with; provided that no power be delegated to the said committee, for the exercise of which, by the articles of confederation, the voice of nine states in the congress of the united states assembled is requisite.

Article XI. Canada acceding to this confederation, and joining in the measures of the united states, shall be admitted into, and entitled to all the advantages of this union: but no other colony shall be admitted into the same, unless such admission be agreed to by nine states.

Article XII. All bills of credit emitted, monies borrowed and debts contracted by, or under the authority of congress, before the assembling of the united states, in pursuance of the present confederation, shall be deemed and considered as a charge against the united states, for payment and satisfaction whereof the said united states, and the public faith are hereby solemnly pledged.

Article XIII. Every state shall abide by the determinations of the united states in congress assembled, on all questions which by this confederation are submitted to them. And the Articles of this confederation shall be inviolably observed by every state, and the union shall be perpetual; nor shall any alteration at any time hereafter be made in any of them; unless such alteration be agreed to in a congress of the united states, and be afterwards confirmed by the legislatures of every state.

And Whereas it has pleased the Great Governor of the World to incline the hearts of the legislatures we respectively represent in congress, to approve of, and to authorize us to ratify the said articles of confederation and perpetual union. Know Ye that we the undersigned delegates, by virtue of the power and authority to us given for that purpose, do by these presents, in the name and in behalf of our respective constituents, fully and entirely ratify and confirm each and every of the said articles of confederation and perpetual union, and all and singular the matters and things therein contained: And we do further solemnly plight and engage the faith of our respective constituents, that they shall abide by the determinations of the united states in congress assembled, on all questions, which by the said confederation are submitted to them. And that the articles thereof shall be inviolably observed by the states we respectively represent, and that the union shall be perpetual. In Witness whereof we have hereunto set our hands in Congress. Done at Philadelphia in the state of Pennsylvania the ninth Day of July in the Year of our Lord one Thousand seven Hundred and Seventy-eight, and in the third year of the independence of America.

New Hampshire:
Josiah Bartlett,
John Wentworth Jr.

Massachusetts:
John Hancock,
Samuel Adams,
Elbridge Gerry,
Francis Dana,
James Lovell,
Samuel Holten.

Rhode Island:
William Ellery,
Henry Marchant,
John Collins.

Connecticut:
Roger Sherman,
Samuel Huntington,
Oliver Wolcott,
Titus Hosmer,
Andrew Adams.

New York:
James Duane,
Francis Lewis,
William Duer,
Gouverneur Morris.

New Jersey:
John Witherspoon,
Nathaniel Scudder.

Pennsylvania:
Robert Morris,
Daniel Roberdeau,
Jonathan Bayard
   Smith,
William Clingan,
Joseph Reed.

Delaware:
Thomas McKean,
John Dickinson,
Nicholas Van Dyke.

Maryland:
John Hanson,
Daniel Carroll.

Virginia:
Richard Henry
   Lee,
John Banister,
Thomas Adams,
John Harvie,
Francis Lightfoot
   Lee.

North Carolina:
John Penn,
Cornelius Harnett,
John Williams.

South Carolina:
Henry Laurens,
William Henry
   Drayton,
John Mathews,
Richard Hutson,
Thomas Heyward Jr.

Georgia:
John Walton,
Edward Telfair,
Edward Langworthy.

Constitution of the United States

The United States Constitution was written at a convention that Congress called on February 21, 1787, for the purpose of recommending amendments to the Articles of Confederation. Every state but Rhode Island sent delegates to Philadelphia, where the convention met that summer. The delegates decided to write an entirely new constitution, completing their labors on September 17. Nine states (the number the Constitution itself stipulated as sufficient) ratified by June 21, 1788.

The Framers of the Constitution included only six paragraphs on the Supreme Court. Article III, Section 1, created the Supreme Court and the federal system of courts. It provided that "[t]he judicial power of the United States, shall be vested in one supreme Court," and whatever inferior courts Congress "from time to time" saw fit to establish. Article III, Section 2, delineated the types of cases and controversies that should be considered by a federal—rather than a state—court. But beyond this, the Constitution left many of the particulars of the Supreme Court and the federal court system for Congress to decide in later years in judiciary acts.

We the People of the United States, in Order to form a more perfect Union, establish Justice, insure domestic Tranquility, provide for the common defence, promote the general Welfare, and secure the Blessings of Liberty to ourselves and our Posterity, do ordain and establish this Constitution for the United States of America.

ARTICLE I

Section 1. All legislative Powers herein granted shall be vested in a Congress of the United States, which shall consist of a Senate and House of Representatives.

Section 2. The House of Representatives shall be composed of Members chosen every second Year by the People of the several States, and the Electors in each State shall have the Qualifications requisite for Electors of the most numerous Branch of the State Legislature.

No Person shall be a Representative who shall not have attained to the age of twenty five Years, and been seven Years a Citizen of the United States, and who shall not, when elected, be an Inhabitant of that State in which he shall be chosen.

[Representatives and direct Taxes shall be apportioned among the several States which may be included within this Union, according to their respective Numbers, which shall be determined by adding to the whole Number of free Persons, including those bound to Service for a Term of Years, and excluding Indians not taxed, three fifths of all other Persons.][1] The actual Enumeration shall be made within three Years after the first Meeting of the Congress of the United States, and within every subsequent Term of ten Years, in such Manner as they shall by Law direct. The Number of Representatives shall not exceed one for every thirty Thousand, but each State shall have at Least one Representative; and until such enumeration shall be made, the State of New Hampshire shall be entitled to chuse three, Massachusetts eight, Rhode-Island and Providence Plantations one, Connecticut five, New-York six, New Jersey four, Pennsylvania eight, Delaware one, Maryland six, Virginia ten, North Carolina five, South Carolina five, and Georgia three.

When vacancies happen in the Representation from any State, the Executive Authority thereof shall issue Writs of Election to fill such Vacancies.

The House of Representatives shall chuse their Speaker and other Officers; and shall have the sole Power of Impeachment.

Section 3. The Senate of the United States shall be composed of two Senators from each State, [chosen by the Legislature thereof,][2] for six Years; and each Senator shall have one Vote.

Immediately after they shall be assembled in Consequence of the first Election, they shall be divided as equally as may be into three Classes. The Seats of the Senators of the first Class shall be vacated at the Expiration of the second Year, of the second Class at the Expiration of the fourth Year, and of the third Class at the Expiration of the sixth Year, so that one third may be chosen every second Year; [and if Vacancies happen by Resignation, or otherwise, during the Recess of the Legislature of any State, the Executive thereof may make temporary Appointments until the next Meeting of the Legislature, which shall then fill such Vacancies.][3]

No Person shall be a Senator who shall not have attained to the Age of thirty Years, and been nine Years a Citizen of the United States, and who shall not, when elected, be an Inhabitant of that State for which he shall be chosen.

The Vice President of the United States shall be President of the Senate, but shall have no Vote, unless they be equally divided.

The Senate shall chuse their other Officers, and also a President pro tempore, in the Absence of the Vice President, or when he shall exercise the Office of President of the United States.

The Senate shall have the sole Power to try all Impeachments. When sitting for that Purpose, they shall be on Oath or Affirmation. When the President of the United States is tried, the Chief Justice shall preside: And no Person shall be convicted without the Concurrence of two thirds of the Members present.

Judgment in Cases of Impeachment shall not extend further than to removal from Office, and disqualification to hold and enjoy any Office of honor, Trust or Profit under the United States: but the Party convicted shall nevertheless be liable and subject to Indictment, Trial, Judgment and Punishment, according to Law.

Section 4. The Times, Places and Manner of holding Elections for Senators and Representatives, shall be prescribed in each State by the Legislature thereof; but the Congress may at any time by Law make or alter such Regulations, except as to the Places of chusing Senators.

The Congress shall assemble at least once in every Year, and such Meeting shall [be on the first Monday in December],[4] unless they shall by Law appoint a different Day.

Section 5. Each House shall be the Judge of the Elections, Returns and Qualifications of its own Members, and a Majority of each shall constitute a Quorum to do Business; but a smaller Number may adjourn from day to day, and may be authorized to compel the Attendance of absent Members, in such Manner, and under such Penalties as each House may provide.

Each House may determine the Rules of its Proceedings, punish its Members for disorderly Behaviour, and, with the Concurrence of two thirds, expel a Member.

Each House shall keep a Journal of its Proceedings, and from time to time publish the same, excepting such Parts as may in their Judgment require Secrecy; and the Yeas and Nays of the Members of either House on any question shall, at the Desire of one fifth of those Present, be entered on the Journal.

Neither House, during the Session of Congress, shall, without the Consent of the other, adjourn for more than three days, nor to any other Place than that in which the two Houses shall be sitting.

Section 6. The Senators and Representatives shall receive a Compensation for their Services, to be ascertained by Law, and paid out of the Treasury of the United States. They shall in all Cases, except Treason, Felony and Breach of the Peace, be privileged from Arrest during their Attendance at the Session of their respective Houses, and in going to and returning from the same; and for any Speech or Debate in either House, they shall not be questioned in any other Place.

No Senator or Representative shall, during the Time for which he was elected, be appointed to any civil Office under the Authority of the United States, which shall have been created, or the Emoluments whereof shall have been encreased during such time; and no Person holding any Office under the United States, shall be a Member of either House during his Continuance in Office.

Section 7. All Bills for raising Revenue shall originate in the House of Representatives; but the Senate may propose or concur with Amendments as on other Bills.

Every Bill which shall have passed the House of Representatives and the Senate, shall, before it become a Law, be presented to the President of the United States; If he approve he shall sign it, but if not he shall return it, with his Objections to that House in which it shall have originated, who shall enter the Objections at large on their Journal, and proceed to reconsider it. If after such Reconsideration two thirds of that House shall agree to pass the Bill, it shall be sent, together with the Objections, to the other House, by which it shall likewise be reconsidered, and if approved by two thirds of that House, it shall become a Law. But in all such Cases the Votes of both Houses shall be determined by yeas and Nays, and the Names of the Persons voting for and against the Bill shall be entered on the Journal of each House respectively. If any Bill shall not be returned by the President within ten Days (Sundays excepted) after it shall have been presented to him, the Same shall be a Law, in like Manner as if he had signed it, unless the Congress by their Adjournment prevent its Return, in which Case it shall not be a Law.

Every Order, Resolution, or Vote to which the Concurrence of the Senate and House of Representatives may be necessary (except on a question of Adjournment) shall be presented to the President of the United States; and before the Same shall take Effect, shall be approved by him, or being disapproved by him, shall be repassed by two thirds of the Senate and House of Representatives, according to the Rules and Limitations prescribed in the Case of a Bill.

Section 8. The Congress shall have Power To lay and collect Taxes, Duties, Imposts and Excises, to pay the Debts and provide for the common Defence and general Welfare of the United States; but all Duties, Imposts and Excises shall be uniform throughout the United States;

To borrow Money on the credit of the United States;

To regulate Commerce with foreign Nations, and among the several States, and with the Indian Tribes;

To establish an uniform Rule of Naturalization, and uniform Laws on the subject of Bankruptcies throughout the United States;

To coin Money, regulate the Value thereof, and of foreign Coin, and fix the Standard of Weights and Measures;

To provide for the Punishment of counterfeiting the Securities and current Coin of the United States;

To establish Post Offices and post Roads;

To promote the Progress of Science and useful Arts, by securing for limited Times to Authors and Inventors the exclusive Right to their respective Writings and Discoveries;

To constitute Tribunals inferior to the supreme Court;

To define and punish Piracies and Felonies committed on the high Seas, and Offences against the Law of Nations;

To declare War, grant Letters of Marque and Reprisal, and make Rules concerning Captures on Land and Water;

To raise and support Armies, but no Appropriation of Money to that Use shall be for a longer Term than two Years;

To provide and maintain a Navy;

To make Rules for the Government and Regulation of the land and naval Forces;

To provide for calling forth the Militia to execute the Laws of the Union, suppress Insurrections and repel Invasions;

To provide for organizing, arming, and disciplining, the Militia, and for governing such Part of them as may be employed in the Service of the United States, reserving to the States respectively, the Appointment of the Officers, and the Authority of training the Militia according to the discipline prescribed by Congress;

To exercise exclusive Legislation in all Cases whatsoever, over such District (not exceeding ten Miles square) as may, by Cession of particular States, and the Acceptance of Congress, become the Seat of the Government of the United States, and to exercise like Authority over all Places purchased by the Consent of the Legislature of the State in which the Same shall be, for the Erection of Forts, Magazines, Arsenals, dock-Yards, and other needful Buildings;—And

To make all Laws which shall be necessary and proper for carrying into Execution the foregoing Powers, and all other Powers vested by this Constitution in the Government of the United States, or in any Department or Officer thereof.

Section 9. The Migration or Importation of such Persons as any of the States now existing shall think proper to admit, shall not be prohibited by the Congress prior to the Year one thousand eight hundred and eight, but a Tax or duty may be imposed on such Importation, not exceeding ten dollars for each Person.

The Privilege of the Writ of Habeas Corpus shall not be suspended, unless when in Cases of Rebellion or Invasion the public Safety may require it.

No Bill of Attainder or ex post facto Law shall be passed.

No Capitation, or other direct, Tax shall be laid, unless in Proportion to the Census or Enumeration herein before directed to be taken.[5]

No Tax or Duty shall be laid on Articles exported from any State.

No Preference shall be given by any Regulation of Commerce or Revenue to the Ports of one State over those of another; nor shall Vessels bound to, or from, one State, be obliged to enter, clear, or pay Duties in another.

No Money shall be drawn from the Treasury, but in Consequence of Appropriations made by Law; and a regular Statement and Account of the Receipts and Expenditures of all public Money shall be published from time to time.

No Title of Nobility shall be granted by the United States: And no Person holding any Office of Profit or Trust under them, shall, without the Consent of the Congress, accept of any present, Emolument, Office, or Title, of any kind whatever, from any King, Prince, or foreign State.

Section 10. No State shall enter into any Treaty, Alliance, or Confederation; grant Letters of Marque and Reprisal; coin Money; emit Bills of Credit; make any Thing but gold and silver Coin a Tender in Payment of Debts; pass any Bill of Attainder, ex post facto Law, or Law impairing the Obligation of Contracts, or grant any Title of Nobility.

No State shall, without the Consent of the Congress, lay any Imposts or Duties on Imports or Exports, except what may be absolutely necessary for executing it's inspection Laws: and the net Produce of all Duties and Imposts, laid by any State on Imports or Exports, shall be for the Use of the Treasury of the United States; and all such Laws shall be subject to the Revision and Controul of the Congress.

No State shall, without the Consent of Congress, lay any Duty of Tonnage, keep Troops, or Ships of War in time of Peace, enter into any Agreement or Compact with another State, or with a foreign Power, or engage in War, unless actually invaded, or in such imminent Danger as will not admit of delay.

ARTICLE II

Section 1. The executive Power shall be vested in a President of the United States of America. He shall hold his Office during the Term of four Years, and, together with the Vice President, chosen for the same Term, be elected, as follows

Each State shall appoint, in such Manner as the Legislature thereof may direct, a Number of Electors, equal to the whole Number of Senators and Representatives to which the State may be entitled in the Congress: but no Senator or Representative, or Person holding an Office of Trust or Profit under the United States, shall be appointed an Elector.

[The Electors shall meet in their respective States, and vote by Ballot for two Persons, of whom one at least shall not be an Inhabitant of the same State with themselves. And they shall make a List of all the Persons voted for, and of the Number of Votes for each; which List they shall sign and certify, and transmit sealed to the Seat of the Government of the United States, directed to the President of the Senate. The President of the Senate shall, in the Presence of the Senate and House of Representatives, open all the Certificates, and the Votes shall then be counted. The Person having the greatest Number of Votes shall be the President, if such Number be a Majority of the whole Number of Electors appointed; and if there be more than one who have such Majority, and have an equal Number of Votes, then the House of Representatives shall immediately chuse by Ballot one of them for President; and if no Person have a Majority, then from the five highest on the list the said House shall in like Manner chuse the President. But in chusing the President, the Votes shall be taken by States, the Representation from each State having one Vote; A quorum for this Purpose shall consist of a Member or Members from two thirds of the States, and a Majority of all the States shall be necessary to a Choice. In every Case, after the Choice of the President, the Person having the greatest Number of Votes of the Electors shall be the Vice President. But if there should remain two or more who have equal Votes, the Senate shall chuse from them by Ballot the Vice President.][6]

The Congress may determine the Time of chusing the Electors, and the Day on which they shall give their Votes; which Day shall be the same throughout the United States.

No Person except a natural born Citizen, or a Citizen of the United States, at the time of the Adoption of this Constitution, shall be eligible to the Office of President; neither shall any Person be eligible to that Office who shall not have attained to the Age of thirty five Years, and been fourteen Years a Resident within the United States.

In Case of the Removal of the President from Office, or of his Death, Resignation, or Inability to discharge the Powers and Duties of the said Office,[7] the Same shall devolve on the Vice President, and the Congress may by Law provide for the Case of Removal, Death, Resignation or Inability, both of the President and Vice President, declaring what Officer shall then act as President, and such Officer shall act accordingly, until the Disability be removed, or a President shall be elected.

The President shall, at stated Times, receive for his Services, a Compensation, which shall neither be encreased nor diminished during the Period for which he shall have been elected, and he shall not receive within that Period any other Emolument from the United States, or any of them.

Before he enter on the Execution of his Office, he shall take the following Oath or Affirmation:—"I do solemnly swear (or affirm) that I will faithfully execute the Office of President of the United States, and will to the best of my Ability, preserve, protect and defend the Constitution of the United States."

Section 2. The President shall be Commander in Chief of the Army and Navy of the United States, and of the Militia of the several States, when called into the actual Service of the United States; he may require the Opinion, in writing, of the principal Officer in each of the executive Departments, upon any Subject relating to the Duties of their respective Offices, and he shall have Power to grant Reprieves and Pardons for Offences against the United States, except in Cases of Impeachment.

He shall have Power, by and with the Advice and Consent of the Senate, to make Treaties, provided two thirds of the Senators present concur; and he shall nominate, and by and with the Advice and Consent of the Senate, shall appoint Ambassadors, other public Ministers and Consuls, Judges of the supreme Court, and all other Officers of the United States, whose Appointments are not herein otherwise provided for, and which shall be established by Law: but the Congress may by Law vest the Appointment of such inferior Officers, as they think proper, in the President alone, in the Courts of Law, or in the Heads of Departments.

The President shall have Power to fill up all Vacancies that may happen during the Recess of the Senate, by granting Commissions which shall expire at the End of their next Session.

Section 3. He shall from time to time give to the Congress Information of the State of the Union, and recommend to their Consideration such Measures as he shall judge necessary and expedient; he may, on extraordinary Occasions, convene both Houses, or either of them, and in Case of Disagreement between them, with Respect to the Time of Adjournment, he may adjourn them to such Time as he shall think proper; he shall receive Ambassadors and other public Ministers; he shall take Care that the Laws be faithfully executed, and shall Commission all the Officers of the United States.

Section 4. The President, Vice President and all civil Officers of the United States, shall be removed from Office on Impeachment for, and Conviction of, Treason, Bribery, or other high Crimes and Misdemeanors.

ARTICLE III

Section 1. The judicial Power of the United States, shall be vested in one supreme Court, and in such inferior Courts as the Congress may from time to time ordain and establish. The Judges, both of the supreme and inferior Courts, shall hold their Offices during good Behaviour, and shall, at stated Times, receive for their Services, a Compensation, which shall not be diminished during their Continuance in Office.

Section 2. The judicial Power shall extend to all Cases, in Law and Equity, arising under this Constitution, the Laws of the United States, and Treaties made, or which shall be made, under their Authority; —to all Cases affecting Ambassadors, other public Ministers and Consuls; —to all Cases of admiralty and maritime Jurisdiction; —to Controversies to which the United States shall be a Party; —to Controversies between two or more States; —between a State and Citizens of another State;[8] —between Citizens of different States; —between Citizens of the same State claiming Lands under Grants of different States, and between a State, or the Citizens thereof, and foreign States, Citizens or Subjects.[8]

In all Cases affecting Ambassadors, other public Ministers and Consuls, and those in which a State shall be Party, the supreme Court shall have original Jurisdiction. In all the other Cases before mentioned, the supreme Court shall have appellate Jurisdiction, both as to Law and Fact, with such Exceptions, and under such Regulations as the Congress shall make.

The Trial of all Crimes, except in Cases of Impeachment, shall be by Jury; and such Trial shall be held in the State where the said Crimes shall have been committed; but when not committed within any State, the Trial shall be at such Place or Places as the Congress may by Law have directed.

Section 3. Treason against the United States, shall consist only in levying War against them, or in adhering to their Enemies, giving them Aid and Comfort. No Person shall be convicted of Treason unless on the Testimony of two Witnesses to the same overt Act, or on Confession in open Court.

The Congress shall have Power to declare the Punishment of Treason, but no Attainder of Treason shall work Corruption of Blood, or Forfeiture except during the Life of the Person attainted.

ARTICLE IV

Section 1. Full Faith and Credit shall be given in each State to the public Acts, Records, and judicial Proceedings of every other State. And the Congress may by general Laws prescribe the Manner in which such Acts, Records and Proceedings shall be proved, and the Effect thereof.

Section 2. The Citizens of each State shall be entitled to all Privileges and Immunities of Citizens in the several States.

A Person charged in any State with Treason, Felony, or other Crime, who shall flee from Justice, and be found in another State, shall on Demand of the executive Authority of the State from which he fled, be delivered up, to be removed to the State having Jurisdiction of the Crime.

[No Person held to Service or Labour in one State, under the Laws thereof, escaping into another, shall, in Consequence of any Law or Regulation therein, be discharged from such Service or Labour, but shall be delivered up on Claim of the Party to whom such Service or Labour may be due.]

Section 3. New States may be admitted by the Congress into this Union; but no new State shall be formed or erected within the Jurisdiction of any other State; nor any State be formed by the Junction of two or more States, or Parts of States, without the Consent of the Legislatures of the States concerned as well as of the Congress.

The Congress shall have Power to dispose of and make all needful Rules and Regulations respecting the Territory or other Property belonging to the United States; and nothing in this Constitution shall be so construed as to Prejudice any Claims of the United States, or of any particular State.

Section 4. The United States shall guarantee to every State in this Union a Republican Form of Government, and shall protect each of them against Invasion; and on Application of the Legislature, or of the Executive (when the Legislature cannot be convened) against domestic Violence.

ARTICLE V

The Congress, whenever two thirds of both Houses shall deem it necessary, shall propose Amendments to this Constitution, or, on the Application of the Legislatures of two thirds of the several States, shall call a Convention for proposing Amendments, which, in either Case, shall be valid to all Intents and Purposes, as Part of this Constitution, when ratified by the Legislatures of three fourths of the several States, or by Conventions in three fourths thereof, as the one or the other Mode of Ratification may be proposed by the Congress; Provided [that no Amendment which may be made prior to the Year One thousand eight hundred and eight shall in any Manner affect the first and fourth Clauses in the Ninth Section of the first Article; and][10]

that no State, without its Consent, shall be deprived of its equal Suffrage in the Senate.

ARTICLE VI

All Debts contracted and Engagements entered into, before the Adoption of this Constitution, shall be as valid against the United States under this Constitution, as under the Confederation.

This Constitution, and the Laws of the United States which shall be made in Pursuance thereof; and all Treaties made, or which shall be made, under the Authority of the United States, shall be the supreme Law of the Land; and the Judges in every State shall be bound thereby, any Thing in the Constitution or Laws of any State to the Contrary notwithstanding.

The Senators and Representatives before mentioned, and the Members of the several State Legislatures, and all executive and judicial Officers, both of the United States and of the several States, shall be bound by Oath or Affirmation, to support this Constitution; but no religious Test shall ever be required as a Qualification to any Office or public Trust under the United States.

ARTICLE VII

The Ratification of the Conventions of nine States, shall be sufficient for the Establishment of this Constitution between the States so ratifying the Same.

Done in Convention by the Unanimous Consent of the States present the Seventeenth Day of September in the Year of our Lord one thousand seven hundred and Eighty seven and of the Independence of the United States of America the Twelfth. IN WITNESS whereof We have hereunto subscribed our Names,

George Washington,
President and deputy from Virginia.

New Hampshire:
John Langdon,
Nicholas Gilman.

Massachusetts:
Nathaniel Gorham,
Rufus King.

Connecticut:
William Samuel Johnson,
Roger Sherman.

New York:
Alexander Hamilton.

New Jersey:
William Livingston,
David Brearley,
William Paterson,
Jonathan Dayton.

Pennsylvania:
Benjamin Franklin,
Thomas Mifflin,
Robert Morris,
George Clymer,
Thomas FitzSimons,
Jared Ingersoll,
James Wilson,
Gouverneur Morris.

Delaware:
George Read,
Gunning Bedford Jr.,
John Dickinson,
Richard Bassett,
Jacob Broom.

Maryland:
James McHenry,
Daniel of St. Thomas Jenifer,
Daniel Carroll.

Virginia:
John Blair,
James Madison Jr.

North Carolina:.
William Blount,
Richard Dobbs Spaight,
Hugh Williamson.

South Carolina:
John Rutledge,
Charles Cotesworth Pinckney,
Charles Pinckney,
Pierce Butler.

Georgia:
William Few,
Abraham Baldwin.

[The language of the original Constitution, not including the Amendments, was adopted by a convention of the states on September 17, 1787, and was subsequently ratified by the states on the following dates: Delaware, December 7, 1787; Pennsylvania, December 12, 1787; New Jersey, December 18, 1787; Georgia, January 2, 1788; Connecticut, January 9, 1788; Massachusetts, February 6, 1788; Maryland, April 28, 1788; South Carolina, May 23, 1788; New Hampshire, June 21, 1788.

Ratification was completed on June 21, 1788.

The Constitution subsequently was ratified by Virginia, June 25, 1788; New York, July 26, 1788; North Carolina, November 21, 1789; Rhode Island, May 29, 1790; and Vermont, January 10, 1791.]

AMENDMENTS

Amendment I

(First ten amendments ratified December 15, 1791.)

Congress shall make no law respecting an establishment of religion, or prohibiting the free exercise thereof; or abridging the freedom of speech, or of the press; or the right of the people peaceably to assemble, and to petition the Government for a redress of grievances.

Amendment II

A well regulated Militia, being necessary to the security of a free State, the right of the people to keep and bear Arms, shall not be infringed.

Amendment III

No Soldier shall, in time of peace be quartered in any house, without the consent of the Owner, nor in time of war, but in a manner to be prescribed by law.

Amendment IV

The right of the people to be secure in their persons, houses, papers, and effects, against unreasonable searches and seizures, shall not be violated, and no Warrants shall issue, but upon probable cause, supported by Oath or affirmation, and particularly describing the place to be searched, and the persons or things to be seized.

Amendment V

No person shall be held to answer for a capital, or otherwise infamous crime, unless on a presentment or indictment of a Grand Jury, except in cases arising in the land or naval forces, or in the Militia, when in actual service in time of War or public danger; nor shall any person be subject for the same offence to be twice put in jeopardy of life or limb; nor shall be compelled in any criminal case to be a witness against himself, nor be deprived of life, liberty, or property, without due process of law; nor shall private property be taken for public use, without just compensation.

Amendment VI

In all criminal prosecutions, the accused shall enjoy the right to a speedy and public trial, by an impartial jury of the State and district wherein the crime shall have been committed, which district shall have been previously ascertained by law, and to be informed of the nature and cause of the accusation; to be confronted with the witnesses against him; to have compulsory process for obtaining witnesses in his favor, and to have the Assistance of Counsel for his defence.

Amendment VII

In Suits at common law, where the value in controversy shall exceed twenty dollars, the right of trial by jury shall be preserved, and no fact tried by a jury, shall be otherwise re-examined in any Court of the United States, than according to the rules of the common law.

Amendment VIII

Excessive bail shall not be required, nor excessive fines imposed, nor cruel and unusual punishments inflicted.

Amendment IX

The enumeration in the Constitution, of certain rights, shall not be construed to deny or disparage others retained by the people.

Amendment X

The powers not delegated to the United States by the Constitution, nor prohibited by it to the States, are reserved to the States respectively, or to the people.

Amendment XI *(Ratified February 7, 1795)*

The Judicial power of the United States shall not be construed to extend to any suit in law or equity, commenced or prosecuted against one of the United States by Citizens of another State, or by Citizens or Subjects of any Foreign State.

Amendment XII *(Ratified June 15, 1804)*

The Electors shall meet in their respective states and vote by ballot for President and Vice-President, one of whom, at least, shall not be an inhabitant of the same state with themselves; they shall name in their ballots the person voted for as President, and in distinct ballots the person voted for as Vice-President, and they shall make distinct lists of all persons voted for as President, and of all persons voted for as Vice-President, and of the number of votes for each, which lists they shall sign and certify, and transmit sealed to the seat of the government of the United States, directed to the President of the Senate; — The President of the Senate shall, in the presence of the Senate and House of Representatives, open all the certificates and the votes shall then be counted; — The person having the greatest number of votes for President, shall be the President, if such number be a majority of the whole number of Electors appointed; and if no person have such majority, then from the persons having the highest numbers not exceeding three on the list of those voted for as President, the House of Representatives shall choose immediately, by ballot, the President. But in choosing the President, the votes shall be taken by states, the representation from each state having one vote; a quorum for this purpose shall consist of a member or members from two-thirds of the states, and a majority of all the states shall be necessary to a choice. [And if the House of Representatives shall not choose a President whenever the right of choice shall devolve upon them, before the fourth day of March next following, then the Vice-President shall act as President, as in the case of the death or other constitutional disability of the President. —][11] The person having the greatest number of votes as Vice-President, shall be the Vice-President, if such number be a majority of the whole number of Electors appointed, and if no person have a majority, then from the two highest numbers on the list, the Senate shall choose the Vice-President; a quorum for the purpose shall consist of two-thirds of the whole number of Senators, and a majority of the whole number shall be necessary to a choice. But no person constitutionally ineligible to the office of President shall be eligible to that of Vice-President of the United States.

Amendment XIII *(Ratified December 6, 1865)*

Section 1. Neither slavery nor involuntary servitude, except as a punishment for crime whereof the party shall have been duly convicted, shall exist within the United States, or any place subject to their jurisdiction.

Section 2. Congress shall have power to enforce this article by appropriate legislation.

Amendment XIV (Ratified July 9, 1868)

Section 1. All persons born or naturalized in the United States, and subject to the jurisdiction thereof, are citizens of the United States and of the State wherein they reside. No State shall make or enforce any law which shall abridge the privileges or immunities of citizens of the United States; nor shall any State deprive any person of life, liberty, or property, without due process of law; nor deny to any person within its jurisdiction the equal protection of the laws.

Section 2. Representatives shall be apportioned among the several States according to their respective numbers, counting the whole number of persons in each State, excluding Indians not taxed. But when the right to vote at any election for the choice of electors for President and Vice President of the United States, Representatives in Congress, the Executive and Judicial officers of a State, or the members of the Legislature thereof, is denied to any of the male inhabitants of such State, being twenty-one years of age,[12] and citizens of the United States, or in any way abridged, except for participation in rebellion, or other crime, the basis of representation therein shall be reduced in the proportion which the number of such male citizens shall bear to the whole number of male citizens twenty-one years of age in such State.

Section 3. No person shall be a Senator or Representative in Congress, or elector of President and Vice President, or hold any office, civil or military, under the United States, or under any State, who, having previously taken an oath, as a member of Congress, or as an officer of the United States, or as a member of any State legislature, or as an executive or judicial officer of any State, to support the Constitution of the United States, shall have engaged in insurrection or rebellion against the same, or given aid or comfort to the enemies thereof. But Congress may by a vote of two-thirds of each House, remove such disability.

Section 4. The validity of the public debt of the United States, authorized by law, including debts incurred for payment of pensions and bounties for services in suppressing insurrection or rebellion, shall not be questioned. But neither the United States nor any State shall assume or pay any debt or obligation incurred in aid of insurrection or rebellion against the United States, or any claim for the loss or emancipation of any slave; but all such debts, obligations and claims shall be held illegal and void.

Section 5. The Congress shall have power to enforce, by appropriate legislation, the provisions of this article.

Amendment XV (Ratified February 3, 1870)

Section 1. The right of citizens of the United States to vote shall not be denied or abridged by the United States or by any State on account of race, color, or previous condition of servitude.

Section 2. The Congress shall have power to enforce this article by appropriate legislation.

Amendment XVI (Ratified February 3, 1913)

The Congress shall have power to lay and collect taxes on incomes, from whatever source derived, without apportionment among the several States, and without regard to any census or enumeration.

Amendment XVII (Ratified April 8, 1913)

The Senate of the United States shall be composed of two Senators from each State, elected by the people thereof, for six years; and each Senator shall have one vote. The electors in each State shall have the qualifications requisite for electors of the most numerous branch of the State legislatures.

When vacancies happen in the representation of any State in the Senate, the executive authority of such State shall issue writs of election to fill such vacancies: *Provided,* That the legislature of any State may empower the executive thereof to make temporary appointments until the people fill the vacancies by election as the legislature may direct.

This amendment shall not be so construed as to affect the election or term of any Senator chosen before it becomes valid as part of the Constitution.

Amendment XVIII (Ratified January 16, 1919)

Section 1. After one year from the ratification of this article the manufacture, sale, or transportation of intoxicating liquors within, the importation thereof into, or the exportation thereof from the United States and all territory subject to the jurisdiction thereof for beverage purposes is hereby prohibited.

Section 2. The Congress and the several States shall have concurrent power to enforce this article by appropriate legislation.

Section 3. This article shall be inoperative unless it shall have been ratified as an amendment to the Constitution by the legislatures of the several States, as provided in the Constitution, within seven years from the date of the submission hereof to the States by the Congress.][13]

Amendment XIX (Ratified August 18, 1920)

The right of citizens of the United States to vote shall not be denied or abridged by the United States or by any State on account of sex.

Congress shall have power to enforce this article by appropriate legislation.

Amendment XX (Ratified January 23, 1933)

Section 1. The terms of the President and Vice President shall end at noon on the 20th day of January, and the terms of Senators and Representatives at noon on the 3d day of January, of the years in which such terms would have ended if this article had not been ratified; and the terms of their successors shall then begin.

Section 2. The Congress shall assemble at least once in every year, and such meeting shall begin at noon on the 3d day of January, unless they shall by law appoint a different day.

Section 3.[14] If, at the time fixed for the beginning of the term of the President, the President elect shall have died, the Vice President elect shall become President. If a President shall not have been chosen before the time fixed for the beginning of his term, or if the President elect shall have failed to qualify, then the Vice President elect shall act as President until a President shall have qualified; and the Congress may by law provide for the case wherein neither a President elect nor a Vice President elect shall have qualified, declaring who shall then act as President, or the manner in which one who is to act shall be selected, and such person shall act accordingly until a President or Vice President shall have qualified.

Section 4. The Congress may by law provide for the case of the death of any of the persons from whom the House of Representatives may choose a President whenever the right of choice shall have devolved upon them, and for the case of the death of any of the persons from whom the Senate may choose a Vice President whenever the right of choice shall have devolved upon them.

Section 5. Sections 1 and 2 shall take effect on the 15th day of October following the ratification of this article.

Section 6. This article shall be inoperative unless it shall have been ratified as an amendment to the Constitution by the legislatures of three-fourths of the several States within seven years from the date of its submission.

Amendment XXI (Ratified December 5, 1933)

Section 1. The eighteenth article of amendment to the Constitution of the United States is hereby repealed.

Section 2. The transportation or importation into any State, Territory, or possession of the United States for delivery or use therein of intoxicating liquors, in violation of the laws thereof, is hereby prohibited.

Section 3. This article shall be inoperative unless it shall have been ratified as an amendment to the Constitution by conventions in the several States, as provided in the Constitution, within seven years from the date of the submission hereof to the States by the Congress.

Amendment XXII (Ratified February 27, 1951)

Section 1. No person shall be elected to the office of the President more than twice, and no person who has held the office of President, or acted as President, for more than two years of a term to which some other person was elected President shall be elected to the office of the President more than once. But this Article shall not apply to any person holding the office of President when this Article was proposed by the Congress, and shall not prevent any person who may be holding the office of President, or acting as President, during the term within which this Article becomes operative from holding the office of President or acting as President during the remainder of such term.

Section 2. This article shall be inoperative unless it shall have been ratified as an amendment to the Constitution by the legislatures of three-fourths of the several States within seven years from the date of its submission to the States by the Congress.

Amendment XXIII (Ratified March 29, 1961)

Section 1. The District constituting the seat of Government of the United States shall appoint in such manner as the Congress may direct:

A number of electors of President and Vice President equal to the whole number of Senators and Representatives in Congress to which the District would be entitled if it were a State, but in no event more than the least populous State; they shall be in addition to those appointed by the States, but they shall be considered, for the purposes of the election of President and Vice President, to be electors appointed by a State; and they shall meet in the District and perform such duties as provided by the twelfth article of amendment.

Section 2. The Congress shall have power to enforce this article by appropriate legislation.

Amendment XXIV (Ratified January 23, 1964)

Section 1. The right of citizens of the United States to vote in any primary or other election for President or Vice President, for electors for President or Vice President, or for Senator or Representative in Congress, shall not be denied or abridged by the United States or any State by reason of failure to pay any poll tax or other tax.

Section 2. The Congress shall have power to enforce this article by appropriate legislation.

Amendment XXV (Ratified February 10, 1967)

Section 1. In case of the removal of the President from office or of his death or resignation, the Vice President shall become President.

Section 2. Whenever there is a vacancy in the office of the Vice President, the President shall nominate a Vice President who shall take office upon confirmation by a majority vote of both Houses of Congress.

Section 3. Whenever the President transmits to the President pro tempore of the Senate and the Speaker of the House of Representa-tives his written declaration that he is unable to discharge the powers and duties of his office, and until he transmits to them a written declaration to the contrary, such powers and duties shall be discharged by the Vice President as Acting President.

Section 4. Whenever the Vice President and a majority of either the principal officers of the executive departments or of such other body as Congress may by law provide, transmit to the President pro tempore of the Senate and the Speaker of the House of Representatives their written declaration that the President is unable to discharge the powers and duties of his office, the Vice President shall immediately assume the powers and duties of the office as Acting President.

Thereafter, when the President transmits to the President pro tempore of the Senate and the Speaker of the House of Representatives his written declaration that no inability exists, he shall resume the powers and duties of his office unless the Vice President and a majority of either the principal officers of the executive departments or of such other body as Congress may by law provide, transmit within four days to the President pro tempore of the Senate and the Speaker of the House of Representatives their written declaration that the President is unable to discharge the powers and duties of his office. Thereupon Congress shall decide the issue, assembling within forty-eight hours for that purpose if not in session. If the Congress, within twenty-one days after receipt of the latter written declaration, or, if Congress is not in session, within twenty-one days after Congress is required to assemble, determines by two-thirds vote of both Houses that the President is unable to discharge the powers and duties of his office, the Vice President shall continue to discharge the same as Acting President; otherwise, the President shall resume the powers and duties of his office.

Amendment XXVI (Ratified July 1, 1971)

Section 1. The right of citizens of the United States, who are eighteen years of age or older, to vote shall not be denied or abridged by the United States or by any State on account of age.

Section 2. The Congress shall have power to enforce this article by appropriate legislation.

Amendment XXVII (Ratified May 7, 1992)

No law varying the compensation for the services of the Senators and Representatives shall take effect, until an election of Representatives shall have intervened.

SOURCE: U.S. Congress, House, Committee on the Judiciary, *The Constitution of the United States of America, as Amended*, 100th Cong., 1st sess., 1987, H Doc 100-94.

NOTES: 1. The part in brackets was changed by section 2 of the Fourteenth Amendment.

2. The part in brackets was changed by the first paragraph of the Seventeenth Amendment.

3. The part in brackets was changed by the second paragraph of the Seventeenth Amendment.

4. The part in brackets was changed by section 2 of the Twentieth Amendment.

5. The Sixteenth Amendment gave Congress the power to tax incomes.

6. The material in brackets was superseded by the Twelfth Amendment.

7. This provision was affected by the Twenty-fifth Amendment.

8. These clauses were affected by the Eleventh Amendment.

9. This paragraph was superseded by the Thirteenth Amendment.

10. Obsolete.

11. The part in brackets was superseded by section 3 of the Twentieth Amendment.

12. See the Nineteenth and Twenty-sixth Amendments.

13. This amendment was repealed by section 1 of the Twenty-first Amendment.

14. See the Twenty-fifth Amendment.

Judiciary Act of 1789

Although the Constitution created the Supreme Court, it said much less about the Court than about Congress and the president. With the Judiciary Act of 1789, Congress set up a system of lower federal courts (district courts and circuit courts with limited jurisdiction), spelled out the appellate jurisdiction of the Supreme Court, and gave the Court the power to review and reverse or affirm state court rulings.

The act also set the number of Supreme Court justices at six: a chief justice and five associates. (Subsequent statutes changed the total number of justices successively to six, seven, nine, ten, seven, and nine.) In addition to establishing the size and jurisdiction of the Supreme Court, the act required the justices to "ride circuit"—a burdensome duty of traveling to and sitting on circuit courts around the country.

JUDICIARY ACT OF 1789

An Act to establish the Judicial Courts of the United States.

STATUTE I
Sept. 24, 1789.

Supreme court to consist of a chief justice, and five associates.
Two sessions annually.

Precedence.

SECTION 1. *Be it enacted by the Senate and House of Representatives of the United States of America in Congress assembled,* That the supreme court of the United States shall consist of a chief justice and five associate justices, any four of whom shall be a quorum, and shall hold annually at the seat of government two sessions, the one commencing the first Monday of February, and the other the first Monday of August. That the associate justices shall have precedence according to the data of their commissions, or when the commissions of two or more of them bear date on the same day, according to the respective ages.

Thirteen districts.

Maine.
N. Hampshire.

Massachusetts.

Connecticut.
New York.

New Jersey.

Pennsylvania.
Delaware.

Maryland.

Virginia.

Kentucky.

South Carolina.
Georgia.

SEC. 2. *And be it further enacted,* That the United States shall be, and they hereby are divided into thirteen districts, to be limited and called as follows, to wit: one to consist of that part of the State of Massachusetts which lies easterly of the State of New Hampshire, and to be called Maine District; one to consist of the State of New Hampshire, and to be called New Hampshire District; one to consist of the remaining part of the State of Massachusetts, and to be called Massachusetts district; one to consist of the State of Connecticut, and to be called Connecticut District; one to consist of the State of New York, and to be called New York District; one to consist of the State of New Jersey, and to be called New Jersey District; one to consist of the State of Pennsylvania, and to be called Pennsylvania District; one to consist of the State of Delaware, and to be called Delaware District; one to consist of the State of Maryland, and to be called Maryland District; one to consist of the State of Virginia, except that part called the District of Kentucky, and to be called Virginia District; one to consist of the remaining part of the State of Virginia, and to be called Kentucky District; one to consist of the State of South Carolina, and to be called South Carolina District; and one to consist of the State of Georgia, and to be called Georgia District.

A district court in each district.

SEC. 3. *And be it further enacted,* That there be a court called a District Court, in each of the aforementioned districts, to consist of one judge, who shall reside in the district for which he is appointed,

Four sessions annually in a district; and when held.

Special district courts.
Stated district courts; when holden.

Special courts, where held.

Where records kept.

and shall be called a District Judge, and shall hold annually four sessions, the first of which to commence as follows, to wit: in the districts of New York and of New Jersey on the first, in the district of Pennsylvania on the second, in the district of Connecticut on the third, and in the district of Delaware on the fourth, Tuesdays of November next; in the districts of Massachusetts, of Maine, and of Maryland, on the first, in the district of Georgia on the second, and in the districts of New Hampshire, of Virginia, and of Kentucky, on the third Tuesdays of December next; and the other three sessions progressively in the respective districts on the like Tuesdays of every third calendar month afterwards, and in the district of South Carolina, on the third Monday in March and September, the first Monday in July, and the second Monday in December of each and every year, commencing in December next; and that the District Judge shall have power to hold special courts at his discretion. That the stated District Court shall be held at the places following, to wit: in the district of Maine, at Portland and Pownalsborough alternately, beginning at the first; in the district of New Hampshire, at Exeter and Portsmouth alternately, beginning at the first; in the district of Massachusetts, at Boston and Salem alternately, beginning at the first; in the district of Connecticut, alternately at Hartford and New Haven, beginning at the first; in the district of Connecticut, alternately at Hartford and New Haven, beginning at the first; in the district of New York, at New York; in the district of New Jersey, alternately at New Brunswick and Burlington, beginning at the first; in the district of Pennsylvania, at Philadelphia and York Town alternately, beginning at the first; in the district of Delaware, alternately at Newcastle and Dover, beginning at the first; in the district of Maryland, alternately at Baltimore and Easton, beginning at the first; in the district of Virginia, alternately at Richmond and Williamsburgh, beginning at the first; in the district of Kentucky, at Harrodsburgh; in the district of South Carolina, at Charleston; and in the district of Georgia, alternately at Savannah and Augusta, beginning at the first; and that the special courts shall be held at the same place in each district as the stated courts, or in districts that have two, at either of them, in the discretion of the judge, or at such other place in the district, as the nature of the business and his discretion shall direct. And that in the districts that have but one place for holding the District Court, the records thereof shall be kept at that place; and in districts that have two, at that place in each district which the judge shall appoint.

Three circuits, and how divided.

SEC. 4. *And be it further enacted,* That the before mentioned districts, except those of Maine and Kentucky, shall be divided into three circuits, and be called the eastern, the middle, and the southern circuit. That the eastern circuit shall consist of the districts of New Hampshire, Massachusetts, Connecticut and New York; that the middle circuit shall consist of the districts of New Jersey, Pennsylvania, Delaware, Maryland and Virginia; and that the southern circuit shall consist of the districts of South Carolina and Georgia, and that there shall be held annually in each district of said circuits, two courts, which shall be called Circuit Courts, and shall consist of any two justices of the Supreme Court, and the district judge of such districts, any two of whom shall constitute a quorum: *Provided,* That no district judge shall give a vote in any case of appeal or error from his own decision; but may assign the reasons of such his decision.

First session of the circuit courts; when holden.

SEC. 5. *And be it further enacted,* That the first session of the said circuit court in the several districts shall commence at the times following, to wit: in New Jersey on the second, in New York on the fourth, in Pennsylvania on the eleventh, in Connecticut on the twenty-second, and in Delaware on the twenty-seventh, days of April next; in Massachusetts on the third, in Maryland on the seventh, in South Carolina on the twelfth, in New Hampshire on the twentieth, in Virginia on the twenty-second, and in Georgia on the twenty-eighth, days of May next, and the subsequent sessions in the respective districts on the like days of every sixth calendar month afterwards, except in South Carolina, where the session of the said court shall commence on the first, and in Georgia where it shall commence on the seventeenth day of October, and except when any of those days shall happen on a Sunday, and then the session shall commence on the next day following. And the sessions of the said circuit court

Where holden.

shall be held in the district of New Hampshire, at Portsmouth and Exeter alternately, beginning at the first; in the district of Massachusetts, at Boston; in the district of Connecticut, alternately at Hartford and New Haven, beginning at the last; in the district of New York, alternately at New York and Albany, beginning at the first; in the district of New Jersey, at Trenton; in the district of Pennsylvania, alternately at Philadelphia and Yorktown, beginning at the first; in the district of Delaware, alternately at New Castle and Dover, beginning at the first; in the district of Maryland, alternately at Annapolis and Easton, beginning at the first; in the district of Virginia, alternately at Charlottesville and Williamsburgh, beginning at the first; in the district of South Carolina, alternately at Columbia and Charleston, beginning at the first; and in the district of Georgia, alternately at Savannah and Augusta, beginning at the first. And

Circuit courts. Special sessions.

the circuit courts shall have power to hold special sessions for the trial of criminal causes at any other

time at their discretion, or at the discretion of the Supreme Court.

Supreme court adjourned by one or more justices; circuit courts adjourned.

SEC. 6. *And be it further enacted,* That the Supreme Court may, by any one or more of its justices being present, be adjourned from day to day until a quorum be convened; and that a circuit court may also be adjourned from day to day by any one of its judges, or if none are present, by the marshal of the district until a quorum be convened; and that a

District courts adjourned.

district court, in case of the inability of the judge to attend at the commencement of a session, may by virtue of a written order from the said judge, directed to the marshal of the district, be adjourned by the said marshal to such day, antecedent to the next stated session of the said court, as in the said order shall be appointed; and in case of the death of the said judge, and his vacancy not being supplied, all process, pleadings and proceedings of what nature soever, pending before the said court, shall be continued of course until the next stated session after the appointment and acceptance of the office by his successor.

The courts have power to appoint clerks.

SEC. 7. *And be it [further] enacted,* That the Supreme Court, and the district courts shall have power to appoint clerks for their respective courts, and that the clerk for each district court shall be clerk also of the circuit court in such district, and each of the said clerks shall, before he enters upon the execu-

Their oath or affirmation.

tion of his office, take the following oath or affirmation, to wit: "I, A. B., being appointed clerk of _____, do solemnly swear, or affirm, that I will truly and faithfully enter and record all the orders, decrees, judgments and proceedings of the said court, and that I will faithfully and impartially discharge and perform all the duties of my said office, according to the best of my abilities and understanding. So help me God." Which words, so help me God, shall be omitted in all cases where an affirmation is admitted instead of an oath. And the said clerks shall also severally give bond, with sufficient sureties, (to be approved of by the Supreme and district courts respectively) to the United States, in the sum of two thousand dollars, faithfully to discharge the duties of his office, and seasonably to record the decrees, judgments and determinations of the court of which he is clerk.

SEC. 8. *And be it further enacted,* That the justices of the Supreme Court, and the district judges, before they proceed to execute the duties of their respective offices, shall take the following oath or affirmation,

Oath of justices of supreme court and judges of the district court.

to wit: "I, A. B., do solemnly swear or affirm, that I will administer justice without respect to persons, and do equal right to the poor and to the rich, and that I will faithfully and impartially discharge and perform all the duties incumbent on me as _____, according to the best of my abilities and understanding, agreeably to the constitution and laws of the United States. So help me God."

District courts exclusive jurisdiction.

SEC. 9. *And be it further enacted,* That the district courts shall have, exclusively of the courts of the several States, cognizance of all crimes and offences that shall be cognizable under the authority of the United States, committed within their respective districts, or upon the high seas; where no other punishment than whipping, not exceeding thirty stripes, a fine not exceeding one hundred dollars, or a term of imprisonment not exceeding six months, is to be inflicted; and shall also have exclusive original cog-

Original cognizance in maritime causes and of seizure under the laws of the United States.

nizance of all civil causes of admiralty and maritime jurisdication, including all seizures under laws of impost, navigation or trade of the United States, where the seizures are made, on waters which are navigable from the sea by vessels of ten or more tons burthen, within their respective districts as well as upon the high seas; saving to suitors, in all cases, the right of a common law remedy, where the common law is competent to give it; and shall also have exclusive original cognizance of all seizures on land, or other waters than as aforesaid, made, and of all suits for penalties and forfeitures incurred, under the laws of the United States. And shall also have cog-

Concurrent jurisdiction.

nizance, concurrent with the courts of the several States, or the circuit courts, as the case may be, of all causes where an alien sues for a tort only in violation of the law of nations or a treaty of the United States. And shall also have cognizance, concurrent as last mentioned, of all suits at common law where the United States sue, and the matter in dispute amounts, exclusive of costs, to the sum or value of one hundred dollars. And shall also have jurisdiction exclusively of the courts of the several States, of all suits against consuls or vice-consuls, except for offences above the description aforesaid. And the

Trial of fact by jury.

trial of issues in fact, in the district courts, in all causes except civil causes of admiralty and maritime jurisdiction, shall be by jury.

Kentucky district court.

SEC. 10. *And be it further enacted,* That the district court in Kentucky district shall, besides the jurisdiction aforesaid, have jurisdiction of all other causes, except of appeals and writs of error, hereinafter made cognizable in a circuit court, and shall proceed therein in the same manner as a circuit court, and writs of error and appeals shall lie from decisions therein to the Supreme Court in the same causes, as from a circuit court to the Supreme Court, and under the same regulations. And the district court in

Maine district court.

Maine district shall, besides the jurisdiction herein before granted, have jurisdiction of all causes, except of appeals and writs of error herein after made cognizable in a circuit court, and shall proceed therein in the same manner as a circuit court: And writs of error shall lie from decisions therein to the circuit court in the district of Massachusetts in the same manner as from other district courts to their respective circuit courts.

Circuit courts original cognizance where the matter in dispute exceeds five hundred dollars.

SEC. 11. *And be it further enacted,* That the circuit courts shall have original cognizance, concurrent with the courts of the several States, of all suits of a civil nature at common law or in equity, where the

matter in dispute exceeds, exclusive of costs, the sum or value of five hundred dollars, and the United States are plaintiffs, or petitioners; or an alien is a party, or the suit is between a citizen of the State where the suit is brought, and a citizen of another

Exclusive cognizance of crimes and offences cognizable under the laws of the United States.

State. And shall have exclusive cognizance of all crimes and offences cognizable under the authority of the United States, except where this act otherwise provides, or the laws of the United States shall otherwise direct, and concurrent jurisdiction with the district courts of the crimes and offences cognizable

No person to be arrested in one district for trial in another on any civil suit.
Limitation as to civil suits.

therein. But no person shall be arrested in one district for trial in another, in any civil action before a circuit or district court. And no civil suit shall be brought before either of said courts against an inhabitant of the United States, by any original process in any other district than that whereof he is an inhabitant, or in which he shall be found at the time of serving the writ, nor shall any district or circuit court have cognizance of any suit to recover the contents

Actions on promissory notes.

of any promissory note or other chose in action in favour of an assignee, unless a suit might have been prosecuted in such court to recover the said contents if no assignment had been made, except in cases of foreign bills of exchange. And the circuit courts shall

Circuit courts shall also have appellate jurisdiction.

also have appellate jurisdiction from the district courts under the regulations and restrictions herein after provided.

Matter in dispute above 500 dollars.

SEC. 12. *And be it further enacted,* That if a suit be commenced in any state court against an alien, or by a citizen of the state in which the suit is brought against a citizen of another state, and the matter in dispute exceeds the aforesaid sum or value of five hundred dollars, exclusive of costs, to be made to appear to the satisfaction of the court; and the defendant shall, at the time of entering his appearance in such state court, file a petition for the removal of

Removal of causes from state courts.

the cause for trial into the next circuit court, to be held in the district where the suit is pending, or if in the district of Maine to the district court next to be holden therein, or if in Kentucky district to the district court next to be holden therein, and offer good and sufficient surety for his entering in such court, on the first day of its session, copies of said process against him, and also for his there appearing and

Special bail.

entering special bail in the cause, if special bail was originally requisite therein, it shall then be the duty of the state court to accept the surety, and proceed no further in the cause, and any bail that may have been originally taken shall be discharged and the said copies being entered as aforesaid, in such court of the United States, the cause shall there proceed in the same manner as if it had been brought there by original process. And any attachment of the goods

Attachment of goods holden to final judgment.

or estate of the defendant by the original process, shall hold the goods or estate so attached, to answer the final judgment in the same manner as by the laws of such state they would have been holden to answer final judgment, had it been rendered by the court in which the suit commenced. And if in any

Title of land where value exceeds 500 dollars.

action commenced in a state court, the title of land be concerned, and the parties are citizens of the same state, and the matter in dispute exceeds the sum or value of five hundred dollars, exclusive of costs, the sum or value being made to appear to the satisfaction of the court, either party, before the trial, shall state to the court and make affidavit if they require it, that he claims and shall rely upon a right or title to the land, under a grant from a state other than that in which the suit is pending, and produce the original grant or an exemplification of it, except where the loss of public records shall put it out of his power, and shall move that the adverse party inform the court, whether he claims a right or title to the land under a grant from the state in which the suit is pending; the said adverse [party] shall give such information, or otherwise not be allowed to plead such grant, or give it in evidence upon the trial, and if he informs that he does claim under such grant, the party claiming under the grant first mentioned may then, on motion, remove the cause for trial to the next circuit court to be holden in such district, or if in the district of Maine, to the court next to be holden therein; or if in Kentucky district, to the district court next to be holden therein; but if he is the defendant, shall do it under the same regulations as in the beforementioned case of the removal of a cause into such court by an alien; and neither party removing the cause, shall be allowed to plead or give evidence of any other title than that by him stated as aforesaid, as the ground of his claim; and the trial of issues in fact in the circuit courts shall, in all suits, except those of equity, and of admiralty, and maritime jurisdiction, be by jury.

If in Maine and Kentucky, where causes are removable.

Issues in fact by jury.

Supreme court exclusive jurisdiction.

SEC. 13. *And be it further enacted,* That the Supreme Court shall have exclusive jurisdiction of all controversies of a civil nature, where a state is a party, except between a state and its citizens; and except also between a state and citizens of other states, or aliens, in which latter case it shall have original but not exclusive jurisdiction. And shall have exclusively all such jurisdiction of suits or proceedings against ambassadors, or other public ministers, or their domestics, or domestic servants, as a court of law can have or exercise consistently with the law of nations; and original, but not exclusive jurisdiction of all suits brought by ambassadors, or other public ministers, or in which a consul, or vice consul, shall be a party. And the trial of issues in fact in the Supreme Court, in all actions at law against citizens of the United States, shall be by jury. The Supreme Court shall also have appellate jurisdiction from the circuit courts and courts of the several states, in the cases herein after specially provided for; and shall have power to issue writs of prohibition to the district courts, when proceeding as courts of admiralty and maritime jurisdiction, and writs of *mandamus,* in cases warranted by the principles and usages of law, to any courts appointed, or persons holding office, under the authority of the United States.

Proceedings against public ministers.

Sup. Court appellate jurisdiction.

Writs of Prohibition.

Of Mandamus.

Courts may issue writs scire facias, habeas corpus, &c.

SEC. 14. *And be it further enacted,* That all the before-mentioned courts of the United States, shall have power to issue writs of *scire facias, habeas cor-*

pus, and all other writs not specially provided for by statute, which may be necessary for the exercise of their respective jurisdictions, and agreeable to the principles and usages of law. And that either of the justices of the supreme court, as well as judges of the district courts, shall have power to grant writs of *habeas corpus* for the purpose of an inquiry into the cause of commitment — *Provided,* That writs of *habeas corpus* shall in no case extend to prisoners in gaol, unless where they are in custody, under or by colour of the authority of the United States, or are committed for trial before some court of the same, or are necessary to be brought into court to testify.

Limitation of writs of habeas corpus.

Parties shall produce books and writings.

SEC. 15. *And be it further enacted,* That all the said courts of the United States, shall have power in the trial of actions at law, on motion and due notice thereof being given, to require the parties to produce books or writings in their possession or power, which contain evidence pertinent to the issue, in cases and under circumstances where they might be compelled to produce the same by the ordinary rules of proceeding in chancery; and if a plaintiff shall fail to comply with such order, to produce books or writings, it shall be lawful for the courts respectively, on motion, to give the like judgment for the defendant as in cases of nonsuit; and if a defendant shall fail to comply with such order, to produce books or writings, it shall be lawful for the courts respectively on motion as aforesaid, to give judgment against him or her by default.

Suits in equity limited.

SEC. 16. *And be it further enacted,* That suits in equity shall not be sustained in either of the courts of the United States, in any case where plain, adequate and complete remedy may be had at law.

Courts may grant new trials.

SEC. 17. *And be it further enacted,* That all the said courts of the United States shall have power to grant new trials, in cases where there has been a trial by jury for reasons for which new trials have usually been granted in the courts of law; and shall have power to impose and administer all necessary oaths or affirmations, and to punish by fine or imprisonment, at the discretion of said courts, all contempts of authority in any cause or hearing before the same; and to make and establish all necessary rules for the orderly conducting business in the said courts, provided such rules are not repugnant to the laws of the United States.

Execution may be stayed on conditions.

SEC. 18. *And be it further enacted,* That when in a circuit court, judgment upon a verdict in a civil action shall be entered, execution may on motion of either party, at the discretion of the court, and on such conditions for the security of the adverse party as they may judge proper, be stayed forty-two days from the time of entering judgment, to give time to file in the clerk's office of said court, a petition for a new trial. And if such petition be there filed within said term of forty-two days, with a certificate thereon from either of the judges of such court, that he allows the same to be filed, which certificate he may make or refuse at his discretion, execution shall of course be further stayed to the next session of said court. And if a new trial be granted, the former judgment shall be thereby rendered void.

Facts to appear on record.

SEC. 19. *And be it further enacted,* That it shall be the duty of circuit courts, in causes in equity and of admiralty and maritime jurisdiction, to cause the facts on which they found their sentence or decree, fully to appear upon the record of either from the pleadings and decree itself, or a state of the case agreed by the parties, or their counsel, or if they disagree by a stating of the case by the court.

Costs not allowed unless 500 dollars recovered.

SEC. 20. *And be it further enacted,* That where in a circuit court, a plaintiff in an action, originally brought there, or a petitioner in equity, other than the United States, recovers less than the sum or value of five hundred dollars, or a libellant, upon his own appeal, less than the sum or value of three hundred dollars, he shall not be allowed, but at the discretion of the court, may be adjudged to pay costs.

Appeals from the district to the circuit court where matter in dispute exceeds 300 dolls.

SEC. 21. *And be it further enacted,* That from final decrees in a district court in causes of admiralty and maritime jurisdiction, where the matter in dispute exceeds the sum or value of three hundred dollars, exclusive of costs, an appeal shall be allowed to the next circuit court, to be held in such district. *Provided nevertheless,* That all such appeals from final decrees as aforesaid, from the district court of Maine, shall be made to the circuit court, next to be holden after each appeal in the district of Massachusetts.

Final decrees re-examined above 50 dollars.

Altered by the 2d section of the act of March 3, 1803, chap. 40.

SEC. 22. *And be it further enacted,* That final decrees and judgments in civil actions in a district court, where the matter in dispute exceeds the sum or value of fifty dollars, exclusive of costs, may be re-examined, and reversed or affirmed in a circuit court, holden in the same distict, upon a writ of error, whereto shall be annexed and returned therewith at the day and place therein mentioned, an authenticated transcript of the record, an assignment of errors, and prayer for reversal, with a citation to the adverse party, signed by the judge of such district court, or a justice of the Supreme Court, the adverse party having at least twenty days' notice. And upon a like process, may final judgments and decrees in civil actions, and suits in equity in a circuit court, brought there by original process, or removed there from courts of the several States, or removed there by appeal from a district court where the matter in dispute exceeds the sum or value of two thousand dollars, exclusive of costs, be re-examined and reversed or affirmed in the Supreme Court, the citation being in such case signed by a judge of such circuit court, or justice of the Supreme Court, and the adverse party having at least thirty days' notice. But there shall be no reversal in either court on such writ of error for error in ruling any plea in abatement, other than a plea to the jurisdiction of the court, or such plea to a petition or bill in equity, as is in the nature of a demurrer, or for any error in fact. And

And suits in equity, exceeding 2000 dollars in value.

Writs of error limited.

writs of error shall not be brought but within five years after rendering or passing the judgment or decree complained of, or in case the person entitled to such writ of error be an infant, *feme covert, non compos mentis,* or imprisoned, then within five years as aforesaid, exclusive of the time of such disability. And every justice or judge signing a citation on any writ of error as aforesaid, shall take good and sufficient security, that the plaintiff in error shall prosecute his writ to effect, and answer all damages and costs if he fail to make his plea good.

Plaintiff to give security.

SEC. 23. *And be it further enacted,* That a writ of error as aforesaid shall be a supersedeas and stay execution in cases only where the writ of error is served, by a copy thereof being lodged for the adverse party in the clerk's office where the record remains, within ten days, Sundays exclusive, after rendering the judgment or passing the decree complained of. Until the expiration of which term of ten days, executions shall not issue in any case where a writ of error may be a supersedeas; and whereupon such writ of error the Supreme or a circuit court shall affirm a judgment or decree, they shall adjudge or decree to the respondent in error just damages for his delay, and single or double costs at their discretion.

Writ of error a supersedeas.

SEC. 24. *And be it further enacted,* That when a judgment or decree shall be reversed in a circuit court, such court shall proceed to render such judgment or pass such decree as the district court should have rendered or passed; and the Supreme Court shall do the same on reversals therein, except where the reversal is in favor of the plaintiff, or petitioner in the original suit, and the damages to be assessed, or matter to be decreed, are uncertain, in which case they shall remand the cause for a final decision. And the Supreme Court shall not issue execution in causes that are removed before them by writs of error, but shall send a special mandate to the circuit court to award execution thereupon.

Judgment or decree reversed.

Supreme court not to issue execution but mandate.

SEC. 25. *And be it further enacted,* That a final judgment or decree in any suit, in the highest court of law or equity of a State in which a decision in the suit could be had, where is drawn in question the validity of a treaty or statute of, or an authority exercised under the United States, and the decision is against their validity; or where is drawn in question the validity of a statute of, or an authority exercised under any State, on the ground of their being repugnant to the constitution, treaties or laws of the United States, and the decision is in favour of such their validity, or where is drawn in question the construction of any clause of the constitution, or of a treaty, or statute of, or commission held under the United States, and the decision is against the title, right, privilege or exemption specially set up or claimed by either party, under such clause of the said Constitution, treaty, statute or commission, may be re-examined and reversed or affirmed in the Supreme Court of the United States upon a writ of error, the

Cases in which judgment and decrees of the highest court of a state may be examined by the supreme court, on writ of error.

citation being signed by the chief justice, or judge or chancellor of the court rendering or passing the judgment or decree complained of, or by a justice of the Supreme Court of the United States, in the same manner and under the same regulations, and the writ shall have the same effect, as if the judgment or decree complained of had been rendered or passed in a circuit court, and the proceeding upon the reversal shall also be the same, except that the Supreme Court, instead of remanding the cause for a final decision as before provided, may at their discretion, if the cause shall have been once remanded before, proceed to a final decision of the same, and award execution. But no other error shall be assigned or regarded as a ground of reversal in any such case as aforesaid, than such as appears on the face of the record, and immediately respects the before mentioned questions of validity or construction of the said constitution, treaties, statutes, commissions, or authorities in dispute.

Proceedings on reversal.

No writs of error but as above mentioned.

SEC. 26. *And be it further enacted,* That in all causes brought before either of the courts of the United States to recover the forfeiture annexed to any articles of agreement, covenant, bond, or other specialty, where the forfeiture, breach or non-performance shall appear, by the default or confession of the defendant, or upon demurrer, the court before whom the action is, shall render judgment therein for the plaintiff to recover so much as is due according to equity. And when the sum for which judgment should be rendered is uncertain, the same shall, if either of the parties request it, be assessed by a jury.

In cases of forfeiture the courts may give judgment according to equity.

Jury to assess damages when the sum is uncertain.

SEC. 27. *And be it further enacted,* That a marshal shall be appointed in and for each district for the term of four years, but shall be removable from office at pleasure, whose duty it shall be to attend the district and circuit courts when sitting therein, and also the Supreme Court in the district in which that court shall sit. And to execute throughout the district, all lawful precepts directed to him, and issued under the authority of the United States, and he shall have power to command all necessary assistance in the execution of his duty, and to appoint as there shall be occasion, one or more deputies, who shall be removable from office by the judge of the district court, or the circuit court sitting within the district, at the pleasure of either; and before he enters on the duties of his office, he shall become bound for the faithful performance of the same, by himself and by his deputies before the judge of the district court to the United States, jointly and severally, with two good and sufficient sureties, inhabitants and freeholders of such district, to be approved by the district judge, in the sum of twenty thousand dollars, and shall take before said judge, as shall also his deputies, before they enter on the duties of their appointment, the following oath of office: "I, A. B., do solemnly swear or affirm, that I will faithfully execute all lawful precepts directed to the marshal of the district of ____ under the authority of the United States, and true returns make, and in all things

Marshal to be appointed. Duration of office.

Deputies removable by the district and circuit courts.

Sureties.

Oath of marshal, and of his deputies.

well and truly, and without malice or partiality, perform the duties of the office of marshal (or marshal's deputy, as the case may be) of the district of ____, during my continuance in said office, and take only my lawful fees. So help me God."

SEC. 28. *And be it further enacted,* That in all causes wherein the marshal or his deputy shall be a party, the writs and precepts therein shall be directed to such disinterested person as the court, or any justice or judge thereof may appoint, and the person so appointed, is hereby authorized to execute and return the same. And in case of the death of any marshal, his deputy or deputies shall continue in office, unless otherwise specially removed; and shall execute the same in the name of the deceased, until another marshal shall be appointed and sworn: And the defaults or misfeasances in office of such deputy or deputies in the mean time, as well as before, shall be adjudged a breach of the condition of the bond given, as before directed, by the marshal who appointed them; and the executor or administrator of the deceased marshal shall have like remedy for the defaults and misfeasances in office of such deputy or deputies during such interval, as they would be entitled to if the marshal had continued in life and in the exercise of his said office, until his successor was appointed, and sworn or affirmed: And every marshal or his deputy when removed from office, or when the term for which the marshal is appointed shall expire, shall have power notwithstanding to execute all such precepts as may be in their hands respectively at the time of such removal or expiration of office; and the marshal shall be held answerable for the delivery to his successor of all prisoners which may be in his custody at the time of his removal, or when the term for which he is appointed shall expire, and for that purpose may retain such prisoners in his custody until his successor shall be appointed and qualified as the law directs.

If marshal, or his deputy, a party to a suit, process to be directed to a person selected by the court.

Deputies to continue in office on the death of the marshal.

Defaults of deputies.

Powers of the executor or administrator of deceased marshals.

Marshal's power after removal.

SEC. 29. *And be it further enacted,* That in cases punishable with death, the trial shall be had in the county where the offence was committed, or where that cannot be done without great inconvenience, twelve petit jurors at least shall be summoned from thence. And jurors in all cases to serve in the courts of the United States shall be designated by lot or otherwise in each State respectively according to the mode of forming juries therein now practised, so far as the laws of the same shall render such designation practicable by the courts or marshals of the United States; and the jurors shall have the same qualifications as are requisite for jurors by the laws of the State of which they are citizens, to serve in the highest courts of law of such State, and shall be returned as there shall be occasion for them, from such parts of the district from time to time as the court shall direct, so as shall be most favourable to an impartial trial, and so as not to incur an unnecessary expense, or unduly to burthen the citizens of any part of the district with such services. And writs of *venire farias* when directed by the court shall issue from the

Trial of cases punishable with death to be had in county.

Jurors by lot.

Writs of venire facias from clerk's office.

clerk's office, and shall be served and returned by the marshal in his proper person, or by his deputy, or in case the marshal or his deputy is not an indifferent person, or is interested in the event of the cause, by such fit person as the court shall specially appoint for that purpose, to whom they shall administer an oath or affirmation that he will truly and impartially serve and return such writ. And when from challenges or otherwise there shall not be a jury to determine any civil or criminal cause, the marshal or his deputy shall, by order of the court where such defect of jurors shall happen, return jurymen *de talibus circumstantibus* sufficient to complete the pannel; and when the marshal or his deputy are disqualified as aforesaid, jurors may be returned by such disinterested person as the court shall appoint.

Juries de talibus, &c.

Mode of proof.

SEC. 30. *And be it further enacted,* That the mode of proof by oral testimony and examination of witnesses in open court shall be the same in all the courts of the United States, as well in the trial of causes in equity and of admiralty and maritime jurisdiction, as of actions at common law. And when the testimony of any person shall be necessary in any civil cause depending in any district in any court of the United States, who shall live at a greater distance from the place of trial than one hundred miles, or is bound on a voyage to sea, or is about to go out of the United States, or out of such district, and to a greater distance from the place of trial than as aforesaid, before the time of trial, or is ancient or very infirm, the deposition of such person may be taken *de bene esse* before any justice or judge of any of the courts of the United States, or before any chancellor, justice or judge of a supreme or superior court, mayor or chief magistrate of a city, or judge of a county court or court of common pleas of any of the United States, not being of counsel or attorney to either of the parties, or interested in the event of the cause, provided that a notification from the magistrate before whom the deposition is to be taken to the adverse party, to be present at the taking of the same, and to put interrogatories, if he think fit, be first made out and served on the adverse party or his attorney as either may be nearest, if either is within one hundred miles of the place of such caption, allowing time for their attendance after notified, not less than at the rate of one day, Sundays exclusive, for every twenty miles travel. And in causes of admiralty and maritime jurisdiction, or other cases of seizure when a libel shall be filed, in which an adverse party is not named, and depositions of persons circumstanced as aforesaid shall be taken before a claim be put in, the like notification as aforesaid shall be given to the person having the agency or possession of the property libelled at the time of the capture or seizure of the same, if known to the libellant. And every person deposing as aforesaid shall be carefully examined and cautioned, and sworn or affirmed to testify the whole truth, and shall subscribe the testimony by him or her given after the same shall be reduced to writing, which shall be done only by the magistrate taking the de-

Depositions de bene esse.

Adverse party to be notified.

Notice in admiralty and maritime causes.

Agent notified.

position, or by the deponent in his presence. And the depositions so taken shall be retained by such magistrate until he deliver the same with his own hand into the court for which they are taken, or shall, together with a certificate of the reasons as aforesaid of their being taken, and of the notice if any given to the adverse party, be by him the said magistrate sealed up and directed to such court, and remain under his seal until opened in court. And any person may be compelled to appear and depose as aforesaid in the same manner as to appear and testify in court. And in the trial of any cause of admiralty or maritime jurisdiction in a district court, the decree in which may be appealed from, if either party shall suggest to and satisfy the court that probably it will not be in his power to produce the witnesses there testifying before the circuit court should an appeal be had, and shall move that their testimony be taken down in writing, it shall be so done by the clerk of the court. And if an appeal be had, such testimony may be used on the trial of the same if it shall appear to the satisfaction of the court which shall try the appeal, that the witnesses are then dead or gone out of the United States, or to a greater distance than as aforesaid from the place where the court is sitting, or that by reason of age, sickness, bodily infirmity or imprisonment, they are unable to travel and appear at court, but not otherwise. And unless the same shall be made to appear on the trial of any cause, with respect to witnesses whose depositions may have been taken therein, such depositions shall not be admitted or used in the cause. *Provided,* That nothing herein shall be construed to prevent any court of the United States from granting a *dedimus potestatem* to take depositions according to common usage, when it may be necessary to prevent a failure or delay of justice, which power they shall severally possess, nor to extend to depositions taken in *perpetuam rei memoriam,* which if they relate to matters that may be cognizable in any court of the United States, a circuit court on application thereto made as a court of equity, may, according to the usages in chancery direct to be taken.

Depositions retained.

Persons may be compelled to appear and testify.

Appeal allowed.

Depositions used in case of sickness, death, &c.

Dedimus potestatem as usual.

SEC. 31. *And be it [further] enacted,* That where any suit shall be depending in any court of the United States, and either of the parties shall die before final judgment, the executor or administrator of such deceased party who was plaintiff, petitioner, or defendant, in case the cause of action doth by law survive, shall have full power to prosecute or defend any such suit or action until final judgment; and the defendant or defendants are hereby obliged to answer thereto accordingly; and the court before whom such cause may be depending, is hereby empowered and directed to hear and determine the same, and to render judgment for or against the executor or administrator, as the case may require. And if such executor or administrator having been duly served with a *scire facias* from the office of the clerk of the court where such suit is depending, twenty days beforehand, shall neglect or refuse to

Executor or administrator may prosecute and defend.

Neglect of executor or administrator to become a party to the suit, judgment to be rendered.

become a party to the suit, the court may render judgment against the estate of the deceased party, in the same manner as if the executor or administrator had voluntarily made himself a party to the suit. And the executor or administrator who shall become a party as aforesaid, shall, upon motion to the court where the suit is depending, be entitled to a continuance of the same until the next term of the said court. And if there be two or more plaintiffs or defendants, and one or more of them shall die, if the cause of action shall survive to the surviving plaintiff or plaintiffs, or against the surviving defendant or defendants, the writ or action shall not be thereby abated; but such death being suggested upon the record, the action shall proceed at the suit of the surviving plaintiff or plaintiffs against the surviving defendant or defendants.

Executor and administrator may have continuance.
Two plaintiffs.
Surviving plaintiff may continue suit.

Writs shall not abate for defect of form.

SEC. 32. *And be it further enacted,* That no summons, writ, declaration, return, process, judgment, or other proceedings in civil causes in any of the courts of the United States, shall be abated, arrested, quashed or reversed, for any defect or want of form, but the said courts respectively shall proceed and give judgment according as the right of the cause and matter in law shall appear unto them, without regarding any imperfections, defects, or want of form in such writ, declaration, or other pleading, return, process, judgment, or course of proceeding whatsoever, except those only in cases of demurrer, which the party demurring shall specially sit down and express together with his demurrer as the cause thereof. And the said courts respectively shall and may, by virtue of this act, from time to time, amend all and every such imperfections, defects and wants of form, other than those only which the party demurring shall express as aforesaid, and may at any time permit either of the parties to amend any defect in the process or pleadings, upon such conditions as the said courts respectively shall in their discretion, and by their rules prescribe.

Exceptions.

Courts may amend imperfections.

Criminals against U.S. arrested by any justice of the peace.

SEC. 33. *And be it further enacted,* That for any crime or offence against the United States, the offender may, by any justice or judge of the United States, or by any justice of the peace, or other magistrate of any of the United States where he may be found agreeably to the usual mode of process against offenders in such state, and at the expense of the United States, be arrested, and imprisoned or bailed, as the case may be, for trial before such court of the United States as by this act has cognizance of the offence. And copies of the process shall be returned as speedily as may be into the clerk's office of such court, together with the recognizances of the witnesses for their appearance to testify in the case; which recognizances the magistrate before whom the examination shall be, may require on pain of imprisonment. And if such commitment of the offender, or the witnesses shall be in a district other than that in which the offence is to be tried, it shall be the duty of the judge of that district where the delinquent is imprisoned, seasonably to issue, and of the

Recognizance to be returned to the clerk's office.

Offender may be removed by warrant.

marshal of the same district to execute, a warrant for the removal of the offender, and the witnesses, or either of them, as the case may be, to the district in which the trial is to be had. And upon all arrests in criminal cases, bail shall be admitted, except where the punishment may be death, in which cases it shall not be admitted but by the supreme or a circuit court, or by a justice of the supreme court, or a judge of a district court, who shall exercise their discretion therein, regarding the nature and circumstances of the offence, and of the evidence, and the usages of law. And if a person committed by a justice of the supreme or a judge of a district court for an offence not punishable with death, shall afterwards procure bail, and there be no judge of the United States in the district to take the same, it may be taken by any judge of the supreme or superior court of law of such state.

Bail admitted.

Bail, how taken.

Laws of States rules of decision.

SEC. 34. *And be it further enacted,* That the laws of the several states, except where the constitution, treaties or statutes of the United States shall otherwise require or provide, shall be regarded as rules of decision in trials at common law in the courts of the United States in cases where they apply.

Parties may manage their own cause.

SEC. 35. *And be it further enacted,* That in all the courts of the United States, the parties may plead and manage their own causes personally or by the assistance of such counsel or attorneys at law as by the rules of the said courts respectively shall be permitted to manage and conduct causes therein. And there shall be appointed in each district a meet person learned in the law to act as attorney for the United States in such district, who shall be sworn or affirmed to the faithful execution of his office, whose duty it shall be to prosecute in such district all delinquents for crimes and offences, cognizable under the authority of the United States, and all civil actions in which the United States shall be concerned, except before the supreme court in the district in which that court shall be holden. And he shall receive as a compensation for his services such fees as shall be taxed therefore in the respective courts before which the suits or prosecutions shall be. And there shall also be appointed a meet person, learned in the law, to act as attorney-general for the United States, who shall be sworn or affirmed to a faithful execution of his office; whose duty it shall be to prosecute and conduct all suits in the Supreme Court in which the United States shall be concerned, and to give his advice and opinion upon questions of law when required by the President of the United States, or when requested by the heads of any of the departments, touching any matters that may concern their departments, and shall receive such compensation for his services as shall by law be provided.

Attorney of the U.S. for each district.

His duties.

Compensation.

Attorney General of the U.S.

Duties.

Compensation.

APPROVED, September 24, 1789.

SOURCE: *Public Statutes at Large of the United States of America,* Vol. I (Boston: Charles C. Little & James Brown, 1845).

Marbury v. Madison (1803)

The most famous decision made by the Court during the tenure of Chief Justice John Marshall, and perhaps the most famous in the Court's history, began as a relatively unimportant controversy over a presidential appointment. Federalist president John Adams, in his final days in office, attempted to entrench Federalists in the judiciary by appointing sixteen new circuit court judges and forty-two new justices of the peace for the District of Columbia. The commissions for four of the new justices of the peace, including William Marbury, were not delivered before Adams's last day in office. When Democratic-Republican secretary of state James Madison refused to give the four men their commissions, Marbury asked the Court to force Madison to do so.

The Court held that Marbury should have received his commission, which had been duly signed and sealed. But, Marshall held, the Court lacked the power to issue the order commanding Madison to deliver it. Congress had added unconstitutionally to the Court's original jurisdiction by authorizing the Court, in the Judiciary Act of 1789, to issue such orders to officers of the federal government. Marbury v. Madison has been called the single most important ruling in the history of the Supreme Court because it established the principle of judicial review, the Court's power to declare an act of Congress unconstitutional.

5 U.S. 137, 1 Cranch 137, 2 L. Ed. 60

William Marbury v. James Madison, SECRETARY OF STATE OF THE UNITED STATES.

February, 1803.

AT the last term, viz. December term, 1801, William Marbury, Dennis Ramsay, Robert Townsend Hooe, and William Harper, by their counsel, Charles Lee, esq. late attorney general of the United States, severally moved the court for a rule to James Madison, secretary of state of the United States, to show cause why a mandamus should not issue commanding him to cause to be delivered to them respectively their several commissions as justices of the peace in the district of Columbia. This motion was supported by affidavits of the following facts; that notice of this motion had been given to Mr. Madison; that Mr. Adams, the late president of the United States, nominated the applicants to the senate for their advice and consent to be appointed justices of the peace of the district of Columbia; that the senate advised and consented to the appointments; that commissions in due form were signed by the said president appointing them justices, &c. and that the seal of the United States was in due form affixed to the said commissions by the secretary of state; that the applicants have requested Mr. Madison to deliver them their said commissions, who has not complied with that request; and that their said commissions are withheld from them; that the applicants have made application to Mr. Madison as secretary of state of the United States at his office, for information whether the commissions were signed and sealed as aforesaid; that explicit and satisfactory information has not been given in answer to that inquiry, either by the secretary of state or any officer in the department of state; that application has been made to the secretary of the Senate for a certificate of the nomination of the applicants, and of the advice and consent of the senate, who has declined giving such a certificate; whereupon a rule was laid to show cause on the fourth day of this term. This rule having been duly served,

Mr. Lee, in support of the rule, observed that it was important to know on what ground a justice of peace in the district of Columbia holds his office, and what proceedings are necessary to constitute an appointment to an office not held at the will of the president. However notorious the facts are, upon the suggestion of which this rule has been laid, yet the applicants have been much embarrassed in obtaining evidence of them. Reasonable information has been denied at the office of the department of state. Although a respectful memorial has been made to the senate praying them to suffer their secretary to give extracts from their executive journals respecting the nomination of the applicants to the senate, and of their advice and consent to the appointments, yet their request has been denied, and their petition rejected. They have therefore been compelled to summon witnesses to attend in court, whose voluntary affidavits they could not obtain. Mr. Lee here read the affidavit of Dennis Ramsay, and the printed journals of the senate of 31 January, 1803, respecting the refusal of the senate to suffer their secretary to give the information requested. He then called Jacob Wagner and Daniel Brent, who had been summoned to attend the court, and who had, as it is understood, declined giving a voluntary affidavit. They objected to being sworn, alleging that they were clerks in the department of state and not bound to disclose any facts relating to the business or transactions in the office. . . .

The court ordered the witnesses to be sworn and their answers taken in writing, but informed them that when the questions were asked they might state their objections to answering each particular question, if they had any. . . .

Mr. Lincoln, attorney general, having been summoned, and now called, objected to answering. He requested that the questions might be put in writing, and that he might afterwards have time to determine whether he would answer. . . . He was acting as secretary of state at the time when this transaction happened. He was of opinion, and his opinion was supported by that of others whom he highly respected, that he was not bound, and ought not to answer, as to any facts which came officially to his knowledge while acting as secretary of state.

The questions being written were then read and handed to him. . . .

The court said, that if Mr. Lincoln wished time to consider what answers he should make, they would give him time; but they had no doubt he ought to answer. There was nothing confidential required to be disclosed. If there had been he was not obliged to answer it; and if he thought that any thing was communicated to him in confidence he was not bound to disclose it; nor was he obliged to state any thing which would criminate himself. . . .

Mr. Lee then observed, that . . . he should confine such further remarks as he had to make in support of the rule to three questions:

1. Whether the supreme court can award the writ of mandamus in any case.

2. Whether it will lie to a secretary of state in any case whatever.

3. Whether in the present case the court may award a mandamus to James Madison, secretary of state. . . .

Opinion of the court.

At the last term on the affidavits then read and filed with the clerk, a rule was granted in this case, requiring the secretary of state to show cause why a mandamus should not issue, directing him to deliver to William Marbury his commission as a justice of the peace for the county of Washington, in the district of Columbia.

No cause has been shown, and the present motion is for a mandamus. The peculiar delicacy of this case, the novelty of some of its circumstances, and the real difficulty attending the points which occur in it, require a complete exposition of the principles, on which the opinion to be given by the court, is founded.

These principles have been, on the side of the applicant, very ably argued at the bar. In rendering the opinion of the court, there will be some departure in form, though not in substance, from the points stated in that argument.

In the order in which the court has viewed this subject, the following questions have been considered and decided.

1. Has the applicant a right to the commission he demands?

2. If he has a right, and that right has been violated, do the laws of his country afford him a remedy?

3. If they do afford him a remedy, is it a *mandamus* issuing from this court?

The first object of inquiry is,

1. Has the applicant a right to the commission he demands?

His right originates in an act of congress passed in February 1801, concerning the district of Columbia.

After dividing the district into two counties, the eleventh section of this law, enacts, "that there shall be appointed in and for each of the said counties, such number of discreet persons to be justices of the peace as the president of the United States shall, from time to time, think expedient, to continue in office for five years.

It appears, from the affidavits, that in compliance with this law, a commission for William Marbury as a justice of peace for the county of Washington, was signed by John Adams, then president of the United States; after which the seal of the United States was affixed to it; but the commission has never reached the person for whom it was made out.

In order to determine whether he is entitled to this commission, it becomes necessary to inquire whether he has been appointed to the office. For if he has been appointed, the law continues him in office for five years, and he is entitled to the possession of those evidences of office, which, being completed, became his property.

The second section of the second article of the constitution declares, "the president shall nominate, and, by and with the advice and consent of the senate, shall appoint ambassadors, other public ministers and consuls, and all other officers of the United States, whose appointments are not otherwise provided for."

The third section declares, that "he shall commission all the officers of the United States."

An act of congress directs the secretary of state to keep the seal of the United States, "to make out and record, and affix the said seal to all civil commissions to officers of the United States to be appointed by the President, by and with the consent of the senate, or by the President alone; provided that the said seal shall not be affixed to any commission before the same shall have been signed by the President of the United States."

These are the clauses of the constitution and laws of the United States, which affect this part of the case. They seem to contemplate three distinct operations:

1. The nomination. This is the sole act of the President, and is completely voluntary.

2. The appointment. This is also the act of the President, and is also a voluntary act, though it can only be performed by and with the advice and consent of the senate.

3. The commission. To grant a commission to a person appointed, might perhaps be deemed a duty enjoined by the constitution. "He shall," says that instrument, "commission all the officers of the United States."

The acts of appointing to office, and commissioning the person appointed, can scarcely be considered as one and the same; since the power to perform them is given in two separate and distinct sections of the constitution. The distinction between the appointment and the commission will be rendered more apparent by adverting to that provision in the second section of the second article of the constitution, which authorises congress "to vest by law the appointment of such inferior officers, as they think proper, in the President alone, in the courts of law, or in the heads of departments;" thus contemplating cases where the law may direct the President to commission an officer appointed by the courts or by the heads of departments. In such a case, to issue a commission would be apparently a duty distinct from the appointment, the performance of which, perhaps, could not legally be refused.

Although that clause of the constitution which requires the President to commission all the officers of the United States, may never have been applied to officers appointed otherwise than by himself, yet it would be difficult to deny the legislative power to apply it to such cases. Of consequence the constitutional distinction between the appointment to an office and the commission of an officer, who has been appointed, remains the same as if in practice the President had commissioned officers appointed by an authority other than his own.

It follows too, from the existence of this distinction, that, if an appointment was to be evidenced by any public act other than the commission, the performance of such public act would create the officer; and if he was not removable at the will of the President, would either give him a right to his commission, or enable him to perform the duties without it.

These observations are premised solely for the purpose of rendering more intelligible those which apply more directly to the particular case under consideration.

This is an appointment made by the President, by and with the advice and consent of the senate, and is evidenced by no act but the commission itself. In such a case therefore the commission and the appointment seem inseparable; it being almost impossible to show an appointment otherwise than by proving the existence of a commission; still the commission is not necessarily the appointment; though conclusive evidence of it.

But at what stage does it amount to this conclusive evidence?

The answer to this question seems an obvious one. The appointment being the sole act of the President, must be completely evidenced, when it is shown that he has done every thing to be performed by him.

Should the commission, instead of being evidence of an appointment, even be considered as constituting the appointment itself; still it would be made when the last act to be done by the President was performed, or, at furthest, when the commission was complete.

The last act to be done by the President, is the signature of the commission. He has then acted on the advice and consent of the senate to his own nomination. The time for deliberation has then passed. He has decided. His judgment, on the advice and consent of the senate concurring with his nomination, has been made, and the officer is appointed. This appointment is evidenced by an open, unequivocal act; and being the last act required from the person making it, necessarily excludes the idea of its being, so far as respects the appointment, an inchoate and incomplete transaction.

Some point of time must be taken when the power of the executive over an officer, not removable at his will, must cease. That point of time must be when the constitutional power of appointment has been exercised. And this power has been exercised when the last act, required from the person possessing the power, has been performed. This last act is the signature of the commission. This idea seems to have prevailed with the legislature, when the act passed, converting the department of foreign affairs into the department of state. By that act it is enacted, that the secretary of state shall keep the seal of the United States, "and shall make out and record, and shall affix the said seal to all civil commissions to officers of the United States, to be appointed by the President:" "Provided that the said seal shall not be affixed to any commission, before the same shall have been signed by the President of the United States; nor to any other instrument or act, without the special warrant of the President therefor."

The signature is a warrant for affixing the great seal to the commission; and the great seal is only to be affixed to an instrument which is complete. It attests, by an act supposed to be of public notoriety, the verity of the Presidential signature.

It is never to be affixed till the commission is signed, because the signature, which gives force and effect to the commission, is conclusive evidence that the appointment is made.

The commission being signed, the subsequent duty of the secretary of state is prescribed by law, and not to be guided by the will of the President. He is to affix the seal of the United States to the commission, and is to record it.

This is not a proceeding which may be varied, if the judgment of the executive shall suggest one more eligible, but is a precise course accurately marked out by law, and is to be strictly pursued. It is the duty of the secretary of state to conform to the law, and in this he is an officer of the United States, bound to obey the laws. He acts, in this respect, as has been very properly stated at the bar, under the authority of law, and not by the instructions of the President. It is a ministerial act which the law enjoins on a particular officer for a particular purpose.

If it should be supposed, that the solemnity of affixing the seal, is necessary not only to the validity of the commission, but even to the completion of an appointment, still when the seal is affixed the appointment is made, and the commission is valid. No other solemnity is required by law; no other act is to be performed on the part of government. All that the executive can do to invest the person with his office, is done; and unless the appointment be then made, the executive cannot make one without the co-operation of others.

After searching anxiously for the principles on which a contrary opinion may be supported, none have been found which appear of sufficient force to maintain the opposite doctrine.

Such as the imagination of the court could suggest, have been very deliberately examined, and after allowing them all the weight which it appears possible to give them, they do not shake the opinion which has been formed.

In considering this question, it has been conjectured that the commission may have been assimilated to a deed, to the validity of which, delivery is essential.

This idea is founded on the supposition that the commission is not merely *evidence* of an appointment, but is itself the actual appointment; a supposition by no means unquestionable. But for the purpose of examining this objection fairly, let it be conceded, that the principle, claimed for its support, is established.

The appointment being, under the constitution, to be made by the President *personally,* the delivery of the deed of appointment, if necessary to its completion, must be made by the President also. It is not necessary that the livery should be made personally to the grantee of the office: It never is so made. The law would seem to contemplate that it should be made to the secretary of state, since it directs the secretary to affix the seal to the commission *after* it shall have been signed by the President. If then the act of livery be necessary to give validity to the commission, it has been delivered when executed and given to the secretary for the purpose of being sealed, recorded, and transmitted to the party.

But in all cases of letters patent, certain solemnities are required by law, which solemnities are the evidences of the validity of the instrument. A formal delivery to the person is not among them. In cases of commissions, the sign manual of the President, and the seal of the United States, are those solemnities. This objection therefore does not touch the case.

It has also occurred as possible, and barely possible, that the transmission of the commission, and the acceptance thereof, might be deemed necessary to complete the right of the plaintiff.

The transmission of the commission is a practice directed by convenience, but not by law. It cannot therefore be necessary to constitute the appointment which must precede it, and which is the mere act of the President. If the executive required that every person appointed to an office, should himself take means to procure his commission, the appointment would not be the less valid on that account. The appointment is the sole act of the President; the transmission of the commission is the sole act of the officer to whom that duty is assigned, and may be accelerated or retarded by circumstances which can have no influence on the appointment. A commission is transmitted to a person already appointed; not to a person to be appointed or not, as the letter enclosing the commission should happen to get into the post-office and reach him in safety, or to miscarry.

It may have some tendency to elucidate this point, to inquire, whether the possession of the original commission be indispensably necessary to authorize a person, appointed to any office, to perform the duties of that office. If it was necessary, then a loss of the commission would lose the office. Not only negligence, but accident or fraud, fire or theft, might deprive an individual of his office. In such a case, I presume it could not be doubted, but that a copy from the record of the office of the secretary of state, would be, to every intent and purpose, equal to the original. The act of congress has expressly made it so. To give that copy validity, it would not be necessary to prove that the original had been transmitted and afterwards lost. The copy would be complete evidence that the original had existed, and that the appointment had been made, but not that the original had been transmitted. If indeed it should appear that the original had been mislaid in the office of state, that circumstance would not affect the operation of the copy. When all the requisites have been performed which authorize a recording officer to record any instrument whatever, and the order for that purpose has been given, the instrument is in law considered as recorded, although the manual labour of inserting it in a book kept for that purpose may not have been performed.

In the case of commissions, the law orders the secretary of state to record them. When therefore they are signed and sealed, the order for their being recorded is given; and whether inserted in the book or not, they are in law recorded.

A copy of this record is declared equal to the original, and the fees to be paid by a person requiring a copy are ascertained by law. Can a keeper of a public record erase therefrom a commission which has been recorded? Or can he refuse a copy thereof to a person demanding it on the terms prescribed by law?

Such a copy would, equally with the original, authorize the justice of peace to proceed in the performance of his duty, because it would, equally with the original, attest his appointment.

If the transmission of a commission be not considered as necessary to give validity to an appointment; still less is its acceptance. The appointment is the sole act of the President; the acceptance is the sole act of the officer, and is, in plain common sense, posterior to the appointment. As he may resign, so may he refuse to accept: but neither the one nor the other is capable of rendering the appointment a nonentity.

That this is the understanding of the government, is apparent from the whole tenor of its conduct.

A commission bears date, and the salary of the officer commences from his appointment; not from the transmission or acceptance of his commission. When a person, appointed to any office, refuses to accept that office, the successor is nominated in the place of the person who has declined to accept, and not in the place of the person who had been previously in office and had created the original vacancy.

It is therefore decidedly the opinion of the court, that when a commission has been signed by the President, the appointment is made; and that the commission is complete when the seal of the United States has been affixed to it by the secretary of state.

Where an officer is removable at the will of the executive, the circumstance which completes his appointment is of no concern; because the act is at any time revocable; and the commission may be arrested, if still in the office. But when the officer is not removable at the will of the executive, the appointment is not revocable and cannot be annulled. It has conferred legal rights which cannot be resumed.

The discretion of the executive is to be exercised until the appointment has been made. But having once made the appointment, his power over the office is terminated in all cases, where, by law, the officer is not removable by him. The right to the office is *then* in the person appointed, and he has the absolute, unconditional, power of accepting or rejecting it.

Mr. Marbury, then, since his commission was signed by the President, and sealed by the secretary of state, was appointed; and as the law creating the office, gave the officer a right to hold for five years, independent of the executive, the appointment was not revocable; but vested in the officer legal rights, which are protected by the laws of his country.

To withhold his commission, therefore, is an act deemed by the court not warranted by law, but violative of a vested legal right.

This brings us to the second inquiry; which is,

2. If he has a right, and that right has been violated, do the laws of his country afford him a remedy?

The very essence of civil liberty certainly consists in the right of every individual to claim the protection of the laws, whenever he receives an injury. One of the first duties of government is to afford that protection. In Great Britain the king himself is sued in the respectful form of a petition, and he never fails to comply with the judgment of his court.

In the 3d vol. of his commentaries, p. 23, Blackstone states two cases in which a remedy is afforded by mere operation of law.

"In all other cases," he says, "it is a general and indisputable rule, that where there is a legal right, there is also a legal remedy by suit or action at law, whenever that right is invaded."

And afterwards, p. 109 of the same vol. he says, "I am next to consider such injuries as are cognizable by the courts of the common law. And herein I shall for the present only remark, that all possible injuries whatsoever, that did not fall within the exclusive cognizance of either the ecclesiastical, military, or maritime tribunals, are for that very reason, within the cognizance of the common law courts of justice; for it is a settled and invariable principle in the laws of England, that every right, when withheld, must have a remedy, and every injury its proper redress."

The government of the United States has been emphatically termed a government of laws, and not of men. It will certainly cease to deserve this high appellation, if the laws furnish no remedy for the violation of a vested legal right.

If this obloquy is to be cast on the jurisprudence of our country, it must arise from the peculiar character of the case.

It behoves us then to inquire whether there be in its composition any ingredient which shall exempt it from legal investigation, or exclude the injured party from legal redress. In pursuing this inquiry the first question which presents itself, is, whether this can be arranged with that class of cases which come under the description of *damnum absque injuria*—a loss without an injury.

This description of cases never has been considered, and it is believed never can be considered, as comprehending offices of trust, of honor or of profit. The office of justice of peace in the district of Columbia is such an office; it is therefore worthy of the attention and guardianship of the laws. It has received that attention and guardianship. It has been created by special act of congress, and has been secured, so far as the laws can give security to the person appointed to fill it, for five years. It is not then on account of the worthlessness of the thing pursued, that the injured party can be alleged to be without remedy.

Is it in the nature of the transaction? Is the act of delivering or withholding a commission to be considered as a mere political act, belonging to the executive department alone, for the performance of which, entire confidence is placed by our constitution in the supreme executive; and for any misconduct respecting which, the injured individual has no remedy.

That there may be such cases is not to be questioned; but that every act of duty, to be performed in any of the great departments of government, constitutes such a case, is not to be admitted.

By the act concerning invalids, passed in June, 1794, vol. 3. p. 112, the secretary at war is ordered to place on the pension list all persons whose names are contained in a report previously made by him to congress. If he should refuse to do so, would the wounded veteran be without remedy? Is it to be contended that where the law in precise terms, directs the performance of an act in which an individual is interested, the law is incapable of securing obedience to its mandate? Is it on account of the character of the person against whom the complaint is made? Is it to be contended that the heads of departments are not amenable to the laws of their country?

Whatever the practice on particular occasions may be, the theory of this principle will certainly never be maintained. No act of the legislature confers so extraordinary a privilege, nor can it derive countenance from the doctrines of the common law. After stating that personal injury from the king to a subject is presumed to be impossible, Blackstone, vol. 3. p. 255, says, "but injuries to the rights of property can scarcely be committed by the crown without the intervention of its officers; for whom, the law, in matters of right, entertains no respect or delicacy; but furnishes various methods of detecting the errors and misconduct of those agents by whom the king has been deceived and induced to do a temporary injustice."

By the act passed in 1796, authorizing the sale of the lands above the mouth of Kentucky river (vol. 3d. p. 299) the purchaser, on paying his purchase money, becomes completely entitled to the property purchased; and on producing to the secretary of state, the receipt of the treasurer upon a certificate required by the law, the president of the United States is authorized to grant him a patent. It is further enacted that all patents shall be countersigned by the secretary of state, and recorded in his office. If the secretary of state should choose to withhold this patent; or the patent being lost, should refuse a copy of it; can it be imagined that the law furnishes to the injured person no remedy?

It is not believed that any person whatever would attempt to maintain such a proposition.

It follows then that the question, whether the legality of an act of the head of a department be examinable in a court of justice or not, must always depend on the nature of that act.

If some acts be examinable, and others not, there must be some rule of law to guide the court in the exercise of its jurisdiction.

In some instances there may be difficulty in applying the rule to particular cases; but there cannot, it is believed, be much difficulty in laying down the rule.

By the constitution of the United States, the President is invested with certain important political powers, in the exercise of which he is to use his own discretion, and is accountable only to his country in his political character, and to his own conscience. To aid him in the performance of these duties, he is authorized to appoint certain officers, who act by his authority and in conformity with his orders.

In such cases, their acts are his acts; and whatever opinion may be entertained of the manner in which executive discretion may be used, still there exists, and can exist, no power to control that discretion. The subjects are political. They respect the nation, not individual rights, and being entrusted to the executive, the decision of the executive is conclusive. The application of this remark will be perceived by adverting to the act of congress for establishing the department of foreign affairs. This officer, as his duties were prescribed by that act, is to conform precisely to the will of the President. He is the mere organ by whom that will is communicated. The acts of such an officer, as an officer, can never be examinable by the courts.

But when the legislature proceeds to impose on that officer other duties; when he is directed peremptorily to perform certain acts; when the rights of individuals are dependent on the performance of those acts; he is so far the officer of the law; is amenable to the laws for his conduct; and cannot at his discretion sport away the vested rights of others.

The conclusion from this reasoning is, that where the heads of departments are the political or confidential agents of the executive, merely to execute the will of the President, or rather to act in cases in which the executive possesses a constitutional or legal discretion, nothing can be more perfectly clear than that their acts are only politically examinable. But where a specific duty is assigned by law, and individual rights depend upon the performance of that duty, it seems equally clear that the individual who considers himself injured has a right to resort to the laws of his country for a remedy.

If this be the rule, let us inquire how it applies to the case under the consideration of the court.

The power of nominating to the senate, and the power of appointing the person nominated, are political powers, to be exercised by the President according to his own discretion. When he has made an appointment, he has exercised his whole power, and his discretion has been completely applied to the case. If, by law, the officer be removable at the will of the President, then a new appointment may be immediately made, and the rights of the officer are terminated. But as a fact which has existed cannot be made never to have existed, the appointment cannot be annihilated; and consequently if the officer is by law not removable at the will of the President the rights he has acquired are protected by the law, and are not resumable by the President. They cannot be extinguished by executive authority, and he has the privilege of asserting them in like manner as if they had been derived from any other source.

The question whether a right has vested or not, is, in its nature, judicial, and must be tried by the judicial authority. If, for example, Mr. Marbury had taken the oaths of a magistrate, and proceeded to act as one; in consequence of which a suit had been instituted against him, in which his defence had depended on his being a magistrate; the validity of his appointment must have been determined by judicial authority.

So, if he conceives that, by virtue of his appointment, he has a legal right, either to the commission which has been made out for him, or to a copy of that commission, it is equally a question examinable in a court, and the decision of the court upon it must depend on the opinion entertained of his appointment.

That question has been discussed, and the opinion is, that the latest point of time which can be taken as that at which the appointment was complete, and evidenced, was when, after the signature of the president, the seal of the United States was affixed to the commission.

It is then the opinion of the court,

1. That by signing the commission of Mr. Marbury, the president of the United States appointed him a justice of peace for the county of Washington in the district of Columbia; and that the seal of the United States, affixed thereto by the secretary of state, is conclusive testimony of the verity of the signature, and of the completion of the appointment; and that the appointment conferred on him a legal right to the office for the space of five years.

2. That, having this legal title to the office, he has a consequent right to the commission; a refusal to deliver which, is a plain violation of that right, for which the laws of his country afford him a remedy.

It remains to be inquired whether,

3. He is entitled to the remedy for which he applies. This depends on,

1. The nature of the writ applied for, and,

2. The power of this court.

1. The nature of the writ.

Blackstone, in the 3d volume of his commentaries, page 110, defines a mandamus to be, "a command issuing in the king's name from the court of king's bench, and directed to any person, corporation, or inferior court of judicature within the king's dominions, requiring them to do some particular thing therein specified, which appertains to their office and duty, and which the court of king's bench has previously determined, or at least supposes, to be consonant to right and justice."

Lord Mansfield, in 3d Burrows 1266, in the case of the *King v. Baker, et al.* states with much precision and explicitness the cases in which this writ may be used.

"Whenever," says that very able judge, "there is a right to execute an office, perform a service, or exercise a franchise (more especially if it be in a matter of public concern, or attended with profit), and a person is kept out of possession, or dispossessed of such right, and has no other specific legal remedy, this court ought to assist by mandamus, upon reasons of justice, as the writ expresses, and upon reasons of public policy, to preserve peace, order and good government." In the same case he says, "this writ ought to be used upon all occasions where the law has established no specific remedy, and where in justice and good government there ought to be one."

In addition to the authorities now particularly cited, many others were relied on at the bar, which show how far the practice has conformed to the general doctrines that have been just quoted.

This writ, if awarded, would be directed to an officer of government, and its mandate to him would be, to use the words of Blackstone, "to do a particular thing therein specified, which appertains to his office and duty and which the court has previously determined, or at least supposes to be consonant to right and justice." Or, in the words of Lord Mansfield, the applicant, in this case, has a right to execute an office of public concern, and is kept out of possession of that right.

These circumstances certainly concur in this case.

Still, to render the mandamus a proper remedy, the officer to whom it is to be directed, must be one to whom, on legal principles, such writ may be directed; and the person applying for it must be without any other specific and legal remedy.

1. With respect to the officer to whom it would be directed. The intimate political relation, subsisting between the president of the

United States and the heads of departments, necessarily renders any legal investigation of the acts of one of those high officers peculiarly irksome, as well as delicate; and excites some hesitation with respect to the propriety of entering into such investigation. Impressions are often received without much reflection or examination, and it is not wonderful that in such a case as this, the assertion, by an individual, of his legal claims in a court of justice; to which claims it is the duty of that court to attend; should at first view be considered by some, as an attempt to intrude into the cabinet, and to intermeddle with the prerogatives of the executive.

It is scarcely necessary for the court to disclaim all pretensions to such a jurisdiction. An extravagance, so absurd and excessive, could not have been entertained for a moment. The province of the court is, solely, to decide on the rights of individuals, not to inquire how the executive, or executive officers, perform duties in which they have a discretion. Questions, in their nature political, or which are, by the constitution and laws, submitted to the executive, can never be made in this court.

But, if this be not such a question; if so far from being an intrusion into the secrets of the cabinet, it respects a paper, which, according to law, is upon record, and to a copy of which the law gives a right, on the payment of ten cents; if it be no intermeddling with a subject, over which the executive can be considered as having exercised any control; what is there in the exalted station of the officer, which shall bar a citizen from asserting, in a court of justice, his legal rights, or shall forbid a court to listen to the claim; or to issue a mandamus, directing the performance of a duty, not depending on executive discretion, but on particular acts of congress and the general principles of law?

If one of the heads of departments commits any illegal act, under color of his office, by which an individual sustains an injury, it cannot be pretended that his office alone exempts him from being sued in the ordinary mode of proceeding, and being compelled to obey the judgment of the law. How then can his office exempt him from this particular mode of deciding on the legality of his conduct, if the case be such a case as would, were any other individual the party complained of, authorize the process?

It is not by the office of the person to whom the writ is directed, but the nature of the thing to be done, that the propriety or impropriety of issuing a mandamus is to be determined. Where the head of a department acts in a case in which executive discretion is to be exercised; in which he is the mere organ of executive will; it is again repeated, that any application to a court to control, in any respect, his conduct, would be rejected without hesitation.

But where he is directed by law to do a certain act affecting the absolute rights of individuals, in the performance of which he is not placed under the particular direction of the President, and the performance of which, the President cannot lawfully forbid, and therefore is never presumed to have forbidden; as for example, to record a commission, or a patent for land, which has received all the legal solemnities; or to give a copy of such record; in such cases, it is not perceived on what ground the courts of the country are further excused from the duty of giving judgment, that right to be done to an injured individual, than if the same services were to be performed by a person not the head of a department.

This opinion seems not now, for the first time, to be taken up in this country.

It must be well recollected that in 1792, an act passed, directing the secretary at war to place on the pension list such disabled officers and soldiers as should be reported to him, by the circuit courts, which act, so far as the duty was imposed on the courts, was deemed unconstitutional; but some of the judges, thinking that the law might be exe-

cuted by them in the character of commissioners, proceeded to act and to report in that character.

This law being deemed unconstitutional at the circuits, was repealed, and a different system was established; but the question whether those persons, who had been reported by the judges, as commissioners, were entitled, in consequence of that report, to be placed on the pension list, was a legal question, properly determinable in the courts, although the act of placing such persons on the list was to be performed by the head of a department.

That this question might be properly settled, congress passed an act in February, 1793, making it the duty of the secretary of war, in conjunction with the attorney general, to take such measures as might be necessary to obtain an adjudication of the supreme court of the United States on the validity of any such rights, claimed under the act aforesaid.

After the passage of this act, a mandamus was moved for, to be directed to the secretary at war, commanding him to place on the pension list a person stating himself to be on the report of the judges.

There is, therefore, much reason to believe, that this mode of trying the legal right of the complainant, was deemed by the head of a department, and by the highest law officer of the United States, the most proper which could be selected for the purpose.

When the subject was brought before the court the decision was, not that a mandamus would not lie to the head of a department, directing him to perform an act, enjoined by law, in the performance of which an individual had a vested interest; but that a mandamus ought not to issue in that case—the decision necessarily to be made if the report of the commissioners did not confer on the applicant a legal right.

The judgment in that case, is understood to have decided the merits of all claims of that description; and the persons on the report of the commissioners found it necessary to pursue the mode prescribed by the law subsequent to that which had been deemed unconstitutional, in order to place themselves on the pension list.

The doctrine, therefore, now advanced, is by no means a novel one.

It is true that the mandamus, now moved for, is not for the performance of an act expressly enjoined by statute.

It is to deliver a commission; on which subjects the acts of congress are silent. This difference is not considered as affecting the case. It has already been stated that the applicant has, to that commission, a vested legal right, of which the executive cannot deprive him. He has been appointed to an office, from which he is not removable at the will of the executive; and being so appointed, he has a right to the commission which the secretary has received from the president for his use. The act of congress does not indeed order the secretary of state to send it to him, but it is placed in his hands for the person entitled to it; and cannot be more lawfully withheld by him, than by another person.

It was at first doubted whether the action of *detinue* was not a specific legal remedy for the commission which has been withheld from Mr. Marbury; in which case a mandamus would be improper. But this doubt has yielded to the consideration that the judgment in *detinue* is for the thing itself, *or* its value. The value of a public office not to be sold, is incapable of being ascertained; and the applicant has a right to the office itself, or to nothing. He will obtain the office by obtaining the commission, or a copy of it from the record.

This, then, is a plain case of a mandamus, either to deliver the commission, or a copy of it from the record; and it only remains to be inquired,

Whether it can issue from this court.

The act to establish the judicial courts of the United States authorizes the supreme court "to issue writs of mandamus, in cases warranted by the principles and usages of law, to any courts appointed, or persons holding office, under the authority of the United States."

The secretary of state, being a person holding an office under the authority of the United States, is precisely within the letter of the description; and if this court is not authorized to issue a writ of mandamus to such an officer, it must be because the law is unconstitutional, and therefore absolutely incapable of conferring the authority, and assigning the duties which its words purport to confer and assign.

The constitution vests the whole judicial power of the United States in one supreme court, and such inferior courts as congress shall, from time to time, ordain and establish. This power is expressly extended to all cases arising under the laws of the United States; and consequently, in some form, may be exercised over the present case; because the right claimed is given by a law of the United States.

In the distribution of this power it is declared that "the supreme court shall have original jurisdiction in all cases affecting ambassadors, other public ministers and consuls, and those in which a state shall be a party. In all other cases, the supreme court shall have appellate jurisdiction."

It has been insisted at the bar, that as the original grant of jurisdiction to the supreme and inferior courts, is general, and the clause, assigning original jurisdiction to the supreme court, contains no negative or restrictive words; the power remains to the legislature, to assign original jurisdiction to that court in other cases than those specified in the article which has been recited; provided those cases belong to the judicial power of the United States.

If it had been intended to leave it in the discretion of the legislature to apportion the judicial power between the supreme and inferior courts according to the will of that body, it would certainly have been useless to have proceeded further than to have defined the judicial power, and the tribunals in which it should be vested. The subsequent part of the section is mere surplussage, is entirely without meaning, if such is to be the construction. If congress remains at liberty to give this court appellate jurisdiction, where the constitution has declared their jurisdiction shall be original; and original jurisdiction where the constitution has declared it shall be appellate; the distribution of jurisdiction, made in the constitution, is form without substance.

Affirmative words are often, in their operation, negative of other objects than those affirmed; and in this case, a negative or exclusive sense must be given to them or they have no operation at all.

It cannot be presumed that any clause in the constitution is intended to be without effect; and therefore such construction is inadmissible, unless the words require it.

If the solicitude of the convention, respecting our peace with foreign powers, induced a provision that the supreme court should take original jurisdiction in cases which might be supposed to affect them; yet the clause would have proceeded no further than to provide for such cases, if no further restriction on the powers of congress had been intended. That they should have appellate jurisdiction in all other cases, with such exceptions as congress might make, is no restriction; unless the words be deemed exclusive of original jurisdiction.

When an instrument organizing fundamentally a judicial system, divides it into one supreme, and so many inferior courts as the legislature may ordain and establish; then enumerates its powers, and proceeds so far to distribute them, as to define the jurisdiction of the supreme court by declaring the cases in which it shall take original jurisdiction, and that in others it shall take appellate jurisdiction, the plain import of the words seems to be, that in one class of cases its jurisdiction is original, and not appellate; in the other it is appellate, and not original. If any other construction would render the clause inoperative, that is an additional reason for rejecting such other construction, and for adhering to the obvious meaning.

To enable this court then to issue a mandamus, it must be shown to be an exercise of appellate jurisdiction, or to be necessary to enable them to exercise appellate jurisdiction.

It has been stated at the bar that the appellate jurisdiction may be exercised in a variety of forms, and that if it be the will of the legislature that a mandamus should be used for that purpose, that will must be obeyed. This is true; yet the jurisdiction must be appellate, not original.

It is the essential criterion of appellate jurisdiction, that it revises and corrects the proceedings in a cause already instituted, and does not create that case. Although, therefore, a mandamus may be directed to courts, yet to issue such a writ to an officer for the delivery of a paper, is in effect the same as to sustain an original action for that paper, and therefore seems not to belong to appellate, but to original jurisdiction. Neither is it necessary in such a case as this, to enable the court to exercise its appellate jurisdiction.

The authority, therefore, given to the supreme court, by the act establishing the judicial courts of the United States, to issue writs of mandamus to public officers, appears not to be warranted by the constitution; and it becomes necessary to inquire whether a jurisdiction, so conferred, can be exercised.

The question, whether an act, repugnant to the constitution, can become the law of the land, is a question deeply interesting to the United States; but, happily, not of an intricacy proportioned to its interest. It seems only necessary to recognise certain principles, supposed to have been long and well established, to decide it.

That the people have an original right to establish, for their future government, such principles as, in their opinion, shall most conduce to their own happiness, is the basis on which the whole American fabric has been erected. The exercise of this original right is a very great exertion; nor can it nor ought it to be frequently repeated. The principles, therefore, so established are deemed fundamental. And as the authority, from which they proceed, is supreme, and can seldom act, they are designed to be permanent.

This original and supreme will organizes the government, and assigns to different departments their respective powers. It may either stop here; or establish certain limits not to be transcended by those departments.

The government of the United States is of the latter description. The powers of the legislature are defined and limited; and that those limits may not be mistaken or forgotten, the constitution is written. To what purpose are powers limited, and to what purpose is that limitation committed to writing; if these limits may, at any time, be passed by those intended to be restrained? The distinction between a government with limited and unlimited powers is abolished, if those limits do not confine the persons on whom they are imposed, and if acts prohibited and acts allowed are of equal obligation. It is a proposition too plain to be contested, that the constitution controls any legislative act repugnant to it; or, that the legislature may alter the constitution by an ordinary act.

Between these alternatives there is no middle ground. The constitution is either a superior, paramount law, unchangeable by ordinary means, or it is on a level with ordinary legislative acts, and like other acts, is alterable when the legislature shall please to alter it.

If the former part of the alternative be true, then a legislative act contrary to the constitution is not law: if the latter part be true, then written constitutions are absurd attempts, on the part of the people, to limit a power in its own nature illimitable.

Certainly all those who have framed written constitutions contemplate them as forming the fundamental and paramount law of the nation, and consequently the theory of every such government must be, that an act of the legislature repugnant to the constitution, is void.

This theory is essentially attached to a written constitution, and is consequently to be considered by this court as one of the fundamental principles of our society. It is not therefore to be lost sight of in the further consideration of this subject.

If an act of the legislature, repugnant to the constitution, is void, does it, notwithstanding its invalidity, bind the courts, and oblige them to give it effect? Or, in other words, though it be not law, does it constitute a rule as operative as if it was a law? This would be to overthrow in fact what was established in theory; and would seem, at first view, an absurdity too gross to be insisted on. It shall, however, receive a more attentive consideration.

It is emphatically the province and duty of the judicial department to say what the law is. Those who apply the rule to particular cases, must of necessity expound and interpret that rule. If two laws conflict with each other, the courts must decide on the operation of each.

So if a law be in opposition to the constitution: if both the law and the constitution apply to a particular case, so that the court must either decide that case conformably to the law, disregarding the constitution; or conformably to the constitution, disregarding the law; the court must determine which of these conflicting rules governs the case. This is of the very essence of judicial duty.

If then the courts are to regard the constitution; and the constitution is superior to any ordinary act of the legislature; the constitution, and not such ordinary act, must govern the case to which they both apply.

Those then who controvert the principle that the constitution is to be considered, in court, as a paramount law, are reduced to the necessity of maintaining that courts must close their eyes on the constitution, and see only the law.

This doctrine would subvert the very foundation of all written constitutions. It would declare that an act, which, according to the principles and theory of our government, is entirely void, is yet, in practice, completely obligatory. It would declare, that if the legislature shall do what is expressly forbidden, such act, notwithstanding the express prohibition, is in reality effectual. It would be giving to the legislature a practical and real omnipotence, with the same breath which professes to restrict their powers within narrow limits. It is prescribing limits, and declaring that those limits may be passed at pleasure.

That it thus reduces to nothing what we have deemed the greatest improvement on political institutions—a written constitution—would of itself be sufficient, in America, where written constitutions have been viewed with so much reverence, for rejecting the construction. But the peculiar expressions of the constitution of the United States furnish additional arguments in favour of its rejection.

The judicial power of the United States is extended to all cases arising under the constitution.

Could it be the intention of those who gave this power, to say that, in using it, the constitution should not be looked into? That a case arising under the constitution should be decided without examining the instrument under which it arises?

This is too extravagant to be maintained.

In some cases then, the constitution must be looked into by the judges. And if they can open it at all, what part of it are they forbidden to read, or to obey?

There are many other parts of the constitution which serve to illustrate this subject.

It is declared that "no tax or duty shall be laid on articles exported from any state." Suppose a duty on the export of cotton, of tobacco, or of flour; and a suit instituted to recover it. Ought judgment to be rendered in such a case? ought the judges to close their eyes on the constitution, and only see the law.

The constitution declares that "no bill of attainder or *ex post facto* law shall be passed."

If, however, such a bill should be passed and a person should be prosecuted under it, must the court condemn to death those victims whom the constitution endeavours to preserve?

"No person," says the constitution, "shall be convicted of treason unless on the testimony of two witnesses to the same overt act, or on confession in open court."

Here the language of the constitution is addressed especially to the courts. It prescribes, directly for them, a rule of evidence not to be departed from. If the legislature should change that rule, and declare *one* witness, or a confession *out* of court, sufficient for conviction, must the constitutional principle yield to the legislative act?

From these and many other selections which might be made, it is apparent, that the framers of the constitution contemplated that instrument as a rule for the government of *courts,* as well as of the legislature.

Why otherwise does it direct the judges to take an oath to support it? This oath certainly applies, in an especial manner, to their conduct in their official character. How immoral to impose it on them, if they were to be used as the instruments, and the knowing instruments, for violating what they swear to support!

The oath of office, too, imposed by the legislature, is completely demonstrative of the legislative opinion on this subject. It is in these words, "I do solemnly swear that I will administer justice without respect to persons, and do equal right to the poor and to the rich; and that I will faithfully and impartially discharge all the duties incumbent on me as according to the best of my abilities and understanding, agreeably to the *constitution,* and laws of the United States."

Why does a judge swear to discharge his duties agreeably to the constitution of the United States, if that constitution forms no rule for his government? if it is closed upon him and cannot be inspected by him?

If such be the real state of things, this is worse than solemn mockery. To prescribe, or to take this oath, becomes equally a crime.

It is also not entirely unworthy of observation, that in declaring what shall be the *supreme* law of the land, the *constitution* itself is first mentioned; and not the laws of the United States generally, but those only which shall be made in *pursuance* of the constitution, have that rank.

Thus, the particular phraseology of the constitution of the United States confirms and strengthens the principle, supposed to be essential to all written constitutions, that a law repugnant to the constitution is void, and that *courts,* as well as other departments, are bound by that instrument.

The rule must be discharged.

McCulloch v. Maryland (1819)

McCulloch v. Maryland *involved a states' rights challenge to the chartering of the second national bank. The bank, chartered in 1816, was extremely unpopular, particularly in the eastern and southern states. Maryland attempted to tax the Baltimore branch out of existence by imposing a hefty tax on the notes issued by the bank. James McCulloch, a bank cashier, refused to pay the tax, claiming it was an unconstitutional infringement on the federally chartered bank. Maryland contended that Congress had exceeded its powers when it chartered the bank and that the state had the power to tax any bank within its borders.*

Chief Justice John Marshall wrote the Court's decision, beginning on p. 1009, which upheld the power of Congress to incorporate the bank. He noted that the national government is "one of enumerated powers," but asserted that "though limited in its powers [it] is supreme within its sphere of action." The creation of the bank was valid under the Constitution's "necessary and proper" clause, which authorized Congress to enact "all Laws which shall be necessary and proper for carrying into "Execution" the powers specifically provided.

17 U.S. 316, 4 L. Ed. 579, 4 Wheat. 316

McCulloch v. State of Maryland et al.

February Term, 1819

Error to the Court of Appeals of the State of Maryland. This was an action of debt, brought by the defendant in error, John James, who sued as well for himself as for the state of Maryland, in the county court of Baltimore county, in the said state, against the plaintiff in error, McCulloch, to recover certain penalties, under the act of the legislature of Maryland, hereafter mentioned. Judgment being rendered against the plaintiff in error, upon the following statement of facts, agreed and submitted to the court by the parties, was affirmed by the court of appeals of the state of Maryland, the highest court of law of said state, and the cause was brought, by writ of error, to this court.

It is admitted by the parties in this cause, by their counsel, that there was passed, on the 10th day of April 1816, by the congress of the United States, an act, entitled, "an act to incorporate the subscribers to the Bank of the United States;" and that there was passed on the 11th day of February 1818, by the general assembly of Maryland, an act, entitled, "an act to impose a tax on all banks, or branches thereof, in the state of Maryland, not chartered by the legislature," which said acts are made part of this statement, and it is agreed, may be read from the statute books in which they are respectively printed. It is further admitted, that the president, directors and company of the Bank of the United States, incorporated by the act of congress aforesaid, did organize themselves, and go into full operation, in the city of Philadelphia, in the state of Pennsylvania, in pursuance of the said act, and that they did on the ___ day of _____ 1817, establish a branch of the said bank, or an office of discount and deposit, in the city of Baltimore, in the state of Maryland, which has, from that time, until the first day of May 1818, ever since transacted and carried on business as a bank, or office of discount and deposit, and as a branch of the said Bank of the United States, by issuing bank-notes and discounting promissory notes, and performing other operations usual and customary for banks to do and perform, under the authority and by the direction of the said president, directors and company of the Bank of the United States, established at Philadelphia as aforesaid. It is further admitted, that the said president, directors and company of the said bank, had no authority to establish the said branch, or office of discount and deposit, at the city of Baltimore, from the state of Maryland, otherwise than the said state having adopted the constitution of the United States and composing one of the states of the Union. It is further admitted, that James William McCulloch, the defendant below, being the cashier of the said branch, or office of discount and deposit, did, on the several days set forth in the declaration in this cause, issue the said respective bank-notes therein described, from the said branch or office, to a certain George Williams, in the city of Baltimore, in part payment of a promissory note of the said Williams, discounted by the said branch or office, which said respective bank-notes were not, nor was either of them, so issued, on stamped paper, in the manner prescribed by the act of assembly aforesaid. It is further admitted, that the said president, directors and company of the Bank of the United States, and the said branch, or office of discount and deposit, have not, nor has either of them, paid in advance, or otherwise, the sum of $15,000, to the treasurer of the Western Shore, for the use of the state of Maryland, before the issuing of the said notes, or any of them, nor since those periods. And it is further admitted, that the treasurer of the Western Shore of Maryland, under the direction of the governor and council of the said state, was ready, and offered to deliver to the said president, directors and company of the said bank, and to the said branch, or office of discount and deposit, stamped paper of the kind and denomination required and described in the said act of assembly.

The question submitted to the court for their decision in this case, is, as to the validity of the said act of the general assembly of Maryland, on the ground of its being repugnant to the constitution of the United States, and the act of congress aforesaid, or to one of them. Upon the foregoing statement of facts, and the pleadings in this cause (all errors in which are hereby agreed to be mutually released), if the court should be of opinion, that the plaintiffs are entitled to recover, then judgment, it is agreed, shall be entered for the plaintiffs for $2500, and costs of suit. But if the court should be of opinion, that the plaintiffs are not entitled to recover upon the statement and pleadings aforesaid, then judgment of *non pros* shall be entered, with costs to the defendant.

It is agreed, that either party may appeal from the decision of the county court, to the court of appeals, and from the decision of the court of appeals to the supreme court of the United States, according to the modes and usages of law, and have the same benefit of this statement of facts, in the same manner as could be had, if a jury had been sworn and impannelled in this cause, and a special verdict had been found, or these facts had appeared and been stated in an exception taken to the opinion of the court, and the court's direction to the jury thereon.

Copy of the act of the Legislature of the State of Maryland, referred to in the preceding statement.

An act to impose a tax on all banks or branches thereof, in the state of Maryland, not chartered by the legislature.

Be it enacted by the general assembly of Maryland, that if any bank has established, or shall, without authority from the state first had and obtained, establish any branch, office of discount and deposit, or office of pay and receipt in any part of this state, it shall not be lawful for the said branch, office of discount and deposit, or office of pay and receipt, to issue notes, in any manner, of any other denomination than five, ten, twenty, fifty, one hundred, five hundred and one thousand dollars, and no note shall be issued, except upon stamped paper of the following denominations; that is to say, every five dollar note shall be upon a stamp of ten cents; every ten dollar note, upon a stamp of twenty cents; every twenty dollar note, upon a stamp of thirty cents; every fifty dollar note, upon a stamp of fifty cents; every one hundred dollar note, upon a stamp of one dollar; every five hundred dollar note, upon a stamp of ten dollars; and every thousand dollar note, upon a stamp of twenty dollars; which paper shall be furnished by the treasurer of the Western Shore, under the direction of the governor and council, to be paid for upon delivery; provided always, that any institution of the above description may relieve itself from the operation of the provisions aforesaid, by paying annually, in advance, to the treasurer of the Western Shore, for the use of state, the sum of $15,000.

And be it enacted, that the president, cashier, each of the directors and officers of every institution established, or to be established as aforesaid, offending against the provisions aforesaid, shall forfeit a sum of $500 for each and every offence, and every person having any agency in circulating any note aforesaid, not stamped as aforesaid directed, shall forfeit a sum not exceeding $100 every penalty aforesaid, to be recovered by indictment, or action of debt, in the county court of the county where the offence shall be committed, one-half to the informer, and the other half to the use of the state.

And be it enacted, that this act shall be in full force and effect from and after the first day of May next.

February 22d–27th, and March 1st–3d.

Webster, for the plaintiff in error,[1] stated: 1. That the question whether congress constitutionally possesses the power to incorporate a bank, might be raised upon this record; and it was in the discretion of the defendant's counsel to agitate it. But it might have been hoped, that it was not now to be considered as an open question. It is a question of the utmost magnitude, deeply interesting to the government itself, as well as to individuals. The mere discussion of such a question may most essentially affect the value of a vast amount of private property. We are bound to suppose, that the defendant in error is well aware of these consequences, and would not have intimated an intention to agitate such question, but with a real design to make it a topic of serious discussion, and with a view of demanding upon it the solemn judgment of this court. This question arose early after the adoption of the constitution, and was discussed and settled, so far as legislative decision could settle it, in the first congress. The arguments drawn from the constitution, in favor of this power, were stated and exhausted in that discussion. They were exhibited, with characteristic perspicuity and force, by the first secretary of the treasury, in his report to the president of the United States. The first congress created and incorporated a bank. Act of 5th February 1791, ch. 84. Nearly each succeeding congress, if not every one, has acted and legislated on the presumption of the legal existence of such a power in the government. Individuals, it is true, have doubted, or thought otherwise; but it cannot be shown, that either branch of the legislature has, at any time, expressed an opinion against the existence of the power. The executive government has acted upon it; and the courts of law have acted upon it. Many of those who doubted or denied the existence of the powers, when first attempted to be exercised, have yielded to the first decision, and acquiesced in it, as a settled question. When all branches of the government have thus been acting on the existence of this power, nearly thirty years, it would seem almost too late to call it in question, unless its repugnancy with the constitution were plain and manifest. Congress, by the constitution, is invested with certain powers; and as to the objects, and within the scope of these powers, it is sovereign. Even without the aid of the general clause in the constitution, empowering congress to pass all necessary and proper laws for carrying its powers into execution, the grant of powers itself necessarily implies the grant of all usual and suitable means for the execution of the powers granted. Congress may declare war; it may consequently carry on war, by armies and navies, and other suitable means

and methods of warfare. So, it has power to raise a revenue, and to apply it in the support of the government, and defence of the country; it may, of course, use all proper and suitable means, not specially prohibited, in the raising and disbursement of the revenue. And if, in the progress of society and the arts, new means arise, either of carrying on war, or of raising revenue, these new means doubtless would be properly considered as within the grant. Steam-frigates, for example, were not in the minds of those who framed the constitution, as among the means of naval warfare; but no one doubts the power of congress to use them, as means to an authorized end. It is not enough to say, that it does not appear that a bank was not in the contemplation of the framers of the constitution. It was not their intention, in these cases, to enumerate particulars. The true view of the subject is, that if it be a fit instrument to an authorized purpose, it may be used, not being specially prohibited. Congress is authorized to pass all laws "necessary and proper" to carry into execution the powers conferred on it. These words, "necessary and proper," in such an instrument, are probably to be considered as synonymous. Necessarily, powers must here intend such powers as are suitable and fitted to the object; such as are best and most useful in relation to the end proposed. If this be not so, and if congress could use no means but such as were absolutely indispensable to the existence of a granted power, the government would hardly exist; at least, it would be wholly inadequate to the purposes of its formation. A bank is a proper and suitable instrument to assist the operations of the government, in the collection and disbursement of the revenue; in the occasional anticipations of taxes and imposts; and in the regulation of the actual currency, as being a part of the trade and exchange between the states. It is not for this court to decide, whether a bank, or such a bank as this, be the best possible means to aid these purposes of government. Such topics must be left to that discussion which belongs to them, in the two houses of congress. Here, the only question is, whether a bank, in its known and ordinary operations, is capable of being so connected with the finances and revenues of the government, as to be fairly within the discretion of congress, when selecting means and instruments to execute its powers and perform its duties. A bank is not less the proper subject for the choice of congress, nor the less constitutional, because it requires to be executed by granting a charter of incorporation. It is not, of itself, unconstitutional in congress to create a corporation. Corporations are but means. They are not ends and objects of government. No government exists for the purpose of creating corporations as one of the ends of its being. They are institutions established to effect certain beneficial purposes; and, as means, take their character generally from their end and object. They are civil or eleemosynary, public or private, according to the object intended by their creation. They are common means, such as all governments use. The state governments create corporations to execute powers confided to their trust, without any specific authority in the state constitutions for that purpose. There is the same reason that congress should exercise its discretion as to the means by which it must execute the powers conferred upon it. Congress has duties to perform and powers to execute. It has a right to the means by which these duties can be properly and most usefully performed, and these powers executed. Among other means, it has established a bank; and before the act establishing it can be pronounced unconstitutional and void, it must be shown, that a bank has no fair connection with the execution of any power or duty of the national government, and that its creation is consequently a manifest usurpation.

2. The second question is, whether, if the bank be constitutionally created, the state governments have power to tax it? The people of the United States have seen fit to divide sovereignty, and to establish a complex system. They have conferred certain powers on the state

governments, and certain other powers on the national government. As it was easy to foresee that question must arise between these governments thus constituted, it became of great moment to determine, upon what principle these questions should be decided, and who should decide them. The constitution, therefore, declares, that the constitution itself, and the laws passed in pursuance of its provisions, shall be the supreme law of the land, and shall control all state legislation and state constitutions, which may be incompatible therewith; and it confides to this court the ultimate power of deciding all questions arising under the constitution and laws of the United States. The laws of the United States, then, made in pursuance of the constitution, are to be the supreme law of the land, anything in the laws of any state to the contrary notwithstanding. The only inquiry, therefore, in this case is, whether the law of the state of Maryland imposing this tax be consistent with the free operation of the law establishing the bank, and the full enjoyment of the privileges conferred by it? If it be not, then it is void; if it be, then it may be valid. Upon the supposition, that the bank is constitutionally created, this is the only question; and this question seems answered, as soon as it is stated. If the states may tax the bank, to what extent shall they tax it, and where shall they stop? An unlimited power to tax involves, necessarily, a power to destroy; because there is a limit beyond which no institution and no property can bear taxation. A question of constitutional power can hardly be made to depend on a question of more or less. If the states may tax, they have no limit but their discretion; and the bank, therefore, must depend on the discretion of the state governments for its existence. This consequence is inevitable. The object in laying this tax, may have been revenue to the state. In the next case, the object may be to expel the bank from the state; but how is this object to be ascertained, or who is to judge of the motives of legislative acts? The government of the United States has itself a great pecuniary interest in this corporation. Can the states tax this property? Under the confederation, when the national government, not having the power of direct legislation, could not protect its own property by its own laws, it was expressly stipulated, that "no impositions, duties or restrictions should be laid by any state on the property of the United States." Is it supposed, that property of the United States is now subject to the power of the state governments, in a greater degree than under the confederation? If this power of taxation be admitted, what is to be its limit? The United States have, and must have, property locally existing in all the states; and may the states impose on this property, whether real or personal, such taxes as they please? Can they tax proceedings in the federal courts? If so, they can expel those judicatures from the states. As Maryland has undertaken to impose a stamp-tax on the notes of this bank, what hinders her from imposing a stamp-tax also on permits, clearances, registers and all other documents connected with imposts and navigation? If, by one, she can suspend the operations of the bank, by the other, she can equally well shut up the custom-house. The law of Maryland, in question, makes a requisition. The sum called for is not assessed on property, nor deducted from profits or income. It is a direct imposition on the power, privilege or franchise of the corporation. The act purports, also, to restrain the circulation of the paper of the bank to bills of certain descriptions. It narrows and abridges the powers of the bank in a manner which, it would seem, even congress could not do. This law of Maryland cannot be sustained, but upon principles and reasoning which would subject every important measure of the national government to the revision and control of the state legislatures. By the charter, the bank is authorized to issue bills of any denomination above five dollars. The act of Maryland purports to restrain and limit their powers in this respect. The charter, as well as the laws of the United States, makes it the duty of all collectors and receivers to receive the notes of

the bank in payment of all debts due the government. The act of Maryland makes it penal, both on the person paying and the person receiving such bills, until stamped by the authority of Maryland. This is a direct interference with the revenue. The legislature of Maryland might, with as much propriety, tax treasury-notes. This is either an attempt to expel the bank from the state; or it is an attempt to raise a revenue for state purposes, by an imposition on property and franchises holden under the national government, and created by that government, for purposes connected with its own administration. In either view, there cannot be a clearer case of interference. The bank cannot exist, nor can any bank established by congress exist, if this right to tax it exists in the state governments. One or the other must be surrendered; and a surrender on the part of the government of the United States would be a giving up of those fundamental and essential powers without which the government cannot be maintained. A bank may not be, and is not, absolutely essential to the existence and preservation of the government. But it is essential to the existence and preservation of the government, that congress should be able to exercise its constitutional powers, at its own discretion, without being subject to the control of state legislation. The question is not, whether a bank be necessary or useful, but whether congress may not constitutionally judge of that necessity or utility; and whether, having so judged and decided, and having adopted measures to carry its decision into effect, the state governments may interfere with that decision, and defeat the operation of its measures. Nothing can be plainer than that, if the law of congress, establishing the bank, be a constitutional act, it must have its full and complete effects. Its operation cannot be either defeated or impeded by acts of state legislation. To hold otherwise, would be to declare, that congress can only exercise its constitutional powers, subject to the controlling discretion, and under the sufferance, of the state governments.

Hopkinson, for the defendants in error, proposed three questions for the consideration of the court. 1. Had congress a constitutional power to incorporate the bank of the United States? 2. Granting this power to congress, has the bank, of its own authority, a right to establish its branches in the several states? 3. Can the bank, and its branches thus established, claim to be exempt from the ordinary and equal taxation of property, as assessed in the states in which they are placed?

1. The first question has, for many years, divided the opinions of the first men of our country. He did not mean to controvert the arguments by which the bank was maintained, on its original establishment. The power may now be denied, in perfect consistency with those arguments. It is agreed, that no such power is expressly granted by the constitution. It has been obtained by implication; by reasoning from the 8th section of the 1st article of the constitution; and asserted to exist, not of and by itself, but as an appendage to other granted powers, as necessary to carry them into execution. If the bank be not "necessary and proper" for this purpose, it has no foundation in our constitution, and can have no support in this court. But it strikes us, at once, that a power, growing out of a necessity which may not be permanent, may also not be permanent. It has relation to circumstances which change; in a state of things which may exist at one period, and not at another. The argument might have been perfectly good, to show the necessity of a bank, for the operations of the revenue, in 1791, and entirely fail now, when so many facilities for money transactions abound, which were wanting then. That some of the powers of the constitution are of this fluctuating character, existing, or not, according to extraneous circumstances, has been fully recognised by this court at the present term, in the case of *Sturges v. Crowninshield* (ante, p. 122). Necessity was the plea and justification of the first Bank of the United States. If the same necessity existed,

when the second was established, it will afford the same justification; otherwise, it will stand without justification, as no other is pretended. We cannot, in making this inquiry, take a more fair and liberal test, than the report of General Hamilton, the father and defender of this power. The uses and advantages he states, as making up the necessity required by the constitution, are three. 1st. The augmentation of the active and productive capital of the country, by making gold and silver the basis of a paper circulation. 2d. Affording greater facility to the government, in procuring pecuniary aids; especially, in sudden emergencies; this, he says, is an indisputable advantage of public banks. 3d. The facility of the payment of taxes, in two ways; by loaning to the citizen, and enabling him to be punctual; and by increasing the quantity of circulating medium, and quickening circulation by bank-bills, easily transmitted from place to place. If we admit, that these advantages or conveniences amount to the necessity required by the constitution, for the creation and exercise of powers not expressly given; yet it is obvious, they may be derived from any public banks, and do not call for a Bank of the United States, unless there should be no other public banks, or not a sufficiency of them for these operations. In 1791, when this argument was held to be valid and effectual, there were but three banks in the United States, with limited capitals, and contracted spheres of operation. Very different is the case now, when we have a banking capital to a vast amount, vested in banks of good credit, and so spread over the country, as to be convenient and competent for all the purposes enumerated in the argument. General Hamilton, conscious that his reasoning must fail, if the state banks were adequate for his objects, proceeds to show they were not. Mr. *Hopkinson* particularly examined all the objections urged by General Hamilton, to the agency of the state banks, then in existence, in the operations required for the revenue; and endeavored to show, that they had no application to the present number, extent and situation of the state banks; relying only on those of a sound and unquestioned credit and permanency. He also contended, that the experience of five years, since the expiration of the old charter of the Bank of the United States, has fully shown the competency of the state banks, to all the purposes and uses alleged as reasons for erecting that bank, in 1791. The loans to the government by the state banks, in the emergencies spoken of; the accommodation to individuals, to enable them to pay their duties and taxes; the creation of a circulating currency; and the facility of transmitting money from place to place, have all been effected, as largely and beneficially, by the state banks, as they could have been done by a bank incorporated by congress. The change in the country, in relation to banks, and an experience that was depended upon, concur in proving, that whatever might have been the truth and force of the bank argument in 1791, they were wholly wanting in 1816.

2. If this Bank of the United States has been lawfully created and incorporated, we next inquire, whether it may, of its own authority, establish its branches in the several states, without the direction of congress, or the assent of the states? It is true, that the charter contains this power, but this avails nothing, if not warranted by the constitution. This power to establish branches, by the directors of the bank, must be maintained and justified, by the same necessity which supports the bank itself, or it cannot exist. The power derived from a given necessity, must be coextensive with it, and no more. We will inquire, 1st. Does this necessity exist in favor of the branches? 2d. Who should be the judge of the necessity, and direct the manner and extent of the remedy to be applied? Branches are not necessary for any of the enumerated advantages. Not for pecuniary aids to the government; since the ability to afford them must be regulated by the strength of the capital of the parent bank, and cannot be increased by scattering and spreading that capital in the branches. Nor are they necessary to create a circulating medium; for they create nothing; but

issue paper on the faith and responsibility of the parent bank, who could issue the same quantity, on the same foundation; the distribution of the notes of the parent bank can as well be done, and in fact, is done, by the state banks. Where, then, is that necessity to be found for the branches, whatever may be allowed to the bank itself? It is undoubtedly true, that these branches are established with a single view to trading, and the profit of the stockholders, and not for the convenience or use of the government; and therefore, they are located at the will of the directors, who represent and regard the interests of the stockholders, and are such themselves. If this is the case, can it be contended, that the state rights of territory and taxation are to yield for the gains of a money-trading corporation; to be prostrated at the will of a set of men who have no concern, and no duty but to increase their profits? Is this the necessity required by the constitution for the creation of undefined powers? It is true, that, by the charter, the government may require a branch in any place it may designate, but if this power is given only for the uses or necessities of the government, then the government only should have the power to order it. In truth, the directors have exercised the power, and they hold it, without any control from the government of the United States; and, as is now contended, without any control of the state governments. A most extravagant power to be vested in a body of men, chosen annually by a very small portion of our citizens, for the purpose of loaning and trading with their money to the best advantage! A state will not suffer its own citizens to erect a bank, without its authority, but the citizens of another state may do so; for it may happen that the state thus used by the bank for one of its branches, does not hold a single share of the stock. 2d. But if these branches are to be supported, on the ground of the constitutional necessity, and they can have no other foundation, the question occurs, who should be the judge of the existence of the necessity, in any proposed case; of the when and the where the power shall be exercised, which the necessity requires? Assuredly, the same tribunal which judges of the original necessity on which the bank is created, should also judge of any subsequent necessity requiring the extension of the remedy. Congress is that tribunal; the only one in which it may be safely trusted; the only one in which the states to be affected by the measure, are all fairly represented. If this power belongs to congress, it cannot be delegated to the directors of a bank, any more than any other legislative power may be transferred to any other body of citizens: if this doctrine of necessity is without any known limits, but such as those who defend themselves by it, may choose, for the time, to give it; and if the powers derived from it, are assignable by the congress to the directors of a bank; and by the directors of the bank to anybody else; we have really spent a great deal of labor and learning to very little purpose, in our attempt to establish a form of government in which the powers of those who govern shall be strictly defined and controlled; and the rights of the government secured from the usurpations of unlimited or unknown powers. The establishment of a bank in a state, without its assent; without regard to its interests, its policy or institutions, is a higher exercise of authority, than the creation of the parent bank; which, if confined to the seat of the government, and to the purposes of the government, will interfere less with the rights and policy of the states, than those widespreading branches, planted everywhere, and influencing all the business of the community. Such an exercise of sovereign power, should, at least, have the sanction of the sovereign legislature, to vouch that the good of the whole requires it, that the necessity exists which justifies it. But will it be tolerated, that twenty directors of a trading corporation, having no object but profit, shall, in the pursuit of it, tread upon the sovereignty of the state; enter it, without condescending to ask its leave; disregard, perhaps, the whole system of its policy; overthrow its institutions, and sacrifice its interests?

3. If, however, the states of this Union have surrendered themselves in this manner, by implication, to the congress of the United States, and to such corporations as the congress, from time to time, may find it "necessary and proper" to create; if a state may no longer decide, whether a trading association, with independent powers and immunities, shall plant itself in its territory, carry on its business, make a currency and trade on its credit, raising capitals for individuals as fictitious as its own; if all this must be granted, the third and great question in this cause presents itself for consideration; that is, shall this association come there with rights of sovereignty, paramount to the sovereignty of the state, and with privileges possessed by no other persons, corporations or property in the state? in other words, can the bank and its branches, thus established, claim to be exempt from the ordinary and equal taxation of property, as assessed in the states in which they are placed? As this overwhelming invasion of state sovereignty is not warranted by any express clause or grant in the constitution, and never was imagined by any state that adopted and ratified that constitution, it will be conceded, that it must be found to be necessarily and indissolubly connected with the power to establish the bank, or it must be repelled. The court has always shown a just anxiety to prevent any conflict between the federal and state powers; to construe both so as to avoid an interference, if possible, and to preserve that harmony of action in both, on which the prosperity and happiness of all depend. If, therefore, the right to incorporate a national bank may exist, and be exercised consistently with the right of the state, to tax the property of such bank within its territory, the court will maintain both rights; although some inconvenience or diminution of advantage may be the consequence. It is not for the directors of the bank to say, you will lessen our profits by permitting us to be taxed; if such taxation will not deprive the government of the uses it derives from the agency and operations of the bank. The necessity of the government is the foundation of the charter; and beyond that necessity, it can claim nothing in derogation of state authority. If the power to erect this corporation were expressly given in the constitution, still, it would not be construed to be an exclusion of any state right, not absolutely incompatible and repugnant. The states need no reservation or acknowledgment of their right; all remain that are not expressly prohibited, or necessarily excluded; and this gives our opponents the broadest ground they can ask. The right now assailed by the bank, is the right of taxing property within the territory of the state. This is the highest attribute of sovereignty, the right to raise revenue; in fact, the right to exist; without which no other right can be held or enjoyed. The general power to tax is not denied to the states, but the bank claims to be exempted from the operation of this power. If this claim is valid, and to be supported by the court, it must be, either, 1. From the nature of the property: 2. Because it is a bank of the United States: 3. From some express provision of the constitution: or 4. Because the exemption is indispensably necessary to the exercise of some power granted by the constitution.

1st. There is nothing in the nature of the property of bank-stock that exonerates it from taxation. It has been taxed, in some form, by every state in which a bank has been incorporated; either annually and directly, or by a gross sum paid for the charter. The United States have not only taxed the capital or stock of the state banks, but their business also, by imposing a duty on all notes discounted by them. The bank paid a tax for its capital; and every man who deals with the bank, by borrowing, paid another tax for the portion of the same capital he borrowed. This species of property, then, so far from having enjoyed any exemption from the calls of the revenue, has been particularly burdened; and been thought a fair subject of taxation both by the federal and state governments.

2d. Is it then exempt, as being a bank of the United States? How is it such? In name only. Just as the Bank of Pennsylvania, or the Bank of

Maryland, are banks of those states. The property of the bank, real or personal, does not belong to the United States only, as a stockholder, and as any other stockholders. The United States might have the same interest in any other bank, turnpike or canal company. So far as they hold stock, they have a property in the institution, and no further; so long, and no longer. Nor is the direction and management of the bank under the control of the United States. They are represented in the board by the directors appointed by them, as the other stockholders are represented by the directors they elect. A director of the government has no more power or right than any other director. As to the control the government may have over the conduct of the bank, by its patronage and deposits, it is precisely the same it might have over any other bank, to which that patronage would be equally important. Strip it of its name, and we find it to be a mere association of individuals, putting their money into a common stock, to be loaned for profit, and to divide the gains. The government is a partner in the firm, for gain also; for, except a participation of the profits of the business, the government could have every other use of the bank, without owning a dollar in it. It is not, then, a bank of the United States, if by that we mean, an institution belonging to the government, directed by it, or in which it has a permanent, indissoluble interest. The convenience it affords in the collection and distribution of the revenue, is collateral, secondary, and may be transferred at pleasure to any other bank. It forms no part of the construction or character of this bank; which, as to all its rights and powers, would be exactly what it now is, if the government was to seek and obtain all this convenience from some other source; if the government were to withdraw its patronage, and sell out its stock. How, then, can such an institution claim the immunities of sovereignty; nay, that sovereignty does not possess? for a sovereign who places his property in the territory of another sovereign, submits it to the demands of the revenue, which are but justly paid, in return for the protection afforded to the property. General Hamilton, in his report on this subject, so far from considering the bank a public institution, connected with, or controlled by, the government, holds it to be indispensable that it should not be so. It must be, says he, under private, not public, direction; under the guidance of individual interest, not public policy. Still, he adds, the state may be holder of part of its stock; and consequently (what? it becomes a public property? no!), a sharer of the profits. He traces no other consequence to that circumstance. No rights are founded on it; no part of its utility or necessity arises from it. Can an institution, then, purely private, and which disclaims any public character, be clothed with the power and rights of the government, and demand subordination from the state government, in virtue of the federal authority, which it undertakes to wield at its own will and pleasure? Shall it be private, in its direction and interests; public, in its rights and privileges: a trading money-lender, in its business; an uncontrolled sovereign, in its powers? If the whole bank, with all its property and business, belonged to the United States, it would not, therefore, be exempted from the taxation of the states. To this purpose, the United States and the several states must be considered as sovereign and independent; and the principle is clear, that a sovereign putting his property within the territory and jurisdiction of another sovereign, and of course, under his protection, submits it to the ordinary taxation of the state, and must contribute fairly to the wants of the revenue. In other words, the jurisdiction of the state extends over all its territory, and everything within or upon it, with a few known exceptions. With a view to this principle, the constitution has provided for those cases in which it was deemed necessary and proper to give the United States jurisdiction within a state, in exclusion of the state authority; and even in these cases, it will be seen, it cannot be done, without the assent of the state. For a seat of government, for forts, arsenals, dock-yards, &c., the assent of the state to surrender its jurisdiction is required; but the bank asks no consent, and is paramount to all state authority, to all the rights of territory, and demands of the public revenue. We have not been told, whether the banking-houses of this corporation, and any other real estate it may acquire, for the accommodation of its affairs, are also of this privileged order of property. In principle, it must be the same; for the privilege, if it exists, belongs to the corporation, and must cover equally all its property. It is understood, that a case was lately decided by the supreme court of Pennsylvania, and from which no appeal has been taken, on the part of the United States, to this court, to show that United States property, as such, has no exemption from state taxation. A fort, belonging to the federal government, near Pittsburgh, was sold by public auction; the usual auction duty was claimed, and the payment resisted, on the ground, that none could be exacted from the United States. The court decided otherwise. In admitting Louisiana into the Union, and so, it is believed, with all the new states, it is expressly stipulated, "that no taxes shall be imposed on lands, the property of the United States." There can, then, be no pretence, that bank property, even belonging to the United States, is, on that account, exonerated from state taxation.[2]

3d. If, then, neither the nature of the property, nor the interest the United States may have in the bank, will warrant the exemption claimed, is there anything expressed in the constitution, to limit and control the state right of taxation, as now contended for? We find but one limitation to this essential right, of which the states were naturally and justly most jealous. In the 10th section of the 1st article, it is declared, that "no state shall, without the consent of congress, lay any imposts or duties on imports or exports, except what may be absolutely necessary for executing its inspection laws;" and there is a like prohibition to laying any duty of tonnage. Here, then, is the whole restriction or limitation, attempted to be imposed by the constitution, on the power of the states to raise revenue, precisely in the same manner, from the same subjects, and to the same extent, that any sovereign and independent state may do; and it never was understood by those who made, or those who received, the constitution, that any further restriction ever would, or could, be imposed. This subject did not escape either the assailants or the defenders of our form of government; and their arguments and commentaries upon the instrument ought not to be disregarded, in fixing its construction. It was foreseen, and objected by its opponents, that under the general sweeping power given to congress, "to make all laws which shall be necessary and proper, for carrying into execution the foregoing powers," &c., the states might be exposed to great dangers, and the most humiliating and oppressive encroachments, particularly in this very matter of taxation. By referring to the Federalist, the great champion of the constitution, the objections will be found stated, together with the answers to them. It is again and again replied, and most solemnly asserted, to the people of these United States, that the right of taxation in the states is sacred and inviolable, with "the sole exception of duties on imports and exports;" that "they retain the authority in the most absolute and unqualified sense; and that an attempt on the part of the national government to abridge them in the exercise of it, would be a violent assumption of power, unwarranted by any article or clause of its constitution." With the exception mentioned, the federal and state powers of taxation are declared to be concurrent; and if the United States are justified in taxing state banks, the same equal and concurrent authority will justify the state in taxing the Bank of the United States, or any other bank.[3] The author begins No. 34, by saying, "I flatter myself it has been clearly shown, in my last number, that the particular states, under the proposed constitution, would have *co-equal* authority with the Union, in the article of revenue, except as to duties on imports." Under such assurances from those who made, who recommended, and carried, the constitution, and who were supposed best to understand it, was it received and adopted by the people of these United States; and now, after a lapse of nearly thirty years, they are to be informed, that all this is a mistake, all these assurances are unwarranted, and that the federal government does possess most productive and important powers of taxation, neither on imports, exports or tonnage, but strictly internal, which are prohibited to the states. The question then was, whether the United States should have any command of the internal revenue; the pretension now is, that they shall enjoy exclusively the best portion of it. The question was then quieted, by the acknowledgment of a co-equal right; it is now to be put at rest, by the prostration of the state power. The federal government is to hold a power by implication, and ingenious inference from general words in the constitution, which it can hardly be believed would have been suffered in an express grant. If, then, the people were not deceived, when they were told that, with the exceptions mentioned, the state right of taxation is sacred and inviolable; and it be also true, that the Bank of the United States cannot exist under the exercise of that right, the consequence ought to be, that the bank must not exist; for if it can live only by the destruction of such a right—if it can live only by the exercise of a power, which this court solemnly declared to be a "violent assumption of power, unwarranted by any clause in the constitution"—we cannot hesitate to say, let it not live.

But, in truth, this is not the state of the controversy. No such extremes are presented for our choice. We only require, that the bank shall not violate state rights, in establishing itself, or its branches; that it shall be submitted to the jurisdiction and laws of the state, in the same manner with other corporations and other property; and all this may be done, without ruining the institution, or destroying its national uses. Its profits will be diminished, by contributing to the revenue of the state; and this is the whole effect that ought, in a fair and liberal spirit of reasoning, to be anticipated. But, at all events, we show, on the part of the state, a clear, general, absolute and unqualified right of taxation (with the exception stated); and protest against such a right being made to yield to implications and obscure constructions of indefinite clauses in the constitution. Such a right must not be defeated, by doubtful pretensions of power, or arguments of convenience or policy to the government; much less to a private corporation. It is not a little alarming, to trace the progress of this argument. 1. The power to raise the bank is founded on no provision of the constitution that has the most distant allusion to such an institution; there is not a word in that instrument that would suggest the idea of a bank, to the most fertile imagination; but the bank is created by implication and construction, made out by a very subtle course of reasoning; then, by another implication, raised on the former, the bank, this creature of construction, claims the right to enter the territory of a state, without its assent; to carry on its business, when it pleases, and where it pleases, against the will, and perhaps, in contravention of the policy, of the sovereign owner of the soil. Having such great success in the acquirement of implied rights, the experiment is now pushed further; and not contented with having obtained two rights in this extraordinary way, the fortunate adventurer assails the sovereignty of the state, and would strip from it its most vital and essential power. It is thus with the famous fig tree of India, whose branches shoot from the trunk to a considerable distance; then drop upon the earth, where they take root and become trees, from which also other branches shoot, and plant and propagate and extend themselves in the same way, until gradually a vast surface is covered, and everything perishes in the spreading shade.

What have we opposed to these doctrines, so just and reasonable? Distressing inconveniences, ingeniously contrived; supposed dangers;

fearful distrusts; anticipated violence and injustice from the states, and consequent ruin to the bank. A right to tax, is a right to destroy, is the whole amount of the argument, however varied by ingenuity, or embellished by eloquence. It is said, the states will abuse the power; and its exercise will produce infinite inconvenience and embarrassment to the bank. Now, if this were true, it cannot help our opponents; because, if the states have the power contended for, this court cannot take it from them, under the fear that they may abuse it; nor, indeed, for its actual abuse; and if they have it not, they may not use it, however moderately and discreetly. Nor is there any more force in the argument, that the bank property will be subjected to double or treble taxation. Each state will tax only the capital really employed in it; and it is always in the power of the bank, to show how its capital is distributed. But it is feared, the capital in a state may be taxed in gross; and the individual stockholders also taxed for the same stock. Is this common case of a double taxation of the same article, to be a cause of alarm now? Our revenue laws abound with similar cases; they arise out of the very nature of our double government. So says the Federalist; and it is the first time it has been the ground of complaint. Poll taxes are paid to the federal and state governments; licenses to retail spirits; land taxes; and the whole round of internal duties, over which both governments have a concurrent, and, until now, it was supposed, a co-equal right. Were not the state banks taxed by the federal, and also by the state governments; in some, by a *bonus* for the charter; in others, directly and annually? The circumstance, that the taxes go to different governments, in these cases, is wholly immaterial to those who pay; unless it is, that it increases the danger of excess and oppression. It is justly remarked, on this subject, by the Federalist, that our security from excessive burdens on any source of revenue, must be found in mutual forbearance and discretion in the use of the power; this is the only security, and the authority of this court can add nothing to it. When that fails, there is an end to the confederation, which is founded on a reasonable and honorable confidence in each other.

It has been most impressively advanced, that the states, under pretence of taxing, may prohibit and expel the banks; that in the full exercise of this power, they may tax munitions of war; ships, about to sail, and armies on their march; nay, the spirit of the court is to be aroused by the fear that judicial proceedings will also come under this all-destroying power. Loans may be delayed for stamps, and the country ruined for the want of the money. But whenever the states shall be in a disposition to uproot the general government, they will take more direct and speedy means; and until they have this disposition, they will not use these. What power may not be abused; and whom or what shall we trust, if we guard ourselves with this extreme caution? The common and daily intercourse between man and man; all our relations in society, depend upon a reasonable confidence in each other. It is peculiarly the basis of our confederation, which lives not a moment, after we shall cease to trust each other. If the two governments are to regard each other as enemies, seeking opportunities of injury and distress, they will not long continue friends. This sort of timid reasoning about the powers of the government, has not escaped the authors so often alluded to; who, in their 31st number, treat it very properly. Surely, the argument is as strong against giving to the United States the power to incorporate a bank with branches. What may be more easily, or more extensively abused; and what more powerful engine can we imagine to be brought into operation against the revenues and rights of the states? If the federal government must have a bank for the purposes of its revenue, all collision will be avoided, by establishing the parent bank in its own district, where it holds an exclusive jurisdiction; and planting its branches in such states as shall assent to it; and using state banks, where such assent cannot be ob-

tained. Speaking practically, and by our experience, it may be safely asserted, that all the uses of the bank to the government might be thus obtained. Nothing would be wanting but profits and large dividends to the stockholders, which are the real object in this contest. Whatever may be the right of the United States to establish a bank, it cannot be better than that of the states. Their lawful power to incorporate such institutions has never yet been questioned; whatever may be in reserve for them, when it may be found "necessary and proper" for the interests of the national bank to crush the state institutions, and curtail the state authority. Granting, that these rights are equal in the two governments; and that the sovereignty of the state, within its territory, over this subject, is but equal to that of the United States; and that all sovereign power remains undiminished in the states, except in those cases in which it has, by the constitution, been expressly and exclusively transferred to the United States; the sovereign power of taxation (except on foreign commerce) being, in the language of the Federalist, co-equal to the two governments; it follows, as a direct and necessary consequence, that having equal powers to erect banks, and equal powers of taxation on property of that description, being neither imports, exports or tonnage, whatever jurisdiction the federal government may exercise in this respect, over a bank created by a state, any state may exercise over a bank created by the United States. Now, the federal government has assumed the right of taxing the state banks, precisely in the manner in which the state of Maryland has proceeded against the Bank of the United States; and as this right has never been resisted or questioned, it may be taken to be admitted by both parties; and must be equal and common to both parties, or the fundamental principles of our confederation have been strangely mistaken, or are to be violently overthrown. It has also been suggested, that the bank may claim a protection from this tax, under that clause of the constitution, which prohibits the states from passing laws, which shall impair the obligation of contracts. The charter is said to be the contract between the government and the stockholders; and the interests of the latter will be injured by the tax which reduces their profits. Many answers offer themselves to this agreement. In the first place, the United States cannot, either by a direct law, or by a contract with a third party, take away any right from the states, not granted by the constitution; they cannot do, collaterally and by implication, what cannot be done directly. Their contracts must conform to the constitution, and not the constitution to their contracts. If, therefore, the states have, in some other way, parted with this right of taxation, they cannot be deprived of it, by a contract between other parties. Under this doctrine, the United States might contract away every right of every state; and any attempt to resist it, would be called a violation of the obligations of a contract. Again, the United States have no more right to violate contracts than the states, and surely, they never imagined they were doing so, when they taxed so liberally the stock of the state banks. Again, it might as well be said, that a tax on real estate, imposed after a sale of it, and not then perhaps contemplated, or new duties imposed on merchandise, after it is ordered, violate the contract between the vendor and the purchaser, and diminishes the value of the property. In fact, all contracts in relation to property, subject to taxation, are presumed to have in view the probability or possibility that they will be taxed; and the happening of the event never was imagined to interfere with the contract, or its lawful obligations.

The *Attorney-General*, for the plaintiff in error, argued: 1. That the power of congress to create a bank ought not now to be questioned, after its exercise ever since the establishment of the constitution, sanctioned by every department of the government: by the legislature, in the charter of the bank, and other laws connected with the incorporation; by the executive, in its assent to those laws; and by the judiciary, in carrying them into effect. After a lapse of time, and so many concurrent acts of the public authorities, this exercise of power must be considered as ratified by the voice of the people, and sanctioned by precedent. In the exercise of criminal judicature, the question of constitutionality could not have been overlooked by the courts, who have so often inflicted punishment for acts which would be no crimes, if these laws were repugnant to the fundamental law.

2. The power to establish such a corporation is implied, and involved in the grant of specific powers in the constitution; because the end involves the means necessary to carry it into effect. A power without the means to use it, is a nullity. But we are not driven to seek for this power in implication: because the constitution, after enumerating certain specific powers, expressly gives to congress the power "to make all laws which shall be necessary and proper for carrying into execution the foregoing powers, and all other powers vested by this constitution in the government of the United States, or in any department or officer thereof." If, therefore, the act of congress establishing the bank was necessary and proper to carry into execution any one or more of the enumerated powers, the authority to pass it is expressly delegated to congress by the constitution. We contend, that it was necessary and proper to carry into execution several of the enumerated powers, such as the powers of levying and collecting taxes throughout this widely-extended empire; of paying the public debts, both in the United States and in foreign countries; of borrowing money, at home and abroad; of regulating commerce with foreign nations, and among the several states; of raising and supporting armies and a navy; and of carrying on war. That banks, dispersed throughout the country, are appropriate means of carrying into execution all these powers, cannot be denied. Our history furnishes abundant experience of the utility of a national bank as an instrument of finance. It will be found in the aid derived to the public cause from the Bank of North America, established by congress, during the war of the revolution; in the great utility of the former Bank of the United States; and in the necessity of resorting to the instrumentality of the banks incorporated by the states, during the interval between the expiration of the former charter of the United States Bank, in 1811, and the establishment of the present bank in 1816; a period of war, the calamities of which were greatly aggravated by the want of this convenient instrument of finance. Nor is it required, that the power of establishing such a moneyed corporation should be indispensably necessary to the execution of any of the specified powers of the government. An interpretation of this clause of the constitution, so strict and literal, would render every law which could be passed by congress unconstitutional; for of no particular law can it be predicated, that it is absolutely and indispensably necessary to carry into effect any of the specified powers; since a different law might be imagined, which could be enacted, tending to the same object, though not equally well adapted to attain it. As the inevitable consequence of giving this very restricted sense to the word "necessary," would be to annihilate the very powers it professes to create; and as so gross an absurdity cannot be imputed to the framers of the constitution, this interpretation must be rejected.

Another not less inadmissible consequence of this construction is, that it is fatal to the permanency of the constitutional powers; it makes them dependent for their being, on extrinsic circumstances, which, as these are perpetually shifting and changing, must produce correspondent changes in the essence of the powers on which they depend. But surely, the constitutionality of any act of congress cannot depend upon such circumstances. They are the subject of legislative discretion, not of judicial cognisance. Nor does this position conflict with the doctrine of the court in *Sturges v. Crowninshield* (*ante*, p. 122). The court has not said, in that case, that the powers of congress are shifting powers, which may or may not be constitutionally exercised, according to extrinsic or temporary circumstances; but it has merely determined, that the power of the state legislatures over the subject of bankruptcies is subordinate to that of congress on the same subject, and cannot be exercised so as to conflict with the uniform laws of bankruptcy throughout the Union which congress may establish. The power, in this instance, resides permanently in congress, whether it chooses to exercise it or not; but its exercise on the part of the states is precarious, and dependent, in certain respects, upon its actual exercise by congress. The convention well knew that it was utterly vain and nugatory, to give to congress certain specific powers, without the means of enforcing those powers. The auxiliary means, which are necessary for this purpose, are those which are useful and appropriate to produce the particular end. "Necessary and proper" are, then, equivalent to needful and adapted; such is the popular sense in which the word necessary is sometimes used. That use of it is confirmed by the best authorities among lexicographers; among other definitions of the word "necessary," Johnson gives "needful;" and he defines "need," the root of the latter, by the words, "want, occasion." Is a law, then, wanted, is there occasion for it, in order to carry into execution any of the enumerated powers of the national government; congress has the power of passing it. To make a law constitutional, nothing more is necessary than that it should be fairly adapted to carry into effect some specific power given to congress. This is the only interpretation which can give effect to this vital clause of the constitution; and being consistent with the rules of the language, is not to be rejected, because there is another interpretation, equally consistent with the same rules, but wholly inadequate to convey what must have been the intention of the convention. Among the multitude of means to carry into execution the powers expressly given to the national government, congress is to select, from time to time, such as are most fit for the purpose. It would have been impossible to enumerate them all in the constitution; and a specification of some, omitting others, would have been wholly useless. The court, in inquiring whether congress had made a selection of constitutional means, is to compare the law in question with the powers it is intended to carry into execution; not in order to ascertain whether other or better means might have been selected, for that is the legislative province, but to see whether those which have been chosen have a natural connection with any specific power; whether they are adapted to give it effect; whether they are appropriate means to an end. It cannot be denied, that this is the character of the Bank of the United States. But it is said, that the government might use private bankers, or the banks incorporated by the states, to carry on their fiscal operations. This, however, presents a mere question of political expediency, which, it is repeated, is exclusively for legislative consideration; which has been determined by the legislative wisdom; and cannot be reviewed by the court.

It is objected, that this act creates a corporation; which, being an exercise of a fundamental power of sovereignty, can only be claimed by congress, under their grant of specific powers. But to have enumerated the power of establishing corporations, among the specific powers of congress, would have been to change the whole plan of the constitution; to destroy its simplicity, and load it with all the complex details of a code of private jurisprudence. The power of establishing corporations is not one of the ends of government; it is only a class of means for accomplishing its ends. An enumeration of this particular class of means, omitting all others, would have been a useless anomaly in the constitution. It is admitted, that this is an act to sovereignty, and so is any other law; if the authority of establishing corporations be a sovereign power, the United States are sovereign, as to all the powers specifically given to their government, and as to all others necessary and proper to carry into effect those specified. If the power of chartering a corporation be necessary and proper for this purpose, congress has it to an extent as ample as any other sovereign legislature. Any government of limited sovereignty can create corporations only with reference to the limited powers that government possesses. The inquiry then reverts, whether the power of incorporating a banking company, be a necessary and proper means of executing the specific powers of the national government. The immense powers incontestably given, show that there was a disposition, on the part of the people, to give ample means to carry those powers into effect. A state can create a corporation, in virtue of its sovereignty, without any specific authority for that purpose, conferred in the state constitutions. The United States are sovereign as to certain specific objects, and may, therefore, erect a corporation for the purpose of effecting those objects. If the incorporating power had been expressly granted as an end, it would have conferred a power not intended; if granted as a means, it would have conferred nothing more than was before given by necessary implication.

Nor does the rule of interpretation we contend for, sanction any usurpation, on the part of the national government; since, if the argument be, that the implied powers of the constitution may be assumed and exercised, for purposes not really connected with the powers specifically granted, under color of some imaginary relation between them, the answer is, that this is nothing more than arguing from the abuse of constitutional powers, which would equally apply against the use of those that are confessedly granted to the national government; that the danger of the abuse will be checked by the judicial department, which, by comparing the means with the proposed end, will decide, whether the connection is real, or assumed as the pretext for the usurpation of powers not belonging to the government; and that, whatever may be the magnitude of the danger from this quarter, it is not equal to that of annihilating the powers of the government, to which the opposite doctrine would inevitably tend.

3. If, then, the establishment of the parent bank itself be constitutional, the right to establish the branches of that bank in the different states of the Union follows, as an incident of the principal power. The expediency of this ramification, congress is alone to determine. To confine the operation of the bank to the district of Columbia, where congress has the exclusive power of legislation, would be as absurd as to confine the courts of the United States to this district. Both institutions are wanted, wherever the administration of justice, or of the revenue, is wanted. The right, then, to establish these branches, is a necessary part of the means. This right is not delegated by congress to the parent bank. The act of congress for the establishment of offices of discount and deposit, leaves the time and place of their establishment to the directors, as a matter of detail. When established, they rest, not on the authority of the parent bank, but on the authority of congress.

4. The only remaining question is, whether the act of the state of Maryland, for taxing the bank thus incorporated, be repugnant to the constitution of the United States? We insist, that any such tax, by authority of a state, would be unconstitutional, and that this act is so, from its peculiar provisions. But it is objected, that, by the 10th amendment of the constitution, all powers not expressly delegated to the United States, nor prohibited to the states, are reserved to the latter. It is said, that this being neither delegated to the one, nor prohibited to the other, must be reserved: and it is also said, that the only prohibition on the power of state taxation, which does exist, excludes this case, and thereby leaves it to the original power of the states. The only prohibition is, as to laying any imposts, or duties on imports and exports, or tonnage duty, and this, not being a tax of that character, is said not to be within the terms of the prohibition; and consequently,

it remains under the authority of the states. But we answer, that this does not contain the whole sum of constitutional restrictions on the authority of the states. There is another clause in the constitution, which has the effect of a prohibition on the exercise of their authority, in numerous cases. The 6th article of the constitution of the United States declares, that the laws made in pursuance of it, "shall be the supreme law of the land, anything in the constitution, or laws of any state to the contrary notwithstanding." By this declaration, the states are prohibited from passing any acts which shall be repugnant to a law of the United States. The court has already instructed us in the doctrine, that there are certain powers, which, from their nature, are exclusively vested in congress.[4] So, we contend here, that the only ground on which the constitutionality of the bank is maintainable, excludes all interference with the exercise of the power by the states. This ground is, that the bank, as ordained by congress, is an instrument to carry into execution its specified powers; and in order to enable this instrument to operate effectually, it must be under the direction of a single head. It cannot be interfered with, or controlled in any manner, by the states, without putting at hazard the accomplishment of the end, of which it is but a means. But the asserted power to tax any of the institutions of the United States, presents directly the question of the supremacy of their laws over the state laws. If this power really exists in the states, its natural and direct tendency is to annihilate any power which belongs to congress, whether express or implied. All the powers of the national government are to be executed in the states, and throughout the states; and if the state legislatures can tax the instruments by which those powers are executed, they may entirely defeat the execution of the powers. If they may tax an institution of finance, they may tax the proceedings in the courts of the United States. If they may tax to one degree, they may tax to any degree; and nothing but their own discretion can impose a limit upon this exercise of their authority. They may tax both the bank and the courts, so as to expel them from the states. But, surely, the framers of the constitution did not intend, that the exercise of all the powers of the national government should depend upon the discretion of the state governments. This was the vice of the former confederation, which it was the object of the new constitution to eradicate. It is a direct collision of powers between the two governments. Congress says, there shall be a branch of the bank in the state of Maryland; that state says, there shall not. Which power is supreme? Besides, the charter, which is a contract between the United States and the corporation, is violated by this act of Maryland. A new condition is annexed by a sovereignty which was no party to the contract. The franchise, or corporate capacity, is taxed by a legislature, between whom and the object of taxation there is no political connection.

Jones, for the defendants in error, contended: 1. That this was to be considered as an open question, inasmuch as it had never before been submitted to judicial determination. The practice of the government, however inveterate, could never be considered as sanctioning a manifest usurpation; still less, could the practice, under a constitution of a date so recent, be put in competition with the contemporaneous exposition of its illustrious authors, as recorded for our instruction, in the "Letters of Publius," or the Federalist. The interpretation of the constitution, which was contended for by the state of Maryland, would be justified from that text-book, containing a commentary, such as no other age or nation furnishes, upon its public law.

It is insisted, that the constitution was formed and adopted, not by the people of the United States at large, but by the people of the respective states. To suppose, that the mere proposition of this fundamental law threw the American people into one aggregate mass, would be to assume what the instrument itself does not profess to establish. It is, therefore, a compact between the states, and all the powers which are not expressly relinquished by it, are reserved to the states. We admit, that the 10th amendment to the constitution is merely declaratory; that it was adopted *ex abundanti cautela;* and that with it, nothing more is reserved, than would have been reserved without it. But it is contended, on the other side, that not only the direct powers, but all incidental powers, partake of the supreme power, which is sovereign. This is an inherent sophism in the opposite argument, which depends on the conversion and ambiguity of terms. What is meant by sovereign power? It is modified by the terms of the grant under which it was given. They do not import sovereign power, generally, but sovereign power, limited to particular cases; and the question again recurs, whether sovereign power was given in this particular case. Is it true, that by conferring sovereign powers on a limited, delegated government, sovereign means are also granted? Is there no restriction as to the means of exercising a general power? Sovereignty was vested in the former confederation, as fully as in the present national government. There was nothing which forbade the old confederation from taxing the people, except that three modes of raising revenue were pointed out, and they could resort to no other. All the powers given to congress, under that system, except taxation, operated as directly on the people, as the powers given to the present government. The constitution does not profess to prescribe the ends merely for which the government was instituted, but also to detail the most important means by which they were to be accomplished. "To levy and collect taxes," "to borrow money," "to pay the public debts," "to raise and support armies," "to provide and maintain a navy," are not the ends for which this or any other just government is established. If a banking corporation can be said to be involved in either of these means, it must be as an instrument to collect taxes, to borrow money, and to pay the public debts. Is it such an instrument? It may, indeed, facilitate the operation of other financial institutions; but in its proper and natural character, it is a commercial institution, a partnership, incorporated for the purpose of carrying on the trade of banking. But we contend, that the government of the United States must confine themselves, in the collection and expenditure of revenue, to the means which are specifically enumerated in the constitution, or such auxiliary means as are naturally connected with the specific means. But what natural connection is there between the collection of taxes, and the incorporation of a company of bankers? Can it possibly be said, that because congress is invested with the power of raising and supporting armies, that it may give a charter of monopoly to a trading corporation, as a bounty for enlisting men? Or that, under its more analogous power of regulating commerce, it may establish an East or a West India company, with the exclusive privilege of trading with those parts of the world? Can it establish a corporation of farmers of the revenue, or burden the internal industry of the states with vexatious monopolies of their staple productions? There is an obvious distinction between those means which are incidental to the particular power, which follow as a corollary from it, and those which may be arbitrarily assumed as convenient to the execution of the power, or usurped under the pretext of necessity.

For example, the power of coining money implies the power of establishing a mint. The power of laying and collecting taxes implies the power of regulating the mode of assessment and collection, and of appointing revenue officers; but it does not imply the power of establishing a great banking corporation, branching out into every district of the country, and inundating it with a flood of paper-money. To derive such a tremendous authority from implication, would be to change the subordinate into fundamental powers; to make the implied powers greater than those which are expressly granted; and to change the whole scheme and theory of the government. It is well known, that many of the powers which are expressly granted to the national government in the constitution, were most reluctantly conceded by the people, who were lulled into confidence, by the assurances of its advocates, that it contained no latent ambiguity, but was to be limited to the literal terms of the grant: and in order to quiet all alarm, the 10th article of amendments was added, declaring "that the powers not delegated to the United States by the constitution, nor prohibited by it to the states, are reserved to the states respectively, or to the people." It would seem, that human language could not furnish words less liable to misconstruction! But it is contended, that the powers expressly granted to the national government in the constitution, are enlarged to an indefinite extent, by the sweeping clause, authorizing congress to make all laws which shall be necessary and proper for carrying into execution the powers expressly delegated to the national government, or any of its departments or officers. Now, we insist, that this clause shows that the intention of the convention was, to define the powers of the government with the utmost precision and accuracy. The creation of a sovereign legislature, implies an authority to pass laws to execute its given powers. This clause is nothing more than a declaration of the authority of congress to make laws, to execute the powers expressly granted to it, and the other departments of the government. But the laws which they are authorized to make, are to be such as are necessary and proper for this purpose. No terms could be found in the language, more absolutely excluding a general and unlimited discretion than these. It is not "necessary or proper," but "necessary and proper." The means used must have both these qualities. It must be, not merely convenient—fit—adapted—proper, to the accomplishment of the end in view; it must likewise be necessary for the accomplishment of that end. Many means may be proper, which are not necessary; because the end may be attained without them. The word "necessary," is said to be a synonyme of "needful." But both these words are defined "indispensably requisite;" and, most certainly, this is the sense in which the word "necessary" is used in the constitution. To give it a more lax sense, would be to alter the whole character of the government as a sovereignty of limited powers. This is not a purpose for which violence should be done to the obvious and natural sense of any terms, used in an instrument drawn up with great simplicity, and with extraordinary precision. The only question, then, on this branch of the argument, will be, whether the establishment of a banking corporation be indispensably requisite to execute any of the express powers of the government? So far as the interest of the United States is concerned, as partners of this company of bankers, or so far as the corporation may be regarded as an executive officer of the government, acquiring real and personal property in trust for the use of the government, it may be asked, what right the United States have to acquire property of any kind, except that purchased by the consent of the legislature of the state in which such property may be, for the erection of forts, magazines, &c.; and ships or munitions of war, constructed or purchased by the United States, and the public treasure? Their right of acquiring property is absolutely limited to the subjects specified, which were the only means, of the nature of wealth or property, with which the people thought it necessary to invest them. The people never intended they should become bankers or traders of any description. They meant to leave to the states the power of regulating the trade of banking, and every other species of internal industry; subject merely to the power of congress to regulate foreign commerce, and the commerce between the different states, with which it is not pretended, that this asserted power is connected. The trade of banking, within the particular states, would then either be left to regulate itself, and carried on as a branch of private trade, as it is in many countries; or banking companies would be incorporated by the state legislatures to carry it on, as has been the usage of this country. But in either case, congress would have nothing to do with the subject. The power of creating corporations is a distinct sovereign power, applicable to a great variety of objects, and not being expressly granted to congress for this, or any other object, cannot be assumed by implication. If it might be assumed for this purpose, it might also be exercised to create corporations for the purpose of constructing roads and canals; a power to construct which has been also lately discovered among other secrets of the constitution, developed by this dangerous doctrine of implied powers. Or it might be exercised to establish great trading monopolies, or to lock up the property of the country in mortmain, by some strained connection between the exercise of such powers, and those expressly given to the government.

3. Supposing the establishment of such a banking corporation, to be implied as one of the means necessary and proper to execute the powers expressly granted to the national government, it is contended by the counsel opposed to us, that its property is exempted from taxation by the state governments, because they cannot interfere with the exercise of any of the powers, express or implied, with which congress is invested. But the radical vice of this argument is, that the taxing power of the states, as it would exist, independent of the constitution, is in no respect limited or controlled by that supreme law, except in the single case of imposts and tonnage duties, which the states cannot lay, unless for the purpose of executing their inspection laws. But their power of taxation is absolutely unlimited in every other respect. Their power to tax the property of this corporation cannot be denied, without at the same time denying their right to tax any property of the United States. The property of the bank cannot be more highly privileged than that of the government. But they are not forbidden from taxing the property of the government, and therefore, cannot be constructively prohibited from taxing that of the bank. Being prohibited from taxing exports and imports, and tonnage, and left free from any other prohibition, in this respect; they may tax everything else but exports, imports and tonnage. The authority of "the Federalist" is express, that the taxing power of congress does not exclude that of the states over any other objects except these. If, then, the exercise of the taxing power of congress does not exclude that of the states, why should the exercise of any other power by congress, exclude the power of taxation by the states? If an express power will not exclude it, shall an implied power have that effect? If a power of the same kind will not exclude it, shall a power of a different kind? The unlimited power of taxation results from state sovereignty. It is expressly taken away only in the particular instances mentioned. Shall others be added by implication? Will it be pretended, that there are two species of sovereignty in our government? Sovereign power is absolute, as to the objects to which it may be applied. But the sovereign power of taxation in the states may be applied to all other objects, except imposts and tonnage: its exercise cannot, therefore, be limited and controlled by the exercise of another sovereign power in congress. The right of both sovereignties are co-equal and co-extensive. The trade of banking may be taxed by the state of Maryland; the United States may incorporate a company to carry on the trade of banking, which may establish a branch in Maryland; the exercise of the one sovereign power, cannot be controlled by the exercise of the other. It can no more be controlled in this case, than if it were the power of taxation in congress, which was interfered with by the power of taxation in the state, both being exerted concurrently on the same object. In both cases, mutual confidence, discretion and forbearance can alone qualify the exercise of the conflicting powers, and prevent the destruction of either. This is an anomaly, and perhaps an imperfection, in our system of government. But neither congress, nor this court, can correct it. That system was established by reciprocal concessions and compromises between the state and federal governments; its harmo-

ny can only be maintained in the same spirit. Even admitting that the property of the United States (such as they have a right to hold), their forts and dock-yards, their ships and military stores, their archives and treasures, public institutions of war, or revenue or justice, are exempt, by necessary implication, from state taxation; does it, therefore, follow, that this corporation, which is a partnership of bankers, is also exempt? They are not collectors of the revenue, any more than any state bank or foreign bankers, whose agency the government may find it convenient to employ as depositaries of its funds. They may be employed to remit those funds from one place to another, or to procure loans, or to buy and sell stock; but it is in a commercial, and not an administrative character, that they are thus employed. The corporate character with which these persons are clothed, does not exempt them from state taxation. It is the nature of their employment, as agents or officers of the government, if anything, which must create the exemption. But the same employment of the state bank or private bankers, would equally entitle them to the same exemption. Nor can the exemption of the stock of this corporation from state taxation, be claimed on the ground of the proprietary interest which the United States have in it as stockholders. Their interest is undistinguishably blended with the general capital stock; if they will mix their funds with those of bankers, or engage as partners in any other branch of commerce, their sovereign character and dignity are lost in the mercantile character which they have assumed; and their property thus employed becomes subject to local taxation, like other capital employed in trade.

Martin, Attorney-General of Maryland.—1. Read several extracts from the Federalist, and the debates of the Virginia and New York conventions, to show that the contemporary exposition of the constitution, by its authors, and by those who supported its adoption, was wholly repugnant to that now contended for by the counsel for the plaintiff in error. That it was then maintained, by the enemies of the constitution, that it contained a vast variety of powers, lurking under the generality of its phraseology, which would prove highly dangerous to the liberties of the people, and the rights of the states, unless controlled by some declaratory amendment, which should negative their existence. This apprehension was treated as a dream of distempered jealousy. The danger was denied to exist; but to provide an assurance against the possibility of its occurrence, the 10th amendment was added to the constitution. This, however, could be considered as nothing more than declaratory of the sense of the people as to the extent of the powers conferred on the new government. We are now called upon to apply that theory of interpretation, which was then rejected by the friends of the new constitution, and we are asked to engraft upon it powers of vast extent, which were disclaimed by them, and which if they had been fairly avowed at the time, would have prevented its adoption. Before we do this, they must, at least, be proved to exist, upon a candid examination of this instrument, as if it were now, for the first time, submitted to interpretation. Although we cannot, perhaps, be allowed to say, that the states have been "deceived in their grant;" yet we may justly claim something like a rigorous demonstration of this power, which nowhere appears upon the face of the constitution, but which is supposed to be tacitly inculcated in its general object and spirit. That the scheme of the framers of the constitution, intended to leave nothing to implication, will be evident, from the consideration, that many of the powers expressly given are only means to accomplish other powers expressly given. For example, the power to declare war involves, by necessary implication, if anything was to be implied, the powers of raising and supporting armies, and providing and maintaining a navy, to prosecute the war then declared. So also, as money is the sinew of war, the powers of laying and collecting taxes, and of borrowing money, are involved in that of declaring war. Yet all these powers are specifically enumerated. If, then, the convention has specified some powers, which being only means to accomplish the ends of government, might have been taken by implication; by what just rule of construction, are other sovereign powers, equally vast and important, to be assumed by implication? We insist, that the only safe rule is, the plain letter of the constitution; the rule which the constitutional legislators themselves have prescribed in the 10th amendment, which is merely declaratory; that the powers not delegated to the United States, nor prohibited to the states, are reserved to the states respectively, or to the people. The power of establishing corporations is not delegated to the United States, nor prohibited to the individual states. It is, therefore, reserved to the states, or to the people. It is not expressly delegated, either as an end, or a means, of national government. It is not to be taken by implication, as a means of executing any or all of the powers expressly granted; because other means, not more important or more sovereign in their character, are expressly enumerated. We still insist, that the authority of establishing corporations is one of the great sovereign powers of government. It may well exist in the state governments, without being expressly conferred in the state constitutions; because those governments have all the usual powers which belong to every political society, unless expressly forbidden, by the letter of the state constitutions, from exercising them. The power of establishing corporations has been constantly exercised by the state governments, and no portion of it has been ceded by them to the government of the United States.

2. But admitting that congress has a right to incorporate a banking company, as one of the means necessary and proper to execute the specific powers of the national government; we insist, that the respective states have the right to tax the property of that corporation, within their territory; that the United States cannot, by such an act of incorporation, withdraw any part of the property within the state from the grasp of taxation. It is not necessary for us to contend, that any part of the public property of the United States, its munitions of war, its ships and treasure, are subject to state taxation. But if the United States hold shares in the stock of a private banking company, or any other trading company, their property is not exempt from taxation, in common with the other capital stock of the company; still less, can it communicate to the shares belonging to private stockholders, an immunity from local taxation. The right of taxation by the state, is co-extensive with all private property within the state. The interest of the United States in this bank is private property, though belonging to public persons. It is held by the government, as an undivided interest with private stockholders. It is employed in the same trade, subject to the same fluctuations of value, and liable to the same contingencies of profit and loss. The shares belonging to the United States, or of any other stockholders, are not subjected to direct taxation by the law of Maryland. The tax imposed, is a stamp tax upon the notes issued by a banking-house within the state of Maryland. Because the United States happen to be partially interested, either as dormant or active partners, in that house, is no reason why the state should refrain from laying a tax which they have, otherwise, a constitutional right to impose, any more than if they were to become interested in any other house of trade, which should issue its notes, or bills of exchange, liable to a stamp duty, by a law of the state. But it is said, that a right to tax, in this case, implies a right to destroy; that it is impossible to draw the line of discrimination between a tax fairly laid for the purposes of revenue, and one imposed for the purpose of prohibition. We answer, that the same objection would equally apply to the right of congress to tax the state banks; since the same difficulty of discriminating occurs in the exercise of that right. The whole of this subject of taxation is full of difficulties, which the convention found it im-

possible to solve, in a manner entirely satisfactory. The first attempt was to divide the subjects of taxation between the state and the national government. This being found impracticable or inconvenient, the state governments surrendered altogether their right to tax imports and exports, and tonnage; giving the authority to tax all other subjects to congress, but reserving to the states a concurrent right to tax the same subjects to an unlimited extent. This was one of the anomalies of the government, the evils of which must be endured, or mitigated by discretion and mutual forbearance. The debates in the state conventions show that the power of state taxation was understood to be absolutely unlimited, except as to imports and tonnage duties. The states would not have adopted the constitution, upon any other understanding. As to the judicial proceedings, and the custom-house papers of the United States, they are not property, by their very nature; they are not the subjects of taxation; they are the proper instruments of national sovereignty, essential to the exercise of its powers, and in legal contemplation altogether extra-territorial as to state authority.

Pinkney, for the plaintiff in error, in reply, stated: 1. That the cause must first be cleared of a question which ought not to have been forced into the argument—whether the act of congress establishing the bank was consistent with the constitution? This question depended both on authority and on principle. No topics to illustrate it could be drawn from the confederation, since the present constitution was as different from that, as light from darkness. The former was a mere federative league; an alliance offensive and defensive between the states, such as there had been many examples of in the history of the world. It had no power of coercion but by arms. Its radical vice, and that which the new constitution was intended to reform, was legislation upon sovereign states in their corporate capacity. But the constitution acts directly on the people, by means of powers communicated directly from the people. No state, in its corporate capacity, ratified it; but it was proposed for adoption to popular conventions. It springs from the people, precisely as the state constitution springs from the people, and acts on them in a similar manner. It was adopted by them in the geographical sections into which the country is divided. The federal powers are just as sovereign as those of the states. The state sovereignties are not the authors of the constitution of the United States. They are preceding in point of time, to the national sovereignty, but they are postponed to it, in point of supremacy, by the will of the people. The means of giving efficacy to the sovereign authorities vested by the people in the national government, are those adapted to the end; fitted to promote, and having a natural relation and connection with, the objects of that government. The constitution, by which these authorities, and the means of executing them, are given, and the laws made in pursuance of it, are declared to be the supreme law of the land; and they would have been such, without the insertion of this declaratory clause; they must be supreme, or they would be nothing. The constitutionality of the establishment of the bank, as one of the means necessary to carry into effect the authorities vested in the national government, is no longer an open question. It has been long since settled by decisions of the most revered authority, legislative, executive and judicial. A legislative construction, in a doubtful case, persevered in for a course of years, ought to be binding upon the court. This, however, is not a question of construction merely, but of political necessity, on which congress must decide. It is conceded, that a manifest usurpation cannot be maintained in this mode; but, we contend, that this is such a doubtful case, that congress may expound the nature and extent of the authority under which it acts, and that this practical interpretation had become incorporated into the constitution. There are two distinguishing points which entitle it to great respect. The first is, that it was a contemporaneous construction; the second is, that it was made by the authors of the constitution themselves. The members of the convention who framed the constitution, passed into the first congress, by which the new government was organized; they must have understood their own work. They determined that the constitution gave to congress the power of incorporating a banking company. It was not required, that this power should be expressed in the text of the constitution; it might safely be left to implication. An express authority to erect corporations generally, would have been perilous; since it might have been constructively extended to the creation of corporations entirely unnecessary to carry into effect the other powers granted; we do not claim an authority in this respect, beyond the sphere of the specific powers. The grant of an authority to erect certain corporations, might have been equally dangerous, by omitting to provide for others, which time and experience might show to be equally, and even more necessary. It is a historical fact, of great importance in this discussion, that amendments to the constitution were actually proposed, in order to guard against the establishment of commercial monopolies. But if the general power of incorporating did not exist, why seek to qualify it, or to guard against its abuse? The legislative precedent, established in 1791, has been followed up by a series of acts of congress, all confirming the authority. Political considerations alone might have produced the refusal to renew the charter in 1811; at any rate, we know that they mingled themselves in the debate, and the determination.

In 1815, a bill was passed by the two houses of congress, incorporating a national bank; to which the president refused his assent, upon political considerations only, waiving the question of constitutionality, as being settled by contemporaneous exposition, and repeated subsequent recognitions. In 1816, all branches of the legislature concurred in establishing the corporation, whose chartered rights are now in judgment before the court. None of these measures ever passed *sub silentio;* the proposed incorporation was always discussed, and opposed, and supported, on constitutional grounds, as well as on considerations of political expediency. Congress is *prima facie* a competent judge of its own constitutional powers. It is not, as in questions of privilege, the exclusive judge; but it must first decide, and that in a proper judicial character, whether a law is constitutional, before it is passed. It had an opportunity of exercising its judgment in this respect, upon the present subject, not only in the principal acts incorporating the former, and the present bank, but in the various incidental statutes subsequently enacted on the same subject; in all of which, the question of constitutionality was equally open to debate, but in none of which was it agitated.

There are, then, in the present case, the repeated determinations of the three branches of the national legislature, confirmed by the constant acquiescence of the state sovereignties, and of the people, for a considerable length of time. Their strength is fortified by judicial authority. The decisions in the courts, affirming the constitutionality of these laws, passed, indeed, *sub silentio;* but it was the duty of the judges, especially in criminal cases, to have raised the question; and we are to conclude, from this circumstance, that no doubt was entertained respecting it. And if the question be examined on principle, it will be found not to admit of doubt. Has congress, abstractedly, the authority to erect corporations? This authority is not more a sovereign power, than many other powers which are acknowledged to exist, and which are but means to an end. All the objects of the government are national objects, and the means are, and must be, fitted to accomplish them. These objects are enumerated in the constitution, and have no limits but the constitution itself. A more perfect union is to be formed; justice to be established; domestic tranquillity insured; the common defence provided for; the general welfare promoted; the blessings of liberty secured to the present generation, and to posteri-

ty. For the attainment of these vast objects, the government is armed with powers and faculties corresponding in magnitude. Congress has power to lay and collect taxes and duties, imposts and excises; to pay the debts, and provide for the common defence and general welfare of the United States; to borrow money on the credit of the nation; to regulate commerce; to establish uniform naturalization and bankrupt laws; to coin money, and regulate the circulating medium, and the standard of weights and measures; to establish post-offices and post-roads; to promote the progress of science and the useful arts, by granting patents and copyrights; to constitute tribunals inferior to the supreme court, and to define and punish offences against the law of nations; to declare and carry on war; to raise and support armies, and to provide and maintain a navy; to discipline and govern the land and naval forces; to call forth the militia to execute the laws, suppress insurrections and repel invasions; to provide for organizing, arming and disciplining the militia; to exercise exclusive legislation, in all cases, over the district where the seat of government is established, and over such other portions of territory as may be ceded to the Union for the erection of forts, magazines, &c.; to dispose of, and make all needful rules and regulations respecting, the territory or other property belonging to the United States; and to make all laws which shall be necessary and proper for carrying into execution these powers, and all other powers vested in the national government, or any of its departments or officers. The laws thus made are declared to be the supreme law of the land; and the judges in every state are bound thereby, anything in the constitution or laws of any state to the contrary notwithstanding. Yet it is doubted, whether a government invested with such immense powers has authority to erect a corporation within the sphere of its general objects, and in order to accomplish some of those objects! The state powers are much less in point of magnitude, though greater in number; yet it is supposed, the states possess the authority of establishing corporations, whilst it is denied to the general government. It is conceded to the state legislatures, though not specifically granted, because it is said to be an incident of state sovereignty; but it is refused to congress, because it is not specifically granted, though it may be necessary and proper to execute the powers which are specifically granted. But the authority of legislation in the state government is not unlimited; there are several limitations to their legislative authority. First, from the nature of all government, especially, of republican government, in which the residuary powers of sovereignty, not granted specifically, by inevitable implication, are reserved to the people. Secondly, from the express limitations contained in the state constitutions. And thirdly, from the express prohibitions to the states contained in the United States constitution. The power of erecting corporations is nowhere expressly granted to the legislatures of the states in their constitutions; it is taken by necessary implication: but it cannot be exercised to accomplish any of the ends which are beyond the sphere of their constitutional authority. The power of erecting corporations is not an end of any government; it is a necessary means of accomplishing the ends of all governments. It is an authority inherent in, and incident to, all sovereignty.

The history of corporations will illustrate this position. They were transplanted from the Roman law into the common law of England, and all the municipal codes of modern Europe. From England, they were derived to this country. But in the civil law, a corporation could be created by a mere voluntary association of individuals. 1 Bl. Com. 471. And in England, the authority of parliament is not necessary to create a corporate body. The king may do it, and may communicate his power to a subject (1 Bl. Com. 474), so little is this regarded as a transcendent power of sovereignty, in the British constitution. So also, in our constitution, it ought to be regarded as but a subordinate power to carry into effect the great objects of government. The state governments cannot establish corporations to carry into effect the national powers given to congress, nor can congress create corporations to execute the peculiar duties of the state governments. But so much of the power or faculty of incorporation as concerns national objects has passed away from the state legislatures, and is vested in the national government. An act of incorporation is but a law, and laws are but means to promote the legitimate end of all government—the felicity of the people. All powers are given to the national government, as the people will. The reservation in the 10th amendment to the constitution, of "powers not delegated to the United States," is not confined to powers not expressly delegated. Such an amendment was indeed proposed; but it was perceived, that it would strip the government of some of its most essential powers, and it was rejected. Unless a specific means be expressly prohibited to the general government, it has it, within the sphere of its specified powers. Many particular means are, of course, involved in the general means necessary to carry into effect the powers expressly granted, and in that case, the general means become the end, and the smaller objects the means.

It was impossible for the framers of the constitution to specify, prospectively, all these means, both because it would have involved an immense variety of details, and because it would have been impossible for them to foresee the infinite variety of circumstances, in such an unexampled state of political society as ours, for ever changing and for ever improving. How unwise would it have been, to legislate immutably for exigencies which had not then occurred, and which must have been foreseen but dimly and imperfectly! The security against abuse is to be found in the constitution and nature of the government, in its popular character and structure. The statute book of the United States is filled with powers derived from implication. The power to lay and collect taxes will not execute itself. Congress must designate in detail all the means of collection. So also, the power of establishing post-offices and post-roads, involves that of punishing the offence of robbing the mail. But there is no more necessary connection between the punishment of mail-robbers, and the power to establish post-roads, than there is between the institution of a bank, and the collection of the revenue and payment of the public debts and expenses. So, light-houses, beacons, buoys and public piers, have all been established, under the general power to regulate commerce. But they are not indispensably necessary to commerce. It might linger on, without these aids, though exposed to more perils and losses. So, congress has authority to coin money, and to guard the purity of the circulating medium, by providing for the punishment of counterfeiting the current coin; but laws are also made for punishing the offence of uttering and passing the coin thus counterfeited. It is the duty of the court to construe the constitutional powers of the national government liberally, and to mould them so as to effectuate its great objects. Whence is derived the power to punish smuggling? It does not collect the impost, but it is a means more effectually to prevent the collection from being diminished in amount, by frauds upon the revenue laws. Powers, as means, may then be implied in many cases. And if so, why not in this case as well as any other?

The power of making all needful rules and regulations respecting the territory of the United States, is one of the specified powers of congress. Under this power, it has never been doubted, that congress had authority to establish corporations in the territorial governments. But this power is derived entirely from implication. It is assumed, as an incident to the principal power. If it may be assumed, in that case, upon the ground, that it is a necessary means of carrying into effect the power expressly granted, why may it not be assumed, in the present case, upon a similar ground? It is readily admitted, there must be a relation, in the nature and fitness of things between the means used and the end to be accomplished. But the question is, whether the necessity which will justify a resort to a certain means, must be an absolute, indispensable, inevitable necessity? The power of passing all laws necessary and proper to carry into effect the other powers specifically granted, is a political power; it is a matter of legislative discretion, and those who exercise it, have a wide range of choice in selecting means. In its exercise, the mind must compare means with each other. But absolute necessity excludes all choice; and therefore, it cannot be this species of necessity which is required. Congress alone has the fit means of inquiry and decision. The more or less of necessity never can enter as an ingredient into judicial decision. Even absolute necessity cannot be judged of here; still less, can practical necessity be determined in a judicial *forum*. The judiciary may, indeed, and must, see that what has been done is not a mere evasive pretext, under which the national legislature travels out of the prescribed bounds of its authority, and encroaches upon state sovereignty, or the rights of the people. For this purpose, it must inquire, whether the means assumed have a connection, in the nature and fitness of things, with the end to be accomplished. The vast variety of possible means, excludes the practicability of judicial determination as to the fitness of a particular means. It is sufficient, that it does not appear to be violently and unnaturally forced into the service, or fraudulently assumed, in order to usurp a new substantive power of sovereignty. A philological analysis of the terms "necessary and proper" will illustrate the argument. Compare these terms as they are used in that part of the constitution now in question, with the qualified manner in which they are used in the 10th section of the same article. In the latter, it is provided that "no state shall, without the consent of congress, lay any imposts or duties on imports or exports, except what may be absolutely necessary for executing its inspection laws." In the clause in question, congress is invested with the power "to make all laws which shall be necessary and proper for carrying into execution the foregoing powers," &c. There is here then, no qualification of the necessity; it need not be absolute; it may be taken in its ordinary grammatical sense. The word *necessary,* standing by itself, has no inflexible meaning; it is used in a sense more or less strict, according to the subject. This, like many other words, has a primitive sense, and another figurative and more relaxed; it may be qualified by the addition of adverbs of diminution or enlargement, such as very, indispensably, more, less, or absolutely necessary; which last is the sense in which it is used in the 10th section of this article of the constitution. But that it is not always used in this strict and rigorous sense, may be proved, by tracing its definition, and etymology in every human language.

If, then, all the powers of the national government are sovereign and supreme; if the power of incorporation is incidental, and involved in the others; if the degree of political necessity which will justify a resort to a particular means, to carry into execution the other powers of the government, can never be a criterion of judicial determination, but must be left to legislative discretion, it only remains to inquire, whether a bank has a natural and obvious connection with other express or implied powers, so as to become a necessary and proper means of carrying them into execution. A bank might be established as a branch of the public administration, without incorporation. The government might issue paper, upon the credit of the public faith, pledged for its redemption, or upon the credit of its property and funds. Let the office where this paper is issued be made a place of deposit for the money of individuals, and authorize its officers to discount, and a bank is created. It only wants the forms of incorporation. But, surely, it will not be pretended, that clothing it with these forms would make such an establishment unconstitutional. In the bank which is actually established and incorporated, the

United States are joint stockholders, and appoint joint directors; the secretary of the secretary of the treasury has a supervising authority over its affairs; it is bound, upon his requisition, to transfer the funds of the government wherever they may be wanted; it performs all the duties of commissioners of the loan-office; it is bound to loan the government a certain amount of money, on demand; its notes are receivable in payment for public debts and duties; it is intimately connected, according to the usage of the whole world, with the power of borrowing money, and with all the financial operations of the government. It has, also, a close connection with the power of regulating foreign commerce, and that between the different states. It provides a circulating medium, by which that commerce can be more conveniently carried on, and exchanges may be facilitated. It is true, there are state banks by which a circulating medium to a certain extent is provided. But that only diminishes the *quantum* of necessity, which is no criterion by which to test the constitutionality of a measure. It is also connected with the power of making all needful regulations for the government of the territory, "and other property of the United States." If they may establish a corporation to regulate their territory, they may establish one to regulate their property. Their treasure is their property, and may be invested in this mode. It is put in partnership; but not for the purpose of carrying on the trade of banking as one of the ends for which the government was established; but only as an instrument or means for executing its sovereign powers. This instrument could not be rendered effectual for this purpose, but by mixing the property of individuals with that of the public. The bank could not otherwise acquire a credit for its notes. Universal experience shows, that, if, altogether a government bank, it could not acquire, or would soon lose, the confidence of the community.

2. As to the branches, they are identical with the parent bank. The power to establish them is that species of subordinate power, wrapped up in the principal power, which congress may place at its discretion.

3. The last and greatest, and only difficult question in the cause, is that which respects the assumed right of the states to tax this bank, and its branches, thus established by congress? This is a question, comparatively of no importance to the individual states, but of vital importance to the Union. Deny this exemption to the bank as an instrument of government, and what is the consequence? There is no express provision in the constitution, which exempts any of the national institutions or property from state taxation. It is only by implication that the army and navy, and treasure, and judicature of the Union are exempt from state taxation. Yet they are practically exempt; and they must be, or it would be in the power of any one state to destroy their use. Whatever the United States have a right to do, the individual states have no right to undo. The power of congress to establish a bank, like its other sovereign powers, is supreme, or it would be nothing. Rising out of an exertion of paramount authority, it cannot be subject to any other power. Such a power in the states, as that contended for on the other side, is manifestly repugnant to the power of congress; since a power to establish, implies a power to continue and preserve.

There is a manifest repugnancy between the power of Maryland to tax, and the power of congress to preserve, this institution. A power to build up, what another may pull down at pleasure, is a power which may provoke a smile, but can do nothing else. This law of Maryland acts directly on the operations of the bank, and may destroy it. There is no limit or check in this respect, but in the discretion of the state legislature. That discretion cannot be controlled by the national councils. Whenever the local councils of Maryland will it, the bank must be expelled from that state. A right to tax, without limit or control, is essentially a power to destroy. If one national institu-

tion may be destroyed in this manner, all may be destroyed in the same manner. If this power to tax the national property and institutions exists in the state of Maryland, it is unbounded in extent. There can be no check upon it, either by congress, or the people of the other states. Is there then any intelligible, fixed, defined boundary of this taxing power? If any, it must be found in this court. If it does not exist here, it is a nonentity. But the court cannot say what is an abuse, and what is a legitimate use of the power. The legislative intention may be so masked, as to defy the scrutinizing eye of the court. How will the court ascertain, *a priori,* that the given amount of tax will crush the bank? It is essentially a question of political economy, and there are always a vast variety of facts bearing upon it. The facts may be mistaken. Some important considerations belonging to the subject may be kept out of sight; they must all vary with times and circumstances. The result, then, must determine, whether the tax is destructive. But the bank may linger on for some time, and that result cannot be known, until the work of destruction is consummated. A criterion which has been proposed, is to see whether the tax has been laid, impartially, upon the state banks, as well as the Bank of the United States. Even this is an unsafe test; for the state governments may wish, and intend, to destroy their own banks. The existence of any national institution ought not to depend upon so frail a security. But this tax is levelled exclusively at the branch of the United States Bank established in Maryland. There is, in point of fact, a branch of no other bank within that state, and there can legally be no other. It is a fundamental article of the state constitution of Maryland, that taxes shall operate on all the citizens impartially and uniformly, in proportion to their property, with the exception, however, of taxes laid for political purposes. This is a tax laid for a political purpose; for the purpose of destroying a great institution of the national government; and if it were not imposed for that purpose, it would be repugnant to the state constitution, as not being laid uniformly on all the citizens, in proportion to their property. So that the legislature cannot disavow this to be its object, without, at the same time, confessing a manifest violation of the state constitution. Compare this act of Maryland with that of Kentucky, which is yet to come before the court, and the absolute necessity of repressing such attempts in their infancy, will be evident. Admit the constitutionality of the Maryland tax, and that of Kentucky follows inevitably. How can it be said, that the office of discount and deposit in Kentucky cannot bear a tax of $60,000 *per annum,* payable monthly? Probably, it could not; but judicial certainty is essential; and the court has no means of arriving at that certainty. There is, then, here, an absolute repugnancy of power to power; we are not bound to show, that the particular exercise of the power in the present case is absolutely repugnant. It is sufficient, that the same power may be thus exercised.

There certainly may be some exceptions out of the taxing power of the states, other than those created by the taxing power of congress; because, if there were no implied exceptions, then, the navy, and other exclusive property of the United States, would be liable to state taxation. If some of the powers of congress, other than its taxing power, necessarily involve incompatibility with the taxing power of the states, this may be incompatible. This is incompatible; for a power to impose a tax *ad libitum* upon the notes of the bank, is a power to repeal the law, by which the bank was created. The bank cannot be useful, it cannot act at all, unless it issues notes. If the present tax does not disable the bank from issuing its notes, another may; and it is the authority itself which is questioned, as being entirely repugnant to the power which established and preserves the bank. Two powers thus hostile and incompatible cannot co-exist. There must be, in this case, an implied exception to the general taxing power of the states, because it is a tax upon the legislative faculty of congress, upon the national property, upon the national institutions. Because the taxing powers of the two governments are concurrent in some respects, it does not follow, that there may not be limitations on the taxing power of the states, other than those which are imposed by the taxing power of congress. Judicial proceedings are practically a subject of taxation in many countries, and in some of the states of this Union. The states are not expressly prohibited in the constitution, from taxing the judicial proceedings of the United States. Yet such a prohibition must be implied, or the administration of justice in the national courts might be obstructed by a prohibitory tax. But such a tax is no more a tax on the legislative faculty of congress than this. The branch bank in Maryland is as much an institution of the sovereign power of the Union, as the circuit court of Maryland. One is established in virtue of an express power; the other by an implied authority; but both are equal, and equally supreme. All the property and all the institutions of the United States are, constructively, without the local, territorial jurisdiction of the individual states, in every respect, and for every purpose, including that of taxation. This immunity must extend to this case, because the power of taxation imports the power of taxation for the purpose of prohibition and destruction. The immunity of foreign public vessels from the local jurisdiction, whether state or national, was established in the case of *The Exchange*, 7 Cranch 116, not upon positive municipal law, nor upon conventional law; but it was implied, from the usage of nations, and the necessity of the case. If, in favor of foreign governments, such an edifice of exemption has been built up, independent of the letter of the constitution, or of any other written law, shall not a similar edifice be raised on the same foundations, for the security of our own national government? So also, the jurisdiction of a foreign power, holding a temporary possession of a portion of national territory, is nowhere provided for in the constitution; but is derived from inevitable implication. *United States v. Rice* (*ante*, p. 246). These analogies show, that there may be exemptions from state jurisdiction, not detailed in the constitution, but arising out of general considerations. If congress has power to do a particular act, no state can impede, retard or burden it. Can there be a stronger ground, to infer a cessation of state jurisdiction?

The Bank of the United States is as much an instrument of the government for fiscal purposes, as the courts are its instruments for judicial purposes. They both proceed from the supreme power, and equally claim its protection. Though every state in the Union may impose a stamp tax, yet no state can lay a stamp tax upon the judicial proceedings or custom-house papers of the United States. But there is no such express exception to the general taxing power of the states contained in the constitution. It arises from the general nature of the government, and from the principle of the supremacy of the national powers, and the laws made to execute them, over the state authorities and state laws.

It is objected, however, that the act of congress, incorporating the bank, withdraws property from taxation by the state, which would be otherwise liable to state taxation. We answer, that it is immaterial, if it does thus withdraw certain property from the grasp of state taxation, if congress had authority to establish the bank, since the power of congress is supreme. But, in fact, it withdraws nothing from the mass of taxable property in Maryland, which that state could tax. The whole capital of the bank, belonging to private stockholders, is drawn from every state in the Union, and the stock belonging to the United States, previously constituted a part of the public treasure. Neither the stock belonging to citizens of other states, nor the privileged treasure of the United States, mixed up with this private property, were previously liable to taxation in Maryland; and as to the stock belonging to its own citizens, it still continues liable to state taxation, as a

portion of their individual property, in common with all the other private property in the state. The establishment of the bank, so far from withdrawing anything from taxation by the state, brings something into Maryland which that state may tax. It produces revenue to the citizens of Maryland, which may be taxed equally and uniformly, with all their other private property. The materials of which the ships of war, belonging to the United States, are constructed, were previously liable to state taxation. But the instant they are converted into public property, for the public defence, they cease to be subject to state taxation. So, here, the treasure of the United States, and that of individuals, citizens of Maryland, and of other states, are undistinguishably confounded in the capital stock of this great national institution, which, it has been before shown, could be made useful as an instrument of finance, in no other mode than by thus blending together the property of the government and of private merchants. This partnership is, therefore, one of necessity, on the part of the United States. Either this tax operates upon the franchise of the bank, or upon its property. If upon the former, then it comes directly in conflict with the exercise of a great sovereign authority of congress; if upon the latter, then it is a tax upon the property of the United States; since the law does not, and cannot, in imposing a stamp tax, distinguish their interest from that of private stockholders.

But it is said, that congress possesses and exercises the unlimited authority of taking the state banks; and therefore, the states ought to have an equal right to tax the Bank of the United States. The answer to this objection is, that, in taxing the state banks, the states in congress exercise their power of taxation. Congress exercises the power of the people; the whole acts on the whole. But the state tax is a part acting on the whole. Even if the two cases were the same, it would rather exempt the state banks from federal taxation, than subject the Bank of the United States to taxation by a particular state. But the state banks are not machines essential to execute the powers of the state sovereignties, and therefore, this is out of the question. The people of the United States, and the sovereignties of the several states, have no control over the taxing power of a particular state. But they have a control over the taxing power of the United States, in the responsibility of the members of the house of representatives to the people of the state which sends them, and of the senators, to the legislature by whom they are chosen. But there is no correspondent responsibility of the local legislature of Maryland, for example, to the people of the other states of the Union. The people of other states are not represented in the legislature of Maryland, and can have no control, directly or indirectly, over its proceedings. The legislature of Maryland is responsible only to the people of that state. The national government can withdraw nothing from the taxing power of the states, which is not for the purpose of national benefit and the common welfare, and within its defined powers. But the local interests of the states are in perpetual conflict with the interests of the Union; which shows the danger of adding power to the partial views and local prejudices of the states. If the tax imposed by this law be not a tax on the property of the United States, it is not a tax on any property; and it must, consequently, be a tax on the faculty or franchise. It is, then, a tax on the legislative faculty of the Union, on the charter of the bank. It imposes a stamp duty upon the notes of the bank, and thus stops the very source of its circulation and life. It is as much a direct interference with the legislative faculty of congress, as would be a tax on patents, or copyrights, or custom-house papers or judicial proceedings.

Since, then, the constitutional government of this republican empire cannot be practically enforced, so as to secure the permanent glory, safety and felicity of this great country, but by a fair and liberal interpretation of its powers; since those powers could not all be expressed in the constitution, but many of them must be taken by implication; since the sovereign powers of the Union are supreme, and, wherever they come in direct conflict and repugnancy with those of the state governments, the latter must give way; since it has been proved, that this is the case as to the institution of the bank, and the general power of taxation by the states; since this power unlimited and unchecked, as it necessarily must be, by the very nature of the subject, is absolutely inconsistent with, and repugnant to, the right of the United States to establish a national bank; if the power of taxation be applied to the corporate property, or franchise, or property of the bank, and might be applied in the same manner, to destroy any other of the great institutions and establishments of the Union, and the whole machine of the national government might be arrested in its motions, by the exertion, in other cases, of the same power which is here attempted to be exerted upon the bank: no other alternative remains, but for this court to interpose its authority, and save the nation from the consequences of this dangerous attempt.

March 7th, 1819. MARSHALL, CH. J., *delivered the opinion of the court.*

—In the case now to be determined, the defendant, a sovereign state, denies the obligation of a law enacted by the legislature of the Union, and the plaintiff, on his part, contests the validity of an act which has been passed by the legislature of that state. The constitution of our country, in its most interesting and vital parts, is to be considered; the conflicting powers of the government of the Union and of its members, as marked in that constitution, are to be discussed; and an opinion given, which may essentially influence the great operations of the government. No tribunal can approach such a question without a deep sense of its importance, and of the awful responsibility involved in its decision. But it must be decided peacefully, or remain a source of hostile legislation, perhaps, of hostility of a still more serious nature; and if it is to be so decided, by this tribunal alone can the decision be made. On the supreme court of the United States has the constitution of our country devolved this important duty.

The first question made in the cause is—has congress power to incorporate a bank? It has been truly said, that this can scarcely be considered as an open question, entirely unprejudiced by the former proceedings of the nation respecting it. The principle now contested was introduced at a very early period of our history, has been recognised by many successive legislatures, and has been acted upon by the judicial department, in cases of peculiar delicacy, as a law of undoubted obligation.

It will not be denied, that a bold and daring usurpation might be resisted, after an acquiescence still longer and more complete than this. But it is conceived, that a doubtful question, one on which human reason may pause, and the human judgment be suspended, in the decision of which the great principles of liberty are not concerned, but the respective powers of those who are equally the representatives of the people, are to be adjusted; if not put at rest by the practice of the government, ought to receive a considerable impression from that practice. An exposition of the constitution, deliberately established by legislative acts, on the faith of which an immense property has been advanced, ought not to be lightly disregarded.

The power now contested was exercised by the first congress elected under the present constitution. The bill for incorporating the Bank of the United States did not steal upon an unsuspecting legislature, and pass unobserved. Its principle was completely understood, and was opposed with equal zeal and ability. After being resisted, first, in the fair and open field of debate, and afterwards, in the executive cabinet, with as much persevering talent as any measure has ever experienced, and being supported by arguments which convinced minds as pure and as intelligent as this country can boast, it became a law. The original act was permitted to expire; but a short experience of the embarrassments to which the refusal to revive it exposed the government, convinced those who were most prejudiced against the measure of its necessity, and induced the passage of the present law. It would require no ordinary share of intrepidity, to assert that a measure adopted under these circumstances, was a bold and plain usurpation, to which the constitution gave no countenance. These observations belong to the cause; but they are not made under the impression, that, were the question entirely new, the law would be found irreconcilable with the constitution.

In discussing this question, the counsel for the state of Maryland have deemed it of some importance, in the construction of the constitution, to consider that instrument, not as emanating from the people, but as the act of sovereign and independent states. The powers of the general government, it has been said, are delegated by the states, who alone are truly sovereign; and must be exercised in subordination to the states, who alone possess supreme dominion. It would be difficult to sustain this proposition. The convention which framed the constitution was indeed elected by the state legislatures. But the instrument, when it came from their hands, was a mere proposal, without obligation, or pretensions to it. It was reported to the then existing congress of the United States, with a request that it might "be submitted to a convention of delegates, chosen in each state by the people thereof, under the recommendation of its legislature, for their assent and ratification." This mode of proceeding was adopted; and by the convention, by congress, and by the state legislatures, the instrument was submitted to the *people*. They acted upon it in the only manner in which they can act safely, effectively and wisely, on such a subject, by assembling in convention. It is true, they assembled in their several states—and where else should they have assembled? No political dreamer was ever wild enough to think of breaking down the lines which separate the states, and of compounding the American people into one common mass. Of consequence, when they act, they act in their states. But the measures they adopt do not, on that account, cease to be the measures of the people themselves, or become the measures of the state governments.

From these conventions, the constitution derives its whole authority. The government proceeds directly from the people; is "ordained and established," in the name of the people; and is declared to be ordained, "in order to form a more perfect union, establish justice, insure domestic tranquillity, and secure the blessings of liberty to themselves and to their posterity." The assent of the states, in their sovereign capacity, is implied, in calling a convention, and thus submitting that instrument to the people. But the people were at perfect liberty to accept or reject it; and their act was final. It required not the affirmance, and could not be negatived, by the state governments. The constitution, when thus adopted, was of complete obligation, and bound the state sovereignties.

It has been said, that the people had already surrendered all their powers to the state sovereignties, and had nothing more to give. But, surely, the question whether they may resume and modify the powers granted to government, does not remain to be settled in this country. Much more might the legitimacy of the general government be doubted, had it been created by the states. The powers delegated to the state sovereignties were to be exercised by themselves, not by a distinct and independent sovereignty, created by themselves. To the formation of a league, such as was the confederation, the state sovereignties were certainly competent. But when, "in order to form a more perfect union," it was deemed necessary to change this alliance into an effective government, possessing great and sovereign powers, and acting directly on the people, the necessity of referring it to the people, and of deriving its powers directly from them, was felt and acknowledged by all. The government of the Union, then (whatever may be the influence of this fact on the case), is, emphatically and truly, a government of the people. In form, and in substance, it emanates from them. Its powers are granted by them, and are to be exercised directly on them, and for their benefit.

This government is acknowledged by all, to be one of enumerated powers. The principle, that it can exercise only the powers granted to it, would seem too apparent, to have required to be enforced by all those arguments, which its enlightened friends, while it was depending before the people, found it necessary to urge; that principle is now universally admitted. But the question respecting the extent of the powers actually granted, is perpetually arising, and will probably continue to arise, so long as our system shall exist. In discussing these questions, the conflicting powers of the general and state governments must be brought into view, and the supremacy of their respective laws, when they are in opposition, must be settled.

If any one proposition could command the universal assent of mankind, we might expect it would be this—that the government of the Union, though limited in its powers, is supreme within its sphere of action. This would seem to result, necessarily, from its nature. It is the government of all; its powers are delegated by all; it represents all, and acts for all. Though any one state may be willing to control its operations, no state is willing to allow others to control them. The nation, on those subjects on which it can act, must necessarily bind its component parts. But this question is not left to mere reason: the people have, in express terms, decided it, by saying, "this constitution, and the laws of the United States, which shall be made in pursuance thereof," "shall be the supreme law of the land," and by requiring that the members of the state legislatures, and the officers of the executive and judicial departments of the states, shall take the oath of fidelity to it. The government of the United States, then, though limited in its powers, is supreme; and its laws, when made in pursuance of the constitution, form the supreme law of the land, "anything in the constitution or laws of any state to the contrary notwithstanding."

Among the enumerated powers, we do not find that of establishing a bank or creating a corporation. But there is no phrase in the instrument which, like the articles of confederation, excludes incidental or implied powers; and which requires that everything granted shall be expressly and minutely described. Even the 10th amendment, which was framed for the purpose of quieting the excessive jealousies which had been excited, omits the word "expressly," and declares only, that the powers "not delegated to the United States, nor prohibited to the states, are reserved to the states or to the people;" thus leaving the question, whether the particular power which may become the subject of contest, has been delegated to the one government, or prohibited to the other, to depend on a fair construction of the whole instrument. The men who drew and adopted this amendment had experienced the embarrassments resulting from the insertion of this word in the articles of confederation, and probably omitted it, to avoid those embarrassments. A constitution, to contain an accurate detail of all the subdivisions of which its great powers will admit, and of all the means by which they may be carried into execution, would partake of the prolixity of a legal code, and could scarcely be embraced by the human mind. It would, probably, never be understood by the public. Its nature, therefore, requires, that only its great outlines should be marked, its important objects designated, and the minor ingredients which compose those objects, be deduced from the nature of the objects themselves. That this idea was entertained by the framers of the American constitution, is not only to be inferred from the nature of the instrument, but from the language. Why else were some of the limitations, found in the 9th section of the 1st article, introduced? It is also, in some degree, warranted by their having omit-

ted to use any restrictive term which might prevent its receiving a fair and just interpretation. In considering this question, then, we must never forget that it is a *constitution* we are expounding.

Although, among the enumerated powers of government, we do not find the word "bank" or "incorporation," we find the great powers, to lay and collect taxes; to borrow money; to regulate commerce; to declare and conduct a war; and to raise and support armies and navies. The sword and the purse, all the external relations, and no inconsiderable portion of the industry of the nation, are intrusted to its government. It can never be pretended, that these vast powers draw after them others of inferior importance, merely because they are inferior. Such an idea can never be advanced. But it may with great reason be contended, that a government, intrusted with such ample powers, on the due execution of which the happiness and prosperity of the nation so vitally depends, must also be intrusted with ample means for their execution. The power being given, it is the interest of the nation to facilitate its execution. It can never be their interest, and cannot be presumed to have been their intention, to clog and embarrass its execution, by withholding the most appropriate means. Throughout this vast republic, from the St. Croix to the Gulf of Mexico, from the Atlantic to the Pacific, revenue is to be collected and expended, armies are to be marched and supported. The exigencies of the nation may require, that the treasure raised in the north should be transported to the south, that raised in the east, conveyed to the west, or that this order should be reversed. Is that construction of the constitution to be preferred, which would render these operations difficult, hazardous and expensive? Can we adopt that construction (unless the words imperiously require it), which would impute to the framers of that instrument, when granting these powers for the public good, the intention of impeding their exercise, by withholding a choice of means? If, indeed, such be the mandate of the constitution, we have only to obey; but that instrument does not profess to enumerate the means by which the powers it confers may be executed; nor does it prohibit the creation of a corporation, if the existence of such a being be essential, to the beneficial exercise of those powers. It is, then, the subject of fair inquiry, how far such means may be employed.

It is not denied, that the powers given to the government imply the ordinary means of execution. That, for example, of raising revenue, and applying it to national purposes, is admitted to imply the power of conveying money from place to place, as the exigencies of the nation may require, and of employing the usual means of conveyance. But it is denied, that the government has its choice of means; or, that it may employ the most convenient means, if, to employ them, it be necessary to erect a corporation. On what foundation does this argument rest? On this alone: the power of creating a corporation, is one appertaining to sovereignty, and is not expressly conferred on congress. This is true. But all legislative powers appertain to sovereignty. The original power of giving the law on any subject whatever, is a sovereign power; and if the government of the Union is restrained from creating a corporation, as a means for performing its functions, on the single reason that the creation of a corporation is an act of sovereignty; if the sufficiency of this reason be acknowledged, there would be some difficulty in sustaining the authority of congress to pass other laws for the accomplishment of the same objects. The government which has a right to do an act, and has imposed on it, the duty of performing that act, must, according to the dictates of reason, be allowed to select the means; and those who contend that it may not select any appropriate means, that one particular mode of effecting the object is excepted, take upon themselves the burden of establishing that exception.

The creation of a corporation, it is said, appertains to sovereignty. This is admitted. But to what portion of sovereignty does it appertain?

Does it belong to one more than to another? In America, the powers of sovereignty are divided between the government of the Union, and those of the states. They are each sovereign, with respect to the objects committed to it, and neither sovereign, with respect to the objects committed to the other. We cannot comprehend that train of reasoning, which would maintain, that the extent of power granted by the people is to be ascertained, not by the nature and terms of the grant, but by its date. Some state constitutions were formed before, some since that of the United States. We cannot believe, that their relation to each other is in any degree dependent upon this circumstance. Their respective powers must, we think, be precisely the same, as if they had been formed at the same time. Had they been formed at the same time, and had the people conferred on the general government the power contained in the constitution, and on the states the whole residuum of power, would it have been asserted, that the government of the Union was not sovereign, with respect to those objects which were intrusted to it, in relation to which its laws were declared to be supreme? If this could not have been asserted, we cannot well comprehend the process of reasoning which maintains, that a power appertaining to sovereignty cannot be connected with that vast portion of it which is granted to the general government, so far as it is calculated to subserve the legitimate objects of that government. The power of creating a corporation, though appertaining to sovereignty, is not, like the power of making war, or levying taxes, or of regulating commerce, a great substantive and independent power, which cannot be implied as incidental to other powers, or used as a means of executing them. It is never the end for which other powers are exercised, but a means by which other objects are accomplished. No contributions are made to charity, for the sake of an incorporation, but a corporation is created to administer the charity; no seminary of learning is instituted, in order to be incorporated, but the corporate character is conferred to subserve the purposes of education. No city was ever built, with the sole object of being incorporated, but is incorporated as affording the best means of being well governed. The power of creating a corporation is never used for its own sake, but for the purpose of effecting something else. No sufficient reason is, therefore, perceived, why it may not pass as incidental to those powers which are expressly given, if it be a direct mode of executing them.

But the constitution of the United States has not left the right of congress to employ the necessary means, for the execution of the powers conferred on the government, to general reasoning. To its enumeration of powers is added, that of making "all laws which shall be necessary and proper, for carrying into execution the foregoing powers, and all other powers vested by this constitution, in the government of the United States, or in any department thereof." The counsel for the state of Maryland have urged various arguments, to prove that this clause, though, in terms, a grant of power, is not so, in effect; but is really restrictive of the general right, which might otherwise be implied, of selecting means for executing the enumerated powers. In support of this proposition, they have found it necessary to contend, that this clause was inserted for the purpose of conferring on congress the power of making laws. That, without it, doubts might be entertained, whether congress could exercise its powers in the form of legislation.

But could this be the object for which it was inserted? A government is created by the people, having legislative, executive and judicial powers. Its legislative powers are vested in a congress, which is to consist of a senate and house of representatives. Each house may determine the rule of its proceedings; and it is declared, that every bill which shall have passed both houses, shall, before it becomes a law, be presented to the president of the United States. The 7th section describes the course of proceedings, by which a bill shall become a law;

and, then, the 8th section enumerates the powers of congress. Could it be necessary to say, that a legislature should exercise legislative powers, in the shape of legislation? After allowing each house to prescribe its own course of proceeding, after describing the manner in which a bill should become a law, would it have entered into the mind of a single member of the convention, that an express power to make laws was necessary, to enable the legislature to make them? That a legislature, endowed with legislative powers, can legislate, is a proposition too self-evident to have been questioned.

But the argument on which most reliance is placed, is drawn from that peculiar language of this clause. Congress is not empowered by it to make all laws, which may have relation to the powers confered on the government, but such only as may be *"necessary and proper"* for carrying them into execution. The word *"necessary"* is considered as controlling the whole sentence, and as limiting the right to pass laws for the execution of the granted powers, to such as are indispensable, and without which the power would be nugatory. That it excludes the choice of means, and leaves to congress, in each case, that only which is most direct and simple.

Is it true, that this is the sense in which the word "necessary" is always used? Does it always import an absolute physical necessity, so strong, that one thing to which another may be termed necessary, cannot exist without that other? We think it does not. If reference be had to its use, in the common affairs of the world, or in approved authors, we find that it frequently imports no more than that one thing is convenient, or useful, or essential to another. To employ the means necessary to an end, is generally understood as employing any means calculated to produce the end, and not as being confined to those single means, without which the end would be entirely unattainable. Such is the character of human language, that no word conveys to the mind, in all situations, one single definite idea; and nothing is more common than to use words in a figurative sense. Almost all compositions contain words, which, taken in a their rigorous sense, would convey a meaning different from that which is obviously intended. It is essential to just construction, that many words which import something excessive, should be understood in a more mitigated sense—in that sense which common usage justifies. The word "necessary" is of this description. It has not a fixed character, peculiar to itself. It admits of all degrees of comparison; and is often connected with other words, which increase or diminish the impression the mind receives of the urgency it imports. A thing may be necessary, very necessary, absolutely or indispensably necessary. To no mind would the same idea be conveyed by these several phrases. The comment on the word is well illustrated by the passage cited at the bar, from the 10th section of the 1st article of the constitution. It is, we think, impossible to compare the sentence which prohibits a state from laying "imposts, or duties on imports or exports, except what may be *absolutely* necessary for executing its inspection laws," with that which authorizes congress "to make all laws which shall be necessary and proper for carrying into execution" the powers of the general government, without feeling a conviction, that the convention understood itself to change materially the meaning of the word "necessary," by prefixing the word "absolutely." This word, then, like others, is used in various senses; and, in its construction, the subject, the context, the intention of the person using them, are all to be taken into view.

Let this be done in the case under consideration. The subject is the execution of those great powers on which the welfare of a nation essentially depends. It must have been the intention of those who gave these powers, to insure, so far as human prudence could insure, their beneficial execution. This could not be done, by confiding the choice of means to such narrow limits as not to leave it in the power of congress to adopt any which might be appropriate, and which were conducive to the end. This provision is made in a constitution, intended to endure for ages to come, and consequently, to be adapted to the various *crises* of human affairs. To have prescribed the means by which government should, in all future time, execute its powers, would have been to change, entirely, the character of the instrument, and give it the properties of a legal code. It would have been an unwise attempt to provide, by immutable rules, for exigencies which, if foreseen at all, must have been seen dimly, and which can be best provided for as they occur. To have declared, that the best means shall not be used, but those alone, without which the power given would be nugatory, would have been to deprive the legislature of the capacity to avail itself of experience, to exercise its reason, and to accommodate its legislation to circumstances.

If we apply this principle of construction to any of the powers of the government, we shall find it so pernicious in its operation that we shall be compelled to discard it. The powers vested in congress may certainly be carried into execution, without prescribing an oath of office. The power to exact this security for the faithful performance of duty, is not given, nor is it indispensably necessary. The different departments may be established; taxes may be imposed and collected; armies and navies may be raised and maintained; and money may be borrowed, without requiring an oath of office. It might be argued, with as much plausibility as other incidental powers have been assailed, that the convention was not unmindful of this subject. The oath which might be exacted—that of fidelity to the constitution—is prescribed, and no other can be required. Yet, he would be charged with insanity, who should contend, that the legislature might not superadd, to the oath directed by the constitution, such other oath of office as its wisdom might suggest.

So, with respect to the whole penal code of the United States: whence arises the power to punish, in cases not prescribed by the constitution? All admit, that the government may, legitimately, punish any violation of its laws; and yet, this is not among the enumerated powers of congress. The right to enforce the observance of law, by punishing its infraction, might be denied, with the more plausibility, because it is expressly given in some cases.

Congress is empowered "to provide for the punishment of counterfeiting the securities and current coin of the United States," and "to define and punish piracies and felonies committed on the high seas, and offences against the law of nations." The several powers of congress may exist, in a very imperfect state, to be sure, but they may exist and be carried into execution, although no punishment should be inflicted, in cases where the right to punish is not expressly given.

Take, for example, the power "to establish post-offices and post-roads." This power is executed, by the single act of making the establishment. But, from this has been inferred the power and duty of carrying the mail along the post-road, from one post-office to another. And from this implied power, has again been inferred the right to punish those who steal letters from the post-office, or rob the mail. It may be said, with some plausibility, that the right to carry the mail, and to punish those who rob it, is not indispensably necessary to the establishment of a post-office and post-road. This right is indeed essential to the beneficial exercise of the power, but not indispensably necessary to its existence. So, of the punishment of the crimes of stealing or falsifying a record or process of a court of the United States, or of perjury in such court. To punish these offences, is certainly conducive to the due administration of justice. But courts may exist, and may decide the causes brought before them, though such crimes escape punishment.

The baneful influence of this narrow construction on all the operations of the government, and the absolute impracticability of maintaining it, without rendering the government incompetent to its great

objects, might be illustrated by numerous examples drawn from the constitution, and from our laws. The good sense of the public has pronounced, without hesitation, that the power of punishment appertains to sovereignty, and may be exercised, whenever the sovereign has a right to act, as incidental to his constitutional powers. It is a means for carrying into execution all sovereign powers, and may be used, although not indispensably necessary. It is a right incidental to the power, and conducive to its beneficial exercise.

If this limited construction of the word "necessary" must be abandoned, in order to punish, whence is derived the rule which would reinstate it, when the government would carry its powers into execution, by means not vindictive in their nature? If the word "necessary" means "needful," "requisite," "essential," "conducive to," in order to let in the power of punishment for the infraction of law; why is it not equally comprehensive, when required to authorize the use of means which facilitate the execution of the powers of government, without the infliction of punishment?

In ascertaining the sense in which the word "necessary" is used in this clause of the constitution, we may derive some aid from that with which it is associated. Congress shall have power "to make all laws which shall be necessary and proper to carry into execution" the powers of the government. If the word "necessary" was used in that strict and rigorous sense for which the counsel for the state of Maryland contend, it would be an extraordinary departure from the usual course of the human mind, as exhibited in composition, to add a word, the only possible effect of which is, to qualify that strict and rigorous meaning; to present to the mind the idea of some choice of means of legislation, not strained and compressed within the narrow limits for which gentlemen contend.

But the argument which most conclusively demonstrates the error of the construction contended for by the counsel for the state of Maryland, is founded on the intention of the convention, as manifested in the whole clause. To waste time and argument in proving that, without it, congress might carry its powers into execution, would be not much less idle, than to hold a lighted taper to the sun. As little can it be required to prove, that in the absence of this clause, congress would have some choice of means. That it might employ those which, in its judgment, would most advantageously effect the object to be accomplished. That any means adapted to the end, any means which tended directly to the execution of the constitutional powers of the government, were in themselves constitutional. This clause, as construed by the state of Maryland, would abridge, and almost annihilate, this useful and necessary right of the legislature to select its means. That this could not be intended, is, we should think, had it not been already controverted, too apparent for controversy.

We think so for the following reasons: 1st. The clause is placed among the powers of congress, not among the limitations on those powers. 2d. Its terms purport to enlarge, not to diminish the powers vested in the government. It purports to be an additional power, not a restriction on those already granted. No reason has been, or can be assigned, for thus concealing an intention to narrow the discretion of the national legislature, under words which purport to enlarge it. The framers of the constitution wished its adoption, and well knew that it would be endangered by its strength, not by its weakness. Had they been capable of using language which would convey to the eye one idea, and, after deep reflection, impress on the mind, another, they would rather have disguised the grant of power, than its limitation. If, then, their intention had been, by this clause, to restrain the free use of means which might otherwise have been implied, that intention would have been inserted in another place, and would have been expressed in terms resembling these. "In carrying into execution the foregoing powers, and all others," &c., "no laws shall be passed but such as are necessary and proper." Had the intention been to make this clause restrictive, it would unquestionably have been so in form as well as in effect.

The result of the most careful and attentive consideration bestowed upon this clause is, that if it does not enlarge, it cannot be construed to restrain the powers of congress, or to impair the right of the legislature to exercise its best judgment in the selection of measures to carry into execution the constitutional powers of the government. If no other motive for its insertion can be suggested, a sufficient one is found in the desire to remove all doubts respecting the right to legislate on that vast mass of incidental powers which must be involved in the constitution, if that instrument be not a splendid bauble.

We admit, as all must admit, that the powers of the government are limited, and that its limits are not to be transcended. But we think the sound construction of the constitution must allow to the national legislature that discretion, with respect to the means by which the powers it confers are to be carried into execution, which will enable that body to perform the high duties assigned to it, in the manner most beneficial to the people. Let the end be legitimate, let it be within the scope of the constitution, and all means which are appropriate, which are plainly adapted to that end, which are not prohibited, but consist with the letter and spirit of the constitution, are constitutional.[5]

That a corporation must be considered as a means not less usual, not of higher dignity, not more requiring a particular specification than other means, has been sufficiently proved. If we look to the origin of corporations, to the manner in which they have been framed in that government from which we have derived most of our legal principles and ideas, or to the uses to which they have been applied, we find no reason to suppose, that a constitution, omitting, and wisely omitting, to enumerate all the means for carrying into execution the great powers vested in government, ought to have specified this. Had it been intended to grant this power, as one which should be distinct and independent, to be exercised in any case whatever, it would have found a place among the enumerated powers of the government. But being considered merely as a means, to be employed only for the purpose of carrying into execution the given powers, there could be no motive for particularly mentioning it.

The propriety of this remark would seem to be generally acknowledged, by the universal acquiescence in the construction which has been uniformly put on the 3d section of the 4th article of the constitution. The power to "make all needful rules and regulations respecting the territory or other property belonging to the United States," is not more comprehensive, than the power "to make all laws which shall be necessary and proper for carrying into execution" the powers of the government. Yet all admit the constitutionality of a territorial government, which is a corporate body.

If a corporation may be employed, indiscriminately with other means, to carry into execution the powers of the government, no particular reason can be assigned for excluding the use of a bank, if required for its fiscal operations. To use one, must be within the discretion of congress, if it be an appropriate mode of executing the powers of government. That it is a convenient, a useful, and essential instrument in the prosecution of its fiscal operations, is not now a subject of controversy. All those who have been concerned in the administration of our finances, have concurred in representing its importance and necessity; and so strongly have they been felt, that statesmen of the first class, whose previous opinions against it had been confirmed by every circumstance which can fix the human judgment, have yielded those opinions to the exigencies of the nation. Under the confederation, congress, justifying the measure by its necessity, tran-

scended, perhaps, its powers, to obtain the advantage of a bank; and our own legislation attests the universal conviction of the utility of this measure. The time has passed away, when it can be necessary to enter into any discussion, in order to prove the importance of this instrument, as a means to effect the legitimate objects of the government.

But were its necessity less apparent, none can deny its being an appropriate measure; and if it is, the decree of its necessity, as has been very justly observed, is to be discussed in another place. Should congress, in the execution of its powers, adopt measures which are prohibited by the constitution; or should congress, under the pretext of executing its powers, pass laws for the accomplishment of objects not intrusted to the government; it would become the painful duty of this tribunal, should a case requiring such a decision come before it, to say, that such an act was not the law of the land. But where the law is not prohibited, and is really calculated to effect any of the objects intrusted to the government, to undertake here to inquire into the degree of its necessity, would be to pass the line which circumscribes the judicial department, and to tread on legislative ground. This court disclaims all pretensions to such a power.

After this declaration, it can scarcely be necessary to say, that the existence of state banks can have no possible influence on the question. No trace is to be found in the constitution, of an intention to create a dependence of the government of the Union on those of the states, for the execution of the great powers assigned to it. Its means are adequate to its ends; and on those means alone was it expected to rely for the accomplishment of its ends. To impose on it the necessity of resorting to means which it cannot control, which another government may furnish or withhold, would render its course precarious, the result of its measures uncertain, and create a dependence on other governments, which might disappoint its most important designs, and is incompatible with the language of the constitution. But were it otherwise, the choice of means implies a right to choose a national bank in preference to state banks, and congress alone can make the election.

After the most deliberate consideration, it is the unanimous and decided opinion of this court, that the act to incorporate the Bank of the United States is a law made in pursuance of the constitution, and is a part of the supreme law of the land.

The branches, proceeding from the same stock, and being conducive to the complete accomplishment of the object, are equally constitutional. It would have been unwise, to locate them in the charter, and it would be unnecessarily inconvenient, to employ the legislative power in making those subordinate arrangements. The great duties of the bank are prescribed; those duties require branches; and the bank itself may, we think, be safely trusted with the selection of places where those branches shall be fixed; reserving always to the government the right to require that a branch shall be located where it may be deemed necessary.

It being the opinion of the court, that the act incorporating the bank is constitutional; and that the power of establishing a branch in the state of Maryland might be properly exercised by the bank itself, we proceed to inquire—

2. Whether the state of Maryland may, without violating the constitution, tax that branch? That the power of taxation is one of vital importance; that it is retained by the states; that it is not abridged by the grant of a similar power to the government of the Union; that it is to be concurrently exercised by the two governments—are truths which have never been denied. But such is the paramount character of the constitution, that its capacity to withdraw any subject from the action of even this power, is admitted. The states are expressly forbidden to lay any duties on imports or exports, except what may be

absolutely necessary for executing their inspection laws. If the obligation of this prohibition must be conceded—if it may restrain a state from the exercise of its taxing power on imports and exports—the same paramount character would seem to restrain, as it certainly may restrain, a state from such other exercise of this power, as is in its nature incompatible with, and repugnant to, the constitutional laws of the Union. A law, absolutely repugnant to another, as entirely repeals that other as if express terms of repeal were used.

On this ground, the counsel for the bank place its claim to be exempted from the power of a state to tax its operations. There is no express provision for the case, but the claim has been sustained on a principle which so entirely pervades the constitution, is so intermixed with the materials which compose it, so interwoven with its web, so blended with its texture, as to be incapable of being separated from it, without rending it into shreds. This great principle is, that the constitution and the laws made in pursuance thereof are supreme; that they control the constitution and laws of the respective states, and cannot be controlled by them. From this, which may be almost termed an axiom, other propositions are deduced as corollaries, on the truth or error of which, and on their application to this case, the cause has been supposed to depend. These are, 1st. That a power to create implies a power to preserve: 2d. That a power to destroy, if wielded by a different hand, is hostile to, and incompatible with these powers to create and to preserve: 3d. That where this repugnancy exists, that authority which is supreme must control, not yield to that over which it is supreme.

These propositions, as abstract truths, would, perhaps, never be controverted. Their application to this case, however, has been denied; and both in maintaining the affirmative and the negative, a splendor of eloquence, and strength of argument, seldom, if ever, surpassed, have been displayed.

The power of congress to create, and of course, to continue, the bank, was the subject of the preceding part of this opinion; and is no longer to be considered as questionable. That the power of taxing it by the states may be exercised so as to destroy it, is too obvious to be denied. But taxation is said to be an absolute power, which acknowledges no other limits than those expressly prescribed in the constitution, and like sovereign power of every other description, is intrusted to the discretion of those who use it. But the very terms of this argument admit, that the sovereignty of the state, in the article of taxation itself, is subordinate to, and may be controlled by the constitution of the United States. How far it has been controlled by that instrument, must be a question of construction. In making this construction, no principle, not declared, can be admissible, which would defeat the legitimate operations of a supreme government. It is of the very essence of supremacy, to remove all obstacles to its action within its own sphere, and so to modify every power vested in subordinate governments, as to exempt its own operations from their own influence. This effect need not be stated in terms. It is so involved in the declaration of supremacy, so necessarily implied in it, that the expression of it could not make it more certain. We must, therefore, keep it in view, while construing the constitution.

The argument on the part of the state of Maryland, is, not that the states may directly resist a law of congress, but that they may exercise their acknowledged powers upon it, and that the constitution leaves them this right, in the confidence that they will not abuse it. Before we proceed to examine this argument, and to subject it to test of the constitution, we must be permitted to bestow a few considerations on the nature and extent of this original right of taxation, which is acknowledged to remain with the states. It is admitted, that the power of taxing the people and their property, is essential to the very existence of government, and may be legitimately exercised on the ob-

jects to which it is applicable, to the utmost extent to which the government may choose to carry it. The only security against the abuse of this power, is found in the structure of the government itself. In imposing a tax, the legislature acts upon its constituents. This is, in general, a sufficient security against erroneous and oppressive taxation.

The people of a state, therefore, give to their government a right of taxing themselves and their property, and as the exigencies of government cannot be limited, they prescribe no limits to the exercise of this right, resting confidently on the interest of the legislator, and on the influence of the constituent over their representative, to guard them against its abuse. But the means employed by the government of the Union have no such security, nor is the right of a state to tax them sustained by the same theory. Those means are not given by the people of a particular state, not given by the constituents of the legislature, which claim the right to tax them, but by the people of all the states. They are given by all, for the benefit of all—and upon theory, should be subjected to that government only which belongs to all.

It may be objected to this definition, that the power of taxation is not confined to the people and property of a state. It may be exercised upon every object brought within its jurisdiction. This is true. But to what source do we trace this right? It is obvious, that it is an incident of sovereignty, and is co-extensive with that to which it is an incident. All subjects over which the sovereign power of a state extends, are objects of taxation; but those over which it does not extend, are, upon the soundest principles, exempt from taxation. This proposition may almost be pronounced self-evident.

The sovereignty of a state extends to everything which exists by its own authority, or is introduced by its permission; but does it extend to those means which are employed by congress to carry into execution powers conferred on that body by the people of the United States? We think it demonstrable, that it does not. Those powers are not given by the people of a single state. They are given by the people of the United States, to a government whose laws, made in pursuance of the constitution, are declared to be supreme. Consequently, the people of a single state cannot confer a sovereignty which will extend over them.

If we measure the power of taxation residing in a state, by the extent of sovereignty which the people of a single state possess, and can confer on its government, we have an intelligible standard, applicable to every case to which the power may be applied. We have a principle which leaves the power of taxing the people and property of a state unimpaired; which leaves to a state the command of all its resources, and which places beyond its reach, all those powers which are conferred by the people of the United States on the government of the Union, and all those means which are given for the purpose of carrying those powers into execution. We have a principle which is safe for the states, and safe for the Union. We are relieved, as we ought to be, from clashing sovereignty; from interfering powers; from a repugnancy between a right in one government to pull down, what there is an acknowledged right in another to build up; from the incompatibility of a right in one government to destroy, what there is a right in another to preserve. We are not driven to the perplexing inquiry, so unfit for the judicial department, what degree of taxation is the legitimate use, and what degree may amount to the abuse of the power. The attempt to use it on the means employed by the government of the Union, in pursuance of the constitution, is itself an abuse, because it is the usurpation of a power which the people of a single state cannot give. We find, then, on just theory, a total failure of this original right to tax the means employed by the government of the Union, for the execution of its powers. The right never existed, and the question whether it has been surrendered, cannot arise.

But, waiving this theory for the present, let us resume the inquiry, whether this power can be exercised by the respective states, consistently with a fair construction of the constitution? That the power to tax involves the power to destroy; that the power to destroy may defeat and render useless the power to create; that there is a plain repugnance in conferring on one government a power to control the constitutional measures of another, which other, with respect to those very measures, is declared to be supreme over that which exerts the control, are propositions not to be denied. But all inconsistencies are to be reconciled by the magic of the word *confidence.* Taxation, it is said, does not necessarily and unavoidably destroy. To carry it to the excess of destruction, would be an abuse, to presume which, would banish that confidence which is essential to all government. But is this a case of confidence? Would the people of any one state trust those of another with a power to control the most insignificant operations of their state government? We know they would not. Why, then, should we suppose, that the people of any one state should be willing to trust those of another with a power to control the operations of a government to which they have confided their most important and most valuable interests? In the legislature of the Union alone, are all represented. The legislature of the Union alone, therefore, can be trusted by the people with the power of controlling measures which concern all, in the confidence that it will not be abused. This, then, is not a case of confidence, and we must consider it is as it really is.

If we apply the principle for which the state of Maryland contends, to the constitution, generally, we shall find it capable of changing totally the character of that instrument. We shall find it capable of arresting all the measures of the government, and of prostrating it at the foot of the states. The American people have declared their constitution and the laws made in pursuance thereof, to be supreme; but this principle would transfer the supremacy, in fact, to the states. If the states may tax one instrument, employed by the government in the execution of its powers, they may tax any and every other instrument. They may tax the mail; they may tax the mint; they may tax patent-rights; they may tax the papers of the custom-house; they may tax judicial process; they may tax all the means employed by the government, to an excess which would defeat all the ends of government. This was not intended by the American people. They did not design to make their government dependent on the states.

Gentlemen say, they do not claim the right to extend state taxation to these objects. They limit their pretensions to property. But on what principle, is this distinction made? Those who make it have furnished no reason for it, and the principle for which they contend denies it. They contend, that the power of taxation has no other limit than is found in the 10th section of the 1st article of the constitution; that, with respect to everything else, the power of the states is supreme, and admits of no control. If this be true, the distinction between property and other subjects to which the power of taxation is applicable, is merely arbitrary, and can never be sustained. This is not all. If the controlling power of the states be established; if their supremacy as to taxation be acknowledged; what is to restrain their exercising control in any shape they may please to give it? Their sovereignty is not confined to taxation; that is not the only mode in which it might be displayed. The question is, in truth, a question of supremacy; and if the right of the states to tax the means employed by the general government be conceded, the declaration that the constitution, and the laws made in pursuance thereof, shall be the supreme law of the land, is empty and unmeaning declamation.

In the course of the argument, the Federalist has been quoted; and the opinions expressed by the authors of that work have been justly supposed to be entitled to great respect in expounding the constitution. No tribute can be paid to them which exceeds their merit; but in applying their opinions to the cases which may arise in the progress of our government, a right to judge of their correctness must be retained; and to understand the argument, we must examine the proposition it maintains, and the objections against which it is directed. The subject of those numbers, from which passages have been cited, is the unlimited power of taxation which is vested in the general government. The objection to this unlimited power, which the argument seeks to remove, is stated with fulness and clearness. It is, "that an indefinite power of taxation in the latter (the government of the Union) might, and probably would, in time, deprive the former (the government of the states) of the means of providing for their own necessities; and would subject them entirely to the mercy of the national legislature. As the laws of the Union are to become the supreme law of the land; as it is to have power to pass all laws that may be necessary for carrying into execution the authorities with which it is proposed to vest it; the national government might, at any time, abolish the taxes imposed for state objects, upon the pretence of an interference with its own. It might allege a necessity for doing this, in order to give efficacy to the national revenues; and thus, all the resources of taxation might, by degrees, become the subjects of federal monopoly, to the entire exclusion and destruction of the state governments."

The objections to the constitution which are noticed in these numbers, were to the undefined power of the government to tax, not to the incidental privilege of exempting its own measures from state taxation. The consequences apprehended from this undefined power were, that it would absorb all the objects of taxation, "to the exclusion and destruction of the state governments." The arguments of the Federalist are intended to prove the fallacy of these apprehensions; not to prove that the government was incapable of executing any of its powers, without exposing the means it employed to the embarrassments of state taxation. Arguments urged against these objections, and these apprehensions, are to be understood as relating to the points they mean to prove. Had the authors of those excellent essays been asked, whether they contended for that construction of the constitution, which would place within the reach of the states those measures which the government might adopt for the execution of its powers; no man, who has read their instructive pages, will hesitate to admit, that their answer must have been in the negative.

It has also been insisted, that, as the power of taxation in the general and state governments is acknowledged to be concurrent, every argument which would sustain the right of the general government to tax banks chartered by the states, will equally sustain the right of the states to tax banks chartered by the general government. But the two cases are not on the same reason. The people of all the states have created the general government, and have conferred upon it the general power of taxation. The people of all the states, and the states themselves, are represented in congress, and, by their representatives, exercise this power. When they tax the chartered institutions of the states, they tax their constituents; and these taxes must be uniform. But when a state taxes the operations of the government of the United States, it acts upon institutions created, not by their own constituents, but by people over whom they claim no control. It acts upon the measures of a government created by others as well as themselves, for the benefit of others in common with themselves. The difference is that which always exists, and always must exist, between the action of the whole on a part, and the action of a part on the whole—between the laws of a government declared to be supreme, and those of a government which, when in opposition to those laws, is not supreme.

But if the full application of this argument could be admitted, it might bring into question the right of congress to tax the state banks, and could not prove the rights of the states to tax the Bank of the United States.

The court has bestowed on this subject its most deliberate consideration. The result is a conviction that the states have no power, by taxation or otherwise, to retard, impede, burden, or in any manner control, the operations of the constitutional laws enacted by congress to carry into execution the powers vested in the general government. This is, we think, the unavoidable consequence of that supremacy which the constitution has declared. We are unanimously of opinion, that the law passed by the legislature of Maryland, imposing a tax on the Bank of the United States, is unconstitutional and void.

This opinion does not deprive the states of any resources which they originally possessed. It does not extend to a tax paid by the real property of the bank, in common with the other real property within the state, nor to a tax imposed on the interest which the citizens of Maryland may hold in this institution, in common with other property of the same description throughout the state. But this is a tax on the operations of the bank, and is, consequently, a tax on the operation of an instrument employed by the government of the Union to carry its powers into execution. Such a tax must be unconstitutional.

JUDGMENT.—This cause came on to be heard, on the transcript of the record of the court of appeals of the state of Maryland, and was argued by counsel: on consideration whereof, it is the opinion of this court, that the act of the legislature of Maryland is contrary to the constitution of the United States, and void; and therefore, that the said court of appeals of the state of Maryland erred, in affirming the judgment of the Baltimore county court, in which judgment was rendered against James W. McCulloch; but that the said court of appeals of Maryland ought to have reversed the said judgment of the said Baltimore county court, and ought to have given judgment for the said appellant, McCulloch: It is, therefore, adjudged and ordered, that the said judgment of the said court of appeals of the state of Maryland in this case, be, and the same hereby is, reversed and annulled. And this court, proceeding to render such judgment as the said court of appeals should have rendered; it is further adjudged and ordered, that the judgment of the said Baltimore county court be reversed and annulled, and that judgment be entered in the said Baltimore county court for the said James W. McCulloch.

1. This case involving a constitutional question of great public importance, and the sovereign rights of the United States and the state of Maryland; and the government of the United States having directed their attorney general to appear for the plaintiff in error, the court dispensed with its general rule, permitting only two counsel to argue for each party.

2. See *Roach v. Philadelphia County,* 2 Am. L.J. 444; *United v. Weise,* 3 Wall. Jr. C. C. 72, 79.

3. Letters of Publius, or *The Federalist,* Nos. 31–36.

4. See *Sturges v. Crowninshield, ante,* p. 122.

5. See *Montague v. Richardson,* 24 Conn. 348.

Circuit Court of Appeals Act of 1891

In 1891 Congress passed the Circuit Court of Appeals Act, which established a new level of federal courts between the circuit and district courts and the Supreme Court. Relieving Supreme Court justices of the duty of sitting as circuit judges, the new circuit court of appeals was to hear all appeals from the decisions of the district and circuit courts.

Prior to the act, Supreme Court justices were required to ride circuit, a hardship for most justices. The justices were often required to travel long distances and deal with difficult conditions. Questions were also raised about the propriety of the justices participating in cases at the circuit level that were then reviewed by the Supreme Court.

The new circuit court of appeals would have final word in almost all diversity, admiralty, patent, revenue, and noncapital criminal cases. The Supreme Court would review such cases, after their decision by the appeals courts, only if the appeals court judges certified a case to the High Court—or if the Supreme Court decided to grant review through issue of a writ of certiorari. Cases involving constitutional questions, matters of treaty law, jurisdictional questions, capital crimes, and conflicting laws were still granted a right to appeal to the Supreme Court.

CIRCUIT COURT OF APPEALS ACT OF 1891

March 3, 1891

An act to establish circuit courts of appeals and to define and regulate in certain cases the jurisdiction of the courts of the United States, and for other purposes.

United States courts. Additional circuit judges to be appointed. Qualifications, etc.

Be it enacted by the Senate and House of Representatives of the United States of America in Congress assembled, That there shall be appointed by the President of the United States, by and with the advice and consent of the Senate, in each circuit an additional circuit judge, who shall have the same qualifications, and shall have the same power and jurisdiction therein that the circuit judges of the United States, within their respective circuits, now have under existing laws, and who shall be entitled to the same compensation as the circuit judges of the United States in their respective circuits now have.

Circuit court of appeals created. Composition.

General powers.

SEC. 2. That there is hereby created in each circuit a circuit court of appeals, which shall consist of three judges, of whom two shall constitute a quorum, and which shall be a court of record with appellate jurisdiction, as is hereafter limited and established. Such court shall prescribe the form and style of its seal and the form of writs and other process and procedure as may be conformable to the exercise of its jurisdiction as shall be conferred by law. It shall have

Marshal.

the appointment of the marshal of the court with the same duties and powers under the regulations of the court as are now provided for the marshal of the Supreme Court of the United States, so far as the same may be applicable. The court shall also appoint

Clerk.

a clerk, who shall perform and exercise the same duties and powers in regard to all matters within its jurisdiction as are now exercised and performed by the clerk of the Supreme Court of the United States, so far as the same may be applicable. The salary of the

Salaries.

marshal of the court shall be twenty-five hundred dollars a year, and the salary of the clerk of the court shall be three thousand dollars a year, to be paid in equal proportions quarterly. The costs and fees in

Costs, etc.

the Supreme Court now provided for by law shall be costs and fees in the circuit courts of appeals; and the same shall be expended, accounted for, and paid for, and paid over to the Treasury Department of the United States in the same manner as is provided in

Rules, etc.

respect to the costs and fees in the Supreme Court.

The court shall have power to establish all rules and regulations for the conduct of the business of the court within its jurisdiction as conferred by law.

Constitution of court.

SEC. 3. That the Chief-Justice and the associate justices of the Supreme Court assigned to each circuit, and the circuit judges within each circuit, and the several district judges within each circuit, shall be competent to sit as judges of the circuit court of appeals within their respective circuits in the manner

Precedence.

hereinafter provided. In case the Chief-Justice or an associate justice of the Supreme Court should attend at any session of the circuit court of appeals he shall preside, and the circuit judges in attendance upon the court in the absence of the Chief-Justice or associate justice of the Supreme Court shall preside in the order of the seniority of their repective commissions.

Service of district judges

In case the full court at any time shall not be made up by the attendance of the Chief-Justice or an associate justice of the Supreme Court and circuit judges, one or more district judges within the circuit shall be competent to sit in the court according to such order or provision among the district judges as either by general or particular assignment

Proviso
No judge to sit on appeal from his court.

shall be designated by the court: *Provided,* That no justice or judge before whom a cause or question may have been tried or heard in a district court, or existing circuit court, shall sit on the trial or hearing of such cause or question in the circuit court of appeals. A term shall be held annually by the circuit

Terms.

court of appeals in the several judicial circuits at the

Regular.

following places: In the first circuit, in the city of Boston; in the second circuit, in the city of New York; in the third circuit, in the city of Philadelphia; in the fourth circuit, in the city of Richmond; in the fifth circuit, in the city of New Orleans; in the sixth circuit, in the city of Cincinnati; in the seventh circuit, in the city of Chicago; in the eighth circuit, in the city of Saint Louis; in the ninth circuit in the city of San Francisco; and in such other places in each of the above circuits as said court may from time to

Additional.
First term.
Post, p. 1115.

time designate. The first terms of said courts shall be held on the second Monday in January, eighteen hundred and ninety-one, and thereafter at such times as may be fixed by said courts.

No appeal allowed from district to circuit courts.

SEC. 4. That no appeal, whether by writ of error or otherwise, shall hereafter be taken or allowed from the district court to the existing circuit courts, and no appellate jurisdiction shall hereafter be exercised or allowed by said existing circuit courts, but all appeals by writ of error otherwise, from said district courts shall only be subject to review in the Supreme Court of the United States or in the circuit court of appeals hereby established, as is hereinafter provided, and the review, by appeal, by writ of error, or otherwise, from the existing circuit courts shall be had only in the Supreme Court of the United States or in the circuit courts of appeals hereby established according to the provisions of this act regulating the same.

Appeals, etc., from circuit court.

SEC. 5. That appeals or writs of error may be taken from the district courts or from the existing circuit courts direct to the Supreme Court in the following cases:

Appeals allowed direct to Supreme Court.

In any case in which the jurisdiction of the court is in issue; in such cases the question of jurisdiction alone shall be certified to the Supreme Court from the court below for decision.

Jurisdiction questions.

From the final sentences and decrees in prize causes.

Prizes.

In cases of conviction of a capital or otherwise infamous crime.

Capital crimes.

In any case that involves the construction or application of the Constitution of the United States.

Constitutional questions.

In any case in which the constitutionality of any law of the United States, or the validity or construction of any treaty made under its authority, is drawn in question.

Construction of law, treaty, etc.

In any case in which the constitution or law of a State is claimed to be in contravention of the Constitution of the United States.

Conflict of laws.

Nothing in this act shall affect the jurisdiction of the Supreme Court in cases appealed from the highest court of a State, nor the construction of the statute providing for review of such cases.

Appeals from highest State court.

SEC. 6. That the circuit courts of appeals established by this act shall exercise appellate jurisdiction to review by appeal or by writ of error final decision in the district court and the existing circuit courts in all cases other than those provided for in the preceding section of this act, unless otherwise provided by law, and the judgments or decrees of the circuit courts of appeals shall be final in all cases in which the jurisdiction is dependent entirely upon the opposite parties to the suit or controversy, being aliens and citizens of the United States or citizens of different States; also in all cases arising under the patent laws, under the revenue laws, and under the criminal laws and in admiralty cases, excepting that in every such subject within its appellate jurisdiction the circuit court of appeals at any time may certify to the Supreme Court of the United States any questions or propositions of law concerning which it desires the instruction of that court for its proper decision. And thereupon the Supreme Court may either give its instruction on the questions and propositions certified to it, which shall be binding upon the

Jurisdiction of court of appeals.

Judgments final.

Certificate for instruction.

Proceedings in Supreme Court.

circuit courts of appeals in such case, or it may require that the whole record and cause may be sent up to it for its consideration, and thereupon shall decide the whole matter in controversy in the same manner as if it had been brought there for review by writ of error or appeal.

And excepting also that in any such case as is hereinbefore made final in the circuit court of appeals it shall be competent for the Supreme Court to require, by certiorari or otherwise, any such case to be certified to the Supreme Court for its review and determination with the same power and authority in the case as if it had been carried by appeal or writ of error to the Supreme Court.

Certiorari to Supreme Court.

In all cases not hereinbefore, in this section, made final there shall be of right an appeal or writ of error or review of the case by the Supreme Court of the United States where the matter in controversy shall exceed one thousand dollars besides costs. But no such appeal shall be taken or writ of error sued out unless within one year after the entry of the order, judgment, or decree sought to be reviewed.

Appeals and writs of error.

Limitation.

SEC. 7. That where, upon a hearing in equity in a district court, or in an existing circuit court, an injunction shall be granted or continued by an interlocutory order or decree, in a cause in which an appeal from a final decree may be taken under the provisions of this act to the circuit court of appeals, an appeal may be taken from such interlocutory order or decree granting or continuing such injunction to the circuit court of appeals: *Provided,* That the appeal must be taken within thirty days from the entry of such order or decree, and it shall take precedence in the appellate court; and the proceedings in other respects in the court below shall not be stayed unless otherwise ordered by that court during the pendency of such appeal.

Appeal in equity causes.

Proviso.
To be taken in 30 days.

SEC. 8. That any justice or judge, who, in pursuance of the provisions of this act, shall attend the circuit court of appeals held at any place other than where he resides shall, upon his written certificate, be paid by the marshal of the district in which the court shall be held his reasonable expenses for travel and attendance, not to exceed ten dollars per day, and such payments shall be allowed the marshal in the settlement of his accounts with the United States.

Expenses of attending judges.

SEC. 9. That the marshals of the several districts in which said circuit court of appeals may be held shall, under the direction of the Attorney-General of the United States, and with his approval, provide such rooms in the public buildings of the United States as may be necessary, and pay all incidental expenses of said court, including criers, bailiffs, and messengers: *Provided, however,* That in case proper rooms cannot be provided in such buildings, then the said marshals, with the approval of the Attorney-General of the United States, may, from time to time, lease such rooms as may be necessary for such

Court rooms in public buildings.

Expenses.
Proviso.

Rent.

Compensation to officers.

courts. That the marshals, criers, clerks, bailiffs, and messengers shall be allowed the same compensation for their respective services as are allowed for similar services in the existing circuit courts.

Remanding causes reviewed by Supreme Court.

SEC. 10. That whenever an appeal or writ of error or otherwise a case coming directly from the district court or existing circuit court shall be reviewed and determined in the Supreme Court the cause shall be remanded to the proper district or circuit court for further proceedings to be taken in pursuance of such determination. And whenever on appeal or

From circuit courts of appeal.

writ of error or otherwise a case coming from a circuit court of appeals shall be reviewed and determined in the Supreme Court the cause shall be remanded by the Supreme Court to the proper district or circuit court for further proceedings in pursuance of such determination. Whenever on appeal or writ or error or otherwise a case coming from a

Review in circuit court of appeals.

district or circuit court shall be reviewed and determined in the circuit court of appeals in a case in which the decision in the circuit court of appeals is final such cause shall be remanded to the said district or circuit court for further proceedings to be there taken in pursuance of such determination.

Appeals, etc., to be brought in six months.

SEC. 11. That no appeal or writ of error by which any order, judgment, or decree may be reviewed in the circuit courts of appeals under the provisions of this act shall be taken or sued out except within six months after the entry of the order, judgment, or decree sought to be reviewed: *Provided however,*

Proviso. Less time in certain cases.

That in all cases in which a lesser time is now by law limited for appeals or writs of error such limits of time shall apply to appeals or writs of error in such cases taken to or sued out from the circuit courts of appeals. And all provisions of law now in force regu-

Rules and regulations, etc.

Issue of writs.

lating the methods and system of review, through appeals or writs of error, shall regulate the methods and system of appeals and writs of error provided for in this act in respect of the circuit courts of appeals, including all provisions for bonds or other securities to be required and taken on such appeals, in respect of cases brought or to be brought to that court, shall have the same powers and duties as to

the allowance of appeals or writs of error, and the conditions of such allowance, as now by law belong to the justices or judges in respect of the existing courts of the United States respectively.

R.S., sec. 716, p. 136.

SEC. 12. That the circuit court of appeals shall have the powers specified in section seven hundred and sixteen of the Revised Statutes of the United States.

Appeals, etc., from Indian Territory Court.

SEC. 13. Appeals and writs of error may be taken and prosecuted from the decisions of the United States court in the Indian Territory to the Supreme Court of the United States, or to the circuit court of appeals in the eighth circuit, in the same manner and under the same regulations as from the circuit or district courts of the United States, under this act.

Appeals to Supreme Court.

R.S., sec. 691, p. 128, repealed.

Vol. 18, p. 316, repealed.

Inconsistent laws repealed.

SEC. 14. That section six hundred and ninety-one of the Revised Statutes of the United States and section three of an act entitled "An act to facilitate the disposition of cases in the Supreme Court, and for other purposes," approved February sixteenth, eighteen hundred and seventy-five, be, and the same are hereby repealed. And all acts and parts of acts relating to appeals or writs of error inconsistent with the provisions for review by appeals or writs of error in the preceding sections five and six of this act are hereby repealed.

Jurisdiction in cases from Territorial supreme courts.

SEC. 15. That the circuit court of appeal in cases in which the judgments of the circuit courts of appeal are made final by this act shall have the same appellate jurisdiction, by writ of error or appeal, to review the judgments, orders, and decrees of the supreme courts of the several Territories as by this act they may have to review the judgments, orders, and decrees of the district court and circuit courts; and for that purpose the several Territories shall, by orders of the Supreme court, to be made from time to time, be assigned to particular circuits.

Approved, March 3, 1891.

SOURCE: *Public Statutes At Large of the United States of America,* Vol. XXVI (Washington, D.C.: U.S. Government Printing Office, 1891).

Judiciary Act of 1925

The Judiciary Act of 1925 established the jurisdictional rules that currently shape the Supreme Court's workload. The act gave the Court greater control of its docket by reducing the types of cases the Court was obliged to hear and by expanding its authority to select cases for review under a writ of certiorari—giving the Court virtually unlimited power in deciding which cases it would review.

Specifically, the act eliminated the right of appeal from appeals court rulings, except where the appeals court held a state law invalid under the Constitution, federal law, or treaties. A right of appeal from district court decisions remained, however, in cases under antitrust or interstate commerce laws; appeals by the government in criminal cases; suits to halt enforcement of state law or other official state action; and suits designed to halt enforcement of Interstate Commerce Commission orders.

The act is also known as the "judges bill"—a reference to the fact that the original legislation was drafted by members of the Court. Chief Justice William Howard Taft was instrumental in lobbying Congress for its passage. Taft maintained that the Court was becoming severely backlogged with cases. The law gave the justices, at least for a time, a more manageable caseload.

JUDICIARY ACT OF 1925

February 13, 1925. [H.R. 8206.] [Public, No. 415.]

An Act To amend the Judicial Code, and to further define the jurisdiction of the circuit courts of appeals and of the Supreme Court, and for other purposes.

Judicial Code.

Be it enacted by the Senate and House of Representatives of the United States of America in Congress assembled, That sections 128, 129, 237, 238, 239, and 240 of the Judicial Code as now existing be, and they are severally, amended and reenacted to read as follows:

Circuit Courts of Appeals. Appeals or writs of error to. Vol. 38, p. 803, amended. In district courts. Exception. Hawaii and Porto Rico district courts. Alaska and Virgin Islands. Cases reviewable.

SEC. 128. (a) The circuit courts of appeal shall have appellate jurisdiction to review by appeal or writ of error final decisions —

"First. In the district courts, in all cases save where a direct review of the decision may be had in the Supreme Court under section 238.

"Second. In the United States district courts for Hawaii and for Porto Rico in all cases.

"Third. In the district courts for Alaska or any division thereof, and for the Virgin Islands, in all cases, civil and criminal, wherein the Constitution or a statute or treaty of the United States or any authority exercised thereunder is involved; in all other civil cases wherein the value in controversy, exclusive of interest and costs, exceeds $1,000; in all other criminal cases where the offense charged is punishable by imprisonment for a term exceeding one year or by death, and in all habeas corpus proceedings;

Canal Zone. Vol. 42, p. 1006.

and in the district court for the Canal Zone in the cases and mode prescribed in the Act approved September 21, 1922, amending prior laws relating to the Canal Zone.

Hawaii and Porto Rico Supreme Courts. Cases reviewable.

"Fourth. In the Supreme Courts of the Territory of Hawaii and of Porto Rico, in all civil cases, civil or criminal, wherein the Constitution or a statute or treaty of the United States or any authority exercised thereunder is involved; in all other civil cases wherein the value in controversy, exclusive of interest and costs, exceeds $5,000, and in all habeas corpus proceedings.

United States Court for China. Other appellate jurisdiction.

"Fifth. In the United States Court for China, in all cases.

(b) The circuit court of appeals shall also have appellate jurisdiction—

Specified orders, etc., of district courts.

"First. To review the interlocutory orders or decrees of the district courts which are specified in section 129.

Awards of railway employees' controversies. Vol. 38, p. 107.

"Second. To review decisions of the district courts sustaining or overruling exceptions to awards in arbitrations, as provided in section 8 of an Act entitled 'An Act providing for mediation, conciliation, and arbitration in controversies between certain employers and their employees,' approved July 15, 1913.

Bankruptcy cases. Vol. 30, p. 553.

"(c) The circuit courts of appeal shall also have an appellate and supervisory jurisdiction under sections 24 and 25 of the Bankruptcy Act of July 1, 1898, over all proceedings, controversies, and cases had or brought in the district courts under that Act or any of its amendments, and shall exercise the same in the manner prescribed in those sections; and the jurisdiction of the Circuit Court of Appeals for the Ninth Circuit in this regard shall cover the courts of bankruptcy in Alaska and Hawaii, and that of the

In Alaska and Hawaii.

Circuit Court of Appeals for the First Circuit shall cover the court of bankruptcy in Porto Rico.

In Porto Rico.

Distribution to circuits.

"(d) The review under this section shall be in the following circuit courts of appeal: The decisions of a district court of the United States within a State in the circuit court of appeals for the circuit embracing such State; those of the District Court of Alaska or any division thereof, the United States district court, and the Supreme Court of Hawaii, and the United States Court for China, in the Circuit Court of Appeals for the Ninth Circuit; those of the United States district court and the Supreme Court of Porto Rico in the Circuit Court of Appeals for the First Circuit; those of the District Court of the Virgin Islands in the Circuit Court of Appeals for the Third Circuit; and those of the District Court of the Canal Zone in the Circuit Court of Appeals for the Fifth Circuit.

Further specified authority. Federal Trade Commission orders. Vol. 38, p. 720.

Orders of Interstate Commerce Commission, etc., under Clayton Act. Vol. 38, p. 735.

"(e) The circuit courts of appeal are further empowered to enforce, set aside, or modify orders of the Federal Trade Commission, as provided in section 5 of 'An Act to create a Federal Trade Commission, to define its powers and duties, and for other purposes,' approved September 26, 1914; and orders of the Interstate Commerce Commission, the Federal Reserve Board, and the Federal Trade Commission, as provided in section 11 of 'An Act to supplement existing laws against unlawful restraints and monopolies, and for other purposes,' approved October 15, 1914.

Appeals allowed from injunctions and interlocutory orders of district courts. Cases specified. Vol. 36, p. 1157, amended.

Authority of Supreme Court.

Provisos. Precedence given.

Additional bond discretionary.

"SEC. 129. Where, upon a hearing in a district court, or by a judge thereof in vacation, an injunction is granted, continued, modified, refused, or dissolved by an interlocutory order or decree, or an application to dissolve or modify an injunction is refused, or an interlocutory order or decree is made appointing a receiver, or refusing an order to wind up a pending receivership or to take the appropriate steps to accomplish the purposes thereof, such as directing a sale or other disposal of property held thereunder, an appeal may be taken from such interlocutory order or decree to the circuit court of appeals; and sections 239 and 240 shall apply to such cases in the circuit courts of appeals as to other cases therein; *Provided*, That the appeal to the circuit court of appeals must be applied for within thirty days from the entry of such order or decree, and shall take precedence in the appellate court; and the proceedings in other respects in the district court shall not be stayed during the pendency of such appeal unless otherwise ordered by the court, or the appellate court, or a judge thereof: *Provided, however,* That the distict court may, in its discretion, require an additional bond as a condition of the appeal."

Supreme Court. Writ of error allowed from decision of State court against validity of treaty or statute of United States. If validity of State statute drawn in question as repugnant to Constitution, etc. Vol. 39, p. 726, amended.

Authority of Supreme Court.

Certiorari to State court where validity of United States treaty or statute drawn in question.

State law as repugnant to the Constitution, etc.

Title, etc., set up under United States authority.

SEC. 237. (a) A final judgment or decree in any suit in the highest court of a State in which a decision in the suit could be had, where is drawn in question the validity of a treaty or statute of the United States, and the decision is against its validity; or where is drawn, in question the validity of a statute of any State, on the ground of its being repugnant to the Constitution, treaties, or laws of the United States, and the decision is in favor of its validity, may be reviewed by the Supreme Court upon a writ of error. The writ shall have the same effect as if the judgment or decree had been rendered or passed in a court of the United States. The Supreme Court may reverse, modify, or affirm the judgment or decree of such State court, and may, in its discretion, award execution or remand the cause to the court from which it was removed by the writ.

"(b) It shall be competent for the Supreme Court, by certiorari, to require that there be certified to it for review and determination, with the same power and authority and with like effect as if brought up by writ of error, any cause wherein a final judgment or decree has been rendered or passed by the highest court of a State in which a decision could be had where is drawn in question the validity of a treaty or statute of the United States; or where is drawn in question the validity of a statute of any State on the ground of its being repugnant to the Constitution, treaties, or laws of the United States; or where any title, right, privilege, or immunity is specially set up or claimed by either party under the Constitution, or any treaty or

Use of writ of error not hereby limited.

statute of, or commission held or authority exercised under, the United States; and the power to review under this paragraph may be exercised as well where the Federal claim is sustained as where it is denied. Nothing in this paragraph shall be construed to limit or detract from the right to a review on a writ of error in a case where such a right is conferred by the preceding paragraph; nor shall the fact that a review on a writ of error might be obtained under the preceding paragraph be an obstacle to granting a review on certiorari under this paragraph.

Writ of error not dismissed if certiorari proper mode of review, etc.

"(c) If a writ of error be improvidently sought and allowed under this section in a case where the proper mode of invoking a review is by a petition for certiorari, this alone shall not be a ground for dismissal; but the papers whereon the writ of error was allowed shall be regarded and acted on as a petition for certiorari and as if duly presented to the Supreme Court at the time they were presented to the court or judge by whom the writ of error was allowed: *Provided,* That where in such a case there appears to be no reasonable ground for granting a petition for certiorari it shall be competent for the Supreme Court to adjudge to the respondent reasonable damages for his delay, and single or double costs, as provided in section 1010 of the Revised Statutes."

Proviso. Damages, etc., if no reasonable ground for certiorari.

R.S., sec. 1010, p. 189.

Direct review of action of district courts in specified Acts limited. Vol. 38, p. 804, amended. Expediting antitrust, etc., cases. Vol. 32, p. 823.

"SEC. 238. A direct review by the Supreme Court of an interlocutory or final judgment or decree of a district court may be had where it is so provided in the following Acts or parts of Acts, and not otherwise:

"(1) Section 2 of the Act of February 11, 1903, 'to expedite the hearing and determination' of certain suits brought by the United States under the antitrust or interstate commerce laws, and so forth.

Adverse decisions in criminal cases. Vol. 34, p. 1246.

"(2) The Act of March 2, 1907, 'providing for writs of error in certain instances in criminal cases' where the decision of the district court is adverse to the United States.

Restricting interlocutory injunctions against State laws, etc. Vol. 37, p. 1013, amended.

"(3) An Act restricting the issuance of interlocutory injunctions to suspend the enforcement of the statute of a State or of an order made by an administrative board or commission created by and acting under the statute of a State, approved March 4, 1913, which Act is hereby amended by adding at the end thereof, 'The requirement respecting the presence of three judges shall also apply to the final hearing in such suit in the district court; and a direct appeal to the Supreme Court may be taken from a final decree granting or denying a permanent injunction in such suit.'

Requirement for presence of three judges, etc.

Judgments, etc., on Interstate Commerce Commission orders. Vol. 38, p. 220.

"(4) So much of 'An Act making appropriations to supply urgent deficiencies in appropriations for the fiscal year 1913, and for other purposes,' approved October 22, 1913, as relates to the review of interlocutory and final judgments and decrees in suits to enforce, suspend, or set aside orders of the Interstate Commerce Commission other than for the payment of money.

Orders by Interstate Commission as to livestock, poultry, etc.
Vol. 42, p. 168.

"(5) Section 316 of 'An Act to regulate interstate and foreign commerce in livestock, livestock products, dairy products, poultry, poultry products, and eggs, and for other purposes' approved August 15, 1921."

Questions certified for instructions by courts of appeals.
Vol. 36, p. 1157, amended.

Authority of court.

"SEC. 239. In any case, civil or criminal, in a circuit court of appeals, or in the Court of Appeals of the District of Columbia, the court at any time may certify to the Supreme Court of the United States any questions or propositions of law concerning which instructions are desired for the proper decision of the cause; and thereupon the Supreme Court may either give binding instructions on the questions and propositions certified or may require that the entire record in the cause be sent up for its consideration, and thereupon shall decide the whole matter in controversy in the same manner as if it had been brought there by writ of error or appeal."

Allowance of certiorari to courts of appeals on petition of either party.
Vol. 36, p. 1157, amended.

Writ of error or appeal allowed, where decision against validity of State law as repugnant to United States Constitution, etc.

Limitation.

No other review by Supreme Court.

SEC. 240. (a) In any case, civil or criminal, in a circuit court of appeals, or in the Court of Appeals of the District of Columbia, it shall be competent for the Supreme Court of the United States, upon the petition of any party thereto, whether Government or other litigant, to require by certiorari, either before or after a judgment or decree by such lower court, that the cause be certified to the Supreme Court for determination by it with the same power and authority, and with like effect, as if the cause had been brought there by unrestricted writ of error or appeal.

(b) Any case in a circuit court of appeals where is drawn in question the validity of a statute of any State, on the ground of its being repugnant to the Constitution, treaties, or laws of the United States, and the decision is against its validity, may, at the election of the party relying on such State statute, be taken to the Supreme Court for review on writ of error or appeal; but in that event a review on certiorari shall not be allowed at the instance of such party, and the review on such writ of error or appeal shall be restricted to an examination and decision of the Federal questions presented in the case.

"(c) No judgment or decree of a circuit court of appeals or of the Court of Appeals of the District of Columbia shall be subject to review by the Supreme Court otherwise than as provided in this section."

Certiorari, etc., allowed.
Railway employees arbitrations.
Vol. 38, p. 107.
Trade Commission orders.
Vol. 38, p. 720.
Clayton Act enforcement.
Vol. 38, p. 735.

SEC. 2. That cases in a circuit court of appeals under section 8 of "An Act providing for mediation, conciliation, and arbitration in controversies between certain employers and their employees," approved July 15, 1913; under section 5 of "An Act to create a Federal Trade Commission, to define its powers and duties, and for other purposes," approved September 26, 1914; and under section 11 of "An Act to supplement existing laws against unlawful restraints and monopolies, and for other purposes," approved October 15, 1914, are included among the cases to which sections 239 and 240 of the Judicial Code shall apply.

Court of Claims. May certify to Supreme Court questions of law for instruction.

Certiorari by either party of any cause for review and determination.

No other review of judgments.

SEC. 3. (a) That in any case in the court of Claims, including those begun under section 180 of the Judicial Code, that court at any time may certify to the Supreme Court any definite and distinct questions of law concerning which instructions are desired for the proper disposition of the cause; and thereupon the Supreme Court may give appropriate instructions on the questions certified and transmit the same to the Court of Claims for its guidance in the further progress of the cause.

(b) In any case in the Court of Claims, including those begun under section 180 of the Judicial Code, it shall be competent for the Supreme Court, upon the petition of either party, whether Government or claimant, to require, by certiorari, that the cause, including the findings of fact and the judgment or decree, but omitting the evidence, be certified to it for review and determination with the same power and authority, and with like effect, as if the cause had been brought there by appeal.

(c) All judgments and decrees of the Court of Claims shall be subject to review by the Supreme Court as provided in this section, and not otherwise.

Claims cases in district courts subject to like review as other judgments.
Ante, p. 938.

SEC. 4. That in cases in the district courts wherein they exercise concurrent jurisdiction with the Court of Claims or adjudicate claims against the United States the judgments shall be subject to review in the circuit courts of appeals like other judgments of the district courts; and sections 239 and 240 of the Judicial Code shall apply to such cases in the circuit courts of appeals as to other cases therein.

District of Columbia Court of Appeals. Jurisdiction of, like circuit court of appeals.

SEC. 5. That the Court of Appeals of the District of Columbia shall have the same appellate and supervisory jurisdiction over proceedings, controversies, and cases in bankruptcy in the District of Columbia that a circuit court of appeals has over such proceedings, controversies, and cases within its circuit, and shall exercise that jurisdiction in the same manner as a circuit court of appeals is required to exercise it.

Habeas corpus. Circuit courts of appeals to review final orders for.

By District of Columbia Court of Appeals.

Authority of Supreme Court.

SEC. 6. (a) In a proceeding in habeas corpus in a district court, or before a district judge or a circuit judge, the final order shall be subject to review, on appeal, by the circuit court of appeals of the circuit wherein the proceeding is had. A circuit judge shall have the same power to grant writs of habeas corpus within his circuit that a district judge has within his district; and the order of the circuit judge shall be entered in the records of the district court of the district wherein the restraint complained of is had.

(b) In such a proceeding in the Supreme Court of the District of Columbia, or before a justice thereof, the final order shall be subject to review, on appeal, by the Court of Appeals of that District.

(c) Sections 239 and 240 of the Judicial Code shall apply to habeas corpus cases in the circuit courts of appeals and in the Court of Appeals of the District of Columbia as to other cases therein.

(d) The provisions of sections 765 and 766 of the Revised Statutes, and the provisions of an Act entitled "An Act restricting in certain cases the right of appeal to the Supreme Court in habeas corpus proceedings," approved March 10, 1908, shall apply to appellate proceedings under this section as they heretofore have applied to direct appeals to the Supreme Court.

SEC. 7. That in any case in the Supreme Court of the Philippine Islands wherein the Constitution, or any statute or treaty of the United States is involved, or wherein the value in controversy exceeds $25,000, or wherein the title or possession of real estate exceeding in value the sum of $25,000 is involved or brought in question, it shall be competent for the Supreme Court of the United States, upon the petition of a party aggrieved by the final judgment or decree, to require, by certiorari, that the cause be certified to it for review and determination with the same power and authority, and with like effect, as if the cause had been brought before it on writ of error or appeal; and, except as provided in this section, the judgments and decrees of the Supreme Court of the Philippine Islands shall not be subject to appellate review.

SEC. 8. (a) That no writ of error, appeal, or writ of certiorari, intended to bring any judgment or decree before the Supreme Court for review shall be allowed or entertained unless application therefor be duly made within three months after the entry of such judgment or decree, excepting that writs of certiorari to the Supreme Court of the Philippine Islands may be granted where application therefor is made within six months: *Provided,* That for good cause shown either of such periods for applying for a writ of certiorari may be extended not exceeding sixty days by a justice of the Supreme Court.

(b) Where an application for a writ of certiorari is made with the purpose of securing a removal of the case to the Supreme Court from a circuit court of appeals or the Court of Appeals of the District of Columbia before the court wherein the same is pending has given a judgment or decree the application may be made at any time prior to the hearing and submission in that court.

(c) No writ of error or appeal intended to bring any judgment or decree before a circuit court of appeals for review shall be allowed unless application therefor be duly made within three months after the entry of such judgment or decree.

(d) In any case in which the final judgment or decree of any court is subject to review by the Supreme Court on writ of certiorari, the execution and enforcement of such judgment or decree may be stayed for a reasonable time to enable the party aggrieved to apply for and to obtain a writ of certiorari from the Supreme Court. The stay may be granted by a judge of the court rendering the judgment or decree or by a justice of the Supreme Court, and may be conditioned on the giving of good and sufficient security, to be approved by such judge or justice, that if the aggrieved party fails to make application for such writ within the period allotted therefor, or fails to obtain an order granting his application, or fails to make his plea good in the Supreme Court, he shall answer for all damage and costs which the other party may sustain by reason of the stay.

SEC. 9. That in any case where the power to review, whether in the circuit courts of appeals or in the Supreme Court, depends upon the amount or value in controversy, such amount or value, if not otherwise satisfactorily disclosed upon the record, may be shown and ascertained by the oath of a party to the cause or by other competent evidence.

SEC. 10. That no court having power to review a judgment or decree of another shall dismiss a writ of error solely because an appeal should have been taken, or dismiss an appeal solely because a writ of error should have been sued out; but where such error occurs the same shall be disregarded and the court shall proceed as if in that regard its power to review were properly invoked.

SEC. 11. (a) That where, during the pendency of an action, suit, or other proceeding brought by or against an officer of the United States, or of the District of Columbia, or the Canal Zone, or of a county, city, or other governmental agency of such Territory or insular possession, and relating to the present or future discharge of his official duties, such officer dies, resigns, or otherwise ceases to hold such office, it shall be competent for the court wherein the action, suit, or proceeding is pending, whether the court be one of first instance or an appellate tribunal, to permit the cause to be continued and maintained by or against the successor in office of such officer, if within six months after his death or separation from the office it be satisfactorily shown to the court that there is a substantial need for so continuing and maintaining the cause and obtaining an adjudication of the questions involved.

(b) Similar proceedings may be had and taken where an action, suit, or proceeding brought by or against an officer of a State, or of a county, city, or other governmental agency of a State, is pending in a court of the United States at the time of the officer's death or separation from the office.

(c) Before a substitution under this section is made, the party or officer to be affected, unless expressly consenting thereto, must be given reasonable notice of the application therefor and accorded an opportunity to present any objection which he may have.

Marginal notes (left column):

Ante, p. 938.

Circuit courts of appeals jurisdiction in State court cases. R.S., secs. 765, 766, p. 144. Vol. 35, p. 40.

Philippine Islands. Cases where certiorari from Supreme Court allowed.

Vol. 36, p. 1158.

No other appellate review allowed.

Time limit for bringing judgments to Supreme Court for review.

Proviso. Extension for cause.

Certiorari allowed prior to hearing in courts of appeals.

Time limit to apply for review by circuit courts of appeals.

Judgments may be stayed in cases subject to certiorari from Supreme Court.

Marginal notes (right column):

Surety to be given, etc.

Ascertainment of value not disclosed upon record, if jurisdiction depends on amount thereof.

Appellate courts. No case dismissed, solely for mistake of procedure. Vol. 39, p. 727.

Action if Federal, etc., officer dies while suit pending.

Cause continued, and successor substituted if substantial need thereof.

Similar action as to State, etc., officer.

Notice of proposed substitution to be given.

Federal incorporation not a ground for action in district courts.

SEC. 12. That no district court shall have jurisdiction of any action or suit by or against any corporation upon the ground that it was incorporated by or under an Act of Congress: *Provided,* That this section shall not apply to any suit, action, or proceeding brought by or against a corporation incorporated by or under an Act of Congress wherein the Government of the United States is the owner of more than one-half of its capital stock.

Proviso.
Except if Government principal owner of stock.

Laws repealed.

SEC. 13. That the following statutes and parts of statutes be, and they are, repealed:

Judicial Code sections.

Sections 130, 131, 133, 134, 181, 182, 236, 241, 242, 243, 244, 245, 246, 247, 248, 249, 250, 251, and 252 of the Judicial Code.

Appellate jurisdiction, court of appeals to Supreme Court.
Vol. 38, pp. 803, 804
Writs of error to Supreme Court.
Vol. 39, p. 726

Sections 2, 4, and 5 of "An Act to amend an Act entitled 'An Act to codify, revise, and amend the laws relating to the judiciary,' approved March 3, 1911," approved January 28, 1915.

Sections 2, 3, 4, 5, and 6 of "An Act to amend the Judicial Code, to fix the time when the annual term of the Supreme Court shall commence, and further to define the jurisdiction of that court," approved September 6, 1916.

Judgments of Philippine Supreme Court.
Vol. 39, p. 555.

Section 27 of "An Act to declare the purpose of the people of the United States as to the future political status of the people of the Philippine Islands, and to provide a more autonomous government for those islands," approved August 29, 1916.

Review by Supreme Court of suits against the United States.
Vol. 24, pp. 506, 507.

So much of sections 4, 9, and 10 of "An Act to provide for the bringing of suits against the Government of the United States," approved March 3, 1887, as provides for a review by the Supreme Court on writ of error or appeal in the cases therein named.

Direct appeal in habeas corpus.
Vol. 35, p. 40.

So much of "An Act restricting in certain cases the right of appeal to the Supreme Court in habeas corpus proceedings," approved March 10, 1908, as permits a direct appeal to the Supreme Court.

Review of bankruptcy cases.
Vol. 30, p. 553.

So much of sections 24 and 25 of the Bankruptcy Act of July 1, 1898, as regulates the mode of review by the Supreme Court in the proceedings, controversies, and cases therein named.

Porto Rico courts.
Vol. 39, p. 966.

So much of "An Act to provide a civil government for Porto Rico, and for other purposes," approved March 2, 1917, as permits a direct review by the Supreme Court of cases in the courts of Porto Rico.

Hawaii courts.
Vol. 42, p. 120.

So much of the Hawaiian Organic Act, as amended by the Act of July 9, 1921, as permits a direct review by the Supreme Court of cases in the courts in Hawaii.

Canal Zone district courts.
Vol. 37, p. 566.

So much of section 9 of the Act of August 24, 1912, relating to the government of the Canal Zone as designates the cases in which, and the courts by which, the judgments and decrees of the district court of the Canal Zone may be reviewed.

Bankruptcy appeals.
R.S., secs. 763, 764, p. 143.
Vol. 23, p. 437.
Actions against Federal officers.
Vol. 30, p. 822.
Contracts repugnant to the Constitution.
Vol. 42, p. 366.
Transfers of appeals and writs of error.
Vol. 42, p. 837.
All other inconsistent Acts, etc.

Sections 763 and 764 of the Revised Statutes.

An Act entitled "An Act amending section 764 of the Revised Statutes," approved March 3, 1885.

An Act entitled "An Act to prevent the abatement of certain actions," approved February 8, 1899.

An Act entitled "An Act to amend section 237 of the Judicial Code," approved February 17, 1922.

An Act entitled "An Act to amend the Judicial Code in reference to appeals and writs of error," approved September 14, 1922.

All other Acts and parts of Acts in so far as they are embraced within and superseded by this Act or are inconsistent therewith.

Effective in three months. Pending cases in Supreme Court, etc., not affected.

SEC. 14. That this Act shall take effect three months after its approval; but it shall not affect cases then pending in the Supreme Court, nor shall it affect the right to a review, or the mode or time for exercising the same, as respects any judgment or decree entered prior to the date when it takes effect.

Approved, February 13, 1925.

SOURCE: *Public Statutes at Large of the United States of America,* Vol. XLIII, Part 1 (Washington, D.C.: U.S. Government Printing Office, 1925).

Roosevelt's 1937 Court Reform Plan

President Franklin D. Roosevelt's plan to increase the Supreme Court's membership in 1937 was an example of a president attempting to change the size of the Court's membership to achieve a judicial consensus more to his liking.

In 1935 and 1936 the Court struck down nearly every important measure of Roosevelt's New Deal program, which called for government spending and work projects to help farmers, labor, and business survive the Great Depression. Encouraged by his overwhelming reelection mandate of 1936, Roosevelt proposed his "Court reform" bill—permitting a president to add a justice to the Supreme Court for every justice over seventy who refused to retire, for a total of fifteen justices. The "Court-packing" plan—as it became known—was extremely unpopular in Congress, and it opened a serious rift in the Democratic Party.

But the potential political confrontation was averted. By the time the bill was unfavorably reported by the Senate Judiciary Committee, Roosevelt had begun to get more cooperation from a Court suddenly more amenable to his legislation. The bill never reached the Senate floor, and the scheme was allowed to die. Roosevelt eventually transformed the Court by making nine appointments to it as vacancies arose during the rest of his presidency.

LETTER OF ATTORNEY GENERAL

FEBRUARY 2, 1937

The President,
The White House.

MY DEAR MR. PRESIDENT: Delay in the administration of justice is the outstanding defect of our Federal judicial system. It has been a cause of concern to practically every one of my predecessors in office. It has exasperated the bench, the bar, the business community, and the public.

The litigant conceives the judge as one promoting justice through the mechanism of the courts. He assumes that the directing power of the judge is exercised over its officers from the time a case is filed with the clerk of the court. He is entitled to assume that the judge is pressing forward litigation in the full recognition of the principle that "justice delayed is justice denied." It is a mockery of justice to say to a person when he files suit that he may receive a decision years later. Under a properly ordered system rights should be determined promptly. The course of litigation should be measured in months and not in years.

Yet in some jurisdictions the delays in the administration of justice are so interminable that to institute suit is to embark on a life-long adventure. Many persons submit to acts of injustice rather than resort to the courts. Inability to secure a prompt judicial adjudication leads to improvident and unjust settlements. Moreover, the time factor is an open invitation to those who are disposed to institute unwarranted litigation or interpose unfounded defenses in the hope of forcing an adjustment which could not be secured upon the merits. This situation frequently results in extreme hardships. The small businessman or the litigant of limited means labors under a grave and constantly increasing disadvantage because of his inability to pay the price of justice.

Statistical data indicate that in many districts a disheartening and unavoidable interval must elapse between the date that issue is joined in a pending case and the time when it can be reached for trial in due course. These computations do not take into account the delays that occur in the preliminary stages of litigation or the postponements after a case might normally be expected to be heard.

The evil is a growing one. The business of the courts is continually increasing in volume, importance, and complexity. The average case load borne by each judge has grown nearly 50 percent since 1913, when the district courts were first organized on their present basis. When the courts are working under such pressure it is inevitable that the character of their work must suffer.

The number of new cases offset those that are disposed of, so that the courts are unable to decrease the enormous backlog of undigested matters. More than 50,000 pending cases, exclusive of bankruptcy proceedings, overhang the Federal dockets—a constant menace to the orderly processes of justice. Whenever a single case requires a protracted trial the routine business of the court is further neglected. It is an intolerable situation and we should make shift to amend it.

Efforts have been made from time to time to alleviate some of the conditions that contribute to the slow rate of speed with which cases move through the courts. The Congress has recently conferred on the Supreme Court the authority to prescribe rules of procedure after verdict in criminal cases and the power to adopt and promulgate uniform rules of practice for civil actions at law in the district courts. It has provided terms of court in certain places at which Federal courts had not previously convened. A small number of judges have been added from time to time.

Despite these commendable accomplishments sufficient progress has not been made. Much remains to be done in developing procedure and administration, but this alone will not meet modern needs. The problem must be approached in a more comprehensive fashion if the United States is to have a judicial system worthy of the Nation. Reason and necessity require the appointment of a sufficient number of judges to handle the business of the Federal courts. These additional judges should be of a type and age which would warrant us in believing that they would vigorously attack their dockets rather than permit their dockets to overwhelm them.

The cost of additional personnel should not deter us. It must be borne in mind that the expense of maintaining the judicial system constitutes hardly three-tenths of 1 percent of the cost of maintaining the Federal establishment. While the estimates for the current fiscal year aggregate over $23,000,000 for the maintenance of the legislative branch of the Government, and over $2,100,000,000 for the permanent agencies of the executive branch, the estimated cost of maintaining the judiciary is only about $6,500,000. An increase in the judicial personnel, which I earnestly recommend, would result in a hardly perceptible percentage of increase in the total annual Budget.

This result should not be achieved, however, merely by creating new judicial positions in specific circuits or districts. The reform should be effectuated on the basis of a consistent system which would revitalize our whole judicial structure and assure the activity of judges at places where the accumulation of business is greatest. As congestion is a varying factor and cannot be foreseen, the system should be flexible and should permit the temporary assignment of judges to points where they appear to be most needed. The newly created personnel should constitute a mobile force, available for service in any part of the country at the assignment and direction of the Chief Justice. A functionary might well be created to be known as proctor, or by some other suitable title, to be appointed by the Supreme Court and to act under its direction, charged with the duty of continuously keeping informed as to the state of Federal judicial business throughout the United States and of assisting the Chief Justice in assigning judges to pressure areas.

I append hereto certain statistical information, which will give point to the suggestions I have made.

These suggestions are designed to carry forward the program for improving the processes of justice which we have discussed and worked upon since the beginning of your first administration.

The time has come when further legislation is essential.

To speed justice, to bring it within the reach of every citizen, to free it of unnecessary entanglements and delays are primary obligations of our Government.

Respectfully submitted.

HOMER CUMMINGS,
Attorney General.

ROOSEVELT'S MESSAGE TO CONGRESS

FEBRUARY 5

February 5, 1937.—Referred to the Committee on the Judiciary and ordered to be printed.

THE WHITE HOUSE, *February 5, 1937*

TO THE CONGRESS OF THE UNITED STATES:

I have recently called the attention of the Congress to the clear need for a comprehensive program to reorganize the administrative machinery of the executive branch of our Government. I now make a similar recommendation to the Congress in regard to the judicial branch of the Government, in order that it also may function in accord with modern necessities.

The Constitution provides that the President "shall from time to time give to the Congress information of the state of the Union, and recommend to their consideration such measures as he shall judge necessary and expedient." No one else is given a similar mandate. It is therefore the duty of the President to advise the Congress in regard to the judiciary whenever he deems such information or recommendation necessary.

I address you for the further reason that the Constitution vests in the Congress direct responsibility in the creation of courts and judicial offices and in the formulation of rules of practice and procedure. It is, therefore, one of the definite duties of the Congress constantly to maintain the effective functioning of the Federal judiciary.

The judiciary has often found itself handicapped by insufficient personnel with which to meet a growing and more complex business. It is true that the physical facilities of conducting the business of the courts have been greatly improved, in recent years, through the erection of suitable quarters, the provision of adequate libraries, and the addition of subordinate court officers. But in many ways these are merely the trappings of judicial office. They play a minor part in the processes of justice.

Since the earliest days of the Republic, the problem of the personnel of the courts has needed the attention of the Congress. For example, from the beginning, over repeated protests to President Washington, the Justices of the Supreme Court were required to "ride circuit" and, as circuit justices, to hold trials throughout the length and breadth of the land—a practice which endured over a century.

In almost every decade since 1789 changes have been made by the Congress whereby the numbers of judges and the duties of judges in Federal courts have been altered in one way or another. The Supreme Court was established with 6 members in 1789; it was reduced to 5 in 1801; it was increased to 7 in 1807; it was increased to 9 in 1837; it was increased to 10 in 1863; it was reduced to 7 in 1866; it was increased to 9 in 1869.

The simple fact is that today a new need for legislative action arises because the personnel of the Federal judiciary is insufficient to meet the business before them. A growing body of our citizens complain of the complexities, the delays, and the expense of litigation in United States courts.

A letter from the Attorney General, which I submit herewith, justifies by reasoning and statistics the common impression created by our overcrowded Federal dockets—and it proves the need for additional judges.

Delay in any court results in injustice.

It makes lawsuits a luxury available only to the few who can afford them or who have property interests to protect which are sufficiently large to repay the cost. Poorer litigants are compelled to abandon valuable rights or to accept inadequate or unjust settlements because of sheer inability to finance or to await the end of a long litigation. Only by speeding up the processes of the law and thereby reducing their cost, can we eradicate the growing impression that the courts are chiefly a haven for the well-to-do.

Delays in the determination of appeals have the same effect. Moreover, if trials of original actions are expedited and existing accumulations of cases are reduced, the volume of work imposed on the circuit courts of appeals will further increase.

The attainment of speedier justice in the courts below will enlarge the task of the Supreme Court itself. And still more work would be added by the recommendation which I make later in this message for the quicker determination of constitutional questions by the highest court.

Even at the present time the Supreme Court is laboring under a heavy burden. Its difficulties in this respect were superficially lightened some years ago by authorizing the Court, in its discretion, to refuse to hear appeals in many classes of cases. This discretion was so freely exercised that in the last fiscal year, although 867 petitions for review were presented to the Supreme Court, it declined to hear 717 cases. If petitions in behalf of the Government are excluded, it appears that the Court permitted private litigants to prosecute appeals in only 108 cases out of 803 applications. Many of the refusals were doubtless warranted. But can it be said that full justice is achieved when a court is forced by the sheer necessity of keeping up with its business to decline, without even an explanation, to hear 87 percent of the cases presented to it by private litigants?

It seems clear, therefore, that the necessity of relieving present congestion extends to the enlargement of the capacity of all the Federal courts.

A part of the problem of obtaining a sufficient number of judges to dispose of cases is the capacity of the judges themselves. This brings forward the question of aged or infirm judges—a subject of delicacy and yet one which requires frank discussion.

In the Federal courts there are in all 237 life tenure permanent judgeships. Twenty-five of them are now held by judges over 70 years of age and eligible to leave the bench on full pay. Originally no pension or retirement allowance was provided by the Congress. When after 80 years of our national history the Congress made provision for pensions, it found a well-entrenched tradition among judges to cling to their posts, in many instances far beyond their years of physical or mental capacity. Their salaries were small. As with other men, responsibilities and obligations accumulated. No alternative had been open to them except to attempt to perform the duties of their offices to the very edge of the grave.

In exceptional cases, of course, judges, like other men, retain to an advanced age full mental and physical vigor. Those not so fortunate are often unable to perceive their own infirmities. "They seem to be tenacious of the appearance of adequacy." The voluntary retirement law of 1869 provided, therefore, only a partial solution. That law, still in force, has not proved effective in inducing aged judges to retire on a pension.

This result had been foreseen in the debates when the measure was being considered. It was then proposed that when a judge refused to retire upon reaching the age of 70, an additional judge should be appointed to assist in the work of the court. The proposal passed the House but was eliminated in the Senate.

With the opening of the twentieth century, and the great increase of population and commerce, and the growth of a more complex type of litigation, similar proposals were introduced in the Congress. To meet the situation, in 1913, 1914, 1915, and 1916, the Attorneys General then in office recommended to the Congress that when a district or a circuit judge failed to retire at the age of 70, an additional judge be appointed in order that the affairs of the court might be promptly and adequately discharged.

In 1919 a law was finally passed providing that the President "may" appoint additional district and circuit judges, but only upon a finding that the incumbent judge over 70 "is unable to discharge efficiently all the duties of his office by reason of mental or physical disability of permanent character." The discretionary and indefinite nature of this legislation has rendered it ineffective. No President should be asked to determine the ability or disability of any particular judge.

The duty of a judge involves more than presiding or listening to testimony or arguments. It is well to remember that the mass of details involved in the average of law cases today is vastly greater and more complicated than even 20 years ago. Records and briefs must be read; statutes, decisions, and extensive material of a technical, scientific, statistical, and economic nature must be searched and studied; opinions must be formulated and written. The modern tasks of judges call for the use of full energies.

Modern complexities call also for a constant infusion of new blood in the courts, just as it is needed in executive functions of the Government and in private business. A lowered mental or physical vigor leads men to avoid an examination of complicated and changed conditions. Little by little, new facts become blurred through old glasses fitted, as it were, for the needs of another generation; older men, assuming that the scene is the same as it was in the past, cease to explore or inquire into the present or the future.

We have recognized this truth in the civil service of the Nation and of many States by compelling retirement on pay at the age of 70. We have recognized it in the Army and Navy by retiring officers at the age of 64. A number of States have recognized it by providing in their constitutions for compulsory retirement of aged judges.

Life tenure of judges, assured by the Constitution, was designed to place the courts beyond temptations or influences which might impair their judgments; it was not intended to create a static judiciary. A constant and systematic addition of younger blood will vitalize the courts and better equip them to recognize and apply the essential concepts of justice in the light of the needs and the facts of an ever changing world.

It is obvious, therefore, from both reason and experience, that some provision must be adopted which will operate automatically to supplement the work of older judges and accelerate the work of the court.

I, therefore, earnestly recommend that the necessity of an increase in the number of judges be supplied by legislation providing for the appointment of additional judges in all Federal courts, without exception, where there are incumbent judges of retirement age who do not choose to retire or to resign. If an elder judge is not in fact incapacitated, only good can come from the presence of an additional judge in the crowded state of the dockets; if the capacity of an elder judge is in fact impaired, the appointment of an additional judge is indispensable. This seems to be a truth which cannot be contradicted.

I also recommend that the Congress provide machinery for taking care of sudden or long-standing congestion in the lower courts. The Supreme Court should be given power to appoint an administrative assistant who may be called a proctor. He would be charged with the duty of watching the calendars and the business of all the courts in the Federal system. The Chief Justice thereupon should be authorized to make a temporary assignment of any circuit or district judge hereafter appointed in order that he may serve as long as needed in any circuit or district where the courts are in arrears.

I attach a carefully considered draft of a proposed bill, which, if enacted, would, I am confident, afford substantial relief. The proposed measure also contains a limit on the total number of judges who might thus be appointed and also a limit on the potential size of any one of our Federal courts.

These proposals do not raise any issue of constitutional law. They do not suggest any form of compulsory retirement for incumbent judges. Indeed, those who have reached the retirement age, but desire to continue their judicial work, would be able to do so under less physical and mental strain and would be able to play a useful part in relieving the growing congestion in the business of our courts. Among them are men of eminence and great ability whose services the Government would be loath to lose. If, on the other hand, any judge eligible for retirement should feel that his court would suffer because of an increase in its membership, he may retire or resign under already existing provisions of law if he wishes so to do. In this connection let me say that the pending proposal to extend to the Justices of the Supreme Court the same retirement privileges now available to other Federal judges, has my entire approval.

One further matter requires immediate attention. We have witnessed the spectacle of conflicting decisions in both trial and appellate courts on the constitutionality of every form of important legislation. Such a welter of uncomposed differences of judicial opinion has brought the law, the courts, and, indeed, the entire administration of justice dangerously near to disrepute.

A Federal statute is held legal by one judge in one district; it is simultaneously held illegal by another judge in another district. An act valid in one judicial circuit is invalid in another judicial circuit. Thus rights fully accorded to one group of citizens may be denied to others. As a practical matter this means that for periods running as long as 1 year or 2 years or 3 years—until final determination can be made by the Supreme Court—the law loses its most indispensable element—equality.

Moreover, during the long processes of preliminary motions, original trials, petitions for rehearings, appeals, reversals on technical grounds requiring retrials, motions before the Supreme Court, and the final hearing by the highest tribunal—during all this time labor, industry, agriculture, commerce, and the Government itself go through an unconscionable period of uncertainty and embarrassment. And it is well to remember that during these long processes the normal operations of society and government are handicapped in many cases by differing and divided opinions in the lower courts and by the lack of any clear guide for the dispatch of business. Thereby our legal system is fast losing another essential of justice—certainty.

Finally, we find the processes of government itself brought to a complete stop from time to time by injunctions issued almost automatically, sometimes even without notice to the Government, and not infrequently in clear violation of the principle of equity that injunctions should be granted only in those rare cases of manifest illegality and irreparable damage against which the ordinary course of the law offers no protection. Statutes which the Congress enacts are set aside or suspended for long periods of time, even in cases to which the Government is not a party.

In the uncertain state of the law, it is not difficult for the ingenious to devise novel reasons for attacking the validity of new legislation or its application. While these questions are laboriously brought to issue and debated through a series of courts, the Government must stand aside. It matters not that the Congress has enacted the law, that the Executive has signed it, and that the administrative machinery is waiting to function. Government by injunction lays a heavy hand upon normal processes; and no important statute can take effect—against any individual or organization with the means to employ lawyers and engaged in wide-flung litigation—until it has passed through the whole hierarchy of the courts. Thus the judiciary, by postponing the effective date of acts of the Congress, is assuming an additional function and is coming more and more to constitute a scattered, loosely organized, and slowly operating third house of the National Legislature.

This state of affairs has come upon the Nation gradually over a period of decades. In my annual message to this Congress I expressed some views and some hopes.

Now, as an immediate step, I recommend that the Congress provide that no decision, injunction, judgment, or decree on any constitutional question be promulgated by any Federal court without previous and ample notice to the Attorney General and an opportunity for the United States to present evidence and be heard. This is to prevent court action on the constitutionality of acts of the Congress in suits between private individuals, where the Government is not a party to the suit, without giving opportunity to the Government of the United States to defend the law of the land.

I also earnestly recommend that, in cases in which any court of first instance determines a question of constitutionality, the Congress provide that there shall be a direct and immediate appeal to the Supreme Court and that such cases take precedence over all other matters pending in that court. Such legislation will, I am convinced, go far to alleviate the inequality, uncertainty, and delay in the disposition of vital questions of constitutionality arising under our fundamental law.

My desire is to strengthen the administration of justice and to make it a more effective servant of public need. In the American ideal of government the courts find an essential and constitutional place. In striving to fulfill that ideal, not only the judges but the Congress and the Executive as well, must do all in their power to bring the judicial organization and personnel to the high standards of usefulness which sound and efficient government and modern conditions require.

This message has dealt with four present needs:

First, to eliminate congestion of calendars and to make the judiciary as a whole less static by the constant and systematic addition of new blood to its personnel; second, to make the judiciary more elastic by providing for temporary transfers of circuit and district judges to those places where Federal courts are most in arrears; third, to furnish the Supreme Court practical assistance in supervising the conduct of business in the lower courts; fourth, to eliminate inequality, uncertainty, and delay now existing in the determination of constitutional questions involving Federal statutes.

If we increase the personnel of the Federal courts so that cases may be promptly decided in the first instance, and may be given adequate and prompt hearing on all appeals; if we invigorate all the courts by the persistent infusion of new blood; if we grant to the Supreme Court further power and responsibility in maintaining the efficiency of the entire Federal judiciary; and if we assure Government participation in the speedier consideration and final determination of all constitutional questions, we shall go a long way toward our high objectives. If these measures achieve their aim, we may be relieved of the necessity of considering any fundamental changes in the powers of the courts or the Constitution of our Government—changes which involve consequences so far reaching as to cause uncertainty as to the wisdom of such course.

FRANKLIN D. ROOSEVELT

WHITE HOUSE BROADCAST

MARCH 9, 1937

Last Thursday I described in detail certain economic problems which everyone admits now face the Nation. For the many messages which have come to me after that speech, and which it is physically impossible to answer individually, I take this means of saying "thank you."

Tonight, sitting at my desk in the White House, I make my first radio report to the people in my second term of office.

I am reminded of that evening in March, four years ago, when I made my first radio report to you. We were then in the midst of the great banking crisis.

Soon after, with the authority of the Congress, we asked the Nation to turn over all of its privately held gold, dollar for dollar, to the Government of the United States.

Today's recovery proves how right that policy was.

But when, almost two years later, it came before the Supreme Court its constitutionality was upheld only by a five-to-four vote. The change of one vote would have thrown all the affairs of this great Nation back into hopeless chaos. In effect, four Justices ruled that the right under a private contract to exact a pound of flesh was more sacred than the main objectives of the Constitution to establish an enduring Nation.

In 1933 you and I knew that we must never let our economic system get completely out of joint again—that we could not afford to take the risk of another great depression.

We also became convinced that the only way to avoid a repetition of those dark days was to have a government with power to prevent and to cure the abuses and the inequalities which had thrown that system out of joint.

We then began a program of remedying those abuses and inequalities—to give balance and stability to our economic system—to make it bomb-proof against the causes of 1929.

Today we are only part-way through that program—and recovery is speeding up to a point where the dangers of 1929 are again becoming possible, not this week or month perhaps, but within a year or two.

National laws are needed to complete that program. Individual or local or state effort alone cannot protect us in 1937 any better than ten years ago.

It will take time—and plenty of time—to work out our remedies administratively even after legislation is passed. To complete our program of protection in time, therefore, we cannot delay one moment in making certain that our National Government has power to carry through.

Four years ago action did not come until the eleventh hour. It was almost too late.

If we learned anything from the depression we will not allow ourselves to run around in new circles of futile discussion and debate, always postponing the day of decision.

The American people have learned from the depression. For in the last three national elections an overwhelming majority of them voted a mandate that the Congress and the President begin the task of providing that protection—not after long years of debate, but now.

The Courts, however, have cast doubts on the ability of the elected Congress to protect us against catastrophe by meeting squarely our modern social and economic conditions.

We are at a crisis in our ability to proceed with that protection. It is a quiet crisis. There are no lines of depositors outside closed banks. But to the far-sighted it is far-reaching in its possibilities of injury to America.

I want to talk with you very simply about the need for present action in this crisis—the need to meet the unanswered challenge of one-third of a Nation ill-nourished, ill-clad, ill-housed.

Last Thursday I described the American form of Government as a three horse team provided by the Constitution to the American people so that their field might be plowed. The three horses are, of course, the three branches of government—the Congress, the Executive and the Courts. Two of the horses are pulling in unison today; the third is not. Those who have intimated that the President of the United States is trying to drive that team overlook the simple fact that the President, as Chief Executive, is himself one of the three horses.

It is the American people themselves who are in the driver's seat.

It is the American people themselves who want the furrow plowed.

It is the American people themselves who expect the third horse to pull in unison with the other two.

I hope that you have re-read the Constitution of the United States. Like the Bible, it ought to be read again and again.

It is an easy document to understand when you remember that it was called into being because the Articles of Confederation under which the original thirteen States tried to operate after the Revolution showed the need of a National Government with power enough to handle national problems. In its Preamble, the Constitution states that it was intended to form a more perfect Union and promote the general welfare; and the powers given to the Congress to carry out those purposes can be best described by saying that they were all the powers needed to meet each and every problem which then had a national character and which could not be met by merely local action.

But the framers went further. Having in mind that in succeeding generations many other problems then undreamed of would become national problems, they gave to the Congress the ample broad powers "to levy taxes . . . and provide for the common defense and general welfare of the United States."

That, my friends, is what I honestly believe to have been the clear and underlying purpose of the patriots who wrote a Federal Constitution to create a National Government with national power, intended as they said, "to form a more perfect union . . . for ourselves and our posterity."

For nearly twenty years there was no conflict between the Congress and the Court. Then, in 1803, Congress passed a statute which the Court said violated an express provision of the Constitution. The Court claimed the power to declare it unconstitutional and did so declare it. But a little later the Court itself admitted that it was an extraordinary power to exercise and through Mr. Justice Washington laid down this limitation upon it: "It is but a decent respect due to the wisdom, the integrity and the patriotism of the Legislative body, by which any law is passed, to presume in favor of its validity until its violation of the Constitution is proved beyond all reasonable doubt."

But since the rise of the modern movement for social and economic progress through legislation, the Court has more and more often and more and more boldly asserted a power to veto laws passed by the Congress and State Legislatures in complete disregard of this original limitation.

In the last four years the sound rule of giving statutes the benefit of all reasonable doubt has been cast aside. The Court has been acting not as a judicial body, but as a policy-making body.

When the Congress has sought to stabilize national agriculture, to improve the conditions of labor, to safeguard business against unfair competition, to protect our national resources, and in many other ways, to serve our clearly national needs, the majority of the Court has been assuming the power to pass on the wisdom of these Acts of the Congress—and to approve or disapprove the public policy written into these laws.

That is not only my accusation. It is the accusation of most distinguished Justices of the present Supreme Court. I have not the time to quote to you all the language used by dissenting Justices in many of these cases. But in the case holding the Railroad Retirement Act unconstitutional, for instance, Chief Justice Hughes said in a dissenting opinion that the majority opinion was "a departure from sound principles," and placed "an unwarranted limitation upon the commerce clause." And three other Justices agreed with him.

In the case holding the A.A.A. unconstitutional, Justice Stone said of the majority opinion that it was a "tortured construction of the Constitution." And two other Justices agreed with him.

In the case holding the New York Minimum Wage Law unconstitutional, Justice Stone said that the majority were actually reading into the Constitution their own "personal economic predilections," and that if the legislative power is not left free to choose the methods of solving the problems of poverty, subsistence and health of large numbers in the community, then "government is to be rendered impotent." And two other Justices agreed with him.

In the face of these dissenting opinions, there is no basis for the claim made by some members of the Court that something in the Constitution has compelled them regretfully to thwart the will of the people.

In the face of such dissenting opinions, it is perfectly clear, that as Chief Justice Hughes has said: "We are under a Constitution but the Constitution is what the Judges say it is."

The Court in addition to the proper use of its judicial functions has improperly set itself up as a third House of the Congress—a super-legislature, as one of the Justices has called it—reading into the Constitution words and implications which are not there, and which were never intended to be there.

We have, therefore, reached the point as a Nation where we must take action to save the Constitution from the Court and the Court from itself. We must find a way to take an appeal from the Supreme Court to the Constitution itself. We want a Supreme Court which will do justice under the Constitution—not over it. In our Courts we want a government of laws and not of men.

I want—as all Americans want—an independent judiciary as proposed by the framers of the Constitution. That means a Supreme Court that will enforce the Constitution as written—that will refuse to amend the Constitution by the arbitrary exercise of judicial power—amendment by judicial say-so. It does not mean a judiciary so independent that it can deny the existence of facts universally recognized.

How then could we proceed to perform the mandate given us? It was said in last year's Democratic platform "If these problems cannot be effectively solved within the Constitution, we shall seek such clarifying amendment as will assure the power to enact those laws, adequately to regulate commerce, protect public health and safety, and safeguard economic security." In other words, we said we would seek an amendment only if every other possible means by legislation were to fail.

When I commenced to review the situation with the problem squarely before me, I came by a process of elimination to the conclusion that short of amendments the only method which was clearly constitutional, and would at the same time carry out other much needed reforms, was to infuse new blood into all our Courts. We must have men worthy and equipped to carry out impartial justice. But, at the same time, we must have Judges who will bring to the Courts a present-day sense of the Constitution—Judges who will retain in the Courts the judicial functions of a court, and reject the legislative powers which the Courts have today assumed.

In forty-five out of the forty-eight States of the Union, Judges are chosen not for life but for a period of years. In many States Judges must retire at the age of seventy. Congress has provided financial security by offering life pensions at full pay for Federal Judges on all Courts who are willing to retire at seventy. In the case of Supreme Court Justices, that pension is $20,000 a year. But all Federal Judges, once appointed, can, if they choose, hold office for life, no matter how old they may get to be.

What is my proposal? It is simply this: whenever a Judge or Justice of any Federal Court has reached the age of seventy and does not avail himself of the opportunity to retire on a pension, a new member shall be appointed by the President then in office, with the approval, as required by the Constitution, of the Senate of the United States.

That plan has two chief purposes. By bringing into the Judicial system a steady and continuing stream of new and younger blood, I hope, first, to make the administration of all Federal justice speedier and, therefore, less costly; secondly, to bring to the decision of social and economic problems younger men who have had personal experience and contact with modern facts and circumstances under which average men have to live and work. This plan will save our national Constitution from hardening of the judicial arteries.

The number of Judges to be appointed would depend wholly on the decision of present Judges now over seventy, or those who would subsequently reach the age of seventy.

If, for instance, any one of the six Justices of the Supreme Court now over the age of seventy should retire as provided under the plan, no additional place would be created. Consequently, although there never can be more than fifteen, there may be only fourteen, or thirteen, or twelve. And there may be only nine.

There is nothing novel or radical about this idea. It seeks to maintain the Federal bench in full vigor. It has been discussed and approved by many persons of high authority ever since a similar proposal passed the House of Representatives in 1869.

Why was the age fixed at seventy? Because the laws of many States, the practice of the Civil Service, the regulations of the Army and Navy, and the rules of many of our Universities and of almost every great private business enterprise, commonly fix the retirement age at seventy years or less.

The statute would apply to all the Courts in the Federal system. There is general approval so far as the lower Federal courts are concerned. The plan has met opposition only so far as the Supreme Court of the United States itself is concerned. If such a plan is good for the lower courts it certainly ought to be equally good for the highest Court from which there is no appeal.

Those opposing this plan have sought to arouse prejudice and fear by crying that I am seeking to "pack" the Supreme Court and that a baneful precedent will be established.

What do they mean by the words "packing the Court"?

Let me answer this question with a bluntness that will end all *honest* misunderstanding of my purposes.

If by that phrase "packing the Court" it is charged that I wish to place on the bench spineless puppets who would disregard the law and would decide specific cases as I wished them to be decided, I make this answer—that no President fit for his office would appoint, and no Senate of honorable men fit for their office would confirm, that kind of appointees to the Supreme Court.

But if by that phrase the charge is made that I would appoint and the Senate would confirm Justices worthy to sit beside present members of the Court who understand those modern conditions—that I will appoint Justices who will not undertake to override the judgment of the Congress on legislative policy—that I will appoint Justices who will act as Justices and not as legislators—if the appointment of such Justices can be called "packing the Courts," then I say that I and with me the vast majority of the American people favor doing just that thing—now.

Is it a dangerous precedent for the Congress to change the number of the Justices? The Congress has always had, and will have, that power. The number of Justices has been changed several times before—in the Administrations of John Adams and Thomas Jefferson,—both signers of the Declaration of Independence—Andrew Jackson, Abraham Lincoln and Ulysses S. Grant.

I suggest only the addition of Justices to the bench in accordance with a clearly defined principle relating to a clearly defined age limit. Fundamentally, if in the future, America cannot trust the Congress it elects to refrain from abuse of our Constitutional usages, democracy will have failed far beyond the importance to it of any kind of precedent concerning the Judiciary.

We think it so much in the public interest to maintain a vigorous judiciary that we encourage the retirement of elderly Judges by offering them a life pension at full salary. Why then should we leave the fulfillment of this public policy to chance or make it dependent upon the desire or prejudice of any individual Justice?

It is the clear intention of our public policy to provide for a constant flow of new and younger blood into the Judiciary. Normally every President appoints a large number of District and Circuit Judges and a few members of the Supreme Court. Until my first term practically every President of the United States had appointed at least one member of the Supreme Court. President Taft appointed five members and named a Chief Justice—President Wilson three—President Harding four including a Chief Justice—President Coolidge one—President Hoover three including a Chief Justice.

Such a succession of appointments should have provided a Court well-balanced as to age. But chance and the disinclination of individuals to leave the Supreme bench have now given us a Court in which five Justices will be over seventy-five years of age before next June and one over seventy. Thus a sound public policy has been defeated.

I now propose that we establish by law an assurance against any such ill-balanced Court in the future. I propose that hereafter, when a Judge reaches the age of seventy, a new and younger Judge shall be added to the Court automatically. In this way I propose to enforce a sound public policy by law instead of leaving the composition of our Federal Courts, including the highest, to be determined by chance or the personal decision of individuals.

If such a law as I propose is regarded as establishing a new precedent—is it not a most desirable precedent?

Like all lawyers, like all Americans, I regret the necessity of this controversy. But the welfare of the United States, and indeed of the Constitution itself, is what we all must think about first. Our difficulty with the Court today rises not from the Court as an institution but from human beings within it. But we cannot yield our constitutional destiny to the personal judgment of a few men who, being fearful of the future, would deny us the necessary means of dealing with the present.

This plan of mine is no attack on the Court; it seeks to restore the Court to its rightful and historic place in our system of Constitutional Government and to have it resume its high task of building anew on the Constitution "a system of living law."

I have thus explained to you the reasons that lie behind our efforts to secure results by legislation within the Constitution. I hope that thereby the difficult process of constitutional amendment may be rendered unnecessary. But let us examine that process.

There are many types of amendment proposed. Each one is radically different from the other. There is no substantial group within the Congress or outside it who are agreed on any single amendment.

It would take months or years to get substantial agreement upon the type and language of an amendment. It would take months and years thereafter to get a two-thirds majority in favor of that amendment in *both* Houses of the Congress.

Then would come the long course of ratification by three-fourths of the States. No amendment which any powerful economic interests or the leaders of any powerful political party have had reason to oppose has ever been ratified within anything like a reasonable time. And thirteen States which contain only five percent of the voting population can block ratification even though the thirty-five States with ninety-five percent of the population are in favor of it.

A very large percentage of newspaper publishers, Chambers of Commerce, Bar Associations, Manufacturers' Associations, who are trying to give the impression that they really do want a constitutional amendment would be the first to exclaim as soon as an amendment was proposed "Oh! I was for an amendment all right, but this amendment that you have proposed is not the kind of an amendment that I was thinking about. I am, therefore, going to spend my time, my efforts and my money to block that amendment, although I would be awfully glad to help get some other kind of amendment ratified."

Two groups oppose my plan on the ground that they favor a constitutional amendment. The first includes those who fundamentally object to social and economic legislation along modern lines. This is the same group who during the campaign last Fall tried to block the mandate of the people.

Now they are making a last stand. And the strategy of that last stand is to suggest the time-consuming process of amendment in order to kill off by delay the legislation demanded by the mandate.

To them I say—I do not think you will be able long to fool the American people as to your purposes.

The other group is composed of those who honestly believe the amendment process is the best and who would be willing to support a reasonable amendment if they could agree on one.

To them I say—we cannot rely on an amendment as the immediate or only answer to our present difficulties. When the time comes for action, you will find that many of those who pretend to support you will sabotage any constructive amendment which is proposed. Look at these strange bed-fellows of yours. When before have you found them really at your side in your fights for progress?

And remember one thing more. Even if an amendment were passed, and even if in the years to come it were to be ratified, its meaning would depend upon the kind of Justices who would be sitting on the Supreme Court bench. An amendment like the rest of the Constitution is what the Justices say it is rather than what its framers or you might hope it is.

This proposal of mine will not infringe in the slightest upon the civil or religious liberties so dear to every American.

My record as Governor and as President proves my devotion to those liberties. You who know me can have no fear that I would tolerate the destruction by any branch of government of any part of our heritage of freedom.

The present attempt by those opposed to progress to play upon the fears of danger to personal liberty brings again to mind that crude and cruel strategy tried by the same opposition to frighten the workers of America in a pay-envelope propaganda against the Social Security Law. The workers were not fooled by that propaganda then. The people of America will not be fooled by such propaganda now.

I am in favor of action through legislation:

First, because I believe that it can be passed at this session of the Congress.

Second, because it will provide a reinvigorated, liberal-minded Judiciary necessary to furnish quicker and cheaper justice from bottom to top.

Third, because it will provide a series of Federal Courts willing to enforce the Constitution as written, and unwilling to assert legislative powers by writing into it their own political and economic policies.

During the past half century the balance of power between the three great branches of the Federal Government, has been tipped out of balance by the Courts in direct contradiction of the high purposes of the framers of the Constitution. It is my purpose to restore that balance. You who know me will accept my solemn assurance that in a world in which democracy is under attack, I seek to make American democracy succeed.

LETTER OF CHIEF JUSTICE HUGHES
MARCH 21

SUPREME COURT OF THE UNITED STATES
Washington, D.C., March 21, 1937

HON. BURTON K. WHEELER,
United States Senate, Washington, D.C.

MY DEAR SENATOR WHEELER: In response to your inquiries, I have the honor to present the following statement with respect to the work of the Supreme Court:

1. The Supreme Court is fully abreast of its work. When we rose on March 15 (for the present recess) we had heard argument in cases in which certiorari had been granted only 4 weeks before—February 15.

During the current term, which began last October and which we call "October term, 1936", we have heard argument on the merits in 150 cases (180 numbers) and we have 28 cases (30 numbers) awaiting argument. We shall be able to hear all these cases, and such others as may come up for argument, before our adjournment for the term. There is no congestion of cases upon our calendar.

This gratifying condition has obtained for several years. We have been able for several terms to adjourn after disposing of all cases which are ready to be heard.

2. The cases on our docket are classified as original and appellate. Our original jurisdiction is defined by the Constitution and embraces cases to which States are parties. There are not many of these. At the present time they number 13 and are in various stages of progress to submission for determination.

Our appellate jurisdiction covers those cases in which appeal is allowed by statute as a matter of right and cases which come to us on writs of certiorari.

The following is a comparative statement of the cases on the dockets for the six terms preceding the current term:

For terms 1930–32

	1930	1931	1932
TOTAL CASES ON DOCKETS	1,039	1,023	1,037
Disposed of during term	900	884	910
Cases remaining on dockets	139	139	127
Distribution of cases:			
Cases disposed of:			
Original cases	8	1	4
Appellate, on merits	326	282	257
Petitions for certiorari	566	601	649
Remaining on dockets:			
Original cases	16	19	17
Appellate, on merits	76	60	56
Petitions for certiorari	47	60	54

For terms 1933–35

	1933	1934	1935
TOTAL CASES ON DOCKETS	1,132	1,040	1,092
Disposed of during term	1,029	931	990
Cases remaining on docket	103	109	102
Distribution of cases:			
Cases disposed of:			
Original cases	4	5	4
Appellate, on merits	293	256	269
Petitions for certiorari	732	670	717
Remaining on dockets:			
Original cases	15	13	12
Appellate, on merits	43	51	56
Petitions for certiorari	45	45	34

Further statistics for these terms, and those for earlier terms, are available if you desire them.

During the present term we have thus far disposed of 666 cases which include petitions for certiorari and cases which have been argued on the merits and already decided.

3. The statute relating to our appellate jurisdiction is the act of February 13, 1925 (43 Stat. 936). That act limits to certain cases the appeals which come to the Supreme Court as a matter of right. Review in other cases is made to depend upon the allowance by the Supreme Court of a writ of certiorari.

Where the appeal purports to lie as a matter of right, the rules of the Supreme Court (rule 12) require the appellant to submit a jurisdictional statement showing that the case falls within that class of appeals and that a substantial question is involved. We examine that statement, and the supporting and opposing briefs, and decide whether the Court had jurisdiction. As a result, many frivolous appeals are forthwith dismissed and the way is open for appeals which disclose substantial questions.

4. The act of 1925, limiting appeals as a matter of right and enlarging the provisions for review only through certiorari was most carefully considered by Congress. I call attention to the reports of the Judiciary Committees of the Senate and House of Representatives (68th Cong., 1st sess.). That legislation was deemed to be essential to enable the Supreme Court to perform its proper function. No single court of last resort, whatever the number of judges, could dispose of all the cases which arise in this vast country and which litigants would seek to bring up if the right of appeal were unrestricted. Hosts of litigants will take appeals so long as there is a tribunal accessible. In protracted litigation, the advantage is with those who command a long purse. Unmeritorious appeals cause intolerable delays. Such appeals clog the calendar and get in the way of those that have merit.

Under our Federal system, when litigants have had their cases heard in the courts of first instance, and the trier of the facts, jury or judge, as the case may require, has spoken and the case on the facts and law has been decided, and when the dissatisfied party has been accorded an appeal to the circuit court of appeals, the litigants, so far as mere private interests are concerned, have had their day in court. If further review is to be had by the Supreme Court it must be because of the public interest in the questions involved. That review, for example, should be for the purpose of resolving conflicts in judicial decisions between different circuit courts of appeals or between circuit courts of appeals and State courts where the question is one of State law; or for the purpose of determining constitutional questions or

settling the interpretation of statutes; or because of the importance of the questions of law that are involved. Review by the Supreme Court is thus in the interest of the law, its appropriate exposition and enforcement, not in the mere interest of the litigants.

It is obvious that if appeal as a matter of right is restricted to certain described cases, the question whether review should be allowed in other cases must necessarily be confided to some tribunal for determination, and, of course, with respect to review by the Supreme Court, that Court should decide.

5. Granting certiorari is not a matter of favor but of sound judicial discretion. It is not the importance of the parties or the amount of money involved that is in any sense controlling. The action of the Court is governed by its rules from which I quote the following (rule 38, par. 5):

"5. A review on writ of certiorari is not a matter of right, but of sound judicial discretion, and will be granted only where there are special and important reasons therefor. The following, while neither controlling nor full measuring the Court's discretion, indicate the character of reason which will be considered:

"(a) Where a State court has decided a Federal question of substance not therefore determined by this Court, or has decided it in a way probably not in accord with applicable decisions of this Court.

"(b) Where a circuit court of appeals has rendered a decision in conflict with the decision of another circuit court of appeals on the same matter; or has decided an important question of local law in a way probably in conflict with applicable local decisions; or has decided an important question of general law in a way probably untenable or in conflict with the weight of authority; or has decided an important question of Federal law which has not been, but should be, settled by this Court; or has decided a Federal question in a way probably in conflict with applicable decisions of this Court; or has so far departed from the accepted and usual course of judicial proceedings, or so far sanctions such a departure by a lower court, as to call for an exercise of this Court's power of supervision.

"(c) Where the United States Court of Appeals for the District of Columbia has decided a question of general importance, or a question of substance relating to the construction or application of the Constitution, or a treaty or statute, of the United States, which has not been, but should be, settled by this Court; or where that court has not given proper effect to an applicable decision of this Court."

These rules are impartially applied, as it is most important that they should be.

I should add that petitions of certiorari are not apportioned among the Justices. In all matters before the Court, except in the more routine of administration, all the Justices—unless for some reason a Justice is disqualified or unable to act in a particular case—participate in the decision. This applies to the grant or refusal of petitions for certiorari. Furthermore, petitions for certiorari are granted if four Justices think they should be. A vote by a majority is not required in such cases. Even if two or three of the Justices are strongly of the opinion that certiorari should be allowed, frequently the other Justices will acquiesce in their view, but the petition is always granted if four so vote.

6. The work of passing upon these applications for certiorari is laborious but the Court is able to perform it adequately. Observations have been made as to the vast number of pages of records and briefs that are submitted in the course of a term. The total is imposing but the suggested conclusion is hasty and rests on an illusory basis. Records are replete with testimony and evidence of facts. But the questions on certiorari are questions of law. So many cases turn on the facts, principles of law not being in controversy. It is only when

the facts are interwoven with the questions of law which we should review that the evidence must be examined and then only to the extent that it is necessary to decide the questions of law.

This at once disposes of a vast number of factual controversies where the parties have been fully heard in the courts below and have no right to burden the Supreme Court with the dispute which interests no one but themselves.

This is also true of controversies over contracts and documents of all sorts which involve only questions of concern to the immediate parties. The applicant for certiorari is required to state in his petition the grounds for his application and in a host of cases that disclosure itself disposes of his request. So that the number of pages of records and briefs afford no satisfactory criterion of the actual work involved. It must also be remembered that Justices who have been dealing with such matters for years have the aid of a long and varied experience in separating the chaff from the wheat.

I think that it is safe to say that about 60 percent of the applications for certiorari are wholly without merit and ought never to have been made. There are probably about 20 percent or so in addition which have a fair degree of plausibility but which fail to survive critical examination. The remainder, falling short, I believe, of 20 percent, show substantial grounds and are granted. I think that it is the view of the members of the Court that if any error is made in dealing with these applications it is on the side of liberality.

7. An increase in the number of Justices of the Supreme Court, apart from any question of policy, which I do not discuss, would not promote the efficiency of the Court. It is believed that it would impair that efficiency so long as the Court acts as a unit. There would be more judges to hear, more judges to confer, more judges to discuss, more judges to be convinced and to decide. The present number of Justices is thought to be large enough so far as the prompt, adequate, and efficient conduct of the work of the Court is concerned. As I have said, I do not speak of any other considerations in view of the appropriate attitude of the Court in relation to questions of policy.

I understand that it has been suggested that with more Justices the Court could hear cases in divisions. It is believed that such a plan would be impracticable. A large proportion of the cases we hear are important and a decision by a part of the Court would be unsatisfactory.

I may also call attention to the provisions of article III, section 1, of the Constitution that the judicial power of the United States shall be vested "in one Supreme Court" and in such inferior courts as the Congress may from time to time ordain and establish. The Constitution does not appear to authorize two or more Supreme Courts or two or more parts of a supreme court functioning in effect as separate courts.

On account of the shortness of time I have not been able to consult with the members of the Court generally with respect to the foregoing statement, but I am confident that it is in accord with the views of the Justices. I should say, however, that I have been able to consult with Mr. Justice Van Devanter and Mr. Justice Brandeis, and I am at liberty to say that the statement is approved by them.

I have the honor to remain,
Respectfully yours,

CHARLES E. HUGHES,
Chief Justice of the United States.

HON. BURTON K. WHEELER,
United States Senate, Washington, D.C.

SENATE JUDICIARY COMMITTEE REPORT
JUNE 7

June 7 (calendar day, June 14), 1937.—ordered to be printed

MR. McCARRAN (*for* MR. KING), *from the committee on the judiciary, submitted the following*

ADVERSE REPORT
[To accompany S. 1392]

The Committee on the Judiciary, to whom was referred the bill (S. 1392) to reorganize the judicial branch of the Government, after full consideration, having unanimously amended the measure, hereby report the bill adversely with the recommendation that it do not pass.

The amendment agreed to by unanimous consent, is as follows:
Page 3, lines 5, 8, and 9, strike out the words "hereafter appointed."

Summary of Proposed Measure

The bill, as thus amended, may be summarized in the following manner:

By section 1 (a) the President is directed to appoint an additional judge to any court of the United States when and only when three contingencies arise:

(a) That a sitting judge shall have attained the age of 70 years;

(b) That he shall have held a Federal judge's commission for at least 10 years;

(c) That he has neither resigned nor retired within 6 months after the happening of the two contingencies first named.

The happening of the three contingencies would not, however, necessarily result in requiring an appointment, for section 1 also contains a specific defeasance clause to the effect that no nomination shall be made in the case of a judge, although he is 70 years of age, has served at least 10 years and has neither resigned nor retired within 6 months after the happening of the first two contingencies, if, before the actual nomination of an additional judge, he dies, resigns, or retires. Moreover, section 6 of the bill provides that "it shall take effect on the 30th day after the date of its enactment."

Thus the bill does not with certainty provide for the expansion of any court or the appointment of any additional judges, for it will not come into operation with respect to any judge in whose case the described contingencies have happened, if such judge dies, resigns, or retires within 30 days after the enactment of the bill or before the President shall have had opportunity to send a nomination to the Senate.

By section 1 (b) it is provided that in event of the appointment of judges under the provisions of section 1 (a), then the size of the court to which such appointments are made is "permanently" increased by that number. But the number of appointments to be made is definitely limited by this paragraph. Regardless of the age or service of the members of the Federal judiciary, no more than 50 judges may be appointed in all; the Supreme Court may not be increased beyond 15 members; no circuit court of appeals, nor the Court of Claims, nor the Court of Customs and Patent Appeals, nor the Customs Court may be increased by more than 2 members; and finally, in the case of district courts, the number of judges now authorized to be appointed for any district or group of districts may not be more than doubled.

Section 1 (c) fixes the quorum of the Supreme Court, the Court of Appeals for the District of Columbia, the Court of Claims, and the Court of Customs and Patent Appeals.

Section 1 (d) provides that an additional judge shall not be appointed in the case of a judge whose office has been abolished by Congress.

Section 2 provides for the designation and assignment of judges to courts other than those in which they hold their commissions. As introduced, it applied only to judges to be appointed after the enactment of the bill. As amended, it applies to all judges regardless of the date of their appointment, but it still alters the present system in a striking manner, as will be more fully indicated later.

Circuit judges may be assigned by the Chief Justice for service in any circuit court of appeals. District judges may be similarly assigned by the Chief Justice to any district court, or by the senior circuit judge of his circuit (but subject to the authority of the Chief Justice) to any district court within the circuit.

After the assignment of a judge by the Chief Justice, the senior circuit judge of the district in which he is commissioned may certify to the Chief Justice any reason deemed sufficient by him to warrant the revocation or termination of the assignment, but the Chief Justice has full discretion whether or not to act upon any such certification. The senior circuit judge of the district to which such assignment will be made is not given similar authority to show why the assignment should not be made effective.

Section 3 gives the Supreme Court power to appoint a Proctor to investigate the volume, character, and status of litigation in the circuit and district courts, to recommend the assignment of judges authorized by section 2, and to make suggestions for expediting the disposition of pending cases. The salary of the Proctor is fixed at $10,000 per year and provision is made for the functions of the office.

Section 4 authorizes an appopriation of $100,000 for the purposes of the act.

Section 5 contains certain definitions.

Section 6, the last section, makes the act effective 30 days after enactment.

The Argument

The committee recommends that the measure be rejected for the following primary reasons:

I. The Bill does not accomplish any one of the objectives for which it was originally offered.

II. It applies force to the judiciary and in its initial and ultimate effect would undermine the independence of the courts.

III. It violates all precedents in the history of our Government and would in itself be a dangerous precedent for the future.

IV. The theory of the bill is in direct violation of the spirit of the American Constitution and its employment would permit alteration of the Constitution without the people's consent or approval; it undermines the protection our constitutional system gives to minorities and is subversive of the rights of individuals.

V. It tends to centralize the Federal district judiciary by the power of assigning judges from one district to another at will.

VI. It tends to expand political control over the judicial department by adding to the powers of the legislative and executive departments respecting the judiciary.

Bill Does Not Deal with Injunctions

This measure was sent to the Congress by the President on February 5, 1937, with a message . . . setting forth the objectives sought to be attained.

It should be pointed out here that a substantial portion of the message was devoted to a discussion of the evils of conflicting decisions by inferior courts on constitutional questions and to the alleged abuse of the power of injunction by some of the Federal courts. These matters, however, have no bearing on the bill before us, for it contains neither a line nor a sentence dealing with either of those problems.

Nothing in this measure attempts to control, regulate, or prohibit the power of any Federal court to pass upon the constitutionality of any law—State or National.

Nothing in this measure attempts to control, regulate, or prohibit the issuance of injunctions by any court, in any case, whether or not the Government is a party to it.

If it were to be conceded that there is need of reform in these respects, it must be understood that this bill does not deal with these problems.

Objectives as Originally Stated

As offered to the Congress, this bill was designed to effectuate only three objectives, described as follows in the President's message:

1. To increase the personnel of the Federal courts "so that cases may be promptly decided in the first instance, and may be given adequate and prompt hearing on all appeals";

2. To "invigorate all the courts by the permanent infusion of new blood";

3. To "grant to the Supreme Court further power and responsibility in maintaining the efficiency of the entire Federal judiciary."

The third of these purposes was to be accomplished by the provisions creating the office of the Proctor and dealing with the assignment of judges to courts other than those to which commissioned.

The first two objectives were to be attained by the provisions authorizing the appointment of not to exceed 50 additional judges when sitting judges of retirement age, as defined in the bill, failed to retire or resign. How totally inadequate the measure is to achieve either of the named objectives, the most cursory examination of the facts reveals.

Bill Fails of Its Purpose

In the first place, as already pointed out, the bill does not provide for any increase of personnel unless judges of retirement age fail to resign or retire. Whether or not there is to be an increase of the number of judges, and the extent of the increase if there is to be one, is dependent wholly upon the judges themselves and not at all upon the accumulation of litigation in any court. To state it another way the increase of the number of judges is to be provided, not in relation to the increase of work in any district or circuit, but in relation to the age of the judges and their unwillingness to retire.

In the second place, as pointed out in the President's message, only 25 of the 237 judges serving in the Federal courts on February 5, 1937, were over 70 years of age. Six of these were members of the Supreme Court at the time the bill was introduced. At the present time there are 24 judges 70 years of age or over distributed among the 10 circuit courts, the 84 district courts, and the 4 courts in the District of Columbia and that dealing with customs cases in New York. Of the 24, only 10 are serving in the 84 district courts, so that the remaining 14 are to be found in 5 special courts and in the 10 circuit courts. . . . Moreover, the facts indicate that the courts with the oldest judges have the best records in the disposition of business. It follows, therefore, that since there are comparatively few aged justices in service and these are among the most efficient on the bench, the age of sitting judges does not make necessary an increase of personnel to handle the business of the courts.

There was submitted with the President's message a report from the Attorney General to the effect that in recent years the number of cases has greatly increased and that delay in the administration of justice is interminable. It is manifest, however, that this condition cannot be remedied by the contingent appointment of new judges to sit beside the judges over 70 years of age, most of whom are either altogether equal to their duties or are commissioned in courts in which congestion of business does not exist. It must be obvious that the way to attack congestion and delay in the courts is directly by legislation which will increase the number of judges in those districts where the accumulation exists, not indirectly by the contingent appointment of new judges to courts where the need does not exist, but where it may happen that the sitting judge is over 70 years of age.

Local Justice Centrally Administered

Perhaps, it was the recognition of this fact that prompted the authors of the bill to draft section 2 providing for the assignment of judges "hereafter appointed" to districts other than those to which commissioned. Such a plan, it will not be overlooked, contemplates the appointment of a judge to the district of his residence and his assignment to duty in an altogether different jurisdiction. It thus creates a flying squadron of itinerant judges appointed for districts and circuits where they are not needed to be transferred to other parts of the country for judicial service. It may be doubted whether such a plan would be effective. Certainly it would be a violation of the salutary American custom that all public officials should be citizens of the jurisdiction in which they serve or which they represent.

Though this plan for the assignment of new judges to the trial of cases in any part of the country at the will of the Chief Justice was in all probability intended for no other purpose than to make it possible to send the new judges into districts where actual congestion exists, it should not be overlooked that most of the plan involves a possibility of real danger.

To a greater and a greater degree, under modern conditions, the Government is involved in civil litigation with its citizens. Are we then through the system devised in this bill to make possible the selection of particular judges to try particular cases?

Under the present system (U.S.C., title 28, sec. 17) the assignment of judges within the circuit is made by the senior circuit judge, or, in his absence, the circuit justice. An assignment of a judge from outside the district may be made only when the senior circuit judge or the circuit justice makes certificate of the need of the district to the Chief Justice. Thus is the principle of local self-government preserved by the present system.

This principle is destroyed by this bill which allows the Chief Justice, at the recommendation of the Proctor, to make assignments anywhere regardless of the needs of any district. Thus is the administration of justice to be centralized by the proposed system.

Measure Would Prolong Litigation

It has been urged that the plan would correct the law's delay, and the President's message contains the statement that "poorer litigants are compelled to abandon valuable rights or to accept inadequate or unjust settlements because of sheer inability to finance or to await the end of long litigation." Complaint is then made that the Supreme Court during the last fiscal year "permitted private litigants to prosecute appeals in only 108 cases out of 803 applications."

It can scarcely be contended that the consideration of 695 more cases in the Supreme Court would have contributed in any degree to curtailing the law's delay or to reducing the expense of litigation. If it be true that the postponement of final decision in cases is a burden on poorer litigants as the President's message contends, then it must be equally true that any change of the present system which would enable wealthy litigants to pursue their cases in the Supreme Court would result only in an added burden on the "poorer litigants" whose "sheer inability to finance or to await the end of long litigation" compels them "to abandon valuable rights or to accept inadequate or unjust settlements."

Of course, there is nothing in this bill to alter the provisions of the act of 1925 by which the Supreme Court was authorized "in its discretion to refuse to hear appeals in many classes of cases." The President has not recommended any change of that law, and the only amendment providing an alteration of the law that was presented to the committee was, on roll call, unanimously rejected by the committee.

It is appropriate, however, to point out here that one of the principal considerations for the enactment of the certiorari law was the belief of Congress that the interests of the poorer litigant would be served and the law's delay reduced if the Supreme Court were authorized to reject frivolous appeals. Congress recognized the fact that wealthy clients and powerful corporations were in a position to wear out poor litigants under the old law. Congress was convinced that, in a great majority of cases, a trial in a nisiprius court and a rehearing in a court of appeals would be ample to do substantial justice. Accordingly, it provided in effect that litigation should end with the court of appeals unless an appellant could show the Supreme Court on certiorari that a question of such importance was involved as to warrant another hearing by the Supreme Court. Few litigated cases were ever decided in which the defeated party thought that justice had been done and in which he would not have appealed from the Supreme Court to Heaven itself, if he thought that by doing so he would wear down his opponent.

The Constitution provides for one Supreme Court (sec. 1, art. III) and authorizes Congress to make such exceptions as it deems desirable to the appellate jurisdiction of the Supreme Court (sec. 2, art. III). One obvious purpose of this provision was to permit Congress to put an end to litigation in the lower courts except in cases of greatest importance, and, also, in the interest of the poorer citizen, to make it less easy for wealthy litigants to invoke delay to defeat justice.

No alteration of this law is suggested by the proponents of this measure, but the implication is made that the Supreme Court has improvidently refused to hear some cases. There is no evidence to maintain this contention. The Attorney General in his statement to the committee presented a mathematical calculation to show how much time would be consumed by the Justices in reading the entire record in each case presented on appeal. The members of the committee and, of course the Attorney General, are well aware of the fact that attorneys are officers of the Court, that it is their duty to summarize the records and the points of appeal, and that the full record is needed only when, after having examined the summary of the attorneys, the court is satisfied there should be a hearing on the merits.

The Chief Justice, in a letter presented to this committee (appendix C), made it clear that "even if two or three of the Justices are strongly of the opinion that certiorari should be allowed, frequently the other judges will acquiesce in their view, but the petition is always granted if four so vote."

It thus appears from the bill itself, from the message of the President, the statement of the Attorney General, and the letter of the Chief Justice that nothing of advantage to litigants is to be derived from this measure in the reduction of the law's delay.

Question of Age Not Solved

The next question is to determine to what extent "the persistent infusion of new blood" may be expected from this bill.

It will be observed that the bill before us does not and cannot compel the retirement of any judge, whether on the Supreme Court or any other court, when he becomes 70 years of age. It will be remembered that the mere attainment of three score and ten by a particular judge does not, under this bill, require the appointment of another. The man on the bench may be 80 years of age, but this bill will not authorize the President to appoint a new judge to sit beside him unless he has served as a judge for 10 years. In other words, age itself is not penalized; the penalty falls only when age is attended with experience.

No one should overlook the fact that under this bill the President, whoever he may be and whether or not he believes in the constant infusion of young blood in the courts, may nominate a man 69 years and 11 months of age to the Supreme Court, or to any court, and, if confirmed, such nominee, if he never had served as a judge, would continue to sit upon the bench unmolested by this law until he had attained the ripe age of 79 years and 11 months.

We are told that "modern complexities call also for a constant infusion of new blood in the courts, just as it is needed in executive functions of the Government and in private business." Does this bill provide for such? The answer is obviously no. As has been just demonstrated, the introduction of old and inexperienced blood into the courts is not prevented by this bill.

More than that, the measure, by its own terms, makes impossible the "constant" or "persistent" infusion of new blood. It is to be observed that the word is "new," not "young."

The Supreme Court may not be expanded to more than 15 members. No more than two additional members may be appointed to any circuit court of appeals, to the Court of Claims, to the Court of Customs and Patent Appeals, or to the Customs Court, and the number of judges now serving in any district or group of districts may not be more than doubled. There is, therefore, a specific limitation of appointment regardless of age. That is to say, this bill, ostensibly designed to provide for the infusion of new blood, sets up insuperable obstacles to the "constant" or "persistent" operation of that principle.

Take the Supreme Court as an example. As constituted at the time this bill was presented to the Congress, there were six members of that tribunal over 70 years of age. If all six failed to resign or retire within 30 days after the enactment of this bill, and none of the members died, resigned, or retired before the President had made a nomination, then the Supreme Court would consist of 15 members. These 15 would then serve, regardless of age, at their own will, during good behavior, in other words, for life. Though as a result we had a court of 15 members 70 years of age or over, nothing could be done about it under this bill, and there would be no way to infuse "new" blood or "young" blood except by a new law further expanding the Court, unless, indeed, Congress and the Executive should be willing to follow the course defined by the framers of the Constitution for such a contingency and submit to the people a constitutional amendment limiting the terms of Justices or making mandatory their retirement at a given age.

It thus appears that the bill before us does not with certainty provide for increasing the personnel of the Federal judiciary, does not remedy the law's delay, does not serve the interest of the "poorer litigant" and does not provide for the "constant" or "persistent infusion of new blood" into the judiciary. What, then, does it do?

The Bill Applies Force to the Judiciary

The answer is clear. It applies force to the judiciary. It is an attempt to impose upon the courts a course of action, a line of decision which, without that force, without that imposition, the judiciary might not adopt.

Can there be any doubt that this is the purpose of the bill? Increasing the personnel is not the object of this measure; infusing young blood is not the object; for if either one of these purposes had been in the minds of the proponents, the drafters would not have written the following clause to be found on page 2, lines 1 to 4, inclusive:

Provided, That no additional judge shall be appointed hereunder if the judge who is of retirement age dies, resigns, or retires prior to the nomination of such additional judge.

Let it also be borne in mind that the President's message submitting this measure contains the following sentence:

If, on the other hand, any judge eligible for retirement should feel that his Court would suffer because of an increase of its membership, he may retire or resign under already existing provisions of law if he wishes to do so.

Moreover, the Attorney General in testifying before the committee (hearings, pt. 1, p. 33) said:

If the Supreme Court feels that the addition of six judges would be harmful to that Court, it can avoid that result by resigning.

Three invitations to the members of the Supreme Court over 70 years of age to get out despite all the talk about increasing personnel to expedite the disposition of cases and remedy the law's delay. One by the bill. One by the President's message. One by the Attorney General.

Can reasonable men by any possibility differ about the constitutional impropriety of such a course?

Those of us who hold office in this Government, however humble or exalted it may be, are creatures of the Constitution. To it we owe all the power and authority we possess. Outside of it we have none. We are bound by it in every official act.

We know that this instrument, without which we would not be able to call ourselves presidents, judges, or legislators, was carefully planned and deliberately framed to establish three coordinate branches of government, every one of them to be independent of the others. For the protection of the people, for the preservation of the rights of the individual, for the maintenance of the liberties of minorities, for maintaining the checks and balances of our dual system, the three branches of the Government were so constituted that the independent expression of honest difference of opinion could never be restrained in the people's servants and no one branch could overawe or subjugate the others. That is the American system. It is immeasurably more important, immeasurably more sacred to the people of America, indeed, to the people of all the world than the immediate adoption of any legislation however beneficial.

That judges should hold office during good behavior is the prescription. It is founded upon historic experience of the utmost significance. Compensation at stated times, which compensation was not to be diminished during their tenure, was also ordained. Those comprehensible terms were the outgrowths of experience which was deepseated. Of the 55 men in the Constitutional Convention, nearly one-half had actually fought in the War for Independence. Eight of the men present had signed the Declaration of Independence, in which, giving their reasons for the act, they had said of their king: "He has made judges dependent upon his will alone for their tenure of office and the amount and payment of their salaries." They sought to correct an abuse and to prevent its recurrence. When these men wrote the Constitution of their new Government, they still sought to avoid such an abuse as had led to such a bloody war as the one through which they had just passed. So they created a judicial branch of government consisting of courts not conditionally but absolutely independent in the discharge of their functions, and they intended that entire and impartial independence should prevail. Interference with this independence was prohibited, not partially but totally. Behavior other than good was the sole and only cause for interference. This judicial system is the priceless heritage of every American.

By this bill another and wholly different cause is proposed for the intervention of executive influence, namely, age. Age and behavior have no connection; they are unrelated subjects. By this bill, judges who have reached 70 years of age may remain on the bench and have their judgment augmented if they agree with the new appointee, or vetoed if they disagree. This is far from the independence intended for the courts by the framers of the Constitution. This is an unwarranted influence accorded the appointing agency, contrary to the spirit of the Constitution. The bill sets up a plan which has as its stability the changing will or inclination of an agency not a part of the judicial system. Constitutionally, the bill can have no sanction. The effect of the bill, as stated by the Attorney General to the committee, and indeed by the President in both his message and speech, is in violation of the organic law.

Object of Plan Acknowledged

No amount of sophistry can cover up this fact. The effect of this bill is not to provide for an increase in the number of Justices composing the Supreme Court. The effect is to provide a forced retirement or, failing in this, to take from the Justices affected a free exercise of their independent judgment.

The President tells us in his address to the Nation of March 9 . . . Congressional Record, March 10, page 2650:

When the Congress has sought to stabilize national agriculture, to improve the conditions of labor, to safeguard business against unfair competition, to protect our national resources, and in many other ways, to serve our clearly national needs, the majority of the Court has been assuming the power to pass on the wisdom of these acts of the Congress and to approve or disapprove the public policy written into these laws. . . . We have, therefore, reached the point as a nation where we must take action to save the Constitution from the Court and the Court from itself. We must find a way to take an appeal from the Supreme Court to the Constitution itself. We want a Supreme Court which will do justice under the Constitution—not over it. In our courts we want a government of laws and not of men.

These words constitute a charge that the Supreme Court has exceeded the boundaries of its jurisdiction and invaded the field reserved by the Constitution to the legislative branch of the Government. At best the accusation is opinion only. It is not the conclusion of judicial process.

Here is the frank acknowledgement that neither speed nor "new blood" in the judiciary is the object of this legislation, but a change in the decisions of the Court—a subordination of the views of the judges to the views of the executive and legislative, a change to be brought about by forcing certain judges off the bench or increasing their number.

Let us, for the purpose of the argument, grant that the Court has been wrong, wrong not only in that it has rendered mistaken opinions but wrong in the far more serious sense that it has substituted its will for the congressional will in the matter of legislation. May we nevertheless safely punish the Court?

Today it may be the Court which is charged with forgetting its constitutional duties. Tomorrow it may be the Congress. The next day it may be the Executive. If we yield to temptation now to lay the lash upon the Court, we are only teaching others how to apply it to ourselves and to the people when the occasion seems to warrant. Manifestly, if we may force the hand of the Court to secure our interpretation of the Constitution, then some succeeding Congress may repeat the process to secure another and a different interpretation and one which may not sound so pleasant in our ears as that for which we now contend.

There is a remedy for usurpation or other judicial wrongdoing. If this bill be supported by the toilers of this country upon the ground that they want a Court which will sustain legislation limiting hours and providing minimum wages, they must remember that the procedure employed in the bill could be used in another administration to lengthen hours and to decrease wages. If farmers want agricultural relief and favor this bill upon the ground that it gives them a Court which will sustain legislation in their favor, they must remember that the procedure employed might some day be used to deprive them of every vestige of a farm relief.

When members of the Court usurp legislative powers or attempt to exercise political power, they lay themselves open to the charge of having lapsed from that "good behavior" which determines the period of their official life. But, if you say, the process of impeachment is difficult and uncertain, the answer is, the people made it so when they framed the Constitution. It is not for us, the servants of the people, to find a more easy way to do that which our masters made difficult.

But, if the fault of the judges is not so grievous as to warrant impeachment, if their offense is merely that they have grown old, and we feel, therefore, that there should be a "constant infusion of new blood", then obviously the way to achieve that result is by constitutional amendment fixing definite terms for the members of the judiciary or making mandatory their retirement at a given age. Such a provision would indeed provide for the constant infusion of new blood, not only now but at all times in the future. The plan before us is but a temporary expedient which operates once and then never again, leaving the Court as permanently expanded to become once more a court of old men, gradually year by year falling behind the times.

What Size the Supreme Court?

How much better to proceed according to the rule laid down by the Constitution itself than by indirection to achieve our purposes. The futility and absurdity of the devious rather than the direct method is illustrated by the effect upon the problem of the retirement of Justice Van Devanter.

According to the terms of the bill, it does not become effective until 30 days after enactment, so the number of new judges to be appointed depends not upon the bill itself, not upon the conditions as they exist now or as they might exist when the bill is enacted, but upon conditions as they exist 30 days thereafter. Because Justice Van Devanter's retirement was effective as of June 2, there were on that date only five rather than six Justices on the Supreme Court of retirement age. The maximum number of appointments, therefore, is now 5 rather than 6 and the size of the Court 14 rather than 15. Now, indeed, we have put an end to 5–to–4 decisions and we shall not be harassed by 8–to–7 decisions. Now instead of making one man on the Court all-powerful, we have rendered the whole Court impotent when it divides 7 to 7 and we have provided a system approving the lower court by default.

But we may have another vacancy, and then the expanded court will be 13 rather than 14. A court of 13 with decisions by a vote of 7 to 6 and the all-powerful one returned to his position of judicial majesty. Meanwhile, the passage of years carries the younger members onward to the age of retirement when, if they should not retire, additional appointments could be made until the final maximum of 15 was reached.

The membership of the Court, between 9 and 15, would not be fixed by the Congress nor would it be fixed by the President. It would not even be fixed by the Court as a court, but would be determined by the caprice or convenience of the Justices over 70 years of age. The size of the Court would be determined by the personal desires of the Justices, and if there be any public advantage in having a court of any certain size, that public advantage in the people's interest would be wholly lost. Is it of any importance to the country that the size of the Court should be definitely fixed? Or are we to shut our eyes to that factor just because we have determined to punish the Justices whose opinions we resent?

But, if you say the process of reform by amendment is difficult and uncertain, the answer is, the people made it so when they framed the Constitution, and it is not for us, the servants of the people, by indirection to evade their will, or by devious methods to secure reforms upon which they only in their popular capacity have the right to pass.

A Measure Without Precedent

This bill is an invasion of judicial power such as has never before been attempted in this country. It is true that in the closing days of the administration of John Adams, a bill was passed creating 16 new circuit judges while reducing by one the number of places on the Supreme Court. It was charged that this was a bill to use the judiciary for a political purpose by providing official positions for members of a defeated party. The repeal of that law was the first task of the Jefferson administration.

Neither the original act nor the repealer was an attempt to change the course of judicial decision. And never in the history of the country has there been such an act. The present bill comes to us, therefore, wholly without precedent.

It is true that the size of the Supreme Court has been changed from time to time, but in every instance after the Adams administration, save one, the changes were made for purely administrative purposes in aid of the Court, not to control it.

Because the argument has been offered that these changes justify the present proposal, it is important to review all of the instances.

They were seven in number.

The first was by the act of 1801 reducing the number of members from six, as originally constituted, to five. Under the Judiciary Act of 1789 the circuit courts were trial courts and the Justices of the Supreme Court sat in them. That onerous duty was removed by the act of 1801 which created new judgeships for the purpose of relieving the members of the Supreme Court of this task. Since the work of the Justices was thereby reduced, it was provided that the next vacancy should not be filled. Jeffersonians explained the provision by saying that it was intended merely to prevent Jefferson from making an appointment of a successor to Justice Cushing whose death was expected.

The next change was in 1802 when the Jefferson administration restored the membership to six.

In neither of these cases was the purpose to influence decisions.

The third change was in 1807 under Jefferson when, three new States having been admitted to the Union, a new judicial circuit had to be created, and since it would be impossible for any of the six sitting Justices of the Supreme Court to undertake the trial work in the new circuit (Ohio, Kentucky, and Tennessee), a seventh Justice was added because of the expansion of the country. Had Jefferson wanted to subjugate John Marshall this was his opportunity to multiply members of the Court and overwhelm him, but he did not do it. We have no precedent here.

Thirty years elapsed before the next change. The country had continued to expand. New States were coming in and the same considerations which caused the increase of 1807 moved the representatives of the new West in Congress to demand another expansion. In 1826 a bill adding three justices passed both Houses but did not survive the conference. Andrew Jackson, who was familiar with the needs of the new frontier States, several times urged the legislation. Finally, it was achieved in 1837 and the Court was increased from 7 to 9 members.

Here again the sole reason for the change was the need of a growing country for a larger Court. We are still without a precedent.

Changes During the Reconstruction Period

In 1863 the western frontiers had reached the Pacific. California had been a State since 1850 without representation on the Supreme Court. The exigencies of the war and the development of the coast region finally brought the fifth change when by the act of 1863 a Pacific circuit was created and consequently a tenth member of the High Court.

The course of judicial opinion had not the slightest bearing upon the change.

Seventy-five years of constitutional history and still no precedent for a legislative attack upon the judicial power.

Now we come to the dark days of the reconstruction era for the sixth and seventh alterations of the number of justices.

The congressional majority in Andrew Johnson's administration had slight regard for the rights of minorities and no confidence in the President. Accordingly, a law was passed in 1866, providing that no appointments should be made to the Court until its membership had been reduced from 10 to 7. Doubtless, Thaddeus Stevens feared that the appointees of President Johnson might not agree with reconstruction policies and, if a constitutional question should arise, might vote to hold unconstitutional an act of Congress. But whatever the motive, a reduction of members at the instance of the bitterest majority that ever held sway in Congress to prevent a President from influencing the Court is scarcely a precedent for the expansion of the Court now.

By the time General Grant had become President in March 1869 the Court had been reduced to 8 members by the operation of the law of 1866. Presidential appointments were no longer resented, so Congress passed a new law, this time fixing the membership at 9. This law was passed in April 1869, an important date to remember, for the *Legal Tender* decision had not yet been rendered. Grant was authorized to make the additional appointment in December. Before he could make it however, Justice Grier resigned, and there were thus two vacancies.

The charge has been made that by the appointment to fill these vacancies Grant packed the Court to affect its decision in the *Legal Tender case*. Now whatever Grant's purpose may have been in making the particular appointments, it is obvious that Congress did not create the vacancies for the purpose of affecting any decision, because the law was passed long before the Court had acted in *Hepburn v. Griswold* and Congress made only one vacancy, but two appointments were necessary to change the opinion.

It was on February 7, 1870, that the court handed down its judgment holding the Legal Tender Act invalid, a decision very much deplored by the administration. It was on the same date that Grant sent down the nomination of the two justices whose votes, on a reconsideration of the issue, caused a reversal of the decision. As it happens, Grant had made two other nominations first, that of his Attorney General, Ebenezer Hoar, who was rejected by the Senate, and Edwin Stanton, who died 4 days after having been confirmed. These appointments were made in December 1869, 2 months before the decision, and Stanton was named, according to Charles Warren, historian of the Supreme Court, not because Grant wanted him but because a large majority of the members of the Senate and the House urged it. So Grant must be acquitted of having packed the Court and Congress is still without a precedent for any act that will tend to impair the independence of the Court.

A Precedent of Loyalty to the Constitution

Shall we now, after 150 years of loyalty to the constitutional ideal of an untrammeled judiciary, duty bound to protect the constitutional rights of the humblest citizen even against the Government itself, create the vicious precedent which must necessarily undermine our system? The only argument for the increase which survives analysis is that Congress should enlarge the Court so as to make the policies of this administration effective.

We are told that a reactionary oligarchy defies the will of the majority, that this is a bill to "unpack" the Court and give effect to the desires of the majority; that is to say, a bill to increase the number of Justices for the express purpose of neutralizing the views of some of the present members. In justification we are told, but without authority, by those who would rationalize this program, that Congress was given the power to determine the size of the Court so that the legislative branch would be able to impose its will upon the judiciary. This amounts to nothing more than the declaration that when the Court stands in the way of a legislative enactment, the Congress may reverse the ruling by enlarging the Court. When such a principle is adopted, our constitutional system is overthrown!

This, then, is the dangerous precedent we are asked to establish. When proponents of the bill assert, as they have done, that Congress in the past has altered the number of Justices upon the Supreme Court and that this is reason enough for our doing it now, they show how important precedents are and prove that we should now refrain from any action that would seem to establish one which could be followed hereafter whenever a Congress and an executive should become dissatisfied with the decisions of the Supreme Court.

This is the first time in the history of our country that a proposal to alter the decisions of the court by enlarging its personnel has been so boldly made. Let us meet it. Let us now set a salutary precedent that will never be violated. Let us, of the Seventy-fifth Congress, in words that will never be disregarded by any succeeding Congress, declare that we would rather have an independent Court, a fearless Court, a Court that will dare to announce its honest opinions in what it believes to be the defense of the liberties of the people, than a Court that, out of fear or sense of obligation to the appointing power, or factional passion, approves any measure we may enact. We are not the judges of the judges. We are not above the Constitution.

Even if every charge brought against the so-called "reactionary" members of this Court be true, it is far better that we await orderly but inevitable change of personnel than that we impatiently overwhelm them with new members. Exhibiting this restraint, thus demonstrating our faith in the American system, we shall set an example that will protect the independent American judiciary from attack as long as this Government stands.

An Independent Judiciary Essential

It is essential to the continuance of our constitutional democracy that the judiciary be completely independent of both the executive and legislative branches of the Government, and we assert that independent courts are the last safeguard of the citizen, where his rights, reserved to him by the express and implied provisions of the Constitution, come in conflict with the power of governmental agencies. We assert that the language of John Marshall, then in his 76th year, in the Virginia Convention (1829–31), was and is prophetic:

Advert, sir, to the duties of a judge. He has to pass between the Government and the man whom the Government is prosecuting; between the most powerful individual in the community and the poorest and most unpopular. It is of the last importance that in the exercise of these duties he should observe the utmost fairness. Need I express the necessity of this? Does not every man feel that his own personal security and the security of his property depends on that fairness? The judicial department comes home in its effect to every man's fireside; it passes on his property, his reputation, his life, his all. Is it not, to the last degree, important that he should be rendered perfectly and completely independent, with nothing to influence or control him but God and his conscience?

The condition of the world abroad must of necessity cause us to hesitate at this time and to refuse to enact any law that would impair the independence of or destroy the people's confidence in an independent judicial branch of our Government. We unhesitatingly assert that any effort looking to the impairment of an independent judiciary of necessity operates toward centralization of power in the other branches of a tripartite form of government. We declare for the continuance and perpetuation of government and rule by law, as distinguished from government and rule by men, and in this we are but reasserting the principles basic to the Constitution of the United States. The converse of this would lead to and in fact accomplish the destruction of our form of government, where the written Constitution

with its history, its spirit, and its long line of judicial interpretation and construction, is looked to and relied upon by millions of our people. Reduction of the degree of the supremacy of law means an increasing enlargement of the degree of personal government.

Personal government, or government by an individual, means autocratic dominance, by whatever name it may be designated. Autocratic dominance was the very thing against which the American Colonies revolted, and to prevent which the Constitution was in every particular framed.

Courts and the judges thereof should be free from a subservient attitude of mind, and this must be true whether a question of constitutional construction or one of popular activity is involved. If the court of last resort is to be made to respond to a prevalent sentiment of a current hour, politically imposed, that Court must ultimately become subservient to the pressure of public opinion of the hour, which might at the moment embrace mob passion abhorrent to a more calm, lasting consideration.

True it is, that courts like Congresses, should take account of the advancing strides of civilization. True it is that the law, being a progressive science, must be pronounced progressively and liberally; but the milestones of liberal progress are made to be noted and counted with caution rather than merely to be encountered and passed. Progress is not a mad mob march; rather, it is a steady, invincible stride. There is ever-impelling truth in the lines of the great liberal jurist, Mr. Justice Holmes, in *Northern Securities v. The United States*, wherein he says:

Great cases like hard cases make bad law. For great cases are called great, not by reason of their real importance in shaping the law of the future, but because of some accident of immediate overwhelming interest which appeals to the feelings and distorts the judgment. These immediate interests exercise a kind of hydraulic pressure which makes what previously was clear, seem doubtful, and before which even well settled principles of law will bend.

If, under the "hydraulic pressure" of our present need for economic justice, we destroy the system under which our people have progressed to a higher degree of justice and prosperity than that ever enjoyed by any other people in all the history of the human race, then we shall destroy not only all opportunity for further advance but everything we have thus far achieved.

The whole bill prophesies and permits executive and legislative interferences with the independence of the Court, a prophecy and a permission which constitute an affront to the spirit of the Constitution.

The complete independence of the courts of justice is peculiarly essential in a limited Constitution. By a limited Constitution, I understand one which contains certain specified exceptions to the legislative authority; such, for instance, as that it shall pass no bills of attainder, no ex-post-facto laws, and the like. Limitations of this kind can be preserved in practice no other way than through the medium of courts of justice, whose duty it must be to declare all acts contrary to the manifest tenor of the Constitution void. Without this, all the reservations of particular rights or privileges would amount to nothing (The Federalist, vol. 2, p. 100, no. 78).

The spirit of the Constitution emphasizing the establishment of an independent judicial branch was reenunciated by Madison in Nos. 47 and 48 (The Federalist, vol. 1, pp. 329, 339) and by John Adams (Adams' Works, vol. 1, p. 186).

If interference with the judgment of an independent judiciary is to be countenanced in any degree, then it is permitted and sanctioned in all degrees. There is no constituted power to say where the degree ends or begins, and the political administration of the hour may apply the essential "concepts of justice" by equipping the courts with one strain of "new blood", while the political administration of another day may use a different light and a different blood test. Thus would influence run riot. Thus perpetuity, independence, and stability belonging to the judicial arm of the Government and relied on by lawyers and laity, are lost. Thus is confidence extinguished.

The President Gives Us Example

From the very beginning of our Government to this hour, the fundamental necessity of maintaining inviolate the independence of the three coordinate branches of government has been recognized by legislators, jurists, and presidents. James Wilson, one of the framers of the Constitution who later became a Justice of the Supreme Court, declared that the independence of each department recognizes that its proceedings "shall be free from the remotest influence, direct or indirect, of either of the other two branches." Thus it was at the beginning. Thus it is now. Thus it was recognized by the men who framed the Constitution and administered the Government under it. Thus it was declared and recognized by the present President of the United States who, on the 19th day of May 1937, in signing a veto message to the Congress of the United States of a measure which would have created a special commission to represent the Federal Government at the World's Fair in New York City in 1939, withheld his approval because he felt that the provision by which it gave certain administrative duties to certain Members of Congress amounted to a legislative interference with executive functions. In vetoing the bill, President Roosevelt submitted with approval the statement of the present Attorney General that:

In my opinion those provisions of the joint resolution establishing a commission composed largely of Members of the Congress and authorizing them to appoint a United States commissioner general and two assistant commissioners for the New York World's Fair, and also providing for the expenditure of the appropriation made by the resolution, and for the administration of the resolution generally, amount to an unconstitutional invasion of the province of the Executive.

The solicitude of the President to maintain the independence of the executive arm of the Government against invasion by the legislative authority should be an example to us in solicitude to preserve the independence of the judiciary from any danger of invasion by the legislative and executive branches combined.

Extent of the Judicial Power

The assertion has been indiscriminately made that the Court has arrogated to itself the right to declare acts of Congress invalid. The contention will not stand against investigation or reason.

Article III of the Federal Constitution provides that the judicial power "shall extend to all cases in law and equity arising under this Constitution, the laws of the United States and treaties made under their authority."

The words "under this Constitution" were inserted on the floor of the Constitutional Convention in circumstances that leave no doubt of their meaning. It is true that the Convention had refused to give the Supreme Court the power to sit as a council of revision over the acts of Congress or the power to veto such acts. That action, however, was merely the refusal to give the Court any legislative power. It was a decision wholly in harmony with the purpose of keeping the judiciary independent. But, while carefully refraining from giving the Court power to share in making laws, the Convention did give it judicial power to construe the Constitution in litigated cases.

After the various forms and powers of the new Government had been determined in principle, the Convention referred the whole matter to the Committee on Detail, the duty of which was to draft a tentative instrument. The report of this committee was then taken up section by section on the floor, debated and perfected, whereupon the instrument was referred to the Committee on Style which wrote the final draft.

When the Committee on Detail reported the provision defining the judicial power, it read as follows:

The jurisdiction of the Supreme Court shall extend to all cases arising under laws passed by the Legislature of the United States, etc. (Elliot's Debates, vol. 5, p. 380).

On August 27, 1787, when this sentence was under consideration of the full Convention, it was changed to read as follows on motion of Dr. Johnson:

The jurisdiction of the Supreme Court shall extend to all cases arising under this Constitution and the laws passed by the Legislature of the United States.

Madison in his notes (Elliot's Debates, vol. 5, p. 483) reports the incident in this language:

Dr. Johnson moved to insert the words, "this Constitution and the" before the word "laws."

Mr. Madison doubted whether it was not going too far, to extend the jurisdiction of the Court generally to cases arising under the Constitution, and whether it ought not to be limited to cases of a judiciary nature. The right of expounding the Constitution, in cases not of this nature, ought not to be given to that department.

The motion of Dr. Johnson was agreed to, nem. con., it being generally supposed that the jurisdiction given was constructively limited to cases of a judiciary nature.

In other words, the framers of the Constitution were not satisfied to give the Court power to pass only on cases arising under the laws but insisted on making it quite clear that the power extends to cases arising "under the Constitution." Moreover, Article VI of the Constitution, clause 2, provides:

This Constitution and the laws of the United States which shall be made in pursuance thereof . . . shall be the supreme law of the land. . . .

Language was never more clear. No doubt can remain. A pretended law which is not "in pursuance" of the Constitution is no law at all.

A citizen has the right to appeal to the Constitution from such a statute. He has the right to demand that Congress shall not pass any act in violation of that instrument, and, if Congress does pass such an act, he has the right to seek refuge in the courts and to expect the Supreme Court to strike down the act if it does in fact violate the Constitution. A written constitution would be valueless if it were otherwise.

The right and duty of the Court to construe the Constitution is thus made clear. The question may, however, be propounded whether in construing that instrument the Court has undertaken to "override the judgment of the Congress on legislative policy." It is not necessary for this committee to defend the Court from such a charge. An invasion of the legislative power by the judiciary would not, as has already been indicated, justify the invasion of judicial authority by the legislative power. The proper remedy against such an invasion is provided in the Constitution.

Very Few Laws Held Unconstitutional

We may, however, point out that neither in this administration nor in any previous administration has the Supreme Court held unconstitutional more than a minor fraction of the laws which have been enacted. In 148 years, from 1789 to 1937, only 64 acts of Congress have been declared unconstitutional—64 acts out of a total of approximately 58,000. . . .

These 64 acts were held invalid in 76 cases, 30 of which were decided by the unanimous vote of all the justices, 9 by the agreement of all but one of the justices, 14 by the agreement of all but two, another

12 by agreement of all but three. In 11 cases only were there as many as four dissenting votes when the laws were struck down.

Only four statutes enacted by the present administration have been declared unconstitutional with three or more dissenting votes. And only 11 statutes, or parts thereof, bearing the approval of the present Chief Executive out of 2,699 signed by him during his first administration, have been invalidated. Of the 11, three—the Municipal Bankruptcy Act, the Farm Mortgage Act, and the Railroad Pension Act—were not what have been commonly denominated administration measures. When he attached his signature to the Railroad Pension Act, the President was quoted as having expressed his personal doubt as to the constitutionality of the measure. The Farm Mortgage Act was later rewritten by the Congress, reenacted, and in its new form sustained by the court which had previously held it void. Both the Farm Mortgage Act in its original form and the National Recovery Administration Act were held to be unconstitutional by a unanimous vote of all the justices. With this record of fact, it can scarcely be said with accuracy that the legislative power has suffered seriously at the hands of the Court.

But even if the case were far worse than it is alleged to be, it would still be no argument in favor of this bill to say that the courts and some judges have abused their power. The courts are not perfect, nor are the judges. The Congress is not perfect, nor are Senators and Representatives. The Executive is not perfect. These branches of government and the office under them are filled by human beings who for the most part strive to live up to the dignity and idealism of a system that was designed to achieve the greatest possible measure of justice and freedom for all the people. We shall destroy the system when we reduce it to the imperfect standards of the men who operate it. We shall strengthen it and ourselves, we shall make justice and liberty for all men more certain when, by patience and self-restraint, we maintain it on the high plane on which it was conceived.

Inconvenience and even delay in the enactment of legislation is not a heavy price to pay for our system. Constitutional democracy moves forward with certainty rather than with speed. The safety and the permanence of the progressive march of our civilization are far more important to us and to those who are to come after us than the enactment now of any particular law. The Constitution of the United States provides ample opportunity for the expression of popular will to bring about such reforms and changes as the people may deem essential to their present and future welfare. It is the people's charter of the powers granted those who govern them.

Guaranties of Individual Liberty Threatened

Let it be recognized that not only is the commerce clause of the Constitution and the clauses having to do with due process and general welfare involved in the consideration of this bill, but every line of the Constitution from the preamble to the last amendment is affected. Every declarative statement in those clauses which we choose to call the Bill of Rights is involved. Guaranties of individual human liberty and the limitation of the governing powers and processes are all reviewable.

During the period in which the writing and the adoption of the Constitution was being considered, it was Patrick Henry who said:

The Judiciary are the sole protection against a tyrannical execution of the laws. They (Congress) cannot depart from the Contitution; and their laws in opposition would be void.

Later, during the discussion of the Bill of Rights, James Madison declared:

If they (the rights specified in the Bill of Rights) were incorporated into the Constitution, independent tribunals of justice will consider themselves in a peculiar manner the guardians of those rights; they will be an impenetrable bulwark against every assumption of power in the legislative or Executive; they will be naturally led to resist every encroachment upon rights stipulated in the Constitution by the Declaration of Rights.

These leaders, who were most deeply imbued with the duty of safeguarding human rights and who were most concerned to preserve the liberty lately won, never wavered in their belief that an independent judiciary and a Constitution defining with clarity the rights of the people, were the only safeguards of the citizen. Familiar with English history and the long struggle for human liberty, they held it to be an axiom of free government that there could be no security for the people against the encroachment of political power save a written Constitution and an uncontrolled judiciary.

This has now been demonstrated by 150 years of progressive American history. As a people, Americans love liberty. It may be with truth and pride also said that we have a sensitive regard for human rights. Notwithstanding these facts, during 150 years the citizen over and over again has been compelled to contend for the plain rights guaranteed in the Constitution. Free speech, a free press, the right of assemblage, the right of a trial by jury, freedom from arbitrary arrest, religious freedom—these are among the great underlying principles upon which our democracy rests. But for all these, there have been occasions when the citizen has had to appeal to the courts for protection as against those who would take them away. And the only place the citizen has been able to go in any of these instances, for protection against the abridgment of his rights, has been to an independent and uncontrolled and incorruptible judiciary. Our law reports are filled with decisions scattered throughout these long years, reassuring the citizen of his constitutional rights, restraining States, restraining the Congress, restraining the Executive, restraining majorities, and preserving the noblest in rights of individuals.

Minority political groups, no less than religious and racial groups, have never failed, when forced to appeal to the Supreme Court of the United States, to find in its opinions the reassurance and protection of their constitutional rights. No finer or more durable philosophy of free government is to be found in all the writings and practices of great statesmen than may be found in the decisions of the Supreme Court when dealing with great problems of free government touching human rights. This would not have been possible without an independent judiciary.

Court Has Protected Human Rights

No finer illustration of the vigilance of the Court in protecting human rights can be found than in a decision wherein was involved the rights of a Chinese person, wherein the Court said:

When we consider the nature and the theory of our institutions of government, the principles upon which they are supposed to rest, and review the history of their development, we are constrained to conclude that they do not mean to leave room for the play and action of purely personal and arbitrary power.... The fundamental rights to life, liberty, and the pursuit of happiness considered as individual possessions are secured by those maxims of constitutional law which are the monuments showing the victorious progress of the race in securing to men the blessings of civilization under the reign of just and equal laws, so that in the famous language of the Massachusetts Bill of Rights, the government of the Commonwealth "may be a government of laws and not of men." For the very idea that one man may be compelled to hold his life or the means of living or any material right essential to the enjoyment of life, at the mere will of another, seems to be intolerable in any country where freedom prevails, as being the essence of slavery itself. (*Yick Wo v. Hopkins*, 118 U.S. 356.)

In the case involving the title to the great Arlington estate of Lee, the Court said:

No man in this country is so high that he is above the law. No officer of the law may set that law at defiance, with impunity. All the officers of the Government, from the highest to the lowest, are creatures of the law and are bound to obey it. (*U.S. v. Lee*, 106 U.S. 196.)

In a noted case where several Negroes had been convicted of the crime of murder, the trial being held in the atmosphere of mob dominance, the Court set aside the conviction, saying:

The State is free to regulate the procedure of its courts in accordance with its own conceptions of policy, unless in so doing it "offends some principle of justice so rooted in the traditions and conscience of our people as to be ranked as fundamental." (*Snyder v. Mass.; Rogers v. Peck*, 199 U.S. 425, 434.)

The State may abolish trial by jury. It may dispense with indictment by a grand jury and substitute complaint or information. (*Walker v. Sauvinet*, 92 U.S. 90; *Hurtado v. California*, 110 U.S. 516; *Snyder v. Mass.*, supra.) But the freedom of the State in establishing its policy is the freedom of constitutional government and is limited by the requirement of due process of law. Because a State may dispense with a jury trial, it does not follow that it may substitute trial by ordeal. The rack and torture chamber may not be substituted for the witness stand. The State may not permit an accused to be hurried to conviction under mob domination—where the whole proceeding is but a mask—without supplying corrective process. . . .

Under a law enacted by a State legislature, it was made possible to censor and control the press through the power of injunction on the charge that the publication of malicious, scandalous, and defamatory matters against officials constituted a nuisance. The Supreme Court, holding the law void, said:

The administration of government has become more complex, the opportunities for malfeasance and corruption have multiplied, crime has grown to most serious proportions, and the danger of its protection by unfaithful officials and of the impairment of the fundamental security of life and property by criminal alliances and official neglect, emphasizes the primary need of a vigilant and courageous press, especially in great cities. The fact that the liberty of the press may be abused by miscreant purveyors of scandal does not make less necessary the immunity of the press from previous restraint in dealing with official misconduct.

Speaking of the rights of labor, the Supreme Court has said:

Labor unions are recognized by the Clayton Act as legal when instituted for mutual help and lawfully carrying out their legitimate objects. They have long been thus recognized by the courts. They were organized out of the necessities of the situation. A single employee was helpless in dealing with an employer. He was dependent ordinarily on his daily wage for the maintenance of himself and family. If the employer refused to pay him the wages that he thought fair, he was nevertheless unable to leave the employ and to resist arbitrary and unfair treatment. Union was essential to give laborers opportunity to deal on equality with their employer. They united to exert influence upon him and to leave him in a body in order by this inconvenience to induce him to make better terms with them. They were withholding their labor of economic value to make him pay what they thought it was worth. The right to combine for such a lawful purpose has in many years not been denied by any court. The strike became a lawful instrument in a lawful economic struggle or competition between employer and employees as to the share or division between them of the joint product of labor and capital (*American Foundries v. Tri City Council*, 257 U.S. 184).

In another instance where the rights of labor were involved, the Court said:

The legality of collective action on the part of employees in order to safeguard their property interests is not to be disputed. It has long been recognized that employees are entitled to organize for the purpose of securing the redress of grievances and to promote agreements with employers relating to rates of pay and conditions of work. Congress . . . could safeguard it and seek to make their appropriate collective action an instrument of peace rather than of strife. Such collective action would be a mockery if representation were made futile by interference with freedom of choice. Thus the prohibition by Congress of interference with the selection of representatives for the purpose of negotiation and conference between employers and employees, instead of being an invasion of the constitutional rights of either, was based on the recognition of the rights of both (*Texas & New Orleans Railway Co. v. Brotherhood of Railway & Steamship Clerks*, 281 U.S. 548).

By the philosophy behind the pending measure it is declared that the Bill of Rights would never be violated, that freedom of speech, freedom of assemblage, freedom of the press, security in life, liberty, and property would never be challenged. Law takes its greatest force and its most secure foundation when it rests on the forum of experience. And how has our court of last resort in the past been called upon to contribute to that great fortification of the law?

In *Cummings v. Missouri* the rights of the lowly citizen were protected in the spirit of the Constitution by declaring that "no State shall pass any bill of attender or ex post fact in law." In the *Milligan case*, in the midst of the frenzied wake of the Civil War, it was the Supreme Court which sustained a citizen against an act of Congress, suspending the right of trial by jury.

In the case of *Pierce v. The Society of Sisters*, it was the Supreme Court that pronounced the inalienable right of the fathers and mothers of America to guide the destiny of their own children, when that power was challenged by an unconstitutional act of a sovereign State.

Only a few months ago in the Scottsboro cases the rights of a Negro to have counsel were upheld by this Court under the due process clause of the Constitution. On March 26 of this year, in the *Herndon case*, the rights of freedom of speech and freedom of assembly were reenunciated. Only a few weeks ago the Supreme Court construed the Constitution to uphold the Wagner Labor Act.

It would extend this report beyond proper limits to pursue this subject and trace out the holdings of the Court on the many different phases of human rights upon which it has had to pass; but the record of the Court discloses, beyond peradventure of doubt, that in preserving and maintaining the rights of American citizens under the Constitution, it has been vigilant, able, and faithful.

If, at the time all these decisions were made, their making had been even remotely influenced by the possibility that such pronouncement would entail the appointment of a co-judge or co-judges to "apply the essential concepts of justice" in the light of what the then prevailing appointing power might believe to be the "needs of an ever-changing world" these landmarks of liberty of the lowly and humble might not today exist; nor would they exist tomorrow. However great the need for human progress and social uplift, their essentials are so interwoven and involved with the individual as to be inseparable.

The Constitution of the United States, courageously construed and upheld through 150 years of history, has been the bulwark of human liberty. It was bequeathed to us in a great hour of human destiny by one of the greatest characters civilization has produced—George Washington. It is in our hands now to preserve or to destroy. If ever there was a time when the people of America should heed the words of the Father of Their Country this is the hour. Listen to his solemn warning from the Farewell Address:

It is important, likewise, that the habits of thinking, in a free country, should inspire caution in those intrusted with its administration, to confine themselves within their respective constitutional spheres, avoiding, in the exercises of the powers of one department, to encroach upon another. The spirit of encroachment tends to consolidate the powers of all the departments in one, and thus to create, whatever the form of government, a real despotism. A first estimate of that love of power, and proneness to abuse it, which predominates in the human heart, is sufficient to satisfy us of the truth of this position. The necessity of reciprocal checks in the exercise of political power, by dividing and distributing it into different depositories, and constituting each the guardian of the public weal, against invasions by the others, has been evinced by experiment, ancient and modern; some of them in our own country, and under our own eyes. To preserve them must be as necessary as to institute them. If, in the opinion of the people, the distribution or modification of the constitutional powers be, in any particular, wrong, let it be corrected by an amendment in the way which the Constitution designates. But let there be no change by usurpation; for though this, in one instance, may be the instrument of good, it is the customary weapon by which free governments are destroyed. The precedent must always greatly overbalance, in permanent evil, any partial or transient benefit which the use can, at any time, yield.

Summary

We recommend the rejection of this bill as a needless, futile, and utterly dangerous abandonment of constitutional principle.

It was presented to the Congress in a most intricate form and for reasons that obscured its real purpose.

It would not banish age from the bench nor abolish divided decisions.

It would not affect the power of any court to hold laws unconstitutional nor withdraw from any judge the authority to issue injunctions.

It would not reduce the expense of litigation nor speed the decision of cases.

It is a proposal without precedent and without justification.

It would subjugate the courts to the will of Congress and the President and thereby destroy the independence of the judiciary, the only certain shield of individual rights.

It contains the germ of a system of centralized administration of law that would enable an executive so minded to send his judges into every judicial district in the land to sit in judgment on controversies between the Government and the citizen.

It points the way to the evasion of the Constitution and establishes the method whereby the people may be deprived of their right to pass upon all amendments of the fundamental law.

It stands now before the country, acknowledged by its proponents as a plan to force judicial interpretation of the Constitution, a proposal that violates every sacred tradition of American democracy.

Under the form of the Constitution it seeks to do that which is unconstitutional.

Its ultimate operation would be to make this Government one of men rather than one of law, and its practical operation would be to make the Constitution what the executive or legislative branches of the Government choose to say it is—an interpretation to be changed with each change of administration.

It is a measure which should be so emphatically rejected that its parallel will never again be presented to the free representatives of the free people of America.

WILLIAM H. KING.   TOM CONNALLY.

FREDERICK VAN NUYS.   JOSEPH C. O'MAHONEY.

PATRICK McCARRAN.   WILLIAM E. BORAH.

CARL A. HATCH.   WARREN R. AUSTIN.

EDWARD R. BURKE.   FREDERICK STEIWER.

INDIVIDUAL VIEWS OF MR. HATCH

In filing this separate brief statement on S. 1392 it is not intended to depart in any degree from the recommendation of the majority report for the committee to the effect that S. 1392 should not pass. In that recommendation I join.

It should be noted that the recommendation and the arguments advanced by the majority are directed against the bill in its present form. It has been my thought that the principal objections set forth in the majority report can be met by proper amendments to the bill; that with sufficient safeguards, it can be made a constructive piece of legislation, not designed for the immediate present, but to provide a permanent plan for the gradual and orderly infusion of new blood into the courts. Such a plan, intended to aid in the better administration of justice and to enable the courts to discharge their judicial function more efficiently, but so safeguarded that it cannot be used to change or control judicial opinions, is within both the spirit and the letter of the constitution.

Intending to offer amendments which it is believed will accomplish this purpose, I desire to make this additional statement to accompany the majority report.

CARL A. HATCH.

PROPOSED BILL

JUNE 7

Be it enacted by the Senate and the House of Representatives of the United States of America in Congress assembled, That —

(a) When any judge of a court of the United States, appointed to hold his office during good behavior, has heretofore or hereafter attained the age of seventy years and has held a commission or commissions as judge of any such court or courts at least ten years, continuously or otherwise, and within six months thereafter has neither resigned nor retired, the President, for each such judge who has not so resigned or retired, shall nominate, and by and with the advice and consent of the Senate, shall appoint one additional judge to the court to which the former is commissioned: *Provided,* That no additional judge shall be appointed hereunder if the judge who is of retirement age dies, resigns, or retires prior to the nomination of such additional judge.

(b) The number of judges of any court shall be permanently increased by the number appointed thereto under the provisions of subsection (a) of this section. No more than fifty judges shall be appointed thereunder, nor shall any judge be so appointed if such appointment would result in (1) more than fifteen members of the Supreme Court of the United States, (2) more than two additional members so appointed to a circuit court of appeals, the Court of Claims, the United States Court of Customs and Patent Appeals, or the Customs Court, or (3) more than twice the number of judges now authorized to be appointed for any district or, in the case of judges appointed for more than one district, for any such group of districts.

(c) That number of judges which is at least two-thirds of the number of which the Supreme Court of the United States consists, or three-fifths of the number of which the United States Court of Appeals for the District of Columbia, the Court of Claims, or the United States Court of Customs and Patent Appeals consists, shall constitute a quorum of such court.

(d) An additional judge shall not be appointed under the provisions of this section when the judge who is of retirement age is commissioned to an office as to which Congress has provided that a vacancy shall not be filled.

Sec. 2 (a) Any circuit judge hereafter appointed may be designated and assigned from time to time by the Chief Justice of the United States for service in the circuit court of appeals for any circuit. Any district judge hereafter appointed may be designated and assigned from time to time by the Chief Justice of the United States for service in any district court, or, subject to the authority of the Chief Justice, by the senior circuit judge of his circuit for service in any district court within the circuit. A district judge designated and assigned to another district hereunder may hold court separately and at the same time as the district judge in such district. All designations and assignments made hereunder shall be filed in the office of the clerk and entered on the minutes of both the court from and to which a judge is designated and assigned, and thereafter the judge so designated and assigned shall be authorized to discharge all the judicial duties (except the power of appointment to a statutory position or of permanent designation of a newspaper or depository of funds) of a judge of the court to which he is designated and assigned. The designation and assignment of a judge shall not impair his authority to perform such judicial duties of the court to which he was commissioned as may be necessary or appropriate. The designation and assignment of any judge may be terminated at any time by order of the Chief Justice or the senior circuit judge, as the case may be.

(b) After the designation and assignment of a judge by the Chief Justice, the senior circuit judge of the circuit in which such judge is commissioned may certify to the Chief Justice any consideration which such senior circuit judge believes to make advisable that the designated judge remain in or return for service in the court to which he was commissioned. If the Chief Justice deems the reasons sufficient he shall revoke or designate the time of termination of such designation and assignment.

(c) In case a trial or hearing has been entered upon but has not been concluded before the expiration of the period of service of a district judge designated and assigned hereunder, the period of service shall, unless terminated under the provisions of subsection (a) of this section, be deemed to be extended until the trial or hearing has been concluded. Any designated and assigned district judge who has held court in another district than his own shall have power, notwithstanding his absence from such district and the expiration of any time limit in his designation, to decide all matters which have been submitted to him within such district, to decide motions for new trials, settle bills of exceptions, certify or authenticate narratives of testimony, or perform any other act required by law or the rules to be performed in order to prepare any case so tried by him for review in an appellate court; and his action thereon in writing filed with the clerk of the court where the trial or hearing was had shall be as valid as if such action had been taken by him within that district and within the period of his designation. Any designated and assigned circuit judge who has sat on another court than his own shall have power, notwithstanding the expiration of any time limit in his designation, to participate in the decision of all matters submitted to the court while he was sitting and to perform or participate in any act appropriate to the disposition or review of matters submitted while he was sitting on such court, and his action thereon shall be as valid as if it had been taken while sitting on such court and within the period of his designation.

Sec. 3. (a) The Supreme Court shall have power to appoint a proctor. It shall be his duty (1) to obtain and, if deemed by the Court to be desirable, to publish information as to the volume, character, and status of litigation in the district courts and circuit courts of appeals, and such other information as the Supreme Court may from time to time require by order, and it shall be the duty of any judge, clerk, or marshal of any court of the United States promptly to furnish such information as may be required by the proctor; (2) to investigate the need of assigning district and circuit judges to other courts and to make recommendations thereon to the Chief Justice; (3) to recommend, with the approval of the Chief Justice, to any court of the United States methods for expediting cases pending on its dockets; and (4) to perform such other duties consistent with his office as the Court shall direct.

(b) The proctor shall, by requisition upon the Public Printer, have any necessary printing and binding done at the Government Printing Office and authority is conferred upon the Public Printer to do such printing and binding.

(c) The salary of the proctor shall be $10,000 per annum, payable out of the Treasury in monthly installments, which shall be in full compensation for the services required by law. He shall also be allowed, in the discretion of the Chief Justice, stationery, supplies, travel expenses, equipment, necessary professional and clerical assistance, and miscellaneous expenses appropriate for performing the duties imposed by this section. The expenses in connection with the maintenance of his office shall be paid from the appropriation of the Supreme Court of the United States.

Sec. 4. There is hereby authorized to be appropriated, out of any money in the Treasury not otherwise appropriated, the sum of $100,000 for the salaries of additional judges and the other purposes of this Act during the fiscal year 1937.

Sec. 5. When used in this Act—

(a) The term "judge of retirement age" means a judge of a court of the United States, appointed to hold his office during good behavior, who has attained the age of seventy years and has held a commission or commissions as judge of any such court or courts at least ten years, continuously or otherwise, and within six months thereafter, whether or not he is eligible for retirement, has neither resigned nor retired.

(b) The term "circuit court of appeals" includes the United States Court of Appeals for the District of Columbia; the term "senior circuit judge" includes the Chief Justice of the United States Court of Appeals for the District of Columbia; and the term "circuit" includes the District of Columbia.

(c) The term "district court" includes the District Court of the District of Columbia but does not include the district court in any territory or insular possession.

(d) The term "judge" includes justice.

Sec. 6. This Act shall take effect on the thirtieth day after the date of its enactment.

SOURCE: U.S. Senate, Committee on the Judiciary, Reorganization of the Federal Judiciary, S. Rept. 711, 75th Congress, 1st session, 1937.

Brown v. Board of Education of Topeka (1954)

Brown v. Board of Education of Topeka *was originally brought in 1951 by Oliver Brown on behalf of his daughter Linda, who was assigned to a segregated public elementary school in Topeka, Kansas. A federal district court found school segregation detrimental to black children but found no constitutional violation because the black and white primary schools were substantially equal.*

The Brown case on appeal was later combined with four other similar cases in which parents of black children had asked lower courts to order school boards to stop enforcing laws requiring or permitting segregated public schools. All five cases were argued before the Supreme Court in 1952 and again in 1953.

In 1954 the Supreme Court issued its historic ruling that prohibited racial segregation in public schools. Chief Justice Earl Warren, writing the unanimous decision for the Court, said that separating children from others solely because of their race, "generates a feeling of inferiority. . . . We conclude that in the field of public education the doctrine of 'separate but equal' has no place. Separate educational facilities are inherently unequal." On that basis he maintained that the plaintiffs had been deprived of equal protection of the laws as guaranteed by the Fourteenth Amendment.

---

74 S. Ct. 686, 347 U.S. 483, 98 L. Ed. 873

Brown et al. v. Board of Education of Topeka et al.

No. 1. Appeal from the United States District Court for the District of Kansas.[1]

Argued December 9, 1952—Reargued December 8, 1953—Decided May 17, 1954.

Robert L. Carter argued the cause for appellants in No. 1 on the original argument and on the reargument. *Thurgood Marshall* argued the cause for appellants in No. 2 on the original argument and *Spottswood W. Robinson, III,* for appellants in No. 4 on the original argument, and both argued the causes for appellants in Nos. 2 and 4 on the reargument. *Louis L. Redding* and *Jack Greenberg* argued the cause for respondents in No. 10 on the original argument and *Jack Greenberg* and *Thurgood Marshall* on the reargument.

On the briefs were *Robert L. Carter, Thurgood Marshall, Spottswood W. Robinson, III, Louis L. Redding, Jack Greenberg, George E. C. Hayes, William R. Ming, Jr., Constance Baker Motley, James M. Nabrit, Jr., Charles S. Scott, Frank D. Reeves, Harold R. Boulware* and *Oliver W. Hill* for appellants in Nos. 1, 2 and 4 and respondents in No. 10; *George M. Johnson* for appellants in Nos. 1, 2 and 4; and *Loren Miller* for appellants in Nos. 2 and 4. *Arthur D. Shores* and *A. T. Walden* were on the Statement as to Jurisdiction and a brief opposing a Motion to Dismiss or Affirm in No. 2.

Paul E. Wilson, Assistant Attorney General of Kansas, argued the cause for appellees in No. 1 on the original argument and on the reargument. With him on the briefs was *Harold R. Fatzer,* Attorney General.

John W. Davis argued the cause for appellees in No. 2 on the original argument and for appellees in Nos. 2 and 4 on the reargument. With him on the briefs in No. 2 were *T. C. Callison,* Attorney General of South Carolina, *Robert McC. Figg, Jr., S. E. Rogers, William R. Meagher* and *Taggart Whipple.*

J. Lindsay Almond, Jr., Attorney General of Virginia, and *T. Justin Moore* argued the cause for appellees in No. 4 on the original argument and for appellees in Nos. 2 and 4 on the reargument. On the

briefs in No. 4 were *J. Lindsay Almond, Jr.,* Attorney General, and *Henry T. Wickham,* Special Assistant Attorney General, for the State of Virginia, and *T. Justin Moore, Archibald G. Robertson, John W. Riely* and *T. Justin Moore, Jr.* for the Prince Edward County School Authorities, appellees.

H. Albert Young, Attorney General of Delaware, argued the cause for petitioners in No. 10 on the original argument and on the reargument. With him on the briefs was *Louis J. Finger,* Special Deputy Attorney General.

By special leave of Court, *Assistant Attorney General Rankin* argued the cause for the United States on the reargument, as *amicus curiae,* urging reversal in Nos. 1, 2 and 4 and affirmance in No. 10. With him on the brief were *Attorney General Brownell, Philip Elman, Leon Ulman, William J. Lamont* and *M. Magdelena Schoch. James P. McGranery,* then Attorney General, and *Philip Elman* filed a brief for the United States on the original argument, as *amicus curiae,* urging reversal in Nos. 1, 2 and 4 and affirmance in No. 10.

Briefs of *amici curiae* supporting appellants in No. 1 were filed by *Shad Polier, Will Maslow* and *Joseph B. Robison* for the American Jewish Congress; by *Edwin J. Lukas, Arnold Forster, Arthur Garfield Hays, Frank E. Karelsen, Leonard Haas, Saburo Kido* and *Theodore Leskes* for the American Civil Liberties Union et al.; and by *John Ligtenberg* and *Selma M. Borchardt* for the American Federation of Teachers. Briefs of *amici curiae* supporting appellants in No. 1 and respondents in No. 10 were filed by *Arthur J. Goldberg* and *Thomas E. Harris* for the Congress of Industrial Organizations and by *Phineas Indritz* for the American Veterans Committee, Inc.

MR. CHIEF JUSTICE WARREN *delivered the opinion of the Court.*

These cases come to us from the States of Kansas, South Carolina, Virginia, and Delaware. They are premised on different facts and different local conditions, but a common legal question justifies their consideration together in this consolidated opinion.[2]

In each of the cases, minors of the Negro race, through their legal representatives, seek the aid of the courts in obtaining admission to the public schools of their community on a nonsegregated basis. In each instance, they had been denied admission to schools attended by white children under laws requiring or permitting segregation according to race. This segregation was alleged to deprive the plaintiffs of the equal protection of the laws under the Fourteenth Amendment. In each of the cases other than the Delaware case, a three-judge federal district court denied relief to the plaintiffs on the so-called "separate but equal" doctrine announced by this Court in *Plessy v. Ferguson,* 163 U. S. 537. Under that doctrine, equality of treatment is accorded when the races are provided substantially equal facilities, even though these facilities be separate. In the Delaware case, the Supreme Court of Delaware adhered to that doctrine, but ordered that the plaintiffs be admitted to the white schools because of their superiority to the Negro schools.

The plaintiffs contend that segregated public schools are not "equal" and cannot be made "equal," and that hence they are deprived of the equal protection of the laws. Because of the obvious importance of the question presented, the Court took jurisdiction.[3] Argument was heard in the 1952 Term, and reargument was heard this Term on certain questions propounded by the Court.[4]

Reargument was largely devoted to the circumstances surrounding the adoption of the Fourteenth Amendment in 1868. It covered exhaustively consideration of the Amendment in Congress, ratification by the states, then existing practices in racial segregation, and the views of proponents and opponents of the Amendment. This discussion and our own investigation convince us that, although these sources cast some light, it is not enough to resolve the problem with which we are faced. At best, they are inconclusive. The most avid proponents of the post-War Amendments undoubtedly intended them to remove all legal distinctions among "all persons born or naturalized in the United States." Their opponents, just as certainly, were antagonistic to both the letter and the spirit of the Amendments and wished them to have the most limited effect. What others in Congress and the state legislatures had in mind cannot be determined with any degree of certainty.

An additional reason for the inconclusive nature of the Amendment's history, with respect to segregated schools, is the status of public education at that time.[5] In the South, the movement toward free common schools, supported by general taxation, had not yet taken hold. Education of white children was largely in the hands of private groups. Education of Negroes was almost nonexistent, and practically all of the race were illiterate. In fact, any education of Negroes was forbidden by law in some states. Today, in contrast, many Negroes have achieved outstanding success in the arts and sciences as well as in the business and professional world. It is true that public school education at the time of the Amendment had advanced further in the North, but the effect of the Amendment on Northern States was generally ignored in the congressional debates. Even in the North, the conditions of public education did not approximate those existing today. The curriculum was usually rudimentary; ungraded schools were common in rural areas; the school term was but three months a year in many states; and compulsory school attendance was virtually unknown. As a consequence, it is not surprising that there should be so little in the history of the Fourteenth Amendment relating to its intended effect on public education.

In the first cases in this Court construing the Fourteenth Amendment, decided shortly after its adoption, the Court interpreted it as proscribing all state-imposed discriminations against the Negro race.[6] The doctrine of "separate but equal" did not make its appearance in this court until 1896 in the case of *Plessy v. Ferguson, supra*, involving not education but transportation.[7] American courts have since labored with the doctrine for over half a century. In this Court, there have been six cases involving the "separate but equal" doctrine in the field of public education.[8] In *Cumming v. County Board of Education*, 175 U. S. 528, and *Gong Lum v. Rice*, 275 U. S. 78, the validity of the doctrine itself was not challenged.[9] In more recent cases, all on the graduate school level, inequality was found in that specific benefits enjoyed by white students were denied to Negro students of the same educational qualifications. *Missouri ex rel. Gaines v. Canada*, 305 U. S. 337; *Sipuel v. Oklahoma*, 332 U. S. 631; *Sweatt v. Painter*, 339 U. S. 629; *McLaurin v. Oklahoma State Regents*, 339 U. S. 637. In none of these cases was it necessary to re-examine the doctrine to grant relief to the Negro plaintiff. And in *Sweatt v. Painter, supra*, the Court expressly reserved decision on the question whether *Plessy v. Ferguson* should be held inapplicable to public education.

In the instant cases, that question is directly presented. Here, unlike *Sweatt v. Painter*, there are findings below that the Negro and white schools involved have been equalized, or are being equalized, with respect to buildings, curricula, qualifications and salaries of teachers, and other "tangible" factors.[10] Our decision, therefore, cannot turn on merely a comparison of these tangible factors in the Negro and white schools involved in each of the cases. We must look instead to the effect of segregation itself on public education.

In approaching this problem, we cannot turn the clock back to 1868 when the Amendment was adopted, or even to 1896 when *Plessy v. Ferguson* was written. We must consider public education in the light of its full development and its present place in American life throughout the Nation. Only in this way can it be determined if segregation in public schools deprives these plaintiffs of the equal protection of the laws.

Today, education is perhaps the most important function of state and local governments. Compulsory school attendance laws and the great expenditures for education both demonstrate our recognition of the importance of education to our democratic society. It is required in the performance of our most basic public responsibilities, even service in the armed forces. It is the very foundation of good citizenship. Today it is a principal instrument in awakening the child to cultural values, in preparing him for later professional training, and in helping him to adjust normally to his environment. In these days, it is doubtful that any child may reasonably be expected to succeed in life if he is denied the opportunity of an education. Such an opportunity, where the state has undertaken to provide it, is a right which must be made available to all on equal terms.

We come then to the question presented: Does segregation of children in public schools solely on the basis of race, even though the physical facilities and other "tangible" factors may be equal, deprive the children of the minority group of equal educational opportunities? We believe that it does.

In *Sweatt v. Painter, supra*, in finding that a segregated law school for Negroes could not provide them equal educational opportunities, this Court relied in large part on "those qualities which are incapable of objective measurement but which make for greatness in a law school." In *McLaurin v. Oklahoma State Regents, supra*, the Court, in requiring that a Negro admitted to a white graduate school be treated like all other students, again resorted to intangible considerations: ". . . his ability to study, to engage in discussions and exchange views with other students, and, in general, to learn his profession." Such considerations apply with added force to children in grade and high schools. To separate them from others of similar age and qualifications solely because of their race generates a feeling of inferiority as to their status in the community that may affect their hearts and minds in a way unlikely ever to be undone. The effect of this separation on their educational opportunities was well stated by a finding in the Kansas case by a court which nevertheless felt compelled to rule against the Negro plaintiffs:

"Segregation of white and colored children in public schools has a detrimental effect upon the colored children. The impact is greater when it has the sanction of the law; for the policy of separating the races is usually interpreted as denoting the inferiority of the negro group. A sense of inferiority affects the motivation of a child to learn. Segregation with the sanction of law, therefore, has a tendency to (retard) the educational and mental development of Negro children and to deprive them of some of the benefits they would receive in a racial[ly] integrated school system."[11]

Whatever may have been the extent of psychological knowledge at the time of *Plessy v. Ferguson*, this finding is amply supported by modern authority.[12] Any language in *Plessy v. Ferguson* contrary to this finding is rejected.

We conclude that in the field of public education the doctrine of "separate but equal" has no place. Separate educational facilities are inherently unequal. Therefore, we hold that the plaintiffs and others similarly situated for whom the actions have been brought are, by reason of the segregation complained of, deprived of the equal protection of the laws guaranteed by the Fourteenth Amendment. This disposition makes unnecessary any discussion whether such segregation also violates the Due Process Clause of the Fourteenth Amendment.[13]

Because these are class actions, because of the wide applicability of this decision, and because of the great variety of local conditions, the formulation of decrees in these cases presents problems of considerable complexity. On reargument, the consideration of appropriate relief was necessarily subordinated to the primary question—the constitutionality of segregation in public education. We have now announced that such segregation is a denial of the equal protection of the laws. In order that we may have the full assistance of the parties in formulating decrees, the cases will be restored to the docket, and the parties are requested to present further argument on Questions 4 and 5 previously propounded by the Court for the reargument this Term.[14] The Attorney General of the United States is again invited to participate. The Attorneys General of the states requiring or permitting segregation in public education will also be permitted to appear as *amici curiae* upon request to do so by September 15, 1954, and submission of briefs by October 1, 1954.[15]

It is so ordered.

1. Together with No. 2, *Briggs et al. v. Elliott et al.,* on appeal from the United States District Court for the Eastern District of South Carolina, argued December 9–10, 1952, reargued December 7–8, 1953; No. 4, *Davis et al. v. County School Board of Prince Edward County, Virginia, et al.,* on appeal from the United States District Court for the Eastern District of Virginia, argued December 10, 1952, reargued December 7–8, 1953; and No. 10, *Gebhart et al. v. Belton et al.,* on certiorari to the Supreme Court of Delaware, argued December 11, 1952, reargued December 9, 1953.

2. In the Kansas case, *Brown v. Board of Education,* the plaintiffs are Negro children of elementary school age residing in Topeka. They brought this action in the United States District Court for the District of Kansas to enjoin enforcement of a Kansas statute which permits, but does not require, cities of more than 15,000 population to maintain separate school facilities for Negro and white students. Kan. Gen. Stat. § 72–1724 (1949). Pursuant to that authority, the Topeka Board of Education elected to establish segregated elementary schools. Other public schools in the community, however, are operated on a nonsegregated basis. The three-judge District Court, convened under 28 U. S. C. §§ 2281 and 2284, found that segregation in public education has a detrimental effect upon Negro children, but denied relief on the ground that the Negro and white schools were substantially equal with respect to buildings, transportation, curricula, and educational qualifications of teachers. 98 F. Supp. 797. The case is here on direct appeal under 28 U. S. C. § 1253.

In the South Carolina case, *Briggs v. Elliott,* the plaintiffs are Negro children of both elementary and high school age residing in Clarendon County. They brought this action in the United States District Court for the Eastern District of South Carolina to enjoin enforcement of provisions in the state constitution and statutory code which require the segregation of Negroes and whites in public schools. S. C. Const. Art. XI, § 7; S. C. Code § 5377 (1942). The three-judge District Court, convened under 28 U. S. C. §§ 2281 and 2284, denied the requested relief. The court found that the Negro schools were inferior to the white schools and ordered the defendants to begin immediately to equalize the facilities. But the court sustained the validity of the contested provisions and denied the plaintiffs admission to the white schools during the equalization program. 98 F. Supp. 529. This Court vacated the District Court's judgment and remanded the case for the purpose of obtaining the court's views on a report filed by the defendants concerning the progress made in the equalization program. 342 U. S. 350. On remand, the District Court found that substantial equality had been achieved except for buildings and that the defendants were proceeding to rectify this inequality as well. 103 F. Supp. 920. The case is again here on direct appeal under 28 U. S. C. § 1253.

In the Virginia case, *Davis v. County School Board,* the plaintiffs are Negro children of high school age residing in Prince Edward County. They brought this action in the United States District Court for the Eastern District of Virginia to enjoin enforcement of provisions in the state constitution and statutory code which require the segregation of Negroes and whites in public schools. Va. Const. § 140; Va. Code § 22–221 (1950). The three-judge District Court, convened under 28 U. S. C. §§ 2281 and 2284, denied the requested relief. The court found the Negro school inferior in physical plant, curricula, and transportation, and ordered the defendants forthwith to provide substantially equal curricula and transportation and to "proceed with all reasonable diligence and dispatch to remove" the inequality in physical plant. But, as in the South Carolina case, the court sustained the validity of the contested provisions and denied the plaintiffs admission to the white schools during the equalization program. 103 F. Supp. 337. The case is here on direct appeal under 28 U. S. C. § 1253.

In the Delaware case, *Gebhart v. Belton,* the plaintiffs are Negro children of both elementary and high school age residing in New Castle County. They brought this action in the Delaware Court of Chancery to enjoin enforcement of provisions in the state constitution and statutory code which require the segregation of Negroes and whites in public schools. Del. Const. Art. X, § 2; Del. Rev. Code, § 2631 (1935). The Chancellor gave judgment for the plaintiffs and ordered their immediate admission to schools previously attended only by white children, on the ground that the Negro schools were inferior with respect to teacher training, pupil-teacher ratio, extracurricular activities, physical plant, and time and distance involved in travel. 87 A. 2d 862. The Chancellor also found that segregation itself results in an inferior education for Negro children (see note 10, *infra*), but did not rest his decision on that ground. *Id.,* at 865. The Chancellor's decree was affirmed by the Supreme Court of Delaware, which intimated, however, that the defendants might be able to obtain a modification of the decree after equalization of the Negro and white schools had been accomplished. 91 A. 2d 137, 152. The defendants, contending only that the Delaware courts had erred in ordering the immediate admission of the Negro plaintiffs to the white schools, applied to this Court for certiorari. The writ was granted, 344 U. S. 891. The plaintiffs, who were successful below, did not submit a cross-petition.

3. 344 U. S. 1, 141, 891.

4. 345 U. S. 972. The Attorney General of the United States participated both Terms as *amicus curiae.*

5. For a general study of the development of public education prior to the Amendment, see Butts and Cremin, A History of Education in American Culture (1953), Pts. I, II; Cubberley, Public Education in the United States (1934 ed.), cc. II–XII. School practices current at the time of the adoption of the Fourteenth Amendment are described in Butts and Cremin, *supra,* at 269–275; Cubberley, *supra,* at 288–339, 408–431; Knight, Public Education in the South (1922), cc. VIII, IX. See also H. Ex. Doc. No. 315, 41st Cong., 2d Sess. (1871). Although the demand for free public schools followed substantially the same pattern in both the North and the South, the development in the South did not begin to gain momentum until about 1850, some twenty years after that in the North. The reasons for the somewhat slower development in the South (*e.g.,* the rural character of the South and the different regional attitudes toward state assistance) are well explained in Cubberley, *supra,* at 408–423. In the country as a whole, but particularly in the South, the War virtually stopped all progress in public education. *Id.,* at 427–428. The low status of Negro education in all sections of the country, both before and immediately after the War, is described in Beale, A History of Freedom of Teaching in American Schools (1941), 112–132, 175–195. Compulsory school attendance laws were not generally adopted until after the ratification of the Fourteenth Amendment, and it was not until 1918 that such laws were in force in all the states. Cubberley, *supra,* at 563–565.

6. *Slaughter-House Cases,* 16 Wall. 36, 67–72 (1873); *Strauder v. West Virginia,* 1880, 100 U. S. 303, 307–308 (1880):

"It ordains that no State shall deprive any person of life, liberty, or property, without due process of law, or deny to any person within its jurisdiction the equal protection of the laws. What is this but declaring that the law in the States shall be the same for the black as for the white; that all persons, whether colored or white, shall stand equal before the laws of the States, and, in regard to the colored race, for whose protection the amendment was primarily designed, that no discrimination shall be made against them by law because of their color? The words of the amendment, it is true, are prohibitory, but they contain a necessary implication of a positive immunity, or right, most valuable to the colored race,—the right to exemption from unfriendly legislation against them distinctively as colored,—exemption from legal discriminations, implying inferiority in civil society, lessening the security of their enjoyment of the rights which others enjoy, and discriminations which are steps towards reducing them to the condition of a subject race."

See also *Virginia v. Rives,* 100 U. S. 313, 318 (1880); *Ex parte Virginia,* 100 U. S. 339, 344–345 (1880).

7. The doctrine apparently originated in *Roberts v. City of Boston,* 59 Mass. 198, 206 (1850), upholding school segregation against attack as being violative of a state constitutional guarantee of equality. Segregation in Boston public schools was eliminated in 1855. Mass. Acts 1855, c. 256. But elsewhere in the North segregation in public education has persisted in some communities until recent years. It is apparent that such segregation has long been a nationwide problem, not merely one of sectional concern.

8. See also *Berea College v. Kentucky,* 211 U. S. 45 (1908).

9. In the *Cumming* case, Negro taxpayers sought an injunction requiring the defendant school board to discontinue the operation of a high school for white children until the board resumed operation of a high school for Negro children. Similarly, in the *Gong Lum* case, the plaintiff, a child of Chinese descent, contended only that state authorities had misapplied the doctrine by classifying him with Negro children and requiring him to attend a Negro school.

10. In the Kansas case, the court below found substantial equality as to all such factors. 98 F. Supp. 797, 798. In the South Carolina case, the court below found that the defendants were proceeding "promptly and in good faith to comply with the court's decree." 103 F. Supp. 920, 921. In the Virginia case, the court below noted that the equalization program was already "afoot and progressing," (103 F. Supp. 337, 341); since then, we have been advised, in the Virginia Attorney General's brief

on reargument, that the program has now been completed. In the Delaware case, the court below similarly noted that the state's equalization program was well under way. 91 A. 2d 137, 149.

11. A similar finding was made in the Delaware case: "I conclude from the testimony that in our Delaware society, State-imposed segregation in education itself results in the Negro children, as a class, receiving educational opportunities which are substantially inferior to those available to white children otherwise similarly situated." 87 A. 2d 862, 865.

12. K. B. Clark, Effect of Prejudice and Discrimination on Personality Development (Midcentury White House Conference on Children and Youth, 1950); Witmer and Kotinsky, Personality in the Making (1952), c. VI; Deutscher and Chein, The Psychological Effects of Enforced Segregation: A Survey of Social Science Opinion, 26 J. Psychol. 259 (1948); Chein, What are the Psychological Effects of Segregation Under Conditions of Equal Facilities?, 3 Int. J. Opinion and Attitude Res. 229 (1949); Brameld, Educational Costs, in Discrimination and National Welfare (MacIver, ed., 1949), 44–48; Frazier, The Negro in the United States (1949), 674–681. And see generally Myrdal, An American Dilemma (1944).

13. See *Bolling v. Sharpe, post,* p. 497, concerning the Due Process Clause of the Fifth Amendment.

14. "4. Assuming it is decided that segregation in public schools violates the Fourteenth Amendment

"(a) would a decree necessarily follow providing that, within the limits set by normal geographic school districting, Negro children should forthwith be admitted to schools of their choice, or

"(b) may this Court, in the exercise of its equity powers, permit an effective gradual adjustment to be brought about from existing segregated systems to a system not based on color distinctions?

"5. On the assumption on which questions 4 *(a)* and *(b)* are based, and assuming further that this Court will exercise its equity powers to the end described in question 4 *(b),*

"(a) should this Court formulate detailed decrees in these cases;

"(b) if so, what specific issues should the decrees reach;

"(c) should this Court appoint a special master to hear evidence with a view to recommending specific terms for such decrees;

"(d) should this Court remand to the courts of first instance with directions to frame decrees in these cases, and if so what general directions should the decrees of this Court include and what procedures should the courts of first instance follow in arriving at the specific terms of more detailed decrees?"

15. See Rule 42, Revised Rules of this Court (effective July 1, 1954).

Bush v. Gore (2000)

With the outcome of the 2000 presidential election hanging in the balance in a month-long battle over a recount of ballots in Florida, the U.S. Supreme Court waded into the controversy and decided the fate of the presidency in Bush v. Gore *on December 12, 2000.*

The case came to the Supreme Court on emergency appeal from the Florida Supreme Court, which had ordered the controversial vote recount to resume. George W. Bush appealed to the Supreme Court to stop it. The Court agreed to hear the appeal, and stopped the recount.

In the historic ruling, the Court held that the recount violated the Fourteenth Amendment's Equal Protection Clause because of the lack of uniform standards for counting disputed ballots in different counties. The 5-4 vote split along conservative/liberal blocs of justices with the majority ruling that there was no time to cure the defects before the scheduled date for choosing presidential electors. The ruling allowed Bush to claim Florida's electoral votes and the presidency.

531 U.S. 98
George W. Bush, et al., Petitioners v. Albert Gore, Jr., et al.

On writ of certiorari to the Florida Supreme Court

Argued December 11, 2000—Decided December 12, 2000
Per Curiam.

I

On December 8, 2000, the Supreme Court of Florida ordered that the Circuit Court of Leon County tabulate by hand 9,000 ballots in Miami-Dade County. It also ordered the inclusion in the certified vote totals of 215 votes identified in Palm Beach County and 168 votes identified in Miami-Dade County for Vice President Albert Gore, Jr., and Senator Joseph Lieberman, Democratic Candidates for President and Vice President. The Supreme Court noted that petitioner, Governor George W. Bush asserted that the net gain for Vice President Gore in Palm Beach County was 176 votes, and directed the Circuit Court to resolve that dispute on remand. ___ So. 2d, at ___ (slip op., at 4, n.6). The court further held that relief would require manual recounts in all Florida counties where so-called "undervotes" had not been subject to manual tabulation. The court ordered all manual recounts to begin at once. Governor Bush and Richard Cheney, Republican Candidates for the Presidency and Vice Presidency, filed an emergency application for a stay of this mandate. On December 9, we granted the application, treated the application as a petition for a writ of certiorari, and granted certiorari. *Post*, p. ___.

The proceedings leading to the present controversy are discussed in some detail in our opinion in *Bush v. Palm Beach County Canvassing Bd., ante*, p. ___ *(per curiam) (Bush I)*. On November 8, 2000, the day following the Presidential election, the Florida Division of Elections reported that petitioner, Governor Bush, had received 2,909,135 votes, and respondent, Vice President Gore, had received 2,907,351 votes, a margin of 1,784 for Governor Bush. Because Governor Bush's margin of victory was less than "one-half of a percent . . . of the votes cast," an automatic machine recount was conducted under §102.141(4) of the election code, the results of which showed Governor Bush still winning the race but by a diminished

margin. Vice President Gore then sought manual recounts in Volusia, Palm Beach, Broward, and Miami-Dade Counties, pursuant to Florida's election protest provisions. Fla. Stat. §102.166 (2000). A dispute arose concerning the deadline for local county canvassing boards to submit their returns to the Secretary of State (Secretary). The Secretary declined to waive the November 14 deadline imposed by statute. §§102.111, 102.112. The Florida Supreme Court, however, set the deadline at November 26. We granted certiorari and vacated the Florida Supreme Court's decision, finding considerable uncertainty as to the grounds on which it was based. *Bush I, ante*, at ___, ___ (slip. op., at 6–7). On December 11, the Florida Supreme Court issued a decision on remand reinstating that date. ___ So. 2d ___, ___ (slip op. at 30–31).

On November 26, the Florida Elections Canvassing Commission certified the results of the election and declared Governor Bush the winner of Florida's 25 electoral votes. On November 27, Vice President Gore, pursuant to Florida's contest provisions, filed a complaint in Leon County Circuit Court contesting the certification. Fla. Stat. §102.168 (2000). He sought relief pursuant to §102.168(3)(c), which provides that "[r]eceipt of a number of illegal votes or rejection of a number of legal votes sufficient to change or place in doubt the result of the election" shall be grounds for a contest. The Circuit Court denied relief, stating that Vice President Gore failed to meet his burden of proof. He appealed to the First District Court of Appeal, which certified the matter to the Florida Supreme Court.

Accepting jurisdiction, the Florida Supreme Court affirmed in part and reversed in part. *Gore v. Harris*, ___ So. 2d. ___ (2000). The court held that the Circuit Court had been correct to reject Vice President Gore's challenge to the results certified in Nassau County and his challenge to the Palm Beach County Canvassing Board's determination that 3,300 ballots cast in that county were not, in the statutory phrase, "legal votes."

The Supreme Court held that Vice President Gore had satisfied his burden of proof under §102.168(3)(c) with respect to his challenge to Miami-Dade County's failure to tabulate, by manual count, 9,000 ballots on which the machines had failed to detect a vote for President ("undervotes"). ___ So. 2d, at ___ (slip. op., at 22–23). Noting the closeness of the election, the Court explained that "[o]n this record, there can be no question that there are legal votes within the 9,000 uncounted votes sufficient to place the results of this election in doubt." *Id.*, at ___ (slip. op., at 35). A "legal vote," as determined by the Supreme Court, is "one in which there is a 'clear indication of the intent of the voter.'" *Id.*, at ___ (slip op., at 25). The court therefore ordered a hand recount of the 9,000 ballots in Miami-Dade County. Observing that the contest provisions vest broad discretion in the circuit judge to "provide any relief appropriate under such circumstances," Fla. Stat. §102.168(8) (2000), the Supreme Court further held that the Circuit Court could order "the Supervisor of Elections and the Canvassing Boards, as well as the necessary public officials, in all counties that have not conducted a manual recount or tabulation of the undervotes . . . to do so forthwith, said tabulation to take place in the individual counties where the ballots are located." ___ So. 2d, at ___ (slip. op., at 38).

The Supreme Court also determined that both Palm Beach County and Miami-Dade County, in their earlier manual recounts, had identified a net gain of 215 and 168 legal votes for Vice President

Gore. *Id.*, at ___ (slip. op., at 33–34). Rejecting the Circuit Court's conclusion that Palm Beach County lacked the authority to include the 215 net votes submitted past the November 26 deadline, the Supreme Court explained that the deadline was not intended to exclude votes identified after that date through ongoing manual recounts. As to Miami-Dade County, the Court concluded that although the 168 votes identified were the result of a partial recount, they were "legal votes [that] could change the outcome of the election." *Id.*, at (slip op., at 34). The Supreme Court therefore directed the Circuit Court to include those totals in the certified results, subject to resolution of the actual vote total from the Miami-Dade partial recount.

The petition presents the following questions: whether the Florida Supreme Court established new standards for resolving Presidential election contests, thereby violating Art. II, §1, cl. 2, of the United States Constitution and failing to comply with 3 U.S.C. §5, and whether the use of standardless manual recounts violates the Equal Protection and Due Process Clauses. With respect to the equal protection question, we find a violation of the Equal Protection Clause.

II

A. The closeness of this election, and the multitude of legal challenges which have followed in its wake, have brought into sharp focus a common, if heretofore unnoticed, phenomenon. Nationwide statistics reveal that an estimated 2% of ballots cast do not register a vote for President for whatever reason, including deliberately choosing no candidate at all or some voter error, such as voting for two candidates or insufficiently marking a ballot. See Ho, *More Than 2M Ballots Uncounted*, AP Online (Nov. 28, 2000); Kelley, *Balloting Problems Not Rare But Only In A Very Close Election Do Mistakes And Mismarking Make A Difference*, Omaha World-Herald (Nov. 15, 2000). In certifying election results, the votes eligible for inclusion in the certification are the votes meeting the properly established legal requirements.

This case has shown that punch card balloting machines can produce an unfortunate number of ballots which are not punched in a clean, complete way by the voter. After the current counting, it is likely legislative bodies nationwide will examine ways to improve the mechanisms and machinery for voting.

B. The individual citizen has no federal constitutional right to vote for electors for the President of the United States unless and until the state legislature chooses a statewide election as the means to implement its power to appoint members of the Electoral College. U.S. Const., Art. II, §1. This is the source for the statement in *McPherson v. Blacker*, 146 U.S. 1, 35 (1892), that the State legislature's power to select the manner for appointing electors is plenary; it may, if it so chooses, select the electors itself, which indeed was the manner used by State legislatures in several States for many years after the Framing of our Constitution. *Id.*, at 28–33. History has now favored the voter, and in each of the several States the citizens themselves vote for Presidential electors. When the state legislature vests the right to vote for President in its people, the right to vote as the legislature has prescribed is fundamental; and one source of its fundamental nature lies in the equal weight accorded to each vote and the equal dignity owed to each voter. The State, of course, after granting the franchise in the special context of Article II, can take back the power to appoint electors. See *id.*, at 35 ("[T]here is no doubt of the right of the legislature to resume the power at any time, for it can neither be taken away nor abdicated") (quoting S. Rep. No. 395, 43d Cong., 1st Sess.).

The right to vote is protected in more than the initial allocation of the franchise. Equal protection applies as well to the manner of its exercise. Having once granted the right to vote on equal terms, the State may not, by later arbitrary and disparate treatment, value one person's vote over that of another. See, *e.g., Harper v. Virginia Bd. of Elections*, 383 U.S. 663, 665 (1966) ("[O]nce the franchise is granted to the electorate, lines may not be drawn which are inconsistent with the Equal Protection Clause of the Fourteenth Amendment"). It must be remembered that "the right of suffrage can be denied by a debasement or dilution of the weight of a citizen's vote just as effectively as by wholly prohibiting the free exercise of the franchise." *Reynolds v. Sims*, 377 U.S. 533, 555 (1964).

There is no difference between the two sides of the present controversy on these basic propositions. Respondents say that the very purpose of vindicating the right to vote justifies the recount procedures now at issue. The question before us, however, is whether the recount procedures the Florida Supreme Court has adopted are consistent with its obligation to avoid arbitrary and disparate treatment of the members of its electorate.

Much of the controversy seems to revolve around ballot cards designed to be perforated by a stylus but which, either through error or deliberate omission, have not been perforated with sufficient precision for a machine to count them. In some cases a piece of the card—a chad—is hanging, say by two corners. In other cases there is no separation at all, just an indentation.

The Florida Supreme Court has ordered that the intent of the voter be discerned from such ballots. For purposes of resolving the equal protection challenge, it is not necessary to decide whether the Florida Supreme Court had the authority under the legislative scheme for resolving election disputes to define what a legal vote is and to mandate a manual recount implementing that definition. The recount mechanisms implemented in response to the decisions of the Florida Supreme Court do not satisfy the minimum requirement for non-arbitrary treatment of voters necessary to secure the fundamental right. Florida's basic command for the count of legally cast votes is to consider the "intent of the voter." *Gore v. Harris*, ___ So. 2d, at ___ (slip op., at 39). This is unobjectionable as an abstract proposition and a starting principle. The problem inheres in the absence of specific standards to ensure its equal application. The formulation of uniform rules to determine intent based on these recurring circumstances is practicable and, we conclude, necessary.

The law does not refrain from searching for the intent of the actor in a multitude of circumstances; and in some cases the general command to ascertain intent is not susceptible to much further refinement. In this instance, however, the question is not whether to believe a witness but how to interpret the marks or holes or scratches on an inanimate object, a piece of cardboard or paper which, it is said, might not have registered as a vote during the machine count. The factfinder confronts a thing, not a person. The search for intent can be confined by specific rules designed to ensure uniform treatment.

The want of those rules here has led to unequal evaluation of ballots in various respects. See *Gore v. Harris*, ___ So. 2d, at ___ (slip op., at 51) (Wells, J., dissenting) ("Should a county canvassing board count or not count a 'dimpled chad' where the voter is able to successfully dislodge the chad in every other contest on that ballot? Here, the county canvassing boards disagree"). As seems to have been acknowledged at oral argument, the standards for accepting or rejecting contested ballots might vary not only from county to county but indeed within a single county from one recount team to another.

The record provides some examples. A monitor in Miami-Dade County testified at trial that he observed that three members of the county canvassing board applied different standards in defining a legal vote. 3 Tr. 497, 499 (Dec. 3, 2000). And testimony at trial also revealed that at least one county changed its evaluative standards during the counting process. Palm Beach County, for example, began the process with a 1990 guideline which precluded counting completely attached chads, switched to a rule that considered a vote to be legal if any light could be seen through a chad, changed back to the 1990 rule, and then abandoned any pretense of a *per se* rule, only to have a court order that the county consider dimpled chads legal. This is not a process with sufficient guarantees of equal treatment.

An early case in our one person, one vote jurisprudence arose when a State accorded arbitrary and disparate treatment to voters in its different counties. *Gray v. Sanders,* 372 U.S. 368 (1963). The Court found a constitutional violation. We relied on these principles in the context of the Presidential selection process in *Moore v. Ogilvie,* 394 U.S. 814 (1969), where we invalidated a county-based procedure that diluted the influence of citizens in larger counties in the nominating process. There we observed that "[t]he idea that one group can be granted greater voting strength than another is hostile to the one man, one vote basis of our representative government." *Id.,* at 819.

The State Supreme Court ratified this uneven treatment. It mandated that the recount totals from two counties, Miami-Dade and Palm Beach, be included in the certified total. The court also appeared to hold *sub silentio* that the recount totals from Broward County, which were not completed until after the original November 14 certification by the Secretary of State, were to be considered part of the new certified vote totals even though the county certification was not contested by Vice President Gore. Yet each of the counties used varying standards to determine what was a legal vote. Broward County used a more forgiving standard than Palm Beach County, and uncovered almost three times as many new votes, a result markedly disproportionate to the difference in population between the counties.

In addition, the recounts in these three counties were not limited to so-called undervotes but extended to all of the ballots. The distinction has real consequences. A manual recount of all ballots identifies not only those ballots which show no vote but also those which contain more than one, the so-called overvotes. Neither category will be counted by the machine. This is not a trivial concern. At oral argument, respondents estimated there are as many as 110,000 overvotes statewide. As a result, the citizen whose ballot was not read by a machine because he failed to vote for a candidate in a way readable by a machine may still have his vote counted in a manual recount; on the other hand, the citizen who marks two candidates in a way discernable by the machine will not have the same opportunity to have his vote count, even if a manual examination of the ballot would reveal the requisite indicia of intent. Furthermore, the citizen who marks two candidates, only one of which is discernable by the machine, will have his vote counted even though it should have been read as an invalid ballot. The State Supreme Court's inclusion of vote counts based on these variant standards exemplifies concerns with the remedial processes that were under way.

That brings the analysis to yet a further equal protection problem. The votes certified by the court included a partial total from one county, Miami-Dade. The Florida Supreme Court's decision thus gives no assurance that the recounts included in a final certification must be complete. Indeed, it is respondent's submission that it would be consistent with the rules of the recount procedures to include whatever partial counts are done by the time of final certi-

cation, and we interpret the Florida Supreme Court's decision to permit this. See ____ So. 2d, at ____, n.21 (slip op., at 37, n.21) (noting "practical difficulties" may control outcome of election, but certifying partial Miami-Dade total nonetheless). This accommodation no doubt results from the truncated contest period established by the Florida Supreme Court in *Bush I,* at respondents' own urging. The press of time does not diminish the constitutional concern. A desire for speed is not a general excuse for ignoring equal protection guarantees.

In addition to these difficulties the actual process by which the votes were to be counted under the Florida Supreme Court's decision raises further concerns. That order did not specify who would recount the ballots. The county canvassing boards were forced to pull together ad hoc teams comprised of judges from various Circuits who had no previous training in handling and interpreting ballots. Furthermore, while others were permitted to observe, they were prohibited from objecting during the recount.

The recount process, in its features here described, is inconsistent with the minimum procedures necessary to protect the fundamental right of each voter in the special instance of a statewide recount under the authority of a single state judicial officer. Our consideration is limited to the present circumstances, for the problem of equal protection in election processes generally presents many complexities.

The question before the Court is not whether local entities, in the exercise of their expertise, may develop different systems for implementing elections. Instead, we are presented with a situation where a state court with the power to assure uniformity has ordered a statewide recount with minimal procedural safeguards. When a court orders a statewide remedy, there must be at least some assurance that the rudimentary requirements of equal treatment and fundamental fairness are satisfied.

Given the Court's assessment that the recount process underway was probably being conducted in an unconstitutional manner, the Court stayed the order directing the recount so it could hear this case and render an expedited decision. The contest provision, as it was mandated by the State Supreme Court, is not well calculated to sustain the confidence that all citizens must have in the outcome of elections. The State has not shown that its procedures include the necessary safeguards. The problem, for instance, of the estimated 110,000 overvotes has not been addressed, although Chief Justice Wells called attention to the concern in his dissenting opinion. See ____ So. 2d, at ____, n.26 (slip op., at 45, n.26).

Upon due consideration of the difficulties identified to this point, it is obvious that the recount cannot be conducted in compliance with the requirements of equal protection and due process without substantial additional work. It would require not only the adoption (after opportunity for argument) of adequate statewide standards for determining what is a legal vote, and practicable procedures to implement them, but also orderly judicial review of any disputed matters that might arise. In addition, the Secretary of State has advised that the recount of only a portion of the ballots requires that the vote tabulation equipment be used to screen out undervotes, a function for which the machines were not designed. If a recount of overvotes were also required, perhaps even a second screening would be necessary. Use of the equipment for this purpose, and any new software developed for it, would have to be evaluated for accuracy by the Secretary of State, as required by Fla. Stat. §101.015 (2000).

The Supreme Court of Florida has said that the legislature intended the State's electors to "participat[e] fully in the federal electoral process," as provided in 3 U.S.C. §5. ___ So. 2d, at ___ (slip op. at 27); see also *Palm Beach Canvassing Bd. v. Harris,* 2000 WL 1725434, *13

(Fla. 2000). That statute, in turn, requires that any controversy or contest that is designed to lead to a conclusive selection of electors be completed by December 12. That date is upon us, and there is no recount procedure in place under the State Supreme Court's order that comports with minimal constitutional standards. Because it is evident that any recount seeking to meet the December 12 date will be unconstitutional for the reasons we have discussed, we reverse the judgment of the Supreme Court of Florida ordering a recount to proceed.

Seven Justices of the Court agree that there are constitutional problems with the recount ordered by the Florida Supreme Court that demand a remedy. See *post*, at 6 (*Souter, J.,* dissenting); *post*, at 2, 15 (*Breyer, J.,* dissenting). The only disagreement is as to the remedy. Because the Florida Supreme Court has said that the Florida Legislature intended to obtain the safe-harbor benefits of 3 U.S.C. §5, *Justice Breyer*'s proposed remedy—remanding to the Florida Supreme Court for its ordering of a constitutionally proper contest until December 18—contemplates action in violation of the Florida election code, and hence could not be part of an "appropriate" order authorized by *Fla. Stat.* §102.168(8) (2000).

* * *

None are more conscious of the vital limits on judicial authority than are the members of this Court, and none stand more in admiration of the Constitution's design to leave the selection of the President to the people, through their legislatures, and to the political sphere. When contending parties invoke the process of the courts, however, it becomes our unsought responsibility to resolve the federal and constitutional issues the judicial system has been forced to confront.

The judgment of the Supreme Court of Florida is reversed, and the case is remanded for further proceedings not inconsistent with this opinion.

Pursuant to this Court's Rule 45.2, the Clerk is directed to issue the mandate in this case forthwith.

It is so ordered.

CHIEF JUSTICE REHNQUIST, **with whom** JUSTICE SCALIA **and** JUSTICE THOMAS *join, concurring.*

We join the *per curiam* opinion. We write separately because we believe that there are additional grounds that require us to reverse the Florida Supreme Court's decision.

I

We deal here not with an ordinary election, but with an election for the President of the United States. In *Burroughs v. United States,* 290 U.S. 534, 545 (1934), we said:

"While presidential electors are not officers or agents of the federal government (*In re Green,* 134 U.S. 377, 379), they exercise federal functions under, and discharge duties in virtue of authority conferred by, the Constitution of the United States. The President is vested with the executive power of the nation. The importance of his election and the vital character of its relationship to and effect upon the welfare and safety of the whole people cannot be too strongly stated."

Likewise, in *Anderson v. Celebrezze,* 460 U.S. 780, 794–795 (1983) (footnote omitted), we said: "[I]n the context of a Presidential election, state-imposed restrictions implicate a uniquely important national interest. For the President and the Vice President of the United States are the only elected officials who represent all the voters in the Nation."

In most cases, comity and respect for federalism compel us to defer to the decisions of state courts on issues of state law. That practice reflects our understanding that the decisions of state courts are definitive pronouncements of the will of the States as sovereigns. Cf. *Erie R. Co. v. Tompkins,* 304 U.S. 64 (1938). Of course, in ordinary cases, the distribution of powers among the branches of a State's government raises no questions of federal constitutional law, subject to the requirement that the government be republican in character. See *U.S. Const.,* Art. IV, §4. But there are a few exceptional cases in which the Constitution imposes a duty or confers a power on a particular branch of a State's government. This is one of them. Article II, §1, cl. 2, provides that "[e]ach State shall appoint, in such Manner as the *Legislature* thereof may direct," electors for President and Vice President. (Emphasis added.) Thus, the text of the election law itself, and not just its interpretation by the courts of the States, takes on independent significance.

In *McPherson v. Blacker,* 146 U.S. 1 (1892), we explained that Art. II, §1, cl. 2, "convey[s] the broadest power of determination" and "leaves it to the legislature exclusively to define the method" of appointment. *Id.,* at 27. A significant departure from the legislative scheme for appointing Presidential electors presents a federal constitutional question.

3 U.S.C. §5 informs our application of Art. II, §1, cl. 2, to the Florida statutory scheme, which, as the Florida Supreme Court acknowledged, took that statute into account. Section 5 provides that the State's selection of electors "shall be conclusive, and shall govern in the counting of the electoral votes" if the electors are chosen under laws enacted prior to election day, and if the selection process is completed six days prior to the meeting of the electoral college. As we noted in *Bush v. Palm Beach County Canvassing Bd., ante,* at 6.

"Since §5 contains a principle of federal law that would assure finality of the State's determination if made pursuant to a state law in effect before the election, a legislative wish to take advantage of the 'safe harbor' would counsel against any construction of the Election Code that Congress might deem to be a change in the law."

If we are to respect the legislature's Article II powers, therefore, we must ensure that postelection state-court actions do not frustrate the legislative desire to attain the "safe harbor" provided by §5.

In Florida, the legislature has chosen to hold statewide elections to appoint the State's 25 electors. Importantly, the legislature has delegated the authority to run the elections and to oversee election disputes to the Secretary of State (Secretary), Fla. Stat. §97.012(1) (2000), and to state circuit courts, §§102.168(1), 102.168(8). Isolated sections of the code may well admit of more than one interpretation, but the general coherence of the legislative scheme may not be altered by judicial interpretation so as to wholly change the statutorily provided apportionment of responsibility among these various bodies. In any election but a Presidential election, the Florida Supreme Court can give as little or as much deference to Florida's executives as it chooses, so far as Article II is concerned, and this Court will have no cause to question the court's actions. But, with respect to a Presidential election, the court must be both mindful of the legislature's role under Article II in choosing the manner of appointing electors and deferential to those bodies expressly empowered by the legislature to carry out its constitutional mandate.

In order to determine whether a state court has infringed upon the legislature's authority, we necessarily must examine the law of the State as it existed prior to the action of the court. Though we generally defer to state courts on the interpretation of state law—see, *e.g., Mullaney v. Wilbur,* 421 U.S. 684 (1975)—there are of course areas in which the Constitution requires this Court to undertake an independent, if still deferential, analysis of state law.

For example, in *NAACP v. Alabama ex rel. Patterson*, 357 U.S. 449 (1958), it was argued that we were without jurisdiction because the petitioner had not pursued the correct appellate remedy in Alabama's state courts. Petitioners had sought a state-law writ of certiorari in the Alabama Supreme Court when a writ of mandamus, according to that court, was proper. We found this state-law ground inadequate to defeat our jurisdiction because we were "unable to reconcile the procedural holding of the Alabama Supreme Court" with prior Alabama precedent. *Id.*, at 456. The purported state-law ground was so novel, in our independent estimation, that "petitioner could not fairly be deemed to have been apprised of its existence." *Id.*, at 457.

Six years later we decided *Bouie v. City of Columbia*, 378 U.S. 347 (1964), in which the state court had held, contrary to precedent, that the state trespass law applied to black sit-in demonstrators who had consent to enter private property but were then asked to leave. Relying upon *NAACP*, we concluded that the South Carolina Supreme Court's interpretation of a state penal statute had impermissibly broadened the scope of that statute beyond what a fair reading provided, in violation of due process. See 378 U.S., at 361–362. What we would do in the present case is precisely parallel: Hold that the Florida Supreme Court's interpretation of the Florida election laws impermissibly distorted them beyond what a fair reading required, in violation of Article II.[1]

This inquiry does not imply a disrespect for state *courts* but rather a respect for the constitutionally prescribed role of state *legislatures*. To attach definitive weight to the pronouncement of a state court, when the very question at issue is whether the court has actually departed from the statutory meaning, would be to abdicate our responsibility to enforce the explicit requirements of Article II.

II

Acting pursuant to its constitutional grant of authority, the Florida Legislature has created a detailed, if not perfectly crafted, statutory scheme that provides for appointment of Presidential electors by direct election. Fla. Stat. §103.011 (2000). Under the statute, "[v]otes cast for the actual candidates for President and Vice President shall be counted as votes cast for the presidential electors supporting such candidates." *Ibid.* The legislature has designated the Secretary of State as the "chief election officer," with the responsibility to "[o]btain and maintain uniformity in the application, operation, and interpretation of the election laws." §97.012. The state legislature has delegated to county canvassing boards the duties of administering elections. §102.141. Those boards are responsible for providing results to the state Elections Canvassing Commission, comprising the Governor, the Secretary of State, and the Director of the Division of Elections. §102.111. Cf. *Boardman v. Esteva*, 323 So. 2d 259, 268, n. 5 (1975) ("The election process . . . is committed to the executive branch of government through duly designated officials all charged with specific duties . . . . [The] judgments [of these officials] are entitled to be regarded by the courts as presumptively correct . . . ").

After the election has taken place, the canvassing boards receive returns from precincts, count the votes, and in the event that a candidate was defeated by .5% or less, conduct a mandatory recount. Fla. Stat. §102.141(4) (2000). The county canvassing boards must file certified election returns with the Department of State by 5 p.m. on the seventh day following the election. §102.112(1). The Elections Canvassing Commission must then certify the results of the election. §102.111(1).

The state legislature has also provided mechanisms both for protesting election returns and for contesting certified election results. Section 102.166 governs protests. Any protest must be filed prior to the certification of election results by the county canvassing board. §102.166(4)(b). Once a protest has been filed, "the county canvassing board may authorize a manual recount." §102.166(4)(c). If a sample recount conducted pursuant to §102.166(5) "indicates an error in the vote tabulation which could affect the outcome of the election," the county canvassing board is instructed to: "(a) Correct the error and recount the remaining precincts with the vote tabulation system; (b) Request the Department of State to verify the tabulation software; or (c) Manually recount all ballots," §102.166(5). In the event a canvassing board chooses to conduct a manual recount of all ballots, §102.166(7) prescribes procedures for such a recount.

Contests to the certification of an election, on the other hand, are controlled by §102.168. The grounds for contesting an election include "[r]eceipt of a number of illegal votes or rejection of a number of legal votes sufficient to change or place in doubt the result of the election." §102.168(3)(c). Any contest must be filed in the appropriate Florida circuit court, Fla. Stat. §102.168(1), and the canvassing board or election board is the proper party defendant, §102.168(4). Section 102.168(8) provides that "[t]he circuit judge to whom the contest is presented may fashion such orders as he or she deems necessary to ensure that each allegation in the complaint is investigated, examined, or checked, to prevent or correct any alleged wrong, and to provide any relief appropriate under such circumstances." In Presidential elections, the contest period necessarily terminates on the date set by 3 U.S.C. §5 for concluding the State's "final determination" of election controversies."

In its first decision, *Palm Beach Canvassing Bd. v. Harris*, ___ So. 2d, ___ (Nov. 21, 2000) (*Harris I*), the Florida Supreme Court extended the 7-day statutory certification deadline established by the legislature.[2] This modification of the code, by lengthening the protest period, necessarily shortened the contest period for Presidential elections. Underlying the extension of the certification deadline and the shortchanging of the contest period was, presumably, the clear implication that certification was a matter of significance: The certified winner would enjoy presumptive validity, making a contest proceeding by the losing candidate an uphill battle. In its latest opinion, however, the court empties certification of virtually all legal consequence during the contest, and in doing so departs from the provisions enacted by the Florida Legislature.

The court determined that canvassing boards' decisions regarding whether to recount ballots past the certification deadline (even the certification deadline established by *Harris I*) are to be reviewed *de novo*, although the election code clearly vests discretion whether to recount in the boards, and sets strict deadlines subject to the Secretary's rejection of late tallies and monetary fines for tardiness. See Fla. Stat. §102.112 (2000). Moreover, the Florida court held that all late vote tallies arriving during the contest period should be automatically included in the certification regardless of the certification deadline (even the certification deadline established by *Harris I*), thus virtually eliminating both the deadline and the Secretary's discretion to disregard recounts that violate it.[3]

Moreover, the court's interpretation of "legal vote," and hence its decision to order a contest-period recount, plainly departed from the legislative scheme. Florida statutory law cannot reasonably be thought to *require* the counting of improperly marked ballots. Each Florida precinct before election day provides instructions on how to properly cast a vote, §101.46; each polling place on election day contains a working model of the voting machine it uses, §101.5611; and each voting booth contains a sample ballot, §101.46. In precincts using punch-card ballots, voters are instructed to punch out the ballot cleanly:

AFTER VOTING, CHECK YOUR BALLOT CARD TO BE SURE YOUR VOTING SELECTIONS ARE CLEARLY AND CLEANLY PUNCHED AND THERE ARE NO CHIPS LEFT HANGING ON THE BACK OF THE CARD.

Instructions to Voters, quoted in *Touchston v. McDermott,* 2000 WL 1781942, *6 & n. 19 (CA11) (Tjoflat, J., dissenting). No reasonable person would call it "an error in the vote tabulation," *Fla. Stat.* §102.166(5), or a "rejection of legal votes," *Fla. Stat.* §102.168(3)(c),[4] when electronic or electromechanical equipment performs precisely in the manner designed, and fails to count those ballots that are not marked in the manner that these voting instructions explicitly and prominently specify. The scheme that the Florida Supreme Court's opinion attributes to the legislature is one in which machines are *required* to be "capable of correctly counting votes," §101.5606(4), but which nonetheless regularly produces elections in which legal votes are predictably *not* tabulated, so that in close elections manual recounts are regularly required. This is of course absurd. The Secretary of State, who is authorized by law to issue binding interpretations of the election code, §§97.012, 106.23, rejected this peculiar reading of the statutes. See DE 00-13 (opinion of the Division of Elections). The Florida Supreme Court, although it must defer to the Secretary's interpretations, see *Krivanek v. Take Back Tampa Political Committee,* 625 So. 2d 840, 844 (Fla. 1993), rejected her reasonable interpretation and embraced the peculiar one. See *Palm Beach County Canvassing Board v. Harris,* No. SC00-2346 (Dec. 11, 2000) (*Harris III*).

But as we indicated in our remand of the earlier case, in a Presidential election the clearly expressed intent of the legislature must prevail. And there is no basis for reading the Florida statutes as requiring the counting of improperly marked ballots, as an examination of the Florida Supreme Court's textual analysis shows. We will not parse that analysis here, except to note that the principal provision of the election code on which it relied, §101.5614(5), was, as the Chief Justice pointed out in his dissent from *Harris II,* entirely irrelevant. See *Gore v. Harris,* No. SC00-2431, slip op., at 50 (Dec. 8, 2000). The State's Attorney General (who was supporting the Gore challenge) confirmed in oral argument here that never before the present election had a manual recount been conducted on the basis of the contention that "undervotes" should have been examined to determine voter intent. Tr. of Oral Arg. in *Bush v. Palm Beach County Canvassing Bd.,* 39–40 (Dec. 1, 2000); cf. *Broward County Canvassing Board v. Hogan,* 607 So. 2d 508, 509 (Fla. Ct. App. 1992) (denial of recount for failure to count ballots with "hanging paper chads"). For the court to step away from this established practice, prescribed by the Secretary of State, the state official charged by the legislature with "responsibility to . . . [o]btain and maintain uniformity in the application, operation, and interpretation of the election laws," §97.012(1), was to depart from the legislative scheme.

III

The scope and nature of the remedy ordered by the Florida Supreme Court jeopardizes the "legislative wish" to take advantage of the safe harbor provided by 3 U.S.C. §5. *Bush v. Palm Beach County Canvassing Bd.,* ante, at 6. December 12, 2000, is the last date for a final determination of the Florida electors that will satisfy §5. Yet in the late afternoon of December 8th—four days before this deadline—the Supreme Court of Florida ordered recounts of tens of thousands of so-called "undervotes" spread through 64 of the State's 67 counties. This was done in a search for elusive—perhaps delusive—certainty as to the exact count of 6 million votes. But no one claims that these bal-

lots have not previously been tabulated; they were initially read by voting machines at the time of the election, and thereafter reread by virtue of Florida's automatic recount provision. No one claims there was any fraud in the election. The Supreme Court of Florida ordered this additional recount under the provision of the election code giving the circuit judge the authority to provide relief that is "appropriate under such circumstances." Fla. Stat. §102.168(8) (2000).

Surely when the Florida Legislature empowered the courts of the State to grant "appropriate" relief, it must have meant relief that would have become final by the cut-off date of 3 U.S.C. §5. In light of the inevitable legal challenges and ensuing appeals to the Supreme Court of Florida and petitions for certiorari to this Court, the entire recounting process could not possibly be completed by that date. Whereas the majority in the Supreme Court of Florida stated its confidence that "the remaining undervotes in these counties can be [counted] within the required time frame," ___ So. 2d. at ___, n. 22 (slip op., at 38, n. 22), it made no assertion that the seemingly inevitable appeals could be disposed of in that time. Although the Florida Supreme Court has on occasion taken over a year to resolve disputes over local elections, see, *e.g., Beckstrom v. Volusia County Canvassing Bd.,* 707 So. 2d 720 (1998) (resolving contest of sheriff's race 16 months after the election), it has heard and decided the appeals in the present case with great promptness. But the federal deadlines for the Presidential election simply do not permit even such a shortened process.

As the dissent noted:

"In [the four days remaining], all questionable ballots must be reviewed by the judicial officer appointed to discern the intent of the voter in a process open to the public. Fairness dictates that a provision be made for either party to object to how a particular ballot is counted. Additionally, this short time period must allow for judicial review. I respectfully submit this cannot be completed without taking Florida's presidential electors outside the safe harbor provision, creating the very real possibility of disenfranchising those nearly 6 million voters who are able to correctly cast their ballots on election day." ___ So. 2d, at ___ (slip op., at 55) (Wells, C. J., dissenting).

The other dissenters echoed this concern: "[T]he majority is departing from the essential requirements of the law by providing a remedy which is impossible to achieve and which will ultimately lead to chaos." *Id.,* at ___ (slip op., at 67 (Harding, J., dissenting, Shaw, J. concurring).

Given all these factors, and in light of the legislative intent identified by the Florida Supreme Court to bring Florida within the "safe harbor" provision of 3 U.S.C. §5, the remedy prescribed by the Supreme Court of Florida cannot be deemed an "appropriate" one as of December 8. It significantly departed from the statutory framework in place on November 7, and authorized open-ended further proceedings which could not be completed by December 12, thereby preventing a final determination by that date.

For these reasons, in addition to those given in the per curiam, *we would reverse.*

JUSTICE STEVENS, **with whom** JUSTICE GINSBURG AND JUSTICE BREYER **join, dissenting.**

The Constitution assigns to the States the primary responsibility for determining the manner of selecting the Presidential electors. See Art. II, §1, cl. 2. When questions arise about the meaning of state laws, including election laws, it is our settled practice to accept the opinions of the highest courts of the States as providing the final answers. On rare occasions, however, either federal statutes or the Federal Constitution may require federal judicial intervention in state elections. This is not such an occasion.

The federal questions that ultimately emerged in this case are not substantial. Article II provides that "[e]ach *State* shall appoint, in such Manner as the Legislature *thereof* may direct, a Number of Electors." *Ibid.* (emphasis added). It does not create state legislatures out of whole cloth, but rather takes them as they come—as creatures born of, and constrained by, their state constitutions. Lest there be any doubt, we stated over 100 years ago in *McPherson v. Blacker,* 146 U.S. 1, 25 (1892), that "[w]hat is forbidden or required to be done by a State" in the Article II context "is forbidden or required of the legislative power under state constitutions as they exist." In the same vein, we also observed that "[t]he [State's] legislative power is the supreme authority except as limited by the constitution of the State." *Ibid.;* cf. *Smiley v. Holm,* 285 U.S. 355, 367 (1932).[5] The legislative power in Florida is subject to judicial review pursuant to Article V of the Florida Constitution, and nothing in Article II of the Federal Constitution frees the state legislature from the constraints in the state constitution that created it. Moreover, the Florida Legislature's own decision to employ a unitary code for all elections indicates that it intended the Florida Supreme Court to play the same role in Presidential elections that it has historically played in resolving electoral disputes. The Florida Supreme Court's exercise of appellate jurisdiction therefore was wholly consistent with, and indeed contemplated by, the grant of authority in Article II.

It hardly needs stating that Congress, pursuant to 3 U.S.C. §5, did not impose any affirmative duties upon the States that their governmental branches could "violate." Rather, §5 provides a safe harbor for States to select electors in contested elections "by judicial or other methods" established by laws prior to the election day. Section 5, like Article II, assumes the involvement of the state judiciary in interpreting state election laws and resolving election disputes under those laws. Neither §5 nor Article II grants federal judges any special authority to substitute their views for those of the state judiciary on matters of state law.

Nor are petitioners correct in asserting that the failure of the Florida Supreme Court to specify in detail the precise manner in which the "intent of the voter," Fla. Stat. §101.5614(5) (Supp. 2001), is to be determined rises to the level of a constitutional violation.[6] We found such a violation when individual votes within the same State were weighted unequally, see, *e.g., Reynolds v. Sims,* 377 U.S. 533, 568 (1964), but we have never before called into question the substantive standard by which a State determines that a vote has been legally cast. And there is no reason to think that the guidance provided to the factfinders, specifically the various canvassing boards, by the "intent of the voter" standard is any less sufficient—or will lead to results any less uniform—than, for example, the "beyond a reasonable doubt" standard employed everyday by ordinary citizens in courtrooms across this country.[7]

Admittedly, the use of differing substandards for determining voter intent in different counties employing similar voting systems may raise serious concerns. Those concerns are alleviated—if not eliminated—by the fact that a single impartial magistrate will ultimately adjudicate all objections arising from the recount process. Of course, as a general matter, "[t]he interpretation of constitutional principles must not be too literal. We must remember that the machinery of government would not work if it were not allowed a little play in its joints." *Bain Peanut Co. of Tex. v. Pinson,* 282 U.S. 499, 501 (1931) (Holmes, J.). If it were otherwise, Florida's decision to leave to each county the determination of what balloting system to employ—despite enormous differences in accuracy[8]—might run afoul of equal protection. So, too, might the similar decisions of the vast majority of state legislatures to delegate to local authorities certain decisions with respect to voting systems and ballot design.

Even assuming that aspects of the remedial scheme might ultimately be found to violate the Equal Protection Clause, I could not subscribe to the majority's disposition of the case. As the majority explicitly holds, once a state legislature determines to select electors through a popular vote, the right to have one's vote counted is of constitutional stature. As the majority further acknowledges, Florida law holds that all ballots that reveal the intent of the voter constitute valid votes. Recognizing these principles, the majority nonetheless orders the termination of the contest proceeding before all such votes have been tabulated. Under their own reasoning, the appropriate course of action would be to remand to allow more specific procedures for implementing the legislature's uniform general standard to be established.

In the interest of finality, however, the majority effectively orders the disenfranchisement of an unknown number of voters whose ballots reveal their intent—and are therefore legal votes under state law—but were for some reason rejected by ballot-counting machines. It does so on the basis of the deadlines set forth in Title 3 of the United States Code. *Ante,* at 11. But, as I have already noted, those provisions merely provide rules of decision for Congress to follow when selecting among conflicting slates of electors. *Supra,* at 2. They do not prohibit a State from counting what the majority concedes to be legal votes until a bona fide winner is determined. Indeed, in 1960, Hawaii appointed two slates of electors and Congress chose to count the one appointed on January 4, 1961, well after the Title 3 deadlines. See Josephson & Ross, Repairing the Electoral College, 22 J. Legis. 145, 166, n. 154 (1996).[9] Thus, nothing prevents the majority, even if it properly found an equal protection violation, from ordering relief appropriate to remedy that violation without depriving Florida voters of their right to have their votes counted. As the majority notes, "[a] desire for speed is not a general excuse for ignoring equal protection guarantees." *Ante,* at 10.

Finally, neither in this case, nor in its earlier opinion in *Palm Beach County Canvassing Bd. v. Harris,* 2000 WL 1725434 (Fla., Nov. 21, 2000), did the Florida Supreme Court make any substantive change in Florida electoral law.[10] Its decisions were rooted in long-established precedent and were consistent with the relevant statutory provisions, taken as a whole. It did what courts do[11]—it decided the case before it in light of the legislature's intent to leave no legally cast vote uncounted. In so doing, it relied on the sufficiency of the general "intent of the voter" standard articulated by the state legislature, coupled with a procedure for ultimate review by an impartial judge, to resolve the concern about disparate evaluations of contested ballots. If we assume—as I do—that the members of that court and the judges who would have carried out its mandate are impartial, its decision does not even raise a colorable federal question.

What must underlie petitioners' entire federal assault on the Florida election procedures is an unstated lack of confidence in the impartiality and capacity of the state judges who would make the critical decisions if the vote count were to proceed. Otherwise, their position is wholly without merit. The endorsement of that position by the majority of this Court can only lend credence to the most cynical appraisal of the work of judges throughout the land. It is confidence in the men and women who administer the judicial system that is the true backbone of the rule of law. Time will one day heal the wound to that confidence that will be inflicted by today's decision. One thing, however, is certain. Although we may never know with complete certainty the identity of the winner of this year's Presidential election, the identity of the loser is perfectly clear. It is the Nation's confidence in the judge as an impartial guardian of the rule of law.

I respectfully dissent.

JUSTICE SOUTER, *with whom* JUSTICE BREYER *joins and with whom* JUSTICE STEVENS *and* JUSTICE GINSBURG *join with regard to all but Part C, dissenting.*

The Court should not have reviewed either *Bush v. Palm Beach County Canvassing Bd., ante,* p. ___ (*per curiam*), or this case, and should not have stopped Florida's attempt to recount all undervote ballots, see *ante* at ___, by issuing a stay of the Florida Supreme Court's orders during the period of this review, see *Bush v. Gore, post* at ____ (slip op., at 1). If this Court had allowed the State to follow the course indicated by the opinions of its own Supreme Court, it is entirely possible that there would ultimately have been no issue requiring our review, and political tension could have worked itself out in the Congress following the procedure provided in 3 U.S.C. §15. The case being before us, however, its resolution by the majority is another erroneous decision.

As will be clear, I am in substantial agreement with the dissenting opinions of *Justice Stevens, Justice Ginsburg* and *Justice Breyer.* I write separately only to say how straightforward the issues before us really are.

There are three issues: whether the State Supreme Court's interpretation of the statute providing for a contest of the state election results somehow violates 3 U.S.C. §5; whether that court's construction of the state statutory provisions governing contests impermissibly changes a state law from what the State's legislature has provided, in violation of Article II, §1, cl. 2, of the national Constitution; and whether the manner of interpreting markings on disputed ballots failing to cause machines to register votes for President (the undervote ballots) violates the equal protection or due process guaranteed by the Fourteenth Amendment. None of these issues is difficult to describe or to resolve.

A. The 3 U.S.C. §5 issue is not serious. That provision sets certain conditions for treating a State's certification of Presidential electors as conclusive in the event that a dispute over recognizing those electors must be resolved in the Congress under 3 U.S.C. §15. Conclusiveness requires selection under a legal scheme in place before the election, with results determined at least six days before the date set for casting electoral votes. But no State is required to conform to §5 if it cannot do that (for whatever reason); the sanction for failing to satisfy the conditions of §5 is simply loss of what has been called its "safe harbor." And even that determination is to be made, if made anywhere, in the Congress.

B. The second matter here goes to the State Supreme Court's interpretation of certain terms in the state statute governing election "contests," Fla. Stat. §102.168 (2000); there is no question here about the state court's interpretation of the related provisions dealing with the antecedent process of "protesting" particular vote counts, §102.166, which was involved in the previous case, *Bush v. Palm Beach County Canvassing Board.* The issue is whether the judgment of the state supreme court has displaced the state legislature's provisions for election contests: is the law as declared by the court different from the provisions made by the legislature, to which the national Constitution commits responsibility for determining how each State's Presidential electors are chosen? See U.S. Const., Art. II, §1, cl. 2. Bush does not, of course, claim that any judicial act interpreting a statute of uncertain meaning is enough to displace the legislative provision and violate Article II; statutes require interpretation, which does not without more affect the legislative character of a statute within the meaning of the Constitution. Brief for Petitioners 48, n. 22, in *Bush v. Palm Beach County Canvassing Bd., et al.,* 531 U.S. ___ (2000). What Bush does argue, as I understand the contention, is that the interpre-

tation of §102.168 was so unreasonable as to transcend the accepted bounds of statutory interpretation, to the point of being a nonjudicial act and producing new law untethered to the legislative act in question.

The starting point for evaluating the claim that the Florida Supreme Court's interpretation effectively re-wrote §102.168 must be the language of the provision on which Gore relies to show his right to raise this contest: that the previously certified result in Bush's favor was produced by "rejection of a number of legal votes sufficient to change or place in doubt the result of the election." Fla. Stat. §102.168(3)(c) (2000). None of the state court's interpretations is unreasonable to the point of displacing the legislative enactment quoted. As I will note below, other interpretations were of course possible, and some might have been better than those adopted by the Florida court's majority; the two dissents from the majority opinion of that court and various briefs submitted to us set out alternatives. But the majority view is in each instance within the bounds of reasonable interpretation, and the law as declared is consistent with Article II.

1. The statute does not define a "legal vote," the rejection of which may affect the election. The State Supreme Court was therefore required to define it, and in doing that the court looked to another election statute, §101.5614(5), dealing with damaged or defective ballots, which contains a provision that no vote shall be disregarded "if there is a clear indication of the intent of the voter as determined by a canvassing board." The court read that objective of looking to the voter's intent as indicating that the legislature probably meant "legal vote" to mean a vote recorded on a ballot indicating what the voter intended. *Gore v. Harris,* ___ So. 2d ___ (slip op., at 23–25) (Dec. 8, 2000). It is perfectly true that the majority might have chosen a different reading. See, *e.g.,* Brief for Respondent Harris et al. 10 (defining "legal votes" as "votes properly executed in accordance with the instructions provided to all registered voters in advance of the election and in the polling places"). But even so, there is no constitutional violation in following the majority view; Article II is unconcerned with mere disagreements about interpretive merits.

2. The Florida court next interpreted "rejection" to determine what act in the counting process may be attacked in a contest. Again, the statute does not define the term. The court majority read the word to mean simply a failure to count. ____ So. 2d, at___ (slip op., at 26–27). That reading is certainly within the bounds of common sense, given the objective to give effect to a voter's intent if that can be determined. A different reading, of course, is possible. The majority might have concluded that "rejection" should refer to machine malfunction, or that a ballot should not be treated as "reject[ed]" in the absence of wrongdoing by election officials, lest contests be so easy to claim that every election will end up in one. Cf. *id.,* at ____ (slip op., at 48) (Wells, C. J., dissenting). There is, however, nothing nonjudicial in the Florida majority's more hospitable reading.

3. The same is true about the court majority's understanding of the phrase "votes sufficient to change or place in doubt" the result of the election in Florida. The court held that if the uncounted ballots were so numerous that it was reasonably possible that they contained enough "legal" votes to swing the election, this contest would be authorized by the statute.[12] While the majority might have thought (as the trial judge did) that a probability, not a possibility, should be necessary to justify a contest, that reading is not required by the statute's text, which says nothing about probability. Whatever people of good will and good sense may argue about the merits of the Florida court's reading, there is no warrant for saying that it transcends the limits of reasonable statutory interpretation to the point of supplanting the statute enacted by the "legislature" within the meaning of Article II.

In sum, the interpretations by the Florida court raise no substantial question under Article II. That court engaged in permissible construction in determining that Gore had instituted a contest authorized by the state statute, and it proceeded to direct the trial judge to deal with that contest in the exercise of the discretionary powers generously conferred by Fla. Stat. §102.168(8) (2000), to "fashion such orders as he or she deems necessary to ensure that each allegation in the complaint is investigated, examined, or checked, to prevent or correct any alleged wrong, and to provide any relief appropriate under such circumstances." As *Justice Ginsburg* has persuasively explained in her own dissenting opinion, our customary respect for state interpretations of state law counsels against rejection of the Florida court's determinations in this case.

C. It is only on the third issue before us that there is a meritorious argument for relief, as this Court's *Per Curiam* opinion recognizes. It is an issue that might well have been dealt with adequately by the Florida courts if the state proceedings had not been interrupted, and if not disposed of at the state level it could have been considered by the Congress in any electoral vote dispute. But because the course of state proceedings has been interrupted, time is short, and the issue is before us, I think it sensible for the Court to address it.

Petitioners have raised an equal protection claim (or, alternatively, a due process claim, see generally *Logan v. Zimmerman Brush Co.,* 455 U.S. 422 (1982)), in the charge that unjustifiably disparate standards are applied in different electoral jurisdictions to otherwise identical facts. It is true that the Equal Protection Clause does not forbid the use of a variety of voting mechanisms within a jurisdiction, even though different mechanisms will have different levels of effectiveness in recording voters' intentions; local variety can be justified by concerns about cost, the potential value of innovation, and so on. But evidence in the record here suggests that a different order of disparity obtains under rules for determining a voter's intent that have been applied (and could continue to be applied) to identical types of ballots used in identical brands of machines and exhibiting identical physical characteristics (such as "hanging" or "dimpled" chads). See, *e.g.,* Tr., at 238–242 (Dec. 2–3, 2000) (testimony of Palm Beach County Canvassing Board Chairman Judge Charles Burton describing varying standards applied to imperfectly punched ballots in Palm Beach County during precertification manual recount); *id.,* at 497–500 (similarly describing varying standards applied in Miami-Dade County); Tr. of Hearing 8–10 (Dec. 8, 2000) (soliciting from county canvassing boards proposed protocols for determining voters' intent but declining to provide a precise, uniform standard). I can conceive of no legitimate state interest served by these differing treatments of the expressions of voters' fundamental rights. The differences appear wholly arbitrary.

In deciding what to do about this, we should take account of the fact that electoral votes are due to be cast in six days. I would therefore remand the case to the courts of Florida with instructions to establish uniform standards for evaluating the several types of ballots that have prompted differing treatments, to be applied within and among counties when passing on such identical ballots in any further recounting (or successive recounting) that the courts might order.

Unlike the majority, I see no warrant for this Court to assume that Florida could not possibly comply with this requirement before the date set for the meeting of electors, December 18. Although one of the dissenting justices of the State Supreme Court estimated that disparate standards potentially affected 170,000 votes, *Gore v. Harris, supra,* ___ So. 2d, at ___ (slip op., at 66), the number at issue is significantly smaller. The 170,000 figure apparently represents all uncounted votes, both undervotes (those for which no Presidential choice was recorded by a machine) and overvotes (those rejected because of votes for more than one candidate). Tr. of Oral Arg. 61–62. But as *Justice Breyer* has pointed out, no showing has been made of legal overvotes uncounted, and counsel for Gore made an uncontradicted representation to the Court that the statewide total of undervotes is about 60,000. *Id.,* at 62. To recount these manually would be a tall order, but before this Court stayed the effort to do that the courts of Florida were ready to do their best to get that job done. There is no justification for denying the State the opportunity to try to count all disputed ballots now.

I respectfully dissent.

JUSTICE GINSBURG, *with whom* JUSTICE STEVENS *joins, and with whom* JUSTICE SOUTER *and* JUSTICE BREYER *join as to Part I, dissenting.*

I

The *Chief Justice* acknowledges that provisions of Florida's Election Code "may well admit of more than one interpretation." *Ante,* at 3. But instead of respecting the state high court's province to say what the State's Election Code means, *The Chief Justice* maintains that Florida's Supreme Court has veered so far from the ordinary practice of judicial review that what it did cannot properly be called judging. My colleagues have offered a reasonable construction of Florida's law. Their construction coincides with the view of one of Florida's seven Supreme Court justices. *Gore v. Harris,* ___ So. 2d ___, ___ (Fla. 2000) (slip op., at 45–55) (Wells, C. J., dissenting); *Palm Beach County Canvassing Bd. v. Harris,* ___ So. 2d ___, ___ (Fla. 2000) (slip op., at 34) (on remand) (confirming, 6-1, the construction of Florida law advanced in *Gore*). I might join *The Chief Justice* were it my commission to interpret Florida law. But disagreement with the Florida court's interpretation of its own State's law does not warrant the conclusion that the justices of that court have legislated. There is no cause here to believe that the members of Florida's high court have done less than "their mortal best to discharge their oath of office," *Sumner v. Mata,* 449 U.S. 539, 549 (1981), and no cause to upset their reasoned interpretation of Florida law.

This Court more than occasionally affirms statutory, and even constitutional, interpretations with which it disagrees. For example, when reviewing challenges to administrative agencies' interpretations of laws they implement, we defer to the agencies unless their interpretation violates "the unambiguously expressed intent of Congress." *Chevron U.S.A. Inc. v. Natural Resources Defense Council, Inc.,* 467 U.S. 837, 843 (1984). We do so in the face of the declaration in Article I of the United States Constitution that "All legislative Powers herein granted shall be vested in a Congress of the United States." Surely the Constitution does not call upon us to pay more respect to a federal administrative agency's construction of federal law than to a state high court's interpretation of its own state's law. And not uncommonly, we let stand state-court interpretations of *federal* law with which we might disagree. Notably, in the habeas context, the Court adheres to the view that "there is 'no intrinsic reason why the fact that a man is a federal judge should make him more competent, or conscientious, or learned with respect to [federal law] than his neighbor in the state courthouse.'" *Stone v. Powell,* 428 U.S. 465, 494, n. 35 (1976) (quoting Bator, Finality in Criminal Law and Federal Habeas Corpus For State Prisoners, 76 Harv. L. Rev. 441, 509 (1963)); see *O'Dell v. Netherland,* 521 U.S. 151, 156 (1997) ("[T]he *Teague* doctrine validates reasonable, good-faith interpretations of existing precedents made by state courts even though they are shown to be contrary to later decisions.") (citing *Butler v. McKellar,* 494 U.S. 407,

414 (1990)); O'Connor, Trends in the Relationship Between the Federal and State Courts from the Perspective of a State Court Judge, 22 Wm. & Mary L. Rev. 801, 813 (1981) ("There is no reason to assume that state court judges cannot and will not provide a 'hospitable forum' in litigating federal constitutional questions.").

No doubt there are cases in which the proper application of federal law may hinge on interpretations of state law. Unavoidably, this Court must sometimes examine state law in order to protect federal rights. But we have dealt with such cases ever mindful of the full measure of respect we owe to interpretations of state law by a State's highest court. In the Contract Clause case, *General Motors Corp. v. Romein*, 503 U.S. 181 (1992), for example, we said that although "ultimately we are bound to decide for ourselves whether a contract was made," the Court "accord[s] respectful consideration and great weight to the views of the State's highest court." *Id.*, at 187 (citation omitted). And in *Central Union Telephone Co. v. Edwardsville*, 269 U.S. 190 (1925), we upheld the Illinois Supreme Court's interpretation of a state waiver rule, even though that interpretation resulted in the forfeiture of federal constitutional rights. Refusing to supplant Illinois law with a federal definition of waiver, we explained that the state court's declaration "should bind us unless so unfair or unreasonable in its application to those asserting a federal right as to obstruct it." *Id.*, at 195.[13]

In deferring to state courts on matters of state law, we appropriately recognize that this Court acts as an " 'outside[r]' lacking the common exposure to local law which comes from sitting in the jurisdiction." *Lehman Brothers v. Schein*, 416 U. S. 386, 391 (1974). That recognition has sometimes prompted us to resolve doubts about the meaning of state law by certifying issues to a State's highest court, even when federal rights are at stake. Cf. *Arizonans for Official English v. Arizona*, 520 U. S. 43, 79 (1997) ("Warnings against premature adjudication of constitutional questions bear heightened attention when a federal court is asked to invalidate a State's law, for the federal tribunal risks friction-generating error when it endeavors to construe a novel state Act not yet reviewed by the State's highest court."). Notwithstanding our authority to decide issues of state law underlying federal claims, we have used the certification devise to afford state high courts an opportunity to inform us on matters of their own State's law because such restraint "helps build a cooperative judicial federalism." *Lehman Brothers*, 416 U.S., at 391.

Just last Term, in *Fiore v. White*, 528 U.S. 23 (1999), we took advantage of Pennsylvania's certification procedure. In that case, a state prisoner brought a federal habeas action claiming that the State had failed to prove an essential element of his charged offense in violation of the Due Process Clause. *Id.*, at 25–26. Instead of resolving the state-law question on which the federal claim depended, we certified the question to the Pennsylvania Supreme Court for that court to "help determine the proper state-law predicate for our determination of the federal constitutional questions raised." *Id.*, at 29; *id.*, at 28 (asking the Pennsylvania Supreme Court whether its recent interpretation of the statute under which Fiore was convicted "was always the statute's meaning, even at the time of Fiore's trial"). *The Chief Justice's* willingness to *reverse* the Florida Supreme Court's interpretation of Florida law in this case is at least in tension with our reluctance in *Fiore* even to interpret Pennsylvania law before seeking instruction from the Pennsylvania Supreme Court. I would have thought the "cautious approach" we counsel when federal courts address matters of state law, *Arizonans*, 520 U.S., at 77, and our commitment to "build[ing] cooperative judicial federalism," *Lehman Brothers*, 416 U.S., at 391, demanded greater restraint.

Rarely has this Court rejected outright an interpretation of state law by a state high court. *Fairfax's Devisee v. Hunter's Lessee*, 7 Cranch 603 (1813), *NAACP v. Alabama ex rel. Patterson*, 357 U.S. 449 (1958), and *Bouie v. City of Columbia*, 378 U.S. 347 (1964), cited by *The Chief Justice*, are three such rare instances. See *ante*, at 4, 5, and n. 2. But those cases are embedded in historical contexts hardly comparable to the situation here. *Fairfax's Devisee*, which held that the Virginia Court of Appeals had misconstrued its own forfeiture laws to deprive a British subject of lands secured to him by federal treaties, occurred amidst vociferous States' rights attacks on the Marshall Court. G. Gunther & K. Sullivan, Constitutional Law 61–62 (13th ed. 1997). The Virginia court refused to obey this Court's *Fairfax's Devisee* mandate to enter judgment for the British subject's successor in interest. That refusal led to the Court's pathmarking decision in *Martin v. Hunter's Lessee*, 1 Wheat. 304 (1816). *Patterson*, a case decided three months after *Cooper v. Aaron*, 358 U.S. 1 (1958), in the face of Southern resistance to the civil rights movement, held that the Alabama Supreme Court had irregularly applied its own procedural rules to deny review of a contempt order against the NAACP arising from its refusal to disclose membership lists. We said that "our jurisdiction is not defeated if the nonfederal ground relied on by the state court is without any fair or substantial support." 357 U.S., at 455. *Bouie*, stemming from a lunch counter "sit-in" at the height of the civil rights movement, held that the South Carolina Supreme Court's construction of its trespass laws—criminalizing conduct not covered by the text of an otherwise clear statute—was "unforeseeable" and thus violated due process when applied retroactively to the petitioners. 378 U.S., at 350, 354.

The Chief Justice's casual citation of these cases might lead one to believe they are part of a larger collection of cases in which we said that the Constitution impelled us to train a skeptical eye on a state court's portrayal of state law. But one would be hard pressed, I think, to find additional cases that fit the mold. As *Justice Breyer* convincingly explains, see *post*, at 5–9 (dissenting opinion), this case involves nothing close to the kind of recalcitrance by a state high court that warrants extraordinary action by this Court. The Florida Supreme Court concluded that counting every legal vote was the overriding concern of the Florida Legislature when it enacted the State's Election Code. The court surely should not be bracketed with state high courts of the Jim Crow South.

The Chief Justice says that Article II, by providing that state legislatures shall direct the manner of appointing electors, authorizes federal superintendence over the relationship between state courts and state legislatures, and licenses a departure from the usual deference we give to state court interpretations of state law. *Ante*, at 5 ("To attach definitive weight to the pronouncement of a state court, when the very question at issue is whether the court has actually departed from the statutory meaning, would be to abdicate our responsibility to enforce the explicit requirements of Article II."). The Framers of our Constitution, however, understood that in a republican government, the judiciary would construe the legislature's enactments. See U.S. Const., Art. III; The Federalist No. 78 (A. Hamilton). In light of the constitutional guarantee to States of a "Republican Form of Government," U.S. Const., Art. IV, §4, Article II can hardly be read to invite this Court to disrupt a State's republican regime. Yet *The Chief Justice* today would reach out to do just that. By holding that Article II requires our revision of a state court's construction of state laws in order to protect one organ of the State from another, *The Chief Justice* contradicts the basic principle that a State may organize itself as it sees fit. See, *e.g.*, *Gregory v. Ashcroft*, 501 U. S. 452, 460 (1991) ("Through the structure of its government, and the character of those who exercise government authority, a State defines itself as a sovereign."); *Highland Farms Dairy, Inc. v. Agnew*, 300 U.S. 608, 612 (1937) ("How power shall be distributed by a state among its governmental organs is commonly, if not always, a question for the state it-self.").[14] Article II does not call for the scrutiny undertaken by this Court.

The extraordinary setting of this case has obscured the ordinary principle that dictates its proper resolution: Federal courts defer to state high courts' interpretations of their state's own law. This principle reflects the core of federalism, on which all agree. "The Framers split the atom of sovereignty. It was the genius of their idea that our citizens would have two political capacities, one state and one federal, each protected from incursion by the other." *Saenz v. Roe,* 526 U.S. 489, 504, n. 17 (1999) (citing *U.S. Term Limits, Inc. v. Thornton,* 514 U.S. 779, 838 (1995) (*Kennedy, J.,* concurring)). *The Chief Justice's* solicitude for the Florida Legislature comes at the expense of the more fundamental solicitude we owe to the legislature's sovereign. U.S. Const., Art. II, §1, cl. 2 ("Each *State* shall appoint, in such Manner as the Legislature *thereof* may direct," the electors for President and Vice President) (emphasis added); *ante,* at 1–2 (*Stevens, J.,* dissenting).[15] Were the other members of this Court as mindful as they generally are of our system of dual sovereignty, they would affirm the judgment of the Florida Supreme Court.

II

I agree with *Justice Stevens* that petitioners have not presented a substantial equal protection claim. Ideally, perfection would be the appropriate standard for judging the recount. But we live in an imperfect world, one in which thousands of votes have not been counted. I cannot agree that the recount adopted by the Florida court, flawed as it may be, would yield a result any less fair or precise than the certification that preceded that recount. See, *e.g., McDonald v. Board of Election Comm'rs of Chicago,* 394 U.S. 802, 807 (1969) (even in the context of the right to vote, the state is permitted to reform "'one step at a time'") (quoting *Williamson v. Lee Optical of Oklahoma, Inc.,* 348 U.S. 483, 489 (1955)).

Even if there were an equal protection violation, I would agree with *Justice Stevens, Justice Souter,* and *Justice Breyer* that the Court's concern about "the December 12 deadline," *ante,* at 12, is misplaced. Time is short in part because of the Court's entry of a stay on December 9, several hours after an able circuit judge in Leon County had begun to superintend the recount process. More fundamentally, the Court's reluctance to let the recount go forward—despite its suggestion that "[t]he search for intent can be confined by specific rules designed to ensure uniform treatment," *ante,* at 8—ultimately turns on its own judgment about the practical realities of implementing a recount, not the judgment of those much closer to the process.

Equally important, as *Justice Breyer* explains, *post,* at 12 (dissenting opinion), the December 12 "deadline" for bringing Florida's electoral votes into 3 U.S.C. §5's safe harbor lacks the significance the Court assigns it. Were that date to pass, Florida would still be entitled to deliver electoral votes Congress *must* count unless both Houses find that the votes "ha[d] not been ... regularly given." 3 U.S.C. §15. The statute identifies other significant dates. See, *e.g.,* §7 (specifying December 18 as the date electors "shall meet and give their votes"); §12 (specifying "the fourth Wednesday in December"—this year, December 27—as the date on which Congress, if it has not received a State's electoral votes, shall request the state secretary of state to send a certified return immediately). But none of these dates has ultimate significance in light of Congress' detailed provisions for determining, on "the sixth day of January," the validity of electoral votes. §15.

The Court assumes that time will not permit "orderly judicial review of any disputed matters that might arise." *Ante,* at 12. But no one has doubted the good faith and diligence with which Florida election officials, attorneys for all sides of this controversy, and the courts of law have performed their duties. Notably, the Florida Supreme Court has produced two substantial opinions within 29 hours of oral argument. In sum, the Court's conclusion that a constitutionally adequate recount is impractical is a prophecy the Court's own judgment will not allow to be tested. Such an untested prophecy should not decide the Presidency of the United States.

I dissent.

JUSTICE BREYER, *with whom* JUSTICE STEVENS *and* JUSTICE GINSBURG *join except as to Part I-A-1, and with whom* JUSTICE SOUTER *joins as to Part I, dissenting.*

The Court was wrong to take this case. It was wrong to grant a stay. It should now vacate that stay and permit the Florida Supreme Court to decide whether the recount should resume.

I

The political implications of this case for the country are momentous. But the federal legal questions presented, with one exception, are insubstantial.

A. 1. The majority raises three Equal Protection problems with the Florida Supreme Court's recount order: first, the failure to include overvotes in the manual recount; second, the fact that *all* ballots, rather than simply the undervotes, were recounted in some, but not all, counties; and third, the absence of a uniform, specific standard to guide the recounts. As far as the first issue is concerned, petitioners presented no evidence, to this Court or to any Florida court, that a manual recount of overvotes would identify additional legal votes. The same is true of the second, and, in addition, the majority's reasoning would seem to invalidate any state provision for a manual recount of individual counties in a statewide election.

The majority's third concern does implicate principles of fundamental fairness. The majority concludes that the Equal Protection Clause requires that a manual recount be governed not only by the uniform general standard of the "clear intent of the voter," but also by uniform subsidiary standards (for example, a uniform determination whether indented, but not perforated, "undervotes" should count). The opinion points out that the Florida Supreme Court ordered the inclusion of Broward County's undercounted "legal votes" even though those votes included ballots that were not perforated but simply "dimpled," while newly recounted ballots from other counties will likely include only votes determined to be "legal" on the basis of a stricter standard. In light of our previous remand, the Florida Supreme Court may have been reluctant to adopt a more specific standard than that provided for by the legislature for fear of exceeding its authority under Article II. However, since the use of different standards could favor one or the other of the candidates, since time was, and is, too short to permit the lower courts to iron out significant differences through ordinary judicial review, and since the relevant distinction was embodied in the order of the State's highest court, I agree that, in these very special circumstances, basic principles of fairness may well have counseled the adoption of a uniform standard to address the problem. In light of the majority's disposition, I need not decide whether, or the extent to which, as a remedial matter, the Constitution would place limits upon the content of the uniform standard.

2. Nonetheless, there is no justification for the majority's remedy, which is simply to reverse the lower court and halt the recount entirely. An appropriate remedy would be, instead, to remand this case with instructions that, even at this late date, would permit the Florida Supreme Court to require recounting *all* undercounted votes in

Florida, including those from Broward, Volusia, Palm Beach, and Miami-Dade Counties, whether or not previously recounted prior to the end of the protest period, and to do so in accordance with a single-uniform substandard.

The majority justifies stopping the recount entirely on the ground that there is no more time. In particular, the majority relies on the lack of time for the Secretary to review and approve equipment needed to separate undervotes. But the majority reaches this conclusion in the absence of *any* record evidence that the recount could not have been completed in the time allowed by the Florida Supreme Court. The majority finds facts outside of the record on matters that state courts are in a far better position to address. Of course, it is too late for any such recount to take place by December 12, the date by which election disputes must be decided if a State is to take advantage of the safe harbor provisions of 3 U.S.C. §5. Whether there is time to conduct a recount prior to December 18, when the electors are scheduled to meet, is a matter for the state courts to determine. And whether, under Florida law, Florida could or could not take further action is obviously a matter for Florida courts, not this Court, to decide. See *ante*, at 13 *(per curiam)*.

By halting the manual recount, and thus ensuring that the uncounted legal votes will not be counted under any standard, this Court crafts a remedy out of proportion to the asserted harm. And that remedy harms the very fairness interests the Court is attempting to protect. The manual recount would itself redress a problem of unequal treatment of ballots. As *Justice Stevens* points out, see *ante*, at 4 and n. 4 *(Stevens, J., dissenting opinion)*, the ballots of voters in counties that use punch-card systems are more likely to be disqualified than those in counties using optical-scanning systems. According to recent news reports, variations in the undervote rate are even more pronounced. See Fessenden, No-Vote Rates Higher in Punch Card Count, N.Y. Times, Dec. 1, 2000, p. A29 (reporting that 0.3% of ballots cast in 30 Florida counties using optical-scanning systems registered no Presidential vote, in comparison to 1.53% in the 15 counties using Votomatic punch card ballots). Thus, in a system that allows counties to use different types of voting systems, voters already arrive at the polls with an unequal chance that their votes will be counted. I do not see how the fact that this results from counties' selection of different voting machines rather than a court order makes the outcome any more fair. Nor do I understand why the Florida Supreme Court's recount order, which helps to redress this inequity, must be entirely prohibited based on a deficiency that could easily be remedied.

B. The remainder of petitioners' claims, which are the focus of the *Chief Justice*'s concurrence, raise no significant federal questions. I cannot agree that the *Chief Justice*'s unusual review of state law in this case, see *ante*, at 5–8 *(Ginsburg, J., dissenting opinion)*, is justified by reference either to Art. II, §1, or to 3 U.S.C. §5. Moreover, even were such review proper, the conclusion that the Florida Supreme Court's decision contravenes federal law is untenable.

While conceding that, in most cases, "comity and respect for federalism compel us to defer to the decisions of state courts on issues of state law," the concurrence relies on some combination of Art. II, §1, and 3 U.S.C. §5 to justify the majority's conclusion that this case is one of the few in which we may lay that fundamental principle aside. *Ante*, at 2 (Opinion of *Rehnquist, C. J.* The concurrence's primary foundation for this conclusion rests on an appeal to plain text: Art. II, §1's grant of the power to appoint Presidential electors to the State "Legislature." *Ibid.* But neither the text of Article II itself nor the only case the concurrence cites that interprets Article II, *McPherson v. Blacker*, 146 U.S. 1 (1892), leads to the conclusion that Article II grants unlimited power to the legislature, devoid of any

state constitutional limitations, to select the manner of appointing electors. See *id.*, at 41 (specifically referring to state constitutional provision in upholding state law regarding selection of electors). Nor, as *Justice Stevens* points out, have we interpreted the Federal constitutional provision most analogous to Art. II, §1—Art. I, §4— in the strained manner put forth in the concurrence. *Ante*, at 1-2 and n. 1 (dissenting opinion).

The concurrence's treatment of §5 as "inform[ing]" its interpretation of Article II, §1, cl. 2, *ante*, at 3 *(Rehnquist, C. J.*, concurring), is no more convincing. The *Chief Justice* contends that our opinion in *Bush v. Palm Beach County Canvassing Bd., ante*, p. ____, *(per curiam) (Bush I)*, in which we stated that "a legislative wish to take advantage of [§5] would counsel against" a construction of Florida law that Congress might deem to be a change in law, *id.*, (slip op. at 6), now means that *this Court* "must ensure that post-election state court actions do not frustrate the legislative desire to attain the 'safe harbor' provided by §5." *Ante*, at 3. However, §5 is part of the rules that govern Congress' recognition of slates of electors. Nowhere in *Bush I* did we establish that *this Court* had the authority to enforce §5. Nor did we suggest that the permissive "counsel against" could be transformed into the mandatory "must ensure." And nowhere did we intimate, as the concurrence does here, that a state court decision that threatens the safe harbor provision of §5 does so in violation of Article II. The concurrence's logic turns the presumption that legislatures would wish to take advantage of § 5's "safe harbor" provision into a mandate that trumps other statutory provisions and overrides the intent that the legislature *did* express.

But, in any event, the concurrence, having conducted its review, now reaches the wrong conclusion. It says that "the Florida Supreme Court's interpretation of the Florida election laws impermissibly distorted them beyond what a fair reading required, in violation of Article II." *Ante*, at 4–5 *(Rehnquist, C. J, concurring)*. But what precisely is the distortion? Apparently, it has three elements. First, the Florida court, in its earlier opinion, changed the election certification date from November 14 to November 26. Second, the Florida court ordered a manual recount of "undercounted" ballots that could not have been fully completed by the December 12 "safe harbor" deadline. Third, the Florida court, in the opinion now under review, failed to give adequate deference to the determinations of canvassing boards and the Secretary.

To characterize the first element as a "distortion," however, requires the concurrence to second-guess the way in which the state court resolved a plain conflict in the language of different statutes. Compare Fla. Stat. §102.166 (2001) (foreseeing manual recounts during the protest period) with §102.111 (setting what is arguably too short a deadline for manual recounts to be conducted); compare §102.112(1) (stating that the Secretary "may" ignore late returns) with §102.111(1) (stating that the Secretary "shall" ignore late returns). In any event, that issue no longer has any practical importance and cannot justify the reversal of the different Florida court decision before us now.

To characterize the second element as a "distortion" requires the concurrence to overlook the fact that the inability of the Florida courts to conduct the recount on time is, in significant part, a problem of the Court's own making. The Florida Supreme Court thought that the recount could be completed on time, and, within hours, the Florida Circuit Court was moving in an orderly fashion to meet the deadline. This Court improvidently entered a stay. As a result, we will never know whether the recount could have been completed.

Nor can one characterize the third element as "impermissibl[e] distort[ing]" once one understands that there are two sides to the opinion's argument that the Florida Supreme Court "virtually eliminated the Secretary's discretion." *Ante,* at 9 (*Rehnquist, C. J,* concurring). The Florida statute in question was amended in 1999 to provide that the "grounds for contesting an election" include the "rejection of a number of legal votes sufficient to … place in doubt the result of the election." Fla. Stat. §§102.168(3), (3)(c) (2000). And the parties have argued about the proper meaning of the statute's term "legal vote." The Secretary has claimed that a "legal vote" is a vote "properly executed in accordance with the instructions provided to all registered voters." Brief for Respondent Harris et al. 10. On that interpretation, punchcard ballots for which the machines cannot register a vote are not "legal" votes. *Id.,* at 14. The Florida Supreme Court did not accept her definition. But it had a reason. Its reason was that a different provision of Florida election laws (a provision that addresses damaged or defective ballots) says that no vote shall be disregarded "if there is a clear indication of the intent of the voter as determined by the canvassing board" (adding that ballots should not be counted "if it is impossible to determine the elector's choice"). Fla. Stat. §101.5614(5) (2000). Given this statutory language, certain roughly analogous judicial precedent, *e.g., Darby v. State ex rel. McCollough,* 75 So. 411 (Fla. 1917) *(per curiam),* and somewhat similar determinations by courts throughout the Nation, see cases cited *infra,* at 9, the Florida Supreme Court concluded that the term "legal vote" means a vote recorded on a ballot that clearly reflects what the voter intended. *Gore v. Harris,* ___ So. 2d ___, ___ (2000) (slip op., at 19). That conclusion differs from the conclusion of the Secretary. But nothing in Florida law requires the Florida Supreme Court to accept as determinative the Secretary's view on such a matter. Nor can one say that the Court's ultimate determination is so unreasonable as to amount to a constitutionally "impermissible distort[ion]" of Florida law.

The Florida Supreme Court, applying this definition, decided, on the basis of the record, that respondents had shown that the ballots undercounted by the voting machines contained enough "legal votes" to place "the results" of the election "in doubt." Since only a few hundred votes separated the candidates, and since the "undercounted" ballots numbered tens of thousands, it is difficult to see how anyone could find this conclusion unreasonable—however strict the standard used to measure the voter's "clear intent." Nor did this conclusion "strip" canvassing boards of their discretion. The boards retain their traditional discretionary authority during the protest period. And during the contest period, as the court stated, "the Canvassing Board's actions [during the protest period] may constitute evidence that a ballot does or does not qualify as a legal vote." *Id.,* at *13. Whether a local county canvassing board's discretionary judgment during the protest period not to conduct a manual recount will be set aside during a contest period depends upon whether a candidate provides additional evidence that the rejected votes contain enough "legal votes" to place the outcome of the race in doubt. To limit the local canvassing board's discretion in this way is not to eliminate that discretion. At the least, one could reasonably so believe.

The statute goes on to provide the Florida circuit judge with authority to "fashion such orders as he or she deems necessary to ensure that each allegation … is *investigated, examined, or checked,* … and to provide any relief appropriate." Fla. Stat. §102.168(8) (2000) (emphasis added). The Florida Supreme Court did just that. One might reasonably disagree with the Florida Supreme Court's interpretation of these, or other, words in the statute. But I do not see how one could call its plain language interpretation of a 1999 statutory change so misguided as no longer to qualify as judicial interpretation or as a usurpation of the authority of the State legislature. Indeed, other state courts have interpreted roughly similar state statutes in similar ways. See, *e.g., In re Election of U.S. Representative for Second Congressional Dist.,* 231 Conn. 602, 621, 653 A. 2d 79, 90–91 (1994) ("Whatever the process used to vote and to count votes, differences in technology should not furnish a basis for disregarding the bedrock principle that the purpose of the voting process is to ascertain the intent of the voters"); *Brown v. Carr,* 130 W.Va. 401, 460, 43 S. E.2d 401, 404–405 (1947) ("[W]hether a ballot shall be counted … depends on the intent of the voter. … Courts decry any resort to technical rules in reaching a conclusion as to the intent of the voter").

I repeat, where is the "impermissible" distortion?

II

Despite the reminder that this case involves "an election for the President of the United States," *ante,* at 1 (*Rehnquist, C. J.,* concurring), no preeminent legal concern, or practical concern related to legal questions, required this Court to hear this case, let alone to issue a stay that stopped Florida's recount process in its tracks. With one exception, petitioners' claims do not ask us to vindicate a constitutional provision designed to protect a basic human right. See, *e.g., Brown v. Board of Education,* 347 U.S. 483 (1954). Petitioners invoke fundamental fairness, namely, the need for procedural fairness, including finality. But with the one "equal protection" exception, they rely upon law that focuses, not upon that basic need, but upon the constitutional allocation of power. Respondents invoke a competing fundamental consideration—the need to determine the voter's true intent. But they look to state law, not to federal constitutional law, to protect that interest. Neither side claims electoral fraud, dishonesty, or the like. And the more fundamental equal protection claim might have been left to the state court to resolve if and when it was discovered to have mattered. It could still be resolved through a remand conditioned upon issuance of a uniform standard; it does not require reversing the Florida Supreme Court.

Of course, the selection of the President is of fundamental national importance. But that importance is political, not legal. And this Court should resist the temptation unnecessarily to resolve tangential legal disputes, where doing so threatens to determine the outcome of the election.

The Constitution and federal statutes themselves make clear that restraint is appropriate. They set forth a road map of how to resolve disputes about electors, even after an election as close as this one. That road map foresees resolution of electoral disputes by *state* courts. See 3 U.S.C. §5 (providing that, where a "State shall have provided, by laws enacted prior to [election day], for its final determination of any controversy or contest concerning the appointment of … electors … by *judicial* or other methods," the subsequently chosen electors enter a safe harbor free from congressional challenge). But it nowhere provides for involvement by the United States Supreme Court.

To the contrary, the Twelfth Amendment commits to Congress the authority and responsibility to count electoral votes. A federal statute, the Electoral Count Act, enacted after the close 1876 Hayes-Tilden Presidential election, specifies that, after States have tried to resolve disputes (through "judicial" or other means), Congress is the body primarily authorized to resolve remaining disputes. See Electoral Count Act of 1887, 24 Stat. 373, 3 U.S.C. §§5, 6, and 15.

The legislative history of the Act makes clear its intent to commit the power to resolve such disputes to Congress, rather than the courts:

"The two Houses are, by the Constitution, authorized to make the count of electoral votes. They can only count legal votes, and in doing so must determine, from the best evidence to be had, what are legal votes. . . . The power to determine rests with the two Houses, and there is no other constitutional tribunal." H. Rep. No. 1638, 49th Cong., 1st Sess., 2 (1886) (report submitted by Rep. Caldwell, Select Committee on the Election of President and Vice-President).

The Member of Congress who introduced the Act added:

"The power to judge of the legality of the votes is a necessary consequent of the power to count. The existence of this power is of absolute necessity to the preservation of the Government. The interests of all the States in their relations to each other in the Federal Union demand that the ultimate tribunal to decide upon the election of President should be a constituent body, in which the States in their federal relationships and the people in their sovereign capacity should be represented." 18 Cong. Rec. 30 (1886).

"Under the Constitution who else could decide? Who is nearer to the State in determining a question of vital importance to the whole union of States than the constituent body upon whom the Constitution has devolved the duty to count the vote?" *Id.,* at 31.

The Act goes on to set out rules for the congressional determination of disputes about those votes. If, for example, a state submits a single slate of electors, Congress must count those votes unless both Houses agree that the votes "have not been . . . regularly given." 3 U.S.C. § 15. If, as occurred in 1876, one or more states submits two sets of electors, then Congress must determine whether a slate has entered the safe harbor of §5, in which case its votes will have "conclusive" effect. *Ibid.* If, as also occurred in 1876, there is controversy about "which of two or more of such State authorities . . . is the lawful tribunal" authorized to appoint electors, then each House shall determine separately which votes are "supported by the decision of such State so authorized by its law." *Ibid.* If the two Houses of Congress agree, the votes they have approved will be counted. If they disagree, then "the votes of the electors whose appointment shall have been certified by the executive of the State, under the seal thereof, shall be counted." *Ibid.*

Given this detailed, comprehensive scheme for counting electoral votes, there is no reason to believe that federal law either foresees or requires resolution of such a political issue by this Court. Nor, for that matter, is there any reason to think that the Constitution's Framers would have reached a different conclusion. Madison, at least, believed that allowing the judiciary to choose the presidential electors "was out of the question." Madison, July 25, 1787 (reprinted in 5 Elliot's Debates on the Federal Constitution 363 (2d ed. 1876)).

The decision by both the Constitution's Framers and the 1886 Congress to minimize this Court's role in resolving close federal presidential elections is as wise as it is clear. However awkward or difficult it may be for Congress to resolve difficult electoral disputes, Congress, being a political body, expresses the people's will far more accurately than does an unelected Court. And the people's will is what elections are about.

Moreover, Congress was fully aware of the danger that would arise should it ask judges, unarmed with appropriate legal standards, to resolve a hotly contested Presidential election contest. Just after the 1876 Presidential election, Florida, South Carolina, and Louisiana each sent two slates of electors to Washington. Without these States, Tilden, the Democrat, had 184 electoral votes, one short of the number required to win the Presidency. With those States, Hayes, his Republican opponent, would have had 185. In order to choose between the two slates of electors, Congress decided to appoint an electoral commission composed of five Senators, five Representatives, and five Supreme Court Justices. Initially the Commission was to be evenly divided between Republicans and Democrats, with Justice David Davis, an Independent, to possess

the decisive vote. However, when at the last minute the Illinois Legislature elected Justice Davis to the United States Senate, the final position on the Commission was filled by Supreme Court Justice Joseph P. Bradley.

The Commission divided along partisan lines, and the responsibility to cast the deciding vote fell to Justice Bradley. He decided to accept the votes by the Republican electors, and thereby awarded the Presidency to Hayes.

Justice Bradley immediately became the subject of vociferous attacks. Bradley was accused of accepting bribes, of being captured by railroad interests, and of an eleventh-hour change in position after a night in which his house "was surrounded by the carriages" of Republican partisans and railroad officials. C. Woodward, Reunion and Reaction 159–160 (1966). Many years later, Professor Bickel concluded that Bradley was honest and impartial. He thought that " 'the great question' for Bradley was, in fact, whether Congress was entitled to go behind election returns or had to accept them as certified by state authorities," an "issue of principle." The Least Dangerous Branch 185 (1962). Nonetheless, Bickel points out, the legal question upon which Justice Bradley's decision turned was not very important in the contemporaneous political context. He says that "in the circumstances the issue of principle was trivial, it was overwhelmed by all that hung in the balance, and it should not have been decisive." *Ibid.*

For present purposes, the relevance of this history lies in the fact that the participation in the work of the electoral commission by five Justices, including Justice Bradley, did not lend that process legitimacy. Nor did it assure the public that the process had worked fairly, guided by the law. Rather, it simply embroiled Members of the Court in partisan conflict, thereby undermining respect for the judicial process. And the Congress that later enacted the Electoral Count Act knew it.

This history may help to explain why I think it not only legally wrong, but also most unfortunate, for the Court simply to have terminated the Florida recount. Those who caution judicial restraint in resolving political disputes have described the quintessential case for that restraint as a case marked, among other things, by the "strangeness of the issue," its "intractability to principled resolution," its "sheer momentousness, . . . which tends to unbalance judicial judgment," and "the inner vulnerability, the self-doubt of an institution which is electorally irresponsible and has no earth to draw strength from." Bickel, *supra,* at 184. Those characteristics mark this case.

At the same time, as I have said, the Court is not acting to vindicate a fundamental constitutional principle, such as the need to protect a basic human liberty. No other strong reason to act is present. Congressional statutes tend to obviate the need. And, above all, in this highly politicized matter, the appearance of a split decision runs the risk of undermining the public's confidence in the Court itself. That confidence is a public treasure. It has been built slowly over many years, some of which were marked by a Civil War and the tragedy of segregation. It is a vitally necessary ingredient of any successful effort to protect basic liberty and, indeed, the rule of law itself. We run no risk of returning to the days when a President (responding to this Court's efforts to protect the Cherokee Indians) might have said, "John Marshall has made his decision; now let him enforce it!" Loth, Chief Justice John Marshall and The Growth of the American Republic 365 (1948). But we do risk a self-inflicted wound — a wound that may harm not just the Court, but the Nation.

I fear that in order to bring this agonizingly long election process to a definitive conclusion, we have not adequately attended to that necessary "check upon our own exercise of power," "our own sense of self-restraint." *United States v. Butler,* 297 U.S. 1, 79 (1936) (Stone, J., dissenting). Justice Brandeis once said of the Court, "The most important thing we do is not doing." Bickel, *supra,* at 71. What it does today, the Court should have left undone. I would repair the damage done as best we now can, by permitting the Florida recount to continue under uniform standards.

I respectfully dissent.

1. Similarly, our jurisprudence requires us to analyze the "background principles" of state property law to determine whether there has been a taking of property in violation of the Takings Clause. That constitutional guarantee would, of course, afford no protection against state power if our inquiry could be concluded by a state supreme court holding that state property law accorded the plaintiff no rights. See *Lucas v. South Carolina Coastal Council,* 505 U.S. 1003 (1992). In one of our oldest cases, we similarly made an independent evaluation of state law in order to protect federal treaty guarantees. In *Fairfax's Devisee v. Hunter's Lessee,* 7 Cranch 603 (1813), we disagreed with the Supreme Court of Appeals of Virginia that a 1782 state law had extinguished the property interests of one Denny Fairfax, so that a 1789 ejectment order against Fairfax supported by a 1785 state law did not constitute a future confiscation under the 1783 peace treaty with Great Britain. See *id.,* at 623; *Hunter v. Fairfax's Devisee,* 1 Munf. 218 (Va. 1809).

2. We vacated that decision and remanded that case; the Florida Supreme Court reissued the same judgment with a new opinion on December 11, 2000, ___ So. 2d, ___.

3. Specifically, the Florida Supreme Court ordered the Circuit Court to include in the certified vote totals those votes identified for Vice President Gore in Palm Beach County and Miami-Dade County.

4. It is inconceivable that what constitutes a vote that must be counted under the "error in the vote tabulation" language of the protest phase is different from what constitutes a vote that must be counted under the "legal votes" language of the contest phase.

5. "Wherever the term 'legislature' is used in the Constitution it is necessary to consider the nature of the particular action in view." 285 U.S., at 367. It is perfectly clear that the meaning of the words "Manner" and "Legislature" as used in Article II, §1, parallels the usage in Article I, §4, rather than the language in Article V. *U.S. Term Limits, Inc. v. Thornton,* 514 U.S. 779, 805 (1995). Article I, §4, and Article II, §1, both call upon legislatures to act in a lawmaking capacity whereas Article V simply calls on the legislative body to deliberate upon a binary decision. As a result, petitioners' reliance on *Leser v. Garnett,* 258 U.S. 130 (1922), and *Hawke v. Smith (No. 1),* 253 U.S. 221 (1920), is misplaced.

6. The Florida statutory standard is consistent with the practice of the majority of States, which apply either an "intent of the voter" standard or an "impossible to determine the elector's choice" standard in ballot recounts. The following States use an "intent of the voter" standard: Ariz. Rev. Stat. Ann. §16-645(A) (Supp. 2000) (standard for canvassing write-in votes); Conn. Gen. Stat. §9-150a(j) (1999) (standard for absentee ballots, including three conclusive presumptions); Ind. Code §3-12-1-1 (1992); Me. Rev. Stat. Ann., Tit. 21-A, §1(13) (1993) (standard for absentee ballots); Md. Ann. Code, Art. 33, §11-302(d) (2000 Supp.) (standard for absentee ballots); Mass. Gen. Laws §70E (1991) (applying standard to Presidential primaries); Mich. Comp. Laws §168.799a(3) (Supp. 2000); Mo. Rev. Stat. §115.453(3) (Cum. Supp. 1998) (looking to voter's intent where there is substantial compliance with statutory requirements); Tex. Elec. Code Ann. §65.009(c) (1986); Utah Code Ann. §20A-4-104(5)(b) (Supp. 2000) (standard for write-in votes), §20A-4-105(6)(a) (standard for mechanical ballots); Vt. Stat. Ann., Tit. 17, §2587(a) (1982); Va. Code Ann. §24.2-644(A) (2000); Wash. Rev. Code §29.62.180(1) (Supp. 2001) (standard for write-in votes); Wyo. Stat. Ann. §22-14-104 (1999). The following States employ a standard in which a vote is counted unless it is "impossible to determine the elector's [or voter's] choice": Ala. Code §11-46-44(c) (1992), Ala. Code §17-13-2 (1995); Ariz. Rev. Stat. Ann. §16-610 (1996) (standard for rejecting ballot); Cal. Elec. Code Ann. §15154(c) (West Supp. 2000); Colo. Rev. Stat. §1-7-309(1) (1999) (standard for paper ballots), §1-7-508(2) (standard

for electronic ballots); Del. Code Ann., Tit. 15, §4972(4) (1999); Idaho Code §34-1203 (1981); Ill. Comp. Stat., ch. 10, §5/7-51 (1993) (standard for primaries), *id.,* ch. 10, §5/17-16 (1993) (standard for general elections); Iowa Code §49.98 (1999); Me. Rev. Stat. Ann., Tit. 21-A §§696(2)(B), (4) (Supp. 2000); Minn. Stat. §204C.22(1) (1992); Mont. Code Ann. §13-15-202 (1997) (not counting votes if "elector's choice cannot be determined"); Nev. Rev. Stat. §293.367(d) (1995); N.Y. Elec. Law §9-112(6) (McKinney 1998); N.C. Gen. Stat. §§163-169(b), 163-170 (1999); N.D. Cent. Code §16.1-15-01(1) (Supp. 1999); Ohio Rev. Code Ann. §3505.28 (1994); 26 Okla. Stat., Tit. 26, §7-127(6) (1997); Ore. Rev. Stat. §254.505(1) (1991); S.C. Code Ann. §7-13-1120 (1977); S.D. Codified Laws §12-20-7 (1995); Tenn. Code Ann. §2-7-133(b) (1994); W. Va. Code §3-6-5(g) (1999).

7. Cf. *Victor v. Nebraska,* 511 U.S. 1, 5 (1994) ("The beyond a reasonable doubt standard is a requirement of due process, but the Constitution neither prohibits trial courts from defining reasonable doubt nor requires them to do so").

8. The percentage of nonvotes in this election in counties using a punch-card system was 3.92%; in contrast, the rate of error under the more modern optical-scan systems was only 1.43%. *Siegel v. LePore,* No. 00-15981, 2000 WL 1781946, *31, *32, *43 (charts C and F) (CA11, Dec. 6, 2000). Put in other terms, for every 10,000 votes cast, punch-card systems result in 250 more nonvotes than optical-scan systems. A total of 3,718,305 votes were cast under punch-card systems, and 2,353,811 votes were cast under optical-scan systems. *Ibid.*

9. Republican electors were certified by the Acting Governor on November 28, 1960. A recount was ordered to begin on December 13, 1960. Both Democratic and Republican electors met on the appointed day to cast their votes. On January 4, 1961, the newly elected Governor certified the Democratic electors. The certification was received by Congress on January 6, the day the electoral votes were counted. Josephson & Ross, 22 J. Legis., at 166, n. 154.

10. When, for example, it resolved the previously unanswered question whether the word "shall" in Fla. Stat. §102.111 or the word "may" in §102.112 governs the scope of the Secretary of State's authority to ignore untimely election returns, it did not "change the law." Like any other judicial interpretation of a statute, its opinion was an authoritative interpretation of what the statute's relevant provisions have meant since they were enacted. *Rivers v. Roadway Express, Inc.,* 511 U.S. 298, 312–313 (1994).

11. "It is emphatically the province and duty of the judicial department to say what the law is." *Marbury v. Madison,* 1 Cranch 137, 177 (1803).

12. When the Florida court ruled, the totals for Bush and Gore were then less than 1,000 votes apart. One dissent pegged the number of uncounted votes in question at 170,000. *Gore v. Harris, supra,* __ So. 2d __ , (slip op., at 66) (opinion of Harding, J.). Gore's counsel represented to us that the relevant figure is approximately 60,000, Tr. of Oral Arg. 62, the number of ballots in which no vote for President was recorded by the machines.

13. See also *Lucas v. South Carolina Coastal Council,* 505 U.S. 1003, 1032, n.18 (1992) (South Carolina could defend a regulatory taking "if an *objectively reasonable application* of relevant precedents [by its courts] would exclude . . . beneficial uses in the circumstances in which the land is presently found"); *Bishop v. Wood,* 426 U.S. 341, 344–345 (1976) (deciding whether North Carolina had created a property interest cognizable under the Due Process Clause by reference to state law as interpreted by the North Carolina Supreme Court). Similarly, in *Gurley v. Rhoden,* 421 U.S. 200 (1975), a gasoline retailer claimed that due process entitled him to deduct a state gasoline excise tax in computing the amount of his sales subject to a state sales tax, on the grounds that the legal incidence of the excise tax fell on his customers and that he acted merely as a collector of the tax. The Mississippi Supreme Court held that the legal incidence of the excise tax fell on petitioner. Observing that "a State's highest court is the final judicial arbiter of the meaning of state statutes," we said that "[w]hen a state court has made its own definitive determination as to the operating incidence, . . . [w]e give this finding great weight in determining the natural effect of a statute, and if it is consistent with the statute's reasonable interpretation it will be deemed conclusive." *Id.,* at 208.

14. Even in the rare case in which a State's "manner" of making and construing laws might implicate a structural constraint, Congress, not this Court, is likely the proper governmental entity to enforce that constraint. See *U.S. Const.,* amend. XII; 3 U.S.C. §§1-15; cf. *Ohio ex rel. Davis v. Hildebrant,* 241 U.S. 565, 569 (1916) (treating as a nonjusticiable political question whether use of a referendum to override a congressional districting plan enacted by the state legislature violates Art. I, §4); *Luther v. Borden,* 7 How. 1, 42 (1849).

15. "[B]ecause the Framers recognized that state power and identity were essential parts of the federal balance, see The Federalist No. 39, the Constitution is solicitous of the prerogatives of the States, even in an otherwise sovereign federal province. The Constitution . . . grants States certain powers over the times, places, and manner of federal elections (subject to congressional revision), Art. I, §4, cl. 1 . . . , and allows States to appoint electors for the President, Art. II, §1, cl. 2." *U.S. Term Limits, Inc. v. Thornton,* 514 U.S. 779, 841–842 (1995) (Kennedy, J., concurring).

Grutter v. Bollinger (2003)

Affirmative action policies designed to ameliorate the effects of racial discrimination have been a source of great public controversy. The Supreme Court's prior rulings had drawn fine lines between permitting narrowly tailored affirmative action policies and programs and casting suspicion on the use of race as the deciding factor in employment and educational admissions decisions (see Regents of University of California v. Bakke*).*

In 2003, the Supreme Court in a landmark 5-4 decision, upheld a race-conscious University of Michigan law school admissions policy that the university justified by its desire to promote racial diversity on campus. In a companion decision the same day, however, the Court ruled the admissions policies at the university's main undergraduate college were unconstitutional violations of the Equal Protection Clause because of the way race was factored into undergraduate admissions decisions (see Gratz v. Bollinger*).*

The majority opinion in Grutter v. Bollinger *ruled "that the Law School has a compelling interest in attaining a diverse student body." But the future of affirmative action programs was cast in doubt: "We expect that 25 years from now, the use of racial preferences will no longer be necessary to further the interest approved today."*

539 U.S. ___

Grutter v. Bollinger, et al.

On Writ of Certiorari to the United States Court of Appeals for the Sixth Circuit

No. 02-241. *Argued April 1, 2003—Decided June 23, 2003*

The University of Michigan Law School (Law School), one of the Nation's top law schools, follows an official admissions policy that seeks to achieve student body diversity through compliance with *Regents of Univ. of Cal. v. Bakke,* 438 U.S. 265. Focusing on students' academic ability coupled with a flexible assessment of their talents, experiences, and potential, the policy requires admissions officials to evaluate each applicant based on all the information available in the file, including a personal statement, letters of recommendation, an essay describing how the applicant will contribute to Law School life and diversity, and the applicant's undergraduate grade point average (GPA) and Law School Admissions Test (LSAT) score. Additionally, officials must look beyond grades and scores to so-called "soft variables," such as recommenders' enthusiasm, the quality of the undergraduate institution and the applicant's essay, and the areas and difficulty of undergraduate course selection. The policy does not define diversity solely in terms of racial and ethnic status and does not restrict the types of diversity contributions eligible for "substantial weight," but it does reaffirm the Law School's commitment to diversity with special reference to the inclusion of African-American, Hispanic, and Native-American students, who otherwise might not be represented in the student body in meaningful numbers. By enrolling a "critical mass" of underrepresented minority students, the policy seeks to ensure their ability to contribute to the Law School's character and to the legal profession.

When the Law School denied admission to petitioner Grutter, a white Michigan resident with a 3.8 GPA and 161 LSAT score, she filed this suit, alleging that respondents had discriminated against her on the basis of race in violation of the Fourteenth Amendment, Title VI of the Civil Rights Act of 1964, and 42 U.S.C. §1981; that she was rejected because the Law School uses race as a "predominant" factor, giving applicants belonging to certain minority groups a significantly

greater chance of admission than students with similar credentials from disfavored racial groups; and that respondents had no compelling interest to justify that use of race. The District Court found the Law School's use of race as an admissions factor unlawful. The Sixth Circuit reversed, holding that Justice Powell's opinion in *Bakke* was binding precedent establishing diversity as a compelling state interest, and that the Law School's use of race was narrowly tailored because race was merely a "potential 'plus' factor" and because the Law School's program was virtually identical to the Harvard admissions program described approvingly by Justice Powell and appended to his *Bakke* opinion.

Held: The Law School's narrowly tailored use of race in admissions decisions to further a compelling interest in obtaining the educational benefits that flow from a diverse student body is not prohibited by the Equal Protection Clause, Title VI, or §1981. Pp. 9–32.

(a) In the landmark *Bakke* case, this Court reviewed a medical school's racial set-aside program that reserved 16 out of 100 seats for members of certain minority groups. The decision produced six separate opinions, none of which commanded a majority. Four Justices would have upheld the program on the ground that the government can use race to remedy disadvantages cast on minorities by past racial prejudice. 438 U.S., at 325. Four other Justices would have struck the program down on statutory grounds. *Id.,* at 408. Justice Powell, announcing the Court's judgment, provided a fifth vote not only for invalidating the program, but also for reversing the state court's injunction against any use of race whatsoever. In a part of his opinion that was joined by no other Justice, Justice Powell expressed his view that attaining a diverse student body was the only interest asserted by the university that survived scrutiny. *Id.,* at 311. Grounding his analysis in the academic freedom that "long has been viewed as a special concern of the First Amendment," *id.,* at 312, 314, Justice Powell emphasized that the " 'nation's future depends upon leaders trained through wide exposure' to the ideas and mores of students as diverse as this Nation." *Id.,* at 313. However, he also emphasized that "[i]t is not an interest in simple ethnic diversity, in which a specified percentage of the student body is in effect guaranteed to be members of selected ethnic groups," that can justify using race. *Id.,* at 315. Rather, "[t]he diversity that furthers a compelling state interest encompasses a far broader array of qualifications and characteristics of which racial or ethnic origin is but a single though important element." *Ibid.* Since *Bakke,* Justice Powell's opinion has been the touchstone for constitutional analysis of race-conscious admissions policies. Public and private universities across the Nation have modeled their own admissions programs on Justice Powell's views. Courts, however, have struggled to discern whether Justice Powell's diversity rationale is binding precedent. The Court finds it unnecessary to decide this issue because the Court endorses Justice Powell's view that student body diversity is a compelling state interest in the context of university admissions. Pp. 9–13.

(b) All government racial classifications must be analyzed by a reviewing court under strict scrutiny. *Adarand Constructors, Inc. v. Peña,* 515 U.S. 200, 227. But not all such uses are invalidated by strict scrutiny. Race-based action necessary to further a compelling governmental interest does not violate the Equal Protection Clause so long as it is narrowly tailored to further that interest. *E.g., Shaw v. Hunt,* 517 U.S. 899, 908. Context matters when reviewing such action. See *Gomillion v. Lightfoot,* 364 U.S. 339, 343–344. Not every decision influenced by race is equally objectionable, and strict scrutiny is designed to provide a framework for carefully examining the importance and the sincerity of the government's reasons for using race in a particular context. 13–15.

(c) The Court endorses Justice Powell's view that student body diversity is a compelling state interest that can justify using race in university admissions. The Court defers to the Law School's educational judgment that diversity is essential to its educational mission. The Court's scrutiny of that interest is no less strict for taking into account complex educational judgments in an area that lies primarily within the university's expertise. See, *e.g., Bakke,* 438 U.S., at 319, n. 53 (opinion of Powell, J.). Attaining a diverse student body is at the heart of the Law School's proper institutional mission, and its "good faith" is "presumed" absent "a showing to the contrary." *Id.,* at 318–319. Enrolling a "critical mass" of minority students simply to assure some specified percentage of a particular group merely because of its race or ethnic origin would be patently unconstitutional. *E.g., id.,* at 307. But the Law School defines its critical mass concept by reference to the substantial, important, and laudable educational benefits that diversity is designed to produce, including cross-racial understanding and the breaking down of racial stereotypes. The Law School's claim is further bolstered by numerous expert studies and reports showing that such diversity promotes learning outcomes and better prepares students for an increasingly diverse workforce, for society, and for the legal profession. Major American businesses have made clear that the skills needed in today's increasingly global marketplace can only be developed through exposure to widely diverse people, cultures, ideas, and viewpoints. High-ranking retired officers and civilian military leaders assert that a highly qualified, racially diverse officer corps is essential to national security. Moreover, because universities, and in particular, law schools, represent the training ground for a large number of the Nation's leaders, *Sweatt v. Painter,* 339 U.S. 629, 634, the path to leadership must be visibly open to talented and qualified individuals of every race and ethnicity. Thus, the Law School has a compelling interest in attaining a diverse student body. 15–21.

(d) The Law School's admissions program bears the hallmarks of a narrowly tailored plan. To be narrowly tailored, a race-conscious admissions program cannot "insulat[e] each category of applicants with certain desired qualifications from competition with all other applicants." *Bakke, supra,* at 315 (opinion of Powell, J.). Instead, it may consider race or ethnicity only as a "'plus' in a particular applicant's file"; *i.e.,* it must be "flexible enough to consider all pertinent elements of diversity in light of the particular qualifications of each applicant, and to place them on the same footing for consideration, although not necessarily according them the same weight," *id.,* at 317. It follows that universities cannot establish quotas for members of certain racial or ethnic groups or put them on separate admissions tracks. See *id.,* at 315–316. The Law School's admissions program, like the Harvard plan approved by Justice Powell, satisfies these requirements. Moreover, the program is flexible enough to ensure that each applicant is evaluated as an individual and not in a way that makes race or ethnicity the defining feature of the application. See *Bakke, supra,* at 317 (opinion of Powell, J.). The Law School engages in a highly individualized, holistic review of each applicant's file, giving serious consideration to all the ways an applicant might contribute to a diverse educational environment. There is no policy, either *de jure* or *de facto,* of automatic acceptance or rejection based on any single "soft" variable. *Gratz v. Bollinger, ante,* p. __, distinguished. Also, the program adequately ensures that all factors that may contribute to diversity are meaningfully considered alongside race. Moreover, the Law School frequently accepts nonmi-

nority applicants with grades and test scores lower than underrepresented minority applicants (and other nonminority applicants) who are rejected. The Court rejects the argument that the Law School should have used other race-neutral means to obtain the educational benefits of student body diversity, *e.g.,* a lottery system or decreasing the emphasis on GPA and LSAT scores. Narrow tailoring does not require exhaustion of every conceivable race-neutral alternative or mandate that a university choose between maintaining a reputation for excellence or fulfilling a commitment to provide educational opportunities to members of all racial groups. See, *e.g., Wygant v. Jackson Bd. of Ed.,* 476 U.S. 267, 280, n. 6. The Court is satisfied that the Law School adequately considered the available alternatives. The Court is also satisfied that, in the context of individualized consideration of the possible diversity contributions of each applicant, the Law School's race-conscious admissions program does not unduly harm nonminority applicants. Finally, race-conscious admissions policies must be limited in time. The Court takes the Law School at its word that it would like nothing better than to find a race-neutral admissions formula and will terminate its use of racial preferences as soon as practicable. The Court expects that 25 years from now, the use of racial preferences will no longer be necessary to further the interest approved today. Pp. 21–31.

(e) Because the Law School's use of race in admissions decisions is not prohibited by the Equal Protection Clause, petitioner's statutory claims based on Title VI and §1981 also fail. See *Bakke, supra,* at 287 (opinion of Powell, J.); *General Building Contractors Assn., Inc. v. Pennsylvania,* 458 U.S. 375, 389-391. Pp. 31–32.

288 F. 3d 732, affirmed.

O'CONNOR, J., *delivered the opinion of the Court, in which* STEVENS, SOUTER, GINSBURG, *and* BREYER, JJ., *joined, and in which* SCALIA *and* THOMAS, JJ., *joined in part insofar as it is consistent with the views expressed in Part VII of the opinion of* THOMAS, J. GINSBURG, J., *filed a concurring opinion, in which* BREYER, J., *joined.* SCALIA, J., *filed an opinion concurring in part and dissenting in part, in which* THOMAS, J., *joined.* THOMAS, J., *filed an opinion concurring in part and dissenting in part, in which* SCALIA, J., *joined as to Parts I–VII.* REHNQUIST, C. J., *filed a dissenting opinion, in which* SCALIA, KENNEDY, *and* THOMAS, JJ., *joined.* KENNEDY, J., *filed a dissenting opinion.*

JUSTICE O'CONNOR *delivered the opinion of the Court.*

This case requires us to decide whether the use of race as a factor in student admissions by the University of Michigan Law School (Law School) is unlawful.

A. The Law School ranks among the Nation's top law schools. It receives more than 3,500 applications each year for a class of around 350 students. Seeking to "admit a group of students who individually and collectively are among the most capable," the Law School looks for individuals with "substantial promise for success in law school" and "a strong likelihood of succeeding in the practice of law and contributing in diverse ways to the well-being of others." App. 110. More broadly, the Law School seeks "a mix of students with varying backgrounds and experiences who will respect and learn from each other." *Ibid.* In 1992, the dean of the Law School charged a faculty committee with crafting a written admissions policy to implement these goals. In particular, the Law School sought to ensure that its efforts to achieve student body diversity complied with this Court's most recent ruling on the use of race in university admissions. See *Regents of Univ. of Cal. v. Bakke,* 438 U.S. 265 (1978). Upon the unanimous adoption of the committee's report by the Law School faculty, it became the Law School's official admissions policy.

The hallmark of that policy is its focus on academic ability coupled with a flexible assessment of applicants' talents, experiences, and potential "to contribute to the learning of those around them." App. 111. The policy requires admissions officials to evaluate each applicant based on all the information available in the file, including a personal statement, letters of recommendation, and an essay describing the ways in which the applicant will contribute to the life and diversity of the Law School. *Id.,* at 83–84, 114–121. In reviewing an applicant's file, admissions officials must consider the applicant's undergraduate grade point average (GPA) and Law School Admissions Test (LSAT) score because they are important (if imperfect) predictors of academic success in law school. *Id.,* at 112. The policy stresses that "no applicant should be admitted unless we expect that applicant to do well enough to graduate with no serious academic problems." *Id.,* at 111.

The policy makes clear, however, that even the highest possible score does not guarantee admission to the Law School. *Id.,* at 113. Nor does a low score automatically disqualify an applicant. *Ibid.* Rather, the policy requires admissions officials to look beyond grades and test scores to other criteria that are important to the Law School's educational objectives. *Id.,* at 114. So-called "'soft' variables" such as "the enthusiasm of recommenders, the quality of the undergraduate institution, the quality of the applicant's essay, and the areas and difficulty of undergraduate course selection" are all brought to bear in assessing an "applicant's likely contributions to the intellectual and social life of the institution." *Ibid.*

The policy aspires to "achieve that diversity which has the potential to enrich everyone's education and thus make a law school class stronger than the sum of its parts." *Id.,* at 118. The policy does not restrict the types of diversity contributions eligible for "substantial weight" in the admissions process, but instead recognizes "many possible bases for diversity admissions." *Id.,* at 118, 120. The policy does, however, reaffirm the Law School's longstanding commitment to "one particular type of diversity," that is, "racial and ethnic diversity with special reference to the inclusion of students from groups which have been historically discriminated against, like African-Americans, Hispanics and Native Americans, who without this commitment might not be represented in our student body in meaningful numbers." *Id.,* at 120. By enrolling a "'critical mass' of [underrepresented] minority students," the Law School seeks to "ensur[e] their ability to make unique contributions to the character of the Law School." *Id.,* at 120–121.

The policy does not define diversity "solely in terms of racial and ethnic status." *Id.,* at 121. Nor is the policy "insensitive to the competition among all students for admission to the [L]aw [S]chool." *Ibid.* Rather, the policy seeks to guide admissions officers in "producing classes both diverse and academically outstanding, classes made up of students who promise to continue the tradition of outstanding contribution by Michigan Graduates to the legal profession." *Ibid.*

B. Petitioner Barbara Grutter is a white Michigan resident who applied to the Law School in 1996 with a 3.8 grade point average and 161 LSAT score. The Law School initially placed petitioner on a waiting list, but subsequently rejected her application. In December 1997, petitioner filed suit in the United States District Court for the Eastern District of Michigan against the Law School, the Regents of the University of Michigan, Lee Bollinger (Dean of the Law School from 1987 to 1994, and President of the University of Michigan from 1996 to 2002), Jeffrey Lehman (Dean of the Law School), and Dennis Shields (Director of Admissions at the Law School from 1991 until 1998). Petitioner alleged that respondents discriminated against her on the basis of race in violation of the Fourteenth Amendment; Title VI of the Civil Rights Act of 1964, 78 Stat. 252, 42 U.S.C. §2000d; and Rev. Stat. §1977, as amended, 42 U.S.C. §1981.

Petitioner further alleged that her application was rejected because the Law School uses race as a "predominant" factor, giving applicants who belong to certain minority groups "a significantly greater chance of admission than students with similar credentials from disfavored racial groups." App. 33–34. Petitioner also alleged that respondents "had no compelling interest to justify their use of race in the admissions process." *Id.,* at 34. Petitioner requested compensatory and punitive damages, an order requiring the Law School to offer her admission, and an injunction prohibiting the Law School from continuing to discriminate on the basis of race. *Id.,* at 36. Petitioner clearly has standing to bring this lawsuit. *Northeastern Fla. Chapter, Associated Gen. Contractors of America v. Jacksonville,* 508 U.S. 656, 666 (1993).

The District Court granted petitioner's motion for class certification and for bifurcation of the trial into liability and damages phases. The class was defined as "'all persons who (A) applied for and were not granted admission to the University of Michigan Law School for the academic years since (and including) 1995 until the time that judgment is entered herein; and (B) were members of those racial or ethnic groups, including Caucasian, that Defendants treated less favorably in considering their applications for admission to the Law School.'" App. to Pet. for Cert. 191a–192a.

The District Court heard oral argument on the parties' cross-motions for summary judgment on December 22, 2000. Taking the motions under advisement, the District Court indicated that it would decide as a matter of law whether the Law School's asserted interest in obtaining the educational benefits that flow from a diverse student body was compelling. The District Court also indicated that it would conduct a bench trial on the extent to which race was a factor in the Law School's admissions decisions, and whether the Law School's consideration of race in admissions decisions constituted a race-based double standard.

During the 15-day bench trial, the parties introduced extensive evidence concerning the Law School's use of race in the admissions process. Dennis Shields, Director of Admissions when petitioner applied to the Law School, testified that he did not direct his staff to admit a particular percentage or number of minority students, but rather to consider an applicant's race along with all other factors. *Id.,* at 206a. Shields testified that at the height of the admissions season, he would frequently consult the so-called "daily reports" that kept track of the racial and ethnic composition of the class (along with other information such as residency status and gender). *Id.,* at 207a. This was done, Shields testified, to ensure that a critical mass of underrepresented minority students would be reached so as to realize the educational benefits of a diverse student body. *Ibid.* Shields stressed, however, that he did not seek to admit any particular number or percentage of underrepresented minority students. *Ibid.*

Erica Munzel, who succeeded Shields as Director of Admissions, testified that "'critical mass'" means "'meaningful numbers'" or "'meaningful representation,'" which she understood to mean a number that encourages underrepresented minority students to participate in the classroom and not feel isolated. *Id.,* at 208a–209a. Munzel stated there is no number, percentage, or range of numbers or percentages that constitute critical mass. *Id.,* at 209a. Munzel also asserted that she must consider the race of applicants because a critical mass of underrepresented minority students could not be enrolled if admissions decisions were based primarily on undergraduate GPAs and LSAT scores. *Ibid.*

The current Dean of the Law School, Jeffrey Lehman, also testified. Like the other Law School witnesses, Lehman did not quantify critical mass in terms of numbers or percentages. *Id.,* at 211a. He indicated that critical mass means numbers such that underrepresented minority students do not feel isolated or like spokespersons for their race. *Ibid.* When asked about the extent to which race is considered in admissions, Lehman testified that it varies from one applicant to another. *Ibid.* In some cases, according to Lehman's testimony, an applicant's race may play no role, while in others it may be a "'determinative'" factor. *Ibid.*

The District Court heard extensive testimony from Professor Richard Lempert, who chaired the faculty committee that drafted the 1992 policy. Lempert emphasized that the Law School seeks students with diverse interests and backgrounds to enhance classroom discussion and the educational experience both inside and outside the classroom. *Id.,* at 213a. When asked about the policy's "'commitment to racial and ethnic diversity with special reference to the inclusion of students from groups which have been historically discriminated against,'" Lempert explained that this language did not purport to remedy past discrimination, but rather to include students who may bring to the Law School a perspective different from that of members of groups which have not been the victims of such discrimination. *Ibid.* Lempert acknowledged that other groups, such as Asians and Jews, have experienced discrimination, but explained they were not mentioned in the policy because individuals who are members of those groups were already being admitted to the Law School in significant numbers. *Ibid.*

Kent Syverud was the final witness to testify about the Law School's use of race in admissions decisions. Syverud was a professor at the Law School when the 1992 admissions policy was adopted and is now Dean of Vanderbilt Law School. In addition to his testimony at trial, Syverud submitted several expert reports on the educational benefits of diversity. Syverud's testimony indicated that when a critical mass of underrepresented minority students is present, racial stereotypes lose their force because nonminority students learn there is no "'minority viewpoint'" but rather a variety of viewpoints among minority students. *Id.,* at 215a.

In an attempt to quantify the extent to which the Law School actually considers race in making admissions decisions, the parties introduced voluminous evidence at trial. Relying on data obtained from the Law School, petitioner's expert, Dr. Kinley Larntz, generated and analyzed "admissions grids" for the years in question (1995–2000). These grids show the number of applicants and the number of admittees for all combinations of GPAs and LSAT scores. Dr. Larntz made "'cell-by-cell'" comparisons between applicants of different races to determine whether a statistically significant relationship existed between race and admission rates. He concluded that membership in certain minority groups "'is an extremely strong factor in the decision for acceptance,'" and that applicants from these minority groups "'are given an extremely large allowance for admission'" as compared to applicants who are members of nonfavored groups. *Id.,* at 218a–220a. Dr. Larntz conceded, however, that race is not the predominant factor in the Law School's admissions calculus. 12 Tr. 11–13 (Feb. 10, 2001).

Dr. Stephen Raudenbush, the Law School's expert, focused on the predicted effect of eliminating race as a factor in the Law School's admission process. In Dr. Raudenbush's view, a race-blind admissions system would have a "'very dramatic,'" negative effect on underrepresented minority admissions. App. to Pet. for Cert. 223a. He testified that in 2000, 35 percent of underrepresented minority applicants were admitted. *Ibid.* Dr. Raudenbush predicted that if race were not considered, only 10 percent of those applicants would have been admitted. *Ibid.* Under this scenario, underrepresented minority students would have comprised 4 percent of the entering class in 2000 instead of the actual figure of 14.5 percent. *Ibid.*

In the end, the District Court concluded that the Law School's use of race as a factor in admissions decisions was unlawful. Applying strict scrutiny, the District Court determined that the Law School's asserted interest in assembling a diverse student body was not compelling because "the attainment of a racially diverse class . . . was not recognized as such by *Bakke* and is not a remedy for past discrimination." *Id.,* at 246a. The District Court went on to hold that even if diversity were compelling, the Law School had not narrowly tailored its use of race to further that interest. The District Court granted petitioner's request for declaratory relief and enjoined the Law School from using race as a factor in its admissions decisions. The Court of Appeals entered a stay of the injunction pending appeal.

Sitting en banc, the Court of Appeals reversed the District Court's judgment and vacated the injunction. The Court of Appeals first held that Justice Powell's opinion in *Bakke* was binding precedent establishing diversity as a compelling state interest. According to the Court of Appeals, Justice Powell's opinion with respect to diversity comprised the controlling rationale for the judgment of this Court under the analysis set forth in *Marks v. United States,* 430 U.S. 188 (1977). The Court of Appeals also held that the Law School's use of race was narrowly tailored because race was merely a "potential 'plus' factor" and because the Law School's program was "virtually identical" to the Harvard admissions program described approvingly by Justice Powell and appended to his *Bakke* opinion. 288 F. 3d 732, 746, 749 (CA6 2002).

Four dissenting judges would have held the Law School's use of race unconstitutional. Three of the dissenters, rejecting the majority's *Marks* analysis, examined the Law School's interest in student body diversity on the merits and concluded it was not compelling. The fourth dissenter, writing separately, found it unnecessary to decide whether diversity was a compelling interest because, like the other dissenters, he believed that the Law School's use of race was not narrowly tailored to further that interest.

We granted certiorari, 537 U.S. 1043 (2002), to resolve the disagreement among the Courts of Appeals on a question of national importance: Whether diversity is a compelling interest that can justify the narrowly tailored use of race in selecting applicants for admission to public universities. Compare *Hopwood v. Texas,* 78 F. 3d 932 (CA5 1996) (*Hopwood I*) (holding that diversity is not a compelling state interest), with *Smith v. University of Wash. Law School,* 233 F. 3d 1188 (CA9 2000) (holding that it is).

II

A. We last addressed the use of race in public higher education over 25 years ago. In the landmark *Bakke* case, we reviewed a racial set-aside program that reserved 16 out of 100 seats in a medical school class for members of certain minority groups. 438 U.S. 265 (1978). The decision produced six separate opinions, none of which commanded a majority of the Court. Four Justices would have upheld the program against all attack on the ground that the government can use race to "remedy disadvantages cast on minorities by past racial prejudice." *Id.,* at 325 (joint opinion of Brennan, White, Marshall, and Blackmun, JJ., concurring in judgment in part and dissenting in part). Four other Justices avoided the constitutional question altogether and struck down the program on statutory grounds. *Id.,* at 408 (opinion of *Stevens, J.,* joined by Burger, C. J., and Stewart and *Rehnquist,* JJ., concurring in judgment in part and dissenting in part). Justice Powell provided a fifth vote not only for invalidating the set-aside program, but also for reversing the state court's injunction against any use of race whatsoever. The only holding for the Court in *Bakke* was that a "State has a substantial interest that legitimately may be served by a properly devised admissions program involving the competitive consideration of race and ethnic origin." *Id.,* at 320. Thus, we reversed that part of the lower court's judgment that enjoined the university "from any consideration of the race of any applicant." *Ibid.*

Since this Court's splintered decision in *Bakke,* Justice Powell's opinion announcing the judgment of the Court has served as the touchstone for constitutional analysis of race-conscious admissions policies. Public and private universities across the Nation have modeled their own admissions programs on Justice Powell's views on permissible race-conscious policies. See, *e.g.,* Brief for Judith Areen et al. as *Amici Curiae* 12-13 (law school admissions programs employ "methods designed from and based on Justice Powell's opinion in *Bakke*"); Brief for Amherst College et al. as *Amici Curiae* 27 ("After *Bakke,* each of the *amici* (and undoubtedly other selective colleges and universities as well) reviewed their admissions procedures in light of Justice Powell's opinion . . . and set sail accordingly"). We therefore discuss Justice Powell's opinion in some detail.

Justice Powell began by stating that "[t]he guarantee of equal protection cannot mean one thing when applied to one individual and something else when applied to a person of another color. If both are not accorded the same protection, then it is not equal." *Bakke,* 438 U.S., at 289–290. In Justice Powell's view, when governmental decisions "touch upon an individual's race or ethnic background, he is entitled to a judicial determination that the burden he is asked to bear on that basis is precisely tailored to serve a compelling governmental interest." *Id.,* at 299. Under this exacting standard, only one of the interests asserted by the university survived Justice Powell's scrutiny.

First, Justice Powell rejected an interest in "'reducing the historic deficit of traditionally disfavored minorities in medical schools and in the medical profession'" as an unlawful interest in racial balancing. *Id.,* at 306–307. Second, Justice Powell rejected an interest in remedying societal discrimination because such measures would risk placing unnecessary burdens on innocent third parties "who bear no responsibility for whatever harm the beneficiaries of the special admissions program are thought to have suffered." *Id.,* at 310. Third, Justice Powell rejected an interest in "increasing the number of physicians who will practice in communities currently underserved," concluding that even if such an interest could be compelling in some circumstances the program under review was not "geared to promote that goal." *Id.,* at 306, 310.

Justice Powell approved the university's use of race to further only one interest: "the attainment of a diverse student body." *Id.,* at 311. With the important proviso that "constitutional limitations protecting individual rights may not be disregarded," Justice Powell grounded his analysis in the academic freedom that "long has been viewed as a special concern of the First Amendment." *Id.,* at 312, 314. Justice Powell emphasized that nothing less than the "'nation's future depends upon leaders trained through wide exposure' to the ideas and mores of students as diverse as this Nation of many peoples." *Id.,* at 313 (quoting *Keyishian v. Board of Regents of Univ. of State of N. Y.,* 385 U.S. 589, 603 (1967)). In seeking the "right to select those students who will contribute the most to the 'robust exchange of ideas,'" a university seeks "to achieve a goal that is of paramount importance in the fulfillment of its mission." 438 U.S., at 313. Both "tradition and experience lend support to the view that the contribution of diversity is substantial." *Ibid.*

Justice Powell was, however, careful to emphasize that in his view race "is only one element in a range of factors a university properly may consider in attaining the goal of a heterogeneous student body."

Id., at 314. For Justice Powell, "[i]t is not an interest in simple ethnic diversity, in which a specified percentage of the student body is in effect guaranteed to be members of selected ethnic groups," that can justify the use of race. *Id.,* at 315. Rather, "[t]he diversity that furthers a compelling state interest encompasses a far broader array of qualifications and characteristics of which racial or ethnic origin is but a single though important element." *Ibid.*

In the wake of our fractured decision in *Bakke,* courts have struggled to discern whether Justice Powell's diversity rationale, set forth in part of the opinion joined by no other Justice, is nonetheless binding precedent under *Marks.* In that case, we explained that "[w]hen a fragmented Court decides a case and no single rationale explaining the result enjoys the assent of five Justices, the holding of the Court may be viewed as that position taken by those Members who concurred in the judgments on the narrowest grounds." 430 U.S., at 193 (internal quotation marks and citation omitted). As the divergent opinions of the lower courts demonstrate, however, "[t]his test is more easily stated than applied to the various opinions supporting the result in [*Bakke*]." *Nichols v. United States,* 511 U.S. 738, 745–746 (1994). Compare, *e.g., Johnson v. Board of Regents of Univ. of Ga.,* 263 F. 3d 1234 (CA11 2001) (Justice Powell's diversity rationale was not the holding of the Court); *Hopwood v. Texas,* 236 F. 3d 256, 274–275 (CA5 2000) (*Hopwood II*) (same); *Hopwood I,* 78 F. 3d 932 (same), with *Smith v. University of Wash. Law School,* 233 F. 3d 1199 (Justice Powell's opinion, including the diversity rationale, is controlling under *Marks*).

We do not find it necessary to decide whether Justice Powell's opinion is binding under *Marks.* It does not seem "useful to pursue the *Marks* inquiry to the utmost logical possibility when it has so obviously baffled and divided the lower courts that have considered it." *Nichols v. United States, supra,* at 745–746. More important, for the reasons set out below, today we endorse Justice Powell's view that student body diversity is a compelling state interest that can justify the use of race in university admissions.

B. The Equal Protection Clause provides that no State shall "deny to any person within its jurisdiction the equal protection of the laws." U.S. Const., Amdt. 14, §2. Because the Fourteenth Amendment "protect[s] *persons,* not *groups,*" all "governmental action based on race—a *group* classification long recognized as in most circumstances irrelevant and therefore prohibited—should be subjected to detailed judicial inquiry to ensure that the *personal* right to equal protection of the laws has not been infringed." *Adarand Constructors, Inc. v. Peña,* 515 U.S. 200, 227 (1995) (emphasis in original; internal quotation marks and citation omitted). We are a "free people whose institutions are founded upon the doctrine of equality." *Loving v. Virginia,* 388 U.S. 1, 11 (1967) (internal quotation marks and citation omitted). It follows from that principle that "government may treat people differently because of their race only for the most compelling reasons." *Adarand Constructors, Inc. v. Peña,* 515 U.S., at 227.

We have held that all racial classifications imposed by government "must be analyzed by a reviewing court under strict scrutiny." *Ibid.* This means that such classifications are constitutional only if they are narrowly tailored to further compelling governmental interests. "Absent searching judicial inquiry into the justification for such race-based measures," we have no way to determine what "classifications are 'benign' or 'remedial' and what classifications are in fact motivated by illegitimate notions of racial inferiority or simple racial politics." *Richmond v. J. A. Croson Co.,* 488 U.S. 469, 493 (1989) (plurality opinion). We apply strict scrutiny to all racial classifications to "'smoke out' illegitimate uses of race by assuring that [government] is pursuing a goal important enough to warrant use of a highly suspect tool." *Ibid.*

Strict scrutiny is not "strict in theory, but fatal in fact." *Adarand Constructors, Inc. v. Peña, supra*, at 237 (internal quotation marks and citation omitted). Although all governmental uses of race are subject to strict scrutiny, not all are invalidated by it. As we have explained, "whenever the government treats any person unequally because of his or her race, that person has suffered an injury that falls squarely within the language and spirit of the Constitution's guarantee of equal protection." 515 U.S., at 229–230. But that observation "says nothing about the ultimate validity of any particular law; that determination is the job of the court applying strict scrutiny." *Id.*, at 230. When race-based action is necessary to further a compelling governmental interest, such action does not violate the constitutional guarantee of equal protection so long as the narrow-tailoring requirement is also satisfied.

Context matters when reviewing race-based governmental action under the Equal Protection Clause. See *Gomillion v. Lightfoot*, 364 U.S. 339, 343–344 (1960) (admonishing that, "in dealing with claims under broad provisions of the Constitution, which derive content by an interpretive process of inclusion and exclusion, it is imperative that generalizations, based on and qualified by the concrete situations that gave rise to them, must not be applied out of context in disregard of variant controlling facts"). In *Adarand Constructors, Inc. v. Peña*, we made clear that strict scrutiny must take " 'relevant differences' into account." 515 U.S., at 228. Indeed, as we explained, that is its "fundamental purpose." *Ibid.* Not every decision influenced by race is equally objectionable and strict scrutiny is designed to provide a framework for carefully examining the importance and the sincerity of the reasons advanced by the governmental decisionmaker for the use of race in that particular context.

III

A. With these principles in mind, we turn to the question whether the Law School's use of race is justified by a compelling state interest. Before this Court, as they have throughout this litigation, respondents assert only one justification for their use of race in the admissions process: obtaining "the educational benefits that flow from a diverse student body." Brief for Respondents Bollinger et al. i. In other words, the Law School asks us to recognize, in the context of higher education, a compelling state interest in student body diversity.

We first wish to dispel the notion that the Law School's argument has been foreclosed, either expressly or implicitly, by our affirmative-action cases decided since *Bakke*. It is true that some language in those opinions might be read to suggest that remedying past discrimination is the only permissible justification for race-based governmental action. See, *e.g., Richmond v. J. A. Croson Co., supra*, at 493 (plurality opinion) (stating that unless classifications based on race are "strictly reserved for remedial settings, they may in fact promote notions of racial inferiority and lead to a politics of racial hostility"). But we have never held that the only governmental use of race that can survive strict scrutiny is remedying past discrimination. Nor, since *Bakke*, have we directly addressed the use of race in the context of public higher education. Today, we hold that the Law School has a compelling interest in attaining a diverse student body.

The Law School's educational judgment that such diversity is essential to its educational mission is one to which we defer. The Law School's assessment that diversity will, in fact, yield educational benefits is substantiated by respondents and their *amici*. Our scrutiny of the interest asserted by the Law School is no less strict for taking into account complex educational judgments in an area that lies primarily within the expertise of the university. Our holding today is in keeping with our tradition of giving a degree of deference to a university's academic decisions, within constitutionally prescribed limits. See *Regents of Univ. of Mich. v. Ewing*, 474 U.S. 214, 225 (1985); *Board of Curators of Univ. of Mo. v. Horowitz*, 435 U.S. 78, 96, n. 6 (1978); *Bakke*, 438 U.S., at 319, n. 53 (opinion of Powell, J.).

We have long recognized that, given the important purpose of public education and the expansive freedoms of speech and thought associated with the university environment, universities occupy a special niche in our constitutional tradition. See, *e.g., Wieman v. Updegraff*, 344 U.S. 183, 195 (1952) (Frankfurter, J., concurring); *Sweezy v. New Hampshire*, 354 U.S. 234, 250 (1957); *Shelton v. Tucker*, 364 U.S. 479, 487 (1960); *Keyishian v. Board of Regents of Univ. of State of N. Y.*, 385 U.S., at 603. In announcing the principle of student body diversity as a compelling state interest, Justice Powell invoked our cases recognizing a constitutional dimension, grounded in the First Amendment, of educational autonomy: "The freedom of a university to make its own judgments as to education includes the selection of its student body." *Bakke, supra*, at 312. From this premise, Justice Powell reasoned that by claiming "the right to select those students who will contribute the most to the 'robust exchange of ideas,' " a university "seek[s] to achieve a goal that is of paramount importance in the fulfillment of its mission." 438 U.S., at 313 (quoting *Keyishian v. Board of Regents of Univ. of State of N. Y., supra*, at 603). Our conclusion that the Law School has a compelling interest in a diverse student body is informed by our view that attaining a diverse student body is at the heart of the Law School's proper institutional mission, and that "good faith" on the part of a university is "presumed" absent "a showing to the contrary." 438 U.S., at 318–319.

As part of its goal of "assembling a class that is both exceptionally academically qualified and broadly diverse," the Law School seeks to "enroll a 'critical mass' of minority students." Brief for Respondents Bollinger et al. 13. The Law School's interest is not simply "to assure within its student body some specified percentage of a particular group merely because of its race or ethnic origin." *Bakke*, 438 U.S., at 307 (opinion of Powell, J.). That would amount to outright racial balancing, which is patently unconstitutional. *Ibid.; Freeman v. Pitts*, 503 U.S. 467, 494 (1992) ("Racial balance is not to be achieved for its own sake"); *Richmond v. J. A. Croson Co.*, 488 U.S., at 507. Rather, the Law School's concept of critical mass is defined by reference to the educational benefits that diversity is designed to produce.

These benefits are substantial. As the District Court emphasized, the Law School's admissions policy promotes "cross-racial understanding," helps to break down racial stereotypes, and "enables [students] to better understand persons of different races." App. to Pet. for Cert. 246a. These benefits are "important and laudable," because "classroom discussion is livelier, more spirited, and simply more enlightening and interesting" when the students have "the greatest possible variety of backgrounds." *Id.*, at 246a, 244a.

The Law School's claim of a compelling interest is further bolstered by its *amici*, who point to the educational benefits that flow from student body diversity. In addition to the expert studies and reports entered into evidence at trial, numerous studies show that student body diversity promotes learning outcomes, and "better prepares students for an increasingly diverse workforce and society, and better prepares them as professionals." Brief for American Educational Research Association et al. as *Amici Curiae* 3; see, *e.g.,* W. Bowen & D. Bok, The Shape of the River (1998); Diversity Challenged: Evidence on the Impact of Affirmative Action (G. Orfield & M. Kurlaender eds. 2001); Compelling Interest: Examining the Evidence on Racial Dynamics in Colleges and Universities (M. Chang, D. Witt, J. Jones, & K. Hakuta eds. 2003).

These benefits are not theoretical but real, as major American businesses have made clear that the skills needed in today's increasingly global marketplace can only be developed through exposure to widely diverse people, cultures, ideas, and viewpoints. Brief for 3M et al. as *Amici Curiae* 5; Brief for General Motors Corp. as *Amicus Curiae* 3-4. What is more, high-ranking retired officers and civilian leaders of the United States military assert that, "[b]ased on [their] decades of experience," a "highly qualified, racially diverse officer corps . . . is essential to the military's ability to fulfill its principle mission to provide national security." Brief for Julius W. Becton, Jr. et al. as *Amici Curiae* 27. The primary sources for the Nation's officer corps are the service academies and the Reserve Officers Training Corps (ROTC), the latter comprising students already admitted to participating colleges and universities. *Id.,* at 5. At present, "the military cannot achieve an officer corps that is *both* highly qualified *and* racially diverse unless the service academies and the ROTC used limited race-conscious recruiting and admissions policies." *Ibid.* (emphasis in original). To fulfill its mission, the military "must be selective in admissions for training and education for the officer corps, *and* it must train and educate a highly qualified, racially diverse officer corps in a racially diverse setting." *Id.,* at 29 (emphasis in original). We agree that "[i]t requires only a small step from this analysis to conclude that our country's other most selective institutions must remain both diverse and selective." *Ibid.*

We have repeatedly acknowledged the overriding importance of preparing students for work and citizenship, describing education as pivotal to "sustaining our political and cultural heritage" with a fundamental role in maintaining the fabric of society. *Plyler v. Doe,* 457 U.S. 202, 221 (1982). This Court has long recognized that "education . . . is the very foundation of good citizenship." *Brown v. Board of Education,* 347 U.S. 483, 493 (1954). For this reason, the diffusion of knowledge and opportunity through public institutions of higher education must be accessible to all individuals regardless of race or ethnicity. The United States, as *amicus curiae,* affirms that "[e]nsuring that public institutions are open and available to all segments of American society, including people of all races and ethnicities, represents a paramount government objective." Brief for United States as *Amicus Curiae* 13. And, "[n]owhere is the importance of such openness more acute than in the context of higher education." *Ibid.* Effective participation by members of all racial and ethnic groups in the civic life of our Nation is essential if the dream of one Nation, indivisible, is to be realized.

Moreover, universities, and in particular, law schools, represent the training ground for a large number of our Nation's leaders. *Sweatt v. Painter,* 339 U.S. 629, 634 (1950) (describing law school as a "proving ground for legal learning and practice"). Individuals with law degrees occupy roughly half the state governorships, more than half the seats in the United States Senate, and more than a third of the seats in the United States House of Representatives. See Brief for Association of American Law Schools as *Amicus Curiae* 5–6. The pattern is even more striking when it comes to highly selective law schools. A handful of these schools accounts for 25 of the 100 United States Senators, 74 United States Courts of Appeals judges, and nearly 200 of the more than 600 United States District Court judges. *Id.,* at 6.

In order to cultivate a set of leaders with legitimacy in the eyes of the citizenry, it is necessary that the path to leadership be visibly open to talented and qualified individuals of every race and ethnicity. All members of our heterogeneous society must have confidence in the openness and integrity of the educational institutions that provide this training. As we have recognized, law schools "cannot be effective in isolation from the individuals and institutions with which

the law interacts." See *Sweatt v. Painter, supra,* at 634. Access to legal education (and thus the legal profession) must be inclusive of talented and qualified individuals of every race and ethnicity, so that all members of our heterogeneous society may participate in the educational institutions that provide the training and education necessary to succeed in America.

The Law School does not premise its need for critical mass on "any belief that minority students always (or even consistently) express some characteristic minority viewpoint on any issue." Brief for Respondent Bollinger et al. 30. To the contrary, diminishing the force of such stereotypes is both a crucial part of the Law School's mission, and one that it cannot accomplish with only token numbers of minority students. Just as growing up in a particular region or having particular professional experiences is likely to affect an individual's views, so too is one's own, unique experience of being a racial minority in a society, like our own, in which race unfortunately still matters. The Law School has determined, based on its experience and expertise, that a "critical mass" of underrepresented minorities is necessary to further its compelling interest in securing the educational benefits of a diverse student body.

B. Even in the limited circumstance when drawing racial distinctions is permissible to further a compelling state interest, government is still "constrained in how it may pursue that end: [T]he means chosen to accomplish the [government's] asserted purpose must be specifically and narrowly framed to accomplish that purpose." *Shaw v. Hunt,* 517 U.S. 899, 908 (1996) (internal quotation marks and citation omitted). The purpose of the narrow tailoring requirement is to ensure that "the means chosen 'fit' . . . th[e] compelling goal so closely that there is little or no possibility that the motive for the classification was illegitimate racial prejudice or stereotype." *Richmond v. J. A. Croson Co.,* 488 U.S., at 493 (plurality opinion).

Since *Bakke,* we have had no occasion to define the contours of the narrow-tailoring inquiry with respect to race-conscious university admissions programs. That inquiry must be calibrated to fit the distinct issues raised by the use of race to achieve student body diversity in public higher education. Contrary to *Justice Kennedy*'s assertions, we do not "abandon[ ] strict scrutiny," see *post,* at 8 (dissenting opinion). Rather, as we have already explained, *ante,* at 15, we adhere to *Adarand*'s teaching that the very purpose of strict scrutiny is to take such " relevant differences into account." 515 U.S., at 228 (internal quotation marks omitted).

To be narrowly tailored, a race-conscious admissions program cannot use a quota system—it cannot "insulat[e] each category of applicants with certain desired qualifications from competition with all other applicants." *Bakke, supra,* at 315 (opinion of Powell, J.). Instead, a university may consider race or ethnicity only as a " 'plus' in a particular applicant's file," without "insulat[ing] the individual from comparison with all other candidates for the available seats." *Id.,* at 317. In other words, an admissions program must be "flexible enough to consider all pertinent elements of diversity in light of the particular qualifications of each applicant, and to place them on the same footing for consideration, although not necessarily according them the same weight." *Ibid.*

We find that the Law School's admissions program bears the hallmarks of a narrowly tailored plan. As Justice Powell made clear in *Bakke,* truly individualized consideration demands that race be used in a flexible, nonmechanical way. It follows from this mandate that universities cannot establish quotas for members of certain racial groups or put members of those groups on separate admissions tracks. See *id.,* at 315-316. Nor can universities insulate applicants who belong to certain racial or ethnic groups from the competition for admission. *Ibid.* Universities can, however, consider race or ethnicity more flexibly as a "plus" factor in the context of individualized consideration of each and every applicant. *Ibid.*

We are satisfied that the Law School's admissions program, like the Harvard plan described by Justice Powell, does not operate as a quota. Properly understood, a "quota" is a program in which a certain fixed number or proportion of opportunities are "reserved exclusively for certain minority groups." *Richmond v. J. A. Croson Co., supra,* at 496 (plurality opinion). Quotas "'impose a fixed number or percentage which must be attained, or which cannot be exceeded,'" *Sheet Metal Workers v. EEOC,* 478 U.S. 421, 495 (1986) (O'Connor, J., concurring in part and dissenting in part), and "insulate the individual from comparison with all other candidates for the available seats." *Bakke, supra,* at 317 (opinion of Powell, J.). In contrast, "a permissible goal . . . require[s] only a good-faith effort . . . to come within a range demarcated by the goal itself," *Sheet Metal Workers v. EEOC, supra,* at 495, and permits consideration of race as a "plus" factor in any given case while still ensuring that each candidate "compete[s] with all other qualified applicants," *Johnson v. Transportation Agency, Santa Clara Cty.,* 480 U.S. 616, 638 (1987).

Justice Powell's distinction between the medical school's rigid 16-seat quota and Harvard's flexible use of race as a "plus" factor is instructive. Harvard certainly had minimum *goals* for minority enrollment, even if it had no specific number firmly in mind. See *Bakke, supra,* at 323 (opinion of Powell, J.) ("10 or 20 black students could not begin to bring to their classmates and to each other the variety of points of view, backgrounds and experiences of blacks in the United States"). What is more, Justice Powell flatly rejected the argument that Harvard's program was "the functional equivalent of a quota" merely because it had some "'plus'" for race, or gave greater "weight" to race than to some other factors, in order to achieve student body diversity. 438 U.S., at 317–318.

The Law School's goal of attaining a critical mass of underrepresented minority students does not transform its program into a quota. As the Harvard plan described by Justice Powell recognized, there is of course "some relationship between numbers and achieving the benefits to be derived from a diverse student body, and between numbers and providing a reasonable environment for those students admitted." *Id.,* at 323. "[S]ome attention to numbers," without more, does not transform a flexible admissions system into a rigid quota. *Ibid.* Nor, as *Justice Kennedy* posits, does the Law School's consultation of the "daily reports," which keep track of the racial and ethnic composition of the class (as well as of residency and gender), "suggest[ ] there was no further attempt at individual review save for race itself" during the final stages of the admissions process. See *post,* at 6 (dissenting opinion). To the contrary, the Law School's admissions officers testified without contradiction that they never gave race any more or less weight based on the information contained in these reports. Brief for Respondents Bollinger et al. 43, n. 70 (citing App. in Nos. 01-1447 and 01-1516 (CA6), p. 7336). Moreover, as *Justice Kennedy* concedes, see *post,* at 4, between 1993 and 2000, the number of African-American, Latino, and Native-American students in each class at the Law School varied from 13.5 to 20.1 percent, a range inconsistent with a quota.

The Chief Justice believes that the Law School's policy conceals an attempt to achieve racial balancing, and cites admissions data to contend that the Law School discriminates among different groups within the critical mass. *Post,* at 3–9 (dissenting opinion). But, as *The Chief Justice* concedes, the number of underrepresented minority students who ultimately enroll in the Law School differs substantially from their representation in the applicant pool and varies considerably for each group from year to year. See *post,* at 8 (dissenting opinion).

That a race-conscious admissions program does not operate as a quota does not, by itself, satisfy the requirement of individualized consideration. When using race as a "plus" factor in university admissions, a university's admissions program must remain flexible enough to ensure that each applicant is evaluated as an individual and not in a way that makes an applicant's race or ethnicity the defining feature of his or her application. The importance of this individualized consideration in the context of a race-conscious admissions program is paramount. See *Bakke, supra,* at 318, n. 52 (opinion of Powell, J.) (identifying the "denial . . . of th[e] right to individualized consideration" as the "principal evil" of the medical school's admissions program).

Here, the Law School engages in a highly individualized, holistic review of each applicant's file, giving serious consideration to all the ways an applicant might contribute to a diverse educational environment. The Law School affords this individualized consideration to applicants of all races. There is no policy, either *de jure* or *de facto,* of automatic acceptance or rejection based on any single "soft" variable. Unlike the program at issue in *Gratz v. Bollinger, ante,* the Law School awards no mechanical, predetermined diversity "bonuses" based on race or ethnicity. See *ante,* at 23 (distinguishing a race-conscious admissions program that automatically awards 20 points based on race from the Harvard plan, which considered race but "did not contemplate that any single characteristic automatically ensured a specific and identifiable contribution to a university's diversity"). Like the Harvard plan, the Law School's admissions policy "is flexible enough to consider all pertinent elements of diversity in light of the particular qualifications of each applicant, and to place them on the same footing for consideration, although not necessarily according them the same weight." *Bakke, supra,* at 317 (opinion of Powell, J.).

We also find that, like the Harvard plan Justice Powell referenced in *Bakke,* the Law School's race-conscious admissions program adequately ensures that all factors that may contribute to student body diversity are meaningfully considered alongside race in admissions decisions. With respect to the use of race itself, all underrepresented minority students admitted by the Law School have been deemed qualified. By virtue of our Nation's struggle with racial inequality, such students are both likely to have experiences of particular importance to the Law School's mission, and less likely to be admitted in meaningful numbers on criteria that ignore those experiences. See App. 120.

The Law School does not, however, limit in any way the broad range of qualities and experiences that may be considered valuable contributions to student body diversity. To the contrary, the 1992 policy makes clear "[t]here are many possible bases for diversity admissions," and provides examples of admittees who have lived or traveled widely abroad, are fluent in several languages, have overcome personal adversity and family hardship, have exceptional records of extensive community service, and have had successful careers in other fields. *Id.,* at 118–119. The Law School seriously considers each "applicant's promise of making a notable contribution to the class by way of a particular strength, attainment, or characteristic—*e.g.,* an unusual intellectual achievement, employment experience, nonacademic performance, or personal background." *Id.,* at 83–84. All applicants have the opportunity to highlight their own potential diversity contributions through the submission of a personal statement, letters of recommendation, and an essay describing the ways in which the applicant will contribute to the life and diversity of the Law School.

What is more, the Law School actually gives substantial weight to diversity factors besides race. The Law School frequently accepts nonminority applicants with grades and test scores lower than underrepresented minority applicants (and other nonminority applicants) who are rejected. See Brief for Respondents Bollinger et al. 10; App. 121–122. This shows that the Law School seriously weighs many other diversity factors besides race that can make a real and dispositive difference for nonminority applicants as well. By this flexible approach, the Law School sufficiently takes into account, in practice as well as in theory, a wide variety of characteristics besides race and ethnicity that contribute to a diverse student body. *Justice Kennedy* speculates that "race is likely outcome determinative for many members of minority groups" who do not fall within the upper range of LSAT scores and grades. *Post,* at 3 (dissenting opinion). But the same could be said of the Harvard plan discussed approvingly by Justice Powell in *Bakke,* and indeed of any plan that uses race as one of many factors. See 438 U.S., at 316 ("'When the Committee on Admissions reviews the large middle group of applicants who are "admissible" and deemed capable of doing good work in their courses, the race of an applicant may tip the balance in his favor'").

Petitioner and the United States argue that the Law School's plan is not narrowly tailored because race-neutral means exist to obtain the educational benefits of student body diversity that the Law School seeks. We disagree. Narrow tailoring does not require exhaustion of every conceivable race-neutral alternative. Nor does it require a university to choose between maintaining a reputation for excellence or fulfilling a commitment to provide educational opportunities to members of all racial groups. See *Wygant v. Jackson Bd. of Ed.,* 476 U.S. 267, 280, n. 6 (1986) (alternatives must serve the interest "'about as well'"); *Richmond v. J. A. Croson Co.,* 488 U.S., at 509–510 (plurality opinion) (city had a "whole array of race-neutral" alternatives because changing requirements "would have [had] little detrimental effect on the city's interests"). Narrow tailoring does, however, require serious, good faith consideration of workable race-neutral alternatives that will achieve the diversity the university seeks. See *id.,* at 507 (set-aside plan not narrowly tailored where "there does not appear to have been any consideration of the use of race-neutral means"); *Wygant v. Jackson Bd. of Ed., supra,* at 280, n. 6 (narrow tailoring "require[s] consideration" of "lawful alternative and less restrictive means").

We agree with the Court of Appeals that the Law School sufficiently considered workable race-neutral alternatives. The District Court took the Law School to task for failing to consider race-neutral alternatives such as "using a lottery system" or "decreasing the emphasis for all applicants on undergraduate GPA and LSAT scores." App. to Pet. for Cert. 251a. But these alternatives would require a dramatic sacrifice of diversity, the academic quality of all admitted students, or both.

The Law School's current admissions program considers race as one factor among many, in an effort to assemble a student body that is diverse in ways broader than race. Because a lottery would make that kind of nuanced judgment impossible, it would effectively sacrifice all other educational values, not to mention every other kind of diversity. So too with the suggestion that the Law School simply lower admissions standards for all students, a drastic remedy that would require the Law School to become a much different institution and sacrifice a vital component of its educational mission. The United States advocates "percentage plans," recently adopted by public undergraduate institutions in Texas, Florida, and California to guarantee admission to all students above a certain class-rank threshold in every high school in the State. Brief for United States as *Amicus Curiae* 14–18. The United States does not, however, explain how such plans could work for graduate and professional schools. Moreover, even assuming such plans are race-neutral, they may preclude the university from conducting the individualized assessments necessary to assemble a student body that is not just racially diverse, but diverse along all the qualities valued by the university. We are satisfied that the Law School adequately considered race-neutral alternatives currently capable of producing a critical mass without forcing the Law School to abandon the academic selectivity that is the cornerstone of its educational mission.

We acknowledge that "there are serious problems of justice connected with the idea of preference itself." *Bakke,* 438 U.S., at 298 (opinion of Powell, J.). Narrow tailoring, therefore, requires that a race-conscious admissions program not unduly harm members of any racial group. Even remedial race-based governmental action generally "remains subject to continuing oversight to assure that it will work the least harm possible to other innocent persons competing for the benefit." *Id.,* at 308. To be narrowly tailored, a race-conscious admissions program must not "unduly burden individuals who are not members of the favored racial and ethnic groups." *Metro Broadcasting, Inc. v. FCC,* 497 U.S. 547, 630 (1990) (O'Connor, J., dissenting).

We are satisfied that the Law School's admissions program does not. Because the Law School considers "all pertinent elements of diversity," it can (and does) select nonminority applicants who have greater potential to enhance student body diversity over underrepresented minority applicants. See *Bakke, supra,* at 317 (opinion of Powell, J.). As Justice Powell recognized in *Bakke,* so long as a race-conscious admissions program uses race as a "plus" factor in the context of individualized consideration, a rejected applicant

"will not have been foreclosed from all consideration for that seat simply because he was not the right color or had the wrong surname. . . . His qualifications would have been weighed fairly and competitively, and he would have no basis to complain of unequal treatment under the Fourteenth Amendment." 438 U.S., at 318.

We agree that, in the context of its individualized inquiry into the possible diversity contributions of all applicants, the Law School's race-conscious admissions program does not unduly harm nonminority applicants.

We are mindful, however, that "[a] core purpose of the Fourteenth Amendment was to do away with all governmentally imposed discrimination based on race." *Palmore v. Sidoti,* 466 U.S. 429, 432 (1984). Accordingly, race-conscious admissions policies must be limited in time. This requirement reflects that racial classifications, however compelling their goals, are potentially so dangerous that they may be employed no more broadly than the interest demands. Enshrining a permanent justification for racial preferences would offend this fundamental equal protection principle. We see no reason to exempt race-conscious admissions programs from the requirement that all governmental use of race must have a logical end point. The Law School, too, concedes that all "race-conscious programs must have reasonable durational limits." Brief for Respondents Bollinger et al. 32.

In the context of higher education, the durational requirement can be met by sunset provisions in race-conscious admissions policies and periodic reviews to determine whether racial preferences are still necessary to achieve student body diversity. Universities in California, Florida, and Washington State, where racial preferences in admissions are prohibited by state law, are currently engaged in experimenting with a wide variety of alternative approaches. Universities in other States can and should draw on the most promising aspects of these race-neutral alternatives as they develop. Cf. *United States v. Lopez,* 514 U.S. 549, 581 (1995) (Kennedy, J., concurring) ("[T]he States may perform their role as laboratories for experimentation to devise various solutions where the best solution is far from clear").

The requirement that all race-conscious admissions programs have a termination point "assure[s] all citizens that the deviation from the norm of equal treatment of all racial and ethnic groups is a temporary matter, a measure taken in the service of the goal of equality itself." *Richmond v. J. A. Croson Co.,* 488 U.S., at 510 (plurality opinion); see also Nathanson & Bartnik, The Constitutionality of Preferential Treatment for Minority Applicants to Professional Schools, 58 Chicago Bar Rec. 282, 293 (May–June 1977) ("It would be a sad day indeed, were America to become a quota-ridden society, with each identifiable minority assigned proportional representation in every desirable walk of life. But that is not the rationale for programs of preferential treatment; the acid test of their justification will be their efficacy in eliminating the need for any racial or ethnic preferences at all").

We take the Law School at its word that it would "like nothing better than to find a race-neutral admissions formula" and will terminate its race-conscious admissions program as soon as practicable. See Brief for Respondents Bollinger et al. 34; *Bakke, supra,* at 317–318 (opinion of Powell, J.) (presuming good faith of university officials in the absence of a showing to the contrary). It has been 25 years since Justice Powell first approved the use of race to further an interest in student body diversity in the context of public higher education. Since that time, the number of minority applicants with high grades and test scores has indeed increased. See Tr. of Oral Arg. 43. We expect that 25 years from now, the use of racial preferences will no longer be necessary to further the interest approved today.

IV

In summary, the Equal Protection Clause does not prohibit the Law School's narrowly tailored use of race in admissions decisions to further a compelling interest in obtaining the educational benefits that flow from a diverse student body. Consequently, petitioner's statutory claims based on Title VI and 42 U.S.C. §1981 also fail. See *Bakke, supra,* at 287 (opinion of Powell, J.) ("Title VI . . . proscribe[s] only those racial classifications that would violate the Equal Protection Clause or the Fifth Amendment"); *General Building Contractors Assn., Inc. v. Pennsylvania,* 458 U.S. 375, 389-391 (1982) (the prohibition against discrimination in §1981 is co-extensive with the Equal Protection Clause). The judgment of the Court of Appeals for the Sixth Circuit, accordingly, is affirmed.

It is so ordered.

JUSTICE GINSBURG, *with whom* JUSTICE BREYER *joins, concurring.*

The Court's observation that race-conscious programs "must have a logical end point," *ante,* at 29, accords with the international understanding of the office of affirmative action. The International Convention on the Elimination of All Forms of Racial Discrimination, ratified by the United States in 1994, see State Dept., Treaties in Force 422–423 (June 1996), endorses "special and concrete measures to ensure the adequate development and protection of certain racial groups or individuals belonging to them, for the purpose of guaranteeing them the full and equal enjoyment of human rights and fundamental freedoms." Annex to G.A. Res. 2106, 20 U.N. GAOR Res. Supp. (No. 14) 47, U.N. Doc. A/6014, Art. 2(2) (1965). But such measures, the Convention instructs, "shall in no case entail as a consequence the maintenance of unequal or separate rights for different racial groups after the objectives for which they were taken have been achieved." *Ibid;* see also Art. 1(4) (similarly providing for temporally limited affirmative action); Convention on the Elimination of All Forms of Discrimination against Women, Annex to G.A. Res. 34/180, 34 U.N. GAOR Res. Supp. (No. 46) 194, U.N. Doc. A/34/46, Art. 4(1) (1979) (authorizing "temporary special measures aimed at accelerating *de facto* equality" that "shall be discontinued when the

objectives of equality of opportunity and treatment have been achieved").

The Court further observes that "[i]t has been 25 years since Justice Powell [in *Regents of Univ. of Cal. v. Bakke,* 438 U.S. 265 (1978)] first approved the use of race to further an interest in student body diversity in the context of public higher education." *Ante,* at 31. For at least part of that time, however, the law could not fairly be described as "settled," and in some regions of the Nation, overtly race-conscious admissions policies have been proscribed. See *Hopwood v. Texas,* 78 F. 3d 932 (CA5 1996); cf. *Wessmann v. Gittens,* 160 F. 3d 790 (CA1 1998); *Tuttle v. Arlington Cty. School Bd.,* 195 F. 3d 698 (CA4 1999); *Johnson v. Board of Regents of Univ. of Ga.,* 263 F. 3d 1234 (CA11 2001). Moreover, it was only 25 years before *Bakke* that this Court declared public school segregation unconstitutional, a declaration that, after prolonged resistance, yielded an end to a law-enforced racial caste system, itself the legacy of centuries of slavery. See *Brown v. Board of Education,* 347 U.S. 483 (1954); cf. *Cooper v. Aaron,* 358 U.S. 1 (1958).

It is well documented that conscious and unconscious race bias, even rank discrimination based on race, remain alive in our land, impeding realization of our highest values and ideals. See, *e.g., Gratz v. Bollinger, ante,* at 1–4 (Ginsburg, J., dissenting); *Adarand Constructors, Inc. v. Peña,* 515 U.S. 200, 272–274 (1995) (Ginsburg, J., dissenting); Krieger, Civil Rights Perestroika: Intergroup Relations after Affirmative Action, 86 Calif. L. Rev. 1251, 1276–1291, 1303 (1998). As to public education, data for the years 2000–2001 show that 71.6% of African-American children and 76.3% of Hispanic children attended a school in which minorities made up a majority of the student body. See E. Frankenberg, C. Lee, & G. Orfield, A Multiracial Society with Segregated Schools: Are We Losing the Dream? p. 4 (Jan. 2003), http://www.civilrightsproject.harvard.edu/research/reseg03/AreWeLosingtheDream.pdf (as visited June 16, 2003, and available in Clerk of Court's case file). And schools in predominantly minority communities lag far behind others measured by the educational resources available to them. See *id.,* at 11; Brief for National Urban League et al. as *Amici Curiae* 11–12 (citing General Accounting Office, Per-Pupil Spending Differences Between Selected Inner City and Suburban Schools Varied by Metropolitan Area, 17 (2002)).

However strong the public's desire for improved education systems may be, see P. Hart & R. Teeter, A National Priority: Americans Speak on Teacher Quality 2, 11 (2002) (public opinion research conducted for Educational Testing Service); The No Child Left Behind Act of 2001, Pub. L. 107-110, 115 Stat. 1425 , 20 U.S.C. A. §7231 (2003 Supp. Pamphlet), it remains the current reality that many minority students encounter markedly inadequate and unequal educational opportunities. Despite these inequalities, some minority students are able to meet the high threshold requirements set for admission to the country's finest undergraduate and graduate educational institutions. As lower school education in minority communities improves, an increase in the number of such students may be anticipated. From today's vantage point, one may hope, but not firmly forecast, that over the next generation's span, progress toward nondiscrimination and genuinely equal opportunity will make it safe to sunset affirmative action.[1]

CHIEF JUSTICE REHNQUIST, *with whom* JUSTICE SCALIA, JUSTICE KENNEDY, *and* JUSTICE THOMAS *join, dissenting.*

I agree with the Court that, "in the limited circumstance when drawing racial distinctions is permissible," the government must ensure that its means are narrowly tailored to achieve a compelling state interest. *Ante,* at 21; see also *Fullilove v. Klutznick,* 448 U.S. 448, 498 (1980) (Powell, J., concurring) ("[E]ven if the government proffers a compelling interest to support reliance upon a suspect classification, the means selected must be narrowly drawn to fulfill the governmental purpose"). I do not believe, however, that the University of Michigan Law School's (Law School) means are narrowly tailored to the interest it asserts. The Law School claims it must take the steps it does to achieve a " 'critical mass' " of underrepresented minority students. Brief for Respondents Bollinger et al. 13. But its actual program bears no relation to this asserted goal. Stripped of its "critical mass" veil, the Law School's program is revealed as a naked effort to achieve racial balancing.

As we have explained many times, " '[a]ny preference based on racial or ethnic criteria must necessarily receive a most searching examination.' " *Adarand Constructors, Inc. v. Peña,* 515 U.S. 200, 223 (1995) (quoting *Wygant v. Jackson Bd. of Ed.,* 476 U.S. 267, 273 (1986) (plurality opinion of Powell, J.)). Our cases establish that, in order to withstand this demanding inquiry, respondents must demonstrate that their methods of using race " 'fit' " a compelling state interest "with greater precision than any alternative means." *Id.,* at 280, n. 6; *Regents of Univ. of Cal. v. Bakke,* 438 U.S. 265, 299 (1978) (opinion of Powell, J.) ("When [political judgments] touch upon an individual's race or ethnic background, he is entitled to a judicial determination that the burden he is asked to bear on that basis is precisely tailored to serve a compelling governmental interest").

Before the Court's decision today, we consistently applied the same strict scrutiny analysis regardless of the government's purported reason for using race and regardless of the setting in which race was being used. We rejected calls to use more lenient review in the face of claims that race was being used in "good faith" because " '[m]ore than good motives should be required when government seeks to allocate its resources by way of an explicit racial classification system.' " *Adarand, supra,* at 226; *Fullilove, supra,* at 537 (Stevens, J., dissenting) ("Racial classifications are simply too pernicious to permit any but the most exact connection between justification and classification"). We likewise rejected calls to apply more lenient review based on the particular setting in which race is being used. Indeed, even in the specific context of higher education, we emphasized that "constitutional limitations protecting individual rights may not be disregarded." *Bakke, supra,* at 314.

Although the Court recites the language of our strict scrutiny analysis, its application of that review is unprecedented in its deference.

Respondents' asserted justification for the Law School's use of race in the admissions process is "obtaining 'the educational benefits that flow from a diverse student body.' " *Ante,* at 15 (quoting Brief for Respondents Bollinger et al. i). They contend that a "critical mass" of underrepresented minorities is necessary to further that interest. *Ante,* at 17. Respondents and school administrators explain generally that "critical mass" means a sufficient number of underrepresented minority students to achieve several objectives: To ensure that these minority students do not feel isolated or like spokespersons for their race; to provide adequate opportunities for the type of interaction upon which the educational benefits of diversity depend; and to challenge all students to think critically and reexamine stereotypes. See App. to Pet. for Cert. 211a; Brief for Respondents Bollinger et al. 26. These objectives indicate that "critical mass" relates to the size of the student body. *Id.,* at 5 (claiming that the Law School has enrolled "critical mass," or "enough minority students to provide meaningful integration of its classrooms and residence halls"). Respondents further claim that the Law School is achieving "critical mass." *Id.,* at 4 (noting that the Law School's goals have been "greatly furthered by the presence of . . . a 'critical mass' of " minority students in the student body).

In practice, the Law School's program bears little or no relation to its asserted goal of achieving "critical mass." Respondents explain that the Law School seeks to accumulate a "critical mass" of *each* underrepresented minority group. See, *e.g., id.,* at 49, n. 79 ("The Law School's . . . current policy . . . provide[s] a special commitment to enrolling a 'critical mass' of 'Hispanics' "). But the record demonstrates that the Law School's admissions practices with respect to these groups differ dramatically and cannot be defended under any consistent use of the term "critical mass."

From 1995 through 2000, the Law School admitted between 1,130 and 1,310 students. Of those, between 13 and 19 were Native American, between 91 and 108 were African-Americans, and between 47 and 56 were Hispanic. If the Law School is admitting between 91 and 108 African-Americans in order to achieve "critical mass," thereby preventing African-American students from feeling "isolated or like spokespersons for their race," one would think that a number of the same order of magnitude would be necessary to accomplish the same purpose for Hispanics and Native Americans. Similarly, even if all of the Native American applicants admitted in a given year matriculate, which the record demonstrates is not at all the case,[2] how can this possibly constitute a "critical mass" of Native Americans in a class of over 350 students? In order for this pattern of admission to be consistent with the Law School's explanation of "critical mass," one would have to believe that the objectives of "critical mass" offered by respondents are achieved with only half the number of Hispanics and one-sixth the number of Native Americans as compared to African-Americans. But respondents offer no race-specific reasons for such disparities. Instead, they simply emphasize the importance of achieving "critical mass," without any explanation of why that concept is applied differently among the three underrepresented minority groups.

These different numbers, moreover, come only as a result of substantially different treatment among the three underrepresented minority groups, as is apparent in an example offered by the Law School and highlighted by the Court: The school asserts that it "frequently accepts nonminority applicants with grades and test scores lower than underrepresented minority applicants (and other nonminority applicants) who are rejected." *Ante,* at 26 (citing Brief for Respondents Bollinger et al. 10). Specifically, the Law School states that "[s]ixty-nine minority applicants were rejected between 1995 and 2000 with at least a 3.5 [Grade Point Average (GPA)] and a [score of] 159 or higher on the [Law School Admissions Test (LSAT)]" while a number of Caucasian and Asian-American applicants with similar or lower scores were admitted. Brief for Respondents Bollinger et al. 10.

Review of the record reveals only 67 such individuals. Of these 67 individuals, 56 were Hispanic, while only 6 were African-American, and only 5 were Native American. This discrepancy reflects a consistent practice. For example, in 2000, 12 Hispanics who scored between a 159-160 on the LSAT and earned a GPA of 3.00 or higher applied for admission and only 2 were admitted. App. 200–201. Meanwhile, 12 African-Americans in the same range of qualifications applied for admission and all 12 were admitted. *Id.,* at 198. Likewise, that same year, 16 Hispanics who scored between a 151-153 on the LSAT and earned a 3.00 or higher applied for admission and only 1 of those applicants was admitted. *Id.,* at 200–201. Twenty-three similarly qualified African-Americans applied for admission and 14 were admitted. *Id.,* at 198.

These statistics have a significant bearing on petitioner's case. Respondents have *never* offered any race-specific arguments explaining why significantly more individuals from one underrepresented minority group are needed in order to achieve "critical mass" or further student body diversity. They certainly have not explained why Hispanics, who they have said are among "the groups most isolated by racial barriers in our country," should have their admission capped out in this manner. Brief for Respondents Bollinger et al. 50. True, petitioner is neither Hispanic nor Native American. But the Law School's disparate admissions practices with respect to these minority groups demonstrate that its alleged goal of "critical mass" is simply a sham. Petitioner may use these statistics to expose this sham, which is the basis for the Law School's admission of less qualified underrepresented minorities in preference to her. Surely strict scrutiny cannot permit these sort of disparities without at least some explanation.

Only when the "critical mass" label is discarded does a likely explanation for these numbers emerge. The Court states that the Law School's goal of attaining a "critical mass" of underrepresented minority students is not an interest in merely "'assur[ing] within its student body some specified percentage of a particular group merely because of its race or ethnic origin.'" *Ante,* at 17 (quoting *Bakke,* 438 U.S., at 307 (opinion of Powell, J.)). The Court recognizes that such an interest "would amount to outright racial balancing, which is patently unconstitutional." *Ante,* at 17. The Court concludes, however, that the Law School's use of race in admissions, consistent with Justice Powell's opinion in *Bakke,* only pays "'[s]ome attention to numbers.'" *Ante,* at 23 (quoting *Bakke, supra,* at 323).

But the correlation between the percentage of the Law School's pool of applicants who are members of the three minority groups and the percentage of the admitted applicants who are members of these same groups is far too precise to be dismissed as merely the result of

the school paying "some attention to [the] numbers." As the tables below show, from 1995 through 2000 the percentage of admitted applicants who were members of these minority groups closely tracked the percentage of individuals in the school's applicant pool who were from the same groups.

For example, in 1995, when 9.7% of the applicant pool was African-American, 9.4% of the admitted class was African-American. By 2000, only 7.5% of the applicant pool was African-American, and 7.3% of the admitted class was African-American. This correlation is striking. Respondents themselves emphasize that the number of underrepresented minority students admitted to the Law School would be significantly smaller if the race of each applicant were not considered. See App. to Pet. for Cert. 223a; Brief for Respondents Bollinger et al. 6 (quoting App. to Pet. for Cert. of Bollinger et al. 299a). But, as the examples above illustrate, the measure of the decrease would differ dramatically among the groups. The tight correlation between the percentage of applicants and admittees of a given race, therefore, must result from careful race based planning by the Law School. It suggests a formula for admission based on the aspirational assumption that all applicants are equally qualified academically, and therefore that the proportion of each group admitted should be the same as the proportion of that group in the applicant pool. See Brief for Respondents Bollinger et al. 43, n. 70 (discussing admissions officers' use of "periodic reports" to track "the racial composition of the developing class").

Not only do respondents fail to explain this phenomenon, they attempt to obscure it. See *id.,* at 32, n. 50 ("The Law School's minority enrollment percentages . . . diverged from the percentages in the

Table 1

Year	Number of law school applicants	Number of African-American applicants	% of applicants who were African-American	Number of applicants admitted by the law school	Number of African-American applicants admitted	% of admitted applicants who were African-American
1995	4147	404	*9.7%*	1130	106	*9.4%*
1996	3677	342	*9.3%*	1170	108	*9.2%*
1997	3429	320	*9.3%*	1218	101	*8.3%*
1998	3537	304	*8.6%*	1310	103	*7.9%*
1999	3400	247	*7.3%*	1280	91	*7.1%*
2000	3432	259	*7.5%*	1249	91	*7.3%*

Table 2

Year	Number of law school applicants	Number of Hispanic applicants	% of applicants who were Hispanic	Number of applicants admitted by the law school	Number of Hispanic applicants admitted	% of admitted applicants who were Hispanic
1995	4147	213	*5.1%*	1130	56	*5.0%*
1996	3677	186	*5.1%*	1170	54	*4.6%*
1997	3429	163	*4.8%*	1218	47	*3.9%*
1998	3537	150	*4.2%*	1310	55	*4.2%*
1999	3400	152	*4.5%*	1280	48	*3.8%*
2000	3432	168	*4.9%*	1249	53	*4.2%*

Table 3

Year	Number of law school applicants	Number of Native American applicants	% of applicants who were Native American	Number of applicants admitted by the law school	Number of Native American applicants admitted	% of admitted applicants who were Native American
1995	4147	45	*1.1%*	1130	14	*1.2%*
1996	3677	31	*0.8%*	1170	13	*1.1%*
1997	3429	37	*1.1%*	1218	19	*1.6%*
1998	3537	40	*1.1%*	1310	18	*1.4%*
1999	3400	25	*0.7%*	1280	13	*1.0%*
2000	3432	35	*1.0%*	1249	14	*1.1%*

applicant pool by as much as 17.7% from 1995–2000"). But the divergence between the percentages of underrepresented minorities in the applicant pool and in the *enrolled* classes is not the only relevant comparison. In fact, it may not be the most relevant comparison. The Law School cannot precisely control which of its admitted applicants decide to attend the university. But it can and, as the numbers demonstrate, clearly does employ racial preferences in extending offers of admission. Indeed, the ostensibly flexible nature of the Law School's admissions program that the Court finds appealing, see *ante*, at 24–26, appears to be, in practice, a carefully managed program designed to ensure proportionate representation of applicants from selected minority groups.

I do not believe that the Constitution gives the Law School such free rein in the use of race. The Law School has offered no explanation for its actual admissions practices and, unexplained, we are bound to conclude that the Law School has managed its admissions program, not to achieve a "critical mass," but to extend offers of admission to members of selected minority groups in proportion to their statistical representation in the applicant pool. But this is precisely the type of racial balancing that the Court itself calls "patently unconstitutional." *Ante*, at 17.

Finally, I believe that the Law School's program fails strict scrutiny because it is devoid of any reasonably precise time limit on the Law School's use of race in admissions. We have emphasized that we will consider "the planned duration of the remedy" in determining whether a race-conscious program is constitutional. *Fullilove*, 448 U.S., at 510 (Powell, J. concurring); see also *United States v. Paradise*, 480 U.S. 149, 171 (1987) ("In determining whether race-conscious remedies are appropriate, we look to several factors, including the . . . duration of the relief"). Our previous cases have required some limit on the duration of programs such as this because discrimination on the basis of race is invidious.

The Court suggests a possible 25-year limitation on the Law School's current program. See *ante*, at 30. Respondents, on the other hand, remain more ambiguous, explaining that "the Law School of course recognizes that race-conscious programs must have reasonable durational limits, and the Sixth Circuit properly found such a limit in the Law School's resolve to cease considering race when genuine race-neutral alternatives become available." Brief for Respondents Bollinger et al. 32. These discussions of a time limit are the vaguest of assurances. In truth, they permit the Law School's use of racial preferences on a seemingly permanent basis. Thus, an important component of strict scrutiny—that a program be limited in time—is casually subverted.

The Court, in an unprecedented display of deference under our strict scrutiny analysis, upholds the Law School's program despite its obvious flaws. We have said that when it comes to the use of race, the connection between the ends and the means used to attain them must be precise. But here the flaw is deeper than that; it is not merely a question of "fit" between ends and means. Here the means actually used are forbidden by the Equal Protection Clause of the Constitution.

JUSTICE KENNEDY, *dissenting.*

The separate opinion by Justice Powell in *Regents of Univ. of Cal. v. Bakke* is based on the principle that a university admissions program may take account of race as one, nonpredominant factor in a system designed to consider each applicant as an individual, provided the program can meet the test of strict scrutiny by the judiciary. 438 U.S. 265, 289–291, 315–318 (1978). This is a unitary formulation. If strict scrutiny is abandoned or manipulated to distort its real and accepted meaning, the Court lacks authority to approve the use of race even in this modest, limited way. The opinion by Justice Powell, in my view, states the correct rule for resolving this case. The Court, however, does not apply strict scrutiny. By trying to say otherwise, it undermines both the test and its own controlling precedents.

Justice Powell's approval of the use of race in university admissions reflected a tradition, grounded in the First Amendment, of acknowledging a university's conception of its educational mission. *Bakke, supra*, at 312–314; *ante*, at 16–17. Our precedents provide a basis for the Court's acceptance of a university's considered judgment that racial diversity among students can further its educational task, when supported by empirical evidence. *Ante*, at 17–19.

It is unfortunate, however, that the Court takes the first part of Justice Powell's rule but abandons the second. Having approved the use of race as a factor in the admissions process, the majority proceeds to nullify the essential safeguard Justice Powell insisted upon as the precondition of the approval. The safeguard was rigorous judicial review, with strict scrutiny as the controlling standard. *Bakke, supra*, at 291 ("Racial and ethnic distinctions of any sort are inherently suspect and thus call for the most exacting judicial examination"). This Court has reaffirmed, subsequent to *Bakke*, the absolute necessity of strict scrutiny when the state uses race as an operative category. *Adarand Constructors, Inc. v. Peña*, 515 U.S. 200, 224 (1995) ("[A]ny person, of whatever race, has the right to demand that any governmental actor subject to the Constitution justify any racial classification subjecting that person to unequal treatment under the strictest judicial scrutiny"); *Richmond v. J.A. Croson Co.*, 488 U.S. 469, 493–494 (1989); see *id.*, at 519 (*Kennedy, J.*, concurring in part and concurring in judgment) ("[A]ny racial preference must face the most rigorous scrutiny by the courts"). The Court confuses deference to a university's definition of its educational objective with deference to the implementation of this goal. In the context of university admissions the objective of racial diversity can be accepted based on empirical data known to us, but deference is not to be given with respect to the methods by which it is pursued. Preferment by race, when resorted to by the State, can be the most divisive of all policies, containing within it the potential to destroy confidence in the Constitution and in the idea of equality. The majority today refuses to be faithful to the settled principle of strict review designed to reflect these concerns.

The Court, in a review that is nothing short of perfunctory, accepts the University of Michigan Law School's assurances that its admissions process meets with constitutional requirements. The majority fails to confront the reality of how the Law School's admissions policy is implemented. The dissenting opinion by *The Chief Justice*, which I join in full, demonstrates beyond question why the concept of critical mass is a delusion used by the Law School to mask its attempt to make race an automatic factor in most instances and to achieve numerical goals indistinguishable from quotas. An effort to achieve racial balance among the minorities the school seeks to attract is, by the Court's own admission, "patently unconstitutional." *Ante*, at 17; see also *Bakke*, 438 U.S., at 307 (opinion of Powell, J.). It remains to point out how critical mass becomes inconsistent with individual consideration in some more specific aspects of the admissions process.

About 80 to 85 percent of the places in the entering class are given to applicants in the upper range of Law School Admissions Test scores and grades. An applicant with these credentials likely will be admitted without consideration of race or ethnicity. With respect to the remaining 15 to 20 percent of the seats, race is likely outcome determinative for many members of minority groups. That is where the competition becomes tight and where any given applicant's chance of admission is far smaller if he or she lacks minority status. At this point the numerical concept of critical mass has the real potential to compromise individual review.

The Law School has not demonstrated how individual consideration is, or can be, preserved at this stage of the application process given the instruction to attain what it calls critical mass. In fact the evidence shows otherwise. There was little deviation among admitted minority students during the years from 1995 to 1998. The percentage of enrolled minorities fluctuated only by 0.3%, from 13.5% to 13.8%. The number of minority students to whom offers were extended varied by just a slightly greater magnitude of 2.2%, from the high of 15.6% in 1995 to the low of 13.4% in 1998.

The District Court relied on this uncontested fact to draw an inference that the Law School's pursuit of critical mass mutated into the equivalent of a quota. 137 F. Supp. 2d 821, 851 (ED Mich. 2001). Admittedly, there were greater fluctuations among enrolled minorities in the preceding years, 1987–1994, by as much as 5 or 6%. The percentage of minority offers, however, at no point fell below 12%, historically defined by the Law School as the bottom of its critical mass range. The greater variance during the earlier years, in any event, does not dispel suspicion that the school engaged in racial balancing. The data would be consistent with an inference that the Law School modified its target only twice, in 1991 (from 13% to 19%), and then again in 1995 (back from 20% to 13%). The intervening year, 1993, when the percentage dropped to 14.5%, could be an aberration, caused by the school's miscalculation as to how many applicants with offers would accept or by its redefinition, made in April 1992, of which minority groups were entitled to race-based preference. See Brief for Respondents Bollinger et al. 49, n. 79.

Year	Percentage of enrolled minority students
1987	12.3%
1988	13.6%
1989	14.4%
1990	13.4%
1991	19.1%
1992	19.8%
1993	14.5%
1994	20.1%
1995	13.5%
1996	13.8%
1997	13.6%
1998	13.8%

The narrow fluctuation band raises an inference that the Law School subverted individual determination, and strict scrutiny requires the Law School to overcome the inference. Whether the objective of critical mass "is described as a quota or a goal, it is a line drawn on the basis of race and ethnic status," and so risks compromising individual assessment. *Bakke*, 438 U.S., at 289 (opinion of Powell, J.). In this respect the Law School program compares unfavorably with the experience of Little Ivy League colleges. *Amicus* Amherst College, for example, informs us that the offers it extended to students of African-American background during the period from 1993 to 2002 ranged between 81 and 125 out of 950 offers total, resulting in a fluctuation from 24 to 49 matriculated students in a class of about 425. See Brief for Amherst College et al. as *Amici Curiae* 10–11. The Law School insisted upon a much smaller fluctuation, both in the offers extended and in the students who eventually enrolled, despite having a comparable class size.

The Law School has the burden of proving, in conformance with the standard of strict scrutiny, that it did not utilize race in an unconstitutional way. *Adarand Constructors,* 515 U.S., at 224. At the very least, the constancy of admitted minority students and the close correlation between the racial breakdown of admitted minorities and the composition of the applicant pool, discussed by *The Chief Justice, ante,* at 3–9, require the Law School either to produce a convincing explanation or to show it has taken adequate steps to ensure individual assessment. The Law School does neither.

The obvious tension between the pursuit of critical mass and the requirement of individual review increased by the end of the admissions season. Most of the decisions where race may decide the outcome are made during this period. See *supra,* at 3. The admissions officers consulted the daily reports which indicated the composition of the incoming class along racial lines. As Dennis Shields, Director of Admissions from 1991 to 1996, stated, "the further [he] went into the [admissions] season the more frequently [he] would want to look at these [reports] and see the change from day-to-day." These reports would "track exactly where [the Law School] st[ood] at any given time in assembling the class," and so would tell the admissions personnel whether they were short of assembling a critical mass of minority students. Shields generated these reports because the Law School's admissions policy told him the racial make-up of the entering class was "something [he] need[ed] to be concerned about," and so he had "to find a way of tracking what's going on."

The consultation of daily reports during the last stages in the admissions process suggests there was no further attempt at individual review save for race itself. The admissions officers could use the reports to recalibrate the plus factor given to race depending on how close they were to achieving the Law School's goal of critical mass. The bonus factor of race would then become divorced from individual review; it would be premised instead on the numerical objective set by the Law School.

The Law School made no effort to guard against this danger. It provided no guidelines to its admissions personnel on how to reconcile individual assessment with the directive to admit a critical mass of minority students. The admissions program could have been structured to eliminate at least some of the risk that the promise of individual evaluation was not being kept. The daily consideration of racial breakdown of admitted students is not a feature of affirmative-action programs used by other institutions of higher learning. The Little Ivy League colleges, for instance, do not keep ongoing tallies of racial or ethnic composition of their entering students. See Brief for Amherst College et al. as *Amici Curiae* 10.

To be constitutional, a university's compelling interest in a diverse student body must be achieved by a system where individual assessment is safeguarded through the entire process. There is no constitutional objection to the goal of considering race as one modest factor among many others to achieve diversity, but an educational institution must ensure, through sufficient procedures, that each applicant receives individual consideration and that race does not become a predominant factor in the admissions decisionmaking. The Law School failed to comply with this requirement, and by no means has it carried its burden to show otherwise by the test of strict scrutiny.

The Court's refusal to apply meaningful strict scrutiny will lead to serious consequences. By deferring to the law schools' choice of minority admissions programs, the courts will lose the talents and resources of the faculties and administrators in devising new and fairer ways to ensure individual consideration. Constant and rigorous judicial review forces the law school faculties to undertake their responsibilities as state employees in this most sensitive of areas with utmost fidelity to the mandate of the Constitution. Dean Allan Stillwagon, who directed the Law School's Office of Admissions from 1979 to 1990, explained the difficulties he encountered in defining racial groups entitled to benefit under the School's affirmative action policy. He testified that faculty members were "breathtakingly cynical" in deciding who would qualify as a member of underrepresented minorities. An example he offered was faculty debate as to whether Cubans should be counted as Hispanics: One professor objected on the grounds that Cubans were Republicans. Many academics at other law schools who are "affirmative action's more forthright defenders readily concede that diversity is merely the current rationale of convenience for a policy that they prefer to justify on other grounds." Schuck, Affirmative Action: Past, Present, and Future, 20 Yale L. & Pol'y Rev. 1, 34 (2002) (citing Levinson, Diversity, 2 U. Pa. J. Const. L. 573, 577–578 (2000); Rubenfeld, Affirmative Action, 107 Yale L. J. 427, 471 (1997)). This is not to suggest the faculty at Michigan or other law schools do not pursue aspirations they consider laudable and consistent with our constitutional traditions. It is but further evidence of the necessity for scrutiny that is real, not feigned, where the corrosive category of race is a factor in decision-making. Prospective students, the courts, and the public can demand that the State and its law schools prove their process is fair and constitutional in every phase of implementation.

It is difficult to assess the Court's pronouncement that race-conscious admissions programs will be unnecessary 25 years from now. *Ante,* at 30–31. If it is intended to mitigate the damage the Court does to the concept of strict scrutiny, neither petitioners nor other rejected law school applicants will find solace in knowing the basic protection put in place by Justice Powell will be suspended for a full quarter of a century. Deference is antithetical to strict scrutiny, not consistent with it.

As to the interpretation that the opinion contains its own self-destruct mechanism, the majority's abandonment of strict scrutiny undermines this objective. Were the courts to apply a searching standard to race-based admissions schemes, that would force educational institutions to seriously explore race-neutral alternatives. The Court, by contrast, is willing to be satisfied by the Law School's profession of its own good faith. The majority admits as much: "We take the Law School at its word that it would 'like nothing better than to find a race-neutral admissions formula' and will terminate its race-conscious admissions program as soon as practicable." *Ante,* at 30 (quoting Brief for Respondent Bollinger et al. 34).

If universities are given the latitude to administer programs that are tantamount to quotas, they will have few incentives to make the existing minority admissions schemes transparent and protective of individual review. The unhappy consequence will be to perpetuate the hostilities that proper consideration of race is designed to avoid. The perpetuation, of course, would be the worst of all outcomes. Other programs do exist which will be more effective in bringing about the harmony and mutual respect among all citizens that our constitutional tradition has always sought. They, and not the program under review here, should be the model, even if the Court defaults by not demanding it.

It is regrettable the Court's important holding allowing racial minorities to have their special circumstances considered in order to improve their educational opportunities is accompanied by a suspension of the strict scrutiny which was the predicate of allowing race to be considered in the first place. If the Court abdicates its constitutional duty to give strict scrutiny to the use of race in university admissions, it negates my authority to approve the use of race in pursuit of student diversity. The Constitution cannot confer the right to classify on the basis of race even in this special context absent searching judicial review. For these reasons, though I reiterate my approval of giving appropriate consideration to race in this one context, I must dissent in the present case.

JUSTICE SCALIA, *with whom* JUSTICE THOMAS *joins, concurring in part and dissenting in part.*

I join the opinion of *The Chief Justice.* As he demonstrates, the University of Michigan Law School's mystical "critical mass" justification for its discrimination by race challenges even the most gullible mind. The admissions statistics show it to be a sham to cover a scheme of racially proportionate admissions.

I also join Parts I through VII of *Justice Thomas*'s opinion.[3] I find particularly unanswerable his central point: that the allegedly "compelling state interest" at issue here is not the incremental "educational benefit" that emanates from the fabled "critical mass" of minority students, but rather Michigan's interest in maintaining a "prestige" law school whose normal admissions standards disproportionately exclude blacks and other minorities. If that is a compelling state interest, everything is.

I add the following: The "educational benefit" that the University of Michigan seeks to achieve by racial discrimination consists, according to the Court, of " 'cross-racial understanding,' " *ante,* at 18, and " 'better prepar[ation of] students for an increasingly diverse workforce and society,' " *ibid.,* all of which is necessary not only for work, but also for good "citizenship," *ante,* at 19. This is not, of course, an "educational benefit" on which students will be graded on their Law School transcript (Works and Plays Well with Others: B+) or tested by the bar examiners (Q: Describe in 500 words or less your cross-racial understanding). For it is a lesson of life rather than law—essentially the same lesson taught to (or rather learned by, for it cannot be "taught" in the usual sense) people three feet shorter and twenty years younger than the full-grown adults at the University of Michigan Law School, in institutions ranging from Boy Scout troops to public-school kindergartens. If properly considered an "educational benefit" at all, it is surely not one that is either uniquely relevant to law school or uniquely "teachable" in a formal educational setting. *And therefore:* If it is appropriate for the University of Michigan Law School to use racial discrimination for the purpose of putting together a "critical mass" that will convey generic lessons in socialization and good citizenship, surely it is no less appropriate—indeed, *particularly* appropriate—for the civil service system of the State of Michigan to do so. There, also, those exposed to "critical masses" of certain races will presumably become better Americans, better Michiganders, better civil servants. And surely private employers cannot be criticized—indeed, should be praised—if they also "teach" good citizenship to their adult employees through a patriotic, all-American system of racial discrimination in hiring. The nonminority individuals who are deprived of a legal education, a civil service job, or any job at all by reason of their skin color will surely understand.

Unlike a clear constitutional holding that racial preferences in state educational institutions are impermissible, or even a clear anti-constitutional holding that racial preferences in state educational institutions are OK, today's *Grutter-Gratz* split double header seems perversely designed to prolong the controversy and the litigation. Some future lawsuits will presumably focus on whether the discriminatory scheme in question contains enough evaluation of the applicant "as an individual," *ante,* at 24, and sufficiently avoids "separate admissions tracks" *ante,* at 22, to fall under *Grutter* rather than *Gratz.* Some will focus on whether a university has gone beyond the bounds of a " 'good faith effort' " and has so zealously pursued its "critical mass" as to make it an unconstitutional *de facto* quota system, rather than merely " 'a permissible goal.' " *Ante,* at 23 (quoting *Sheet Metal Workers v. EEOC,* 478 U.S 421, 495 (1986) (*O'Connor, J.,* concurring in part and dissenting in part)). Other lawsuits may focus on whether, in the particular setting at issue, any educational benefits flow from racial diversity. (That issue was not contested in *Grutter;* and while the opinion accords "a degree of deference to a university's academic decisions," *ante,* at 16, "deference does not imply abandonment or abdication of judicial review," *Miller-El v. Cockrell,* 537 U.S. 322, 340

(2003).) Still other suits may challenge the bona fides of the institution's expressed commitment to the educational benefits of diversity that immunize the discriminatory scheme in *Grutter*. (Tempting targets, one would suppose, will be those universities that talk the talk of multiculturalism and racial diversity in the courts but walk the walk of tribalism and racial segregation on their campuses—through minority-only student organizations, separate minority housing opportunities, separate minority student centers, even separate minority-only graduation ceremonies.) And still other suits may claim that the institution's racial preferences have gone below or above the mystical *Grutter*-approved "critical mass." Finally, litigation can be expected on behalf of minority groups intentionally short changed in the institution's composition of its generic minority "critical mass." I do not look forward to any of these cases. The Constitution proscribes government discrimination on the basis of race, and state-provided education is no exception.

JUSTICE THOMAS, *with whom* JUSTICE SCALIA *joins as to Parts I–VII, concurring in part and dissenting in part.*

Frederick Douglass, speaking to a group of abolitionists almost 140 years ago, delivered a message lost on today's majority:

"[I]n regard to the colored people, there is always more that is benevolent, I perceive, than just, manifested towards us. What I ask for the negro is not benevolence, not pity, not sympathy, but simply *justice*. The American people have always been anxious to know what they shall do with us. . . . I have had but one answer from the beginning. Do nothing with us! Your doing with us has already played the mischief with us. Do nothing with us! If the apples will not remain on the tree of their own strength, if they are worm-eaten at the core, if they are early ripe and disposed to fall, let them fall! . . . And if the negro cannot stand on his own legs, let him fall also. All I ask is, give him a chance to stand on his own legs! Let him alone! . . . [Y]our interference is doing him positive injury." What the Black Man Wants: An Address Delivered in Boston, Massachusetts, on 26 January 1865, reprinted in 4 The Frederick Douglass Papers 59, 68 (J. Blassingame & J. McKivigan eds. 1991) (emphasis in original).

Like Douglass, I believe blacks can achieve in every avenue of American life without the meddling of university administrators. Because I wish to see all students succeed whatever their color, I share, in some respect, the sympathies of those who sponsor the type of discrimination advanced by the University of Michigan Law School (Law School). The Constitution does not, however, tolerate institutional devotion to the status quo in admissions policies when such devotion ripens into racial discrimination. Nor does the Constitution countenance the unprecedented deference the Court gives to the Law School, an approach inconsistent with the very concept of "strict scrutiny."

No one would argue that a university could set up a lower general admission standard and then impose heightened requirements only on black applicants. Similarly, a university may not maintain a high admission standard and grant exemptions to favored races. The Law School, of its own choosing, and for its own purposes, maintains an exclusionary admissions system that it knows produces racially disproportionate results. Racial discrimination is not a permissible solution to the self-inflicted wounds of this elitist admissions policy.

The majority upholds the Law School's racial discrimination not by interpreting the people's Constitution, but by responding to a faddish slogan of the cognoscenti. Nevertheless, I concur in part in the Court's opinion. First, I agree with the Court insofar as its decision, which approves of only one racial classification, confirms that further use of race in admissions remains unlawful. Second, I agree with the Court's holding that racial discrimination in higher education admissions will be illegal in 25 years. See *ante*, at 31 (stating that racial discrimination will no longer be narrowly tailored, or "necessary to further" a compelling state interest, in 25 years). I respectfully dissent from the remainder of the Court's opinion and the judgment, however, because I believe that the Law School's current use of race violates the Equal Protection Clause and that the Constitution means the same thing today as it will in 300 months.

I

The majority agrees that the Law School's racial discrimination should be subjected to strict scrutiny. *Ante*, at 14. Before applying that standard to this case, I will briefly revisit the Court's treatment of racial classifications.

The strict scrutiny standard that the Court purports to apply in this case was first enunciated in *Korematsu v. United States*, 323 U.S. 214 (1944). There the Court held that "[p]ressing public necessity may sometimes justify the existence of [racial discrimination]; racial antagonism never can." *Id.*, at 216. This standard of "pressing public necessity" has more frequently been termed "compelling governmental interest,"[4] see, *e.g.*, *Regents of Univ. of Cal. v. Bakke*, 438 U.S. 265, 299 (1978) (opinion of Powell, J.). A majority of the Court has validated only two circumstances where "pressing public necessity" or a "compelling state interest" can possibly justify racial discrimination by state actors. First, the lesson of *Korematsu* is that national security constitutes a "pressing public necessity," though the government's use of race to advance that objective must be narrowly tailored. Second, the Court has recognized as a compelling state interest a government's effort to remedy past discrimination for which it is responsible. *Richmond v. J. A. Croson Co.*, 488 U.S. 469, 504 (1989).

The contours of "pressing public necessity" can be further discerned from those interests the Court has rejected as bases for racial discrimination. For example, *Wygant v. Jackson Bd. of Ed.*, 476 U.S. 267 (1986), found unconstitutional a collective-bargaining agreement between a school board and a teachers' union that favored certain minority races. The school board defended the policy on the grounds that minority teachers provided "role models" for minority students and that a racially "diverse" faculty would improve the education of all students. See Brief for Respondents, O.T. 1984, No. 84-1340, pp. 27–28; 476 U.S., at 315 (Stevens, J., dissenting) ("[A]n integrated faculty will be able to provide benefits to the student body that could not be provided by an all-white, or nearly all-white faculty"). Nevertheless, the Court found that the use of race violated the Equal Protection Clause, deeming both asserted state interests insufficiently compelling. *Id.*, at 275–276 (plurality opinion); *id.*, at 295 (White, J., concurring in judgment) ("None of the interests asserted by the [school board] … justify this racially discriminatory layoff policy").[5]

An even greater governmental interest involves the sensitive role of courts in child custody determinations. In *Palmore v. Sidoti*, 466 U.S. 429 (1984), the Court held that even the best interests of a child did not constitute a compelling state interest that would allow a state court to award custody to the father because the mother was in a mixed-race marriage. *Id.*, at 433 (finding the interest "substantial" but holding the custody decision could not be based on the race of the mother's new husband).

Finally, the Court has rejected an interest in remedying general societal discrimination as a justification for race discrimination. See *Wygant, supra*, at 276 (plurality opinion); *Croson*, 488 U.S., at 496–498 (plurality opinion); *id.*, at 520–521 (Scalia, J., concurring in judgment). "Societal discrimination, without more, is too amorphous a basis for imposing a racially classified remedy" because a "court could uphold remedies that are ageless in their reach into the past, and timeless in their ability to affect the future." *Wygant, supra*, at 276 (plurality opinion). But see *Gratz v. Bollinger, ante*, p. ___ (Ginsburg, J., dissenting).

Where the Court has accepted only national security, and rejected even the best interests of a child, as a justification for racial discrimination, I conclude that only those measures the State must take to provide a bulwark against anarchy, or to prevent violence, will constitute a "pressing public necessity." Cf. *Lee v. Washington,* 390 U.S. 333, 334 (1968) *(per curiam)* (Black, J., concurring) (indicating that protecting prisoners from violence might justify narrowly tailored racial discrimination); *Croson, supra,* at 521 (*Scalia, J.,* concurring in judgment) ("At least where state or local action is at issue, only a social emergency rising to the level of imminent danger to life and limb … can justify [racial discrimination]").

The Constitution abhors classifications based on race, not only because those classifications can harm favored races or are based on illegitimate motives, but also because every time the government places citizens on racial registers and makes race relevant to the provision of burdens or benefits, it demeans us all. "Purchased at the price of immeasurable human suffering, the equal protection principle reflects our Nation's understanding that such classifications ultimately have a destructive impact on the individual and our society." *Adarand Construction, Inc. v. Peña,,* 515 U.S. 200, 240 (1995) (*Thomas, J.,* concurring in part and concurring in judgment).

II

Unlike the majority, I seek to define with precision the interest being asserted by the Law School before determining whether that interest is so compelling as to justify racial discrimination. The Law School maintains that it wishes to obtain "educational benefits that flow from student body diversity," Brief for Respondents Bollinger et al. 14. This statement must be evaluated carefully, because it implies that both "diversity" and "educational benefits" are components of the Law School's compelling state interest. Additionally, the Law School's refusal to entertain certain changes in its admissions process and status indicates that the compelling state interest it seeks to validate is actually broader than might appear at first glance.

Undoubtedly there are other ways to "better" the education of law students aside from ensuring that the student body contains a "critical mass" of underrepresented minority students. Attaining "diversity," whatever it means,[6] is the mechanism by which the Law School obtains educational benefits, not an end of itself. The Law School, however, apparently believes that only a racially mixed student body can lead to the educational benefits it seeks. How, then, is the Law School's interest in these allegedly unique educational "benefits" *not* simply the forbidden interest in "racial balancing," *ante,* at 17, that the majority expressly rejects?

A distinction between these two ideas (unique educational benefits based on racial aesthetics and race for its own sake) is purely sophistic—so much so that the majority uses them interchangeably. Compare *ante,* at 16 ("[T]he Law School has a compelling interest in attaining a diverse student body"), with *ante,* at 21 (referring to the "compelling interest in securing the *educational benefits* of a diverse student body" (emphasis added)). The Law School's argument, as facile as it is, can only be understood in one way: Classroom aesthetics yields educational benefits, racially discriminatory admissions policies are required to achieve the right racial mix, and therefore the policies are required to achieve the educational benefits. It is the *educational benefits* that are the end, or allegedly compelling state interest, not "diversity." But see *ante,* at 20 (citing the need for "openness and integrity of the educational institutions that provide [legal] training" without reference to any consequential educational benefits).

One must also consider the Law School's refusal to entertain changes to its current admissions system that might produce the same educational benefits. The Law School adamantly disclaims any race-neutral alternative that would reduce "academic selectivity," which would in turn "require the Law School to become a very different institution, and to sacrifice a core part of its educational mission." Brief for Respondents Bollinger et al. 33–36. In other words, the Law School seeks to improve marginally the education it offers without sacrificing too much of its exclusivity and elite status.[7]

The proffered interest that the majority vindicates today, then, is not simply "diversity." Instead the Court upholds the use of racial discrimination as a tool to advance the Law School's interest in offering a marginally superior education while maintaining an elite institution. Unless each constituent part of this state interest is of pressing public necessity, the Law School's use of race is unconstitutional. I find each of them to fall far short of this standard.

III

A. A close reading of the Court's opinion reveals that all of its legal work is done through one conclusory statement: The Law School has a "compelling interest in securing the educational benefits of a diverse student body." *Ante,* at 21. No serious effort is made to explain how these benefits fit with the state interests the Court has recognized (or rejected) as compelling, see Part I, *supra,* or to place any theoretical constraints on an enterprising court's desire to discover still more justifications for racial discrimination. In the absence of any explanation, one might expect the Court to fall back on the judicial policy of *stare decisis.* But the Court eschews even this weak defense of its holding, shunning an analysis of the extent to which Justice Powell's opinion in *Regents of Univ. of Cal. v. Bakke,* 438 U.S. 265 (1978), is binding, *ante,* at 13, in favor of an unfounded wholesale adoption of it.

Justice Powell's opinion in *Bakke* and the Court's decision today rest on the fundamentally flawed proposition that racial discrimination can be contextualized so that a goal, such as classroom aesthetics, can be compelling in one context but not in another. This "we know it when we see it" approach to evaluating state interests is not capable of judicial application. Today, the Court insists on radically expanding the range of permissible uses of race to something as trivial (by comparison) as the assembling of a law school class. I can only presume that the majority's failure to justify its decision by reference to any principle arises from the absence of any such principle. See Part VI, *infra.*

B. Under the proper standard, there is no pressing public necessity in maintaining a public law school at all and, it follows, certainly not an elite law school. Likewise, marginal improvements in legal education do not qualify as a compelling state interest.

1. While legal education at a public university may be good policy or otherwise laudable, it is obviously not a pressing public necessity when the correct legal standard is applied. Additionally, circumstantial evidence as to whether a state activity is of pressing public necessity can be obtained by asking whether all States feel compelled to engage in that activity. Evidence that States, in general, engage in a certain activity by no means demonstrates that the activity constitutes a pressing public necessity, given the expansive role of government in today's society. The fact that some fraction of the States reject a particular enterprise, however, creates a presumption that the enterprise itself is not a compelling state interest. In this sense, the absence of a public, American Bar Association (ABA) accredited, law school in Alaska, Delaware, Massachusetts, New Hampshire, and Rhode Island, see ABA-LSAC Official Guide to ABA-Approved Law Schools (W. Margolis, B. Gordon, J. Puskarz, & D. Rosenlieb, eds. 2004) (hereinafter ABA-LSAC Guide), provides further evidence that Michigan's maintenance of the Law School does not constitute a compelling state interest.

2. As the foregoing makes clear, Michigan has no compelling interest in having a law school at all, much less an *elite* one. Still, even

assuming that a State may, under appropriate circumstances, demonstrate a cognizable interest in having an elite law school, Michigan has failed to do so here.

This Court has limited the scope of equal protection review to interests and activities that occur within that State's jurisdiction. The Court held in *Missouri ex rel. Gaines v. Canada,* 305 U.S. 337 (1938), that Missouri could not satisfy the demands of "separate but equal" by paying for legal training of blacks at neighboring state law schools, while maintaining a segregated law school within the State. The equal protection

> obligation is imposed by the Constitution upon the States severally as governmental entities—each responsible for its own laws establishing the rights and duties of persons within its borders. It is an obligation the burden of which cannot be cast by one State upon another, and no State can be excused from performance *by what another State may do or fail to do.* That separate responsibility of each State within its own sphere is of the essence of statehood maintained under our dual system. *Id.,* at 350 (emphasis added).

The Equal Protection Clause, as interpreted by the Court in *Gaines,* does not permit States to justify racial discrimination on the basis of what the rest of the Nation "may do or fail to do." The only interests that can satisfy the Equal Protection Clause's demands are those found within a State's jurisdiction.

The only cognizable state interests vindicated by operating a public law school are, therefore, the education of that State's citizens and the training of that State's lawyers. James Campbell's address at the opening of the Law Department at the University of Michigan on October 3, 1859, makes this clear:

"It not only concerns *the State* that every one should have all reasonable facilities for preparing himself for any honest position in life to which he may aspire, but it also concerns *the community* that the Law should be taught and understood.... There is not an office *in the State* in which serious legal inquiries may not frequently arise.... In all these matters, public and private rights are constantly involved and discussed, and ignorance of the Law has frequently led to results deplorable and alarming.... [I]n the history of *this State,* in more than one instance, that ignorance has led to unlawful violence, and the shedding of innocent blood." E. Brown, Legal Education at Michigan 1859–1959, pp. 404–406 (1959) (emphasis added).

The Law School today, however, does precious little training of those attorneys who will serve the citizens of Michigan. In 2002, graduates of the University of Michigan Law School made up less than 6% of applicants to the Michigan bar, Michigan Lawyers Weekly, available at http://www.michiganlawyersweekly.com/barpassers0202.cfm,barpassers0702.cfm (all Internet materials as visited June 13, 2003, and available in Clerk of Court's case file), even though the Law School's graduates constitute nearly 30% of all law students graduating in Michigan. *Ibid.* Less than 16% of the Law School's graduating class elects to stay in Michigan after law school. ABA-LSAC Guide 427. Thus, while a mere 27% of the Law School's 2002 entering class are from Michigan, see University of Michigan Law School Website, available at http://www.law.umich.edu/prospectivestudents/Admissions/index.htm, only half of these, it appears, will stay in Michigan.

In sum, the Law School trains few Michigan residents and overwhelmingly serves students, who, as lawyers, leave the State of Michigan. By contrast, Michigan's other public law school, Wayne State University Law School, sends 88% of its graduates on to serve the people of Michigan. ABA-LSAC Guide 775. It does not take a social scientist to conclude that it is precisely the Law School's status as an elite institution that causes it to be a way-station for the rest of the country's lawyers, rather than a training ground for those who will remain in Michigan. The Law School's decision to be an elite institution does little to advance the welfare of the people of Michigan or any cognizable interest of the State of Michigan.

Again, the fact that few States choose to maintain elite law schools raises a strong inference that there is nothing compelling about elite status. Arguably, only the public law schools of the University of Texas, the University of California, Berkeley (Boalt Hall), and the University of Virginia maintain the same reputation for excellence as the Law School.[8] Two of these States, Texas and California, are so large that they could reasonably be expected to provide elite legal training at a separate law school to students who will, in fact, stay in the State and provide legal services to its citizens. And these two schools far outshine the Law School in producing in-state lawyers. The University of Texas, for example, sends over three-fourths of its graduates on to work in the State of Texas, vindicating the State's interest (compelling or not) in training Texas' lawyers. *Id.,* at 691.

3. Finally, even if the Law School's racial tinkering produces tangible educational benefits, a marginal improvement in legal education cannot justify racial discrimination where the Law School has no compelling interest in either its existence or in its current educational and admissions policies.

IV

The interest in remaining elite and exclusive that the majority thinks so obviously critical requires the use of admissions "standards" that, in turn, create the Law School's "need" to discriminate on the basis of race. The Court validates these admissions standards by concluding that alternatives that would require "a dramatic sacrifice of . . . the academic quality of all admitted students," *ante,* at 27, need not be considered before racial discrimination can be employed.[9] In the majority's view, such methods are not required by the "narrow tailoring" prong of strict scrutiny because that inquiry demands, in this context, that any race-neutral alternative work "'about as well.'" *Ante,* at 26–27 (quoting *Wygant,* 476 U.S., at 280, n. 6). The majority errs, however, because race-neutral alternatives must only be "workable," *ante,* at 27, and do "about as well" *in vindicating the compelling state interest.* The Court never explicitly holds that the Law School's desire to retain the status quo in "academic selectivity" is itself a compelling state interest, and, as I have demonstrated, it is not. See Part III-B, *supra.* Therefore, the Law School should be forced to choose between its classroom aesthetic and its exclusionary admissions system—it cannot have it both ways.

With the adoption of different admissions methods, such as accepting all students who meet minimum qualifications, see Brief for United States as *Amicus Curiae* 13-14, the Law School could achieve its vision of the racially aesthetic student body without the use of racial discrimination. The Law School concedes this, but the Court holds, implicitly and under the guise of narrow tailoring, that the Law School has a compelling state interest in doing what it wants to do. I cannot agree. First, under strict scrutiny, the Law School's assessment of the benefits of racial discrimination and devotion to the admissions status quo are not entitled to any sort of deference, grounded in the First Amendment or anywhere else. Second, even if its "academic selectivity" must be maintained at all costs along with racial discrimination, the Court ignores the fact that other top law schools have succeeded in meeting their aesthetic demands without racial discrimination.

A. The Court bases its unprecedented deference to the Law School—a deference antithetical to strict scrutiny—on an idea of "educational autonomy" grounded in the First Amendment. *Ante,* at

17. In my view, there is no basis for a right of public universities to do what would otherwise violate the Equal Protection Clause.

The constitutionalization of "academic freedom" began with the concurring opinion of Justice Frankfurter in *Sweezy v. New Hampshire,* 354 U.S. 234 (1957). Sweezy, a Marxist economist, was investigated by the Attorney General of New Hampshire on suspicion of being a subversive. The prosecution sought, *inter alia,* the contents of a lecture Sweezy had given at the University of New Hampshire. The Court held that the investigation violated due process. *Id.,* at 254.

Justice Frankfurter went further, however, reasoning that the First Amendment created a right of academic freedom that prohibited the investigation. *Id.,* at 256–267 (opinion concurring in result). Much of the rhetoric in Justice Frankfurter's opinion was devoted to the personal right of Sweezy to free speech. See, *e.g., id.,* at 265 ("For a citizen to be made to forgo even a part of so basic a liberty as his political autonomy, the subordinating interest of the State must be compelling"). Still, claiming that the United States Reports "need not be burdened with proof," Justice Frankfurter also asserted that a "free society" depends on "free universities" and "[t]his means the exclusion of governmental intervention in the intellectual life of a university." *Id.,* at 262. According to Justice Frankfurter: "[I]t is the business of a university to provide that atmosphere which is most conducive to speculation, experiment and creation. It is an atmosphere in which there prevail 'the four essential freedoms' of a university—to determine for itself on academic grounds who may teach, what may be taught, how it shall be taught, and who may be admitted to study.'" *Id.,* at 263 (citation omitted).

In my view, "[i]t is the business" of this Court to explain itself when it cites provisions of the Constitution to invent new doctrines—including the idea that the First Amendment authorizes a public university to do what would otherwise violate the Equal Protection Clause. The majority fails in its summary effort to prove this point. The only source for the Court's conclusion that public universities are entitled to deference even within the confines of strict scrutiny is Justice Powell's opinion in *Bakke.* Justice Powell, for his part, relied only on Justice Frankfurter's opinion in *Sweezy* and the Court's decision in *Keyishian v. Board of Regents of Univ. of State of N. Y.,* 385 U.S. 589 (1967), to support his view that the First Amendment somehow protected a public university's use of race in admissions. *Bakke,* 438 U.S., at 312. *Keyishian* provides no answer to the question whether the Fourteenth Amendment's restrictions are relaxed when applied to public universities. In that case, the Court held that state statutes and regulations designed to prevent the "appointment or retention of 'subversive' persons in state employment," 385 U.S., at 592, violated the First Amendment for vagueness. The statutes covered all public employees and were not invalidated only as applied to university faculty members, although the Court appeared sympathetic to the notion of academic freedom, calling it a "special concern of the First Amendment." *Id.,* at 603. Again, however, the Court did not relax any independent constitutional restrictions on public universities.

I doubt that when Justice Frankfurter spoke of governmental intrusions into the independence of universities, he was thinking of the Constitution's ban on racial discrimination. The majority's broad deference to both the Law School's judgment that racial aesthetics leads to educational benefits and its stubborn refusal to alter the status quo in admissions methods finds no basis in the Constitution or decisions of this Court.

B. 1. The Court's deference to the Law School's conclusion that its racial experimentation leads to educational benefits will, if adhered to, have serious collateral consequences. The Court relies heavily on social science evidence to justify its deference. See *ante,* at

18–20; but see also Rothman, Lipset, & Nevitte, Racial Diversity Reconsidered, 151 Public Interest 25 (2003) (finding that the racial mix of a student body produced by racial discrimination of the type practiced by the Law School in fact hinders students' perception of academic quality). The Court never acknowledges, however, the growing evidence that racial (and other sorts) of heterogeneity actually impairs learning among black students. See, *e.g.,* Flowers & Pascarella, Cognitive Effects of College Racial Composition on African American Students After 3 Years of College, 40 J. of College Student Development 669, 674 (1999) (concluding that black students experience superior cognitive development at Historically Black Colleges (HBCs) and that, even among blacks, "a substantial diversity moderates the cognitive effects of attending an HBC"); Allen, The Color of Success: African-American College Student Outcomes at Predominantly White and Historically Black Public Colleges and Universities, 62 Harv. Educ. Rev. 26, 35 (1992) (finding that black students attending HBCs report higher academic achievement than those attending predominantly white colleges).

At oral argument in *Gratz v. Bollinger, ante,* p. ___, counsel for respondents stated that "most every single one of [the HBCs] do have diverse student bodies." Tr. of Oral Arg. in No. 02-516, p. 52. What precisely counsel meant by "diverse" is indeterminate, but it is reported that in 2000 at Morehouse College, one of the most distinguished HBC's in the Nation, only 0.1% of the student body was white, and only 0.2% was Hispanic. College Admissions Data Handbook 2002-2003, p. 613 (43d ed. 2002) (hereinafter College Admissions Data Handbook). And at Mississippi Valley State University, a public HBC, only 1.1% of the freshman class in 2001 was white. *Id.,* at 603. If there is a "critical mass" of whites at these institutions, then "critical mass" is indeed a very small proportion.

The majority grants deference to the Law School's "assessment that diversity will, in fact, yield educational benefits," *ante,* at 16. It follows, therefore, that an HBC's assessment that racial homogeneity will yield educational benefits would similarly be given deference.[10] An HBC's rejection of white applicants in order to maintain racial homogeneity seems permissible, therefore, under the majority's view of the Equal Protection Clause. But see *United States v. Fordice,* 505 U.S. 717, 748 (1992) (*Thomas, J.,* concurring) ("Obviously, a State cannot maintain ... traditions by closing particular institutions, historically white or historically black, to particular racial groups"). Contained within today's majority opinion is the seed of a new constitutional justification for a concept I thought long and rightly rejected—racial segregation.

2. Moreover one would think, in light of the Court's decision in *United States v. Virginia,* 518 U.S. 515 (1996), that before being given license to use racial discrimination, the Law School would be required to radically reshape its admissions process, even to the point of sacrificing some elements of its character. In *Virginia,* a majority of the Court, without a word about academic freedom, accepted the all-male Virginia Military Institute's (VMI) representation that some changes in its "adversative" method of education would be required with the admission of women, *id.,* at 540, but did not defer to VMI's judgment that these changes would be too great. Instead, the Court concluded that they were "manageable." *Id.,* at 551, n. 19. That case involved sex discrimination, which is subjected to intermediate, not strict, scrutiny. *Id.,* at 533; *Craig v. Boren,* 429 U.S. 190, 197 (1976). So in *Virginia,* where the standard of review dictated that greater flexibility be granted to VMI's educational policies than the Law School deserves here, this Court gave no deference. Apparently where the status quo being defended is that of the elite establishment—here the Law School—rather than a less fashionable Southern military institution, the Court will defer without serious inquiry and without regard to the applicable legal standard.

C. *Virginia* is also notable for the fact that the Court relied on the "experience" of formerly single-sex institutions, such as the service academies, to conclude that admission of women to VMI would be "manageable." 518 U.S., at 544–545. Today, however, the majority ignores the "experience" of those institutions that have been forced to abandon explicit racial discrimination in admissions.

The sky has not fallen at Boalt Hall at the University of California, Berkeley, for example. Prior to Proposition 209's adoption of Cal. Const., Art. 1, §31(a), which bars the State from "grant[ing] preferential treatment . . . on the basis of race . . . in the operation of . . . public education," [11] Boalt Hall enrolled 20 blacks and 28 Hispanics in its first-year class for 1996. In 2002, without deploying express racial discrimination in admissions, Boalt's entering class enrolled 14 blacks and 36 Hispanics.[12] University of California Law and Medical School Enrollments, available at http://www.ucop.edu/acadadv/datamgmt/lawmed/law-enrolls-eth2.html. Total underrepresented minority student enrollment at Boalt Hall now exceeds 1996 levels. Apparently the Law School cannot be counted on to be as resourceful. The Court is willfully blind to the very real experience in California and elsewhere, which raises the inference that institutions with "reputation[s] for excellence," *ante,* at 16, 26, rivaling the Law School's have satisfied their sense of mission without resorting to prohibited racial discrimination.

V

Putting aside the absence of any legal support for the majority's reflexive deference, there is much to be said for the view that the use of tests and other measures to "predict" academic performance is a poor substitute for a system that gives every applicant a chance to prove he can succeed in the study of law. The rallying cry that in the absence of racial discrimination in admissions there would be a true meritocracy ignores the fact that the entire process is poisoned by numerous exceptions to "merit." For example, in the national debate on racial discrimination in higher education admissions, much has been made of the fact that elite institutions utilize a so-called "legacy" preference to give the children of alumni an advantage in admissions. This, and other, exceptions to a "true" meritocracy give the lie to protestations that merit admissions are in fact the order of the day at the Nation's universities. The Equal Protection Clause does not, however, prohibit the use of unseemly legacy preferences or many other kinds of arbitrary admissions procedures. What the Equal Protection Clause does prohibit are classifications made on the basis of race. So while legacy preferences can stand under the Constitution, racial discrimination cannot.[13] I will not twist the Constitution to invalidate legacy preferences or otherwise impose my vision of higher education admissions on the Nation. The majority should similarly stay its impulse to validate faddish racial discrimination the Constitution clearly forbids.

In any event, there is nothing ancient, honorable, or constitutionally protected about "selective" admissions. The University of Michigan should be well aware that alternative methods have historically been used for the admission of students, for it brought to this country the German certificate system in the late-19th century. See H. Wechsler, The Qualified Student 16–39 (1977) (hereinafter Qualified Student). Under this system, a secondary school was certified by a university so that any graduate who completed the course offered by the school was offered admission to the university. The certification regime supplemented, and later virtually replaced (at least in the Midwest), the prior regime of rigorous subject-matter entrance examinations. *Id.,* at 57–58. The facially race-neutral "percent plans" now used in Texas, California, and Florida, see *ante,* at 28, are in many ways the descendents of the certificate system.

Certification was replaced by selective admissions in the beginning of the 20th century, as universities sought to exercise more control over the composition of their student bodies. Since its inception, selective admissions has been the vehicle for racial, ethnic, and religious tinkering and experimentation by university administrators. The initial driving force for the relocation of the selective function from the high school to the universities was the same desire to select racial winners and losers that the Law School exhibits today. Columbia, Harvard, and others infamously determined that they had "too many" Jews, just as today the Law School argues it would have "too many" whites if it could not discriminate in its admissions process. See Qualified Student 155–168 (Columbia); H. Broun & G. Britt, Christians Only: A Study in Prejudice 53–54 (1931) (Harvard).

Columbia employed intelligence tests precisely because Jewish applicants, who were predominantly immigrants, scored worse on such tests. Thus, Columbia could claim (falsely) that "'[w]e have not eliminated boys because they were Jews and do not propose to do so. We have honestly attempted to eliminate the lowest grade of applicant [through the use of intelligence testing] and it turns out that a good many of the low grade men are New York City Jews.'" Letter from Herbert E. Hawkes, dean of Columbia College, to E. B. Wilson, June 16, 1922 (reprinted in Qualified Student 160–161). In other words, the tests were adopted with full knowledge of their disparate impact. Cf. *DeFunis v. Odegaard,* 416 U.S. 312, 335 (1974) *(per curiam)* (Douglas, J., dissenting).

Similarly no modern law school can claim ignorance of the poor performance of blacks, relatively speaking, on the Law School Admissions Test (LSAT). Nevertheless, law schools continue to use the test and then attempt to "correct" for black underperformance by using racial discrimination in admissions so as to obtain their aesthetic student body. The Law School's continued adherence to measures it knows produce racially skewed results is not entitled to deference by this Court. See Part IV, *supra.* The Law School itself admits that the test is imperfect, as it must, given that it regularly admits students who score at or below 150 (the national median) on the test. See App. 156–203 (showing that, between 1995 and 2000, the Law School admitted 37 students—27 of whom were black; 31 of whom were "underrepresented minorities"—with LSAT scores of 150 or lower). And the Law School's *amici* cannot seem to agree on the fundamental question whether the test itself is useful. Compare Brief for Law School Admission Council as *Amicus Curiae* 12 ("LSAT scores . . . are an effective predictor of students' performance in law school") with Brief for Harvard Black Law Students Association et al. as *Amici Curiae* 27 ("Whether [the LSAT] measure[s] objective merit . . . is certainly questionable").

Having decided to use the LSAT, the Law School must accept the constitutional burdens that come with this decision. The Law School may freely continue to employ the LSAT and other allegedly merit-based standards in whatever fashion it likes. What the Equal Protection Clause forbids, but the Court today allows, is the use of these standards hand-in-hand with racial discrimination. An infinite variety of admissions methods are available to the Law School. Considering all of the radical thinking that has historically occurred at this country's universities, the Law School's intractable approach toward admissions is striking.

The Court will not even deign to make the Law School try other methods, however, preferring instead to grant a 25-year license to violate the Constitution. And the same Court that had the courage to order the desegregation of all public schools in the South now fears, on the basis of platitudes rather than principle, to force the Law School to abandon a decidedly imperfect admissions regime that provides the basis for racial discrimination.

VI

The absence of any articulated legal principle supporting the majority's principal holding suggests another rationale. I believe what lies beneath the Court's decision today are the benighted notions that one can tell when racial discrimination benefits (rather than hurts) minority groups, see *Adarand*, 515 U.S., at 239 (*Scalia, J.*, concurring in part and concurring in judgment), and that racial discrimination is necessary to remedy general societal ills. This Court's precedents supposedly settled both issues, but clearly the majority still cannot commit to the principle that racial classifications are *per se* harmful and that almost no amount of benefit in the eye of the beholder can justify such classifications.

Putting aside what I take to be the Court's implicit rejection of *Adarand*'s holding that beneficial and burdensome racial classifications are equally invalid, I must contest the notion that the Law School's discrimination benefits those admitted as a result of it. The Court spends considerable time discussing the impressive display of *amicus* support for the Law School in this case from all corners of society. *Ante*, at 18–19. But nowhere in any of the filings in this Court is any evidence that the purported "beneficiaries" of this racial discrimination prove themselves by performing at (or even near) the same level as those students who receive no preferences. Cf. Thernstrom & Thernstrom, Reflections on the Shape of the River, 46 UCLA L. Rev. 1583, 1605-1608 (1999) (discussing the failure of defenders of racial discrimination in admissions to consider the fact that its "beneficiaries" are underperforming in the classroom).

The silence in this case is deafening to those of us who view higher education's purpose as imparting knowledge and skills to students, rather than a communal, rubber-stamp, credentialing process. The Law School is not looking for those students who, despite a lower LSAT score or undergraduate grade point average, will succeed in the study of law. The Law School seeks only a facade—it is sufficient that the class looks right, even if it does not perform right.

The Law School tantalizes unprepared students with the promise of a University of Michigan degree and all of the opportunities that it offers. These overmatched students take the bait, only to find that they cannot succeed in the cauldron of competition. And this mismatch crisis is not restricted to elite institutions. See T. Sowell, Race and Culture 176–177 (1994) ("Even if most minority students are able to meet the normal standards at the 'average' range of colleges and universities, the systematic mismatching of minority students begun at the top can mean that such students are generally overmatched throughout all levels of higher education"). Indeed, to cover the tracks of the aestheticists, this cruel farce of racial discrimination must continue—in selection for the Michigan Law Review, see University of Michigan Law School Student Handbook 2002–2003, pp. 39–40 (noting the presence of a "diversity plan" for admission to the review), and in hiring at law firms and for judicial clerkships—until the "beneficiaries" are no longer tolerated. While these students may graduate with law degrees, there is no evidence that they have received a qualitatively better legal education (or become better lawyers) than if they had gone to a less "elite" law school for which they were better prepared. And the aestheticists will never address the real problems facing "underrepresented minorities,"[14] instead continuing their social experiments on other people's children.

Beyond the harm the Law School's racial discrimination visits upon its test subjects, no social science has disproved the notion that this discrimination "engender[s] attitudes of superiority or, alternatively, provoke[s] resentment among those who believe that they have been wronged by the government's use of race." *Adarand*, 515 U.S., at 241 (*Thomas, J.*, concurring in part and concurring in judgment).

"These programs stamp minorities with a badge of inferiority and may cause them to develop dependencies or to adopt an attitude that they are 'entitled' to preferences." *Ibid.*

It is uncontested that each year, the Law School admits a handful of blacks who would be admitted in the absence of racial discrimination. See Brief for Respondents Bollinger et al. 6. Who can differentiate between those who belong and those who do not? The majority of blacks are admitted to the Law School because of discrimination, and because of this policy all are tarred as undeserving. This problem of stigma does not depend on determinacy as to whether those stigmatized are actually the "beneficiaries" of racial discrimination. When blacks take positions in the highest places of government, industry, or academia, it is an open question today whether their skin color played a part in their advancement. The question itself is the stigma—because either racial discrimination did play a role, in which case the person may be deemed "otherwise unqualified," or it did not, in which case asking the question itself unfairly marks those blacks who would succeed without discrimination. Is this what the Court means by "visibly open"? *Ante*, at 20.

Finally, the Court's disturbing reference to the importance of the country's law schools as training grounds meant to cultivate "a set of leaders with legitimacy in the eyes of the citizenry," *ibid.*, through the use of racial discrimination deserves discussion. As noted earlier, the Court has soundly rejected the remedying of societal discrimination as a justification for governmental use of race. *Wygant*, 476 U.S., at 276 (plurality opinion); *Croson*, 488 U.S., at 497 (plurality opinion); *id.*, at 520–521 (*Scalia, J.*, concurring in judgment). For those who believe that every racial disproportionality in our society is caused by some kind of racial discrimination, there can be no distinction between remedying societal discrimination and erasing racial disproportionalities in the country's leadership caste. And if the lack of proportional racial representation among our leaders is not caused by societal discrimination, then "fixing" it is even less of a pressing public necessity.

The Court's civics lesson presents yet another example of judicial selection of a theory of political representation based on skin color—an endeavor I have previously rejected. See *Holder v. Hall*, 512 U.S. 874, 899 (1994) (*Thomas, J.*, concurring in judgment). The majority appears to believe that broader utopian goals justify the Law School's use of race, but "[t]he Equal Protection Clause commands the elimination of racial barriers, not their creation in order to satisfy our theory as to how society ought to be organized." *DeFunis*, 416 U.S., at 342 (*Douglas, J.*, dissenting).

VII

As the foregoing makes clear, I believe the Court's opinion to be, in most respects, erroneous. I do, however, find two points on which I agree.

A. First, I note that the issue of unconstitutional racial discrimination among the groups the Law School prefers is not presented in this case, because petitioner has never argued that the Law School engages in such a practice, and the Law School maintains that it does not. See Brief for Respondents Bollinger et al. 32, n. 50, and 6–7, n. 7. I join the Court's opinion insofar as it confirms that this type of racial discrimination remains unlawful. *Ante*, at 13–15. Under today's decision, it is still the case that racial discrimination that does not help a university to enroll an unspecified number, or "critical mass," of underrepresented minority students is unconstitutional. Thus, the Law School may not discriminate in admissions between similarly situated blacks and Hispanics, or between whites and Asians. This is so because preferring black to Hispanic applicants, for instance, does nothing to further the interest recognized by the majority today.[15] Indeed, the majority describes such racial balancing as "patently unconstitutional." *Ante,* at 17. Like the Court, *ante,* at 24, I express no opinion as to whether the Law School's current admissions program runs afoul of this prohibition.

B. The Court also holds that racial discrimination in admissions should be given another 25 years before it is deemed no longer narrowly tailored to the Law School's fabricated compelling state interest. *Ante,* at 30. While I agree that in 25 years the practices of the Law School will be illegal, they are, for the reasons I have given, illegal now. The majority does not and cannot rest its time limitation on any evidence that the gap in credentials between black and white students is shrinking or will be gone in that timeframe.[16] In recent years there has been virtually no change, for example, in the proportion of law school applicants with LSAT scores of 165 and higher who are black.[17] In 1993 blacks constituted 1.1% of law school applicants in that score range, though they represented 11.1% of all applicants. Law School Admission Council, National Statistical Report (1994) (hereinafter LSAC Statistical Report). In 2000 the comparable numbers were 1.0% and 11.3%. LSAC Statistical Report (2001). No one can seriously contend, and the Court does not, that the racial gap in academic credentials will disappear in 25 years. Nor is the Court's holding that racial discrimination will be unconstitutional in 25 years made contingent on the gap closing in that time.[18]

Indeed, the very existence of racial discrimination of the type practiced by the Law School may impede the narrowing of the LSAT testing gap. An applicant's LSAT score can improve dramatically with preparation, but such preparation is a cost, and there must be sufficient benefits attached to an improved score to justify additional study. Whites scoring between 163 and 167 on the LSAT are routinely rejected by the Law School, and thus whites aspiring to admission at the Law School have every incentive to improve their score to levels above that range. See App. 199 (showing that in 2000, 209 out of 422 white applicants were rejected in this scoring range). Blacks, on the other hand, are nearly guaranteed admission if they score above 155. *Id.,* at 198 (showing that 63 out of 77 black applicants are accepted with LSAT scores above 155). As admission prospects approach certainty, there is no incentive for the black applicant to continue to prepare for the LSAT once he is reasonably assured of achieving the requisite score. It is far from certain that the LSAT test-taker's behavior is responsive to the Law School's admissions policies.[19] Nevertheless, the possibility remains that this racial discrimination will help fulfill the bigot's prophecy about black underperformance—just as it confirms the conspiracy theorist's belief that "institutional racism" is at fault for every racial disparity in our society.

I therefore can understand the imposition of a 25-year time limit only as a holding that the deference the Court pays to the Law School's educational judgments and refusal to change its admissions policies will itself expire. At that point these policies will clearly have failed to "'eliminat[e] the [perceived] need for any racial or ethnic'" discrimination because the academic credentials gap will still be there. *Ante,* at 30 (quoting Nathanson & Bartnika, The Constitutionality of Preferential Treatment for Minority Applicants to Professional Schools, 58 Chicago Bar Rec. 282, 293 (May-June 1977)). The Court defines this time limit in terms of narrow tailoring, see *ante,* at 30, but I believe this arises from its refusal to define rigorously the broad state interest vindicated today. Cf. Part II, *supra.* With these observations, I join the last sentence of Part III of the opinion of the Court.

* * *

For the immediate future, however, the majority has placed its *imprimatur* on a practice that can only weaken the principle of equality embodied in the Declaration of Independence and the Equal Protection Clause. "Our Constitution is color-blind, and neither knows nor tolerates classes among citizens." *Plessy v. Ferguson,* 163 U.S. 537, 559 (1896) (Harlan, J., dissenting). It has been nearly 140 years since Frederick Douglass asked the intellectual ancestors of the Law School to "[d]o nothing with us!" and the Nation adopted the Fourteenth Amendment. Now we must wait another 25 years to see this principle of equality vindicated. I therefore respectfully dissent from the remainder of the Court's opinion and the judgment.

1. As the Court explains, the admissions policy challenged here survives review under the standards stated in *Adarand Constructors, Inc . v. Peña,* 515 U.S. 200 (1995), *Richmond v. J. A. Croson Co.,* 488 U.S. 469 (1989), and Justice Powell's opinion in *Regents of Univ. of Cal. v. Bakke,* 438 U.S. 265 (1978). This case therefore does not require the Court to revisit whether all governmental classifications by race, whether designed to benefit or to burden a historically disadvantaged group, should be subject to the same standard of judicial review. Cf. *Gratz, ante,* at 4–5 (Ginsburg, J., dissenting); *Adarand,* 515 U.S., at 274, n. 8 (Ginsburg, J., dissenting). Nor does this case necessitate reconsideration whether interests other than "student body diversity," *ante,* at 13, rank as sufficiently important to justify a race-conscious government program. Cf. *Gratz, ante,* at 5 (Ginsburg, J., dissenting); *Adarand,* 515 U.S., at 273–274 (Ginsburg, J., dissenting).

2. Indeed, during this 5-year time period, enrollment of Native American students dropped to as low as *three* such students. Any assertion that such a small group constituted a "critical mass" of Native Americans is simply absurd.

3. Part VII of *Justice Thomas's* opinion describes those portions of the Court's opinion in which I concur. See *post,* at 27–31.

4. Throughout I will use the two phrases interchangeably.

5. The Court's refusal to address *Wygant's* rejection of a state interest virtually indistinguishable from that presented by the Law School is perplexing. If the Court defers to the Law School's judgment that a racially mixed student body confers educational benefits to all, then why would the *Wygant* Court not defer to the school board's judgment with respect to the benefits a racially mixed faculty confers?

6. "[D]iversity," for all of its devotees, is more a fashionable catch-phrase than it is a useful term, especially when something as serious as racial discrimination is at issue. Because the Equal Protection Clause renders the color of one's skin constitutionally irrelevant to the Law School's mission, I refer to the Law School's interest as an "aesthetic." That is, the Law School wants to have a certain appearance, from the shape of the desks and tables in its classrooms to the color of the students sitting at them.

I also use the term "aesthetic" because I believe it underlines the ineffectiveness of racially discriminatory admissions in actually helping those who are truly underprivileged. Cf. *Orr v. Orr,* 440 U.S. 268, 283 (1979) (noting that suspect classifications are especially impermissible when "the choice made by the State appears to redound . . . to the benefit of those without need for special solicitude"). It must be remembered that the Law School's racial discrimination does nothing for those too poor or uneducated to participate in elite higher education and therefore presents only an illusory solution to the challenges facing our Nation.

7. The Law School believes both that the educational benefits of a racially engineered student body are large and that adjusting its overall admissions standards to achieve the same racial mix would require it to sacrifice its elite status. If the Law School is correct that the educational benefits of "diversity" are so great, then achieving them by altering admissions standards should not compromise its elite status. The Law School's reluctance to do this suggests that the educational benefits it alleges are not significant or do not exist at all.

8. Cf. U.S. News & World Report, America's Best Graduate Schools 28 (2004 ed.) (placing these schools in the uppermost 15 in the Nation).

9. The Court refers to this component of the Law School's compelling state interest variously as "academic quality," avoiding "sacrifice [of] a vital component of its educational mission," and "academic selectivity." *Ante,* at 27–28.

10. For example, North Carolina A&T State University, which is currently 5.4% white, College Admissions Data Handbook 643, could seek to reduce the representation of whites in order to gain additional educational benefits.

11. Cal. Const., Art. 1, §31(a), states in full:

"The state shall not discriminate against, or grant preferential treatment to, any individual or group on the basis of race, sex, color, ethnicity, or national origin in the operation of public employment, public education, or public contracting." See *Coalition for Economic Equity v. Wilson,* 122 F. 3d 692 (CA9 1997).

12. Given the incredible deference the Law School receives from the Court, I think it appropriate to indulge in the presumption that Boalt Hall operates without violating California law.

13. Were this Court to have the courage to forbid the use of racial discrimination in admissions, legacy preferences (and similar practices) might quickly become less popular—a possibility not lost, I am certain, on the elites (both individual and institutional) supporting the Law School in this case.

14. For example, there is no recognition by the Law School in this case that even with their racial discrimination in place, black *men* are "underrepresented" at the Law School. See ABA-LSAC Guide 426 (reporting that the Law School has 46 black women and 28 black men). Why does the Law School not also discriminate in favor of black men over black women, given this underrepresentation? The answer is, again, that all the Law School cares about is its own image among know-it-all elites, not solving real problems like the crisis of black male underperformance.

15. That interest depends on enrolling a "critical mass" of underrepresented minority students, as the majority repeatedly states. *Ante,* at 3, 5, 7, 17, 20, 21, 23, 28; cf. *ante,* at 21 (referring to the unique experience of being a "racial minority," as opposed to being black, or Native American); *ante,* at 24 (rejecting argument that the Law School maintains a disguised quota by referring to the total number of enrolled underrepresented minority students, not specific races). As it relates to the Law School's racial discrimination, the Court clearly approves of only one use of race—the distinction between underrepresented minority applicants and those of all other races. A relative preference awarded to a black applicant over, for example, a simi-

larly situated Native American applicant, does not lead to the enrollment of even one more underrepresented minority student, but only balances the races within the "critical mass."

16. I agree with *Justice Ginsburg* that the Court's holding that racial discrimination in admissions will be illegal in 25 years is not based upon a "forecast," *post,* at 3 (concurring opinion). I do not agree with *Justice Ginsburg's* characterization of the Court's holding as an expression of "hope." *Ibid.*

17. I use a score of 165 as the benchmark here because the Law School feels it is the relevant score range for applicant consideration (absent race discrimination). See Brief for Respondents Bollinger et al. 5; App. to Pet. for Cert. 309a (showing that the median LSAT score for all accepted applicants from 1995–1998 was 168); *id.,* at 310a–311a (showing the median LSAT score for accepted applicants was 167 for the years 1999 and 2000); University of Michigan Law School Website, available at http://www.law.umich.edu/prospectivestudents/Admissions/index.htm (showing that the median LSAT score for accepted applicants in 2002 was 166).

18. The majority's non sequitur observation that since 1978 the number of blacks that have scored in these upper ranges on the LSAT has grown, *ante,* at 30, says nothing about current trends. First, black participation in the LSAT until the early 1990's lagged behind black representation in the general population. For instance, in 1984 only 7.3% of law school applicants were black, whereas in 2000 11.3% of law school applicants were black. See LSAC Statistical Reports (1984 and 2000). Today, however, unless blacks were to begin applying to law school in proportions greater than their representation in the general population, the growth in absolute numbers of high scoring blacks should be expected to plateau, and it has. In 1992, 63 black applicants to law school had LSAT scores above 165. In 2000, that number was 65. See LSAC Statistical Reports (1992 and 2000).

19. I use the LSAT as an example, but the same incentive structure is in place for any admissions criteria, including undergraduate grades, on which minorities are consistently admitted at thresholds significantly lower than whites.

Lawrence v. Texas (2003)

In 2003, the Supreme Court ruled in a historic 6-3 decision that state laws banning private consensual sexual conduct between persons of the same sex were invalid on due process grounds under the Fourteenth Amendment. The decision was controversial as it potentially opens new constitutional grounds for the expansion of gay rights.

The emotionally charged issue reached the Court on appeal from the Texas Court of Criminal Appeals in a case brought by two gay men arrested under a Texas statute that banned "deviate sexual intercourse" between persons of the same sex.

The Court used the right of privacy as the basis for striking down such laws. "The petitioners are entitled to respect for their private lives," Justice Kennedy wrote for the majority. "The State cannot demean their existence or control their destiny by making their private sexual conduct a crime. Their right to liberty under the Due Process Clause gives them the full right to engage in their conduct without the intervention of the government."

The decision expressly overruled the controversial 1986 Bowers v. Hardwick, *precedent. "Bowers was not correct when it was decided, and it is not correct today," Kennedy concluded.*

539 U.S. ____

Lawrence et al. v. Texas

On Writ of Certiorari to the Court of Appeals of Texas, Fourteenth District

No. 02-102. *Argued March 26, 2003—Decided June 26, 2003*

Responding to a reported weapons disturbance in a private residence, Houston police entered petitioner Lawrence's apartment and saw him and another adult man, petitioner Garner, engaging in a private, consensual sexual act. Petitioners were arrested and convicted of deviate sexual intercourse in violation of a Texas statute forbidding two persons of the same sex to engage in certain intimate sexual conduct. In affirming, the State Court of Appeals held, *inter alia,* that the statute was not unconstitutional under the Due Process Clause of the Fourteenth Amendment. The court considered *Bowers v. Hardwick,* 478 U.S. 186, controlling on that point.

Held: The Texas statute making it a crime for two persons of the same sex to engage in certain intimate sexual conduct violates the Due Process Clause. Pp. 3–18.

(a) Resolution of this case depends on whether petitioners were free as adults to engage in private conduct in the exercise of their liberty under the Due Process Clause. For this inquiry the Court deems it necessary to reconsider its *Bowers* holding. The *Bowers* Court's initial substantive statement—"The issue presented is whether the Federal Constitution confers a fundamental right upon homosexuals to engage in sodomy . . . ," 478 U.S., at 190—discloses the Court's failure to appreciate the extent of the liberty at stake. To say that the issue in *Bowers* was simply the right to engage in certain sexual conduct demeans the claim the individual put forward, just as it would demean a married couple were it said that marriage is just about the right to have sexual intercourse. Although the laws involved in *Bowers* and here purport to do no more than prohibit a particular sexual act, their penalties and purposes have more far-reaching consequences, touching upon the most private human conduct, sexual behavior, and in the most private of places, the home. They seek to control a personal relationship that, whether or not entitled to formal recognition in the law, is within the liberty of persons to choose without being punished as criminals. The liberty protected by the Constitution allows homosexual persons the right to choose to enter upon relationships in the confines of their homes and their own private lives and still retain their dignity as free persons. Pp. 3–6.

(b) Having misapprehended the liberty claim presented to it, the *Bowers* Court stated that proscriptions against sodomy have ancient roots. 478 U.S., at 192. It should be noted, however, that there is no longstanding history in this country of laws directed at homosexual conduct as a distinct matter. Early American sodomy laws were not directed at homosexuals as such but instead sought to prohibit nonprocreative sexual activity more generally, whether between men and women or men and men. Moreover, early sodomy laws seem not to have been enforced against consenting adults acting in private. Instead, sodomy prosecutions often involved predatory acts against those who could not or did not consent: relations between men and minor girls or boys, between adults involving force, between adults implicating disparity in status, or between men and animals. The longstanding criminal prohibition of homosexual sodomy upon which *Bowers* placed such reliance is as consistent with a general condemnation of nonprocreative sex as it is with an established tradition of prosecuting acts because of their homosexual character. Far from possessing "ancient roots," *ibid.,* American laws targeting same-sex couples did not develop until the last third of the 20th century. Even now, only nine States have singled out same-sex relations for criminal prosecution. Thus, the historical grounds relied upon in *Bowers* are more complex than the majority opinion and the concurring opinion by Chief Justice Burger there indicated. They are not without doubt and, at the very least, are overstated. The *Bowers* Court was, of course, making the broader point that for centuries there have been powerful voices to condemn homosexual conduct as immoral, but this Court's obligation is to define the liberty of all, not to mandate its own moral code, *Planned Parenthood of Southeastern Pa. v. Casey,* 505 U.S. 833, 850. The Nation's laws and traditions in the past half century are most relevant here. They show an emerging awareness that liberty gives substantial protection to adult persons in deciding how to conduct their private lives in matters pertaining to sex. See *County of Sacramento v. Lewis,* 523 U.S. 833, 857. Pp. 6–12.

(c) *Bowers'* deficiencies became even more apparent in the years following its announcement. The 25 States with laws prohibiting the conduct referenced in *Bowers* are reduced now to 13, of which 4 enforce their laws only against homosexual conduct. In those States, including Texas, that still proscribe sodomy (whether for same-sex or heterosexual conduct), there is a pattern of nonenforcement with respect to consenting adults acting in private. *Casey, supra,* at 851—which confirmed that the Due Process Clause protects personal decisions relating to marriage, procreation, contraception, family relationships, child rearing, and education—and *Romer v. Evans,* 517 U.S. 620, 624—which struck down class-based legislation directed at homosexuals—cast *Bowers'* holding into even more doubt. The stigma the Texas criminal statute imposes, moreover, is not trivial. Although the offense is but a minor misdemeanor, it remains a criminal offense with all that imports for the dignity of the persons charged, including notation of convictions on their records and on job application forms, and registration as sex offenders under state law. Where a case's foundations have sustained serious erosion, criticism from other sources is of greater significance. In the United States, criticism of *Bowers* has been substantial and continuing, disapproving of its reasoning in all respects, not just as to its historical assumptions. And, to the extent *Bowers* relied on values shared with a wider civilization, the case's reasoning and holding have been rejected by the European Court of Human Rights, and that other nations have taken action consistent with an affirmation of the protected right of homosexual adults to engage in intimate, consensual conduct. There has been no showing that in this country the governmental interest in circumscribing personal choice is somehow more legitimate or urgent. *Stare decisis* is not an inexorable command. *Payne v. Tennessee,* 501 U.S. 808, 828. *Bowers'* holding has not induced detrimental reliance of the sort that could counsel against overturning it once there are compelling reasons to do so. *Casey, supra,* at 855–856. *Bowers* causes uncertainty, for the precedents before and after it contradict its central holding. Pp. 12–17.

(d) *Bowers'* rationale does not withstand careful analysis. In his dissenting opinion in *Bowers, Justice Stevens* concluded that (1) the fact a State's governing majority has traditionally viewed a particular practice as immoral is not a sufficient reason for upholding a law prohibiting the practice, and (2) individual decisions concerning the intimacies of physical relationships, even when not intended to produce offspring, are a form of "liberty" protected by due process. That analysis should have controlled *Bowers,* and it controls here. *Bowers* was not correct when it was decided, is not correct today, and is hereby overruled. This case does not involve minors, persons who might be injured or coerced, those who might not easily refuse consent, or public conduct or prostitution. It does involve two adults who, with full and mutual consent, engaged in sexual practices common to a homosexual lifestyle. Petitioners' right to liberty under the Due Process Clause gives them the full right to engage in private conduct without government intervention. *Casey, supra,* at 847. The Texas statute furthers no legitimate state interest which can justify its intrusion into the individual's personal and private life. Pp. 17–18.

41 S.W. 3d 349, reversed and remanded.

KENNEDY, J., *delivered the opinion of the Court, in which* STEVENS, SOUTER, GINSBURG, *and* BREYER, JJ., *joined.* O'CONNOR, J., *filed an opinion concurring in the judgment.* SCALIA, J., *filed a dissenting opinion, in which* REHNQUIST, C.J., *and* THOMAS, J., *joined.* THOMAS, J., *filed a dissenting opinion.*

JUSTICE KENNEDY *delivered the opinion of the Court.*

Liberty protects the person from unwarranted government intrusions into a dwelling or other private places. In our tradition the State is not omnipresent in the home. And there are other spheres of our lives and existence, outside the home, where the State should not be a dominant presence. Freedom extends beyond spatial bounds. Liberty presumes an autonomy of self that includes freedom of thought, belief, expression, and certain intimate conduct. The instant case involves liberty of the person both in its spatial and more transcendent dimensions.

I

The question before the Court is the validity of a Texas statute making it a crime for two persons of the same sex to engage in certain intimate sexual conduct.

In Houston, Texas, officers of the Harris County Police Department were dispatched to a private residence in response to a reported weapons disturbance. They entered an apartment where one of the petitioners, John Geddes Lawrence, resided. The right of the police to enter does not seem to have been questioned. The officers observed Lawrence and another man, Tyron Garner, engaging in a sexual act. The two petitioners were arrested, held in custody overnight, and charged and convicted before a Justice of the Peace.

The complaints described their crime as "deviate sexual intercourse, namely anal sex, with a member of the same sex (man)." App. to Pet. for Cert. 127a, 139a. The applicable state law is Tex. Penal Code Ann. §21.06(a) (2003). It provides: "A person commits an offense if he engages in deviate sexual intercourse with another individual of the same sex." The statute defines "[d]eviate sexual intercourse" as follows:

"(A) any contact between any part of the genitals of one person and the mouth or anus of another person; or

"(B) the penetration of the genitals or the anus of another person with an object." §21.01(1).

The petitioners exercised their right to a trial *de novo* in Harris County Criminal Court. They challenged the statute as a violation of the Equal Protection Clause of the Fourteenth Amendment and of a like provision of the Texas Constitution. Tex. Const., Art. 1, §3a. Those contentions were rejected. The petitioners, having entered a plea of *nolo contendere,* were each fined $200 and assessed court costs of $141.25. App. to Pet. for Cert. 107a–110a.

The Court of Appeals for the Texas Fourteenth District considered the petitioners' federal constitutional arguments under both the Equal Protection and Due Process Clauses of the Fourteenth Amendment. After hearing the case en banc the court, in a divided opinion, rejected the constitutional arguments and affirmed the convictions. 41 S.W. 3d 349 (Tex. App. 2001). The majority opinion indicates that the Court of Appeals considered our decision in *Bowers v. Hardwick,* 478 U.S. 186 (1986), to be controlling on the federal due process aspect of the case. *Bowers* then being authoritative, this was proper.

We granted certiorari, 537 U.S. 1044 (2002), to consider three questions:

"1. Whether Petitioners' criminal convictions under the Texas 'Homosexual Conduct' law—which criminalizes sexual intimacy by same-sex couples, but not identical behavior by different-sex couples—violate the Fourteenth Amendment guarantee of equal protection of laws?

"2. Whether Petitioners' criminal convictions for adult consensual sexual intimacy in the home violate their vital interests in liberty and privacy protected by the Due Process Clause of the Fourteenth Amendment?

"3. Whether *Bowers v. Hardwick,* 478 U.S. 186 (1986), should be overruled?" Pet. for Cert. i.

The petitioners were adults at the time of the alleged offense. Their conduct was in private and consensual.

II

We conclude the case should be resolved by determining whether the petitioners were free as adults to engage in the private conduct in the exercise of their liberty under the Due Process Clause of the Fourteenth Amendment to the Constitution. For this inquiry we deem it necessary to reconsider the Court's holding in *Bowers.*

There are broad statements of the substantive reach of liberty under the Due Process Clause in earlier cases, including *Pierce v. Society of Sisters,* 268 U.S. 510 (1925), and *Meyer v. Nebraska,* 262 U.S. 390 (1923); but the most pertinent beginning point is our decision in *Griswold v. Connecticut,* 381 U.S. 479 (1965).

In *Griswold* the Court invalidated a state law prohibiting the use of drugs or devices of contraception and counseling or aiding and abetting the use of contraceptives. The Court described the protected interest as a right to privacy and placed emphasis on the marriage relation and the protected space of the marital bedroom. *Id.,* at 485.

After *Griswold* it was established that the right to make certain decisions regarding sexual conduct extends beyond the marital relationship. In *Eisenstadt v. Baird,* 405 U.S. 438 (1972), the Court invalidated a law prohibiting the distribution of contraceptives to unmarried persons. The case was decided under the Equal Protection Clause, *id.,* at 454; but with respect to unmarried persons, the Court went on to state the fundamental proposition that the law impaired the exercise of their personal rights, *ibid.* It quoted from the statement of the Court of Appeals finding the law to be in conflict with fundamental human rights, and it followed with this statement of its own:

"It is true that in *Griswold* the right of privacy in question inhered in the marital relationship.... If the right of privacy means anything, it is the right of the *individual,* married or single, to be free from unwarranted governmental intrusion into matters so fundamentally affecting a person as the decision whether to bear or beget a child." *Id.,* at 453.

The opinions in *Griswold* and *Eisenstadt* were part of the background for the decision in *Roe v. Wade,* 410 U.S. 113 (1973). As is well known, the case involved a challenge to the Texas law prohibiting abortions, but the laws of other States were affected as well. Although the Court held the woman's rights were not absolute, her right to elect an abortion did have real and substantial protection as an exercise of her liberty under the Due Process Clause. The Court cited cases that protect spatial freedom and cases that go well beyond it. *Roe* recognized the right of a woman to make certain fundamental decisions affecting her destiny and confirmed once more that the protection of liberty under the Due Process Clause has a substantive dimension of fundamental significance in defining the rights of the person.

In *Carey v. Population Services Int'l,* 431 U.S. 678 (1977), the Court confronted a New York law forbidding sale or distribution of contraceptive devices to persons under 16 years of age. Although there was no single opinion for the Court, the law was invalidated. Both *Eisenstadt* and *Carey,* as well as the holding and rationale in *Roe,* confirmed that the reasoning of *Griswold* could not be confined to the protection of rights of married adults. This was the state of the law with respect to some of the most relevant cases when the Court considered *Bowers v. Hardwick.*

The facts in *Bowers* had some similarities to the instant case. A police officer, whose right to enter seems not to have been in question, observed Hardwick, in his own bedroom, engaging in intimate sexual conduct with another adult male. The conduct was in violation of a Georgia statute making it a criminal offense to engage in sodomy. One difference between the two cases is that the Georgia statute prohibited the conduct whether or not the participants were of the same sex, while the Texas statute, as we have seen, applies only to participants of the same sex. Hardwick was not prosecuted, but he brought an action in federal court to declare the state statute invalid. He alleged he was a practicing homosexual and that the criminal prohibition violated rights guaranteed to him by the Constitution. The Court, in an opinion by Justice White, sustained the Georgia law. Chief Justice Burger and Justice Powell joined the opinion of the Court and filed separate, concurring opinions. Four Justices dissented. 478 U.S., at 199 (opinion of Blackmun, J., joined by Brennan, Marshall, and *Stevens,* JJ.); *id.,* at 214 (opinion of *Stevens,* J., joined by Brennan and Marshall, JJ.).

The Court began its substantive discussion in *Bowers* as follows: "The issue presented is whether the Federal Constitution confers a fundamental right upon homosexuals to engage in sodomy and hence invalidates the laws of the many States that still make such conduct illegal and have done so for a very long time." *Id.,* at 190. That statement, we now conclude, discloses the Court's own failure to appreciate the extent of the liberty at stake. To say that the issue in *Bowers* was simply the right to engage in certain sexual conduct demeans the claim the individual put forward, just as it would demean a married couple were it to be said marriage is simply about the right to have sexual intercourse. The laws involved in *Bowers* and here are, to be sure, statutes that purport to do no more than prohibit a particular sexual act. Their penalties and purposes, though, have more far-

reaching consequences, touching upon the most private human conduct, sexual behavior, and in the most private of places, the home. The statutes do seek to control a personal relationship that, whether or not entitled to formal recognition in the law, is within the liberty of persons to choose without being punished as criminals.

This, as a general rule, should counsel against attempts by the State, or a court, to define the meaning of the relationship or to set its boundaries absent injury to a person or abuse of an institution the law protects. It suffices for us to acknowledge that adults may choose to enter upon this relationship in the confines of their homes and their own private lives and still retain their dignity as free persons. When sexuality finds overt expression in intimate conduct with another person, the conduct can be but one element in a personal bond that is more enduring. The liberty protected by the Constitution allows homosexual persons the right to make this choice.

Having misapprehended the claim of liberty there presented to it, and thus stating the claim to be whether there is a fundamental right to engage in consensual sodomy, the *Bowers* Court said: "Proscriptions against that conduct have ancient roots." *Id.,* at 192. In academic writings, and in many of the scholarly *amicus* briefs filed to assist the Court in this case, there are fundamental criticisms of the historical premises relied upon by the majority and concurring opinions in *Bowers.* Brief for Cato Institute as *Amicus Curiae* 16–17; Brief for American Civil Liberties Union et al. as *Amici Curiae* 15–21; Brief for Professors of History et al. as *Amici Curiae* 3–10. We need not enter this debate in the attempt to reach a definitive historical judgment, but the following considerations counsel against adopting the definitive conclusions upon which *Bowers* placed such reliance.

At the outset it should be noted that there is no longstanding history in this country of laws directed at homosexual conduct as a distinct matter. Beginning in colonial times there were prohibitions of sodomy derived from the English criminal laws passed in the first instance by the Reformation Parliament of 1533. The English prohibition was understood to include relations between men and women as well as relations between men and men. See, *e.g., King v. Wiseman,* 92 Eng. Rep. 774, 775 (K. B. 1718) (interpreting "mankind" in Act of 1533 as including women and girls). Nineteenth-century commentators similarly read American sodomy, buggery, and crime-against-nature statutes as criminalizing certain relations between men and women and between men and men. See, *e.g.,* 2 J. Bishop, Criminal Law §1028 (1858); 2 J. Chitty, Criminal Law 47–50 (5th Am. ed. 1847); R. Desty, A Compendium of American Criminal Law 143 (1882); J. May, The Law of Crimes §203 (2d ed. 1893). The absence of legal prohibitions focusing on homosexual conduct may be explained in part by noting that according to some scholars the concept of the homosexual as a distinct category of person did not emerge until the late 19th century. See, *e.g.,* J. Katz, The Invention of Heterosexuality 10 (1995); J. D'Emilio & E. Freedman, Intimate Matters: A History of Sexuality in America 121 (2d ed. 1997) ("The modern terms *homosexuality* and *heterosexuality* do not apply to an era that had not yet articulated these distinctions"). Thus early American sodomy laws were not directed at homosexuals as such but instead sought to prohibit nonprocreative sexual activity more generally. This does not suggest approval of homosexual conduct. It does tend to show that this particular form of conduct was not thought of as a separate category from like conduct between heterosexual persons.

Laws prohibiting sodomy do not seem to have been enforced against consenting adults acting in private. A substantial number of sodomy prosecutions and convictions for which there are surviving records were for predatory acts against those who could not or did not consent, as in the case of a minor or the victim of an assault. As to these, one purpose for the prohibitions was to ensure there would be no lack of coverage if a predator committed a sexual assault that did not constitute rape as defined by the criminal law. Thus the model sodomy indictments presented in a 19th-century treatise, see 2 Chitty, *supra*, at 49, addressed the predatory acts of an adult man against a minor girl or minor boy. Instead of targeting relations between consenting adults in private, 19th-century sodomy prosecutions typically involved relations between men and minor girls or minor boys, relations between adults involving force, relations between adults implicating disparity in status, or relations between men and animals.

To the extent that there were any prosecutions for the acts in question, 19th-century evidence rules imposed a burden that would make a conviction more difficult to obtain even taking into account the problems always inherent in prosecuting consensual acts committed in private. Under then-prevailing standards, a man could not be convicted of sodomy based upon testimony of a consenting partner, because the partner was considered an accomplice. A partner's testimony, however, was admissible if he or she had not consented to the act or was a minor, and therefore incapable of consent. See, *e.g.,* F. Wharton, Criminal Law 443 (2d ed. 1852); 1 F. Wharton, Criminal Law 512 (8th ed. 1880). The rule may explain in part the infrequency of these prosecutions. In all events that infrequency makes it difficult to say that society approved of a rigorous and systematic punishment of the consensual acts committed in private and by adults. The longstanding criminal prohibition of homosexual sodomy upon which the *Bowers* decision placed such reliance is as consistent with a general condemnation of nonprocreative sex as it is with an established tradition of prosecuting acts because of their homosexual character.

The policy of punishing consenting adults for private acts was not much discussed in the early legal literature. We can infer that one reason for this was the very private nature of the conduct. Despite the absence of prosecutions, there may have been periods in which there was public criticism of homosexuals as such and an insistence that the criminal laws be enforced to discourage their practices. But far from possessing "ancient roots," *Bowers,* 478 U.S., at 192, American laws targeting same-sex couples did not develop until the last third of the 20th century. The reported decisions concerning the prosecution of consensual, homosexual sodomy between adults for the years 1880–1995 are not always clear in the details, but a significant number involved conduct in a public place. See Brief for American Civil Liberties Union et al. as *Amici Curiae* 14–15, and n. 18.

It was not until the 1970's that any State singled out same-sex relations for criminal prosecution, and only nine States have done so. See 1977 Ark. Gen. Acts no. 828; 1983 Kan. Sess. Laws p. 652; 1974 Ky. Acts p. 847; 1977 Mo. Laws p. 687; 1973 Mont. Laws p. 1339; 1977 Nev. Stats. p. 1632; 1989 Tenn. Pub. Acts ch. 591; 1973 Tex. Gen. Laws ch. 399; see also *Post v. State,* 715 P. 2d 1105 (Okla. Crim. App. 1986) (sodomy law invalidated as applied to different-sex couples). Post-*Bowers* even some of these States did not adhere to the policy of suppressing homosexual conduct. Over the course of the last decades, States with same-sex prohibitions have moved toward abolishing them. See, *e.g., Jegley v. Picado,* 349 Ark. 600, 80 S. W. 3d 332 (2002); *Gryczan v. State,* 283 Mont. 433, 942 P. 2d 112 (1997); *Campbell v. Sundquist,* 926 S. W. 2d 250 (Tenn. App. 1996); *Commonwealth v. Wasson,* 842 S. W. 2d 487 (Ky. 1992); see also 1993 Nev. Stats. p. 518 (repealing Nev. Rev. Stat. § 201.193).

In summary, the historical grounds relied upon in *Bowers* are more complex than the majority opinion and the concurring opinion by Chief Justice Burger indicate. Their historical premises are not without doubt and, at the very least, are overstated.

It must be acknowledged, of course, that the Court in *Bowers* was making the broader point that for centuries there have been powerful voices to condemn homosexual conduct as immoral. The condemnation has been shaped by religious beliefs, conceptions of right and acceptable behavior, and respect for the traditional family. For many persons these are not trivial concerns but profound and deep convictions accepted as ethical and moral principles to which they aspire and which thus determine the course of their lives. These considerations do not answer the question before us, however. The issue is whether the majority may use the power of the State to enforce these views on the whole society through operation of the criminal law. "Our obligation is to define the liberty of all, not to mandate our own moral code." *Planned Parenthood of Southeastern Pa. v. Casey,* 505 U.S. 833, 850 (1992).

Chief Justice Burger joined the opinion for the Court in *Bowers* and further explained his views as follows: "Decisions of individuals relating to homosexual conduct have been subject to state intervention throughout the history of Western civilization. Condemnation of those practices is firmly rooted in Judeao-Christian moral and ethical standards." 478 U.S., at 196. As with Justice White's assumptions about history, scholarship casts some doubt on the sweeping nature of the statement by Chief Justice Burger as it pertains to private homosexual conduct between consenting adults. See, *e.g.,* Eskridge, Hardwick and Historiography, 1999 U. Ill. L. Rev. 631, 656. In all events we think that our laws and traditions in the past half century are of most relevance here. These references show an emerging awareness that liberty gives substantial protection to adult persons in deciding how to conduct their private lives in matters pertaining to sex. "[H]istory and tradition are the starting point but not in all cases the ending point of the substantive due process inquiry." *County of Sacramento v. Lewis,* 523 U.S. 833, 857 (1998) (*Kennedy, J.,* concurring).

This emerging recognition should have been apparent when *Bowers* was decided. In 1955 the American Law Institute promulgated the Model Penal Code and made clear that it did not recommend or provide for "criminal penalties for consensual sexual relations conducted in private." ALI, Model Penal Code §213.2, Comment 2, p. 372 (1980). It justified its decision on three grounds: (1) The prohibitions undermined respect for the law by penalizing conduct many people engaged in; (2) the statutes regulated private conduct not harmful to others; and (3) the laws were arbitrarily enforced and thus invited the danger of blackmail. ALI, Model Penal Code, Commentary 277–280 (Tent. Draft No. 4, 1955). In 1961 Illinois changed its laws to conform to the Model Penal Code. Other States soon followed. Brief for Cato Institute as *Amicus Curiae* 15–16.

In *Bowers* the Court referred to the fact that before 1961 all 50 States had outlawed sodomy, and that at the time of the Court's decision 24 States and the District of Columbia had sodomy laws. 478 U.S., at 192–193. Justice Powell pointed out that these prohibitions often were being ignored, however. Georgia, for instance, had not sought to enforce its law for decades. *Id.,* at 197–198, n. 2 ("The history of nonenforcement suggests the moribund character today of laws criminalizing this type of private, consensual conduct").

The sweeping references by Chief Justice Burger to the history of Western civilization and to Judeo-Christian moral and ethical standards did not take account of other authorities pointing in an opposite direction. A committee advising the British Parliament recommended in 1957 repeal of laws punishing homosexual conduct. The Wolfenden Report: Report of the Committee on Homosexual Offenses and Prostitution (1963). Parliament enacted the substance of those recommendations 10 years later. Sexual Offences Act 1967, §1.

Of even more importance, almost five years before *Bowers* was decided the European Court of Human Rights considered a case with parallels to *Bowers* and to today's case. An adult male resident in Northern Ireland alleged he was a practicing homosexual who desired to engage in consensual homosexual conduct. The laws of Northern Ireland forbade him that right. He alleged that he had been questioned, his home had been searched, and he feared criminal prosecution. The court held that the laws proscribing the conduct were invalid under the European Convention on Human Rights. *Dudgeon v. United Kingdom,* 45 Eur. Ct. H. R. (1981) ¶ ; 52. Authoritative in all countries that are members of the Council of Europe (21 nations then, 45 nations now), the decision is at odds with the premise in *Bowers* that the claim put forward was insubstantial in our Western civilization.

In our own constitutional system the deficiencies in *Bowers* became even more apparent in the years following its announcement. The 25 States with laws prohibiting the relevant conduct referenced in the *Bowers* decision are reduced now to 13, of which 4 enforce their laws only against homosexual conduct. In those States where sodomy is still proscribed, whether for same-sex or heterosexual conduct, there is a pattern of nonenforcement with respect to consenting adults acting in private. The State of Texas admitted in 1994 that as of that date it had not prosecuted anyone under those circumstances. *State v. Morales,* 869 S. W. 2d 941, 943.

Two principal cases decided after *Bowers* cast its holding into even more doubt. In *Planned Parenthood of Southeastern Pa. v. Casey,* 505 U.S. 833 (1992), the Court reaffirmed the substantive force of the liberty protected by the Due Process Clause. The *Casey* decision again confirmed that our laws and tradition afford constitutional protection to personal decisions relating to marriage, procreation, contraception, family relationships, child rearing, and education. *Id.,* at 851. In explaining the respect the Constitution demands for the autonomy of the person in making these choices, we stated as follows:

"These matters, involving the most intimate and personal choices a person may make in a lifetime, choices central to personal dignity and autonomy, are central to the liberty protected by the Fourteenth Amendment. At the heart of liberty is the right to define one's own concept of existence, of meaning, of the universe, and of the mystery of human life. Beliefs about these matters could not define the attributes of personhood were they formed under compulsion of the State." *Ibid.*

Persons in a homosexual relationship may seek autonomy for these purposes, just as heterosexual persons do. The decision in *Bowers* would deny them this right.

The second post-*Bowers* case of principal relevance is *Romer v. Evans,* 517 U.S. 620 (1996). There the Court struck down class-based legislation directed at homosexuals as a violation of the Equal Protection Clause. *Romer* invalidated an amendment to Colorado's constitution which named as a solitary class persons who were homosexuals, lesbians, or bisexual either by "orientation, conduct, practices or relationships," *id.,* at 624 (internal quotation marks omitted), and deprived them of protection under state antidiscrimination laws. We concluded that the provision was "born of animosity toward the class of persons affected" and further that it had no rational relation to a legitimate governmental purpose. *Id.,* at 634.

As an alternative argument in this case, counsel for the petitioners and some *amici* contend that *Romer* provides the basis for declaring the Texas statute invalid under the Equal Protection Clause. That is a tenable argument, but we conclude the instant case requires us to address whether *Bowers* itself has continuing validity. Were we to hold the statute invalid under the Equal Protection Clause some might question whether a prohibition would be valid if drawn differently, say, to prohibit the conduct both between same-sex and different-sex participants.

Equality of treatment and the due process right to demand respect for conduct protected by the substantive guarantee of liberty are linked in important respects, and a decision on the latter point advances both interests. If protected conduct is made criminal and the law which does so remains unexamined for its substantive validity, its stigma might remain even if it were not enforceable as drawn for equal protection reasons. When homosexual conduct is made criminal by the law of the State, that declaration in and of itself is an invita-

tion to subject homosexual persons to discrimination both in the public and in the private spheres. The central holding of *Bowers* has been brought in question by this case, and it should be addressed. Its continuance as precedent demeans the lives of homosexual persons.

The stigma this criminal statute imposes, moreover, is not trivial. The offense, to be sure, is but a class C misdemeanor, a minor offense in the Texas legal system. Still, it remains a criminal offense with all that imports for the dignity of the persons charged. The petitioners will bear on their record the history of their criminal convictions. Just this Term we rejected various challenges to state laws requiring the registration of sex offenders. *Smith v. Doe,* 538 U.S. __ (2003); *Connecticut Dept. of Public Safety v. Doe,* 538 U.S. 1 (2003). We are advised that if Texas convicted an adult for private, consensual homosexual conduct under the statute here in question the convicted person would come within the registration laws of a least four States were he or she to be subject to their jurisdiction. Pet. for Cert. 13, and n. 12 (citing Idaho Code §§18-8301 to 18-8326 (Cum. Supp. 2002); La. Code Crim. Proc. Ann., §§15:540-15:549 (West 2003); Miss. Code Ann. §§45-33-21 to 45-33-57 (Lexis 2003); S. C. Code Ann. §§23-3-400 to 23-3-490 (West 2002)). This underscores the consequential nature of the punishment and the state-sponsored condemnation attendant to the criminal prohibition. Furthermore, the Texas criminal conviction carries with it the other collateral consequences always following a conviction, such as notations on job application forms, to mention but one example.

The foundations of *Bowers* have sustained serious erosion from our recent decisions in *Casey* and *Romer.* When our precedent has been thus weakened, criticism from other sources is of greater significance. In the United States criticism of *Bowers* has been substantial and continuing, disapproving of its reasoning in all respects, not just as to its historical assumptions. See, *e.g.,* C. Fried, Order and Law: Arguing the Reagan Revolution—A Firsthand Account 81–84 (1991); R. Posner, Sex and Reason 341–350 (1992). The courts of five different States have declined to follow it in interpreting provisions in their own state constitutions parallel to the Due Process Clause of the Fourteenth Amendment, see *Jegley v. Picado,* 349 Ark. 600, 80 S. W. 3d 332 (2002); *Powell v. State,* 270 Ga. 327, 510 S. E. 2d 18, 24 (1998); *Gryczan v. State,* 283 Mont. 433, 942 P. 2d 112 (1997); *Campbell v. Sundquist,* 926 S. W. 2d 250 (Tenn. App. 1996); *Commonwealth v. Wasson,* 842 S. W. 2d 487 (Ky. 1992).

To the extent *Bowers* relied on values we share with a wider civilization, it should be noted that the reasoning and holding in *Bowers* have been rejected elsewhere. The European Court of Human Rights has followed not *Bowers* but its own decision in *Dudgeon v. United Kingdom.* See *P. G. & J. H. v. United Kingdom,* App. No. 00044787/98, ¶ ; 56 (Eur. Ct. H. R., Sept. 25, 2001); *Modinos v. Cyprus,* 259 Eur. Ct. H. R. (1993); *Norris v. Ireland,* 142 Eur. Ct. H. R. (1988). Other nations, too, have taken action consistent with an affirmation of the protected right of homosexual adults to engage in intimate, consensual conduct. See Brief for Mary Robinson et al. as *Amici Curiae* 11–12. The right the petitioners seek in this case has been accepted as an integral part of human freedom in many other countries. There has been no showing that in this country the governmental interest in circumscribing personal choice is somehow more legitimate or urgent.

The doctrine of *stare decisis* is essential to the respect accorded to the judgments of the Court and to the stability of the law. It is not, however, an inexorable command. *Payne v. Tennessee,* 501 U.S. 808, 828 (1991) ("*Stare decisis* is not an inexorable command; rather, it 'is a principle of policy and not a mechanical formula of adherence to the latest decision'") (quoting *Helvering v. Hallock,* 309 U.S. 106, 119 (1940))). In *Casey* we noted that when a Court is asked to overrule a precedent recognizing a constitutional liberty interest, individual or societal reliance on the existence of that liberty cautions with particular strength against reversing course. 505 U.S., at 855–856; see also *id.,* at 844 ("Liberty finds no refuge in a jurisprudence of doubt"). The holding in *Bowers,* however, has not induced detrimental reliance comparable to some instances where recognized individual rights are involved. Indeed, there has been no individual or societal reliance on *Bowers* of the sort that could counsel against overturning its holding once there are compelling reasons to do so. *Bowers* itself causes uncertainty, for the precedents before and after its issuance contradict its central holding.

The rationale of *Bowers* does not withstand careful analysis. In his dissenting opinion in *Bowers, Justice Stevens* came to these conclusions:

Our prior cases make two propositions abundantly clear. First, the fact that the governing majority in a State has traditionally viewed a particular practice as immoral is not a sufficient reason for upholding a law prohibiting the practice; neither history nor tradition could save a law prohibiting miscegenation from constitutional attack. Second, individual decisions by married persons, concerning the intimacies of their physical relationship, even when not intended to produce offspring, are a form of 'liberty' protected by the Due Process Clause of the Fourteenth Amendment. Moreover, this protection extends to intimate choices by unmarried as well as married persons. 478 U.S., at 216 (footnotes and citations omitted).

Justice Stevens' analysis, in our view, should have been controlling in *Bowers* and should control here.

Bowers was not correct when it was decided, and it is not correct today. It ought not to remain binding precedent. *Bowers v. Hardwick* should be and now is overruled.

The present case does not involve minors. It does not involve persons who might be injured or coerced or who are situated in relationships where consent might not easily be refused. It does not involve public conduct or prostitution. It does not involve whether the government must give formal recognition to any relationship that homosexual persons seek to enter. The case does involve two adults who, with full and mutual consent from each other, engaged in sexual practices common to a homosexual lifestyle. The petitioners are entitled to respect for their private lives. The State cannot demean their existence or control their destiny by making their private sexual conduct a crime. Their right to liberty under the Due Process Clause gives them the full right to engage in their conduct without intervention of the government. "It is a promise of the Constitution that there is a realm of personal liberty which the government may not enter." *Casey, supra,* at 847. The Texas statute furthers no legitimate state interest which can justify its intrusion into the personal and private life of the individual.

Had those who drew and ratified the Due Process Clauses of the Fifth Amendment or the Fourteenth Amendment known the components of liberty in its manifold possibilities, they might have been more specific. They did not presume to have this insight. They knew times can blind us to certain truths and later generations can see that laws once thought necessary and proper in fact serve only to oppress. As the Constitution endures, persons in every generation can invoke its principles in their own search for greater freedom.

The judgment of the Court of Appeals for the Texas Fourteenth District is reversed, and the case is remanded for further proceedings not inconsistent with this opinion.

It is so ordered.

JUSTICE O'CONNOR, *concurring in the judgment.*

The Court today overrules *Bowers v. Hardwick,* 478 U.S. 186 (1986). I joined *Bowers,* and do not join the Court in overruling it. Nevertheless, I agree with the Court that Texas' statute banning same-sex sodomy is unconstitutional. See Tex. Penal Code Ann. §21.06 (2003).

Rather than relying on the substantive component of the Fourteenth Amendment's Due Process Clause, as the Court does, I base my conclusion on the Fourteenth Amendment's Equal Protection Clause.

The Equal Protection Clause of the Fourteenth Amendment "is essentially a direction that all persons similarly situated should be treated alike." *Cleburne v. Cleburne Living Center, Inc.,* 473 U.S. 432, 439 (1985); see also *Plyler v. Doe,* 457 U.S. 202, 216 (1982). Under our rational basis standard of review, "legislation is presumed to be valid and will be sustained if the classification drawn by the statute is rationally related to a legitimate state interest." *Cleburne v. Cleburne Living Center, supra,* at 440; see also *Department of Agriculture v. Moreno,* 413 U.S. 528, 534 (1973); *Romer v. Evans,* 517 U.S. 620, 632–633 (1996); *Nordlinger v. Hahn,* 505 U.S. 1, 11–12 (1992).

Laws such as economic or tax legislation that are scrutinized under rational basis review normally pass constitutional muster, since "the Constitution presumes that even improvident decisions will eventually be rectified by the democratic processes." *Cleburne v. Cleburne Living Center, supra,* at 440; see also *Fitzgerald v. Racing Assn. of Central Iowa, ante,* p. ___; *Williamson v. Lee Optical of Okla., Inc.,* 348 U.S. 483 (1955). We have consistently held, however, that some objectives, such as "a bare . . . desire to harm a politically unpopular group," are not legitimate state interests. *Department of Agriculture v. Moreno, supra,* at 534. See also *Cleburne v. Cleburne Living Center, supra,* at 446–447; *Romer v. Evans, supra,* at 632. When a law exhibits such a desire to harm a politically unpopular group, we have applied a more searching form of rational basis review to strike down such laws under the Equal Protection Clause.

We have been most likely to apply rational basis review to hold a law unconstitutional under the Equal Protection Clause where, as here, the challenged legislation inhibits personal relationships. In *Department of Agriculture v. Moreno,* for example, we held that a law preventing those households containing an individual unrelated to any other member of the household from receiving food stamps violated equal protection because the purpose of the law was to " 'discriminate against hippies.' " 413 U.S., at 534. The asserted governmental interest in preventing food stamp fraud was not deemed sufficient to satisfy rational basis review. *Id.,* at 535–538. In *Eisenstadt v. Baird,* 405 U.S. 438, 447–455 (1972), we refused to sanction a law that discriminated between married and unmarried persons by prohibiting the distribution of contraceptives to single persons. Likewise, in *Cleburne v. Cleburne Living Center, supra,* we held that it was irrational for a State to require a home for the mentally disabled to obtain a special use permit when other residences—like fraternity houses and apartment buildings—did not have to obtain such a permit. And in *Romer v. Evans,* we disallowed a state statute that "impos[ed] a broad and undifferentiated disability on a single named group"—specifically, homosexuals. 517 U.S., at 632. The dissent apparently agrees that if these cases have *stare decisis* effect, Texas' sodomy law would not pass scrutiny under the Equal Protection Clause, regardless of the type of rational basis review that we apply. See *post,* at 17–18 (opinion of Scalia, J.).

The statute at issue here makes sodomy a crime only if a person "engages in deviate sexual intercourse with another individual of the same sex." Tex. Penal Code Ann. §21.06(a) (2003). Sodomy between opposite-sex partners, however, is not a crime in Texas. That is, Texas treats the same conduct differently based solely on the participants. Those harmed by this law are people who have a same-sex sexual orientation and thus are more likely to engage in behavior prohibited by §21.06.

The Texas statute makes homosexuals unequal in the eyes of the law by making particular conduct—and only that conduct—subject to criminal sanction. It appears that prosecutions under Texas' sodomy law are rare. See *State v. Morales,* 869 S. W. 2d 941, 943 (Tex. 1994) (noting in 1994 that §21.06 "has not been, and in all probability will not be, enforced against private consensual conduct between adults"). This case shows, however, that prosecutions under §21.06 *do* occur. And while the penalty imposed on petitioners in this case was relatively minor, the consequences of conviction are not. As the Court notes, see *ante,* at 15, petitioners' convictions, if upheld, would disqualify them from or restrict their ability to engage in a variety of professions, including medicine, athletic training, and interior design. See, *e.g.,* Tex. Occ. Code Ann. §164.051(a)(2)(B) (2003 Pamphlet) (physician); §451.251 (a)(1) (athletic trainer); §1053.252(2) (interior designer). Indeed, were petitioners to move to one of four States, their convictions would require them to register as sex offenders to local law enforcement. See, *e.g.,* Idaho Code §18-8304 (Cum. Supp. 2002); La. Stat. Ann. §15:542 (West Cum. Supp. 2003); Miss. Code Ann. §45-33-25 (West 2003); S. C. Code Ann. §23-3-430 (West Cum. Supp. 2002); cf. *ante,* at 15.

And the effect of Texas' sodomy law is not just limited to the threat of prosecution or consequence of conviction. Texas' sodomy law brands all homosexuals as criminals, thereby making it more difficult for homosexuals to be treated in the same manner as everyone else. Indeed, Texas itself has previously acknowledged the collateral effects of the law, stipulating in a prior challenge to this action that the law "legally sanctions discrimination against [homosexuals] in a variety of ways unrelated to the criminal law," including in the areas of "employment, family issues, and housing." *State v. Morales,* 826 S. W. 2d 201, 203 (Tex. App. 1992).

Texas attempts to justify its law, and the effects of the law, by arguing that the statute satisfies rational basis review because it furthers the legitimate governmental interest of the promotion of morality. In *Bowers,* we held that a state law criminalizing sodomy as applied to homosexual couples did not violate substantive due process. We rejected the argument that no rational basis existed to justify the law, pointing to the government's interest in promoting morality. 478 U.S., at 196. The only question in front of the Court in *Bowers* was whether the substantive component of the Due Process Clause protected a right to engage in homosexual sodomy. *Id.,* at 188, n. 2. *Bowers* did not hold that moral disapproval of a group is a rational basis under the Equal Protection Clause to criminalize homosexual sodomy when heterosexual sodomy is not punished.

This case raises a different issue than *Bowers:* whether, under the Equal Protection Clause, moral disapproval is a legitimate state interest to justify by itself a statute that bans homosexual sodomy, but not heterosexual sodomy. It is not. Moral disapproval of this group, like a bare desire to harm the group, is an interest that is insufficient to satisfy rational basis review under the Equal Protection Clause. See, *e.g., Department of Agriculture v. Moreno, supra,* at 534; *Romer v. Evans,* 517 U.S., at 634–635. Indeed, we have never held that moral disapproval, without any other asserted state interest, is a sufficient rationale under the Equal Protection Clause to justify a law that discriminates among groups of persons.

Moral disapproval of a group cannot be a legitimate governmental interest under the Equal Protection Clause because legal classifications must not be "drawn for the purpose of disadvantaging the group burdened by the law." *Id.,* at 633. Texas' invocation of moral disapproval as a legitimate state interest proves nothing more than Texas' desire to criminalize homosexual sodomy. But the Equal Protection Clause prevents a State from creating "a classification of persons undertaken for its own sake." *Id.,* at 635. And because Texas so rarely enforces its sodomy law as applied to private, consensual acts, the law serves more as a statement of dislike and disapproval against homosexuals than as a tool to stop criminal behavior. The Texas sodomy law "raise[s] the inevitable inference that the disadvantage imposed is born of animosity toward the class of persons affected." *Id.,* at 634.

Texas argues, however, that the sodomy law does not discriminate against homosexual persons. Instead, the State maintains that the law discriminates only against homosexual conduct. While it is true that the law applies only to conduct, the conduct targeted by this law is conduct that is closely correlated with being homosexual. Under such circumstances, Texas' sodomy law is targeted at more than conduct. It is instead directed toward gay persons as a class. "After all, there can hardly be more palpable discrimination against a class than making the conduct that defines the class criminal." *Id.,* at 641 (*Scalia, J.,* dissenting) (internal quotation marks omitted). When a State makes homosexual conduct criminal, and not "deviate sexual intercourse" committed by persons of different sexes, "that declaration in and of itself is an invitation to subject homosexual persons to discrimination both in the public and in the private spheres." *Ante,* at 14.

Indeed, Texas law confirms that the sodomy statute is directed toward homosexuals as a class. In Texas, calling a person a homosexual is slander *per se* because the word "homosexual" "impute[s] the commission of a crime." *Plumley v. Landmark Chevrolet, Inc.,* 122 F. 3d 308, 310 (CA5 1997) (applying Texas law); see also *Head v. Newton,* 596 S. W. 2d 209, 210 (Tex. App. 1980). The State has admitted that because of the sodomy law, *being* homosexual carries the presumption of being a criminal. See *State v. Morales,* 826 S. W. 2d, at 202–203 ("[T]he statute brands lesbians and gay men as criminals and thereby legally sanctions discrimination against them in a variety of ways unrelated to the criminal law"). Texas' sodomy law therefore results in discrimination against homosexuals as a class in an array of areas outside the criminal law. See *ibid.* In *Romer v. Evans,* we refused to sanction a law that singled out homosexuals "for disfavored legal status." 517 U.S., at 633. The same is true here. The Equal Protection Clause " 'neither knows nor tolerates classes among citizens.' " *Id.,* at 623 (quoting *Plessy v. Ferguson,* 163 U.S. 537, 559 (1896) (Harlan, J. dissenting)).

A State can of course assign certain consequences to a violation of its criminal law. But the State cannot single out one identifiable class of citizens for punishment that does not apply to everyone else, with moral disapproval as the only asserted state interest for the law. The Texas sodomy statute subjects homosexuals to "a lifelong penalty and stigma. A legislative classification that threatens the creation of an underclass ... cannot be reconciled with" the Equal Protection Clause. *Plyler v. Doe,* 457 U.S., at 239 (Powell, J., concurring).

Whether a sodomy law that is neutral both in effect and application, see *Yick Wo v. Hopkins,* 118 U.S. 356 (1886), would violate the substantive component of the Due Process Clause is an issue that need not be decided today. I am confident, however, that so long as the Equal Protection Clause requires a sodomy law to apply equally to the private consensual conduct of homosexuals and heterosexuals alike, such a law would not long stand in our democratic society. In the words of Justice Jackson:

"The framers of the Constitution knew, and we should not forget today, that there is no more effective practical guaranty against arbitrary and unreasonable government than to require that the principles of law which officials would impose upon a minority be imposed generally. Conversely, nothing opens the door to arbitrary action so effectively as to allow those officials to pick and choose only a few to whom they will apply legislation and thus to escape the political retribution that might be visited upon them if larger numbers were affected." *Railway Express Agency, Inc. v. New York,* 336 U.S. 106, 112–113 (1949) (concurring opinion).

That this law as applied to private, consensual conduct is unconstitutional under the Equal Protection Clause does not mean that other laws distinguishing between heterosexuals and homosexuals would similarly fail under rational basis review. Texas cannot assert any legitimate state interest here, such as national security or preserving the traditional institution of marriage. Unlike the moral disapproval of same-sex relations—the asserted state interest in this case—

other reasons exist to promote the institution of marriage beyond mere moral disapproval of an excluded group.

A law branding one class of persons as criminal solely based on the State's moral disapproval of that class and the conduct associated with that class runs contrary to the values of the Constitution and the Equal Protection Clause, under any standard of review. I therefore concur in the Court's judgment that Texas' sodomy law banning "deviate sexual intercourse" between consenting adults of the same sex, but not between consenting adults of different sexes, is unconstitutional.

JUSTICE SCALIA, *with whom* THE CHIEF JUSTICE *and* JUSTICE THOMAS *join, dissenting.*

"Liberty finds no refuge in a jurisprudence of doubt." *Planned Parenthood of Southeastern Pa. v. Casey,* 505 U.S. 833, 844 (1992). That was the Court's sententious response, barely more than a decade ago, to those seeking to overrule *Roe v. Wade,* 410 U.S. 113 (1973). The Court's response today, to those who have engaged in a 17-year crusade to overrule *Bowers v. Hardwick,* 478 U.S. 186 (1986), is very different. The need for stability and certainty presents no barrier.

Most of the rest of today's opinion has no relevance to its actual holding—that the Texas statute "furthers no legitimate state interest which can justify" its application to petitioners under rational-basis review. *Ante,* at 18 (overruling *Bowers* to the extent it sustained Georgia's anti-sodomy statute under the rational-basis test). Though there is discussion of "fundamental proposition[s]," *ante,* at 4, and "fundamental decisions," *ibid.* nowhere does the Court's opinion declare that homosexual sodomy is a "fundamental right" under the Due Process Clause; nor does it subject the Texas law to the standard of review that would be appropriate (strict scrutiny) if homosexual sodomy *were* a "fundamental right." Thus, while overruling the *outcome* of *Bowers,* the Court leaves strangely untouched its central legal conclusion: "[R]espondent would have us announce . . . a fundamental right to engage in homosexual sodomy. This we are quite unwilling to do." 478 U.S., at 191. Instead the Court simply describes petitioners' conduct as "an exercise of their liberty"—which it undoubtedly is—and proceeds to apply an unheard-of form of rational-basis review that will have far-reaching implications beyond this case. *Ante,* at 3.

I

I begin with the Court's surprising readiness to reconsider a decision rendered a mere 17 years ago in *Bowers v. Hardwick.* I do not myself believe in rigid adherence to *stare decisis* in constitutional cases; but I do believe that we should be consistent rather than manipulative in invoking the doctrine. Today's opinions in support of reversal do not bother to distinguish—or indeed, even bother to mention—the paean to *stare decisis* coauthored by three Members of today's majority in *Planned Parenthood v. Casey.* There, when *stare decisis* meant preservation of judicially invented abortion rights, the widespread criticism of *Roe* was strong reason to *reaffirm* it:

"Where, in the performance of its judicial duties, the Court decides a case in such a way as to resolve the sort of intensely divisive controversy reflected in *Roe*[,] . . . its decision has a dimension that the resolution of the normal case does not carry. . . . [T]o overrule under fire in the absence of the most compelling reason . . . would subvert the Court's legitimacy beyond any serious question." 505 U.S., at 866–867.

Today, however, the widespread opposition to *Bowers,* a decision resolving an issue as "intensely divisive" as the issue in *Roe,* is offered as a reason in favor of *overruling* it. See *ante,* at 15–16. Gone, too, is any "enquiry" (of the sort conducted in *Casey*) into whether the decision sought to be overruled has "proven 'unworkable,'" *Casey, supra,* at 855.

Today's approach to *stare decisis* invites us to overrule an erroneously decided precedent (including an "intensely divisive" decision) *if:* (1) its foundations have been "eroded" by subsequent decisions,

ante, at 15; (2) it has been subject to "substantial and continuing" criticism, *ibid.;* and (3) it has not induced "individual or societal reliance" that counsels against overturning, *ante,* at 16. The problem is that *Roe* itself—which today's majority surely has no disposition to overrule—satisfies these conditions to at least the same degree as *Bowers.*

(1) A preliminary digressive observation with regard to the first factor: The Court's claim that *Planned Parenthood v. Casey, supra,* "casts some doubt" upon the holding in *Bowers* (or any other case, for that matter) does not withstand analysis. *Ante,* at 10. As far as its holding is concerned, *Casey* provided a *less* expansive right to abortion than did *Roe,* which was already on the books when *Bowers* was decided. And if the Court is referring not to the holding of *Casey,* but to the dictum of its famed sweet-mystery-of-life passage, *ante,* at 13 ("'At the heart of liberty is the right to define one's own concept of existence, of meaning, of the universe, and of the mystery of human life'"): That "casts some doubt" upon either the totality of our jurisprudence or else (presumably the right answer) nothing at all. I have never heard of a law that attempted to restrict one's "right to define" certain concepts; and if the passage calls into question the government's power to regulate *actions based on* one's self-defined "concept of existence, etc.," it is the passage that ate the rule of law.

I do not quarrel with the Court's claim that *Romer v. Evans,* 517 U.S. 620 (1996), "eroded" the "foundations" of *Bowers*' rational-basis holding. See *Romer, supra,* at 640–643 (Scalia, J., dissenting).) But *Roe* and *Casey* have been equally "eroded" by *Washington v. Glucksberg,* 521 U.S. 702, 721 (1997), which held that *only* fundamental rights which are "'deeply rooted in this Nation's history and tradition'" qualify for anything other than rational basis scrutiny under the doctrine of "substantive due process." *Roe* and *Casey,* of course, subjected the restriction of abortion to heightened scrutiny without even attempting to establish that the freedom to abort *was* rooted in this Nation's tradition.

(2) *Bowers,* the Court says, has been subject to "substantial and continuing [criticism], disapproving of its reasoning in all respects, not just as to its historical assumptions." *Ante,* at 15. Exactly what those nonhistorical criticisms are, and whether the Court even agrees with them, are left unsaid, although the Court does cite two books. See *ibid.* (citing C. Fried, Order and Law: Arguing the Reagan Revolution—A Firsthand Account 81–84 (1991); R. Posner, Sex and Reason 341–350 (1992)).[1] Of course, *Roe* too (and by extension *Casey*) had been (and still is) subject to unrelenting criticism, including criticism from the two commentators cited by the Court today. See Fried, *supra,* at 75 ("*Roe* was a prime example of twisted judging"); Posner, *supra,* at 337 ("[The Court's] opinion in *Roe* . . . fails to measure up to professional expectations regarding judicial opinions"); Posner, Judicial Opinion Writing, 62 U. Chi. L. Rev. 1421, 1434 (1995) (describing the opinion in *Roe* as an "embarrassing performanc[e]").

(3) That leaves, to distinguish the rock-solid, unamendable disposition of *Roe* from the readily overrulable *Bowers,* only the third factor. "[T]here has been," the Court says, "no individual or societal reliance on *Bowers* of the sort that could counsel against overturning its holding. . . ." *Ante,* at 16. It seems to me that the "societal reliance" on the principles confirmed in *Bowers* and discarded today has been overwhelming. Countless judicial decisions and legislative enactments have relied on the ancient proposition that a governing majority's belief that certain sexual behavior is "immoral and unacceptable" constitutes a rational basis for regulation. See, *e.g., Williams v. Pryor,* 240 F. 3d 944, 949 (CA11 2001) (citing *Bowers* in upholding Alabama's prohibition on the sale of sex toys on the ground that "[t]he crafting and safeguarding of public morality . . . indisputably is a legitimate government interest under rational basis scrutiny"); *Milner v. Apfel,* 148 F. 3d 812, 814 (CA7 1998) (citing *Bowers* for the proposition that "[l]egislatures are

permitted to legislate with regard to morality . . . rather than confined to preventing demonstrable harms"); *Holmes v. California Army National Guard* 124 F. 3d 1126, 1136 (CA9 1997) (relying on *Bowers* in upholding the federal statute and regulations banning from military service those who engage in homosexual conduct); *Owens v. State*, 352 Md. 663, 683, 724 A. 2d 43, 53 (1999) (relying on *Bowers* in holding that "a person has no constitutional right to engage in sexual intercourse, at least outside of marriage"); *Sherman v. Henry*, 928 S. W. 2d 464, 469–473 (Tex. 1996) (relying on *Bowers* in rejecting a claimed constitutional right to commit adultery). We ourselves relied extensively on *Bowers* when we concluded, in *Barnes v. Glen Theatre, Inc.*, 501 U.S. 560, 569 (1991), that Indiana's public indecency statute furthered "a substantial government interest in protecting order and morality," *ibid.*, (plurality opinion); see also *id.*, at 575 (Scalia, J., concurring in judgment). State laws against bigamy, same-sex marriage, adult incest, prostitution, masturbation, adultery, fornication, bestiality, and obscenity are likewise sustainable only in light of *Bowers*' validation of laws based on moral choices. Every single one of these laws is called into question by today's decision; the Court makes no effort to cabin the scope of its decision to exclude them from its holding. See *ante*, at 11 (noting "an emerging awareness that liberty gives substantial protection to adult persons in deciding how to conduct their private lives *in matters pertaining to sex*" (emphasis added)). The impossibility of distinguishing homosexuality from other traditional "morals" offenses is precisely why *Bowers* rejected the rational-basis challenge. "The law," it said, "is constantly based on notions of morality, and if all laws representing essentially moral choices are to be invalidated under the Due Process Clause, the courts will be very busy indeed." 478 U.S., at 196.[2]

What a massive disruption of the current social order, therefore, the overruling of *Bowers* entails. Not so the overruling of *Roe,* which would simply have restored the regime that existed for centuries before 1973, in which the permissibility of and restrictions upon abortion were determined legislatively State-by-State. *Casey*, however, chose to base its *stare decisis* determination on a different "sort" of reliance. "[P]eople," it said, "have organized intimate relationships and made choices that define their views of themselves and their places in society, in reliance on the availability of abortion in the event that contraception should fail." 505 U.S., at 856. This falsely assumes that the consequence of overruling *Roe* would have been to make abortion unlawful. It would not; it would merely have *permitted* the States to do so. Many States would unquestionably have declined to prohibit abortion, and others would not have prohibited it within six months (after which the most significant reliance interests would have expired). Even for persons in States other than these, the choice would not have been between abortion and childbirth, but between abortion nearby and abortion in a neighboring State.

To tell the truth, it does not surprise me, and should surprise no one, that the Court has chosen today to revise the standards of *stare decisis* set forth in *Casey*. It has thereby exposed *Casey*'s extraordinary deference to precedent for the result-oriented expedient that it is.

II

Having decided that it need not adhere to *stare decisis*, the Court still must establish that *Bowers* was wrongly decided and that the Texas statute, as applied to petitioners, is unconstitutional.

Texas Penal Code Ann. §21.06(a) (2003) undoubtedly imposes constraints on liberty. So do laws prohibiting prostitution, recreational use of heroin, and, for that matter, working more than 60 hours per week in a bakery. But there is no right to "liberty" under the Due Process Clause, though today's opinion repeatedly makes that claim. *Ante*, at 6 ("The

liberty protected by the Constitution allows homosexual persons the right to make this choice"); *ante*, at 13 ("'These matters . . . are central to the liberty protected by the Fourteenth Amendment'"); *ante*, at 17 ("Their right to liberty under the Due Process Clause gives them the full right to engage in their conduct without intervention of the government"). The Fourteenth Amendment *expressly allows* States to deprive their citizens of "liberty," *so long as "due process of law" is provided:*

"No state shall . . . deprive any person of life, liberty, or property, *without due process of law*." Amdt. 14 (emphasis added).

Our opinions applying the doctrine known as "substantive due process" hold that the Due Process Clause prohibits States from infringing *fundamental* liberty interests, unless the infringement is narrowly tailored to serve a compelling state interest. *Washington* v. *Glucksberg*, 521 U.S., at 721. We have held repeatedly, in cases the Court today does not overrule, that *only* fundamental rights qualify for this so-called "heightened scrutiny" protection—that is, rights which are "'deeply rooted in this Nation's history and tradition,'" *ibid.* See *Reno v. Flores*, 507 U.S. 292, 303 (1993) (fundamental liberty interests must be "so rooted in the traditions and conscience of our people as to be ranked as fundamental" (internal quotation marks and citations omitted)); *United States v. Salerno*, 481 U.S. 739, 751 (1987) (same). See also *Michael H. v. Gerald D.*, 491 U.S. 110, 122 (1989) ("[W]e have insisted not merely that the interest denominated as a 'liberty' be 'fundamental' . . . but also that it be an interest traditionally protected by our society"); *Moore v. East Cleveland*, 431 U.S. 494, 503 (1977) (plurality opinion); *Meyer v. Nebraska*, 262 U.S. 390, 399 (1923) (Fourteenth Amendment protects "those privileges *long recognized at common law* as essential to the orderly pursuit of happiness by free men" (emphasis added)).[3] All other liberty interests may be abridged or abrogated pursuant to a validly enacted state law if that law is rationally related to a legitimate state interest.

Bowers held, first, that criminal prohibitions of homosexual sodomy are not subject to heightened scrutiny because they do not implicate a "fundamental right" under the Due Process Clause, 478 U.S., at 191–194. Noting that "[p]roscriptions against that conduct have ancient roots," *id.*, at 192, that "[s]odomy was a criminal offense at common law and was forbidden by the laws of the original 13 States when they ratified the Bill of Rights," *ibid.*, and that many States had retained their bans on sodomy, *id.*, at 193, *Bowers* concluded that a right to engage in homosexual sodomy was not "'deeply rooted in this Nation's history and tradition,'" *id.*, at 192.

The Court today does not overrule this holding. Not once does it describe homosexual sodomy as a "fundamental right" or a "fundamental liberty interest," nor does it subject the Texas statute to strict scrutiny. Instead, having failed to establish that the right to homosexual sodomy is "'deeply rooted in this Nation's history and tradition,'" the Court concludes that the application of Texas's statute to petitioners' conduct fails the rational-basis test, and overrules *Bowers'* holding to the contrary, see *id.*, at 196. "The Texas statute furthers no legitimate state interest which can justify its intrusion into the personal and private life of the individual." *Ante*, at 18.

I shall address that rational-basis holding presently. First, however, I address some aspersions that the Court casts upon *Bowers'* conclusion that homosexual sodomy is not a "fundamental right"—even though, as I have said, the Court does not have the boldness to reverse that conclusion.

III

The Court's description of "the state of the law" at the time of *Bowers* only confirms that *Bowers* was right. *Ante*, at 5. The Court points to *Griswold v. Connecticut*, 381 U.S. 479, 481–482 (1965). But that case *expressly disclaimed* any reliance on the doctrine of "substantive due process," and grounded the so-called "right to privacy" in penumbras of constitutional provisions *other than* the Due Process Clause. *Eisenstadt v. Baird*, 405 U.S. 438 (1972), likewise had nothing to do with "substantive due process"; it invalidated a Massachusetts law prohibiting the distribution of contraceptives to unmarried persons solely on the basis of the Equal Protection Clause. Of course *Eisenstadt* contains well known dictum relating to the "right to privacy," but this referred to the right recognized in *Griswold*—a right penumbral to the *specific* guarantees in the Bill of Rights, and not a "substantive due process" right.

Roe v. Wade recognized that the right to abort an unborn child was a "fundamental right" protected by the Due Process Clause. 410 U.S., at 155. The *Roe* Court, however, made no attempt to establish that this right was "'deeply rooted in this Nation's history and tradition'"; instead, it based its conclusion that "the Fourteenth Amendment's concept of personal liberty . . . is broad enough to encompass a woman's decision whether or not to terminate her pregnancy" on its own normative judgment that anti-abortion laws were undesirable. See *id.,* at 153. We have since rejected *Roe*'s holding that regulations of abortion must be narrowly tailored to serve a compelling state interest, see *Planned Parenthood v. Casey,* 505 U.S., at 876 (joint opinion of *O'Connor, Kennedy,* and *Souter, JJ.*); *id.,* at 951–953 (*Rehnquist, C. J.,* concurring in judgment in part and dissenting in part)—and thus, by logical implication, *Roe*'s holding that the right to abort an unborn child is a "fundamental right." See 505 U.S., at 843–912 (joint opinion of *O'Connor, Kennedy,* and *Souter, JJ.*) (not once describing abortion as a "fundamental right" or a "fundamental liberty interest").

After discussing the history of antisodomy laws, *ante,* at 7–10, the Court proclaims that, "it should be noted that there is no longstanding history in this country of laws directed at homosexual conduct as a distinct matter," *ante,* at 7. This observation in no way casts into doubt the "definitive [historical] conclusion," *id.,* on which *Bowers* relied: that our Nation has a longstanding history of laws prohibiting *sodomy in general*—regardless of whether it was performed by same-sex or opposite-sex couples:

"It is obvious to us that neither of these formulations would extend a fundamental right to homosexuals to engage in acts of consensual sodomy. Proscriptions against that conduct have ancient roots. *Sodomy* was a criminal offense at common law and was forbidden by the laws of the original 13 States when they ratified the Bill of Rights. In 1868, when the Fourteenth Amendment was ratified, all but 5 of the 37 States in the Union had *criminal sodomy laws.* In fact, until 1961, all 50 States outlawed *sodomy,* and today, 24 States and the District of Columbia continue to provide criminal penalties for *sodomy* performed in private and between consenting adults. Against this background, to claim that a right to engage in such conduct is 'deeply rooted in this Nation's history and tradition' or 'implicit in the concept of ordered liberty' is, at best, facetious." 478 U.S., at 192–194 (citations and footnotes omitted; emphasis added).

It is (as *Bowers* recognized) entirely irrelevant whether the laws in our long national tradition criminalizing homosexual sodomy were "directed at homosexual conduct as a distinct matter." *Ante,* at 7. Whether homosexual sodomy was prohibited by a law targeted at same-sex sexual relations or by a more general law prohibiting both homosexual and heterosexual sodomy, the only relevant point is that it *was* criminalized—which suffices to establish that homosexual sodomy is not a right "deeply rooted in our Nation's history and tradition." The Court today agrees that homosexual sodomy was criminalized and thus does not dispute the facts on which *Bowers actually* relied.

Next the Court makes the claim, again unsupported by any citations, that "[l]aws prohibiting sodomy do not seem to have been enforced against consenting adults acting in private." *Ante,* at 8. The key qualifier here is "acting in private"—since the Court admits that sodomy laws *were* enforced against consenting adults (although the Court contends that prosecutions were "infrequent," *ante,* at 9). I do not know what "acting in private" means; surely consensual sodomy, like heterosexual intercourse, is rarely performed on stage. If all the Court means by "acting in private" is "on private premises, with the doors closed and windows covered," it is entirely unsurprising that evidence of enforcement would be hard to come by. (Imagine the circumstances that would enable a search warrant to be obtained for a residence on the ground that there was probable cause to believe that consensual sodomy was then and there occurring.) Surely that lack of evidence would not sustain the proposition that consensual sodomy on private premises with the doors closed and windows covered was regarded as a "fundamental right," even though all other consensual sodomy was criminalized. There are 203 prosecutions for consensual, adult homosexual sodomy reported in the West Reporting system and official state reporters from the years 1880–1995. See W. Eskridge, Gaylaw: Challenging the Apartheid of the Closet 375 (1999) (hereinafter Gaylaw). There are also records of 20 sodomy prosecutions and 4 executions during the colonial period. J. Katz, Gay/Lesbian Almanac 29, 58, 663 (1983). *Bowers'* conclusion that homosexual sodomy is not a fundamental right "deeply rooted in this Nation's history and tradition" is utterly unassailable.

Realizing that fact, the Court instead says: "[W]e think that our laws and traditions in the past half century are of most relevance here. These references show *an emerging awareness* that liberty gives substantial protection to adult persons in deciding how to conduct their private lives *in matters pertaining to sex.*" *Ante,* at 11 (emphasis added). Apart from the fact that such an "emerging awareness" does not establish a "fundamental right," the statement is factually false. States continue to prosecute all sorts of crimes by adults "in matters pertaining to sex": prostitution, adult incest, adultery, obscenity, and child pornography. Sodomy laws, too, have been enforced "in the past half century," in which there have been 134 reported cases involving prosecutions for consensual, adult, homosexual sodomy. Gaylaw 375. In relying, for evidence of an "emerging recognition," upon the American Law Institute's 1955 recommendation not to criminalize "'consensual sexual relations conducted in private,'" *ante,* at 11, the Court ignores the fact that this recommendation was "a point of resistance in most of the states that considered adopting the Model Penal Code." Gaylaw 159.

In any event, an "emerging awareness" is by definition not "deeply rooted in this Nation's history and tradition[s]," as we have said "fundamental right" status requires. Constitutional entitlements do not spring into existence because some States choose to lessen or eliminate criminal sanctions on certain behavior. Much less do they spring into existence, as the Court seems to believe, because *foreign nations* decriminalize conduct. The *Bowers* majority opinion *never* relied on "values we share with a wider civilization," *ante,* at 16, but rather rejected the claimed right to sodomy on the ground that such a right was not "'deeply rooted in *this Nation's* history and tradition,'" 478 U.S., at 193–194 (emphasis added). *Bowers'* rational-basis holding is likewise devoid of any reliance on the views of a "wider civilization," see *id.,* at 196. The Court's discussion of these foreign views (ignoring, of course, the many countries that have retained criminal prohibitions on sodomy) is therefore meaningless dicta. Dangerous dicta, however, since "this Court . . . should not impose foreign moods, fads, or fashions on Americans." *Foster v. Florida,* 537 U.S. 990, n. (2002) (*Thomas, J.,* concurring in denial of certiorari).

IV

I turn now to the ground on which the Court squarely rests its holding: the contention that there is no rational basis for the law here under attack. This proposition is so out of accord with our jurisprudence—indeed, with the jurisprudence of *any* society we know—that it requires little discussion.

The Texas statute undeniably seeks to further the belief of its citizens that certain forms of sexual behavior are "immoral and unacceptable," *Bowers, supra,* at 196—the same interest furthered by criminal laws against fornication, bigamy, adultery, adult incest, bestiality, and obscenity. *Bowers* held that this *was* a legitimate state interest. The Court today reaches the opposite conclusion. The Texas statute, it says, "furthers *no legitimate state interest* which can justify its intrusion into the personal and private life of the individual," *ante,* at 18 (emphasis addded). The Court embraces instead *Justice Stevens'* declaration in his *Bowers* dissent, that "the fact that the governing majority in a State has traditionally viewed a particular practice as immoral is not a sufficient reason for upholding a law prohibiting the practice," *ante,* at 17. This effectively decrees the end of all morals legislation. If, as the Court asserts, the promotion of majoritarian sexual morality is not even a *legitimate* state interest, none of the above-mentioned laws can survive rational-basis review.

V

Finally, I turn to petitioners' equal-protection challenge, which no Member of the Court save *Justice O'Connor, ante,* at 1 (opinion concurring in judgment), embraces: On its face §21.06(a) applies equally to all persons. Men and women, heterosexuals and homosexuals, are all subject to its prohibition of deviate sexual intercourse with someone of the same sex. To be sure, §21.06 does distinguish between the sexes insofar as concerns the partner with whom the sexual acts are performed: men can violate the law only with other men, and women only with other women. But this cannot itself be a denial of equal protection, since it is precisely the same distinction regarding partner that is drawn in state laws prohibiting marriage with someone of the same sex while permitting marriage with someone of the opposite sex.

The objection is made, however, that the antimiscegenation laws invalidated in *Loving v. Virginia,* 388 U.S. 1, 8 (1967), similarly were applicable to whites and blacks alike, and only distinguished between the races insofar as the *partner* was concerned. In *Loving,* however, we correctly applied heightened scrutiny, rather than the usual rational-basis review, because the Virginia statute was "designed to maintain White Supremacy." *Id.,* at 6, 11. A racially discriminatory purpose is always sufficient to subject a law to strict scrutiny, even a facially neutral law that makes no mention of race. See *Washington v. Davis,* 426 U.S. 229, 241–242 (1976). No purpose to discriminate against men or women as a class can be gleaned from the Texas law, so rational-basis review applies. That review is readily satisfied here by the same rational basis that satisfied it in *Bowers*—society's belief that certain forms of sexual behavior are "immoral and unacceptable," 478 U.S., at 196. This is the same justification that supports many other laws regulating sexual behavior that make a distinction based upon the identity of the partner—for example, laws against adultery, fornication, and adult incest, and laws refusing to recognize homosexual marriage.

Justice O'Connor argues that the discrimination in this law which must be justified is not its discrimination with regard to the sex of the partner but its discrimination with regard to the sexual proclivity of the principal actor.

"While it is true that the law applies only to conduct, the conduct targeted by this law is conduct that is closely correlated with being homosexual. Under such circumstances, Texas' sodomy law is targeted at more than conduct. It is instead directed toward gay persons as a class." *Ante,* at 5.

Of course the same could be said of any law. A law against public nudity targets "the conduct that is closely correlated with being a nudist," and hence "is targeted at more than conduct"; it is "directed toward nudists as a class." But be that as it may. Even if the Texas law *does* deny equal protection to "homosexuals as a class," that denial *still* does not need to be justified by anything more than a rational basis, which our cases show is satisfied by the enforcement of traditional notions of sexual morality.

Justice O'Connor simply decrees application of "a more searching form of rational basis review" to the Texas statute. *Ante,* at 2. The cases she cites do not recognize such a standard, and reach their conclusions only after finding, as required by conventional rational-basis analysis, that no conceivable legitimate state interest supports the classification at issue. See *Romer v. Evans,* 517 U.S., at 635; *Cleburne v. Cleburne Living Center, Inc.,* 473 U.S. 432, 448–450 (1985); *Department of Agriculture v. Moreno,* 413 U.S. 528, 534–538 (1973). Nor does *Justice O'Connor* explain precisely what her "more searching form" of rational-basis review consists of. It must at least mean, however, that laws exhibiting " 'a … desire to harm a politically unpopular group,' " *ante,* at 2, are invalid *even though* there may be a conceivable rational basis to support them.

This reasoning leaves on pretty shaky grounds state laws limiting marriage to opposite-sex couples. *Justice O'Connor* seeks to preserve them by the conclusory statement that "preserving the traditional institution of marriage" is a legitimate state interest. *Ante,* at 7. But "preserving the traditional institution of marriage" is just a kinder way of describing the State's *moral disapproval* of same-sex couples. Texas's interest in §21.06 could be recast in similarly euphemistic terms: "preserving the traditional sexual mores of our society." In the jurisprudence *Justice O'Connor* has seemingly created, judges can validate laws by characterizing them as "preserving the traditions of society" (good); or invalidate them by characterizing them as "expressing moral disapproval" (bad).

* * *

Today's opinion is the product of a Court, which is the product of a law-profession culture, that has largely signed on to the so-called homosexual agenda, by which I mean the agenda promoted by some homosexual activists directed at eliminating the moral opprobrium that has traditionally attached to homosexual conduct. I noted in an earlier opinion the fact that the American Association of Law Schools (to which any reputable law school *must* seek to belong) excludes from membership any school that refuses to ban from its job-interview facilities a law firm (no matter how small) that does not wish to hire as a prospective partner a person who openly engages in homosexual conduct. See *Romer, supra,* at 653.

One of the most revealing statements in today's opinion is the Court's grim warning that the criminalization of homosexual conduct is "an invitation to subject homosexual persons to discrimination both in the public and in the private spheres." *Ante,* at 14. It is clear from this that the Court has taken sides in the culture war, departing from its role of assuring, as neutral observer, that the democratic rules of engagement are observed. Many Americans do not want persons who openly engage in homosexual conduct as partners in their business, as scoutmasters for their children, as teachers in their children's schools, or as boarders in their home. They view this as protecting themselves and their families from a lifestyle that they believe to be immoral and destructive. The Court views it as "discrimination" which it is the function of our judgments to deter. So imbued is the Court with the law profession's anti-anti-homosexual culture, that it is seemingly unaware that the attitudes of that culture are not obviously "mainstream"; that in most States what the Court calls "discrimination" against those who engage in homosexual acts is perfectly legal; that proposals to ban such "discrimination" under Title VII have repeatedly been rejected by Congress, see Employment Non-Discrimination Act of 1994, S. 2238, 103d Cong., 2d Sess. (1994); Civil Rights Amendments, H. R. 5452, 94th Cong., 1st Sess. (1975); that in some cases such "discrimination" is *mandated* by federal statute, see 10 U.S.C. §654(b)(1) (mandating discharge from the armed forces of any service member who engages in or intends to engage in homosexual acts); and that in some cases such "discrimination" is a constitutional right, see *Boy Scouts of America v. Dale,* 530 U.S. 640 (2000).

Let me be clear that I have nothing against homosexuals, or any other group, promoting their agenda through normal democratic means. Social perceptions of sexual and other morality change over time, and every group has the right to persuade its fellow citizens that its view of such matters is the best. That homosexuals have achieved some success in that enterprise is attested to by the fact that Texas is one of the few remaining States that criminalize private, consensual homosexual acts. But persuading one's fellow citizens is one thing, and imposing one's views in absence of democratic majority will is something else. I would no more *require* a State to criminalize homosexual acts—or, for that matter, display *any* moral disapproval of them—than I would *forbid* it to do so. What Texas has chosen to do is well within the range of traditional democratic action, and its hand should not be stayed through the invention of a brand-new "constitutional right" by a Court that is impatient of democratic change. It is indeed true that "later generations can see that laws once thought necessary and proper in fact serve only to oppress," *ante,* at 18; and when that happens, later generations can repeal those laws. But it is the premise of our system that those judgments are to be made by the people, and not imposed by a governing caste that knows best.

One of the benefits of leaving regulation of this matter to the people rather than to the courts is that the people, unlike judges, need not carry things to their logical conclusion. The people may feel that their disapprobation of homosexual conduct is strong enough to disallow homosexual marriage, but not strong enough to criminalize private homosexual acts—and may legislate accordingly. The Court today pretends that it possesses a similar freedom of action, so that we need not fear judicial imposition of homosexual marriage, as has recently occurred in Canada (in a decision that the Canadian Government has chosen not to appeal). See *Halpern v. Toronto,* 2003 WL 34950 (Ontario Ct. App.); Cohen, Dozens in Canada Follow Gay Couple's Lead, Washington Post, June 12, 2003, p. A25. At the end of its opinion—after having laid waste the foundations of our rational-basis jurisprudence—the Court says that the present case "does not involve whether the government must give formal recognition to any relationship that homosexual persons seek to enter." *Ante,* at 17. Do not believe it. More illuminating than this bald, unreasoned disclaimer is the progression of thought displayed by an earlier passage in the Court's opinion, which notes the constitutional protections afforded to "personal decisions relating to *marriage,* procreation, contraception, family relationships, child rearing, and education," and then declares that "[p]ersons in a homosexual relationship may seek autonomy for these purposes, just as heterosexual persons do." *Ante,* at 13 (emphasis added). Today's opinion dismantles the structure of constitutional law that has permitted a distinction to be made between heterosexual and homosexual unions, insofar as formal recognition in marriage is concerned. If moral disapproval of homosexual conduct is "no legitimate

state interest" for purposes of proscribing that conduct, *ante,* at 18; and if, as the Court coos (casting aside all pretense of neutrality), "[w]hen sexuality finds overt expression in intimate conduct with another person, the conduct can be but one element in a personal bond that is more enduring," *ante,* at 6; what justification could there possibly be for denying the benefits of marriage to homosexual couples exercising "[t]he liberty protected by the Constitution," *ibid.*? Surely not the encouragement of procreation, since the sterile and the elderly are allowed to marry. This case "does not involve" the issue of homosexual marriage only if one entertains the belief that principle and logic have nothing to do with the decisions of this Court. Many will hope that, as the Court comfortingly assures us, this is so.

The matters appropriate for this Court's resolution are only three: Texas's prohibition of sodomy neither infringes a "fundamental right" (which the Court does not dispute), nor is unsupported by a rational relation to what the Constitution considers a legitimate state interest, nor denies the equal protection of the laws. I dissent.

JUSTICE THOMAS, *dissenting.*

I join *Justice Scalia*'s dissenting opinion. I write separately to note that the law before the Court today "is … uncommonly silly." *Griswold v. Connecticut,* 381 U.S. 479, 527 (1965) (Stewart, J., dissenting). If I were a member of the Texas Legislature, I would vote to repeal it. Punishing someone for expressing his sexual preference through noncommercial consensual conduct with another adult does not appear to be a worthy way to expend valuable law enforcement resources.

Notwithstanding this, I recognize that as a member of this Court I am not empowered to help petitioners and others similarly situated. My duty, rather, is to "decide cases 'agreeably to the Constitution and laws of the United States.'" *Id.*, at 530. And, just like Justice Stewart, I "can find [neither in the Bill of Rights nor any other part of the Constitution a] general right of privacy," *ibid.*, or as the Court terms it today, the "liberty of the person both in its spatial and more transcendent dimensions," *ante,* at 1.

1. This last-cited critic of *Bowers* actually writes: "*[Bowers]* is correct nevertheless that the right to engage in homosexual acts is not deeply rooted in America's history and tradition." Posner, Sex and Reason, at 343.

2. While the Court does not overrule *Bowers'* holding that homosexual sodomy is not a "fundamental right," it is worth noting that the "societal reliance" upon that aspect of the decision has been substantial as well. See 10 U.S.C. §654(b)(1) ("A member of the armed forces shall be separated from the armed forces … if … the member has engaged in … a homosexual act or acts"); *Marcum v. McWhorter,* 308 F. 3d 635, 640–642 (CA6 2002) (relying on *Bowers* in rejecting a claimed fundamental right to commit adultery); *Mullins v. Oregon,* 57 F. 3d 789, 793–794 (CA9 1995) (relying on *Bowers* in rejecting a grandparent's claimed "fundamental liberty interes[t]" in the adoption of her grandchildren); *Doe v. Wigginton,* 21 F. 3d 733, 739–740 (CA6 1994) (relying on *Bowers* in rejecting a prisoner's claimed "fundamental right" to on-demand HIV testing); *Schowengerdt v. United States,* 944 F. 2d 483, 490 (CA9 1991) (relying on *Bowers* in upholding a bisexual's discharge from the armed services); *Charles v. Baesler,* 910 F. 2d 1349, 1353 (CA6 1990) (relying on *Bowers* in rejecting fire department captain's claimed "fundamental" interest in a promotion); *Henne v. Wright,* 904 F. 2d 1208, 1214–1215 (CA8 1990) (relying on *Bowers* in rejecting a claim that state law restricting surnames that could be given to children at birth implicates a "fundamental right"); *Walls v. Petersburg,* 895 F. 2d 188, 193 (CA4 1990) (relying on *Bowers* in rejecting substantive-due-process challenge to a police department questionnaire that asked prospective employees about homosexual activity); *High Tech Gays v. Defense Industrial Security Clearance Office,* 895 F. 2d 563, 570–571 (CA9 1988) (relying on *Bowers'*

holding that homosexual activity is not a fundamental right in rejecting—on the basis of the rational-basis standard—an equal-protection challenge to the Defense Department's policy of conducting expanded investigations into backgrounds of gay and lesbian applicants for secret and top-secret security clearance).

3.The Court is quite right that "history and tradition are the starting point but not in all cases the ending point of the substantive due process inquiry," *ante,* at 11. An asserted "fundamental liberty interest" must not only be "deeply rooted in this Nation's history and tradition," *Washington v. Glucksberg,* 521 U.S. 702, 721 (1997), but it must *also* be "implicit in the concept of ordered liberty," so that "neither liberty nor justice would exist if [it] were sacrificed," *ibid.* Moreover, liberty interests unsupported by history and tradition, though not deserving of "heightened scrutiny," are *still* protected from state laws that are not rationally related to any legitimate state interest. *Id.,* at 722. As I proceed to discuss, it is this latter principle that the Court applies in the present case.

Rules of the Supreme Court (1995)

The Supreme Court, empowered by Title 28, section 2071 of the U.S. Code, sets its own rules covering the activities of the Court. These rules, first established in 1790, are revised from time to time, generally by a consensus of the justices. The current rules were adopted July 26, 1995, and went into effect October 2, 1995.

There are currently forty-eight rules governing the presentation of cases to the Court. These rules cover the activities of Court officers (Part I), the requirements for attorneys and counselors (Part II), the jurisdiction of the Court (Parts III and IV), procedures that must be followed in the presentation of cases (Parts V, VI, and VII), Court procedures and litigant requirements at the disposition of cases (Part VIII), and definitions and the effective date of the rules (Part IX).

The rules go into specific detail on many matters, such as the time allotted for oral argument, the preparation of documents, and the printing of appendices.

RULES OF THE SUPREME COURT OF THE UNITED STATES

Adopted July 26, 1995
Effective October 2, 1995

PART I. THE COURT

RULE 1. CLERK

1. The Clerk receives documents for filing with the Court and has authority to reject any submitted filing that does not comply with these Rules.

2. The Clerk maintains the Court's records and will not permit any of them to be removed from the Court building except as authorized by the Court. Any document filed with the Clerk and made a part of the Court's records may not thereafter be withdrawn from the official Court files. After the conclusion of proceedings in this Court, original records and documents transmitted to this Court by any other court will be returned to the court from which they were received.

3. Unless the Court or the Chief Justice orders otherwise, the Clerk's office is open from 9 A.M. to 5 P.M., Monday through Friday, except on federal legal holidays listed in 5 U.S.C. §6103.

RULE 2. LIBRARY

1. The Court's library is available for use by appropriate personnel of this Court, members of the Bar of this Court, Members of Congress and their legal staffs, and attorneys for the United States and for federal departments and agencies.

2. The library's hours are governed by regulations made by the Librarian with the approval of the Chief Justice or the Court.

3. Library books may not be removed from the Court building, except by a Justice or a member of a Justice's staff.

RULE 3. TERM

The Court holds a continuous annual Term commencing on the first Monday in October and ending on the day before the first Monday in October of the following year. See 28 U.S.C. §2. At the end of each Term, all cases pending on the docket are continued to the next Term.

RULE 4. SESSIONS AND QUORUM

1. Open sessions of the Court are held beginning at 10 A.M. on the first Monday in October of each year, and thereafter as announced by the Court. Unless it orders otherwise, the Court sits to hear arguments from 10 A.M. until noon and from 1 P.M. until 3 P.M.

2. Six Members of the Court constitute a quorum. See 28 U.S.C. §1. In the absence of a quorum on any day appointed for holding a session of the Court, the Justices attending, or if no Justice is present, the Clerk or a Deputy Clerk may announce that the Court will not meet until there is a quorum.

3. When appropriate, the Court will direct the Clerk or the Marshal to announce recesses.

PART II. ATTORNEYS AND COUNSELORS

RULE 5. ADMISSION TO THE BAR

1. To qualify for admission to the Bar of this Court, an applicant must have been admitted to practice in the highest court of a State, Commonwealth, Territory or Possession, or the District of Columbia for a period of at least three years immediately before the date of application; must not have been the subject of any adverse disciplinary action pronounced or in effect during that 3 year period; and must appear to the Court to be of good moral and professional character.

2. Each applicant shall file with the Clerk (1) a certificate from the presiding judge, clerk, or other authorized official of that court evidencing the applicant's admission to practice there and the applicant's current good standing, and (2) a completely executed copy of the form approved by this Court and furnished by the Clerk containing (a) the applicant's personal statement, and (b) the statement of two sponsors endorsing the correctness of the applicant's statement, stating that the applicant possesses all the qualifications required for admission, and affirming that the applicant is of good moral and professional character. Both sponsors must be members of the Bar of this Court who personally know, but are not related to, the applicant.

3. If the documents submitted demonstrate that the applicant possesses the necessary qualifications, and if the applicant has signed the oath or affirmation and paid the required fee, the Clerk will notify the applicant of acceptance by the Court as a member of the Bar and issue a certificate of admission. An applicant who so wishes may be admitted in open court on oral motion by a member of the Bar of this Court, provided that all other requirements for admission have been satisfied.

4. Each applicant shall sign the following oath or affirmation: I, _____, do solemnly swear (or affirm) that as an attorney and as a counselor of this Court, I will conduct myself uprightly and according to law, and that I will support the Constitution of the United States.

5. The fee for admission to the Bar and a certificate bearing the seal of the Court is $100, payable to the United States Supreme Court. The Marshal will deposit such fees in a separate fund to be disbursed by the Marshal at the direction of the Chief Justice for the costs of admissions, for the benefit of the Court and its Bar, and for related purposes.

6. The fee for a duplicate certificate of admission to the Bar bearing the seal of the Court is $15, payable to the United States Supreme Court. The proceeds will be maintained by the Marshal as provided in paragraph 5 of this Rule.

RULE 6. ARGUMENT *PRO HAC VICE*

1. An attorney not admitted to practice in the highest court of a State, Commonwealth, Territory or Possession, or the District of

Columbia for the requisite three years, but otherwise eligible for admission to practice in this Court under Rule 5.1, may be permitted to argue *pro hac vice.*

2. An attorney qualified to practice in the courts of a foreign state may be permitted to argue *pro hac vice.*

3. Oral argument *pro hac vice* is allowed only on motion of the counsel of record for the party on whose behalf leave is requested. The motion shall state concisely the qualifications of the attorney who is to argue *pro hac vice.* It shall be filed with the Clerk, in the form required by Rule 21, no later than the date on which the respondent's or appellee's brief on the merits is due to be filed and it shall be accompanied by proof of service as required by Rule 29.

RULE 7. PROHIBITION AGAINST PRACTICE

No employee of this Court shall practice as an attorney or counselor in any court or before any agency of government while employed by the Court; nor shall any person after leaving such employment participate in any professional capacity in any case pending before this Court or in any case being considered for filing in this Court, until two years have elapsed after separation; nor shall a former employee ever participate in any professional capacity in any case that was pending in this Court during the employee's tenure.

RULE 8. DISBARMENT AND DISCIPLINARY ACTION

1. Whenever a member of the Bar of this Court has been disbarred or suspended from practice in any court of record, or has engaged in conduct unbecoming a member of the Bar of this Court, the Court will enter an order suspending that member from practice before this Court and affording the member an opportunity to show cause, within 40 days, why a disbarment order should not be entered. Upon response, or if no response is timely filed, the Court will enter an appropriate order.

2. After reasonable notice and an opportunity to show cause why disciplinary action should not be taken, and after a hearing if material facts are in dispute, the Court may take any appropriate disciplinary action against any attorney who is admitted to practice before it for conduct unbecoming a member of the Bar or for failure to comply with these Rules or any Rule or order of the Court.

RULE 9. APPEARANCE OF COUNSEL

1. An attorney seeking to file a document in this Court in a representative capacity must first be admitted to practice before this Court as provided in Rule 5, except that admission to the Bar of this Court is not required for an attorney appointed under the Criminal Justice Act of 1964, see 18 U.S.C. §3006A(d)(6), or under any other applicable federal statute. The attorney whose name, address, and telephone number appear on the cover of a document presented for filing is considered counsel of record, and a separate notice of appearance need not be filed. If the name of more than one attorney is shown on the cover of the document, the attorney who is counsel of record shall be clearly identified.

2. An attorney representing a party who will not be filing a document shall enter a separate notice of appearance as counsel of record indicating the name of the party represented. A separate notice of appearance shall also be entered whenever an attorney is substituted as counsel of record in a particular case.

PART III. JURISDICTION ON WRIT OF CERTIORARI

RULE 10. CONSIDERATIONS GOVERNING REVIEW ON WRIT OF CERTIORARI

Review on a writ of certiorari is not a matter of right, but of judicial discretion. A petition for a writ of certiorari will be granted only for compelling reasons. The following, although neither controlling nor fully measuring the Court's discretion, indicate the character of the reasons the Court considers:

(a) a United States court of appeals has entered a decision in conflict with the decision of another United States court of appeals on the same important matter; has decided an important federal question in a way that conflicts with a decision by a state court of last resort; or has so far departed from the accepted and usual course of judicial proceedings, or sanctioned such a departure by a lower court, as to call for an exercise of this Court's supervisory power;

(b) a state court of last resort has decided an important federal question in a way that conflicts with the decision of another state court of last resort or of a United States court of appeals;

(c) a state court or a United States court of appeals has decided an important question of federal law that has not been, but should be, settled by this Court, or has decided an important federal question in a way that conflicts with relevant decisions of this Court.

A petition for a writ of certiorari is rarely granted when the asserted error consists of erroneous factual findings or the misapplication of a properly stated rule of law.

RULE 11. CERTIORARI TO A UNITED STATES COURT OF APPEALS BEFORE JUDGMENT

A petition for a writ of certiorari to review a case pending in a United States court of appeals, before judgment is entered in that court, will be granted only upon a showing that the case is of such imperative public importance as to justify deviation from normal appellate practice and to require immediate determination in this Court. See 28 U.S.C. §2101(e).

RULE 12. REVIEW ON CERTIORARI: HOW SOUGHT; PARTIES

1. Except as provided in paragraph 2 on this Rule, the petitioner shall file 40 copies of a petition for a writ of certiorari, prepared as required by Rule 33.1, and shall pay the Rule 38(a) docket fee.

2. A petitioner proceeding *in forma pauperis* under Rule 39 shall file an original and 10 copies of a petition for a writ of certiorari prepared as required by Rule 33.2, together with an original and 10 copies of the motion for leave to proceed *in forma pauperis.* A copy of the motion shall precede and be attached to each copy of the petition, and shall preface and be attached to the petition for a writ of certiorari. An inmate confined in an institution, if proceeding *in forma pauperis* and is not represented by counsel, need file only an original petition and motion.

3. Whether prepared under to Rule 33.1 or Rule 33.2, the petition shall comply in all respects with Rule 14 and shall be submitted with proof of service as required by Rule 29. The case then will be placed on the docket. It is the petitioner's duty to notify all respondents promptly, on a form supplied by the Clerk, of the date of filing, the date the case was placed on the docket, and the docket number of the case. The notice shall be served as required by Rule 29.

4. Parties interested jointly, severally, or otherwise in a judgment may petition separately for a writ of certiorari; or any two or more may join in a petition. A party not shown on the petition as joined therein at the time the petition is filed may not later join in that petition. When two or more judgments are sought to be reviewed on a writ of certiorari to the same court and involve identical or closely related questions, a single petition for a writ of certiorari covering all the judgments suffices. A petition for a writ of certiorari may not be joined with any other pleading, except that any motion for leave to proceed *in forma pauperis* shall be attached.

5. No more than 30 days after a case has been placed on the docket, a respondent seeking to file a conditional cross-petition (*i.e.,* a cross-petition that otherwise would be untimely) shall file, with proof of

service as required by Rule 29, 40 copies of the cross-petition prepared as required by Rule 33.1, except that a cross-petitioner proceeding *in forma pauperis* under Rule 39 shall comply with Rule 12.2. The cross-petition shall comply in all respects with this Rule and Rule 14, except that material already reproduced in the appendix to the opening petition need not be reproduced again. A cross-petitioning respondent shall pay the Rule 38(a) docket fee or submit a motion for leave to proceed *in forma pauperis*. The cover of the cross-petition shall indicate clearly that it is a conditional cross-petition. The cross-petition then will be placed on the docket, subject to the provisions of Rule 13.4. It is the cross-petitioner's duty to notify all cross-respondents promptly, on a form supplied by the Clerk, of the date of filing, the date the cross-petition was placed on the docket, and the docket number of the cross-petition. The notice shall be served as required by Rule 29. A cross-petition for a writ of certiorari may not be joined with any other pleading, except that any motion for leave to proceed *in forma pauperis* shall be attached. The time to file a cross-petition will not be extended.

6. All parties to the proceeding in the court whose judgment is sought to be reviewed are deemed parties entitled to file documents in this Court, unless the petitioner notifies the Clerk of this Court in writing of the petitioner's belief that one or more of the parties below have no interest in the outcome of the petition. A copy of such notice shall be served as required by Rule 29 on all parties to the proceeding below. A party noted as no longer interested may remain a party by notifying the Clerk promptly, with service on the other parties, of an intention to remain a party. All parties other than the petitioner are considered respondents, but any respondent who supports the position of a petitioner shall meet the petitioner's time schedule for filing documents, except that a response supporting the petition shall be filed within 20 days after the case is placed on the docket, and that time will not be extended. Parties who file no document will not qualify for any relief from this Court.

7. The clerk of the court having possession of the record shall keep it until notified by the Clerk of this Court to certify and transmit it. In any document filed with this Court, a party may cite or quote from the record, even if it has not been transmitted to this Court. When requested by the Clerk of this Court to certify and transmit the record, or any part of it, the clerk of the court having possession of the record shall number the documents to be certified and shall transmit therewith a numbered list specifically identifying each document transmitted. If the record, or stipulated portions, have been printed for the use of the court below, that printed record, plus the proceedings in the court below, may be certified as the record unless one of the parties or the Clerk of this Court requests otherwise. The record may consist of certified copies, but if the lower court is of the view that original documents of any kind should be seen by this Court, that court may provide by order for the transport, safekeeping, and return of such originals.

RULE 13. REVIEW ON CERTIORARI: TIME FOR PETITIONING

1. Unless otherwise provided by law, a petition for a writ of certiorari to review a judgment in any case, civil or criminal, entered by a state court of last resort or a United States court of appeals (including the United States Court of Appeals for the Armed Forces) is timely when it is filed with the Clerk of this Court within 90 days after entry of the judgment. A petition for a writ of certiorari seeking review of a judgment of a lower state court that is subject to discretionary review by the state court of last resort is timely when it is filed with the Clerk within 90 days after entry of the order denying discretionary review.

2. The Clerk will not file any petition for a writ of certiorari that is jurisdictionally out of time. See, *e.g.,* 28 U.S.C. §2101(c).

3. The time to file a petition for a writ of certiorari runs from the date of entry of the judgment or order sought to be reviewed, and not from the issuance date of the mandate (or its equivalent under local practice). But if a petition for rehearing is timely filed in the lower court by any party, the time to file the petition for a writ of certiorari for all parties (whether or not they requested rehearing or joined in the petition for rehearing) runs from the date of the denial of the petition for rehearing or, if the petition for rehearing is granted, the subsequent entry of judgment. A suggestion made to a United States court of appeals for a rehearing en banc is not a petition for rehearing within the meaning of this Rule unless so treated by the United States court of appeals.

4. A cross-petition for a writ of certiorari is timely when it is filed with the Clerk as provided in paragraphs 1, 3, and 5 of this Rule, or in Rule 12.5. However, a conditional cross-petition (which except for Rule 12.5 would be untimely) will not be granted unless another party's timely petition for a writ of certiorari is granted.

5. For good cause, a Justice may extend the time to file a petition for a writ of certiorari for a period not exceeding 60 days. An application to extend the time to file shall set out the basis for jurisdiction in this Court, identify the judgment sought to be reviewed, include a copy of the opinion and any order respecting rehearing, and set out specific reasons why an extension of time is justified. The application must be received by the Clerk at least 10 days before the date the petition is due, except in extraordinary circumstances. For the time and manner of presenting the application, see Rules 21, 22, 30, and 33.2. An application to extend the time to file a petition for a writ of certiorari is not favored.

RULE 14. CONTENT OF A PETITION FOR A WRIT OF CERTIORARI

1. A petition for a writ of certiorari shall contain, in the order indicated:

(a) The questions presented for review, expressed concisely in relation to the circumstances of the case, without unnecessary detail. The questions should be short and should not be argumentative or repetitive. If the petitioner or respondent is under a death sentence that may be affected by the disposition of the petition, the notation "capital case" shall precede the questions presented. The questions shall be set out on the first page following the cover, and no other information may appear on that page. The statement of any question presented is deemed to comprise every subsidiary question fairly included therein. Only the questions set out in the petition, or fairly included therein, will be considered by the Court.

(b) A list of all parties to the proceeding in the court whose judgment is sought to be reviewed (unless the caption of the case contains the names of all the parties), and a list of parent companies and non-wholly owned subsidiaries as required by Rule 29.6.

(c) If the petition exceeds five pages, a table of contents and a table of cited authorities.

(d) Citations of the official and unofficial reports of the opinions and orders entered in the case by courts or administrative agencies.

(e) A concise statement of the basis for jurisdiction in this Court, showing:

(i) the date the judgment or order sought to be reviewed was entered (and, if applicable, a statement that the petition is filed under this Court's Rule 11);

(ii) the date of any order respecting rehearing, and the date and terms of any order granting an extension of time to file the petition for a writ of certiorari;

(iii) express reliance on Rule 12.5, when a cross-petition for a writ of certiorari is filed under that Rule, and the date of docketing of the petition for a writ of certiorari in connection with which the cross-petition is filed;

(iv) the statutory provision believed to confer on this Court jurisdiction to review on a writ of certiorari the judgment or order in question; and

(v) if applicable, a statement that the notifications required by Rule 29.4(b) or (c) have been made.

(f) The constitutional provisions, treaties, statutes, ordinances, and regulations involved in the case, set out verbatim with appropriate citation. If the provisions involved are lengthy, their citation alone suffices at this point, and their pertinent text shall be set out in the appendix referred to in subparagraph 1(i).

(g) A concise statement of the case setting out the facts material to consideration of the questions presented, and also containing the following:

(i) If review of a state-court judgment is sought, specification of the stage in the proceedings, both in the court of first instance and in the appellate courts, when the federal questions sought to be reviewed were raised; the method or manner of raising them and the way in which they were passed on by those courts; and pertinent quotations of specific portions of the record or summary thereof, with specific reference to the places in the record where the matter appears (*e.g.*, court opinion, ruling on exception, portion of court's charge and exception thereto, assignment of error), so as to show that the federal question was timely and properly raised and that this Court has jurisdiction to review the judgment on a writ of certiorari. When the portions of the record relied on under this subparagraph are voluminous, they shall be included in the appendix referred to in subparagraph 1(i).

(ii) If review of a judgment of a United States court of appeals is sought, the basis for federal jurisdiction in the court of first instance.

(h) A direct and concise argument amplifying the reasons relied on for allowance of the writ. See Rule 10.

(i) An appendix containing, in the order indicated:

(i) the opinions, orders, findings of fact, and conclusions of law, whether written or orally given and transcribed, entered in conjunction with the judgment sought to be reviewed;

(ii) any other opinions, orders, findings of fact, and conclusions of law entered in the case by courts or administrative agencies, and, if reference thereto is necessary to ascertain the grounds of the judgment, of those in companion cases (each document shall include the caption showing the name of the issuing court or agency, the title and number of the case, and the date of entry);

(iii) any order on rehearing, including the caption showing the name of the issuing court, the title and number of the case, and the date of entry;

(iv) the judgment sought to be reviewed if the date of its entry is diVerent from the date of the opinion or order required in sub subparagraph (i) of this subparagraph;

(v) material required by subparagraphs 1(f) or 1(g)(i); and

(vi) any other material the petitioner believes essential to understand the petition.

If the material required by this subparagraph is voluminous, it may be presented in a separate volume or volumes with appropriate covers.

2. All contentions in support of a petition for a writ of certiorari shall be set out in the body of the petition, as provided in subparagraph 1(h) of this Rule. No separate brief in support of a petition for a writ of certiorari may be filed, and the Clerk will not file any petition for a writ of certiorari to which any supporting brief is annexed or appended.

3. A petition for a writ of certiorari should be stated briefly and in plain terms and may not exceed the page limitations specified in Rule 33.

4. The failure of a petitioner to present with accuracy, brevity, and clarity whatever is essential to ready and adequate understanding of the points requiring consideration is sufficient reason for the Court to deny a petition.

5. If the Clerk determines that a petition submitted timely and in good faith is in a form that does not comply with this Rule or with Rule 33 or Rule 34, the Clerk will return it with a letter indicating the deficiency. A corrected petition received no more than 60 days after the date of the Clerk's letter will be deemed timely.

RULE 15. BRIEFS IN OPPOSITION; REPLY BRIEFS; SUPPLEMENTAL BRIEFS

1. A brief in opposition to the petition for a writ of certiorari may be filed by the respondent in any case, but is not mandatory except in a capital case, see Rule 14.1(a) or when ordered by the Court.

2. A brief in opposition should be stated briefly and in plain terms and may not exceed the page limitations specified in Rule 33. In addition to presenting other arguments for denying the petition, the brief in opposition should address any perceived misstatement of fact or law in the petition that bears on what issues properly would be before the Court if certiorari were granted. Counsel are admonished that they have an obligation to the Court to point out in the brief in opposition, and not later, any perceived misstatement made in the petition. Any objection to consideration of a question presented based on what occurred in the proceedings below, if the objection does not go to jurisdiction, may be deemed waived unless called to the Court's attention in the brief in opposition.

3. Any brief in opposition shall be filed within 30 days after the case is placed on the docket, unless the time is extended by the Court or a Justice, or by the Clerk under Rule 30.4. Forty copies shall be filed, except that a respondent proceeding *in forma pauperis* under Rule 39, including an inmate of an institution, shall file the number of copies required for a petition by such a person under Rule 12.2, together with a motion for leave to proceed *in forma pauperis*, a copy of which shall precede and be attached to each copy of the brief in opposition. If the petitioner is proceeding *in forma pauperis*, the respondent may file an original and 10 copies of a brief in opposition prepared as required by Rule 33.2. Whether prepared under Rule 33.1 or Rule 33.2, the brief in opposition shall comply with the requirements of Rule 24 governing a respondent's brief, except that no summary of the argument is required. A brief in opposition may not be joined with any other pleading, except that any motion for leave to proceed *in forma pauperis* shall be attached. The brief in opposition shall be served as required by Rule 29.

4. No motion by a respondent to dismiss a petition for a writ of certiorari may be filed. Any objections to the jurisdiction of the Court to grant a petition for a writ of certiorari shall be included in the brief in opposition.

5. The Clerk will distribute the petition to the Court for its consideration upon receiving an express waiver of the right to file a brief in opposition, or, if no waiver or brief in opposition is filed, upon the expiration of the time allowed for filing. If a brief in opposition is timely filed, the Clerk will distribute the petition, brief in opposition, and any reply brief to the Court for its consideration no less than 10 days after the brief in opposition is filed.

6. Any petitioner may file a reply brief addressed to new points raised in the brief in opposition, but distribution and consideration by the Court under paragraph 5 of this Rule will not be deferred pending its receipt. Forty copies shall be filed, except that petitioner proceeding *in forma pauperis* under Rule 39, including an inmate of an institution, shall file the number of copies required for a petition

by such a person under Rule 12.2. The reply brief shall be served as required by Rule 29.

7. If a cross-petition for a writ of certiorari has been docketed, distribution of both petitions will be deferred until the cross-petition is due for distribution under this Rule.

8. Any party may file a supplemental brief at any time while a petition for a writ of certiorari is pending, calling attention to new cases, new legislation, or other intervening matter not available at the time of the party's last filing. A supplemental brief shall be restricted to new matter and shall follow, insofar as applicable, the form for a brief in opposition prescribed by this Rule. Forty copies shall be filed, except that a party proceeding *in forma pauperis* under Rule 39, including an inmate of an institution, shall file the number of copies required for a petition by such a person under Rule 12.2. The supplemental brief shall be served as required by Rule 29.

RULE 16. DISPOSITION OF A PETITION FOR A WRIT OF CERTIORARI

1. After considering the documents distributed under Rule 15, the Court will enter an appropriate order. The order may be a summary disposition on the merits.

2. Whenever the Court grants a petition for a writ of certiorari, the Clerk will prepare, sign, and enter an order to that effect and will notify forthwith counsel of record and the court whose judgment is to be reviewed. The case then will be scheduled for briefing and oral argument. If the record has not previously been filed in this Court, the Clerk will request the clerk of the court having possession of the record to certify and transmit it. A formal writ will not issue unless specially directed.

3. Whenever the Court denies a petition for a writ of certiorari, the Clerk will prepare, sign, and enter an order to that effect and will notify forthwith counsel of record and the court whose judgment was sought to be reviewed. The order of denial will not be suspended pending disposition of a petition for rehearing except by order of the Court or a Justice.

PART IV. OTHER JURISDICTION

RULE 17. PROCEDURE IN AN ORIGINAL ACTION

1. This Rule applies only to an action invoking the Court's original jurisdiction under Article III of the Constitution of the United States. See also 28 U.S.C. §1251 and U.S. Const., Amdt. 11. A petition for an extraordinary writ in aid of the Court's appellate jurisdiction shall be filed as provided in Rule 20.

2. The form of pleadings and motions prescribed by the Federal Rules of Civil Procedure is followed. In other respects, those Rules and the Federal Rules of Evidence may be taken as guides.

3. The initial pleading shall be preceded by a motion for leave to file, and may be accompanied by a brief in support of the motion. Forty copies of each document shall be filed, with proof of service. Service shall be as required by Rule 29, except that when an adverse party is a State, service shall be made on both the Governor and the Attorney General of that State.

4. The case will be placed on the docket when the motion for leave to file and the initial pleading are filed with the Clerk. The Rule 38(a) docket fee shall be paid at that time.

5. No more than 60 days after receiving the motion for leave to file and the initial pleading, an adverse party shall file 40 copies of any brief in opposition to the motion, with proof of service as required by Rule 29. The Clerk will distribute the filed documents to the Court for its consideration upon receiving an express waiver of the right to file a brief in opposition, or, if no waiver or brief is filed, upon the

expiration of the time allowed for filing. If a brief in opposition is timely filed, the Clerk will distribute the filed documents to the Court for its consideration no less than 10 days after the brief in opposition is filed. A reply brief may be filed, but consideration of the case will not be deferred pending its receipt. The Court thereafter may grant or deny the motion, set it for oral argument, direct that additional documents be filed, or require that other proceedings be conducted.

6. A summons issued out of this Court shall be served on the defendant 60 days before the return day specified therein. If the defendant does not respond by the return day, the plaintiff may proceed *ex parte.*

7. Process against a State issued out of this Court shall be served on both the Governor and the Attorney General of that State.

RULE 18. APPEAL FROM A UNITED STATES DISTRICT COURT

1. When a direct appeal from a decision of a United States district court is authorized by law, the appeal is commenced by filing a notice of appeal with the clerk of the district court within the time provided by law after entry of the judgment sought to be reviewed. The time to file may not be extended. The notice of appeal shall specify the parties taking the appeal, designate the judgment, or part thereof, appealed from and the date of its entry, and specify the statute or statutes under which the appeal is taken. A copy of the notice of appeal shall be served on all parties to the proceeding as required by Rule 29, and proof of service shall be filed in the district court together with the notice of appeal.

2. All parties to the proceeding in the district court are deemed parties entitled to file documents in this Court, but a party having no interest in the outcome of the appeal may so notify the Clerk of this Court and shall serve a copy of the notice on all other parties. Parties interested jointly, severally, or otherwise in the judgment may appeal separately, or any two or more may join in an appeal. When two or more judgments involving identical or closely related questions are sought to be reviewed on appeal from the same court, a notice of appeal for each judgment shall be filed with the clerk of the district court, but a single jurisdictional statement covering all the judgments suffices. Parties who file no document will not qualify for any relief from this Court.

3. No more than 60 days after filing the notice of appeal in the district court, the appellant shall file 40 copies of a jurisdictional statement and shall pay the Rule 38 docket fee, except that an appellant proceeding *in forma pauperis* under Rule 39, including an inmate of an institution, shall file the number of copies required for a petition by such a person under Rule 12.2, together with a motion for leave to proceed *in forma pauperis,* a copy of which shall precede and be attached to each copy of the jurisdictional statement. The jurisdictional statement shall follow, insofar as applicable, the form for a petition for a writ of certiorari prescribed by Rule 14, and shall be served as required by Rule 29. The appendix shall include a copy of the notice of appeal showing the date it was filed in the district court. For good cause, a Justice may extend the time to file a jurisdictional statement for a period not exceeding 60 days. An application to extend the time to file a jurisdictional statement shall set out the basis for jurisdiction in this Court; identify the judgment sought to be reviewed; include a copy of the opinion, any order respecting rehearing, and the notice of appeal; and set out specific reasons why an extension of time is justified. For the time and manner of presenting the application, see Rules 21, 22, and 30. An application to extend the time to file a jurisdictional statement is not favored.

4. No more than 30 days after a case has been placed on the docket, an appellee seeking to file a conditional cross-appeal (*i.e.,* a cross-appeal

that otherwise would be untimely) shall file, with proof of service as required by Rule 29, a jurisdictional statement that complies in all respects (including number of copies filed) with paragraph 3 of this Rule, except that material already reproduced in the appendix to the opening jurisdictional statement need not be reproduced again. A cross-appealing appellee shall pay the Rule 38 docket fee or submit a motion for leave to proceed *in forma pauperis*. The cover of the cross-appeal shall indicate clearly that it is a conditional cross-appeal. The cross-appeal then will be placed on the docket. It is the cross-appellant's duty to notify all cross-appellees promptly, on a form supplied by the Clerk, of the date of filing, the date the cross-appeal was placed on the docket, and the docket number of the cross-appeal. The notice shall be served as required by Rule 29. A cross-appeal may not be joined with any other pleading, except that any motion for leave to proceed *in forma pauperis* shall be attached. The time to file a cross-appeal will not be extended.

5. After a notice of appeal has been filed in the district court, but before the case is placed on this Court's docket, the parties may dismiss the appeal by stipulation filed in the district court, or the district court may dismiss the appeal on the appellant's motion, with notice to all parties. If a notice of appeal has been filed, but the case has not been placed on this Court's docket within the time prescribed for docketing, the district court may dismiss the appeal on the appellee's motion, with notice to all parties, and may make any just order with respect to costs. If the district court has denied the appellee's motion to dismiss the appeal, the appellee may move this Court to docket and dismiss the appeal by filing an original and 10 copies of a motion presented in conformity with Rules 21 and 33.2. The motion shall be accompanied by proof of service as required by Rule 29, and by a certificate from the clerk of the district court, certifying that a notice of appeal was filed and that the appellee's motion to dismiss was denied. The appellant may not thereafter file a jurisdictional statement without special leave of the Court, and the Court may allow costs against the appellant.

6. Within 30 days after the case is placed on this Court's docket, the appellee may file a motion to dismiss, to affirm, or in the alternative to affirm or dismiss. Forty copies of the motion shall be filed, except that an appellee proceeding *in forma pauperis* under Rule 39, including an inmate of an institution, shall file the number of copies required for a petition by such a person under Rule 12.2, together with a motion for leave to proceed *in forma pauperis,* a copy of which shall precede and be attached to each copy of the motion to dismiss, to affirm, or in the alternative to affirm or dismiss. The motion shall follow, insofar as applicable, the form for a brief in opposition prescribed by Rule 15, and shall comply in all respects with Rule 21.

7. The Clerk will distribute the jurisdictional statement to the Court for its consideration upon receiving an express waiver of the right to file a motion to dismiss or to affirm or, if no waiver or motion is filed, upon the expiration of the time allowed for filing. If a motion to dismiss or to affirm is timely filed, the Clerk will distribute the jurisdictional statement, motion, and any brief opposing the motion to the Court for its consideration no less than 10 days after the motion is filed.

8. Any appellant may file a brief opposing a motion to dismiss or to affirm, but distribution and consideration by the Court under paragraph 7 of this Rule will not be deferred pending its receipt. Forty copies shall be filed, except that an appellant proceeding *in forma pauperis* under Rule 39, including an inmate of an institution, shall file the number of copies required for a petition by such a person under Rule 12.2. The brief shall be served as required by Rule 29.

9. If a cross-appeal has been docketed, distribution of both jurisdictional statements will be deferred until the cross-appeal is due for distribution under this Rule.

10. Any party may file a supplemental brief at any time while a jurisdictional statement is pending, calling attention to new cases, new legislation, or other intervening matter not available at the time of the party's last filing. A supplemental brief shall be restricted to new matter and shall follow, insofar as applicable, the form for a brief in opposition prescribed by Rule 15. Forty copies shall be filed, except that a party proceeding *in forma pauperis* under Rule 39, including an inmate of an institution, shall file the number of copies required for a petition by such a person under Rule 12.2. The supplemental brief shall be served as required by Rule 29.

11. The clerk of the district court shall retain possession of the record until notified by the Clerk of this Court to certify and transmit it. See Rule 12.7.

12. After considering the documents distributed under this Rule, the Court may dispose summarily of the appeal on the merits, note probable jurisdiction, or postpone consideration of jurisdiction until a hearing of the case on the merits. If not disposed of summarily, the case stands for briefing and oral argument on the merits. If consideration of jurisdiction is postponed, counsel, at the outset of their briefs and at oral argument, shall address the question of jurisdiction. If the record has not previously been filed in this Court, the Clerk of this Court will request the clerk of the court in possession of the record to certify and transmit it.

13. If the Clerk determines that a jurisdictional statement submitted timely and in good faith is in a form that does not comply with this Rule or with Rule 33 or Rule 34, the Clerk will return it with a letter indicating the deficiency. If a corrected jurisdictional statement is received no more than 60 days after the date of the Clerk's letter, its filing will be deemed timely.

RULE 19. PROCEDURE ON A CERTIFIED QUESTION

1. A United States court of appeals may certify to this Court a question or proposition of law on which it seeks instruction for the proper decision of a case. The certificate shall contain a statement of the nature of the case and the facts on which the question or proposition of law arises. Only questions or propositions of law may be certified, and they shall be stated separately and with precision. The certificate shall be prepared as required by Rule 33.2 and shall be signed by the clerk of the court of appeals.

2. When a question is certified by a United States court of appeals, this Court, on its own motion or that of a party, may consider and decide the entire matter in controversy. See 28 U.S.C. §1254(2).

3. When a question is certified, the Clerk will notify the parties and docket the case. Counsel shall then enter their appearances. After docketing, the Clerk will submit the certificate to the Court for a preliminary examination to determine whether the case should be briefed, set for argument, or dismissed. No brief may be filed until the preliminary examination of the certificate is completed.

4. If the Court orders the case briefed or set for argument, the parties will be notified and permitted to file briefs. The Clerk of this Court then will request the clerk of the court in possession of the record to certify and transmit it. Any portion of the record to which the parties wish to direct the Court's particular attention should be printed in a joint appendix, prepared in conformity with Rule 26 by the appellant or petitioner in the court of appeals, but the fact that any part of the record has not been printed does not prevent the parties or the Court from relying on it.

5. A brief on the merits in a case involving a certified question shall comply with Rules 24, 25, and 33.1, except that the brief for the

party who is the appellant or petitioner below shall be filed within 45 days of the order requiring briefs or setting the case for argument.

RULE 20. PROCEDURE ON A PETITION FOR AN EXTRAORDINARY WRIT

1. Issuance by the Court of an extraordinary writ authorized by 28 U.S.C. §1651(a) is not a matter of right, but of discretion sparingly exercised. To justify the granting of any such writ, the petition must show that the writ will be in aid of the Court's appellate jurisdiction, that exceptional circumstances warrant the exercise of the Court's discretionary powers, and that adequate relief cannot be obtained in any other form or from any other court.

2. A petition seeking a writ authorized by 28 U.S.C. §1651(a), §2241, or §2254(a) shall be prepared in all respects as required by Rules 33 and 34. The petition shall be captioned "*In re* [name of petitioner]" and shall follow, insofar as applicable, the form of a petition for a writ of certiorari prescribed by Rule 14. All contentions in support of the petition shall be included in the petition. The case will be placed on the docket when 40 copies of the petition are filed with the Clerk and the docket fee is paid, except that a petitioner proceeding *in forma pauperis* under Rule 39, including an inmate of an institution, shall file the number of copies required for a petition by such a person under Rule 12.2, together with a motion for leave to proceed *in forma pauperis*, a copy of which shall precede and be attached to each copy of the petition. The petition shall be served as required by Rule 29 (subject to subparagraph 4(b) of this Rule).

3. (a) A petition seeking a writ of prohibition, a writ of mandamus, or both in the alternative shall state the name and office or function of every person against whom relief is sought and shall set out with particularity why the relief sought is not available in any other court. A copy of the judgment with respect to which the writ is sought, including any related opinion, shall be appended to the petition together with any other document essential to understanding the petition.

(b) The petition shall be served on every party to the proceeding with respect to which relief is sought. Within 30 days after the petition is placed on the docket, a party shall file 40 copies of any brief or briefs in opposition thereto, which shall comply fully with Rule 15. If a party named as a respondent does not wish to respond to the petition, that party may so advise the Clerk and all other parties by letter. All persons served are deemed respondents for all purposes in the proceedings in this Court.

4. (a) A petition seeking a writ of habeas corpus shall comply with the requirements of 28 U.S.C. §§2241 and 2242, and in particular with the provision in the last paragraph of §2242, which requires a statement of the "reasons for not making application to the district court of the district in which the applicant is held." If the relief sought is from the judgment of a state court, the petition shall set out specifically how and where the petitioner has exhausted available remedies in the state courts or otherwise comes within the provisions of 28 U.S.C. §2254(b). To justify the granting of a writ of habeas corpus, the petitioner must show that exceptional circumstances warrant the exercise of the Court's discretionary powers, and that adequate relief cannot be obtained in any other form or from any other court. This writ is rarely granted.

(b) Habeas corpus proceedings are *ex parte,* unless the Court requires the respondent to show cause why the petition for a writ of habeas corpus should not be granted. A response, if ordered, shall comply fully with Rule 15. Neither the denial of the petition, without more, nor an order of transfer to a district court under the authority of 28 U.S.C. §2241(b), is an adjudication on the merits, and therefore does not preclude further application to another court for the relief sought.

5. The Clerk will distribute the documents to the Court for its consideration when a brief in opposition under subparagraph 3(b) of this Rule has been filed, when a response under subparagraph 4(b) has been ordered and filed, when the time to file has expired, or when the right to file has been expressly waived.

6. If the Court orders the case set for argument, the Clerk will notify the parties whether additional briefs are required, when they shall be filed, and, if the case involves a petition for a common-law writ of certiorari, that the parties shall prepare a joint appendix in accordance with Rule 26.

PART V. MOTIONS AND APPLICATIONS

RULE 21. MOTIONS TO THE COURT

1. Every motion to the Court shall clearly state its purpose and the facts on which it is based and may present legal argument in support thereof. No separate brief may be filed. A motion should be concise and shall comply with any applicable page limits. Rule 22 governs an application addressed to a single Justice.

2. (a) A motion in any action within the Court's original jurisdiction shall comply with Rule 17.3.

(b) A motion to dismiss as moot (or a suggestion of mootness), a motion for leave to file a brief as *amicus curiae,* and any motion the granting of which would dispose of the entire case or would affect the final judgment to be entered (other than a motion to docket and dismiss under Rule 18.5 or a motion for voluntary dismissal under Rule 46) shall be prepared as required by Rule 33.1, and 40 copies shall be filed, except that a movant proceeding *in forma pauperis* under Rule 39, including an inmate of an institution, shall file a motion prepared as required by Rule 33.2, and shall file the number of copies required for a petition by such a person under Rule 12.2. The motion shall be served as required by Rule 29.

(c) Any other motion to the Court shall be prepared as required by Rule 33.2; the moving party shall file an original and 10 copies. The Court subsequently may order the moving party to prepare the motion as required by Rule 33.1; in that event, the party shall file 40 copies.

3. A motion to the Court shall be filed with the Clerk and shall be accompanied by proof of service as required by Rule 29. No motion may be presented in open Court, other than a motion for admission to the Bar, except when the proceeding to which it refers is being argued. Oral argument on a motion will not be permitted unless the Court so directs.

4. Any response to a motion shall be filed as promptly as possible considering the nature of the relief sought and any asserted need for emergency action, and, in any event, within 10 days of receipt, unless the Court or a Justice, or the Clerk under Rule 30.4, orders otherwise. A response to a motion prepared as required by Rule 33.1 shall be prepared in the same manner if time permits. In an appropriate case, the Court may act on a motion without waiting for a response.

RULE 22. APPLICATIONS TO INDIVIDUAL JUSTICES

1. An application addressed to an individual Justice shall be filed with the Clerk, who will transmit it promptly to the Justice concerned if an individual Justice has authority to grant the sought relief.

2. The original and two copies of any application addressed to an individual Justice shall be prepared as required by Rule 33.2, and shall be accompanied by proof of service as required by Rule 29.

3. An application shall be addressed to the Justice allotted to the Circuit from which the case arises. When the Circuit Justice is

unavailable for any reason, the application addressed to that Justice will be distributed to the Justice then available who is next junior to the Circuit Justice; the turn of the Chief Justice follows that of the most junior Justice.

4. A Justice denying an application will note the denial thereon. Thereafter, unless action thereon is restricted by law to the Circuit Justice or is untimely under Rule 30.2, the party making an application, except in the case of an application for an extension of time, may renew it to any other Justice, subject to the provisions of this Rule. Except when the denial is without prejudice, a renewed application is not favored. Renewed application is made by a letter to the Clerk, designating the Justice to whom the application is to be directed, and accompanied by 10 copies of the original application and proof of service as required by Rule 29.

5. A Justice to whom an application for a stay or for bail is submitted may refer it to the Court for determination.

6. The Clerk will advise all parties concerned, by appropriately speedy means, of the disposition made of an application.

RULE 23. STAYS

1. A stay may be granted by a Justice as permitted by law.

2. A party to a judgment sought to be reviewed may present to a Justice an application to stay the enforcement of that judgment. See 28 U.S.C. §2101(f).

3. An application for a stay shall set out with particularity why the relief sought is not available from any other court or judge. Except in the most extraordinary circumstances, an application for a stay will not be entertained unless the relief requested was first sought in the appropriate court or courts below or from a judge or judges thereof. An application for a stay shall identify the judgment sought to be reviewed and have appended thereto a copy of the order and opinion, if any, and a copy of the order, if any, of the court or judge below denying the relief sought, and shall set out specific reasons why a stay is justified. The form and content of an application for a stay are governed by Rules 22 and 33.2.

4. A judge, court, or Justice granting an application for a stay pending review by this Court may condition the stay on the filing of a supersedeas bond having an approved surety or sureties. The bond will be conditioned on the satisfaction of the judgment in full, together with any costs, interest, and damages for delay that may be awarded. If a part of the judgment sought to be reviewed has already been satisfied, or is otherwise secured, the bond may be conditioned on the satisfaction of the part of the judgment not otherwise secured or satisfied, together with costs, interest, and damages.

PART VI. BRIEFS ON THE MERITS AND ORAL ARGUMENT

RULE 24. BRIEFS ON THE MERITS: IN GENERAL

1. A brief on the merits for a petitioner or an appellant shall comply in all respects with Rules 33.1 and 34 and shall contain in the order here indicated:

(a) The questions presented for review under Rule 14.1(a). The questions shall be set out on the first page following the cover, and no other information may appear on that page. The phrasing of the questions presented need not be identical with that in the petition for a writ of certiorari or the jurisdictional statement, but the brief may not raise additional questions or change the substance of the questions already presented in those documents. At its option, however, the Court may consider a plain error not among the questions presented but evident from the record and otherwise within its jurisdiction to decide.

(b) A list of all parties to the proceeding in the court whose judgment is under review (unless the caption of the case in this Court contains the names of all parties). Any amended list of parent companies and nonwholly owned subsidiaries as required by Rule 29.6 shall be placed here.

(c) If the brief exceeds five pages, a table of contents and a table of cited authorities.

(d) Citations of the official and unofficial reports of the opinions and orders entered in the case by courts and administrative agencies.

(e) A concise statement of the basis for jurisdiction in this Court, including the statutory provisions and time factors on which jurisdiction rests.

(f) The constitutional provisions, treaties, statutes, ordinances, and regulations involved in the case, set out verbatim with appropriate citation. If the provisions involved are lengthy, their citation alone suffices at this point, and their pertinent text, if not already set out in the petition for a writ of certiorari, jurisdictional statement, or an appendix to either document, shall be set out in an appendix to the brief.

(g) A concise statement of the case, setting out the facts material to the consideration of the questions presented, with appropriate references to the joint appendix, e.g., App. 12, or to the record, e.g., Record 12.

(h) A summary of the argument, suitably paragraphed. The summary should be a clear and concise condensation of the argument made in the body of the brief; mere repetition of the headings under which the argument is arranged is not sufficient.

(i) The argument, exhibiting clearly the points of fact and of law presented and citing the authorities and statutes relied on.

(j) A conclusion specifying with particularity the relief the party seeks.

2. A brief on the merits for a respondent or an appellee shall conform to the foregoing requirements, except that items required by subparagraphs 1(a), (b), (d), (e), (f), and (g) of this Rule need not be included unless the respondent or appellee is dissatisfied with their presentation by the opposing party.

3. A brief on the merits may not exceed the page limitations specified in Rule 33.1(g). An appendix to a brief may include only relevant material, and counsel are cautioned not to include in an appendix arguments or citations that properly belong in the body of the brief.

4. A reply brief shall conform to those portions of this Rule applicable to the brief for a respondent or an appellee, but, if appropriately divided by topical headings, need not contain a summary of the argument.

5. A reference to the joint appendix or to the record set out in any brief shall indicate the appropriate page number. If the reference is to an exhibit, the page numbers at which the exhibit appears, at which it was offered in evidence, and at which it was ruled on by the judge shall be indicated, e.g., Pl. Exh. 14, Record 199, 2134.

6. A brief shall be concise, logically arranged with proper headings, and free of irrelevant, immaterial, or scandalous matter. The Court may disregard or strike a brief that does not comply with this paragraph.

RULE 25. BRIEFS ON THE MERITS: NUMBER OF COPIES AND TIME TO FILE

1. The petitioner or appellant shall file 40 copies of the brief on the merits within 45 days of the order granting the writ of certiorari, noting probable jurisdiction, or postponing consideration of jurisdiction.

2. The respondent or appellee shall file 40 copies of the brief on the merits within 30 days after receiving the brief for the petitioner or appellant.

3. The petitioner or appellant shall file 40 copies of the reply brief, if any, within 30 days after receiving the brief for the respondent or appellee, but any reply brief must actually be received by the Clerk no more than one week before the date of oral argument.

4. The time periods stated in paragraphs 1 and 2 of this Rule may be extended as provided in Rule 30. An application to extend the time to file a brief on the merits is not favored. If a case is advanced for hearing, the time to file briefs on the merits may be abridged as circumstances require pursuant to an order of the Court on its own motion or that of a party.

5. A party wishing to present late authorities, newly enacted legislation, or other intervening matter that was not available in time to be included in a brief may file 40 copies of a supplemental brief, restricted to such new matter and otherwise presented in conformity with these Rules, up to the time the case is called for oral argument or by leave of the Court thereafter.

6. After a case has been argued or submitted, the Clerk will not file any brief, except that of a party filed by leave of the Court.

7. The Clerk will not file any brief that is not accompanied by proof of service as required by Rule 29.

RULE 26. JOINT APPENDIX

1. Unless the Clerk has allowed the parties to use the deferred method described in paragraph 4 of this Rule, the petitioner or appellant, within 45 days after entry of the order granting the writ of certiorari, noting probable jurisdiction, or postponing consideration of jurisdiction, shall file 40 copies of a joint appendix, prepared as required by Rule 33.1. The joint appendix shall contain: (1) the relevant docket entries in all the courts below; (2) any relevant pleadings, jury instructions, findings, conclusions, or opinions; (3) the judgment, order, or decision under review; and (4) any other parts of the record that the parties particularly wish to bring to the Court's attention. Any of the foregoing items already reproduced in a petition for a writ of certiorari, jurisdictional statement, brief in opposition to a petition for a writ of certiorari, motion to dismiss or affirm, or any appendix to the foregoing, that was prepared as required by Rule 33.1, need not be reproduced again in the joint appendix. The petitioner or appellant shall serve three copies of the joint appendix on each of the other parties to the proceeding as required by Rule 29.

2. The parties are encouraged to agree on the contents of the joint appendix. In the absence of agreement, the petitioner or appellant, within 10 days after entry of the order granting the writ of certiorari, noting probable jurisdiction, or postponing consideration of jurisdiction, shall serve on the respondent or appellee a designation of parts of the record to be included in the joint appendix. Within 10 days after receiving the designation, a respondent or appellee who considers the parts of the record so designated insufficient shall serve on the petitioner or appellant a designation of additional parts to be included in the joint appendix, and the petitioner or appellant shall include the parts so designated. If the Court has permitted the respondent or appellee to proceed *in forma pauperis*, the petitioner or appellant may seek by motion to be excused from printing portions of the record the petitioner or appellant considers unnecessary. In making these designations, counsel should include only those materials the Court should examine; unnecessary designations should be avoided. The record is on file with the Clerk and available to the Justices, and counsel may refer in briefs and in oral argument to relevant portions of the record not included in the joint appendix.

3. When the joint appendix is filed, the petitioner or appellant immediately shall file with the Clerk a statement of the cost of printing 50 copies and shall serve a copy of the statement on each of the other parties as required by Rule 29. Unless the parties agree otherwise, the cost of producing the joint appendix shall be paid initially by the petitioner or appellant; but a petitioner or appellant who considers that parts of the record designated by the respondent or appellee are unnecessary for the determination of the issues presented may so advise the respondent or appellee, who then shall advance the cost of printing the additional parts, unless the Court or a Justice otherwise fixes the initial allocation of the costs. The cost of printing the joint appendix is taxed as a cost in the case, but if a party unnecessarily causes matter to be included in the joint appendix or prints excessive copies, the Court may impose these costs on that party.

4. (a) On the parties' request, the Clerk may allow preparation of the joint appendix to be deferred until after the briefs have been filed. In that event, the petitioner or appellant shall file the joint appendix no more than 14 days after receiving the brief for the respondent or appellee. The provisions of paragraphs 1, 2, and 3 of this Rule shall be followed, except that the designations referred to therein shall be made by each party when that party's brief is served. Deferral of the joint appendix is not favored.

(b) If the deferred method is used, the briefs on the merits may refer to the pages of the record. In that event, the joint appendix shall include in brackets on each page thereof the page number of the record where that material may be found. A party wishing to refer directly to the pages of the joint appendix may serve and file copies of its brief prepared as required by Rule 33.2 within the time provided by Rule 25, with appropriate references to the pages of the record. In that event, within 10 days after the joint appendix is filed, copies of the brief prepared as required by Rule 33.1 containing references to the pages of the joint appendix in place of, or in addition to, the initial references to the pages of the record, shall be served and filed. No other change may be made in the brief as initially served and filed, except that typographical errors may be corrected.

5. The joint appendix shall be prefaced by a table of contents showing the parts of the record that it contains, in the order in which the parts are set out, with references to the pages of the joint appendix at which each part begins. The relevant docket entries shall be set out after the table of contents, followed by the other parts of the record in chronological order. When testimony contained in the reporter's transcript of proceedings is set out in the joint appendix, the page of the transcript at which the testimony appears shall be indicated in brackets immediately before the statement that is set out. Omissions in the transcript or in any other document printed in the joint appendix shall be indicated by asterisks. Immaterial formal matters (*e.g.,* captions, subscriptions, acknowledgments) shall be omitted. A question and its answer may be contained in a single paragraph.

6. Exhibits designated for inclusion in the joint appendix may be contained in a separate volume or volumes suitably indexed. The transcript of a proceeding before an administrative agency, board, commission, or officer used in an action in a district court or court of appeals is regarded as an exhibit for the purposes of this paragraph.

7. The Court, on its own motion or that of a party, may dispense with the requirement of a joint appendix and may permit a case to be heard on the original record (with such copies of the record, or relevant parts thereof, as the Court may require) or on the appendix used in the court below, if it conforms to the requirements of this Rule. 8. For good cause, the time limits specified in this Rule may be shortened or extended by the Court or a Justice, or by the Clerk under Rule 30.4.

RULE 27. THE CALENDAR

1. From time to time, the Clerk will prepare a calendar of cases ready for argument. A case ordinarily will not be called for argument less than two weeks after the brief on the merits for the respondent or appellee is due.

2. The Clerk will advise counsel when they are required to appear for oral argument and will publish a hearing list in advance of each argument session for the convenience of counsel and the information of the public.

3. The Court, on its own motion or that of a party, may order that two or more cases involving the same or related questions be argued together as one case or on such other terms as the Court may prescribe.

RULE 28. ORAL ARGUMENT

1. Oral argument should emphasize and clarify the written arguments in the briefs on the merits. Counsel should assume that all Justices have read the briefs before oral argument. Oral argument read from a prepared text is not favored.

2. The petitioner or appellant shall open and may conclude the argument. A cross writ of certiorari or cross-appeal will be argued with the initial writ of certiorari or appeal as one case in the time allowed for that one case, and the Court will advise the parties who shall open and close.

3. Unless the Court directs otherwise, each side is allowed one-half hour for argument. Counsel is not required to use all the allotted time. Any request for additional time to argue shall be presented by motion under Rule 21 no more than 15 days after the petitioner's or appellant's brief on the merits is filed, and shall set out specifically and concisely why the case cannot be presented within the half hour limitation. Additional time is rarely accorded.

4. Only one attorney will be heard for each side, except by leave of the Court on motion filed no more than 15 days after the respondent's or appellee's brief on the merits is filed. Any request for divided argument shall be presented by motion under Rule 21 and shall set out specifically and concisely why more than one attorney should be allowed to argue. Divided argument is not favored.

5. Regardless of the number of counsel participating in oral argument, counsel making the opening argument shall present the case fairly and completely and not reserve points of substance for rebuttal.

6. Oral argument will not be allowed on behalf of any party for whom a brief has not been filed.

7. By leave of the Court, and subject to paragraph 4 of this Rule, counsel for an *amicus curiae* whose brief has been filed as provided in Rule 37 may argue orally on the side of a party, with the consent of that party. In the absence of consent, counsel for an *amicus curiae* may seek leave of the Court to argue orally by a motion setting out specifically and concisely why oral argument would provide assistance to the Court not otherwise available. Such a motion will be granted only in the most extraordinary circumstances.

PART VII. PRACTICE AND PROCEDURE

RULE 29. FILING AND SERVICE OF DOCUMENTS SPECIAL NOTIFICATIONS; CORPORATE LISTING

1. Any document required or permitted to be presented to the Court or to a Justice shall be filed with the Clerk.

2. A document is timely filed if it is sent to the Clerk through the United States Postal Service by first-class mail (including express or priority mail), postage prepaid, and bears a postmark showing that the document was mailed on or before the last day for filing. Commercial postage meter labels alone are not acceptable. If submitted by an inmate confined in an institution, a document is timely filed if it is deposited in the institution's internal mail system on or before the last day for filing and is accompanied by a notarized statement or declaration in compliance with 28 U.S.C. §1746 setting out the date of deposit and stating that first-class postage has been prepaid. If the

postmark is missing or not legible, the Clerk will require the person who mailed the document to submit a notarized statement or declaration in compliance with 28 U.S.C. §1746 setting out the details of the mailing and stating that the mailing took place on a particular date within the permitted time. A document also is timely filed if it is forwarded through a private delivery or courier service and is actually received by the Clerk within the time permitted for filing.

3. Any document required by these Rules to be served may be served personally or by mail on each party to the proceeding at or before the time of filing. If the document has been prepared as required by Rule 33.1, three copies shall be served on each other party separately represented in the proceeding. If the document has been prepared as required by Rule 33.2, service of a single copy on each other separately represented party suffices. If personal service is made, it shall consist of delivery at the office of the counsel of record, either to counsel or to an employee therein. If service is by mail, it shall consist of depositing the document with the United States Postal Service, with no less than first-class postage prepaid, addressed to counsel of record at the proper post office address. When a party is not represented by counsel, service shall be made on the party, personally or by mail.

4.(a) If the United States or any federal department, office, agency, officer, or employee is a party to be served, service shall be made on the Solicitor General of the United States, Room 5614, Department of Justice, 10th St. and Constitution Ave., N.W., Washington, DC 20530. When an agency of the United States that is a party is authorized by law to appear before this Court on its own behalf, or when an officer or employee of the United States is a party, the agency, officer, or employee shall be served in addition to the Solicitor General.

(b) In any proceeding in this Court in which the constitutionality of an Act of Congress is drawn into question, and neither the United States nor any federal department, office, agency, officer, or employee is a party, the initial document filed in this Court shall recite that 28 U.S.C. §2403(a) may apply and shall be served on the Solicitor General of the United States, Room 5614, Department of Justice, 10th St. and Constitution Ave., N.W., Washington, DC 20530. In such a proceeding from any court of the United States, as defined by 28 U.S.C. §451, the initial document also shall state whether that court, pursuant to 28 U.S.C. §2403(a), certified to the Attorney General the fact that the constitutionality of an Act of Congress was drawn into question. See Rule 14.1(e)(v).

(c) In any proceeding in this Court in which the constitutionality of any statute of a State is drawn into question, and neither the State nor any agency, officer, or employee thereof is a party, the initial document filed in this Court shall recite that 28 U.S.C. §2403(b) may apply and shall be served on the Attorney General of that State. In such a proceeding from any court of the United States, as defined by 28 U.S.C. §451, the initial document also shall state whether that court, pursuant to 28 U.S.C. §2403(b), certified to the State Attorney General the fact that the constitutionality of a statute of that State was drawn into question. See Rule 14.1(e)(v).

5. Proof of service, when required by these Rules, shall accompany the document when it is presented to the Clerk for filing and shall be separate from it. Proof of service shall contain, or be accompanied by, a statement that all parties required to be served have been served, together with a list of the names, addresses, and telephone numbers of counsel indicating the name of the party or parties each counsel represents. It is not necessary that service on each party required to be served be made in the same manner or evidenced by the same proof. Proof of service may consist of any one of the following:

(a) an acknowledgment of service, signed by counsel of record for the party served;

(b) a certificate of service, reciting the facts and circumstances of service in compliance with the appropriate paragraph or paragraphs of this Rule, and signed by a member of the Bar of this Court representing the party on whose behalf service is made or by an attorney appointed to represent that party under the Criminal Justice Act of 1964, see 18 U.S.C. §3006A(d)(6), or under any other applicable federal statute; or

(c) a notarized affidavit or declaration in compliance with 28 U.S.C. §1746, reciting the facts and circumstances of service in accordance with the appropriate paragraph or paragraphs of this Rule, whenever service is made by any person not a member of the Bar of this Court and not an attorney appointed to represent a party under the Criminal Justice Act of 1964, see 18 U.S.C. §3006A(d)(6), or under any other applicable federal statute.

6. Every document, except a joint appendix or *amicus curiae* brief, filed by or on behalf of one or more corporations shall list all parent companies and nonwholly owned subsidiaries of each of the corporate filers. If there is no parent or subsidiary company to be listed, a notation to this effect shall be included in the document. If a list has been included in a document filed earlier in the case, reference may be made to the earlier document (except when the earlier list appeared in an application for an extension of time or for a stay), and only amendments to the list to make it current need be included in the document being filed.

RULE 30. COMPUTATION AND EXTENSION OF TIME

1. In the computation of any period of time prescribed or allowed by these Rules, by order of the Court, or by an applicable statute, the day of the act, event, or default from which the designated period begins to run is not included. The last day of the period shall be included, unless it is a Saturday, Sunday, federal legal holiday listed in 5 U.S.C. §6103, or day on which the Court building is closed by order of the Court or the Chief Justice, in which event the period shall extend until the end of the next day that is not a Saturday, Sunday, federal legal holiday, or day on which the Court building is closed.

2. Whenever a Justice or the Clerk is empowered by law or these Rules to extend the time to file any document, an application seeking an extension shall be filed within the period sought to be extended. An application to extend the time to file a petition for a writ of certiorari or to file a jurisdictional statement must be received by the Clerk at least 10 days before the specified final filing date as computed under these Rules; if received less than 10 days before the final filing date, such application will not be granted except in the most extraordinary circumstances.

3. An application to extend the time to file a petition for a writ of certiorari, to file a jurisdictional statement, to file a reply brief on the merits, or to file a petition for rehearing shall be made to an individual Justice and presented and served on all other parties as provided by Rule 22. Once denied, such an application may not be renewed.

4. An application to extend the time to file any document or paper other than those specified in paragraph 3 of this Rule may be presented in the form of a letter to the Clerk setting out specific reasons why an extension of time is justified. The letter shall be served on all other parties as required by Rule 29. The application may be acted on by the Clerk in the first instance, and any party aggrieved by the Clerk's action may request that the application be submitted to a Justice or to the Court. The Clerk will report action under this paragraph to the Court as instructed.

RULE 31. TRANSLATIONS

Whenever any record to be transmitted to this Court contains material written in a foreign language without a translation made under the authority of the lower court, or admitted to be correct, the clerk of the court transmitting the record shall advise the Clerk of this Court immediately so that this Court may order that a translation be supplied and, if necessary, printed as part of the joint appendix.

RULE 32. MODELS, DIAGRAMS, AND EXHIBITS

1. Models, diagrams, and exhibits of material forming part of the evidence taken in a case and brought to this Court for its inspection shall be placed in the custody of the Clerk at least two weeks before the case is to be heard or submitted.

2. All models, diagrams, and exhibits of material placed in the custody of the Clerk shall be removed by the parties no more than 40 days after the case is decided. If this is not done, the Clerk will notify counsel to remove the articles forthwith. If they are not removed within a reasonable time thereafter, the Clerk will destroy them or dispose of them in any other appropriate way.

RULE 33. DOCUMENT PREPARATION: BOOKLET FORMAT; 8½- BY 11-INCH PAPER FORMAT

1. Booklet Format:

(a) Except for a document expressly permitted by these Rules to be submitted on 8½- by 11-inch paper, see, *e.g.,* Rules 21, 22, and 39, every document filed with the Court shall be prepared using typesetting (*e.g.,* word-processing, electronic publishing, or image setting) and reproduced by offset printing, photocopying, or similar process. The process used must produce a clear, black image on white paper.

(b) The text of every document, including any appendix thereto, except a document permitted to be produced on 8½- by 11-inch paper, shall be typeset in standard 11 point or larger type with 2 point or more leading between lines. The type size and face shall be no smaller than that contained in the United States Reports beginning with Volume 453. Type size and face shall be consistent throughout. No attempt should be made to reduce, compress, or condense the typeface in a manner that would increase the content of a document. Quotations in excess of three lines shall be indented. Footnotes shall appear in print as standard 9 point or larger type with 2 point or more leading between lines. The text of the document must appear on both sides of the page.

(c) Every document, except one permitted to be produced on 8½- by 11-inch paper, shall be produced on paper that is opaque, unglazed, 6⅛ by 9¼ inches in size, and not less than 60 pounds in weight, and shall have margins of at least three fourths of an inch on all sides. The text field, including footnotes, should be approximately 4⅛ by 7⅛ inches. The document shall be bound firmly in at least two places along the left margin (saddle stitch or perfect binding preferred) so as to permit easy opening, and no part of the text should be obscured by the binding. Spiral, plastic, metal, and string bindings may not be used. Copies of patent documents, except opinions, may be duplicated in such size as is necessary in a separate appendix.

(d) Every document, except one permitted to be produced on 8½- by 11-inch paper, shall comply with the page limits shown on the chart in subparagraph 1(g) of this Rule. The page limits do not include the pages containing the questions presented, the list of parties and corporate affiliates of the filing party, the table of contents, the table of cited authorities, or any appendix. Verbatim quotations required under Rule 14.1(f), if set out in the text of a brief rather than in the appendix, are also excluded. For good cause, the Court or a Justice may grant leave to file a document in excess of the page limits, but application for such leave is not favored. An application to exceed page limits shall comply with Rule 22 and must be received by the Clerk at least 15 days before the filing date of the document in question, except in the most extraordinary circumstances.

(e) Every document, except one permitted to be produced on 8½-by 11-inch paper, shall have a suitable cover consisting of 65-pound weight paper in the color indicated on the chart in subparagraph 1(g) of this Rule. If a separate appendix to any document is filed, the color of its cover shall be the same as that of the cover of the document it supports. The Clerk will furnish a color chart upon request. Counsel shall ensure that there is adequate contrast between the printing and the color of the cover. A document filed by the United States, or by any other federal party represented by the Solicitor General, shall have a gray cover. A joint appendix, answer to a bill of complaint, motion for leave to intervene, and any other document not listed in subparagraph 1(g) of this Rule shall have a tan cover.

(f) Forty copies of a document prepared under this paragraph shall be filed.

(g) Page limits and cover colors for booklet-format documents are as follows [see table below]:

2. 8½- by 11-Inch Paper Format:

(a) The text of every document, including any appendix thereto, expressly permitted by these Rules to be presented to the Court on 8½- by 11-inch paper shall appear double spaced, except for indented quotations, which shall be single spaced, on opaque, unglazed, white paper. The document shall be stapled or bound at the upper left hand corner. Copies, if required, shall be produced on the same type of paper and shall be legible. The original of any such document (except a motion to dismiss or affirm under Rule 18.6) shall be signed by the party proceeding *pro se* or by counsel of record who must be a member of the Bar of this Court or an attorney appointed under the Criminal Justice Act of 1964, see 18 U.S.C. §3006A(d)(6), or under any other applicable federal statute. Subparagraph 1(g) of this Rule does not apply to documents prepared under this paragraph.

(b) Page limits for documents presented on 8½- by 11-inch paper are: 40 pages for a petition for a writ of certiorari, jurisdictional statement, petition for an extraordinary writ, brief in opposition, or motion to dismiss or affirm; and 15 pages for a reply to a brief in opposition, brief opposing a motion to dismiss or affirm, supplemental brief, or petition for rehearing. The page exclusions specified in subparagraph 1(d) of this Rule apply.

RULE 34. DOCUMENT PREPARATION: GENERAL REQUIREMENTS

Every document, whether prepared under Rule 33.1 or Rule 33.2, shall comply with the following provisions:

1. Each document shall bear on its cover, in the order indicated, from the top of the page:

(a) the docket number of the case or, if there is none, a space for one;

(b) the name of this Court;

(c) the October Term in which the document is filed (see Rule 3);

(d) the caption of the case as appropriate in this Court;

(e) the nature of the proceeding and the name of the court from which the action is brought (*e.g.,* "On Petition for Writ of Certiorari to the United States Court of Appeals for the Fifth Circuit"; or, for a merits brief, "On Writ of Certiorari to the United States Court of Appeals for the Fifth Circuit");

(f) the title of the document (*e.g.,* "Petition for Writ of Certiorari," "Brief for Respondent," "Joint Appendix");

(g) the name of the attorney who is counsel of record for the party concerned (who must be a member of the Bar of this Court except as provided in Rule 33.2), and on whom service is to be made, with a notation directly thereunder identifying the attorney as counsel of record and setting out counsel's office address and telephone number. Only one counsel of record may be noted on a single document. The names of other members of the Bar of this Court or of the bar of the highest court of a State acting as counsel, and, if desired, their

Type of Document	Page Limits	Color of Cover
i. Petition for a Writ of Certiorari (Rule 14); Motion for Leave to file a Bill of Complaint and Brief in Support (Rule 17.3); Jurisdictional Statement (Rule 18.3); Petition for an Extraordinary Writ (Rule 20.2)	30	white
ii. Brief in Opposition (Rule 15.3); Brief in Opposition to Motion for Leave to file an Original Action (Rule 17.5); Motion to Dismiss or Affirm (Rule 18.6); Brief in Opposition to Mandamus or Prohibition (Rule 20.3 (b)); Response to a Petition for Habeas Corpus (Rule 20.4)	30	orange
iii. Reply to Brief in Opposition (Rules 15.6 and 17.5); Brief Opposing a Motion to Dismiss or Affirm (Rule 18.8)	10	tan
iv. Supplemental Brief (Rules 15.8, 17, 18.10, and 25.5)	10	tan
v. Brief on the Merits by Petitioner or Appellant (Rule 24); Exceptions by Plaintiff to Report of Special Master (Rule 17)	50	light blue
vi. Brief on the Merits by Respondent or Appellee (Rule 24.2); Brief on the Merits for Respondent	50	light red

Type of Document	Page Limits	Color of Cover
or Appellee Supporting Petitioner or Appellant (Rule 12.6); Exceptions by Party Other than Plaintiff to Report of Special Master (Rule 17)		
vii. Reply Brief on the Merits (Rule 24.4)	20	yellow
viii. Reply to Plaintiff's Exceptions to Report of Special Master (Rule 17)	50	orange
ix. Reply to Exceptions by Party Other Than Plaintiff to Report of Special Master (Rule 17)	50	yellow
x. Brief for an *Amicus Curiae* at the Petition Stage (Rule 37.2)	20	cream
xi. Brief for an *Amicus Curiae* in Support of the Plaintiff, Petitioner, or Appellant, or in Support of Neither Party, on the Merits, or in an Original Action at the Exceptions Stage (Rule 37.3)	30	light green
xii. Brief for an *Amicus Curiae* in Support of the Defendant, Respondent, or Appellee, on the Merits or in an Original Action at the Exceptions Stage (Rule 37.3)	30	dark green
xiii. Petition for Rehearing (Rule 44)	10	tan

addresses, may be added, but counsel of record shall be clearly identified. Names of persons other than attorneys admitted to a state bar may not be listed, unless the party is appearing *pro se,* in which case the party's name, address, and telephone number shall appear. The foregoing shall be displayed in an appropriate typographic manner and, except for the identification of counsel, may not be set in type smaller than standard 11 point, if the document is prepared as required by Rule 33.1.

2. Every document exceeding five pages (other than a joint appendix), whether prepared under Rule 33.1 or Rule 33.2, shall contain a table of contents and a table of cited authorities (*i.e.,* cases alphabetically arranged, constitutional provisions, statutes, treatises, and other materials) with references to the pages in the document where such authorities are cited.

3. The body of every document shall bear at its close the name of counsel of record and such other counsel, identified on the cover of the document in conformity with subparagraph 1(g) of this Rule, as may be desired.

RULE 35. DEATH, SUBSTITUTION, AND REVIVOR; PUBLIC OFFICERS

1. If a party dies after filing a petition for a writ of certiorari to this Court, or after filing a notice of appeal, the authorized representative of the deceased party may appear and, on motion, be substituted as a party. If the representative does not voluntarily become a party, any other party may suggest the death on the record and, on motion, seek an order requiring the representative to become a party within a designated time. If the representative then fails to become a party, the party so moving, if a respondent or appellee, is entitled to have the petition for a writ of certiorari or the appeal dismissed, and if a petitioner or appellant, is entitled to proceed as in any other case of nonappearance by a respondent or appellee. If the substitution of a representative of the deceased is not made within six months after the death of the party, the case shall abate.

2. Whenever a case cannot be revived in the court whose judgment is sought to be reviewed, because the deceased party's authorized representative is not subject to that court's jurisdiction, proceedings will be conducted as this Court may direct.

3. When a public officer who is a party to a proceeding in this Court in an official capacity dies, resigns, or otherwise ceases to hold office, the action does not abate and any successor in office is automatically substituted as a party. The parties shall notify the Clerk in writing of any such successions. Proceedings following the substitution shall be in the name of the substituted party, but any misnomer not affecting substantial rights of the parties will be disregarded.

4. A public officer who is a party to a proceeding in this Court in an official capacity may be described as a party by the officer's official title rather than by name, but the Court may require the name to be added.

RULE 36. CUSTODY OF PRISONERS IN HABEAS CORPUS PROCEEDINGS

1. Pending review in this Court of a decision in a habeas corpus proceeding commenced before a court, Justice, or judge of the United States, the person having custody of the prisoner may not transfer custody to another person unless the transfer is authorized under this Rule.

2. Upon application by a custodian, the court, Justice, or judge who entered the decision under review may authorize transfer and the substitution of a successor custodian as a party.

3.(a) Pending review of a decision failing or refusing to release a prisoner, the prisoner may be detained in the custody from which release is sought or in other appropriate custody or may be enlarged on personal recognizance or bail, as may appear appropriate to the court, Justice, or judge who entered the decision, or to the court of appeals, this Court, or a judge or Justice of either court.

(b) Pending review of a decision ordering release, the prisoner shall be enlarged on personal recognizance or bail, unless the court, Justice, or judge who entered the decision, or the court of appeals, this Court, or a judge or Justice of either court, orders otherwise.

4. An initial order respecting the custody or enlargement of the prisoner, and any recognizance or surety taken, shall continue in effect pending review in the court of appeals and in this Court unless for reasons shown to the court of appeals, this Court, or a judge or Justice of either court, the order is modified or an independent order respecting custody, enlargement, or surety is entered.

RULE 37. BRIEF FOR AN *AMICUS CURIAE*

1. An *amicus curiae* brief that brings to the attention of the Court relevant matter not already brought to its attention by the parties may be of considerable help to the Court. An *amicus curiae* brief that does not serve this purpose burdens the Court, and its filing is not favored.

2. (a) An *amicus curiae* brief submitted before the Court's consideration of a petition for a writ of certiorari, motion for leave to file a bill of complaint, jurisdictional statement, or petition for an extraordinary writ, may be filed if accompanied by the written consent of all parties, or if the Court grants leave to file under subparagraph 2(b) of this Rule. The brief shall be submitted within the time allowed for filing a brief in opposition or for filing a motion to dismiss or affirm. The *amicus curiae* brief shall specify whether consent was granted, and its cover shall identify the party supported.

(b) When a party to the case has withheld consent, a motion for leave to file an *amicus curiae* brief before the Court's consideration of a petition for a writ of certiorari, motion for leave to file a bill of complaint, jurisdictional statement, or petition for an extraordinary writ may be presented to the Court. The motion, prepared as required by Rule 33.1 and as one document with the brief sought to be filed, shall be submitted within the time allowed for filing an *amicus curiae* brief, and shall indicate the party or parties who have withheld consent and state the nature of the movant's interest. Such a motion is not favored.

3. (a) An *amicus curiae* brief in a case before the Court for oral argument may be filed if accompanied by the written consent of all parties, or if the Court grants leave to file under subparagraph 3(b) of this Rule. The brief shall be submitted within the time allowed for filing the brief for the party supported, or if in support of neither party, within the time allowed for filing the petitioner's or appellant's brief. The *amicus curiae* brief shall specify whether consent was granted, and its cover shall identify the party supported or indicate whether it suggests affirmance or reversal. The Clerk will not file a reply brief for an *amicus curiae,* or a brief for an *amicus curiae* in support of, or in opposition to, a petition for rehearing.

(b) When a party to a case before the Court for oral argument has withheld consent, a motion for leave to file an *amicus curiae* brief may be presented to the Court. The motion, prepared as required by Rule 33.1 and as one document with the brief sought to be filed, shall be submitted within the time allowed for filing an *amicus curiae* brief, and shall indicate the party or parties who have withheld consent and state the nature of the movant's interest.

4. No motion for leave to file an *amicus curiae* brief is necessary if the brief is presented on behalf of the United States by the Solicitor General; on behalf of any agency of the United States allowed by law

to appear before this Court when submitted by the agency's authorized legal representative; on behalf of a State, Commonwealth, Territory, or Possession when submitted by its Attorney General; or on behalf of a city, county, town, or similar entity when submitted by its authorized law officer.

5. A brief or motion filed under this Rule shall be accompanied by proof of service as required by Rule 29, and shall comply with the applicable provisions of Rules 21, 24, and 33.1 (except that it suffices to set out in the brief the interest of the *amicus curiae,* the summary of the argument, the argument, and the conclusion). A motion for leave to file may not exceed five pages. A party served with the motion may file an objection thereto, stating concisely the reasons for withholding consent; the objection shall be prepared as required by Rule 33.2.

RULE 38. FEES

Under 28 U.S.C. §1911, the fees charged by the Clerk are:

(a) for docketing a case on a petition for a writ of certiorari or on appeal or for docketing any other proceeding, except a certified question or a motion to docket and dismiss an appeal under Rule 18.5, $300;

(b) for filing a petition for rehearing or a motion for leave to file a petition for rehearing, $200;

(c) for reproducing and certifying any record or paper, $1 per page; and for comparing with the original thereof any photographic reproduction of any record or paper, when furnished by the person requesting its certification, $.50 per page;

(d) for a certificate bearing the seal of the Court, $10; and

(e) for a check paid to the Court, Clerk, or Marshal that is returned for lack of funds, $35.

RULE 39. PROCEEDINGS *IN FORMA PAUPERIS*

1. A party seeking to proceed *in forma pauperis* shall file a motion for leave to do so, together with the party's notarized affidavit or declaration (in compliance with 28 U.S.C. §1746) in the form prescribed by the Federal Rules of Appellate Procedure, Form 4. See 28 U.S.C. §1915. The motion shall state whether leave to proceed *in forma pauperis* was sought in any other court and, if so, whether leave was granted. If the United States district court or the United States court of appeals has appointed counsel under the Criminal Justice Act, see 18 U.S.C. §3006A, or under any other applicable federal statute, no affidavit or declaration is required, but the motion shall cite the statute under which counsel was appointed.

2. If leave to proceed *in forma pauperis* is sought for the purpose of filing a document, the motion, and affidavit or declaration if required, shall be filed with that document and shall comply in every respect with Rule 21. As provided in that rule, it suffices to file an original and 10 copies, unless the party is an inmate confined in an institution and is not represented by counsel, in which case the original, alone, suffices. A copy of the motion shall precede and be attached to each copy of the accompanying document.

3. Except when these Rules expressly provide that a document shall be prepared as required by Rule 33.1, every document presented by a party proceeding under this Rule shall be prepared as required by Rule 33.2 (unless such preparation is impossible). Every document shall be legible. While making due allowance for any case presented under this Rule by a person appearing *pro se,* the Clerk will not file any document if it does not comply with the substance of these Rules or is jurisdictionally out of time.

4. When the documents required by paragraphs 1 and 2 of this Rule are presented to the Clerk, accompanied by proof of service as required by Rule 29, they will be placed on the docket without the payment of a docket fee or any other fee.

5. The respondent or appellee in a case filed *in forma pauperis* shall respond in the same manner and within the same time as in any other case of the same nature, except that the filing of an original and 10 copies of a response prepared as required by Rule 33.2, with proof of service as required by Rule 29, suffices. The respondent or appellee may challenge the grounds for the motion for leave to proceed *in forma pauperis* in a separate document or in the response itself.

6. Whenever the Court appoints counsel for an indigent party in a case set for oral argument, the briefs on the merits submitted by that counsel, unless otherwise requested, shall be prepared under the Clerk's supervision. The Clerk also will reimburse appointed counsel for any necessary travel expenses to Washington, D. C., and return in connection with the argument.

7. In a case in which certiorari has been granted, probable jurisdiction noted, or consideration of jurisdiction postponed, this Court may appoint counsel to represent a party financially unable to afford an attorney to the extent authorized by the Criminal Justice Act of 1964, 18 U.S.C. §3006A, or by any other applicable federal statute.

8. If satisfied that a petition for a writ of certiorari, jurisdictional statement, or petition for an extraordinary writ is frivolous or malicious, the Court may deny leave to proceed *in forma pauperis.*

RULE 40. VETERANS, SEAMEN, AND MILITARY CASES

1. A veteran suing to establish reemployment rights under 38 U.S.C. §2022, or under any other provision of law exempting veterans from the payment of fees or court costs, may file a motion for leave to proceed on papers prepared as required by Rule 33.2. The motion shall ask leave to proceed as a veteran and be accompanied by an affidavit or declaration setting out the moving party's veteran status. A copy of the motion shall precede and be attached to each copy of the petition for a writ of certiorari or other substantive document filed by the veteran.

2. A seaman suing under 28 U.S.C. §1916 may proceed without prepayment of fees or costs or furnishing security therefor, but is not entitled to proceed under Rule 33.2, except as authorized by the Court on separate motion under Rule 39.

3. An accused person petitioning for a writ of certiorari to review a decision of the United States Court of Appeals for the Armed Forces under 28 U.S.C. §1259 may proceed without prepayment of fees or costs or furnishing security therefor and without filing an affidavit of indigency, but is not entitled to proceed on papers prepared as required by Rule 33.2, except as authorized by the Court on separate motion under Rule 39.

PART VIII. DISPOSITION OF CASES

RULE 41. OPINIONS OF THE COURT

Opinions of the Court will be released by the Clerk immediately upon their announcement from the bench, or as the Court otherwise directs. Thereafter, the Clerk will cause the opinions to be issued in slip form, and the Reporter of Decisions will prepare them for publication in the preliminary prints and bound volumes of the United States Reports.

RULE 42. INTEREST AND DAMAGES

1. If a judgment for money in a civil case is affirmed, any interest allowed by law is payable from the date the judgment under review was entered. If a judgment is modified or reversed with a direction that a judgment for money be entered below, the mandate will contain instructions with respect to the allowance of interest. Interest

in cases arising in a state court is allowed at the same rate that similar judgments bear interest in the courts of the State in which judgment is directed to be entered. Interest in cases arising in a court of the United States is allowed at the interest rate authorized by law.

2. When a petition for a writ of certiorari, an appeal, or an application for other relief is frivolous, the Court may award the respondent or appellee just damages, and single or double costs under Rule 43. Damages or costs may be awarded against the petitioner, appellant, or applicant, against the party's counsel, or against both party and counsel.

RULE 43. COSTS

1. If the Court affirms a judgment, the petitioner or appellant shall pay costs unless the Court otherwise orders.

2. If the Court reverses or vacates a judgment, the respondent or appellee shall pay costs unless the Court otherwise orders.

3. The Clerk's fees and the cost of printing the joint appendix are the only taxable items in this Court. The cost of the transcript of the record from the court below is also a taxable item, but shall be taxable in that court as costs in the case. The expenses of printing briefs, motions, petitions, or jurisdictional statements are not taxable.

4. In a case involving a certified question, costs are equally divided unless the Court otherwise orders, except that if the Court decides the whole matter in controversy, as permitted by Rule 19.2, costs are allowed as provided in paragraphs 1 and 2 of this Rule.

5. To the extent permitted by 28 U.S.C. §2412, costs under this Rule are allowed for or against the United States or an officer or agent thereof, unless expressly waived or unless the Court otherwise orders.

6. When costs are allowed in this Court, the Clerk will insert an itemization of the costs in the body of the mandate or judgment sent to the court below. The prevailing side may not submit a bill of costs.

7. In extraordinary circumstances the Court may adjudge double costs.

RULE 44. REHEARING

1. Any petition for the rehearing of any judgment or decision of the Court on the merits shall be filed within 25 days after entry of the judgment or decision, unless the Court or a Justice shortens or extends the time. The petitioner shall file 40 copies of the rehearing petition and shall pay the filing fee prescribed by Rule 38(b), except that a petitioner proceeding *in forma pauperis* under Rule 39, including an inmate of an institution, shall file the number of copies required for a petition by such a person under Rule 12.2. The petition shall state its grounds briefly and distinctly and shall be served as required by Rule 29. The petition shall be presented together with certification of counsel (or of a party unrepresented by counsel) that it is presented in good faith and not for delay; one copy of the certificate shall bear the signature of counsel (or of a party unrepresented by counsel). A copy of the certificate shall follow and be attached to each copy of the petition. A petition for rehearing is not subject to oral argument and will not be granted except by a majority of the Court, at the instance of a Justice who concurred in the judgment or decision.

2. Any petition for the rehearing of an order denying a petition for a writ of certiorari or extraordinary writ shall be filed within 25 days after the date of the order of denial and shall comply with all the form and filing requirements of paragraph 1 of this Rule, including the payment of the filing fee if required, but its grounds shall be limited to intervening circumstances of a substantial or controlling effect or to other substantial grounds not previously presented. The petition shall be presented together with certification of counsel (or of a party unrepresented by counsel) that it is restricted to the grounds specified in this paragraph and that it is presented in good faith and not for delay; one copy of the certificate shall bear the signature of counsel (or of a party unrepresented by counsel). A copy of the certificate shall follow and be attached to each copy of the petition. The Clerk will not file a petition without a certificate. The petition is not subject to oral argument.

3. The Clerk will not file any response to a petition for rehearing unless the Court requests a response. In the absence of extraordinary circumstances, the Court will not grant a petition for rehearing without first requesting a response.

4. The Clerk will not file consecutive petitions and petitions that are out of time under this Rule.

5. The Clerk will not file any brief for an *amicus curiae* in support of, or in opposition to, a petition for rehearing.

RULE 45. PROCESS; MANDATES

1. All process of this Court issues in the name of the President of the United States.

2. In a case on review from a state court, the mandate issues 25 days after entry of the judgment, unless the Court or a Justice shortens or extends the time, or unless the parties stipulate that it issue sooner. The filing of a petition for rehearing stays the mandate until disposition of the petition, unless the Court orders otherwise. If the petition is denied, the mandate issues forthwith.

3. In a case on review from any court of the United States, as defined by 28 U.S.C. §451, a formal mandate does not issue unless specially directed; instead, the Clerk of this Court will send the clerk of the lower court a copy of the opinion or order of this Court and a certified copy of the judgment. The certified copy of the judgment, prepared and signed by this Court's Clerk, will provide for costs if any are awarded. In all other respects, the provisions of paragraph 2 of this Rule apply.

RULE 46. DISMISSING CASES

1. At any stage of the proceedings, whenever all parties file with the Clerk an agreement in writing that a case be dismissed, specifying the terms for payment of costs, and pay to the Clerk any fees then due, the Clerk, without further reference to the Court, will enter an order of dismissal.

2. (a) A petitioner or appellant may file a motion to dismiss the case, with proof of service as required by Rule 29, tendering to the Clerk any fees due and costs payable. No more than 15 days after service thereof, an adverse party may file an objection, limited to the amount of damages and costs in this Court alleged to be payable or to showing that the moving party does not represent all petitioners or appellants. The Clerk will not file any objection not so limited.

(b) When the objection asserts that the moving party does not represent all the petitioners or appellants, the party moving for dismissal may file a reply within 10 days, after which time the matter will be submitted to the Court for its determination.

(c) If no objection is filed, or if upon objection going only to the amount of damages and costs in this Court, the party moving for dismissal tenders the additional damages and costs in full within 10 days of the demand therefor, the Clerk, without further reference to the Court, will enter an order of dismissal. If, after objection as to the amount of damages and costs in this Court, the moving party does not respond by a tender within 10 days, the Clerk will report the matter to the Court for its determination.

3. No mandate or other process will issue on a dismissal under this Rule without an order of the Court.

PART IX. DEFINITIONS AND EFFECTIVE DATE

RULE 47. REFERENCE TO "STATE COURT" AND "STATE LAW"

The term "state court," when used in these Rules, includes the District of Columbia Court of Appeals and the Supreme Court of the Commonwealth of Puerto Rico. See 28 U.S.C. §§1257 and 1258. References in these Rules to the common law and statutes of a State include the common law and statutes of the District of Columbia and of the Commonwealth of Puerto Rico.

RULE 48. EFFECTIVE DATE OF RULES

1. These Rules, adopted July 26, 1995, will be effective October 2, 1995.

2. The Rules govern all proceedings after their effective date except to the extent that, in the opinion of the Court, their application to a pending matter would not be feasible or would work an injustice, in which event the former procedure applies.

APPENDIX B Tables, Lists, and Graphical Data

Natural Courts

Natural court [a]	Justices [b]	Dates	U.S. Reports [c]
Jay 1	Jay (*o* October 19, 1789), J. Rutledge (*o* February 15, 1790), Cushing (*o* February 2, 1790), Wilson (*o* October 5, 1789), Blair (*o* February 2, 1790)	October 5, 1789–May 12, 1790	2
Jay 2	Jay, Rutledge (*r* March 5, 1791), Cushing, Wilson, Blair, Iredell (*o* May 12, 1790)	May 12, 1790–August 6, 1792	2
Jay 3	Jay, Cushing, Wilson, Blair, Iredell, T. Johnson (*o* August 6, 1792; *r* January 16, 1793)	August 6, 1792–March 11, 1793	2
Jay 4	Jay (*r* June 29, 1795), Cushing, Wilson, Blair, Iredell, Paterson (*o* March 11, 1793)	March 11, 1793–August 12, 1795	2–3
Rutledge 1	J. Rutledge (*o* August 12, 1795; *rj* December 15, 1795), Cushing, Wilson, Blair (*r* January 27, 1796), Iredell, Paterson	August 12, 1795–February 4, 1796	3
No chief justice	Cushing, Wilson, Iredell, Paterson, S. Chase (*o* February 4, 1796)	February 4, 1796–March 8, 1796	3
Ellsworth 1	Ellsworth (*o* March 8, 1796), Cushing, Wilson (*d* August 21, 1798), Iredell, Paterson, S. Chase	March 8, 1796–February 4, 1799	3
Ellsworth 2	Ellsworth, Cushing, Iredell (*d* October 20, 1799), Paterson, S. Chase, Washington (*o* February 4, 1799)	February 4, 1799–April 21, 1800	3–4
Ellsworth 3	Ellsworth (*r* December 15, 1800), Cushing, Paterson, S. Chase, Washington, Moore (*o* April 21, 1800)	April 21, 1800–February 4, 1801	4
Marshall 1	Marshall (*o* February 4, 1801), Cushing, Paterson, S. Chase, Washington, Moore (*r* January 26, 1804)	February 4, 1801–May 7, 1804	5–6
Marshall 2	Marshall, Cushing, Paterson (*d* September 9, 1806), S. Chase, Washington, W. Johnson (*o* May 7, 1804)	May 7, 1804–January 20, 1807	6–7
Marshall 3	Marshall, Cushing, S. Chase, Washington, W. Johnson, Livingston (*o* January 20, 1807)	January 20, 1807–May 4, 1807	8
Marshall 4	Marshall, Cushing (*d* September 13, 1810), S. Chase (*d* June 19, 1811), Washington, W. Johnson, Livingston, Todd (*o* May 4, 1807)	May 4, 1807–November 23, 1811	8–10
Marshall 5	Marshall, Washington, W. Johnson, Livingston, Todd, Duvall (*o* November 23, 1811)	November 23, 1811–February 3, 1812	11
Marshall 6	Marshall, Washington, W. Johnson, Livingston (*d* March 18, 1823), Todd, Duvall, Story (*o* February 3, 1812)	February 3, 1812–February 10, 1824	11–21
Marshall 7	Marshall, Washington, W. Johnson, Todd (*d* February 7, 1826), Duvall, Story, Thompson (*o* February 10, 1824)	February 10, 1824–June 16, 1826	22–24
Marshall 8	Marshall, Washington (*d* November 26, 1829), W. Johnson, Duvall, Story, Thompson, Trimble (*o* June 16, 1826; *d* August 25, 1828)	June 16, 1826–January 11, 1830	25–27
Marshall 9	Marshall, W. Johnson (*d* August 4, 1834), Duvall (*r* January 14, 1835), Story, Thompson, McLean (*o* January 11, 1830), Baldwin (*o* January 18, 1830)	January 11, 1830–January 14, 1835	28–33
Marshall 10	Marshall (*d* July 6, 1835), Story, Thompson, McLean, Baldwin, Wayne (*o* January 14, 1835)	January 14, 1835–March 28, 1836	34–35
Taney 1	Taney (*o* March 28, 1836), Story, Thompson, McLean, Baldwin, Wayne	March 28, 1836–May 12, 1836	35
Taney 2	Taney, Story, Thompson, McLean, Baldwin, Wayne, Barbour (*o* May 12, 1836)	May 12, 1836–May 1, 1837	35–36
Taney 3	Taney, Story, Thompson, McLean, Baldwin, Wayne, Barbour, Catron (*o* May 1, 1837)	May 1, 1837–January 9, 1838	36

Natural court[a]	Justices[b]	Dates	U.S. Reports[c]
Taney 4	Taney, Story, Thompson, McLean, Baldwin, Wayne, Barbour (*d* February 25, 1841), Catron, McKinley (*o* January 9, 1838)	January 9, 1838–January 10, 1842	37–40
Taney 5	Taney, Story, Thompson (*d* December 18, 1843), McLean, Baldwin (*d* April 21, 1844), Wayne, Catron, McKinley, Daniel (*o* January 10, 1842)	January 10, 1842–February 27, 1845	40–44
Taney 6	Taney, Story (*d* September 10, 1845), McLean, Wayne, Catron, McKinley, Daniel, Nelson (*o* February 27, 1845)	February 27, 1845–September 23, 1845	44
Taney 7	Taney, McLean, Wayne, Catron, McKinley, Daniel, Nelson, Woodbury (*o* September 23, 1845)	September 23,1845–August 10, 1846	44–45
Taney 8	Taney, McLean, Wayne, Catron, McKinley, Daniel, Nelson, Woodbury (*d* September 4, 1851), Grier (*o* August 10, 1846)	August 10, 1846–October 10, 1851	46–52
Taney 9	Taney, McLean, Wayne, Catron, McKinley (*d* July 19, 1852), Daniel, Nelson, Grier, Curtis (*o* October 10, 1851)	October 10, 1851–April 11, 1853	53–55
Taney 10	Taney, McLean, Wayne, Catron, Daniel, Nelson, Grier, Curtis (*r* September 30, 1857), Campbell (*o* April 11, 1853)	April 11, 1853–January 21, 1858	56–61
Taney 11	Taney, McLean (*d* April 4, 1861), Wayne, Catron, Daniel (*d* May 31, 1860), Nelson, Grier, Campbell (*r* April 30, 1861), Clifford (*o* January 21, 1858)	January 21, 1858–January 27, 1862	61–66
Taney 12	Taney, Wayne, Catron, Nelson, Grier, Clifford, Swayne (*o* January 27, 1862)	January 27, 1862–July 21, 1862	66
Taney 13	Taney, Wayne, Catron, Nelson, Grier, Clifford, Swayne, Miller (*o* July 21, 1862)	July 21, 1862–December 10, 1862	67
Taney 14	Taney, Wayne, Catron, Nelson, Grier, Clifford, Swayne, Miller, Davis (*o* December 10, 1862)	December 10, 1862–May 20, 1863	67
Taney 15	Taney (*d* October 12, 1864), Wayne, Catron, Nelson, Grier, Clifford, Swayne, Miller, Davis, Field (*o* May 20, 1863)	May 20, 1863–December 15, 1864	67–68
Chase 1	S. P. Chase (*o* December 15, 1864), Wayne (*d* July 5, 1867), Catron (*d* May 30, 1865), Nelson, Grier (*r* January 31, 1870), Clifford, Swayne, Miller, Davis, Field	December 15, 1864–March 14, 1870	69–76
Chase 2	S. P. Chase, Nelson (*r* November 28, 1872), Clifford, Swayne, Miller, Davis, Field, Strong (*o* March 14, 1870), Bradley (*o* March 23, 1870)	March 14, 1870–January 9, 1873	76–82
Chase 3	S. P. Chase (*d* May 7, 1873), Clifford, Swayne, Miller, Davis, Field, Strong, Bradley, Hunt (*o* January 9, 1873)	January 9, 1873–March 4, 1874	82–86
Waite 1	Waite (*o* March 4, 1874), Clifford, Swayne, Miller, Davis (*r* March 4, 1877), Field, Strong, Bradley, Hunt	March 4, 1874–December 10, 1877	86–95
Waite 2	Waite, Clifford, Swayne, Miller, Field, Strong (*r* December 14, 1880), Bradley, Hunt, Harlan I (*o* December 10, 1877)	December 10, 1877–January 5, 1881	95–103
Waite 3	Waite, Clifford, Swayne (*r* January 24, 1881), Miller, Field, Bradley, Hunt, Harlan I, Woods (*o* January 5, 1881)	January 5, 1881–May 17, 1881	103
Waite 4	Waite, Clifford (*d* July 25, 1881), Miller, Field, Bradley, Hunt, Harlan I, Woods, Matthews (*o* May 17, 1881)	May 17, 1881–January 9, 1882	103–104
Waite 5	Waite, Miller, Field, Bradley, Hunt (*r* January 27, 1882), Harlan I, Woods, Matthews, Gray (*o* January 9, 1882)	January 9, 1882–April 3, 1882	104–105
Waite 6	Waite, Miller, Field, Bradley, Harlan I, Woods (*d* May 14, 1887), Matthews, Gray, Blatchford (*o* April 3, 1882)	April 3, 1882–January 18, 1888	105–124
Waite 7	Waite (*d* March 23, 1888), Miller, Field, Bradley, Harlan I, Matthews, Gray, Blatchford, L. Lamar (*o* January 18, 1888)	January 18, 1888–October 8, 1888	124–127
Fuller 1	Fuller (*o* October 8, 1888), Miller, Field, Bradley, Harlan I, Matthews (*d* March 22, 1889), Gray, Blatchford, L. Lamar	October 8, 1888–January 6, 1890	128–132
Fuller 2	Fuller, Miller (*d* October 13, 1890), Field, Bradley, Harlan I, Gray, Blatchford, L. Lamar, Brewer (*o* January 6, 1890)	January 6, 1890–January 5, 1891	132–137

Natural court [a]	Justices [b]	Dates	U.S. Reports [c]
Fuller 3	Fuller, Field, Bradley (*d* January 22, 1892), Harlan I, Gray, Blatchford, L. Lamar, Brewer, Brown (*o* January 5, 1891)	January 5, 1891– October 10, 1892	137–145
Fuller 4	Fuller, Field, Harlan I, Gray, Blatchford, L. Lamar (*d* January 23, 1893), Brewer, Brown, Shiras (*o* October 10, 1892)	October 10, 1892– March 4, 1893	146–148
Fuller 5	Fuller, Field, Harlan I, Gray, Blatchford (*d* July 7, 1893), Brewer, Brown, Shiras, H. Jackson (*o* March 4, 1893)	March 4, 1893– March 12, 1894	148–151
Fuller 6	Fuller, Field, Harlan I, Gray, Brewer, Brown, Shiras, H. Jackson (*d* August 8, 1895), E. White (*o* March 12, 1894)	March 12, 1894– January 6, 1896	152–160
Fuller 7	Fuller, Field (*r* December 1, 1897), Harlan I, Gray, Brewer, Brown, Shiras, E. White, Peckham (*o* January 6, 1896)	January 6, 1896– January 26, 1898	160–169
Fuller 8	Fuller, Harlan I, Gray (*d* September 15, 1902), Brewer, Brown, Shiras, E. White, Peckham, McKenna (*o* January 26, 1898)	January 26, 1898– December 8, 1902	169–187
Fuller 9	Fuller, Harlan I, Brewer, Brown, Shiras (*r* February 23, 1903), E. White, Peckham, McKenna, Holmes (*o* December 8, 1902)	December 8, 1902– March 2, 1903	187–188
Fuller 10	Fuller, Harlan I, Brewer, Brown (*r* May 28, 1906), E. White, Peckham, McKenna, Holmes, Day (*o* March 2, 1903)	March 2, 1903– December 17, 1906	188–203
Fuller 11	Fuller, Harlan I, Brewer, E. White, Peckham (*d* October 24, 1909), McKenna, Holmes, Day, Moody (*o* December 17, 1906)	December 17, 1906– January 3, 1910	203–215
Fuller 12	Fuller (*d* July 4, 1910), Harlan I, Brewer (d March 28, 1910), E. White, McKenna, Holmes, Day, Moody, Lurton (*o* January 3, 1910)	January 3, 1910– October 10, 1910	215–217
No chief justice	Harlan I, E. White (*p* December 18, 1910), McKenna, Holmes, Day, Moody (*r* November 20, 1910), Lurton, Hughes (*o* October 10, 1910)	October 10, 1910– December 19, 1910	218
White 1	E. White (*o* December 19, 1910), Harlan I (*d* October 14, 1911), McKenna, Holmes, Day, Lurton, Hughes, Van Devanter (*o* January 3, 1911), J. Lamar (*o* January 3, 1911)	December 19, 1910– March 18, 1912	218–223
White 2	E. White, McKenna, Holmes, Day, Lurton (*d* July 12, 1914), Hughes, Van Devanter, J. Lamar, Pitney (*o* March 18, 1912)	March 18, 1912– October 12, 1914	223–234
White 3	E. White, McKenna, Holmes, Day, Hughes, Van Devanter, J. Lamar (*d* January 2, 1916), Pitney, McReynolds (*o* October 12, 1914)	October 12, 1914– June 5, 1916	235–241
White 4	E. White, McKenna, Holmes, Day, Hughes (*r* June 10, 1916), Van Devanter, Pitney, McReynolds, Brandeis (*o* June 5, 1916)	June 5, 1916– October 9, 1916	241
White 5	E. White (*d* May 19, 1921), McKenna, Holmes, Day, Van Devanter, Pitney, McReynolds, Brandeis, Clarke (*o* October 9, 1916)	October 9, 1916– July 11, 1921	242–256
Taft 1	Taft (*o* July 11, 1921), McKenna, Holmes, Day, Van Devanter, Pitney, McReynolds, Brandeis, Clarke (*r* September 18, 1922)	July 11, 1921– October 2, 1922	257–259
Taft 2	Taft, McKenna, Holmes, Day (*r* November 13, 1922), Van Devanter, Pitney (*r* December 31, 1922), McReynolds, Brandeis, Sutherland (*o* October 2, 1922)	October 2, 1922– January 2, 1923	260
Taft 3	Taft, McKenna, Holmes, Van Devanter, McReynolds, Brandeis, Sutherland, Butler (*o* January 2, 1923)	January 2, 1923– February 19, 1923	260
Taft 4	Taft, McKenna (*r* January 5, 1925), Holmes, Van Devanter, McReynolds, Brandeis, Sutherland, Butler, Sanford (*o* February 19, 1923)	February 19, 1923– March 2, 1925	260–267
Taft 5	Taft (*r* February 3, 1930), Holmes, Van Devanter, McReynolds, Brandeis, Sutherland, Butler, Sanford, Stone (*o* March 2, 1925)	March 2, 1925– February 24, 1930	267–280
Hughes 1	Hughes (*o* February 24, 1930), Holmes, Van Devanter, McReynolds, Brandeis, Sutherland, Butler, Sanford (*d* March 8, 1930), Stone	February 24, 1930– June 2, 1930	280–281
Hughes 2	Hughes, Holmes (*r* January 12, 1932), Van Devanter, McReynolds, Brandeis, Sutherland, Butler, Stone, Roberts (*o* June 2, 1930)	June 2, 1930– March 14, 1932	281–285

Natural court [a]	Justices [b]	Dates	U.S. Reports [c]
Hughes 3	Hughes, Van Devanter (r June 2, 1937), McReynolds, Brandeis, Sutherland, Butler, Stone, Roberts, Cardozo (o March 14, 1932)	March 14, 1932–August 19, 1937	285–301
Hughes 4	Hughes, McReynolds, Brandeis, Sutherland (r January 17, 1938), Butler, Stone, Roberts, Cardozo, Black (o August 19, 1937)	August 19, 1937 January 31, 1938	302–303
Hughes 5	Hughes, McReynolds, Brandeis, Butler, Stone, Roberts, Cardozo (d July 9, 1938), Black, Reed (o January 31, 1938)	January 31, 1938–January 30, 1939	303–305
Hughes 6	Hughes, McReynolds, Brandeis (r February 13, 1939), Butler, Stone, Roberts, Black, Reed, Frankfurter (o January 30, 1939)	January 30, 1939–April 17, 1939	306
Hughes 7	Hughes, McReynolds, Butler (d November 16, 1939), Stone, Roberts, Black, Reed, Frankfurter, Douglas (o April 17, 1939)	April 17, 1939–February 5, 1940	306–308
Hughes 8	Hughes (r July 1, 1941), McReynolds (r January 31, 1941), Stone (p July 2, 1941), Roberts, Black, Reed, Frankfurter, Douglas, Murphy (o February 5, 1940)	February 5, 1940–July 3, 1941	308–313
Stone 1	Stone (o July 3, 1941), Roberts, Black, Reed, Frankfurter, Douglas, Murphy, Byrnes (o July 8, 1941; r October 3, 1942), R. Jackson (o July 11, 1941)	July 3, 1941–February 15, 1943	314–318
Stone 2	Stone, Roberts (r July 31, 1945), Black, Reed, Frankfurter, Douglas, Murphy, R. Jackson, W. Rutledge (o February 15, 1943)	February 15, 1943–October 1, 1945	318–326
Stone 3	Stone (d April 22, 1946), Black, Reed, Frankfurter, Douglas, Murphy, R. Jackson, W. Rutledge, Burton (o October 1, 1945)	October 1, 1945–June 24, 1946	326–328
Vinson 1	Vinson (o June 24, 1946), Black, Reed, Frankfurter, Douglas, Murphy (d July 19, 1949), R. Jackson, W. Rutledge, Burton	June 24, 1946–August 24, 1949	329–338
Vinson 2	Vinson, Black, Reed, Frankfurter, Douglas, R. Jackson, W. Rutledge (d September 10, 1949), Burton, Clark (o August 24, 1949)	August 24, 1949–October 12, 1949	338
Vinson 3	Vinson (d September 8, 1953), Black, Reed, Frankfurter, Douglas, R. Jackson, Burton, Clark, Minton (o October 12, 1949)	October 12, 1949–October 5, 1953	338–346
Warren 1	Warren (o October 5, 1953), Black, Reed, Frankfurter, Douglas, R. Jackson (d October 9, 1954), Burton, Clark, Minton	October 5, 1953–March 28, 1955	346–348
Warren 2	Warren, Black, Reed, Frankfurter, Douglas, Burton, Clark, Minton (r October 15, 1956), Harlan II (o March 28, 1955)	March 28, 1955–October 16, 1956	348–352
Warren 3	Warren, Black, Reed (r February 25, 1957), Frankfurter, Douglas, Burton, Clark, Harlan II, Brennan (o October 16, 1956)	October 16, 1956–March 25, 1957	352
Warren 4	Warren, Black, Frankfurter, Douglas, Burton (r October 13, 1958), Clark, Harlan II, Brennan, Whittaker (o March 25, 1957)	March 25, 1957–October 14, 1958	352–358
Warren 5	Warren, Black, Frankfurter, Douglas, Clark, Harlan II, Brennan, Whittaker (r March 31, 1962), Stewart (o October 14, 1958)	October 14, 1958–April 16, 1962	358–369
Warren 6	Warren, Black, Frankfurter (r August 28, 1962), Douglas, Clark, Harlan II, Brennan, Stewart, B. White (o April 16, 1962)	April 16, 1962–October 1, 1962	369–370
Warren 7	Warren, Black, Douglas, Clark, Harlan II, Brennan, Stewart, B. White, Goldberg (o October 1, 1962; r July 25, 1965)	October 1, 1962–October 4, 1965	371–381
Warren 8	Warren, Black, Douglas, Clark (r June 12, 1967), Harlan II, Brennan, Stewart, B. White, Fortas (o October 4, 1965)	October 4, 1965–October 2, 1967	382–388
Warren 9	Warren (r June 23, 1969), Black, Douglas, Harlan II, Brennan, Stewart, B. White, Fortas (r May 14, 1969), T. Marshall (o October 2, 1967)	October 2, 1967–June 23, 1969	389–395
Burger 1	Burger (o June 23, 1969), Black, Douglas, Harlan II, Brennan, Stewart, B. White, T. Marshall	June 23, 1969–June 9, 1970	395–397
Burger 2	Burger, Black (r September 17, 1971), Douglas, Harlan II (r September 23, 1971), Brennan, Stewart, B. White, T. Marshall, Blackmun (o June 9, 1970)	June 9, 1970–January 7, 1972	397–404

Natural court [a]	Justices [b]	Dates	U.S. Reports [c]
Burger 3	Burger, Douglas (r November 12, 1975), Brennan, Stewart, B. White, T. Marshall, Blackmun, Powell (o January 7, 1972), Rehnquist (o January 7, 1972)	January 7, 1972– December 19, 1975	404–423
Burger 4	Burger, Brennan, Stewart (r July 3, 1981), B. White, T. Marshall, Blackmun, Powell, Rehnquist, Stevens (o December 19, 1975)	December 19, 1975– September 25, 1981	423–453
Burger 5	Burger (r September 26, 1986), Brennan, B. White, T. Marshall, Blackmun, Powell, Rehnquist (p September 26, 1986), Stevens, O'Connor (o September 25, 1981)	September 25, 1981– September 26, 1986	453–478
Rehnquist 1	Rehnquist (o September 26, 1986), Brennan, B. White, T. Marshall, Blackmun, Powell (r June 26, 1987), Stevens, O'Connor, Scalia (o September 26, 1986)	September 26, 1986– February 18, 1988	478–484
Rehnquist 2	Rehnquist, Brennan (r July 20, 1990), B. White, T. Marshall, Blackmun, Stevens, O'Connor, Scalia, Kennedy (o February 18, 1988)	February 18, 1988– October 9, 1990	484–498
Rehnquist 3	Rehnquist, B. White, T. Marshall (r October 1, 1991), Blackmun, Stevens, O'Connor, Scalia, Kennedy, Souter (o October 9, 1990)	October 9, 1990– October 23, 1991	498–
Rehnquist 4	Rehnquist, B. White (r July 1, 1993), Blackmun, Stevens, O'Connor, Scalia, Kennedy, Souter, Thomas (o October 23, 1991)	October 23, 1991– August 10, 1993	
Rehnquist 5	Rehnquist, Blackmun (r August 3, 1994), Stevens, O'Connor, Scalia, Kennedy, Souter, Thomas, Ginsburg (o August 10, 1993)	August 10, 1993– August 3, 1994	
Rehnquist 6	Rehnquist, Stevens, O'Connor, Scalia, Kennedy, Souter, Thomas, Ginsburg, Breyer (o August 3, 1994)	August 3, 1994	

SOURCE: Lee Epstein, Jeffrey A. Segal, Harold J. Spaeth, Thomas G. Walker, *The Supreme Court Compendium: Data, Decisions, and Developments* (Washington, D.C.: Congressional Quarterly, 1994), Table 5-2.

a. The term *natural court* refers to a period of time during which the membership of the Court remains stable. There are a number of ways to determine the beginning and end of a natural court. Here a natural court begins when a new justice takes the oath of office and continues until the next new justice takes the oath. When two or more justices join the Court within a period of fifteen or fewer days, we treat it as the beginning of a single natural court (for example, Marshall 9, Chase 2, White 1, and Stone 1).

Natural courts in the table are numbered sequentially within the tenure of each chief justice.

b. The name of the chief justice appears first, with associate justices following in order of descending seniority. In addition, the date a justice left the Court, creating a vacancy for the next justice to be appointed, is given, as well as the date the new justice took the oath of office. o=oath of office taken, d=died, r=resigned or retired, rj=recess appointment rejected by Senate, p=promoted from associate justice to chief justice.

c. Volumes of *United States Reports* in which the actions of each natural court generally may be found. Because of the way decisions were published prior to the twentieth century, these volume numbers may not contain all of the decisions of a given natural court. They do, however, provide a general guide to the location of each natural court's published decisions. Natural courts of short duration may have little business published in the reports.

Supreme Court Nominations, 1789–2003

Name	State	Date of Birth	To Replace	Date of Appointment	Confirmation or Other Action *	Date Resigned	Date of Death	Years of Service
WASHINGTON								
John Jay	N.Y.	12/12/1745		9/24/1789	9/26/1789	6/29/1795	5/17/1829	6
John Rutledge	S.C.	9/1739		9/24/1789	9/26/1789	3/5/1791	7/18/1800	1
William Cushing	Mass.	3/1/1732		9/24/1789	9/26/1789		9/13/1810	21
Robert H. Harrison	Md.	1745		9/24/1789	9/26/1789 (D)		4/20/1790	
James Wilson	Pa.	9/14/1742		9/24/1789	9/26/1789		8/21/1798	9
John Blair	Va.	1732		9/24/1789	9/26/1789	1/27/1796	8/31/1800	6
James Iredell	N.C.	10/5/1751	Harrison	2/8/1790	2/10/1790		10/20/1799	9
Thomas Johnson	Md.	11/4/1732	Rutledge	11/1/1791	11/7/1791	3/4/1793	10/26/1819	1
William Paterson	N.J.	12/24/1745	Johnson	2/27/1793	2/28/1793 (W)			
William Paterson†			Johnson	3/4/1793	3/4/1793		9/9/1806	13
John Rutledge ‡			Jay	7/1/1795	12/15/1795 (R, 10–14)			
William Cushing ‡			Jay	1/26/1796	1/27/1796 (D)			
Samuel Chase	Md.	4/17/1741	Blair	1/26/1796	1/27/1796		6/19/1811	15
Oliver Ellsworth	Conn.	4/29/1745	Jay	3/3/1796	3/4/1796 (21–1)	12/15/1800	11/26/1807	4
ADAMS								
Bushrod Washington	Va.	6/5/1762	Wilson	12/19/1798	12/20/1798		11/26/1829	31
Alfred Moore	N.C.	5/21/1755	Iredell	12/6/1799	12/10/1799	1/26/1804	10/15/1810	4
John Jay ‡			Ellsworth	12/18/1800	12/19/1800 (D)			
John Marshall	Va.	9/24/1755	Ellsworth	1/20/1801	1/27/1801		7/6/1835	34
JEFFERSON								
William Johnson	S.C.	12/27/1771	Moore	3/22/1804	3/24/1804		8/4/1834	30
H. Brockholst Livingston	N.Y.	11/25/1757	Paterson	12/13/1806	2/17/1806		3/18/1823	16
Thomas Todd	Ky.	1/23/1765	New seat	2/28/1807	3/3/1807		2/7/1826	19
MADISON								
Levi Lincoln	Mass.	5/15/1749	Cushing	1/2/1811	1/3/1811 (D)		4/14/1820	
Alexander Wolcott	Conn.	9/15/1758	Cushing	2/4/1811	2/13/1811 (R, 9–24)		6/26/1828	
John Quincy Adams	Mass.	7/11/1767	Cushing	2/21/1811	2/22/1811 (D)		2/23/1848	
Joseph Story	Mass.	9/18/1779	Cushing	11/15/1811	11/18/1811		9/10/1845	34
Gabriel Duvall	Md.	12/6/1752	Chase	11/15/1811	11/18/1811	1/14/1835	3/6/1844	23
MONROE								
Smith Thompson	N.Y.	1/17/1768	Livingston	12/8/1823	12/19/1823		12/18/1843	20
J. Q. ADAMS								
Robert Trimble	Ky.	11/17/1776	Todd	4/11/1826	5/9/1826 (27–5)		8/25/1828	2
John J. Crittenden	Ky.	9/10/1787	Trimble	12/17/1828	2/12/1829 (P)		7/26/1863	
JACKSON								
John McLean	Ohio	3/11/1785	Trimble	3/6/1829	3/7/1829		4/4/1861	32
Henry Baldwin	Pa.	1/14/1780	Washington	1/4/1830	1/6/1830 (41–2)		4/21/1844	14
James M. Wayne	Ga.	1790	Johnson	1/7/1835	1/9/1835		7/5/1867	32
Roger B. Taney	Md.	3/17/1777	Duvall	1/15/1835	3/3/1835 (P)			
Roger B. Taney †			Marshall	12/28/1835	3/15/1836 (29–15)		10/12/1864	28
Philip P. Barbour	Va.	5/25/1783	Duvall	12/28/1835	3/15/1836 (30–11)		2/25/1841	5
William Smith	Ala.	1762	New seat	3/3/1837	3/8/1837 (23–18) (D)		6/10/1840	
John Catron	Tenn.	1786	New seat	3/3/1837	3/8/1837 (28–15)		5/30/1865	28
VAN BUREN								
John McKinley	Ala.	5/1/1780	New seat	9/18/1837	9/25/1837		7/19/1852	15
Peter V. Daniel	Va.	4/24/1784	Barbour	2/26/1841	3/2/1841 (22–5)		5/31/1860	19
TYLER								
John C. Spencer	N.Y.	1/8/1788	Thompson	1/9/1844	1/31/1844 (R, 21–26)		5/18/1855	
Reuben H. Walworth	N.Y.	10/26/1788	Thompson	3/13/1844	6/17/1844 (W)		11/27/1867	
Edward King	Pa.	1/31/1794	Baldwin	6/5/1844	6/15/1844 (P)			

Name	State	Date of Birth	To Replace	Date of Appointment	Confirmation or Other Action *	Date Resigned	Date of Death	Years of Service
TYLER *(Continued)*								
Edward King [†]			Baldwin	12/4/1844	2/7/1845 (W)		5/8/1873	
Samuel Nelson	N.Y.	11/10/1792	Thompson	2/4/1845	2/14/1845	11/28/1872	12/13/1873	27
John M. Read	Pa.	2/21/1797	Baldwin	2/7/1845	No action		11/29/1874	
POLK								
George W. Woodward	Pa.	3/26/1809	Baldwin	12/23/1845	1/22/1846 (R, 20–29)		5/10/1875	
Levi Woodbury	N.H.	12/22/1789	Story	12/23/1845	1/3/1846		9/4/1851	5
Robert C. Grier	Pa.	3/5/1794	Baldwin	8/3/1846	8/4/1846	1/31/1870	9/25/1870	23
FILLMORE								
Benjamin R. Curtis	Mass.	11/4/1809	Woodbury	12/11/1851	12/29/1851	9/30/1857	9/15/1874	5
Edward A. Bradford	La.	9/27/1813	McKinley	8/16/1852	No action1`		11/22/1872	
George E. Badger	N.C.	4/13/1795	McKinley	1/10/1853	2/11/1853 (P)		5/11/1866	
William C. Micou	La.	1806	McKinley	2/24/1853	No action		4/16/1854	
PIERCE								
John A. Campbell	Ala.	6/24/1811	McKinley	3/22/1853	3/25/1853	4/30/1861	3/12/1889	8
BUCHANAN								
Nathan Clifford	Maine	8/18/1803	Curtis	12/9/1857	1/12/1858 (26–23)		7/25/1881	23
Jeremiah S. Black	Pa.	1/10/1810	Daniel	2/5/1861	2/21/1861 (R, 25–26)		8/19/1883	
LINCOLN								
Noah H. Swayne	Ohio	12/7/1804	McLean	1/21/1862	1/24/1862 (38–1)	1/24/1881	6/8/1884	19
Samuel F. Miller	Iowa	4/5/1816	Daniel	7/16/1862	7/16/1862		10/13/1890	28
David Davis	Ill.	3/9/1815	Campbell	12/1/1862	12/8/1862	3/4/1877	6/26/1886	14
Stephen J. Field	Calif.	11/4/1816	New seat	3/6/1863	3/10/1863	12/1/1897	4/9/1899	34
Salmon P. Chase	Ohio	1/13/1808	Taney	12/6/1864	12/6/1864		5/7/1873	8
JOHNSON								
Henry Stanbery	Ohio	2/20/1803	Catron	4/16/1866	No action		6/26/1881	
GRANT								
Ebenezer R. Hoar	Mass.	2/21/1816	New seat	12/15/1869	2/3/1870 (R, 24–33)		1/31/1895	
Edwin M. Stanton	Pa.	12/19/1814	Grier	12/20/1869	12/20/1869 (46–11)		12/24/1869	
William Strong	Pa.	5/6/1808	Grier	2/7/1870	2/18/1870	12/14/1880	8/19/1895	10
Joseph P. Bradley	N.J.	3/14/1813	New seat	2/7/1870	3/21/1870 (46–9)		1/22/1892	21
Ward Hunt	N.Y.	6/14/1810	Nelson	12/3/1872	12/11/1872	1/27/1882	3/24/1886	9
George H. Williams	Ore.	3/23/1823	Chase	12/1/1873	1/8/1874 (W)		4/4/1910	
Caleb Cushing	Mass.	1/17/1800	Chase	1/9/1874	1/13/1874 (W)		1/2/1879	
Morrison R. Waite	Ohio	11/29/1816	Chase	1/19/1874	1/21/1874 (63–0)		3/23/1888	14
HAYES								
John M. Harlan	Ky.	6/1/1833	Davis	10/17/1877	11/29/1877		10/14/1911	34
William B. Woods	Ga.	8/3/1824	Strong	12/15/1880	12/21/1880 (39–8)		5/14/1887	6
Stanley Matthews	Ohio	7/21/1824	Swayne	1/26/1881	No action			
GARFIELD								
Stanley Matthews [†]			Swayne	3/14/1881	5/12/1881 (24–23)		3/22/1889	7
ARTHUR								
Horace Gray	Mass.	3/24/1828	Clifford	12/19/1881	12/20/1881 (51–5)		9/15/1902	20
Roscoe Conkling	N.Y.	10/30/1829	Hunt	2/24/1882	3/2/1882 (39–12) (D)		4/18/1888	
Samuel Blatchford	N.Y.	3/9/1820	Hunt	3/13/1882	3/27/1882		7/7/1893	11
CLEVELAND								
Lucius Q. C. Lamar	Miss.	9/17/1825	Woods	12/6/1887	1/16/1888 (32–28)		1/23/1893	5
Melville W. Fuller	Ill.	2/11/1833	Waite	4/30/1888	7/20/1888 (41–20)		7/4/1910	22

Name	State	Date of Birth	To Replace	Date of Appointment	Confirmation or Other Action *	Date Resigned	Date of Death	Years of Service
HARRISON								
David J. Brewer	Kan.	6/20/1837	Matthews	12/4/1889	12/18/1889 (53–11)		3/28/1910	20
Henry B. Brown	Mich.	3/2/1836	Miller	12/23/1890	12/29/1890	5/28/1906	9/4/1913	15
George Shiras, Jr.	Pa.	1/26/1832	Bradley	7/19/1892	7/26/1892	2/23/1903	8/2/1924	10
Howell E. Jackson	Tenn.	4/8/1832	Lamar	2/2/1893	2/18/1893		8/8/1895	2
CLEVELAND								
William B. Hornblower	N.Y.	5/13/1851	Blatchford	9/19/1893	1/15/1894 (R, 24–30)		6/16/1914	
Wheeler H. Peckham	N.Y.	1/1/1833	Blatchford	1/22/1894	2/16/1894 (R, 32–41)		9/27/1905	
Edward D. White	La.	11/3/1845	Blatchford	2/19/1894	2/19/1894		5/19/1921	17
Rufus W. Peckham	N.Y.	11/8/1838	Jackson	12/3/1895	12/9/1895		10/24/1909	13
McKINLEY								
Joseph McKenna	Calif.	8/10/1843	Field	12/16/1897	1/21/1898	1/5/1925	11/21/1926	26
ROOSEVELT								
Oliver W. Holmes	Mass.	3/8/1841	Gray	12/2/1902	12/4/1902	1/12/1932	3/6/1935	29
William R. Day	Ohio	4/17/1849	Shiras	2/19/1903	2/23/1903	11/13/1922	7/9/1923	19
William H. Moody	Mass.	12/23/1853	Brown	12/3/1906	12/12/1906	11/20/1910	7/2/1917	3
TAFT								
Horace H. Lurton	Tenn.	2/26/1844	Peckham	12/13/1909	12/20/1909		7/12/1914	4
Charles E. Hughes	N.Y.	4/11/1862	Brewer	4/25/1910	5/2/1910	6/10/1916	8/27/1948	6
Edward D. White ‡			Fuller	12/12/1910	12/12/1910		5/19/1921	10‡
Willis Van Devanter	Wyo.	4/17/1859	White	12/12/1910	12/15/1910	6/2/1937	2/8/1941	26
Joseph R. Lamar	Ga.	10/14/1857	Moody	12/12/1910	12/15/1910		1/2/1916	5
Mahlon Pitney	N.J.	2/5/1858	Harlan	2/19/1912	3/13/1912 (50–26)	12/31/1922	12/9/1924	10
WILSON								
James C. McReynolds	Tenn.	2/3/1862	Lurton	8/19/1914	8/29/1914 (44–6)	1/31/1941	8/24/1946	26
Louis D. Brandeis	Mass.	11/13/1856	Lamar	1/28/1916	6/1/1916 (47–22)	2/13/1939	10/5/1941	22
John H. Clarke	Ohio	9/18/1857	Hughes	7/14/1916	7/24/1916	9/18/1922	3/22/1945	6
HARDING								
William H. Taft	Ohio	9/15/1857	White	6/30/1921	6/30/1921	2/3/1930	3/8/1930	8
George Sutherland	Utah	3/25/1862	Clarke	9/5/1922	9/5/1922	1/17/1938	7/18/1942	15
Pierce Butler	Minn.	3/17/1866	Day	11/23/1922	12/21/1922 (61–8)		11/16/1939	17
Edward T. Sanford	Tenn.	7/23/1865	Pitney	1/24/1923	1/29/1923		3/8/1930	7
COOLIDGE								
Harlan F. Stone	N.Y.	10/11/1872	McKenna	1/5/1925	2/5/1925 (71–6)		4/22/1946	16
HOOVER								
Charles E. Hughes ‡			Taft	2/3/1930	2/13/1930 (52–26)	7/1/1941	8/27/1948	11‡
John J. Parker	N.C.	11/20/1885	Sanford	3/21/1930	5/7/1930 (R, 39–41)		3/17/1958	
Owen J. Roberts	Pa.	5/2/1875	Sanford	5/9/1930	5/20/1930	7/31/1945	5/17/1955	15
Benjamin N. Cardozo	N.Y.	5/24/1870	Holmes	2/15/1932	2/24/1932		7/9/1938	6
ROOSEVELT								
Hugo L. Black	Ala.	2/27/1886	Van Devanter	8/12/1937	8/17/1937 (63–16)	9/17/1971	10/25/1971	34
Stanley F. Reed	Ky.	12/31/1884	Sutherland	1/15/1938	1/25/1938	2/25/1957	4/2/1980	19
Felix Frankfurter	Mass.	11/15/1882	Cardozo	1/5/1939	1/17/1939	8/28/1962	2/22/1965	23
William O. Douglas	Conn.	10/16/1898	Brandeis	3/20/1939	4/4/1939 (62–4)	11/12/1975	1/19/1980	36‡
Frank Murphy	Mich.	4/13/1890	Butler	1/4/1940	1/15/1940		7/19/1949	9
Harlan F. Stone ‡			Hughes	6/12/1941	6/27/1941		4/22/1946	5‡
James F. Byrnes	S.C.	5/2/1879	McReynolds	6/12/1941	6/12/1941	10/3/1942	4/9/1972	1
Robert H. Jackson	N.Y.	2/13/1892	Stone	6/12/1941	7/7/1941		10/9/1954	13
Wiley B. Rutledge	Iowa	7/20/1894	Byrnes	1/11/1943	2/8/1943		9/10/1949	6
TRUMAN								
Harold H. Burton	Ohio	6/22/1888	Roberts	9/19/1945	9/19/1945	10/13/1958	10/28/1964	13
Fred M. Vinson	Ky.	1/22/1890	Stone	6/6/1946	6/20/1946		9/8/1953	7

Name	State	Date of Birth	To Replace	Date of Appointment	Confirmation or Other Action *	Date Resigned	Date of Death	Years of Service
TRUMAN *(Continued)*								
Tom C. Clark	Texas	9/23/1899	Murphy	8/2/1949	8/18/1949 (73–8)	6/12/1967	6/13/1977	18
Sherman Minton	Ind.	10/20/1890	Rutledge	9/15/1949	10/4/1949 (48–16)	10/15/1956	4/9/1965	7
EISENHOWER								
Earl Warren	Calif.	3/19/1891	Vinson	9/30/1953	3/1/1954	6/23/1969	6/9/1974	15
John M. Harlan	N.Y.	5/20/1899	Jackson	1/10/1955	3/16/1955 (71–11)	9/23/1971	12/29/1971	16
William J. Brennan, Jr.	N.J.	4/25/1906	Minton	1/14/1957	3/19/1957	7/23/1990		33
Charles E. Whittaker	Mo.	2/22/1901	Reed	3/2/1957	3/19/1957	3/31/1962	11/26/1973	5
Potter Stewart	Ohio	1/23/1915	Burton	1/17/1959	5/5/1959 (70–17)	7/3/1981	12/7/1985	22
KENNEDY								
Byron R. White	Colo.	6/8/1917	Whittaker	3/30/1962	4/11/1962	6/28/1993		31
Arthur J. Goldberg	Ill.	8/8/1908	Frankfurter	8/29/1962	9/25/1962	7/25/1965	1/19/1990	3
JOHNSON								
Abe Fortas	Tenn.	6/19/1910	Goldberg	7/28/1965	8/11/1965	5/14/1969	4/5/1982	4
Thurgood Marshall	N.Y.	6/2/1908	Clark	6/13/1967	8/30/1967 (69–11)	10/1/1991	1/24/1993	24
Abe Fortas ‡			Warren	6/26/1968	10/4/1968 (W)			
Homer Thornberry	Texas	1/9/1909	Fortas	6/26/1968	No action			
NIXON								
Warren E. Burger	Minn.	9/17/1907	Warren	5/21/1969	6/9/1969 (74–3)	9/26/1986	6/25/95	17
Clement Haynsworth, Jr.	S.C.	10/30/1912	Fortas	8/18/1969	11/21/1969 (R, 45–55)		11/22/1989	
G. Harrold Carswell	Fla.	12/22/1919	Fortas	1/19/1970	4/8/1970 (R, 45–51)		7/31/1992	
Harry A. Blackmun	Minn.	11/12/1908	Fortas	4/14/1970	5/12/1970 (94–0)	8/3/1994		24
Lewis F. Powell, Jr.	Va.	9/19/1907	Black	10/21/1971	12/6/1971 (89–1)	6/26/1987		16
William H. Rehnquist	Ariz.	10/1/1924	Harlan	10/21/1971	12/10/1971 (68–26)			
FORD								
John Paul Stevens	Ill.	4/20/1920	Douglas	11/28/1975	12/17/1975 (98–0)			
REAGAN								
Sandra Day O'Connor	Ariz.	3/26/1930	Stewart	8/19/1981	9/21/1981 (99–0)			
William H. Rehnquist ††			Burger	6/20/1986	9/17/1986 (65–33)			
Antonin Scalia	Va.	3/11/1936	Rehnquist	6/24/1986	9/17/1986 (98–0)			
Robert H. Bork	D.C.	3/1/1927	Powell	7/1/1987	10/23/1987 (R, 42–58)			
Anthony M. Kennedy	Calif.	7/23/1936	Powell	11/30/1987	2/3/1988 (97–0)			
BUSH								
David Hackett Souter	N.H.	9/17/1939	Brennan	7/23/1990	10/2/1990 (90–9)			
Clarence Thomas	Ga.	6/23/1948	Marshall	7/1/1991	10/15/1991 (52–48)			
CLINTON								
Ruth Bader Ginsburg	N.Y.	3/15/1933	White	6/22/1993	8/3/1993 (96–3)			
Stephen G. Breyer	Mass.	8/15/1938	Blackmun	5/13/1994	7/29/1994 (87–9)			

SOURCES: Leon Friedman and Fred L. Israel, eds., *The Justices of the United States Supreme Court, 1789–1969, Their Lives and Major Opinions,* 5 vols. (New York and London: Chelsea House Publishers, 1969–1978); U.S. Senate, Executive Journal of the U.S. Senate, 1789–1975 (Washington, D.C.: Government Printing Office); Congressional Quarterly *Almanacs,* 1971, 1975, 1981, 1986, 1987 (Washington, D.C.: Congressional Quarterly, 1972, 1976, 1982, 1987, 1988); Clare Cushman, ed., *The Supreme Court Justices: Illustrated Biographies, 1789–1995,* 2d ed. (Washington, D.C.: Congressional Quarterly, 1995).

NOTE: Boldface—Chief justice; Italics—Did not serve; *—Where no vote is listed, confirmation was by voice or otherwise unrecorded; †—Earlier nomination not confirmed. See above; ††—Earlier court service. See above; W—Withdrawn; P—Postponed; R—Rejected; D—Declined.

Glossary of Common Legal Terms

Accessory. In criminal law, a person not present at the commission of an offense who commands, advises, instigates, or conceals the offense.

Acquittal. Discharge of a person from a charge of guilt. A person is acquitted when a jury returns a verdict of not guilty. A person may also be acquitted when a judge determines that there is insufficient evidence to convict him or that a violation of due process precludes a fair trial.

Adjudicate. To determine finally by the exercise of judicial authority to decide a case.

Affidavit. A voluntary written statement of facts or charges affirmed under oath.

A fortiori. With stronger force, with more reason.

Amicus curiae. A friend of the court, a person not a party to litigation, who volunteers or is invited by the court to give his views on a case.

Appeal. To take a case to a higher court for review. Generally, a party losing in a trial court may appeal once to an appellate court as a matter of right. If he loses in the appellate court, appeal to a higher court is within the discretion of the higher court. Most appeals to the U.S. Supreme Court are within the Court's discretion. However, when the highest court in a state rules that a U.S. statute is unconstitutional or upholds a state statute against the claim that it is unconstitutional, appeal to the Supreme Court is a matter of right.

Appellant. The party that appeals a lower court decision to a higher court.

Appellee. One who has an interest in upholding the decision of a lower court and is compelled to respond when the case is appealed to a higher court by the appellant.

Arraignment. The formal process of charging a person with a crime, reading him the charge, asking whether he pleads guilty or not guilty, and entering his plea.

Attainder, Bill of. A legislative act pronouncing a particular individual guilty of a crime without trial or conviction and imposing a sentence upon him.

Bail. The security, usually money, given as assurance of a prisoner's due appearance at a designated time and place (as in court) in order to procure in the interim his release from jail.

Bailiff. A minor officer of a court usually serving as an usher or a messenger.

Brief. A document prepared by counsel to serve as the basis for an argument in court, setting out the facts of and the legal arguments in support of his case.

Burden of proof. The need or duty of affirmatively proving a fact or facts that are disputed.

Case Law. The law as defined by previously decided cases, distinct from statutes and other sources of law.

Cause. A case, suit, litigation, or action, civil or criminal.

Certiorari, Writ of. A writ issued from the Supreme Court, at its discretion, to order a lower court to prepare the record of a case and send it to the Supreme Court for review.

Civil law. Body of law dealing with the private rights of individuals, as distinguished from criminal law.

Class action. A lawsuit brought by one person or group on behalf of all persons similarly situated.

Code. A collection of laws, arranged systematically.

Comity. Courtesy, respect; usually used in the legal sense to refer to the proper relationship between state and federal courts.

Common law. Collection of principles and rules of action, particularly from unwritten English law, which derive their authority from longstanding usage and custom or from courts recognizing and enforcing these customs. Sometimes used synonymously with case law.

Consent decree. A court-sanctioned agreement settling a legal dispute and entered into by the consent of the parties.

Contempt (civil and criminal). Civil contempt consists in the failure to do something that the party is ordered by the court to do for the benefit of another party. Criminal contempt occurs when a person willfully exhibits disrespect for the court or obstructs the administration of justice.

Conviction. Final judgment or sentence that the defendant is guilty as charged.

Criminal law. That branch of law which deals with the enforcement of laws and the punishment of persons who, by breaking laws, commit crimes.

Declaratory judgment. A court pronouncement declaring a legal right or interpretation but not ordering a specific action.

De facto. In fact, in reality.

Defendant. In a civil action, the party denying or defending itself against charges brought by a plaintiff. In a criminal action, the person indicted for commission of an offense.

De jure. As a result of law, as a result of official action.

Deposition. Oral testimony from a witness taken out of court in response to written or oral questions, committed to writing, and intended to be used in the preparation of a case.

Dicta. See Obiter dictum.

Dismissal. Order disposing of a case without a trial.

Docket. See Trial docket.

Due process. Fair and regular procedure. The Fifth and Fourteenth Amendments guarantee persons that they will not be deprived of life, liberty, or property by the government until fair and usual procedures have been followed.

Error, Writ of. A writ issued from an appeals court to a lower court requiring it to send to the appeals court the record of a case in which it has entered a final judgment and which the appeals court will now review for error.

Ex parte. Only from, or on, one side. Application to a court for some ruling or action on behalf of only one party.

Ex post facto. After the fact; an ex post facto law makes an action a crime after it has already been committed, or otherwise changes the legal consequences of some past action.

Ex rel. Upon information from; usually used to describe legal proceedings begun by an official in the name of the state, but at the instigation of, and with information from, a private individual interested in the matter.

Grand jury. Group of twelve to twenty-three persons impaneled to hear in private evidence presented by the state against persons accused of crime and to issue indictments when a majority of the jurors find probable cause to believe that the accused has committed a crime. Called a "grand" jury because it comprises a greater number of persons than a "petit" jury.

Grand jury report. A public report released by a grand jury after an investigation into activities of public officials that fall short of criminal actions. Grand jury reports are often called "presentments."

Guilty. A word used by a defendant in entering a plea or by a jury in returning a verdict, indicating that the defendant is legally responsible as charged for a crime or other wrongdoing.

Habeas corpus. Literally, "you have the body"; a writ issued to inquire whether a person is lawfully imprisoned or detained. The writ demands that the persons holding the prisoner justify his detention or release him.

Immunity. A grant of exemption from prosecution in return for evidence or testimony.

In camera. "In chambers." Refers to court hearings in private without spectators.

In forma pauperis. In the manner of a pauper, without liability for court costs.

In personam. Done or directed against a particular person.

In re. In the affair of, concerning. Frequent title of judicial proceedings in which there are no adversaries, but rather where the matter itself—as a bankrupt's estate—requires judicial action.

In rem. Done or directed against the thing, not the person.

Indictment. A formal written statement based on evidence presented by the prosecutor from a grand jury decided by a majority vote, charging one or more persons with specified offenses.

Information. A written set of accusations, similar to an indictment, but filed directly by a prosecutor.

Injunction. A court order prohibiting the person to whom it is directed from performing a particular act.

Interlocutory decree. A provisional decision of the court that temporarily settles an intervening matter before completion of a legal action.

Judgment. Official decision of a court based on the rights and claims of the parties to a case that was submitted for determination.

Jurisdiction. The power of a court to hear a case in question, which exists when the proper parties are present, and when the point to be decided is within the issues authorized to be handled by the particular court.

Juries. See Grand jury and Petit jury.

Magistrate. A judicial officer having jurisdiction to try minor criminal cases and conduct preliminary examinations of persons charged with serious crimes.

Mandamus. "We command." An order issued from a superior court directing a lower court or other authority to perform a particular act.

Moot. Unsettled, undecided. A moot question is also one that is no longer material; a moot case is one that has become hypothetical.

Motion. Written or oral application to a court or a judge to obtain a rule or an order.

Nolo contendere. "I will not contest it." A plea entered by a defendant at the discretion of the judge with the same legal effect as a plea of guilty, but it may not be cited in other proceedings as an admission of guilt.

Obiter dictum. Statement by a judge or justice expressing an opinion and included with, but not essential to, an opinion resolving a case before the court. Dicta are not necessarily binding in future cases.

Parole. A conditional release from imprisonment under conditions that if the prisoner abides by the law and other restrictions that may be placed upon him, he will not have to serve the remainder of his sentence. But if he does not abide by specified rules, he will be returned to prison.

Per curiam. "By the court." An unsigned opinion of the court or an opinion written by the whole court.

Petit jury. A trial jury, originally a panel of twelve persons who tried to reach a unanimous verdict on questions of fact in criminal and civil proceedings. Since 1970 the Supreme Court has upheld the legality of state juries with fewer than twelve persons. Because it comprises fewer persons than a "grand" jury, it is called a "petit" jury.

Petitioner. One who files a petition with a court seeking action or relief, including a plaintiff or an appellant. But a petitioner is also a person who files for other court action where charges are not necessarily made; for example, a party may petition the court for an order requiring another person or party to produce documents. The opposite party is called the respondent.

When a writ of certiorari is granted by the Supreme Court, the parties to the case are called petitioner and respondent in contrast to the appellant and appellee terms used in an appeal.

Plaintiff. A party who brings a civil action or sues to obtain a remedy for injury to his rights. The party against whom action is brought is termed the defendant.

Plea Bargaining. Negotiations between prosecutors and the defendant aimed at exchanging a plea of guilty from the defendant for concessions by the prosecutors, such as reduction of charges or a request for leniency.

Pleas. See Guilty and Nolo contendere.

Presentment. See Grand jury report.

Prima facie. At first sight; referring to a fact or other evidence presumably sufficient to establish a defense or a claim unless otherwise contradicted.

Probation. Process under which a person convicted of an offense, usually a first offense, receives a suspended sentence and is given his freedom, usually under the guardianship of a probation officer.

Quash. To overthrow, annul, or vacate; as to quash a subpoena.

Recognizance. An obligation entered into before a court or magistrate requiring the performance of a specified act—usually to appear in court at a later date. It is an alternative to bail for pretrial release.

Remand. To send back. In the event of a decision being remanded, it is sent back by a higher court to the court from which it came for further action.

Respondent. One who is compelled to answer the claims or questions posed in court by a petitioner. A defendant and an appellee may be called respondents, but the term also includes those parties who answer in court during actions where charges are not necessarily brought or where the Supreme Court has granted a writ of certiorari.

Seriatim. Separately, individually, one by one.

Stare Decisis. "Let the decision stand." The principle of adherence to settled cases, the doctrine that principles of law established in earlier judicial decisions should be accepted as authoritative in similar subsequent cases.

Statute. A written law enacted by a legislature. A collection of statutes for a particular governmental division is called a code.

Stay. To halt or suspend further judicial proceedings.

Subpoena. An order to present one's self before a grand jury, court, or legislative hearing.

Subpoena duces tecum. An order to produce specified documents or papers.

Tort. An injury or wrong to the person or property of another.

Transactional immunity. Protects a witness from prosecution for any offense mentioned in or related to his testimony, regardless of independent evidence against him.

Trial docket. A calendar prepared by the clerks of the court listing the cases set to be tried.

Use immunity. Protects a witness against the use of his own testimony against him in prosecution.

Vacate. To make void, annul, or rescind.

Writ. A written court order commanding the designated recipient to perform or not perform acts specified in the order.

Acts of Congress Held Unconstitutional

1. ACT OF SEPTEMBER 24, 1789 (1 STAT. 81, § 13, IN PART).

Provision that ". . . [the Supreme Court] shall have power to issue . . . writs of mandamus, in cases warranted by the principles and usages of law, to any . . . persons holding office, under authority of the United States" as applied to the issue of mandamus to the Secretary of State requiring him to deliver to plaintiff a commission (duly signed by the President) as justice of the peace in the District of Columbia *held* an attempt to enlarge the original jurisdiction of the Supreme Court, fixed by Article III, § 2.

Marbury v. Madison, 1 Cr. (5 U.S.) 137 (1803).

2. ACT OF FEBRUARY 20, 1812 (2 STAT. 677).

Provisions establishing board of revision to annul titles conferred many years previously by governors of the Northwest Territory were *held* violative of the due process clause of the Fifth Amendment.

Reichart v. Felps, 6 Wall. (73 U.S.) 160 (1868).

3. ACT OF MARCH 6, 1820 (3 STAT. 548, § 8, PROVISO).

The Missouri Compromise, prohibiting slavery within the Louisiana Territory north of 36° 30′ except Missouri, *held* not warranted as a regulation of Territory belonging to the United States under Article IV, § 3, clause 2 (and *see* Fifth Amendment).

Scott v. Sandford, 19 How. (60 U.S.) 393 (1857).

4. ACT OF FEBRUARY 25, 1862 (12 STAT. 345, § 1); JULY 11, 1862 (12 STAT. 532, § 1); MARCH 3, 1863 (12 STAT. 711, § 3), EACH IN PART ONLY.

"Legal tender clauses," making noninterest-bearing United States notes legal tender in payment of "all debts, public and private," so far as applied to debts contracted before passage of the act, *held* not within express or implied powers of Congress under Article I, § 8, and inconsistent with Article I, § 10, and Fifth Amendment.

Hepburn v. Griswold, 8 Wall. (75 U.S.) 603 (1870); overruled in *Knox v. Lee (Legal Tender Cases),* 12 Wall. (79 U.S.) 457 (1871).

5. ACT OF MAY 20, 1862 (§ 35, 12 STAT.); ACT OF MAY 21, 1862 (12 STAT. 407); ACT OF JUNE 25, 1864 (13 STAT. 187); ACT OF JULY 23, 1866 (14 STAT. 216); REVISED STATUTES RELATING TO THE DISTRICT OF COLUMBIA, ACT OF JUNE 22, 1874 (§§ 281, 282, 294, 304, 18 STAT. PT. 2).

Provisions of law requiring, or construed to require, racial separation in the schools of the District of Columbia, *held* to violate the equal protection component of the due process clause of the Fifth Amendment.

Bolling v. Sharpe, 347 U.S. 497 (1954).

6. ACT OF MARCH 3, 1863 (12 STAT. 756, § 5).

"So much of the fifth section . . . as provides for the removal of a judgment in a State court, and in which the cause was tried by a jury to the circuit court of the United States for a retrial on the facts and law, is not in pursuance of the Constitution, and is void" under the Seventh Amendment.

The Justices v. Murray, 9 Wall. (76 U.S.) 274 (1870).

7. ACT OF MARCH 3, 1863 (12 STAT. 766, § 5).

Provision for an appeal from the Court of Claims to the Supreme Court—there being, at the time, a further provision (§ 14) requiring an estimate by the Secretary of the Treasury before payment of final judgment, *held* to contravene the judicial finality intended by the Constitution, Article III.

Gordon v. United States, 2 Wall. (69 U.S.) 561 (1865). (Case was dismissed without opinion; the grounds upon which this decision was made were stated in a posthumous opinion by Chief Justice Taney printed in the appendix to volume 117 U.S. 697.)

8. ACT OF JUNE 30, 1864 (13 STAT. 311, § 13).

Provision that "any prize cause now pending in any circuit court shall, on the application of all parties in interest . . . be transferred by that court to the Supreme Court. . .," as applied in a case where no action had been taken in the Circuit Court on the appeal from the district court, *held* to propose an appeal procedure not within Article III, § 2.

The Alicia, 7 Wall. (74 U.S.) 571 (1869).

9. ACT OF JANUARY 24, 1865 (13 STAT. 424).

Requirement of a test oath (disavowing actions in hostility to the United States) before admission to appear as attorney in a federal court by virtue of any previous admission, *held* invalid as applied to an attorney who had been pardoned by the President for all offenses during the Rebellion—as *ex post facto* (Article I, § 9, clause 3) and an interference with the pardoning power (Article II, § 2, clause 1).

Ex parte Garland, 4 Wall. (71 U.S.) 333 (1867).

10. ACT OF MARCH 2, 1867 (14 STAT. 484, § 29).

General prohibition on sale of naphtha, etc., for illuminating purposes, if inflammable at less temperature than 110 F., *held* invalid "except so far as the section named operates within the United States, but without the limits of any State," as being a mere police regulation.

United States v. Dewitt, 9 Wall. (76 U.S.) 41 (1870).

11. REVISED STATUTES 5132, SUBDIVISION 9 (ACT OF MARCH 2, 1867, 14 STAT. 539).

Provision penalizing "any person respecting whom bankruptcy proceedings are commenced . . . who, within 3 months before the commencement of proceedings in bankruptcy, under the false color and pretense of carrying on business and dealing in the ordinary course of trade, obtains on credit from any person any goods or chattels with intent to defraud. . .," *held* a police regulation not within the bankruptcy power (Article I, § 4, clause 4).

United States v. Fox, 95 U.S. 670 (1878).

12. ACT OF MAY 31, 1870 (16 STAT. 140, §§ 3, 4).

Provisions penalizing (1) refusal of local election official to permit voting by persons offering to qualify under State laws, applicable to any citizens; and (2) hindering of any person from qualifying or voting, *held* invalid under Fifteenth Amendment.

United States v. Reese, 92 U.S. 214 (1876).

13. REVISED STATUTES 5507 (ACT OF MAY 31, 1870, 16 STAT. 141, § 4).

Provision penalizing "every person who prevents, hinders, controls, or intimidates another from exercising . . . the right of suffrage, to whom that right is guaranteed by the Fifteenth Amendment to the

Constitution of the United States, by means of bribery. . .," *held* not authorized by the Fifteenth Amendment.

James v. Bowman, 190 U.S. 127 (1903).

14. REVISED STATUTES 1977 (ACT OF MAY 31, 1870, 16 STAT. 144).

Provision that "all persons within the jurisdiction of the United States shall have the same right in every State and Territory to make and enforce contracts . . . as is enjoyed by white citizens. . .," *held* invalid under the Thirteenth Amendment.

Hodges v. United States, 203 U.S. 1 (1906), overruled in *Jones v. Alfred H. Mayer Co.,* 392 U.S. 409, 441-443 (1968).

15. REVISED STATUTES OF THE DISTRICT OF CO-LUMBIA, § 1064 (ACT OF JUNE 17, 1870, 16 STAT. 154 § 3).

Provision that "prosecutions in the police court [of the District of Columbia] shall be by information under oath, without indictment by grand jury or trial by petit jury," as applied to punishment for conspiracy *held* to contravene Article III, § 2, requiring jury trial of all crimes.

Callan v. Wilson, 127 U.S. 540 (1888).

16. REVISED STATUTES 4937–4947 (ACT OF JULY 8, 1870, 16 STAT. 210), AND ACT OF AUGUST 14, 1876 (19 STAT. 141).

Original trademark law, applying to marks "for exclusive use within the United States," and a penal act designed solely for the protection of rights defined in the earlier measure, *held* not supportable by Article I, § 8, clause 8 (copyright clause), nor Article I, § 8, clause 3, by reason of its application to intrastate as well as interstate commerce.

Trade-Mark Cases, 100 U.S. 82 (1879).

17. ACT OF JULY 12, 1870 (16 STAT. 235).

Provision making Presidential pardons inadmissible in evidence in Court of Claims, prohibiting their use by that court in deciding claims or appeals, and requiring dismissal of appeals by the Supreme Court in cases where proof of loyalty had been made otherwise than as prescribed by law, *held* an interference with judicial power under Article III, § 1, and with the pardoning power under Article II, § 2, clause 1.

United States v. Klein, 13 Wall. (80 U.S.) 128 (1872).

18. REVISED STATUTES 5519 (ACT OF APRIL 20, 1871, 17 STAT. 13, § 2).

Section providing punishment in case "two or more persons in any State . . . conspire . . . for the purpose of depriving . . . any person . . . of the equal protection of the laws . . . or for the purpose of preventing or hindering the constituted authorities of any State . . . from giving or securing to all persons within such State . . . the equal protection of the laws. . .," *held* invalid as not being directed at state action proscribed by the Fourteenth Amendment.

United States v. Harris, 106 U.S. 629 (1883).

In *Baldwin v. Franks,* 120 U.S. 678 (1887), an attempt was made to distinguish the *Harris* case and to apply the statute to a conspiracy directed at aliens within a State, but the provision was *held* not enforceable in such limited manner.

19. ACT OF MARCH 3, 1873 (CH. 258 § 2, 17 STAT. 599, RECODIFIED IN 39 U.S.C. § 3001(E)(2)).

Comstock Act provision barring from the mails any unsolicited advertisement for contraceptives, as applied to circulars and flyers promoting prophylactics or containing information discussing the desirability and availability of prophylactics, violates the free speech clause of the First Amendment.

Bolger v. Youngs Drug Products Corp. 463 U.S. 60 (1983).

20. ACT OF JUNE 22, 1874 (18 STAT. 1878, § 4).

Provision authorizing federal courts, in suits for forfeitures under revenue and custom laws, to require production of documents, with allegations expected to be proved therein to be taken as proved on failure to produce such documents, was *held* violative of the search and seizure provision of the Fourth Amendment and the self-incrimination clause of the Fifth Amendment.

Boyd v. United States, 116 U.S. 616 (1886).

21. ACT OF MARCH 1, 1875 (18 STAT. 336, §§ 1, 2).

Provision "That all persons within the jurisdiction of the United States shall be entitled to the full and equal enjoyment of the accommodations . . . of inns, public conveyances on land or water, theaters, and other places of public amusement; subject only to the conditions and limitations established by law, and applicable alike to citizens of every race and color, regardless of any previous condition of servitude"—subject to penalty, *held* not to be supported by the Thirteenth or Fourteenth Amendments.

Civil Rights Cases, 109 U.S. 3 (1883), as to operation within States.

22. ACT OF MARCH 3, 1875 (18 STAT. 479, § 2).

Provision that "if the party [i.e., a person stealing property from the United States] has been convicted, then the judgment against him shall be conclusive evidence in the prosecution against [the] receiver that the property of the United States therein described has been embezzled, stolen, or purloined," *held* to contravene the Sixth Amendment.

Kirby v. United States, 174 U.S. 47 (1899).

23. ACT OF JULY 12, 1876 (19 STAT. 80, SEC. 6, IN PART).

Provision that "postmasters of the first, second, and third classes . . . may be removed by the President by and with the advice and consent of the Senate," *held* to infringe the executive power under Article II, § 1, clause 1.

Myers v. United States, 272 U.S. 52 (1926).

24. ACT OF AUGUST 11, 1888 (25 STAT. 411).

Clause, in a provision for the purchase or condemnation of a certain lock and dam in the Monongahela River, that ". . . in estimating the sum to be paid by the United States, the franchise of said corporation to collect tolls shall not be considered or estimated. . .," *held* to contravene the Fifth Amendment.

Monongahela Navigation Co. v. United States, 148 U.S. 312 (1893).

25. ACT OF MAY 5, 1892 (27 STAT. 25, § 4).

Provision of a Chinese exclusion act, that Chinese persons "convicted and adjudged to be not lawfully entitled to be or remain in the United States shall be imprisoned at hard labor for a period not exceeding 1 year and thereafter removed from the United States . . . (such conviction and judgment being had before a justice, judge, or commissioner upon a summary hearing), *held* to contravene the Fifth and Sixth Amendments.

Wong Wing v. United States, 163 U.S. 228 (1896).

26. JOINT RESOLUTION OF AUGUST 4, 1894 (28 STAT. 1018, NO. 41).

Provision authorizing the Secretary of the Interior to approve a second lease of certain land by an Indian chief in Minnesota (granted to lessor's ancestor by art. 9 of a treaty with the Chippewa Indians), *held* an interference with judicial interpretation of treaties under Article III, § 2, clause 1 (and repugnant to the Fifth Amendment).

Jones v. Meehan, 175 U.S. 1 (1899).

27. ACT OF AUGUST 27, 1894 (28 STAT. 553–560, §§ 27-37).

Income tax provisions of the tariff act of 1894. "The tax imposed by §§ 27 and 37, inclusive . . . so far as it falls on the income of real estate and of personal property, being a direct tax within the meaning of the Constitution, and, therefore, unconstitutional and void because not apportioned according to representation [Article I, § 2, clause 3], all those sections, constituting one entire scheme of taxation, are necessarily invalid" (158 U.S. 601, 637).

Pollock v. Farmers' Loan & Trust Co., 157 U.S. 429 (1895), and rehearing, 158 U.S. 601 (1895).

28. ACT OF JANUARY 30, 1897 (29 STAT. 506).

Prohibition on sale of liquor ". . . to any Indian to whom allotment of land has been made while the title to the same shall be held in trust by the Government. . .," *held* a police regulation infringing state powers, and not warranted by the commerce clause, Article I, § 8, clause 3.

Matter of Heff, 197 U.S. 488 (1905), overruled in *United States v. Nice,* 241 U.S. 591 (1916).

29. ACT OF JUNE 1, 1898 (30 STAT. 428).

Section 10, penalizing "any employer subject to the provisions of this act" who should "threaten any employee with loss of employment . . . because of his membership in . . . a labor corporation, association, or organization" (the act being applicable "to any common carrier . . . engaged in the transportation of passengers or property . . . from one State . . . to another State. . .," etc.), *held* an infringement of the Fifth Amendment and not supported by the commerce clause.

Adair v. United States, 208 U.S. 161 (1908).

30. ACT OF JUNE 13, 1898 (30 STAT. 448, 459).

Stamp tax on foreign bills of lading, *held* a tax on exports in violation of Article I, § 9.

Fairbank v. United States, 181 U.S. 283 (1901).

31. SAME (30 STAT. 448, 460).

Tax on charter parties, as applied to shipments exclusively from ports in United States to foreign ports, *held* a tax on exports in violation of Article I, § 9.

United States v. Hvoslef, 237 U.S. 1 (1915).

32. SAME (30 STAT. 448, 461).

Stamp tax on policies of marine insurance on exports, *held* a tax on exports in violation of Article I, § 9.

Thames & Mersey Marine Ins. Co. v. United States, 237 U.S. 19 (1915).

33. ACT OF JUNE 6, 1900 (31 STAT. 359, § 171).

Section of the Alaska Code providing for a six-person jury in trials for misdemeanors, *held* repugnant to the Sixth Amendment, requiring "jury" trial of crimes.

Rassmussen v. United States, 197 U.S. 516 (1905).

34. ACT OF MARCH 3, 1901 (31 STAT. 1341, § 935).

Section of the District of Columbia Code granting the same right of appeal, in criminal cases, to the United States or the District of Columbia as to the defendant, but providing that a verdict was not to

be set aside for error found in rulings during trial, *held* an attempt to take an advisory opinion, contrary to Article III, § 2.

United States v. Evans, 213 U.S. 297 (1909).

35. ACT OF JUNE 11, 1906 (34 STAT. 232).

Act providing that "every common carrier engaged in trade or commerce in the District of Columbia . . . or between the several States . . . shall be liable to any of its employees . . . for all damages which may result from the negligence of any of its officers . . . or by reason of any defect . . . due to its negligence in its cars, engines . . . roadbed," etc., *held* not supportable under Article I, § 8, clause 3 because it extended to intrastate as well as interstate commercial activities.

The Employers' Liability Cases, 207 U.S. 463 (1908). (The act was upheld as to the District of Columbia in *Hyde v. Southern R. Co.,* 31 App. D.C. 466 (1908); and as to the Territories, in *El Paso & N.E. Ry. v. Gutierrez,* 215 U.S. 87 (1909).)

36. ACT OF JUNE 16, 1906 (34 STAT. 269, § 2).

Provision of Oklahoma Enabling Act restricting relocation of the State capital prior to 1913, *held* not supportable by Article IV, § 3, authorizing admission of new States.

Coyle v. Smith, 221 U.S. 559 (1911).

37. ACT OF FEBRUARY 20, 1907 (34 STAT. 889, § 3).

Provision in the Immigration Act of 1907 penalizing "whoever . . . shall keep, maintain, control, support, or harbor in any house or other place, for the purpose of prostitution . . . any alien woman or girl, within 3 years after she shall have entered the United States," *held* an exercise of police power not within the control of Congress over immigration (whether drawn from the commerce clause or based on inherent sovereignty).

Keller v. United States, 213 U.S. 138 (1909).

38. ACT OF MARCH 1, 1907 (34 STAT. 1028).

Provisions authorizing certain Indians "to institute their suits in the Court of Claims to determine the validity of any acts of Congress passed since . . . 1902, insofar as said acts . . . attempt to increase or extend the restrictions upon alienation . . . of allotments of lands of Cherokee citizens. . .," and giving a right of appeal to the Supreme Court, *held* an attempt to enlarge the judicial power restricted by Article III, § 2, to cases and controversies.

Muskrat v. United States, 219 U.S. 346 (1911).

39. ACT OF MAY 27, 1908 (35 STAT. 313, § 4).

Provision making locally taxable "all land [of Indians of the Five Civilized Tribes] from which restrictions have been or shall be removed," *held* a violation of the Fifth Amendment, in view of the Atoka Agreement, embodied in the Curtis Act of June 28, 1898, providing tax-exemption for allotted lands while title in original allottee, not exceeding 21 years.

Choate v. Trapp, 224 U.S. 665 (1912).

40. ACT OF FEBRUARY 9, 1909, § 2, 35 STAT. 614, AS AMENDED.

Provision of Narcotic Drugs Import and Export Act creating a presumption that possessor of cocaine knew of its illegal importation into the United States, *held,* in light of the fact that more cocaine is produced domestically than is brought into the country and in absence of any showing that defendant could have known his cocaine was imported, if it was, inapplicable to support conviction from mere possession of cocaine.

Turner v. United States, 396 U.S. 398 (1970).

41. ACT OF AUGUST 19, 1911 (37 STAT. 28).

A proviso in § 8 of the Federal Corrupt Practices Act fixing a maximum authorized expenditure by a candidate for Senator "in any campaign for his nomination and election," as applied to a primary election, *held* not supported by Article I, § 4, giving Congress power to regulate the manner of holding elections for Senators and Representatives.

Newberry v. United States, 256 U.S. 232 (1921), overruled in *United States v. Classic*, 313 U.S. 299 (1941).

42. ACT OF JUNE 18, 1912 (37 STAT. 136, § 8).

Part of § 8 giving the Juvenile Court of the District of Columbia (proceeding upon information) concurrent jurisdiction of desertion cases (which were, by law, punishable by fine or imprisonment in the workhouse at hard labor for 1 year), *held* invalid under the Fifth Amendment which gives right to presentment by a grand jury in case of infamous crimes.

United States v. Moreland, 258 U.S. 433 (1922).

43. ACT OF MARCH 4, 1913 (37 STAT. 988, PART OF PAR. 64).

Provision of the District of Columbia Public Utility Commission Act authorizing appeal to the United States Supreme Court from decrees of the District of Columbia Court of Appeals modifying valuation decisions of the Utilities Commission, *held* an attempt to extend the appellate jurisdiction of the Supreme Court to cases not strictly judicial within the meaning of Article III, § 2.

Keller v. Potomac Elec. Co., 261 U.S. 428 (1923).

44. ACT OF SEPTEMBER 1, 1916 (39 STAT. 675).

The original Child Labor Law, providing "that no producer . . . shall ship . . . in interstate commerce . . . any article or commodity the product of any mill . . . in which within 30 days prior to the removal of such product therefrom children under the age of 14 years have been employed or permitted to work more than 8 hours in any day or more than 6 days in any week. . .," *held* not within the commerce power of Congress.

Hammer v. Dagenhart, 247 U.S. 251 (1918).

45. ACT OF SEPTEMBER 8, 1916 (39 STAT. 757, § 2(A), IN PART).

Provision of the income tax law of 1916, that a "stock dividend shall be considered income, to the amount of its cash value," *held* invalid (in spite of the Sixteenth Amendment) as an attempt to tax something not actually income, without regard to apportionment under Article I, § 2, clause 3.

Eisner v. Macomber, 252 U.S. 189 (1920).

46. ACT OF OCTOBER 6, 1917 (40 STAT. 395).

The amendment of §§ 24 and 256 of the Judicial Code (which prescribe the jurisdiction of district courts) "saving . . . to claimants the rights and remedies under the workmen's compensation law of any State," *held* an attempt to transfer federal legislative powers to the States—the Constitution, by Article III, § 2, and Article I, § 8, having adopted rules of general maritime law.

Knickerbocker Ice Co. v. Stewart, 253 U.S. 149 (1920).

47. ACT OF SEPTEMBER 19, 1918 (40 STAT. 960).

Specifically, that part of the Minimum Wage Law of the District of Columbia which authorized the Wage Board "to ascertain and declare . . . (a) Standards of minimum wages for women in any occupation within the District of Columbia, and what wages are inadequate to supply the necessary cost of living to any such women workers to maintain them in good health and to protect their morals. . .," *held* to interfere with freedom of contract under the Fifth Amendment.

Adkins v. Children's Hospital, 261 U.S. 525 (1923), overruled in *West Coast Hotel Co. v. Parrish*, 300 U.S. 379 (1937).

48. ACT OF FEBRUARY 24, 1919 (40 STAT. 1065, § 213, IN PART).

That part of § 213 of the Revenue Act of 1919 which provided that ". . . for the purposes of the title . . . the term 'gross income' . . . includes gains, profits, and income derived from salaries, wages, or compensation for personal service (including in the case of . . . judges of the Supreme and inferior courts of the United States . . . the compensation received as such) . . ." as applied to a judge in office when the act was passed, *held* a violation of the guaranty of judges' salaries, in Article III, § 1.

Evans v. Gore, 253 U.S. 245 (1920).

Miles v. Graham, 268 U.S. 501 (1925), held it invalid as applied to a judge taking office subsequent to the date of the act. Both cases were overruled by *O'Malley v. Woodrough*, 307 U.S. 227 (1939).

49. ACT OF FEBRUARY 24, 1919 (40 STAT. 1097, § 402(C)).

That part of the estate tax law providing that "gross estate" of a decedent should include value of all property "to the extent of any interest therein of which the decedent has at any time made a transfer or with respect to which he had at any time created a trust, in contemplation of or intended to take effect in possession or enjoyment at or after his death (whether such transfer or trust is made or created before or after the passage of this act), except in case of a *bona fide* sale . . ." as applied to a transfer of property made prior to the act and intended to take effect "in possession or enjoyment" at death of grantor, but not in fact testamentary or designed to evade taxation, *held* confiscatory, contrary to Fifth Amendment.

Nicholds v. Coolidge, 274 U.S. 531 (1927).

50. ACT OF FEBRUARY 24, 1919, TITLE XII (40 STAT. 1138, ENTIRE TITLE).

The Child Labor Tax Act, providing that "every person . . . operating . . . any . . . factory . . . in which children under the age of 14 years have been employed or permitted to work . . . shall pay . . . in addition to all other taxes imposed by law, an excise tax equivalent to 10 percent of the entire net profits received . . . for such year from the sale . . . of the product of such . . . factory. . .," *held* beyond the taxing power under Article I, § 8, clause 1, and an infringement of state authority.

Bailey v. Drexel Furniture Co. (Child Labor Tax Case), 259 U.S. 20 (1922).

51. ACT OF OCTOBER 22, 1919 (41 STAT. 298, § 2), AMENDING ACT OF AUGUST 10, 1917 (40 STAT. 277, § 4).

(a) § 4 of the Lever Act, providing in part "that it is hereby made unlawful for any persons willfully . . . to make any unjust or unreasonable rate or charge in handling or dealing in or with any necessaries . . ." and fixing a penalty, *held* invalid to support an indictment for charging an unreasonable price on sale—as not setting up an ascertainable standard of guilt within the requirement of the Sixth Amendment.

United States v. L. Cohen Grocery Co., 255 U.S. 81 (1921).

(b) That provision of § 4 making it unlawful "to conspire, combine, agree, or arrange with any other person to . . . exact excessive prices for any necessaries" and fixing a penalty, *held* invalid to support an indictment, on the reasoning of the *Cohen Grocery* case.

Weeds, Inc. v. United States, 255 U.S. 109 (1921).

52. ACT OF AUGUST 24, 1921 (42 STAT. 187, FUTURES TRADING ACT).

(a) § 4 (and interwoven regulations) providing a "tax of 20 cents a bushel on every bushel involved therein, upon each contract of sale of grain for future delivery, except . . . where such contracts are made by or through a member of a board of trade which has been designated by the Secretary of Agriculture as a 'contract market'. . .," *held* not within the taxing power under Article I, § 8.

Hill v. Wallace, 259 U.S. 44 (1922).

(b) § 3, providing "That in addition to the taxes now imposed by law there is hereby levied a tax amounting to 20 cents per bushel on each bushel involved therein, whether the actual commodity is intended to be delivered or only nominally referred to, upon each . . . option for a contract either of purchase or sale of grain. . .," *held* invalid on the same reasoning.

Trusler v. Crooks, 269 U.S. 475 (1926).

53. ACT OF NOVEMBER 23, 1921 (42 STAT. 261, § 245, IN PART).

Provision of Revenue Act of 1921 abating the deduction (4 percent of mean reserves) allowed from taxable income of life insurance companies in general by the amount of interest on their tax-exempts, and so according no relative advantage to the owners of the tax-exempt securities, *held* to destroy a guaranteed exemption.

National Life Ins. v. United States, 277 U.S. 508 (1928).

54. ACT OF JUNE 10, 1922 (42 STAT. 634).

A second attempt to amend §§ 24 and 256 of the Judicial Code, relating to jurisdiction of district courts, by saving "to claimants for compensation for injuries to or death of persons other than the master or members of the crew of a vessel, their rights and remedies under the workmen's compensation law of any State . . ." *held* invalid on authority of *Knickerbocker Ice Co. v. Stewart.*

Washington v. Dawson & Co., 264 U.S. 219 (1924).

55. ACT OF JUNE 2, 1924 (43 STAT. 313).

The gift tax provisions of the Revenue Act of 1924, applicable to gifts made during the calendar year, were *held* invalid under the Fifth Amendment insofar as they applied to gifts made before passage of the act.

Untermeyer v. Anderson, 276 U.S. 440 (1928).

56. ACT OF FEBRUARY 26, 1926 (44 STAT. 70, § 302, IN PART).

Stipulation creating a conclusive presumption that gifts made within two years prior to the death of the donor were made in contemplation of death of donor and requiring the value thereof to be included in computing the death transfer tax on decedent's estate was *held* to effect an invalid deprivation of property without due process.

Heiner v. Donnan, 285 U.S. 312 (1932).

57. ACT OF FEBRUARY 26, 1926 (44 STAT. 95, § 701).

Provision imposing a special excise tax of $1,000 on liquor dealers operating in States where such business is illegal, was *held* a penalty, without constitutional support following repeal of the Eighteenth Amendment.

United States v. Constantine, 296 U.S. 287 (1935).

58. ACT OF MARCH 20, 1933 (48 STAT. 11, § 17, IN PART).

Clause in the Economy Act of 1933 providing ". . . all laws granting or pertaining to yearly renewable term war risk insurance are hereby repealed," *held* invalid to abrogate an outstanding contract of insurance, which is a vested right protected by the Fifth Amendment.

Lynch v. United States, 292 U.S. 571 (1934).

59. ACT OF MAY 12, 1933 (48 STAT. 31).

Agricultural Adjustment Act providing for processing taxes on agricultural commodities and benefit payments therefor to farmers, *held* not within the taxing power under Article I, § 8, clause 1.

United States v. Butler, 297 U.S. 1 (1936).

60. ACT OF JOINT RESOLUTION OF JUNE 5, 1933 (48 STAT. 113, § 1).

Abrogation of gold clause in Government obligations, *held* a repudiation of the pledge implicit in the power to borrow money (Article 1, § 8, clause 2), and within the prohibition of the Fourteenth Amendment, against questioning the validity of the public debt. (The majority of the Court, however, held plaintiff not entitled to recover under the circumstances.)

Perry v. United States, 294 U.S. 330 (1935).

61. ACT OF JUNE 16, 1933 (48 STAT. 195, THE NATIONAL INDUSTRIAL RECOVERY ACT).

(a) Title I, except § 9.

Provisions relating to codes of fair competition, authorized to be approved by the President in his discretion "to effectuate the policy" of the act, *held* invalid as a delegation of legislative power (Article I, § 1) and not within the commerce power (Article I, § 8, clause 3).

Schechter Poultry Corp. v. United States, 295 U.S. 495 (1935).

(b) § 9(c).

Clause of the oil regulation section authorizing the President "to prohibit the transportation in interstate . . . commerce of petroleum . . . produced or withdrawn from storage in excess of the amount permitted . . . by any State law . . ." and prescribing a penalty for violation of orders issued thereunder, *held* invalid as a delegation of legislative power.

Panama Refining Co. v. Ryan, 293 U.S. 388 (1935).

62. ACT OF JUNE 16, 1933 (48 STAT. 307, § 13).

Temporary reduction of 15 percent in retired pay of judges, retired from service but subject to performance of judicial duties under the Act of March 1, 1929 (45 Stat. 1422), was *held* a violation of the guaranty of judges' salaries in Article III, § 1.

Booth v. United States, 291 U.S. 339 (1934).

63. ACT OF APRIL 27, 1934 (48 STAT. 646, § 6) AMENDING § 5(I) OF HOME OWNERS' LOAN ACT OF 1933.

Provision for conversion of state building and loan associations into federal associations, upon vote of 51 percent of the votes cast at a meeting of stockholders called to consider such action, *held* an encroachment on reserved powers of State.

Hopkins Savings Assn. v. Cleary, 296 U.S. 315 (1935).

64. ACT OF MAY 24, 1934 (48 STAT. 798).

Provision for readjustment of municipal indebtedness, though "adequately related" to the bankruptcy power, was *held* invalid as an interference with state sovereignty.

Ashton v. Cameron County Dist., 298 U.S. 513 (1936).

65. ACT OF JUNE 27, 1934 (48 STAT. 1283).

The Railroad Retirement Act, establishing a detailed compulsory retirement system for employees of carriers subject to the Interstate Commerce Act, *held* not a regulation of commerce within the meaning of Article I, § 8, clause 3, and violative of the due process clause (Fifth Amendment).

Railroad Retirement Board v. Alton R. Co., 295 U.S. 330 (1935).

66. ACT OF JUNE 28, 1934 (48 STAT. 1289, CH. 869).

The Frazier-Lemke Act, adding subsection (5) to § 75 of the Bankruptcy Act, designed to preserve to mortgagors the ownership and enjoyment of their farm property and providing specifically, in paragraph 7, that a bankrupt left in possession has the option at any time within 5 years of buying at the appraised value—subject meanwhile to no monetary obligation other than payment of reasonable rental, *held* a violation of property rights, under the Fifth Amendment.

Louisville Bank v. Radford, 295 U.S. 555 (1935).

67. ACT OF AUGUST 24, 1935 (49 STAT. 750).

Amendments of Agricultural Adjustment Act *held* not within the taxing power.

Rickert Rice Mills v. Fontenot, 297 U.S. 110 (1936).

68. ACT OF AUGUST 29, 1935 (CH. 814 § 5(E), 49 STAT. 982, 27 U.S.C. § 205(E)).

The prohibition in section 5(e)(2) of the Federal Alcohol Administration Act of 1935 on the display of alcohol content on beer labels is inconsistent with the protections afforded to commercial speech by the First Amendment. The government's interest in curbing strength wars among brewers is substantial, but, given the "overall irrationality" of the regulatory scheme, the labeling prohibition does not directly and materially advance that interest.

Rubin v. Coors Brewing Co., 115 S. Ct. 1585 (1995).

69. ACT OF AUGUST 30, 1935 (49 STAT. 991).

Bituminous Coal Conservation Act of 1935, *held* to impose, not a tax within Article I, § 8, but a penalty not sustained by the commerce clause (Article I, § 8, clause 3).

Carter v. Carter Coal Co., 298 U.S. 238 (1936).

70. ACT OF FEBRUARY 15, 1938 (CH. 29, 52 STAT. 30).

District of Columbia Code § 22-1115, prohibiting the display of any sign within 500 feet of a foreign embassy if the sign tends to bring the foreign government into "public odium" or "public disrepute," violates the First Amendment.

Boos v. Barry, 312, (1988).

71. ACT OF JUNE 25, 1938 (52 STAT. 1040).

Federal Food, Drug, and Cosmetic Act of 1938, § 301(f), prohibiting the refusal to permit entry or inspection of premises by federal officers *held* void for vagueness and as violative of the due process clause of the Fifth Amendment.

United States v. Cardiff, 344 U.S. 174 (1952).

72. ACT OF JUNE 30, 1938 (52 STAT. 1251).

Federal Firearms Act, § 2(f), establishing a presumption of guilt based on a prior conviction and present possession of a firearm, *held* to violate the test of due process under the Fifth Amendment.

Tot v. United States, 319 U.S. 463 (1943).

73. ACT OF AUGUST 10, 1939 (§ 201(D), 53 STAT. 1362, AS AMENDED, 42 U.S.C. § 402(G)).

Provision of Social Security Act that grants survivors' benefits based on the earnings of a deceased husband and father covered by the Act to his widow and to the couple's children in her care but that grants benefits based on the earnings of a covered deceased wife and mother only to the minor children and not to the widower *held* violative of the right to equal protection secured by the Fifth Amendment's due process clause, since it unjustifiably discriminates against female wage earners required to pay social security taxes by affording them less protection for their survivors than is provided for male wage earners.

Weinberger v. Wiesenfeld, 420 U.S. 636 (1975).

74. ACT OF OCTOBER 14, 1940 (54 STAT. 1169, § 401(G)); AS AMENDED BY ACT OF JANUARY 20, 1944 (58 STAT. 4, § 1).

Provision of Aliens and Nationality Code (8 U.S.C. § 1481(a) (8)), derived from the Nationality Act of 1940, as amended, that citizenship shall be lost upon conviction by court martial and dishonorable discharge for deserting the armed services in time of war, *held* invalid as imposing a cruel and unusual punishment barred by the Eighth Amendment and not authorized by the war powers conferred by Article I, § 8, clauses 11 to 14.

Trop v. Dulles, 356 U.S. 86 (1958).

75. ACT OF NOVEMBER 15, 1943 (57 STAT. 450).

Urgent Deficiency Appropriation Act of 1943, § 304, providing that no salary should be paid to certain named federal employees out of moneys appropriated, *held* to violate Article I, § 9, clause 3, forbidding enactment of bill of attainder or *ex post facto* law.

United States v. Lovett, 328 U.S. 303 (1946).

76. ACT OF SEPTEMBER 27, 1944 (58 STAT. 746, § 401(J)); AND ACT OF JUNE 27, 1952 (66 STAT. 163, 267-268, § 349(A)(10)).

§ 401(J) of Immigration and Nationality Act of 1940, added in 1944, and § 49(a)(10) of the Immigration and Nationality Act of 1952 depriving one of citizenship, without the procedural safeguards guaranteed by the Fifth and Sixth Amendments, for the offense of leaving or remaining outside the country, in time of war or national emergency, to evade military service *held* invalid.

Kennedy v. Mendoza-Martinez, 372 U.S. 144 (1963).

77. ACT OF JULY 31, 1946 (CH. 707, § 7, 60 STAT. 719).

District court decision *holding* invalid under First and Fifth Amendments statute prohibiting parades or assemblages on United States Capitol grounds is summarily affirmed.

Chief of Capitol Police v. Jeannette Rankin Brigade, 409 U.S. 972 (1972).

78. ACT OF JUNE 25, 1948 (62 STAT. 760).

Provision of Lindbergh Kidnapping Act which provided for the imposition of the death penalty only if recommended by the jury *held* unconstitutional inasmuch as it penalized the assertion of a defendant's Sixth Amendment right to jury trial.

United States v. Jackson, 390 U.S. 570 (1968).

79. ACT OF AUGUST 18, 1949 (63 STAT. 617, 40 U.S.C. § 13K)

Provision, insofar as it applies to the public sidewalks surrounding the Supreme Court building, which bars the display of any flag, banner, or device designed to bring into public notice any party, organization, or movement *held* violative of the free speech clause of the First Amendment.

United States v. Grace, 461 U.S. 171 (1983)

80. ACT OF MAY 5, 1950 (64 STAT. 107).

Article 3(a) of the Uniform Code of Military Justice subjecting civilian ex-servicemen to court martial for crime committed while in military service *held* to violate Article III, § 2, and the Fifth and Sixth Amendments.

Toth v. Quarles, 350 U.S. 11 (1955).

81. ACT OF MAY 5, 1950 (64 STAT. 107).

Insofar as Article 2(11) of the Uniform Code of Military Justice subjects civilian dependents accompanying members of the armed forces overseas in time of peace to trial, in capital cases, by court martial, it is violative of Article III, § 2, and the Fifth and Sixth Amendments.

Reid v. Covert, 354 U.S. 1 (1957).

Insofar as the aforementioned provision is invoked in time of peace for the trial of noncapital offenses committed on land bases overseas by employees of the armed forces who have not been inducted or who have not voluntarily enlisted therein, it is violative of the Sixth Amendment.

McElroy v. United States, 361 U.S. 281 (1960).

Insofar as the aforementioned provision is invoked in time of peace for the trial of noncapital offenses committed by civilian dependents accompanying members of the armed forces overseas, it is violative of Article III, § 2, and the Fifth and Sixth Amendments.

Kinsella v. United States, 361 U.S. 234 (1960).

Insofar as the aforementioned provision is invoked in time of peace for the trial of a capital offense committed by a civilian employee of the armed forces overseas, it is violative of Article III, § 2, and the Fifth and Sixth Amendments.

Grisham v. Hagan, 361 U.S. 278 (1960).

82. ACT OF AUGUST 16, 1950 (64 STAT. 451, AS AMENDED).

Statutory scheme authorizing the Postmaster General to close the mails to distributors of obscene materials *held* unconstitutional in the absence of procedural provisions which would assure prompt judicial determination that protected materials were not being restrained.

Blount v. Rizzi, 400 U.S. 410 (1971).

83. ACT OF AUGUST 28, 1950 (§ 202(C)(1)(D), 64 STAT. 483, 42 U.S.C. § 402(C)(1)(C)).

District court decision *holding* invalid as a violation of the equal protection component of the Fifth Amendment's due process clause a Social Security provision entitling a husband to insurance benefits through his wife's benefits, provided he received at least one-half of his support from her at the time she became entitled, but requiring no such showing of support for the wife to qualify for benefits through her husband, is summarily affirmed.

Califano v. Silbowitz, 430 U.S. 934 (1977).

84. ACT OF AUGUST 28, 1950 § 202(F)(1)(E), 64 STAT. 485, 42 U.S.C. § 402(F)(1)(D)).

Social Security Act provision awarding survivors' benefits based on earnings of a deceased wife to widower only if he was receiving at least half of his support from her at the time of her death, whereas widow receives benefits regardless of dependency, *held* violative of

equal protection element of Fifth Amendment's due process clause because of its impermissible gender classification.

Califano v. Goldfarb, 430 U.S. 199 (1977).

85. ACT OF SEPTEMBER 23, 1950 (TITLE 1, § 5, 64 STAT. 992).

Provision of Subversive Activities Control Act making it unlawful for member of Communist front organization to work in a defense plant *held* to be an overbroad infringement of the right of association protected by the First Amendment.

United States v. Robel, 389 U.S. 258 (1967).

86. ACT OF SEPTEMBER 23, 1950 (64 STAT. 993, § 6).

Subversive Activities Control Act of 1950, § 6, providing that any member of a Communist organization, which has registered or has been ordered to register, commits a crime if he attempts to obtain or use a passport, *held* violative of due process under the Fifth Amendment.

Aptheker v. Secretary of State, 378 U.S. 500 (1964).

87. ACT OF SEPTEMBER 28, 1950 (TITLE I, §§ 7, 8, 64 STAT. 993).

Provisions of Subversive Activities Control Act of 1950 requiring in lieu of registration by the Communist Party registration by Party members may not be applied to compel registration or to prosecute for refusal to register of alleged members who have asserted their privilege against self-incrimination inasmuch as registration would expose such persons to criminal prosecution under other laws.

Albertson v. Subversive Activities Control Board, 382 U.S. 70 (1965).

88. ACT OF OCTOBER 30, 1951 (§ 5(F)(II), 65 STAT. 683, 45 U.S.C. § 231A(C)(3)(II)).

Provision of Railroad Retirement Act similar to section voided in *Goldfarb.* (ns. 81).

Railroad Retirement Bd. v. Kalina, 431 U.S. 909 (1977).

89. ACT OF JUNE 27, 1952 (CH. 477, § 244(E)(2), 66 STAT. 214, 8 U.S.C. § 1254 (C)(2)).

Provision of the immigration law that permits either House of Congress to veto the decision of the Attorney General to suspend the deportation of certain aliens violates the bicameralism and presentation requirements of lawmaking imposed upon Congress by Article I, §§ 1 and 7.

INS v. Chadha, 462 U.S. 919 (1983).

90. ACT OF JUNE 27, 1952 (TITLE III, § 349, 66 STAT. 267).

Provision of Immigration and Nationality Act of 1952 providing for revocation of United States citizenship of one who votes in a foreign election *held* unconstitutional under § 1 of the Fourteenth Amendment.

Afroyim v. Rusk, 387 U.S. 253 (1967).

91. ACT OF JUNE 27, 1952 (66 STAT. 163, 269, § 352(A)(1)).

§ 352(a)(1) of the Immigration and Nationality Act of 1952 depriving a naturalized person of citizenship for "having a continuous residence for three years" in state of his birth or prior nationality *held* violative of the due process clause of the Fifth Amendment.

Schneider v. Rusk, 377 U.S. 163 (1964).

92. ACT OF AUG. 16, 1954 (CH. 736, 68A STAT. 521, 26 U.S.C. § 4371(1)).

A federal tax on insurance premiums paid to foreign insurers not subject to the federal income tax violates the Export Clause, Art. I, § 9, cl. 5, as applied to casualty insurance for losses incurred during the shipment of goods from locations within the United States to purchasers abroad.

United States v. IBM Corp., 116 S. Ct. 1793 (1996).

93. ACT OF AUGUST 16, 1954 (68A STAT. 525, INT. REV. CODE OF 1954, §§ 4401-4423).

Provisions of tax laws requiring gamblers to pay occupational and excise taxes may not be used over an assertion of one's privilege against self-incrimination either to compel extensive reporting of activities, leaving the registrant subject to prosecution under the laws of all the States with the possible exception of Nevada, or to prosecute for failure to register and report, because the scheme abridged the Fifth Amendment privilege.

Marchetti v. United States, 390 U.S. 39 (1968), and *Grosso v. United States,* 390 U.S. 62 (1968).

94. ACT OF AUGUST 16, 1954 (68A STAT. 560, MARIJUANA TAX ACT, §§ 4741, 4744, 4751, 4753).

Provisions of tax laws requiring possessors of marijuana to register and to pay a transfer tax may not be used over an assertion of the privilege against self-incrimination to compel registration or to prosecute for failure to register.

Leary v. United States, 395 U.S. 6 (1969).

95. ACT OF AUGUST 16, 1954 (68A STAT. 728, INT. REV. CODE OF 1954, §§ 5841, 5851).

Provisions of tax laws requiring the possessor of certain firearms, which it is made illegal to receive or to possess, to register with the Treasury Department may not be used over an assertion of the privilege against self-incrimination to prosecute one for failure to register or for possession of an unregistered firearm since the statutory scheme abridges the Fifth Amendment privilege.

Haynes v. United States, 390 U.S. 85 (1968).

96. ACT OF AUGUST 16, 1954 (68A STAT. 867, INT. REV. CODE OF 1954, § 7302).

Provision of tax laws providing for forfeiture of property used in violating internal revenue laws may not be constitutionally used in face of invocation of privilege against self-incrimination to condemn money in possession of gambler who had failed to comply with the registration and reporting scheme held void in *Marchetti v. United States,* 390 U.S. 39 (1968).

United States v. United States Coin & Currency, 401 U.S. 715 (1971).

97. ACT OF JULY 18, 1956 (§ 106, STAT. 570).

Provision of Narcotic Drugs Import and Export Act creating a presumption that possessor of marijuana knew of its illegal importation into the United States *held,* in absence of showing that all marijuana in United States was of foreign origin and that domestic users could know that their marijuana was more likely than not of foreign origin, unconstitutional under the due process clause of the Fifth Amendment.

Leary v. United States, 395 U.S. 6 (1969).

98. ACT OF AUGUST 10, 1956 (70A STAT. 35, § 772(F)).

Proviso of statute permitting the wearing of United States military apparel in theatrical productions only if the portrayal does not tend to discredit the armed force imposes an unconstitutional restraint upon First Amendment freedoms and precludes a prosecution under 18 U.S.C. § 702 for unauthorized wearing of uniform in a street skit disrespectful of the military.

Schacht v. United States, 398 U.S. 58 (1970).

99. ACT OF AUGUST 10, 1956 (70A STAT. 65, UNIFORM CODE OF MILITARY JUSTICE, ARTICLES 80, 130, 134).

Servicemen may not be charged under the Act and tried in military courts because of the commission of non-service connected crimes committed off-post and off-duty which are subject to civilian court jurisdiction where the guarantees of the Bill of Rights are applicable.

O'Callahan v. Parker, 395 U.S. 258 (1969).

100. ACT OF SEPTEMBER 2, 1958 (§ 5601(B)(1), 72 STAT. 1399).

Provision of Internal Revenue Code creating a presumption that one's presence at the site of an unregistered still shall be sufficient for conviction under a statute punishing possession, custody, or control of an unregistered still unless defendant otherwise explained his presence at the site to the jury *held* unconstitutional because the presumption is not a legitimate, rational, or reasonable inference that defendant was engaged in one of the specialized functions proscribed by the statute.

United States v. Romano, 382 U.S. 136 (1965).

101. ACT OF SEPTEMBER 2, 1958 (§ 1(25)(B), 72 STAT. 1446), AND ACT OF SEPTEMBER 7, 1962 (§ 401, 76 STAT. 469).

Federal statutes providing that spouses of female members of the Armed Forces must be dependent in fact in order to qualify for certain dependent's benefits, whereas spouses of male members are statutorily deemed dependent and automatically qualified for allowances, whatever their actual status, *held* an invalid sex classification under the equal protection principles of the Fifth Amendment's due process clause.

Frontiero v. Richardson, 411 U.S. 677 (1973).

102. ACT OF SEPTEMBER 2, 1958 (PUB. L. 85-921, § 1, 72 STAT. 1771, 18 U.S.C. § 504(1)).

Exemptions from ban on photographic reproduction of currency "for philatelic, numismatic, educational, historical, or newsworthy purposes" violates the First Amendment because it discriminates on the basis of the content of a publication.

Regan v. Time, Inc., 468 U.S. 641 (1984).

103. ACT OF SEPTEMBER 14, 1959 (§ 504, 73 STAT. 536).

Provision of Labor-Management Reporting and Disclosure Act of 1959 making it a crime for a member of the Communist Party to serve as an officer or, with the exception of clerical or custodial positions, as an employee of a labor union *held* to be a bill of attainder and unconstitutional.

United States v. Brown, 381 U.S. 437 (1965).

104. ACT OF OCTOBER 11, 1962 (§ 305, 76 STAT. 840).

Provision of Postal Services and Federal Employees Salary Act of 1962 authorizing Post Office Department to detain material determined to be "communist political propaganda" and to forward it to the addressee only if he requested it after notification by the Department, the material to be destroyed otherwise, *held* to impose on the addressee an affirmative obligation which amounted to an abridgment of First Amendment rights.

Lamont v. Postmaster General, 381 U.S. 301 (1965).

105. ACT OF OCTOBER 15, 1962 (76 STAT. 914).

Provision of District of Columbia laws requiring that a person to be eligible to receive welfare assistance must have resided in the District for at least one year impermissibly classified persons on the basis of an assertion of the right to travel interstate and therefore *held* to violate the due process clause of the Fifth Amendment.

Shapiro v. Thompson, 394 U.S. 618 (1969).

106. ACT OF DECEMBER 16, 1963 (77 STAT. 378, 20 U.S.C. § 754).

Provision of Higher Education Facilities Act of 1963 which in effect removed restriction against religious use of facilities constructed with federal funds after 20 years *held* to violate the establishment clause of the First Amendment inasmuch as the property will still be of considerable value at the end of the period and removal of the restriction would constitute a substantial governmental contribution to religion.

Tilton v. Richardson, 403 U.S. 672 (1971).

107. ACT OF JULY 30, 1965 (§ 339, 79 STAT. 409).

Section of Social Security Act qualifying certain illegitimate children for disability insurance benefits by presuming dependence but disqualifying other illegitimate children, regardless of dependency, if the disabled wage earner parent did not contribute to the child's support before the onset of the disability or if the child did not live with the parent before the onset of disability held to deny latter class of children equal protection as guaranteed by the due process clause of the Fifth Amendment.

Jimenez v. Weinberger, 417 U.S. 628 (1974).

108. ACT OF SEPTEMBER 3, 1966 (§ 102(B), 80 STAT. 831), AND ACT OF APRIL 8, 1974 (§§ 6(A)(1) AMENDING § 3(D) OF ACT, 6(A)(2) AMENDING § 3(E)(2)(C), 6(A)(5) AMENDING § 3(S)(5), AND 6(A) (6) AMENDING § 3(X)).

Those sections of the Fair Labor Standards Act extending wage and hour coverage to the employees of state and local governments *held* invalid because Congress lacks the authority under the commerce clause to regulate employee activities in areas of traditional governmental functions of the States.

National League of Cities v. Usery, 426 U.S. 833 (1976).

109. ACT OF NOVEMBER 7, 1967 (PUB. L. 90-129, § 201(8), 81 STAT. 368), AS AMENDED BY ACT OF AUGUST 13, 1981 (PUB. L. 97-35, § 1229, 95 STAT. 730, 47 U.S.C. § 399).

Communications Act provision banning noncommercial educational stations receiving grants from the Corporation for Public Broadcasting from engaging in editorializing violates the First Amendment.

FCC v. League of Women Voters, 468 U.S. 364 (1984).

110. ACT OF JANUARY 2, 1968 (§ 163(A)(2), 81 STAT. 872).

District court decisions *holding* unconstitutional under Fifth Amendment's due process clause section of Social Security Act that reduced, perhaps to zero, benefits coming to illegitimate children upon death of parent in order to satisfy the maximum payment due the wife and legitimate children are summarily affirmed.

Richardson v. Davis, 409 U.S. 1069 (1972).

111. ACT OF JANUARY 2, 1968 (§ 203, 81 STAT. 882).

Provision of Social Security Act extending benefits to families whose dependent children have been deprived of parental support because of the unemployment of the father but not giving benefits when the mother becomes unemployed *held* to impermissibly classify on the basis of sex and violate the Fifth Amendment's due process clause.

Califano v. Westcott, 443 U.S. 76 (1979).

112. ACT OF JUNE 22, 1970 (CH. III, 84 STAT. 318).

Provision of Voting Rights Act Amendments of 1970 which set a minimum voting age qualification of 18 in state and local elections *held* to be unconstitutional because beyond the powers of Congress to legislate.

Oregon v. Mitchell, 400 U.S. 112 (1970).

113. ACT OF DECEMBER 29, 1970 (§ 8(A), 84 STAT. 1598, 29 U.S.C. § 637 (A)).

Provision of Occupational Safety and Health Act authorizing inspections of covered work places in industry without warrants *held* to violate Fourth Amendment.

Marshall v. Barlow's, Inc., 436 U.S. 307 (1978).

114. ACT OF JANUARY 11, 1971 (§ 2, 84 STAT. 2048).

Provision of Food Stamp Act disqualifying from participation in program any household containing an individual unrelated by birth, marriage, or adoption to any other member of the household violates the due process clause of the Fifth Amendment.

Department of Agriculture v. Moreno, 413 U.S. 528 (1973).

115. ACT OF JANUARY 11, 1971 (§ 4, 84 STAT. 2049).

Provision of Food Stamp Act disqualifying from participation in program any household containing a person 18 years or older who had been claimed as a dependent child for income tax purposes in the present or preceding tax year by a taxpayer not a member of the household violates the due process clause of the Fifth Amendment.

Dept. of Agriculture v. Murry, 413 U.S. 508 (1973).

116. ACT OF DECEMBER 10, 1971 (PUB. L. 92-178, § 801, 85 STAT. 570, 26 U.S.C. § 9012(F)).

Provision of Presidential Election Campaign Fund Act limiting to $1,000 the amount that independent committees may expend to further the election of a presidential candidate financing his campaign with public funds is an impermissible limitation of freedom of speech and association protected by the First Amendment.

FEC v. National Conservative Political Action Comm., 470 U.S. 480 (1985).

117. FEDERAL ELECTION CAMPAIGN ACT OF FEBRUARY 7, 1972 (86 STAT. 3), AS AMENDED BY THE FEDERAL CAMPAIGN ACT AMENDMENTS OF 1974 (88 STAT. 1263), ADDING OR AMENDING 18 U.S.C. §§ 608(A), 608(E), AND 2 U.S.C. § 437(C).

Provisions of election law that forbid a candidate or the members of his immediate family from expending personal funds in excess of specified amounts, that limit to $1,000 the independent expenditures of any person relative to an identified candidate, and that forbid expenditures by candidates for federal office in excess of specified amounts violate the First Amendment speech guarantees; provisions of the law creating a commission to oversee enforcement of the Act are an invalid infringement of constitutional separation of powers in that they devolve responsibilities upon a commission four of whose six members are appointed by Congress and all six of whom are confirmed by the House of Representatives as well as by the Senate, not in compliance with the appointments clause.

Buckley v. Valeo, 424 U.S. 1 (1976).

118. ACT OF MAY 11, 1976 (PUB. L. 92-225, § 316, 90 STAT. 490, 2 U.S.C. § 441)(B)).

Provision of Federal Election Campaign Act requiring that independent corporate campaign expenditures be financed by voluntary contributions to a separate segregated fund violates the First Amendment as applied to a corporation organized to promote political ideas, having no stockholders, and not serving as a front for a business corporation or union.

FEC v. Massachusetts Citizens for Life, Inc., 479 U.S. 238 (1986).

119. ACT OF MAY 11, 1976 (PUB. L. 94-283, § 112(2), 90 STAT. 489, 2 U.S.C. 6 441A(D)(3)).

The Party Expenditure Provision of the Federal Election Campaign Act, which limits expenditures by a political party "in connection with the general election campaign of a [congressional] candidate," violates the First Amendment when applied to expenditures that a political party makes independently, without coordination with the candidate.

Colo. Repub. Campaign Comm. v. FEC, 116 S. Ct. ____, 64 USLW 4663 (1996).

120. ACT OF OCTOBER 1, 1976 (TITLE II, 90 STAT. 1446); ACT OF OCTOBER 12, 1979 (101(C), 93 STAT. 657).

Provisions of appropriations laws rolling back automatic pay increases for federal officers and employees is unconstitutional as to Article III judges because, the increases having gone into effect, they violate the security of compensation clause of Article III, § 1.

United States v. Will, 449 U.S. 200 (1980).

121. ACT OF OCT. 19, 1976 (PUB. L. 94-553, § 101 C, 17 U.S.C. § 504-C.)

Section 504 c of the Copyright Act, which authorizes a copyright owner to recover statutory damages, in lieu of actual damages, "in a sum of not less than $500 or more than $20,000 as the court considers just," does not grant the right to a jury trial on the amount of statutory damages. The Seventh Amendment, however, requires a jury determination of the amount of statutory damages.

Felner v Columbia Pictures Television, 523 U.S. 340 (1998)

122. ACT OF NOVEMBER 6, 1978 (§ 241(A), 92 STAT. 2668, 28 U.S.C. § 1471)

Assignment to judges who do not have tenure and guarantee of compensation protections afforded Article III judges of jurisdiction over all proceedings arising under or in the bankruptcy act and over all cases relating to proceedings under the bankruptcy act is invalid, inasmuch as judges without Article III protection may not receive at least some of this jurisdiction.

Northern Pipeline Const. Co. v. Marathon Pipe Line Co., 458 U.S. 50 (1982).

123. ACT OF NOVEMBER 9, 1978 (PUB. L. 95-621, § 202(C)(1), 92 STAT. 3372, 15 U.S.C. § 3342(C)(1)).

Decision of Court of Appeals holding unconstitutional provision giving either House of Congress power to veto rules of Federal Energy Regulatory Commission on certain natural gas pricing matters is summarily affirmed on the authority of *Chadha.*

Process Gas Consumers Group v. Consumer Energy Council, 463 U.S. 1216 (1983).

124. ACT OF MAY 30, 1980 (94 STAT. 399, 45 U.S.C. § 1001 ET. SEQ.) AS AMENDED BY THE ACT OF OCTOBER 14, 1980 (94 STAT. 1959).

Acts of Congress applying to bankruptcy reorganization of one railroad and guaranteeing employee benefits is repugnant to the requirement of Article I, § 8, cl. 4, that bankruptcy legislation be "uniform."

Railway Labor Executives' Assn. v. Gibbons, 455 U.S. 457 (1982).

125. ACT OF MAY 28, 1980 (PUB. L. 96-252, § 21(A), 94 STAT. 393, 15 U.S.C. § 57A-1(A)).

Decision of Court of Appeals holding unconstitutional provision of FTC Improvements Act giving Congress power by concurrent resolution to veto final rules of the FTC is summarily affirmed on the basis of *Chadha.*

United States Senate v. FTC, 463 U.S. 1216 (1983).

126. ACT OF JANUARY 12, 1983 (PUB. L. 97-459, § 207, 96 STAT. 2519, 25 U.S.C. § 2206).

Section of Indian Land Consolidation Act providing for escheat to tribe of fractionated interests in land representing less than 2% of a tract's total acreage violates the Fifth Amendment's takings clause by completely abrogating rights of intestacy and devise.

Hodel v. Irving, 481 U.S. 704, 107 S. Ct. 2076, 95 L.Ed.2d 668 (1987).

127. ACT OF APRIL 20, 1983, (PUB. L. NO. 98-21, 97 STAT. 69, § 101 B-1) AMENDING 26 U.S.C. § 3121 (B) (5).

The 1983 extension of the Social Security tax to then-sitting judges violates the Compensation Clause of Article III, S.1. The Clause "does not prevent Congress from imposing a non-discriminatory tax laid generally upon judges and other citizens...but it does prohibit taxation that singles out judges for specially unfavorable treatment." The 1983 Social Security law gave 96% of federal employees "total freedom" of choice about whether to participate in the system, and structured the system in such a way that "virtually all" of the remaining 4% of employees—except judges—could opt to retain existing coverage. By requiring then-sitting judges to join the Social Security System and pay Social Security taxes, the 1983 law discriminated against judges in violation of the Compensation Clause.

United States v. Hatter, 532 U.S. 557 (2001)

128. ACT OF OCT. 30, 1984 (PUB L. 98-608, § 1 (4), 98 STAT. 3173, 25 U.S.C. § 2206.

Section 207 of the Indian Land Consolidation Act, as amended in 1984, effects an unconstitutional taking of property without compensation by restricting a property owner's right to pass on property to his heirs. The amended section, like an earlier version held unconstitutional in Hodel v Irving (1987), provides that certain small interests in Indian land will escheat to the tribe upon death of the owner. None of the changes made in 1984 cures the constitutional defect.

Babbitt v Youpee, 519 U.S. 234 (1997)

129. ACT OF JAN. 15, 1985 (PUB. L. 99-240, § 5(D)(2)(C), 99 STAT. 1842, 42 U.S.C. § 2021E(D)(2)(C)).

"Take-title" incentives contained in the Low-Level Radioactive Waste Policy Amendments Act of 1985, designed to encourage states to cooperate in the federal regulatory scheme, offend principles of federalism embodied in the Tenth Amendment. These incentives, which require that non-participating states take title to waste or become liable for generators' damages, cross the line distinguishing encouragement from coercion. Congress may not simply commandeer the legislative and regulatory processes of the states, nor may it force a transfer from generators to state governments. A required choice between two unconstitutionally coercive regulatory techniques is also impermissible.

New York v. United States, 505 U.S. 144(1992).

130. ACT OF DECEMBER 12, 1985 (PUB. L. 99-177, § 251, 99 STAT. 1063, 2 U.S.C. § 901).

That portion of the Balanced Budget and Emergency Deficit Control Act which authorizes the Comptroller General to determine the amount of spending reductions which must be accomplished each year to reach congressional targets and which authorizes him to report a figure to the President which the President must implement violates the constitutional separation of powers inasmuch as the Comptroller General is subject to congressional control (removal) and cannot be given a role in the execution of the laws.

Bowsher v. Synar, 478 U.S. 714 (1986).

131. ACT OF OCT. 30, 1986 (PUB. L. 99-591, TITLE VI, § 6007(F), 100 STAT. 3341, 49 U.S.C. APP. § 2456(F)).

The Metropolitan Washington Airports Act of 1986, which transferred operating control of two Washington, D.C., area airports from the Federal Government to a regional airports authority, violates separation of powers principles by conditioning that transfer on the establishment of a Board of Review, composed of Members of Congress and having veto authority over actions of the airports authority's board of directors.

Metropolitan Washington Airports Auth. v. Citizens for the Abatement of Aircraft Noise, 501 U.S. 252 (1991).

132. ACT OF NOV. 17, 1986 (PUB. L. 99-662, TITLE IVC, § 1402 (A), 26 U.S.C. 4461, 4462.

The Harbor Maintenance Tax (HMT) violates the Export Clause of the Constitution, Art. I, S 9, cl. 5 to the extent that the tax applies to goods loaded for export at United States ports. The HMT, which requires shippers to pay a uniform charge of 0.125% of cargo value on commercial cargo shipped through the Nation's ports, is an impermissible tax rather than a permissible user fee. The value of export cargo does not correspond reliably with federal harbor services used

by exporters, and the tax does not, therefore, represent compensation for services rendered.

United States vs. United States Shoe Corp., 523 U.S. 360, 1998

133. ACT OF APRIL 28, 1988 (PUB. L. 100-297, § 6101, 102 STAT. 424, 47 U.S.C. § 223(B)).

Provision insofar as it bans indecent as well as obscene commercial interstate telephone messages violates the speech clause of the First Amendment.

Sable Communications v. FCC, 492 U.S. 115(1989).

134. ACT OF OCT. 17, 1988 (PUB. L. 100-497, § 11(D)(7), 102 STAT. 2472, 25 U.S.C. § 2710(D)(7)).

A provision of the Indian Gaming Regulatory Act authorizing an Indian tribe to sue a State in federal court to compel performance of a duty to negotiate in good faith toward the formation of a compact violates the Eleventh Amendment. In exercise of its powers under Article I, Congress may not abrogate States' Eleventh Amendment immunity from suit in federal court. *Pennsylvania v. Union Gas Co.,* 491 U.S. 1 (1989), is overruled.

Seminole Tribe of Florida v. Florida, 517 U.S. 44 (1996).

135. ACT OF OCT. 28, 1989 (PUB. L. 101-131, 103 STAT. 777, 18 U.S.C. § 700).

The Flag Protection Act of 1989, criminalizing burning and certain other forms of destruction of the United States flag, violates the First Amendment. Most of the prohibited acts involve disrespectful treatment of the flag, and evidence a purpose to suppress expression out of concern for its likely communicative impact.

United States v. Eichman, 496 U.S. 310 (1990).

136. ACT OF NOV. 30, 1989 (PUB. L. 101-194, § 601, 103 STAT. 1760, 5 U.S.C. APP. § 501).

Section 501(b) of the Ethics in Government Act, as amended in 1989 to prohibit Members of Congress and federal employees from accepting honoraria, violates the First Amendment as applied to Executive Branch employees below grade GS-16. The ban is limited to expressive activity and does not include other outside income, and the "speculative benefits" of the ban do not justify its "crudely crafted burden" on expression.

United States v. National Treasury Employees Union, 513 U.S. 454 (1995).

137. ACT OF JULY 26, 1990 (PUB L. NO. 101-336, TITLE I), 104 STAT. 330, 42 U.S.C. §§ 12111-12117.

Title I of the Americans with Disabilities Act of 1990 (ADA) exceeds congressional power to enforce the Fourteenth Amendment and violates the Eleventh Amendment, by subjecting states to suits brought by state employees in federal courts to collect money damages for the state's failure to make reasonable accommodations for qualified individuals with disabilities.

Board of Trustees of the Univ. of Alabama v. Garrett, 531 U.S. 356 (2001)

138. ACT OF NOV. 28, 1990 (PUB. L. NO. 101-624, TITLE XIX, SUBTITLE B), 104 STAT. 3854, 7 U.S.C. §§ 6101.

The Mushroom Promotion, Research and Consumer Information Act violates the First Amendment by imposing mandatory assessments on mushroom handlers for the purpose of funding generic advertising to promote mushroom sales.

United States v. United Foods Inc., 533 U.S. 405, 2001)

139. ACT OF NOV. 29, 1990 (PUB. L. 101-647, § 1702, 104 STAT. 4844, 18 U.S.C. § 922Q).

The Gun Free School Zones Act of 1990, which makes it a criminal offense to knowingly possess a firearm within a school zone, exceeds congressional power under the Commerce Clause. It is "a criminal statute that by its terms has nothing to do with 'commerce' or any sort of economic enterprise." Possession of a gun at or near a school "is in no sense an economic activity that might, through repetition elsewhere, substantially affect any sort of interstate commerce."

United States v. Lopez, 514 U.S. 549 (1995).

140. ACT OF DEC. 19, 1991 (PUB. L. 102-242 § 476, 105 STAT. 2387, 15 U.S.C. § 78AA-1).

Section 27A(b) of the Securities Exchange Act of 1934, as added in 1991, requiring reinstatement of any section 10(b) actions that were dismissed as time barred subsequent to a 1991 Supreme Court decision, violates the Constitution's separation of powers to the extent that it requires federal courts to reopen final judgments in private civil actions. The provision violates a fundamental principle of Article III that the federal judicial power comprehends the power to render dispositive judgments.

Plaut v. Spendthrift Farm, Inc., 514 U.S. 211 (1995)

141. ACT OF OCT. 5, 1992 (PUB. L. 102-385, §§ 10(B) AND 10(C), 106 STAT. 1487, 1503; 47 U.S.C. § 532(J) AND § 531 NOTE, RESPECTIVELY).

Section 10(b) of the Cable Television Consumer Protection and Competition Act of 1992, which requires cable operators to segregate and block indecent programming on leased access channels if they do not prohibit it, violates the First Amendment. Section 10(c) of the Act, which permits a cable operator to prevent transmission of "sexually explicit" programming on public access channels, also violates the First Amendment.

Denver Area Educ. Tel. Consortium v. FCC, 518 U.S. 727 (1996)

142. ACT OF OCT. 24, 1992, TITLE XIX, 106 STAT. 3037 (PUB. L. 102-486, 26 U.S.C. §§ 9701-9722).

The Coal Industry Retiree Health Benefit Act of 1992 is unconstitutional as applied to the petitioner Eastern Enterprises. Pursuant to the act, the Social Security Commissioner had imposed liability on Eastern for funding health care benefits of retirees from the coal industry who had worked for Eastern prior to 1966. Eastern had transferred its coal-related business to a subsidiary in 1965.

Eastern Enterprises v. Apfel, 524 U.S. 498 (1998)

143. ACT OF OCT. 27, 1992 (PUB. L. 102-542, 15 U.S.C. § 1122).

The Trademark Remedy Clarification Act, which provided that states shall not be immune from suit under the Lanham Act, did not validly abrogate state sovereign immunity. Congress lacks the power to do so in exercise of Article I powers or under section 5 of the Fourteenth Amendment.

College Savings Bank v. Florida Prepaid Postsecondary Education Expense Board, 527 U.S. 666 (1999)

144. ACT OF OCT. 28, 1992 (PUB. L. 102-560, 106 STAT. 4230, 29 U.S.C. § 296).

The Patent and Plant Variety Clarification Act, which subjected states to suit for patent infringement, is invalid. Congress lacks power

to abrogate state immunity in exercise of its Article I powers and section 5 of the Fourteenth Amendment.

Florida Prepaid Postsecondary Education Expense Board v. College Savings Bank, 527 U.S. 627 (1999)

145. ACT OF NOV. 16, 1993 (PUB. L. 103-141, 107 STAT. 1488., 42 U.S.C. §§ 2000BB TO 2000 BB-4).

The Religious Freedom Restoration Act, which directed use of the compelling interest test against laws that substantially burden the free exercise of religion, exceeds congressional power under section 5 of the Fourteenth Amendment. Congress's power to "enforce" the Fourteenth Amendment does not extend to defining the substance of the amendment's provisions.

City of Boerne v. Flores, 521 U.S. 507 (1997)

146. ACT OF NOV. 30, 1993 (PUB. L. 103-159, 107 STAT. 1536).

Interim provisions of the Brady Handgun Violence Prevention Act that require state and local law enforcement officers to conduct background checks on prospective handgun purchasers are inconsistent with the Constitution's allocation of power between federal and state governments.

Printz v. United States, 521 U.S. 898 (1997)

147. ACT OF SEPT. 13, 1994 (PUB. L. 103-322, § 40302, 108 STAT. 1941, 42 U.S.C. § 13981).

A provision of the Violence Against Women Act that creates a federal civil remedy for victims of gender-motivated violence exceeds congressional power under the Commerce Clause and under section 5 of the Fourteenth Amendment.

United States v. Morrison, 529 U.S. 598 (2000)

148. ACT OF FEB. 8, 1996 (PUB. L. 104-104 TITLE V, § 502, 110 STAT. 56, 133-34, 47 U.S.C. §§ 223 A, 223 D.

Two provisions of the Communications Decency Act of 1996—prohibiting knowing transmission on the Internet of obscene or indecent messages to any recipient under eighteen years of age and prohibiting the knowing sending or displaying of patently offensive messages in a manner that is available to anyone under eighteen years of age—violate the First Amendment.

Reno v. American Civil Liberties Union, 521 U.S. 844 (1997)

149. ACT OF FEB. 8, 1996 (PUB. L. 104-104, § 505, 110 STAT. 136, 47 U.S.C. § 561).

Section 505 of the Telecommunications Act of 1996, which required operators of cable TV who were unable to prevent signal bleed of sexually explicit channels to transmit those channels only in late hours, when children would not be watching, violates the First Amendment.

United States v. Playboy Entertainment Group Inc. 529 U.S. 803 (2000)

150. ACT OF APRIL 9, 1996 (PUB. L. 104-130, 110 STAT. 1200, 2 U.S.C. §§ 691).

The Line Item Veto Act, which gave the president the authority to "cancel" three types of provisions that signed into law, violates the Presentment Clause of Article I, section 7.

Clinton v. City of New York, 524 U.S. 417 (1998)

151. ACT OF APRIL 26, 1996 (PUB. L. 104-134 § 504 A, 16, 110 STAT. 1321–55).

A restriction in the appropriations act for the Legal Services Corporation that prohibits funding for any organization that participates in litigation that challenges a federal or state welfare law constitutes viewpoint discrimination and violates the First Amendment.

Legal Services Corp. v. Velazquez, 531 U.S. 533 (2001)

152. ACT OF SEPT. 30, 1996 (PUB. L. 104028, § 121, 110 STAT. 3009-26, 18 U.S.C § 2252, 2256).

Two sections of the Child Pornography Prevention Act of 1996 that extend the prohibition on child pornography to sexually explicit images that appear to depict minors but are "virtual" images and do not use real children violate the First Amendment.

Ashcroft v. Free Speech Coalition, 535 U.S. 234 (2002)

153. ACT OF NOV. 21, 1997 (PUB. L. 105-115 § 127, 111 STAT. 2328, 21 U.S.C. § 353A).

Section 127 of the Food and Drug Administration Modernization Act of 1997, which prohibited makers of "compounded drugs" from advertising or promoting these products, violate the First Amendment.

Thompson v. Western States Medical Center, 535 U.S. 357 (2002)

SOURCES: Compiled from Library of Congress, *The Constitution of the United States of America: Analysis and Interpretation,* S. Doc. 103-6, 1992; Library of Congress, Congressional Research Service.

Chronology of Major Decisions of the Court, 1790–2003

Every Supreme Court decision begins with a dispute between two people. The interests they assert and defend may be personal, corporate, or official, but they all arise from a fundamental clash between two points of view.

Early on, the Court made clear that it would adhere to the language of the Constitution in Article III, Section 2, and refuse to rule on theoretical situations or hypothetical cases. It would only resolve actual "cases and controversies" in which there were real collisions of rights and powers. To decide a hypothetical case, said the justices, would be to exceed their constitutional function.

The individuals who bring their complaints before the justices are as diverse as the nation. William Marbury wished to secure his appointment as a justice of the peace. Dred Scott sought his freedom. Linda Brown wanted to attend her neighborhood school. Clarence Gideon believed he should have a lawyer to defend him in court. Richard Nixon wanted to keep his White House tapes confidential. The Court resolved their cases, as it has done each case of the thousands that have arrived before it, on the basis of their particular facts.

The immediate impact of each is simply to answer the claims of Marbury, Scott, Brown, Gideon, or Nixon, settling one particular situation. Many of the Court's rulings have no further effect. But often—as in these cases—the decision has a larger significance, upholding or striking down similar laws or practices or claims, establishing the Court's authority in new areas, or finding that some areas lie outside its competence.

To the Supreme Court, wrote Richard Kluger in the foreword to *Simple Justice,*

the nation has increasingly brought its most vexing social and political problems. They come in the guise of private disputes between only the litigating parties, but everybody understands that this is a legal fiction and merely a convenient political device. American society thus reduces its most troubling controversies to the scope—and translates them into the language—of a lawsuit.

Although the progress of cases to the Supreme Court is slow, the body of issues before the Court in a particular period does reflect public concerns. "Virtually all important decisions of the Supreme Court are the beginnings of conversations between the Court and the people and their representatives," Alexander M. Bickel wrote in *The Supreme Court and the Idea of Progress.*

Most major cases decided by the Court from 1790 until 1860 involved the balance between state and federal power. Questions of war powers and policies came to the Court during the Civil War; matters of civil rights and state powers questions followed during the era of Reconstruction. As the nation's economy flourished and grew, cases concerning the relationship of government and business became everyday matters at the Court. For the contemporary Court, questions of individual rights and liberties dominate its work.

Following are summary descriptions of the Supreme Court's major rulings from the first, *Chisholm v. Georgia* in 1793, through those issued in the summer of 1996. The summaries consist of a general subject heading, the case name, its citation, the vote by which it was decided, the date it was announced, the justice writing the major opinion, the dissenting justices, and a summary statement of the ruling. (In some early cases, the vote or the exact date of its announcement is unavailable.)

HOW TO READ A COURT CITATION

The official version of each Supreme Court decision and opinion is contained in a series of volumes entitled *United States Reports,* published by the U.S. Government Printing Office.

While there are several unofficial compilations of Court opinions, including *United States Law Week,* published by the Bureau of National Affairs; *Supreme Court Reporter,* published by West Publishing Company; and *United States Supreme Court Reports, Lawyers' Edition,* published by Lawyers Cooperative Publishing Company, it is the official record that is generally cited. An unofficial version or the official slip opinion might be cited if a decision has not yet been officially reported.

A citation to a case includes, in order, the name of the parties to the case, the volume of *United States Reports* in which the decision appears, the page in the volume on which the opinion begins, the page from which any quoted material is taken, and the year of the decision.

For example, *Colegrove v. Green,* 328 U.S. 549 at 553 (1946) means that the Supreme Court decision in the case of Colegrove against Green can be found in volume 328 of *United States Reports* beginning on page 549. The specific quotation in question will be found on page 553. The case was decided in 1946.

Until 1875 the official reports of the Court were published under the names of the Court reporters, and it is their names, or abbreviated versions, that appear in cites for those years, although U.S. volume numbers have been assigned retroactively to them. A citation such as *Marbury v. Madison,* 1 Cranch 137 (1803) means that the opinion in the case of Marbury against Madison is in the first volume of reporter Cranch beginning on page 137. (Between 1875 and 1883 a Court reporter named William T. Otto compiled the decisions and opinions; his name appears on the volumes for those years as well as the *United States Reports* volume number, but Otto is seldom cited.)

The titles of the volumes to 1875, the full names of the reporters, and the corresponding *United States Reports* volumes are:

1–4 Dall.	Dallas	1–4 U.S.
1–9 Cranch or Cr.	Cranch	5–13 U.S.
1–12 Wheat.	Wheaton	14–25 U.S.
1–16 Pet.	Peters	26–41 U.S.
1–24 How.	Howard	42–65 U.S.
1–2 Black	Black	66–67 U.S.
1–23 Wall.	Wallace	68–90 U.S.

1790–1799

EX POST FACTO LAWS

Calder v. Bull, 3 Dall. 386, decided by a 4–0 vote, August 8, 1798. Chase wrote the Court's opinion.

The Constitution's ban on ex post facto laws does not forbid a state to nullify a man's title to certain property. The ban applies only to laws making certain actions criminal after they had been committed. It was not intended to protect property rights.

FEDERAL COURTS

Chisholm v. Georgia, 2 Dall. 419, decided by a 4–1 vote, February 18, 1793. Jay wrote the Court's major opinion; Iredell dissented.

Citizens of one state have the right to sue another state in federal court, without the consent of the defendant state.

Adoption of the Eleventh Amendment reversed this ruling, barring such suits from federal court unless the defendant state consented.

TAXES

Hylton v. United States, 3 Dall. 171, decided without dissent, March 8, 1796. The participating justices—Chase, Paterson, and Iredell—submitted opinions; Cushing, Wilson, and Ellsworth did not participate; Wilson filed an opinion.

The Court upheld Congress's power to tax carriages. It declared that the only "direct" taxes required by the Constitution to be apportioned among the states were head taxes and taxes on land.

This definition remained in force until 1895 when the Court held that income taxes were direct and must be apportioned. The addition of the Sixteenth Amendment to the Constitution overturned that ruling.

TREATIES

Ware v. Hylton, 3 Dall. 199, decided by a 4–0 vote, March 7, 1796. Chase delivered the major opinion for the Court; Iredell did not participate in the decision, but placed an opinion in the record.

Treaties made by the United States override conflicting state laws. The 1783 Treaty of Paris with Britain, ending the Revolutionary War, provided that neither Britain nor the United States would block the efforts of the other nation's citizens to secure repayment of debts in the other country. This provision rendered invalid Virginia's law allowing debts owed by Virginians to British creditors to be "paid off" through payments to the state.

1800–1809

FEDERAL COURTS

Bank of the United States v. Deveaux, 5 Cr. 61, decided without dissent, March 15, 1809. Marshall wrote the Court's opinion; Livingston did not participate.

The Court strictly interpreted the "diversity" requirement in federal cases—the rule that certain cases could be heard in federal, not state, courts simply because the two parties were residents of different states. Cases involving corporations, the Court held, could only come into federal courts for this reason if all the stockholders of the corporation lived in a state other than that of the opposing party. This strict rule resulted in very little corporate litigation in the federal courts until 1844 when it was revised.

JUDICIAL REVIEW

Marbury v. Madison, 1 Cr. 137, decided without dissent, February 24, 1803. Marshall wrote the Court's opinion.

Congress may not expand or contract the Supreme Court's original jurisdiction. Therefore, Congress exceeded its power when, in Section 13 of the Judiciary Act of 1789, it authorized the Supreme Court to issue writs of mandamus in original cases ordering federal officials to perform particular acts. Although William Marbury had a right to receive his commission as a justice of the peace—already signed and sealed, but not delivered—the Court lacked the power, under its original jurisdiction, to order its delivery.

The immediate effect of the decision was to absolve the Jefferson administration of the duty to install several of President Adams's last-minute appointments in such posts.

The more lasting significance was the establishment of the Court's power of judicial review, the power to review Acts of Congress and declare invalid those it found in conflict with the Constitution.

1810–1819

CONTRACTS

Fletcher v. Peck, 6 Cr. 87, decided without dissent, March 16, 1810. Marshall wrote the Court's opinion; Johnson filed a separate opinion.

The Constitution forbids a state to impair the obligation of contracts. This prohibition denies a state legislature the power to annul titles to land secured under a land grant approved by a previous session of the legislature.

Dartmouth College v. Woodward, 4 Wheat. 519, decided by a 5–1 vote, February 2, 1819. Marshall wrote the Court's opinion; Duvall dissented.

The Constitution's ban on state action impairing the obligation of contracts denies a state the power to alter or repeal private corporate charters, such as that between New Hampshire and the trustees of Dartmouth College establishing that institution.

Sturges v. Crowninshield, 4 Wheat. 122, decided without dissent, February 17, 1819. Marshall wrote the Court's opinion.

The Constitution's grant of power to Congress to enact a uniform bankruptcy law does not deny states the power to pass insolvency statutes, at least until Congress enacts a bankruptcy law.

However, the constitutional ban on state action impairing the obligation of contracts denies a state the power to enact a law freeing debtors from liability for debts contracted before the law's passage.

JUDICIAL REVIEW

Martin v. Hunter's Lessee, 1 Wheat. 304, decided without dissent, March 20, 1816. Story wrote the Court's opinion; Marshall did not participate.

The Court upheld as constitutional Section 25 of the Judiciary Act of 1789, which gave the Supreme Court the power to review the rejection, by state courts, of federally based challenges to a state law or state action.

POWERS OF CONGRESS

McCulloch v. Maryland, 4 Wheat. 316, decided without dissent, March 6, 1819. Marshall wrote the Court's opinion.

In a broad definition of the Constitution's grant to Congress of the power to enact all laws that are "necessary and proper" to execute the responsibilities given the legislative branch by the Constitution, the Court ruled that Congress had the authority to charter a national bank in the exercise of its fiscal and monetary powers.

The necessary and proper clause empowered Congress to adopt any appropriate and legitimate means for achieving a legislative goal; it was not confined to using only those means that were indispensable to reaching the desired end.

The Court also held that the national bank was immune to state taxation. Observing that the "power to tax involves the power to destroy," the Court began to develop the doctrine that one government may not tax certain holdings of another government.

1820–1829

COMMERCE

Gibbons v. Ogden, 9 Wheat. 1, decided without dissent, March 2, 1824. Marshall wrote the Court's opinion.

In its first definition of Congress's power over interstate commerce, the Court ruled that Congress could regulate all commerce affecting more than one state. The Court defined commerce as intercourse, including navigation and other modes of transportation, as well as commercial transactions. The Court also declared that the congressional authority to regulate commerce is superior to state power to regulate the same commerce.

This decision laid the foundation for the modern interpretation of the power that gives Congress virtually exclusive control over all business, even that which only indirectly affects interstate commerce.

Willson v. Blackbird Creek Marsh Co., 2 Pet. 245, decided without dissent, March 20, 1829. Marshall wrote the Court's opinion.

A state may exercise its police power to regulate matters affecting interstate commerce if Congress has not enacted conflicting legislation.

CONTRACTS

Ogden v. Saunders, 12 Wheat. 213, decided by a 4–3 vote, February 18, 1827. Washington wrote the Court's major opinion; Marshall, Story, and Duvall dissented.

The contract clause does not deny states the power to enact insolvency statutes that provide for the discharge of debts contracted after its passage.

Mason v. Haile, 12 Wheat. 370, decided by a 6–1 vote in the January 1827 term. Thompson wrote the Court's opinion; Washington dissented.

The contract clause does not prevent a state from abolishing imprisonment as a punishment for debtors who fail to pay their obligations. Modifying the remedy for defaulting on a contract does not inevitably impair the obligation incurred under the contract.

FEDERAL COURTS

Osborn v. Bank of the United States, 9 Wheat. 738, decided with one dissenting vote, March 18, 1824. Marshall wrote the Court's opinion; Johnson dissented.

The Court upheld the right of the Bank of the United States to sue state officials in federal court. It held that the Eleventh Amendment—allowing states to be sued in federal court by citizens of another state only with the consent of the defendant state—did not deny federal courts jurisdiction over a case brought against a state official for actions under an unconstitutional state law or in excess of his legal authority. (See *Chisholm v. Georgia,* above.)

Foster v. Neilson, 2 Pet. 253, decided without dissent in the January 1829 term. Marshall delivered the Court's opinion.

The Court refused to rule in a boundary dispute involving territory east of the Mississippi River claimed by both the United States and Spain. Marshall described the matter as a "political question" that was not the business of the judiciary to resolve.

JUDICIAL REVIEW

Cohens v. Virginia, 6 Wheat. 264, decided without dissent, March 3, 1821. Marshall delivered the Court's opinion.

For the second time, the Court reaffirmed the constitutionality of Section 25 of the Judiciary Act of 1789, under which the Supreme Court was empowered to review state court rulings denying federal claims. (See *Martin v. Hunter's Lessee,* above.)

POWERS OF CONGRESS

Wayman v. Southard, 10 Wheat. 1, decided without dissent, February 12, 15, 1825. Marshall wrote the Court's opinion.

The Court for the first time recognized the power of Congress to delegate portions of its legislative authority. In this case the Court sanctioned the right of Congress to set an objective and then authorize an administrator to promulgate rules and regulations to achieve that objective. The right to delegate such authority provides the basis for creation of the federal regulatory agencies.

POWERS OF THE PRESIDENT

Martin v. Mott, 12 Wheat. 19, decided without dissent, February 2, 1827. Story wrote the Court's opinion.

A president's decision to call out the militia is not subject to judicial review and is binding on state authorities. As a result of congressional delegation of power to the president, the decision to call out the militia, the Court said, "belongs exclusively to the President, and . . . his decision is conclusive upon all other persons."

TAXES

Brown v. Maryland, 12 Wheat. 419, decided by a 6–1 vote, March 12, 1827. Marshall wrote the Court's opinion; Thompson dissented.

The Court reinforced its broad interpretation of congressional power over commerce, ruling that a state unconstitutionally infringed on that power when it taxed imported goods still the property of the importer and in their original package.

Weston v. City Council of Charleston, 2 Pet. 449, decided by a 4–2 vote, March 18, 1829. Marshall wrote the Court's opinion; Johnson and Thompson dissented.

A city tax on United States stock impermissibly hinders the exercise of the federal power to borrow money.

1830–1839

BILLS OF CREDIT

Craig v. Missouri, 4 Pet. 410, decided by a 4–3 vote, March 12, 1830. Marshall wrote the Court's opinion; Johnson, Thompson, and McLean dissented.

The constitutional provision barring states from issuing bills of credit denies a state the power to issue state loan certificates.

Briscoe v. Bank of the Commonwealth of Kentucky, 11 Pet. 257, decided by a 6–1 vote, February 11, 1837. McLean wrote the Court's opinion; Story dissented.

The constitutional ban on state bills of credit is not violated by a state law authorizing issuance of notes by a state-chartered bank, in which the state owns all the stock.

COMMERCE

New York v. Miln, 11 Pet. 102, decided by a 6–1 vote, February 16, 1837. Barbour wrote the Court's opinion; Story dissented.

The Court upheld a New York statute, which required all ships arriving in New York to report lists of passengers, against a challenge that the statute interfered with federal power to regulate foreign commerce. The state law was a valid exercise of state police power to protect public welfare against an influx of paupers, the majority said.

CONTRACTS

Charles River Bridge v. Warren Bridge, 11 Pet. 420, decided by a 4–3 vote, February 12, 1837. Taney wrote the Court's opinion; Story, Thompson, and McLean dissented.

Charters granted by a state should never be assumed to limit the state's power of eminent domain. Absent an explicit grant of exclusive privilege, a corporate charter granted by the state should not be interpreted as granting such a privilege and thereby limiting the state's power to charter a competing corporation.

The Court rejected the claim of the owners of the Charles River Bridge that their charter implicitly granted them a monopoly of the foot passenger traffic across the river and was impaired by state action authorizing construction of a second bridge over that same river.

FEDERAL COURTS

Kendall v. United States ex rel. Stokes, 12 Pet. 524, decided by votes of 9–0 and 6–3, March 12, 1838. Thompson wrote the Court's opinion; Taney, Barbour, and Catron dissented in part.

Federal courts—if they have jurisdiction over a controversy—have the power to issue a writ of mandamus to an executive branch official ordering him to take some ministerial action, which he is required by law to perform. The Court distinguished between ministerial actions of executive officials, which are prescribed by law or regulation and about which there is little discretion, and policy or political actions of those officials, which are beyond the reach of the courts.

INDIVIDUAL RIGHTS

Barron v. Baltimore, 7 Pet. 243, decided without dissent, February 16, 1833. Marshall wrote the Court's opinion.

The Bill of Rights was added to the Constitution to protect persons only against the action of the federal, not state, government. The Court rejected the effort of a wharf owner to invoke the Fifth Amendment to compel the city of Baltimore to compensate him for the value of his wharf which, he claimed, was rendered useless as a result of city action.

STATE POWERS

Worcester v. Georgia, 6 Pet. 515, decided by a 5–1 vote, March 3, 1832. Marshall wrote the Court's opinion; Baldwin dissented; Johnson did not participate.

Federal jurisdiction over Indian affairs is exclusive, leaving no room for state authority. States lack any power to pass laws affecting Indians living in Indian territory within their borders. The Court reversed the conviction, under Georgia law, of two missionaries who had failed to comply with a state law requiring the licensing of all white persons living in Indian territory. (This case is one of a pair known as the *Cherokee Cases.*)

1840–1849

COMMERCE

Thurlow v. Massachusetts, Fletcher v. Rhode Island, Peirce v. New Hampshire (License Cases), 5 How. 504, decided without dissent, March 6, 1847. Taney, McLean, Catron, Daniel, Woodbury, and Grier wrote separate opinions.

States may require that all sales of intoxicating liquors within their borders be licensed, including imported liquor. This requirement is a valid exercise of state police power.

Smith v. Turner, Norris v. Boston (Passenger Cases), 7 How. 283, decided by a 5–4 vote, February 7, 1849. McLean wrote the Court's opinion; Taney, Daniel, Nelson, and Woodbury dissented.

In apparent contradiction of *New York v. Miln,* the Court struck down state laws that placed a head tax on each passenger brought into a U.S. port. The revenue was intended to support immigrant paupers, but the majority held that such laws conflicted with federal power to regulate interstate and foreign commerce—even though Congress had not acted in this area.

FEDERAL COURTS

Louisville Railroad Company v. Letson, 2 How. 497, decided without dissent, March 15, 1844. Wayne wrote the Court's opinion. Taney did not participate.

Effectively overruling *Bank of the United States v. Deveaux* (1809), the Court declared that a corporation would be assumed to be a citizen of the state in which it was chartered. This assumed citizenship, for purposes of diversity jurisdiction, facilitated the movement of corporate litigation into federal courts.

Luther v. Borden, 7 How. 1, decided by a 5–1 vote, January 3, 1849. Taney delivered the Court's opinion; Woodbury dissented; Catron, McKinley, and Daniel did not participate.

The guaranty clause of the Constitution—stating that the United States will guarantee to each state a republican form of government—is enforceable only through the political branches, not the judiciary.

The Court refused to resolve a dispute between two competing political groups, each of which asserted it was the lawful government of Rhode Island. This dispute was a "political question," held the Court, that it would leave to Congress.

FOREIGN AFFAIRS

Holmes v. Jennison, 14 Pet. 540, decided by a 4–4 vote, March 4, 1840. Taney wrote an opinion for himself, Story, McLean, and Wayne; Barbour, Baldwin, Catron, and Thompson filed separate opinions; McKinley did not participate.

A fugitive from Canada, detained in Vermont, sought release through a petition for a writ of habeas corpus. After the state supreme court denied his petition, he asked the U.S. Supreme Court to review that action. The Court divided 4–4 over whether it had jurisdiction in the case. Taney, Story, McLean, and Wayne held that the Court did have jurisdiction; Barbour, Baldwin, Catron, and Thompson disagreed.

The 4–4 vote meant that the Court dismissed the case. But its significance came in Taney's declaration that states were forbidden by the Constitution to take any independent role in foreign affairs, and therefore a state governor could not surrender a fugitive within his jurisdiction to a foreign country who sought the fugitive's return.

INTERSTATE BOUNDARIES

Rhode Island v. Massachusetts, 4 How. 591, decided by 8–0 and 7–1 votes in the January 1846 term. McLean wrote the Court's opinion; Taney dissented in part.

This decision was the Court's first resolving an interstate boundary dispute. The Court affirmed its jurisdiction over these matters, a point upon which Taney dissented, and then resolved the dispute in favor of Massachusetts, the state that had challenged the Court's jurisdiction to hear the case.

SLAVERY

Prigg v. Pennsylvania, 16 Pet. 539, decided by 8–1 and 5–4 votes, March 1, 1842. Story wrote the Court's opinion. McLean dissented; Taney, Thompson, and Daniel dissented in part.

The Court struck down a Pennsylvania law concerning procedures for the return of fugitive slaves to owners in other states, finding the law in conflict with the federal Fugitive Slave Act. McLean dissented on this point. Story declared that federal power over fugitive slaves was exclusive, denying states any power to enact any laws on that subject. On this point the three justices dissented.

TAXES

Dobbins v. Erie County, 16 Pet. 435, decided without dissent, March 4, 1842. Wayne wrote the Court's opinion.

Extending the principle adopted in *McCulloch v. Maryland* (1819) that the power to tax involves the power to destroy, the Court held that states could not tax the income of federal officials.

This decision, together with that in *Collector v. Day,* 11 Wall. 113, (1871), which held that the federal government could not tax the incomes of state officials, led to numerous intergovernmental tax immunities that were not removed until 1939 when *Dobbins* and *Collector* were overruled.

1850–1859

COMMERCE

Cooley v. Board of Wardens of Port of Philadelphia, 12 How. 299, decided by a 7–2 vote, March 2, 1852. Curtis wrote the Court's opinion; McLean and Wayne dissented.

Adopting the "selective exclusiveness doctrine," the majority ruled that Congress had exclusive power to regulate commerce that was national in nature and demanded uniform regulation. The states retained the authority to regulate commerce that was local in nature.

Pennsylvania v. Wheeling and Belmont Bridge, 13 How. 518, decided by a 7–2 vote, February 6, 1852. McLean wrote the Court's opinion; Taney and Daniel dissented.

A bridge built across the Ohio River was so low that it obstructed interstate commerce, the Court ruled, and so it must either be raised so that ships could pass under it or be taken down.

In its first legislative reversal of a Supreme Court decision, Congress passed a law declaring that the bridge did not interfere with interstate commerce and requiring ships to be refitted so that they could pass under the bridge. The Court upheld this statute in 1856.

CONTRACTS

Dodge v. Woolsey, 18 How. 331, decided by a 6–3 vote, April 8, 1856. Wayne wrote the majority opinion; Campbell, Catron, and Daniel dissented.

A state may not revoke a tax exemption included in a charter, grant, or contract. The Constitution's ban on state action impairing the obligation of contracts forbids revocation. With this ruling the Court declared unconstitutional part of the Ohio constitution, the first time it had nullified part of a state's constitution.

DUE PROCESS

Murray's Lessee v. Hoboken Land and Improvement Co., 18 How. 272, decided by a unanimous vote, February 19, 1856. Curtis wrote the Court's opinion.

The due process clause of the Fifth Amendment limits the legislature as well as the executive and the judiciary. The Fifth Amendment "cannot be construed as to leave Congress free to make any process 'due process of law' by its mere will."

With this decision the Court began to define due process, stating that any process in conflict with specific constitutional provisions or the "settled modes and usages" of proceedings in English and early American practice was not due process of law.

FEDERAL COURTS

Ableman v. Booth, United States v. Booth, 21 How. 506, decided by a unanimous Court, March 7, 1859. Taney wrote the Court's opinion.

State courts lack the power to issue writs of habeas corpus ordering federal courts or federal officers to release a prisoner whose detention they cannot justify.

The Court overturned state court action using the writ to order federal officials to release a man convicted in federal courts of violating the Federal Fugitive Slave Act.

SLAVERY

Scott v. Sandford, 19 How. 393, decided by a 7–2 vote, March 6, 1857. Each justice submitted a separate opinion. Taney's is considered the formal opinion of the Court; McLean and Curtis dissented.

In what many think the most ill-considered decision in Supreme Court history, the majority declared unconstitutional the already repealed Missouri Compromise of 1820. Congress, the Court declared, did not have the authority to prohibit slavery in the territories. The majority also held that blacks were not and could not become citizens of the United States and therefore were not entitled to its privileges and immunities. This part of the decision was overturned by ratification of the Fourteenth Amendment.

1860–1869

COMMERCE

Paul v. Virginia, 8 Wall. 168, decided by a unanimous vote, November 1, 1869. Field wrote the opinion.

Insurance is a local business, not interstate commerce. The states, not Congress, are responsible for regulating insurance practices, even though insurance transactions crossed state lines. The Court reversed this ruling in 1944, but Congress quickly returned authority to regulate insurance to the states.

EX POST FACTO LAWS

Cummings v. Missouri, 4 Wall. 277, *Ex parte Garland,* 4 Wall. 333, decided by votes of 5–4, January 14, 1867. Field wrote the majority opinion; Chase, Swayne, Davis, and Miller dissented.

Neither the states nor the federal government may constitutionally require persons who wish to practice certain professions or exercise certain civil rights to take a "test oath" affirming past as well as present loyalty to the United States.

The Court held invalid state and federal test oaths, enacted to exclude persons who had supported the Confederacy from certain offices and certain professions. These requirements, held the Court, violated the constitutional prohibitions on ex post facto laws and bills of attainder.

EXTRADITION

Kentucky v. Dennison, 24 How. 66, decided by a unanimous Court, March 14, 1861. Taney wrote the opinion.

The federal government lacks the power to enforce the constitutional provision that a "person charged in any state with treason, felony or other crime, who shall flee from justice, and be found in another state, shall, on demand of the executive authority of the state from which he fled, be delivered up, to be removed to the state having jurisdiction of the crime."

The Constitution imposes a moral obligation upon a governor to surrender a fugitive sought and requested by another governor, but that obligation cannot be enforced in the federal courts.

FEDERAL COURTS

Mississippi v. Johnson, 4 Wall. 475, decided by a unanimous Court, April 15, 1867. Chase wrote the opinion.

The Supreme Court lacks jurisdiction over the political acts of the president; it has no power to issue an order directing him to stop enforcing acts of Congress, even if those acts are challenged as unconstitutional.

Ex parte McCardle, 7 Wall. 506, decided by a unanimous vote, April 12, 1869. Chase wrote the opinion.

The Constitution authorizes Congress to make exceptions to the appellate jurisdiction of the Supreme Court. That grant includes the power to revoke the Court's appellate jurisdiction over cases already argued and awaiting decision before it. Without jurisdiction over a case, the Court can do nothing but dismiss it.

Congress had revoked the Court's jurisdiction over cases in which lower courts denied prisoners' petitions for release through a writ of habeas corpus. Congress did so because it feared that in this particular case, seeking release of a southern editor held by military authorities for "impeding" the Reconstruction effort, the Court would declare the Reconstruction Acts unconstitutional.

POWERS OF THE PRESIDENT

The Prize Cases, 2 Black 635, decided by a 5–4 vote, March 10, 1863. Grier wrote the majority opinion; Taney, Catron, Clifford, and Nelson dissented.

These cases arose out of the capture of four ships seized while trying to run the Union blockade of Confederate ports that Lincoln instituted in April and Congress sanctioned in July 1861.

The Court sustained the president's power to proclaim the blockade without a congressional declaration of war. A state of war already existed, the majority said, and the president was obligated "to meet it in the shape it presented itself, without waiting for Congress to baptize it with a name."

Ex parte Milligan, 4 Wall. 2, decided by 9–0 and 5–4 votes, April 3, 1866. Full opinions in the case were not announced until December 17, 1866. Davis wrote the majority opinion; Chase, Miller, Swayne, and Wayne dissented in part.

The president lacks the power to authorize military tribunals to try civilians in areas where civil courts are still functioning.

Five justices said that even Congress and the president acting together lacked this power.

STATE POWERS

Texas v. White, 7 Wall. 700, decided by a 5–3 vote, April 12, 1869. Chase wrote the majority opinion; Grier, Swayne, and Miller dissented in part.

States lack the power to secede from the Union. From a legal point of view, Texas and the other states that had approved ordinances of secession had never left the Union.

TAXES

Woodruff v. Parham, 8 Wall. 123, decided without dissent, November 8, 1869. Miller wrote the majority opinion.

States may tax goods "imported" from other states. The constitutional ban on state taxes on imports or exports applies only to goods coming from or going to foreign countries.

States may tax goods from other states, once interstate transportation of those goods has ended, even if they are still in their original packages.

Veazie Bank v. Fenno, 8 Wall. 533, decided by a 7–2 vote, December 31, 1869. Chase wrote the majority opinion; Nelson and Davis dissented.

Congress may use its power to tax as a regulatory tool to support or enforce exercise of another constitutional power, even if the tax is designed to eliminate the matter taxed.

The Court sustained a federal statute that placed a 10 percent tax on the circulation of state bank notes in order to give the untaxed national bank notes a competitive edge and drive the state notes out of the market. The Court said the tax was a legitimate means through which Congress could regulate currency.

1870–1879

CIVIL RIGHTS

Hall v. DeCuir, 95 U.S. 485, decided without dissent, January 14, 1878. Waite wrote the opinion.

A state law forbidding racial discrimination on common carriers operating in the state impermissibly infringes upon the federal power to regulate interstate commerce. Equal access to steamboat accommodations is a matter that requires national, uniform regulation and thus is outside the proper scope of state regulation.

COMMERCE

Henderson v. Wickham, Commissioners of Immigration v. The North German Lloyd, 92 U.S. 259, *Chy Lung v. Freeman,* 92 U.S. 275, decided without dissent, March 20, 1876. Miller wrote the opinion.

A state may not require shipowners to give bond for each alien their ships bring into its ports. Despite the argument that this requirement would reduce the potential burden that immigrants place upon state finances, this bond requirement impermissibly interferes with the federal power to regulate foreign commerce.

This ruling resulted in the first general federal immigration law in U.S. history, enacted in 1882.

CURRENCY

Hepburn v. Griswold (First Legal Tender Case), 8 Wall. 603, decided by a 4–3 vote, February 7, 1870. Chase wrote the majority opinion; Davis, Miller, and Swayne dissented.

The Court declared unconstitutional acts of Congress that substituted paper money for gold as legal tender for the payment of debts contracted prior to adoption of the first legal tender act in 1862.

The statute had been enacted to help the Union finance the Civil War, but the Court held it an improper exercise of Congress's implied powers under the "necessary and proper" clause.

Knox v. Lee, Parker v. Davis (Second Legal Tender Case), 12 Wall. 457, decided by a 5–4 vote, May 1, 1871. Strong wrote the majority opinion; Chase, Nelson, Clifford, and Field dissented.

Overturning *Hepburn v. Griswold,* the majority held that Congress had exercised its implied powers properly when it made paper money legal tender for the payment of debts. The fact that the two justices appointed to the Court since the first decision supported the reversal led to charges that the Court had been "packed."

FEDERAL COURTS

Bradley v. Fisher, 13 Wall. 335, decided by a 7–2 vote, April 8, 1872. Field wrote the majority opinion; Davis and Clifford dissented.

Setting out the doctrine of judicial immunity, the Court ruled that judges may not be sued for their official actions, no matter how erroneous or injurious those actions may be.

JURY TRIALS

Walker v. Sauvinet, 92 U.S. 90, decided by a 7–2 vote, April 24, 1876. Waite wrote the majority opinion; Clifford and Field dissented.

The Seventh Amendment guarantee of a jury trial in suits involving more than $20, affects only federal, not state, trials.

PRIVILEGES AND IMMUNITIES

The Butchers' Benevolent Association of New Orleans v. The Crescent City Livestock Landing and Slaughterhouse Co., Esteben v. Louisiana (Slaughterhouse Cases), 16 Wall. 36, decided by a 5–4 vote, April 14, 1873. Miller wrote the majority opinion; Chase, Field, Swayne, and Bradley dissented.

Louisiana did not violate the Fourteenth Amendment when it granted a monopoly on the slaughterhouse business to one company for all of New Orleans. The right of other butchers to do business is neither a "privilege and immunity" of U.S. citizenship protected by the Fourteenth Amendment nor an aspect of the "property" protected by the amendment's due process guarantee.

Bradwell v. Illinois, 16 Wall. 130, decided by an 8–1 vote, April 15, 1873. Miller wrote the majority opinion; Chase dissented.

A state does not violate the Fourteenth Amendment's guarantee of the privileges and immunities of U.S. citizenship when it refuses on the grounds of gender to license a woman to practice law in its courts. The right to practice law is not a privilege or immunity of U.S. citizenship.

Minor v. Happersett, 21 Wall. 162, decided by a unanimous vote, March 29, 1875. Waite wrote the opinion.

The privileges and immunities clause of the Fourteenth Amendment does not guarantee women the right to vote. A state therefore does not violate that amendment's guarantee when it denies a woman the right to vote. "[T]he Constitution of the United States does not confer the right of suffrage on anyone," the Court said.

STATE POWERS

Munn v. Illinois, 94 U.S. 113, decided by a 7–2 vote, March 1, 1877. Waite wrote the majority opinion; Field and Strong dissented.

The state police power includes the right of states to regulate private business. The Court sustained a state law setting the maximum rate that grain elevator operators could charge for grain storage. Private property dedicated to public use was subject to government regulation.

TAXES

Low v. Austin, 13 Wall. 29, decided by a unanimous vote, January 29, 1872. Field wrote the opinion.

The constitutional ban on state taxes on imports or exports prohibits state taxes on goods imported from foreign countries so long as those goods retain their character as imports.

VOTING RIGHTS

United States v. Reese, 92 U.S. 214, decided by an 8–1 vote, March 27, 1876. Waite wrote the majority opinion; Hunt dissented.

The Fifteenth Amendment, forbidding states to deny anyone the right to vote because of race, color, or previous condition of servitude, did not give anyone the right to vote. It simply guaranteed the right to be free from racial discrimination in the exercise of the right to vote—a right granted under state, not federal, laws.

Congress therefore exceeded its power to enforce the Fifteenth Amendment when it enacted laws that penalized state officials who denied blacks the right to vote, refused to count votes, or obstructed citizens from voting.

United States v. Cruikshank, 92 U.S. 542, decided by a unanimous vote, March 27, 1876. Waite wrote the Court's opinion.

The Court dismissed indictments brought against Louisiana citizens accused of using violence and fraud to prevent blacks from voting. Because the indictments did not charge that these actions were motivated by racial discrimination, they were not federal offenses. "We may suspect," Waite wrote, "that race was the cause of the hostility but it is not so averred."

1880–1889

CIVIL RIGHTS

Civil Rights Cases, 109 U.S. 3, decided by an 8–1 vote, October 15, 1883. Bradley wrote the Court's opinion; Harlan dissented.

Neither the Thirteenth nor the Fourteenth Amendment empowers Congress to enact a law barring discrimination against blacks in privately owned public accommodations. The Fourteenth Amendment prohibits only state-sponsored discrimination, not private discriminatory acts, the Court held. Private discrimination does not violate the Thirteenth Amendment because "such an act of refusal has nothing to do with slavery or involuntary servitude."

The decision effectively blocked further attempts by Congress in the post–Civil War period to end private racial discrimination; not until 1964 did Congress enact and the Court sustain a federal law prohibiting discrimination in privately owned public accommodations.

COMMERCE

Wabash, St. Louis and Pacific Railway Co. v. Illinois, 118 U.S. 557, decided by a 6–3 vote, October 25, 1886. Miller wrote the majority opinion; Waite, Bradley, and Gray dissented.

States may not regulate the rates charged by railroads which form part of an interstate network, even if the state regulates only for the intrastate portion of a trip. Such state regulation infringes upon the federal power to regulate interstate commerce.

Kidd v. Pearson, 128 U.S. 1, decided without dissent, October 22, 1888. Lamar wrote the opinion.

The Court upheld a state law that forbade the manufacture of liquor in the state—even if it was for sale and consumption outside the state. This law did not infringe federal power to regulate interstate commerce, held the Court. Manufacture of goods is not commerce and cannot be regulated as interstate commerce.

CONTRACTS

Stone v. Mississippi, 101 U.S. 814, decided without dissent, May 10, 1880. Waite wrote the opinion.

A state may not permanently contract away any portion of its police power, its power to act to protect the general welfare. Mississippi therefore did not act in violation of the contract clause when it amended its constitution to ban lotteries. This state action had been challenged as impairing the earlier obligation of another legislature that chartered a state lottery corporation.

DUE PROCESS

Hurtado v. California, 110 U.S. 516, decided by a 7–1 vote, March 3, 1884. Matthews wrote the majority opinion; Harlan dissented; Field did not participate.

The due process clause of the Fourteenth Amendment does not require states to use grand jury indictments or presentments in capital offenses.

EQUAL PROTECTION

Yick Wo v. Hopkins, 118 U.S. 356, decided by a unanimous vote, May 10, 1886. Matthews wrote the Court's opinion.

The Fourteenth Amendment protects persons, not just citizens. Holding that a city's arbitrary enforcement of a fire hazard ordinance had discriminated against Chinese laundry owners in violation of the amendment's equal protection clause, the Court said that guarantee applied "to all persons within the territorial jurisdiction, without regard to any differences of race, of color, or of nationality."

Santa Clara County v. Southern Pacific Railroad Co., 118 U.S. 394, decided by a unanimous vote, May 10, 1886. Harlan wrote the opinion; Waite made a preliminary announcement.

Before the Court heard arguments in this case, involving a tax dispute between a county, a state, and a railroad, Waite announced that the equal protection clause of the Fourteenth Amendment applied to protect corporations as well as individuals. Corporations were established to be "persons" within the meaning of that amendment and able to invoke its protection.

FEDERAL COURTS

Wisconsin v. Pelican Insurance Company, 127 U.S. 265, decided without dissent, May 14, 1888. Gray wrote the opinion.

States may not invoke the original jurisdiction of the Supreme Court to enforce their criminal laws against nonresidents. The Supreme Court refused to enforce the order of a Wisconsin court against a Louisiana corporation for failing to comply with Wisconsin laws.

IMMIGRATION

Chae Chan Ping v. United States (Chinese Exclusion Case), 130 U.S. 581, decided by a unanimous vote, May 13, 1889. Field wrote the opinion.

The power of Congress over the entry of aliens, derived from the need to preserve the nation's sovereign status, is exclusive and absolute. The Court sustained an act of Congress that barred the entry of Chinese aliens into the United States.

POWERS OF CONGRESS

Kilbourn v. Thompson, 103 U.S. 168, decided by a unanimous vote, January 24, February 28, 1881. Miller wrote the opinion.

The power of Congress to investigate is not unlimited, nor is its power to punish witnesses who refuse to cooperate with such an investigation. Investigations must be confined to subject areas over which Congress has jurisdiction, their purpose must be enactment of legislation, and they may not merely inquire into the private affairs of citizens. Contempt citations issued against witnesses who refuse to cooperate in investigations that do not meet these standards are invalid.

This assertion was the first of the Court's authority to review the propriety of congressional investigations. The Court subsequently modified the standards laid out in this case, but its basic limitations on the power of Congress to investigate remain in effect.

SEARCH AND SEIZURE

Boyd v. United States, 116 U.S. 616, decided without dissent, February 1, 1886. Bradley wrote the opinion.

The Court held that a revenue statute compelling a defendant to produce in court his private papers was unconstitutional as an unreasonable search and seizure violating the Fourth Amendment and as compelled self-incrimination in violation of the Fifth Amendment.

STATE POWERS

Mugler v. Kansas, 123 U.S. 623, decided by an 8–1 vote, December 5, 1887. Harlan wrote the majority opinion; Field dissented.

The Court upheld a state law that forbade the manufacture and sale of intoxicating liquor in the state. Rejecting a challenge to this law as abridging the privileges and immunities of U.S. citizenship, as well as the due process guarantee of the Fourteenth Amendment, the Court held the law a proper exercise of the state police power to safeguard the public health and morals.

TAXES

Head Money Cases, 112 U.S. 580, decided by a unanimous vote, December 8, 1884. Miller wrote the opinion.

The constitutional requirement that indirect taxes be uniform is met if the tax operates the same upon all subjects being taxed; an indirect tax is not unconstitutional simply because the subject being taxed is not distributed uniformly throughout the United States.

VOTING RIGHTS

Ex parte Siebold, 100 U.S. 371, decided by a 7–2 vote, March 8, 1880. Bradley wrote the majority opinion; Field and Clifford dissented.

Confirming federal power to protect the electoral process in congressional elections in the states, the Court upheld federal laws making it a federal crime for state election officers to neglect their duty in congressional elections. The Court upheld the convictions of two state officials tried and convicted for stuffing the ballot box.

Ex parte Yarbrough, 110 U.S. 651, decided by a unanimous Court, March 3, 1884; Miller wrote the opinion.

The Court upheld as a valid exercise of congressional power to enforce the Fifteenth Amendment legislation penalizing persons who conspired to stop blacks from exercising their right to vote. The Court upheld the convictions of several members of the Ku Klux Klan for intimidating a black man to stop him from voting. In some cases, the Court held, the Fifteenth Amendment does confer the right to vote, as well as the right to be free of racial discrimination in voting, and Congress has the power to enforce that right.

1890–1899

CITIZENSHIP

United States v. Wong Kim Ark, 169 U.S. 649, decided by a 6–2 vote, March 28, 1898. Gray wrote the majority opinion; Fuller and Harlan dissented; McKenna did not participate.

Children born in the United States to resident alien parents are citizens of the United States even if their parents are barred from becoming citizens because of their race.

This decision was the Court's first interpreting the Fourteenth Amendment's clause that defines U.S. citizens as all persons born in the United States.

CIVIL RIGHTS

Louisville, New Orleans and Texas Railway Co. v. Mississippi, 133 U.S. 587, decided by a 7–2 vote, March 3, 1890. Brewer wrote the majority opinion; Harlan and Bradley dissented.

Mississippi does not infringe on the federal commerce power when it requires railroads doing business in the state to provide separate accommodations for black and white passengers. The state supreme court viewed this as applying solely to intrastate railroad operations. The Supreme Court accepted those findings and held the requirement no burden on interstate commerce.

Plessy v. Ferguson, 163 U.S. 537, decided by an 7–1 vote, May 18, 1896. Brown wrote the Court's opinion; Harlan dissented; Brewer did not participate.

A state law requiring trains to provide separate but equal facilities for black and white passengers does not infringe upon federal authority to regulate interstate commerce nor is it in violation of the Thirteenth or Fourteenth Amendments. The train was local; a legal distinction between the two races did not destroy the legal equality of the two races guaranteed by the Thirteenth Amendment, and the Fourteenth Amendment protected only political, not social, equality, the majority said.

In dissent, Harlan declared that the "Constitution is color-blind, and neither knows nor tolerates classes among citizens." The "separate but equal" doctrine remained in effect until *Brown v. Board of Education* (1954).

COMMERCE

United States v. E. C. Knight Co., 156 U.S. 1, decided by an 8–1 vote, January 21, 1895. Fuller wrote the majority opinion; Harlan dissented.

In its first interpretation of the Sherman Antitrust Act, the Court ruled that the act did not apply to a trust that refined more than 90 percent of the sugar sold in the country.

Congress had no constitutional power to regulate manufacture, the Court stated, even though much of the refined sugar was intended for sale in interstate commerce. Such sales would affect interstate commerce only indirectly. Congressional authority extended only to regulation of matters that directly affected interstate commerce.

This distinction between matters affecting interstate commerce directly or indirectly significantly modified the Court's decision in *Gibbons v. Ogden* (1824), which held that the Constitution gave Congress authority to regulate intrastate matters that affected other states.

The holding in *Knight* was gradually eroded by later decisions.

In re Debs, 158 U.S. 564, decided by a 9–0 vote, May 27, 1895. Brewer wrote the Court's opinion.

Eugene V. Debs and other leaders of the 1894 Pullman strike challenged their contempt convictions for violating a federal court injunction that was intended to break the strike. A lower court upheld the validity of the injunction under the Sherman Antitrust Act.

The Supreme Court affirmed the validity of the injunction—and Debs's conviction—but on the broader grounds of national sovereignty, which the Court said gave the federal government authority to remove obstructions to interstate commerce and transportation of the mails.

COMPACTS

Virginia v. Tennessee, 148 U.S. 503, decided without dissent, April 3, 1893. Field wrote the opinion.

A compact to resolve a boundary dispute between two states need not be approved formally by Congress in order to be permissible. The Constitution does declare that "no state shall, without the consent of Congress, . . . enter into any Agreement or Compact with another state," but this requirement of formal consent applies only to compacts tending to increase the political power of the states at the expense of national authority or the federal government.

DUE PROCESS

Chicago, Milwaukee & St. Paul Railway Co. v. Minnesota, 134 U.S. 418, decided by a 6–3 vote, March 24, 1890. Blatchford wrote the majority opinion; Bradley, Gray, and Lamar dissented.

If a state deprives a company of the power to charge reasonable rates without providing judicial review of those rate limitations, the state is depriving the company of its property without due process of law.

Courts have the power to decide on the reasonableness of rates set by states for companies to charge and due process requires that an opportunity for judicial review be provided.

Allgeyer v. Louisiana, 165 U.S. 578, decided without dissent, March 1, 1897. Peckham wrote the opinion.

The liberty protected by the due process clause of the Fourteenth Amendment against denial by states included the freedom to make a contract. The Court struck down a state law that forbade its citizens to obtain insurance from out-of-state companies.

This decision was the first recognition by the Court of the protected "freedom of contract" that the justices would use subsequently to strike down minimum wage and maximum hour laws.

Chicago, Burlington & Quincy Railroad Company v. Chicago, 166 U.S. 226, decided by a 7–1 vote, March 1, 1897. Harlan wrote the majority opinion; Brewer dissented; Fuller did not participate.

The Fourteenth Amendment guarantee of due process requires a state, when it takes private property for public use, to provide just compensation to the property owner.

Holden v. Hardy, 169 U.S. 366, decided by a 7–2 vote, February 28, 1898. Brown wrote the majority opinion; Brewer and Peckham dissented.

The Court upheld, against a due process challenge, Utah's law that limited the number of hours that miners could work in underground mines. The "freedom of contract" is subject to certain limitations imposed by the state in the exercise of its police power to protect the health of workers in hazardous conditions.

Smyth v. Ames, 169 U.S. 466, decided by a 7–0 vote, March 7, 1898. Harlan wrote the opinion; Fuller and McKenna did not participate.

Corporations are persons within the protection of the Fourteenth Amendment's guarantee of due process. That guarantee requires states to set railroad rates sufficiently high to ensure the railroad companies a fair return on the value of the investment and just compensation for the use of their property. To ensure compliance with this standard, federal courts have the power to review the rates.

FEDERAL COURTS

United States v. Texas, 143 U.S. 621, decided by a 7–2 vote, February 29, 1892. Harlan wrote the majority opinion; Fuller and Lamar dissented.

By joining the Union, states acquiesce in the constitutional provision extending federal judicial power over all cases in which the United States is a party, including those brought by the United States against a state. The Court rejected Texas's argument that the Court lacked jurisdiction over such a case.

California v. Southern Pacific Railway Co., 157 U.S. 220, decided by a 7–2 vote, March 18, 1895. Fuller wrote the majority opinion; Harlan and Brewer dissented.

The Supreme Court does not have original jurisdiction over cases brought by a state against its own citizens; such suits are generally to be brought in state courts, not federal courts.

SELF-INCRIMINATION

Counselman v. Hitchcock, 142 U.S. 547, decided by a unanimous vote, January 11, 1892. Blatchford wrote the opinion.

Only a grant of complete and absolute immunity against prosecution for an offense revealed in compelled testimony is sufficient to justify waiver of the Fifth Amendment privilege against compelled self-incrimination.

The Court struck down as insufficient the existing federal immunity statute that protected a witness only against the actual use of his testimony as evidence against him, not against its indirect use to obtain other evidence against him.

TAXES

Pollock v. Farmers' Loan and Trust Co., 158 U.S. 601, decided by a 5–4 vote, May 20, 1895. Fuller wrote the majority opinion; Harlan, Jackson, Brown, and White dissented.

Taxes on income derived from real estate and personal property are direct taxes. They therefore must be apportioned among the states according to population. The Court struck down the first general income tax law enacted by Congress and overruled earlier decisions that defined head taxes and taxes on land as the only two forms of direct taxation.

The decision led to adoption and ratification in 1913 of the Sixteenth Amendment, which exempted income taxes from the Constitution's apportionment requirement.

TREATIES

Geofroy v. Riggs, 133 U.S. 258, decided by a unanimous vote, February 3, 1890. Field wrote the opinion.

It is within the scope of the treaty power of the United States to regulate the inheritance by aliens of land and other property in the United States. The Court declared that the treaty power was unlimited except by the Constitution. Field observed: "It would not be contended that it extends so far as to authorize what the Constitution forbids."

VOTING RIGHTS

Williams v. Mississippi, 170 U.S. 213, decided by a unanimous vote, April 25, 1898. McKenna delivered the opinion.

A state does not violate the equal protection clause of the Fourteenth Amendment when it requires eligible voters to be able to read, write, and interpret or understand any part of the Constitution.

1900–1905

COMMERCE

Champion v. Ames, 188 U.S. 321, decided by a 5–4 vote, February 23, 1903. Harlan wrote the majority opinion; Fuller, Brewer, Peckham, and Shiras dissented.

In its first recognition of a federal "police" power, the Court sustained a federal law banning the shipment of lottery tickets in interstate commerce. Just as states might regulate intrastate matters to protect the health, welfare, and morals of their residents, so might Congress exercise its authority to regulate interstate commerce for the same purposes.

Northern Securities Co. v. United States, 193 U.S. 197, decided by a 5–4 vote, March 14, 1904. Harlan wrote the majority opinion; Fuller, White, Holmes, and Peckham dissented.

A holding company formed solely to eliminate competition between two railroad lines was a combination in restraint of trade and therefore in violation of the federal antitrust act.

This was a major modification of the *Knight* decision (1895). The majority now held that although the holding company itself was not in interstate commerce, it sufficiently affected that commerce by restraining it and therefore came within the scope of the federal antitrust statute.

Swift and Co. v. United States, 196 U.S. 375, decided by a unanimous vote, January 30, 1905. Holmes wrote the opinion.

Congress can regulate local commerce that is part of an interstate current of commerce. This opinion was the first enunciation of the "stream-of-commerce" doctrine.

The Court held that meatpackers who combined to fix the price of livestock and meat bought and sold in Chicago stockyards were in violation of the federal antitrust act because the meatpacking operation was the middle part of an interstate transaction in which cattle were shipped from out of the state into Chicago for slaughter and packing and then shipped to other states for sale.

DUE PROCESS

Lochner v. New York, 198 U.S. 45, decided by a 5–4 vote, April 17, 1905. Peckham wrote the majority opinion for the Court; Day, Harlan, Holmes, and White dissented.

The Court struck down a New York law limiting the hours bakery employees could work. The majority found the law a denial of due process, infringing upon the freedom of contract. Because there was no sufficient health reason for the limit, it could not be justified as an exercise of the state's police power.

PRIVILEGES AND IMMUNITIES

Maxwell v. Dow, 176 U.S. 581, decided by an 8–1 vote, February 26, 1900. Peckham wrote the majority opinion; Harlan dissented.

The right to be tried by a jury of twelve persons is not one of the privileges and immunities of U.S. citizenship protected by the Fourteenth Amendment against violation by states.

The Court upheld a state court judgment reached by a jury composed of eight persons, instead of twelve as required in federal courts.

TAXES

Knowlton v. Moore, 178 U.S. 41, decided by a 5–3 vote, May 14, 1900. White wrote the majority opinion; Harlan and McKenna dissented; Brewer dissented in part; Peckham did not participate.

The constitutional requirement that indirect taxes be uniform does not require that the tax rate be uniform, only that the same rate be applied to the same class in the same manner throughout the United States.

McCray v. United States, 195 U.S. 27, decided by a 6–3 vote, May 31, 1904. White wrote the Court's opinion; Fuller, Brown, and Peckham dissented.

Congress may use its taxing power as a regulatory "police" power. So long as the tax produces some revenue, the Court will not examine the motivation for imposing the tax.

The Court upheld a federal statute that placed a high tax on oleomargarine colored yellow to resemble butter. That tax was obviously designed to eliminate the competition to butter, but it was lawful on its face. The Court had no power to "restrain the exercise of a lawful power on the assumption that a wrongful purpose or motive has caused the power to be exerted."

This ruling came little more than a year after the Court held that Congress could also use its interstate commerce power as a police power; the two decisions substantially increased congressional power to regulate commerce in the United States.

TERRITORIES

The Insular Cases, decided May 27, 1901.

DeLima v. Bidwell, 182 U.S. 1, decided by a 5–4 vote; Brown wrote the majority opinion; Gray, McKenna, Shiras, and White dissented.

Downes v. Bidwell, 182 U.S. 244, decided by a 5–4 vote; Brown wrote the majority opinion; Fuller, Harlan, Brewer, and Peckham dissented.

In these two cases the Court ruled that as a result of U.S. annexation of Puerto Rico, the island was no longer a foreign country, but neither was it a part of the United States included within the full protection of the Constitution. The Constitution applied automatically only to states, the Court held, and it was up to Congress, in the exercise of its power to govern territories, to determine whether the Constitution should apply in particular territories.

In a third case, *Dorr v. United States,* 195 U.S. 138 (1904), the Court adopted the "incorporation theory," still in effect, under which the Constitution automatically applies in territories that have been formally incorporated into the United States either through ratified treaty or act of Congress, but not to unincorporated territories.

1906–1910

COMMERCE

Adair v. United States, 208 U.S. 161, decided by a 6–2 vote, January 27, 1908. Harlan wrote the majority opinion; Holmes and McKenna dissented; Moody did not participate.

A federal law prohibiting contracts that required an employee to promise not to join a labor union as a condition of employment exceeded federal authority to regulate interstate commerce and violated the "freedom of contract."

This decision, later overruled, placed "yellow dog" contracts beyond the reach of federal power. It was one of several decisions of the early twentieth century in which the Court ruled against the interests of the labor movement.

Loewe v. Lawler (Danbury Hatters Case), 208 U.S. 274, decided by a unanimous vote, February 3, 1908. Fuller wrote the opinion.

A union attempting to organize workers in a factory in one state by boycotting stores elsewhere that sell its products (secondary boycotts) is a combination in restraint of trade and in violation of the federal antitrust law.

This decision led to adoption of provisions in the Clayton Antitrust Act of 1914 exempting labor unions from suits brought under the antitrust laws.

CRUEL AND UNUSUAL PUNISHMENT

Weems v. United States, 217 U.S. 349, decided by a 4–2 vote, May 2, 1910. McKenna wrote the majority opinion; White and Harlan dissented; Moody and Lurton did not participate.

A Philippine law providing for a punishment of twelve years at hard labor in chains for the crime of falsifying an official document was "cruel and unusual punishment" prohibited by the Eighth Amendment.

FEDERAL COURTS

Ex parte Young, 209 U.S. 123, decided by an 8–1 vote, March 23, 1908. Peckham wrote the majority opinion; Harlan dissented.

Federal judges may properly enjoin, temporarily, the enforcement of a state law challenged as unconstitutional. The injunction may remain in effect until the validity of the law is determined.

SELF-INCRIMINATION

Twining v. New Jersey, 211 U.S. 78, decided by an 8–1 vote, November 9, 1908. Moody delivered the majority opinion; Harlan dissented.

The Fourteenth Amendment does not automatically extend the Fifth Amendment privilege against compelled self-incrimination—or other provisions of the Bill of Rights—to state defendants. The constitutional rights of state defendants are not impaired when a judge or prosecutor comments adversely upon their failure to testify in their own defense.

STATE POWERS

Georgia v. Tennessee Copper Co., 206 U.S. 230, decided by a unanimous vote, May 13, 1907. Holmes wrote the opinion.

In one of the first environmental cases to come to the Court, the justices declared that a state could ask a federal judge to order a company in another state to cease polluting the air shared by the two states.

Muller v. Oregon, 208 U.S. 412, decided by a unanimous vote, February 24, 1908. Brewer wrote the opinion.

The Court upheld Oregon's law setting maximum hours for women working in laundries. The Court relied on the argument that longer working hours might impair the childbearing function of women. State limitation of those hours was therefore justified as a health measure, properly within the state police power.

1911–1915

COMMERCE

Standard Oil Co. v. United States, 221 U.S. 1, decided by an 8–1 vote, May 15, 1911. White wrote the majority opinion; Harlan dissented in part.

Only unreasonable combinations and undue restraints of trade are illegal under the federal antitrust act. In this decision, which resulted in the breakup of the Standard Oil monopoly, a majority of the Court for the first time adopted the so-called "rule of reason." Previously, the Court had held that any combination that restrained trade, whether "reasonable" or "unreasonable," was a violation of the federal statute.

Houston, East and West Texas Railway Co. v. United States; Texas and Pacific Railway Co. v. United States (Shreveport Rate Cases), 234 U.S. 342, decided by a 7–2 vote, June 8, 1914. Hughes wrote the majority opinion; Lurton and Pitney dissented.

Congress may regulate intrastate rail rates if they are so intertwined with interstate rail rates that it is impossible to regulate the one without regulating the other. This so-called "Shreveport Doctrine" was eventually expanded to allow regulation of other intrastate matters that affected interstate commerce.

CONTEMPT

Gompers v. Buck's Stove and Range Co., 221 U.S. 418, decided by a unanimous Court, May 15, 1911. Lamar wrote the opinion.

Civil contempt and criminal contempt are distinguished by the character and purpose of the penalty imposed for them. The purpose of a punishment for civil contempt is remedial—to convince a witness to testify, for example—while the purpose of punishment for criminal contempt is clearly punitive, to vindicate the authority of the court.

Civil contempt ends whenever the person held in contempt decides to comply with the court; criminal contempt is punished by a fixed sentence.

DUE PROCESS

Frank v. Mangum, 237 U.S. 309, decided by a 7–2 vote, April 12, 1915. Pitney wrote the majority opinion; Holmes and Hughes dissented.

The Court upheld a state conviction for murder although the trial court atmosphere was dominated by anti-Semitism and hostility. The majority reasoned that review of the conviction by Georgia's highest state court guaranteed the defendant due process.

FEDERAL COURTS

Muskrat v. United States, 219 U.S. 346, decided by a unanimous vote, January 23, 1911. Day wrote the opinion.

The Court dismissed a case that Congress had authorized certain Indians to bring in order to test the constitutionality of certain laws. No actual dispute or conflict of rights and interests existed here, the Court held, and therefore there was no "case or controversy" properly within its power to resolve.

INTERSTATE RELATIONS

Virginia v. West Virginia, 238 U.S. 202, decided by a unanimous vote, June 14, 1915. Hughes wrote the opinion.

In one of the longest-running disputes to come before the Court, the justices held in 1915 that West Virginia owed Virginia some $12 million—its share of the pre–Civil War state debts of Virginia, which West Virginia had agreed to assume upon its becoming a separate state.

SEARCH AND SEIZURE

Weeks v. United States, 232 U.S. 383, decided by a unanimous vote, February 24, 1914. Day wrote the opinion.

A person whose Fourth Amendment rights to be secure against unreasonable search and seizure are violated by federal agents has the right to require that evidence obtained in the search be excluded from use against him in federal courts.

This was the Court's first decision adopting the so-called exclusionary rule.

STATE POWERS

Coyle v. Smith, 221 U.S. 559, decided by a 7–2 vote, May 29, 1911. Lurton wrote the Court's opinion; McKenna and Holmes dissented.

States are admitted into the Union on an equal footing with all other states; Congress may not place any restrictions on matters wholly under the state's control as a condition of entry. This ruling invalidated a congressional requirement that Oklahoma's state capital remain in Guthrie for seven years after statehood was granted.

Hadacheck v. Los Angeles, 239 U.S. 394, decided by a unanimous vote, December 12, 1915. McKenna wrote the opinion.

Zoning power is part of the state police power, enabling the state to control the use to which certain lands are put. A city's use of this power to forbid brickmaking in a certain area is valid and does not deny due process to a brickmaker, even if it puts him out of business.

VOTING RIGHTS

Guinn v. United States, 238 U.S. 347, decided by an 8–0 vote, June 21, 1915. White wrote the opinion; McReynolds did not participate.

The Court declared an Oklahoma "grandfather clause" for voters an unconstitutional evasion of the Fifteenth Amendment guarantee that states would not deny citizens the right to vote because of their race. Oklahoma law imposed a literacy test upon potential voters, but exempted all persons whose ancestors voted in 1866. The Court said that although race, color, or previous servitude were not mentioned in the law, selection of a date prior to adoption of the Fifteenth Amendment was intended to disenfranchise blacks in "direct and positive disregard" of the amendment.

United States v. Mosley, 238 U.S. 383, decided by a 7–1 vote, June 21, 1915. Holmes wrote the opinion; Lamar dissented; McReynolds did not participate.

The Court upheld congressional power to regulate elections tainted with fraud and corruption, sustaining provisions of the 1870 Enforcement Act implementing the Fifteenth Amendment. In *Ex parte Yarbrough* (1884) the Court had backed congressional power to penalize persons who used violence and intimidation to prevent blacks from voting.

1916–1920

COMMERCE

Hammer v. Dagenhart, 247 U.S. 251, decided by a 5–4 vote, June 3, 1918. Day wrote the majority opinion; Holmes, McKenna, Brandeis, and Clarke dissented.

Narrowing the federal "police" power, the Court struck down a federal statute that prohibited the shipment in interstate commerce of any goods produced by child labor.

Labor was an aspect of manufacture, an intrastate matter not subject to federal control, the majority held. Furthermore, Congress could prohibit shipments in interstate commerce only of goods that were in themselves harmful. Because products made by children were not themselves harmful, Congress had no authority to forbid their shipment.

This decision and a 1922 ruling that Congress had used its taxing power unconstitutionally in a second law intended to bring an end to child labor were overruled in 1941. (See *United States v. Darby Lumber Co.*)

DUE PROCESS

Bunting v. Oregon, 243 U.S. 426, decided by a 5–3 vote, April 9, 1917. McKenna wrote the majority opinion; White, McReynolds, and Van Devanter dissented; Brandeis did not participate.

Extending its decision in *Muller v. Oregon* (1908), the Court upheld an Oregon law setting ten hours as the maximum permissible workday for all industrial workers.

Buchanan v. Warley, 245 U.S. 60, decided by a 9–0 vote, November 5, 1917. Day wrote the opinion.

City ordinances that segregate neighborhoods by restricting some blocks to white residents only and other blocks to black residents only violate the Fourteenth Amendment guarantee of due process.

This decision led to the growth of private restrictive covenants under which neighbors would agree to sell or rent their homes only to persons of the same race. The Court upheld such private covenants in *Corrigan v. Buckley,* 271 U.S. 323 (1926).

FREEDOM OF EXPRESSION

Schenck v. United States, 249 U.S. 47, decided by a 9–0 vote, March 3, 1919. Holmes wrote the opinion.

In its first decision dealing with the extent of the First Amendment's protection for speech, the Court sustained the Espionage Act of 1917 against a challenge that it violated the guarantees of freedom of speech and press.

The First Amendment is not an absolute guarantee, the Court said. Freedom of speech and press may be constrained if "the words used are used in such circumstances and are of such a nature as to create a clear and present danger that they will bring about the substantive evils that Congress has a right to prevent."

POWERS OF CONGRESS

Clark Distilling Co. v. Western Maryland Railway, 242 U.S. 311, decided by a 7–2 vote, January 8, 1917. White wrote the majority opinion; Holmes and Van Devanter dissented.

States have the power, under the federal Webb-Kenyon Act of 1913, to ban the entry of intoxicating liquor into their territory. The act had been challenged as an unconstitutional delegation of power, but the Court held it permissible because the statute established the precise conditions under which states might act.

Selective Draft Law Cases, 245 U.S. 366, decided by a 9–0 vote, January 7, 1918. White wrote the opinion.

Congress is authorized to institute a compulsory draft of persons into the armed forces under its power to raise armies and under the necessary and proper clause. Moreover, service in the military is one of the duties of a citizen in a "just government." Compulsory conscription is not involuntary servitude in violation of the Thirteenth Amendment.

TAXES

Brushaber v. Union Pacific Railroad Co., 240 U.S. 1, decided by a 7–2 vote, January 24, 1916. White wrote the majority opinion; McKenna and Pitney dissented.

With two other cases decided the same day, the Court sustained the 1913 general income tax law enacted after ratification of the Sixteenth Amendment. This decision completed the action necessary to nullify the Court's 1895 ruling that income taxes were direct taxes that must be apportioned among the states according to population. The Sixteenth Amendment exempted income taxes from the apportionment requirement.

TREATIES

Missouri v. Holland, 252 U.S. 416, decided by a 7–2 vote, April 19, 1920. Holmes wrote the majority opinion; Van Devanter and Pitney dissented.

In order to implement a treaty, Congress may enact legislation that otherwise might be an unconstitutional invasion of state sovereignty.

After lower courts ruled an act of Congress protecting migratory birds an unconstitutional invasion of state powers, the U.S. government negotiated a treaty with Canada for the protection of the birds. After the Senate ratified it, Congress again enacted protective legislation to fulfill the terms of the treaty. Sustaining this second act, the Court wrote: "It is obvious that there may be matters of the sharpest exigency for the national well-being that an act of Congress could not deal with but that a treaty followed by such an act could."

1921–1925

COMMERCE

Duplex Printing Press Co. v. Deering, 254 U.S. 443, decided by a 6–3 vote, January 3, 1921. Pitney wrote the majority opinion. Brandeis, Holmes, and Clarke dissented.

Reading the Clayton Act narrowly, the majority held that federal courts were prohibited from issuing injunctions only against normal labor union operations. A secondary boycott was a combination in restraint of trade, which was illegal, and could therefore be the target of a federal court injunction.

DOUBLE JEOPARDY

United States v. Lanza, 260 U.S. 377, decided by an 8–0 vote, December 11, 1922. Taft delivered the opinion.

Where both federal and state law make the same act a crime, the double jeopardy guarantee of the Fifth Amendment does not prohibit a federal prosecution and a state prosecution of the same defendant for the same crime.

DUE PROCESS

Moore v. Dempsey, 261 U.S. 86, decided by a 6–2 vote, February 19, 1923. Holmes wrote the majority opinion; McReynolds and Sutherland dissented.

Mob domination of the atmosphere of a trial can deny a defendant his right to a fair trial guaranteed by the Sixth Amendment.

Adkins v. Children's Hospital, 261 U.S. 525, decided by a 5–3 vote, April 9, 1923. Sutherland wrote the majority opinion; Taft, Holmes, and Sanford dissented; Brandeis did not participate.

The Court struck down an act of Congress setting a minimum wage for women and children workers in the District of Columbia. The majority found this law a price-fixing measure, in violation of the freedom of contract protected by the Fifth Amendment against infringement by federal action.

FEDERAL COURTS

Massachusetts v. Mellon, Frothingham v. Mellon, 262 U.S. 447, decided by a unanimous Court, June 4, 1923. Sutherland wrote the opinion.

Rejecting state and taxpayer challenges to a federal grant-in-aid program as unconstitutional, the Court held that the taxpayer lacked "standing" to sue, because her share of the federal revenues expended in the challenged program was too minute to constitute the personal interest one must have in a matter in order to bring a challenge in federal court.

FREEDOM OF SPEECH

Gitlow v. New York, 268 U.S. 652, decided by a 7–2 vote, June 8, 1925. Sanford wrote the majority opinion; Holmes and Brandeis dissented.

The First Amendment prohibition against government abridgment of the freedom of speech applies to the states as well as to the federal government. The freedoms of speech and press "are among the fundamental personal rights and 'liberties' protected by the due process clause of the Fourteenth Amendment from impairment by the states," the Court asserted, even though it rejected Gitlow's free speech claim. This ruling was the first of a long line of rulings holding that the Fourteenth Amendment extended the guarantees of the Bill of Rights to state, as well as federal, action.

PERSONAL LIBERTY

Pierce v. Society of Sisters, 268 U.S. 510, decided by a unanimous vote, June 1, 1925. McReynolds wrote the Court's opinion.

A state law that requires all children in the first eight grades to attend public, rather than private or parochial, schools violates the Fourteenth Amendment due process guarantee of "personal liberty." Implicit in this liberty is the right of parents to choose the kind of education they want for their children.

POWERS OF CONGRESS

Newberry v. United States, 256 U.S. 232, decided by a 5–4 vote, May 2, 1921. McReynolds wrote the majority opinion; White, Pitney, Brandeis, and Clark dissented in part.

The Court reversed the conviction of Truman H. Newberry for violating a federal law limiting campaign expenditures in a primary election. Congress, the Court held, lacks power to regulate primary campaigns because a primary was "in no real sense part of the manner of holding the election."

Dillon v. Gloss, 256 U.S. 368, decided by a unanimous vote, May 16, 1921. Van Devanter wrote the opinion.

The power of Congress to designate the manner in which the states shall ratify proposed amendments to the Constitution includes the power to set a "reasonable" time period within which the states must act.

SEARCH AND SEIZURE

Carroll v. United States, 267 U.S. 132, decided by a 7–2 vote, March 2, 1925. Taft delivered the majority opinion; McReynolds and Sutherland dissented.

The Court enlarged the scope of permissible searches conducted without a warrant. Federal agents could make warrantless searches of automobiles when they had a reasonable suspicion of illegal actions.

STATE POWERS

Ponzi v. Fessenden, 258 U.S. 254, decided by a unanimous vote, March 27, 1922. Taft wrote the opinion.

With federal consent, a state court may issue a writ of habeas corpus to federal officials, directing them to present a federal prisoner to state court for trial.

TAXES

Bailey v. Drexel Furniture Co., 259 U.S. 20, decided by an 8–1 vote, May 15, 1922. Taft wrote the majority opinion; Clarke dissented.

In its second decision frustrating congressional efforts to end child labor, the Court invalidated a federal law that imposed a 10 percent tax on the net profits of any company that employed children under a certain age. The Court said the tax was an impermissible use of Congress's police power because Congress intended it as a penalty rather than a source of revenue. The Court overruled this decision and that in *Hammer v. Dagenhart* (1918) in *United States v. Darby Lumber Co.* in 1941.

1926–1930

CIVIL RIGHTS

Corrigan v. Buckley, 271 U.S. 323, decided by a unanimous vote, May 24, 1926. Sanford wrote the opinion.

Civil rights are not protected by the Fifth, Thirteenth, or Fourteenth Amendments against the discriminatory actions of private individuals. Therefore no constitutional protection exists for individuals who have been discriminated against by private restrictive covenants, under which residents of one race living in a neighborhood agree among themselves not to sell or rent their homes to members of another race.

DUE PROCESS

Tumey v. Ohio, 273 U.S. 510, decided by a unanimous vote, March 7, 1927. Taft wrote the opinion.

The Fourteenth Amendment due process guarantee assures a defendant a trial before an impartial judge. A state, therefore, may not allow a city's mayor to serve as judge in cases, when half the fines collected go into the city treasury. A defendant is denied due process when he is tried before a judge with a direct, personal, pecuniary interest in ruling against him.

Buck v. Bell, 274 U.S. 200, decided by an 8–1 vote, May 2, 1927. Holmes wrote the majority opinion; Butler dissented.

Virginia did not violate the Fourteenth Amendment's due process guarantee when it sterilized, without her consent, a mentally defective mother.

FREEDOM OF ASSOCIATION

Whitney v. California, 274 U.S. 357, decided by a unanimous vote, May 26, 1927. Sanford wrote the opinion.

The Court upheld a state law that made it a crime to organize and participate in a group that advocated the overthrow by force of the established political system. The law was challenged as a violation of the First Amendment freedoms of speech and assembly.

JURY TRIALS

Patton v. United States, 281 U.S. 276, decided by a 7–0 vote, April 14, 1930. Sutherland wrote the opinion; Hughes did not participate.

The three essential elements of a jury trial required in federal courts by the Sixth Amendment are a panel of twelve jurors, supervision by a judge, and a unanimous verdict.

POWERS OF THE PRESIDENT

Myers v. United States, 272 U.S. 52, decided by a 6–3 vote, October 25, 1926. Taft wrote the majority opinion; Holmes, Brandeis, and McReynolds dissented.

This decision upheld the president's power to remove certain postmasters from office without congressional consent. The Court held that the statute creating the positions—which also provided for removal only with congressional consent—was an unconstitutional incursion upon executive power. The Court implied that the removal power was virtually unlimited, extending even to members of independent regulatory agencies.

SEARCH AND SEIZURE

Olmstead v. United States, 277 U.S. 438, decided by a 5–4 vote, June 4, 1928. Taft wrote the majority opinion; Brandeis, Holmes, Butler, and Stone dissented.

Wiretaps do not violate the Fourth Amendment's prohibition against unreasonable searches and seizures where no entry of private premises occurred.

STATE POWERS

Euclid v. Ambler Realty Co., 272 U.S. 365, decided by a 6–3 vote, November 22, 1926. Sutherland wrote the majority opinion; Butler, McReynolds, and Van Devanter dissented.

A city's zoning ordinance excluding apartment houses from certain neighborhoods is an appropriate use of the police power and does not violate due process in denying an individual the right to use his property as he desires. If the classification of land use in a zoning ordinance is "fairly debatable," it will be upheld.

TAXES

J. W. Hampton Jr. & Co. v. United States, 276 U.S. 394, decided by a unanimous vote, April 9, 1928. Taft wrote the opinion.

Imposition of protective tariffs is a permissible exercise of the power to tax, a power that may be used to regulate as well as to raise revenue.

VOTING RIGHTS

Nixon v. Herndon, 273 U.S. 536, decided by a unanimous vote, March 7, 1927. Holmes wrote the opinion.

The Court invalidated a Texas law that excluded blacks from voting in primary elections of the Democratic Party. The Court declared the Texas "white primary" law unconstitutional as a violation of the equal protection clause of the Fourteenth Amendment.

1931–1934

CONTRACTS

Home Building and Loan Assn. v. Blaisdell, 290 U.S. 398, decided by a 5–4 vote, January 8, 1934. Hughes wrote the majority opinion; Sutherland, Van Devanter, Butler, and McReynolds dissented.

The Court upheld an emergency state mortgage moratorium law against challenge that it violated the constitutional ban on state action impairing the obligation of contracts.

FREEDOM OF SPEECH

Stromberg v. California, 283 U.S. 359, decided by a 7–2 vote, May 18, 1931. Hughes wrote the majority opinion; McReynolds and Butler dissented.

A state violates the First Amendment guarantee of free speech when it penalizes persons who raise a red flag as a symbol of opposition to organized government. The Court did not directly address the First Amendment issue in this case but held instead that the language of the statute was impermissibly vague. Although aimed at curbing symbolic speech that advocated the unlawful overthrow of the government, the statute's language conceivably permitted punishment for the flying of any banner symbolizing advocacy of a change in government, even through peaceful means.

FREEDOM OF THE PRESS

Near v. Minnesota, 283 U.S. 697, decided by a 5–4 vote, June 1, 1931. Hughes wrote the majority opinion; Butler, Van Devanter, McReynolds, and Sutherland dissented.

A state law that bars continued publication of a newspaper that prints malicious or defamatory articles is a prior restraint of the press in violation of the First Amendment.

This decision marked the first time the Court specifically enforced the First Amendment's guarantee of freedom of the press to strike down a state law because it infringed too far on that freedom.

RIGHT TO COUNSEL

Powell v. Alabama, 287 U.S. 45, decided by a 7–2 vote, November 7, 1932. Sutherland wrote the majority opinion; Butler and McReynolds dissented.

Under the particular circumstances of this, the "First Scottsboro Case," in which a number of young black men charged with raping two white women were tried in a hostile community atmosphere, the failure of the trial court to provide the defendants the effective aid of an attorney for their defense constituted a denial of due process.

STATE POWERS

Nebbia v. New York, 291 U.S. 502, decided by a 5–4 vote, March 5, 1934. Roberts wrote the majority opinion; McReynolds, Butler, Van Devanter, and Sutherland dissented.

The Court abandoned its "public interest" rationale for determining which areas of business were properly subject to state regulation—a line of cases begun in *Munn v. Illinois* (1877).

In this case the Court upheld a New York law that set an acceptable range of prices to be charged for milk. States could regulate almost any business in the interest of the public good, so long as the regulation was reasonable and effected through appropriate means, the Court said.

VOTING RIGHTS

Nixon v. Condon, 286 U.S. 73, decided by a 5–4 vote, May 2, 1932. Cardozo wrote the majority opinion; McReynolds, Butler, Sutherland, and Van Devanter dissented.

Exclusion of blacks from primary elections—as a result of action by the Democratic Party—denies them equal protection of the laws and is impermissible under the Fourteenth Amendment.

The political party, the Court held, acted as the agent of the state when it denied blacks the opportunity to participate in primary elections.

After the Court's decision in *Nixon v. Herndon* (1927), the Texas legislature authorized the state party executive committee to set voting qualifications for its primary, and the party excluded blacks. The Court held this action unconstitutional, saying that neither the state nor political parties could exclude blacks from primaries on the basis of race alone.

Wood v. Broom, 287 U.S. 1, decided by a 5–4 vote, October 18, 1932. Hughes wrote the majority opinion; Brandeis, Stone, Cardozo, and Roberts dissented.

When Congress in the Apportionment Act of 1929 omitted the requirement that electoral districts for congressional elections be contiguous, compact, and equal, it effectively repealed similar requirements in previous laws.

Lacking statutory authority, federal courts therefore could not act to correct malapportionment in state districts.

1935

COMMERCE

Railroad Retirement Board v. Alton Railroad Co., 295 U.S. 330, decided by a 5–4 vote, May 6, 1935. Roberts wrote the majority opinion; Hughes, Brandeis, Cardozo, and Stone dissented.

Congress exceeded its authority when it enacted the Railroad Retirement Act of 1934, which set up a comprehensive pension system for railroad workers, the Court held, invalidating the act. The pension plan was unrelated to interstate commerce, the majority said, and several parts of the act violated the guarantee of due process.

Schechter Poultry Corp. v. United States, 295 U.S. 495, decided by a unanimous vote, May 27, 1935. Hughes wrote the opinion.

Congress exceeded its powers to delegate legislative powers and to regulate interstate commerce when it enacted the National Industrial Recovery Act. The section of the statute that permitted the president to approve "fair competition" codes under certain conditions left the chief executive with too much discretionary power. Furthermore, the statute regulated matters that affected interstate commerce indirectly and so were not within federal power to regulate.

CURRENCY

Norman v. Baltimore and Ohio Railroad Co., 294 U.S. 240, **Nortz v. United States,** 294 U.S. 317, **Perry v. United States,** 294 U.S. 330 **(Gold Clause Cases),** decided by a 5–4 vote, February 18, 1935. Hughes wrote the majority opinion; McReynolds, Butler, Sutherland, and Van Devanter dissented.

The power of Congress to regulate the value of currency permits it to abrogate clauses in private contracts requiring payment in gold. But the federal power to borrow money "on the credit of the United States" prohibits Congress from abrogating such clauses contained in government bonds and other federal contracts.

JURY TRIALS

Norris v. Alabama, 294 U.S. 587, decided by an 8–0 vote, April 1, 1935. Hughes wrote the opinion; McReynolds did not participate.

In the "Second Scottsboro Case," the Court set aside the conviction of the black defendant because blacks had been consistently barred from service on both the grand jury and trial jury in this case.

POWERS OF CONGRESS

Panama Refining Co. v. Ryan, 293 U.S. 388, decided by an 8–1 vote, January 7, 1935. Hughes wrote the majority opinion; Cardozo dissented.

The Court declared invalid a provision of the National Industrial Recovery Act that authorized the president to prohibit from interstate commerce oil produced in violation of state regulations controlling the amount of production. The Court said this congressional delegation of power was unconstitutionally broad, leaving too much to the discretion of the president. This ruling was the first of the Court's decisions striking down New Deal legislation.

POWERS OF THE PRESIDENT

Humphrey's Executor v. United States, 295 U.S. 602, decided by a unanimous vote, May 27, 1935. Sutherland wrote the opinion.

The Court denied the president the power to remove members of independent regulatory agencies without the consent of Congress and limited sharply the executive removal power given such broad scope in *Myers v. United States* (1926).

VOTING RIGHTS

Grovey v. Townsend, 295 U.S. 45, decided by a unanimous vote, April 1, 1935. Roberts wrote the opinion.

The Texas Democratic Party did not violate the Fourteenth Amendment by deciding to confine membership in the party to white citizens. A political party was a private organization, the Court ruled, and the Fourteenth Amendment's guarantee did not reach private action. (See *Nixon v. Herndon,* 1927; *Nixon v. Condon,* 1932.)

1936

DUE PROCESS

Brown v. Mississippi, 297 U.S. 278, decided by a unanimous Court, February 17, 1936. Hughes wrote the opinion.

States may not use coerced confessions as evidence at the trial of persons from whom the confessions were obtained by torture. Use of a person's involuntary statements to convict him is a clear denial of due process of law.

Morehead v. New York ex rel. Tipaldo, 298 U.S. 587, decided by a 5–4 vote, June 1, 1936. Butler wrote the majority opinion; Hughes, Brandeis, Cardozo, and Stone dissented.

The Court struck down a New York minimum wage law for women and children workers, declaring all minimum wage laws a violation of due process. The decision was overruled the following year with *West Coast Hotel Co. v. Parrish.*

FREE PRESS

Grosjean v. American Press Co., 297 U.S. 233, decided by a unanimous vote, February 10, 1936. Sutherland wrote the opinion.

A state law that taxes the gross receipts of certain newspapers and not others is a prior restraint on the press in violation of the First Amendment. Although labeled a tax on the privilege of doing business, the law had actually been written so that the tax fell only on those newspapers that opposed the governor.

POWERS OF CONGRESS

Ashwander v. Tennessee Valley Authority, 297 U.S. 288, decided by votes of 8–1 and 5–4, February 17, 1936. Hughes wrote the majority opinion; McReynolds, Brandeis, Stone, Roberts, and Cardozo dissented in part.

The Court implicitly upheld the statute authorizing the establishment of the Tennessee Valley Authority. It sustained the authority of the TVA to enter into a contract for the sale of the excess energy generated by a TVA-operated dam. Construction of the dam was within the federal power to defend the nation and improve navigation, the Court said. The Constitution gave the federal government unfettered power to dispose of government property.

This statute was one of only two major early New Deal laws declared valid by the Court.

Carter v. Carter Coal Co., 298 U.S. 238, decided by a 6–3 vote, May 18, 1936. Sutherland wrote the majority opinion; Hughes wrote a separate opinion; Cardozo, Brandeis, and Stone dissented.

Striking down the Bituminous Coal Conservation Act of 1935, the Court found that Congress had unconstitutionally delegated its legislative powers to private parties in that statute when it allowed a majority of coal mine operators to set mandatory wage and hours standards for the entire coal industry.

The Court also held unconstitutional those provisions giving miners collective bargaining rights. Such labor relations were local in nature and not subject to regulation by Congress under its interstate commerce powers.

POWERS OF THE PRESIDENT

United States v. Curtiss-Wright Export Corp., 299 U.S. 304, decided by a 7–1 vote, December 21, 1936. Sutherland wrote the majority opinion; McReynolds dissented; Stone did not participate.

The Court upheld an act of Congress authorizing the president, at his discretion, to embargo arms shipments to foreign belligerents in a South American war.

The plenary nature of the federal government's power over foreign affairs permitted Congress greater latitude in delegating power to the president in international relations than in internal matters. Sutherland described the power of the president in foreign affairs as "plenary and exclusive." The president is "the sole organ of the federal government in the field of international relations."

SPENDING POWER

United States v. Butler, 297 U.S. 1, decided by a 6–3 vote, January 6, 1936. Roberts wrote the majority opinion; Stone, Brandeis, and Cardozo dissented.

In its first interpretation of Congress's power to spend for the general welfare, the Court held that Congress could not combine that power with the power to tax in order to regulate a matter that was outside the scope of federal authority—in this instance, agricultural production.

The ruling declared unconstitutional the Agricultural Adjustment Act of 1933, which sought to regulate agricultural production by taxing processors of basic food commodities and then using the revenue from that tax to pay benefits to farmers who reduced their production of those commodities.

1937

COMMERCE

National Labor Relations Board v. Jones & Laughlin Steel Corp., 301 U.S. 1, decided by a 5–4 vote, April 12, 1937. Hughes wrote the majority opinion; McReynolds, Butler, Sutherland, and Van Devanter dissented.

The federal power to regulate interstate commerce permits Congress to regulate intrastate matters that directly burden or obstruct interstate commerce. In this case, the Court found that a dispute between management and labor that threatened to close down a Pennsylvania steel factory directly affected interstate commerce because the factory was in a stream of commerce.

This decision, in which the Court finally abandoned its narrow view of the federal power to regulate interstate commerce, sustained the constitutionality of the National Labor Relations Act of 1935.

DUE PROCESS

West Coast Hotel Co. v. Parrish, 300 U.S. 379, decided by a 5–4 vote, March 29, 1937. Hughes wrote the majority opinion; Butler, McReynolds, Sutherland, and Van Devanter dissented.

The Court upheld Washington State's law setting minimum wages for women and children workers. The Court overruled *Adkins v. Children's Hospital* (1923) in which it had declared minimum wage laws to be in violation of freedom of contract, and *Morehead v. Tipaldo* (1936).

Palko v. Connecticut, 302 U.S. 319, decided by an 8–1 vote, December 6, 1937. Cardozo wrote the majority opinion; Butler dissented.

The due process clause of the Fourteenth Amendment does not require states to observe the double jeopardy guarantee of the Fifth Amendment. The promise that an individual will not be tried twice for the same crime is "not of the very essence of a scheme of ordered liberty," and therefore due process does not mandate its application to the states.

FREEDOM OF ASSEMBLY

DeJonge v. Oregon, 299 U.S. 353, decided by an 8–0 vote, January 4, 1937. Hughes wrote the opinion; Stone did not participate.

The First Amendment guarantee of the freedom of assembly prohibits a state from making it a crime to organize and participate in a meeting at which no illegal action was discussed, even if the meeting was held under the auspices of an association that had as its goal the forcible overthrow of the government.

For the first time, the Court recognized that the right of assembly was on an equal footing with the rights of free speech and free press and that the First Amendment guarantee of freedom of assembly was applicable to the states through the due process clause of the Fourteenth Amendment.

SPENDING POWER

Steward Machine Co. v. Davis, 301 U.S. 548, decided by a 5–4 vote, May 24, 1937. Cardozo wrote the majority opinion; McReynolds, Butler, Sutherland, and Van Devanter dissented.

A system to induce employers to participate in the federal unemployment compensation program by taxing them and then giving those who participate a tax credit is a valid exercise of the taxing and spending powers to regulate interstate commerce. While not in commerce, employment affects commerce and therefore falls within the reach of federal regulation.

Helvering v. Davis, 301 U.S. 619, decided by a 7–2 vote, May 24, 1937. Cardozo wrote the majority opinion; McReynolds and Butler dissented.

Effectively overturning its ruling in *United States v. Butler* (1936), the Court sustained the Social Security Act of 1935. This statute placed a tax on employees and employers, the revenue from which was used to pay benefits to retired employees. Such a program was an appropriate combination of the power to tax and the power to spend for the general welfare, the Court said.

VOTING RIGHTS

Breedlove v. Suttles, 302 U.S. 277, decided by a unanimous vote, December 6, 1937. Butler wrote the opinion.

The Court upheld a Georgia law that required all inhabitants of the state between the ages of twenty-one and sixty to pay an annual poll tax of $1.00. Under the state constitution payment of the tax was a prerequisite to voting in any election. The Court ruled that the tax did not constitute denial of equal protection in violation of the Fourteenth Amendment, nor did it violate the Fifteenth Amendment ban on racial discrimination in voting.

1938

CIVIL RIGHTS

Missouri ex rel. Gaines v. Canada, 305 U.S. 337, decided by a 6–2 vote, December 12, 1938. Hughes wrote the majority opinion; McReynolds and Butler dissented.

A state denies equal protection of the laws to a black student when it refuses him admission to its all-white law school, even though it volunteers to pay his tuition at any law school in an adjacent state. By providing a law school for whites but not for blacks the state has created a privilege for one race and denied it to another.

This decision was the first in a series that culminated in abandonment of the "separate but equal" doctrine of *Plessy v. Ferguson* (1896).

FREEDOM OF THE PRESS

Lovell v. City of Griffin, 303 U.S. 444, decided by an 8–0 vote, March 28, 1938. Hughes wrote the opinion; Cardozo did not participate.

A city ordinance that prohibits circulation on public streets of handbills or literature of any kind without written permission from the city manager is an unconstitutional prior restraint on freedom of the press. (In subsequent cases, the Court said that a city could regulate the manner of distributing handbills.)

RIGHT TO COUNSEL

Johnson v. Zerbst, 304 U.S. 458, decided by a 6–2 vote, May 23, 1938. Black wrote the majority opinion; McReynolds and Butler dissented; Cardozo did not participate.

The Sixth Amendment guarantee that in "all criminal prosecutions, the accused shall enjoy the right . . . to have the Assistance of Counsel for his defence" means that federal courts may not deprive anyone of liberty or life unless he has been provided the aid of an attorney at his trial or has explicitly waived his right to that aid.

1939

COMMERCE

Mulford v. Smith, 307 U.S. 38, decided by a 7–2 vote, April 17, 1939. Roberts wrote the majority opinion; Butler and McReynolds dissented.

Congress has authority to limit the amount of any commodity shipped in interstate commerce. The imposition of marketing quotas on certain agricultural commodities is valid; such quotas are at the "throat" of interstate commerce.

The Court sustained the validity of the second agricultural adjustment act against challenge that the marketing quotas limited production, an area which Congress had no authority to regulate.

FEDERAL COURTS

Coleman v. Miller, 307 U.S. 433, decided by a 7–2 vote, June 5, 1939. Hughes wrote the majority opinion; Butler and McReynolds dissented.

It is up to Congress, not the Court, to resolve political questions such as, what is a "reasonable" time period for the ratification by states of proposed constitutional amendments and whether a state that has rejected a constitutional amendment may later reverse itself and ratify the amendment.

FREEDOM OF ASSEMBLY

Hague v. Congress of Industrial Organizations, 307 U.S. 496, decided by a 5–2 vote, June 5, 1939. There was no Court opinion; Roberts, Stone, and Hughes wrote separate concurring opinions; McReynolds and Butler dissented; Frankfurter and Douglas did not participate.

The right to speak and assemble in public may not be arbitrarily prohibited by federal, state, or local governments. Three members of the majority found this right to be a privilege and immunity of national citizenship; two justices found it implicit in the personal liberty protected by the Fourteenth Amendment's due process clause. This latter, broader view, which secured the right to all persons, not just citizens, was eventually accepted by a majority of the Court's members.

TAXES

Graves v. New York ex rel. O'Keefe, 306 U.S. 466, decided by a 7–2 vote, March 27, 1939. Stone wrote the Court's opinion; Butler and McReynolds dissented.

The Court specifically overruled two earlier decisions, *Collector v. Day* (1871) and *Dobbins v. Erie County* (1842), that held that the income of state and federal government employees was immune from taxation by the nonemploying governing body. *Graves* led to the demise of most intergovernmental tax immunities.

VOTING RIGHTS

Lane v. Wilson, 307 U.S. 268, decided by a 6–2 vote, May 22, 1939. Frankfurter wrote the majority opinion; McReynolds and Butler dissented; Douglas did not participate.

In ***Guinn v. United States*** (1915) the Court had held unconstitutional an Oklahoma "grandfather clause" exemption to a literacy test requirement for voters. The state legislature then adopted a second voting registration law that exempted from registration all those who had voted in the 1914 election, conducted while the "grandfather clause" was still in effect. The new law required all other potential voters to register within a two-week period. The Supreme Court held the second law invalid as a violation of the Fifteenth Amendment ban on racial discrimination in voting.

1940

FREEDOM OF RELIGION

Cantwell v. Connecticut, 310 U.S. 296, decided by a unanimous vote, May 20, 1940. Roberts wrote the opinion.

States may limit the free exercise of religion only by statutes that are narrowly drawn and applied in a nondiscriminatory manner. Therefore, a state may not convict a sidewalk preacher for breach of the peace under a general ordinance which sweeps in "a great variety of conduct under a general and indefinite characterization" and leaves too much discretion to the officials applying it. Furthermore, such activity may not be penalized under a general breach of the peace statute if there is no evidence that this speech, although insulting to some religions, caused any disturbance or threatened any "clear and present menace to public peace."

Likewise, a state statute that requires persons who wish to solicit for religious causes to obtain permits, but allows state officials discretion in determining which causes are religious is arbitrary and therefore violates the First Amendment guarantee of the free exercise of religion.

This case was the first in which the Court specifically applied the First Amendment's guarantee of free exercise of religion against state action.

Minersville School District v. Gobitis, 310 U.S. 586, decided by an 8–1 vote, June 3, 1940. Frankfurter wrote the majority opinion; Stone dissented.

In this first "flag-salute" case, the Court sustained a state law requiring all school children to pledge allegiance to the U.S. flag. The requirement had been challenged by Jehovah's Witnesses, for whom the pledge conflicted with their religious beliefs. They argued that the compulsory pledge violated their First Amendment freedom of religion.

Religious liberty must give way to political authority so long as that authority is not used directly to promote or restrict religion, the Court said. The "mere possession of religious convictions . . . does not relieve the citizen from the discharge of political responsibilities."

In 1943 the Court reversed this decision with its ruling in *West Virginia State Board of Education v. Barnette.*

TAXES

Sunshine Anthracite Coal Co. v. Adkins, 310 U.S. 381, decided by an 8–1 vote, May 20, 1940. Douglas wrote the majority opinion; McReynolds dissented.

The use of the tax power as a penalty is an appropriate means for Congress to employ in regulating interstate commerce. The Court upheld the second coal conservation act, which placed a high tax on coal sold in interstate commerce but exempted from payment those producers who agreed to abide by industry price and competition regulations.

1941

COMMERCE

United States v. Darby Lumber Co., 312 U.S. 100, decided by a unanimous vote, February 3, 1941. Stone wrote the opinion.

Congress has authority to prohibit the shipment in interstate commerce of any goods manufactured in violation of federally established minimum wage and maximum hours standards. This decision overruled *Hammer v. Dagenhart* (1918), in which the Court held that Congress had no power to prohibit the shipment in interstate commerce of goods made by children.

Edwards v. California, 314 U.S. 160, decided by a unanimous vote, November 24, 1941. Byrnes wrote the opinion.

A state impermissibly obstructs interstate commerce when it penalizes persons who bring indigent persons into the state to reside there. The Court in this ruling struck down California's "anti-Okie" law.

In a concurring opinion, four justices held the right to travel to be one of the privileges and immunities of national citizenship protected by the Fourteenth Amendment from abridgment by the states.

FREEDOM OF ASSEMBLY

Cox v. New Hampshire, 312 U.S. 569, decided by a unanimous vote, March 31, 1941. Hughes wrote the Court's opinion.

The First Amendment guarantees of free speech and assembly do not bar states from setting the time, place, and manner of parades on public streets so that they do not interfere unduly with other use of the streets. Such ordinances must be precisely drawn and applied in a nondiscriminatory fashion.

VOTING RIGHTS

United States v. Classic, 313 U.S. 299, decided by a 5–3 vote, May 26, 1941. Stone wrote the majority opinion; Black, Murphy, and Douglas dissented. Hughes did not participate.

Congress has the power to regulate primary elections when the primary is an integral part of the process of selecting candidates for federal office.

This decision overruled *Newberry v. United States* (1921), which had limited congressional regulation to general elections.

1942

COMMERCE

Wickard v. Filburn, 317 U.S. 111, decided by a unanimous vote, November 9, 1942. Jackson wrote the opinion.

The federal power to prevent burdens on interstate commerce permits the federal government to regulate matters that are neither interstate nor commerce. The Court made this point in sustaining a penalty levied against a farmer who had produced for his own consumption more wheat than he was allotted under the 1938 Agricultural Adjustment Act. The Court held that Congress had the power to prevent homegrown wheat from competing with wheat sold in interstate commerce.

This decision is regarded as the high point in the Court's broad interpretation of federal regulatory powers authorized under the interstate commerce clause of the Constitution.

EQUAL PROTECTION

Skinner v. Oklahoma, 316 U.S. 535, decided by a unanimous vote, June 1, 1942. Douglas wrote the opinion.

A state law that provides for involuntary sterilization of certain felons violates the equal protection clause of the Fourteenth Amendment because it does not treat all persons convicted of the same crime in the same manner.

This decision was the first recognition by the Court that individuals have certain constitutionally protected "fundamental interests"— in this case, procreation—with which a state may interfere only if it shows a compelling need.

FREEDOM OF SPEECH

Chaplinsky v. New Hampshire, 315 U.S. 568, decided by a unanimous vote, March 9, 1942. Murphy wrote the opinion.

A state does not violate the First Amendment by enacting a precisely drawn and narrowly applied law making it a crime to use, in public, "fighting words"—words so insulting as to provoke violence from the person to whom they are directed. Fighting words, the lewd and obscene, profanity, and libelous statements are among the classes of speech that have so little value in advancing thought or ideas that they fall outside the protection of the First Amendment guarantees of freedom of speech and press.

RIGHT TO COUNSEL

Betts v. Brady, 316 U.S. 455, decided by a 6–3 vote, June 1, 1942. Roberts wrote the majority opinion; Black, Douglas, and Murphy dissented.

The Fourteenth Amendment's due process clause does not require states to supply defense counsel to defendants too poor to employ their own attorney.

This decision was overturned by *Gideon v. Wainwright* in 1963.

WAR POWERS

Ex parte Quirin, 317 U.S. 1, decided by a unanimous vote, July 31, 1942. Stone wrote the opinion; Murphy did not participate.

The Supreme Court upheld the conviction of seven Nazi saboteurs by a presidentially established military commission, instead of by a civilian jury. Congress had already provided for the trial of spies by military commission, and the acts charged against the saboteurs were acts of war. The guarantee of jury trial under the Sixth Amendment applies to civilian—not military—courts.

This decision firmly established the power of civil courts to review the jurisdiction of presidential military commissions.

1943

DUE PROCESS

McNabb v. United States, 318 U.S. 332, decided by a 7–1 vote, March 1, 1943. Frankfurter wrote the majority opinion; Reed dissented; Rutledge did not participate.

A person accused of a federal crime must be taken before a judicial officer for arraignment without delay after arrest.

FREEDOM OF RELIGION

Murdock v. Pennsylvania, 319 U.S. 105, decided by a 5–4 vote, May 3, 1943. Douglas wrote the majority opinion; Reed, Frankfurter, Roberts, and Jackson dissented.

A city ordinance that requires licenses for all persons taking orders for or delivering goods door-to-door and imposes a daily tax of $1.50 on the privilege is unconstitutional when applied to Jehovah's Witnesses who go from house to house soliciting new members and selling religious literature. "A state may not impose a charge for the enjoyment of a right granted by the federal Constitution," the majority said.

This decision overruled that of the previous year in *Jones v. Opelika,* 316 U.S. 584 (1942), in which the Court upheld such license fees as applied to Jehovah's Witnesses on the grounds that these activities were primarily commercial and so outside the protection of the First Amendment.

West Virginia State Board of Education v. Barnette, 319 U.S. 624, decided by a 6–3 vote, June 14, 1943. Jackson wrote the majority opinion; Roberts, Reed, and Frankfurter dissented.

The First Amendment guarantee of the free exercise of religion protects the right of persons to remain silent and forbids the government to compel them to participate in a symbolic display of patriotic unity that conflicts with their religious beliefs.

The Court upheld the right of Jehovah's Witnesses' children to refuse to participate in compulsory flag salute ceremonies in public schools. The decision overruled *Minersville School District v. Gobitis* (1940).

WAR POWERS

Hirabayashi v. United States, 320 U.S. 81, decided by a unanimous vote, June 21, 1943. Stone wrote the Court's opinion.

The Court upheld the wartime curfew law placed on Japanese-Americans living on the West Coast as an appropriate exercise by the president and Congress of the federal war powers.

The curfew law, by making a classification based solely on race, did not violate the Fifth Amendment. In this instance, consideration of race was relevant to the national security.

1944

COMMERCE

United States v. South-Eastern Underwriters Assn., 322 U.S. 533, decided by a 4–3 vote, June 5, 1944. Black wrote the majority opinion;

Stone and Frankfurter dissented; Jackson dissented in part; Roberts and Reed did not participate.

Insurance transactions are matters in interstate commerce subject to regulation under the federal antitrust act.

This ruling overturned a long line of decisions, beginning in 1869, that held that purely financial and contractual transactions, such as insurance, were not in commerce, even if they involved parties in different states, and were therefore not subject to federal regulation.

Because this ruling called into question the validity of all state insurance regulations, Congress quickly passed a statute permitting states to continue to regulate insurance. The Court upheld that statute in *Prudential Insurance Co. v. Benjamin,* 328 U.S. 408 (1946).

POWERS OF CONGRESS

Yakus v. United States, 321 U.S. 414, decided by a 6–3 vote, March 27, 1944. Stone wrote the majority opinion; Roberts, Murphy, and Rutledge dissented.

The Court sustained portions of the Emergency Price Control Act of 1942 giving the federal price administrator discretionary power to enforce the act, including the maximum prices set under it. The law was challenged as an unconstitutional delegation of legislative power. The Court held that the standards for decisions under the law were "sufficiently definite and precise" and said it was "unable to find in them an unauthorized delegation of legislative power."

VOTING RIGHTS

Smith v. Allwright, 321 U.S. 649, decided by an 8–1 vote, April 3, 1944. Reed wrote the majority opinion; Roberts dissented.

When party primaries are part of the machinery for choosing state and national officials, the action of any political party to exclude blacks from voting in primaries is "state action" within the prohibitions of the Fourteenth and Fifteenth Amendments. This ruling reversed *Grovey v. Townsend* (1935).

WAR POWERS

Korematsu v. United States, 323 U.S. 214, decided by a 6–3 vote, December 18, 1944. Black wrote the majority opinion; Roberts, Murphy, and Jackson dissented.

The Court upheld the removal of Japanese-Americans to relocation centers at inland camps away from the West Coast. It held that the removal program was within the combined war powers of the president and Congress.

In this case, for the first time, a majority of the Court said it would give classifications by race increased attention to ensure that racial antagonism did not lie at the base of the classification. In this instance, however, the Court held that military necessity warranted the racial classification.

1946

BILLS OF ATTAINDER

United States v. Lovett, 328 U.S. 303, decided by an 8–0 vote, June 3, 1946. Black wrote the Court's opinion; Jackson did not participate.

Congress violated the ban on bills of attainder by passing a section of an appropriations law that prohibited payment of salaries to three specifically named federal employees until they were reappointed and reconfirmed to their positions.

CIVIL RIGHTS

Morgan v. Virginia, 328 U.S. 373, decided by a 7–1 vote, June 3, 1946. Reed wrote the Court's opinion; Burton dissented; Jackson did not participate.

A state law requiring segregated seating on interstate buses is an unconstitutional burden on interstate commerce. Where interstate commerce is involved, bus seating requires uniform national rules; otherwise the constant shifting of seats and rearrangement demanded by various state laws will burden interstate commerce.

FREEDOM OF RELIGION

Girouard v. United States, 328 U.S. 61, decided by a 5–3 vote, April 22, 1946. Douglas wrote the majority opinion; Stone, Reed, and Frankfurter dissented; Jackson did not participate.

The oath that persons must swear to become naturalized citizens does not expressly require them to swear to bear arms in defense of the United States. Therefore, a person who meets all other qualifications for naturalization should not be barred from citizenship because he is unwilling to bear arms, an activity that conflicts with his religious beliefs.

This decision overturned three earlier rulings in which the Court had interpreted the naturalization oath to require a willingness to bear arms. The decisions had barred from citizenship two women, who would not have been required to serve in the armed forces in any event, and a fifty-four-year-old divinity school professor unlikely to be called for duty because of his age.

VOTING RIGHTS

Colegrove v. Green, 328 U.S. 549, decided by a 4–3 vote, June 10, 1946. Frankfurter wrote the majority opinion; Black, Douglas, and Murphy dissented; Jackson did not participate.

The Court declined to compel the rural-dominated Illinois legislature to redraw congressional districts. The districts had not been reconfigured since 1901, resulting in population disparities of as much as nine to one between rural and urban regions within the state. The Court said this matter was a political question beyond judicial power to resolve.

1947

CONTEMPT

United States v. United Mine Workers, 330 U.S. 258, decided by a divided Court, March 6, 1947. Vinson wrote the majority opinion; Murphy and Rutledge dissented; Black, Frankfurter, Douglas, and Jackson dissented in part.

The same action may constitute civil and criminal contempt. The justices upheld the conviction of the United Mine Workers of America and its president, John L. Lewis, for both types of contempt for failure to obey a court order forbidding a strike.

CRUEL AND UNUSUAL PUNISHMENT

Louisiana ex rel. Francis v. Resweber, 329 U.S. 459, decided by a 5–4 vote, January 13, 1947. Reed wrote the majority opinion; Burton, Douglas, Murphy, and Rutledge dissented.

Assuming without argument that the Eighth Amendment ban on cruel and unusual punishment applied to state as well as federal actions, the Court nevertheless held that this ban was not violated by the state's execution of a man whose first execution attempt failed because the electric chair did not work.

FREEDOM OF RELIGION

Everson v. Board of Education of Ewing Township, 330 U.S. 1, decided by a 5–4 vote, February 10, 1947. Black wrote the majority opinion; Jackson, Frankfurter, Rutledge, and Burton dissented.

State reimbursement of parents for the cost of transporting their children to parochial schools does not violate the First Amendment clause barring government establishment of religion. Such reimbursements aid parents and children, not the church-affiliated schools.

This decision was the first in which the Court specifically applied the First Amendment's establishment clause to state action.

JURY TRIALS

Fay v. New York, 332 U.S. 261, decided by a 5–4 vote, June 23, 1947. Jackson wrote the majority opinion; Murphy, Black, Douglas, and Rutledge dissented.

The Court upheld New York's "blue ribbon" jury system saying that panels of specially qualified jurors disproportionately representing upper economic and social strata were not deliberately discriminatory and did not violate the Constitution.

OFFSHORE LANDS

United States v. California, 332 U.S. 19, decided by a 6–2 vote, June 23, 1947. Black wrote the majority opinion; Frankfurter and Reed dissented; Jackson did not participate.

The federal government, not the states, owns the tidelands immediately adjacent to the states and the oil therein. The Court reaffirmed this ruling in two subsequent cases, but then sustained—as an exercise of Congress's unrestricted power to dispose of government property—an act of Congress giving coastal states rights to the tidelands oil (*Alabama v. Texas,* 347 U.S. 272, 1954).

POWERS OF CONGRESS

United Public Workers v. Mitchell, 330 U.S. 75, decided by a 4–3 vote, February 10, 1947. Reed wrote the majority opinion; Black, Douglas, and Rutledge dissented; Murphy and Jackson did not participate.

The Court sustained the 1939 Hatch Act, upholding the power of Congress to impose limitations on the political activity of government employees.

1948

EQUAL PROTECTION

Shelley v. Kraemer, 334 U.S. 1, decided by a 6–0 vote, May 3, 1948. Vinson wrote the opinion; Reed, Jackson, and Rutledge did not participate.

The Fourteenth Amendment does not bar private parties from entering into racially restrictive covenants, which exclude blacks from buying or renting homes in "covenanted" neighborhoods, but it does prohibit state courts from enforcing such covenants. Such enforcement constitutes state action denying equal protection of the laws.

FREEDOM OF RELIGION

Illinois ex rel. McCollum v. Board of Education, 333 U.S. 203, decided by an 8–1 vote, March 8, 1948. Black wrote the majority opinion; Reed dissented.

The First Amendment clause barring establishment of religion is violated by a voluntary "released time" program in which religious instruction is given to public school students in the public school during school time.

The Court in 1952 sustained a released time program in which students left the school premises to receive religious instruction (*Zorach v. Clauson,* 343 U.S. 306).

1949

FREEDOM OF SPEECH

Terminiello v. Chicago, 337 U.S. 1, decided by a 5–4 vote, May 16, 1949. Douglas wrote the majority opinion; Vinson, Frankfurter, Jackson, and Burton dissented.

The Court reversed the conviction, for breach of the peace, of a speaker whose remarks in a meeting hall provoked a near-riot among protesters gathered outside.

Without deciding whether the First Amendment guarantee of free speech protected such inciteful speech, the majority held that the trial court's definition of breach of the peace was so broad that it included speech that was clearly protected by the First Amendment.

SEARCH AND SEIZURE

Wolf v. Colorado, 338 U.S. 25, decided by a 6–3 vote, June 27, 1949. Frankfurter wrote the majority opinion; Douglas, Murphy, and Rutledge dissented.

The Fourth Amendment protection of individuals against unreasonable searches and seizures by government agents applies against searches by state, as well as federal, agents.

State judges, however, are not required to exclude from use evidence obtained by searches in violation of this guarantee.

1950

CIVIL RIGHTS

Sweatt v. Painter, 339 U.S. 629, decided by a unanimous vote, June 5, 1950. Vinson wrote the opinion.

A state may not deny admission to its law school to a black even if there is a "black" law school available. The Court found the facilities of the "black" school inferior to those provided by the "white" school, therefore violating the "separate but equal" doctrine.

McLaurin v. Oklahoma State Regents for Higher Education, 339 U.S. 637, decided by a unanimous vote, June 5, 1950. Vinson wrote the opinion.

Going beyond *Sweatt* and eroding the "separate but equal" doctrine even more, the Court ruled that once a black was admitted to a state university, the state could not deny him the right to use all its facilities, including the library, lunchroom, and classrooms.

FREEDOM OF ASSOCIATION

American Communications Assn. v. Douds, 339 U.S. 382, decided by a 5–1 vote, May 8, 1950. Vinson wrote the majority opinion; Black dissented. Douglas, Clark, and Minton did not participate.

The Taft-Hartley Act can properly require each officer of a labor union to file an affidavit swearing that he was not a member of or affiliated with the Communist Party. The Court held that Congress could properly impose this requirement as part of its power to prevent political strikes obstructing interstate commerce.

SEARCH AND SEIZURE

United States v. Rabinowitz, 339 U.S. 56, decided by a 5–3 vote, February 20, 1950. Minton wrote the majority opinion; Frankfurter, Jackson, and Black dissented; Douglas did not participate.

The Fourth Amendment guarantee of security against unreasonable searches permits a warrantless search, incident to a lawful arrest, of the person arrested and the premises where the arrest occurs.

1951

EXCESSIVE BAIL

Stack v. Boyle, 342 U.S. 1, decided by an 8–0 vote, November 5, 1951. Vinson wrote the opinion; Minton did not participate.

The amount of bail required of twelve Communist Party leaders prosecuted under the Smith Act of 1940 was excessive and violated the Eighth Amendment's prohibition of excessive bail.

FREEDOM OF ASSOCIATION

Joint Anti-Fascist Refugee Committee v. McGrath, 341 U.S. 123, decided by a 5–3 vote, April 30, 1951. Burton wrote the majority opinion; Vinson, Reed, and Minton dissented; Clark did not participate.

The attorney general has the power to prepare and distribute a list of subversive organizations to aid the work of the federal Loyalty Review Board. But, the Court ruled, to list an organization without affording it a hearing violated the organization's constitutional rights.

Garner v. Board of Public Works, 341 U.S. 716, decided by a 5–4 vote, June 4, 1951. Clark wrote the majority opinion; Burton, Frankfurter, Black, and Douglas dissented.

A loyalty oath for public employees was not a denial of due process or invalid as a bill of attainder or an ex post facto law.

FREEDOM OF SPEECH

Kunz v. New York, 340 U.S. 290, decided by an 8–1 vote, January 15, 1951. Vinson wrote the majority opinion; Jackson dissented.

A New York City ordinance that barred worship services on public streets without a permit is an unconstitutional prior restraint on the exercise of the First Amendment rights of free speech and free exercise of religion.

Feiner v. New York, 340 U.S. 315, decided by a 6–3 vote, January 15, 1951. Vinson wrote the majority opinion; Black, Douglas, and Minton dissented.

The First Amendment is not violated by the conviction, for breach of the peace, of a street speaker who refused to stop speaking after police asked him to desist. The police had acted not to suppress speech but to preserve public order, a legitimate reason for limiting speech.

This decision, read with the decisions in *Terminiello v. Chicago* (1949) and *Kunz v. New York* (1951) demonstrate the Court's difficulty in defining precisely the circumstances in which a state might properly curtail free speech.

Dennis v. United States, 341 U.S. 494, decided by a 6–2 vote, June 4, 1951. Vinson wrote the majority opinion; Black and Douglas dissented; Clark did not participate.

Convictions under the Smith Act of 1940 for speaking and teaching about communist theory advocating forcible overthrow of the government do not abridge First Amendment rights.

1952

EXCESSIVE BAIL

Carlson v. Landon, 342 U.S. 524, decided by a 5–4 vote, March 10, 1952. Reed wrote the majority opinion; Black, Frankfurter, Burton, and Douglas dissented.

Five alien members of the Communist Party could be detained without bail pending the outcome of deportation proceedings. Denial of bail was justified because deportation was not a criminal proceeding.

POWERS OF THE PRESIDENT

Youngstown Sheet and Tube Co. v. Sawyer (Steel Seizure Case), 343 U.S. 579, decided by a 6–3 vote, June 2, 1952. Black wrote the majority opinion; Vinson, Reed, and Minton dissented.

President Truman exceeded his power in seizing the nation's steel mills to prevent a strike. The president had based the seizure order on his general powers as commander in chief and chief executive. But the Court held he could not take such action without express authorization from Congress.

SEARCH AND SEIZURE

Rochin v. California, 342 U.S. 165, decided by an 8–0 vote, January 2, 1952. Frankfurter wrote the opinion; Minton did not participate.

State police officers who used a stomach pump to obtain evidence of drugs—which a suspect had swallowed in their presence—violated Fourth Amendment prohibitions against unreasonable searches and seizures.

1953

VOTING RIGHTS

Terry v. Adams, 345 U.S. 461, decided by an 8–1 vote, May 4, 1953. Black wrote the majority opinion; Minton dissented.

The all-white Texas Jaybird Party primary, held before the regular Democratic Party primary, whose winners usually then won the Democratic nomination and election to county offices, is unconstitutional. It was an integral part of the election process and the exclusion of blacks from this primary violated the Fifteenth Amendment.

WAR POWERS

Rosenberg v. United States, 346 U.S. 273, decided by a 6–3 vote, June 19, 1953. Vinson wrote the majority opinion; Frankfurter, Black, and Douglas dissented.

The Court, after meeting in special session, lifted a stay of execution for Julius and Ethel Rosenberg, convicted of violating the Espionage Act of 1917 and sentenced to death.

Justice Douglas had granted the stay so that lower courts might consider the argument of the Rosenbergs' attorney that the espionage act had been repealed by subsequent passage of the Atomic Energy Act of 1946. The Rosenbergs were convicted of having conveyed atomic secrets to the Soviet Union. They were executed as soon as the Court lifted the stay.

1954

CIVIL RIGHTS

Brown v. Board of Education of Topeka, 347 U.S. 483, decided by a unanimous vote, May 17, 1954. Warren wrote the opinion.

Separate public schools for black and white students are inherently unequal, and their existence violates the equal protection guarantee of the Fourteenth Amendment.

In the companion case of *Bolling v. Sharpe* (347 U.S. 497), the Court ruled that the congressionally mandated segregated public school system in the District of Columbia violated the Fifth Amendment's due process guarantee of personal liberty.

In *Brown* the Court specifically overruled the "separate but equal" doctrine first enunciated in *Plessy v. Ferguson* (1896) so far as it applied to public schools. The ruling also led to the abolition of state-sponsored segregation in other public facilities.

1955

CIVIL RIGHTS

Brown v. Board of Education of Topeka, 349 U.S. 294, decided by a unanimous vote, May 31, 1955. Warren wrote the opinion.

The Court laid out guidelines for ending segregation in public schools. The Court placed primary responsibility on local school officials, recognizing that local factors would call for different treatment and timing, but admonishing the boards to proceed toward desegregation "with all deliberate speed."

Federal district courts were to retain jurisdiction over school desegregation cases. They could grant school districts additional time to complete desegregation once the process was begun, but the school boards had the burden of justifying such delays.

1956

SELF-INCRIMINATION

Ullmann v. United States, 350 U.S. 422, decided by a 7–2 vote, March 26, 1956. Frankfurter wrote the majority opinion; Douglas and Black dissented.

The Court sustained the Immunity Act of 1950, which provided that witnesses cannot claim their privilege against self-incrimination if the government grants them immunity from prosecution.

Slochower v. Board of Education of New York City, 350 U.S. 551, decided by a 5–4 vote, April 9, 1956. Clark wrote the majority opinion; Reed, Burton, Harlan, and Minton dissented.

The provision of New York City's charter that provided for summary dismissal of employees who invoked the Fifth Amendment privilege against self-incrimination violated the due process guarantee of the Fourteenth Amendment.

STATE POWERS

Pennsylvania v. Nelson, 350 U.S. 497, decided by a 6–3 vote, April 2, 1956. Warren wrote the majority opinion; Reed, Minton, and Burton dissented.

States may not punish persons for seditious activity against the federal government.

Congress has preempted that field by passing federal legislation on that subject.

1957

DUE PROCESS

Mallory v. United States, 354 U.S. 449, decided by a unanimous vote, June 24, 1957. Frankfurter delivered the opinion.

The Court reversed the criminal conviction of a man interrogated without being informed of his constitutional rights and held for an unnecessarily long period between arrest and arraignment. Such practices deprived him of his liberty without due process of law.

FREEDOM OF SPEECH

Yates v. United States, 354 U.S. 298, decided by votes of 6–1 and 4–3, June 17, 1957. Harlan wrote the majority opinion; Clark dissented; Black and Douglas dissented in part; Brennan and Whittaker did not participate.

To prosecute persons for violating the Smith Act by advocating the forcible overthrow of the government, the United States must show active engagement on the part of the defendant—overt acts, not just abstract arguments. The decision made it much more difficult for the government to obtain convictions under the Smith Act.

OBSCENITY

Roth v. United States, Alberts v. California, 354 U.S. 476, decided by votes of 6–3 and 7–2, June 24, 1957. Brennan wrote the majority opinion; Harlan dissented in Roth, but concurred in Alberts; Black and Douglas dissented.

Obscene material is not protected by the First Amendment guarantees of freedom of speech and press. Material is obscene, the Court said, if the average person would consider that its dominant theme appealed to prurient interest.

This definition of obscenity was the first offered by the Court. It was modified in several subsequent decisions and finally replaced with another standard in *Miller v. California* (1973).

POWERS OF CONGRESS

Watkins v. United States, 354 U.S. 178, decided by a 6–1 vote, June 17, 1957. Warren wrote the majority opinion; Clark dissented; Burton and Whittaker did not participate.

Declaring that "there is no congressional power to expose for the sake of exposure," the Court held that congressional investigations may be undertaken only in aid of the legislative function. House and Senate instructions to their investigating committees must therefore fully spell out the investigating committee's purpose and jurisdiction.

Furthermore, a witness may refuse with impunity to answer questions if they are not pertinent to the investigation. "It is the duty of the investigative body, upon objection of the witness on grounds of pertinency, to state . . . the subject under inquiry at the time and the manner in which the propounded questions are pertinent thereto," the majority said.

This reversed the contempt conviction of a labor union officer who answered questions about his own association with the Communist Party but refused to answer similar questions about other people.

1958

CIVIL RIGHTS

Cooper v. Aaron, 358 U.S. 1, decided by a unanimous vote, September 12, 1958. Warren wrote the opinion; each justice personally signed it.

Standing firm against defiance of its 1954 and 1955 decisions declaring public school segregation unconstitutional, the Court refused a request by Little Rock, Arkansas, school officials for a delay in desegregation of their public schools. Local school officials had made the request after Gov. Orval Faubus called out the state national guard to block the entrance to a Little Rock high school to prevent entry by black students. Federal troops were eventually sent to the city to restore order and protect the black students, and the school board asked for delay of further desegregation efforts. The Court convened a special session in late summer of 1958 to hear the case.

In a sharp rebuke to Faubus and state legislators, the Court said that the rights of black children could "neither be nullified openly and directly by state legislators or state executive officials nor nullified indirectly by them by evasive schemes for segregation."

CRUEL AND UNUSUAL PUNISHMENT

Trop v. Dulles, 356 U.S. 86, decided by a 5–4 vote, March 31, 1958. Warren wrote the majority opinion; Frankfurter, Burton, Clark, and Harlan dissented.

The Eighth Amendment ban on cruel and unusual punishment prohibits the use of expatriation or denaturalization as punishment for persons found guilty of desertion from the armed forces in wartime.

FREEDOM OF ASSOCIATION

National Association for the Advancement of Colored People v. Alabama ex rel. Patterson, 357 U.S. 449, decided by a unanimous vote, June 30, 1958. Harlan wrote the opinion.

The freedom to associate with others is implicit in the freedoms of speech and assembly guaranteed by the First Amendment. The right to associate carries with it the right of privacy in that association.

A state court order requiring the NAACP to produce its membership lists is therefore an unconstitutional restraint on NAACP members' right of association. The state did not show a sufficient interest in the disclosure of the lists to justify the limitation such disclosure placed on freedom of association.

PERSONAL LIBERTY

Kent v. Dulles, 357 U.S. 116, decided by a 5–4 vote, June 16, 1958. Douglas wrote the majority opinion; Clark, Harlan, Burton, and Whittaker dissented.

The freedom to travel is part of the personal liberty protected by the due process guarantee of the Fifth and Fourteenth Amendments.

Congress has not authorized the secretary of state to withhold passports from citizens because of their beliefs or associations.

POWERS OF THE PRESIDENT

Wiener v. United States, 357 U.S. 349, decided by a unanimous vote, June 30, 1958. Frankfurter wrote the opinion.

This decision reinforced the "nature of the office" approach to the presidential removal power. The Court held that where the duties of the office included quasi-judicial functions, and, where there was no statutory provision for removal, the president lacked the power to remove an incumbent official from his post simply to replace him with a person of his own choice.

1959

POWERS OF CONGRESS

Barenblatt v. United States, 360 U.S. 109, decided by a 5–4 vote, June 8, 1959. Harlan wrote the majority opinion; Warren, Black, Brennan, and Douglas dissented.

Retreating from *Watkins,* the Court held that the First Amendment rights of witnesses appearing before congressional investigating committees may be limited when the public interest outweighs the private interest.

In this case, the federal government's interest in preserving itself against those who advocated the forceful overthrow of that government outweighed the right of the witness, a teacher, to conduct a classroom discussion on the theoretical nature of communism.

VOTING RIGHTS

Lassiter v. Northampton County Board of Elections, 360 U.S. 45, decided by a unanimous vote, June 8, 1959. Douglas delivered the opinion.

North Carolina can require that all persons must be able to read and write a section of the state constitution in English before being allowed to vote. Such a provision, applied in a nondiscriminatory way, did not violate the Fourteenth, Fifteenth, or Seventeenth Amendments, the Court held.

1960

SEARCH AND SEIZURE

Elkins v. United States, 364 U.S. 206, decided by a 5–4 vote, June 27, 1960. Stewart wrote the majority opinion; Frankfurter, Clark, Harlan, and Whittaker dissented.

The Court abandoned the "silver platter" doctrine that permitted use—in federal court—of evidence illegally seized by state authorities and handed over to federal authority. The Court held that such a practice violated the Fourth Amendment prohibition against unreasonable search and seizure.

VOTING RIGHTS

Gomillion v. Lightfoot, 364 U.S. 339, decided by a unanimous vote, November 14, 1960. Frankfurter wrote the opinion.

It is unconstitutional, a violation of the Fifteenth Amendment guarantee of the right to vote, for a state legislative districting plan to exclude almost all black voters from voting in city elections in Tuskegee, Alabama.

1961

EQUAL PROTECTION

Hoyt v. Florida, 368 U.S. 57, decided by a unanimous vote, November 20, 1961. Harlan wrote the opinion.

States do not violate the equal protection guarantee by generally excluding women from jury duty. The exclusion was rational in light of the state's interest in preventing interference with women's traditional functions as wives, homemakers, and mothers, the Court said.

FREEDOM OF ASSOCIATION

Communist Party v. Subversive Activities Control Board, 367 U.S. 1, decided by a 5–4 vote, June 5, 1961. Frankfurter wrote the majority opinion; Warren, Black, Douglas, and Brennan dissented.

The Court upheld provisions of the Subversive Activities Control Act of 1950 requiring the Communist Party to register with the Justice Department, list its officials, and file financial statements. The Court rejected the party's arguments that the registration provisions were unconstitutional as a bill of attainder and a violation of the First Amendment guarantees of freedom of speech and association.

Scales v. United States, 367 U.S. 203, *Noto v. United States,* 367 U.S. 290, decided by 5–4 votes, June 5, 1961. Harlan wrote the majority opinions; Warren, Black, Douglas, and Brennan dissented.

The First Amendment freedoms of speech and association are not violated by laws providing penalties for active membership in a group specifically intending to bring about the violent overthrow of the government. The Court upheld Scales's conviction, but reversed Noto's, finding insufficient evidence in the latter case to justify the conviction.

SEARCH AND SEIZURE

Mapp v. Ohio, 367 U.S. 643, decided by a 5–4 vote, June 19, 1961. Clark wrote the majority opinion; Stewart, Harlan, Frankfurter, and Whittaker dissented.

Evidence obtained in violation of the Fourth Amendment guarantee against unreasonable search and seizure must be excluded from use at state as well as federal trials. With this decision, the Court overruled *Wolf v. Colorado* (1949).

1962

CRUEL AND UNUSUAL PUNISHMENT

Robinson v. California, 370 U.S. 660, decided by a 6–2 vote, June 25, 1962. Stewart wrote the majority opinion; Clark and White dissented; Frankfurter did not participate.

It is a violation of the Eighth Amendment ban on cruel and unusual punishment for a state to make narcotics addiction a criminal offense.

FREEDOM OF RELIGION

Engel v. Vitale, 370 U.S. 421, decided by a 6–1 vote, June 25, 1962. Black wrote the majority opinion; Stewart dissented; Frankfurter and White did not participate.

Public school officials may not require pupils to recite a state-composed prayer at the beginning of each school day, even though the prayer is denominationally neutral and pupils who so desire may be excused from reciting it.

Official state-sanctioned prayers, the Court held, are unconstitutional attempts by government to establish religion.

VOTING RIGHTS

Baker v. Carr, 369 U.S. 186, decided by a 6–2 vote, March 26, 1962. Brennan wrote the majority opinion; Frankfurter and Harlan dissented; Whittaker did not participate.

The Court for the first time held that constitutional challenges to the maldistribution of voters among legislative districts might properly be resolved by federal courts. The Court rejected the doctrine set out in *Colgrove v. Green* (1946) that all such apportionment challenges were "political questions" beyond the proper reach of the federal courts.

1963

FEDERAL COURTS

Fay v. Noia, 372 U.S. 391, decided by a 6–3 vote, March 18, 1963. Brennan wrote the majority opinion; Harlan, Clark, and Stewart dissented.

In some circumstances, a state prisoner may challenge his imprisonment by obtaining a federal writ of habeas corpus even if he has not appealed his conviction through the state court system.

The requirement that a state prisoner "exhaust" all state remedies before challenging his conviction in federal courts simply means that a state prisoner must have tried all state remedies still available to him at the time he comes into federal court seeking the writ.

FREEDOM OF ASSOCIATION

National Association for the Advancement of Colored People v. Button, 371 U.S. 415, decided by a 6–3 vote, January 14, 1963. Brennan wrote the majority opinion; Harlan, Clark, and Stewart dissented.

A state law, directed against the NAACP, which forbids solicitation of clients by an agent of an organization that litigates cases in which it is not a party and has no pecuniary interest, impermissibly infringes on the First Amendment right of association. "Abstract discussion is not the only species of communication which the Constitution protects; the First Amendment also protects vigorous advocacy, certainly of lawful ends, against government intrusion," the Court wrote.

FREEDOM OF RELIGION

School District of Abington Township v. Schempp, 374 U.S. 203, decided by an 8–1 vote, June 17, 1963. Clark wrote the opinion; Stewart dissented.

State-ordered recitation of the Lord's Prayer and the reading of the Bible in the public school system as a devotional exercise violates the establishment clause.

FREEDOM OF SPEECH

Edwards v. South Carolina, 372 U.S. 229, decided by an 8–1 vote, February 25, 1963. Stewart wrote the majority opinion; Clark dissented.

The Court reversed the breach-of-the-peace convictions of student demonstrators who had marched peacefully to protest racial discrimination. The Court held that the breach-of-the-peace statute was unconstitutionally broad and had been used in this case to penalize the exercise of free speech, assembly, and petition for redress of grievances "in their most pristine and classic form," a clear violation of the First Amendment.

RIGHT TO COUNSEL

Gideon v. Wainwright, 372 U.S. 335, decided by a unanimous vote, March 18, 1963. Black delivered the Court's opinion.

The due process clause of the Fourteenth Amendment extends to state as well as federal defendants the Sixth Amendment guarantee that all persons charged with serious crimes will be provided the aid of an attorney. *Betts v. Brady* (1942) is overruled. States are required to appoint counsel for defendants who can not afford to pay their own attorneys' fees.

SEARCH AND SEIZURE

Ker v. California, 374 U.S. 23, decided by a 5–4 vote, June 10, 1963. Clark wrote the majority opinion; Warren, Brennan, Douglas, and Goldberg dissented in part.

The same standards apply to determine whether federal and state searches and seizures are reasonable and therefore permissible under the Fourth Amendment. (The justices disagreed over whether the warrantless search at issue in this case was reasonable.)

VOTING RIGHTS

Gray v. Sanders, 372 U.S. 368, decided by an 8–1 vote, March 18, 1963. Douglas wrote the majority opinion; Harlan dissented.

Georgia's "county unit" system of electing officers to state posts violates the equal protection guarantee of the Fourteenth Amendment by giving more weight to the votes of people in rural counties than urban counties. The idea of political equality, inherent in the U.S. system, held the Court, "can mean only one thing—one person, one vote."

1964

CIVIL RIGHTS

Griffin v. County School Board of Prince Edward County, 377 U.S. 218, decided by a 7–2 vote, May 25, 1964. Black wrote the majority opinion; Clark and Harlan dissented in part.

Losing patience with state defiance of its school desegregation decisions, the Court declared that there had been "entirely too much deliberation and not enough speed." It was unconstitutional, a violation of the Fourteenth Amendment's equal protection clause, for Prince Edward County, Virginia, to close its schools, to avoid the impact of desegregation.

Heart of Atlanta Motel v. United States, 379 U.S. 241, decided by a unanimous vote, December 14, 1964. Clark wrote the opinion.

The commerce power may be used to prohibit racial discrimination in privately owned public accommodations. This decision effectively overturned the Court's 1883 *Civil Rights Cases* and sustained Title II of the Civil Rights Act of 1964. That section prohibited discrimination, on the basis of race, religion, or national origin, in accommodations that catered to interstate travelers or that served food or provided entertainment, a substantial portion of which was shipped through interstate commerce.

FREEDOM OF ASSOCIATION

Aptheker v. Secretary of State, 378 U.S. 500, decided by a 6–3 vote, June 22, 1964. Goldberg wrote the majority opinion; Clark, Harlan, and White dissented.

The Court declared unconstitutional a section of the Subversive Activities Control Act of 1950 that denied passports—and thus the right to travel—to persons who belonged to organizations listed as subversive by the attorney general. The law was too broad; it failed to distinguish between persons who joined such organizations with the full knowledge of their subversive purpose and persons who joined with less knowledge.

FREEDOM OF THE PRESS

New York Times Co. v. Sullivan, 376 U.S. 254, decided by a unanimous vote, March 9, 1964. Brennan wrote the opinion.

The First Amendment guarantee of freedom of the press protects the press from libel suits for defamatory reports on public officials unless the officials prove that the reports were made with actual malice. Actual malice is defined as "with knowledge that it [the defamatory statement] was false or with reckless disregard of whether it was false or not."

Until this decision, libelous statements were not protected by the First Amendment.

RIGHT TO COUNSEL

Escobedo v. Illinois, 378 U.S. 478, decided by a 5–4 vote, June 22, 1964. Goldberg wrote the majority opinion; Harlan, Stewart, White, and Clark dissented.

The Court expanded a suspect's right to counsel under the Sixth Amendment, holding that confessions obtained by police who had not advised the suspect of his right to counsel—or acceded to his requests for counsel—were inadmissible as evidence.

SELF-INCRIMINATION

Malloy v. Hogan, 378 U.S. 1, decided by a 5–4 vote, June 15, 1964. Brennan wrote the majority opinion; Harlan, Clark, White, and Stewart dissented.

The Fifth Amendment protection against self-incrimination is extended to state defendants through the due process clause of the Fourteenth Amendment.

Murphy v. Waterfront Commission of New York, 378 U.S. 52, decided by a unanimous vote, June 15, 1964. Goldberg wrote the opinion.

The Fifth Amendment privilege against compelled self-incrimination protects witnesses immunized by either state or federal officials from prosecution in either jurisdiction based on their testimony.

VOTING RIGHTS

Wesberry v. Sanders, 376 U.S. 1, decided by a 6–3 vote, February 17, 1964. Black wrote the majority opinion; Clark dissented in part; Harlan and Stewart dissented.

Substantial disparity in the population of congressional districts within a state is unconstitutional, violating the provision for election of members of the House of Representatives "by the people of the several states." Congressional voting districts within a state must be as nearly equal in population as possible.

Reynolds v. Sims, 377 U.S. 533, decided by an 8–1 vote, June 15, 1964. Warren wrote the majority opinion; Harlan dissented.

The equal protection clause of the Fourteenth Amendment requires application of the "one person, one vote" apportionment rule to both houses of a state legislature.

1965

DUE PROCESS

Pointer v. Texas, 380 U.S. 400, decided by a unanimous vote, April 5, 1965. Black wrote the opinion.

The Sixth Amendment guarantee of the right to confront and cross-examine witnesses is applied to state defendants by the Fourteenth Amendment's due process clause.

FEDERAL COURTS

Dombrowski v. Pfister, 380 U.S. 479, decided by a 5–2 vote, April 26, 1965. Brennan wrote the majority opinion; Harlan and Clark dissented; Black and Stewart did not participate.

Federal courts need not abstain from ordering state officials to halt enforcement of a law justifiably attacked as in violation of the First Amendment, even if the person seeking the order has not yet exhausted all state procedures for challenging that law.

PERSONAL PRIVACY

Griswold v. Connecticut, 381 U.S. 479, decided by a 7–2 vote, June 7, 1965. Douglas wrote the majority opinion; Stewart and Black dissented.

A state unconstitutionally interferes with personal privacy when it prohibits anyone, including married couples, from using contraceptives. There is a right of personal privacy implicit in the Constitution, although there is disagreement on its exact source.

SELF-INCRIMINATION

Griffin v. California, 380 U.S. 609, decided by a 6–2 vote, April 28, 1965. Douglas wrote the majority opinion; Stewart and White dissented; Warren did not participate.

The Fifth Amendment privilege against compelled self-incrimination, as applied to the states through the due process guarantee of the Fourteenth Amendment, is infringed when a judge or prosecutor comments adversely during a trial upon a defendant's failure to testify in his own behalf.

Albertson v. Subversive Activities Control Board, 382 U.S. 70, decided by an 8–0 vote, November 15, 1965. Brennan wrote the opinion; White did not participate.

The Court overturned convictions of Communist Party members who were ordered to register personally with the attorney general by the Subversive Activities Control Act of 1950. The registration orders violated the Fifth Amendment privilege against self-incrimination.

VOTING RIGHTS

Harman v. Forssenius, 380 U.S. 528, decided by a unanimous vote, April 27, 1965. Warren wrote the opinion.

A Virginia law imposing special registration requirements on persons not paying the state's poll tax violates the Twenty-fourth Amendment's ban on poll taxes in federal elections.

1966

FREEDOM OF ASSOCIATION

Elfbrandt v. Russell, 384 U.S. 11, decided by a 5–4 vote, April 18, 1966. Douglas wrote the majority opinion; White, Clark, Harlan, and Stewart dissented.

An Arizona loyalty oath violates the First Amendment freedom of association by penalizing persons for membership in certain groups whether or not they joined the group with the specific intent of engaging in unlawful acts.

SELF-INCRIMINATION

Miranda v. Arizona, 384 U.S. 436, decided by a 5–4 vote, June 13, 1966. Warren wrote the majority opinion; Clark, Harlan, Stewart, and White dissented.

The due process guarantee requires that suspects in police custody be informed of their right to remain silent, that anything they say may be used against them, and that they have the right to counsel—before any interrogation can permissibly take place.

VOTING RIGHTS

South Carolina v. Katzenbach, 383 U.S. 301, decided by an 8–1 vote, March 7, 1966. Warren wrote the majority opinion; Black dissented.

The Voting Rights Act of 1965 is a proper exercise of congressional power to enforce the Fifteenth Amendment ban on racial discrimination in voting.

Harper v. Virginia State Board of Elections, 383 U.S. 663, decided by a 6–3 vote, March 24, 1966. Douglas wrote the majority opinion; Black, Harlan, and Stewart dissented.

State laws that condition the right to vote upon payment of a tax violate the equal protection clause of the Fourteenth Amendment.

1967

CIVIL RIGHTS

Loving v. Virginia, 388 U.S. 1, decided by a unanimous vote, June 12, 1967. Warren wrote the opinion.

A state law punishing persons who enter into interracial marriages violates both the equal protection and due process clauses of the Fourteenth Amendment. "Under our Constitution, the freedom to marry or not marry a person of another race resides with the individual and cannot be infringed by the state," the Court declared.

This decision was the first in which the Court explicitly held classifications by race "inherently suspect" and justifiable only by compelling reasons.

DUE PROCESS

Klopfer v. North Carolina, 386 U.S. 213, decided by a unanimous vote, March 13, 1967. Warren wrote the Court's opinion.

The Sixth Amendment right to a speedy trial applies in state, as well as federal, proceedings.

In re Gault, 387 U.S. 1, decided by a 7–2 vote, May 15, 1967. Fortas wrote the majority opinion; Harlan and Stewart dissented.

Juveniles have some—but not all—due process privileges in juvenile court proceedings. The privilege against self-incrimination and the right to counsel do apply.

Washington v. Texas, 388 U.S. 14, decided by a unanimous vote, June 12, 1967. Warren wrote the opinion.

Compulsory process to obtain witnesses in the defendant's favor is so fundamental to the Sixth Amendment guarantee of a fair trial that it is applicable to state trials through the Fourteenth Amendment.

FREEDOM OF ASSOCIATION

Keyishian v. Board of Regents, 385 U.S. 589, decided by a 5–4 vote, January 23, 1967. Brennan wrote the majority opinion; Clark, Harlan, Stewart, and White dissented.

New York State's teacher loyalty oath requirement is invalid as too vague and uncertain. Membership in the Communist Party alone is not sufficient reason to disqualify a teacher from public school employment.

United States v. Robel, 389 U.S. 258, decided by a 6–2 vote, December 11, 1967. Warren wrote the majority opinion; White and Harlan dissented; Marshall did not participate.

The Subversive Activities Control Act of 1950 violates the First Amendment freedom of association by forbidding a member of a group listed as subversive by the attorney general to take a job in a defense industry.

RIGHT TO COUNSEL

United States v. Wade, 388 U.S. 218, decided by a unanimous vote, June 12, 1967. Brennan wrote the opinion.

A police line-up identification of a suspect—made without the suspect's attorney present—is inadmissible as evidence at trial.

SEARCH AND SEIZURE

Warden v. Hayden, 387 U.S. 294, decided by an 8–1 vote, May 29, 1967. Brennan wrote the majority opinion; Douglas dissented.

Law enforcement searches for "mere evidence" are just as constitutional and reasonable as searches for implements and products of crime.

Katz v. United States, 389 U.S. 347, decided by a 7–1 vote, December 18, 1967. Stewart wrote the majority opinion for the Court; Black dissented; Marshall did not participate.

The Court abandoned its view, set out in *Olmstead v. United States* (1928), that electronic surveillance and wiretapping were not "searches and seizures" within the scope of the Fourth Amendment. The amendment protects people, not places; it protects what an individual seeks to preserve as private, even in a place accessible to the public.

1968

CIVIL RIGHTS

Green v. County School Board of New Kent County, 391 U.S. 430, decided by a unanimous vote, May 27, 1968. Brennan wrote the opinion.

Local school district officials have an affirmative duty to eliminate segregation "root and branch" from public schools, the Court said, striking down a "freedom-of-choice" plan that would have maintained segregated schools in New Kent County, Virginia. "The burden on a school board today is to come forward with a [desegregation] plan that promises realistically to work and . . . to work *now,*" the Court declared.

Jones v. Alfred H. Mayer Co., 392 U.S. 409, decided by a 7–2 vote, June 17, 1968. Stewart wrote the majority opinion; Harlan and White dissented.

The 1866 Civil Rights Act bars private as well as state-backed discrimination on the basis of race in the sale and rental of housing.

This decision reinterpreted congressional authority to enforce the Thirteenth Amendment, which was intended to remove "the badges of slavery." In the *Civil Rights Cases* of 1883, the Court had held that Congress had no authority to enforce the guarantees of the Thirteenth Amendment against private acts of discrimination.

DUE PROCESS

Duncan v. Louisiana, 391 U.S. 145, decided by a 7–2 vote, May 20, 1968. White wrote the majority opinion; Harlan and Stewart dissented.

The Fourteenth Amendment's guarantee of due process requires states to provide trial by jury to persons accused of serious crimes.

FEDERAL COURTS

Flast v. Cohen, 392 U.S. 83, decided by an 8–1 vote, June 10, 1968. Warren wrote the majority opinion; Harlan dissented.

Modifying *Frothingham v. Mellon* (1923), the Court held that a federal taxpayer may have the requisite standing to bring a federal challenge to federal spending and taxing programs as unconstitutional.

To prove the necessary personal interest in such programs, the Court ruled, the taxpayer must establish a logical connection between his taxpayer status and the claim before the court. This connection or "nexus" must be shown so that the federal courts not become merely forums for the airing of generalized grievances about government programs and policies.

SEARCH AND SEIZURE

Terry v. Ohio, 392 U.S. 1, decided by an 8–1 vote, June 10, 1968. Warren wrote the majority opinion; Douglas dissented.

The Court upheld the police practice of "stop and frisk," saying that when a police officer observes unusual conduct and suspects a crime is about to be committed, he may "frisk" a suspect's outer clothing for dangerous weapons. Such searches do not violate the Fourth Amendment's prohibition against unreasonable searches and seizures.

1969

DUE PROCESS

Benton v. Maryland, 395 U.S. 784, decided by a 6–2 vote, June 23, 1969. Marshall wrote the opinion; Stewart and Harlan dissented.

Overruling *Palko v. Connecticut* (1937), the Court declared that the Fourteenth Amendment due process guarantee extends the double jeopardy guarantee of the Fifth Amendment against state, as well as federal, action.

FREEDOM OF SPEECH

Tinker v. Des Moines Independent Community School District, 393 U.S. 503, decided by a 7–2 vote, February 24, 1969. Fortas wrote the majority opinion; Harlan and Black dissented.

Students have the right to engage in peaceful nondisruptive protest, the Court said, recognizing that the First Amendment guarantee of freedom of speech protects symbolic as well as oral speech.

The wearing of black armbands to protest the Vietnam War is "closely akin" to the "pure speech" protected by the First Amendment, the majority said, and therefore a public school ban on this form of protest, which did not disrupt the school's work or offend the rights of others, violated these students' rights.

PERSONAL LIBERTY

Shapiro v. Thompson, Washington v. Legrant, Reynolds v. Smith, 394 U.S. 618, decided by a 6–3 vote, April 21, 1969. Brennan wrote the majority opinion; Warren, Black, and Harlan dissented.

The right to travel is constitutionally protected. State or federal requirements that a person reside within a jurisdiction for one year before becoming eligible for welfare assistance violate individual rights to due process and equal protection of the laws.

No compelling government interest was presented to justify this infringement on the right to travel.

POWERS OF CONGRESS

Powell v. McCormack, 395 U.S. 486, decided by a 7–1 vote, June 16, 1969. Warren wrote the opinion; Stewart dissented.

The House of Representatives lacks authority to exclude a duly elected representative who meets the constitutional qualifications of age, residence, and citizenship. The House acted unconstitutionally when it voted to exclude Rep. Adam Clayton Powell, D-N.Y., for misconduct and misuse of public funds.

The Court did not deny the interest of Congress in maintaining its own integrity, but said such interest could be maintained by the use of each chamber's power to punish and expel its members.

The Court rejected the argument that the case presented a "political question," holding that a determination of Powell's right to his seat required only the interpretation of the Constitution, the traditional function of the Court.

SEARCH AND SEIZURE

Chimel v. California, 395 U.S. 752, decided by a 6–2 vote, June 23, 1969. Stewart wrote the opinion; White and Black dissented.

Overruling *United States v. Rabinowitz* (1950), the Court narrowed the limits of permissible searches conducted without a warrant incident to lawful arrest to the immediate area around the suspect from which he could obtain a weapon or destroy evidence. A person's entire dwelling cannot be searched simply because he is arrested there.

VOTING RIGHTS

Kirkpatrick v. Preisler, 394 U.S. 526, decided by a 6–3 vote, April 7, 1969. Brennan wrote the majority opinion; Harlan, Stewart, and White dissented.

Congressional districts with population variances of 3.1 percent from mathematical equality are unconstitutional unless the state can show that such variations are unavoidable.

Gaston County v. U.S., 395 U.S. 285, decided by a 7–1 vote, June 2, 1969. Harlan wrote the majority opinion; Black dissented.

The Court denied a county's request—under provisions of the 1965 Voting Rights Act—to reinstate a literacy test for voters. The combination of such a test, the Court ruled, with previous deprivation of educational opportunity for blacks in the county, would abridge the right to vote on account of race.

1970

DUE PROCESS

In re Winship, 397 U.S. 358, decided by a 5–3 vote, March 31, 1970. Brennan wrote the majority opinion; Burger, Black, and Stewart dissented.

The Fourteenth Amendment guarantee of due process requires that juveniles, like adult defendants, be found guilty "beyond a reasonable doubt." The Supreme Court forbade states to use a lesser standard of proof in juvenile proceedings.

Williams v. Florida, 399 U.S. 78, decided by a 7–1 vote, June 22, 1970. White wrote the majority opinion; Marshall dissented; Blackmun did not participate.

A six-member jury in noncapital state cases is constitutional. The number twelve is a "historical accident"; a jury can perform just as well with six members as it can with twelve.

VOTING RIGHTS

Oregon v. Mitchell, Texas v. Mitchell, United States v. Idaho, United States v. Arizona, 400 U.S. 112, decided by a 5–4 vote on lowered voting age, by an 8–1 vote on residency requirements, and by a unanimous vote on literacy test ban, December 21, 1970.

Black wrote the opinion; Burger, Harlan, Stewart, and Blackmun dissented on the question of age; Harlan dissented on the residency issue.

Congress has the power to lower the voting age for federal—but not for state and local—elections, to restrict state residency requirements to thirty days for voters in presidential elections, and to ban literacy tests as voter qualification devices in any election.

1971

CIVIL RIGHTS

Griggs v. Duke Power Co., 401 U.S. 424, decided by an 8–0 vote, March 8, 1971. Burger wrote the opinion; Brennan did not participate.

In its first case implicitly upholding the right of Congress to bar employment discrimination based on race, the Court held that the Civil Rights Act of 1964 prohibits employers from requiring a high school diploma or score on a general intelligence test as a condition for employment or promotion if neither test is related to job skills and if both tend to disqualify more black than white applicants.

Swann v. Charlotte-Mecklenburg County Board of Education, 402 U.S. 1, decided by a unanimous vote, April 20, 1971. Burger wrote the opinion.

Busing, racial balance ratios, and gerrymandered school districts are all permissible interim methods of eliminating the vestiges of state-imposed segregation from southern schools.

There were limits to the remedies that might be used to eliminate the remnants of segregation, the Court said, but no fixed guidelines setting such limits could be established. The Court acknowledged that there might be valid objections to busing when so much time or distance is involved as to risk the children's health or to impinge significantly on the education process.

DUE PROCESS

McKeiver v. Pennsylvania, In re Burrus, 403 U.S. 528, decided by votes of 6–3 and 5–4, June 21, 1971. Blackmun wrote the majority opinion; Douglas, Black, and Marshall dissented, joined in *Burrus* by Brennan.

The Sixth Amendment right to trial by jury does not extend to juvenile defendants.

EQUAL PROTECTION

Graham v. Richardson, 403 U.S. 365, decided by a unanimous vote, June 14, 1971. Blackmun wrote the Court's opinion.

Extending the equal protection guarantee to aliens, the Court struck down an Arizona law denying welfare benefits to aliens who lived in the United States less than fifteen years and a Pennsylvania law denying benefits to all resident aliens. The Court held that all classification by alienage was "suspect," requiring especially close scrutiny to ensure compliance with the equal protection guarantee.

Reed v. Reed, 404 U.S. 71, decided by a 7–0 vote, November 22, 1971. Burger wrote the opinion.

The Fourteenth Amendment guarantee of equal protection invalidates a state law that automatically prefers a father over a mother as executor of a son's estate. "To give a mandatory preference to members of either sex over members of the other . . . is to make the very kind of arbitrary legislative choice forbidden by the equal protection clause," the Court said in its first opinion declaring a state law unconstitutional on the grounds that it discriminated against women.

FEDERAL COURTS

Younger v. Harris, 401 U.S. 37, decided by an 8–1 vote, February 23, 1971. Black wrote the majority opinion; Douglas dissented.

Federal judges should not normally issue orders to state officials to halt enforcement of a state law or ongoing state proceedings—at least without a showing that continued enforcement of the law threatens to do irreparable injury to the person seeking the order.

FREEDOM OF RELIGION

Lemon v. Kurtzman, 403 U.S. 602, decided by a unanimous vote, June 28, 1971. Burger wrote the opinion; Marshall did not participate.

In this case the Court established a three-part test to determine whether state aid to parochial schools violated the First Amendment's ban on government action "establishing" religion.

State aid is permissible, the Court said, if it is intended to achieve a secular legislative purpose, if its primary effect neither advances nor inhibits religion, and if it does not foster excessive government entanglement with religion.

Applying this test, the Court declared invalid a state law authorizing supplemental salary grants to certain parochial school teachers and another state law authorizing reimbursement to parochial schools for teachers' salaries, textbooks, and instructional materials; the Court found that both laws fostered an excessive entanglement between government and religion.

FREEDOM OF THE PRESS

New York Times Co. v. United States, United States v. The Washington Post, 403 U.S. 713, decided by a 6–3 vote, June 30, 1971. The opinion was unsigned; each justice wrote a separate opinion. Burger, Blackmun, and Harlan dissented.

The Court in its brief per curiam opinion denied the government's request for a court order barring continued publication in the *New York Times* and the *Washington Post* of articles based on classified documents detailing the history of U.S. involvement in Indochina, popularly known as the Pentagon Papers.

Any request for prior restraint of the press bears a "heavy presumption against its constitutional validity," the Court said, and the government had failed to show sufficient justification for imposing such restraint.

SELF-INCRIMINATION

Harris v. New York, 401 U.S. 222, decided by a 5–4 vote, February 24, 1971. Burger wrote the majority opinion; Black, Douglas, Brennan, and Marshall dissented.

Voluntary statements made by a defendant not properly warned of his constitutional rights may be used in court to impeach his credibility if he takes the witness stand in his own defense and contradicts the earlier statements.

1972

DUE PROCESS

Johnson v. Louisiana, 406 U.S. 356, Apodaca v. Oregon, 406 U.S. 404, decided by a 5–4 vote, May 22, 1972. White wrote the majority opinion; Douglas, Brennan, Stewart, and Marshall dissented.

The constitutional guarantee of a jury trial applied to state courts does not require that the jury's verdict be unanimous. Lack of unanimity on the question of guilt does not constitute evidence of a reasonable doubt of guilt.

Furman v. Georgia, Jackson v. Georgia, Branch v. Texas, 408 U.S. 238, decided by a 5–4 vote, June 29, 1972. The Court's opinion was unsigned; each justice filed a separate opinion. Burger, Blackmun, Powell, and Rehnquist dissented.

The Court nullified all death penalty statutes in the United States. It held that the procedures the statutes provided for judges and juries to follow in deciding when and whether to impose a sentence of death upon a defendant left so much discretion to the judge and jury that the result was arbitrary, irrational, and deprived defendants of due process of law.

FREEDOM OF THE PRESS

Branzburg v. Hayes, In re Pappas, United States v. Caldwell, 408 U.S. 665, decided by a 5–4 vote, June 29, 1972. White wrote the majority opinion; Douglas, Brennan, Stewart, and Marshall dissented.

The constitutional guarantee of freedom of the press does not privilege news reporters to refuse—without risking contempt charges—to provide information to grand juries concerning a crime or the sources of evidence concerning a crime.

OFFICIAL IMMUNITY

United States v. Brewster, 408 U.S. 501, decided by a 6–3 vote, June 29, 1972. Burger wrote the opinion; Brennan, Douglas, and White dissented.

The constitutional immunity conferred on members of Congress by the "speech or debate clause" does not protect them from prosecution for accepting a bribe to vote a certain way on a legislative matter.

The holding cleared the way for prosecution of former senator Daniel B. Brewster, D-Md., (1963–1969), who had been indicted in 1969 on charges of accepting $24,000 in bribes from the mail order firm of Spiegel Incorporated to influence his vote on changes in postal rates. Taking a bribe is illegal, the majority wrote, and is no part of the legislative process. It is therefore subject to prosecution and punishment in the nation's courts.

RIGHT TO COUNSEL

Argersinger v. Hamlin, 407 U.S. 25, decided by a unanimous vote, June 12, 1972. Douglas wrote the opinion.

The right of counsel applies in trials for all offenses, state and federal, where a jail sentence is a possible penalty.

SELF-INCRIMINATION

Kastigar v. United States, 406 U.S. 441, decided by a 5–2 vote, May 22, 1972. Powell wrote the opinion; Douglas and Marshall dissented; Rehnquist and Brennan did not participate.

The narrowed witness immunity provisions of the 1970 Organized Crime Control Act do not infringe upon the Fifth Amendment privilege against self-incrimination. In any subsequent prosecution of an immunized witness, the government must demonstrate that the evidence is derived from sources independent of testimony given under a grant of immunity.

1973

CIVIL RIGHTS

Keyes v. Denver School District No. 1, 413 U.S. 921, decided by a 7–1 vote, June 21, 1973. Brennan wrote the majority opinion; Rehnquist dissented; White did not participate.

This decision was the Court's first definition of the responsibility of school officials to act to desegregate public schools in a district where racial segregation had never been required by law (de jure).

The Court held that school officials were constitutionally obligated to desegregate a school system if the segregation there had resulted from intentional school board policies. In the case of racially segregated schools within a system, the burden of proof was on the school board to prove such segregation was not a result of intentional board actions.

EQUAL PROTECTION

San Antonio Independent School District v. Rodriguez, 411 U.S. 1, decided by a 5–4 vote, March 21, 1973. Powell wrote the majority opinion; Marshall, Douglas, Brennan, and White dissented.

The right to an education is not a fundamental right guaranteed by the Constitution. Wealth is not a suspect way of classifying persons. Therefore, the equal protection guarantee does not require that courts give the strictest scrutiny to state decisions to finance public schools from local property taxes, a decision resulting in wide disparities among districts in the amount spent per pupil.

States do not deny anyone the opportunity for an education by adopting this means of financing public education. Financing public schools from local property taxes rationally furthers a legitimate state purpose and so is upheld.

OBSCENITY

Miller v. California, 413 U.S. 15, decided by a 5–4 vote, June 21, 1973. Burger wrote the majority opinion; Brennan, Stewart, Marshall, and Douglas dissented.

States have the power, without violating the First Amendment, to regulate material that is obscene in its depiction or description of sexual conduct. Material is obscene if the average person, applying contemporary local community standards, would find that it appeals to the prurient interest, and if it depicts in a patently offensive way, sexual conduct specifically defined by the applicable state law, and if the work, taken as a whole, lacks serious literary, artistic, political, or scientific value.

This definition of obscenity was the first approved by of a majority of the justices since 1957; it was less stringent than the prevailing standard and consequently gave the states more control over obscene materials.

PERSONAL PRIVACY

Roe v. Wade, 410 U.S. 113, *Doe v. Bolton,* 410 U.S. 179, decided by 7–2 votes, January 22, 1973. Blackmun wrote the majority opinions; Rehnquist and White dissented.

The right to privacy, grounded in the Fourteenth Amendment's due process guarantee of personal liberty, encompasses and protects a woman's decision whether or not to bear a child. This right is impermissibly abridged by state laws that make abortion a crime.

During the first trimester of pregnancy, the decision to have an abortion should be left entirely to a woman and her physician. The state can forbid abortions by nonphysicians. During the second trimester, the state may regulate the abortion procedure in ways reasonably related to maternal health. And during the third trimester, the state may, if it wishes, forbid all abortions except those necessary to save the mother's life.

VOTING RIGHTS

Mahan v. Howell, City of Virginia Beach v. Howell, Weinberg v. Prichard, 410 U.S. 315, decided by a 5–3 vote, February 21, 1973. Rehnquist wrote the opinion; Brennan, Douglas, and Marshall dissented; Powell did not participate.

The Court's decision in this case relaxed the requirement that state legislative districts be as nearly equal as possible—holding that states may apply more flexible standards in drawing new state legislative districts than in congressional redistricting.

The decision approved a Virginia plan permitting a 16 percent variation between the largest and smallest population districts.

1974

CIVIL RIGHTS

Milliken v. Bradley, 418 U.S. 717, decided by a 5–4 vote, July 25, 1974. Burger wrote the majority opinion; Douglas, Brennan, Marshall, and White dissented.

A multidistrict remedy for school segregation, such as busing school children across district lines, can be ordered by a federal court only when there has been a finding that all the districts involved have been responsible for the segregation to be remedied.

The Court reversed a lower court's order directing busing across city, county, and district lines to desegregate the schools of Detroit, Michigan. The majority ordered the lower court to devise a remedy that would affect only the city schools.

EQUAL PROTECTION

Geduldig v. Aiello, 417 U.S. 484, decided by a 6–3 vote, June 17, 1974. Stewart wrote the majority opinion; Douglas, Brennan, and Marshall dissented.

California did not violate the constitutional guarantee of equal protection by excluding from its disability insurance program women unable to work because of pregnancy-related disabilities.

Women were not denied equal protection by this exclusion because, the majority said, "there is no risk from which men are protected and women are not." The decision to exclude the risk of pregnancy from the risks insured by the state plan was a rational one in light of the state interest in maintaining a low-cost, self-supporting insurance fund.

FEDERAL COURTS

Edelman v. Jordan, 415 U.S. 651, decided by a 5–4 vote, March 25, 1974. Rehnquist wrote the majority opinion; Brennan, Douglas, Marshall, and Blackmun dissented.

The Eleventh Amendment immunity of states from federal lawsuits brought by citizens without the state's consent protects a state from a federal court order directing it to spend money to remedy past abuses.

Federal judges may order a state to halt enforcement of a law that violates due process and equal protection, but that order may only reach future action—it may not require the state to remedy past damages inflicted under the invalid law.

In 1976 the Court substantially modified the reach of this decision, holding unanimously in *Fitzpatrick v. Bitzer, Bitzer v. Matthews,* 427 U.S. 445, that federal courts could order states to pay retroactive benefits to persons against whom the state had discriminated in violation of the Fourteenth Amendment.

POWERS OF THE PRESIDENT

United States v. Nixon, 418 U.S. 683, decided by an 8–0 vote, July 24, 1974. Burger wrote the opinion; Rehnquist did not participate.

Neither the separation of powers nor the need to preserve the confidentiality of presidential communications alone can justify an absolute executive privilege of immunity from judicial demands for evidence to be used in a criminal trial.

The Court held that President Richard Nixon must comply with a subpoena for tapes of certain White House conversations, sought for use as evidence against White House aides charged with obstruction of justice in regard to the investigation of the break-in at the Democratic National Headquarters in the Watergate Office Building in June 1972.

1975

CIVIL RIGHTS

Albemarle Paper Co. v. Moody, 422 U.S. 405, decided by a 7–1 vote, June 25, 1975. Stewart wrote the majority opinion; Burger dissented; Powell did not participate.

Back pay awards to victims of employment discrimination are the rule, not the exception, in cases won under Title VII of the 1964 Civil Rights Act. Back pay awards carry out the intent of Congress to make persons whole for injuries suffered on account of unlawful discrimination and should not be restricted to cases in which the employer is found to have acted in bad faith.

EQUAL PROTECTION

Weinberger v. Wiesenfeld, 420 U.S. 636, decided by an 8–0 vote, March 19, 1975. Brennan wrote the opinion; Douglas did not participate.

Social Security law that provides survivors' benefits for widows with small children, but not for widowers with small children, violates the guarantee of due process by providing working women with fewer benefits for their Social Security contributions than it provides to working men. "It is no less important for a child to be cared for by its sole surviving parent when that parent is male rather than female," wrote Brennan, pointing out that the intended purpose of this benefit was to allow a mother not to work, but to stay home and care for her children.

FREE SPEECH

Bigelow v. Virginia, 421 U.S. 809, decided by a 7–2 vote, June 16, 1975. Blackmun wrote the opinion; Rehnquist and White dissented.

Commercial advertising enjoys some First Amendment protection; *Valentine v. Chrestensen,* 316 U.S. 52 (1942), held that the manner in which such ads were distributed could be regulated—not advertising itself.

The Court reversed the conviction of a newspaper editor in Virginia for violating a state law against "encouraging" abortions by running an advertisement including information on legal abortions available in New York. This law was an improper effort by the state to control what its citizens could hear or read, the Court held.

JURY TRIALS

Taylor v. Louisiana, 419 U.S. 522, decided by an 8–1 vote, January 21, 1975. White wrote the opinion; Rehnquist dissented.

State laws generally exempting women from jury duty are unconstitutional because they violate the Sixth Amendment requirement that juries be drawn from a fair cross-section of the community.

The Court overruled its 1961 decision in *Hoyt v. Florida,* which upheld this general exclusion of women from jury duty as rational in light of the state's interest in preventing interference with women's traditional functions as wives, homemakers, and mothers.

1976

CIVIL RIGHTS

Washington v. Davis, 426 U.S. 229, decided by a 7–2 vote, June 7, 1976. White wrote the majority opinion; Brennan and Marshall dissented.

Job qualification tests are not unconstitutional simply because more black than white job applicants fail them. Some racially discriminatory purpose must be found in order for such a test to be in violation of the constitutional guarantees of due process and equal protection. "Disproportionate impact is not irrelevant, but it is not the sole touchstone of an invidious racial discrimination forbidden by the Constitution."

Runyon v. McCrary, Fairfax-Brewster School Inc. v. Gonzales, Southern Independent School Association v. McCrary, 427 U.S. 160, decided by a 7–2 vote, June 25, 1976. Stewart wrote the opinion; White and Rehnquist dissented.

Racially segregated private schools that refuse to admit black students violate the Civil Rights Act of 1866, which gave "all persons within the jurisdiction of the United States the same right . . . to make and enforce contracts . . . as is enjoyed by white citizens." That law bans this type of private discrimination.

Pasadena Board of Education v. Spangler, 427 U.S. 424, decided by a 6–2 vote, June 28, 1976. Rehnquist wrote the opinion; Brennan and Marshall dissented; Stevens did not participate.

Once a school board has implemented a racially neutral plan for assignment of students to city schools, it is not constitutionally required to continue juggling student assignments in order to maintain a certain racial balance in the student body of each school.

COMMERCE

National League of Cities v. Usery, California v. Usery, 426 U.S. 833, decided by a 5–4 vote, June 24, 1976. Rehnquist wrote the opinion; Brennan, White, Marshall, and Stevens dissented.

Congress exceeded its power to regulate interstate commerce when it extended federal minimum wage and overtime standards to cover state and local government employees by its 1974 amendments to the Fair Labor Standards Act. Determination of state government employees' wages and hours is one of the "attributes of sovereignty attaching to every state government, which may not be impaired by Congress."

CRUEL AND UNUSUAL PUNISHMENT

Gregg v. Georgia, 428 U.S. 153, ***Proffitt v. Florida,*** 428 U.S. 242, ***Jurek v. Texas,*** 428 U.S. 262, decided by 7–2 votes, July 2, 1976. Stewart wrote the opinion in *Gregg;* Stevens wrote the opinion in *Jurek;* Powell wrote the opinion in *Proffitt;* Brennan and Marshall dissented.

As a punishment for persons convicted of first degree murder, death is not in and of itself cruel and unusual punishment in violation of the Eighth Amendment.

The Eighth Amendment requires the sentencing judge or jury to consider the individual character of the offender and the circumstances of the particular crime before deciding whether to impose a death sentence. A two-part proceeding—one for the determination of guilt or innocence and a second for determining the sentence—provides an opportunity for such individualized consideration prior to sentencing.

Woodson v. North Carolina, 428 U.S. 280, ***Roberts v. Louisiana,*** 428 U.S. 325, decided by votes of 5–4, July 2, 1976. Stewart wrote the opinion in *Woodson;* Stevens wrote the opinion in *Roberts;* Burger, White, Rehnquist, and Blackmun dissented.

States may not make death the mandatory penalty for first degree murder. Such mandatory sentences fail to meet the constitutional requirement for consideration of the individual offender and offense prior to the decision to impose the death penalty.

EQUAL PROTECTION

Craig v. Boren, 429 U.S. 190, decided by a 7–2 vote, December 20, 1976. Brennan wrote the opinion; Burger and Rehnquist dissented.

A classification based on gender is invalid unless it is substantially related to the achievement of an important government objective.

Using this rule, the Court declared unconstitutional a state law that permitted the sale of 3.2 beer to women at age eighteen but not to men until age twenty-one. The law was not substantially related to the state's expressed goal of promoting traffic safety.

FEDERAL COURTS

Stone v. Powell, Wolff v. Rice, 428 U.S. 465, decided by a 6–3 vote, July 6, 1976. Powell wrote the opinion; Brennan, Marshall, and White dissented.

A state prisoner's claim that illegally obtained evidence was used to convict him cannot serve as a basis for a federal court order of his release through a writ of habeas corpus—unless the state failed to provide the prisoner an opportunity for full and fair hearing of his challenge to the evidence.

FREEDOM OF ASSOCIATION

Elrod v. Burns, 427 U.S. 347, decided by a 5–3 vote, June 28, 1976. Brennan wrote the opinion; Burger, Powell, and Rehnquist dissented; Stevens did not participate.

Patronage firing—the discharge by an official of the public employees who do not belong to his party—violates the First Amendment freedom of political association.

FREEDOM OF SPEECH

Buckley v. Valeo, 424 U.S. 1, decided by votes of 8–0, 7–1, and 6–2, January 31, 1976. The opinion was unsigned; Burger, Blackmun, Rehnquist, White, and Marshall all dissented in part; Stevens did not participate.

The First Amendment guarantee of freedom of expression is impermissibly infringed by the limits placed by the 1974 Federal Election Campaign Act Amendments on the amount a candidate for federal office may spend. The vote was 7–1; White dissented.

The majority did find limits permissible for candidates who accepted public financing of their campaigns for the presidency.

The Court upheld, 6–2, the law's limits on the amount individuals and political committees could contribute to candidates. The limit was only a marginal restriction on a contributor's First Amendment freedom, justified by the interest in preventing corruption, the majority said. Burger and Blackmun dissented.

The Court upheld, 6–2, the system of public financing set up for presidential campaigns and elections. Burger and Rehnquist dissented. Burger also dissented from the majority's decision to uphold the law's requirements for public disclosure of campaign contributions of more than $100 and campaign expenditures of more than $10.

The Court unanimously agreed that the Federal Election Commission, as set up by the 1974 law, was unconstitutional as a violation of the separation of powers.

FREEDOM OF THE PRESS

Nebraska Press Association v. Stuart, 427 U.S. 539, decided by a unanimous vote, June 30, 1976. Burger wrote the opinion.

A gag order severely limiting what the press can report about pretrial proceedings in a mass murder case violates the First Amendment guarantee of a free press.

If ever permissible, this sort of prior restraint of publication can be justified only by the most extreme circumstances. In most situations, judges concerned about preserving a defendant's right to a fair trial by an unbiased jury have many less drastic means of ensuring that potential jurors are not prejudiced by publicity.

TAXES

Michelin Tire Corp. v. Wages, 423 U.S. 276, decided by an 8–0 vote, January 14, 1976. Brennan wrote the opinion; Stevens did not participate.

The Court overruled *Low v. Austin* (1872), which forbade states to tax imported goods so long as those goods retained their character as imports.

The export-import clause of the Constitution, the Court held, did not bar a county from imposing a property tax on imported goods stored prior to sale, so long as the tax did not discriminate against imported goods.

1977

CIVIL RIGHTS

Village of Arlington Heights v. Metropolitan Housing Development Corporation, 429 U.S. 252, decided by a 5–3 vote, January 11, 1977. Powell wrote the opinion; White dissented; Brennan and Marshall dissented in part; Stevens did not participate.

Without any showing of discriminatory motive, the refusal of a village to rezone property to permit building of a housing development for low- and moderate-income persons of both races does not violate the Fourteenth Amendment guarantee of equal protection.

CRUEL AND UNUSUAL PUNISHMENT

Coker v. Georgia, 433 U.S. 584, decided by a 7–2 vote, June 29, 1977. White wrote the opinion; Burger and Rehnquist dissented.

A death sentence for the crime of rape is an excessive and disproportionate penalty forbidden by the Eighth Amendment ban on cruel and unusual punishments.

TAXES

Complete Auto Transit Inc. v. Brady, 430 U.S. 274, decided by a unanimous vote, March 8, 1977. Blackmun wrote the opinion.

The commerce clause—granting Congress the power to regulate interstate and foreign commerce—does not forbid a state to tax an interstate enterprise doing business within the state for the "privilege" of doing business there.

Such taxes are permissible so long as the taxed activity has a sufficient nexus with the taxing state, the tax does not discriminate against interstate commerce, is fairly apportioned, and is related to services provided by the state.

VOTING RIGHTS

United Jewish Organizations of Williamsburgh v. Carey, 430 U.S. 144, decided by a 7–1 vote, March 1, 1977. White wrote the opinion; Burger dissented; Marshall did not participate.

The Court upheld the use of racial criteria by the state of New York in its 1974 state legislative redistricting plan drawn to comply with the 1965 Voting Rights Act. Even if the result of the redistricting dilutes the vote of a white ethnic minority—in this case the Hasidic Jewish community of Brooklyn—the Constitution "does not prevent a state subject to the Voting Rights Act from deliberately creating or preserving black majorities in particular districts in order to ensure that its reapportionment plan" complies with the act.

1978

CIVIL RIGHTS

Regents of the University of California v. Bakke, 438 U.S. 265, decided by a 5–4 vote, June 28, 1978. Powell announced the judgment of the Court; Stevens and Brennan filed separate opinions; Stevens was joined by Burger, Rehnquist, and Stewart; Brennan was joined by Marshall, White, and Blackmun.

A special state medical school admissions program under which a certain number of slots were set aside for minority group members, and white applicants were denied the opportunity to compete for them, violates Title VI of the 1964 Civil Rights Act. Title VI forbids exclusion of anyone, because of race, from participation in a federally funded program.

Admissions programs that consider race as one of several factors involved in the decision to admit an applicant are not unconstitutional in and of themselves. "Government may take race into account when it acts not to demean or insult any racial group, but to remedy disadvantages cast on minorities by past racial prejudice, at least when appropriate findings have been made by judicial, legislative, or administrative bodies with competence to act in this area."

FEDERAL COURTS

Monell v. Department of Social Services, 436 U.S. 658, decided by a 7–2 vote, June 6, 1978. Brennan wrote the opinion; Burger and Rehnquist dissented.

City officials, municipalities, and municipal agencies are not immune from civil rights damage suits filed under the Civil Rights Act of 1871.

Cities may be held liable for damages if action pursuant to official policy violates someone's constitutional rights. Cities are not liable if their employees or agents infringe someone's rights in the course of their duties.

FREEDOM OF SPEECH

First National Bank of Boston v. Bellotti, 435 U.S. 765, decided by a 5–4 vote, April 26, 1978. Powell wrote the opinion; White, Brennan, Marshall, and Rehnquist dissented.

State law banning corporate expenditures relative to a referendum issue that does not materially affect corporate business impermissibly abridges political speech protected by the First Amendment. "If the speakers here were not corporations, no one would suggest that the state could silence their proposed speech. It is the type of speech indispensable to decisionmaking in a democracy, and this is no less true because the speech comes from a corporation rather than an individual," the majority said.

JURY TRIALS

Ballew v. Georgia, 435 U.S. 223, decided by a unanimous vote, March 21, 1978. Blackmun wrote the opinion.

In order to fulfill the constitutional guarantee of trial by jury, state juries must be composed of at least six members.

OFFICIAL IMMUNITY

Butz v. Economou, 438 U.S. 478, decided by a 5–4 vote, June 29, 1978. White wrote the opinion; Burger, Rehnquist, Stewart, and Stevens dissented.

Federal officials are not absolutely immune from damage suits based upon actions taken in the performance of their official duties. Even when carrying out directives from Congress, federal officials are subject to the restraints of the Constitution.

SEARCH AND SEIZURE

Zurcher v. The Stanford Daily, 436 U.S. 547, decided by a 5–3 vote, May 31, 1978. White wrote the opinion; Stewart, Marshall, and Stevens dissented; Brennan did not participate.

The Fourth Amendment does not preclude or limit the use of search warrants for searches of places owned or occupied by innocent third parties not suspected of any crime.

The First Amendment guarantee of freedom of the press does not require that information concerning a crime in the possession of a newspaper be sought by a subpoena rather than a search warrant.

1979

CIVIL RIGHTS

United Steelworkers of America v. Weber, Kaiser Aluminum v. Weber, United States v. Weber, 443 U.S. 193, decided by a 5–2 vote, June 27, 1979. Brennan wrote the opinion; Burger and Rehnquist dissented; Powell and Stevens did not participate.

Title VII of the 1964 Civil Rights Act forbids racial discrimination in employment but does not forbid employers to adopt voluntarily race-conscious affirmative action programs to encourage minority participation in areas of work in which they have traditionally been underrepresented.

Columbus Board of Education v. Penick, Dayton Board of Education v. Brinkman, 443 U.S. 449, decided by votes of 7 to 2 and 5 to 4, July 2, 1979. White wrote the opinion; Rehnquist and Powell dissented in both; Burger and Stewart dissented in *Dayton.*

School boards operating segregated school systems at the time of the 1954 decision in *Brown v. Board of Education* are under an affirmative duty to end that segregation—even if it was not imposed as a result of state law. The Court upheld systemwide busing orders for Dayton and Columbus, Ohio, where segregated schools had not been required by law since 1888.

DUE PROCESS

Davis v. Passman, 442 U.S. 228, decided by a 5–4 vote, June 5, 1979. Brennan wrote the opinion; Burger, Powell, Rehnquist, and Stewart dissented.

An individual denied due process and equal protection by federal action can bring a federal suit for damages based on the Fifth Amendment guarantee.

For the first time, the Court provided a constitutional basis for job discrimination charges by congressional employees, who are not protected by the guarantees of the federal civil rights laws.

EQUAL PROTECTION

Orr v. Orr, 440 U.S. 268, decided by a 6–3 vote, March 5, 1979. Brennan wrote the opinion; Powell, Rehnquist, and Burger dissented.

States violate the Fourteenth Amendment guarantee of equal protection when they allow women, but not men, to receive alimony as part of a divorce settlement.

JURY TRIAL

Burch v. Louisiana, 441 U.S. 130, decided by a unanimous vote, April 17, 1979. Rehnquist wrote the opinion.

A state deprives a defendant of his constitutional right to a jury trial when it allows him to be convicted by the nonunanimous vote of a six-person jury.

OFFICIAL IMMUNITY

United States v. Helstoski, 442 U.S. 477, decided by a 5–3 vote, June 18, 1979. Burger wrote the opinion, Brennan dissented; Stevens and Stewart dissented in part; Powell did not participate.

The Constitution's provision immunizing members of Congress from being questioned outside Congress "for any Speech or Debate in either House" forbids the government, in prosecuting a member for accepting a bribe in return for a legislative act, to introduce evidence of the legislative act. The constitutional provision was intended to preclude prosecution of members for legislative acts.

Hutchinson v. Proxmire, 443 U.S. 111, decided by a 7–2 vote, June 26, 1979. Burger wrote the opinion; Brennan dissented; Stewart dissented in part.

The Constitution's speech or debate clause does not protect a senator from being sued for libel as a result of statements made in press releases and newsletters.

An individual who does not seek to thrust himself into the public eye or otherwise draw public attention, but who is drawn into public notice by events outside his control, is not a public figure subject to the "actual malice" standard set out by the Supreme Court for libel suits brought by public officials.

RIGHT OF ACCESS

Gannett Co. Inc. v. DePasquale, 443 U.S. 368, decided by a 5–4 vote, July 2, 1979. Stewart wrote the opinion; Blackmun, Brennan, White, and Marshall dissented in part.

The Constitution's guarantee of the right to a public trial is intended for the benefit of the defendant, not the public. Members of the public cannot use that guarantee as the basis for their constitutional right to attend a criminal trial.

A judge may constitutionally exclude press and public from a pretrial hearing to avoid publicity prejudicial to the defendant and to protect his right to a fair trial.

1980

CIVIL RIGHTS

Fullilove v. Klutznick, 448 U.S. 448, decided by a 6–3 vote, July 2, 1980. Burger announced the Court's decision; Stewart, Rehnquist, and Stevens dissented.

Congress may make limited use of racial quotas to remedy past discrimination. The Court upheld as constitutional a provision in the 1977 Public Works Employment Act that set aside for minority businesses 10 percent of federal funds provided for local public works projects.

POWERS OF CONGRESS

Harris v. McRae, 448 U.S. 297, decided by a 5–4 vote, June 30, 1980. Stewart wrote the opinion; Brennan, Marshall, Blackmun, and Stevens dissented.

Congress did not act unconstitutionally when it restricted federal funding of medically necessary abortions. The Court upheld the so-called Hyde Amendment, which denies federal reimbursement for abortions under the Medicaid program except when the abortion is necessary to save the pregnant woman's life or to terminate a pregnancy caused by promptly reported rape or incest.

In a companion decision the same day, the Court upheld similar state restrictions on public funding of abortions, *Williams v. Zbaraz, Miller v. Zbaraz, United States v. Zbaraz,* 448 U.S. 358.

RIGHT OF ACCESS

Richmond Newspapers Inc. v. Virginia, 448 U.S. 555, decided by a 7–1 vote, July 2, 1980. Burger announced the Court's decision; Rehnquist dissented; Powell did not participate.

The First Amendment guarantees citizens and members of the press the right to attend criminal trials. In some situations, a judge may limit that access to protect the defendant's right to a fair trial, but such closure should be explained and limited.

RIGHT TO COUNSEL

Rhode Island v. Innis, 446 U.S. 291, decided by 9–0 and 6–3 votes, May 12, 1980. Stewart wrote the opinion; Marshall, Brennan, and Stevens dissented.

The Court defined "interrogation"—a critical word in *Miranda v. Arizona* (1966)—as meaning the direct questioning of a suspect *and* the use of other "techniques of persuasion." Interrogation, said the Court, includes "words or actions on the part of police officers that they *should have known* were reasonably likely to elicit an incriminating response." The Court was unanimous in that holding although it declined, 6–3, to find that interrogation had occurred in this particular case.

SEARCH AND SEIZURE

Payton v. New York, Riddick v. New York, 445 U.S. 573, decided by a 6–3 vote, April 15, 1980. Stevens wrote the opinion; Burger, White, and Rehnquist dissented.

Police may not enter a home to arrest its occupant without an arrest warrant or the consent of the occupant—unless an immediate arrest is imperative under emergency circumstances.

VOTING RIGHTS

Mobile v. Bolden, 446 U.S. 55, decided by a 6–3 vote, April 22, 1980. Stewart wrote the opinion; Brennan, White, and Marshall dissented.

The Mobile, Alabama, at-large system for electing city commissioners is constitutional unless it is shown to be intentionally discriminatory. Its effect—the fact that no black officials had been elected—is not enough to prove it unconstitutional.

1981

DUE PROCESS

Chandler v. Florida, 449 U.S. 560, decided by an 8–0 vote, January 26, 1981. Burger wrote the opinion; Stevens did not participate.

Nothing in the Constitution—neither the guarantee of due process nor the promise of a fair trial—forbids states from permitting television cameras in a courtroom to broadcast criminal trials.

EQUAL PROTECTION

Rostker v. Goldberg, 453 U.S. 57, decided by a 6–3 vote, June 25, 1981. Rehnquist wrote the opinion; White, Marshall, and Brennan dissented.

Congress did not violate the Constitution by excluding women from the military draft. Because they are barred by law and policy from combat, they are not "similarly situated" with men for purposes of draft registration, and therefore Congress may treat the sexes differently in this context.

PERSONAL PRIVACY

H. L. v. Matheson, 450 U.S. 398, decided by a 6–3 vote, March 23, 1981. Burger wrote the opinion; Marshall, Brennan, and Blackmun dissented.

A pregnant minor's right of privacy is not violated by a Utah law requiring a doctor to notify her parents before providing her with an abortion. The law does not give parents a veto, but does require that they be notified.

POWERS OF THE PRESIDENT

Dames & Moore v. Regan, 453 U.S. 654, decided by a 9–0 vote, July 2, 1981. Rehnquist wrote the opinion.

President Jimmy Carter acted within the scope of his authority over foreign affairs when he reached a financial agreement with Iran that resulted in the release of Americans held hostage in that country, including the agreement to nullify all federal court orders attaching Iranian assets in the United States and to transfer them back to Iran.

It was also within the president's power to agree that all pending claims against Iran be transferred to an international tribunal for resolution. Congress in the International Emergency Economic Powers Act of 1977, and a number of other earlier laws, gave the president powers broad enough to authorize these actions.

1982

CRUEL AND UNUSUAL PUNISHMENT

Enmund v. Florida, 458 U.S. 782, decided by a 5–4 vote, July 2, 1982. White wrote the Court's opinion; Burger, O'Connor, Powell, and Rehnquist dissented.

It is cruel and unusual punishment, disproportionate to the actions of the defendant, for the driver of a getaway car to be sentenced to death after he is convicted of first-degree murder for his role in killings he neither committed nor witnessed.

EQUAL PROTECTION

Plyler v. Doe, Texas v. Certain Named and Unnamed Undocumented Alien Children, 457 U.S. 202, decided by a 5–4 vote, June 15, 1982. Brennan wrote the opinion; Burger, Rehnquist, White, and O'Connor dissented.

Aliens in the United States are guaranteed the equal protection of the law by the Fourteenth Amendment, even if they have entered the country illegally. Texas may not deny illegal alien children a free public education; there is neither national policy nor sufficient state interest to justify this action.

Youngberg v. Romeo, 457 U.S. 307, decided by a 9–0 vote, June 18, 1982. Powell wrote the opinion.

Mentally retarded persons in state institutions have a constitutional right to safe conditions, freedom of movement, and sufficient training to enable them to move freely and safely within that institution.

FREEDOM OF EXPRESSION

Board of Education, Island Trees Union Free School District No. 26 v. Pico, 457 U.S. 853, decided by a 5–4 vote, June 25, 1982. Brennan announced the Court's decision; Burger, Powell, Rehnquist, and O'Connor dissented.

The First Amendment limits a local school board's power to remove certain books from public school libraries. It is impermissible for a board to remove a book because it contains unpopular ideas; it is permissible to remove vulgar and irrelevant books.

National Association for the Advancement of Colored People v. Claiborne Hardware Co., 458 U.S. 886, decided by an 8–0 vote, July 2, 1982. Stevens wrote the opinion; Marshall did not participate.

The First Amendment protection for speech and expressive conduct includes a nonviolent boycott by civil rights demonstrators of the stores of white merchants. Violence, however, is not protected, and a state court may assess damages against those responsible for violence in such a setting. But any liability for damages must be based on the individual's participation in violent activity, not simply on his membership in the boycotting group.

OFFICIAL IMMUNITY

Nixon v. Fitzgerald, 457 U.S. 731, decided by a 5–4 vote, June 24, 1982. Powell wrote the opinion; White, Brennan, Marshall, and Blackmun dissented.

Presidents are absolutely immune from civil damages suits for all official actions taken while in office. The electoral process and the impeachment mechanism provide sufficient remedy for presidential wrongdoing.

Harlow v. Fitzgerald, 457 U.S. 800, decided by an 8–1 vote, June 24, 1982. Powell wrote the Court's opinion; Burger dissented.

Presidential aides do not have absolute immunity from civil rights damage suits by individuals who claim to have been denied their rights by those aides acting in their official capacity. Like other executive officials, they enjoy qualified immunity from such damage suits. Immunity attaches when the challenged conduct does not violate clearly established statutory or constitutional rights of which a reasonable person would have known.

1983

CIVIL RIGHTS

Bob Jones University v. United States, Goldsboro Christian Schools v. United States, 461 U.S. 574, decided by an 8–1 vote, May 24, 1983. Burger wrote the opinion; Rehnquist dissented.

The Internal Revenue Service acted within its authority when it denied tax-exempt status to private schools that discriminate against blacks. In light of the clear national policy against racial discrimination in education, the IRS was correct in its 1970 declaration that it would no longer grant tax-exempt status to discriminatory private schools.

The national interest in eradicating racial discrimination in education "substantially outweighs whatever burden denial of tax benefits places" on the exercise of First Amendment freedom of religion.

CRUEL AND UNUSUAL PUNISHMENT

Solem v. Helm, 463 U.S. 277, decided by a 5–4 vote, June 28, 1983. Powell wrote the opinion; Burger, White, Rehnquist, and O'Connor dissented.

South Dakota violated the constitutional ban on cruel and unusual punishment when it imposed a life sentence without possibility of parole on a man convicted on seven separate occasions of nonviolent felonies. This was the first time the Court had used this constitutional provision to judge the relative severity of a prison sentence.

FREEDOM OF RELIGION

Mueller v. Allen, 463 U.S. 388, decided by a 5–4 vote, June 29, 1983. Rehnquist wrote the opinion; Marshall, Brennan, Blackmun, and Stevens dissented.

The First Amendment permits Minnesota to grant parents a state income tax deduction for the cost of tuition, textbooks, and transportation for their elementary and secondary school children. The deduction is available to public school patrons as well as private school patrons, and therefore any benefit to church-run schools is the result of individual choices, not state design.

PERSONAL PRIVACY

Akron v. Akron Center for Reproductive Health Inc., Akron Center for Reproductive Health Inc. v. Akron, 462 U.S. 416, decided by a 6–3 vote, June 15, 1983. Powell wrote the opinion; White, Rehnquist, and O'Connor dissented.

An Akron, Ohio, ordinance unconstitutionally required that all abortions after the first trimester be performed in full-service hospitals; that physicians obtain parental consent before performing an abortion on a patient younger than sixteen; that physicians recite to women seeking abortions certain information about fetal development, alternatives to abortion, and possible abortion complications; that the attending physician inform a patient of the risks associated with her own pregnancy or abortion; that there be a twenty-four-hour waiting period between the time consent is signed for an abortion and the time it is performed; and that fetal remains be given a "humane" disposal.

Planned Parenthood Association of Kansas City, Missouri v. Ashcroft, Ashcroft v. Planned Parenthood Association of Kansas City, Missouri, 462 U.S. 476, decided by 5–4 and 6–3 votes, June 15, 1983. Powell wrote the opinion; Blackmun, Brennan, Marshall, and Stevens dissented in part; O'Connor, White, and Rehnquist dissented in part.

Missouri law requiring "unemancipated" minors to have parental or judicial consent for abortion is permissible, because it provides an alternative to parental consent. It is also appropriate for the law to require pathological examination of tissue from an abortion and that a second physician be present at late-term abortions. But the law is unconstitutional in requiring that all abortions after the first trimester be performed in a hospital.

POWERS OF CONGRESS

Immigration and Naturalization Service v. Chadha, United States House of Representatives v. Chadha, United States Senate v. Chadha, 462 U.S. 919, decided by a 7–2 vote, June 23, 1983. Burger wrote the opinion; White and Rehnquist dissented.

The one-house legislative veto, under which Congress claimed the power to review and veto executive branch decisions implementing laws, is unconstitutional. It violates the separation of powers between executive and legislative branches, and it runs counter to the "single, finely wrought and exhaustively considered procedure" the Constitution prescribes for the enactment of legislation: approval by both chambers and signature of the president.

With this decision, invalidating a device included in one form or another in more than two hundred laws enacted since 1932, the Court struck down at one time more provisions in more federal laws than it had invalidated in its entire history.

VOTING RIGHTS

Karcher v. Daggett, 462 U.S. 725, decided by a 5–4 vote, June 22, 1983. Brennan wrote the opinion; Burger, Powell, Rehnquist, and White dissented.

A state must adhere as closely as possible to the "one person, one vote" standard of reapportionment. When precise equality is not achieved, the state must prove the variations are necessary to achieve some other important state goal. New Jersey did not prove this for its congressional redistricting plan that had a variation of less than 1 percent between the least and most populous districts. Therefore, its plan was invalid.

Brown v. Thomson, 462 U.S. 835, decided by a 5–4 vote, June 22, 1983. Powell wrote the opinion; Brennan, White, Marshall, and Blackmun dissented.

Wyoming law, requiring that each county have at least one representative in the state House of Representatives, is constitutional even though there is an 89 percent population variance between the largest and smallest counties. That result is permissible because the state has a legitimate interest in assuring each county its own representative.

1984

CIVIL RIGHTS

Firefighters Local Union No. 1794 v. Stotts, 467 U.S. 561, decided by a 6–3 vote, June 11, 1984. White wrote the Court's opinion; Brennan, Marshall, and Stevens dissented.

Federal judges may not override valid seniority systems to preserve the jobs of black workers hired under an affirmative action plan. Such good-faith seniority systems are expressly immunized from challenge as discriminatory under the Civil Rights Act of 1964.

DUE PROCESS

Schall v. Martin, Abrams v. Martin, 467 U.S. 253, decided by a 6–3 vote, June 4, 1984. Rehnquist wrote the opinion; Brennan, Marshall, and Stevens dissented.

For the first time, the Court upheld as constitutional a law providing for the preventive pretrial detention of suspects. The Court held that New York's law permitting pretrial detention of juveniles, when there is a serious risk that the juvenile may commit a serious crime before trial, falls within the bounds set by the constitutional guarantee of due process.

EQUAL PROTECTION

Grove City College v. Bell, 465 U.S. 555, decided by a 6–3 vote, February 28, 1984. White wrote the opinion; Brennan, Marshall, and Stevens dissented.

Title IX of the 1972 Education Amendments—barring sex discrimination in any "program or activity" receiving federal aid, does not apply to every program at an institution—but only to the particular program receiving aid.

FREEDOM OF ASSOCIATION

Roberts v. U.S. Jaycees, 468 U.S. 609, decided by a 7–0 vote, July 3, 1984. Brennan wrote the opinion; Burger and Blackmun did not participate.

Minnesota may invoke its public accommodations law to require the Jaycees, a large, nonexclusive membership organization, to admit women as full members. The state's interest in equal treatment for women outweighs any First Amendment freedom the Jaycees might assert.

FREEDOM OF RELIGION

Lynch v. Donnelly, 465 U.S. 668, decided by a 5–4 vote, March 5, 1984. Burger wrote the opinion; Brennan, Marshall, Blackmun, and Stevens dissented.

The inclusion of a nativity scene in a city-sponsored holiday display does not violate the First Amendment ban on establishment of religion. The Constitution, held the Court, "affirmatively mandates accommodation, not merely tolerance, of all religions, and forbids hostility toward any."

RIGHT TO COUNSEL

Nix v. Williams, 467 U.S. 431, decided by a 7–2 vote, June 11, 1984. Burger wrote the opinion; Brennan and Marshall dissented.

The Court approved an "inevitable discovery" exception to the exclusionary rule, permitting the use of evidence taken illegally if the prosecution shows that it would ultimately have been discovered by lawful means.

SEARCH AND SEIZURE

United States v. Leon, 468 U.S. 897, decided by a 6–3 vote, July 5, 1984. White wrote the opinion; Brennan, Marshall, and Stevens dissented.

Illegally obtained evidence may be used by the prosecution at trial if the police who seized it had a search warrant and thought they were acting legally. This ruling was the Court's first adoption of a "good faith" exception to the exclusionary rule it had adopted seventy years earlier in *Weeks v. United States,* barring all use of such evidence at trial.

This decision was limited to a situation in which police had a warrant and executed a search in accord with it, only to have the warrant later found defective. In such a case, there was no deterrent effect to excluding the evidence, and exclusion exacted too high a price from society, the Court held.

SELF-INCRIMINATION

New York v. Quarles, 467 U.S. 649, decided by 5–4 and 6–3 votes, June 12, 1984. Rehnquist wrote the opinion; O'Connor, Stevens, Marshall, and Brennan dissented.

The Court recognized a "public safety" exception to the rule set out in *Miranda v. Arizona* (1966), which denies prosecutors use of evidence obtained from a suspect who was not advised first of his constitutional rights. This decision was the first exception to that rule.

The Court reasoned that in some situations, concern for the public safety dictates that police immediately ask a suspect a particular question, such as "Where's the gun?" In these cases, the suspect's reply and any evidence it leads to may be used against him.

1985

EQUAL PROTECTION

Cleburne v. Cleburne Living Center Inc., 473 U.S. 432, decided by 9–0 and 6–3 votes, July 1, 1985. White wrote the opinion; Brennan, Marshall, and Stevens dissented in part.

Laws that treat the mentally retarded differently from other citizens are constitutional so long as they are a rational means to a legitimate end. Using that test, the Court struck down a city's zoning ordinance-based denial of a permit for a group home for mentally retarded adults in a residential neighborhood. That requirement was based on an irrational prejudice against the retarded, an impermissible basis for a city's action.

FREEDOM OF EXPRESSION

Federal Election Commission v. National Conservative Political Action Committee, Democratic Party of the United States v. National Conservative Political Action Committee, 470 U.S. 480, decided by a 7–2 vote, March 18, 1985. Rehnquist wrote the opinion; Marshall and White dissented.

Congress cannot limit independent spending by political action committees in presidential campaigns. The First Amendment guarantee of free speech is violated by the $1,000 limit imposed by the Federal Election Campaign Act Amendments on independent expenditures by PACs to promote or prevent the election of publicly funded presidential candidates.

FREEDOM OF RELIGION

Wallace v. Jaffree, 472 U.S. 38, decided by a 6–3 vote, June 4, 1985. Stevens wrote the opinion; Burger, Rehnquist, and White dissented.

Moment-of-silence laws intended to restore prayer to the nation's public schools are unconstitutional. The Court struck down an Alabama law that permitted a moment of silence for prayer or meditation at the beginning of each school day. The history of the law made clear that it was intended as an endorsement of religion, to encourage students to pray. Such state endorsement of religion is a violation of the First Amendment's establishment clause.

Aguilar v. Felton, 473 U.S. 402, decided by a 5–4 vote, July 1, 1985. Brennan wrote the opinion; Burger, White, Rehnquist, and O'Connor dissented.

New York's system for providing remedial and counseling services to disadvantaged students who attend nonpublic schools violates the First Amendment because it uses federal funds to send teachers and other educational personnel into private and parochial schools to provide services to these students during the regular school day. Therefore, like the Grand Rapids system held unconstitutional the same day in *Grand Rapids School District v. Ball,* 473 U.S. 373, it practically and symbolically advances religion by providing services the private or parochial school would otherwise have to provide itself.

POWERS OF CONGRESS

Garcia v. San Antonio Metropolitan Transit Authority, 469 U.S. 528, decided by a 5–4 vote, February 19, 1985. Blackmun wrote the opinion; Burger, Powell, Rehnquist, and O'Connor dissented.

Neither the Tenth Amendment nor any other specific provision of the Constitution limits Congress when it exercises its power to regulate commerce in such a fashion as to curtail the power of the states. The federal minimum wage and overtime law, the Fair Labor Standards Act, applies to the employees of a city owned and operated transit system. The Court overruled its 1976 decision in *National League of Cities v. Usery,* which found that the Tenth Amendment forbade the application of this law to employees of state and local governments.

The Framers of the Constitution intended for the political process and the structure of the federal government to protect state prerogatives. States must use their political power to persuade Congress, not the courts, to change federal laws they find too burdensome.

RIGHT TO COUNSEL

Ake v. Oklahoma, 470 U.S. 68, decided by an 8–1 vote, February 26, 1985. Marshall wrote the opinion; Rehnquist dissented.

Indigents seeking to defend themselves with a claim of insanity are entitled to the aid of a court-appointed psychiatrist, paid for by the government. Defendants in capital cases must also be provided psychiatric counsel when their sentence depends in part upon a finding that they pose a future danger to the community.

SEARCH AND SEIZURE

Tennessee v. Garner, 471 U.S. 1, decided by a 6–3 vote, March 27, 1985. White wrote the opinion; O'Connor, Burger, and Rehnquist dissented.

Police may not use deadly force to stop a fleeing felon unless they have reason to believe that he might kill or seriously injure persons nearby. "A police officer may not seize an unarmed, nondangerous suspect by shooting him dead," declared the Court.

1986

CIVIL RIGHTS

Wygant v. Jackson Board of Education, 476 U.S. 267, decided by a 5–4 vote, May 19, 1986. Powell announced the decision; Brennan, Marshall, Stevens, and Blackmun dissented.

An affirmative action plan voluntarily adopted by a school board, under which white teachers with more seniority were laid off to preserve the jobs of newly hired black teachers, is unconstitutional, a denial to the white teachers of the equal protection of the law. The primary flaw was that the plan was adopted without any showing that the school board had previously discriminated against black teachers. In a separate opinion, O'Connor emphasized that affirmative action,

carefully used, was an appropriate remedy for past or present discrimination by a public employer.

Local 28 of Sheet Metal Workers International Assn. v. Equal Employment Opportunity Commission, 478 U.S. 421, decided by a 5–4 vote, July 2, 1986. Brennan wrote the opinion; Burger, White, Rehnquist, and O'Connor dissented.

Court-ordered minority quotas for union admission do not violate Title VII of the 1964 Civil Rights Act, which bans discrimination in employment based on race, sex, religion, or national origin.

Local 93 of International Association of Firefighters v. City of Cleveland, 478 U.S. 501, decided by a 6–3 vote, July 2, 1986. Brennan wrote the opinion; Burger, White, and Rehnquist dissented.

Race-based promotions do not violate Title VII of the 1964 Civil Rights Act when they are part of a consent decree settling a job bias case against a city, and when the promotion plan is for a limited period of time.

CRUEL AND UNUSUAL PUNISHMENT

Lockhart v. McCree, 476 U.S. 162, decided by a 6–3 vote, May 5, 1986. Rehnquist wrote the opinion; Brennan, Marshall, and Stevens dissented.

Opponents of the death penalty may be excluded from juries in capital cases if they oppose capital punishment so strongly that they cannot objectively assess the evidence in the case. They may be excluded even if their exclusion increases the likelihood that the jury will convict the defendant.

Neither the requirement that a jury be drawn from a fair cross-section of the community nor the requirement that the jury be impartial is offended by excluding opponents of capital punishment. An impartial jury is simply one composed of jurors who will conscientiously apply the law and find the facts.

Ford v. Wainwright, 477 U.S. 399, decided by 7–2 and 5–4 votes, June 26, 1986. Marshall wrote the opinion; Rehnquist and Burger dissented; White and O'Connor dissented in part.

The Constitution forbids the execution of an insane prisoner, the Court ruled, 5–4. By a 7–2 vote, it also held inadequate Florida's procedures for deciding whether a death row inmate had lost the ability to understand the reason for his execution. Current procedures permitted that decision to be made entirely within the executive branch without any judicial participation.

EQUAL PROTECTION

Vasquez v. Hillery, 474 U.S. 254, decided by a 6–3 vote, January 14, 1986. Marshall wrote the Court's opinion; Burger, Powell, and Rehnquist dissented.

Anyone indicted by a grand jury selected in a racially discriminatory fashion has the right to a new trial, regardless of how long ago the indictment occurred.

Batson v. Kentucky, 476 U.S. 79, decided by a 7–2 vote, April 30, 1986. Powell wrote the opinion; Burger and Rehnquist dissented.

Prosecutors may not use peremptory challenges to exclude someone from jury service on the basis of race. The Court ruled that such action, when based on racial stereotypes, including the assumption that black jurors will not fairly consider the state's case against a black defendant, violates the right to a fair trial and equal right to jury service.

FREEDOM OF ASSOCIATION

Tashjian v. Republican Party of Connecticut, 479 U.S. 208, decided by a 5–4 vote, December 10, 1986. Marshall wrote the opinion; Rehnquist, Stevens, O'Connor, and Scalia dissented.

States violate the First Amendment guarantee of freedom of association by requiring political parties to hold "closed" primary elections in which only party members may vote. Parties themselves may make that decision, but they may not be required to do so by the states.

PERSONAL PRIVACY

Thornburgh v. American College of Obstetricians and Gynecologists, 476 U.S. 747, decided by a 5–4 vote, June 11, 1986. Blackmun wrote the opinion; White, Rehnquist, O'Connor, and Burger dissented.

Reaffirming *Roe v. Wade,* 1973, the Court struck down a Pennsylvania law designed to discourage women from having abortions. Among the provisions invalidated as unduly burdening a woman's private decision to have an abortion were those that set out specific methods for ensuring that a woman gave "informed consent," required physicians to report certain information about the abortion and to take special care to preserve the life of the fetus in abortions performed after a certain point in pregnancy.

Bowers v. Hardwick, 478 U.S. 186, decided by a 5–4 vote, June 30, 1986. White wrote the opinion; Blackmun, Brennan, Marshall, and Stevens dissented.

The Constitution's guarantees of personal liberty and privacy do not protect private consensual homosexual conduct between consenting adults. The Court upheld Georgia's law against sodomy, which banned oral and anal sex.

POWERS OF CONGRESS

Bowsher v. Synar, Senate v. Synar, O'Neill v. Synar, 478 U.S. 714, decided by a 7–2 vote, July 7, 1986. Burger wrote the opinion; White and Blackmun dissented.

Congress violated the constitutional separation of powers among the judicial, legislative, and executive branches when it included in the 1985 Gramm-Rudman-Hollings deficit reduction law a provision giving the comptroller general the power to tell the president what fixed-percentage cuts he must make in federal spending to meet the targets set by the bill. The comptroller general is removable from office only at the initiative of Congress, which places this position under congressional, not executive, control.

VOTING RIGHTS

Davis v. Bandemer, 478 U.S. 109, decided by 6–3 and 7–2 votes, June 30, 1986. White wrote the opinion; Burger, O'Connor, and Rehnquist dissented in part; Powell and Stevens dissented in part.

Political gerrymanders are subject to constitutional challenge and review by federal courts, even if the disputed districts meet the "one person, one vote" test, the Court held. But, 7–2, it upheld Indiana's 1981 reapportionment plan that heavily favored Republicans, saying that more than one election's results are necessary to prove a gerrymander unconstitutional.

1987

CIVIL RIGHTS

United States v. Paradise, 480 U.S. 149, decided by a 5–4 vote, February 25, 1987. Brennan wrote the opinion; Rehnquist, O'Connor, Scalia, and White dissented.

A federal judge acted constitutionally when he imposed a one-black-for-one-white promotion quota on Alabama's state police. The action was appropriate in light of the state agency's long resistance to efforts to remedy past discrimination against blacks.

Johnson v. Transportation Agency of Santa Clara County, 480 U.S. 616, decided by a 6–3 vote, March 25, 1987. Brennan wrote the opinion; Rehnquist, Scalia, and White dissented.

The Court upheld an affirmative action plan adopted voluntarily by a county agency that resulted in the promotion of a woman over a man who had scored somewhat higher during the qualifying process.

Affirmative action, carefully used, does not violate Title VII of the 1964 Civil Rights Act or the Fourteenth Amendment.

CRUEL AND UNUSUAL PUNISHMENT

Tison v. Arizona, 481 U.S. 137, decided by a 5–4 vote, April 21, 1987. O'Connor wrote the opinion; Brennan, Marshall, Blackmun, and Stevens dissented.

It is not unconstitutional to execute persons convicted of being accomplices to murder if their participation in the crime was major and they displayed reckless indifference to the value of human life.

McCleskey v. Kemp, 481 U.S. 279, decided by a 5–4 vote, April 22, 1987. Powell wrote the opinion; Brennan, Marshall, Blackmun, and Stevens dissented.

Statistics showing that black defendants are more likely than white defendants to be sentenced to death are not enough to establish that a particular black defendant was denied equal protection when he was given the death penalty.

DUE PROCESS

United States v. Salerno, 481 U.S. 739, decided by a 6–3 vote, May 26, 1987. Rehnquist wrote the opinion; Brennan, Marshall, and Stevens dissented.

The preventive detention provisions of a 1984 federal anticrime statute are constitutional. It does not violate either due process or the ban on excessive bail for a judge to invoke the law to keep in jail, before trial, a suspect who is considered a danger to the community.

FREEDOM OF RELIGION

Edwards v. Aguillard, 482 U.S. 578, decided by a 7–2 vote, June 19, 1987. Brennan wrote the opinion; Rehnquist and Scalia dissented.

A Louisiana law requiring public schools that teach the theory of evolution also to teach "creation science," violates the establishment clause because the state legislature enacted it for the purpose of promoting religion.

1988

CRUEL AND UNUSUAL PUNISHMENT

Thompson v. Oklahoma, 487 U.S. 815, decided by a 5–3 vote, June 29, 1988. Stevens wrote the opinion; Rehnquist, White, and Scalia dissented; Kennedy did not participate.

It is unconstitutional for a state to execute a capital defendant who was younger than sixteen at the time of his offense, if his sentence was imposed under a law that does not set a minimum age at which defendants are subject to the death penalty.

FREEDOM OF ASSOCIATION

New York State Club Association v. City of New York, 487 U.S. 1, decided by a 9–0 vote, June 20, 1988. White wrote the opinion.

Cities can constitutionally forbid discrimination in any place of public accommodation, including large private clubs used by their members for business purposes.

POWERS OF CONGRESS

South Carolina v. Baker, 485 U.S. 505, decided by a 7–1 vote, April 20, 1988. Brennan wrote the opinion; O'Connor dissented; Kennedy did not participate.

Neither the Tenth Amendment nor the doctrine of intergovernmental tax immunity is violated by the decision of Congress, in the 1982 Tax Equity and Fiscal Responsibility Act, to deny a federal income tax exemption for interest earned on state and local government bonds issued in unregistered form.

Morrison v. Olson, 487 U.S. 654, decided by a 7–1 vote, June 29, 1988. Rehnquist wrote the opinion; Scalia dissented; Kennedy did not participate.

Congress did not violate the separation of powers or usurp executive power when it authorized, as part of the 1978 Ethics in Government Act, the appointment of independent counsels to investigate and prosecute high government officials. The Constitution permits Congress to vest the appointment power of such officials in the judicial branch.

1989

CIVIL RIGHTS

Richmond v. J. A. Croson Co. 488 U.S. 469, decided by a 6–3 vote, January 23, 1989. O'Connor wrote the opinion; Marshall, Brennan, and Blackmun dissented.

A minority set-aside plan adopted by Richmond, Virginia, to assure that 30 percent of city funds granted for construction projects went to minority-owned firms was too rigid and insufficiently justified by past findings of specific discrimination. The Court said a state or local government's affirmative action plan could survive constitutional scrutiny only if the government had a compelling interest in creating the program and it was narrowly tailored to that interest.

Wards Cove Packing Co. v. Atonio, 490 U.S. 642, decided by a 5–4 vote, June 5, 1989. White wrote the Court's opinion; Blackmun, Brennan, Marshall, and Stevens dissented.

Citing statistics that show a particular group is underrepresented in a particular workforce is not sufficient to demonstrate racial discrimination, the Court held. The decision made it more difficult for workers to prove discrimination and made it easier for employers to rebut charges by demonstrating that there is a reasonable business justification for their policies. Congress overturned parts of this decision by passing the Civil Rights Act of 1991.

CRUEL AND UNUSUAL PUNISHMENT

Stanford v. Kentucky, 492 U.S. 361, decided by a 5–4 vote, June 26, 1989. Scalia announced the Court's decision; Brennan, Marshall, Blackmun, and Stevens dissented.

Imposition of the death penalty upon a defendant convicted of a capital crime committed when he or she was only sixteen or seventeen years old does not violate the ban on cruel and unusual punishment simply because of the defendant's youth.

Penry v. Lynaugh, 492 U.S. 302, decided by a 5–4 vote, June 26, 1989. O'Connor announced the Court's decision; Stevens, Blackmun, Brennan, and Marshall dissented.

The constitutional ban on cruel and unusual punishment does not categorically deny a state the power to execute a mentally retarded person who was found competent to stand trial, whose defense of legal insanity was rejected, and who was properly convicted.

FREEDOM OF EXPRESSION

Texas v. Johnson, 491 U.S. 397, decided by a 5–4 vote, June 21, 1989. Brennan wrote the opinion; Rehnquist, White, O'Connor, and Stevens dissented.

The First Amendment guarantee of freedom of expression precludes a state from punishing someone for desecrating the American flag in the course of a peaceful political demonstration.

FREEDOM OF RELIGION

Allegheny County v. American Civil Liberties Union, Greater Pittsburgh Chapter, 492 U.S. 573, decided by votes of 5–4 and 6–3, July 3, 1989. Blackmun wrote the opinion; Brennan, Marshall, and Stevens dissented on one point; Kennedy, Rehnquist, White, and Scalia dissented on another.

Allegheny County violated the First Amendment's establishment clause when it placed a crèche in the center of its courthouse staircase with a banner declaring "Gloria in Excelsis Deo." The vote on this point was 5–4.

But it was not unconstitutional establishment of religion for the county to include a menorah as part of a display outside another government building along with a Christmas tree. The vote on this point was 6–3. Taken together, the rulings suggested that a display that includes secular holiday symbols along with religious items can legitimately be viewed as having a secular purpose and not endorsing religion.

PERSONAL PRIVACY

Webster v. Reproductive Health Services, 492 U.S. 490, decided by a 5–4 vote, July 3, 1989. Rehnquist announced the Court's decision; Blackmun, Brennan, Marshall, and Stevens dissented.

Without overturning *Roe v. Wade,* 1973, the Court upheld Missouri's law barring the use of public facilities or public employees to perform abortions and requiring physicians to test for the viability of any fetus believed to be more than twenty weeks old.

POWERS OF CONGRESS

Mistretta v. United States, 488 U.S. 361, decided by an 8–1 vote, January 18, 1989. Blackmun wrote the opinion; Scalia dissented.

Congress did not unconstitutionally delegate authority to the U.S. Sentencing Commission when it authorized it to set binding guidelines for sentencing federal defendants.

The delegation was specific and detailed. The constitutional separation of powers does not deny Congress the power to delegate this function to a body within the judicial branch, including judges, or to direct the president to select the members of the commission.

SEARCH AND SEIZURE

Skinner v. Railway Labor Executives Association, 489 U.S. 602, decided by a 7–2 vote, March 21, 1989. Kennedy wrote the opinion; Marshall and Brennan dissented.

The Court upheld the Federal Railroad Administration's requirement that railroad workers be subjected to tests for drug and alcohol use after major accidents and other safety violations.

Such tests are a search, but they are reasonable in light of the government's compelling interest in protecting public safety, and warrants are not required.

National Treasury Employees Union v. Von Raab, 489 U.S. 656, decided by a 5–4 vote, March 21, 1989. Kennedy wrote the opinion; Marshall, Brennan, Scalia, and Stevens dissented.

The Court upheld the mandatory drug testing required by the U.S. Customs Service for employees who apply for promotions to positions involving drug-interdiction duties or carrying firearms.

In light of the government's interest in the integrity of the law enforcement process, this "search" is reasonable and may be conducted without a warrant and without any particularized suspicion of an employee.

1990

CIVIL RIGHTS

Metro Broadcasting Inc. v. Federal Communications Commission, Astroline Communications Co. v. Shurberg Broadcasting of Hartford Inc., 497 U.S. 547, decided by a 5–4 vote, June 27, 1990. Brennan wrote the opinion; O'Connor, Rehnquist, Scalia, and Kennedy dissented.

Congress may order preferential treatment of blacks and other minorities to increase their ownership of broadcast licenses. Racial preferences, including those not specifically intended to compensate victims of past discrimination, are constitutional as long as they serve important government objectives.

The Court rejected an argument that the broadcast set-aside programs at issue violated the constitutional guarantee of equal protection of the laws. It stressed Congress's determination that race-based preferences are necessary for broadcast diversity. Distinguishing the case from a 1989 decision in *City of Richmond v. J. A. Croson Co.,* which struck down a city's set-aside program, the Court said the federal government has more power to legislate racial preferences than do state and local governments.

FREEDOM OF ASSOCIATION

Rutan v. Republican Party of Illinois, Frech v. Rutan, 497 U.S. 62, decided by a 5–4 vote, June 21, 1990. Brennan wrote the opinion; Scalia, Rehnquist, Kennedy, and O'Connor dissented.

It is unconstitutional to hire, promote, or transfer most public employees based on party affiliation. Such patronage infringes on the First Amendment rights of public employees unless party membership is an appropriate requirement for the job, for example, in a policy or confidential position. The ruling expanded a 1976 decision, *Elrod v. Burns,* that patronage firing violates the First Amendment right of free association.

FREEDOM OF EXPRESSION

United States v. Eichman, United States v. Haggerty, 496 U.S. 310, decided by a 5–4 vote, June 11, 1990. Brennan wrote the opinion; Rehnquist, White, Stevens, and O'Connor dissented.

The federal Flag Protection Act making it a crime to burn, mutilate, or otherwise destroy a U.S. flag infringes on free speech rights. The First Amendment forbids government from stopping such political protest by asserting an interest in the physical integrity of the flag. This statute was passed by Congress in response to the Court's 1989 ruling in *Texas v. Johnson,* which invalidated a state statute making it illegal to burn a flag.

FREEDOM OF RELIGION

Employment Division, Department of Human Resources of Oregon v. Smith, 494 U.S. 872, decided by 6–3 and 5–4 votes, April 17, 1990. Scalia wrote the opinion; Blackmun, Brennan, and Marshall dissented; O'Connor dissented in part of the opinion.

States may outlaw the sacramental use of the drug peyote without violating the First Amendment guarantee of free exercise of religion. In so deciding, a five-justice majority said no constitutional violation occurs when a criminal law is applied generally to all people and it has only the incidental effect of infringing on religious exercise. The Court declined to invoke a test used in earlier cases that required a state to prove it had a "compelling interest" in enforcing a statute that infringed on religious freedom. Justice O'Connor sought to keep the stricter constitutional standard.

In 1993 Congress passed the Religious Freedom Restoration Act to counteract the effects of this decision and to reinstate the "compelling interest" test in cases involving free exercise of religion.

Board of Education of the Westside Community Schools (Dist. 66) v. Mergens, 496 U.S. 226, decided by a 8–1 vote, June 4, 1990. O'Connor wrote the opinion; Stevens dissented.

Student religious groups may meet in public high schools on the same basis as other extracurricular clubs. The Equal Access Act, a 1984 federal law, does not breach the Constitution's required separation of church and state.

The Equal Access Act prohibits schools that receive federal funds and that allow extracurricular groups to meet at school from dis-

criminating against any group because of the subject it wants to discuss. The Court said that because the law grants equal access to both secular and religious speech, it was not intended to endorse or disapprove of religion.

PERSONAL PRIVACY

Cruzan v. Director, Missouri Department of Health, 497 U.S. 261, decided by a 5–4 vote, June 25, 1990. Rehnquist wrote the opinion; Brennan, Marshall, Blackmun, and Stevens dissented.

States may stop the family of a comatose patient from disconnecting life support systems unless the family shows clear and convincing evidence of the patient's previously expressed wish to die under such circumstances. Because the choice between life and death is a personal decision of overwhelming finality, the Court said, a state may require clear and convincing evidence of that personal choice.

The Court said for the first time that an individual has a constitutionally protected right to decline lifesaving food and water. All of the justices except Scalia agreed that the due process guarantee protects an interest in life as well as an interest in refusing life-sustaining treatment.

Hodgson v. Minnesota, Minnesota v. Hodgson, 497 U.S. 417, decided by separate 5–4 votes, June 25, 1990. Stevens wrote the opinion striking down a statute that required a teenage girl to notify both biological parents of her decision to have an abortion; Scalia, Kennedy, Rehnquist and White dissented. A separate majority found the statute ultimately constitutional because it provided the alternative of a judicial hearing for girls who did not want to tell their parents. Brennan, Blackmun, Marshall, and Stevens dissented.

States may compel an unmarried woman under age eighteen to tell both parents before obtaining an abortion as long as states provide a judicial hearing on her decision as an alternative to parental notice. The Minnesota statute said no abortion could be performed on a minor until at least forty-eight hours after both biological parents had been notified. Part of the statute said that if the law was ever suspended by a court, it would automatically be amended to allow a judicial hearing as an alternative to a young woman's telling both parents. The so-called judicial bypass is intended to allow a teenager to show either that she is mature enough and well-informed enough to make the abortion decision herself or that the abortion would be in her best interest.

The Court said a required notification of both parents, without exception, does not further legitimate state interests and noted that Minnesota made no exception for a divorced parent, parent without custody, or a biological parent who never married or lived with the pregnant woman's mother.

Ohio v. Akron Center for Reproductive Health, 497 U.S. 502, decided by a 6–3 vote, June 25, 1990. Kennedy wrote the opinion; Blackmun, Brennan, and Marshall dissented.

A state may require an unmarried woman under eighteen who seeks an abortion to notify at least one parent before having an abortion. The Court upheld an Ohio law that barred a physician from performing an abortion on a teenager without giving twenty-four hours' notice to one of the girl's parents or guardians. The law gave young women who did not wish to tell a parent the alternative of appearing before a judge.

The Court said the one-parent notification did not impose an undue or otherwise unconstitutional burden on a minor seeking an abortion. It did not address whether a judicial bypass is necessary in all notice statutes.

SEARCH AND SEIZURE

Michigan Department of State Police v. Sitz, 496 U.S. 444, decided by a 6–3 vote, June 14, 1990. Rehnquist wrote the opinion; Brennan, Marshall, and Stevens dissented.

Police may stop and examine drivers for signs of drunkenness at highway checkpoints. The sobriety checkpoints are not unreasonable "seizures" under the Fourth Amendment because states have a strong interest in deterring drunk driving and the intrusion on motorists stopped is slight.

1991

CIVIL RIGHTS

International Union, United Automobile, Aerospace & Agricultural Implement Workers of America, UAW v. Johnson Controls Inc., 499 U.S. 187, decided by 9–0 and 5–4 votes, March 20, 1991. Blackmun wrote the opinion; White, Rehnquist, Kennedy, and Scalia dissented from a portion of the opinion.

Companies may not exclude women from jobs that might harm a developing fetus, the Court ruled unanimously. The justices divided over how to interpret standards in federal antidiscrimination law. Five justices, led by Blackmun, said Congress had intended to forbid all hiring practices based on a worker's ability to have children. The four dissenting justices said situations could arise in which a company, because of personal injury liability and workplace costs, could lawfully exclude women based on hazards to the unborn.

CRUEL AND UNUSUAL PUNISHMENT

Payne v. Tennessee, 501 U.S. 808, decided by a 6–3 vote, June 27, 1991. Rehnquist wrote the opinion; Marshall, Blackmun, and Stevens dissented.

Evidence of a victim's character and the impact of a crime on the victim's family may be considered by the jury deciding upon the sentence of a convicted murderer who could be sentenced to die. The Eighth Amendment ban on cruel and unusual punishment does not bar a jury from considering such factors.

DUE PROCESS

Arizona v. Fulminante, 499 U.S. 279, decided by a 5–4 decision, March 26, 1991. White and Rehnquist wrote opinions for separate majorities; White, Marshall, Blackmun, and Stevens dissented.

Use of a coerced confession at trial does not automatically taint a conviction that results. If there is other evidence sufficient to convict the defendant, use of a compelled confession may be harmless error—and therefore not require a new trial. With this decision, the Court reversed a 1967 decision, *Chapman v. California,* establishing the rule that due process is always denied when a forced confession is used against a defendant.

FREEDOM OF EXPRESSION

Barnes v. Glen Theatre, 501 U.S. 560, decided by a 5–4 vote, June 21, 1991. Rehnquist wrote the opinion; White, Marshall, Blackmun, and Stevens dissented.

A state may outlaw nude dancing without violating the First Amendment's guarantee of freedom of expression. Although nude dancing may be entitled to some First Amendment protection as communication of an erotic message, other community interests in safety and morality are overriding.

FREEDOM OF THE PRESS

Masson v. New Yorker Magazine, 501 U.S. 496, decided by a 7–2 vote, June 20, 1991. Kennedy wrote the opinion; White and Scalia dissented.

Fabricated quotes may be libelous if they materially change the speaker's meaning. The question for a jury in a libel case is whether a writer acted with knowledge of falsity or reckless disregard for the truth of the passages in question.

Cohen v. Cowles Media Co., 501 U.S. 663, decided by a 5–4 vote, June 24, 1991. White wrote the opinion; Souter, Marshall, Blackmun, and O'Connor dissented.

The First Amendment does not shield the news media from lawsuits charging reporters with breaking promises of confidentiality to sources. State law may permit an individual to recover damages caused by publication of information.

Simon & Schuster v. Members of New York State Crime Victims Board, 502 U.S. 105, decided by an 8–0 vote, December 10, 1991. O'Connor wrote the opinion; Thomas did not participate.

A state law prohibiting publishers from paying criminals for their stories violates the First Amendment guarantees of free press and free speech. The Court said New York's "Son of Sam" law, which redirected criminals' book proceeds to a victims' fund, was too broadly worded. The law covered works on any subject that expressed an author's thoughts about his crime, however incidentally, and it applied to writers who admitted to crimes even if they never were charged or convicted.

FREEDOM OF SPEECH

Rust v. Sullivan, 500 U.S. 173, decided by a 5–4 vote, May 23, 1991. Rehnquist wrote the opinion; Blackmun, Marshall, Stevens, and O'Connor dissented.

Congress may forbid workers at publicly funded clinics from counseling pregnant women on abortion. The Court upheld the administration's interpretation of Title X of the Public Health Service Act of 1970 as barring not only abortions but abortion counseling. The Court said Congress may regulate the content of the speech it funds.

Rejecting a First Amendment challenge, the justices said the restriction on a clinic worker's speech accompanies a worker's decision to be employed in a project financed by the government. It observed that government is not required to subsidize abortions and said the regulations ensure that federal money is spent on services for which it has been granted.

VOTING RIGHTS

Chisom v. Roemer, United States v. Roemer, 501 U.S. 380, decided by a 6–3 vote, June 20, 1991. Stevens wrote the opinion; Scalia, Rehnquist, and Kennedy dissented.

The Voting Rights Act of 1965, as amended in 1982, applies to elections for judges. The law enacted in 1965 unquestionably applied to judicial elections, despite 1982 amendments that referred to the election of "representatives."

1992

CIVIL RIGHTS

United States v. Fordice, Ayers v. Fordice, 505 U.S. 717, decided by an 8–1 vote, June 26, 1992. White wrote the opinion; Scalia dissented.

A state has not fulfilled its constitutional obligation to desegregate a public university system if its seemingly race-neutral policies continue to foster racial discrimination. Judges assessing whether a state has made sufficient effort to desegregate its colleges and universities must ask whether the racial identity of a school stems from state policies and must examine a range of factors to determine whether the state has perpetuated segregation. The state must justify potentially discriminatory practices and explain why a high percentage of whites attend certain schools and a high percentage of blacks attend other schools.

FREEDOM OF RELIGION

Lee v. Weisman, 505 U.S. 577, decided by a 5–4 vote, June 24, 1992. Kennedy wrote the opinion; Scalia, Rehnquist, White, and Thomas dissented.

Prayer at a public school graduation ceremony violates the constitutional requirement of separation of church and state. Elementary and secondary students should not be made to feel coerced to be part of the prayer exercises. In pointing to the constitutional flaws in a Rhode Island school's graduation prayer, the justices stressed that school officials organized the prayer exercise and students were obliged to attend the graduation.

FREEDOM OF SPEECH

R. A. V. v. City of St. Paul, 505 U.S. 377, decided by 9–0 and 5–4 votes, June 22, 1992. Scalia wrote the opinion; White, Blackmun, O'Connor, and Stevens dissented in part.

A city's "hate crime" ordinance, which includes a ban on cross-burning and the display of swastikas, violates the First Amendment's free speech guarantee. The Court ruled that cities may not target "hate speech" tied to race, color, creed, religion, or gender.

The ruling striking down a St. Paul, Minnesota, ordinance was unanimous, but the justices split in their rationale. A five-justice majority said if a municipality wants to outlaw speech that would be considered "fighting words," it must outlaw all fighting words, not just race-, religion-, or gender-based epithets. It said the ordinance's content-based distinctions were impermissible.

PERSONAL PRIVACY

Planned Parenthood of Southeastern Pennsylvania v. Casey, 505 U.S. 833, decided by 5–4 and 7–2 votes, June 29, 1992. O'Connor, Kennedy, and Souter wrote the opinion; Rehnquist, White, Scalia, and Thomas dissented from the part of the opinion upholding a woman's right to an abortion; Blackmun and Stevens dissented from the part of the opinion allowing Pennsylvania abortion restrictions to stand.

The Court affirmed the central holding of *Roe v. Wade,* 1973, which established a constitutional right to abortion and said states may not prohibit abortions at least until a fetus becomes viable. But a plurality of justices instituted a new standard for testing whether state restrictions infringe on the abortion right and upheld Pennsylvania regulations that had earlier been found to conflict with the "fundamental" right to abortion.

The plurality said the standard should be whether a regulation puts an "undue burden" on a woman seeking an abortion. An undue burden exists when a regulation places substantial obstacles in the path of a woman seeking an abortion before the fetus is viable. The Court said a state may adopt regulations to further the health or safety or a woman seeking an abortion but may not impose unnecessary health regulations.

The Pennsylvania provisions that were upheld required a woman seeking an abortion to wait twenty-four hours after being given certain information about the medical procedure and alternatives; required minors to obtain permission from one parent or, alternatively, to go before a judge to get a waiver; imposed reporting requirements on facilities providing abortions; and defined a "medical emergency" that excused compliance with the foregoing requirements. The Court struck down a provision requiring that a woman seeking an abortion sign a statement that she has notified her husband.

1993

CIVIL RIGHTS

Harris v. Forklift Systems, 510 U.S. 17, decided by a 9–0 vote, November 9, 1993. O'Connor wrote the opinion.

A worker who claims sexual harassment must prove the existence of a hostile or abusive work environment but need not show that he or she suffered serious psychological injury as a result of the harassment. The Court said the prohibition on sex discrimination in Title VII of the Civil Rights Act of 1964 "comes into play before the harassing conduct leads to a nervous breakdown."

CRUEL AND UNUSUAL PUNISHMENT

Herrera v. Collins, 506 U.S. 390, decided by a 6–3 vote, January 25, 1993. Rehnquist wrote the opinion; Blackmun, Stevens, and Souter dissented.

A death row prisoner ordinarily is not entitled to federal review of his case based only on an assertion that he is innocent. To obtain a writ of habeas corpus, the inmate must make an independent claim that a constitutional error occurred in his trial or other state proceedings. Federal habeas courts sit not to correct errors of fact but to ensure that individuals are not imprisoned because of constitutional violations.

EXCESSIVE FINES

Austin v. United States, 509 U.S. 602, decided by a 9–0 vote, June 28, 1993. Blackmun wrote the opinion.

The government's power to seize the property of criminals in civil forfeiture proceedings is subject to the Eighth Amendment's prohibition against excessive fines. Confiscation arising from drug trafficking, racketeering, and other criminal allegations must stand in some proportion to the crime at issue, said the Court, but it left unanswered what standard should be used to determine when a forfeiture is "excessive."

FREEDOM OF RELIGION

Lamb's Chapel v. Center Moriches Union Free School District, 508 U.S. 384, decided by a 9–0 vote, June 7, 1993. White wrote the opinion.

A school district policy that denies a religious group access to school facilities after hours for a film presentation, but allows secular groups to use the premises for similar presentations, violates the First Amendment's free speech guarantee. The Court said government cannot deny a speaker the use of public facilities based on the speaker's identity or point of view. The Court rejected an argument that a neutral policy permitting religious groups as well as nonreligious groups to use school property as a meeting place is an unconstitutional establishment of religion.

Zobrest v. Catalina Foothills School District, 509 U.S. 1, decided by a 5–4 vote, June 18, 1993. Rehnquist wrote the opinion; Blackmun, Stevens, O'Connor, and Souter dissented.

The government does not violate the constitutional requirement of separation of church and state when it pays for a sign-language interpreter to accompany a deaf student who attends a parochial school. Providing an interpreter, the Court said, is permissible under the federal Individuals with Disabilities Education Act that distributes benefits neutrally to disabled children in both public and sectarian schools.

VOTING RIGHTS

Shaw v. Reno, 509 U.S. 630, decided by a 5–4 vote, June 28, 1993. O'Connor wrote the opinion; White, Blackmun, Stevens, and Souter dissented.

White voters may challenge black-majority congressional districts that are "highly irregular" in shape and lack "sufficient justification." While the race of voters may be a consideration in redistricting, the Court said, some districts could be so bizarrely drawn that they only can be understood as an effort to segregate voters by race and, therefore, violate the Fourteenth Amendment's guarantee of equal protection of the laws.

The Court said racial gerrymanders may exacerbate the racial bloc voting that "majority-minority" districts originally were intended to counteract. Governments may justify a minority district that is irregular in shape by showing it is narrowly tailored to serve a compelling government interest.

1994

DUE PROCESS

Dolan v. City of Tigard, 512 U.S. 374, decided by a 5–4 vote, June 24, 1994. Rehnquist wrote the opinion; Stevens, Blackmun, Souter, and Ginsburg dissented.

Municipalities that require property owners to turn over some of their land for public use in return for permission to develop the land must show a connection and a "rough proportionality" between conditions exacted and any asserted public harm caused by the development. Without that showing, the actions of local governments could amount to an uncompensated taking of property in violation of the guarantee of due process.

EQUAL PROTECTION

J. E. B. v. Alabama ex rel. T. B., 511 U.S. 127, decided by a 6–3 vote, April 19, 1994. Blackmun wrote the opinion; Scalia, Rehnquist, and Thomas dissented.

Lawyers may not exclude people from serving on juries solely because of their gender. The constitutional guarantee of equal protection of the laws prohibits sexual discrimination in jury selection. This ruling extended the reasoning of a line of cases beginning in 1986 that had barred lawyers from eliminating potential jurors on account of race.

FREEDOM OF EXPRESSION

Turner Broadcasting System Inc. v. Federal Communications Commission, 512 U.S. 622, decided by 9–0 and 5–4 votes, June 27, 1994. Kennedy wrote the opinion; Stevens dissented in one part; O'Connor, Scalia, Thomas, and Ginsburg dissented in another part.

Cable television is entitled to First Amendment protections comparable to those enjoyed by newspapers and other print media rather than those protections afforded broadcasters. The reason that broadcasters have lesser protection and therefore stricter regulation—the scarcity of radio and television channels—does not apply to cable television. The Court said restrictions on cable television should be reviewed under an "intermediate scrutiny" standard, which would allow a regulation of speech if it is narrowly tailored to further an important government interest.

The Court left unresolved a constitutional challenge to the 1992 law requiring cable systems to carry local broadcast stations, voting 5–4 to order a lower court to hear more evidence in the case. The dissenting justices said "must carry" rules were an inappropriate restraint on the cable operator's editorial discretion and freedom of speech.

FREEDOM OF RELIGION

Board of Education of Kiryas Joel Village School District v. Grumet, 512 U.S. 687, decided by a 6–3 vote, June 27, 1994. Souter wrote the opinion; Scalia, Rehnquist, and Thomas dissented.

A New York law creating a special school district to serve the disabled children of a Hasidic sect violates the constitutional requirement of separation of church and state. The law designated the village of Kiryas Joel, inhabited exclusively by the Satmar Hasidim, as a state school district. The Court said New York's action wrongly favored a single religious group and there was no assurance that the state would provide the same benefit equally to other religious and nonreligious groups.

FREEDOM OF SPEECH

Madsen v. Women's Health Center Inc., 512 U.S. 753, decided by a 6–3 vote, June 30, 1994. Rehnquist wrote the opinion; Scalia, Kennedy, and Thomas dissented.

Judges may establish "buffer zones" to prevent antiabortion protesters from getting too close to clinics where abortions are performed. But judges may not restrict "more speech than necessary" to protect access to clinics or other government interests. The Court upheld an injunction prohibiting demonstrations within thirty-six feet of a clinic because it was aimed at protesters who had violated an earlier court order by blocking access, not at their particular anti-abortion message, and because it curtailed no more speech than necessary.

VOTING RIGHTS

Holder v. Hall, 512 U.S. 874, decided by a 5–4 vote, June 30, 1994. Kennedy wrote the opinion; Blackmun, Stevens, Souter, and Ginsburg dissented.

The size of a governing body—in this case a single county commissioner with executive and legislative authority—is not subject to challenge under the federal Voting Rights Act. The Court barred a lawsuit against the unusual government structure used in rural Bleckley County, Georgia. Blacks, who made up about 20 percent of the county's population, claimed the single-member commission violated the Voting Rights Act by "diluting" their opportunity to elect a black to the office.

1995

CIVIL RIGHTS

Adarand Constructors Inc. v. Peña, 515 U.S. 200, decided by a 5–4 vote, June 12, 1995. O'Connor wrote the opinion; Stevens, Souter, Ginsburg, and Breyer dissented.

Federal affirmative action programs are unconstitutional unless they serve a compelling government interest and are narrowly tailored to address that interest. Federal policies based on race should undergo the strictest judicial scrutiny to ensure that an individual's right to equal protection of the laws has not been infringed.

The Court did not decide whether the particular affirmative action program before it—a federal highway contracting program that gave bonuses to companies that subcontracted with minority-owned firms—was constitutional or not, leaving that to lower courts to resolve based on its new, heightened standard of scrutiny. With this decision the Court overturned its 1990 ruling in *Metro Broadcasting Inc. v. Federal Communications Commission,* which said minority set-asides are constitutional as long as they serve important government objectives.

Missouri v. Jenkins, 515 U.S. 70, decided by a 5–4 vote, June 12, 1995. Rehnquist wrote the opinion; Stevens, Souter, Ginsburg, and Breyer dissented.

A federal district judge overseeing a school desegregation plan exceeded his authority when he ordered extra public spending to make the district more attractive to students in other districts and to reverse the trend of "white flight." Desegregation remedies must be tailored to address specific constitutional violations within a district.

COMMERCE

United States v. Lopez, 514 U.S. 549, decided by a 5–4 vote, April 26, 1995. Rehnquist wrote the opinion; Breyer, Stevens, Souter, and Ginsburg dissented.

Congress exceeded its authority to regulate interstate commerce when it passed a law banning guns within one thousand feet of a school. The Court said the statute had "nothing to do with commerce or any sort of economic enterprise." The simple possession of a gun in or near a school is an essentially local, noncommercial activity that does not have a substantial effect on interstate commerce, the Court said.

FREEDOM OF EXPRESSION

McIntyre v. Ohio Elections Commission, 514 U.S. 334, decided by a 7–2 vote, April 19, 1995. Stevens wrote the opinion; Scalia and Rehnquist dissented.

States cannot prohibit the distribution of anonymous leaflets and other campaign literature without impinging the First Amendment. Anonymous pamphleteering is part of the nation's heritage, the Court said, and a way to ensure that the voices of the minority are protected from the majority.

Hurley v. Irish-American Gay, Lesbian and Bisexual Group of Boston, 515 U.S. 557, decided by a 9–0 vote, June 19, 1995. Souter wrote the opinion.

The organizers of a parade cannot be required by state law to include participants with whom they disagree, in this case, marchers who wish to proclaim their homosexual identity. A parade is a form of private expression protected by the First Amendment's guarantee of free speech.

FREEDOM OF RELIGION

Rosenberger v. University of Virginia, 515 U.S. 819, decided by a 5–4 vote, June 29, 1995. Kennedy wrote the opinion; Stevens, Souter, Ginsburg, and Breyer dissented.

A university violated the First Amendment by refusing to provide funds for a student group's Christian magazine while at the same time subsidizing nonreligious student publications. The Court rejected an argument that the constitutional requirement of separation of church and state prohibits a university from providing funds for a religious group. A university that sets up a general policy for disbursing student activity funds must subsidize secular and religious publications on the same basis.

Capital Square Review and Advisory Board v. Pinette, 515 U.S. 753, decided by a 7–2 vote, June 29, 1995. Scalia wrote the opinion; Stevens and Ginsburg dissented.

Government officials cannot exclude a privately sponsored religious message from a public forum so long as the forum is open to other privately sponsored messages. Ohio officials denied members of the Ku Klux Klan their free speech rights when they barred them from putting up a large wooden cross in front of the state capitol. Such exclusion was not required to preserve the separation of church and state, the Court said, reasoning that a privately erected cross in a public forum would not cause an observer to think that the state endorsed its message.

SEARCH AND SEIZURE

Vernonia School District 47J v. Acton, 515 U.S. 646, decided by a 6–3 vote, June 26, 1995. Scalia wrote the opinion; O'Connor, Stevens, and Souter dissented.

Public schools may require all student participants in sports to undergo drug tests, regardless of whether any are suspected of drug use. A school district's urinalysis requirement does not violate the constitutional protection against unreasonable searches because children do not have the full fundamental rights of adults and can be subjected to more regulation by school officials, who act as substitute parents.

STATE POWERS

U.S. Term Limits, Inc. v. Thornton, 514 U.S. 779, decided by a 5–4 vote, May 22, 1995. Stevens wrote the opinion; Rehnquist, O'Connor, Scalia, and Thomas dissented.

States may not set a limit on the number of terms their representatives serve in Congress. The Constitution sets three qualifications for members of Congress: age, citizenship, and residency. To allow states to adopt term limits would create a patchwork of tenure qualifications and undermine the uniform national character of Congress sought by the Founders.

VOTING RIGHTS

Miller v. Johnson, 515 U.S. 900, decided by a 5–4 vote, June 29, 1995. Kennedy wrote the opinion; Stevens, Souter, Ginsburg, and Breyer dissented.

A judge should strictly scrutinize any redistricting plan in which the race of voters has been a "predominant factor" in drawing boundaries. Strict scrutiny is required by the Constitution to ensure that "majority minority" districts do not violate white voters' right to equal protection. A state must prove that it has a compelling interest in drawing districts in which race was a predominant factor and that the districts have been narrowly tailored to meet that interest.

1996

CIVIL RIGHTS

Romer v. Evans, 517 U.S. 620, decided by a 6–3 vote, May 20, 1996. Kennedy wrote the opinion; Scalia, Rehnquist, and Thomas dissented.

An amendment to the Colorado state constitution prohibiting local laws that protect homosexuals from discrimination violates the federal Constitution's guarantee of equal protection. The amendment, adopted by voters in 1992, barred any legislative, executive, or judicial action designed to protect Coloradans based on their "homosexual, lesbian or bisexual orientation, conduct, practices or relationships."

The Court said the amendment lacked a rational relationship to any legitimate state interest. Indeed, it "seems inexplicable by anything but animus toward the class that it affects," the majority said.

DUE PROCESS

Bennis v. Michigan, 516 U.S. 442, decided by a 5–4 vote, March 4, 1996. Rehnquist wrote the opinion; Stevens, Souter, Breyer, and Kennedy dissented.

A state law that allows an innocent co-owner to forfeit property because of the other owner's criminal activity does not violate the Fourteenth Amendment's due process clause or the Fifth Amendment protection against takings. The case involved a woman whose car was seized after her husband was caught in the car engaging in a sex act with a prostitute. The wife protested the forfeiture, saying she did not know her husband would use the car to violate state law. But the Court said that a co-owner's lack of knowledge of the wrongdoing is not an adequate defense.

BMW of North America v. Gore, 517 U.S. 559, decided by a 5-4 vote, May 20, 1996. Stevens wrote the opinion; Rehnquist, Scalia, Thomas, and Ginsburg dissented.

A state court jury award of punitive damages against an auto manufacturer for $2 million is "grossly excessive" and in violation of the standards for punitive damages under the Due Process Clause of the Fourteenth Amendment.

EQUAL PROTECTION

United States v. Virginia, 518 U.S. 515, decided by a 7–1 vote, June 26, 1996. Ginsburg wrote the opinion; Scalia dissented; Thomas did not participate.

The exclusion of women from the state-funded Virginia Military Institute breaches the constitutional guarantee of equal protection. When government defends sex-based distinctions, it must demonstrate an "exceedingly persuasive justification" for them.

Emphasizing that government may not rely on stereotypes of the talents and preferences of men and women, the Court reinforced its view that a state policy that separates people by sex is constitutional only if it serves important governmental objectives and is substantially related to the achievement of those objectives.

Colorado Republican Federal Campaign Commission v. Federal Election Commission, 518 U.S. 604, decided by a 7-2 vote, June26, 1996. Breyer wrote the opinion; Stevens and Ginsburg dissented.

The First Amendment prohibits application of monetary limits under federal campaign finance law to an expenditure that a state political party has made independently, without coordination with any candidate. Because the government did not point to evidence or legislative findings suggesting any special corruption problem in respect to political parties' independent expenditures, the Court's prior cases forbid regulation of such expenditures.

Denver Area Educational Telecommunications Consortium, Inc. v. Federal Communications Commission, 518 U.S. 727, decided by a split 7-2 decision, June 28, 1996. Breyer wrote the opinion; Kennedy and Ginsburg dissented.

The provision of the Cable Television Consumer Protection and Competition Act of 1992 allowing cable operators to prohibit sexually explicit programming on leased channels is valid. The Court, however, held the public access provision of the law unconstitutional by a 5-4 vote and overturned the "segregate and block" provision by a 6-3 vote. The Court recognized the government's interest in dealing with "an extraordinarily important problem"—"protecting children from exposure to patently offensive depictions of sex." The government may regulate speech to address "extraordinary problems" if the regulations are "appropriately tailored to resolve those problems without imposing an unnecessarily great restriction on speech." The act's blocking requirement is unconstitutional because the government has less restrictive ways of accomplishing its goal.

FREEDOM OF EXPRESSION

O'Hare Truck Service v. Northlake, 518 U.S. 712, decided by a 7–2 vote, June 28, 1996. Kennedy wrote the opinion; Scalia and Thomas dissented.

Government officials may not retaliate against a contractor for voting for a political opponent or otherwise refusing to pledge political allegiance. The Court extended to contractors First Amendment associational protections articulated in past cases to protect regular payroll employees from being fired because they declined to adopt the policies of the government for which they worked.

FREEDOM OF SPEECH

44 Liquormart v. Rhode Island, 517 U.S. 484, decided 9–0, May 13, 1996. Stevens wrote the opinion.

A Rhode Island prohibition on the advertisement of retail liquor prices violates the First Amendment guarantee of free speech. While the justices splintered in their reasoning over four separate opinions, the majority offered broad protections for commercial speech and said advertising that is neither false nor misleading should be especially scrutinized. Regarding the law's regulation of liquor prices, Stevens, joined by three justices, said courts should be especially skeptical of regulations "that seek to keep people in the dark for . . . their own good."

Board of County Commissioners, Wabaunsee County v. Umbehr, 518 U.S. 668, decided by a 7–2 vote, June 28, 1996. O'Connor wrote the opinion; Scalia and Thomas dissented.

The First Amendment protects independent contractors from being terminated for speaking out on public issues. The Court extended free speech protections similar to those enjoyed by regular payroll employees to independent contractors, finding that, although an individual's and the government's interests are typically less strong in an independent contractor case, contractors are similar in most relevant respects. The majority said lower courts should weigh the public employer's legitimate interests against the contractor's free speech rights.

HABEAS CORPUS

Felker v. Turpin, 518 U.S. 1051, decided 9–0, June 28, 1996. Rehnquist wrote the opinion.

A federal law limiting successive habeas corpus petitions, intended by Congress to eliminate protracted appeals from death row prisoners, is constitutional. The Court said that while Congress changed the standards for the justices' review of most second and successive petitions, lawmakers did not constrain the Court's ability to hear habeas petitions as an original matter (petitions made directly to the Supreme Court, rather than coming from lower courts) and therefore did not affect the Court's constitutional jurisdiction.

STATE SOVEREIGNTY

Seminole Tribe of Florida v. Florida, 517 U.S. 44, decided by a 5–4 vote, March 27, 1996. Rehnquist wrote the opinion; Stevens, Souter, Ginsburg, and Breyer dissented.

The Eleventh Amendment prevents Congress from authorizing lawsuits by Indian tribes to enforce federal legislation relating to Indian gambling compacts. The Indian Gaming Regulatory Act allowed tribes to run commercial gambling operations under valid agreements with a state. The act required states to negotiate in good faith with a tribe toward a compact and said a tribe could sue a state in federal court to compel the negotiations.

The Court ruled that Congress infringed on state sovereignty in allowing states to be sued. Congress may abrogate state sovereign immunity only when it acts pursuant to a valid exercise of power; the Indian Commerce Clause does not provide such authority.

VOTING RIGHTS

Bush v. Vera, 517 U.S. 952, decided by a 5–4 vote, June 13, 1996. O'Connor wrote the opinion; Stevens, Ginsburg, Breyer, and Souter dissented.

Two Texas majority-black congressional voting districts and one majority-Hispanic district violate the equal protection guarantee because residents' race was the predominant factor in drawing boundaries and state officials lacked a compelling reason for the emphasis on race. The Court adopted findings from a special three-judge panel that Texas had substantially neglected traditional districting criteria, such as compactness, and had been committed from the outset to creating minority districts.

Shaw v. Hunt, 517 U.S. 899, decided by a 5–4 vote, June 13, 1996. Rehnquist wrote the opinion; Stevens, Ginsburg, Breyer, and Souter dissented.

A North Carolina majority-black congressional voting district is unconstitutional because race was the predominant factor in drawing the lines and the state lacked a compelling interest for the action. The Court rejected North Carolina's arguments that the majority black district was required under federal voting rights law to eliminate the lingering effects of discrimination.

1997

CIVIL LAW

Amchem Products, Inc. v. Windsor, 521 U.S. 591, decided by a 6–2 vote, June 25, 1997. Ginsburg wrote the opinion; Stevens and Breyer dissented. O'Connor did not participate.

An asbestos settlement scheme establishing a $1.3 billion fund for claims is invalid because it had "no structural assurance of fair and adequate representation for the diverse groups and individuals affected." The ruling limits the defensive use of class-action settlements to resolve mass torts under the Federal Rules of Civil Procedure. The "sprawling" class did not meet the federal rules' requirements, and judges were "not free to amend a rule" for the convenience of managing a complex case. The Court acknowledged that while a uniform administrative claims system would be "the most secure, fair, and efficient means of compensating victims of asbestos exposure … Congress has not adopted such a solution."

DUE PROCESS

Kansas v. Hendricks, 521 U.S. 346, decided by a 5–4 vote, June 23, 1997. Thomas wrote the opinion; Stevens, Souter, Ginsburg, and Breyer dissented.

States can lock up sex offenders for treatment after they have served their prison terms. Kansas law said "sexual predators" who have a "mental abnormality" are a danger to the public and should be confined for treatment. Leroy Hendricks, a pedophile who had served his full ten-year prison term, contended that the added confinement violated his rights to due process of law and his protection against double jeopardy and ex post facto laws. Disagreeing, Thomas said civil confinement is not criminal punishment and is therefore not double jeopardy or an ex post facto violation.

ESTABLISHMENT OF RELIGION

Agostini v. Felton, 521 U.S. 203, decided by a 5–4 vote, June 23, 1997. O'Connor wrote the opinion; Stevens, Souter, Ginsburg, and Breyer dissented.

Federal funds can be used to send public school tutors into parochial schools to give instruction to low-income students. The federal education law known as Chapter 1 requires public school districts to tutor poor students in need, regardless of where they attend school, but in *Aguilar v. Felton* (1985) the Court ruled that sending public teachers into religious schools wrongly abridged the separation of church and state. Two dissenters from 1985, Rehnquist and O'Connor, joined with three others to overrule the decision. *Aguilar* "is no longer good law," O'Connor said.

EXECUTIVE IMMUNITIY

Clinton v. Jones, 520 U.S. 681, decided by a 9–0 vote, May 27, 1997. Stevens wrote the opinion; Breyer concurred.

A president is not immune from being sued and forced to stand trial for alleged private wrongdoing. In *Nixon v. Fitzgerald* (1982) the court ruled that a president is forever shielded from being sued over "official acts," but the justices refused to extend that shield of immunity to the president's private life. In 1994 President Bill Clinton was sued for sexual harassment by Paula Corbin Jones, a former Arkansas state employee. He claimed a "temporary immunity" from being sued while serving as president. After the Court allowed Jones' lawsuit to proceed, her lawyers learned of Monica Lewinsky, a former White House intern. When asked about her during a deposition in the Jones case, Clinton gave misleading answers, which led the House of Representatives to impeach him. He was acquitted by the Senate.

FREEDOM OF EXPRESSION

Reno v. American Civil Liberties Union, 521 U.S. 844, decided by a 9–0 vote, June 26, 1997. Stevens wrote the opinion; Rehnquist and O'Connor concurred.

Congress cannot make it a crime to post on the Internet "indecent" and sexually explicit material. This restriction—part of the Communications Decency Act passed in 1996 as part of the wideranging Telecommunications Act—was so broad and its terms so vague that libraries and art galleries could violate it by posting paintings and photographs on their Web sites, the Court held. Stevens described the Internet as a "unique and wholly new medium of worldwide human communication" and said the Court should be cautious about upholding criminal restrictions on this form of free speech. This case was the Court's first ruling concerning the Internet.

Turner Broadcasting System, Inc. v. Federal Communications Commission, 520 U.S. 180, decided by a 5–4 vote, March 31, 1997. Kennedy wrote the opinion; O'Connor, Scalia, Thomas, and Ginsburg dissented.

Congress did not violate the First Amendment rights of cable broadcasting companies by passing a federal law requiring cable systems to carry the signals of local television stations. The Cable Television Consumer Protection and Competition Act of 1992, which included a "must-carry provision," was narrowly tailored to further Congress's goals of preserving local broadcasting, promoting media diversity, and promoting fair competition.

PERSONAL PRIVACY

Vacco v. Quill, 521 U.S. 793, and *Washington v. Glucksberg,* 571 U.S. 702, decided by 9–0 votes, June 26, 1997. Rehnquist wrote the opinions; Stevens, O'Connor, Souter, Ginsburg, and Breyer concurred.

States may enforce their traditional laws against assisted suicide. The rulings rejected "right to die" claims brought by doctors and terminally ill patients in Washington and New York. In the case from Washington, the Court said this claimed right to die with the assistance of a doctor was not a liberty or privacy right recognized in the Fourteenth Amendment. The New York case held that it was not a denial of equal protection of the laws to deny this right to terminally ill patients, but persons sustained by life-supporting medical equipment can choose to "pull the plug" and end their lives.

POWERS OF CONGRESS

City of Boerne v. Flores, 521 U.S. 507, decided by a 6–3 vote, June 25, 1997. Kennedy wrote the opinion; O'Connor and Breyer dissented. Souter dissented on jurisdictional grounds.

The Religious Freedom Restoration Act of 1993 is an unconstitutional violation of the separation of powers. Under RFRA Congress sought to define the extent of the First Amendment's Free Exercise Clause—by authority of section 5 of the Fourteenth Amendment granting Congress power to pass civil rights legislation—and require that states accommodate the free exercise of religion. The law was a direct response to the Court's opinion in *Employment Division, Department of Human Resources of Oregon v. Smith* (1990). A Catholic archbishop had invoked the federal law after city officials in Boerne, Texas, blocked his church's plans to tear down a small but historic cathedral on the town's main street. The Court asserted that the powers of Congress, while extensive, are also limited and that it is emphatically the function of the Court to determine the meaning of the Constitution. The Fourteenth Amendment grants Congress the power to pass legislation protecting civil rights against state action, an area that had never encompassed rights protected under the First Amendment.

POWERS OF THE EXECUTIVE

United States v. O'Hagan, 521 U.S. 642, decided by a 6–3 vote, June 25, 1997. Ginsburg wrote the opinion; Rehnquist, Scalia, and Thomas dissented.

It is permissible to prosecute based on the "misappropriation theory." Someone who learns of confidential information through a fiduciary relationship and then uses it to trade in securities has committed a "deception" for purposes of prosecuting under securities antifraud laws. The ruling upholds the "misappropriation theory," one of the Security and Exchange Commissions main legal strategies for combating insider trading. The Court also upheld SEC Rule 14e-3(a), or "tender offer" rule, which prohibits anyone from using information to trade in the stock of a company that is the subject of a planned tender offer if the individual knows that the information is, directly or indirectly, from either the offering company, the target company, or any of its officers, directors, or employees.

STATE SOVEREIGNTY

Printz v. United States, 521 U.S. 898, decided by a 5–4 vote, June 27, 1997. Scalia wrote the opinion; Stevens, Souter, Ginsburg, and Breyer dissented.

Congress may not require county sheriffs to conduct background checks of buyers of handguns. The decision voided a provision of the Brady Handgun Violence Prevention Act of 1993 that sought to prevent felons, drug users, and mentally ill persons from buying handguns. While Congress planned to have a national system of instant background checks, state and county sheriffs were given the duty in the interim. The Court, however, ruled that Congress cannot "commandeer" local officials and put them to work for the federal government.

1998

ATTORNEY-CLIENT PRIVILEGE

Swidler & Berlin v. United States, 524 U.S. 399, decided by a 6–3 vote, June 25, 1998. Rehnquist wrote the opinion; O'Connor, Scalia, and Thomas dissented.

The attorney-client privilege remains in effect even after the death of the client.

EXCESSIVE FINES

United States v. Bajakajian, 524 U.S. 321, decided by a 5–4 vote, June 22, 1998. Thomas wrote the opinion; Rehnquist, Scalia, Kennedy, and O'Connor dissented.

A government seizure of property was grossly disproportionate to the offense for which it was prescribed. The decision voided the seizure of $357,144 in cash that a Syrian immigrant living in Los Angeles had stuffed into his luggage before boarding a flight from Los Angeles to Cyprus. He was charged with violating a federal currency reporting law that carries a $10,000 fine. Although a judge found that the money was legally the property of Hosep Bajakajian, federal authorities demanded that the cash be forfeited to the government as smuggled goods. It was the first time that the Court ruled a government seizure to be excessive.

FREEDOM OF EXPRESSION

National Endowment for the Arts v. Finley, 524 U.S. 569, decided by a 8–1 vote, June 25, 1998. O'Connor wrote the opinion; Souter dissented.

Congress can require the federal arts endowment to consider "general standards of decency and respect for the diverse beliefs and values of the American public" before it awards grants to controversial artists. Four "performance artists" had claimed this mandate violated their right to freedom of expression. Outraged members of Congress added the mandate after they learned that federal arts funds had paid for an exhibit of homoerotic photographs by the late Robert Mapplethorpe and another by Andres Serrano that portrayed a crucifix in urine.

POWERS OF THE EXECUTIVE

Clinton v. City of New York, 524 U.S. 417, decided by a 6–3 vote, June 25, 1998. Stevens wrote the opinion; O'Connor, Scalia, and Breyer dissented.

The Line Veto Act of 1996 is unconstitutional because it allows the president to amend laws passed by Congress. Stevens said the Constitution gives the president an all-or-nothing choice when presented with a bill passed by the House and Senate—sign it into law or veto it. Passed as a reform favored by Republicans as well as Democrats, the Line Item Veto Act authorized the chief executive to "cancel" select items in large spending bills.

SEX DISCRIMINATION

Burlington Industries, Inc. v. Ellerth, 524 U.S. 742, and *Faragher v. City of Boca Raton,* 524 U.S. 775, decided by 7–2 votes, June 26, 1998. Kennedy wrote the in Ellerth; Souter wrote the opinion in Faragher; Thomas and Scalia dissented.

Companies and other employers can be held liable for sexual harassment of an employee by a mid-level supervisor unless they have taken steps to stop or prevent such harassment. The pair of 7-2 rulings made clear that employers have the duty to prevent sexual harassment of their employees. Companies can, however, shield themselves by having a strong policy against such harassment as well as a complaint procedure that allows employees to report violations.

Oncale v. Sundowner Offshore Services, 523 U.S. 75, decided by a 9-0 vote, March 4, 1998. Scalia wrote the opinion.

Federal law against sexual harassment in the workplace covers same-sex harassment, in this case a male employee by a male supervisor. The ruling revived a lawsuit brought by a worker on an offshore oil rig who said he was forced to quit because of repeated harassment and crude advances from a male supervisor. Scalia said the law forbids employment discrimination based on sex, and it is not limited to harassment of women by men.

Gebser v. Lago Vista School District, 524 U.S. 274, decided by a 5–4 vote, on June 22, 1998. O'Connor wrote the opinion; Stevens, Souter, Ginsburg, and Breyer dissented.

A school district or college cannot be held liable for a teacher's sexual harassment or abuse of a student unless a school official knew of the abuse and did nothing to stop it. The decision interpreted Title IX of the federal education code that forbids sex discrimination in schools that receive federal funds. A former high school student and her mother sued a Texas school district over a sexual affair the girl had had with her ninth grade teacher. O'Connor said the school officials did not have "actual notice" of the teacher's abusive behavior and therefore could not be held liable for it.

TAKINGS

Eastern Enterprises v. Apfel, 524 U.S. 498, decided by a 5–4 vote, June 25, 1998. O'Connor wrote the opinion; Stevens, Souter, Ginsburg, and Breyer dissented.

The required payments (totaling millions of dollars) from companies no longer contributing to an industry-wide health insurance program for retired coal miners is "an unconstitutional taking" prohibited by the Taking Clause of the Constitution. The ruling concerned the Coal Industry Retiree Health Benefit Act passed in 1992.

1999

CIVIL RIGHTS

Sutton v. United Air Lines, Inc., 527 U.S. 471, *Murphy v. United Parcel Service,* 527 U.S. 516, and *Albertsons v. Kirkingburg,* 527 U.S. 555, decided by a 7–2 vote, June 22, 1999. O'Connor wrote the opinion; Stevens and Breyer dissented.

Employees and job applicants who are capable of working are not "persons with disabilities" even if they are rejected for a particular job because of a physical impairment. The three decisions sharply limited who qualifies for protection under the Americans with Disabilities Act of 1990. Karen Sutton and her sister Kimberly Hinton, computer pilots who wear glasses, were turned down by United Air Lines because of their poor eyesight. Vaughn Murphy, a veteran truck mechanic, was fired after UPS learned he had unusually high blood pressure. Hallie Kirkinburg, an Oregon truck driver, was fired because he could see from only one eye. None of them qualified for protection from discrimination because they were not truly disabled.

DUE PROCESS

City of Chicago v. Morales, 527 U.S. 41, decided by a 6–3 vote, June 10, 1999. Stevens wrote the opinion; O'Connor, Kennedy, and Breyer concurred; Rehnquist, Scalia, and Thomas dissented.

A city cannot arrest suspected gang members for "loitering" simply because they fail to disperse when told to do so by a police officer. Such a law gives police too much authority over persons who may be standing innocently on a street corner. "Freedom to loiter for innocent purposes is part of the 'liberty' protected by … the 14th Amendment," said Stevens, Souter, and Ginsburg. O'Connor, Kennedy, and Breyer said Chicago's ordinance was "unconstitutionally vague," but could be revived if it focused on gang members who gather and intimidate others.

FUNDAMENTAL RIGHTS

Saenz v. Roe, 526 U.S. 489, decided by a 7–2 vote, May 17, 1999. Stevens wrote the opinion; Rehnquist and Thomas dissented.

States may not pay lower welfare benefits to their new residents than they pay to longer established residents. "Citizens of the United States have the right to choose" where they live, Stevens said. "The states, however, do not have any right to select their citizens." California had adopted the two-tiered welfare system in 1992 to discourage poor people from moving there. For one year, these new residents would receive the same benefits as paid in the state they left. Constitutional scholars took note because the Court's opinion relied on the all-but-forgotten Privileges and Immunities Clause of the Fourteenth Amendment.

POWERS OF THE EXECUTIVE

Department of Commerce v. United States House of Representatives, 525 U.S. 316, decided by a 6–3 vote, January 25, 1999. O'Connor wrote the opinion; Stevens, Souter, Ginsburg, and Breyer dissented.

The Census Bureau may not use statistical sampling to supplement the actual headcount. Statisticians assert that about 2 percent of the population go uncounted in the census, but the accuracy of the totals can be improved through sampling techniques. A partisan dispute arose over the Census Bureau's plan to adjust the 2000 census. House Republicans said sampling would boost the size and strength of Democrat-dominated neighborhoods. The Constitution calls for an "actual enumeration" of the population. Though not relying entirely on this provision, O'Connor said an actual headcount is required for dividing up the seats in the House of Representatives.

SEX DISCRIMINATION

Davis v. Monroe County Board of Education, 526 U.S. 629, decided by a 5–4 vote, May 24, 1999. O'Connor wrote the opinion; Rehnquist, Scalia, Kennedy, and Thomas dissented.

A student who is crudely harassed and fondled in class by another student can sue the school district for damages if the principal is told of the harassment but takes no action to stop it. "Damages are not available for simple acts of teasing and name-calling," O'Connor said, but "severe, pervasive" abuse can make it impossible for a child to learn. Aurelia Davis, the mother of LaShonda Davis, had gone to the school repeatedly to complain about a fellow fifth grader who tried to fondle LaShonda in class. O'Connor had spoken for the Court a year earlier in rejecting a lawsuit brought by a ninth grader who had been involved in a sexual relationship with a teacher. In the Davis lawsuit, unlike in the earlier case, school officials knew of the abuse.

Kolstad v. American Dental Association, 527 U.S. 526, decided by split 5–4 decision, June 22, 1999. O'Connor wrote the opinion; Stevens, Souter, Ginsburg, and Breyer dissented.

Employers can be held liable for punitive damages, in addition to the established remedies of back pay and reinstatement, in job bias suits under the Civil Rights Act of 1991. The Court established a standard for punitive damages that requires a showing of "malice" or "reckless indifference" on the part of the employer and gives employers a chance to show whether they "had been making good faith efforts to enforce an antidiscrimination policy."

STATE SOVEREIGNTY

Alden v. Maine, 527 U.S. 706, decided by a 5–4 vote, June 23, 1999. Kennedy wrote the opinion; Stevens, Souter, Ginsburg and Breyer dissented.

States cannot be sued in their own courts for failing to pay their employees the overtime pay required by the Fair Labor Standards Act. The principle of "sovereign immunity" shields states from such claims, whether in federal or state court. John Alden and his fellow probation officers in Maine said they were owed time and a half for overtime under federal law, but their lawsuit was blocked in federal and state courts. Kennedy said, however, that the United States and the Labor Department could sue on the workers' behalf.

College Savings Bank v. Florida Prepaid Postsecondary Educational Expenses Board, 527 U.S. 666, and *Florida Prepaid Postsecondary Education Expense Board v. College Savings Bank,* 527 U.S. 627, decided by 5–4 votes, June 23, 1999. Scalia wrote the opinion in *College Savings Bank;* Rehnquist wrote the opinion in *Florida Prepaid;* Stevens, Breyer, Souter, and Ginsburg dissented.

State agencies have a "sovereign immunity" that shields them from being sued by private plaintiffs for infringing a patent or a trademark. The rulings were setbacks for businesses that have as competitors state agencies, universities, or hospitals. While state agencies can sue businesses that steal one of their patented ideas, a business that has been a victim of such a theft cannot sue the state in return. College Savings Bank of New Jersey patented the idea of prepaid college tuition and sued for patent and trademark infringement when a Florida state agency adopted the program. The Court blocked the bank from pursuing its claims.

2000

DUE PROCESS

Dickerson v. United States, 530 U.S. 428, decided by a 7–2 vote, June 26, 2000. Rehnquist wrote the opinion; Scalia and Thomas dissented.

Congress does not have the authority to change "a constitutional rule" announced by the Supreme Court. The justices struck down a provision of a 1968 law in which Congress sought to reverse *Miranda v. Arizona* (1966). Because Miranda is "a constitutional decision of this Court," it "may not be in effect overruled by an Act of Congress" wrote Rehnquist, a long-time critic of the original Miranda ruling. It has "become embedded in routine police practice to the point where the warnings have become part of our national culture," he stated. Charles Dickerson, who was indicted for taking part in a bank robbery, was questioned by an FBI agent but not given his Miranda warnings. When a trial judge suppressed his statements, a U.S. court of appeals disagreed and cited the 1968 law as allowing the use of confessions that are "voluntarily given," regardless of the Miranda warnings. The Court reversed that ruling.

ESTABLISHMENT OF RELIGION

Mitchell v. Helms, 530 U.S. 793, decided by a 6–3 vote, June 28, 2000. Thomas wrote the opinion; O'Connor and Breyer concurred; Stevens, Souter, and Ginsburg dissented.

Federal funds can be spent to buy computers for use in private religious schools. Chapter 1, a federal school aid program, pays for tutoring and instructional equipment to help disadvantaged children, regardless of where they attend school. Allowing parochial schools to benefit from the money is an example of "neutrality" toward religion, not favoritism, Thomas argued. Further, the strict ban on aid for "sectarian" schools arose from anti-Catholic "bigotry" in the nineteenth century, he continued. This "hostility" to aiding parochial schools "has a shameful pedigree that we do not hesitate to disavow," Thomas wrote. In addition to upholding the use of federal aid in parochial schools, the Court overruled *Meek v. Pittenger* (1975) and *Wolman v. Walter* (1977), decisions that had struck down state laws that provided textbooks to parochial schools:

Santa Fe Independent School District v. Doe, 530 U.S. 290, decided by a 6-3 vote, June 19, 2000. Stevens wrote the opinion; Rehnquist, Scalia, and Thomas dissented.

Student-led prayers at school functions violate the First Amendment's Establishment Clause. The Court struck down a Texas school board's policy allowing high school seniors to elect one student to deliver a prayer over the stadium microphone at football games. While nothing stops "any public school student from voluntarily praying at any time before, during or after the school day," Stevens said, "school sponsorship of a religious message is impermissible." The pregame invocations were sponsored and organized by school authorities, so they are not private prayers, Stevens said. In dissent, Rehnquist said the Court's opinion "bristles with hostility to all things religious in public life."

FREEDOM OF ASSOCIATION

Boy Scouts of America v. Dale, 530 U.S. 640, decided by a 5–4 vote, June 28, 2000. Rehnquist wrote the opinion; Stevens, Souter, Ginsburg, and Breyer dissented

A New Jersey antidiscrimination statute cannot override a Boy Scouts of America policy barring homosexuals as troop leaders. The group's policy was sustained under the freedom of association the Court previously recognized under the First Amendment. James Dale, an Eagle Scout, became an adult scoutmaster and later became a leader of a campus gay rights group at Rutgers University. When the local scout troop revoked his adult membership, he sued and won a ruling in New Jersey courts that his exclusion violated the state's civil rights law.

FREEDOM OF EXPRESSION

Nixon v. Shrink Missouri Government PAC, 528 U.S. 377, decided by a 6–3 vote, January 24, 2000. Souter wrote the opinion; Scalia, Kennedy, and Thomas dissented.

A state may limit money contributions to candidates running for state office to $1,000, rejecting a free speech challenge supported by the Republican National Committee. The Court upheld the standards established in *Buckley v. Valeo* (1976), and its decision spurred reformers in Congress to pass a new campaign finance law.

FUNDAMENTAL RIGHTS

Troxel v. Granville, 530 U.S. 57, decided by a 6–3 vote, June 5, 2000. O'Connor wrote the opinion; Stevens, Scalia, and Kennedy dissented.

A state cannot require that a parent allow grandparents regular visits with his or her children. In a setback for the "grandparents' rights" movement, the Court overturned a Washington state judge's order that a mother send her two daughters to visit their grandparents monthly. The Constitution protects "the fundamental right of parents to make decisions concerning the care, custody and control of their children," O'Connor said, and the judge's visitation order violated the mother's right. Jenifer and Gary Troxel are the grandparents of Isabelle and Natalie Troxel. After their son Brad committed suicide, the girl's mother, Tommie Granville, remarried. The Troxels sued seeking visitation rights under the terms of a Washington state law that authorized judges to order visitation whenever it would "serve the best interest of the child."

PERSONAL PRIVACY

Stenberg v. Carhart, 530 U.S. 914, decided by a 5–4 vote, June 28, 2000. Breyer wrote the opinion; Rehnquist, Scalia, Kennedy, and Thomas dissented.

A Nebraska law making it a crime for doctors to perform a "partial birth abortion" is invalid. The law defined a "partial birth abortion" as "partially delivering vaginally a living unborn child before killing the unborn child." Dr. Leroy Carhart, at the time the only physician who performed second-trimester abortions in Nebraska, challenged the law. He said he sometimes performed "an intact delivery" on women who were between sixteen and twenty weeks pregnant because there was less bleeding and less risk of injury compared to using instruments to dismember the fetus. Justice Breyer said Nebraska's law was unclear because it could apply to several abortion procedures. In addition, the state may not "force women to use riskier methods of abortion" for fetuses that cannot live on their own, he said.

POWERS OF THE EXECUTIVE

Food and Drug Administration v. Brown & Williamson Tobacco Corp., 529 U.S. 120, decided by a 5–4 vote, March 21, 2000. O'Connor wrote the opinion; Stevens, Souter, Ginsburg, and Breyer dissented.

Congress had not given the Food and Drug Administration the authority to regulate cigarettes or tobacco products. The ruling voided Clinton administration rules barring sales practices and advertising designed to appeal to youthful smokers. The Court majority said Congress had considered the problem of cigarettes over many years, but had "clearly precluded the FDA from asserting jurisdiction to regulate tobacco products," O'Connor said.

STATE SOVEREIGNTY

Kimel v. Florida Board of Regents, 528 U.S. 62, decided in a split 5–4 decision, January 11, 2000. O'Connor wrote the opinion; Stevens, Souter, Ginsburg, and Breyer dissented.

State employees who are victims of age discrimination cannot sue their employers in federal court. States have a "sovereign immunity" that shields them from claims. Daniel Kimel, a professor at Florida State University, sued under the federal Age Discrimination in Employment Act, but his suit was dismissed. The ruling left nearly 5 million state employees without the full protection of federal antidiscrimination laws.

United States v. Morrison, 529 U.S. 598, decided by a 5–4 vote, May 15, 2000. Rehnquist wrote the opinion; Stevens, Souter, Ginsburg, and Breyer dissented.

Because a sexual assault is not an act of commerce, Congress exceeded its power in passing that part of the Violence Against Women Act of 1994 allowing victims of sexual assaults to sue their attackers in federal court. Moreover, because sexual assaults are private acts, not offenses by state officials, they are not acts of discrimination covered by the Fourteenth Amendment. The ruling sharply limited Congress's power to punish "hate crimes" that take place in one state.

VOTING RIGHTS

Bush v. Gore, 531 U.S. 98, decided by a 5–4 vote, December 12, 2000. An unsigned per curiam opinion. Rehnquist, Scalia, and Thomas concurred; Stevens, Souter, Ginsburg, and Breyer dissented.

A county-by-county recount of votes violates the Equal Protection Clause because the state failed to set "specific rules designed to ensure uniform treatment" of the ballots. The Court thus blocked a statewide recount of thousands of ballots in Florida that went uncounted by tabulating machines. The ruling overturned an order of the Florida Supreme Court and preserved a narrow victory in Florida—and in the electoral college—for the Republican presidential candidate, George W. Bush. Rehnquist, Scalia and Thomas said the recount was unconstitutional because the state judges had revised the election law after the election. The four dissenters in separate opinions said the Court was wrong to halt the recount. Two of them—Souter and Breyer—said they agreed on the need for uniform standards and said the recount should proceed under tighter standards.

2001

CIVIL RIGHTS

PGA Tour, Inc. v. Martin, 532 U.S. 661, decided by a 7–2 vote, May 29, 2001. Stevens wrote the opinion; Scalia and Thomas dissented.

The professional golfers' tour violated the Americans with Disabilities Act when it refused to accommodate disabled golfer Casey Martin and allow him to ride in a cart. Martin has a circulatory disorder that makes it difficult for him to walk. He is not an employee of the tour, but its tournaments are public events and are covered by the law's section on "public accommodations." The justices agreed with Martin's argument that walking is not fundamental to golf. "From early on, the essence of the game has been shot-making," Stevens said.

COMMERCE POWER

Lorillard Tobacco Co. v. Reilly, 533 U.S. 525, decided by a 5–4 vote, June 28, 2001. O'Connor wrote the opinion; Stevens, Souter, Ginsburg, and Breyer dissented.

State officials could not place limits on the advertising of cigarettes, cigars, and smokeless tobacco to protect children. The decision struck down a series of Massachusetts regulations prohibiting billboard ads for tobacco products. O'Connor said these measures were preempted by the Federal Cigarette Labeling and Advertising Act of 1965, which put warnings label on cigarette packs. The advertising restrictions also violate the First Amendment because they prohibit nearly all public promotions of a legal product.

FREEDOM OF EXPRESSION

Federal Election Commission v. Colorado Republican Federal Campaign Commission, 533 U.S. 431, decided by a 5–4 vote, June 25, 2001. Souter wrote the opinion; Rehnquist, Scalia, Kennedy, and Thomas dissented.

The provisions of the Federal Election Campaign Act limiting "coordinated expenditure" between candidates and political parties or individuals do not violate First Amendment free speech rights.

Good News Club v. Milford Central School, 533 U.S. 98, decided by a 6-3 vote, June 11, 2001. Thomas wrote the opinion; Stevens, Souter, and Ginsburg dissented.

School districts that allow private groups to use their classrooms after hours cannot exclude religious groups from using them. Milford's refusal to allow the Good News Club, a private Christian group, to meet with elementary children after class violates the group's free speech rights, and allowing them to meet on school grounds does not violate the Establishment Clause of the First Amendment.

SEARCH AND SEIZURE

Atwater v. Lago Vista, 532 U.S. 318, decided by a 5–4 vote, April 24, 2001. Souter wrote the opinion; Stevens, O'Connor, Ginsburg, and Breyer dissented.

A police officer who observes a violation of the law may make an arrest and take the offender to jail for booking, even if the offense is as minor as driving without a buckled seatbelt. The Court rejected the claim that the Fourth Amendment's ban on "unreasonable seizures" forbids police from making arrests without a warrant for minor offenses that do not call for jail time. Souter said the history of England and the colonial period shows that constables were empowered to make arrests whenever they observed violations. Gail Atwater was driving her pickup truck with her two children in the front seat when an officer pulled her over. He had previously warned her about not wearing a seat belt. This time he handcuffed her and took her to jail. She paid a $50 fine and later sued for an unconstitutional arrest.

Ferguson v. Charleston, 532 U.S. 67, decided by a 6–3 vote, March 21, 2001. Stevens wrote the opinion; Rehnquist, Scalia, and Thomas dissented.

A South Carolina hospital's policy of screening pregnant women for drugs and referring suspected women for prosecution violates the Fourth Amendment prohibition on warrantless searches.

STATE SOVEREIGNTY

Board of Trustees of University of Alabama v. Garrett, 531 U.S. 356, decided by a 5–4 vote, February 21, 2001. Rehnquist wrote the opinion; Stevens, Souter, Ginsburg, and Breyer dissented.

The provisions of the Americans with Disabilities Act of 1990 that prohibit discrimination against disabled persons in employment by state and local governments are invalid. Congress lacked the authority under section 5 of the Fourteenth Amendment to contravene the Eleventh Amendment, which bars suits against states in federal courts, absent a pattern of discrimination by the states. Patricia Garrett, a nursing supervisor at the University of Alabama Hospital in Birmingham, was demoted after being treated for breast cancer. She sued her employer under the ADA, but her suit was dismissed by the Court.

Kyllo v. United States, 533 U.S. 27, decided by a 5–4 vote, June 11, 2001. Scalia wrote the opinion; Rehnquist, Stevens, O'Connor, and Kennedy dissented.

The use of thermal imaging devices by federal agents to detect illegal activity in a private residence and secure a search warrant is a warrantless search in violation of the Fourth Amendment.

2002

CRUEL AND UNUSUAL PUNISHMENT

Atkins v. Virginia, 536 U.S. 304, decided by a 6–3 vote, June 20, 2002. Stevens wrote the opinion; Rehnquist, Scalia, and Thomas dissented.

The death penalty for a mentally retarded defendant is cruel and unusual punishment and is therefore prohibited. Persons who have an I.Q. under 70 are more likely to act on impulse and less likely to consider the consequences, Stevens noted. Opinion polls and a series of exemptions for the mentally retarded enacted by states with capital punishment show "a national consensus has developed" against executing such persons, said Stevens. Daryl Atkins robbed and killed an air force serviceman, and a Virginia jury sentenced him to die, despite testimony that he had an I.Q. of 59. After overturning his sentence, the Court sent the case back to Virginia authorities to set his punishment.

DUE PROCESS

Ring v. Arizona, 536 U.S. 584, decided by a 7–2 vote, June 24, 2002.Ginsburg wrote the opinion; Rehnquist and O'Connor dissented.

A jury, not a judge, must find beyond a reasonable doubt any aggravating factor that would increase the jail time a defendant faces for a particular crime. The Court overturned the Arizona death sentence of a defendant whose death sentence was imposed by the judge rather than the jury at the sentencing hearing.

ESTABLISHMENT OF RELIGION

Zelman v. Simmons-Harris, 536 U.S. 639, decided by a 5–4 vote, June 27, 2002. Rehnquist wrote the opinion; Stevens, Souter, Ginsburg, and Breyer dissented.

States may use taxpayers' money to provide parents with vouchers to send their children to religious schools. The decision upheld an Ohio voucher law that gives low-income parents in Cleveland the option of sending their children to private or parochial schools. The Court rejected the claim that such aid to religious schools violates the Establishment Clause of the First Amendment. The flow of public money depends on "true private choice," and therefore, does not amount to government favoritism for religion or religious schools, Rehnquist said.

FREEDOM OF EXPRESSION

Ashcroft v. Free Speech Coalition, 535 U.S. 234, decided Apr. 16, 2002 with a 6–3 vote. Kennedy wrote the opinion; Rehnquist and Scalia dissented. O'Connor dissented in part.

That part of the Child Pornography Prevention Act of 1996 that makes it a crime to own or sell computer-generated images of children engaged in sex is invalid. Child pornography is outside the protections of the First Amendment because it involves the sexual abuse of children, but the same is not true of purely imaginary or computer-created images. Kennedy said the law was written so broadly that it could brand as illegal any films that used adult actresses to play the part of teenage girls.

FREEDOM OF RELIGION

Watchtower Bible & Tract Society v. Village of Stratton, 536 U.S. 150, decided by an 8–1 vote, June 17, 2002. Stevens wrote the opinion; Rehnquist dissented.

Ordinances regulating door-to-door solicitation must be narrowly drawn in order not to infringe on the religious rights of religious or other groups, including nonreligious groups and individuals, who are poorly financed and rely extensively upon this method of communication. A Stratton, Ohio, ordinance prohibiting canvassers from going door-to-door without a permit from the mayor's office was struck down under the Free Exercise Clause.

PERSONAL PRIVACY

Board of Education of Independent School District No. 92 of Pottawatomie County v. Earls, 536 U.S. 822, decided by a 5–4 vote, June 27, 2002. Thomas wrote the opinion; Stevens, O'Connor, Souter, and Ginsburg dissented.

School authorities may require students participating in extracurricular activities to undergo regular and random drug testing. A Tecumseh, Oklahoma, school board policy subjected all students engaged in extracurricular activities to random drug testing. The justices rejected the claim that these tests amount to unreasonable searches without evidence that an individual is using drugs or the school itself has a serious drug problem. The nation has a serious drug problem, and school officials act reasonably when they act to deter drug use, Thomas said. Lindsay Earls, who sang in the choir and played an instrument in the marching band, objected to the drug tests as an invasion of her privacy. The Court had upheld drug testing for student athletes in *Vernonia School District v. Acton*) (1995). The new ruling cleared the way for testing of all students who volunteer for extracurricular activities.

POWERS OF THE EXECUTIVE

New York v. Federal Energy Regulatory Commission, 535 U.S. 1, decided by 9–0 and 6–3 votes, March 4, 2002. Stevens wrote the opinion; Thomas, Scalia, and Kennedy dissented in part.

The Federal Energy Regulatory Commission's order is valid in requiring some but not all electric utilities to transmit competitors' electricity over its lines on the same terms that the utility applies to its own transmissions.

PROPERTY RIGHTS

Tahoe-Sierra Preservation Council v. Tahoe Regional Planning Agency, 535 U.S. 302, decided by a 6–3 vote, April 23, 2002. Stevens wrote the opinion; Rehnquist, Scalia and Thomas dissented.

A government's temporary "moratorium" on private building is not a "taking" of property that entitles the owner to just compensation. The decision upholds the government's power to plan development. The Court rejected the claim that an owner's property rights are taken when he is barred from using his land for a few months or a few years. A regional planning agency had halted new building around Lake Tahoe, and the "moratorium" lasted thirty-two months. More than 700 lot owners sued, contending that the order violated their rights under the Fifth Amendment.

STATE SOVEREIGNTY

Federal Maritime Commission v. South Carolina Ports Authority, 535 U.S. 743, decided by a 5–4 vote, May 28, 2002. Thomas wrote the opinion; Stevens, Souter, Ginsburg, and Breyer dissented.

The Eleventh Amendment bars federal agency adjudications in private suits against a state.

Republican Party of Minnesota v. White, 536 U.S. 765, decided by a 5–4 vote, June 27, 2002. Scalia wrote the opinion; Stevens, Souter, Ginsburg, and Breyer dissented.

States that elect judges cannot enforce ethics rules that prohibit judicial candidates from "announcing" their views on controversial issues. The decision upheld the free speech rights of prospective judges to criticize the courts and to take stands on such issues as abortion and the death penalty. Minnesota, like most states, has ethics rules that prohibit judges from taking public stands on issues that might come before their courts. The law was successfully challenged by Gregory Wersal, an unsuccessful Republican candidate for the state supreme court.

2003

AFFIRMATIVE ACTION

Grutter v. Bollinger, Gratz v. Bollinger, 539 U.S ___ , decided by 5–4 and 6–3 votes, June 23, 2003. O'Connor wrote the *Grutter* opinion; Rehnquist, Scalia, Kennedy, and Thomas dissented. Rehnquist wrote the *Gratz* opinion; Ginsburg, Stevens, and Souter dissented.

The "compelling interest" in racial diversity validates college and university's use of a minority student's race as a "plus factor" in admissions. The decisions affirmed the rule set in *Regents of the University of California v. Bakke* (1978) allowing a limited use of race. The Court upheld the admissions policy at the University of Michigan Law School because officials "engage in a highly individualized, holistic review of each applicant's file." It, however, struck down the undergraduate admissions policy at the university because all minority applicants received twenty bonus points. O'Connor said this "mechanized selection" system violates the Equal Protection Clause by putting too much emphasis on race.

CRUEL AND UNUSUAL PUNISHMENT

Ewing v. California, 538 U.S. 11, and *Lockyer v. Andrade,* 538 U.S. ___ , decided by 5–4 votes, March 5, 2003. O'Connor wrote the opinions; Stevens, Souter, Ginsburg, and Breyer dissented.

It is not cruel and unusual punishment to sentence a repeat offender to decades in prison even if such a long sentence is triggered by a petty crime. The pair of rulings upheld California's "three strikes and you're out" law. Although the law was enacted in response to the highly publicized kidnapping and murder of twelve-year-old Polly Klass by a paroled kidnapper, the statute may be triggered by a minor crime if the offender has prior felonies. Gary Ewing had a long record of thefts and was given a twenty-five-year term for trying to steal golf clubs from a pro shop. Leandro Andrade had two burglary convictions and received a fifty-year sentence for stealing videotapes from a K-Mart.

DUE PROCESS

Demore v. Kim, 538 U.S. 510, decided by a split 6–3 decision, April 29, 2003. Rehnquist wrote the opinion; Stevens, Souter, Ginsburg, and Breyer dissented.

Immigrants previously convicted of certain crimes can be detained during deportation proceedings without an individual hearing to show that they are neither a flight risk nor a danger to the community.

Smith v. Doe, 538 U.S. 84, decided by a 6–3 vote, March 5, 2003. Kennedy wrote the opinion; Stevens, Ginsburg, and Breyer dissented.

A state law requiring previously convicted sex offenders to register with law enforcement authorities and provide current information about their residence and employment does not amount to retroactive punishment in violation of Article I's Ex Post Facto Clause because it is not punitive in intent or effect.

State Farm Mutual Automobile Insurance Co. v. Campbell, 538 U.S. 408, decided by a 6–3 vote, April 7, 2003. Kennedy wrote the opinion; Scalia, Thomas, and Ginsburg dissented.

Punitive damages should bear some reasonable proportion to a compensatory damage award in a civil suit. The Court threw out as "excessive" under due process standards a $145 million punitive damage award against a major insurance company for bad faith in mishandling an automobile accident claim against one of its policyholders. Without setting a fixed ratio, the Court suggested that punitive damages should rarely if ever be as much as ten times the amount of a compensatory damage award.

FREEDOM OF EXPRESSION

Eldred v. Ashcroft, 537 U.S. ___ , decided by a 7–2 vote, January 15, 2003. Ginsburg wrote the opinion; Stevens and Breyer dissented.

Congress may extend the time for existing copyrights for another twenty years. The ruling rejected a challenge brought by Internet archivists who post books, poems, and other writings that are in the public domain. They argued that Congress has ignored the Constitution's mandate that copyrights are monopolies for "limited times." The decision upheld the Copyright Term Extension Act of 1998, which extended the terms for most copyrights to ninety-five years from the publication date.

McConnell v. Federal Election Commission, ___ U.S. ___ , decided by a 5–4 vote on major issues, December 10, 2003. Stevens and O'Connor wrote the main opinion; Rehnquist and Breyer wrote opinions for the Court on secondary issues; Rehnquist, Scalia, Kennedy, and Thomas wrote opinions dissenting on the major issues.

Most of the important provisions of the Bipartisan Campaign Reform Act of 2002 (also known as McCain-Feingold) do not violate the First Amendment. In a monumental opinion reflecting deference to Congress' attempts to regulate campaign money, the Court upheld the BCRA's ban on "soft money" contributions channeled through political parties and restrictions on "electioneering communication" or broadcast ads funded by corporations or unions that target specific candidates close to an election. The majority opinion noted that the law was "designed to purge national politics of what was conceived to be the pernicious influence of 'big money' campaign contributions." The law will "protect the integrity of the political process" and have "only a marginal impact on the ability of contributors, candidates, officeholders and parties to engage in effective political speech." "Congress has a fully legitimate interest in maintaining the integrity of federal office holders and preventing corruption of the federal electoral process."

United States v. American Library Association, Inc., 539 U.S. ___ , decided by a 6–3 vote, June 23, 2003. Rehnquist wrote the opinion; Stevens, Souter, and Ginsburg dissented.

Public libraries must install software filters on computers to prevent juveniles from viewing sexually explicit materials on the Internet. The Court ruled that the Children's Internet Protection Act of 2000 is a constitutional exercise of Congress's spending powers and does not impose unconstitutional conditions on public libraries or free expression. Rehnquist noted that adults could request that filters be removed while they used the computers.

Virginia v. Black, 538 U.S. 343, decided by a 6–3 vote, April 7, 2003 O'Connor wrote the opinion; Kennedy, Souter, and Ginsburg dissented.

Blanket banning of cross burning violates the First Amendment's protection for freedom of speech. States can, however, make it a crime to burn a cross with an intent to intimidate if prosecutors prove that the action was meant as a threat and not solely as symbolic speech.

PRIVACY

Lawrence v. Texas, 539 U.S. ___ , decided by a 6–3 vote, June 26, 2003. Kennedy wrote the opinion; O'Connor concurred; Rehnquist, Scalia, and Thomas dissented.

State laws that criminalize private sexual conduct between consenting adults are unconstitutional. The ruling struck down a Texas sodomy law as well as similar laws in twelve other states. It also overruled *Bowers v. Hardwick* (1986), which had upheld a Georgia sodomy law. Kennedy said these laws violate the right to liberty in the Fourteenth Amendment and "demean the lives of homosexual persons."

O'Connor said they violate the Equal Protection Clause because they "brand one class of persons as criminal solely based on the State's moral disapproval."

SEX DISCRIMINATION

Nevada Department of Human Resources v. Hibbs, 538 U.S. 721, decided by a 6–3 vote, May 27, 2003.

Rehnquist wrote the opinion; Scalia, Kennedy, and Thomas dissented.

State agencies can be sued for damages by employees who are denied the right to take unpaid leave to care for a sick relative. Rehnquist rejected the state's claim that it had a "sovereign immunity" from the federal Family and Medical Leave Act of 1993. This law "aims to protect the right to be free from gender-based discrimination in the workplace," he said, and under the Fourteenth Amendment, Congress has the authority to remedy race and sex discrimination by states.

SOURCES: *United States Reports* (Washington, D.C.: U.S. Government Printing Office); *United States Law Week* (Washington, D.C.: Bureau of National Affairs); *Supreme Court Reporter* (Saint Paul, Minn.: West Publishing Company); *United States Supreme Court Reports, Lawyers' Edition* (Rochester, N.Y.: Lawyers Cooperative Publishing Company; Paul A. Freund and Stanley N. Katz, gen. eds., *History of the Supreme Court of the United States.* vol. 1, *Antecedents and Beginnings to 1801*, by Julius Goebel Jr., 1971; vol. 2, *Foundations of Power: John Marshall, 1801–1815*, by George L. Haskins and Herbert A. Johnson, 1981; vols. 3–4, *The Marshall Court and Cultural Change, 1815–1835*, by G. Edward White, 1988; vol. 5, *The Taney Period, 1836–1864*, by Carl B. Swisher, 1974; vol. 6: *Reconstruction and Reunion, 1864–1888*, part one, by Charles Fairman, 1971; vol. 7, *Reconstruction and Reunion, 1864–1888*, part two, by Charles Fairman, 1987; Supplement to vol. 7, *Five Justices and the Electoral Commission of 1877*, by Charles Fairman, 1988; vol. 8, *Troubled Beginnings of the Modern State, 1888–1910*, by Owen M. Fiss, 1993; vol. 9, *The Judiciary and Responsible Government, 1910–1921*, by Alexander M. Bickel and Benno C. Schmidt Jr., 1984 (New York: Macmillan); and Charles Warren, *The Supreme Court in United States History,* rev. ed., 2 vols. (Boston: Little, Brown, 1922, 1926).

NOTE: Any discrepancy between the votes reported for decisions in this list and those reported by other sources may be explained by the fact that this chronology summarizes the most important point of a decision and reports the vote on that point. Votes on other issues resolved in that case may differ, especially in a highly contentious case.

The Federal Court System

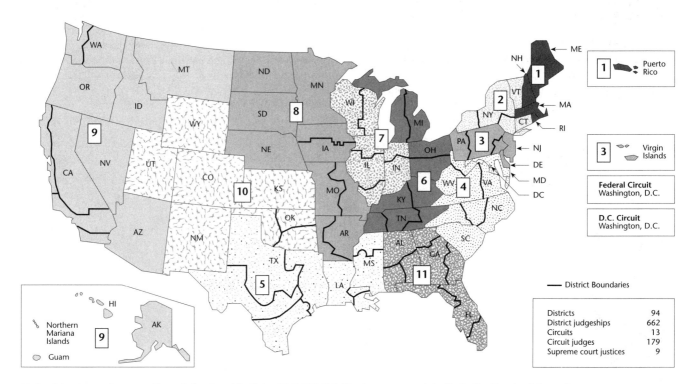

Note: Number and composition of circuits set forth by 28 U.S.C. § 4. The large numerals indicate the Courts of Appeals.

Source: Administrative Office of the United States Courts.

Illustration Credits and Acknowledgments

699   AP/Wide World Photos
702   George Harris
716   (top) Mike Peters. Reprinted by
       permission: Tribune Media Services;
       (bottom) (c) 1995 John Trever,
       Albuquerque Journal. Reprinted by
       permission.
718   AP/Wide World Photos
720   Library of Congress
732   AP/Wide World Photos
740   UPI/Bettmann
743   AP/Wide World Photos
749   AP/Wide World Photos

13. Congressional Pressure

757   Collection of the Curator, Supreme Court
       of the United States
765   (top) Library of Congress, (bottom)
       R. Michael Jenkins, Congressional
       Quarterly
767   (left) Library of Congress, (right) The
       National Portrait Gallery
769   Library of Congress
778   Library of Congress
780   Karl Hubenthal, *Los Angeles Herald
       Examiner*
787   Ohman, *The Oregonian.* (c) 1990 by
       Tribune

14. Presidential Pressure

796   LBJ Library Collection
804   *HERBLOCK: A CARTOONIST'S LIFE*
       (Macmillan, 1993)
805   (left) Library of Congress; (right) Y. R.
       Okamoto, LBJ Library Collection
808   Library of Congress

15. The Court, the Press, and the Public

816   Library of Congress
818   Library of Congress
826   Library of Congress
829   Library of Congress
835   R. Michael Jenkins, Congressional
       Quarterly

16. Operations and Traditions of the Court

841   Collection of the Curator, Supreme Court
       of the United States
851   Library of Congress
853   Franz Jantzen. Collection of the Curator,
       Supreme Court of the United States

17. The People of the Court

868   Collection of the Supreme Court of the
       United States
869   Theodore Roosevelt Collection, Harvard
       College Library
873   Library of Congress
875   Collection of the Supreme Court of the
       United States
876   Collection of the Supreme Court of the
       United States
887   Library of Congress

18. Courtrooms and Costs

894   Library of Congress
896   Library of Congress
897   R. Michael Jenkins, Congressional
       Quarterly

898   Collection of the Supreme Court of the
       United States

19. Members of the Court

903   Library of Congress

20. Brief Biographies

915   National Portrait Gallery
917   Library of Congress
918   Independence National Historical Park
       Collection
919   The Historical Society of Pennsylvania
920   Colonial Williamsburg Foundation
922   James Iredell Association
923   Collection of the Supreme Court of the
       United States
924   Collection of the Supreme Court of the
       United States
925   National Portrait Gallery
926   Independence National Historical Park
927   Library of Congress
928   Collection of the Supreme Court of the
       United States
929   Collection of the Supreme Court of the
       United States
930   Collection of the Supreme Court of the
       United States
931   New York Historical Society
932   Collection of the Supreme Court of the
       United States
933   Library of Congress
934   Collection of the Supreme Court of the
       United States
935   Collection of the Supreme Court of the
       United States
936   Library of Congress
937   (top) Collection of the Supreme Court of
       the United States, (bottom) Collection
       of the Supreme Court of the United
       States
938   Collection of the Supreme Court of the
       United States
939   Library of Congress
940   Library of Congress
941   Collection of the Supreme Court of the
       United States
942   Collection of the Supreme Court of the
       United States
943   Collection of the Supreme Court of the
       United States
944   (top) Collection of the Supreme Court of
       the United States, (bottom) Library of
       Congress
945   Collection of the Supreme Court of the
       United States
946   Collection of the Supreme Court of the
       United States
947   Collection of the Supreme Court of the
       United States
948   Collection of the Supreme Court of the
       United States
949   Library of Congress
950   (top) Collection of the Supreme Court of
       the United States, (bottom) Library of
       Congress
951   Collection of the Supreme Court of the
       United States
952   Collection of the Supreme Court of the
       United States
953   Collection of the Supreme Court of the
       United States

954   Library of Congress
955   Library of Congress
956   Collection of the Supreme Court of the
       United States
957   Library of Congress
958   Collection of the Supreme Court of the
       United States
959   Collection of the Supreme Court of the
       United States
960   Collection of the Supreme Court of the
       United States
961   Collection of the Supreme Court of the
       United States
962   Library of Congress
963   Library of Congress
964   Collection of the Supreme Court of the
       United States
965   Harvard Law Library
966   Collection of the Supreme Court of the
       United States
967   Collection of the Supreme Court of the
       United States
968   Collection of the Supreme Court of the
       United States
969   Collection of the Supreme Court of the
       United States
970   Collection of the Supreme Court of the
       United States
971   Library of Congress
972   Library of Congress
973   Library of Congress
975   (top) Collection of the Supreme Court of
       the United States, (bottom) Collection
       of the Supreme Court of the United
       States
977   Library of Congress
978   Collection of the Supreme Court of the
       United States
979   Collection of the Supreme Court of the
       United States
980   Library of Congress
981   Collection of the Supreme Court of the
       United States
982   Collection of the Supreme Court of the
       United States
983   Library of Congress
984   Library of Congress
985   Library of Congress
986   Library of Congress
987   Library of Congress
988   Collection of the Supreme Court of the
       United States
989   Collection of the Supreme Court of the
       United States
990   Collection of the Supreme Court of the
       United States
991   Library of Congress
992   Collection of the Supreme Court of the
       United States
993   Library of Congress
994   Collection of the Supreme Court of the
       United States
995   Library of Congress
997   Collection of the Supreme Court of the
       United States
998   Collection of the Supreme Court of the
       United States
999   Collection of the Supreme Court of the
       United States
1000   Collection of the Supreme Court of the
       United States

1001 Collection of the Supreme Court of the United States
1002 (both) Collection of the Supreme Court of the United States
1003 Collection of the Supreme Court of the United States
1004 Library of Congress
1005 Collection of the Supreme Court of the United States
1006 Collection of the Supreme Court of the United States
1007 Collection of the Supreme Court of the United States
1008 Collection of the Supreme Court of the United States
1009 Library of Congress
1011 Supreme Court Historical Society
1012 National Geographic Society
1013 Collection of the Supreme Court of the United States
1014 Collection of the Supreme Court of the United States
1015 Collection of the Supreme Court of the United States
1016 Collection of the Supreme Court of the United States
1017 Collection of the Supreme Court of the United States
1018 Collection of the Supreme Court of the United States
1019 Collection of the Supreme Court of the United States
1021 National Geographic Society
1022 (top) Collection of the Supreme Court of the United States, (bottom) Supreme Court Historical Society

Selected Bibliography

PART I ORIGINS AND DEVELOPMENT OF THE COURT

Bickel, Alexander M. *The Least Dangerous Branch.* Indianapolis: Bobbs-Merrill, 1962.

Cranch, William. Preface to Vol. 1 of *Reports of Cases Argued and Adjudged in the Supreme Court of the United States in August and December Terms, 1801, and February Term, 1803.*

de Tocqueville, Alexis. *Democracy in America.* New York: Knopf and Random House, Vintage Books, 1945.

Fairman, Charles. *History of the Supreme Court of the United States.* Vol. 4, *Reconstruction and Reunion, 1864–1888.* New York: Macmillan, 1971.

Friedman, Leon, and Fred L. Israel, eds. *Justices of the United States Supreme Court, 1789–1991.* 5 vols., rev. ed. New York: Chelsea House, 1992.

Goebel, Julius, Jr. *History of the Supreme Court of the United States.* Vol. 1, *Antecedents and Beginnings to 1801.* New York: Macmillan, 1971.

Greenhouse, Linda. "The Year the Court Turned to the Right." *New York Times,* July 7, 1989.

Haines, Charles G. *The American Doctrine of Judicial Supremacy.* 2d ed. Berkeley: University of California Press, 1932; reprint ed. New York: Da Capo Press, 1973.

Harriger, Katy J., ed. *Separation of Powers: Documents and Commentary.* Washington, D.C.: CQ Press, 2003.

Haskins, George L., and Herbert A. Johnson. *History of the Supreme Court of the United States.* Vol. 2, *Foundations of Power: John Marshall, 1801–1815.* New York: Macmillan, 1981.

Hughes, Charles Evans. *The Supreme Court of the United States.* New York: Columbia University Press, 1928.

Jackson, Robert H. *The Struggle for Judicial Supremacy.* New York: Knopf, 1941.

———. *The Supreme Court in the American System of Government.* Cambridge: Harvard University Press, 1955.

Madison, James, Alexander Hamilton, and John Jay. *The Federalist Papers.* Edited by Clinton Rossiter. New York: New American Library, 1961.

Mason, Alpheus T. *The Supreme Court from Taft to Warren.* Baton Rouge: Louisiana State University, 1958.

McCloskey, Robert G., and Sanford Levinson. *The Modern Supreme Court.* 2d ed. Chicago: University of Chicago Press, 1994.

Miller, Samuel F. *Lectures on the Constitution of the United States.* New York and Albany: Banks & Brothers, 1891.

Pfeffer, Leo. *This Honorable Court: A History of the United States Supreme Court.* Boston: Beacon Press, 1965.

Schlesinger, Arthur M., Jr. *The Politics of Upheaval.* Cambridge, Mass.: Houghton Mifflin, 1960.

Swindler, William F. *Court and Constitution in the 20th Century: The New Legality, 1932–1968.* Indianapolis: Bobbs-Merrill, 1970.

———. *Court and Constitution in the 20th Century: The Old Legality, 1889–1932.* Indianapolis: Bobbs-Merrill, 1969.

Swisher, Carl B. *History of the Supreme Court of the United States.* Vol. 5, *The Taney Period, 1836–1864.* New York: Macmillan, 1974.

Warren, Charles. *Congress, the Constitution and the Supreme Court.* Boston: Little, Brown, 1925.

———. *The Supreme Court in United States History.* rev. ed., 2 vols. Boston: Little, Brown, 1926.

White, G. Edward. *History of the Supreme Court of the United States.* Vols. 3–4, *The Marshall Court and Cultural Change, 1815–1835.* New York: Macmillan, 1988.

PART II THE COURT AND THE FEDERAL SYSTEM

THE COURT AND CONGRESS

Baxter, Maurice G. *The Steamboat Monopoly: Gibbons v. Ogden, 1824.* Borzoi Series in United States Constitutional History. New York: Knopf, Borzoi Books, 1972.

Beth, Loren P. *The Development of the American Constitution, 1877–1917.* New York: Harper and Row, 1971.

Black, Charles L., Jr. *Perspectives in Constitutional Law.* Englewood Cliffs, N.J.: Prentice-Hall, 1963.

Carr, Robert K. *The Supreme Court and Judicial Review.* American Government in Action Series. New York: Farrar and Rinehart, 1942.

Claude, Richard. *The Supreme Court and the Electoral Process.* Baltimore: Johns Hopkins University Press, 1970.

Commager, Henry Steele, and Milton Cantor, eds. *Documents of American History.* 10th ed., 2 vols. Englewood Cliffs, N.J.: Prentice-Hall, 1988.

Congressional Quarterly. *Guide to Congress.* 4th ed. Washington, D.C.: Congressional Quarterly, 1991; 5th ed., 1999.

Cortner, Richard C. *The Jones & Laughlin Case.* Borzoi Series in United States Constitutional History. New York: Knopf, Borzoi Books, 1970.

———. *The Iron Horse and the Constitution: Railroads and the Transformation of the Fourteenth Amendment.* Westport, Conn.: Greenwood Press, 1993.

Corwin, Edward S. *The Constitution and What It Means Today.* 14th ed. Revised by Harold W. Chase and Craig R. Ducat. Princeton, N.J.: Princeton University Press, 1978.

———. *The Doctrine of Judicial Review: Its Legal and Historical Basis and other Essays.* Princeton, N.J.: Princeton University Press, 1914; reprint ed., Gloucester, Mass.: Peter Smith, 1963.

Coyle, Dennis J. *Property Rights and the Constitution.* Albany: State University of New York Press, 1993.

Cushman, Robert F. *Leading Constitutional Decisions.* 15th ed. Englewood Cliffs, N.J.: Prentice-Hall, 1977.

Cushman, Robert E., and Robert F. Cushman. *Cases in Constitutional Law.* 4th ed. New York: Appleton-Century-Crofts, 1975.

Dimock, Marshall E. *Congressional Investigating Committees.* Baltimore: Johns Hopkins University Press, 1929; reprint ed., New York: AMS Press, 1971.

Epstein, Lee, and Thomas G. Walker. *Rights, Liberties, and Justice: Constitutional Law for a Changing America.* 5th ed. Washington, D.C.: CQ Press, 2004.

Fisher, Louis. *Constitutional Dialogues: Interpretation as Political Process.* Princeton, N.J.: Princeton University Press, 1988.

Frankfurter, Felix. *The Commerce Clause under Marshall, Taney and Waite.* Chapel Hill: University of North Carolina Press, 1937.

Freund, Paul A., and Stanley N. Katz, gen. eds. *History of the Supreme Court of the United States.* Vol. 1, *Antecedents and Beginnings to 1801,* by Julius Goebel Jr., 1971; Vol. 2, *Foundations of Power: John Marshall, 1801–1815,* by George L. Haskins and Herbert A. Johnson, 1981; Vols. 3–4, *The Marshall Court and Cultural Change, 1815–1835,* by G. Edward White, 1988; Vol. 5, *The Taney Period, 1836–1864,* by Carl B. Swisher, 1974; Vol. 6, *Reconstruction and Reunion, 1864–1888,* Part One, by Charles Fairman, 1971; Vol. 7,

Reconstruction and Reunion, 1864–1888, Part Two, by Charles Fairman, 1987; Supplement to Vol. 7, *Five Justices and the Electoral Commission of 1877*, by Charles Fairman, 1988; Vol. 8, *Troubled Beginnings of the Modern State, 1888–1910*, by Owen M. Fiss, 1993; Vol. 9, *The Judiciary and Responsible Government, 1910–1921*, by Alexander M. Bickel and Benno C. Schmidt Jr., 1984. New York: Macmillan.

Garraty, John A., ed. *Quarrels That Have Shaped the Constitution.* rev. ed. New York: Perennial Library, 1987.

Gillman, Howard. *The Constitution Besieged: The Rise and Demise of* Lochner *Era Police Powers Jurisprudence.* Baltimore: Johns Hopkins University Press, 1993.

Henkin, Louis. *Foreign Affairs and the Constitution.* New York: Norton, 1975.

Hughes, Charles Evans. *The Supreme Court of the United States: Its Foundations, Methods and Achievements, An Interpretation.* New York: Columbia University Press, 1928.

Jackson, Robert H. *The Struggle for Judicial Supremacy: A Study of a Crisis in American Power Politics.* New York: Random House, Vintage Books, 1941.

James, Leonard F. *The Supreme Court in American Life.* 2d ed. Glenview, Ill.: Scott, Foresman, 1971.

Kauper, Paul G. *Constitutional Law: Cases and Materials.* 5th ed. Boston: Little, Brown, 1980.

Kelly, Alfred H., and Winfred A. Harbison. *The American Constitution: Its Origins and Development.* 7th ed., 2 vols. New York: Norton, 1991.

Kurland, Philip B. *Politics, the Constitution and the Warren Court.* Chicago: University of Chicago Press, 1970.

Kutler, Stanley I., ed. *The Supreme Court and the Constitution: Readings in American Constitutional History.* 3d ed. New York: Norton, 1984.

Library of Congress. Congressional Research Service. *The Constitution of the United States of America: Analysis and Interpretation.* Washington, D.C.: Government Printing Office, 1973; together with the 1976 Supplement. Washington, D.C.: U.S. Government Printing Office, 1982.

Madison, James, Alexander Hamilton, John Jay. *The Federalist Papers.* Edited by Clinton Rossiter. New York: New American Library, 1961.

Mason, Alpheus T. *The Supreme Court from Taft to Warren.* rev. ed. Baton Rouge: Louisiana State University Press, 1979.

Mason, Alpheus T., and William M. Beaney. *The Supreme Court in a Free Society.* New York: Norton, 1968.

McCloskey, Robert G., with Sanford Levinson. *The Modern Supreme Court.* Chicago History of American Civilization Series. Chicago: University of Chicago Press, 1994.

Melone, Albert P. *Researching Constitutional Law.* 2d ed. Liberty Heights, Ill.: Waveland Press, 2000.

Miller, Arthur Selwyn. *The Supreme Court and American Capitalism.* The Supreme Court in American Life Series. New York: Free Press, 1968.

Morgan, Donald G. *Congress and the Constitution: A Study of Responsibility.* Cambridge, Mass.: The Belknap Press of Harvard University Press, 1966.

Murphy, Walter F. *Congress and the Court: A Case Study in the American Political Process.* Chicago: University of Chicago Press, 1962.

O'Brien, David M. *Constitutional Law and Politics: Struggles for Power and Governmental Accountability.* 4th ed. New York: Norton, 2000.

Pfeffer, Leo. *This Honorable Court: A History of the United States Supreme Court.* Boston: Beacon Press, 1965.

Pollak, Louis H., ed. *The Constitution and the Supreme Court: A Documentary History.* 2 vols. Cleveland: World Publishing, 1966.

Pritchett, C. Herman. *Congress Versus the Supreme Court, 1957–1960.* Minneapolis: University of Minnesota Press, 1961.

———. *The American Constitution.* 3d ed. New York: McGraw-Hill, 1977.

Ratner, Sidney. *American Taxation: Its History as a Social Force in Democracy.* New York: Norton, 1942.

Schmidhauser, John R., and Larry L. Berg. *The Supreme Court and Congress: Conflict and Interaction, 1945–1968.* Supreme Court in American Life Series. New York: Free Press, 1972.

Schwartz, Bernard. *A History of the Supreme Court.* New York: Oxford University Press, 1993.

Swindler, William F. *Court and Constitution in the Twentieth Century: The Old Legality, 1889–1932.* Indianapolis: Bobbs-Merrill, 1969.

———. *Court and Constitution in the Twentieth Century: The New Legality, 1932–1968.* Indianapolis: Bobbs-Merrill, 1970.

Swisher, Carl B. *American Constitutional Development.* reprint ed. Westport, Conn.: Greenwood Press, 1978.

Twiss, Benjamin R. *Lawyers and the Constitution: How Laissez-Faire Came to the Supreme Court.* Princeton, N.J.: Princeton University Press, 1942.

Warren, Charles. *The Supreme Court in United States History.* rev. ed., 2 vols. Boston: Little, Brown, 1926.

THE COURT AND THE PRESIDENCY

Abernethy, Thomas P. *The Burr Conspiracy.* New York: Oxford University Press, 1954.

Alsop, Joseph, and Turner Catledge. *The 168 Days.* New York: Da Capo Press, 1973.

Anderson, Frank M. "Contemporary Opinion of the Virginia and Kentucky Resolutions." *American Historical Review* 5: 45–63, 225–252.

Baker, Leonard. *Back to Back: The Duel Between F.D.R. and the Supreme Court.* New York: Macmillan, 1967.

———. *John Marshall: A Life in Law.* New York: Collier Books, 1981.

Bassett, John S. *Life of Andrew Jackson.* 2 vols. Hamden, Conn.: Archon Books, 1967.

Bemis, Samuel F. *A Diplomatic History of the United States.* 5th ed. New York: Holt, Rinehart, and Winston, 1965.

Berger, Raoul. *Executive Privilege: A Constitutional Myth.* Cambridge: Harvard University Press, 1974.

Beveridge, Albert. *The Life of John Marshall.* 4 vols. Boston and New York: Houghton Mifflin, 1916–1919.

Binkley, Wilfred E. *The Powers of the President: Problems of American Democracy.* New York: Russell & Russell, 1973.

Burke, Joseph C. "The Cherokee Cases: A Study in Law, Politics and Morality." *Stanford Law Review* 21: 500–531.

Burns, James M. *Roosevelt: The Lion and the Fox.* New York: Harcourt Brace Jovanovich, 1960.

———. *Roosevelt: The Soldier of Freedom.* New York: Harcourt Brace Jovanovich, 1970.

Chapin, Bradley. *The American Law of Treason: Revolutionary and Early National Origins.* Seattle: University of Washington Press, 1964.

Commager, Henry Steele, and Milton Cantor, eds. *Documents of American History.* 10th ed., 2 vols. Englewood Cliffs, N.J.: Prentice-Hall, 1988.

Congressional Quarterly. *Congress and the Nation, 1973–1976.* Vol. 4. Washington, D.C.: Congressional Quarterly, 1977; Vol. 10, 1997–2001, 2002.

———. *CQ Almanac 1970.* Washington, D.C.: Congressional Quarterly, 1971.

———. *CQ Almanac 2002.* Washington, D.C.: Congressional Quarterly, 2003.

———. *Guide to Congress.* 4th ed. Washington, D.C.: Congressional Quarterly, 1991; 5th ed., 1999.

———. *Guide to the Presidency.* 2d ed. Washington, D.C.: Congressional Quarterly, 1996; 3d ed., 2002.

———. *Members of Congress since 1789.* 3d ed. Washington, D.C.: Congressional Quarterly, 1985.

———. *Nixon, The Fifth Year of His Presidency.* Washington, D.C.: Congressional Quarterly, 1974.

———. *Watergate: Chronology of a Crisis.* Washington, D.C.: Congressional Quarterly, 1975.

Corwin, Edward S. *The Constitution and What It Means Today.* 14th ed. Revised by Harold W. Chase and Craig R. Ducat. Princeton, N.J.: Princeton University Press, 1978.

———. *The President: Offices and Powers.* 5th rev. ed. New York: New York University Press, 1984.

Cox, Archibald. *The Role of the Supreme Court in American Government.* New York: Oxford University Press, 1976.

Cunningham, Noble E., Jr. *The Jeffersonian Republicans: The Formation of Party Organization, 1789–1801.* Chapel Hill: University of North Carolina Press, 1957.

Cushman, Robert F. *Cases in Civil Liberties.* 6th ed. Englewood Cliffs, N.J.: Prentice-Hall, 1984.

DeConde, Alexander. *The Quasi-War: The Politics and Diplomacy of the Undeclared War with France, 1797–1801.* New York: Scribner's, 1966.

Dewey, Donald O. *Marshall versus Jefferson: The Political Background of* Marbury v. Madison. New York: Knopf, 1970.

Dorson, Norman, and John H. F. Shattuck. "Executive Privilege, the Congress and the Court." *Ohio State Law Journal* 34: 1–40.

Doyle, Elisabeth Joan. "The Conduct of the War, 1861." In *Congress Investigates 1792–1974.* Edited by Arthur M. Schlesinger Jr. and Roger Bruns. New York: Chelsea House, 1975.

Eisenhower, Dwight D. *Public Papers of the Presidents.* Washington, D.C.: U.S. Government Printing Office, 1950.

Ellis, Richard E. *The Jeffersonian Crisis: Courts and Politics in the Young Republic.* New York: Oxford University Press, 1971.

Ely, John Hart. *War and Responsibility: Constitutional Lessons of Vietnam and Its Aftermath.* Princeton, N.J.: Princeton University Press, 1993.

Farrand, Max, ed. *The Records of the Federal Convention of 1787.* rev. ed., 4 vols. New Haven, Conn.: Yale University Press, 1966.

Faulkner, Robert K. *The Jurisprudence of John Marshall.* Princeton, N.J.: Greenwood Press, 1980.

Fisher, Louis. *Constitutional Dialogues: Interpretation as Political Process.* Princeton, N.J.: Princeton University Press, 1988.

———. *Presidential War Power.* Lawrence: University of Kansas Press, 1995.

Fisher, Louis, and Neal Devins. *Political Dynamics of Constitutional Law.* St. Paul: West Publishing, 1992.

Ford, Paul L., ed. *The Writings of Thomas Jefferson.* 10 vols. New York: Putnam's, 1892–1899.

Freedman, Max, ann. *Roosevelt and Frankfurter: Their Correspondence, 1928–45.* Boston: Little, Brown, 1968.

Freund, Paul A., and Stanley N. Katz, gen. eds., *History of the Supreme Court of the United States.* Vol. 1, *Antecedents and Beginnings to 1801,* by Julius Goebel Jr., 1971; Vol. 2, *Foundations of Power: John Marshall, 1801–1815,* by George L. Haskins and Herbert A. Johnson, 1981; Vols. 3–4, *The Marshall Court and Cultural Change, 1815–1835,* by G. Edward White, 1988; Vol. 5, *The Taney Period, 1836–1864,* by Carl B. Swisher, 1974; Vol. 6: *Reconstruction and Reunion, 1864– 1888,* Part One, by Charles Fairman, 1971; Vol. 7, *Reconstruction and Reunion, 1864–1888,* Part Two, by Charles Fairman, 1987; Supplement to Vol. 7, *Five Justices and the Electoral Commission of 1877,* by Charles Fairman, 1988; Vol. 8, *Troubled Beginnings of the Modern State, 1888–1910,* by Owen M. Fiss, 1993; Vol. 9, *The Judiciary and Responsible Government, 1910–1921,* by Alexander M. Bickel and Benno C. Schmidt Jr., 1984. New York: Macmillan.

Friedman, Leon, and Fred L. Israel, eds. *The Justices of the United States Supreme Court, 1789–1995, Their Lives and Major Opinions.* 5 vols. New York and London: Chelsea House, 1969–1995.

Garraty, John A., ed. *Quarrels That Have Shaped the Constitution.* rev. ed. New York: Perennial Library, 1987.

Hamilton, John C., ed. *The Works of Alexander Hamilton.* 7 vols. New York: John F. Trow, 1850–1851.

Henkin, Louis. *Foreign Affairs and the Constitution.* New York: Norton, 1975.

Ickes, Harold L. *The Secret Diary of Harold L. Ickes.* 3 vols. New York: Simon and Schuster, 1954.

Israel, Fred L., ed. *The State of the Union Messages of the Presidents, 1790–1966.* 13 vols. New York: Chelsea House, Robert Hector Publishers, 1966.

Jackson, Percival E. *Dissent in the Supreme Court: A Chronology.* Norman: University of Oklahoma Press, 1969.

Jackson, Robert H. *The Struggle for Judicial Supremacy.* New York: Random House, 1941.

Johnson, Lyndon B. *Public Papers of the Presidents, 1963–1964.* 2 vols. Washington, D.C.: U.S. Government Printing Office, 1965.

Kelly, Alfred H., and Winfred A. Harbison. *The American Constitution: Its Origins and Development.* 7th ed., 2 vols. New York: Norton, 1991.

Kennedy, John F. *Public Papers of the Presidents, 1962.* Washington, D.C.: U.S. Government Printing Office, 1963.

Key, V.O., Jr. *Politics, Parties and Pressure Groups.* 5th ed. New York: Crowell, 1964.

Koch, Adrienne. *Jefferson and Madison: The Great Collaboration.* Lanham, Md.: University Press of America, 1986.

Koenig, Louis. *The Chief Executive.* 5th. ed. San Diego: Harcourt Brace Jovanovich, 1986.

Kramer, Robert, and Herman Marcuse. "Executive Privilege: A Study of the Period 1953–1960." *George Washington Law Review* 29: 623–827.

Krislov, Samuel. *The Supreme Court in the Political Process.* New York: Macmillan, 1965.

Kurland, Philip B. *Politics, the Constitution and the Warren Court.* Chicago: University of Chicago Press, 1970.

Kutler, Stanley I. "*Ex Parte McCardle:* Judicial Impotency? The Supreme Court and Reconstruction Reconsidered." *American Historical Review* 72: 835–851.

Laski, Harold J. *The American Presidency: An Interpretation.* New Brunswick: Transaction Books, 1980.

Lasser, William. *The Limits of Judicial Power: The Supreme Court in American Politics.* Chapel Hill: University of North Carolina Press, 1988.

Leopold, Richard W. *The Growth of American Foreign Policy.* New York: Knopf, 1962.

Leuchtenburg, William E. *Franklin D. Roosevelt and the New Deal: 1932–1940.* New York: Harper and Row, 1963.

———. *The Supreme Court Reborn: The Constitutional Revolution in the Age of Roosevelt.* New York: Oxford University Press, 1995.

Levy, Leonard. *Legacy of Suppression: Freedom of Speech and Press in Early American History.* New York: Harper and Row, 1963.

———. *Jefferson and Civil Liberties: The Darker Side.* New York: Quadrangle Books, 1973.

Library of Congress. Congressional Research Service. *The Constitution of the United States of America: Analysis and Interpretation.* Washington, D.C.: Government Printing Office, 1973; together with the 1976 Supplement. Washington, D.C.: U.S. Government Printing Office, 1982.

Library of Congress. "The Present Limits of Executive Privilege." A Study Prepared by the Government and General Research Division of the Library of Congress. *Congressional Record.* March 28, 1973. H. 2243–64.

Lillich, Richard B. "The Chase Impeachment." *American Journal of Legal History* 4: 49–72.

Link, Arthur. *Wilson the Diplomatist: A Look at His Major Foreign Policies.* New York: New Viewpoints, 1974.

Link, Eugene P. *Democratic Republican Societies, 1790–1800.* New York: Columbia University Press, 1942.

Lofgren, Charles A. "*United States v. Curtiss-Wright:* An Historical Assessment." *Yale Law Journal* 83: 1–32.

Longaker, Richard P. "Andrew Jackson and the Judiciary." *Political Science Quarterly* 71: 341–364.

Madison, James, Alexander Hamilton, and John Jay. *The Federalist Papers.* Edited by Clinton Rossiter. New York: New American Library, 1961.

Mason, Alpheus T., and William M. Beaney. *The Supreme Court in a Free Society.* New York: Norton, 1968.

McClure, William. *International Executive Agreements: Democratic Procedure u the Constitution of the United States.* New York: AMS Press, 1941.

Meeker, Leonard. "The Legality of United States' Participation in the Defense of Vietnam." United States Department of State, *Bulletin* 474 (1966).

Morgan, Donald G. *Congress and the Constitution.* Cambridge: Harvard University Press, 1966.

Morison, Samuel E., Henry S. Commager, and William E. Leuchtenberg. *The Growth of the American Republic.* 7th ed., 2 vols. New York: Oxford University Press, 1980.

Murphy, Paul L. *The Constitution in Crisis Times, 1918-1969.* New York: Harper and Row, 1972.

Neustadt, Richard E. *Presidential Power.* New York: Wiley, 1960.

Nicolay, John G., and John Hay, eds. *The Complete Works of Abraham Lincoln.* 12 vols. New York: Francis D. Tandy, 1905.

Patterson, James T. *Congressional Conservatism and the New Deal, 1933–1939.* Lexington: University of Kentucky Press, 1967.

Peltason, Jack W. *Corwin & Peltason's Understanding the Constitution.* 13th ed. Fort Worth: Harcourt Brace College Publishers, 1994.

Post, Gordon C. *The Supreme Court and Political Questions.* Baltimore: Johns Hopkins University Press, 1936.

Pritchett, C. Herman. *The Tennessee Valley Authority: A Study in Public Administration.* Chapel Hill: University of North Carolina Press, 1943.

———. *The American Constitution.* 3d ed. New York: McGraw-Hill, 1977.

Pritchett, C. Herman, and Alan F. Westin. *The Third Branch of Government.* New York: Harcourt, Brace, and World, 1963.

Randall, James G. *Constitutional Problems under Lincoln.* rev. ed. Urbana: University of Illinois Press, 1951.

Reveley, W. Taylor, III. "Presidential War-Making: Constitutional Prerogative or Usurpation?" *Virginia Law Review* 55: 1243–1305.

Richardson, James D., ed. *Messages and Papers of the Presidents.* 10 vols. Washington, D.C.: Bureau of National Literature, 1904.

Rodell, Fred. *Nine Men: A Political History of the Supreme Court of the United States from 1790–1955.* New York: Random House, 1955.

Rosenman, Samuel I., comp. *The Public Papers and Addresses of Franklin D. Roosevelt.* 13 vols. New York: Russell & Russell, 1969.

Rossiter, Clinton. *The Supreme Court and the Commander in Chief.* expanded ed. Ithaca, N.Y.: Cornell University Press, 1976.

Rostow, Eugene V. "The Japanese American Cases: A Disaster." *Yale Law Journal* 54 (June 1945): 489–533.

Schlesinger, Arthur M., Jr. *The Imperial Presidency.* New York: Popular Library, 1973.

Schubert, Glendon A. *The Presidency in the Courts.* Minneapolis: University of Minnesota Press, 1957.

Smith, James M. *Freedom's Fetters: The Alien and Sedition Laws and American Civil Liberties.* Ithaca, N.Y.: Cornell University Press, 1956.

Stinchcombe, William. "The Diplomacy of the WXYZ Affair." *William and Mary Quarterly.* 3d Series, 34: 590–617.

Surrency, Erwin C. "The Judiciary Act of 1801." *American Journal of Legal History* II: 53–65.

Sutherland, George. *Constitutional Power and World Affairs.* New York: Columbia University Press, 1919.

Swindler, William F. *Court and Constitution in the Twentieth Century: The New Legality, 1932–1968.* New York and Indianapolis: Bobbs-Merrill, 1954.

———. *Court and Constitution in the Twentieth Century: The Old Legality, 1889–1932.* Indianapolis: Bobbs-Merrill, 1970.

Tribe, Laurence H. *God Save This Honorable Court.* New York: Random House, 1985.

Truman, Harry S. *Memoirs.* 2 vols. Garden City, N.Y.: Doubleday, 1956.

Turner, Kathryn. "Federalist Policy and the Judiciary Act of 1801." *William and Mary Quarterly* 22: 32.

U.S. Congress. *Debates and Proceedings, First Congress, First Session. March 3, 1789, to Eighteenth Congress, First Session, May 27, 1824. [Annals of Congress]* 42 vols. Washington, D.C.: Gales and Seaton, 1834–1856.

U.S. Congress. Senate. "A Decade of American Foreign Policy, Basic Documents, 1941–1949," Senate Document No. 123, 81st Cong., 1st sess., 1950, pt. 1.

U.S. Congress. Senate. Committee on the Judiciary. Subcommittee on the Separation of Powers. *Executive Privilege: The Withholding of Information by the Executive.* Hearings. 92d Cong., 1st sess. Washington, D.C.: U.S. Government Printing Office, 1971.

U.S. Congress. Senate. *Hearings on S.J. Res. 1 and S.J. Res. 43 before a Subcommittee of the Senate Judiciary Committee.* 83d Cong., 1st sess., 1953.

U.S. Congress. Senate. *Hearings on U.S. Commitments to Foreign Powers before the Senate Committee on Foreign Relations.* 90th Cong., 1st sess., 1967.

U.S. Department of State. "Authority of the President to Repel the Attack in Korea." *Bulletin* 23 (1950).

Warren, Charles. *The Supreme Court in United States History.* rev. ed., 2 vols. Boston: Little, Brown, 1926.

Wiggins, J. Russell. "Government Operations and the Public's Right to Know." *Federal Bar Journal* 19: 62.

Wilson, Woodrow. *Congressional Government: A Study in American Politics.* Boston: Houghton, Mifflin, 1885.

———. *The State.* Boston: D. C. Heath, 1889.

———. *Constitutional Government in the United States.* New York: Columbia University Press, 1908.

Wolkinson, Herman. "Demand of Congressional Committees for Executive Papers." *Federal Bar Journal* 10 (April, July, October 1949): 103–150.

Wormuth, Francis D. "The Nixon Theory of the War Power: A Critique." *California Law Review* 60: 623–703.

Younger, Irving. "Congressional Investigations and Executive Secrecy: A Study in Separation of Powers." *University of Pittsburgh Law Review* 20: 755.

THE COURT AND JUDICIAL POWER

Abraham, Henry J. *The Judicial Process.* 6th ed. New York: Oxford University Press, 1993.

Beth, Loren P. *Politics, the Constitution and the Supreme Court.* Evanston, Ill.: Row, Peterson, 1962.

Bickel, Alexander M. *The Least Dangerous Branch.* 2d ed. New Haven: Yale University Press, 1986.

Black, Charles L., Jr. *Perspectives in Constitutional Law.* Englewood Cliffs, N.J.: Prentice-Hall, 1963.

Carp, Robert A., and Ronald Stidham. *The Federal Courts.* 4th ed. Washington, D.C.: CQ Press, 2001.

Carp, Robert A., Ronald Stidham, and Kenneth L. Manning. *Judicial Process in America.* Washington, D.C.: CQ Press, 2001.

Carr, Robert K. *The Supreme Court and Judicial Review.* New York: Farrar and Rinehart, 1942.

Corwin, Edward S. *The Constitution of the United States of America.* Washington, D.C.: U.S. Government Printing Office, 1953.

Early, Stephen T. *Constitutional Courts of the United States.* Totowa, N.J.: Littlefield, Adams, 1977.

Fisher, Louis. *American Constitutional Law: Separated Powers and Federalism.* 4th ed. Durham, N.C.: Carolina Academic Press, 2001.

Frankfurter, Felix. *The Commerce Clause under Marshall, Taney and Waite.* Chapel Hill: University of North Carolina Press, 1937.

Frankfurter, Felix, and James M. Landis. *The Business of the Supreme Court: A Study in the Federal Judicial System.* New York: Macmillan, 1928.

Freund, Paul A., and Stanley N. Katz, gen. eds. *History of the Supreme Court of the United States.* Vol. 1, *Antecedents and Beginnings to 1801,* by Julius Goebel Jr., 1971; Vol. 2, *Foundations of Power: John Marshall, 1801–1815,* by George L. Haskins and Herbert A. Johnson, 1981; Vols. 3–4, *The Marshall Court and Cultural Change, 1815–1835,* by G. Edward White, 1988; Vol. 5, *The Taney Period, 1836–1864,* by Carl B. Swisher, 1974; Vol. 6: *Reconstruction and Reunion, 1864–1888,* Part One, by Charles Fairman, 1971; Vol. 7, *Reconstruction and Reunion, 1864–1888,* Part Two, by Charles Fairman, 1987; Supplement to Vol. 7, *Five Justices and the Electoral Commission of 1877,* by Charles Fairman, 1988; Vol. 8, *Troubled Beginnings of the Modern State, 1888–1910,* by Owen M. Fiss, 1993; Vol. 9, *The Judiciary and Responsible Government, 1910–1921,* by Alexander M. Bickel and Benno C. Schmidt Jr., 1984. New York: Macmillan.

Graber, Mark A., and Michael Perhac, eds. *Marbury versus Madison: Documents and Commentary.* Washington, D.C.: CQ Press, 2002.

Haines, Charles G. *The American Doctrine of Judicial Supremacy.* 2d ed. Berkeley: University of California Press, 1932.

Hart, Henry M., Jr., and Herbert Wechsler. *The Federal Courts and the Federal System.* 3d ed. Westbury, N.Y.: Foundation Press, 1988.

Hughes, Charles Evans. *The Supreme Court of the United States: Its Foundation, Methods and Achievements: An Interpretation.* New York: Columbia University Press, 1928.

Ivers, Gregg. *American Constitutional Law: Power and Politics.* Vol. 1, *Constitutional Structure and Political Power.* Boston: Houghton and Mifflin, 2001.

Library of Congress. Congressional Research Service. *The Constitution of the United States of America: Analysis and Interpretation.* Washington, D.C.: Government Printing Office, 1973; together with the 1976 Supplement. Washington, D.C.: U.S. Government Printing Office, 1982.

Madison, James, Alexander Hamilton, and John Jay. *The Federalist Papers.* Edited by Clinton Rossiter. New York: New American Library, 1961.

Mason, Alpheus T. *The Supreme Court from Taft to Burger.* 3d ed. Baton Rouge: Louisiana State University Press, 1979.

McDowell, Gary L., and Eugene W. Hickok Jr. *Justice vs. Law: The Courts in America.* New York: Free Press, 1993.

Post, C. Gordon. *Supreme Court and Political Questions.* Baltimore: Johns Hopkins University Press, 1936; reprint ed. New York: Da Capo Press, 1969.

Powell, Thomas Reed. *Vagaries and Varieties in Constitutional Interpretation.* New York: Columbia University Press, 1956; reprint ed. New York: AMS Press, 1967.

Scigliano, Robert, ed. *The Courts: A Reader in the Judicial Process.* Boston: Little, Brown, 1962.

Stern, Robert L., and Eugene Gressman. *Supreme Court Practice.* 7th ed. Washington, D.C.: Bureau of National Affairs, 1993.

Swisher, Carl B. *American Constitutional Development.* reprint ed. Westport, Conn.: Greenwood Press, 1978.

Warren, Charles. *The Supreme Court in United States History.* rev. ed., 2 vols. Boston: Little, Brown, 1926.

Westin, Alan F., ed. *The Supreme Court: Views from Inside.* New York: Norton, 1961.

THE COURT AND THE STATES

Beth, Loren P. *The Development of the American Constitution: 1877–1917.* New York: Harper and Row, 1971.

Black, Charles L., Jr. *The People and the Court.* New York: Macmillan, 1960.

Carr, Robert K. *The Supreme Court and Judicial Review.* New York: Farrar & Rinehart, 1942.

Carson, Hampton L. *The Supreme Court of the United States: Its History.* Philadelphia: A.R. Keller, 1892.

Corwin, Edward S. *The Constitution and What It Means Today.* 14th ed. Revised by Harold W. Chase and Craig R. Ducat. Princeton, N.J.: Princeton University Press, 1978.

Frankfurter, Felix. *The Commerce Clause under Marshall, Taney and Waite.* Chapel Hill: University of North Carolina Press, 1937.

Freund, Paul A. *The Supreme Court of the United States: Its Business, Purposes, and Performances.* Cleveland: Meridian Books, World Publishing Co., 1961.

Haines, Charles G. *The American Doctrine of Judicial Supremacy.* 2d ed. Berkeley: University of California Press, 1932.

Jackson, Robert H. *The Struggle for Judicial Supremacy.* New York: Knopf, 1941.

Kelly, Alfred H., and Winfred A. Harbison. *The American Constitution: Its Origins and Development.* 7th ed., 2 vols. New York: Norton, 1991.

Kruman, Marc. *Between Authority and Liberty: State Constitution Making in Revolutionary America.* Chapel Hill: University of North Carolina Press, 1997.

Mason, Alpheus T. *The Supreme Court from Taft to Burger.* 3d ed. Baton Rouge: Louisiana State University Press, 1979.

Mason, Alpheus T., and William M. Beaney. *The Supreme Court in a Free Society.* New York: Norton, 1968.

Powell, Thomas Reed. *Vagaries and Varieties in Constitutional Interpretation.* New York: Columbia University Press, 1956; reprint ed. New York: AMS Press, 1967.

Pritchett, C. Herman. *The American Constitution.* 3d ed. New York: McGraw-Hill, 1977.

Swindler, William F. *Court and Constitution in the Twentieth Century.* 3 vols. Indianapolis: Bobbs-Merrill, 1969, 1970, 1974.

Swisher, Carl B. *American Constitutional Development.* reprint ed. Westport, Conn.: Greenwood Press, 1978.

Warren, Charles. *The Supreme Court in United States History.* rev. ed., 2 vols. Boston: Little, Brown, 1926.

———. *The Supreme Court and Sovereign States.* Princeton, N.J.: Princeton University Press, 1924.

Westin, Alan F., ed. *The Supreme Court: Views from Inside.* New York: Norton, 1961.

PART III THE COURT AND THE INDIVIDUAL

FREEDOM OF EXPRESSION

Barker, Lucius J., and Twiley W. Barker Jr. *Civil Liberties and the Constitution: Cases and Commentaries.* 7th ed. Englewood Cliffs, N.J.: Prentice-Hall, 1994.

Bearinger, David, ed. *The Bill of Rights, the Courts, and the Law: Landmark Cases That Have Shaped American History.* 3d ed. Charlottesville: Virginia Foundation for the Humanities, 1999.

Berman, Harold J. "Religion and Law: The First Amendment in Historical Perspective." *Emory Law Journal* 35 (1986): 777–793.

Beth, Loren P. *The American Theory of Church and State.* Gainesville: University of Florida Press, 1958.

Bodenhamer, David J., and James W. Ely Jr. *The Bill of Rights in Modern America After 200 Years.* Bloomington: Indiana University Press, 1993.

Bogen, David S. *Bulwark of Liberty: The Court and the First Amendment.* Port Washington, N.Y.: Associated Faculty Press, 1984.

Bollinger, Lee C. *The Tolerant Society: Freedom of Speech and Extremist Speech in America.* New York: Oxford University Press, 1986.

———. *Images of a Free Press.* Chicago: University of Chicago Press, 1991.

Branit, James R. "Reconciling Free Speech and Equality: What Justifies Censorship?" *Harvard Journal of Law and Public Policy* 9 (1986): 429–460.

Choper, Jess H. *Securing Religious Liberty.* Chicago: University of Chicago Press, 1995.

Congressional Quarterly. *Guide to Congress.* 4th ed. Washington, D.C.: Congressional Quarterly, 1991; 5th ed., 1999.

Cushman, Robert F. *Cases in Civil Liberties.* 6th ed. Englewood Cliffs, N.J.: Prentice-Hall, 1994.

Dowling, Noel T. *Cases on Constitutional Law.* 7th ed. Brooklyn, N.Y.: The Foundation Press, 1965.

Emerson, Thomas I. *The System of Freedom of Expression.* New York: Random House, Vintage, 1970.

Epstein, Lee, and Thomas G. Walker. *Constitutional Law for a Changing America.* 5th ed. Washington, D.C.: CQ Press, 2003.

Esbeck, Carl H. "1985 Survey of Trends and Developments on Religious Liberty in the Courts." *Journal of Law and Religion* 4 (1986): 211–240.

Forer, Lois G. *A Chilling Effect: The Mounting Threat of Libel and Invasion of Privacy Actions to the First Amendment.* New York: Norton, 1987.

Hemmer, Joseph J. *The Supreme Court and the First Amendment.* New York: Praeger, 1986.

Kalven, Harry, Jr. *The Negro and the First Amendment.* Chicago: University of Chicago Press, Phoenix Books, 1966.

Kelly, Alfred H., and Winfred A. Harbison. *The American Constitution: Its Origin and Development.* 7th ed. New York: Norton, 1991.

Konvitz, Milton R. *Fundamental Liberties of a Free People: Religion, Speech, Press, Assembly.* Ithaca, N.Y.: Cornell University Press, 1978. Reprint of 1957 ed.

Lewis, Anthony. *Make No Law: The Sullivan Case and the First Amendment.* New York: Random House, 1991.

Madison, James. *The Federalist Papers.* Edited by Isaac Kramnick. New York: Penguin Books, 1987.

Marshall, William P. "Discrimination and the Right of Association." *Northwestern Law Review* 81 (1986): 68–105.

Mason, Alpheus T., and William M. Beaney. *The Supreme Court in a Free Society.* New York: Norton, 1968.

Miller, William Lee. *The First Liberty: Religion and the American Republic.* New York: Knopf, 1985.

Miller, William, and Charles Cureton. *Supreme Court Decisions on Church and State.* Charlottesville, Va.: Ibis Publications, 1986.

Murphy, Paul L. *The Constitution in Crisis Times, 1918–1969.* New York: Harper and Row, 1972.

Peters, Shawn Francis. *The Yoder Case: Religious Freedom, Education, and Parental Rights.* Landmark Law Cases and American Society. Lawrence: University Press of Kansas, 2003.

Pfeffer, Leo. *Church, State and Freedom.* 2 vols. rev. ed. Boston: Beacon Press, 1967.

Redish, Martin H. *Freedom of Expression: A Critical Analysis.* Charlottesville, Va.: Michie, 1984.

Spitzer, Matthew Laurence. *Seven Dirty Words and Six Other Stories: Controlling the Content of Print and Broadcast.* New Haven, Conn.: Yale University Press, 1986.

Sunstein, Cass R. *Democracy and the Problem of Free Speech.* New York: Free Press, 1993.

Tedford, Thomas L. *Freedom of Speech in the United States.* New York: Random House, 1985.

Van Alstyne, William W. *Interpretations of the First Amendment.* Durham, N.C.: Duke University Press, 1984.

POLITICAL PARTICIPATION

Anzalone, Christopher A., ed. *Supreme Court Cases on Political Representation, 1787–2001.* Armonk, N.Y.: M. E. Sharpe, 2002.

Atleson, James B. "The Aftermath of *Baker v. Carr:* An Adventure in Judicial Experimentation." *California Law Review* 51 (1963): 535–572.

Auerbach, Carl E. "The Reapportionment Cases: One Person, One Vote—One Vote, One Value." In *Supreme Court Review 1964,* ed. Philip B. Kurland. Chicago: University of Chicago Press, 1964.

Banzhaf, John F., III. "Multi-Member Electoral Districts—Do They Violate the 'One Man, One Vote' Principle?" *Yale Law Journal* 75 (1966): 1309–1338.

Bickel, Alexander M. "The Voting Rights Cases." In *Supreme Court Review 1966,* ed. Philip B. Kurland. Chicago: University of Chicago Press, 1966.

Bontecou, Eleanor. *The Federal Loyalty-Security Program.* Westport, Conn.: Greenwood Press, 1974. Reprint of 1953 ed.

Brown, Ralph S., Jr. *Loyalty and Security: Employment Tests in the United States.* Jersey City, N.J.: Da Capo, 1972. Reprint of 1958 ed.

Cushman, Robert E. *Civil Liberties in the United States.* Ithaca, N.Y.: Cornell University Press, 1969. Reprint of 1956 ed.

Davidson, Chandler, and Bernard Grofman, eds. *Quiet Revolution in the South: The Impact of the Voting Rights Act, 1965–1990.* Princeton, N.J.: Princeton University Press, 1994.

DeGrazia, Alfred. *Essay on Apportionment and Representative Government.* Westport, Conn.: Greenwood Press, 1983. Reprint of 1963 ed.

Elliott, Ward E. Y. *The Rise of Guardian Democracy: The Supreme Court's Role in Voting Rights Disputes, 1845–1969.* Cambridge: Harvard University Press, 1974.

Irwin, William P. "Representation and Election: The Reapportionment Cases in Retrospect." *Michigan Law Review* 67 (1969): 73–82.

Konvitz, Milton R. *Fundamental Liberties of a Free People.* Westport, Conn.: Greenwood Press, 1978. Reprint of 1957 ed.

Lahava, Prina. *Press Law in Modern Democracies: A Comparative Study.* New York: Longman, 1985.

Latham, Earl. *The Communist Controversy in Washington.* Ann Arbor, Mich.: UMI, Books on Demand, 1966.

McKay, Robert. *Reapportionment: The Law and Politics of Equal Representation.* New York: Twentieth Century Fund, 1965.

Meiklejohn, Alexander. *Political Freedom: The Constitutional Powers of the People.* Westport, Conn.: Greenwood Press, 1979. Reprint of 1960 ed.

Mendelson, Wallace E. "Clear and Present Danger—From *Schenck* to *Dennis.*" *Columbia Law Review* 52 (1952): 313–333.

Murray, Robert K. *Red Scare: A Study in National Hysteria, 1919–1920.* Minneapolis: University of Minnesota Press, 1955.

Nathanson, Nathaniel L. "The Communist Trial and the Clear and Present Danger Test." *Harvard Law Review* 63 (1950): 1167–1175.

Polsby, Nelson W., ed. *Reapportionment in the 1970s.* Berkeley: University of California Press, 1971.

Pritchett, C. Herman. *Congress versus the Supreme Court, 1957–1960.* New York: Da Capo Press, 1973. Reprint.

Thompson, Kenneth. *The Voting Rights Act and Black Electoral Participation.* Washington, D.C.: Joint Center for Political Studies, 1984.

Woodward, C. Vann. *Origins of the New South, 1877–1913.* Baton Rouge, La.: Louisiana State University Press, 1971.

———. *The Strange Career of Jim Crow.* 3d rev. ed. New York: Oxford University Press, 1974.

DUE PROCESS

Alexander, Frederick, and John L. Amsden. "Scope of the Fourth Amendment." *Georgetown Law Journal* 75 (1987): 713–727.

Allen, Francis A. "Federalism and the Fourth Amendment: A Requiem for Wolf." In *Supreme Court Review 1961,* ed. Philip B. Kurland. Chicago: University of Chicago Press, 1961.

Amsterdam, Anthony. "Perspectives on the Fourth Amendment." *Minnesota Law Review* 58 (1974): 349.

Angotti, Donna Louise, and Michael D. Warden. "Warrantless Searches and Seizures." *Georgetown Law Journal* 75 (1987): 742–790.

Barnett, Edward L., Jr. "Personal Rights, Property Rights and the Fourth Amendment." In *Supreme Court Review 1960,* ed. Philip B. Kurland. Chicago: University of Chicago Press, 1960.

Beaney, William M. "The Constitutional Right to Privacy in the Supreme Court." In *Supreme Court Review 1962,* ed. Philip B. Kurland. Chicago: University of Chicago Press, 1962.

———. *The Right to Counsel in American Courts.* Westport, Conn.: Greenwood Press, 1972.

Black, Charles L. *Capital Punishment: The Inevitability of Caprice and Mistake.* rev. ed. New York: Norton, 1982.

Epstein, Lee, and Joseph F. Kobylka. *The Supreme Court and Legal Change: Abortion and the Death Penalty.* Chapel Hill: University of North Carolina Press, 1992.

Essaye, Anne. "Cruel and Unusual Punishment." *Georgetown Law Journal* 75 (1987): 1168–1195.

Fellman, David. *The Defendant's Rights Today.* Madison: University of Wisconsin Press, 1976.

Fingarette, Herbert. "Addiction and Criminal Responsibility." *Yale Law Journal* 84 (1975): 413.

Fisher, George. *Plea Bargaining's Triumph: A History of Plea Bargaining in America.* Stanford, Calif.: Stanford University Press, 2003.

Fisher, Louis. "Congress and the Fourth Amendment." *Georgia Law Review* 21 (1986): 107–170.

Goldberger, Peter. "A Guide to Identifying Fourth Amendment Issues." *Search and Seizure Law Report* 13 (1986): 33–40.

Green, John Raeburn. "The Bill of Rights, the Fourteenth Amendment, and the Supreme Court." *Michigan Law Review* 46 (1948): 869.

Griswold, Erwin N. *Search and Seizure: A Dilemma of the Supreme Court.* Lincoln: University of Nebraska Press, 1975.

Hall, Livingston, et al. *Modern Criminal Procedure.* 6th ed. St. Paul, Minn.: West, 1986.

Herman, Michele G. *Search and Seizure Checklists.* 4th ed. New York: Boardman, 1985.

Israel, Jerrold H. "*Gideon v. Wainwright:* The Art of Overruling." *Supreme Court Review 1963,* ed. Philip B. Kurland. Chicago: University of Chicago Press, 1963.

James, Joseph B. *The Ratification of the Fourteenth Amendment.* Macon, Ga.: Mercer University Press, 1984.

Kalven, Harry A., Jr., and Hans Zeisel. *The American Jury.* Chicago: University of Chicago Press, 1986.

Kroll, Robert. "Can the Fourth Amendment Go High Tech?" *American Bar Association* 73 (1987): 70–74.

LaFave, Wayne R. "'Case-by-Case Adjudication' versus 'Standardized Procedures': The *Robinson* Dilemma." *Supreme Court Review 1974,* ed. Philip B. Kurland. Chicago: University of Chicago Press, 1974.

———. *Search and Seizure: A Treatise on the Fourth Amendment.* 2d ed. St. Paul, Minn.: West, 1986.

Landynski, Jacob W. *Searches and Seizures and the Supreme Court: A Study in Constitutional Interpretation.* Ann Arbor, Mich.: UMI, Books on Demand. Reprint of 1965 ed.

Leo, Richard A., and George C. Thomas III, eds. *The Miranda Debate: Law, Justice, and Policing.* Boston: Northeastern University Press, 2000.

Levy, Leonard W. *Origins of the Fifth Amendment: The Right against Self-Incrimination.* New York: Macmillan, 1986.

Lewis, Anthony. *Gideon's Trumpet.* New York: Random House, 1964.

Marshaw, Jerry L. *Due Process in the Administrative State.* New Haven, Conn.: Yale University Press, 1985.

Mason, Alpheus T., and Donald G. Stephenson, Jr. *American Constitutional Law.* 11th ed. Englewood Cliffs, N.J.: Prentice-Hall, 1995.

Moore, Tim. "Constitutional Law: The Fourth Amendment and Drug Testing in the Workplace." *Harvard Journal of Law and Public Policy* 10 (1987): 762–768.

Oaks, Dallin. "Studying the Exclusionary Rule in Searches and Seizures." *University of Chicago Law Review* 37 (1970): 665.

Port, Joseph Clinton, Jr., and James D. Mathias. "Right to Counsel." *Georgetown Law Journal* 75 (1987): 1029–1052.

Rossum, Ralph A. "New Rights and Old Wrongs: The Supreme Court and the Problem of Retroactivity." *Emory Law Journal* 23 (1974): 381.

Sit, Po Yin. "Double Jeopardy, Due Process, and the Breach of Plea Agreements." *Columbia Law Review* 87 (1987): 142–160.

Strong, Frank R. *Substantive Due Process of Law: A Dichotomy of Sense and Nonsense.* Durham, N.C.: Carolina Academic Press, 1986.

White, James B. "The Fourth Amendment as a Way of Talking About People: A Study of *Robinson* and *Matlock.*" In *Supreme Court Review 1974,* ed. Philip B. Kurland. Chicago: University of Chicago Press, 1974.

White, Welsh S. *The Death Penalty in the Eighties: An Examination of the Modern System of Capital Punishment.* Ann Arbor, Mich.: University of Michigan Press, 1987.

EQUAL RIGHTS

Abernathy, M. Glenn. *Civil Liberties under the Constitution.* 4th ed. Columbia: University of South Carolina Press, 1985.

Amar, Akhil Reed. *The Bill of Rights: Creation and Reconstruction.* New Haven, Conn.: Yale University Press, 1998.

Anzalone, Christopher A., ed. *Supreme Court Cases on Gender and Sexual Equality, 1787 2001.* Armonk, N.Y.: M.E. Sharpe, 2002.

Berger, Morroe. *Equality by Statute: The Revolution in Civil Rights.* New York: Hippocrene Books, 1978. Reprint of 1967 ed.

Bickel, Alexander M. *Politics and the Warren Court.* Jersey City, N.J.: Da Capo, 1973. Reprint of 1955 ed.

Blaustein, Albert P., and Clarence Clyde Ferguson Jr. *Desegregation and the Law: The Meaning and Effect of the School Segregation Cases.* Littleton, Colo.: Rothman, 1985. Reprint of 1957 ed.

Carter, Stephen L. *Reflections of an Affirmative Action Baby.* New York: Basic Books, 1991.

Craig, Barbara Hinkson, and David M. O'Brien. *Abortion and American Politics.* Chatham, N.J.: Chatham House, 1993.

Cushman, Clare, ed. *Supreme Court Decisions and Women's Rights: Milestones to Equality.* Washington, D.C.: CQ Press, 2001.

"Developments in the Law: Equal Protection." *Harvard Law Review* 82 (March 1969): 1065.

Dworkin, Ronald. *Life's Dominion: An Argument about Abortion, Euthanasia and Individual Freedom.* New York: Knopf, 1993.

Esdall, Thomas Byrne. *The New Politics of Inequality.* New York: Norton, 1984.

Fisher, Louis. *American Constitutional Law: Civil Rights and Civil Liberties.* 4th ed. Durham, NC: Carolina Academic Press, 2001.

Franklin, John Hope. *From Slavery to Freedom: A History of African Americans.* 7th ed. New York: McGraw-Hill, 1994.

Galloway, Russell W. *Justice for All? The Rich and Poor in Supreme Court History, 1790–1990.* Durham, N.C.: Carolina Academic Press, 1991.

Garraty, John A., ed. *Quarrels That Have Shaped the Constitution.* rev. ed. New York: Harper and Row, 1987.

Garrow, David J. *Liberty and Sexuality: The Right to Privacy and the Making of* Roe v. Wade. New York: Macmillan, 1994.

Glick, Henry R. "The Impact of Permissive Judicial Policies: The U.S. Supreme Court and the Right to Die." *Political Research Quarterly* 47 (1994): 207–222.

Gunther, Gerald. "In Search of Evolving Doctrine on a Changing Court: A Model for a Newer Equal Protection." *Harvard Law Review* 86 (November 1972): 1.

Hartmann, Heidi I. *Comparable Worth: New Direction for Research.* Washington, D.C.: National Academy Press, 1985.

Hull, Elizabeth. *Without Justice for All: The Constitutional Rights of Aliens.* Westport, Conn.: Greenwood Press, 1985.

Ivers, Gregg. *American Constitutional Law: Power and Politics.* Vol. 2, *Civil Rights and Liberties.* Boston: Houghton and Mifflin, 2002.

Karst, Kenneth L. "Equal Citizenship under the Fourteenth Amendment." *Harvard Law Review* 91 (November 1977): 1.

Kelly, Alfred H., and Winfred A. Harbison. *The American Constitution: Its Origins and Development.* 7th ed. New York: Norton, 1991.

Kirp, David L., Mark G. Yudof, and Marlene Strong Franks. *Gender Justice.* Chicago: University of Chicago Press, 1985.

Kluger, Richard. *Simple Justice: The History of* Brown v. Board of Education *and Black America's Struggle for Equality.* New York: Knopf, 1976.

Konvitz, Milton R., and Theodore Leskes. *A Century of Civil Rights, with a Study of State Law against Discrimination.* Westport, Conn.: Greenwood Press, 1983. Reprint of 1961 ed.

Lawson, Steven F. *In Pursuit of Power: Southern Blacks and Electoral Politics, 1965–1982.* New York: Columbia University Press, 1985.

Levin-Epstein, Michael D., and Howard J. Anderson. *Primer of Equal Employment Opportunity.* 3d ed. Washington, D.C.: Bureau of National Affairs, 1984.

Morris, Frank C. *Judicial Wage Determination: A Volatile Spectre: Perspectives on Comparable Worth.* Washington, D.C.: National Legal Center for the Public Interest, 1984.

Murdoch, Joyce, and Deb Price. *Courting Justice: Gay Men and Lesbians v. the Supreme Court.* New York: Basic Books, 2001.

Phelps, Glenn A., and Robert A. Poirer. *Contemporary Debates on Civil Liberties: Enduring Constitutional Questions.* Lexington, Mass.: Lexington Books, 1985.

Remick, Helen. *Comparable Worth and Wage Discrimination: Technical Possibilities and Political Realities.* Philadelphia: Temple University Press, 1984.

Reskin, Barbara F., and Heidi I. Hartmann. *Women's Work, Men's Work: Sex Segregation on the Job.* Washington, D.C.: National Academy Press, 1985.

Schiller, Bradley R. *The Economics of Poverty and Discrimination.* 4th ed. Englewood Cliffs, N.J.: Prentice-Hall, 1984.

Schmid, Gunther, and Renata Weitzel. *Sex Discrimination and Equal Opportunity: The Labor Market and Employment Policy.* New York: St. Martin's Press, 1984.

Schuman, Howard, Charlotte Steeh, and Lawrence Bobo. *Racial Attitudes in America: Trends and Interpretations.* Cambridge: Harvard University Press, 1985.

Sunstein, Cass. *One Case at a Time.* Cambridge, Mass.: Harvard University Press, 1999.

Tushnet, Mark V. *Making Civil Rights Law: Thurgood Marshall and the Supreme Court, 1936–1961.* New York: Oxford University Press, 1994.

Tussman, Joseph, and Jacobus tenBroek. "The Equal Protection of the Laws." *California Law Review* 37 (1949): 341.

U.S. Commission on Civil Rights. *Comparable Worth: Issue for the 80's—A Consultation of the U.S. Commission on Civil Rights, June 6–7, 1984.* Washington, D.C.: Commission on Civil Rights, 1984.

Wechsler, Herbert. "Toward Neutral Principles of Constitutional Law." *Harvard Law Review* 73 (November 1959): 31.

Woodward, C. Vann. *The Strange Career of Jim Crow.* 3d rev. ed. New York: Oxford University Press, 1974.

PART IV PRESSURES ON THE COURT

CONGRESSIONAL PRESSURE

Abraham, Henry J. *Justices and Presidents: A Political History of Appointments to the Supreme Court.* 3d ed. New York: Oxford University Press, 1992.

Baker, Leonard. *Back to Back: The Duel Between FDR and the Supreme Court.* New York: Macmillan, 1967.

———. *John Marshall: A Life in Law.* New York: Macmillan, 1974.

Beveridge, Albert J. *The Life of John Marshall.* 4 vols. Cambridge, Mass.: Houghton Mifflin, The Riverside Press, 1919.

Black, Charles L., Jr. *Perspectives in Constitutional Law.* Englewood Cliffs, N.J.: Prentice-Hall, 1973.

Brant, Irving. *Impeachment: Trials and Errors.* New York: Knopf, 1972.

———. "Appellate Jurisdiction: Congressional Abuse of the Exceptions Clause." *Oregon Law Review* 53 (Fall 1973): 3.

Carter, Stephen L. *The Confirmation Mess: Cleaning Up the Federal Appointments Process.* New York: Basic Books, 1994.

Casper, Gerhard, and Richard A. Posner. *The Workload of the Supreme Court.* Chicago: American Bar Foundation, 1976.

Choper, J. H. "Supreme Court and the Political Branches: Democratic Theory and Practice." *University of Pennsylvania Law Review* 122 (April 1974): 810.

"Congress vs. Court: The Legislative Arsenal." *Villanova Law Review* 10 (Winter 1965): 347.

Curtis, Charles P., Jr. *Lions under the Throne.* Cambridge, Mass.: Houghton Mifflin, The Riverside Press, 1947.

Elliott, Shelden D. "Court Curbing Proposals in Congress." *Notre Dame Lawyer* 33 (August 1958): 597.

Fite, Katherine B., and Louis Baruch Rubinstein. "Curbing the Supreme Court—State Experiences and Federal Proposals." *Michigan Law Review* 35 (March 1937): 762.

Frankfurter, Felix, and James M. Landis. *The Business of the Supreme Court: A Study in the Federal Judicial System.* New York: Macmillan, 1928.

Freund, Paul A., and Stanley N. Katz, gen. eds. *History of the Supreme Court of the United States.* Vol. 1, *Antecedents and Beginnings to 1801,* by Julius Goebel Jr., 1971; Vol. 2, *Foundations of Power: John Marshall, 1801–1815,* by George L. Haskins and Herbert A. Johnson, 1981; Vols. 3–4, *The Marshall Court and Cultural Change, 1815–1835,* by G. Edward White, 1988; Vol. 5, *The Taney Period, 1836–1864,* by Carl B. Swisher, 1974; Vol. 6, *Reconstruction and Reunion, 1864–1888,* Part One, by Charles Fairman, 1971; Vol. 7, *Reconstruction and Reunion, 1864–1888,* Part Two, by Charles Fairman, 1987; Supplement to Vol. 7, *Five Justices and the Electoral Commission of 1877,* by Charles Fairman, 1988; Vol. 8, *Troubled Beginnings of the Modern State, 1888–1910,* by Owen M. Fiss, 1993; Vol. 9, *The Judiciary and Responsible Government, 1910–1921,* by Alexander M. Bickel and Benno C. Schmidt Jr., 1984. New York: Macmillan.

Gimpel, James G., and Robin M. Wolpert. "Rationalizing Support and Opposition to Supreme Court Nominees: The Role of Credentials. *Polity* 28 (1995): 67–82.

Hart, Henry M., Jr. "The Power of Congress to Limit the Jurisdiction of Federal Courts: An Exercise in Dialectic." *Harvard Law Review* 66 (June 1953): 1362.

Hughes, Charles Evans. *The Supreme Court of the United States; Its Foundations, Methods and Achievements, An Interpretation.* New York: Columbia University Press, 1928.

Ignagni, Joseph, and James Meernilo. "Explaining Congressional Attempts to Reverse Supreme Court Decisions." *Political Research Quarterly* 47 (1994): 353–371.

Jackson, Robert H. *The Struggle for Judicial Supremacy: A Study of a Crisis in American Power Politics.* New York: Random House, Vintage Books, 1941.

Kelly, Alfred H., and Winfred A. Harbison. *The American Constitution: Its Origins and Development.* 7th ed. New York: Norton, 1991.

Kurland, Philip B. *Politics, the Constitution and the Warren Court.* Chicago: University of Chicago Press, 1970.

Levinson, Sanford, ed. *Responding to Imperfection: The Theory and Practice of Constitutional Amendment.* Princeton, N.J.: Princeton University Press, 1995.

Marke, Julius J. *Vignettes of Legal History.* South Hackensack, N.J.: Fred B. Rothman, 1965.

Martig, Ralph R. "Congress and the Appellate Jurisdiction of the Supreme Court." *Michigan Law Review* 34 (March 1936): 650.

Murphy, Walter F. *Congress and the Court: A Case Study in the American Political Process.* Chicago: University of Chicago Press, 1962.

Nagel, Stuart S. "Court-Curbing Periods in American History." *Vanderbilt Law Review* 18 (June 1955): 925.

Pritchett, C. Herman. *Congress Versus the Supreme Court, 1957–60.* Minneapolis: University of Minnesota Press, 1961; reprint ed. New York: Da Capo Press, 1973.

Ratner, Leonard G. "Congressional Power over the Appellate Jurisdiction of the Supreme Court." *University of Pennsylvania Law Review* 109 (December 1960): 157.

Ruckman, P. S. "The Supreme Court, Critical Nominations, and the Senate Confirmation Process." *Journal of Politics* 55 (1993): 793–805.

Schmidhauser, John R., and Larry L. Berg. *The Supreme Court and Congress: Conflict and Interaction, 1945–1968.* New York: Free Press, 1972.

Stumpf, Harry P. "Congressional Response to Supreme Court Rulings: The Interaction of Law and Politics." *Journal of Public Law* 14 (1965): 382.

Swindler, William F. *Court and Constitution in the Twentieth Century: The Old Legality, 1889–1932.* Indianapolis: Bobbs-Merrill, 1969.

———. *Court and Constitution in the Twentieth Century: The New Legality, 1932–1968.* Indianapolis: Bobbs-Merrill, 1970.

Swisher, Carl Brent. *American Constitutional Development.* 2d ed. Cambridge, Mass.: Houghton Mifflin, Riverside Press, 1954.

Vose, Clement E. *Constitutional Change: Amendment Politics and Supreme Court Litigation Since 1900.* Lexington, Mass: D.C. Heath, Lexington Books, 1972.

Warren, Charles. "Legislative and Judicial Attacks on the Supreme Court of the United States." *American Law Review* 47 (January–February 1913): 4.

———. *The Supreme Court in United States History.* rev. ed., 2 vols. Boston: Little, Brown, 1926.

———. *Congress, the Constitution and the Supreme Court.* Boston: Little, Brown, 1925.

PRESIDENTIAL PRESSURE

Abraham, Henry J. *Justices and Presidents: A Political History of Appointments to the Supreme Court.* 3d ed. New York: Oxford University Press, 1992.

Danielski, David J. *A Supreme Court Justice Is Appointed.* New York: Random House, 1964.

Dunne, Gerald T. *Hugo Black and the Judicial Revolution.* New York: Simon and Schuster, 1977.

Kelly, Alfred H., and Winfred A. Harbison. *The American Constitution: Its Origins and Development.* 7th ed. New York: Norton, 1991.

Lasser, William. *The Limits of Judicial Power: The Supreme Court in American Politics.* Chapel Hill: University of North Carolina Press, 1988.

Leuchtenberg, William E. *The Supreme Court Reborn: The Constitutional Revolution in the Age of Roosevelt.* New York: Oxford University Press, 1995.

Mason, Alpheus T. *Harlan Fiske Stone: Pillar of the Law.* New York: Viking Press, 1956.

———. *William Howard Taft: Chief Justice.* New York: Simon and Schuster, 1965.

Massaro, John. *Supremely Political: The Role of Ideology and Presidential Management in Unsuccessful Supreme Court Nominations.* Albany: SUNY Press, 1990.

McHargue, Daniel S. "Appointments to the Supreme Court of the United States: The Factors that Have Affected Appointments, 1789–1932." Ph.D. diss., University of California at Los Angeles, 1949.

O'Brien, David M. *Storm Center: The Supreme Court in American Politics.* New York: Norton, 1986.

Odegaard, Peter. *American Politics.* 2d ed. New York: Harper and Bros., 1947.

Pacelle, Richard L., Jr. *The Transformation of the Supreme Court's Agenda: From the New Deal to the Reagan Administration.* Boulder: Westview Press, 1991.

Perry, Barbara A. *A "Representative" Supreme Court? The Impact of Race, Religion and Gender on Appointments.* Westport, Conn.: Greenwood Press, 1991.

Pringle, Henry F. *The Life and Times of William Howard Taft.* New York: Farrar and Rinehart, 1939.

Pusey, Merlo F. *Charles Evans Hughes.* 2 vols. New York: Macmillan, 1951.

Ratner, Sidney F. "Was the Supreme Court Packed by President Grant?" *Political Science Quarterly* 50 (September 1935): 343.

Schlesinger, Arthur M., Jr., and Fred L. Israel, eds. *History of American Presidential Elections.* 9 vols. New York: Chelsea House Publishers, 1985.

Schwartz, Herman. *Packing the Courts: The Conservatives' Campaign to Rewrite the Constitution.* New York: Scribner's, 1988.

Scigliano, Robert G. *The Supreme Court and the Presidency.* New York: Free Press, 1971.

Shogan, Robert. *A Question of Judgment: The Fortas Case and the Struggle for the Supreme Court.* Indianapolis: Bobbs-Merrill, 1972.

Steamer, Robert J. *The Supreme Court in Crisis: A History of Conflict.* Amherst, Mass.: University of Massachusetts Press, 1971.

Swindler, William F. *Court and Constitution in the Twentieth Century.* 3 vols. Indianapolis: Bobbs-Merrill, 1969–1974.

Tribe, Laurence H. *God Save This Honorable Court.* New York: Random House, 1985.

Warren, Charles. *The Supreme Court in United States History.* rev. ed., 2 vols. Boston: Little, Brown, 1926.

Wasby, Stephen J. *The Supreme Court in the Federal Judicial System.* 4th ed. Chicago: Nelson-Hall, 1993.

Witt, Elder. *A Different Justice: Reagan and the Supreme Court.* Washington, D.C.: Congressional Quarterly, 1986.

THE COURT, THE PRESS, AND THE PUBLIC

Arnold, Thurman. *The Symbols of Government.* New York: Harcourt Brace and World, 1935; reprint ed., 1962.

Cook, Beverly B. "Measuring the Significance of U.S. Supreme Court Decisions." *Journal of Politics* 56 (1993): 1127–1139.

Davis, Richard. *Decisions and Images: The Supreme Court and the Press.* Englewood Cliffs, N.J.: Prentice-Hall, 1994.

Epstein, Lee. *Conservatives in Court.* Knoxville: University of Tennessee Press, 1985.

Freund, Paul A., and Stanley N. Katz, gen. eds. *History of the Supreme Court of the United States.* Vol. 1, *Antecedents and Beginnings to 1801,* by Julius Goebel Jr., 1971; Vol. 2, *Foundations of Power: John Marshall, 1801–1815,* by George L. Haskins and Herbert A. Johnson, 1981; Vols. 3–4, *The Marshall Court and Cultural Change, 1815–1835,* by G. Edward White, 1988; Vol. 5, *The Taney Period, 1836–1864,* by Carl B. Swisher, 1974; Vol. 6, *Reconstruction and Reunion, 1864–1888,* Part One, by Charles Fairman, 1971; Vol. 7, *Reconstruction and Reunion, 1864–1888,* Part Two, by Charles Fairman, 1987; Supplement to Vol. 7, *Five Justices and the Electoral Commission of 1877,* by Charles Fairman, 1988; Vol. 8, *Troubled Beginnings of the Modern State, 1888–1910,* by Owen M. Fiss, 1993; Vol. 9, *The Judiciary and Responsible Government, 1910–1921,* by Alexander M. Bickel and Benno C. Schmidt Jr., 1984. New York: Macmillan.

Garraty, John A., ed. *Quarrels that Have Shaped the Constitution.* rev. ed. New York: Perennial Library, 1987.

Hirschfield, Robert S. *The Constitution and the Court.* New York: Random House, 1962.

Lasser, William. *The Limits of Judicial Power: The Supreme Court in American Politics.* Chapel Hill: University of North Carolina Press, 1988.

Leuchtenburg, William E. *Franklin D. Roosevelt and the New Deal.* New York: Harper and Row, Harper Torchbooks, 1963.

Link, Michael W. "Tracking Public Mood in the Supreme Court: Cross-Time Analyses of Criminal Procedure and Civil Rights Cases." *Political Research Quarterly* 48 (1995): 61–78.

McCloskey, Robert G., with Sanford Levinson.*The Modern Supreme Court.* Chicago: University of Chicago Press, 1994.

McGuire, Kevin T., and Barbara Palmer. "Issue Fluidity on the U.S. Supreme Court." *American Political Science Review* 89 (1995): 691–702.

Murphy, Paul L. *The Constitution in Crisis Times: 1918–1969.* New York: Harper and Row, Harper Torchbooks, 1972.

Warren, Charles. *The Supreme Court in United States History.* rev. ed., 2 vols. Boston: Little, Brown, 1926.

PART V THE COURT AT WORK

American Bar Association. "The Supreme Court—Its Homes Past and Present." *American Bar Association Journal* 27 (1941).

Anzalone, Christopher A. *Encyclopedia of Supreme Court Quotations.* Armonk, N.Y.: M. E. Sharpe, 2000.

Baker, Liva. *Felix Frankfurter.* New York: Coward-McCann, 1969.

Baum, Lawrence. *The Supreme Court.* 8th ed. Washington, D.C.: CQ Press, 2003.

Bickel, Alexander M. *The Caseload of the Supreme Court.* Washington, D.C.: American Enterprise Institute for Public Policy Research, 1973.

———. *The Unpublished Opinions of Justice Brandeis.* Cambridge: Harvard University Press, 1957.

———. *Politics and the Warren Court.* New York: Harper and Row, 1965.

Brennan, William J., Jr. "State Court Decisions and the Supreme Court." *Pennsylvania Bar Association Quarterly* 31 (1960).

Brenner, Saul, and Harold J. Spaeth. *Stare Indecisis: The Alteration of Precedent on the Supreme Court, 1946–1992.* Cambridge: Cambridge University Press, 1995.

Caplan, Lincoln. *The Tenth Justice: The Solicitor General and the Rule of Law.* New York: Knopf, 1987.

Cranberg, Gilbert. "What Did the Supreme Court Say?" *Saturday Review.* April 8, 1967.

Curtis, Charles P., Jr. *Lions under the Throne.* Boston: Houghton Mifflin, 1947.

Elsasser, Glenn, and Jack Fuller. "The Hidden Face of the Supreme Court." *Chicago Tribune Magazine,* April 23, 1978.

Epstein, Lee, et al. *The Supreme Court Compendium: Data, Decisions & Development.* 3d ed. Washington, D.C., CQ Press, 2002.

Fairman, Charles. *Mr. Justice Miller.* Cambridge: Harvard University Press, 1939.

Finkelman, Paul, and Melvin I. Urofsky. *Landmark Decisions of the United States Supreme Court.* Washington, D.C.: CQ Press, 2002.

Frank, John P. *Marble Palace: The Supreme Court in American Life.* New York: Knopf, 1961.

Friedman, Lawrence M. *American Law in the 20th Century.* New Haven, Conn.: Yale University Press, 2002.

Freund, Paul A. *The Supreme Court of the United States.* Cleveland: World Publishing, 1961.

Freund, Paul A., and Stanley N. Katz, gen. eds. *History of the Supreme Court of the United States.* Vol. 1, *Antecedents and Beginnings to 1801,* by Julius Goebel Jr., 1971; Vol. 2, Foundations of Power: John Marshall, 1801–1815, by George L. Haskins and Herbert A. Johnson, 1981; Vols. 3–4, *The Marshall Court and Cultural Change, 1815–1835,* by G. Edward White, 1988; Vol. 5, *The Taney Period, 1836–1864,* by Carl B. Swisher, 1974; Vol. 6: *Reconstruction and*

Reunion, 1864–1888, Part One, by Charles Fairman, 1971; Vol. 7, *Reconstruction and Reunion, 1864–1888,* Part Two, by Charles Fairman, 1987; Supplement to Vol. 7, *Five Justices and the Electoral Commission of 1877,* by Charles Fairman, 1988; Vol. 8, *Troubled Beginnings of the Modern State, 1888–1910,* by Owen M. Fiss, 1993; Vol. 9, *The Judiciary and Responsible Government, 1910–1921,* by Alexander M. Bickel and Benno C. Schmidt Jr., 1984. New York: Macmillan.

Hand, Learned. *The Bill of Rights.* New York: Atheneum, 1964.

Harrell, Mary Ann. *Equal Justice under Law: The Supreme Court in American Life.* 5th ed. Washington, D.C.: The Foundation of the Federal Bar Association, with the cooperation of the National Geographic Society, 1988.

Hughes, Charles Evans. *The Supreme Court of the United States: Its Foundations, Methods and Achievements, An Interpretation.* New York: Columbia University Press, 1928.

Jackson, Robert H. "Advocacy Before the Supreme Court: Suggestions for Effective Case Presentations." *American Bar Association Journal* 101 (1951).

King, Willard L. *Melville Weston Fuller.* New York: Macmillan, 1950.

Kluger, Richard. *Simple Justice:* Brown v. Board of Education *and Black America's Struggle for Equality.* New York: Knopf, 1976.

Lash, Joseph P. *From the Diaries of Felix Frankfurter.* Norton, 1975.

Lasser, William. *The Limits of Judicial Power: The Supreme Court in American Politics.* Chapel Hill: University of North Carolina Press, 1988.

Lazarus, Edward. *Closed Chambers : The First Eyewitness Account of the Epic Struggles inside the Supreme Court.* New York : Times Books, 1998.

Lively, Donald E. *Foreshadows of the Law: Supreme Court Dissents and Constitutional Development.* Westport, Conn.: Praeger, 1993.

Mason, Alpheus T. *Harlan Fiske Stone: Pillar of the Law.* New York: Viking, 1956.

McCune, Wesley. *The Nine Young Men.* New York: Harper and Brothers, 1947.

McGuire, Kevin T. *The Supreme Court Bar: Legal Elites in the Washington Community.* Charlottesville: University of Virginia Press, 1993.

Murphy, Bruce Allen. *The Brandeis/Frankfurter Connection: The Secret Political Activities of Two Supreme Court Justices.* New York: Oxford University Press, 1982.

O'Brien, David M. *Storm Center: The Supreme Court in American Politics.* New York: Norton, 1986.

Perry, H. W., Jr. *Deciding to Decide: Agenda Setting in the United States Supreme Court.* Cambridge: Harvard University Press, 1992.

Pfeffer, Leo. *This Honorable Court: A History of the United States Supreme Court.* Boston: Beacon Press, 1965.

Pringle, Henry F. *Life and Times of William Howard Taft.* New York: Farrar and Rinehart, 1939.

Pusey, Merlo F. *Charles Evans Hughes.* New York: Columbia University Press, 1963.

Rehnquist, William H. *The Supreme Court: How It Was, How It Is.* New York: Morrow, 1987.

Schwartz, Bernard. *Super Chief: Earl Warren and His Supreme Court, A Judicial Biography.* New York: New York University Press, 1983.

Simon, James F. *In His Own Image: The Supreme Court in Richard Nixon's America.* New York: McKay, 1973.

Steamer, Robert J. *Chief Justice: Leadership and the Supreme Court.* Columbia: University of South Carolina Press, 1986.

Stern, Robert L., Eugene Gressman, Stephen M. Shapiro, and Kenneth S. Geller. *Supreme Court Practice.* 7th ed. Washington, D.C.: Bureau of National Affairs, 1993.

Tribe, Laurence H. *God Save This Honorable Court.* New York: Random House, 1985.

Warren, Charles. *The Supreme Court in United States History.* rev. ed., 2 vols. Boston: Little, Brown, 1926.

Williams, Richard L. "Justices Run 'Nine Little Law Firms' at Supreme Court." *Smithsonian,* February 1977.

———. "Supreme Court of the United States: The Staff That Keeps It Operating." *Smithsonian,* January 1977.

Zobell, Karl M. "Division of Opinion in the Supreme Court: A History of Judicial Disintegration." *Cornell Law Quarterly* 44 (1959).

Case Index

State Farm, Fire & Casualty Co. v. Tashire, 386 U.S. 523 (1967), 322 n. 23

State Farm Mutual Automobile Insurance Co. v. Campbell, __ U.S. __ (2003), 402 (box)

State Freight Tax Case (Philadelphia & Reading RR v. Pennsylvania), 15 Wall. 232 (1873), 408 n. 158

State Tax on Railroad Gross Receipts (Philadelphia & Reading RR v. Pennsylvania), 15 Wall. 284 (1873), 408 n. 159

Stearns v. Minnesota, 179 U.S. 223 (1900), 197 n. 7

Steele v. Louisville and Nashville Railroad Company, 323 U.S. 192 (1944), 707

Steel Seizure Case. *See* Youngstown Sheet and Tube Co. v. Sawyer

Stefanelli v. Minard, 342 U.S. 117 (1951), 621 (box)

Steffel v. Thompson, 415 U.S. 452 (1974), 305 (box), 324 n. 117

Steffens; United States v. (Trademark Cases), 100 U.S. 82 (1879), 385 (box)

Stein v. New York, 346 U.S. 156 (1953), 665 n. 44

Stenberg v. Carhart, 530 U.S. 914 (1992), 72 n. 165, 743

Steward Machine Co. v. Davis, 301 U.S. 548 (1937), 48, 134, 139 (box), 265, 275 n. 101, 410 n. 9

Stewart v. Kahn, 11 Wall. (78 U.S.) 493 (1871), 196 n. 40

Stilson v. United States, 250 U.S. 583 (1919), 444 n. 21

Stolar, In re, 401 U.S. 23 (1971), 587 (box), 595 n. 103

Stone v. Graham, 449 U.S. 39 (1980), 529 (box)

Stone v. Mississippi, 101 U.S. 814 (1880), 29, 343, 344

Stone v. Powell, 428 U.S. 465 (1976), 71 n. 111, 324 n. 59, 621 (box)

Stone v. Wisconsin, 94 U.S. 181 (1877), 407 n. 72

Storer v. Brown, 415 U.S. 724 (1974), 596 n. 108

Strader v. Graham, 10 How. (51 U.S.) 82 (1851), 21, 22, 151, 152, 419 (box)

Strauder v. West Virginia, 100 U.S. 303 (1880), 283 (box), 429 n. 62, 663 n. 25, 673, 731 (box), 753 n. 3

Strawbridge v. Curtiss, 3 Cr. (7 U.S.) 267 (1806), 322 n. 22

Street v. New York, 394 U.S. 576 (1969), 458

Strickland v. Washington, 466 U.S. 668 (1984), 647–648, 666 n. 46

Stroble v. California, 343 U.S. 181 (1951), 497

Strogner v. California, __ U.S. __ (2003), 366

Stromberg v. California, 283 U.S. 359 (1938), 42, 374, 422 (box), 428 n. 37, 534 n. 51, 595 n. 8, 667

Strunk v. United States, 412 U.S. 434 (1973), 609

Stuart v. Laird, 1 Cr. (5 U.S.) 299 (1803), 11, 775, 792 n. 9

Stump v. Sparkman, 435 U.S. 349 (1978), 317 (box)

Sturges v. Crowninshield, 4 Wheat. 122 (1819), 13, 14, 15, 31 n. 56, 341, 407 n. 25

Sugarman v. Dougall, 413 U.S. 634 (1973), 410 n. 128, 722

Sugarman v. United States, 249 U.S. 182 (1919), 444 n. 21

Sugar Trust Case. *See* United States v. E. C. Knight Co.

Sullivan; United States v., 274 U.S. 259 (1927), 131 (box)

Sullivan v. Little Hunting Park, Inc., 396 U.S. 229 (1969), 752 n. 146

Summers, In re, 325 U.S. 561 (1945), 309 (box), 537 n. 66

Sumner v. Shuman, 483 U.S. 66 (1987), 666 n. 39

Sunshine Anthracite Coal Co. v. Adkins, 310 U.S. 381 (1940), 70 n. 15, 192 n. 39, 195 n. 32, 410 n. 9, 789

Supreme Court of New Hampshire v. Piper, 470 U.S. 274 (1985), 412 n. 9

Swaim v. United States, 165 U.S. 553 (1897), 215 (box)

Swain v. Alabama, 380 U.S. 202 (1965), 606

Swann v. Adams, 385 U.S. 440 (1967), 561

Swann v. Charlotte-Mecklenburg County Board of Education, 402 U.S. 1 (1971), 59, 410 n. 111, 689

Sweatt v. Painter, 339 U.S. 629 (1950), 53, 380, 679

Swift v. Tyson, 16 Pet. (41 U.S.) 1 (1842), 32 n. 90, 287 (box), 412 n. 126

Swift & Co. v. United States, 196 U.S. 375 (1905), 37, 103, 107 (box)

Syres v. Oil Workers International Union, 350 U.S. 892 (1955), 752 n. 160

T

Tahoe-Sierra Preservation Council v. Tahoe Regional Planning Agency, 535 U.S. 302 (2002), 156 (box), 411 n. 106

Takahashi v. Fish & Game Commission, 334 U.S. 410 (1948), 410 n. 126, 721

Talbot v. Seeman, 1 Cr. 1 (1801), 270 n. 15

Talley v. California, 362 U.S. 60 (1960), 480

Tashjian v. Republican Party of Connecticut, 479 U.S. 208 (1986), 411 n. 63

Tate v. Short, 401 U.S. 395 (1971), 753 n. 50

Taylor; United States v., 485 U.S. 902 (1988), 663 n. 62

Taylor v. Carryl, 20 How. 583 (1858), 412 n. 128

Taylor v. Georgia, 315 U.S. 25 (1942), 752 n. 155

Taylor v. Louisiana, 419 U.S. 522 (1975), 410 n. 134, 606, 663 n. 23, 727, 731 (box)

Teague v. Lane, 489 U.S. 225 (1989), 298, 299

Teamsters v. United States, 431 U.S. 324 (1977), 710

10 East 40th St. Bldg. v. Callus, 325 U.S. 578 (1945), 194 n. 174

Tennessee v. Davis, 100 U.S. 257 (1880), 283 (box)

Tennessee v. Garner, 471 U.S. 1 (1985), 629 (box)

Tennessee Coal, Iron and Railroad Co. v. Muscola Local 123, 321 U.S. 590 (1944), 811 n. 11

Tennessee Electric Power Co. v. Tennessee Valley Authority, 306 U.S. 118 (1939), 196 n. 66

Tennessee Valley Authority v. Hill, 437 U.S. 153 (1978), 793 n. 50

Tenney v. Brandhove, 341 U.S. 367 (1951), 185

Terlinden v. Ames, 184 U.S. 270 (1992), 272 n. 20

Terminiello v. Chicago, 337 U.S. 1 (1949), 452, 462, 533 n. 36

Terrace v. Thompson, 263 U.S. 197 (1923), 410 n. 124, 720

Terry, Ex parte, 128 U.S. 289 (1888), 324 (nn. 123, 146)

Terry v. Adams, 346 U.S. 461 (1953), 547

Terry v. Ohio, 392 U.S. 1 (1968), 409 n. 78, 616 (box)

Test Oath Cases. *See* Cummings v. Missouri; Ex parte Garland

Texas; United States v., 143 U.S. 621 (1892), 322 n. 14

Texas; United States v., 339 U.S. 707 (1950), 146 (box), 197 n. 5, 793 n. 42

Texas v. Certain Named and Unnamed Undocumented Alien Children, 457 U.S. 202 (1982), 722

Texas v. Cobb, 532 U.S. 162 (2001), 665 n. 34

Texas v. Eastern Texas R. Co., 258 U.S. 204 (1922), 314 (box)

Texas v. Johnson, 491 U.S. 397 (1989), 65, 460, 534 n. 63, 787

Texas v. McCullough, 475 U.S. 134 (1986), 666 n. 18

Texas v. Mitchell, 400 U.S. 112 (1970), 409 n. 42, 411 n. 61, 546 (box)

Texas v. White, 7 Wall. (74 U.S.) 700 (1869), 25, 26, 328 (box), 406 n. 1, 412 n. 134

Texas and Pacific Railway Co. v. United States. *See* Shreveport Rate Cases

Thermstron Products v. Hermansdorfer, 423 U.S. 336 (1976), 324 n. 85

Thirty-seven Photographs; United States v., 402 U.S. 363 (1971), 486 (box)

Thomas v. Collins, 323 U.S. 516 (1945), 436, 453, 468, 534 n. 116, 537 n. 60

Thomas v. Review Board of the Indiana Employment Security Division, 450 U.S. 707 (1981), 537 n. 61

Thompson v. Missouri, 171 U.S. 380 (1898), 409 n. 3

Thompson v. Oklahoma, 487 U.S. 815 (1988), 662

Thompson v. Utah, 170 U.S. 343 (1898), 409 n. 3

Thomson v. Union Pacific Railroad Co., 9 Wall. (76 U.S.) 579 (1870), 195 n. 60

Thornburg v. Gingles, 478 U.S. 30 (1986), 553, 793 n. 53

Thornburgh v. American College of Obstetricians and Gynecologists, 476 U.S. 747 (1986), 71 n. 116, 742, 754 n. 20

Thornhill v. Alabama, 310 U.S. 88 (1940), 50, 465, 467, 468, 533 n. 34

Thornton, Estate of v. Caldor Inc., 472 U.S. 703 (1985), 516

Thurlow v. Massachusetts. *See* License Cases

Tibbs v. Florida, 457 U.S. 31 (1982), 666 n. 5

Tileston v. Ullman, 318 U.S. 44 (1943), 325 n. 34

Tillman v. Wheaton-Haven Recreational Association, Inc., 410 U.S. 431 (1973), 700 (box), 705

Tilton v. Richardson, 403 U.S. 672 (1971), 530, 532–533

T.I.M.E.-D.C. v. United States, 431 U.S. 324 (1977), 710

Time Inc. v. Firestone, 424 U.S. 448 (1976), 494

Time Inc. v. Hill, 385 U.S. 374 (1967), 492 (box)

Time Inc. v. Pape, 401 U.S. 279 (1971), 535 n. 52

Times Film Corp. v. Chicago, 365 U.S. 43 (1961), 484 (box)

Times-Mirror Co. v. Superior Court of California, 314 U.S. 252 (1941), 496

Tinker v. Des Moines Independent Community School District, 393 U.S. 503 (1969), 71 n. 95, 457

Tison v. Arizona, 481 U.S. 137 (1987), 661

Toledo Newspaper Co. v. United States, 247 U.S. 402 (1918), 307, 536 n. 85

Tollett v. Henderson, 411 U.S. 258 (1973), 636 (box), 666 n. 38

Tomkins v. Missouri, 323 U.S. 485 (1945), 665 n. 17

Tony and Susan Alamo Foundation v. Secretary of Labor, 471 U.S. 290 (1985), 537 n. 75

Toomer v. Witsell, 334 U.S. 385 (1948), 412 n. 8

Torcaso v. Watkins, 367 U.S. 488 (1961), 508 (box), 516–517

Totten v. United States, 92 U.S. 105 (1876), 215 (box)

Toucey v. New York Life Insurance Co., 314 U.S. 118 (1941), 324 n. 93

Townsend v. Burk, 334 U.S. 736 (1948), 665 n. 17

Townsend v. Sain, 372 U.S. 293 (1963), 297, 299, 665 n. 43

Townsend v. Yeomans, 301 U.S. 441 (1937), 408 n. 123

Township of. *See* name of township

Trademark Cases, 100 U.S. 82 (1879), 314 (box). *See also* United States v. Steffens

Trafficante v. Metropolitan Life Insurance Company, 409 U.S. 295 (1972), 704 (box)

Train v. Campaign Clean Water, 420 U.S. 136 (1975), 276 n. 129

Train v. City of New York, 420 U.S. 35 (1975), 276 n. 129

Trainor v. Hernandez, 431 U.S. 434 (1976), 324 n. 107

Trans-Missouri Freight Assn.; United States v., 166 U.S. 290 (1897), 104

Travis v. United States, 385 U.S. 491 (1967), 575 (box)

Subject Index

Page numbers in italics indicate illustrations and photographs. For case names, see separate Case Index.

A

ABA. *See* American Bar Association
Abduction. *See* Kidnapping
Abernathy, Ralph A., 487
Abernathy, Thomas G., 765
Ableman, Stephen, 401 (box)
Abortion
  advertising, 472
  Catholic justices, 910 (box)
  consent, notice requirements, 65, 741–742
  constitutional amendment proposed, 162, 786
  exclusionary rule, 620 (box)
  federal counseling ban, 65, 474 (box)
  hospital limits, 65
  intracourt relations, 854
  partial birth, 70, 742–744
  presidential opposition, 60, 61, 803 (box), 809
  press coverage of issue, 831–832
  public funding ban, 741, 789
  right to choose, 70
  Roe v. Wade
    fundamental privacy right, 374 (box), 671, 737, 741
    mootness exception, 315
    news leak, 825 (box)
    substantive due process, 739 (box)
    upheld in *Casey*, 67, 321, 321 (box), 374 (box), 426, 742
    state restrictions, 374 (box), 741, 742, 810, 854
    nonresidents, 405
Abraham, Henry J., 306 (box), 797, 803 (box)
Abrams, Jacob, *442*
Abstention doctrine, 303, 305, 322
Accountants, 473
Acquittal, 649, 651
Act to Improve the Administration of Justice (1988), 280 (box)
"Actual malice" standard, 58, 433
  private individuals, 476, 491–493
  public figures, 58, 491–493
  public officials, 58, 433, 487, 489
Adams, John (Army counsel), 253
Adams, John (President), *81*
  chief justice appointments, 10
  Eleventh Amendment ratification, 783
  foreign policy, 219, 807
  pardons, 767
  sedition prosecutions, 256
  Supreme Court appointments, 9, 80, 256, 334, 759, 766–767, 773, 800, 867, 910, 924 (box)
  Supreme Court relations
    Chase politics, impeachment, 877–878
    diplomatic missions, 872
    size of Court, 873
Adams, John Quincy
  Amistad decision, 674 (box)
  campaign supporters, 878
  judicial appointments
    size of Court, 772
    social associations, 874
    Trimble, Robert, 15

nomination, decline of, 13
  Supreme Court appointments, 806, 924 (box)
    confirmation controversy, 762 (box)
Adams, Samuel, 94
Adarand Constructors, 716–717
Adjournment, 240, 241, 243 (box)
Administrative Office of the United States Courts, 871, 880, 885, 891, 899
Administrative searches, 625 (box)
Admiralty law, 279, 281, 281 (box), 401
Adolescents. *See also* Children; Juvenile justice
  parental consent, notice of abortion, 65, 741, 742
Adoption, 730 (box)
Advertising
  commercial speech protections, 433, 439, 471–475, 489
  contraceptives, 473, 486 (box)
  federal-state preemption, 334 (box)
  gender-based "help wanted," 481 (box)
  political ads, 470, 481–483
  solicitation for litigation, 309 (box)
Advisory opinions, 8, 304–305, 313–314, 871
Affirmative action
  broadcast licenses, 716
  college admissions, 61, 70, 315, 711–712
  employment
    layoff policies, 63, 713
    promotion quotas, 714–715
    training programs, 712
    women, 714–715
  minority preferences, 424
    city contracts, 65, 710–711, 714–715
    federal contracts, 61, 712–713, 715–718
  Reagan criticism of Court, 809
  summary, 61, 424, 676–677, 710–711
  recent Court trends, 65, 68
Afroyim, Beys, 160
Age
  of justices, 911
  minimum drinking age, 133, 382, 731
  retirement age, 709, 735–736
  voting rights, 394, 541, 546 (box), 784
Age Discrimination in Employment Act, 168, 790
Agee, Philip, 575 (box)
Agricultural Adjustment Act of 1933, 44
  background of, 139 (box)
  press coverage, 827
  reversal of, 125, 133, 262, 385 (box)
  United States v. Butler, 788
Agricultural Adjustment Act of 1938, 115, 351, 788
Agricultural Marketing Act of 1937, 115–116
Agriculture
  farm mortgage relief, 44, 45, 261, 263, 788
  New Deal
    marketing quotas, 93, 115–116, 351
    production controls, 76, 131, 133–134, 139 (box), 261
Aguinaldo, Emilio, 206
AIDS, 745
Air Quality Act of 1967, 119
Aircraft, drug trafficking, 631

Airline Deregulation Act of 1978, 91, 334 (box)
Airlines, employment discrimination, 707
Airport solicitation, 470
Aitken, Robert, 898
Akron, Ohio, 63, 703
Alabama
  boundary dispute, 406
  death penalty, 662
  election day editorials, 481–483
  labor picketing, 465
  legislative apportionment, 559, 562
  libel of public officials, 487–490
  loitering and vagrancy, 622 (box)
  moment-of-silence law, 521
  prison conditions, 655
  punitive damage awards, 402 (box)
  racial discrimination
    affirmative action, 714
    black voting rights, 548, 549, 551
    NAACP membership disclosure, 445 (box)
    racial gerrymanders, 548
    school desegregation, 686, 688
  school prayer, 63
  Scottsboro Boys case, 42–43, 642–643
  sex discrimination, 382–383, 733
Alameda County, Calif., Jail, 501
Alaska
  jury size, 155
  oil tax exemption, 128
  voting rights, 550
Albany, N.Y., 444
Albert Parvin Foundation, 769–770, 878
Alcohol regulation
  Eighteenth Amendment challenges, 162
  federal taxes, 131, 395
  licenses for discriminatory clubs, 700 (box)
  search and seizure, 625 (box), 627
  sex discrimination, 727, 731
  state commerce regulation, 20
    delegated powers, 90
    legislative reversals of Court decisions, 787
    manufacture prohibition, 350
    police powers, 30, 346, 355–356
    wartime controls, 145, 215 (box)
Alcohol use
  advertising, 473
  minimum drinking age, 133, 382, 731
  naturalization denial, 157
  public drunkenness, 654
Alden, John, 123, 391
Aldrich, Charles H., 889 (box)
Alexandria Advertiser, 815
Alien Act of 1798
  Chase impeachment, 766, 913
  enactment of, 432
  protests against, 329
  violations of, 571
Alien Registration Act. *See* Smith Act of 1940
Aliens. *See also* Deportation; Immigration and emigration; Naturalization
  bar admissions, 309 (box)

21

Municipal Bankruptcy Act of 1934, 263, 385 (box), 788
Municipal Bankruptcy Act of 1937, 788
Murder
  death penalty, 659–662
  double jeopardy, 649–650
  mandatory sentences, 660
  non-killer participants, 661
  racial bias, 660
  sentence commutation, 246
  victim impact statements, 661
Murphy, Frank W., *49, 50, 994*
  biography, 994–995
  cabinet experience, 267 (box)
  citizenship, 158
  concurring opinions, 858
  criminal rights decisions
    blue ribbon juries, 607
    cruel, unusual punishment, 653
    right to counsel, 51, 644
    search and seizure, 624
  death of, 52
  due process, 601
  education, 909
  First Amendment rights
    flag salute, 51, 514
    labor union picketing, 465
    religious freedom, 514
  law clerks, 885
  nomination of, 48
  political experience, 546, 910, 911
  political rights
    federal employee politics, 588 (box)
    redistricting, 555
  religion, 796, 910 (box)
Murphy, William, 634
Murray, Madalyn and William, 520
Music, expression rights, 456 (box)

N

NAACP. *See* National Association for the Advancement of Colored People
Nabrit, James M., *683*
Narcotics, 40, 57, 129
"Narrow-tailoring test," 717
Nashville Daily Union and American, 821
Natchez Press, 818
Nation, 822, 824, 825
National Association for the Advancement of Colored People
  history, 674
  membership disclosure, 56, 437, 445 (box)
  school desegregation, 679, 686, 690
    Brown case, 58, 682, 1107 (full text)
  segregation challenges, 424
  solicitation of litigants, 421 (box)
  Supreme Court nominee opposition, 763
  teachers' associations, 445 (box)
  white primaries, 547
National Association of Manufacturers, 190
National bank. *See* Bank of the United States
National Broadcasting Company (NBC), 837
National Endowment for the Humanities, 851
National Farm Committee, 190
National Firearms Act of 1934, 131
National Gallery of Art, 872
National Gazette, 819
National Grange, 27–28, 348
National Guard, 218 (box)
National Industrial Recovery Act of 1933, 93, 261, 788
  hot oil ban, 87
  invalidation by Supreme Court, 44
  press coverage, 827
  purposes of, 110, 139 (box)
National Intelligencer, 14, 815, 817, 818, 819, 895

National Labor Relations Act of 1935, 44, 467 (box), 788
  enactment of, 112
  manufacturing, 351
  press as business, 479 (box)
  union officers, 437
National Labor Relations Board, 585
National parks, 464
National Public Radio, 825 (box), 836
  Supreme Court coverage, 738
National Right to Life Committee, 743
National security issues. *See also* Subversive activity
  association rights, 540
  balancing test for speech restraints, 437
  communists in defense jobs, 582
  congressional investigation power, 79
  electronic surveillance, 268, 631
  executive privilege, 253
  federal loyalty programs, 583–584
  passport denials, 575 (box)
  press restraints, 478
    Pentagon Papers, 266–268, 483–486
    postal circulation, 486 (box)
  seditious speech, 439–450
  Supreme Court jurisdiction repeal plan, 777–781
National Traffic and Motor Vehicle Safety Act of 1985, 334 (box)
National Urban League, 674
Native American Church, 509
Nativity scenes, 63, 529 (box)
Natural gas, 101, 396
Natural resources
  state regulation, 396, 720, 721
Naturalization
  Communist Party members, 157, 573 (box)
  congressional powers, 157
  conscientious objectors, 51, 157, 517
  exclusion, 157
  fraud, 89 (box), 157, 160
  revocation, 79, 159–161
Naval War with France, 141
Navigation. *See* Shipping and navigation
Nazis
  denaturalization, 158
  saboteurs, 51, 211–212, 440 (box), 845
  war crimes trials, 804, 879
Neagle, David, 235, 875 (box)
Near, J. M., *477, 477*–478
Near riot, 452
Neas, Ralph G., 835
Nebbia, Leo, *357*
Nebraska
  election of 2000, 566
  ERA rescission, 163 (box)
  foreign language teaching, 737–740
  partial birth abortion, 743
  slavery crisis, 150
Necessary and proper clause
  enabling legislation for treaties, 145
  Marshall Court's broad interpretation, 75
  military draft, 142
  national bank, 14, 85–86
  war powers, 140
Nelson, Samuel, *24,* 908 (box), *944*
  age, 911
  appointment, 907
  biography, 943–944
  Legal Tender decision, 26
  nomination of, 20, 762
  party affiliation, 797
  resignation of, 27
  retirement, 900
  Scott v. Stanford, 22

slavery, 151, 152
  war powers opposition, 24, 207–208
Nelson, Steve, 580 (box)
Neutrality Acts of 1935, 1936, and 1937, 210
Neutrality laws
  War of 1812, 13
  Washington administration, 219
Nevada
  search and seizure, 623
  zoning, 399
New Castle County, Del., 680
New Deal
  commerce regulation, 76, 93, 110–116, *826*
  congressional-judicial relations, 759
  Court development, 44–45, 261–265
  delegated powers, 87
  general welfare spending, 133–134
  legislative reversals of Court decisions, 788
  press coverage of Supreme Court, 826–829
New Hampshire
  corporate charters, 13, 817
  fighting words, 454 (box)
  license plate mottoes, 457 (box)
New Hampshire Gazette, 818
New Hyde Park, N.Y., 520
New Jersey
  commerce regulation
    garbage disposal, 350 (box)
    steamboat monopoly, 94–96, 344–345
  Fourteenth Amendment ratification, 164
  homosexuals, 748
  justices' state of origin, 798, 911
  legislative apportionment, redistricting, 394, 560, 562
  moment-of-silence laws, 524
  New York harbor dispute, 405
  oyster fishery, 404
  religious school aid, 524
  sentence, enhancement by judge not allowed, 608–609
  student, search and seizure, 598 (box)
  waterways diversion, 396
New Kent County, Va., 688–689
New Orleans, La.
  French quarters, 398
  racial discrimination in public accommodations, 699
  Slaughterhouse decision, 27–28, 369–370, 738 (box)
New Orleans Times-Picayune, 830
New River dam, 98
New York
  abortion counseling ban, 474 (box)
  association right, 445 (box)
  bankruptcy law, 13–14, 341, 815
  commerce regulation
    bakery hours, 357–358
    milk prices, 43
    minimum wage, 45, 359
    steamboat monopoly, 15, 94–96, 338, 344–345, 819
    stock transaction taxes, 365
  commercial speech, 473
  crime story profits, 478
  employment discrimination, 707
    aliens, 382, 722
  historic landmark preservation, 398
  immigration regulation, 346, 348, 354
  justices' state of origin, 796, 907, 908 (box), 911
  juvenile detention, 378, 609 (box)
  legislative apportionment, redistricting, 559, 560
  Line Item Veto Act, 242
  New York harbor dispute, 405
  obscenity prior restraint, 483 (box)